FAMOUS PLAYS OF CRIME
AND DETECTION

Famous Plays of Crime and Detection

From SHERLOCK HOLMES
to ANGEL STREET

Compiled by *Van H. Cartmell*, 1896–

AND

Bennett Cerf, 1898–1971.

INTRODUCTION BY JOHN CHAPMAN

Play Anthology Reprint Series

 BOOKS FOR LIBRARIES PRESS
FREEPORT, NEW YORK

INTERNATIONAL STANDARD BOOK NUMBER:
0-8369-8220-7

LIBRARY OF CONGRESS CATALOG CARD NUMBER:
76-173621

PRINTED IN THE UNITED STATES OF AMERICA
BY
NEW WORLD BOOK MANUFACTURING CO., INC.
HALLANDALE, FLORIDA 33009

FOREWORD

IT IS HARD to believe that in a period when mystery and murder stories in book form are selling four or five times better than they ever did before, and when the hills of Hollywood are echoing the horrendous shrieks of countless motion picture gang molls, zombies, hatchet men, and monsters (all of whom look suspiciously like Boris Karloff), there should not be a single play of this genre on the Broadway boards. In the past three years, in fact, with the public, prosperous and thrill-hungry, literally begging for cops-and-robbers, body-in-the-closet entertainment, all that the legitimate theater has been able to whip up was one single exhibit, "Ten Little Indians," so feeble in comparison with the stalwarts in this collection that we never even considered it for inclusion.

On behalf of those countless theater-goers who prefer an old-fashioned murder to a revival of "Blossom Time" and a bony hand reaching out of a panelled wall to the fleshy thigh of a blasé strip tease artiste, we have assembled these thirteen thrillers of earlier and more crime-conscious days in the theater. We hope that the public will make such a fuss over them that at least one competent playwright will decide it's high time to make another killing. Our motto is "More Corpses and Less Corps de Ballet!"

This is the sixth anthology in a series that already includes the best American, English, and European plays, a collection of thirty one-act pieces, and "S.R.O.," the fourteen most successful plays (from a box-office point of view) of the American stage. We have reached a point in our relentless collaboration where we ourselves sometimes are confused over which one is Cerf and which one is Cartmell. One lady bookseller in Jacksonville, Florida, insists upon regarding "Cartmell Cerf" as the name of a single person. It is a heavy cross, but we believe we can continue to bear it as long as you can. Incidentally, in case you have wondered, a full share of the spoils quite rightfully goes to the authors and proprietors of the plays we include, but there is sufficient left for the editors, particularly when the idea for the anthology came from someone else (in this case it was that connoisseur of tales of terror and the supernatural, Miss Phyllis Fraser). Contrast the happy state of mind of the anthologists, if you will, with that of the writers of murder stories who, despite their unprecedented prosperity, have just organized a protective association, or union, with the motto, "Crime Doesn't Pay—Enough!"

And so we turn you over to John Chapman, who will provide the footnotes on the thirteen thrillers in this collection, and then to the plays themselves, superlative examples, we believe, of the school of drama made to order for audiences who want to hiss and tell. They stand up well. Most of them are as thrilling in book form as they were on the stage. The proofreader of this volume was so carried away by the contents, in fact, that it took him three days to get back.

Off with the house lights (except the lamp over your shoulder)! Silence please (except the creak on the stair and the low moan of the wind outside)! Settle down for the evening with a good crook!

VAN H. CARTMELL AND BENNETT CERF

New York, June 1946.

CONTENTS

INTRODUCTION

IN ASSEMBLING thirteen plays of crime and detection, not to mention horror, Mr. Cartmell and Mr. Cerf have culled not only some good things but also the proper number of them—for 13 bodes ill. One of the nicest of the affairs of death in this volume is, indeed, "The Thirteenth Chair." If you should chance to curl up with this collection—or lie flat on your tummy on the floor, if that is your habit—on a stormy and lonely night, you will be most deliciously ill-boden-by, come the dawn.

You will remember some, if not all, of the dramas herein, and the people who played them. Your memory will put you in Baldpate Inn, or Mr. Manningham's baleful house on Angel Street, or Mr. Holmes' digs on Baker Street, or in the hideous little Dulwich house where William Marble spent so much of his time fretting at the living-room window. Remembering will help; but when you cannot remember, imagine: read carefully about the settings, bring them into being in your mind, and turn loose the villains therein to perform their acts of desperation.

Crime *does* pay—in the fiction of page and stage. It richly pays the authors, the publishers, the producers, the actors . . . and the audiences. The cops-and-robbers games of our childhood never quite leave us, so we still would like to be either a cop or a robber. I should not mind being Arsene Lupin or Dick Tracy, Robin Hood or Sherlock Holmes. Had I had foreknowledge of all the delicious literature I would inspire, I'd not have objected to being Lizzie Borden, for Lizzie is infinitely more arresting than our modern Elsie Borden. If I could act one-tenth as well as Leo G. Carroll, I'd rather be Inspector Rough than a drama critic.

It was Wolfe Kaufman, who recently collapsed to the point of writing a mystery novel, who coined the word "whodunit" when he was on the great slangmaking staff of *Variety*. He did a service, for so pithy a word is immediately taken into the language because it is brilliantly useful; but he also performed a disservice, in that something which really is worth respect can be dismissed, offhand and without hearing, by that same single word. There is some art and a deal of craft in the writing of the thirteen thrillers herein, and there was art in the playing. You will find such hallowed theatrical names as Jane Cowl, William Gillette, Dame May Whitty, Grace George and Charles Laughton involved in this volume.

The collection takes you from the last year of the Nineteenth Century, when Gillette adapted Conan Doyle's "Sherlock Holmes" for himself, to the last moment of today—for at the time of writing and, I will wager, at the time of publication, there has been no more expert thriller than Patrick Hamilton's "Angel Street." The years between 1899 and now have brought a change in method—a change from the direct to the indirect. We have had for some seasons the "psychological" thriller in place of the obvious melodrama; the trick of the modern playwright is to make you scare yourself. The maker of today's whodunit does not ask who done it; he tells you at the beginning—and then, having laid his cards on the table, he makes your hair curl anyway.

Now and then, of course, we do get a melodrama in which a body falls out of a closet or a clutching claw emerges from a trick bookcase—but it doesn't seem to last long. We prefer associating with known maniacs like Dan, the head-lugging bellhop of "Night Must Fall," or Mr. Manningham, the cunning sadist of "Angel Street."

William Gillette, whose father had been a U.S. Senator, was a Connecticut Yankee who took in not only Yale but also Harvard and the Massachusetts Fine Arts Institute. He began acting in 1875 when he was still on the Yale roster, and he appeared in scores of plays including most of Shakespeare. He wrote or adapted a good number of dramas for himself, including the well-remembered "Secret Service." But playgoers here and in Britain will always remember him as Sherlock Holmes because he *was* Sherlock.

Gillette adapted the Doyle story in 1899 and Charles Frohman presented it. It did splendidly against such competition as Mrs. Fiske's "Becky Sharp," Viola Allen's "The Christian" and the spectacular "Ben Hur." It ran for 256 performances, then toured, then had a run in London. It was revived in 1902, 1905 and 1910. In 1928 there was a revival with another Sherlock, Robert Warwick; and again in 1929 the old master, Gillette, came back for forty-five performances. In 1931 he gave the play its farewell tour.

The late Bayard (Bidey) Veiller had always an eye for melodrama and so, naturally, he became a movie executive in those golden silent days. Once Veiller's film employers wired him to fix up a movie—not one of his own —which was so bad it couldn't be released. They said he could spend $10,000 on the fixing. Veiller had just read about the invention of two brothers named Johnson, a camera which could make pictures under water, and had mentally noted the melodramatic possibilities of same. He figured that a fight to the death between hero and villain on the ocean's floor would fix any film.

Veiller prepared such a sequence, in which the battle was over a chest of gold ingots. The shooting began. In their diving suits the antagonists went through their slow-motion struggle. At last, of course, the hero did the villain in, and, triumphant but exhausted, lifted the lid of the treasure chest. Whereupon all of the gold ingots floated gracefully surfaceward. Nobody had told the property man about this underwater stuff and he had followed the standard prop-faking procedure by making his gold bars out of wood and gilding them.

"Within the Law" was produced by the Selwyns in 1912, and even then Veiller had a modern melodramatic trick for it—a Maxim silencer for a revolver. "Some class to that, eh?" boasts Garson when the cops finally get him. "Say, them things cost sixty dollars and they're worth the money, too. They'll remember me as the first to spring one of them, won't they?"

In the Veiller meller there is something more sound than a silencer. It is the old standby, the poor working girl—a girl who has been railroaded to prison by a heartless uppercrust society. The girl was Jane Cowl . . . and she got even when she had done her stretch by operating a clever blackmailing gang that was always within the law—and she got even, too, by marrying the son of the wealthy scoundrel who had caused her conviction.

What a second-act curtain line Miss Cowl had! "Four years ago," she told the man who owned the department store, "you took away my name and gave me a number. Now"—and you can imagine the triumph in her voice and the applause from the audience—"now I've given up that number and I've got *your* name!" Life is really satisfying in plays like this.

The year following the production of "Within the Law" George M. Cohan came up with a melodramatic comedy adapted from Earl Derr Biggers' popular novel, "Seven Keys to Baldpate." On reading the play one is hit by the suspicion that here, in the central character of a nimble-witted novelist, is a role tailor-made by Cohan for Cohan. Yet it was not George M., but the late Wallace Eddinger, who had a resounding success in the last year of peace before World War I. There is a small story in this connection.

George was about to begin a second season in "Broadway Jones" when he and Sam Harris produced "Seven Keys." The tryout of the new play was scheduled for Hartford, Conn., and Cohan, Eddinger and two companions motored up from New York. On the Post Road their car turned over in a ditch, giving Eddinger a bad shaking-up and Cohan a broken collar bone. Eddinger seemed more shaken than Cohan was broken, so Georgie pinch-hit for Wallace at the Hartford opening. Not until twenty-two years later, when The Players revived "Seven Keys," did Cohan again assume the role of William Hallowell Magee, the writer who bet he could write a novel in twenty-four hours in the dead of Winter in a Summer hotel.

The Players' revival was a success, not alone because it had Cohan but also because "Seven Keys" stands up admirably well. It could be done again, now . . . if Cohan or Eddinger were alive. The stage trick upon which it depends is a sound trick, and the Cohan pace and the Cohan humor are not yet dated.

A very important stage trick appeared in 1914—the flashback. The theater could hardly get along nowadays without a few flashbacks per season, and without this device the movies would still be hand-cranked and the operator would have a lantern slide handy saying, "One Moment Please While We Change Reels."

The innovator was a young law clerk, Elmer Rice, and his play was "On Trial." When Rice sold it to Arthur Hopkins it was called "According to the Evidence" and it was about a Kentucky mountain feud killing. Hopkins got Rice to rewrite it, shifting the locale to the metropolitan banking area which, even now, has in it more playwrights than bankers. When Hopkins found he couldn't produce the play on account of a lack of money the firm of Cohan & Harris took it over and Elmer Rice quit law-clerking for good. For the theater's good as well as his own, one may now add.

There have been other courtroom dramas, such as "The Trial of Mary

Dugan" and "The Night of January 16," but none is any tighter and more suspenseful than Rice's story of a man who admits a killing and wants to be sentenced without a trial. It has in it, besides melodrama, sex—and when you've put murder and sex together you have hit the boxoffice jackpot. As played by Frederick Perry and Mary Ryan, "On Trial" was an absorbing story of a noble assassin and a much-harassed female.

You will note, I think, that this early courtroom thriller is shrewdly done, in that the trial scenes seem perfectly authentic without the "I object" and "Objection overruled" which clutters the works of modern fictioneers. Elmer Rice had the good sense to use the law as a background, not as a principal character.

Roi Cooper Megrue's "Under Cover," also dated 1914, *does* take one back—back to times when wealthy playfolk were crossing back and forth on the Atlantic in luxury liners and worrying about their customs declarations. Smuggling was an exciting sport from then right through the Tourist Twenties, and many a girl stuffed two-ounce nips of Cointreau into her bloomers until her knees clanked as she innocently passed the inspector on the Cunard Line dock. Here in this play are the days of BVDs, phrases like "Ta-ta, old sport," and the resounding drinking slogan, "What's a quart among three?" This is when a man declared his passion by saying, "Do you know, Nora, for the last year there's been something trembling on my lips." To which Nora replied, "Oh, Monty, don't shave it off—I love it."

"Under Cover" had in it an upcoming supporting cast for its featured player, the handsome William Courtenay. Ralph Morgan was the one who had something trembling on his lips and the ladies involved included Lily Cahill, Phoebe Foster and Lucile Watson.

When Bidey Veiller came up with "The Thirteenth Chair" in 1916 he had another fine gadget—a disappearing knife. Who will ever forget the first spine-curling thrill of seeing that nasty skewer stuck in the ceiling, or the chunk with which it fell downward and stuck, quivering, in the table-top? (It took two knives in the ceiling to manage this, by the way: one pointed upward, as if wedged in the rafters, and another, unseen, pointed downward. They were worked by a stagehand pulling strings. Veiller's mechanical genius was considerable.) To many of us, including myself, "The Thirteenth Chair" remains the best of all the shriek-in-the-dark dramas, even though we know very well that later technicians have made improvements in the business of fashioning thrillers.

As you go through this volume you will observe the ungentlemanliness, the positive deliberate cruelty, of playwrights. They are, the fiends, continually putting upon elderly women—submitting them to cunning mental tortures, scaring the daylights out of them and even killing the poor old things. None of them, these thrill-makers, ever heard the late Don Skene sing his favorite ballad: "Don't beat your mother just 'cause she's old, don't bounce a rock off her bean . . ."

Take, if you will, the instance of a spinster of 60 named Cornelia Van Gorder. She innocently rented the Summer home of a rich man who supposedly had died some months before and she figured on a nice holiday. She had no vacation. Some bank money was missing, and everybody was looking for it right in the old lady's house. The bank cashier wanted it, and so did a detective, and so did a doctor of dubious mien, and so did an arch-criminal known as The Bat.

"The Bat," by Mary Roberts Rinehart and Avery Hopwood, was the thriller of 1920, and in it was the best of all comedy servants—May Vokes. The killings in "The Bat" have passed to nothingness in my memory, but the comic terrors of Miss Vokes are as vivid now as they were the first night I heard her shriek.

Another female—this time a young 'un—was given a rugged time in 1922. She had inherited a fortune and a house, with the proviso that she be of sound mind in order to keep her heritage. So, naturally, others tried to drive her crazy in order that the legacy might pass along to someone else. The girl maintained her sanity, all right, for she was the heroine—but audiences didn't. The play was "The Cat and the Canary."

There were sliding panels and clutching claws; there was a corpse flopping from behind a piece of plywood, which disappeared later; there was a colored woman who believed in voodoo and gave everybody the jumps. The property list for a production of "The Cat and the Canary" includes such delicious items as two automatics, a bottle of smelling salts, a necklace of sapphires and rubies, a mask and a block of wood covered with sandpaper —the last-mentioned item for making the sound of dragging a body across the floor.

The girl whom they tried to make insane in "The Cat and the Canary" was Florence Eldridge, now Mrs. Fredric March, and the trembling hero who protected her in spite of his Milquetoast nature was Henry Hull. They were quite a pair and John Willard had written quite a play. Mr. Willard had a part in it for himself, too.

In 1926 there were gangsters and the Capone mob who had made anybody from Chicago suspect, even if he was just a district representative for Grand Rapids furniture. There was prohibition then, and there were night clubs—night clubs which had an air of excitement which is lacking in the overstuffed joints of today.

In 1926 there was also a young man named Philip Dunning, who had done song-and-dance acts, played Summer stock and written some plays. One of the plays he peddled around was called "A White Little Guy" for a while. Then it was titled "Bright Lights," and again "The Roaring Forties." By the time Jed Harris bought it and called in George Abbott to do some work on it, Mr. Dunning's piece was called "Broadway." Burns Mantle picked "Broadway" for one of the ten best plays of the season.

It had about everything a melodrama should have—taut construction, plenty of action, inside dope on the theatrical business, inside dope on the liquor racket, a lot of comedy and plenty of pathos. The character of Roy

Lane, the small-time hoofer with the big ideas, was a gallant one, and it was given a top-flight performance by Lee Tracy.

From here on we encounter the "psychological" thriller. Playwrights seem to have decided that everything has been done which can be done with spring panels, clawing hands, poor working girls and such riffraff as smugglers, political crooks and mobsters from Cicero. The movies can turn out so frightening a Frankenstein's monster, so sinister a chamber of torture, that there is not much sense in the stage trying to remain in the cinema's game. The movies, of course, are in turn going psychological as all get-out, with Alfred Hitchcock and his ilk preying upon the public mind. Where it all will end Freud only knows.

The arrival on Broadway of "Payment Deferred" in 1931 was a subject for history. Not only was it a superb melodrama in the modern manner; it also introduced to America a British actor, Charles Laughton. It was not many years later that Mr. Laughton was introducing Lincoln's Gettysburg address and passages from the Bible to America.

"Payment Deferred" was adapted by Jeffrey Dell from a novel by C. S. Forester, who is much better known for the seagoing saga of Captain Horatio Hornblower. The play was—and is, as you read it—a study in remorse and terror. There are two murders in it, but you do not see them. The fact of murder is not important here; it is the consequence of it in the mind of the killer which counts. The play is one of lovely anguish and delicious suspense, and no one who saw Mr. Laughton's first performance here will forget the chills it offered.

By 1935 it was time for someone to pick on a nice old lady again, so Edward Chodorov adapted "Kind Lady" from a story by Hugh Walpole. The result was that dear Grace George had a terrible time.

Miss George was a wealthy widow with a house full of art treasures and a heart full of compassion, so when a hungry wayfarer came by she took him in. The wayfarer, in turn, took her over, gently but diabolically. A man who knew art and also knew what he liked, he moved in his gang and kept Miss George a prisoner up to the last part of the last act. He was quite a one, this wayfaring stranger, and he was very well played by Henry Daniell —who later did another slick, sinister job in a thriller which deserved a better fate than it got, "Murder Without Crime." "Kind Lady" was revived by Miss George in 1940, and both she and the play were still in good shape.

Of all the murderers to be found between these covers, the most sinister is Dan, the bellboy in "Night Must Fall." He is so cocky, so annoyingly glib and so insane that I loathe him, and right now I should like to warn the nasty old woman he smothers in time to save her life.

Here again is a case of a woman being put upon. This time she is no kind lady and no doubt she deserves what she gets. Put upon, too, is a nice girl who falls in love with Dan the bellboy, and I think she is a fool. But mostly I hate Dan.

"Night Must Fall" came here from England in 1936 with the author, Emlyn Williams, in the role of what the script calls the page boy. Mr.

Williams can write and he also can act. Entirely able to act, too, is Dame May Whitty, who played the old fussbudget who got murdered. Dame May and Mr. Williams made an exquisite evening of quiet alarm.

Clever also is another Briton, Patrick Hamilton. Of him *The Times'* Brooks Atkinson wrote, "He understands his horrors. He never strays outside the bailiwick of dark, soft-footed nervousness." Mr. Hamilton wrote what is to me the best of the tales of mental torture, "Angel Street." He wrote it under the title of "Gaslight," which is what it was called in a movie version. The movie rights having been tied up, Producer Shepard Traube dreamed up "Angel Street" for his memorable Broadway production.

The play opened two days before Pearl Harbor, and its enthusiastic reviews were printed on the same morning the papers carried word of the Jap attack on our fleet. Hardly anybody got as far back as the drama pages that Monday morning, so "Angel Street" had to coast along for a spell; but soon enough it got rolling and it did not stop until it had played 1,295 performances. This record places it sixth on Broadway's long-run list, with "Tobacco Road," "Life With Father," "Abie's Irish Rose," "Arsenic and Old Lace" and "Hellzapoppin" ahead of it.

The most admirable thing about Mr. Hamilton's play is its economy—its economy of characters, of action, of words. There are five players and there is one set. There is a murder, all right—but it happened years ago. The action is such slight stuff as the dimming of the gas mantles, the lock picking of a desk. Anything resembling violent action is avoided until the triumphant finale, in which the villain is tied to a chair and given a dose of his own medicine by the woman he tried to drive insane. (Note: here is another play in which somebody tries to put a poor female out of her mind.)

Splendid were the performances of Vincent Price as the evil Mr. Manningham, Judith Evelyn as the collapsing heroine, and Leo Carroll as the comforting man from Scotland Yard. But Mr. Hamilton had written so soundly that "Angel Street" was actor-proof. As the seasons passed replacements were necessary, and a succession of actors gave complete satisfaction on Broadway and more recently on tour.

Curl up, now. Turn low the lights. Forget bedtime and revel in dark and direful doings.

JOHN CHAPMAN

Sherlock Holmes

A Melodrama in Four Acts By

WILLIAM GILLETTE

Based on Sir Arthur Conan Doyle's
Incomparable Stories

THE CAST

SHERLOCK HOLMES *was first presented at the Garrick Theatre, New York, November 6, 1899, with the following cast:*

SHERLOCK HOLMES	William Gillette
DR. WATSON	Bruce McRae
BENJ. FORMAN	Ruben Fax
BILLY	Henry McArdle
SIR EDWARD LEIGHTON	Harold Heaton
COUNT VON STALBURG	Thos. McGrath
PROFESSOR MORIARTY	Geo. Wessells
JAMES LARRABEE	Ralph Delmore
SIDNEY PRINCE	Geo. Honey
ALF BASSICK	Henry Harman
CRAIGIN	Thos. McGrath
TIM LEARY	Elwyn Eaton
McTAGUE	Soldene Powell
JOHN	William Postance
PARSONS	Soldene Powell
ALICE FAULKNER	Katherine Florence
MRS. FAULKNER	Kate Ten Eyck
MADGE LARRABEE	Judith Berolde
TERESE	Hilda Englund
MRS. SMEEDLEY	Kate Ten Eyck

ACT ONE

Drawing Room at the Larrabees'   *Evening*

ACT TWO

Scene I: Professor Moriarty's Underground Office   *Morning*
Scene II: Sherlock Holmes's Apartments in Baker Street   *Evening*

ACT THREE

The Stepney Gas Chamber   *Midnight*

ACT FOUR

Doctor Watson's Consulting Room—Kensington   *The following evening*

THE PLACE IS LONDON

SHERLOCK HOLMES

ACT ONE

SCENE I

The drawing room at Edelweiss Lodge, an old house, gloomy and decayed, situated in a lonely street in a little frequented part of London. Wide door or open columns up L. and L.C. to entrance hall. Heavily carved fireplace in large wide alcove up C. By window up R.C. are window seats. Old furniture, decayed, worn, though once very magnificent. A new piano. A heavy desk or cabinet down R., very solid, with doors in front of lower part which, opened, show a strongbox or safe with combination lock such as might be in use in private houses. Heavily beamed ceiling of a dark color. Many places are out of repair in the walls and ceiling; the carvings are somewhat broken, as if by age—not violence.

The music stops an instant before the rise of the curtain. There is a short pause after the curtain is up. MADGE LARRABEE *is discovered near the piano anxiously waiting. She is a large and strikingly handsome woman with a somewhat hard face. Black hair. Richly dressed.*

Enter FORMAN *at door C. with evening paper. He is a quiet, perfectly trained servant or butler. He hands the paper to* MADGE *who takes it listlessly.*

FORMAN (*speaks always very quietly*). I beg pardon, ma'am, but one of the maids wished to know if she could speak with you. (MADGE, *scanning the paper, sinks onto a seat near the piano.*)

MADGE (*not looking up from paper*). I can't spare the time now.

FORMAN. Very well, ma'am. (*Turns to go.*)

MADGE (*still without looking up from paper*). Which maid was it?

FORMAN (*turning toward* MADGE *again*). Terese, ma'am.

MADGE (*looking up. Very slight surprise in her tone*). Terese!

FORMAN. Yes ma'am.

MADGE. Have you any idea what she wants?

FORMAN. Not the least, ma'am.

MADGE. She must tell you. I'm very busy and can't see her unless I know.

FORMAN. I'll say so, ma'am. (*Turns and exits carefully and quietly, closing the door after him, immediately coming in again and watching* MADGE.)

(MADGE, *rustling the leaves of the paper, finds what she has been looking for and starts eagerly to read it. As if not seeing the print well, she leans closer to the light and resumes reading with the greatest avidity.* FORMAN *quietly shuts door. He stands a moment at the door looking at* MADGE *as she reads the paper. His eyes are upon her sharply and intensely, yet he does not assume any expression otherwise. She finishes and angrily rises, casting the paper violently on the piano; turns and goes over to R. near the large desk, her eyes upon it—pauses—then away to L. angrily. Suddenly sees* FORMAN *and calms herself at once.* FORMAN *times it so that just as* MADGE *turns he seems to be coming into the room.*)

FORMAN (*half down C.*). I could get nothing from her, ma'am. She insists that she must speak to you herself.

MADGE. Tell her to wait till tomorrow. (*Turns and moves toward R.*)

FORMAN. I asked her to do so, ma'am, and she said that she would not be here tomorrow.

(MADGE *turns toward* FORMAN *with some surprise.*)

MADGE. Tell her to come here. (FORMAN *bows and turns to go.* MADGE *goes toward chair she occupied and near which the paper lies. She sees it and stops with hand on piano.*) Oh—Judson! (FORMAN *stops and comes back. Everything is quiet, subdued, catlike in his manner.*) How did you happen to imagine that I would be interested in this marriage announcement? (*Taking up paper and glancing at it carelessly.*)

FORMAN. I could 'ardly 'elp it, ma'am.

(MADGE *turns and looks hard at him for an instant.* FORMAN *stands deferentially.*)

MADGE. We know the—the parties concerned and are naturally interested in the event. Of course you did not imagine there was anything more. (*She does not look at him as she says this.*)

FORMAN (*not looking at* MADGE). Certainly not, ma'am—and may I add that if I *did* imagine there was anything more I'm sure you'd find it to your interest, ma'am, to remember my faithful service in 'elpin' to keep it quiet.

MADGE (*after a slight pause*). Judson, what sort of a fool *are* you? (FORMAN *turns to her with feigned astonishment.* MADGE *speaks with sharp, caustic utterance, almost between her teeth. Turns to* FORMAN.) Do you imagine I would take a house and bring this girl and her mother here and keep up the establishment for nearly two years without protecting myself against the chance of petty blackmail by my own servants?

FORMAN (*protestingly*). Ah—ma'am —you misunderstand me—I——

MADGE (*rising*). I understand you too well! And now I beg you to understand *me*. I have had a trifle of experience in the selection of my servants and can recognize certain things when I see them! It was quite evident from your behavior that you had *been in something yourself* and it didn't take me long to get it out of you. You are a *self-confessed forger.*

FORMAN (*with a quick movement of apprehension*). No! No! (*He looks around.*) Don't speak out like that! (*Recovers a little.*) It was—it was in confidence—I told you in *confidence*, ma'am!

MADGE. Well, I'm telling *you* in confidence that at the first sign of any underhand conduct on *your* part this little episode of yours will——

FORMAN (*hurriedly—to prevent her from speaking it*). Yes, yes! I—I'll—bear it in mind, ma'am!

MADGE (*after a cold look at him*). Very well. . . . (*Moves down R.*) Now as to the maid—Terese—— (FORMAN *inclines his head for instruction.*) Do you think of anything which might explain her assertion that she will not be here tomorrow?

FORMAN (*His eyes turned away from* MADGE. *He speaks in low tones, and his behavior is subdued, as if completely humiliated.*) It has occurred to me, ma'am, since you first asked me regarding the matter, that she may 'ave taken exceptions to some occurrences which she thinks she 'as seen going on in this 'ouse. That is, seen or 'eard, ma'am.

MADGE. Raise her wages if you find it necessary. If it isn't money she wants I'll see her myself.

FORMAN. Very well, ma'am. (*He turns and exits quietly at door up C.*)

(MADGE *stands motionless a moment. Sounds of heavy door outside L.* MADGE *makes a quick motion of listening. Hurries to door up C. and*

then to L., *looking off. Enter* JIM LARRABEE *door up L., passing her in some excitement. He is a tall, heavily built man with a hard face full of determination and of strong character. He is well dressed and attractive in some respects—a fine-looking man with dark hair and eyes but with the hard sinister appearance of a criminal.*)

MADGE (*as he passes her*). Didn't you find him?

LARRABEE. No. (*Goes to the heavy desk safe and throws open the wooden doors of lower part, showing the iron door and combination lock of a safe or strongbox. Gives knob a turn or two nervously and works at it.* MADGE *follows, watching him.*) He wasn't there! (*Rises from desk.*) We'll have to get a locksmith in.

MADGE (*quickly*). We can't do that!

LARRABEE. We've got to do something, haven't we? (*Down quickly before door of safe again.*) There's no time to waste either. They've put Holmes on the case!

MADGE. Sherlock Holmes?

LARRABEE. Yes. (*At safe. Trying knob.*)

MADGE. Where did you hear that?

LARRABEE. I heard it at Leary's.

MADGE. What could he do?

LARRABEE (*rises and faces her*). How do I know?—but he'll make some move—he never waits long! (*Moves about restlessly but stops when* MADGE *speaks.*)

MADGE. Can't you think of someone else—as we can't find Sid?

LARRABEE. He may turn up yet. I left word with Billy Rounds, and he's on the hunt for him. (*Between his teeth.*) What a cussed, rotten—— Holding on for two good years, just for this—and now the time comes and she's blocked us! (*Looks off and up stairway from where he stands.*) Look here! I'll just get at her for a minute! (*Starting toward L.*)

MADGE (*quickly*). Wait, Jim! (LARRABEE *stops and turns to her. She goes close to him.*) What's the use of hurting the girl? We've tried all that!

LARRABEE. We'll try something else! (*Turns and goes to door L.*)

MADGE (*in a quick half-whisper*). Jim! (LARRABEE *turns at door.* MADGE *approaches him.*) Remember —nothing that'll show! No marks!

LARRABEE (*going doggedly*). I'll look out for that. (LARRABEE *exits at door L. and is seen running upstairs with a fierce haste.*)

(*As* MADGE *looks after him anxiously at door L. enter* TERESE. *She is a quiet-looking French maid with a pleasant face. She stands near the door up* C. MADGE *turns back into the room and sees her; she stands an instant then moves toward* C. *and seats herself.*)

MADGE. Come here! (TERESE *comes down a little way with some hesitation.*) What is it?

TERESE. Meester Judson said I vas to come.

MADGE. I told Judson to arrange with you himself.

TERESE. He could not, madame. I do not veesh longer to remain.

MADGE. What is it? You must give me some reason!

TERESE. It is zat I *veesh* to go.

MADGE. You've been here for months and made no complaint!

TERESE. Ah, madame—it is not so before!—It is now beginning zat I do not like!

MADGE (*rising and turning on her sharply*). What? What *is* it that you do not like?

TERESE (*with some spirit but in a low voice*). *I do not like eet*, mad-ame—*eet—here—zis place*—what you do—ze young lady you have up zere. (*Indicating above.*) Eet eez not well! I cannot remain to see!

MADGE. You know nothing about it! The young lady is ill—she is not right here—(*touching forehead*)— she is a great trouble to us, but we take every care of her and treat her with the utmost kindness and——

(*A piercing scream, as if muffled by something, is heard in a distant part of house above. There is a pause. Both are motionless.* TERESE *does not assume a horrified expression; she simply stands motionless. Enter at door up L., coming down stairway rapidly,* MRS. FAULKNER, *a white-haired lady dressed in an old black gown which is almost in shreds.*)

MRS. FAULKNER. My child! My child! They are hurting my child!

(*She stands just within the door looking helplessly at* MADGE *who goes quickly to her.*)

MADGE (*between her teeth*). What are you doing here? Didn't I tell you *never* to come down? (*The old lady stares vacantly, but a vague expression of trouble is upon her face.*) Come with me! (*Taking* MRS. FAULKNER *by the left arm and drawing her toward the door. The old lady hangs back in a frightened way. The scream sounds again— more muffled—from above.*) Come, I say! (*Takes* MRS. FAULKNER *off with some force up stairway.*)

(TERESE *stands looking after them. Enter* FORMAN *quietly at door up* C. *He looks toward door up* L. *a moment, where* MADGE *has just taken the old lady off.* TERESE *is looking the same way, and there is a significant pause.* FORMAN *goes down to* TERESE. *They look at one another an instant in silence. Then he speaks to her in a low voice.*)

FORMAN. She's made it quite satisfactory, I suppose? (TERESE *looks at* FORMAN.) You will not leave her— *now?*

TERESE. More zan evaire before! Do you hear ze young ladee? What is eet they make to her?

FORMAN (*in a low voice*). Maybe she is ill.

TERESE. Indeed I sink it is so zat zay *make* her eel! I weel not remain to see! (*Moving away.*) I can find another place—eet eez not so *dee-*ficult.

FORMAN. Not if you know where to go!

TERESE. Ah—zhat eez eet!

FORMAN. I have one address——

TERESE (*turns to him quickly*). Bien!—You know one? (FORMAN *nods, then looks quickly toward the door* L.) Est-ce sérieux? What you call re-li-ah-ble?

FORMAN (*goes to her*). Here—on this card—— (*Quickly takes card from pocket and pushes it into her hands.*) Go to that address! (*Looks apprehensively to door* L.)

TERESE (*looking at card and beginning slowly to read*). Meester— Sheer-lock——

(FORMAN, *with a warning exclamation, turns and seizes her, covering her mouth with one hand. They stand rigid a moment. He looks slowly round without releasing her.*)

FORMAN. Someone might hear you! Go to that address in the morning.

(*The doorbell rings in a distant part of the house.* FORMAN *releases* TERESE *and both listen. He motions her off with a quick gesture. She exits at* door up C. FORMAN *exits at door up* L. *to open the house door quickly. Sound of house door outside* L., *a solid heavy sound. Enter* SID PRINCE, *walking in quickly at door up* L. *He is a short, stoutish dapper little fellow. He carries a small black satchel, wears an overcoat and hat, gloves, etc., is well dressed and jaunty. Wears a diamond scarfpin and rings. Is quick in his movements, always on the alert.* FORMAN *follows him on, standing near door at* L.)

PRINCE (*moving toward piano* R.C.). Don't wyste time, you fool—tell 'em

I'm 'ere, cawn't yer? (PRINCE *speaks always in an undertone, as if to keep from being overheard.*)

FORMAN. Did you wish to see *Mr.* Chetwood, sir, ór was it *Miss* Chetwood?

PRINCE (*stopping and turning to* FORMAN). Well, I'll be blowed—you act as if I'd never been 'ere befoŕe! 'Ow do you know but I was born in this 'ere 'ouse? Go on an' tell 'em as it's Mr. Sidney Prince, Hesquire. (*He puts his satchel, which is apparently heavy, on an ottoman near the piano.*)

FORMAN. I beg pardon, sir!—I'll announce you immediate. (*Exits at door L.*)

(PRINCE *takes off hat, gloves, and overcoat, placing them on a chair so as to cover the satchel. Looks about the room. Walks over to the heavy desk R. and glances at it. Then swings open the lower door in an easy businesslike way.*)

PRINCE. Ah! (*As if he had found what he was looking for, he drops on one knee and gives the lock a turn, then rises and goes over to his satchel which he uncovers and opens. He feels about for something.* MADGE *and* LARRABEE *come down the stairway and enter at door up L.* PRINCE *sees them but does not stop what he is doing.*)

MADGE (*moving toward* PRINCE). Is that you, Sid?—I'm so glad you've come! (*All now speak in lowered voices, confidentially.*)

LARRABEE. Hullo, Sid! . . . Did you get my note?

PRINCE (*going right on with what he is doing*). Well, I'm 'ere, ain't I? (*Fumbling in his satchel.*) That's wat it is, I tyke it! (*Nods toward desk.*)

MADGE (*nods*). We're awfully glad you turned up, Sid. We might have had to get a stranger in. (*Moves across to stand in front of* PRINCE.)

PRINCE (*standing up and looking at* LARRABEE *and* MADGE). Stranger! That *would* be nice now, wouldn't it—if your game 'appens to be anything off color!

LARRABEE. Oh—it isn't so 'specially dark.

PRINCE. Mph! That's different. (*Crosses to desk with tools from satchel.*) I say, Larrabee—— (*Quick* "Sh!" *from* MADGE *just behind him.*)

LARRABEE (*at the same time*). Shut up! (*They look anxiously round.* PRINCE *looks up surprised.*) My name is Chetwood here!

PRINCE. Beg pardon, I'm sure—my mistyke! Chetwood, eh? Wot a nice nifty little nyme you've 'it on this time! I was only goin' to ask, Chetty ole man, w'ere you picked up such a relic as *that*. Ole-timer an' no mistyke! (*About to try some tools on the lock, he looks about.*) All clear, you say? No danger lurking?

LARRABEE (*shaking head*). Not the least! (MADGE *moves away a little, glancing cautiously about her.* PRINCE *tries his tools and keys.*)

PRINCE (*they watch him as he tries to open the lock*). Not robbin' yourselves, I trust?

LARRABEE. It does look a little like it!

PRINCE. I knew you was on some rum lay—squatting down in this place for over a year; but I never could seem to—(*working at safe*)—get a line on you. (*He works a moment and then crosses to get a tool out of satchel, stopping and looking sharply at* MADGE *and* LARRABEE.) What do we get here—oof, I trust?

MADGE (*shakes head*). Only a bundle of papers, Sid.

(PRINCE *works at tool an instant before speaking.*)

PRINCE. Pipers!

LARRABEE. Um!

PRINCE. Realize, I trust?

MADGE. We can't tell. It may be something—it may be nothing.

PRINCE. Well, if it's something, I'm in it, I hope? (*Moving a step or so toward* MADGE.)

MADGE. Why, of course, Sid.

PRINCE. Fair enough! (*Glances round quickly.*) Before we starts 'er goin', what's the general surroundin's?

LARRABEE. What's the good of wasting time on——

PRINCE. See 'ere! If I'm in this I'm *in* it, ain't I? An' I want to know *wot* I'm in.

MADGE. Tell him, Jimmie.

LARRABEE. Well—I'm willing to give him an idea of what it is, but I won't give the name of the—— (*Hesitates, then speaking lower.*) You know we've been working the Continent—resorts and all that.

PRINCE. So I've 'eard.

(MADGE *motions them to wait. She is looking off quietly. After a moment she nods for them to proceed.*)

LARRABEE. It was over there—Homburg was the place—we ran across a young girl who'd been having trouble. Sister just died. Mother seemed wrong here. (*Touches forehead.*)

PRINCE. Well—you run acrost 'er.

LARRABEE. Madge took hold and found that this sister of hers had been having some kind of a love affair with a—well—with a foreign gentleman of exceedingly high rank —or at least—well, expectations that way.

PRINCE. 'Ow much was there to it?

LARRABEE. Promise of marriage.

PRINCE. I see—broke it, of course!

LARRABEE. Yes—and the girl's heart with it. I don't know what more she expected—anyway, she *did* expect more. She and her child died together.

PRINCE. Oh—*dead!*

LARRABEE. *She's* dead—but the *case isn't!* There are evidences, letters, photographs, jewelry with inscriptions, that he gave her. The sister's been keeping them! . . . (*He glances about.*) *We've* been keeping the sister! . . . See?

PRINCE (whistles). An' all the truck with 'er?—That the tot gave 'er sister? What's 'er little gyme?

LARRABEE. To get even. Waits till he wants to marry—then plugs him with it!

PRINCE (meditatively). These papers an' things ought to be worth a little something—wot?

LARRABEE (emphatically). I tell you it wouldn't be safe for him to marry until he gets them out of the way! He knows it very well. But what's more, the family knows it!

PRINCE. Oh—family! . . . Rich, I tyke it?

LARRABEE. Rich isn't quite the word. They're something else.

PRINCE. You don't mean—— (LARRABEE moves nearer to PRINCE and whispers a name in his ear.) My Gawd! Which of 'em?

LARRABEE (shakes his head). I don't tell you that.

PRINCE (thinking it over). Well, we are a-movin' among the swells now, ain't we? But this 'ere girl now—the sister o' the one that died—'ow did you manage to get 'er into it?

LARRABEE. We did the Generous Friendly.

MADGE (moving closer). I picked her up, of course, and sympathized and consoled. I invited her to stay with me at my house in London— Jimmie came over and got this place —and when I brought her along a week later it was all ready. And a private desk safe for the packet of letters and jewelry.

LARRABEE (turning). Yes—combination lock and all!—Everything worked smooth until a couple of weeks ago, when we began to hear from a firm of London solicitors. Some veiled proposals were made—which showed that the time was coming. They wanted the things out of the way. Suddenly all negotiations on their side stopped. The next thing for me to do was to threaten. I wanted the letters for this, but when I went to get them—I found that in some way the girl had managed to change the lock on us. The numbers were wrong—and we couldn't frighten or starve her into opening the thing.

PRINCE. I see. You've got the stuff in there!

LARRABEE. That's what I'm telling you! It's in there and we can't get it out! She's juggled the lock!

PRINCE (going at once to safe). Oh well—it won't take long to rectify that triflin' little error—— (Looking front.) But wot gets me is w'y they broke off with their offers.

LARRABEE. It's simple enough— they've given it up themselves and have got in Sherlock Holmes on the case.

PRINCE (suddenly starting up). Wot's that! (Pause.) Is 'Olmes in this?

LARRABEE. That's what Leary told me—half an hour ago.

MADGE. But what can he do, Sid? We haven't——

PRINCE. 'Ere! Don't stand talkin' about that—I'll get the box open. (*Goes to piano in front of* LARRABEE.) You send a telegram, that's all I want! (PRINCE *tears a page out of his notebook. He writes hurriedly with the other two watching.* LARRABEE *remains at R., a little suspicious.*) Where's your nearest telegraph office?

MADGE. Around the corner in Rincon Street.

PRINCE (*gives* LARRABEE *the telegram he has written*). Run for it! Mind what I say—*run for it!* (LARRABEE *is looking at him hard.*) That's to Alf Bassick—'e's Professor Moriarty's confidential man. Moriarty is king of 'em all in London. 'E runs everything that's shady—an' 'Olmes 'as been settin' lines all round him for months—and 'e didn't know it—an' now 'e's wakin' up to it an' there's the devil to pay! 'E wants any case 'Olmes is on—it's a dead fight between 'em. 'E'll take the case just to get at 'Olmes! 'E'll *kill* him before he's finished with him, you can lay all you've got on it.

LARRABEE. What are you telling him?

PRINCE. Nothin' whatever except I've got a job on as I wants to see 'im about in the mornin'! . . . Read it yourself. (LARRABEE *looks at what* PRINCE *has written.*) But don't take all night over it! You cawn't tell wot might 'appen! (*Crosses to safe.*)

MADGE. Go on, Jim!

(LARRABEE *crosses to door L.,* MADGE *following him.*)

LARRABEE (*to* MADGE *near door*). Keep your eyes open!

MADGE. Don't you worry!

(*Exit* LARRABEE. *Quick sound of door closing outside L. As* LARRABEE *and* MADGE *move,* PRINCE *has dropped down to work—real work now—at the desk. There is a short pause.* MADGE *stands watching him for a moment. She moves over to the piano and picks up a book carelessly, at which she glances with perfect nonchalance. After a time she speaks without taking her eyes from the book.*) I've *heard* of this Professor Moriarty.

PRINCE. If you 'aven't you must've been *out in the woods!*

MADGE. You say he's king of them all.

PRINCE (*working*). Bloomin' H'emperor—that's wot *I* call 'im!

MADGE. He must be in a good many different things!

PRINCE. You might see it that way if you looked around an' didn't breathe too 'ard!

MADGE. What does he do?

PRINCE. I'll tell you one thing he does! (*Turns to her and rests a moment from his work.*) He sits at 'ome —quiet an' easy—an' runs nearly every big operation that's on. An' if there's a slip an' the police get wind of it there ain't never any 'old on 'im —they can't touch 'im—an' wot's more they wouldn't want to do it if they could.

MADGE. Why not?

PRINCE. Because they've *tried* it— that's w'y! An' the men as did try it was always found shortly after a-floatin' in the river—that is, if they was found at all! The moment a man's marked there ain't a street that's safe for 'im! No—nor yet an alley! (*Resumes drilling.*)

MADGE (*after pause*). How about him?

PRINCE. Square as a die an' liberal into the bargain!

MADGE. But this isn't such a big case. He might not want——

PRINCE (*turning to her*). I tell yer 'e'll take *anything* that gives him a chance at 'Olmes! He wants to trap 'im—that's what it is! an' that's just what 'e'll do! (*Resumes work.*)

(PRINCE *works rapidly, and the drill suddenly sinks through. He tries a few tools in it and quickly starts another hole.* MADGE *starts forward.*)

MADGE. Have you got it, Sid?

PRINCE. Not yet—but I'll be there soon. (*Works.*) I know where I am now.

(*Sound of door closing outside L. Enter* LARRABEE *hurriedly. He is breathless from running.*)

LARRABEE. Well, Sid! How goes it?

PRINCE. So-so (*working*).

LARRABEE. Now what about this Professor Moriarty? (*Gets a chair from near the piano and sits behind* PRINCE.)

PRINCE. Ask 'er (*working*).

MADGE. It's all right, Jim. It was the proper thing to do!

(MADGE *and* LARRABEE *move nearer* PRINCE, *looking over him eagerly.* PRINCE *quickly introduces a small punch and hammers rapidly. There is a sound of bolts falling inside the lock and the eagerness of all three increases.* PRINCE *pulls open the iron doors and all three look quickly within.* MADGE *and* LARRABEE *start back with subdued exclamations.* PRINCE *looks in more carefully, then turns to them. There is a pause, then* LARRABEE's *chair rasps along the floor.*)

MADGE. *Gone!*

LARRABEE. She's taken them out!

PRINCE. What do you mean? (*Rising to his feet.*)

LARRABEE. The girl!

(MADGE *goes quickly to the safe in front of* PRINCE *and, dropping down, feels carefully about inside. Their dialogue since the opening of the safe has dropped to low, excited tones, almost to whispers.*)

MADGE. She's got them! (*Rises and turns to* LARRABEE.)

PRINCE. 'Ow can you tell as she 'asn't done the trick *already?*

LARRABEE (*turns quickly to* PRINCE). What's that?

PRINCE. —An' sent 'em along to the girl 'e wants to marry!

MADGE. She hasn't had the chance.

LARRABEE. She couldn't get them out of this room. We've watched her too close for that.

MADGE. Wait! (*Turns and looks rapidly about the piano among the books and music.*)

(LARRABEE *crosses to* L. *and hurriedly looks about under the cushions.* PRINCE *raises the piano lid and looks inside.*)

LARRABEE. Here! (*Suddenly turning.*) I'll get her down! She'll tell us where she put them or strangle for it! Wait here! (*Exit at door up* L.)

PRINCE. Wot's 'e goin' to do?

MADGE. We've got to get it out of her or the whole two years' work is wasted.

(*Muffled cry of pain from* ALICE *in the distance.*)

PRINCE (*after a pause anxiously*). Look 'ere. I don't so much fancy this sort of thing. (*Goes to safe and collects tools.*)

MADGE. You don't have to worry—we'll attend to it! (*Sounds of* LARRABEE *approaching, then speaking angrily. He comes nearer and nearer. The footsteps are heard just before the entrance.* LARRABEE *pushes* ALICE FAULKNER *into the room, shoving her before him.*)

LARRABEE (*as he brings* ALICE *on*). Now we'll *see* whether you will or not! (*To* MADGE.) Tell her what we want!

ALICE (*in a low voice, with a slight shake of her head*). You needn't tell me. I know well enough.

MADGE (*drawing nearer to* ALICE *with a catlike glide and smiling*). Oh no, dear, you *don't* know! It isn't anything about locks or keys or numbers this time! (*Points slowly to the open safe.*) We want to know what you've *done* with them! (ALICE *looks at* MADGE *calmly; there is neither defiance nor suffering in her expression.* MADGE *comes closer and speaks with set teeth.*) Do you *hear*? We want to. know what you've done with them!

ALICE (*in a low voice but clearly and distinctly*). You will never know from me.

LARRABEE (*with sudden violence*). We *will* know from you—and we'll know before——

MADGE (*interrupting him with a gesture*). Wait, Jim!

LARRABEE (*to* MADGE *violently*). They're in this room—she couldn't have got them out—and I'm going to make her—— (*Turning as if to seize* ALICE.)

MADGE (*detaining him*). No! Let me speak to her first! (LARRABEE, *after an instant's sullen pause, turns and walks up stage. He stands watching them.* MADGE *turns to* ALICE *again.*) Don't you think, dear, it's about time to remember that you owe *us* a little consideration? Wasn't it something—just a little something that we found you friendless and ill in Homburg and befriended you?

ALICE. It was only to *rob* me!

MADGE. My dear *child*—you have nothing of value! That package of letters wouldn't bring sixpence——

ALICE. Then why do you want it?

LARRABEE (*who has controlled himself with difficulty*). No matter why we want it—(*he moves toward her*) —you're going to tell us what you've done with it before you leave this room tonight!   o

ALICE (*frightened but still calm*). Not if·you kill me!

LARRABEE (*seizing* ALICE *violently by the arms as he stands behind her*). It isn't *killing* that's going to do it— it's something else! (*He gets both her arms behind her and holds her as if wrenching or twisting them from behind.* ALICE *gives a slight cry of pain as* MADGE *comes toward her.* PRINCE *looks away, appearing not to like the scene, but he does not move.*)

MADGE (*in a sharp, hard voice*). Tell us where it is!

LARRABEE (*wrenching at* ALICE'S *arms*). Out with it!

ALICE (*moans*). Oh!

LARRABEE. I'll give you a turn next time that'll take it out of you!

MADGE (*in a low voice*). Be careful, Jimmie!

LARRABEE (*angrily*). I tell you we've got to get it out of her—and we'll do it too! (*Twisting.*) Will you tell! (*Twisting.*) Will you tell! (*Twisting.*) Will you—— (*There is a loud ringing of the doorbell in a distant part of the house.*)

PRINCE (*turns quickly, speaks in a short, sharp whisper*). Look out! (ALL *stand listening, except* ALICE, *who has heard nothing; the pain has made her faint although not unconscious.*)

LARRABEE (*to* MADGE *in a low, hoarse half-whisper*). See who it is! (*He quickly pushes* ALICE *into a chair facing the fireplace and stands before it.* MADGE *goes quickly to one side and cautiously draws a picture away from a small concealed window on the extreme left; she peers cautiously out. Steps are heard outside.* LARRABEE *turns quickly. The steps are slow and distinct but not loud.*) Here! (*Enter* FORMAN *at door* L. *He stands waiting.*) Don't go to that door!

(FORMAN *waits.* MADGE *turns and speaks in a low, clear voice.* LARRABEE *stands so that* FORMAN *will not see* ALICE.)

MADGE (*standing on ottoman*). Tall slim man in a long coat—soft hat —smooth face—carries a hunting crop—— (*There is a short quick exclamation from* PRINCE.)

PRINCE. That's 'im! *Sherlock 'Olmes!* (*Conceals his satchel and closes safe door.*)

LARRABEE. Here! Turn off the lights! (*Moving as if to do so.*) We won't answer the bell.

PRINCE (*stopping him quickly*). Now! that won't do, ye know! Looks crooked at the start!

(MADGE *moves quickly away from the window.*)

LARRABEE. You're right! We'll have him in—and come the easy innocent!

MADGE. Here's the girl!

LARRABEE. Take her up the back stairway!

(MADGE *takes* ALICE *quickly and forces her back to the door as they speak.*)

MADGE (*to* LARRABEE). She's in poor health and can't see anyone—*you understand!*

LARRABEE. Yes! Yes! Lock her in the room—and stay by the door! (MADGE *and* ALICE *quickly exit at door up C.* LARRABEE *opens lid of settle near fireplace and gets a loaded club—an ugly-looking weapon. He shoves it into* PRINCE's *hand.*) You get out at that terrace window! (*Indicating.*) Keep quiet till he gets into the house —then come round to the front.

PRINCE. I come round to the front after 'e's in the 'ouse—that's plain!

LARRABEE. Be ready for him when he comes out! If he's got the things in spite of us I'll give you a rap on the front window glass. If you don't hear it let him pass!

PRINCE. An' if I *do* 'ear it——?

LARRABEE. Let him have it! (PRINCE *gets out at window and closes it behind him.*) (*To* FORMAN.) Go on, answer the bell. (FORMAN *bows slightly and* ·*exits at door up L.* LARRABEE *stands near the piano, leaning on it carelessly. There are sounds of a heavy door closing outside, then a brief silence. Enter* SHERLOCK HOLMES *at door up L., his hat and stick in his hand. He wears a long coat and carries gloves. He lingers near the door, apparently seeing nothing in particular, then moves to a seat close at hand, not far from the door. There is an embarrassing silence. At length* LARRABEE *clears his throat and tosses his book* onto the piano. He saunters toward HOLMES *in rather an ostentatious manner and when close at hand bows.* HOLMES *does not look at him.*) Mr. Holmes, I believe?

HOLMES (*Rises slowly and turns to* LARRABEE *as if mildly surprised.*) Yes—quite so.

LARRABEE. Who did you wish to see, Mr. Holmes?

HOLMES. Oh, thank you so much! I *sent* my card—by the butler.

(LARRABEE *stands motionless for an instant.*)

LARRABEE (*after a pause*). Oh—very well. (*Turns and strolls away, then stands motionless. There is a long pause.*)

(*Enter* FORMAN *coming down the stairway and to the door.*)

FORMAN (*to* HOLMES). Miss Faulkner begs Mr. Holmes to excuse her. She is not well enough to see anyone this evening.

(LARRABEE's *gesture seems to say,* "*I could have told you so!*" HOLMES *quietly places his hat and stick on the couch and drops his gloves into his pocket. He removes his overcoat and adds it to the pile. Deliberately but rapidly he takes out a card and a pencil and writes, then glances at his watch and hands the card to* FORMAN.)

HOLMES. Hand this to Miss Faulkner and say that I have——

LARRABEE. I beg your pardon, Mr. Holmes, but it's quite useless— really!

(HOLMES *turns quietly to* LARRABEE *and looks at him.*)

HOLMES. Oh—I'm so sorry to hear it!

LARRABEE. Yes—Miss Faulkner is—I regret to say—quite an invalid. She is unable to see anyone—her health is so poor.

HOLMES. Has it ever occurred to you that she might be confined to the house too much? (*An instant's pause.*)

LARRABEE (*suddenly, in a low threatening tone*). How does that concern you?

HOLMES (*carelessly*). It doesn't—I simply make the suggestion. You might like to think it over.

(*The two look at one another for an instant.* HOLMES *turns quietly to* FORMAN.)

HOLMES. That's all. Go on! Take it up.

(*Exit* FORMAN *up stairway.* HOLMES *picks up a magazine from the seat and reads. After a moment* LARRABEE *turns, breaking into hearty laughter.*)

LARRABEE. Ha! Ha!—this is really too good! (*Strolling away still laughing.*) Why of *course* he can take up your card—or your note—or whatever it is, if you wish it so much! I was only trying to save you the trouble!

HOLMES (*who has been watching him*). Thanks—it's hardly any trouble at all to send up a card. (*Seats himself easily and resumes his reading.*)

LARRABEE (*endeavors to be easy, careless, and patronizing*). Do you know, Mr. Holmes, you interest me very much!

HOLMES (*looking up*). Oh, really?

LARRABEE. Upon my word, yes! We've all heard of your wonderful methods—(*coming towards* HOLMES) —and the astonishing manner in which you gain information from the most trifling details. Now I daresay—in this brief moment or two—you've discovered any number of things about *me!*

HOLMES. Nothing of consequence, Mr. Chetwood. I have scarcely more than asked myself why you rushed off and sent that telegram in such a frightful hurry—why your friend with the auburn hair left so suddenly by the terrace window—and what there can possibly be about the safe in the lower part of that desk to cause you such painful anxiety. (LARRABEE *stands motionless.* HOLMES *again picks up paper and reads.*)

LARRABEE (*laughs hollowly*). Ha! Ha!—Very good! Very* good indeed! If those things were only true now, I'd be wonderfully impressed! It would be absolutely—— (*Enter* FORMAN, *coming down stairway. He quietly crosses to* LARRABEE, *who is watching him, and extends salver with a note upon it.* LARRABEE *takes note.*) You'll excuse me, I trust. (HOLMES *remains silent, glancing over his paper and looking quietly at* FORMAN.) Ah—it's from—er—Miss Faulkner!—Well, really! She begs to be allowed to see you, Mr. Holmes.

She absolutely *implores* it! (HOLMES *looks slowly up as though scarcely interested.*) Well, I suppose I shall have to give way! (*Turns to* FOR-MAN.) Judson—ask Miss Faulkner to come down to the drawing room. Say that Mr. Holmes is waiting to see her. (FORMAN *bows and vanishes up the stairway.*) It's quite remarkable, upon my soul! May I ask —(*turns toward* HOLMES)—if it's not an impertinent question, what message you sent up that could have so aroused Miss Faulkner's desire to come down?

HOLMES (*looking up innocently*). Merely that if she wasn't down here in five minutes I'd go up.

LARRABEE (*slightly knocked*). Oh! Er—*that* was it!

HOLMES. Quite so. (*Rises.*) And unless I am greatly mistaken I hear the young lady on the stairs. In which case—(*looks at his watch*)—she has a minute and a half to spare. (*Taking the stage near the piano and seizing the opportunity to look at keys, music, etc.*)

(*Enter* MADGE LARRABEE, *coming down the stairway as if not quite strong. She has made her face pale and steadies herself by clinging to the furniture as she advances. She has changed into a white dress.*)

LARRABEE (*advancing*). Alice—er—that is, Miss Faulkner—let me introduce Mr. Sherlock Holmes.

MADGE. Mr. Holmes! (*Coming toward him with extended hand.*)

HOLMES. Ah! Miss Faulkner!

MADGE. I'm really most charmed to meet you, although it does look as if

you had made me come down in spite of myself, doesn't it?

HOLMES. I thank you very much indeed for consenting to see me, Miss Faulkner, but regret to observe that you were put to the trouble of making such a very rapid change of dress. (MADGE *gives the slightest possible start but recovers at once.*)

MADGE. Oh yes! I *did* hurry a trifle, I confess! (*Crosses toward* LARRA-BEE.) Mr. Holmes is quite living up to his reputation, isn't he, Freddie?

LARRABEE. Yes—but he didn't quite live up to it a moment ago!

MADGE. Oh, didn't he! I'm so sorry! (*Sits.*)

LARRABEE (*laughing*). He's been telling me the most astonishing things!

MADGE. And weren't they true?

LARRABEE. Well, hardly! He wanted to know what there was about the safe in the lower part of that desk that caused me such horrible anxiety! Ha! Ha! Ha!

MADGE. Why, there isn't *anything*.

LARRABEE. That's just it! Ha! Ha! (*With a quick motion swings back the doors.*) There's a safe there—but nothing in it! (MADGE *joins him in laughter.* HOLMES, *easily seated L. among the cushions, regards* MADGE *and* LARRABEE *with a whimsical look.*) Perhaps you'll do better next time, Mr. Holmes.

MADGE. Yes; next time you might try on *me*, Mr. Holmes! (*Looking playfully at* HOLMES *as if greatly enjoying the lark.*)

LARRABEE. Yes, what do you think of her?

HOLMES. It's very easy to . discern one thing about Miss Faulkner, and that is that she is particularly fond of the piano. While she likes light music very well, she is extremely fond of some of the great masters, among them Chopin, Liszt, and Schubert. She plays a great deal; indeed I see it is her chief diversion, which makes it all the more remarkable *that she has not touched the piano for three days!* (*There is a dead pause.*)

MADGE (*turning to* LARRABEE, *a trifle disconcerted, but nearly hiding it with success*). Why, that's quite surprising, isn't it?

LARRABEE. Certainly better than he did for me.

HOLMES (*rising*). I am glad to repair somewhat my shattered reputation, and as a reward, will Miss Faulkner be so good as to play me something of which I am particularly fond?

MADGE. I shall be delighted, if I *can!* (*Looks questioningly at* HOLMES.)

HOLMES. If you can! Something tells me that Chopin's Prelude No. 15 is at your finger ends. (LARRABEE *looks uneasy.*)

MADGE. Oh yes! (*Rising and forgetting her illness, she goes to the keyboard.*) I can give you that!

HOLMES. It would please me so much. (*He strolls toward her.*)

MADGE (*stopping suddenly as she is about to sit at the piano*). But tell me, Mr. Holmes, how did you know so much about my playing—the things I'm so fond of, I mean?

HOLMES. Your hands—and your music rack.

MADGE (*smiling*). How simple! But you said I hadn't played for three days! How did——

HOLMES. The keys.

MADGE. The keys?

HOLMES. A light touch of London's smoky atmosphere.

MADGE. Dust? Oh dear! (*She quickly rubs her handkerchief on the keyboard.*) I never knew Terese to forget before. (*To* HOLMES.) You must think us very untidy, I'm sure.

HOLMES. Quite the reverse, Miss Faulkner. I observe from many things that you are not untidy *in the least*; and therefore I am compelled to conclude that the failure of Terese is due to something else. (*He approaches the end of the piano.*)

MADGE (*a little under her breath and hesitatingly, yet compelled by* HOLMES's *pointed statement to ask*). Wh-what do you mean?

HOLMES. To some unusual excitement or disturbance that has recently taken place in this house.

MADGE (*after an instant's pause*). You're doing very well, Mr. Holmes —and you deserve your Chopin. (*Sits and makes hurried preparations to play in order to change the subject.*)

HOLMES. How kind you are!

(LARRABEE, *leaning on the piano, looks at the safe, far from easy in his mind.* MADGE *strikes a few preliminary chords and begins to play the composition asked for. Shortly after the music begins and while* LARRABEE *is looking elsewhere,* HOLMES *reaches quietly back and pulls the bell crank, then sinks into a seat. After a short time,* FORMAN *enters and stands waiting just within the door.* LARRABEE *does not see* FORMAN *at first, then he discovers him and speaks a warning word to* MADGE *under his breath.*)

LARRABEE. Madge! Madge! (MADGE *looks up and sees* FORMAN. *She stops playing in the midst of a phrase and looks at him. There is a peculiar pause.*)

MADGE. What are you doing here, Judson? (FORMAN *seems surprised.*)

FORMAN. I beg pardon, ma'am. I was answering the bell.

LARRABEE (*savagely*). What bell?

FORMAN. The drawing-room bell, sir.

LARRABEE. What do you mean, you blockhead? No one rang the bell.

FORMAN. I'm quite sure it rung, sir!

LARRABEE (*in a loud voice*). Well, I tell you it did *not* ring! (*The* LARRABEES *are looking angrily at* FORMAN.)

HOLMES (*after a slight pause, in a clear, incisive voice*). Your butler is right, Mr. Chetwood, the bell *did* ring.

(LARRABEE *and* MADGE *look at* HOLMES, *amazed.* MADGE, *after a short pause, rises slowly.*)

LARRABEE. How do you know?

HOLMES. I rang it.

LARRABEE (*roughly*). What do you want?

(HOLMES *rises quietly, taking a card from his pocket.*)

HOLMES. I want to send my card to Miss Faulkner. (*Gives card to* FORMAN, *who stands apparently paralyzed, but he mechanically presents the salver.*)

LARRABEE (*angrily approaching* HOLMES). What right have you to ring for servants and give orders in my house!

HOLMES (*turning on* LARRABEE *sharply*). What right have you to prevent my cards from reaching their destination? And how does it happen that you and this woman are resorting to trickery and deceit to prevent me from seeing Alice Faulkner? (*Turns quietly to* FORMAN.) Through some trifling oversight, Judson, neither of the cards I handed you has been delivered. Kindly see that this *error*—does not occur again.

(FORMAN *stands apparently uncertain what to do.*)

FORMAN. My orders, sir——

HOLMES (*sharply*). Ah! You have orders!

FORMAN. I can't say, sir, as I——

HOLMES (*interrupting*). You were told *not to deliver my card!*

LARRABEE. What business is this of yours, I'd like to know!

HOLMES (*wheeling quickly*). I shall satisfy your curiosity on that point in a *very short time.*

LARRABEE. Yes—and you'll find out in a very short time that it isn't safe to meddle with me! It wouldn't be any trouble at all for me to throw you out into the street!

HOLMES (*sauntering easily toward him and shaking his finger ominously*). Possibly not—but trouble would swiftly follow such an experiment on your part!

LARRABEE. It's a cursed lucky thing for you I'm not armed!

HOLMES (*wearily*). Yes—well, when Miss Faulkner comes down you can go and arm yourself.

LARRABEE. Arm myself! I'll call the police! And what's more, I'll do it now! (*Turns to go.*)

HOLMES (*with sudden intensity*). Oh no! You will *not* do it now! You will remain where you are until the lady I came here to see has entered this room!

LARRABEE. What makes you so sure of that?

HOLMES (*into* LARRABEE's *face*). Because you will prefer to avoid an investigation of your very suspicious conduct, Mr. James Larrabee— (LARRABEE *and* MADGE *start sharply*) —an investigation that shall certainly

take place if you or your wife presume further to interfere with my business. (*He turns to* FORMAN.) As for you, my man—it gives me pleasure to recall the features of an old acquaintance. Your recent connection with the signing of another man's name to a small piece of paper has made your presence at headquarters much desired. You will either deliver that card to Miss Faulkner at once—or you sleep in the police station tonight. It's a matter of small consequence to me which you do. (*Turns and strolls to the fire, picking up a book from the mantelpiece, and seats himself.*)

(FORMAN *stands motionless, torn with conflicting fears.*)

FORMAN (*in a low, painful voice*). Shall I—shall I go, sir?

LARRABEE. Go on. Take up the card —it makes no difference to me.

MADGE (*in a quick sharp aside to* LARRABEE). If she comes down, can't he get them away from her?

LARRABEE (*to* MADGE). If he does, Sid Prince is waiting for him outside.

(FORMAN *exits* q u i c k l y w i t h HOLMES's *card. There is a long pause during which no one moves. Enter* ALICE FAULKNER *at door up L. She comes down a little, very weak, looking at* LARRABEE *as she passes, then sees* HOLMES *for first time.* HOLMES *rises and puts his book on the mantel.*)

HOLMES (*after a brief pause turns and comes down to* LARRABEE). A short time since, you displayed an acute anxiety to leave the room. Pray do not let me detain you or your wife—*any longer.* (*The* LARRABEES *do not move.* HOLMES *shrugs slightly and goes over to* ALICE. *They regard each other a moment.*)

ALICE. This is Mr. Holmes?

HOLMES (*nodding*). Yes.

ALICE. You wished to see me?

HOLMES. Very much indeed, Miss Faulkner; but I am sorry to see that —(*placing a chair near her*)—you are far from well.

ALICE (LARRABEE *casts a quick glance across at her threateningly*). Oh, no—I—— (*Stops as she catches* LARRABEE'S *angry glance.*)

HOLMES. No? (*Pauses.*) I beg your pardon—but—(*goes to her and takes her hand delicately, looking at some red marks on the wrist*)—what does *this* mean?

ALICE (*shrinking a little*). Oh— nothing.

(HOLMES *looks steadily at her an instant.*)

HOLMES. Nothing?

ALICE (*shaking head*). No!

HOLMES. And the—(*pointing lightly*) —mark here on your neck—plainly showing the clutch of a man's fingers? (*Indicating.*) Does that mean nothing—also? (ALICE *turns slightly away without answering.*) It occurs to me that I should like to have an explanation of this. Possibly—(*turns slowly toward* LARRABEE)—you can furnish one, Mr. Larrabee!

LARRABEE (*doggedly*). How should I know?

HOLMES. It seems to have occurred in your own house.

LARRABEE (*becoming violently angry*). What if it did? You'd better understand that it isn't healthy for you or anyone else to interfere with my business.

HOLMES (*quickly, incisively*). Ah! Then it *is* your business! We have that much at least! (LARRABEE *stops suddenly, holding himself in.*) Pray be seated, Miss Faulkner.

(ALICE *hesitates an instant, then decides to remain standing.* LARRABEE *moves nearer and openly stands watching and listening to the interview between* HOLMES *and* ALICE.)

ALICE. I don't know who you are, Mr. Holmes, or why you are here.

HOLMES. I shall be very glad indeed to explain. So far as the question of my identity is concerned, you have my name and address, as well as the announcement of my profession, on the card—which I observe you still hold clasped tightly in the fingers of your left hand.

(ALICE *looks at the card in her hand.*)

ALICE. A—detective! (*Sinks slowly on the ottoman, looking at* HOLMES.)

HOLMES (*draws a chair near to her and sits*). Quite so. And my business is this: I have been consulted as to the possibility of obtaining from you certain letters, and other things, which are supposed to be in your possession, and which—I need not tell you—are , a source of the greatest anxiety. (ALICE *moves suddenly.*) I am able to assure you of the sincere penitence, the deep regret, of the one who inflicted the injury, and of his earnest desire to make—*any reparation* in his power.

ALICE. How can reparation be made to the dead?

HOLMES. How indeed! And for that very reason, whatever injury you yourself may be able to inflict by means of these—things—can be no reparation—no satisfaction—no indemnity to the one no longer here. You will be acting for the *living*—not the dead!—For *your own* satisfaction, Miss Faulkner—your *own* gratification—your own revenge!

(ALICE *starts slightly at the idea suggested. She rises and there is a brief pause.* HOLMES *rises also, moving back his chair.*)

ALICE (*in a low voice*). I know—from this—and from other things that have happened—that a—a marriage is—contemplated.

HOLMES (*inclines his head*). It is quite true.

ALICE (*slowly*). I *cannot* give up what I intend to do, Mr. Holmes. There are other things besides revenge—there is punishment! If I am not able to communicate with the family—to which this man proposes to ally himself—in time to prevent such a thing—the punishment will come later. But you may be perfectly sure that it will come! (*She motions for him not to speak.*) There is nothing more to say! (HOLMES *gives a sudden signal,*

thumping the back legs of his chair twice upon the floor.) Good night, Mr. Holmes! (*She turns and starts away.*)

HOLMES. But, my dear Miss Faulkner, before you—— (*There is a confused noise of shouting and terrified screams from below followed by sounds of people running up a stairway and through the halls.*) What's that? What's that? (ALL *stop and listen. The noise is louder.*) What's going on in your house here?

(*Enter* FORMAN *at door up L., running; he is breathless and white. A volume of smoke is now pouring in through the door.* HOLMES *is watching* ALICE *sharply.*)

FORMAN (*gasping*). Mr. Chetwood! Mr. Chetwood!

LARRABEE (*moving toward him*). What is it? Speak out!

(HOLMES *moves quietly up, keeping his eyes on* ALICE. ALICE *stands back alarmed.*)

FORMAN. The lamp! The lamp in the kitchen, sir! It fell off the table —and everything down there is *blazing*, sir!

ALICE. Oh! (*Looks quickly, in panic, to a chair in the center of the room, then moves toward it. Catching* HOLMES's *eye upon her, she checks herself and stands looking at him.*)

MADGE. The house is on fire! (*She gives an involuntary start and a glance toward the safe, forgetting that the package is gone, but instantly recovers and hurries toward the door.*)

(LARRABEE *with one bound exits at door,* MADGE *after him.* FORMAN *also disappears. There is a sound of people running downstairs. Then the noise grows less and ultimately dies away.* HOLMES *and* ALICE *stand looking at each other.*)

HOLMES. Don't alarm yourself, Miss Faulkner—(*with a slight shake of his head*)—there is no fire.

ALICE (*steps back, and her voice betrays that she fears something*). No fire! (*She stands dreading what may come.*)

HOLMES. The smoke was all I arranged for.

ALICE (*looks at* HOLMES *in alarm*). Arranged for? (HOLMES *moves quickly to the large upholstered chair.*) What does it mean, Mr. Holmes?°

(HOLMES *feels rapidly over the chair, then rips away the upholstery. With a cry* ALICE *attempts to stop him, but it is too late.* HOLMES *stands erect with a package in his hand.*)

HOLMES. That I wanted this package of letters, Miss Faulkner.

(ALICE *stands looking at* HOLMES, *speechless. Then suddenly she covers her face with her hands, crying.* HOLMES *steps quickly and in a businesslike way to the seat where his coat, hat, and stick are lying and picks up the coat, throwing it over his arm as if to go at once. As he is about to take his hat he catches sight of* ALICE'S *face and stops dead. He stands looking at her, motionless. She*

looks up, brushing her hand across her face as if to clear away any sign of crying. HOLMES'S *eyes leave her face; he glances downward. After a moment he lays his coat, hat, and stick back on the seat, pauses for an instant, then turns toward her.*)

HOLMES (*in a low voice*). I won't take them, Miss Faulkner. (*Her eyes are upon his face steadily.*) As you—(*still looking down*)—as you —very likely conjecture, the—alarm of fire was only to make you betray their hiding place—which you did. And I—availed myself of that betrayal—as you see. But now that I witness your great distress—I find that I cannot keep them—unless— (*looking up at her*)—you can—possibly—change your mind and let me have them—of your own free will. . . . (*He looks at her a moment. She shakes her head very slightly.*) I hardly supposed you could. I will therefore—return them to you. (*He is about to hand her the package when there is a sound of quick footsteps outside. Enter* LARRABEE *at door up L. with a revolver in his hand, followed by* MADGE.)

LARRABEE. So! You've got them, have you? Now I suppose we're going to see you walk out of the house with them! (*Handling his revolver with meaning.*)

(HOLMES *looks quietly at* LARRABEE *for an instant.*)

HOLMES (*shakes his head mildly*). On the contrary, you are going to see me return them to their rightful owner.

LARRABEE (*shaking revolver menacingly*). Yes—I think·that will be the safest thing for Mr. Sherlock Holmes to do!

(HOLMES *stops dead and looks at* LARRABEE, *then walks quietly down to face him.*)

HOLMES. You flatter yourself, Mr. Larrabee. The reason I do not leave the house with this package of papers is not because of you, or what you may do—or say—or think—or feel! It is on account of this young lady! (*Looks at revolver and smiles.*) *Really!* (*Turns and goes ·to* MISS FAULKNER.) Miss Faulkner, permit me to place this in your hands. (*Gives her the package.* ALICE *takes the package with sudden eagerness —then turns and keeps her eyes steadily on* HOLMES.) Should you ever change your mind and be so generous—so forgiving—as to wish to return these letters to the one who wrote them—you have my address. In any event, rest assured there will be no more cruelty, no more persecution in this house. You are perfectly safe with your property now—for I shall so arrange it that your faintest cry of distress will be heard! And if that cry *is* heard—it will be a very unfortunate thing for those who are responsible! Good night, Miss Faulkner. (ALICE *looks at* HOLMES *for an instant, uncertain what to do. After a slight pause she crosses in front of* HOLMES *and exits at door up* L. LARRABEE *makes a slight move toward* ALICE *as she passes him but is checked by a look from* HOLMES. HOLMES *waits, motionless, until* ALICE *has disappeared, then turns and takes up his coat and hat. He turns to* LARRABEE *and* MADGE.) As for you, sir, and you, madam, I beg you to understand that you continue your perse-cution of that young lady—*at your peril!* (*Looks at them for an instant.*) Good evening. (*Walks out at door up* L. *and the sound of heavy door opening and closing is heard outside.* LARRABEE *and* MADGE *stand where* HOLMES *left them.* SID PRINCE *hurries in at window up* R.)

PRINCE (*sharp, but subdued*). 'E didn't get it, did 'e? (LARRABEE *shakes head.* PRINCE *looks at him puzzled, then turns toward* MADGE.) Well—wot is it?—Wot's to pay if 'e didn't?

MADGE. He gave it to *her!*

PRINCE. *What!*—'E found it! (MADGE *indicates "yes" by a slight movement.*) An' gave it to the girl! (MADGE *repeats the slight affirmative motion.*) Well, 'ere—I say!— Wot are you waitin' for? Now's the chance—before she 'ides it again! (*Starting as if to go after the package himself.*)

MADGE. No!—Wait! (*Glances round nervously.*)

PRINCE. Wot's the matter? (*Going to* LARRABEE.) Do you want to lose it?

LARRABEE (*with a sudden turn*). No!—You're right! It's all a cursed bluff!

MADGE (*stops him*). No, no, Jim!

LARRABEE (*pushing her aside*). I tell you we will! Now's our chance to get hold of it! (*Moves toward stairway.*)

PRINCE (*following him*). Well, I should *say!* (*Just as* PRINCE *and*

LARRABEE *reach the door L. a distant sound reverberates through the house, as if three heavy blows had been struck against the floor from beneath.* ALL *stop motionless.*)

LARRABEE (*in a low voice*). What's that?

MADGE (*softly*). Someone at the door!

LARRABEE (*in the same low voice*). No—it was on that side! (*Indicating.*)

(PRINCE *glances round alarmed.* MADGE *rings bell and stands waiting. Enter* FORMAN *at door up C.* ALL *stand easily as if nothing out of the usual had occurred.*)

MADGE. I think someone knocked, Judson. (FORMAN *at once crosses quietly but quickly and exits at door L. Sound of door outside opening and closing again.* FORMAN *re-enters.*)

FORMAN. I beg pardon, ma'am, but there's no one at the door.

MADGE. That's all.

(*Exit* FORMAN *at door L.*)

PRINCE (*speaks almost in whisper*). 'E's got us *watched!* Wot we want to do is leave it alone an' let the H'emperor 'ave it!

MADGE (*in a low voice, taking a step towards* PRINCE). ·Do you mean—Professor Moriarty?

PRINCE (*gets his satchel*). That's 'oo I mean. Once let '*im* get at it an' 'e'll settle it with 'Olmes pretty quick! (*Turns to* LARRABEE.) Meet me at Leary's—nine sharp—in the morning. (*Looks at door L. and up stage R. quickly. Goes up R. and turns to them again.*) Don't you worry a minute! I tell you the Professor'll get at 'im before tomorrow night! 'E don't wait long either!—An' when 'e strikes—it means *death!* (*Exit* PRINCE *at window up R.*)

CURTAIN

ACT TWO

SCENE I

PROFESSOR MORIARTY'S *underground office, a large vaultlike room with rough masonry walls and vaulted ceiling. The general idea of the place is that it has been converted from a cellar room of a warehouse into a fairly comfortable office or headquarters. There are no windows. Maps and charts have been tacked as high up as someone could reach—a marked map of London and many charts of buildings. Books are visible on impoverished shelves—ledgers, railway guides, etc. The effect of this set is of masonry that has long ago been whitewashed and is now old, stained, and grimy.*

There is a large, solid-looking door, fitted with mechanical devices for opening, closing, and lowering, up L.C.

PROFESSOR ROBERT MORIARTY *is seated at a large circular desk up R. facing front. He is looking over letters, telegrams, papers: a middle-aged man with massive head, gray hair, and a face full of character; overhanging brow and heavy jaw. A man of great intellectual force. The room is dark but a light falls upon his face as if from a lamp.*

MORIARTY *rings a gong on his desk; it has a peculiar sound. In a second a buzzer outside door replies twice.* MORIARTY *picks up speaking tube and puts it to his mouth.*

MORIARTY (*speaking into tube in a low voice*). Number. (*He places tube to his ear and listens, then speaks into it again.*) Correct! (*Drops tube and moves a lever against wall; the bolt of a door slides back with a solid heavy sound.*)

(*Enter* JOHN *at door up L. noiselessly. He stands just within the door in the half-darkness.*)

MORIARTY. Has any report come in from Chibley?

JOHN. Nothing yet, sir.

MORIARTY. All the others are heard from?

JOHN. Yes sir.

MORIARTY. I was afraid we'd have trouble there. If anything happened, we lose Hickson—one of our best men. Send Bassick!

JOHN. Yes sir. (*A peculiar signal sounds from another electric buzzer outside.*) He's here now, sir!

(MORIARTY *touches a lever on his desk and a bolt slides back at side of door. Enter* BASSICK, *with a packet of papers which he places on desk. He is a solid-looking man of fine appearance—about forty—with* black hair and eyes. Strong and alert and a bit sinister. He goes at once to MORIARTY *at desk. At a gesture, he seats himself.*)

MORIARTY. Before we go into anything else, I want to refer to Davidson.

BASSICK. I've made a note of him myself, sir. He's holding back!

MORIARTY. Something like six hundred short on that last haul, isn't it?

BASSICK. Yes sir.

MORIARTY. Have him attended to. Craigin is the one to do it. (BASSICK *scratches a memorandum.*) And see that his disappearance is noticed; have it spoken of. That finishes Davidson. Now as to this Blaisdell matter——

BASSICK. The whole thing was a trap!—set and baited by an expert.

MORIARTY. But those letters and papers of instructions——

BASSICK (*shakes his head*). Manning has disappeared and the papers are gone!

MORIARTY (*with sudden vehemence*). Gone! (*After a moment he quiets down, holding his wrath in check.*) Sherlock Holmes a̐gain! (*Turns suddenly and savagely on* BASSICK.) Haven't I told you to get some line on him?

BASSICK. Every man on the force is working on it, sir!

MORIARTY (*more quietly*). That's bad for the Underwood trial.

BASSICK. I thought Shackelford was going to get a postponement.

MORIARTY. He found he was blocked!

BASSICK. Who could have done it?

(MORIARTY *turns and looks at* BASSICK, *his head vibrating from side to side, as if forcing him to speak the name.*)

MORIARTY. Say it yourself.

BASSICK. Sherlock Holmes!

(MORIARTY *nods slowly several times, his eyes still fixing* BASSICK.)

MORIARTY. Sherlock Holmes. (JOHN *and* BASSICK *look at* MORIARTY, *fascinated during the speech that follows.*) He's got hold of between twenty and thirty papers and instructions in as many different jobs —and some as to putting a man or two out of the way—and he's gradually completing chains of evidence that, if we let him go on, will reach to *me* as surely as the sun will rise. Reach to *me!—Ha!* (*Sneers.*) He's playing rather a dangerous game, Bassick! Inspector Wilson tried it seven years ago. Wilson is dead. Two years later Henderson took it up. We haven't heard anything of Henderson lately. *Eh?*

BASSICK (*shaking his head*). Not a thing, sir!

MORIARTY. Ha! (*Sneers.*) We'll see about that! This Holmes is rather a talented man but he doesn't realize that there isn't a street in London that'll be safe for him if I whisper his name to Craigin! I might even make him a little call myself —just for the satisfaction of it—(*his head swaying*)—just for the satisfaction of it! (BASSICK *watches* MORIARTY *with some anxiety.*) Baker Street, isn't it? His place—Baker Street—*eh?*

BASSICK. Baker Street, sir.

MORIARTY. We could make it safe. We could make it absolutely secure for three streets in every direction.

BASSICK. Yes sir, but——

MORIARTY. We could! We've done it over and over again elsewhere!—Police decoyed! Men in every doorway! (*Turns suddenly on* BASSICK.) Do this tonight—in Baker Street! At nine o'clock call his attendants out on one pretext and another and keep them out—you understand? I'll see this Sherlock Holmes myself. I'll give him a chance for his life. If he declines to treat with me—— (*He takes a savage-looking bulldog revolver from under the desk and examines it carefully, slowly placing it in his breast pocket. There is a peculiar ring of the telephone bell.* MORIARTY *gives a nod to* BASSICK, *who goes quickly to telephone and picks up earpiece.* MORIARTY *resumes his examination of papers on his desk.*)

BASSICK (*speaks into receiver and listens*). Yes—— Yes, Bassick—what name did you say? Oh, Prince, yes —put him on! (*Longer wait.*) Yes— I got your telegram, Prince, but I have an important matter on. You'll have to wait—— Who? (*Suddenly becomes very much interested.*) Where is he now?—Wait a minute! (*To* MORIARTY.) Here's something, sir! Sid Prince has come here with some job and he says he's got Holmes fighting against him.

MORIARTY (*turns quickly*). Eh? Ask him what it is—ask him what it is! (BASSICK *is about to speak through the telephone.*) Wait! Let him come in here! (BASSICK *turns in surprise.*)

BASSICK. No one sees you—no one knows you! That has meant safety for years!

MORIARTY. No one sees me now! You talk with him—I'll listen from the next room. (BASSICK *looks at him an instant, hesitatingly.*) This is *your office*—you understand? *Your office*—I'll be there!

BASSICK (*speaking into telephone*). Is that you, Prince?—Yes. I find I can't come out—but I'll see you here —in my office. What interest have they got? What's the name? (*Looks round at* MORIARTY.) He says there's two with him—a man and a woman named Larrabee. They won't consent to any interview unless they're present.

MORIARTY. Send them in!

BASSICK (*speaking into telephone*). Eh, Prince—ask Beads to come to the telephone—Beads—eh—— (*In a lower voice.*) Those people with Prince, do they seem to be all right? Well, take them out through the warehouse and down by the circu-lar stairway, then bring them here by the long tunnel—yes, here!— Look them over as you go along to see they're not carrying anything! —Yes. (*Hangs up and turns and looks at* MORIARTY.) I don't like this, sir!

MORIARTY (*rises*). Whether you like it or not, I must take every chance to find the weak spot—every chance! (*The peculiar electric buzzer rings three times, then twice.* MORIARTY *moves toward opening R. Turns at door.*) Your office, you understand, *your* office!

(BASSICK *takes* MORIARTY'S *place back of counter. Speaks in a low voice.*)

BASSICK. John!

JOHN (*in the same tone*). Yes sir.

BASSICK. There's a gang of people coming in here. You stand over there and keep your eye on them from behind. If you see anything suspicious drop your handkerchief. If it's the woman, pick it up—if it's the man, leave it on the floor. (*Three knocks are heard distinctly on the door.*)

JOHN. Yes sir. (*Goes.*)

(BASSICK *pushes lever across and the bolt slides back; the door slowly swings open. Enter* SID PRINCE, *followed by* MADGE *and* LARRABEE. *The door closes and the bolts slide back with a clang. At the sound of bolts* LARRABEE *looks round at the door, realizing that they are all locked within.* BASSICK *motions* MADGE *to a chair.* LARRABEE, *standing near her, is suspicious and does not like the look of the place.* BASSICK *sits behind the desk.*)

BASSICK. I understood you to say just now that you've got something with Sherlock Holmes against you.

PRINCE. Yes sir—we 'ave.

BASSICK. What is it?

PRINCE. Jim and Madge Larrabee 'ere, which I used to know in early days, they picked up a girl at 'Omburg, w'ere 'er sister 'ad been 'avin' a strong affair of the 'eart with a very 'igh young foreign nobs who promised to marry 'er—but the family stepped in and threw the whole thing down. 'E'd be'aved very bad to 'er, an' 'ad let 'imself out, an' written 'er letters an' given 'er rings an' tokens, ye see—and there was photographs too—an' as these various things showed as 'ow 'e'd deceived an' betrayed 'er, they wouldn't look nice at all considerin' of wot the young man was an' wot 'igh titles 'e was comin' into. So w'en this girl ups an' dies of it all, these letters an' things all falls into the 'ands of the sister, which is the one my friends 'ere 'as béen nursin' along, together with 'er mother.

BASSICK (to LARRABEE). Where have you had these people?

LARRABEE. In a house on the Norrington Road.

BASSICK. Your home?

LARRABEE. No, we took it for this job.

BASSICK. How long have you been there?

LARRABEE. Two years the fourteenth of next month.

BASSICK. And those letters and—other evidences of the young man's misconduct—when will they reach their full value?

(LARRABEE *is about to answer, but* PRINCE *jumps in quickly.*)

PRINCE. It's *now*, don't you see? It's *now!*—There's a marriage comin' on, an' there's been offers! An' the problem is to get the papers in our 'ands!

BASSICK. Where are they?

PRINCE. Why, the girl's got 'old of 'em, sir!

(BASSICK *turns for an explanation of this to* LARRABEE.)

LARRABEE. We had a safe for her to keep them in, supposing that when the time came we could open it. But the lock was out of order and we got Prince in to help us. He opened it last night and the package containing the things was gone.

BASSICK. What did you do?

PRINCE. Do!—I 'adn't any more than got the box open, sir, an' given one look in it when Sherlock 'Olmes rings the front-door bell!

BASSICK (*intent*). *There*—at your house?

LARRABEE. At my house.

BASSICK. He *didn't get those letters?*

LARRABEE. Well, he did get them, but he passed them back to the Faulkner girl.

BASSICK (*surprised*). Passed them back? What did that mean?

LARRABEE (*with a slight shrug of his shoulders*). There's another thing that puzzles me. There was an accident below in the kitch—a lamp fell off the table and scattered burning oil about; and the butler came running up the stairs yelling fire! We ran down there and a few buckets of water put it out.

(MORIARTY *suddenly appears at the door R. All look up in surprise and* BASSICK *hurriedly gives up his chair at the desk.* LARRABEE *and* MADGE *also stand.*)

MORIARTY. The first thing we must do is to get rid of your butler—not discharge him—*get rid of him.* (*To* BASSICK.) Craigin for that! *Today!* As soon as it's dark. Give him two others to help—Mr. Larrabee will send the man into the cellar for something—they'll be ready for him there. Doulton's van will get the body to the river. (MADGE *shudders slightly.*) It need not inconvenience you at all, madam. We do these things quietly. (BASSICK *is writing orders at the desk.* MORIARTY *addresses him.*) What's the Seraph doing?

BASSICK. He's on that Reading job tomorrow night.

MORIARTY. Put him on with Craigin today to help with that butler. (*To* LARRABEE.) But there's something else we want! Have you seen those letters—the photographs and whatever else there may be? Have you seen them? Do you know what they're like?

MADGE. I have, sir! I've looked them through carefully several times.

MORIARTY. Oh, you have! (*Sharply and at the same time admiringly.*) That is well! (*Takes her arm and leads her forward.*) Do you think you could make me a counterfeit set of these things and tie them up

so they will look precisely like the package this Holmes man held in his hand last night?

MADGE. I could manage the letters —but——

MORIARTY. If you can manage the *letters*, I'll send someone who can manage the rest—from your description. Bassick—that old German artist—eh?

BASSICK. Leuftner?

MORIARTY. Precisely! Send Leuftner to Mrs. Larrabee at eleven. (*Looks at his watch.*) A quarter past ten —that gives you three quarters of an hour to reach home. I shall want that counterfeit package at eleven tonight—twelve hours to make it!

MADGE. I'll have it ready, sir!

MORIARTY. Bassick—notify the Lascar that I may require the Gas Chamber at Stepney tomorrow night —and have Craigin there at a quarter before twelve with his crew. Mr. Larrabee, I shall want you to write a letter to Mr. Sherlock Holmes, which I shall dictate—and tomorrow night I may require a little assistance from you both. (*Taking in* PRINCE *with his glance.*) Meet me here at eleven.

LARRABEE. This is all very well, sir, but you have said nothing about— the business arrangements. I'm not sure that I——

MORIARTY (*turning sharply*). You have no choice.

LARRABEE. No choice!

MORIARTY. No choice. *No choice! No choice!!!* (PRINCE *is aghast.*) I do what I please! It pleases me to take hold of this case!

LARRABEE (*angry*). Well, what about pleasing me? (BASSICK *moves toward* MORIARTY *and looks across at* LARRABEE.)

MORIARTY (*speaks in* LARRABEE'S *face*). I am not sure but that I shall be able to do that as well. I will obtain the original letters from Miss Faulkner and negotiate them for much more than you could possibly obtain. In addition—you will have an opportunity to sell the counterfeit package to Holmes for a good round sum. And the money obtained from both these sources shall be divided between us as follows: You will take one hundred per cent and I—nothing!

LARRABEE (*astounded*). *Nothing!*

MORIARTY. Nothing.

BASSICK. But we cannot negotiate those letters until we know who they incriminate. Mr. Larrabee has not yet informed us.

MORIARTY. Mr. Larrabee—(LARRABEE *looks round*)—is wise in exercising caution. But he will consent to let me know.

(LARRABEE *looks at* MADGE. *He is disturbed.*)

MADGE (*going to* MORIARTY). Professor Moriarty, that information we would like to give—only to you.

MORIARTY (*handing her a card and pencil from the desk*). Write the name on that card. (*She writes and gives him back the card. He glances at the name and looks at* LARRABEE *and* MADGE, *astonished.*) This is an absolute certainty?

LARRABEE. Absolute.

MORIARTY. It means that you have a fortune. (PRINCE *drinks in every word and look.*) Had I known this, you should hardly have had such terms.

LARRABEE. Oh well—we don't object to a——

MORIARTY (*interrupting*). The arrangement is made, Mr. Larrabee! —I bid you good morning! (*Bowing with dignity and pulling back the lever.*)

(LARRABEE, PRINCE, *and* MADGE *move toward the door as the bolts slide back.* BASSICK *motions to* JOHN, *who stands ready to conduct the party.* ALL *bow a little and exit at door L.C. followed by* JOHN. BASSICK *turns at door and looks at* MORIARTY.)

MORIARTY. Bassick, place your men at nine tonight, for Sherlock Holmes' house in Baker Street.

BASSICK. You will still go there *yourself*, sir?

MORIARTY. I will still go there myself!

BASSICK. But this meeting tomorrow night, sir! To get him in the Gas Chamber!

MORIARTY. If I fail to kill him in Baker Street, we'll have him in Swandem Lane. Either way I have him, Bassick! Two strings to our bow—two strings—eh, Bassick? (*His evil grin is almost the last thing visible as the lights fade and vanish.*)

DARK CHANGE

ACT TWO

SCENE II

SHERLOCK HOLMES'S *rooms in Baker Street, the large drawing room of his apartments. An open, cheerful room, not too much decorated. The furniture is comfortable and good but not elegant. Easy chairs, books, music, violins, tobacco pouches, pipes, tobacco, etc., are scattered about the room in some disorder. Various odd things hang on the walls, including some choice pictures in plain wooden frames. All is rather simple; the room has more the appearance of an artist's studio than a parlor. Some chests covered with rugs, and on shelves a number of lacquered tin boxes for documents. A wide door up right side to hall (and thus by stairway to street door). Door up L. communicating with bedroom or dining room. A fireplace down or half down left side with cheerful grate fire burning and throwing a red glow into room. The mantelpiece is littered with pipes, tobacco, and various knickknacks. Up L. a table with chemicals and chemical apparatus; shelves with phials above it. A big bay window up C. with window seats and cushions. Street lights outside. A blue spirit flame is burning under a glass retort on the chemical table up L. A large round table down stage near C. Cigarettes, matches, etc., on this table; also alarm bell. Books, papers, and writing materials are on the table.*

SHERLOCK HOLMES *is discovered seated among the cushions on the floor before the fire at L.C. He is in dressing gown and slippers and is smoking his pipe. He has pulled up a lounge in back of him and leans against it. A violin leans against the lounge and a bow has recently been laid down. He sits smoking awhile in deep thought.*

Enter BILLY *the pageboy at door up R.*

BILLY. Mrs. 'Udson's compliments, sir, an' she wants to know if she can see you?

HOLMES (*without moving*). Where is Mrs. Hudson?

BILLY. Downstairs in the back kitchen, sir.

HOLMES. My compliments and I don't think she can—from where she is

BILLY. She'll be very sorry, sir.

HOLMES. Our regret will be mutual.

BILLY (*hesitating*). It was most terrible important, sir, bein' as she wants to know what you'll 'ave for your breakfast in the mornin'.

HOLMES. The same.

BILLY. Same as when, sir?

HOLMES. This morning.

BILLY (*pause of astonishment*). You didn't 'ave *nothink*, sir—you wasn't 'ere!

HOLMES. I won't be here tomorrow.

BILLY. Yes sir. Was that all, sir?

HOLMES. Quite so.

BILLY. Thank you, sir. (*Exits at door up R. After a long pause the doorbell rings. Re-enter* BILLY.) It's Dr. Watson, sir.

HOLMES. What! (*He leans over as if to rise.*)

BILLY. You told me as I could always show 'im up.

HOLMES. Well! I should think so. (*He scrambles to his feet, bringing a cushion with him which he tosses onto the lounge.*)

BILLY. Yes sir—thank you, sir!—Dr. Watson, sir!

(*Enter* DR. WATSON *at door up R.* BILLY *is grinning with pleasure as he passes in.* BILLY *exits up R.*)

HOLMES (*cordially and affectionately*). Ah, Watson, my dear fellow! (*Shaking hands.*)

WATSON. How are you, Holmes?

HOLMES. I'm delighted to see you—perfectly delighted, upon my word I am—but—— (*Stops suddenly and looks him over with assumed sympathy.*) Oh! I'm so sorry to observe that your wife has left you in this way!

WATSON (*laughing*). Ha! Ha! She *has* gone on a little visit—(*tosses coat and hat down on lounge*)—but how did you know?

HOLMES. How did I—— Well, I like that! (*Goes to chemical table and puts spirit lamp out.*) How did I know! How do I *know anything?* (*Sniffs.*) How do I know that you've opened an office and resumed the practice of medicine—without letting me hear a word about it? How do I know you've been getting yourself very wet lately—that you have an extremely careless servant girl—and that you've moved your dressing table to the other side of your room? (*He puffs at his pipe as he talks.*)

WATSON (*looks at* HOLMES *in astonishment*). Holmes, if you'd lived a few centuries ago, they'd have burned you alive! (*Sits in chair R. of table and prepares to light a cigar.*)

HOLMES. Such a conflagration would have saved me a great deal of trouble and expense. (*He pretends to tidy up the room.*)

WATSON (*crossing his legs*). Tell me now, how *did* you know all that?

HOLMES (*gestures*). Ho! Too simple to talk about! (*Pointing at* WATSON's *shoe.*) Scratches and clumsy cuts, my dear fellow—on the inner side of your shoe there—just where the firelight strikes it. Scratches! Cuts! Somebody scraped away crusted mud—and did it badly—*badly!* Scraped the shoe along with it. There's your wet feet and your careless servant all on one shoe! Face badly shaved on right side—always used to be on left—light must come from other side—couldn't very well move your window—must have moved your dressing table. (*Sits on edge of table for a moment, then strolls to mantel and comes back with a hypodermic syringe in its case.*)

WATSON. Yes—but my medical practice—I don't see how you——

HOLMES (*placing syringe on table*). Now, Watson! How perfectly absurd of you—*absurd!*—to come stumping in here fairly reeking with the odor of iodoform, and with the black mark of nitrate of silver on the forefinger of your right hand, and ask me how I know——

WATSON (*interrupting with a laugh*). Ha, ha! Of course! But how the deuce did you know my wife was away and——

HOLMES. Where the deuce is your second waistcoat button, and what the deuce is yesterday's boutonniere doing in today's lapel—and why the deuce do you wear the expression of a——

WATSON. Ha, ha, ha!—Marvelous!

HOLMES. Elementary, my dear fellow! Elementary! The child's play of deduction! I'm only doing it for your amusement. (*Opens the case and takes out the syringe. Carefully adjusts the delicate needle and fills it from the phial. Rolls back left shirt cuff a little. Pauses, looking at wrist. Throughout this action he continues to speak.*) Sometimes we apply these principles to more serious matters but then we have to be a little more careful with our guessing or we'd get into trouble! (*Inserts needle in arm.*) Sometimes we get into trouble anyway——

(WATSON *has watched him with an expression of anxiety and disapproval but with an effort has restrained himself from speaking.*)

WATSON (*finally speaks*). Which is it today? Cocaine or morphine?

HOLMES. Cocaine, my dear fellow; I'm back to my old love! A seven-per-cent solution. (*Offering syringe and phial.*) Would you like to try some?

WATSON (*emphatically*). Certainly not!

HOLMES (*as if surprised*). Oh! I'm so sorry!

WATSON. I have no wish to break my system down before its time.

HOLMES. Quite right, my dear fellow—quite right! But you see my time has come! (*Replaces case, then throws himself languidly onto the sofa, leaning back in luxurious enjoyment of the drug.*)

WATSON. Holmes, for months I have seen you using these deadly drugs in ever-increasing doses. When they once lay hold of you there is no end! It must go on and on and on—until the finish!

HOLMES (*dreamily*). So must you go on and on eating your breakfast—until the finish.

WATSON (*approaching and laying a hand on* HOLMES'S *shoulder*). Ah, Holmes—I'm trying to save you!

HOLMES (*smiles and immediately is serious*). You can't do it, old fellow —so don't waste your time. (WATSON *turns away dejectedly, resumes his seat.*) Watson, my dear fellow

—to change the subject a trifle! In the enthusiasm which has prompted you to chronicle, and, if you will excuse my saying so, to somewhat embellish a few of my little—er—adventures, you have occasionally seen fit to introduce a certain element of romance which struck me as being *just a trifle*—out of place! Something like working an elopement into the fifth proposition of Euclid. I merely refer to this in case you should see fit at some future time—to chronicle the most important and far-reaching piece of work in my entire career—the case of Professor Robert Moriarty.

WATSON. Moriarty? I don't remember ever having heard of the fellow!

HOLMES (*emphasizing his words with a violin bow*). The Napoleon of crime! Sitting motionless like an ugly venomous spider in the center of his web—but that web having a thousand radiations and the spider knowing every quiver of every one of them. And within forty-eight hours we'll have the lines drawn so tightly around him that he can't move! We'll arrest him and his entire gang!

WATSON. Why, Holmes, this is a very dangerous thing! (*Rises.*)

HOLMES. My dear fellow, it's perfectly delightful! My whole life is spent in a series of frantic endeavors to escape from the dreary commonplaces of existence. For a brief period I escape. You should congratulate me.

WATSON. But you could escape them without such serious risks! Your other cases have not been so dangerous and they were even more interesting! Now the one you spoke of the last time I saw you—the recovery of those damaging letters and gifts from a young girl who—— (HOLMES *suddenly rises and stands motionless.* WATSON *looks at him surprised.*) A most peculiar affair, as I remember it. You were going to try the experiment of making her betray their hiding place by an alarm of fire in her own house—and after that——

HOLMES. Precisely—after that!

WATSON. Didn't the plan succeed?

HOLMES (*shortly*). Yes—as far as I've gone.

WATSON (*seats himself in armchair*). You got Forman into the house as butler?

HOLMES (*nods*). Yes, Forman was in as butler.

WATSON. And upon your signal he overturned a lamp in the kitchen, scattered the smoke balls, and gave an alarm of fire! (HOLMES *nods.*) And the young lady—did she——

HOLMES (*interrupting*). Yes, she did, Watson! The young lady did. It all transpired precisely as I planned. She betrayed the hiding place, in her fright, and I took the packet of papers and—handed it back to Miss Faulkner.

WATSON. But why did you hand it back after going to all that trouble to get it?

HOLMES. For the very simple reason, my dear Watson, that it would have been theft for me to keep it. The contents of the packet are the absolute property of the young lady. My only chance is to induce her to give me the package of her own free will. Its return to her after I had laid hands on it was the first move in this direction. The second will depend upon what transpirés today. I expect Forman to report here in half an hour. (*There is a light hurried step outside, then a short, quick knock at the door. Enter* TERESE *at door up* R. *in great haste and excitement.*)

TERESE. I beg you to pardon me, sir; ze boy he say to come right up as soon as I come!

HOLMES. Quite right! Quite right!

TERESE. Ah! I fear me zere ees trouble. Messieur—ze butlair—your asseestant—ze one who sent me to you——

HOLMES. Forman?

TERESE. Heem! *Forman!* Zere ees somesing done to heem! I fear to go down and see.

HOLMES (*clutching her shoulder*). Down where?

TERESE. Ze *down!* Ze cellaire of zat house! Oh, eet ees a dreadful place. He deed not come back. He went down—he deed not return.

(HOLMES *springs to the table and rings the bell. He pulls open a drawer and takes out a revolver. After a quick glance at it slides it into his hip pocket at the same time unfastening his dressing gown. He takes out a second revolver and puts it on the table.*)

HOLMES. Who sent him down?

TERESE. M'sieur of ze house! M'sieur Chetvood!

HOLMES. Larrabee!

TERESE. Yes.

HOLMES. Has he been down there long?

TERESE. No, for I soon suspect! Ze dreadful noise was heard—*oh!* (*Covers her face.*) Ze noise! Ze noise!

HOLMES. *What noise?* (*Seizes her arm.*) Here, here—look at me! What did it sound like?

TERESE. Ze dreadful cry of a man who eez struck down by some deadly seeng!

(*Enter* BILLY.)

HOLMES. Billy! Coat! Boots! Order a cab! Quick!

BILLY (*darting off at door up* L.). Yes sir.

HOLMES (*to* TERESE). Now answer me! Did anyone follow him down?

(BILLY *is back in a few seconds.*)

TERESE. I did not see.

HOLMES. Don't wait, Billy. The cab! (BILLY *shoots off at door up* R.) Take this, Watson, and come with me. (*Handing him a revolver.*)

TERESE. I had not better go also?

HOLMES. No, no! Great God, no! We don't want *you!* Wait here. (*Hurried footsteps are heard outside.*) Ha! I hear Forman coming now.

(*Enter* FORMAN *up* R.)

TERESE (*under her breath*). Ah!

FORMAN (*in matter-of-fact tones*). Nothing more last night, sir. After you left, Prince came in and they made a start for her room to get the package away; but I gave the three knocks with an axe on the floor beams, as you directed, and they didn't go any further. This morning, a little after nine——

HOLMES. One moment.

FORMAN. Yes sir!

HOLMES (*quietly turns to* TERESE). Mademoiselle—step into that room and rest yourself.

TERESE (*who has been deeply interested.*) I am not tired, monsieur.

HOLMES. Step in and walk about then. I'll let you know when you are required.

TERESE (*after an instant's pause*). Oui, monsieur. (*Exit* TERESE *at door down* R. HOLMES *quietly closes the door after her, then turns to* WATSON, *but remains at the door with right ear alert to catch any sound from within.*)

HOLMES. Take a look at his head, Watson. (*Listens at door.*)

FORMAN. It's nothing at all.

HOLMES (*coming back*). Take a look at his head, Watson.

WATSON. An ugly bruise—but not dangerous (*examining head*).

HOLMES. Ah—very well—a little after nine, you say——

FORMAN. Yes sir. This morning, a little after nine, Larrabee and his wife drove away in a four-wheeler. She returned about eleven without him—a little later old Leuftner came and the two went to work at something in the library. I got a look at them from the outside and found they were making up a *counterfeit of the package we're working for!*

HOLMES. *Counterfeit?*—Good thing! —I think I can use that. And Larrabee—what of him?

FORMAN. He came back a little after three.

HOLMES. How did he seem?

FORMAN. Under great excitement, sir!

HOLMES. Any marked resentment toward *you?*

FORMAN. I think there was, sir— though he tried not to show it!

HOLMES. Ah! Tried not to show it! They've consulted someone outside. In fact I'm inclined to think they've taken in a partner, and a dangerous one, at that! It was on his advice they sent you down into the coal cellar, where you doubtless had a bit of a fight.

FORMAN. That's what I did, sir.

(*Enter* BILLY *with a letter.*)

HOLMES. It was fortunate that you got away alive. (*Perceives* BILLY *approaching.*)

BILLY. Letter, sir! Most important, sir!

HOLMES (*passes letter lightly beneath his nose*). Read it, Watson, there's a good fellow—my eyes, you know—cocaine, and all those things you like so much. (WATSON *takes letter and goes to lamp as* HOLMES *drops onto the ottoman among the cushions.*)

WATSON. "Dear Sir."

HOLMES. Who—thus—addresses me?

WATSON (*glances at signature*). "James Larrabee."

HOLMES (*whimsically*). And what has James to say this evening?

WATSON (*repeats*). "Dear Sir."

HOLMES. I hope he won't say that again.

WATSON. "I have the honor to inform you that Miss Faulkner has changed her mind regarding the letters, etc., which you wish to obtain and has decided to dispose of them for a monetary consideration. She has placed them in my hands for this purpose and if you are in a position to offer a good round sum and to pay it down at once in cash the entire lot is yours. If you wish to negotiate, however, it must be tonight, at the house of a friend of mine in the city. At eleven o'clock you will be at the Guards Monument at the foot of Waterloo Place. You will see a four-wheeler with wooden shutters to the windows. Enter it and the driver will bring you to my friend's house. If you have the cab followed or try any other underhand trick you won't get what you want. Let me know your decision. Yours truly, James Larrabee."

(HOLMES, *during the reading of the letter, begins to write something in a leisurely way. Light of fire upon him—on his left—as he writes.*)

HOLMES. H'm! Mine truly. Well, later perhaps!

WATSON. What does the fellow mean?

HOLMES. The fellow means to sell me a base imitation—for a large sum of money. Now see if I have the points. Tonight—eleven o'clock—Guards Monument—cab with wooden shutters. No one to come with me. No one to follow—or I don't get what I want.

WATSON. Quite right.

HOLMES. Ah!

WATSON. But this cab with the wooden shutters——

HOLMES. Merely a little device to keep me from seeing where they are taking me. Billy!

BILLY. Yes sir.

HOLMES (*hands him a letter*). Give this to the man—and——

BILLY. It was a woman, sir.

HOLMES (*withdraws letter*). Ah!— Young or old?

BILLY. Looked quite young, sir.

HOLMES. Hansom?

BILLY. Four-wheeler, sir!

HOLMES. Seen the driver before?

BILLY. Yes sir—but I can't think w'ere.

HOLMES (*rising*). Hand this to the lady—apologize for the delay—and *look at the driver again!*

BILLY. Yes sir. (BILLY *exits at door up R.*)

WATSON. But, my dear Holmes— you didn't say you would *go!*

HOLMES. But I certainly did! (*Moves toward door R.*) Oh—mademoiselle! Mademoiselle! (*Pushes door open and beckons.*) One moment, if you please.

WATSON. But this fellow means mischief!

(*Enter* TERESE *at door R.*)

HOLMES (*touching himself lightly*). This fellow means the same! (*To* TERESE.) Be so good, mademoiselle, as to listen to every word. Tonight at twelve o'clock I meet Mr. James Larrabee and purchase from him the false bundle of letters to which you just now overheard us refer as you were listening at the keyhole of that door.

TERESE (*slightly confused but staring blankly*). Oui, monsieur.

HOLMES. I wish Miss Faulkner to know *at once* that I propose to buy this package tonight.

TERESE. I will tell her, monsieur.

HOLMES. That is my wish. But do *not* tell her that I know this packet and its contents to be counterfeit. She is to suppose that I think I am buying the genuine.

TERESE. Oui, monsieur. When you purchase you think you have the *real!*

HOLMES. Quite so! (*Moving toward door with her.*) Oh, one thing more! *Tomorrow* evening I shall want you to accompany her to this place— here. However, you will receive further instructions as to this in the morning.

TERESE. Oui, monsieur. (*Exits at door up R. as* HOLMES *bows her out.*)

HOLMES (*sharply*). Forman!

FORMAN. Yes sir.

HOLMES. Change to your beggar disguise No. 14 and go through every place in the Riverside District. Don't stop till you get a clue to this new partner of Larrabee's. I *must* have it!

FORMAN. Very well, sir.

(*Enter* BILLY *at door up R.*)

BILLY. If you please, sir, there's a man a-waitin' down at the street door—an' 'e says 'e must speak to Mr. Forman, sir, as quick as 'e can.

(HOLMES *stops suddenly and stands motionless.*)

HOLMES (*after a pause*). I think we'd better have a look at that man. Billy, show him up.

BILLY. 'E can't come up, sir—'e's a-watchin' of a man in the street. 'E says 'e's from Scotland Yard.

(HOLMES *is suspicious.*)

FORMAN (*going toward door*). I'd better see what it is, sir.

HOLMES No! (FORMAN *stops.* HOLMES *stands motionless a moment.*) Well, take a look at him first. *Be ready for anything!*

FORMAN. Trust me for that, sir! (*Exits.*)

HOLMES. See what he does, Billy.

BILLY. Yes sir. (*Exits after* FORMAN.)

(HOLMES *stands an instant thinking.*)

WATSON. This is becoming interesting! (*He goes to door and listens, then moves to window and glances down into the street.*) Look here, Holmes, you've been so kind as to give me a halfway look into this case——

HOLMES. One moment, my dear fellow! (*Rings bell. After slight wait enter* BILLY *at door up* R.) Mr. Forman—is he still there?

BILLY. No sir—'e's gone.

HOLMES. That's all.

BILLY. Yes sir. Thank you sir. (*Exits.*)

HOLMES. As you were saying, Watson, this strange case—of——

WATSON. Of Miss Faulkner.

HOLMES (*abandoning further anxiety and giving attention to* WATSON). Precisely! This strange case of Miss Faulkner.

WATSON. You've given me some idea of it—but I would certainly like to know what you propose to do with that counterfeit package which you are going to risk your life to obtain!

HOLMES. I intend with the aid of the counterfeit to make her willingly hand me the genuine. I shall accomplish this by a piece of trickery and deceit of which I am heartily ashamed—and which I would never have undertaken if I—if I had known her—as I do now. It's too bad! She's—she's rather a nice girl, Watson. (*Crosses to mantel and gets his pipe.*)

WATSON (*following* HOLMES *with his eyes*). Nice girl, is she? Then you think that possibly——

(*Enter* BILLY *quickly at door up* R.)

BILLY. I beg pardon, sir, Mr. Forman's just sent over from the chemist's on the corner to say 'is 'ead is a-painin' 'im a bit, an' would Dr. Watson kindly step over an' get 'im somethin' to put on it.

WATSON (*moving at once toward door*). Yes—certainly! I'll go at once! (*Picking up hat off sofa.*) That's singular!—It didn't look like anything serious! (*At door.*) I'll be back in a minute, Holmes! (*Exits.*)

HOLMES. Billy!

BILLY. Yes sir!

HOLMES (*lighting his pipe*). Who brought that message from Forman?

BILLY. Boy from the chemist's, sir.

HOLMES. Yes, of course! But *which* boy?

BILLY. Must a been a new one, sir —I ain't never seen 'im before.

HOLMES (*snatching his pipe from his mouth*). Billy! Get downstairs *quickly* and look after the doctor! If the boy's gone and there's a man with him, it means mischief! Let me know! Don't stop to come up; ring the doorbell! I'll hear it! Ring it *loud*!

BILLY. Yes sir! (*Exits quickly at door up R.* HOLMES *waits motionless a moment, listening. After a moment he relights his pipe. Suddenly there is a loud ring of the bell followed by a muffled shout from* BILLY.) Look out, sir! Look out! (*A door slams.*)

(HOLMES *seizes his revolver from the table and slips it into the pocket of his dressing gown, with his hand still clasping it. He at once assumes an easy attitude but keeps his eyes on the door. Enter* MORIARTY *at door up R. He stands just within the doorway and looks fixedly at* HOLMES. *His right hand is behind him.*)

MORIARTY (*in a quiet voice*). It is a dangerous habit to finger loaded firearms in the pocket of one's dressing gown.

HOLMES. I give you my word you'll be taken from here to the hospital if you keep your hand behind you like that! (*After a slight pause* MORIARTY *slowly takes his hand from behind his back and holds it with the other in front.*) That's better! In that case, the table will do quite as well. (*Places his revolver on the table.*)

MORIARTY. You evidently don't know me.

HOLMES (*with slight motion toward the revolver*). I think it quite evident that I *do!* Pray have a chair, Professor (*indicating*). I can spare you five minutes—if you have anything to say.

(MORIARTY *moves his right hand as if to take something from inside his coat but stops instantly as* HOLMES *covers him with the revolver.*)

HOLMES. What were you about to do?

MORIARTY. Look at my watch.

HOLMES. I'll tell you when your five minutes is up.

(MORIARTY *slowly pulls away a woolen muffler from his throat and stands again with his hands before him.*)

MORIARTY. It is your intention to pursue this case against me?

HOLMES (*nods*). That is my intention—to the very end.

MORIARTY. I regret this—not so much on my own account—but on yours.

HOLMES. I share your regret, Professor, but solely because of the rather uncomfortable position it will cause you to occupy.

MORIARTY. May I inquire to what position you are pleased to allude, Mr. Holmes? (HOLMES *takes his pipe from his mouth with his left hand and moves the stem in a circular motion close to his neck. He jerks his head in a shocking suggestion of a hanged man.*) And have you the faintest idea that you would be permitted to *live to see that day?* (MORIARTY's *eyes are blazing with anger.*)

HOLMES. As to that I do not particularly care—so that I bring *you* to see it!

MORIARTY (*passionately*). *You will never bring me to see it! You will find——* (*He stops, recollecting himself, and speaks in a quieter tone.*) You are a bold man, Mr. Holmes, to insinuate such a thing to my face; but it is the boldness born of ignorance. (*He is again stopped with his hand close to his breast pocket by* HOLMES's *revolver, but passes the matter off by feeling for his muffler, as if adjusting it.*) You'll never bring me to see it, you'll never bring me to see it! (*Slowly seats himself.*) Do you think that I would be here if I had not made the streets *quite safe in every respect?*

HOLMES (*shaking his head*). I could never so grossly overestimate your courage as that!

MORIARTY. Do you imagine that your friend the doctor and your man Forman will soon return?

HOLMES. Possibly not.

MORIARTY. So—it leaves us quite alone—doesn't it, Mr. Holmes? Quite alone—so that we can talk the matter over *quietly* and not be disturbed. In the first place I wish to call your attention to a few memoranda which I have jotted down—(*suddenly putting both hands to his breast pocket*) —which you will find——

HOLMES. *Look out!* Don't do that! Put your hands down—*quickly!*

(*Cheerfully.*) A little farther away from that memorandum book you are talking about!

MORIARTY (*slowly lowers his hands*). I was merely about to take out a small notebook.

HOLMES. Well, merely don't do it! I don't want it. I've got one of my own. If you want it we'll have someone get it for you. (*Rings bell on table with left hand.*) I always like to save my guests unnecessary trouble.

MORIARTY (*after quite a pause*). I observe that your boy does not answer the bell.

HOLMES (*puffing now at his pipe*). No—but I have an idea that he *will* before long.

MORIARTY (*leaning towards* HOLMES *significantly*). It may possibly be longer than you think, Mr. Holmes!

HOLMES (*intensely*). *What!* That boy! (*He scowls dangerously.*)

MORIARTY (*hissing it*). Yes, that boy! (HOLMES *slowly reaches his left hand out to ring the bell again.*)

HOLMES. At least we'll try the bell once more, Professor. (*Rings.*)

MORIARTY (*after a pause*). Doesn't it occur to you that he may possibly have been *detained,* Mr. Holmes?

HOLMES. It does, Professor. But it also occurs to me that you are in very much the same predicament, Professor Moriarty! (*Rings bell for the third time. There is a noise on the stairway outside. Enter* BILLY *up*

R. *without his coat and with the sleeves of his shirt and waistcoat badly torn.*)

BILLY. I beg pardon, sir—someone tried to 'old me, sir! (*Panting for breath.*)

HOLMES (*pipe in mouth*). It's quite evident, however, that he failed to do so.

BILLY. Yes sir—'e's got my coat, sir, but 'e 'asn't got *me!*

HOLMES. Billy!

BILLY (*cheerfully*). Yes sir! (*He is still out of breath.*)

HOLMES. The gentleman I am carefully pointing out to you with this .42 desires to have us get something out of his left-hand inside coat pocket. (MORIARTY *gives a very slight start.*) Ah, I thought so! Left-hand coat pocket. As he is not feeling quite himself today, and the consequence of his trying to do it himself might prove fatal, suppose you attend to it for him.

BILLY. Yes sir. (*He goes quickly to* MORIARTY, *puts a hand in his pocket, and draws out a bulldog revolver.*) Is this it, sir?

HOLMES. Quite so! Put it on the table. (MORIARTY *makes a grab for it.*) Not there, Billy! Look out! Push it a little further this way. (BILLY *places the weapon within easy reach of* HOLMES.) That's more like it.

BILLY. Shall I see if he's got another, sir?

HOLMES (*laughs*). Why, Billy, you surprise me! After the gentleman has taken the trouble to inform us that he *hasn't!*

BILLY. When, sir?

HOLMES. When he made a snatch for *this* one. And now, Professor— (*toying with the revolver*)—now that we have your little memorandum book—do you think of anything else you'd like before Billy goes? (MORIARTY *does not reply.*) Any little thing you've got that you don't want? Oh—I'm so sorry! That's all, Billy. (MORIARTY *is motionless, his eyes on* HOLMES.)

BILLY. Thank you, sir. (*Exits at door up R.*)

(*As* MORIARTY'S *eyes follow Billy out of the room,* HOLMES *extracts the cartridges from* MORIARTY'S *revolver, below the table line, then tosses it back on the table again.*)

HOLMES (*tapping the revolver with his pipe*). Rather a rash project of yours, Moriarty, to make use of that thing so early in the evening and in this part of the town.

MORIARTY. Listen, you, to me! On the 4th of January you crossed my path. On the 23rd you incommoded me. And now, at the close of April, I find myself placed in such a position through your continual interference that I am in positive danger of losing my liberty.

HOLMES (*smoking*). Have you any suggestion to make?

MORIARTY (*head swaying from side to side*). No! I have no suggestion to make. I have a fact to state. If you do not drop it *at once*, your life is not worth *that!* (*A snap of his fingers.*)

HOLMES (*rising, as if rather bored*). I'm afraid, Professor, that in the pleasure of this conversation I am neglecting more important business. (*Turns away to mantel at left.*)

(MORIARTY *rises slowly and picks up his hat. Suddenly catches sight of the revolver on the table and puts down his hat.*)

MORIARTY (*nearing* HOLMES). I came here this evening to see if *peace* could not be arranged between us!

HOLMES. Ha! Yes—(*smiling pleasantly and pressing tobacco into his pipe*)—I saw that! That's rather good!

MORIARTY (*passionately*). You have seen fit not only to reject my proposals but to make insulting references coupled with threats of arrest!

HOLMES. Quite so! Quite so! (*Lights a match and holds it to his pipe.*)

MORIARTY. You have been warned of your danger—you do not heed that warning. Perhaps you will heed this! (*Making a sudden plunge, he seizes the revolver from the table and, at the same instant aiming at* HOLMES's *head, rapidly snaps the trigger in quick attempts to fire.*)

(HOLMES *turns quietly toward him, still holding a match to his pipe, so that the last snaps of the hammer are directly in his face.*)

HOLMES. Oh!—Here! (*As if recollecting something. Tosses away his match and, feeling quickly in the left pocket of his dressing gown, brings out some cartridges, which he throws carelessly onto the table.*) I didn't suppose you'd want to use that thing again—so I took your cartridges out and put them in my pocket. You'll find them all there, Professor! (*Reaches over and rings bell on table with his right hand. Enter* BILLY *door up R.*) Billy!

BILLY. Yes sir!

HOLMES. The door.

BILLY. Yes sir!—This way, sir!

(PROFESSOR MORIARTY *looks at* HOLMES *a moment, then flings the revolver down and across the table. Boiling with rage, he picks up his hat and rushes out at door up R.*)

HOLMES. Billy! Come here!

BILLY. Yes sir! (*Moves quickly forward.*)

HOLMES (*scowling*). Billy!—You're a good boy!

BILLY (*grinning*). Yes sir! Thank you, sir!

CURTAIN

ACT THREE

SCENE I

The Gas Chamber at Stepney, a large, dark grimy room on an upper floor of an old building backing on the wharves. The plaster is cracking off and the general appearance of the place is uncanny and gruesome. Wide door down L. Door up L.C. leading to small cupboard, the walls of which may be seen when door is opened. Large window up R.C. closed; its glass is grimy and dirty, so nothing can be seen through it, but all the panes are in place.

CRAIGIN is discovered sitting on a box R., glum and motionless—waiting. A miner's safety lamp hangs near him on a bit of projecting stone.

After a long wait LEARY enters at door L. and glides noiselessly to table R.C. upon which he half leans and half sits. After a pause he fills his pipe and prepares to strike a match.

CRAIGIN (*without looking around, in a low, deep voice*). Are you a-lightin' matches 'ere?

LEARY. That's wot I'm doing!

CRAIGIN. Well, *chuck* it!

LEARY (*after a pause*). W'y should I chuck it?

CRAIGIN. There might be gas, ye fool!

LEARY. There's no gas. It's four days since we 'ad it in.

CRAIGIN. An' I still say there might be gas.

(LEARY *strikes a match which burns flickeringly for a moment.*)

LEARY. You're too particular. (*Lights his pipe.*)

(*Door at L. opens and* MCTAGUE *enters with a safety lamp. He stops just within for a moment, glancing around in the dimness, then moves to a masonry pier L. a little above the door and leans against it, waiting.* CRAIGIN, LEARY, *and* MCTAGUE *are dressed in dark clothes and wear felt-soled shoes.*)

LEARY (*in a low voice*). Wot's McTague doing 'ere?

MCTAGUE. I was sent 'ere.

LEARY. I thought the Seraph was with us in this job?

CRAIGIN. 'E ain't.

LEARY (*after a pause*). 'Oo was the last you put the gas on?

CRAIGIN. I didn't 'ear 'is name. (*Pause.*) 'E'd been 'oldin' back money on a 'aul—that's all I know.

MCTAGUE (*after a long pause*). Wot's this 'ere job he wants done?

CRAIGIN. I ain't been told.

LEARY. As long as it's 'ere we know wot it's likely to be.

(*There is a sound of footsteps outside, then the door opens slowly and hesitatingly. Enter* SID PRINCE *at door L. He stands just within the door and looks about a little suspiciously, as if uncertain what to do.*)

PRINCE. Does any of you blokes know whether this is the plyce w'ere I'm to meet Alf Bassick? (*There is a long silence. None of the men notice* PRINCE.)

PRINCE (*after waiting a moment*). From wot you sye, I tyke it you don't! (*Comes a little further into room and lets the door close.*) Nice old plyce to find, this 'ere is! (*No one answers him.*) And w'en you do find it—(*looks about*)—I can't sye as it's any too cheerful. (*He pulls out a cigarette case, puts a cigarette in his mouth, and feels in his pocket for matches. Finds one and is about to light it.*)

CRAIGIN. *Don't light that!* (PRINCE *stops motionless and looks at* CRAIGIN.) *It ain't safe!*

PRINCE. If it ain't askin' too much, wot's the matter with the plyce? It looks all right to *me!*

CRAIGIN. Well, don't light no matches an' it'll stay lookin' the same. (*There are footsteps outside; then the door opens and* BASSICK *enters hurriedly. He looks quickly about him.*)

BASSICK. Oh, Prince, you're here!

PRINCE. Yes sir.

BASSICK. You'll stand by Larrabee. He'll be here soon. (*Glancing about to see that the other men are present.*) You've got the rope, Craigin? (*All voices are still low.*)

CRAIGIN (*pointing*). It's 'ere.

BASSICK. That you, Leary?

LEARY. 'Ere, sir!

BASSICK. And McTague?

MCTAGUE. 'Ere, sir!

BASSICK. Be careful now, you boys. You've got a tough one tonight!

CRAIGIN. You ain't said who, as I've 'eard!

BASSICK (*in a low voice*). Sherlock Holmes.

(CRAIGIN *rises and approaches* BASSICK *as* LEARY *and* MCTAGUE *draw nearer. There is a brief pause.*)

CRAIGIN. You mean that, sir?

BASSICK. God's truth!

CRAIGIN. We're goin' to count '*im* out?

BASSICK. Well, if you *don't*, and he gets away—I'm sorry for you—that's all!

CRAIGIN. I'll be cursed glad to put the gas on 'im—I can tell you *that!*

LEARY. An' I says the same meself! (*Footsteps are heard outside as two men approach the door.*)

BASSICK. Tack it! The gov'nor's here!

LEARY. Not the gov'nor '*imself!*

BASSICK. *Sh!* Shut up! (*The door opens, and enter* MORIARTY *followed by* LARRABEE.)

MORIARTY (*sharply*). Where's Craigin? (CRAIGIN *steps forward, pulling off his cap.*) Have you got your full crew?

CRAIGIN. All 'ere, sir.

MORIARTY. No mistakes tonight.

CRAIGIN. I'll be careful o' that!

MORIARTY (*after a quick glance about*). That door, Bassick?

BASSICK. A small cupboard, sir! (BASSICK *quickly opens the door, and* LEARY *catches up a lantern and swings it before the cupboard.*)

MORIARTY. No outlet?

BASSICK. None whatever, sir.

MORIARTY (*turns and points*). That window?

BASSICK. Nailed down, sir!

(LEARY *turns R. and swings the lantern near the window.*)

MORIARTY. A man might break the glass?

BASSICK. If he did that he'd come against heavy iron bars outside.

CRAIGIN. Huh! We'll 'ave 'im tied down afore 'e can break any glass, sir!

MORIARTY. Ah! You've used it before! Of course you know it's airtight?

BASSICK. Every crevice is caulked, sir.

MORIARTY. M'm! (*With satisfaction.*) And when the men have turned the gas on him they leave by that door?

BASSICK. Yes sir.

MORIARTY. It can be made quite *secure?*

BASSICK. Heavy bolts on the outside, sir, and solid oak bars over all.

MORIARTY. Let me see how quick you can operate them.

BASSICK. They tie the man down, sir —there's no need to hurry!

MORIARTY. Let me see how quick you can operate them.

BASSICK (*quickly*). Leary!

LEARY (*setting down the lamp*). Yes sir! (*He jumps to door L. and goes out, closing it at once, and immediately the sounds of sliding bolts and the dropping of bars is heard from outside.*)

MORIARTY. That's all. (*Sounds of bolts being withdrawn and* LEARY *re-enters and waits.*) Craigin—you'll take your men outside that door and wait till Mr. Larrabee has had a little business interview with the gentleman. Take them up the passage to the left so Holmes doesn't see them as he comes in. (*To* BASSICK.) Who's driving the cab tonight?

BASSICK. I sent O'Hagan, sir.

MORIARTY. The cab windows were covered, of course?

BASSICK. Wooden shutters, sir. Bolted on secure.

MORIARTY (*satisfied*). Ah—(*looks about*)—we must have a lamp here.

BASSICK. Better not, sir! There might be some gas left.

MORIARTY. You've got a light there (*pointing . to the miner's safety lamp*).

BASSICK. It's a safety lamp, sir.

MORIARTY. A safety lamp! You mustn't have that here! The moment he sees it he'll know what you're doing! (*Sniffs.*) There's hardly any gas. Go and tell the Lascar we must have a good lamp. (BASSICK *exits L.*) Put that table over there! (CRAIGIN *and* MCTAGUE *bring table from up C. and place it.*) Now, Craigin—and the rest of you—one thing, remember. No shooting to-night! Not a single shot! It can be heard in the alley below. The first thing is to get his revolver away before he has a chance to use it. Two of you attract his attention in front—the other come up on him from behind and snatch it out of his pocket. Then you have him. Arrange that, Craigin.

CRAIGIN. I'll attend to it, sir.

(*Enter* BASSICK *with a large lamp. He crosses to the table and sets it down.*)

BASSICK (*to* MCTAGUE). Put out that safety lamp.

CRAIGIN. Stop! We'll want it when the other's taken away.

BASSICK. He mustn't see it, you understand.

MORIARTY. Don't put it out. Cover it with something.

CRAIGIN. Here! (*Takes safety lantern from* MCTAGUE *and, pulling out a large box, places the lantern within, pushing the open side against the wall.*)

MORIARTY. That will do.

BASSICK (*approaching* MORIARTY). You mustn't stay any longer, sir. ·O'Hagan might be a little early. (*Crosses to door and stands waiting.*)

MORIARTY. Mr. Larrabee—you understand? *They wait for you!*

LARRABEE (*in a low voice*). I understand, sir.

MORIARTY. I give you this opportunity to sell him the packet and get what you can for your trouble. But anything that is found on him after you have finished—is subject— (*glances at* CRAIGIN *and the others*) —to the usual division.

LARRABEE. That's all I want.

MORIARTY. When you have quite finished and got your money, suppose you blow that little whistle which I observe hanging from your watch chain—and these gentlemen will take *their* turn. (*He crosses to the door.*) And, Craigin—at the proper moment present my compliments to Mr. Sherlock Holmes and say that I wished him a pleasant ·journey to the other side.

(MORIARTY *exits, followed by* BAS-SICK.)

LARRABEE. You'd better put that rope out of sight.

(CRAIGIN *picks it up as* LEARY *and* MCTAGUE *move across noiselessly at the back.* LARRABEE *is examining his package.*)

CRAIGIN (*joins* LEARY *and* MCTAGUE *at door, then speaks to* LARRABEE). You understand, sir, we're on this floor just around the far turn of the passage—so 'e won't see us as 'e's comin' up.

LARRABEE. I understand.

CRAIGIN. An' we comes in for it w'en we 'ears that whistle, eh?

LARRABEE. That's it.

(*Exit* CRAIGIN, LEARY, *and* MC-TAGUE *noiselessly at door L. which remains open.* PRINCE, *who has been very quiet, begins to move a little, nervously. He looks at his watch and glances about him.* LARRABEE *is near the lamp, looking at the package of papers which he took from his pocket.*)

PRINCE (*head down*). Look 'ere, Jim, this sort o' thing ain't so much in my line!

LARRABEE. I suppose not.

PRINCE (*still without looking at* LARRABEE). W'en it comes to a shy at a safe or drillin' into bank vaults I feels perfectly at 'ome, but I don't so much care to see a man—— (*Hesitates.*) Well, it ain't my line!

LARRABEE (*turning*). Here! (*Going to him and urging him toward the door.*) All I want of you is to go down on the corner below and let me know when he comes!

PRINCE. 'Ow will I let you know?

LARRABEE. Have you got a cab whistle?

PRINCE (*pulls one out of pocket*). Cert'nly.

LARRABEE. Well, when you see O'Hagan driving up with him, come down the alley there and blow it three times.

PRINCE. Ain't it likely to call a cab at the same time?

LARRABEE. What more do you want? Take the cab and go home.

PRINCE. Then you won't need me 'ere again?

LARRABEE. No—(*sarcastically*)—it ain't your line.

PRINCE (*going to door*). Oh! very well—then I'll tear myself away. (*Exit* PRINCE *in haste.*)

(LARRABEE *crosses to the table and looks at the lamp. He gets two chairs and places them on either side of the table, then takes out a cigar and holds it a moment, unlighted, as he thinks. Enter* ALICE FAULKNER *at door L.* LARRABEE *looks at her in astonishment.*)

LARRABEE (*after a pause*). What do *you* want?

ALICE. It's true then!

LARRABEE. How did you get to this place?

ALICE. I followed you—in a cab.

LARRABEE. What have you been doing since I came up here? Informing the police perhaps!

ALICE. No—I was afraid *he'd* come— so I waited.

LARRABEE. To warn him, I suppose.

ALICE. Yes—(*pause*)—to warn him. (*She looks about the room.*) You're going to swindle and deceive him—I know that! *Is there anything more?*

LARRABEE. What could you do if there was?

ALICE. I could buy you off!

LARRABEE. How much would you give?

ALICE. The genuine package—the *real* ones—all the proofs—*everything!*

LARRABEE (*advancing eagerly*). Have you got it with you?

ALICE. I can get it in a few moments.

LARRABEE. Oh (*disappointed*). So you'll do all that for this man? You think he's your friend, I suppose!

ALICE. I haven't thought of it.

LARRABEE. Look what he's doing now! Coming here to *buy* those things of *me!*

ALICE. They're false! They're counterfeit!

LARRABEE. Yes, but he doesn't know that.

ALICE. He may ask my permission still!

LARRABEE. Ha! (*Sneers and turns away.*) He won't get the chance!

ALICE (*suspicious again*). Won't get the—— Then there *is* something else!

LARRABEE. You see me here by myself, don't you? I'm going to talk to him on a little business. How could I do him any harm?

ALICE (*advancing*). Where are those men who came up here?

LARRABEE. What men?

ALICE. Three terrible-looking men— I saw them go in at the street door.

LARRABEE. Oh—*those* men! They went up the other stairway! You can see them in the next building—if you look out of this window.

(ALICE *goes rapidly toward the window as* LARRABEE *crosses to the door. She tries to look out but, failing, turns to find she has been trapped.*)

ALICE (*starting toward the door*). I'll look in the passageway, if you please!

LARRABEE (*before the door*). Yes— but I don't please!

ALICE. Where are those men?

LARRABEE. Stay just where you are and you'll see them very soon. (LARRABEE *pushes the door open and blows his whistle as quietly as possible. There is a short silence. No footsteps are heard as the men move noiselessly. Enter then* CRAIGIN, MCTAGUE, *and* LEARY. *They stand looking in astonishment at* ALICE.)

ALICE. I knew it! (*Moving back a step. After a slight pause she turns and hurries to the window, trying to look out or to give an alarm, then runs to the cupboard door. At length she just stands looking at them, at bay.* LARRABEE *waits, watching her movements.*)

ALICE (*desperately*). You're going to do him some harm!

LARRABEE. Oh no, it's only a little *joke*—at his expense.

ALICE (*moving toward him*). You wanted the letters, the package I had in the safe! I'll get it for you! Let me go and I'll bring it here—or whatever you tell me—(LARRABEE *sneers*)—I'll give you my word not to say anything to anyone—not to him—not to the policemen—not to *anyone!*

LARRABEE (*without moving*). You needn't take the trouble to *get it*—but you can *tell me where it is*—and you'll have to be quick about it too!

ALICE. Yes—if you'll promise not to go on with this! *Not to do him any harm!*

LARRABEE. Of course! That's understood.

ALICE (*excitedly*). You promise?

LARRABEE. Certainly I promise! Now where is it?

ALICE. Just outside my chamber window—just outside on the left—fastened between the shutter and the wall—you can easily find it!

LARRABEE. Yes—I can easily find it.

ALICE. Now tell them—tell them to go!

LARRABEE (*stepping toward the men*). Tie her up so she can't make a noise. Keep her out there with you until we have Holmes in here and then let O'Hagan keep her in his cab!

(ALICE *listens dazed, astonished.*)

CRAIGIN (*speaks low*). Go an' get a-hold Leary. Hand me a piece of that rope!

(MCTAGUE *brings a rope out from under his coat and takes a handkerchief from his pocket.*)

LARRABEE. Now then, my pretty bird——

(ALICE *begins to move back in alarm.*)

ALICE. You said—you said if I *told* you——

LARRABEE. Well—we haven't done him any harm yet, have we?

(LEARY *is quietly stealing round behind her.*)

ALICE. Then send them away!

LARRABEE. Certainly! Go away now, boys, there's no more work for you tonight!

ALICE (*looking at them, terrified*). They don't obey you! They are——

(LEARY *seizes her. She screams and resists, but* CRAIGIN *and* MCTAGUE *come up at once and she is quickly subdued, gagged with a handkerchief, and her hands tied. Just as they finish a shrill whistle is heard in the distance.* ALL *stop, listening. The prolonged whistle is heard again and then again.*)

LARRABEE. By God, he's *here!*

CRAIGIN. What!

LARRABEE. That's Sid Prince! I put him on the watch!

CRAIGIN. We won't have time to get her out!

LARRABEE. Shut her in there! (*Pointing to cupboard.*)

LEARY. Yes—that'll do.

CRAIGIN. In with her! (*Almost on the word they have her in the cupboard and are standing before it.*)

LEARY. There ain't no lock to this 'ere door!

LARRABEE. No lock!—Drive something in!

CRAIGIN. 'Ere, this knife! (*He hands* LEARY *a large clasp knife, opened and ready.*)

LARRABEE. A knife won't hold it.

CRAIGIN. Yes, it will—if you drive it in strong.

(LEARY *drives the blade into the doorframe with all his force.*)

LEARY. 'E'll 'ave to find us 'ere!

CRAIGIN. Yes—and we won't wait either—we'll go on and do 'im up! (*Moving to the door.*)

LARRABEE. No, you won't—I'll see him first, if you please!

(CRAIGIN *and* LARRABEE *face each other savagely.*)

MCTAGUE. Them was orders, Craigin.

LEARY. So it was!

MCTAGUE. There might be time to get back into the passage! (*He lis-*

tens at the door.) They ain't up the first flight yet.

LEARY. Quick then!

(*Exit* MCTAGUE, LEARY, *and* CRAIGIN. LARRABEE *glances at cupboard door anxiously. He makes a quick dash to it and forces the knife in with all his strength, then comes quickly back to the table, draws out his papers, and sits looking at them. Enter* SHERLOCK HOLMES *at door L., walking easily as though on some ordinary business.*)

HOLMES (*chuckles*). Well, really! I certainly thought after all this driving about in a closed cab you'd show me something new!

LARRABEE (*looking up nonchalantly*). Seen it before, have you?

HOLMES. Well, a time or two. Now that I come to think of it, I nabbed a friend of yours in this place while he was trying to drop himself out of that window—Ed Colvin the cracksman. (*Taking off his gloves.*)

LARRABEE. Colvin! Never heard of him before!

HOLMES (*good-naturedly*). Well, you certainly never heard of him *after!*—I'm sure of that! A brace of counterfeiters used these luxurious chambers in the spring of '89. One of them hid in that cupboard. We pulled him out by the heels.

LARRABEE (*drawling*). Quite interesting! But times have changed since then!

(HOLMES *darts a lightning glance at* LARRABEE *but instantly is easy again and glancing about him as before.*)

HOLMES (*dropping down near* LAR-RABEE). So they have, Mr. Larrabee—so they have! (*Confidentially.*) Then it was only cracksmen, counterfeiters, pickpockets, and petty swindlers of various kinds! But now——

LARRABEE. Well? What now?

HOLMES. Well—(*mysteriously*)—between you and me, Mr. Larrabee—we've heard some not altogether agreeable rumors—rumors of some pretty shady work not far from here—a murder or two of a very peculiar kind—and I've always had a suspicion—— (*Stops and sniffs very delicately, then nods ominously at* LAR-RABEE, *who is watching him.*) That's it! (*Moves quickly to window and runs his hand lightly along the frame before returning to table.*) My surmise was correct—*it is!*

LARRABEE. It is what?

HOLMES. *Caulked!*

LARRABEE. What does that signify to us?

HOLMES. Nothing to *us*, Mr. Larrabee—nothing to us—but it might signify a good deal to some poor devil who's been caught in this trap!

LARRABEE. Well, if it's nothing to us, suppose we leave it alone and get to business. My time is limited.

HOLMES. Of course! I should have realized that these reflections could not possibly appeal to you.

LARRABEE (*tossing a cigar onto the table between them*). Smoke?

HOLMES. Thanks! (*Takes the cigar and shortly drops it unseen upon the floor, at the same moment producing one of his own from his coat pocket; this he lights.*) Fine cigar!

LARRABEE. Glad you like it! (*Takes out the counterfeit package and tosses it on the table before them.*) Now here is the little packet which is the object of this meeting. (HOLMES *looks at it calmly as he smokes.*)

LARRABEE. I haven't opened it yet, but Miss Faulkner tells me everything is there.

HOLMES (*pointedly*). Suppose, Mr. Larrabee, that as Miss Faulkner knows nothing whatever about this affair, we omit her name from the discussion.

LARRABEE. What do you mean?—Who told you she doesn't know?

HOLMES. You did. Every look, tone, gesture—everything you have said and done since I have been in this room has informed me that Miss Faulkner has never consented to this transaction. *It is a little speculation of your own!*

LARRABEE. Huh! (*Sneering.*) I suppose you think you can read me like a book!

HOLMES. Oh no—like a Primer.

LARRABEE (*another sneer*). Well, let it pass. How much'll you give?

HOLMES. A thousand pounds.

LARRABEE. I couldn't take it!

HOLMES. What do you ask?

LARRABEE. Five thousand

HOLMES (*shakes his head*). I couldn't give it.

LARRABEE. Very well. (*Rises.*) We've had all this trouble for nothing (*as if about to pick up the packet*).

HOLMES (*remonstrating*). Oh—don't say that, Mr. Larrabee! Don't say that! To me the occasion has been doubly interesting. I have not only had the pleasure of meeting you again but I have also availed myself of the opportunity to make some observations regarding this place which may not come.amiss.

LARRABEE. Why, I've been offered four thousand for this little——

HOLMES (*calmly smoking*). Why didn't you take it?

LARRABEE. Because I intend to get *more*.

HOLMES. Oh—that's too bad!

LARRABEE. If they offered four thousand they'll give five!

HOLMES. They won't give anything.

LARRABEE. Why not?

HOLMES. They've turned the case over to me.

LARRABEE. Will you give three thousand?

HOLMES (*rising*). Mr. Larrabee, strange as it may appear, *my* time is limited as well as yours. I have brought with me the sum of one thousand pounds, which is all that I wish to pay. If it is your desire to sell *at* this figure kindly apprise me

of the fact at once. If not, permit me to wish you a very good evening.

(LARRABEE *looks at him, then ill-naturedly tosses the package onto the table.*)

LARRABEE. You can have it. It's too small a matter to haggle over!

(HOLMES *reseats himself at once and takes a wallet from his pocket from which he produces a bundle of bank notes,* LARRABEE *watching him with glittering eyes.* HOLMES *counts out ten one-hundred-pound notes, then lays the remainder of the notes on the table with his elbow on them while he counts the first over again.*)

LARRABEE (*sneeringly*). Oh—I thought you said you had brought *just a thousand*.

HOLMES (*without looking up*). I did —this is it.

LARRABEE. You brought a trifle more, I see!

HOLMES (*still counting the notes*). Quite so! I didn't say I hadn't brought any *more*.

LARRABEE. Ha! (*Sneering.*) You can do *your* little tricks when it comes to it, can't you?

HOLMES. It depends on who I'm dealing with. (*Hands* LARRABEE *one thousand pounds in notes.* LARRABEE *takes the money and keeps a close watch at the same time on the remaining pile of notes lying at* HOLMES's *left.* HOLMES, *after handing the notes to* LARRABEE, *lays the cigar he was smoking on the table and* LARRABEE *makes a sudden lunge and snatches the pile of bank notes.* HOLMES *springs to his feet at same time.*)

HOLMES. *Now* I've got you where I want you, James Larrabee! You've been so cunning and so cautious and so wise we couldn't find a thing to hold you for—but this little slip will get you in *for robbery!*

LARRABEE. Ha, ha! You'll have me in, will you? What are your views about being able to get away from here yourself?

HOLMES. I do not now anticipate any particular difficulty.

LARRABEE. Ha, ha! Robbery, eh? Why, even if you got away from here you haven't got a witness! *You haven't got a witness to your name!*

HOLMES. I'm not so sure of that, Mr. Larrabee! (*Pointing.*) Do you usually fasten that door with a *knife?*

(*There is a faint moan from within the cupboard.* HOLMES *listens motionless for an instant, then makes a quick dash to the door and, seizing the knife, wrenches it out and flings it to the floor.*)

LARRABEE. Come away from that door!

(*But* HOLMES *has torn open the door, and* ALICE FAULKNER *pitches out before* LARRABEE *can get near.*)

HOLMES (*turning on* LARRABEE *and supporting* ALICE *at same time*). Stand back! You contemptible scoundrel, what does this mean?

LARRABEE. I'll show you what it means cursed quick! (*Blows the*

little silver whistle attached to his watch chain.)

HOLMES (*untying* ALICE *quickly*). I'm afraid you're badly hurt, Miss Faulkner.

(*Enter* CRAIGIN. *He stands for a moment near the door, watching* HOLMES, *then makes a signal with his hand to the others outside the door.* MCTAGUE *enters noiselessly and remains a little behind* CRAIGIN. ALICE *shakes her head quickly and tries to call* HOLMES'S *attention to* CRAIGIN *and* MCTAGUE.)

ALICE. Mr. Holmes! (*Points to* CRAIGIN *and* MCTAGUE.)

HOLMES (*glances around*). Ah, Craigin—delighted to see you! (CRAIGIN *gives a slight start.*) And you too, McTague. (*To* ALICE.) I hope you're beginning to feel a little more like yourself, Miss Faulkner—because we shall leave here very soon.

ALICE (*who has been shrinking from the sight of* CRAIGIN *and* MC-TAGUE). Oh yes—do let us go, Mr. Holmes!

CRAIGIN (*in a low deep voice*). You'll 'ave to wait a bit, Mr. 'Olmes! We've a little matter o' business we'd like to talk h'over!

(*Enter* LEARY *at door L. He glides across the room in shadow and begins to move toward* HOLMES.)

HOLMES. All right, Craigin—I'll see you tomorrow morning—in your cell at Bow Street.

(*At this instant* ALICE *sees* LEARY *approaching rapidly from behind;*

she screams. HOLMES *turns, but* LEARY *is upon him. There is a short struggle, and* HOLMES *throws* LEARY *violently off; but* LEARY *has got* HOLMES'S *revolver. There is a short and deadly pause.*)

CRAIGIN (*in a low voice to* LEARY). 'Ave yer got his revolver?

LEARY (*on the floor*). 'Ere it is! (*Getting slowly to his feet.*)

HOLMES. Ah, Leary! This is a pleasure indeed! It needed only your blithe personality to make the party complete! (*Sits and writes rapidly in a notebook taken from his pocket. Picks up his cigar, which he had left on the table, and keeps it in his mouth as he writes.*)

CRAIGIN (*to* LARRABEE). Now we got 'is gun, ain't we goin' on with it?

LARRABEE. Why not? (*To* HOLMES.) Writing your will, I suppose?

HOLMES (*writing*). No—(*shakes his head*)—only a brief description of one or two of you gentlemen—for the police. (*Rising and putting the notebook in his pocket.*) I'm ready now! (*Buttoning up his coat.*)

(CRAIGIN, MCTAGUE, *and* LEARY *suddenly brace themselves for action and stand ready to spring.* LARRABEE *also is ready to join in the struggle if necessary.*)

CRAIGIN. Wait a bit! You'd better listen to me, Mr. 'Olmes. We're goin' to tie yer down nice and tight to the top o' that table.

HOLMES (*jovially*). Ha! Thank you very much indeed—but I don't think you *will!* That's my *idea*, you know!

CRAIGIN. An' you'll save yourself a deal o' trouble if yer submit quiet and easy like—because if yer don't yer might get knocked about some.

ALICE (*coming to his side*). Oh—Mr. Holmes!

LARRABEE (*to* ALICE). Come away from him! Come over here if you don't want to get hurt!

HOLMES (*to* ALICE, *without looking round but reaching her with his left hand*). My child, if you don't want to get hurt *don't leave me* for a second!

CRAIGIN. You'd better look out, miss —he might get *killed!*

ALICE. Then you can kill me too! (HOLMES *moves sharply.*)

HOLMES (*in a low voice, without taking his eyes from the men before him*). I'm afraid you don't mean that, Miss Faulkner!

ALICE. Ah, but I *do!*

HOLMES. No, no! (*Shakes his head a trifle.*) You wouldn't say it at another time and place!

ALICE. I would say it anywhere—always.

(HOLMES *looks down at her for an instant, then turns quickly back to confront his assailants.*)

CRAIGIN. So you'll 'ave it out with us, eh?

HOLMES. Something like that, my good Craigin!

CRAIGIN. Well, then—I'll 'ave to give yer one—same as I did yer right-'and man this afternoon! (*Approaching Holmes.*)

HOLMES (*to* ALICE, *without turning*). Ah! You heard him say that! *The same as he did my right-hand man this afternoon!* (*Pointing · to* CRAIGIN).

ALICE (*under her breath*). Yes! Yes!

HOLMES. Don't forget that face! (*Pointing.*) In three days I shall ask you to identify it in the prisoners' dock!

CRAIGIN (*enraged*). Ha! (*Turning away as if to hide his face.*)

HOLMES (*sharply*). Why, you surprise me, gentlemen—thinking you're sure of anybody in this room —and three bars gone out of that window! (*There is a pause. His assailants are surprised.*)

LARRABEE. Bars or no bars, you're not going to get out of here as easy as you expect.

HOLMES. There are so many ways, Mr. Larrabee, that I hardly know which one to choose. (*He is caressing a chair back.*)

CRAIGIN (*advancing*). Well, you'd better choose quick—I can tell you that.

HOLMES (*suddenly*). I'll choose at once, Mr. Craigin—and my choice— (*quickly seizing the chair*)—falls on this! (*On the word he brings the chair down upon the lamp with a frightful crash, extinguishing the light instantly. Only the glow of* HOLMES'S *cigar remains visible where he stands at the table. He at once begins to move toward the window, keeping the cigar so that its light will show.*)

CRAIGIN (*in a loud, sharp voice*). Track 'im by the cigar!

LARRABEE. Watch his cigar! Look out! He's going for the window! (*MCTAGUE and LEARY hurry in that direction.*)

CRAIGIN (*loudly*). The safety light! Where is it?

(*MCTAGUE kicks over the box which has concealed it.* HOLMES *and* ALICE *are at the door and* ALICE *is just going out.*)

HOLMES (*turning and pointing to the window*). Er—I left that cigar for you on the window sill! (*He exits with* ALICE, *slamming the door in the faces of the men who rush to seize them. The heavy bolts and bars outside fall into place as* MC-TAGUE *and* LEARY *hurl themselves upon the door.*)

CURTAIN

ACT FOUR

SCENE I

DR. WATSON's *house in Kensington, the consulting room. Wide double doors on right opening to hall and street door, and door L.C. communicating with the doctor's inner office. A door up C. a little to R. which opens to private hallway of house. Two windows L. which open at side of house upon an area or lawn facing the street. The shades are down so that no one can see into the room. A large and comfortable lounge up R.C, with high back and cushions.*

DR. WATSON *is discovered at his desk L.*

WATSON (*turns and rings bell, then busies himself with some papers. Enter* PARSONS, *a servant, at door R.*). Oh—Parsons! Is there anyone waiting?

PARSONS. There's one person in the waiting room, sir—a gentleman.

WATSON (*looks at his watch*). Very well, I'll see him, but if any more come you must send them·over to Dr. Anstruther. I have an important appointment at nine.

PARSONS. Yes sir. (*Exits at door R. There is a pause during which* WATSON *is busy at his desk.* PARSONS *opens door and remains outside. Enter* SID PRINCE. *He comes in a little way and pauses.* WATSON *looks up.*)

PRINCE (*speaking in a husky whisper*). Good evenin', sir!

WATSON. Good evening. (*Indicating a chair.*) Pray be seated.

PRINCE. Thanks. I don't mind if I do! (*Coughs and sits in chair near desk.*)

WATSON (*looking at him with professional interest*). What seems to be the trouble?

PRINCE. Throat, sir . (*Indicating.*) Most dreadful sore throat!

WATSON. Sore throat, eh? (*Glancing about for an instrument.*)

PRINCE. Well, I should think it is! It's the most 'arrowing thing I ever 'ad! It pains me that much to swallow that I——

WATSON. Hurts you to swallow, does it? (*Instrument in hand.*)

PRINCE. Indeed it does! Why, I can 'ardly get a bit of food down! (WATSON *rises and goes to a small table up L.C. Pushes gas burner out into position and lights it.*)

WATSON. Just step this way a moment, please. (PRINCE *rises.* WATSON *adjusts a reflector over his eye and peers into* PRINCE's *throat.*) Now—mouth open, please. Wide as possible! (PRINCE *opens his mouth and* WATSON *places a depressor on his tongue.*) Say "Ah!" (PRINCE *does so.*) That's it—*h'm!* Where do you feel this pain?

PRINCE (*indicating with his finger*). Just about there, Doctor. Inside about there.

WATSON. That's singular. I don't find anything wrong. (*Pushes gas burner back to usual position and returns to desk.*)

PRINCE. You may not find anything wrong but I *feel* it wrong! If you would only give me something to take away this awful h'agony.

WATSON. Odd thing it should have affected your voice in this way! I'll give you a gargle—it may help you a little!

PRINCE. If you only would, Doctor!

(WATSON *goes into his surgery,* PRINCE *watching him like a cat. He does not completely close the door of the room.* PRINCE *moves toward the door, watching* WATSON *through it. He suddenly turns and runs up the shades of both windows, then is back watching* WATSON *through the door again. Still having time to spare, he goes to door up C. and opens it, looking and listening. A distant sound of piano playing when the door is open which stops when it is closed.* PRINCE *quickly turns back into the room but returns again to the door, leaving it open so that he is seen peering up above and listening. He turns to come back but sees* WATSON *suddenly enter at door up L. with a vial in his hand.* PRINCE *gives forth a violent wheezy cough.* WATSON *goes quickly to his desk and rings the bell. Enter* PARSONS *at door R.*)

WATSON. Show this gentleman the shortest way to the street door and close it after him.

PRINCE. But, Doctor, yer don't understand!

WATSON. I understand quite enough. Good evening, sir!

PRINCE. Yer know a draught plays 'ob with my throat, sir—and seems to affect my——

WATSON. Good evening, sir! (WATSON *sits down and pays no further attention to* PRINCE.)

PARSONS. This way, sir, *h'iff* you please!

PRINCE. I consider, sir, that you've treated me damned outrageous—that's wot I do! And yer won't 'ear the last of this very soon!

PARSONS (*approaching him*). Come, none o' that now! (*Takes* PRINCE *by the arm.*)

PRINCE (*loudly, in his natural voice*). You keep yer 'ands off me, do ye 'ear! (*Over his shoulder.*) Yer call yerself a doctor an' treat sick people as comes to see yer this 'ere way! A bloomin' nice doctor, *you* are! (PARSONS *forces* PRINCE *out by the arm during his impassioned speech. The outside door closes smartly.* WATSON, *after a short pause, looks round the room but does not observe that the window shades are up. He rings the bell. Enter* PARSONS.)

WATSON (*rises and gathers up a few things, as if to go*). I shall be at Mr. Holmes' place in Baker Street. If there's anything special you'll know where to find me. (*Looks at his watch.*) I'm going to walk over.

PARSONS. Very well, sir. (*Bell of outside door rings.* PARSONS *looks at* WATSON, *who shakes his head.*)

WATSON. No, I won't see any more tonight. They must go to Dr. Anstruther.

PARSONS. Very good, sir.

WATSON. Parsons! Why aren't those blinds down?

PARSONS. They was down a few moments ago, sir!

WATSON. That's strange! Well, you'd better pull them down now—again.

PARSONS. Yes sir. (*Bell rings twice as* PARSONS *pulls down second blind. He exits R. to answer it. Reenter* PARSONS *quickly, in a peculiar manner.*) If you please, sir—it *ain't* a patient at all, sir!

WATSON. Well, what is it?

PARSONS. A lady, sir—— (WATSON *looks up.*) And she wants to see you —most particular, sir.

WATSON. What about?

PARSONS. She didn't say, sir. Only she said it was of the h'utmost h'importance to 'er if you could see 'er, sir.

WATSON. Very well—I was going to walk for the exercise—but I can take a cab.

PARSONS. Then you'll see the lady, sir?

WATSON. Yes (*He goes on with his preparations.*) And call a cab for me at the same time—have it wait.

PARSONS. Yes sir. (*Exit at door R. Then reappears, ushering in a young lady, and exits when she has entered. Enter* MADGE LARRABEE, *removing a veil. She is now an impetuous, gushing society woman with trouble on her mind.*)

MADGE (*as she comes in*). Ah, Doctor—it's awfully good of you to see me! I'm Mrs. H. de Witte Seaton. (*Trying to find a cardcase.*) Dear me! I didn't bring my cardcase—or if I did I've lost it!

WATSON. Don't trouble about a card, Mrs. Seaton. (*With a gesture to indicate a chair.*)

MADGE. Oh, thank you so much! (*Sitting as she continues to talk.*) It's something that has happened, Doctor—it has *just simply happened*—I know it wasn't his fault! I *know* it!

WATSON. Whose fault?

MADGE. My brother's—my poor dear youngest brother—he *couldn't* have done such a thing, he simply *couldn't*, and——

WATSON. Such a thing as what, Mrs. Seaton?

MADGE. As to take the plans of our defenses at Gibraltar from the Admiralty office. You see, he works there. He was the only one who knew about them in the whole office! (*Overcome, she takes out her handkerchief and wipes her eyes.*)

WATSON. I'm very sorry indeed, Mrs. Seaton——

MADGE (*sobbing*). Oh, thank you so much! They said you were Mr. Holmes' friend—several people told me that, several. They advised me to ask you where I could find him—and everything depends on it, Doctor—*everything!*

WATSON. Holmes, of course! He's just the one you want!

MADGE. That's it! He's just the one! (*Choking down her sobs.*) Oh, thank you so much! Now what would you advise me to do?

WATSON. I'd go to Mr. Holmes at once!

MADGE. But I've *been!* I've been and he wasn't *there!*

WATSON. You went to his house?

MADGE. Yes—in Baker Street. That's why I came to you! They said he might be here!

WATSON. No—he isn't here.

(MADGE *looks deeply discouraged.*)

MADGE. But don't you expect him sometime this evening?

WATSON. No. (*Shaking his head.*) There's no possibility of his coming —so far as I know.

MADGE. But couldn't you *get* him to come? It would be *such* a great favor to me—I'm almost worn out with going about—and with this dreadful anxiety! If you could get word to him to—(*sees that* WATSON *is looking at her strangely*)—to come.

WATSON (*rising and speaking in a hard voice*). I could *not* get him to

come, madam. And I beg you to excuse me. I am going out myself—(*looks at his watch*)—on urgent business.

MADGE (*rising*). Then you think I had better call at his house again?

WATSON (*coldly*). That will be the wisest thing to do. (*He rings his.* bell. *There is an awkward pause, then enter* PARSONS *at door R. He stands waiting.*)

MADGE. Well—good night, Doctor!

(WATSON *bows coldly.* MADGE *turns to go. As she turns there is a loud noise in the distance, outside, as if in the street beyond the front door of the house—a noise of hoofs and the crash of a capsizing vehicle, followed by the excited shouts of men.*)

WATSON. What's that, Parsons?

PARSONS. H'it sounded to me like a h'accident, sir!

MADGE (*turning to* WATSON). Oh *dear!* I do hope it isn't anything serious! It affects me terribly to know that anyone is hurt!

WATSON. ·Probably nothing more than a broken-down hansom. See what it is, Parsons.

(MADGE *turns and looks toward door anxiously. As* PARSONS *turns to go there is a sudden vigorous ringing of the doorbell followed by a loud rapping on the door.*)

PARSONS. There's the bell, sir! Somebody's 'urt, sir, an' they're a-wantin' *you!*

WATSON. Well, don't allow anybody to come in! I have no more time! (*Hurriedly gathers his papers.*)

PARSONS. Very well, sir! (*Exits leaving door open.*)

(MADGE *turns and looks at* WATSON *anxiously, then toward the door again.*)

MADGE. But they're coming *in,* Doctor!

WATSON (*moving toward door*). Parsons! Parsons! (*There is a sound of voices outside.*)

VOICE. Let the ol' man come in, carn't yer?

ANOTHER VOICE. We 'ad to bring 'im in, man! There's nowhere else fer 'im to go! Wot kind of a doctor's office is this if 'e carn't come in when 'e's 'urt?

PARSONS (*outside*). The doctor can't see anybody!

VOICE. 'E's got to come in! We carn't tyke 'im out in the street, can we?

VOICES. Yes! Yes! Let him stay!

(*Enter* PARSONS.)

PARSONS. They *would* bring 'im in, sir! It's the old gentleman as was 'urt a bit w'en the 'ansom upset!

MADGE. *Oh!*

WATSON. Oh well—let them put him here—(*indicating an operating chair*) —and send at once for Dr. Anstruther.

PARSONS. Yes sir.

WATSON. Help him in, Parsons.

(*Parsons exits at door R.*)

MADGE. Oh, Doctor! Isn't it frightful!

WATSON (*turning to door up C.*). Mrs. Seaton, if you will be so good as to step this way you can reach the hall by taking the first door to your left.

MADGE (*hesitating*). But I—I may be of some use, Doctor!

WATSON (*impatiently*). None whatever! (*Holds door open.*)

MADGE. But, Doctor—I *must* see the poor fellow—I haven't the *power* to go!

WATSON (*facing her*). Madam, I believe you have some ulterior motive in coming here! You will kindly——

(*Enter at door R. a white-haired old gentleman in black clerical clothes assisted by* PARSONS *and a cabdriver. He limps as though his leg were hurt, and he is considerably soiled, as if he had been rolled in the street.*)

HOLMES (*as he comes in*). Oh, oh! (*He limps so that he hardly touches his right foot to the floor.*)

PARSONS. Right this way, sir! Be careful of the sill, sir! That's it!

CABMAN (*as he comes in*). Now we'll go right in 'ere! You'll see the doctor an' it'll be all right!

HOLMES. No, it won't be all right.

CABMAN. It was a h'accident. Yer carn't 'elp a h'accident.

HOLMES. *You* can't—that's plain enough!

CABMAN. 'E was on the wrong side of the street. I turned h'up——

PARSONS. Now over to this chair.

HOLMES (*pushing back and trying to stop at another chair*). No, I'll sit here.

PARSONS. No, this is the chair, sir.

HOLMES. Don't you suppose I know *where I want to sit down?*

CABMAN (*impatiently*). You'll sit 'ere! (*They lead him to chair R.C.*) Now the doctor'll 'ave a look at yer—'ere's the doctor!

HOLMES. That isn't a doctor!

CABMAN. It is a doctor! 'Ere, Doctor! Will you just come an' 'ave a look at this old party? (HOLMES *is trying to stop him.*) He's 'urt 'imself a little an'—an'——

HOLMES. Wait, wait, wait!

CABMAN. Well?

HOLMES. Are you the cabman?

CABMAN. Yes, I'm the cabman.

HOLMES. Well, I'll have you arrested for this!

CABMAN. Arrested?

HOLMES. Arrested, arrested, arrested!

CABMAN. Yer carn't arrest *me!*

HOLMES. No—I can't—but somebody else can.

CABMAN. 'Ere, 'ere! (*Trying to urge* HOLMES *into the chair.*)

HOLMES. You are a very disagreeable man! You are totally uninformed on every subject! I wonder you are able to live in the same house with yourself. (*Turns suddenly on* PARSONS.) Are *you* a cabman?

PARSONS. No sir.

HOLMES (*screaming*). Well, what *are* you?

PARSONS. I'm the butler, sir.

HOLMES. Butler! Butler! You're *not* —you're a cabman in disguise! Who'd have such a looking butler as you? What fool would——

CABMAN (*turning* HOLMES *toward him roughly*). He's the doctor's servant!

HOLMES. Who asked *you* who he was?

CABMAN. Never mind who asked me—I'm *telling* you!

HOLMES. Well, go and tell somebody else.

CABMAN (*trying to push* HOLMES *into the chair*). Sit down here! Sit down and be quiet!

HOLMES (*resisting*). Quiet! Quiet! Where's my hat? Where's my hat? My hat! *My hat!*

CABMAN. Never mind your 'at!

HOLMES. I will mind my hat!—and I hold you responsible——

CABMAN. There's your 'at in your 'and.

HOLMES (*looks at hat*). That isn't my hat! Here! (*The* CABMAN *is trying to push him into the chair.*) You're responsible! (*In the chair.*) I'll have you arrested! (*Clinging to the* CABMAN's *coattail as he tries to get away.*) Here! Come back! (*Choking with rage.*) Oh!

CABMAN (*wrenching away from* HOLMES's *grasp*). I carn't stay around 'ere, yer know! I've got to go and attend to me 'orse! (*Exit* CABMAN.)

HOLMES (*screaming after him*). Bring your horse in here—I want to speak to him! I want—— (*Lapses into groans and remonstrances.*) Oh! —Why didn't somebody stop him? These cabmen! What did he bring me in here for? I know where I am. It's a conspiracy! I won't stay in this place! If I ever get out of here alive——

WATSON (*to* PARSONS). Have a cab ready for me. I must see if he is badly hurt.

PARSONS. Yes sir. (*Exits quickly.*)

WATSON (*steps quickly to door*). And, Parsons—take that cabman's number. Now, sir, if you'll sit quiet for one moment I'll have a look at you! (*Goes to his desk.*)

(MADGE *advances nearer to the old gentleman, looking at him closely. She suddenly seems to be satisfied of something and backs away, turning and reaching out as if to get to the window and give a signal. Coming face to face with* WATSON, *she*

smiles *pleasantly at him and begins to move around toward the door as if to get out.* MADGE *shows by her expression that she has recognized* HOLMES *and is trying to evade suspicion. Quick as a flash the old gentleman springs to the door and stands facing her. She stops suddenly on finding him before her, stands for an instant, then wheels quickly about and goes rapidly across toward the window.*)

HOLMES (*sharply*). Don't let her get to that window!

(WATSON *instantly springs before her and* MADGE *stops.*)

WATSON. Good Lord! Is that *you*. Holmes?

HOLMES. Quite so, my dear fellow. (*He leisurely pushes back his wig and takes off his shawl.* MADGE *stands motionless.*)

WATSON. What do you want me to do?

HOLMES. That's all. You've done it! Don't do anything more just now.

(MADGE *gives them a sharp look, then suddenly turns and makes a dash for the door up C.*)

WATSON. Look out, Holmes! *She can get out that way!* (*A step or two up.*)

(MADGE *runs off at door up C.* HOLMES *is unmoved.*)

HOLMES. I don't think so. (*Saunters over to* WATSON's *desk.*) Well, well! What remarkable weather we're having, Doctor! Ah! I'm glad to see that you keep a few prescriptions carefully done up. (*Picks up a cigarette and sits on a corner of the desk.*) First aid to the injured, eh? (*Finds matches and lights his cigarette.*) Have you ever observed, Watson, that those people are always making——

(*Enter* CABMAN *at door up C.*)

CABMAN. I've got her, sir.

WATSON. Good heavens! Is that *Forman?*

HOLMES (*nods*). It's Forman, all right. Has Inspector Bradstreet come with his men?

FORMAN. Yes sir. One of 'em's in the hall here, holding her. The others are in the kitchen garden. They came in over the back wall from Mortimer Street.

HOLMES. One moment! (*Sits in thought.*) Watson, my dear fellow—as you doubtless gather from the little episode that has just taken place, we are making the arrests. We've made a pretty good haul already—four last night in the Gas Chamber—eleven this afternoon in various places, and one more just now. But I regret to say that up to this present time Professor Moriarty himself has not risen to the bait.

WATSON. Where do you think he is?

HOLMES. In the open streets—under some clever disguise—watching for a chance to get at me.

WATSON. And was this woman sent in here to——

HOLMES. Quite so! A spy—to let them know by some signal—probably at that window—if she found me in the house. And it has just occurred to me that it might not be such a very bad idea to try the Professor with *that* bait. *Forman!*

FORMAN. Yes sir!

HOLMES. One moment! Bring that Larrabee woman back here for a minute. When you see me light a fresh cigarette let go your hold on her—carelessly—as if your attention was attracted to something else. Pick her up again when I tell you.

FORMAN. Yes sir! (*Exits quickly at door up C. After a pause, re-enter* FORMAN, *bringing with him* MADGE LARRABEE. MADGE *is calm but looks venomous; she looks at* HOLMES *with the utmost hatred.*)

HOLMES. My dear Mrs. Larrabee— (MADGE, *who has looked away, turns to him angrily*)—I took the liberty of having you brought in for a moment—in order to convey to you —my sincere sympathy in your rather—unpleasant—predicament.

MADGE (*hissing it out angrily between her teeth*). It's a lie! It's a lie! There's no predicament!

HOLMES. Ah—I'm pleased to gather —from your somewhat forcible—er —observation—that you do not regard it—as such. Quite right too! Our prisons are so well conducted now!

MADGE. How your prisons may be conducted is no concern of mine! There is nothing they can hold me for—nothing!

HOLMES. To be sure! There may be something in that! Still—(*rises and moves to gas bracket*)—it occurred to me that you might prefer to be near your unfortunate husband. (*A good-natured chuckle.*) We hear a great deal about the heroic devotion of wives and all that—(*lights his cigarette at the gas*)—rubbish. You know, Mrs. Larrabee, when we come right down to it——

(*FORMAN carelessly relinquishes his hold on MADGE's arm and stands as if listening to something outside.*)

HOLMES (*apparently not noticing anything*). You know, Mrs. Larrabee, it's sometimes difficult to foresee the turns that Fortune's wheel—— (*MADGE makes a sudden dash for window down L., quickly snaps up the blind, and makes a rapid gesture up and down with her right hand, then turns and faces HOLMES with triumphant defiance.*) Ah, many thanks! (*To FORMAN.*) That's all, Forman. Pick her up again! Doctor, would you kindly pull the blind down once more? I don't care to be shot from the street.

MADGE (*in cruel triumph*). It's too late!

HOLMES. Too late, eh?

MADGE. The signal is given—you will hear from him soon!

HOLMES. It wouldn't surprise me at all!

(*The doorbell rings violently, and the voices of BILLY and PARSONS are heard outside the door. BILLY comes in a little way but is held back by PARSONS. He breaks away. BILLY is* dressed as a street gamin and is carrying a bunch of pink evening papers.*)

HOLMES. I think I shall hear from him now! Let him go, Parsons. Quick, Billy!

BILLY (*breathless*). He's just come, sir!

HOLMES. From where?

BILLY. The house across the street. He was in there a-watching these windows. He must 'ave seen something, for he's just come out. There was a cab waitin' in front of this house, sir—and he's climbed up an' changed places with the driver!

HOLMES (*with an amused glance at FORMAN*). Aha! Another cabman tonight! (*To BILLY.*) Where did the first driver go?

BILLY. He slunk away in the dark, sir—but he ain't gone far! An' there's two or three more 'anging about. They're a-layin' for to get you into that cab, sir!—But don't you do it, sir!

HOLMES. On the contrary, sir, I'll have that new cabman *in here*, sir! Get out again, quick, Billy, and keep your eye on him!

BILLY. Yes sir—thank you, sir! (*Runs off.*)

HOLMES. Watson, could you let me have a rather heavy portmanteau for a few moments? I won't do it any harm.

WATSON. Parsons—my large Gladstone—bring it here!

PARSONS. Yes sir. (*Exits.*)

WATSON. I'm afraid it's a pretty shabby-looking——

(MADGE *suddenly tries to break away from* FORMAN *and make a dash for the window, but* FORMAN *stops her.*)

HOLMES. Ah—many thanks, Mrs. Larrabee!—but your first signal was all that we required. By it you informed your friend Moriarty that I was here in the house. You are now aware of the fact that he is impersonating a cabdriver and that it is my intention to have him in here. You wish to signal that there is danger. There *is* danger, Mrs. Larrabee—but we don't care to have you let him know it. Take her out, Forman, and make her comfortable and happy. (FORMAN *leads* MADGE *toward the door.*) And by the way, Forman, you might tell the inspector to wait a few minutes—and I'll send him another lot.

FORMAN. Come along now! (*Takes her out at door up C. As* MADGE *exits she sneers and snaps her fingers in* HOLMES'S *face, then goes off laughing hysterically.*)

HOLMES. Fine woman! (*Enter* PARSONS *at door · R. carrying a large Gladstone valise.*) Ah!—put it down there. (*Pointing.*) Thank you so much. Parsons, you ordered a cab for the doctor a short time ago. It has been waiting, I believe?

PARSONS. Yes sir, I think it 'as, sir.

HOLMES. Be so good as to tell the driver to come in here and get a valise. When he comes tell him that's the one.

PARSONS. Very good, sir. (*Exits at door R.*)

HOLMES. My dear fellow—my dear fellow! In times like these you should tell your man never to take the first cab that comes on a call—nor yet the second—the third may be safe! (*He smokes placidly.*)

WATSON (*after· a pause*). But, Holmes——

(*The door opens and* PARSONS *enters, pointing the portmanteau out to someone who is following.*)

PARSONS. 'Ere it is—right in this way!

HOLMES (*in a loud voice to* WATSON). Well, good-by, old fellow! (*Shakes hands with him warmly.*) I'll write you from Paris—and I hope you'll keep me fully informed of the progress of events——

(MORIARTY *enters at door R. in the disguise of a cabman and goes at once to the valise which* PARSONS *points out, trying to hurry it through. He keeps his face away from* HOLMES.)

HOLMES (*goes right on, apparently paying no attention to* MORIARTY). As for those papers, I'll attend to them personally. Here, my man— (*to* MORIARTY)—just help me to tighten up these straps a bit—— (*He slides over to the valise and kneels, pulling at a strap, and* MORIARTY *bends over and does the same.*) There are a few little things in this bag—that I wouldn't like to lose. And it's just as well to—eh? (*Looking round for an instant.*) Who's that at the window?

(MORIARTY *looks quickly round without lifting his hands from the valise; at the same instant the snap of handcuffs is heard and he springs up with the irons on his wrists, roaring with rage. In rising his hat has been knocked off and he stands bareheaded, facing the audience.* HOLMES *drops quietly into a chair, his cigarette still in his mouth.*)

HOLMES (*lazily*). Doctor, will you kindly strike that bell of yours—two or three times—in rapid succession?

(WATSON *steps to the desk and gives several rapid strokes.*)

HOLMES. Many thanks.

(*Enter* FORMAN *at door up C. He crosses to* MORIARTY *and fastens the handcuff which he has on his own wrist to a chain attached to* MORIARTY'S. *The two men look at each other.*)

HOLMES. Forman!

FORMAN. Yes sir!

HOLMES. Got a man there with you?

FORMAN. Yes sir, the inspector came in himself.

HOLMES. Ah—suppose you introduce the professor to the inspector. I'm sure they'll be pleased to meet.

(FORMAN *starts to force* MORIARTY *off, but the prisoner hangs back and endeavors to get at* HOLMES. *There is a slight struggle.*)

HOLMES. Here! Here! Let's see what he wants!

MORIARTY (*in a low voice*). Do you imagine, Sherlock Holmes, that this is the end?

HOLMES (*seriously, after a pause*). I ventured to dream that it might be.

MORIARTY. Are you quite sure the police will be able to hold me?

HOLMES (*smiles slightly*). I am quite sure of nothing.

MORIARTY. *Ah!* (*After a pause.*) I have heard that you are planning to take a little trip—you and your friend here—a little trip on the Continent.

HOLMES. And if I do?

MORIARTY. I shall meet you there. (*There is another pause.*)

HOLMES. That's all, Forman.

(FORMAN *moves to the door quietly with* MORIARTY. *Once more the professor stops and turns toward* HOLMES; *he gives him a long earnest look—without malice—then moves on.* MORIARTY *and* FORMAN *exit at door up C.*)

HOLMES. Did you hear that, Watson?

WATSON. Yes—but surely you don't place any importance on such——

HOLMES (*stopping him with wave of the hand*). Oh—no importance! No importance! But, do you know, I have a fancy that he spoke the truth!

WATSON. Good heavens! We'll give up the trip!

HOLMES. Good heavens, we'll do nothing of the kind. What does it matter, here or there—if it must come! (*He sits meditating for a moment.*) If it must come!

WATSON (*after a long pause*). Parsons! (*Points to the valise.* PARSONS *removes it.*) Good heavens, Holmes! (*Looking at his watch.*) We've barely five minutes!

HOLMES (*innocently*). For what?

WATSON. To get to Baker Street—your rooms! (HOLMES *still looks at him.*) Your appointment with Sir Edward and the Count! They were to receive that packet of letters from you.

HOLMES. They're coming here.

WATSON. *Here!*

HOLMES. That is—if you'll be so good as to permit it.

WATSON. Of course! But why not there?

HOLMES. The scoundrels have burned me out.

WATSON. Good heavens! Burned out —— (HOLMES *nods*). Oh, that's too bad! And you lost everything?

HOLMES (*with an upward toss of both arms*). Everything! Everything! I'm glad of it. I'm glad of it, Watson! *I've had enough!*—This one thing—that I shall do here, in a few moments—is the finish!

WATSON. You mean—Miss Faulkner? (HOLMES *nods slightly.*)

HOLMES (*turning suddenly*). Why, Watson—she trusted me! She—

clung to me! (WATSON *has been watching him narrowly.*) What does it matter? Life is a small affair at the most—a little while—a few sunrises and sunsets—the warm breath of a few summers—the cold chill of a few winters—and then——

WATSON. And then——? (HOLMES *turns and looks steadily in* WATSON'S *eyes.*)

HOLMES. And *then.*

WATSON (*going to him*). My dear Holmes—I'm afraid that plan of—gaining her confidence and regard —went a little further than you intended? (HOLMES *nods assent.*) But —if you both love each other——

HOLMES (*quickly—his hand on* WATSON'S *shoulder*). No, no! Don't say it, Watson! Don't tempt me with such a thought! That girl! Young—exquisite—just beginning her sweet life. I—seared, drugged, poisoned—nearly at the end! Oh no! I must cure her! I must stop it—*now*—before it's too late! She's coming here, Watson—yes, a little before Sir Edward and the Count. In fact, it's because they're coming that I want her here. (*He turns and walks rapidly to the door up L., getting a book on the way and placing it in the way of the door's closing.*) When she comes let her wait in that room. You can manage that, I'm sure.

WATSON. Certainly. (*Pointing.*) Did you intend to leave that book there?

HOLMES (*nods*). To keep the door from closing. She is to overhear.

WATSON. I see.

HOLMES. Sir Edward and the Count are quite likely to become excited.

I shall endeavor to make them so. They may even use strong language. Don't be alarmed, old fellow! (*Bell of outside door rings.* HOLMES *and* WATSON *look at each other.*)

HOLMES. She may be here now. I'll go to your dressing room for a moment, if you'll allow me, and brush away a little of this dust.

WATSON. By all means! Mrs. Watson is in the drawing room. Do look in on her a moment—it will please her so much.

HOLMES. It will more than please me! (*Opens door and the sound of a piano is heard playing in another room.*) Mrs. Watson! Home—love—life! Ah, Watson—— (*He sighs a little, then turns and exits at door up C.* WATSON *turns and goes to his desk but remains standing. Enter* PARSONS.)

PARSONS. A lady, sir, wants to know if she can speak to you. If there's anyone 'ere she won't come in.

WATSON. Any name?

PARSONS. No sir. I ast 'er an' she said it was unnecessary—as you wouldn't know 'er. She 'as 'er maid with 'er, sir.

WATSON. Show her in here—let the maid wait in the reception room. (PARSONS *turns to go.*) And Parsons—(*in a lower voice*)—two gentlemen, Count Von Stalburg and Sir Edward Leighton, will call. Bring them here to this room at once and then tell Mr. Holmes. You'll find him in my dressing room.

PARSONS. Yes sir.

WATSON. Send everybody else away —I'll see that lady.

PARSONS. Yes sir.

(*Exits at door R., leaving it open. A moment later he reappears with* ALICE FAULKNER. *She glances apprehensively about, fearing she will see* HOLMES. *Sensing that* WATSON *is alone, she is relieved and goes toward him.* PARSONS *closes the door from outside.*)

ALICE (*with some timidity*). Is this —is this Dr. Watson's?

WATSON (*encouragingly, advancing a step or two*). Yes—and I am Dr. Watson.

ALICE. Is—would you mind telling me if Mr. Holmes—Mr.—Sherlock Holmes—is here?

WATSON. He *will* be before long, Miss—er——

ALICE. My name is Faulkner.

WATSON. Miss Faulkner. He came a short time ago but has gone upstairs for a few moments.

ALICE. Oh! (*With an apprehensive look.*) And is he coming down—soon?

WATSON. Well, the fact is, Miss Faulkner, he has an appointment with two gentlemen here, and I was to let him know as soon as they arrived.

ALICE. Do you suppose I could wait, without troubling you too much— and see him—*afterward?*

WATSON. Why, certainly.

ALICE. Thank you—and I—I don't want him to know—that—I—that I came.

WATSON. Of course, if you wish, there's no need of my telling him.

ALICE. It's—very important *indeed* that you *don't*, Dr. Watson. I can explain it all to you afterward.

WATSON. No explanation is necessary, Miss Faulkner.

ALICE. Thank you. (*Glances about.*) I suppose there is a waiting room for—for *patients?*

WATSON. Yes, or you could sit in there (*indicating door*). You'll be less likely to be disturbed—if you don't mind a few medicine bottles about!

ALICE. Yes, I'd prefer that. (*She glances toward door up L. Bell of front door rings.*)

WATSON. Then step this way. I think the gentlemen have arrived.

ALICE (*turns at door*). And when the business between the gentlemen is over, would you please have someone tell me?

WATSON. I'll tell you myself, Miss Faulkner. ˙

ALICE. Thank you. (*She exits at door up L.* PARSONS *enters at door R.*)

PARSONS. Count Von Stalburg. Sir Edward Leighton. (*Enter* SIR EDWARD *and the* COUNT VON STALBURG. *Exit* PARSONS.)

WATSON. Count—Sir Edward—— (*bowing and coming forward*).

SIR EDWARD. Dr. Watson! (*Bows.*) Good evening. (VON STALBURG *bows slightly.*) Our appointment with Mr. Holmes was changed to your house, I believe.

WATSON. Quite right, Sir Edward. Pray be seated, gentlemen.

SIR EDWARD *takes a chair and seats himself, as does* WATSON.)

VON STALBURG (*standing*). Mr. Holmes is a trifle late.

WATSON. He has already arrived, Count. I have sent for him.

VON STALBURG. Ugh! (*He saunters to the wall R. and examines a picture.*)

SIR EDWARD. It was quite a surprise to receive his message an hour ago, changing the place of meeting. We should otherwise have gone to his house.

VON STALBURG (*coming forward*). Did I understand you to say, Doctor, that you had sent for Mr. Holmes?

WATSON. Yes, Count, and he will be here shortly—indeed, I think I hear him on the stairs now.

(*Enter* HOLMES *at door up C. He is very pale. His clothing has been rearranged and cleansed, though he still wears the clerical suit.* SIR EDWARD *rises and turns to him.*)

HOLMES (*coming forward. He speaks in low clear voice*). Gentlemen, be seated again, I beg. (*After a pause.*) Our business this evening can be quickly disposed of. You were notified to come here in order that I might deliver into your hands the packet which you engaged me on behalf of your—*exalted client*—to recover. Let me say, in justice to myself, that but for that agreement on my part I would never have continued with the work. As it was, however, I felt bound to do so—and I now have the honor to place the papers in your hands. (*Both gentlemen rise.*)

SIR EDWARD (*formally*). Permit me to congratulate you, Mr. Holmes, upon the marvelous skill you have displayed and the promptness with which you have fulfilled your agreement.

(HOLMES *bows slightly and turns away.* SIR EDWARD *at once breaks the seals of the packet and looks at the contents. He begins to show surprise as he glances at one or two letters, and quickly motions to the* COUNT, *who goes to him. Their subdued exclamations of astonishment are audible.*)

COUNT. Oh no, no, no!

SIR EDWARD (*stopping his examination and looking across at* HOLMES). What does this mean? (HOLMES *turns in apparent surprise.*) These letters! And these—other things! *Where did you get them?*

HOLMES. I purchased them last night.

SIR EDWARD. Purchased them?

HOLMES. Quite so.

VON STALBURG. From whom, if I may ask?

HOLMES. From the parties interested, by the consent of Miss Faulkner.

SIR EDWARD. You have been deceived!

HOLMES. *What!*

(WATSON *rises and stands at his desk.*)

SIR EDWARD (*excitedly*). This packet contains *nothing*—not a single letter or paper that we wanted! All clever imitations! The photographs are of another person. You have been *duped!* With all your supposed cleverness they have *tricked you!*

(HOLMES *stands motionless.*)

VON STALBURG. Most decidedly duped, Mr. Holmes!

HOLMES. Why, this is terrible! (*Turns back to L. and to* WATSON. *Stands looking in his face.*) .

SIR EDWARD (*astonished*). Terrible? Terrible? You surely do not mean, by that, that there is a possibility you may not be able to recover them?

(*Enter* ALICE *at door up L. and stands listening up L.*)

HOLMES. It's quite true!

SIR EDWARD. After your positive assurances! After the steps we have taken in the matter by your advice! Why—why, this is outrageous. Why, I—— (*Turns to* COUNT *too indignant to go on.*)

VON STALBURG (*indignantly*). Do you mean to say there is no hope of it?

HOLMES. None whatever, Count! It's too late now! I can't begin all over again!

SIR EDWARD (*throws package on the floor*). Why, this is scandalous! It is criminal, sir! You had no right to mislead us in this way, and you shall certainly suffer the consequences. I shall see that you are brought into court to answer for it.

HOLMES. There is nothing to do, Sir Edward. I am ruined—ruined!

(ALICE *crosses quickly toward* SIR EDWARD, *passing above* HOLMES *and* WATSON. *She is entirely calm and self-possessed.*)

ALICE. It's all a mistake, Sir Edward. I'm so sorry. This is the packet you wanted. (*Giving it to* SIR EDWARD.) Mr. Holmes didn't know that—that he had the wrong one.

SIR EDWARD (*astounded*). Well, this is—er—this is certainly kind of you —Miss—er—Miss——

ALICE. My name is Faulkner.

SIR EDWARD. Yes, very kind indeed, Miss Faulkner—e—e—eh, Count?

VON STALBURG. Surely kind—if it isn't another swindle!

SIR EDWARD. Will you mind if we—— (*Indicates opening package to examine.*)

ALICE. Oh, not at all! (*She backs a step or two, bringing her near up C. Business* SIR EDWARD *and* COUNT *quickly opening and examining contents of package. They show that they are satisfied.*)

SIR EDWARD. This is certainly what we wanted!

VON STALBURG. Quite genuine— quite genuine!

SIR EDWARD. We are greatly indebted to you, Miss Faulkner!

VON STALBURG. To be sure!

SIR EDWARD. And to you too, Mr. Holmes—if this was a part of your general scheme! (HOLMES *turns to* SIR EDWARD *on cue "you too, Mr. Holmes," and stands rather stiffly facing him.*) It was certainly an extraordinary method of obtaining possession of valuable documents!

VON STALBURG. Quite extraordinary!

SIR EDWARD (*going to* HOLMES). You have only to notify me of the charge for your invaluable services and you will receive a check.

HOLMES. Kind, I'm sure, Sir Edward.

SIR EDWARD (*shaking hands with* HOLMES). Good night, sir.

(HOLMES, *shaking hands with* SIR EDWARD, *murmurs a good night in reply to him, and* COUNT VON STALBURG *bows punctiliously to* HOLMES. HOLMES *returns the bow.* SIR EDWARD *shakes hands with* WATSON.)

SIR EDWARD. Good night, Doctor. It was most kind of you to allow us the use of your consulting room.

(PARSONS *enters at door R. and stands just within.*)

VON STALBURG. Entirely so—entirely so. (*Exits with* SIR EDWARD. DR.

WATSON *stands at door as the two pass out and follows them off.* PARSONS, *when they are well off, exits at door R. and closes it after him. After his slight bow of good night to the* COUNT, HOLMES *turns away and, while the party is making ready to leave, turns away and moves L., sinking rather wearily into* DR. WATSON's *chair at desk L.C. He glances absently at book or railway guide on desk and once or twice raises his eyes with a pained expression, dreading what is to come. After exit of* SIR EDWARD, COUNT, WATSON, *and* PARSONS, ALICE *remains a moment where she was near up C. Then, after a glance at* HOLMES, *she moves toward him.*)

ALICE. Aren't you—aren't you going to say good night?

HOLMES (*quickly rises to his feet and slight pause as he faces* ALICE. *Low voice*). Miss Faulkner—you have no reason to allow me to do such a thing.

ALICE (*surprised*). But why?

HOLMES. Because by now you must begin to realize the trick and—and the deception I've practiced on you in order to make you give up your property. I couldn't take it out of the house that first night like a straightforward thief, because it could have been recovered at law. And for that reason I—(*with an effort*)—I swindled you out of it. (*Looks down on desk at last words.*)

ALICE (*surprised*). Swindled me!

HOLMES (*turning toward her and speaking emphatically*). Precisely!—That's just what I did—swindled you out of it!—Now that you know this, Miss Faulkner, and now that you realize what—what sort of a person I am, it must be sufficient to make you—to make you turn away from me with loathing and disgust! (*On last word he turns away and is moving toward door up L. when he is stopped by* ALICE *speaking.*)

ALICE. But it isn't sufficient!

(HOLMES *turns quickly, toward her and the two stand facing each other in silence for an instant.* ALICE *at back of chair near right of desk,* HOLMES *halfway to door.*)

HOLMES (*slightly uncertain at first*). Yes—well—I—I'm sorry, but I must be going!—I suppose mademoiselle is waiting to take you home. (*Is turning to go.*)

ALICE (*quickly*). But, Mr. Holmes!

HOLMES (*stops and turns toward* ALICE). Yes?

ALICE. I—— (*she lowers her eyes for a moment—then looks up in his face*)—I want to ask you something. (*She looks down with slight embarrassment.*)

HOLMES. Certainly. (*He moves down near upper left end of desk and stands facing her.*) What is it?

(*A pause.* HOLMES *looking at* ALICE. ALICE *stands with eyes lowered. Soon she raises her eyes to his.*)

ALICE (*looking in his face*). Don't you care for me—at all?

HOLMES (*after very slight pause*). It can make no difference whatever whether I do or not.

ALICE (*low voice*). It can make a—a great deal of difference—to me. (*She turns away as she speaks the last word or two and moves a little way toward C.* HOLMES *watches* ALICE *as she moves away and after an instant of hesitation goes to her—crossing between the chair and the desk—and takes her left hand gently in his. As* HOLMES *touches her hand* ALICE *turns to him quickly.*)

HOLMES. Miss Faulkner—— (*He hesitates.*)

ALICE (*looking up in his face and speaking in hardly more than a whisper*). Yes?

HOLMES. This is—this is a trying situation, isn't it?—Of course we—we must find some way out of it.

ALICE. But I don't want any way out of it!

HOLMES (*looks down into her face before speaking*). Do you remember that you asked me a question just now? (ALICE *nods a little.*) Well, this is the answer—I do care for you—I do!—But I'm not telling you anything—you knew it perfectly well before.

ALICE. But I think it's just as well for you to say it.

HOLMES. I *do* say it—but, dearest one, that must be the end of it! Do you fancy for one second that I'd allow your young life to be tangled up with a life like mine?—You at the very beginning—I only a few years from the end at the very most.—Why, it would be simply a——

ALICE (*interrupting*). But listen, please!—I want you to—oh, I want to tell you!—All that is nothing—nothing—because whatever life you have left is my life too—all my life—all the life I want! (HOLMES *looks down in her eyes for an instant—then puts his arms around her and draws her close to him, her head against his breast and her face turned to front or near it, for final spotlight which holds the two faces for a moment, then slowly fades out.*)

CURTAIN

Within the Law

A Melodrama in Four Acts By

BAYARD VEILLER

THE CAST

Within the Law *was first produced by Messrs. Selwyn & Company at the Eltinge Theatre, New York, September 11, 1912.*

Sarah, *Edward Gilder's private secretary*	Georgia Lawrence
Smithson, *floorwalker at The Emporium*	S. V. Phillips
Richard Gilder, *Edward Gilder's son*	Orme Caldara
Edward Gilder, *proprietor of The Emporium*	Dodson Mitchell
George Demarest, *Edward Gilder's lawyer*	Brandon Hurst
Helen Morris, *a salesgirl in The Emporium*	Catherine Tower
Detective Sergeant Cassidy *of the New York police*	John Willard
Mary Turner, *a saleswoman in The Emporium*	Jane Cowl
Agnes Lynch, *a confidence woman*	Florence Nash
Joe Garson, *a forger*	William B. Mack
Fannie, *a maid*	Martha White
William Irwin, *a lawyer*	William A. Norton
Eddie Griggs, *a crook known as "English Eddie"*	Kenneth Hill
Police Inspector Burke *of the New York police*	Wilton Taylor
Thomas, *a butler*	Arthur Moore
Chicago Red, *a crook*	Arthur Spaulding
Tom Dacey, *a crook*	John Camp
Williams, *a stenographer at police headquarters*	Joseph Nickson
Thompson, *a detective of the New York police*	Edward Bolton
Dan, *doorman at police headquarters*	Frederick Howe

WITHIN THE LAW

ACT ONE

TIME—*About noon. Early spring.*

SCENE—*Office of* EDWARD GILDER, *proprietor of The Emporium. There is a door down L. leading into the store and another door up C. leading into the hall. The door down L. opens off and up stage, and the door up C. opens up and to the L. Down R., almost to the curtain line, is* MR. GILDER'S *desk, set at an angle. so that anyone coming in the door C. or the door L. can be observed by anyone sitting at the desk, without moving. The angle of the desk is from down R. to up R.C. Up R., set obliquely, is a large table covered with department-store samples. The angle of this desk is from down L. to up C. A hat tree is just left of Center door. There is an office chair in upper Right corner and a large leather rocker right of Center door, and above* GILDER'S *desk; another leather chair is down L. just below door L. There is an office chair just below sample table and facing up stage. Another office chair is R. of* GILDER'S *desk. There is a plain green carpet on the floor. All of this furniture, with the exception of the two leather chairs, is mahogany. The leather chairs are green leather. The walls of the office are paneled in mahogany halfway up and the upper half is plain green.*

AT RISE—SARAH *is discovered seated at* GILDER'S *desk opening mail. When the curtain is well up* SMITHSON *enters left and crosses to L.C.* SARAH *just looks up and then goes on with her work.*

SMITHSON. Has Mr. Gilder come down yet?

SARAH. He's down at the Court of General Sessions.

SMITHSON (*as he crosses to L. of desk*). Ah! Yes, I remember now. Well, I hope the girl gets off. She's a nice little thing.

SARAH. Oh, did you know her?

SMITHSON. Naturally one doesn't know salespeople; but they put her in my department when she first came to work here. She's a good saleswoman, as saleswomen go; in fact, I thought her a very worthy person. She's the last girl in the world I'd take for a thief (*going toward door L.*). Will you please let me know when Mr. Gilder arrives? I have several little matters I want to discuss with him.

(SMITHSON *exits L. Door at C. is thrown open and* DICK GILDER *rushes in and down C. with a suitcase in his hand as he speaks.*)

DICK. Hello, Dad!

(SARAH *looks up and, as she sees* DICK, *quickly rises and goes around lower end of desk to meet* DICK *at C. as she speaks.*)

SARAH. Why, Mr. Dick!

DICK (DICK *stops at C. as he shows his displeasure at not finding his father in. He drops his suitcase and extends both his hands to* SARAH, *who takes them).* Oh, hello, Sadie. I'm home. Where's Dad?

SARAH. In court.

DICK (*as he drops* SARAH's *hands*). In court? (*Laughingly.*) What's he done this time? (SARAH *laughs and, going to lower end of desk, sits and continues her work as* DICK *removes his hat and, crossing to the opposite side of the desk, half sits on it.*) Remember the time that fresh cop arrested him for speeding? I thought he'd have the whole police force discharged.

SARAH. We didn't expect you for two or three months yet.

DICK (*crossing to desk and half sitting on it*). Sadie, don't ever let the old man know it, he'd be all swelled up, and we can't afford to let our parents swell up. It's bad for them, but I got kind of homesick for Dad.

SARAH (*looking up at* DICK *with a laugh*). Oh!

DICK. That's the truth. I went broke, too.

(SARAH *laughs.*)

DICK. What's Father doing in court?

SARAH. One of the girls was arrested for stealing.

DICK. And Dad went down to court to get her out of the scrape. Isn't that just like the old man.

SARAH. She was tried last week and convicted. The judge sent for Mr.

Gilder to come down this morning and have a talk with him about the sentence.

DICK. Oh well, it'll be all right. Dad's heart is as big as a barrel. He'll get her off. (DICK *gives a sudden start, jumps off desk, and, as he goes hurriedly towards door at C.*) Oh Lord! I forgot all about it.

SARAH. About what, Mr. Dick?

DICK (*as he turns to* SARAH). My taxi's been waiting all this time. (SARAH *goes on with her work, not noticing* DICK. DICK *goes all through his pockets, then looking at* SARAH *with some hesitation.*) Sadie—Sadie, have you got five dollars?

SARAH (*looking at* DICK *with a laugh*). Five dollars?

DICK. Yes. I'm broke.

SARAH. Wait a minute. (SARAH *turns up stage and starts for her stocking.* DICK, *as he realizes what* SARAH *is about to do, turns away towards sample table and puts his hand over his eyes.* SARAH *gets the money from her stocking and, as she offers one bill across the desk to* DICK.) Here you are.

DICK (*as he quickly crosses to* SARAH *and takes the money*). Thanks. Say, Sadie, remember when I used to borrow nickels from you to buy candy?

SARAH. Yes, and you're not much older now than you were ten years ago.

DICK (*as he crosses over and picks up his suitcase*). I'll be right back, but I won't come until I know Dad's here. I want to give him the surprise of his young life. (*Starts toward door at C., but stops and looks at his suitcase, then turns to* SARAH.) Where can I put this so he won't see it?

SARAH (*as she goes on with her work*). Oh, anywhere.

DICK (*looks around, then*). Oh, I know. (*Crosses and puts suitcase under sample table and starts to door C.*) Don't give him a hint, will you, Sadie?

SARAH. No indeed!

DICK (*in the doorway at C.*). That's an old dear. I'm tickled to death to see you again, Sadie, really I am.

SARAH. Me too, Mr. Dick. (DICK *exits at C. Phone bell rings.* SARAH *rises and, going around to upper end of desk so that she faces front, picks up phone.*) Hello—hello? No sir, he hasn't reached the office yet. (*Pause.*) At four this afternoon. Wait till I see. (SARAH *leans across the desk and looks at memo pad, then back into phone.*) Yes, he'll be free at four, but he has another engagement at four-thirty—— (MR. GILDER *enters at C. and, as* SARAH *continues, bangs his hat on hat tree and crosses to phone.*) Just a minute, Mr. Hastings. Here's Mr. Gilder now. (*To* GILDER, *as she sets the phone down and· steps back.*) Mr. Hastings of the Empire wants to know if you can see him at four this afternoon.

(MR. GILDER *picks up phone as* SARAH *crosses to sample table and examines samples.*)

MR. GILDER (*into phone*). Oh, good morning. (*Pause.*) Yes, certainly, four will suit me admirably. (*Pause.*) Sunday? Why, yes, if you like. We can stop at the Claremont for a highball and have a lunch at the Country Club; yes, we can go out right after church. (*Pause.*) My dear fellow, you couldn't beat me in a thousand years. Why, I made the eighteen holes in ninety-two last week. (*Pause.*) For fifty, all right, you're on! (*With a laugh he bangs up receiver and goes to his chair at desk, sits and starts to work at his mail.*)

SARAH (*as* GILDER *sits*). What did they do to the Turner girl?

MR. GILDER (*impatiently and going on sorting the mail*). I don't know. I couldn't wait. I don't see why Judge Lawler bothered me about the matter. He's the one to impose sentence, not me. I'm hours behind with my work now, and I had to stop on my way and talk for nearly an hour with old Cushing. Sarah, he's getting more fussy every year. Sarah! (SARAH *crosses quickly to L. of desk,* GILDER *handing her a pile of opened letters.*) Give these to Smith to attend to (*handing her another pile of mail*). These go to Osgood. (GILDER *picks up another pile of letters and looking through them hurriedly.*) I'll reply to this lot myself this afternoon. (*Drops the letters into letter basket.* SARAH *starts door L. and* GILDER *takes back one letter from the basket.*) Oh, Sarah. (SARAH *stops.*) Take this before I forget it. (SARAH *comes back to the desk, seats herself in chair L., and picks up her notebook and pencil, taking* MR. GILDER'S *dictation.*) "Mr. Gilden, Editor New York Herald—Dear Sir: Enclosed please find my check for one thousand dollars for your Free Ice Fund. It's going to be a very hard summer for the poor and I hope by starting the contributions to your noble charity at this early date that you will be able to accomplish even more good than ever before. Very truly yours." (*To Sarah.*) That's what I usually give, isn't it, Sarah?

SARAH (*without looking up*). That's what you've given every year for the last ten years.

MR. GILDER (*settling back in his chair with a self-satisfied air*). Ten thousand to this one charity alone. Ah, it's splendid to be able to help those less fortunate than ourselves!

SARAH (*without looking away from her notebook*). Yes sir, especially when we make so much we don't miss it.

GILDER (*looking at* SARAH *rather sternly*). The profits from my store are large, I admit, but I neither smuggle my goods, take rebates from railroads, conspire against small competitors, nor do any of the dishonest things that disgrace other lines of business. As long as I make my profits honestly, I'm honestly entitled to them, no matter how large they are.

SARAH (*rising and starting towards door L.*). Yes sir.

GILDER. Have the cashier send my usual five hundred to the Charity Organization Society. (SARAH *starts toward door L.*) And, Sarah— (SARAH *stops and turns. She is just at C.*)—I don't like your remark about my not missing the money I give. What difference does that make?

SARAH (*at C.*). Oh, I didn't mean anything wrong, Mr. Gilder.

GILDER. Just the same, I don't like it. (SARAH *crosses to door L.* DEMAREST *enters at C.*) Well, Demarest? (*As* SARAH *reaches door L. she stops and turns.*)

DEMAREST (*at door C.*). Judge Lawler gave her three years.

GILDER. Three years? Good. Take this, Sarah. (*During* GILDER'S *next speech* SARAH *crosses to L. of desk and stands with notebook open.* DEMAREST *goes to hat tree and hangs his hat up.*) Have Smithson post a copy of it conspicuously in all the girls' dressing rooms, and in the reading room, lunch room, and assembly room. (*Dictating.* SARAH *takes the dictation, while* DEMAREST *comes down C. on a level with* SARAH.) "Mary Turner, formerly employed in this store, was today sent to prison for three years, having been convicted of the theft of goods valued at over four hundred dollars. The management wishes again to draw the attention of its employees to the fact that honesty is always the best policy." Got that?

SARAH. Yes sir.

GILDER. Take it to Smithson and tell him I want it attended to immediately.

SARAH. Yes sir.

(SARAH *crosses to door L. and exits.* GILDER *opens right top drawer of his desk and takes out a box of cigars, which he offers to* DEMAREST.)

GILDER. Smoke, Demarest?

DEMAREST (*crossing to back of chair L. of* GILDER'S *desk*). No, thanks.

GILDER (*as he takes a cigar from the box, returns the box to the drawer, and lights the cigar. Thoughtfully*). Three years—three years. Well, that ought to be a warning to the rest of the girls.

DEMAREST (*over the back of the chair of* GILDER'S *desk*). Funny thing, this case. One of the most unusual I have seen since I began practicing law.

CILDER (*sitting down in his chair and smoking cigar*). Very—(*puff*)—sad—(*puff*)—case—(*puff*)—I call it.

DEMAREST. Very sad case! The girl persists in declaring that she's innocent.

GILDER. But the stolen goods were found in her locker—some of them even in the pocket of her coat.

DEMAREST. She says someone must have put them there.

GILDER. Who, and for what reason? It's too absurd to talk about.

DEMAREST. She says, as well, that her record of five years in your employ ought to count.

GILDER (*with finality*). A court of justice has declared her guilty.

DEMAREST. Nowadays we don't call them courts of justice, we call them courts of law.

GILDER. Anyway, it's out of our hands. There's nothing we can do.

DEMAREST (*as he comes around from the back of the chair and sits in the chair L. of* GILDER'S *desk*). Although I helped to prosecute the case, I am not proud of the verdict.

GILDER. Why?

DEMAREST. Because, in spite of the evidence, I'm not sure she's guilty.

GILDER. But the goods were found——

DEMAREST (*interrupting him*). I admit it.

GILDER (*triumphantly*). Then there you are.

DEMAREST (*slowly and seriously*). Gilder, she wants to *see* you.

GILDER. What's the use? I can't have a woman crying all over the place and begging for mercy.

DEMAREST. The girl isn't begging for mercy. She's a very unusual girl —very unusual—much above the average saleswoman, both in brain and education. Just before the judge imposed sentence he asked her if she had anything to say—you know, the usual form—and she surprised us all by saying that she had. You should have waited, Gilder; she made a damn fine speech.

GILDER (*with some eagerness*). Did she say anything against me or the store?

DEMAREST. Not a word; she told how her father died when she was in high school and how she had to earn her own living since she was sixteen, and how she worked for you for five years without there being a thing against her; she said she'd never even seen the goods found in her locker, and then asked the judge if he knew what it meant for a girl to be sent to prison for three years for something she hadn't done. It took brains and courage to do it, and it all rang true. I believe Lawler would have suspended the sentence if it hadn't been for your talk with him.

GILDER (*rising*). I simply did my duty—(*crossing around in front of desk up to sample table*)—I didn't seek the interview (*turning and coming down C.*). Judge Lawler sent for me and asked me what I thought about the case; whether I thought it would be right to let the girl go on suspended sentence. (*Turning to* DEMAREST.) I told him frankly I thought an example should be made of her, for the sake of the others who might be tempted to steal. (*Takes stage down L., then, turning to* DEMAREST.) Property has some rights, Demarest, although it's getting so nowadays that nobody seems to think so. (*A pause as* GILDER *smokes a puff or two and crosses to C.*) I can't understand why the girl wants to see me.

DEMAREST (*as he rises and crosses to* GILDER, C.). She said if you'd see her for ten minutes, she'd tell you how to stop the thefts in this store.

GILDER (*triumph*). There you are. She wants to confess. It's the first sign of decent feeling she has shown. There may have been others mixed up in this thing.

DEMAREST. Perhaps. Anyway, it can do no harm. I've seen the district attorney and he's given orders to have her brought here on her way to Grand Central. They are taking her up to Auburn. Better have a little talk with her. (*As* DEMAREST *goes up to hat tree and gets his hat,* GILDER *takes a step or two down L.*) Let me know what the girl tells you. I'm curious about it.

(*Door at C. is thrown violently open and* DICK *rushes in.*)

DICK. Hello, Dad! (DICK *rushes down to* GILDER, *dropping his hat on sample table at L.C. as he passes. They embrace.*)

GILDER. Dick! (*After the embrace, as* DICK *draws back.*) What brought you back?

DICK (*as he steps back from* GILDER). Oh, I just wanted to come home. Say, Dad, I'm broke. (DEMAREST *comes slowly down C. with his hat in his hand.*)

GILDER. Poker on the ship?

DICK. Nope. They hired Captain Kidd and a bunch of his pirates as stewards, and what they did to little Richard—— (DICK *turns away from* GILDER *as if to cross to desk and sees* DEMAREST. DICK *puts out his hand and they shake hands as* DICK *continues.*) Why, hello, Mr. Demarest. You're looking fine. How's business?

DEMAREST. Pretty good, Dick, pretty good.

DICK. Glad to hear it.

DEMAREST (DEMAREST *starts for the door up C.* DICK *crosses to upper end of desk at R.C. and* GILDER *crosses below the desk to his chair back of it, and sits, as he lays his cigar in the ash tray. As* DEMAREST *goes.*) I'll get along now, Gilder. (DEMAREST, *about to go out, turns in the doorway.*) Oh, come down and see me, Dick, any time you need legal advice.

DICK (*at the upper end of the desk at R.C. and facing* DEMAREST). I'm not going to need any legal advice.

DEMAREST. I hope not. Good-by. (*Exits through door C.*)

DICK (*comes around to the side of desk and sits on it, facing* GILDER, *and pats his shoulder*). Well, Dad, how goes it?

GILDER. Pretty well, Son. I'm glad to see you home again, my boy.

DICK. And I'm glad to be home—to see you.

GILDER. Have a good time?

DICK. I had the time of my young life. I nearly broke the bank at Monte Carlo.

GILDER (*with a laugh*). Oh-oh!

DICK. I'd have done it, too—if my money had lasted.

GILDER (*with mock seriousness*). So that's where it went?

DICK. Yes sir.

GILDER. Why didn't you cable me? (SARAH *enters door L. and crosses to L.C.*)

DICK (*sincerely, and leaning across and placing his hand on his father's shoulder*). Because it gave me a good excuse for coming home.

SARAH (*at L.C., with notebook and pencil*). I see you found him.

GILDER. Yes.

DICK (*off the desk, passes around upper end of it to C., facing* SARAH). Sadie, you're looking finer than ever; and how thin you've grown!

SARAH (*sincerely*). Really! (*As she takes stage, down L.*) How much do you think I've lost?

DICK (*eyeing her, with a laugh*). Let me see. I should say about—two —ounces.

SARAH (*as she turns and faces him with a laugh*). Oh, you!

DICK. You're not angry with me, are you?

SARAH. Why, no. Of course not. Then——

DICK. Then give me a little kiss. (DICK *starts towards* SARAH. SARAH *crosses in front of* DICK *and up towards door C. As* SARAH *passes* DICK, *he catches her left arm and she keeps him protesting and drawing closer to door C. with* DICK *trying to draw her to him.*) Oh, come on, Sadie. (GILDER *rises and comes up above his desk towards* DICK *and* SARAH.)

SARAH. No, no, please, Mr. Dick.

DICK. Just to show there's no ill-feeling.

SARAH. Oh, please stop, Mr. Dick.

GILDER (*as he takes* DICK's *right arm and starts him walking down stage.*

DICK *releases* SARAH, *who exits at C.*) Now, Dick. That will do. Why, you're making Sarah blush!

DICK. A little kiss never hurts anyone. Here, I'll show you. (DICK *suddenly throws his right arm around* GILDER'S *neck, who is facing down stage, and kisses his left cheek and then quickly takes a step from* GILDER.)

GILDER (*in surprise, as he rubs his cheek. Quickly.*) God bless my soul! (*Thoughtfully.*) Why, I don't believe you've kissed me since you were a little boy! God bless my soul.

DICK (*going to* GILDER *and putting his right arm around* GILDER'S *shoulder, with his right hand on* GILDER'S *right shoulder*). I'm awfully glad to see you again, Dad.

GILDER (*affectionately, and as he reaches up his left hand and puts it on* DICK'S *right*). Are you, Son? (*Then quickly changes his manner, pushes* DICK *away from him in mock seriousness.*) You chase out of here! (*As* GILDER *starts to go around to his desk and* DICK *starts up for his suitcase.*) I'm a hard-working man. (*As* GILDER *stops and puts his hand in his pocket.*) Wait a minute. Here it is. (DICK *stops and turns at center.*) Here's some carfare for you. (GILDER *takes out a roll of bills, takes off a couple, and with his left hand offers them to* DICK. DICK *comes down stage to his father's side, reaches across* GILDER, *and takes the big roll of money out of* GILDER'S *right hand.*)

DICK. Thanks. (GILDER *laughs and passes around the lower end of his desk and sits.* DICK *takes a step or*

two up C. and watches GILDER *and as* GILDER *sits.*) You can always get rid of me on the same terms. (GILDER *starts to work on his mail, and* DICK *goes quickly up and gets his suitcase from under sample table and, as he is going to the door C.*) See you later. (DICK, *about to go out, stops and turns to* GILDER.) Oh, Dad, for the love of heaven, give Sadie five dollars. I just borrowed it from her to pay for the taxi. (DICK *exits quickly through* C. GILDER *chuckles at his desk and goes back to his work.*)

GILDER (*to himself*). Finest boy in the world—that's all. (*Picks up his cigar. As* SMITHSON *enters L. and quickly crosses to the L. of* GILDER'S *desk,* GILDER *just looks up and sees who it is and goes on with his work as he speaks.*) Well, Smithson, what is it?

SMITHSON. McCracken, the store detective, has detained a *lady*, sir. She's been searched and we have found about a hundred dollars' worth of lace on her.

GILDER (*without looking up*). Well?

SMITHSON. I thought it better to bring the matter to your attention, sir.

GILDER. Not at all necessary, Smithson. You know my views on the subject of property. Tell McCracken to have the thief arrested.

SMITHSON. She's not exactly a thief, Mr. Gilder.

GILDER (*looking up in surprise*). Not a thief? In heaven's name, what would you call her?

SMITHSON. I'd call her a klepto-maniac, sir. You see, the lady happens to be the wife of J. W. Gaskell.

GILDER. Gaskell? Gaskell? President of the Central National Bank?

SMITHSON. Yes sir.

GILDER. That's very awkward. (*Pause.*) You were quite right in coming to me. (*Pause, as* GILDER *stops and thinks.*) Of course there's nothing we can do. Put the stuff back on the counter and let her go. (*Returns to his work.*)

SMITHSON. She's very angry, sir; she demands an apology.

GILDER (*irritable and without raising his head*). Well, apologize to her.

SMITHSON (*coming to door L.*). Yes sir.

GILDER (*pause, until* SMITHSON *gets to door L.*). And—er—Smithson—— (SMITHSON *stops at door and turns to* GILDER. GILDER *presses button as he looks at* SMITHSON *and continues.*) I'll take it as a personal favor if you will tactfully advise the lady that the goods at Stern's and Altman's are even finer than ours.

SMITHSON (*with a knowing smile*). Yes sir. I'll see what I can do, Mr. Gilder. (*Exits L.* SARAH *enters up C. door with notebook and pencil.*)

GILDER (*as* SARAH *enters, up - C. door*). Now then, Sarah. (SARAH *comes down quickly to chair L. of* GILDER'S *desk and takes* GILDER'S *dictation in shorthand notes.* GILDER *dictating.*) "J. W. Gaskell, Central

National Bank, New York. My dear Mr. Gaskell, I feel that I shall be doing less than my duty as a man if I did not let you know that Mrs. Gaskell is in urgent need of medical attention. She came into our store today and——" No, wait a minute, put it this way. (SARAH *scratches out a mark or two.*) "We found her wandering about our store today in a very nervous condition. In her excitement she carried away about a hundred dollars' worth of lace. Not recognizing her, our store detective arrested her." No—no—make that "detained her for a short time." (SARAH *scratches out a note or two in her book.*) "Fortunately for us all, Mrs. Gaskell was able to explain who she was, and she has just gone to her home. Hoping for your wife's speedy recovery and with all good wishes, I remain, Yours very truly——" (*To* SARAH.) Sarah, I can't understand the theft—it's entirely beyond my comprehension. (SMITHSON *enters door L. and advances a few steps inside the door and above it.*) Now, Smithson, what is it?

SMITHSON. Mrs. Gaskell wants you to apologize to her.

GILDER (*rising and stepping to lower end of his desk*). What?

SMITHSON. And she wants the store detective discharged.

GILDER (*crossing to C.*). Discharge McCracken?

SMITHSON. She seems slightly hysterical, sir.

GILDER (*crossing to door L.*). Well, I'll apologize to her, but I'll be damned if I discharge McCracken. (GILDER *exits L., followed by* SMITHSON, *who closes the door.* SARAH *laughingly rises and crosses to upper right corner of sample table, picking up a sample and examining it. As* SARAH *picks up sample the door at L. opens and* HELEN *enters quietly. She glances at* SARAH *and, as she turns to close the door, looks off stage and speaks.*)

HELEN. Sadie! (HELEN, *receiving no answer, turns and crosses quickly up to L. of table and appears nervous.*) Sadie!

SARAH (*as she sees who it is*). Now what do you want?

HELEN (*with forced calm*). I just saw the boss go out. (*Anxiously.*) What did they do to Mary Turner?

SARAH (*as she crosses to L. of* GILDER'S *desk, with her back to* HELEN). You'll know soon enough.

HELEN (*as she starts to cross to* SARAH *and gets as far as the chair in front of sample table*). Tell me now.

SARAH (*without turning*). They sent her to prison for three years.

HELEN. Three years?

SARAH. Yes.

HELEN (*as she turns a step backwards and turning so that she faces front*). Good God!

SARAH (*as she turns and crosses to* HELEN). See here, what are you so anxious about it for? This is the third time you've asked me about Mary Turner today. What is it to you? (*During* SARAH'S *speech* HELEN

shows she is trying to recover her self-control.)

HELEN (*without looking at* SARAH). Nothing—nothing at all—only she's a friend of mine, a great friend.— Three years! (*Turning and taking a step toward door L.*) I didn't understand—— (*Another step toward door.*) It's awful. (*Another step.*) It's· awful. (*Exits through door L. As* HELEN *goes out,* SARAH *watches her with a puzzled look, then, turning, crosses to* GILDER'S *desk; she pushes the chair L. of the desk down stage to the lower end of desk. Just as* SARAH *reaches desk, several firm, hard knocks are heard at the door up C.*)

SARAH (*as she picks up a letter from the desk and, without turning, says*). Come in.

(*The door is opened by* CASSIDY, *and* MARY TURNER *is discovered in the doorway, head hanging and handcuffs attached to her left wrist. On her left hand, and holding the other end of the handcuff, is* CASSIDY. *They slowly enter,* MARY *slightly in front.* CASSIDY *closes door afterward. Then they slowly come down C. and are on a line with the middle of* GILDER'S *desk. At* CASSIDY'S *first word* SARAH *turns and faces them.* CASSIDY *speaks as they come to a stop, C.*)

CASSIDY. The district attorney told me to bring this girl here on my way to Grand Central.

SARAH (*to* CASSIDY). Mr. Gilder will be right back. (*Crossing to Mary. and taking her right hand impulsively.*) I'm terribly sorry, Mary, terribly sorry.

MARY (*dully*). Are you? Nobody's been near me the whole time I've been in the Tombs. Nobody's been near me.

SARAH (*as she drops* MARY's *hand*). Helen·Morris was just asking about you. She's all broke up.

MARY. Who's Helen Morris? I don't know her. Why should she care?

SARAH. Why, she said she was a friend of yours, and——

(GILDER *enters L., smoking his cigar, and starts to cross to his desk. As he sees the group he pauses, takes the cigar from his mouth, then to* SARAH.)

GILDER. You may go, Sarah.

SARAH. Yes sir! (*Up to door C. and exits.* GILDER *looks at* MARY *a minute, and as she returns the look,* GILDER *crosses over to the lower R. corner of his desk, stops, and turns to* MARY, *speaking.* MARY *has followed him with her eyes.*)

GILDER. I am very sorry about this, my girl.

MARY. You should be.

GILDER. Come, come, that's no tone to take!

MARY. What did you expect?

GILDER. A decent amount of humility from one in your position.

MARY. Would you be humble if you were being sent to prison for three years for something you didn't do?

CASSIDY. Don't mind her, Mr. Gilder, they all talk like that—it don't do them no good, but they all swear their innocence to the very last—no matter how right we got 'em. Not guilty? Huh! Why, she tried to make a getaway comin' uptown this mornin'. Sure. That's why she's wearing these. (*Just indicating handcuffs.*)

MARY. I tell you, I didn't do it.

GILDER. What's the use of all this pretense? You were given a fair trial.

MARY. Oh no, I wasn't. If it had been fair, I shouldn't be here.

CASSIDY. That's another thing they all say.

MARY. Do you call it fair when the only lawyer I had was a boy the court told me to take—a boy trying his first case—getting experience. they call it—yes, getting it at my expense!

GILDER. The jury found you guilty.

MARY. Because they had been out for three hours and the judge threatened to lock them up all night! The men were tired and wanted to get home, and the easy thing to do was to find me guilty and let it go at that. Was that fair? Was it fair for you to come down to the court this morning and tell the judge that I ought to be sent to prison as a warning to the others?

GILDER. You mean——

MARY. Oh! I heard you. It wasn't did I do it or didn't I do it? It was to be a warning to the others. (*A pause.* MARY *sobs softly.*) Mr. Gilder—(*crossing halfway toward*

GILDER)—as God is my judge, you are sending me to prison for three years for something I didn't do. (*A pause, plaintively.*) Why did you ask the judge to send me to prison?

GILDER. The thieving that has been going on in this store for over a year has got to stop.

MARY. Sending me to prison won't stop it.

GILDER. Perhaps not; but the discovery and punishment of the other guilty ones will! Now, you sent me word that you could tell me how to stop the thefts here. Do this, and while I can make you no definite promises, I will see what can be done about getting you out of your present difficulty. (GILDER *moves around the corner of his desk as he continues.*) Come now, tell me, who were your accomplices?

MARY (*losing control of herself*). I have no accomplices! I never stole anything in my life! Must I go on telling you over and over again? Why won't anyone believe me?

GILDER (*pause, as* GILDER *moves to back corner of desk; then sternly and sharply*). Unless you control yourself you must go. (*Softening.*) Why did you send me that message if you have nothing to tell me?

MARY (*pause, as she regains her self-control*). I have some things to tell you, only I—sort of lost my grip, walking through the streets with this man by my side.

CASSIDY. Most of them do—the first time.

GILDER. Well?

MARY. Well, when you sit in a cell for three months waiting trial like I did, and then for another month wondering what your sentence is going to be, you think a lot, so I got the idea if I could talk to you, I might be able to make you understand what's really wrong. And if I could do that and so help out the other girls, what's happened to me wouldn't be quite so awful. (*Pleadingly and slowly crossing to* GILDER's *desk,* CASSIDY *following.*) Mr. Gilder, do you really want to stop the girls from stealing?

GILDER. Most certainly I do.

MARY. Then give them a fair chance.

GILDER. What do you mean?

MARY. Give them a living chance to be honest.

GILDER. A living chance?

MARY. A living chance to get enough food to eat and a decent room to sleep in, and shoes that will keep their feet off the sidewalks on winter mornings. Do you think any girl wants to steal? Do you think she wants to *risk*——

GILDER. So, this is what you're taking my time up for? To make a maudlin plea for a lot of dishonest girls when I thought you were bringing me facts!

MARY (*pause, as* MARY *straightens up and takes a step back from the desk, then in a low clear tone*). We work nine hours a day for six dollars a week. That's a fact, isn't it? And an honest girl can't live decently on six dollars a week—and buy food and clothes and pay room rent and carfare, that's another fact, isn't it?

GILDER (*as he sits at his desk and starts to attend to his mail*). I don't care to discuss these things.

MARY (*moving up close to the desk, pleadingly*). And I don't want to discuss anything; I only want to give you what you ask for—facts. (*Pause.*) When they first locked me up I just sat and hated you.

GILDER. Of course.

MARY. And then I thought perhaps you didn't understand, and if I told you how things really are, maybe you'd change them somehow.

GILDER (*looking up at MARY in amazement*). Change my business policy because you ask me?

MARY (*pleadingly*). Do you know how we girls live? Of course you don't. (GILDER *stops work and sits back in his chair, showing his annoyance.*) Three of us in one room doing our own cooking over a two-burner gas stove, and our own washing and ironing evenings—after being on our feet for nine hours.

GILDER. I have provided chairs behind the counters.

MARY. But have you ever seen a girl sit on one of them? (GILDER *turns away.*) Well, have you? Of course not, because she knows the manager of the department would think he could get along without her, and she'd be discharged. And so, after being on her feet for nine hours, the girl walks home, to save carfare—walks whether she's sick or whether

she's well—and you're generally so tired that it don't make much difference which you are.

GILDER. What has that got to do with——

MARY. And when you're real sick and have to stop work, what are you going to do then? (*Pause.*) Do you know that the first time an honest girl steals, it's often because she needs a doctor or some luxury like that? And some of them do worse than steal; and they started straight; too, and wanted to stay that way. Some get so tired of the whole grind that——

GILDER (*rising and interrupting her sharply*). I'm not their guardian. I can't watch over them after they leave the store. They are paid the current rate of wages, as much as any other store pays.

MARY. Yes, I know that, Mr. Gilder, but——

GILDER (*virtuously indignant*). No man living does more for his employees than I do! Who gave the girls the fine rest room upstairs? I did. Who gave them the cheap lunchroom? I did.

MARY. But you won't pay them enough to live on.

GILDER. I pay the same as other stores.

MARY (*slower and with more weight than the first time*). But you won't pay them enough to live on.

GILDER. So that's the plea you make for yourself and your friends, that you are forced to steal!

MARY (*leaning across* GILDER's *desk*). I wasn't forced to steal and I didn't steal! But that's the plea, as you call it, that I'm making for the other girls. There are hundreds of them stealing or going on the streets because they don't get enough to eat. You asked me to tell you how to stop the thefts; well, I've done it. Give the girls a living chance to be honest. You asked me for names—there's only one name I know of to put the blame for the whole business on—Edward Gilder!

GILDER (*indignantly*). What!

MARY (*pleadingly*). Now won't you do something about it?

GILDER. How dare you talk to me like this?

MARY. Won't you do something about it?

GILDER. How dare you?

MARY (*as she backs to center*). Why not? You've done all the harm you can to me. I'm trying to give you a chance to be—to do better by the others. You ask me how I dare? I've been straight all my life. I've wanted decent food and warm clothes, and

a little happiness, all the time I've worked for you, and I've gone without them to stay straight, and now you're sending me to prison for three years for something I didn't do!

GILDER. Take her away, Officer.

MARY. That's why I dare!

GILDER. Take her away. (CASSIDY *draws* MARY *two or three steps toward C.*)

MARY. Oh, he can take me now. Three years isn't forever, and when I come out you're going to pay me for every minute of them. There won't be a day or an hour that I won't remember that it was your word at the last that sent me to prison, and you're going to pay me for that, you're going to pay me for the five years I've starved making money for you—you're going to pay me for everything I'm losing today—(CASSIDY *shakes the handcuffs and starts toward door C.* MARY *takes a step or two down C., sticking her hand out and dragging that of* CASSIDY *with it, showing the handcuffs*)—and you're going to pay me for this—you're going to pay—you're going to——

CURTAIN

ACT TWO

TIME—*Four years later. Spring.*

SCENE—*Room in* MARY TURNER'S *apartment in Gramercy Square. It is a well-furnished room with a door down L., leading into* MARY'S *bedroom. Another door up L.C. leading into a hall, and a door up R. leading into another hall. Up L. is a bay window, and up R. is a fireplace.*

LIGHTS—*The sunlight is coming in through the bay window, and the stage is bright. There is plenty of light coming in at all of the doors as they are opened.*

AT RISE—AGNES *enters through the door at up R.C. with a vase of buttercups in her hand. She closes the doors, and as she comes down stage glances over towards* MARY'S *room at L., the door of which is open. She comes down stage to R. of the trick table and places the vase of buttercups on the table, picks up a magazine from the table, passes around the table to the chair L. of it and, as she sits, she speaks.*

AGNES. What are you doin', Mary, dolling up?

MARY (*off stage L., in room, the door of which is opened*). I've an important engagement.

AGNES (*as she reads her magazine*). Are you goin' out again with that young Gilder?

MARY. Yes.

AGNES. Nice boy, isn't he? (*Starts to read magazine.*)

MARY. I suppose so.

AGNES (*looking up towards* MARY'S *door. Sharply*). Suppose so? He's here so much we ought to be charging him for his meals—and you don't know whether he's the goods or not. (*Returns to reading magazine.*)

MARY (*as she enters from room L., dressed for the street, crosses back of table L. to R. of it and continues putting on her gloves*). I know he's the son of Edward Gilder, and that's enough for me.

AGNES (*turning in her chair toward* MARY). I can't get you, Mary. You never looked at a man—why, from the way you acted when I first ran into you after we left Auburn prison, I thought you'd become a suffragette, and then you meet young Gilder—and—good night, nurse! (*Returns to reading magazine.*)

MARY. Well?

AGNES (*turning to* MARY, *sharply*). His old man sends you up for a stretch for something you didn't do and you take up with his son like——

MARY. Yes, perhaps that's the reason.

AGNES. Gee, I'm getting wise. (*Looking back to her magazine.*)

MARY. Agnes, whatever there is between young Gilder and me is my affair. I don't want to talk about it, but—I do want to know what you were doing with that pickpocket yesterday. (AGNES *turns to* MARY *as if about to speak.*) Oh, I saw you. (AGNES *sheepishly returns to reading her magazine.*) Joe Garson told me who he was. A common pickpocket.

AGNES (*looking up quickly*). Common? (*Then turning to* MARY.) He's the best dip in the business. I guess I've got a right to speak to my own brother if I want to. (*Turning back again to read her magazine.*)

MARY. Oh, your brother. What did he want, money?

AGNES (*turning to* MARY). Nix. Business is immense. This has been a great year for crooks. (*Back to reading magazine.*)

MARY. How can it be? With the dead line at John Street and——

AGNES (*turning to* MARY). Dead line? Wake up, my dear. Why, Jim takes lunch every day at the Wall Street Delmonico's. Yes, and he went down to Police Headquarters yesterday. (*Laugh.*) Say, they've got a mat at the front door with "Welcome" on it in letters three feet high. (*Pauses as* AGNES *laughs.*) He lifted a leather from a bull that was standing in the hallway. (*Back to reading magazine.*)

MARY. It's no use, Agnes. I can't remember your slang. What did he do?

AGNES (*still reading magazine*). He copped the copper's kale.

MARY. He what?

AGNES (*turning to Mary and with a great deal of emphasis and in her ladylike manner*). He gently removed a leather wallet containing a large sum of money from the coat pocket of a member of the detective force. (*Naturally.*) Say, he says Inspector Burke got a gold watch that weighs a ton, all set with diamonds. It was gave to him by admiring friends. (*Goes back to reading.*)

MARY. Given, now, Agnes, please: given.

AGNES (*looking up in surprise*). What difference does that make. He's got it. (*Turning to* MARY.) When I get time I'm going after that watch. (*Back to reading magazine.*)

MARY. Oh no, you're not. (AGNES *looks up.*) As long as you're working with us you'll break no laws.

AGNES (*turning to* MARY). But I can't see——

MARY. Now, Agnes, when you worked alone, did you have a home like this?

AGNES (*as she looks around the room*). No.

MARY. Or good clothes, or proper food, or safety from the police?

AGNES. No, but I can't see——

MARY (*crossing to center*). Agnes, the richest men in this country have made their fortunes not because of the law, but in spite of it. They made up their minds what they wanted to do and they engaged lawyers clever enough to show them how they could do it and still stay inside the law. Anyone with brains can get rich in this country if he'll engage the right lawyer. I have the brains, and my attorney, Harris, is showing me the law—the wonderful twisted law that was made for the rich. As long as we keep inside the law we're safe.

AGNES (*taking her magazine with her, rising and crossing to* MARY). Gee, that's funny, you and me and Joe Garson handin' it to 'em right and left and the bulls can't touch us. The next you know, Harris will be havin' us incorporated as the American Legal Crime Company.

MARY (*with her arm around* AGNES' *shoulder*). I shouldn't be in the least surprised. (*Phone rings. Both look toward phone, then* MARY *crosses to phone to answer it and* AGNES *crosses down R. with her magazine and sits and starts reading.* MARY, *at the upper side of table, down L., answers the phone as she stands facing the front.*) Hello. (*Tenderly.*) Oh, Dick. (*Pause.*) Yes, I'm ready. (*Pause.*) I understand—why, it's just around the corner from here. I won't be five minutes. By the way, I read the papers very carefully this morning. I didn't see anything about our going down there together, did you? (*Pause.*) I thought, of course, when you mentioned your father's name it was bound to come out. (*Pause. Strong and hard.*) Oh, I see. It's wonderful what money will do, isn't it? (*Pause. Lovingly.*) Do you suppose, if I didn't care for you, I'd be coming to you now? (*Pause.*) No, please, stay where you are. I really won't be five minutes. (MARY *hangs up receiver.*)

AGNES (*looking up from magazine*). Say, what's all this?

MARY. Secrets, Agnes, secrets. (*Starting toward door up L.C.*) I shan't be gone over—— (GARSON *enters up L.C. and steps in, to* MARY'S *right, and removes his hat.*) Oh, good morning, Joe.

GARSON. Good morning.

MARY. You're around early?

GARSON. Oh, a little bit. Going out?

AGNES. No, she's putting in a ton of coal. (MARY *and* JOE *both laugh.*)

MARY. Wait for me, Joe. I shan't be gone more than ten or fifteen minutes. (MARY *exits up* L.C. GARSON *turns and drops his hat on couch up C. and crosses down right toward* AGNES *as far as the trick table.* AGNES *is seated in the chair down right reading her magazine.*)

GARSON. Where's she going?

AGNES (*without looking up*). Had a date with young Gilder.

GARSON. M'm. She's been with him a good deal lately.

AGNES. That's what.

GARSON. Think she's stuck on him?

AGNES (*looking up at* GARSON). Why not? Bet your life I'd be if I had the chance. (GARSON *turns and crosses to chair R. of table at L.C., sits and picks up magazine from table.*) He's one swell boy and entirely surrounded by money. (*Pause.* GARSON'S *manner shows that he's un-*

easy.) Say, Joe, if there's anything on your mind, shoot it.

GARSON. It's Mary and young Gilder.

AGNES. Well?

GARSON. Well, I can't see any good in it for her.

AGNES. Why?

GARSON. Old man Gilder's got a big pull and if he gets wise to his son going around with Mary he'll send the bulls down after us strong. Believe me, I ain't looking for any trip up the river.

AGNES. We ain't done anything they can touch us for—Mary says so.

GARSON. Whether you done anything or you ain't, once the bulls set out to get yer, they'll get yer. Why, Russia ain't in it with some o' the things I've seen pulled off in this town. (*Doorbell rings off L.C.*)

AGNES. Yes, but they can't touch us; we got our fingers crossed.

GARSON (*with a laugh*). Can't, eh?

CASSIDY (CASSIDY *starts speaking outside, opens the door, and comes just inside during his line.* FANNIE *is following closely and comes to a standstill at* CASSIDY's *left. At the first sound of* CASSIDY's *voice* GARSON *rises and turns and faces the door and takes the stage a little to the* L. CASSIDY *does not remove his hat during the following scene*). Never mind that announcing thing.

FANNIE (*angrily*). You get out of here. What do you mean by pushing your way in here like this?

CASSIDY (*watching* GARSON). Beat it!

GARSON. It's all right, Fannie. (FANNIE *turns and exits up L.C., closing the door after her.*)

CASSIDY (*without moving and in a familiar tone*). Hello, Joe. Hello, Aggie!

GARSON. Well?

CASSIDY (*coming down C.*). Oh, just a friendly little call. Where's the lady of the house?

GARSON (*as he turns with his back against the front of the table at L. C.*). Why, she's out.

CASSIDY (*in a little sharper tone*). Well, when she gets back, Joe, you tell her it's up to her to make her getaway and make it quick.

AGNES. Say, you can't throw a scare into us. You haven't got anything on us. (*At first word from* AGNES, CASSIDY *turns to her.*)

GARSON. Right.

CASSIDY (*to* AGNES). Nothing on you, eh? (*To* GARSON.) You're Joe Garson, ain't yer?

GARSON. Well, what of it?

CASSIDY (*feels his pockets quickly and takes out a notebook from his vest pocket and opens it and reads*). Joe Garson, forger. First arrested in '91, for forging the name of Edwin Goodsell for a check for ten thousand dollars; again arrested in '98, for forging the signature of Oscar Hemmingway to a series of counterfeit bonds; arrested as the man back of the Reilly gang in '03; arrested in '08 for forgery. (CASSIDY *returns book to his pocket.*)

GARSON (*quietly*). Haven't got any records of convictions, have you?

CASSIDY. No—but we got the right dope on you. (*Turning to* AGNES *with sarcasm.*) And you're little Aggie Lynch, posin' as Mary Turner's cousin. Did two years for blackmail. Was arrested in Buffalo and served yer time in Auburn. Nothin' on yer? (*Looking at* GARSON.) Well? (*Looking at* AGNES.) Well?

AGNES. My Gawd, it looks as tho' you'd actually been working. (*During the laugh* CASSIDY *looks "mad," turns to* GARSON, *and quickly turns and gives* AGNES *another look—then turns to* GARSON.)

CASSIDY. And the head of the gang is Mary Turner. Arrested four years ago for robbin' The Emporium. Done a stretch of three years.

GARSON (*quietly crossing to* CASSIDY). That all you got about her?

CASSIDY. That's enough, ain't it?

GARSON. Got anything in your record about her coming out of the stir without a friend in the world and tryin' to go straight? (*Pause. As* CASSIDY *does not answer.*) I suppose you forgot about going to that millinery store where she finally got a job and tippin' them off to where she came from?

CASSIDY. Sure they were tipped off. We got to protect the city.

GARSON. Yes. Got anything in that record of yours about her gettin' another job an' you followin' up again an' havin' her thrown out? Got anything in that record about the letter you had old Gilder write tellin' the next people she was workin' for what she'd done to him, or what he thought she'd done?

CASSIDY. Oh, we had her right the first time.

GARSON. Yes, you did—not. She was railroaded for a job she'd never done. She went in honest and came out honest.

CASSIDY. And now she's here with a gang of crooks.

GARSON. Where else should she be? You got anything in that record about us jumpin' into the river after her? That's where I found her—a girl that never done any harm to anyone—starving because you bulls wouldn't give her a chance to work —in the river, because she wouldn't take the only other way left her to make a livin'. Have you got any of that in your little book?

CASSIDY. Guess you must be kinder stuck on her, eh?

GARSON (*turning away from* CASSIDY; *quietly*). Cut that.

CASSIDY (*sharply*). What?

GARSON (*turning to* CASSIDY, *and stronger*). Cut it!

CASSIDY (*stronger*). Why, you don't mean——

GARSON (*quickly up to* CASSIDY *and looking him straight in the eye and speaking savagely*). I mean, cut it. (*Pause. Then slowly and quietly.*) Do you get me? (*Pause. Then* CASSIDY *sinks back a step.* GARSON *holds his position without moving. Just as* CASSIDY *shows the first sign of sinking,* AGNES *speaks.*)

AGNES. He's got yer.

CASSIDY (*looking at* GARSON *in admiration*). Gee, you'd been a big man, Joe, if it hadn't been for that temper of yours. It's got you into trouble a lot of times; someday it'll get you in so wrong you'll never get out.

GARSON (*quietly but firmly*). That's my business. (*Pause, as* GARSON *crosses left to front of table.*)

CASSIDY (*after pause*). Well, anyway, you've got to clear out—the whole gang of you—and do it quick.

AGNES (*rising, dropping magazine in chair, and crossing to* CASSIDY). Say, listen, we don't scare worth a cent—you can't do anything to us. (*As she turns away.*) We ain't broke the law.

CASSIDY (*in amazement*). What?

AGNES (*stopping suddenly and as she smiles over her shoulder at* CASSIDY). Well, maybe we've bent it.

CASSIDY. It don't make any difference what you've done.

AGNES (*freshly*). No?

CASSIDY (*positively*). No. (*Looking from* AGNES *to* GARSON.) Gee, things are comin' to a pretty pass when a couple of crooks gets to arguing about their rights.

GARSON. Yes.

CASSIDY. That's funny.

AGNES. Then laugh, Ha! Ha!

CASSIDY (*sharply*). Well, you've got the tip and it's up to you to take it. If you don't, one of you will make a long visit with some people out of town. (*To* GARSON.) And it'll probably be—Mary. Remember, Joe, I'm givin' it to you straight. (*Starts up C. toward door. Only gets a couple of steps when* AGNES' *voice stops him and he turns to* AGNES.)

AGNES (*as she follows* CASSIDY *up stage and stops at his right side—then in her ladylike manner*). Do come again soon, won't you, little one? I've enjoyed your visit so much. Good afternoon. (AGNES *kisses the tips of her fingers and quickly puts them on* CASSIDY's *lips.* CASSIDY *turns quickly away in disgust and exits up L.C.* AGNES *standing still and looking after* CASSIDY.) The truck-horse detective. An 18-inch collar, a 6½ hat. (*Crossing down toward* GARSON *as far as chair R. at table, at L.C. Seriously.*) He was right about one thing, too.

GARSON (*as he starts across to chair L. of trick table*). I know—my temper.

AGNES. Yes.

GARSON. I can't help it. (*Sitting in chair L. of trick table and picking up newspaper from floor.*) I know I shouldn't let it break out, but I can't help it.

AGNES. He had his nerve; tryin' to bluff us.

GARSON. Perhaps it wasn't a bluff.

AGNES (*as she takes a step toward* GARSON). What have we done?

GARSON. It ain't what you've done—it's what they can make the jury think you've done; and once they set out to get you, how they can frame things. If they ever set out after Mary——

AGNES (*crossing a little nearer* GARSON). Joe, you're a grand little forger, but Mary's got the brains and I'll string along with her as far as she wants to go. She's educated me. She talks like a lady and she acts like a lady. (*As she does an exaggerated ladylike walk up to back of chair R. of table at L.C.—*GARSON *watching her—in her ladylike manner.*) She's trying to make a lady out of me.

GARSON (*as he continues to read his paper*). She's got a swell chance.

AGNES. Is that so? Pipe the tea stuff! (*In rather exaggerated society manner at the back of table at L.C.* GARSON *watches her. As she pretends to shake hands.*) How do you do, Mrs. Jones? So good of you to call! (*Turning to the other side.*) Oh, my dear Miss Smith, this *is* a pleasure! (*Pretending to put sugar in a cup of tea.*) One lump or two? (*As if she had cream in her hand.*) No cream? Oh dear, and it's so expensive this year! (*As she pretends to hand cup of tea to someone.*) Yes, I just love bridge. No, I don't play it, but just the same I love it. (*As she crosses toward* GARSON *just beyond chair R. of table, talking naturally.*) That's the kind of stuff she's been havin' me do. (*Turning and crossing to table*

at L.C. *and below chair at its right.*) And, believe me, it's pretty damn near killed me! (*Picks up magazine from table.*)

GARSON (*as he returns to reading*). Mary's refined all right.

AGNES (*turning to* GARSON *quickly*). Sure she is, but she does some things that certainly get me. (*As she looks around room.*) Look at this room. (*To* GARSON.) It's supposed to be swell. Well, I can't see it—(*as she sits in chair right of table at L.C. and faces front*)—why, she ain't got one gold chair in the whole place!

GARSON. I'll bet it's the goods just the same. (*Doorbell rings.*)

AGNES (*as she turns in her chair so as to face* GARSON). Sure—I'm for Mary strong. Stick to her and you'll wear diamonds. (*Regretfully.*) I wish to God she'd let me wear mine —but she won't—she says they're vulgar. Now how can anything be vulgar that costs two hundred and fifty a carat? (FANNIE *opens door and closes it after her and stands just inside the door.*)

GARSON. Search me! I don't know.

FANNIE. There's a girl wants to see Miss Turner.

AGNES (*in her society manner*). Has she a card?

FANNIE. No, but she says it's very important.

GARSON (*to* AGNES, *dropping his paper to the floor between his chair and trick table*). Better have her come in and wait.

AGNES (*in her society manner*). Fannie, tell the young lady to come in. (AGNES *looks at* GARSON *and* GARSON *watches* AGNES, *smiles as she gets up and does her society walk down to the front of the table at L.C.* AGNES *then turns to* GARSON *with a knowing smile.*)

GARSON (*after* AGNES *looks at him, rises, and as he goes up to door at up R.C.*). I wonder who it is?

AGNES (*naturally*). No idea—but it can't do no harm to have her in and pipe her off.

GARSON. Right. (FANNIE *opens door at up L.C. and* HELEN, *pale and shabbily dressed, enters and stops just inside the door, and* FANNIE *closes the door.*)

AGNES (*as* HELEN *stops. In her society manner*). Won't you come in, please?

HELEN (HELEN *walks down C. in silence until she faces* AGNES). Are you Miss Turner?

AGNES (*in her society manner*). Oh, I'm awfully sorry, I'm only her cousin Agnes Lynch.

HELEN (*as she slightly drops her head in disappointment*). Oh!

AGNES (*quickly and in her society manner*). Miss Turner will be back almost any moment now.

HELEN (*a little anxiously*). Could I wait?

AGNES (*as she indicates chair left of trick table, then in her society manner*). Oh yes. Won't you sit down,

please? (HELEN *crosses to chair indicated.* AGNES *crosses to chair right of table at L.C. and* GARSON *quietly comes down to back of trick table.* HELEN *does not notice* GARSON. *As* HELEN *sits in the chair* AGNES *sits and* GARSON *speaks to* HELEN *a little sharply.*)

GARSON. You don't know Miss Turner? (*At* GARSON's *first word* HELEN *slightly turns to* GARSON *and shrinks a little.*)

HELEN. No sir.

GARSON. What do you want to see her for?

HELEN. She once helped a girl friend of mine, and I thought——

GARSON. She might help you!

HELEN (*as she bows her head*). Yes.

AGNES (*quickly rising and starting toward* HELEN *and naturally*). Then you've been in stir—— (*A quick look of warning from* GARSON *and a look of surprise stops* AGNES *shortly at center and then in her ladylike tone.*) Prison, I mean?

HELEN (*dropping her head with shame.*) Yes, miss.

AGNES (*in her affected manner and taking the stage to the front of table at L.C.*). How sad, how very very sad!

(FANNIE *opens the door at up L. for* MARY, *who stops in the doorway and gives her hat, parasol, and gloves to* FANNIE, *then steps into the room and sees* HELEN *as* FANNIE *closes the door.*)

MARY (*coming down C. To* AGNES). A visitor, Agnes? (AGNES *nods as* MARY *takes a step or two toward* HELEN. *On* MARY'S *first word* HELEN *turns in her chair toward* MARY *and slowly recognizes her.*)

HELEN (*rising and turning toward* MARY). You—you are Miss Turner?

MARY. Yes.

HELEN (*as she faces front*). Mary Turner! (*As she sinks into chair.*) Oh, my God! (MARY *crosses quickly to* HELEN, *then to* GARSON, *who is still back of trick table.*)

MARY. Joe, have Fannie bring a glass of milk with an egg in it, quick, please. (GARSON *crosses quickly to up L.C. and exits.*)

HELEN. I didn't know.

MARY (*with her arms around* HELEN'S *shoulders*). Don't try to talk until you've had something to eat.

AGNES (*crossing part way toward* HELEN). She's hungry and I never even thought of it. Ain't I the simp?

HELEN. I'm starving.

MARY (*helping* HELEN *to rise*). I understand. (*To* AGNES, *quickly crossing to* HELEN'S *right and putting her arms around* HELEN *and helping her.*) Take her to my room. (*All three start across stage L., and as they get to table at L.C.* MARY *drops back and follows.*) Have her drink the egg and milk slowly, then lie down for a while.

AGNES. Sure. You come along with me. We'll fix you up, all right. Come along with me.

(HELEN *and* AGNES *exit through door at L.* MARY *stops at door watching them.* GARSON *enters at up L.C. door, coming down to back of table at L.C. as he speaks.*)

GARSON. Mary.

MARY (*turning away from door and crossing to back of chair L. of table at L.C.*). Yes.

GARSON. There's a man named Irwin out there——

MARY. Oh! General Hastings' lawyer.

GARSON. Yes. He says he wants to see you.

MARY (*after a moment's thought*). Would you mind asking him to come in, Joe? (GARSON *starts toward door at up L.C.*) Fannie's busy getting something for that poor girl in there. (GARSON *exits, closing door.*) Agnes, oh, Aggie, just a minute, please. (AGNES *enters and crosses to* MARY. MARY *puts her arms around* AGNES' *shoulders.*) Mr. Irwin, General Hastings' lawyer is here. He wants to see you. When I call, come in, please, but you'd better leave everything to me. Just follow my lead. (AGNES *smiles and starts toward door L.* MARY *stops her.*) And, Agnes, be very ingénue.

AGNES. I'm wise. (*Crosses to door L. and turns.*) I'll be a squab.

(AGNES *exits and* GARSON *opens door, and* IRWIN, *dropping his hat on table, steps into the room and stops just at the head of the couch.* IRWIN *is followed by* FANNIE, *who carries a glass of milk on a tray and stops just above table at L.C.* GARSON *closes door and* MARY *passes around to the front of chair, L. of table at L.C.*)

MARY (*to* IRWIN). You wanted to see me?

IRWIN. Yes. (IRWIN *comes slowly down C.*)

MARY (*to* FANNIE). Take it to my room, please. (FANNIE *crosses and exits through door L.*)

IRWIN. I hope no one is ill?

MARY. No. Just a poor girl half starved—that's all. (*To* IRWIN.) Won't you sit down. (*Pause as* IRWIN *sits in chair R. of table and* MARY *sits on chair L. of table. Each watching the other.*)

IRWIN. I called in reference to the suit which Miss Agnes Lynch threatens to bring against my client, General Hastings.

MARY. It isn't a threat, Mr. Irwin. The suit will be brought.

IRWIN. Of course you realize that it's blackmail.

(FANNIE *enters at door L. and crosses up toward door at up L.C.*)

MARY. If it's blackmail, Mr. Irwin, why don't you consult the pol—— Oh, Fannie—(FANNIE *stops and turns to* MARY)—will you ask Miss Lynch to come in, please? (FANNIE *crosses to door L. and exits.*) Really, Mr. Irwin, I think you'd better take this matter to the police.

IRWIN. You know perfectly well that General Hastings cannot afford such publicity.

MARY. I'm quite sure the police would keep your complaint a secret. Really, Mr. Irwin, why don't you tell your troubles to a policeman?

IRWIN. Very well, then. (*Rising and crossing quickly up toward door at up L.C.*) I will.

MARY (*rising and pushing phone toward* IRWIN). 3100 Spring will bring an officer almost immediately.

(IRWIN *comes down quickly, picks up phone, and is about to lift off receiver when* MARY *laughs. He quickly sets it down and crosses down C.*)

IRWIN. Nevertheless General Hastings did not promise to marry that girl.

AGNES (AGNES *appears in doorway followed by* FANNIE, *who quickly crosses to door up L.C. and exits. Shyly and slowly coming toward* MARY.) Did you want me, dear?

MARY (*putting her arm around* AGNES' *shoulder and bringing her forward toward* IRWIN). Yes, Agnes, this is Mr. Irwin, who has come to see us in behalf of General Hastings.

AGNES (*shrinkingly and burying her face in* MARY'S *shoulder*). Oh, I'm frightened.

MARY (*petting her*). Nonsense, dear, there's nothing to be frightened about. (MARY *takes* AGNES *by the shoulders and looking her in the eye with an occasional side glance at* IRWIN). Of course you know, my dear, that under no circumstances must you say anything that isn't true, and if General Hastings did not promise to marry you, you have no case. (*Pause, as* MARY *backs* AGNES *up and sits in chair L. of table at L.C. and* AGNES *kneels at* MARY'S *left, and a little below her, facing* IRWIN.) Now, tell me, did the general promise to marry you?

AGNES. Oh yes, oh yes, and I wish he would; he's such a delightful old gentleman.

IRWIN. Was that promise made in writing?

AGNES. No—— (*Pause, as* IRWIN *turns away with a smile.*) But all his letters were in writing. (*Pause as* IRWIN *turns back to look sharply at* AGNES *and the smile leaves his face.*) Oh, such wonderful letters— so tender and—er—interesting. (AGNES *buries her face in* MARY'S *lap.*)

IRWIN. Yes. I dare say, I dare say.

MARY (*as* AGNES *raises her head and looks at* MARY). But you are quite sure the general did promise to marry you?

AGNES. Oh yes, I'd swear to that.

MARY (*to* IRWIN). You see, sir? She'd swear to that.

IRWIN (*pause, as he thinks*). Well, we're beaten. (*A quick look between* MARY *and* AGNES. *As* IRWIN *crosses to R. of table at L.C. and* MARY *watches him warily.*) I'm going to be quite frank with you, Miss Turner, quite frank. (IRWIN, *during the following speech, takes a wallet from his inside pocket, extracts a package of money, returns wallet to his pocket.*) We can't afford any scandal, so we're going to settle at your own terms. (IRWIN *riffles the*

package of yellowbacks and AGNES *leans forward eagerly.* MARY *watches* IRWIN.) We can't fight where ladies are involved, so if you just hand over General Hastings' letters, why, here's your ten thousand dollars. (*Drops package of money on table and turns away taking stage C. As his back turns* AGNES *makes a grab for the money and* MARY *quickly grabs her wrist and pushes her back to her former position as* IRWIN *turns to them again.*) You have the letters, haven't you?

AGNES (*putting her hand over her heart*). They never leave me.

IRWIN (*crossing toward* AGNES *as far as the table at L.C. and with hand outstretched*). They can now. (AGNES *about to reach into her dress and take them out when* MARY *lays a restraining hand on* AGNES' *hand and rises at the same time, facing* IRWIN. AGNES *rises and stands back of* MARY.)

MARY. Not quite yet, I'm afraid.

IRWIN (*as he turns and takes stage C.*). But there's your money, waiting for you.

MARY (*as she crosses part way over to* IRWIN, *and in a doubtful tone*). I think you'd better see our lawyer, Mr. Harris, first.

IRWIN. Oh, there's no need of all that formality. Just a friendly little arrangement between ourselves.

MARY (*all doubt gone—with a smile, as she crosses up to* IRWIN *and* AGNES *moves to C. of the table at L.C.*). Now I'm quite certain you'd better see Mr. Harris first.

IRWIN (*seeing he has been tricked*). Oh, I see.

MARY (*with meaning*). Yes, I thought you would. If you'll take your money to Mr. Harris, Miss Lynch—(MARY *turns to* AGNES, *then back to* IRWIN)—will meet you in his office at four o'clock, and when her suit for breach of promise is legally settled out of court, you will get those letters, Mr. Irwin. Good afternoon. (IRWIN *bows gravely and starts to door at up L.C.* MARY *crosses to chair at L. of trick table. Just as* IRWIN *is about to go out the door,* MARY *speaks.*) Oh—(IRWIN *stops*)—you forgot your marked money.

(MARY *sits in chair.* IRWIN *crosses down below chair R. of table at L.C., picks up money, then crosses quickly up to door, up L.C., then turns to* MARY.)

IRWIN (*sharply*). Young woman, you should have been a lawyer! (IRWIN *exits and* MARY *laughs.*)

MARY (*laughingly*). Thank you.

AGNES (*crossing quickly to* MARY). Say, you darned near broke my heart lettin' all that money get out of the house. How'd you know it was marked?

MARY. I didn't, but it was a pretty good guess, wasn't it? Couldn't you see that all he wanted was to have us take the money, get the letters, and then we'd have been arrested for blackmail.

AGNES. Where do we get off now?

MARY. Now he'll go to our lawyer—hand over the same marked bills, get the letters he wants so much, and because it's a transaction between two lawyers with everything done according to legal ethics——

AGNES. What are legal ethics?

MARY. Get it legally and get twice as much.

AGNES. But it's the same game.

MARY. Agnes, a shameless old roué makes love to you and writes you silly letters——

AGNES. He might have ruined my life!

MARY. If you'd asked him for ten thousand dollars for the return of his letters, it would have been blackmail and we'd have gone to jail; but a lawyer threatens a suit for breach of promise for ten thousand dollars —his lawyer steps in; they have conferences, they run up bills of expenses, and in the end we get our ten thousand, he gets his letters, and we're safely within the law and there you are. (MARY *rises and crosses down R. to armchair.*)

AGNES. All too much for me. (*Goes up to chair in front of desk at R.*)

GARSON (*enters up L.C. and as he crosses down C. To* MARY). Is it all right?

MARY. Certainly.

GARSON (*at C.*). Did you get ten thousand?

(HELEN *enters at door L., takes a quick look, and as no one is looking her way starts quickly for door up L.C.*)

MARY (*turning to* GARSON). Yes.

GARSON. Fine! (*Starts to cross L. and just gets as far as front of table at L.C. as* MARY *discovers* HELEN. HELEN *is about to put her hand on the knob of door at up L.C. As* MARY *speaks* GARSON *stops and watches* HELEN *with his back down stage and* AGNES, *who is about to sit at desk R., stops and watches.*)

MARY (*quickly, crossing up to* HELEN). Why, you ought to rest. (HELEN *stops.*)

HELEN (*without looking up*). I'm all right.

MARY. Quite sure?

HELEN. Yes.

MARY (*putting her arm around* HELEN's *shoulder and bringing her to chair L. of trick table.* GARSON *crosses around to chair L. of table at L.C. and* AGNES *brings the desk chair down to the R. of trick table and slightly above it*). Then come over and sit down and tell us all about it. (HELEN *sits L. of trick table.* GARSON *sits L. of table at L.C., watching the whole scene and never taking his eyes off* MARY. AGNES *sits in chair she has brought down to R. of trick table.* MARY *crosses over and takes chair from R. of table at L.C., brings chair back to C. and sets it a little above* HELEN *and half facing her and stands back of it. As* MARY *gets the chair she gives* GARSON *a look.*) Now then, what's your name?

HELEN (*facing down stage and half huddled in chair*). Helen—Helen Morris.

MARY. There's no need my asking if you've been in prison. Your face shows that.

HELEN. I came out three months ago.

MARY. And you've made up your mind to go straight?

HELEN. Yes.

MARY. You are going to do what the chaplain told you—start all over again—begin a new life? (HELEN *nods "Yes."*) It doesn't work very well, does it? (*Comes around chair and sits so that she is half facing* HELEN.)

HELEN. No, I'm beaten.

MARY (*first giving* GARSON *a look*). Well, how would you like to work with us?

HELEN (*as she turns toward* MARY *in surprise*). You are——

MARY. Certainly, it pays to when you know how. Look at us.

AGNES (HELEN *turns and looks at* AGNES *on her first word*). Hats from Joseph's, gowns from Lucille's, and cracked ice from Tiffany's. (HELEN *continues to look at* AGNES *until* MARY's *first word, then she looks straight front and shows during* MARY's *following speech that it is not to her liking.*)

MARY (*watching* HELEN *closely*). Suppose I stake you for the present and put you in with the right people? All you'll have to do is answer ads for servant girls—I'll see that you have the best of references, and then when you get in with the right people, you'll open the front door some night and let in the gang. Of course you'll make your getaway when they do and get your bit as well. (HELEN *half turns to* MARY, *as if about to speak, then turns away.* MARY *gives* GARSON *a smile.*) Doesn't suit you? (HELEN *shakes her head—no.* MARY *rises and crosses to* HELEN.) Good! I hoped you wouldn't. Now here's my real plan. (HELEN *is all attention and at first suspicious, gradually shows that* MARY'S *following speech is to her liking.* MARY *steps a little back from* HELEN.) Suppose you go West— where you'd have a fair chance— with money enough to live like a human being until you get a start. (HELEN *looks up at* MARY.) I'll give you that chance if you really want it.

HELEN (*rising and turning to* MARY). Oh, I do—I do.

MARY (*taking* HELEN'S *hands*). Then I've just one thing to say to you first. If you're going to start fresh, go through with it. Do you know what that means?

HELEN (*turning away from* MARY *and looking out front*). You mean, keep straight?

MARY. I mean forget that you've ever been in prison. I don't know what you've done, but whatever it was, you've paid for it—a pretty big price, too.

HELEN. I have, I have!

MARY. Well, then, stand up for your rights; don't let them make you pay again and don't tell the first people who are kind to you that you've been crooked. If they think you're straight—be it; will you promise me that?

HELEN (*very seriously and turning to* MARY). Yes, I promise.

MARY. Good. Then wait a minute. (MARY *takes her chair, returns it to its place at* R. *of table* L.C., *crosses behind table around to other side. To* GARSON.) Excuse me, Joe. (GARSON *draws his chair back and* MARY *opens drawer, takes out purse from which she takes a roll of money, returns purse to drawer and closes it; and, as she speaks, crosses stage to* HELEN, *counting money, reaching* HELEN *on her last word.* HELEN *has been watching* MARY.) Take this— it will pay your fare West and keep you quite a while if you're careful.

HELEN (*about to take it, looks up at* MARY *and shrinks away a step and turns front*). I can't take it—I can't.

MARY. Why, didn't you come here for help?

HELEN. Yes, but I didn't know it was you. (HELEN *realizes she has made a mistake in admitting she knows* MARY.)

MARY. Oh, then you've met me before?

HELEN. No.

AGNES (*rising quickly and stepping down on a level with* HELEN *at the side of trick table*).

GARSON (*as he rises and crosses to* C.). Yes.

HELEN. No.

MARY (after a quick look at GAR-SON). You've met me before. Where?

HELEN. I can't tell you.

MARY. You must.

HELEN. I can't.

MARY. Why not?

HELEN. Because—because——

MARY. Well?

HELEN. Oh, I can't.

MARY (pause). What were you sent up for? (Pause.) Tell me. (Pause and harder.) Tell me.

HELEN (HELEN turns her eyes to MARY, then front again, then answers slowly). For stealing.

MARY. Stealing, what?

HELEN (another look, then front before answering). Goods!

MARY. Where from?

HELEN (another glance from HELEN, then, as she turns front, she swallows, her lips tremble, and finally she answers). The Emporium.

MARY (now convinced of what she suspects). Then you are the girl who——

HELEN (turning to MARY). I'm not, I'm not!

MARY. You are, you are! (Turning to GARSON.) She did it. (GARSON starts quickly forward to HELEN.

MARY just stops him before he crosses her.) Joe! (GARSON stops and steps back with his face up stage. At GARSON's first move HELEN shrinks into chair L. of trick table and buries her head in her hands on the trick table. To HELEN.) Why did you throw the blame on me?

HELEN (taking her hands from her face and facing front). I found out they were watching me and I was afraid they'd catch me, so I took 'em and ran into the cloakroom and put 'em in a locker that wasn't close to mine and some in the pocket of a coat that was hangin' there. (Turning to MARY pleadingly.) I didn't know whose it was, I just put them there—(turning front)—I was frightened.

MARY. And you let me go to prison for three years!

HELEN (turning to MARY). I was scared (turning front). I didn't dare tell.

MARY. But they caught you later. Why didn't you tell then?

HELEN. I was afraid. I told 'em it was the first I took and they let me off with a year. (On the last word she cries and buries her face in her hands.)

MARY (turning up stage). You cried and lied and they let you off with a year! I wouldn't cry and told the truth and——(MARY starts to break down.)

GARSON. Mary, don't!

HELEN (turning half to MARY). I'll never forgive myself—never.

MARY. Oh yes, you will. (HELEN *again buries her face in her hands.* MARY *turns and looks at* HELEN, *having controlled herself.*) People forgive themselves pretty easily. (HELEN *cries aloud.*) Oh, stop crying, no one's going to hurt you. (HELEN *continues to cry softly with her hands up to her face.* MARY *offers the money.*) Here, take it and get out.

HELEN. I can't take it.

MARY (*forcing it into her hand, and crossing to armchair down R. with her back to C.*). Take it before I change my mind, and get out.

(HELEN *rises with her hands over her face, crosses L. until she almost runs into* GARSON *at C., then looks and sees an awful look on his face and quickly slinks up to door up L. with her hands over her face and, sobbing softly, exits. At* HELEN'S *exit* AGNES *turns to look at* MARY.)

MARY (*kneeling in armchair at the closing of the door and crying*). A girl I didn't know—to smash my life like that—if it wasn't so awful, it would be funny—it is funny. (*Slipping down into chair with her head on the down-stage arm, and, hysterically.*) It is funny.

(AGNES *and* GARSON *both cross quickly to* MARY, AGNES *above* MARY *and puts her hands on her shoulders.* GARSON *goes over to* MARY *as he speaks.*)

GARSON. Mary, don't do that. That's no good. (*Pause as* MARY *regains her self-control and* GARSON *crosses to front of trick table quietly and faces up stage.*)

MARY (*through her tears and sobs*). You're right. It's done and it can't be undone; but the sight of that girl—you understand.

GARSON (*crossing as far as chair L. of trick table with his face still up stage*). Sure we do.

AGNES (*bending over* MARY, *with her right cheek close to* MARY'S *left, quietly*). Yes, but if a dame sent me up for three years and then wanted money from me, do you think she'd get it? Not much.

(MARY *pats* AGNES' *cheek, then slowly rises and crosses to chair L. of table at L.C. and sits facing down stage.* AGNES *sits on chair down R. vacated by* MARY. *As* MARY *passes* GARSON, *he turns and follows her across stage to the upper end of the table at L.C.*)

GARSON (*as* MARY *passes him*). Mary, I've got something to tell you. Cassidy was up here from headquarters. He didn't put a name to it—but I'm on. I guess you'll have to quit seeing young Gilder. The bulls are wise. (*As* GARSON *crosses down C.*) His father's made a holler.

MARY (*pause, then quietly*). Don't let that trouble you. I was married to Dick less than an hour ago.

GARSON (*turning to* MARY). Married?

MARY. Yes.

AGNES. Well, I'm glad you landed him.

GARSON (*to* AGNES). Wait a minute. (*Then crossing to R. of table at L.C.*) Do you love him?

MARY. No.

GARSON (*persistently*). Do you love him?

MARY (*pause*). No, NO!

AGNES. Then why did you marry him?

MARY. I married him to get even with his father. I've been working and scheming for nearly a year to do this and now it's done. It's only beginning, too.

GARSON (*crosses up back of chair at R. of table at L.C.*). Then everything's goin' on as before—you won't leave us?

MARY. Leave? Certainly not!

AGNES. You'll live here in this house with me?

MARY. Yes!

AGNES. Well, where will hubby live?

MARY. Anywhere but here.

GARSON. Does he understand the arrangement?

MARY. No, not yet.

AGNES. Well, when you tell him—break it to him gently.

GARSON (*coming down C. To* AGNES). Pretty tough on him. He's a fine young fellow. (*Goes up back of chair R. of table at L.C.*) He must think a lot of you! Don't he?

MARY. Yes, I suppose so.

AGNES. Only enough to marry her. (*Pause.*) And when a man thinks enough of you to marry you—believe me, that's some thinkin'.

GARSON (*crossing up back of table at L.C.*). Well, I'd say chuck up the whole game and go to him if you cared—and you don't, do you?

MARY. I married him to get even with his father. That's all there is to it. I expect he'll be here in a minute or two and when he comes —— (*Doorbell rings and* GARSON *crosses to door up R.C. and with his left hand on the knob.*)

MARY (*rising*). If that's he, Agnes, don't forget all I've tried to teach you.

AGNES (*rising and crossing up C.*). Don't worry about me. Whenever it's really wanted I'm always there with a full line of lady stuff.

FANNIE (*enters at up L.C. door and closes it after her*). Mr. Gilder, miss.

MARY (*eagerly*). Anyone with him?

FANNIE. No, miss.

MARY (*showing disappointment*). Have Mr. Gilder come in. (FANNIE *exits L.C. and closes door after her.*)

GARSON. I guess you can excuse me. I'll see you when I'm wanted. (*Exits at up R. door.*)

MARY (*as she starts across stage R., stops and turns to meet* DICK *in front of chair L. of trick table.* AGNES *starts crossing L. at the same time and does not stop until she is standing in front of chair L. of table at L.C.*) Don't forget, Agnes.

AGNES (*as she is crossing*). I'm there—I'm there.

DICK (DICK *enters at up L. door and, dropping his hat on the head of couch, rushes down to* MARY. MARY *receives him with one hand extended, which he takes and attempts to draw to him and kiss her*). Hello, dear.

MARY (*holding him off*). Don't, don't—please, Agnes. (DICK *releases* MARY *and turns to* AGNES. MARY *goes across R. below armchair down R. and to the back of it.*)

DICK. I beg your pardon, Miss Lynch. But you could hardly expect me to see anyone but Mary under the circumstances, could you?

AGNES (*in her society manner*). Under what circumstances, Mr. Gilder?

DICK. Why, hasn't Mary told you? We were married this morning.

AGNES. Goodness gracious! How perfectly lovely! (*Sits in chair L. of table at L.C.*)

DICK. You bet, it's lovely. (*Crosses to* MARY *and kneels in chair down R. with his arm around* MARY'S *shoulder.*) Now listen, dear, I've got the honeymoon trip all arranged. The *Mauretania* sails at five in the morning, so we'll——

MARY (*interrupting*). Where's your father?

DICK. Oh Lord, I'd forgotten all about Dad. I'm awfully sorry—I'll tell you what we'll do; we'll send him a wireless and write him from Paris.

MARY. What was your promise? I told you I wouldn't go away with you until you brought your father to me and he'd wished us happiness.

DICK. You're going to be stubborn and hold me to my promise?

MARY (*with meaning*). I'm going to hold you to that promise.

DICK (*off chair and taking a step back toward C. and looking at his watch*). All right, Mrs. Gilder (*with a laugh*). Sounds fine, doesn't it?

MARY (*with meaning*). Yes.

DICK (*returning to his former position at chair*). You pack up what things you need—not much, because they sell clothes in Paris—and I'll run over to Dad's office and have him back here in half an hour. You'll be all ready, won't you?

MARY. Yes—I'll be ready. Go and bring your father.

DICK (*as he tightens his arms about* MARY *and attempts to draw her to him*). You bet I will. (MARY *holding away from him.*) What's the matter?

MARY. Nothing.

DICK. But, Mary, just one.

MARY. No—NO. Please.

DICK (*releasing her*). For a married woman you are certainly shy. (*Then off chair quickly, speaking to* AGNES *as he goes up C. and gets his hat.*) You'll excuse me, won't you, Miss Lynch? (*Turning to* MARY *with his hand on doorknob.*) Good-by, Mrs.

Gilder—Mrs. Gilder, doesn't that sound immense? (*Exits at L.C. door, closing it after him. As the door closes* MARY *leans against the back of the chair down R. and then crosses up and picks up small mirror from top of desk at R. and arranges her hair.*)

AGNES. Oh gee, the poor simp.

(GARSON *enters at up R. door, closes it after him, and looks around room quickly, then, as he crosses down to chair L. of trick table.*)

GARSON. Where's he gone?

MARY. To bring his father.

AGNES. I suppose I'll miss that—I've got to be at that lawyer's at four. (*A look of amusement passes between* GARSON *and* MARY.)

MARY (*as she starts across stage L. and below trick table toward* AGNES). Yes, and you'd better be getting ready, too.

AGNES (*rising*). I know it. (*Crossing up to door at L.*) That's what I'm kicking about.

MARY (*as she sits in chair L. of table at L.C. and* GARSON *sits in chair L. of trick table, picks up newspaper, and starts reading it*). Have you that release for me to look over?

AGNES (*as she turns in doorway at L.*). Yes, but I don't see the use of it; all I want is the coin. (AGNES *exits through door L.*)

GARSON. It's a good thing for her she met you.

MARY (*as she takes a memo book from drawer and makes memos in it*). Why?

GARSON. She hasn't got the brains of a knot.

MARY. Brains are useful, even in our business.

GARSON. I should say they were. You've proved that.

(AGNES *re-enters from door L. with her hat on and gloves and purse and legal paper in her hand. She crosses back of* MARY'S *chair and stands at the back of the table at L.C.*)

AGNES. Here it is. (*Hands* MARY *legal paper.*)

MARY (*opens legal paper and reads it a moment*). Tell Harris it's splendid. (*Hands legal paper to* AGNES.) Just what we wanted.

AGNES. Seems to me we're goin' through a lot of red tape.

MARY. Agnes—the last time you tried to separate an old gentleman from part of his money you got two years.

AGNES. But that way was so exciting.

MARY. And this way is so safe. Your way didn't get the money. Mine will—your way was blackmail, mine isn't. Understand?

AGNES. Sure. (*Turns and as she goes toward door up L.C.*) It's as clear as Pittsburgh. (AGNES *exits at up L.C. door.* GARSON *and* MARY *both laugh.*)

GARSON. Solid · ivory. (*Doorbell rings.*)

MARY (*making notes in notebook*). She's a dear, anyway. You don't half appreciate her, Joe.

GARSON. Why, sure she is. Did you pipe that lid?

(FANNIE *enters up L.C. door and closes it after her.*)

FANNIE (*smiling*). Mr. Griggs, miss.

MARY. Well, have Mr. Griggs come in. (FANNIE *exits up L.C. door, closing it after her.*)

GARSON. English Eddie?

MARY (*laying notebook on the table in front of her*). I wonder what he wants.

GARSON. Probably got a trick for me. We used to work together.

MARY. Joe, nothing without my consent!

GARSON. Oh no, sure not.

(FANNIE *goes up L.C. door and* GRIGGS *enters coming just over the doorsill.* FANNIE *is smiling broadly and closes door after him.*)

GRIGGS (*to* MARY). How do you do? (*As he crosses to center.*) Hello, Joe.

GARSON (*drops newspaper to the floor between chair and trick table, rises smiling*). Hello, English. (GARSON *moves a few steps up stage.*)

MARY (*looking at* GRIGGS's *swagger clothes, he standing C. for her to admire him.* MARY *is laughing*). Really, you overcome me.

GRIGGS. Well, I think it rather neat myself.

MARY. Even for you.

GRIGGS. Yes. (*Turning and laying his silk hat on couch and returning to his former position.*) Even for me.

MARY. Is this a social call?

GRIGGS. Well, no, not exactly.

MARY. That's what I thought. Sit down, please.

GRIGGS. Thanks. (GRIGGS *takes the chair from R. of table at L.C. and turns it with his left hand so that it is just opposite* MARY *and points slightly down stage and a little away from table and with the chair back to* MARY. *He then straddles the chair with his left arm across the back.*)

MARY (*after* GRIGGS *is settled*). What's the game?

GRIGGS. The greatest game in the world. (*Half turns his head toward* GARSON.) Get in on this, Joe.

(GARSON *crosses to the back of the table at L.C. as* GRIGGS *continues.*)

GRIGGS. Two years ago a set of Gothic tapestry worth three hundred thousand dollars and some Fragonard panels, worth nearly as much, were plucked from a château in France and smuggled into this country.

MARY. I've never heard of that.

GRIGGS. Why, no, certainly not—it's been kept on the dead quiet.

GARSON (*to* MARY). Are them things worth that much?

MARY. Sometimes more. The Metropolitan has a set of Gothic tapestries worth half a million.

GARSON. Half a million for a set of rugs to hang on its wall—(*starting toward chair at down L.*)—and they wonder at crime! (*Sits in chair down L., facing* GRIGGS.)

GRIGGS. Now about a month ago the things I was telling you about were hung in the library of a millionaire in this city. (*To* GARSON.) Let's go after them. They were smuggled, mind you, and he can't squeal no matter what happens. (*Pause.*) Well, what do you say?

GARSON. It's up to Mary.

GRIGGS (*to* MARY). Well?

MARY. It's out of our line.

GRIGGS. Well, I don't know any easier way to get half a million.

MARY (*rising*). It wouldn't make any difference if it were fifty million. It's against the law.

GRIGGS. I know, but if we can——

MARY. My friends and I never do anything that's illegal! (*With a smile.*) Thanks for coming to us, Mr. Griggs, but we can't go in. (*Picks up notebook and starts down L.* GRIGGS *rises and turns chair around so that he is standing at the back of chair without changing his position.*)

GRIGGS. Now wait a minute, this chap Gilder is—— (*as* MARY *turns to* GRIGGS *and* GARSON *rises from his chair*).

MARY *and* GARSON. Gilder?

GRIGGS. Yes, you know, that linen-draper chap.

GARSON. There's a chance for you, Mary.

MARY (*facing* GARSON). No, I won't be mixed up in anything that's outside the law.

(GRIGGS *during the following couple of speeches steps back up stage, watching* MARY *and* GARSON *and drawing the chair he was standing behind with him.*)

GARSON. But it's Gilder, the man you——

MARY. I know, but it's illegal, and I won't touch it, and that's all there is to it. (GARSON *with a growl starts up stage, and just as he is alongside of* MARY *she puts her right hand on his arm as she speaks.*) Joe!

GARSON (*pauses*). Yes.

(GARSON *goes up to back window with his back down stage.* MARY *turns and looks at* GRIGGS *a moment, then drops the notebook on the table and, crossing to the door L., exits, closing the door after her. At the close of the door,* GARSON *starts down stage slowly and does not stop until he is in front of table at L.C.*)

GRIGGS (*who is watching* GARSON *closely, speaks on* GARSON's *first move. Insinuatingly*). Half a million!

GARSON (*while walking, half to himself*). Half a million.

GRIGGS (*temptingly*). There's a stake worth playing for. (GRIGGS *down to*

GARSON's *right a little above him during the following line.*) Think of it, Joe, a half a million!

GARSON (*half to himself and walking front*). Half a million.

GRIGGS. And it's the softest money you ever saw. (*As he takes paper from his pocket and unfolds it.*) Here's a plan of the house. (GRIGGS *looks at* GARSON. GARSON *slowly turns and looks at* GRIGGS. *As* GARSON *looks at* GRIGGS *he slowly offers the paper to* GARSON. GARSON *slowly takes it, then, as he turns front to look at it,* GRIGGS *backs a step or two up stage, watching* GARSON.)

GARSON (*slowly*). It looks easy.

GRIGGS (*eagerly*). It is easy. What do you say?

GARSON (*as he crosses in front of* GRIGGS *to R.C. and handing* GRIGGS *the paper*). No, I promised Mary ——

GRIGGS (*following* GARSON *to C., a little above him, and returning the paper to his pocket. Persuasively*). But a chance like this—a chance with one play to get all you'll ever want.

GARSON (*with his back to* GRIGGS). It sounds good.

GRIGGS. Why, this is so big that if it comes off we can quit. (*Pause.*) All of us.

GARSON (*turning to* GRIGGS). By God, that's right. We can quit. (*Pause. With a quick glance at door L. and turning his back to* GRIGGS.) All of us.

GRIGGS. What do you say?

GARSON (*crossing L. to front of table at L. C. Pause*). How'll we split it?

GRIGGS (*with relief in his tone*). I think three ways would be right. one to me, one to you, and one to the bunch we'll have to take in. (*Pause.*)

GARSON (*as he offers his hand*). You're on.

GRIGGS (*as he takes* GARSON's *hand*). Fine, now I'll get——

GARSON (*as he drops* GRIGGS's *hand*). You'll get nothing. I'll get my own men. Chicago Red's in town. So is Dacey. They'll do.

GRIGGS. Yes.

GARSON. I'll get them to meet you at —Scanlan's at—two tomorrow afternoon, and if it looks right, we'll turn the trick tomorrow night.

(GRIGGS *with a snap of his fingers and a half turn away to the right as* GARSON *stops him.*)

GARSON. Eh! (GRIGGS *turns back to him.*) She mustn't know.

GRIGGS. She'll never know—Joe, I give you my word of honor as a gentleman, I'll never tell—— (MARY *enters at door L. and comes to the front of L. C. table. At the sound of the door opening,* GARSON *stands at C. and* GRIGGS *takes stage R. In a changed tone.*) I tell you, after all, it's the only way to do.

MARY (*at front of L.C. table*). What is?

GRIGGS (*turning and pretending he didn't know* MARY *was there*). I was just saying that when there's a leader, the only way is to follow the leader.

(*A look passes between* GARSON *and* GRIGGS *as* GARSON *answers and goes up stage to the foot of couch, watching* GRIGGS.)

GARSON. Yes. Sure.

GRIGGS. And since you're against it, why, that's all there is to it.

MARY (*as she picks magazine up from table*). Well, I am against it.

GRIGGS. I'm sorry, but we must all play the game as we see it. Well, that was the business I was after, and, as it's finished—(*starting up stage for his hat*)—so good afternoon.

MARY. Won't you stay and have tea?

GRIGGS (*at the head of couch*). No, thanks.

MARY. Then good afternoon.

GRIGGS (*in doorway at up L.C.*). So long, Joe. (*A look between* GARSON *and* GRIGGS. GRIGGS *nods to* MARY *and as he puts on his hat slowly exits at up left door closing it after him.*)

(*Pause as* MARY *and* GARSON *catch each other's eye and* GARSON *crosses and, picking up chair that* GRIGGS *has left up stage, replaces it L. of L.C. table, then speaks.*)

GARSON. That's a big stake he's playing for, ain't it?

MARY. Yes, and a big chance he's taking, too. (*As she starts to cross R. to the front of the trick table and looking through the magazine.*) No, Joe, we'll play the game that's safe and sure.

GARSON (*coming down C.*) It's sure enough, but is it safe?

MARY (*looking at* GARSON). What do you mean?

GARSON (*crossing to* MARY). Suppose the bulls got tired of you putting it over on 'em and tried some rough work?

MARY (*with a laugh, returning to her magazine*). Don't worry. I know a way to stop it.

GARSON (*as he takes revolver from his pocket*). Yes, and so do I.

MARY (*in alarm and taking hold of* GARSON'S *right arm*). No, Joe, no, none of that—ever.

GARSON. Even if I used it, they'd never get on to me.

MARY (*as she removes her hand from his arm*). What do you mean?

GARSON (*with revolver in his right hand hanging straight down by his side, and with his left hand taking silencer from his left coat pocket*). See this? (*Hands* MARY *silencer, which she looks at and turns over.*)

MARY. I've never seen anything like that before.

GARSON (*as he takes the silencer and adjusts it to the revolver*). No, I'll bet you didn't. I'm the first man in the business to get one and I'll bet on it. I'm a scientific guy. That's what they call a Maxim Silencer. With smokeless powder and the silencer I can fire a shot from my coat pocket and you'd never know it had been done. (*Drops his gun hand down straight by his side.*)

MARY (*with a laugh*). Impossible.

GARSON. No, it ain't; here, I'll show you. (*Turns toward bay window and is about to raise his arm to fire as* MARY *grabs his arm.*)

MARY. Joe, you'd have the whole place down on us.

GARSON (*turning to* MARY *with a laugh and transferring revolver to left hand*). No, I won't. You stand over there (*indicating down L.*).

MARY. NO! NO!

GARSON. Go ahead, it's all right. (MARY *crosses L. around table at L.C. with* GARSON *following as far as the front of the table at L.C. and talking. As* MARY *is halfway over she turns around and gives the gun a final scared look. As* GARSON *follows he again takes revolver in his right hand.*) If you can tell when I fire I'll eat the gun.

MARY (*as she goes up toward bay window up L.*). Nonsense.

GARSON. No, it ain't nonsense. (*Turning toward vase on trick table and taking aim at vase of flowers.*) You turn your back and you won't hear. (*Snaps revolver. Vase of flowers breaks.* MARY *drops magazine, looks at* GARSON, *and crosses to vase of flowers. As* MARY *crosses,* GARSON *follows to C. and up to* MARY.)

MARY (*after a pause*). I wouldn't have believed it.

GARSON (*as he removes silencer*). Neat little thing, ain't it?

MARY (*crossing around R. of trick table and down stage*). Where did you get it?

GARSON (*replacing revolver in his pocket and crossing down L.C.*). Oh, I got it—over in Boston last week. (*Doorbell. At the sound of the doorbell* GARSON *turns and faces the door.*)

MARY. That can't be Agnes back already.

FANNIE (*off stage L.C.*). I'll see if Miss Turner's at home.

BURKE (*off stage L.C.*). That's all right. We'll see for ourselves.

GARSON (*turning to* MARY). That's Burke.

MARY (*standing in front of chair down R.*). Don't worry: he can't touch us. (BURKE *opens up L.C. door and just hesitates on doorsill as* MARY *sits in chair down R.*). An inspector!

BURKE (*as he quickly crosses down toward* MARY *as far as chair to L. of trick table without removing his hat.* DEMAREST *follows* BURKE *in, closing the door after him, removes his hat, and quietly comes down to the back of the chair R. of L.C. table*). Oh! here you are.

MARY. Yes, Inspector. To what do I owe the pleasure?

BURKE. I've come for a few quiet words with you.

MARY. Then you don't want Joe?

BURKE (*pause as he turns and looks at* GARSON). Not yet.

GARSON (*as he quietly advances a step or two and with a sneer*). I'm much obliged.

MARY. Will you excuse us, Joe?

GARSON (*as he crosses to* BURKE *with menace both in his action and words,* BURKE *looking him in the eye and just a slight movement of straightening up*). But suppose they——

MARY. Please!

GARSON (*quietly*). All right. (*Crossing to door up L.C., then as he turns in doorway.*) But if you want me, just call. (GARSON *exits up L.C. door.* BURKE *has just turned his head and watches* GARSON *out. At the closing of the door* BURKE *crosses L. below table at L.C., then up stage as far as the doorway L., and during the following scene back down stage again as far as the front of the table at L.C. At the closing of the door by* GARSON, DEMAREST *crosses over to* MARY *as far as the front of the chair L. of trick table.*)

MARY (*as* DEMAREST *comes toward her*). Ah, Mr. Demarest, it's four years since I saw you last, and they've made you District Attorney since then. Allow me to congratulate you.

DEMAREST (*a little puzzled*). There is a—— Where have I seen you?

MARY (*rising*). Can't you guess? (*Crossing to* DEMAREST *and looking into his face.*) Try.

DEMAREST (*pause*). Why, you're the girl—why, you're the Mary Turner that—— Oh, I know you now.

MARY. I'm the girl you mean, Mr. Demarest, but you don't know me at all. (*Turns away from* DEMAREST *with her back to trick table.*)

BURKE (*interrupting. During* BURKE'S *speech* DEMAREST *quietly turns away and crosses up C.*) Young woman, the Twentieth Century leaves the Grand Central at four o'clock. It arrives in Chicago at eight fifty-five tomorrow morning. (*Looks at his watch.*) You'll just have time to catch that train.

MARY. Working for the New York Central now?

BURKE (*sternly*). I'm working for the good of New York City.

MARY (*with a laugh*). Since when?

DEMAREST (*quietly*). I think a different tone will serve you better.

BURKE. Oh, let her talk—she's only got a few minutes anyway.

MARY (*as she indicates a chair R. of table at L.C. and sits in chair left of trick table*). Let's be comfortable then.

BURKE. You'd better be packing your trunk.

MARY. Why? I'm not going away!

BURKE (*as he crosses to* MARY). On the Twentieth Century this afternoon.

MARY (*with a smile*). Oh! dear no! (DEMAREST *quietly drops down to the position* BURKE *has just left.*)

BURKE (*a little louder than usual*). I say, yes.

MARY. I thought you wanted quiet words.

BURKE (*in his natural tone*). Now, look here, Mollie——

MARY (*sharply*). Miss Turner, if you please—(*with a laugh*)—for the present anyway.

BURKE (*sternly*). I'm givin' you your orders. You'll go to Chicago, or you'll go up the river.

MARY. If you can convict me—notice that•little word, if.

DEMAREST (*suavely*). I did it once, remember.

MARY. But you can't do it again.

BURKE. How do you know he can't?

MARY. Because if he could, you'd have had me in prison some time ago.

BURKE (*with a look at* DEMAREST *and a cynical smile*). I've seen 'em go up pretty easy.

MARY (*seriously*). The poor ones, yes—but not those who have money, and I have money now.

BURKE. Money you stole.

MARY (*in mock seriousness*). Oh dear, no——

BURKE. What about that thirty thousand you got in that partnership swindle? (*Sarcastically.*) I suppose you didn't steal that?

MARY (*with a laugh*). Certainly not! (*Seriously.*) A man advertised for a partner in a business sure to bring large and safe returns. I answered the advertisement. What the businessman proposed was to buy a tract of land and subdivide it. The deeds to the land were all forged and the supposed seller was his confederate with whom he was to divide my money. We formed a partnership with a capital of sixty thousand dollars—he put the money in the bank and I promptly drew it out. He wanted to get my money illegally, instead of which I managed to get his legally, for it was legal. (*Turning to* DEMAREST.) Wasn't it, Mr. Demarest?

DEMAREST. Yes, unfortunately! A partner has the right to draw out any or all of the partnership funds.

MARY. And I was his partner. So you see you wrong me, Inspector. I'm not a swindler—(*with a laugh*)—I'm a financier.

BURKE (*sarcastically*). Yes. Well you'll never pull another one on me, you can gamble on that.

MARY. Won't I? Miss Lynch, at the present moment, is painlessly extracting ten thousand dollars from General Hastings, in a perfectly legal manner, Inspector Burke.

BURKE (*with a sneer*). Oh, she is, eh? (*Sternly.*) Well, you may stay within the law but you've got to get outside the city. (*Coaxingly.*) On the level now, did you think you could get away with that young Gilder scheme you're planning?

MARY (*innocently*). What young Gilder scheme?

BURKE. That's all right—I'm wise—I'm wise.

MARY (*with a laugh*). Yes, you are.

BURKE (*sternly*). Once for all, you leave town this afternoon or you'll be in the Tombs in the morning.

MARY (*as she rises and crosses to C., DEMAREST steps back out of the way*). It can't be done, Inspector. (*Turns and looks back over her shoulder at BURKE.*) It can't be done. (*Then crosses to drawer in left side of table at L.C. and opens the drawer.*)

BURKE (*following MARY as far as the lower L. corner. As soon as BURKE is in position DEMAREST drops quietly down to BURKE's right*). Who says it can't?

MARY (*as she is getting paper from drawer*). This.

BURKE. And what's—this?

MARY (*handing BURKE legal paper and coming down to the lower end of table. While he proceeds to open the paper and glances at it*). A temporary restraining order from the Supreme Court instructing you to let me alone until you have legal proof that I have broken the law.

BURKE. Another new one. (*Folding up paper.*) But you can't do it.

MARY (*seriously and earnestly*). Oh, can't I? A gambling house can get one and go on breaking the law, a race track can get one and laugh at the law, a railroad can restrain their employees from striking. Why shouldn't I get one too? I have money, I can buy all the LAW I want; and there's nothing you can't do with the law if you have money. (*With a laugh.*) Ask Mr. Demarest, he knows. (MARY *crosses up to the side of the chair L. of table at L.C. with her face up stage.*)

BURKE (*looking at DEMAREST*). Can you tie that? (*Hands DEMAREST legal paper which DEMAREST opens and looks at and then folds up. Then as BURKE crosses up to back of chair R. of table at L.C.*). A crook appealing to the law.

MARY. And getting justice—that's the remarkable part of it! (*Turning so that she faces both BURKE and DEMAREST and with a challenge in her voice.*) Well, gentlemen, what are you going to do about it?

BURKE (*sternly*). This is what I'm going to do, one way or the other. I'm going to get you.

DEMAREST (*crossing to table and laying paper on it, then stepping back. Gently and persuasively*). I'm going to appeal to your sense of fair play.

MARY (*as she turns away*). That was killed four years ago.

DEMAREST. Let young Gilder alone.

MARY (*turning to DEMAREST, strong*). His father sent me away for three years, and he's got to pay me.

BURKE (*quietly*). Don't fool yourself, my girl, you can't go through with it. There's always a weak link in the chain somewhere, and I'm going to find it.

MARY (*turning and looking at* BURKE. *Seriously*). Now you sound really dangerous. (GARSON *enters up L. door, closing it after him, and speaks as he is crossing down to* BURKE'S *L. just above* MARY.)

GARSON. Mary, I want to see you a minute.

MARY (*to* BURKE). Excuse me, please.

BURKE (*to* MARY). Nothing doin'. (*To* GARSON.) What is it?

GARSON. Something private.

BURKE. Private things don't go. (*Sternly*.) Out with it.

MARY. Tell then, Joe. There's nothing we need be afraid of.

GARSON. Old man Gilder's here.

BURKE (*as he crosses back of* DEMAREST *to down R. in front of trick table. Surprised*). Gilder!

DEMAREST (*surprised*). Here?

GARSON. That's what I said.

MARY (*as she shows pleasure*). Have Mr. Gilder come in, Joe. (GARSON *crosses to door up L.C., holds it open, and nods to* GILDER. MARY *taking stage down L.*) It seems I am having quite a number of distinguished callers today.

DEMAREST (*to* BURKE). He shouldn't have come. (*Starting to door up L.C. and gets as far as the head of the couch.*) Burke and I will attend to this, Mr. Gilder. (GILDER *enters and drops his hat on the table in the*

hall, *passes* DEMAREST, *and comes down before table at L.C. and to R. of it, facing* MARY, *who has her back half to him.* DEMAREST *comes down to upper end of table at L.C. as soon as* GILDER *passes him.*)

GILDER (*in a hard mechanical tone*). So you are the woman.

MARY. I am the woman. What do you want?

GILDER. My son.

MARY. Have you seen him lately?

GILDER. No.

MARY. Then why do you come?

GILDER. Because I intend to save my boy from a great folly. I am informed that he is infatuated with you, and Inspector Burke tells me—tells me——

BURKE (*starting a step or two forward*). I tell you she's an ex-convict.

GILDER. Is this true?

MARY (*positively*). It is.

BURKE. You'd better leave her to me. (*Crosses toward* MARY, *but just as he reaches* GILDER *on his last word* GILDER *checks him with a slight movement of his arm without taking his eyes off* MARY.) Now see here, you——

GILDER (*stopping him*). If you please, Inspector—— Of course you don't really care for my son—(BURKE *turns in disgust and crosses right to his former position*)—so how much will you take to go away—how much?

MARY. I don't want money. Inspector Burke can tell you how easy it is for me to get it.

DEMAREST. If you'll permit me, Mr. Gilder——

GILDER (*calmly and without taking his eyes off* MARY). I think this matter can be settled between this woman and me. (DEMAREST *crosses R. to back of chair L. of trick table as* GILDER *continues.*) Do you want my son to learn what you are?

MARY. Why not? I'll tell him myself.

GILDER. I don't want him to know. I've spared the boy all his life. If he really loves you——

DICK (*speaking outside and entering up L.C. door during the line, closes door after him and puts his hat on the couch. At the sound of* DICK'S *voice* GILDER *takes a step or two back and half turns toward door*). I didn't see Father but I left him—— (*Turns and sees his father and comes down stage and as he passes chair R. of table at L.C. draws it with him by the back until he stands facing his father with his back leaning against the chair. This business is done as he is speaking his next line.*) Hello, Dad, you got my note?

GILDER. No, I've had no note.

DICK. Then why—— (DICK *looks over his father's shoulder and sees* BURKE *and* DEMAREST.) What are they doing here?

MARY. Never mind them. Tell your father your news.

DICK (*as he crosses down to* MARY *and puts his hands on her shoulders and looks over her shoulders into her face*). Dad, we're married. Mary and I were married this morning.

GILDER. What!

MARY (*in exultation*). I married your son this morning. Do you understand, Mr. Gilder, I married him.

BURKE (*tempestuously*). It's a frame-up! Tell your father it ain't true. Why, do you know what she is? She's done time, and by God she'll do it again.

DICK (*turning to them*). That's a lie. (*To* MARY.) Mary, say it's a lie.

MARY (*as she turns to* DICK *and takes a step back*). It's the truth.

BURKE. What did I tell you?

DICK. You have——

MARY (*looking squarely at* DICK). I have served three years.

GILDER (*to* DICK). I wanted to save you from this.

DICK (*facing front*). But there's a mistake.

DEMAREST. There isn't.

DICK. I say there is. (*Pleading.*) Mary, say there's a mistake—say there's a mistake.

MARY. It's all quite true. (*Pause as* DICK *staggers back, with his hand over his eyes, against L. side of table at L.C. and sinks into a sitting position with bowed head on the table.*)

GILDER. Do you see what you've done to my boy?

MARY (*controlling her emotion and starting toward* GILDER). And what is that compared to what you have done to me?

GILDER. What I have done to you?

MARY (*up to* GILDER; GILDER *breaks ground a step or two during the speech*). Yes, do you remember what I said to you the day you had me sent away?

GILDER (*as he starts to cross in front of her to* DICK). I don't remember you at all.

MARY (*stepping in front of him and blocking him*). Don't you remember Mary Turner, who was arrested four years ago for robbing your store? (GILDER *shows he begins to remember and breaks ground a step or two and a little up stage.*) Who swore she was innocent, and who would have got off if you hadn't asked the judge to make an example of her?

GILDER. You are that girl?

MARY. I am that girl. (DICK *starts to take notice of what is being said and slowly rises and turns and drops to lower side of table at L.C.*). You helped smash my life, you put me behind the bars; you owe me for all that, and I have just begun to collect.

GILDER. And that is why you married my boy?

MARY. It is.

DICK. It's not.

BURKE (*as he takes a step toward* MARY). Now see here——

DICK. You keep out of this. (BURKE *turns and takes his former position.*)

DEMAREST. But, Dick——

DICK. And you. (*As he puts his hands on* MARY's *shoulders. She is standing facing* GILDER.) This is my affair. (*To* MARY *as he turns her slightly down stage, speaking over her shoulder.* MARY *keeps her eyes on* GILDER.) You married me because you loved me.

MARY. I didn't.

DICK. And you love me now.

MARY. No! NO!

DICK. You love me now.

MARY. I don't.

DICK. Look me in the face and say that. (DICK *turns* MARY *so that she faces him and holding both her arms.*) Look me in the face and say that.

MARY. I don't love you.

DICK (*as his hands slip down to both her wrists and he tries to draw her to him*). Just the same, you're my wife and I'm going to make you love me.

MARY. You can't. You're his son.

DICK. I'm going to make you love me. I don't care what you've done.

BURKE. She's a crook!

DICK (*to* BURKE). I don't give a damn what she's been. (*To* MARY.) Do you hear, I don't care what you've been? From now on you'll go straight. You'll walk the straightest line a woman ever walked. (MARY, *who has had her head turned away from him during this speech, now starts to draw* DICK *up stage until they reach the chair that* DICK *placed on his entrance, then* DICK *puts his right knee on the chair and as* MARY *continues to draw away she gets around the chair and above* DICK, *and on the last few words of his speech he draws her around in front of him again and on his last word forces her hands to the back of the chair, thus forcing her to look at him.*) You'll put all thoughts of revenge out of your heart—(DICK *kneels on chair*)—because I'm going to make—(DICK *draws* MARY *around to face him*)—you love me. (*A pause as* MARY *gives* DICK *one look of wonder, when* BURKE *breaks in sharply.*)

BURKE. She's no good, I tell you, she's a crook.

MARY (*turning quickly to face* BURKE *and forcing her wrists away from* DICK. DICK *off chair and back against table at L.C.*). And if I am, who made me one? You can't send a decent girl to prison and have her come out anything else.

BURKE (*sarcastically*). She didn't even get her time off for good behavior.

MARY. And I'm proud of it. (*To* GILDER.) Do you know what goes on behind those stone walls? (*To* DEMAREST *as she takes a couple of steps up stage.*) Do you, Mr. District Attorney, whose business it is to send girls there? Do you know what a girl is expected to do so that she can get time off for good behavior? If you don't—(*starts down stage and with horror in her voice*) —ask the keepers.

GILDER. And you?

MARY (*as she turns to face* GILDER *and with her back to the chair* DICK *placed on his entrance*). I served every minute of my time: three full, whole years. Do you wonder I want to get even—that someone has got to pay? (*A step to* GILDER.) Four years ago you took away my name and gave me a number. Now I've given up—(*ring curtain down*)— that number and I've got your name.

CURTAIN

ACT THREE

SCENE I

TIME—*The next night at half-past ten.*
SCENE—*Library in* EDWARD GILDER'S *house. At R. is a practical bay window with tapestry portieres. Across the back at C. is a fireplace. R. of the fireplace is a door leading into another room. L. of the fireplace is a bookcase. The*

walls over the door up R., fireplace, and both bookcases are covered with tapestry. At L. second entrance is a door which leads into the hall. Below this door is another bookcase. To L. of the fireplace and between it and the bookcase is a chair, and another chair is in front of the fireplace. Down R. is a library table with a practical lamp on the R. middle side and a phone on the R. upper end. On the surbase just below the bay window is the practical bell box of the phone. Down L. is a couch set diagonally. Back of the couch is a small square table with a practical lamp, box of cigarettes, and box of matches on it. On the wall L. between the door and the bookcase is a push-button switch which is supposed to control chandelier but does not.

LIGHTS—*Foots up, amber, no borders. Both table lamps lit, with amber shades and globes. Chandeliers not on in* SCENE I *but on and off with foots on cues in* SCENE II. *Chandelier has amber shades and amber globes. Moonlight in bay window to be flashed on and off on cue, once in* SCENE I *and once in* SCENE II.

AT RISE—MR. GILDER, *wearing dinner clothes, is discovered seated at the table at R.C. reading a book. After a short pause the door at L. opens and* DICK *enters, closing the door after him and coming to back of couch above table. He is in dinner clothes. As he enters* MR. GILDER *looks up, then goes on with his reading.*

DICK (*as* DICK *speaks he comes around to the front of couch*). ·I'm awfully sorry I'm so late, Dad.

GILDER (*without raising his eyes*). Where have you been? With that woman again?

DICK (*coming around upper end of couch to front of it*). She won't see me.

GILDER. Naturally. She's got all she wants from you: my name!

DICK (*to lower end of couch and sits*). It's mine, too, you know, sir.

GILDER (*turning to* DICK). Dick, you're all I have, my boy. You'll have to free yourself from this woman somehow. You owe me that much.

DICK. Dear old dad, I owe you everything in the world, but I owe something to her too——

GILDER. What can you owe her? She tricked you into this marriage —it's not even that, she's simply fooled you into a wedding ceremony. Now it's for us to get you out of this scrape——

DICK. I'm not certain that I want to get out of it.

GILDER. You want to stay married to this jailbird?

DICK (*rising sharply*). I'm very fond of her, Dad.

GILDER. Now that you know?

DICK. Now that I know. (*As* DICK *crosses to* GILDER *at the table.*) Don't you see she's justified in a way, in her own mind, I mean? She was innocent when she was sent to prison. She feels that society owes her something——

GILDER. Don't talk nonsense. I suppose you'll argue next that because she's clever enough to keep within the law since she got out of State's Prison that she's not a criminal. (DICK *crosses to* C.) A crime's a crime whether the law touches it or not. There's only one course open to you, my boy: you must give this girl up.

DICK (*crossing to* L.C.). I've told you, Dad, that I can't.

GILDER (*rising and crossing to* DICK). You must, I tell you. (*Pause, then softly.*) If you don't, what are you going to do the day your wife is thrown into a patrol wagon and carried down to police headquarters? (DICK *turns to* GILDER *as if about to speak.*) For it's sure to happen. The cleverest people make mistakes, and someday she'll make one!

DICK. But she isn't going to——

GILDER (DICK *turns away*). They'll stand her in a line and the detectives will walk past her with masks on their faces; her picture is already in the Rogues' Gallery, but they'll take another—yes, and the imprints of her fingers, and the measurements of her body.

DICK (*turning quickly to* GILDER). Father!

GILDER. That's what they'll do to your wife, the woman who bears your name and mine; now what are you going to do about it?

DICK. It will never happen. She'll go straight. You don't know her as I do. (*Sits on lower end of couch.*)

GILDER (*crossing to* DICK). Be sensible, my boy, be sensible.

DICK. Why, Dad, she's young—she's just like a child in a hundred ways. She loves everything that's simple and real! And as for her heart, Dad—I've seen her pick up a baby that had fallen in the street and mother it in a way that—well, no one could do it as she did unless her soul was clean.

GILDER. After what you heard her say yesterday, you still think that?

DICK. I don't think—I know.

GILDER. Do you realize what you are doing? Don't go to smash just at the beginning of your life. Put this woman out of your thoughts and start afresh.

DICK. I can't.

GILDER (*putting his left hand on* DICK's *right shoulder*). You're all I have, my boy.

DICK (*rising*). Dad, I know, I'm sorry—if I could avoid it, I wouldn't hurt you for anything in the world—but I've got to fight this out in my own way. (*Crossing in front of* GILDER *and above the table at* R. *to bay window.*) And I'm going to. (GILDER *starts toward* DICK. THOMAS *enters* R. *door and* GILDER *stops as* THOMAS *stands with card tray and card just inside the door, which he closes after him.*)

GILDER (*at* C.). Well, Thomas?

THOMAS. A man to see you, sir.

GILDER. I can't see anyone tonight. (*Starts to cross to* DICK *at first word of* THOMAS.)

THOMAS (*as he crosses down to* GILDER's *L.*). He says it's very important, sir. (*Offers* GILDER *a card on a tray.*)

GILDER (*takes card and reads*). Inspector Burke. (*To* THOMAS.) Show him in. (THOMAS *crosses to door L. and exits leaving door open.*)

DICK. Burke! (*Starts toward door up R.*)

GILDER. Better wait a minute. You may as well get used to visits from the police. (DICK *comes down to R. upper corner of table at R. Enter* THOMAS, *stands above door facing down stage.* BURKE *follows* THOMAS *in and crosses to table at back of couch and puts his hat on it, then goes around upper end of couch to* GILDER. THOMAS *exits L., closing door after him.*)

GILDER (*at* BURKE's *entrance*). Good evening, Inspector—you wish to see me?

BURKE. Yes. (DICK *starts for door up R.*) I want to see you too, young man. (DICK *stops and, turning, comes down to R. side of table at R.C.*)

GILDER. Well, Burke?

BURKE. Well, she's skipped.

DICK. I don't believe it.

BURKE (*to* GILDER). She left this afternoon for Chicago. I told you she'd go. Now all we have to do is to get this boy out of this scrape and we're all right.

GILDER. If we only could.

BURKE. Oh, I guess we can find some way to have the marriage an-

nulled—(DICK *gives* BURKE *a look of anger*)—or whatever they do to marriages that don't take.

DICK (*angrily*). Don't you interfere in this.

BURKE. Interfere? (*As he crosses to L. of table at R.C.*) Huh! That's what I'm paid to do. (*Quietly, with meaning.*) Listen to me, Son: the minute you begin mixing up with crooks you ain't in a position to give orders to anyone. A crook's got no rights in the eyes of the police. Just remember that.

DICK (*all anger gone*). So she's going to Chicago.

BURKE. Yes.

DICK. Where's she going in Chicago?

BURKE. I'm no mind reader, but she's a swell little girl; I've got to hand it to her for that anyway—she'll probably stop at the Blackstone—that is until the Chicago police are tipped off that she's in town.

DICK. Burke, give me a chance—I'll leave for Chicago in the morning. Give me twenty-four hours' start before you begin hounding her.

BURKE. That sounds reasonable.

GILDER (*as he quietly comes down to* BURKE's *L.*) You shan't go, Dick. You shan't go.

BURKE (*to* GILDER). Why not? It's a fair gamble and I like the boy's nerve.

DICK (*to* BURKE). And you'll agree?

BURKE. Yes.

DICK (*as he starts for door up R.*). Thank you.

GILDER (*turning toward* DICK). You shan't go.

BURKE (*aside to* GILDER *as he crosses to down R. corner of table at R. and then turns to face* GILDER). Keep still, it's all right.

DICK (*turns at door up R. and then crosses down to lower L. corner of table at right and faces* BURKE). You give me your word that you won't notify the police in Chicago until I've been there twenty-four hours?

BURKE. You're on. They won't get a whisper out of me until the time's up.

DICK (*as he starts to door up R.*). Thank you.

GILDER. But, Dick——

DICK (DICK *is just on a level with his father and turns to him with his back to the audience*). I'm sorry, Dad, but I've got to do what I think is the right thing. (*Up to door up R. and exits closing door after him.*)

BURKE (*as he starts across stage L. to the lower end of couch*). Sure you have. (DICK *exits.*) That's the best any of us can do. (*Pause as* GILDER *goes to armchair back of table at R. and sits.* BURKE *turns at lower end of couch and looks at him.*)

BURKE (*as he crosses up C.*). He'll go to Chicago in the morning?

GILDER. Certainly.

BURKE. Best thing that could happen. (*Pause.*) He won't find her there.

GILDER (*in surprise*). What makes you think that?

BURKE (*with a chuckle*). Because she didn't go there.

GILDER. Where did she go then?

BURKE. Nowhere—yet. But just about the time he's starting for the west, I'll have her down to police headquarters, Demarest will have her indicted before noon, she'll get on trial in the afternoon, and tomorrow night she'll be sleeping up the river. That's where she's going.

GILDER (*rising*). But how can you do that?

BURKE (*as he crosses to* GILDER). Maybe I can't—but I will. Think I'm going to let this girl make a joke of the Police Department? Listen—this is where I'll get her— her gang is going to break into your house tonight.

GILDER. She's—(*stepping toward window at R.*)—coming here. (*Looking out window, then back to R. side of table facing* BURKE.) A thief?

BURKE. Not if I know her she won't. She's too clever for that. Why, if she even knew what Garson was up to tonight, there isn't anything in the world she wouldn't do to stop him. (*Pause as* BURKE *shows that he has thought of something.*) By God, I've got her. (*As he drops quickly into chair back of table R.*

and pulls the phone toward him.)
Can I use your phone?

GILDER. Certainly.

BURKE (*into phone*). Give me thirty-one hundred Spring. (*To* GILDER.) Maybe it isn't too late. I must have been out of my head not to have thought of it before. (*Into phone.*) Headquarters? Inspector Burke speaking. Who's in my office? (*Short pause.*) I want him quick. (*To* GILDER.) Smith's the best man I've got. We're in some luck anyhow. (*Into phone.*) Oh, Ed, send someone up to the Turner woman's flat—tip her off that Joe Garson, Chicago Red, and Tom Dacey are going to break into Edward Gilder's house tonight. Get some stool to hand her the information, and you've got to work quick. Hold on—— (*Pause as* BURKE *looks at his watch.*) It's ten-thirty now. She went to the Eltinge Theatre with some woman. Try to get her as she's leaving there; you'll have to hustle. If you miss her at the theater, have the man go to the house for her. That's all. (*Hangs up receiver.*)

GILDER. What good will all that do?

BURKE. She'll come here to stop them and we'll grab her when we get the rest of the gang. (*As he slaps the table and rises and crosses to C.*) God, I'll be glad to get Garson. (*Turning to* GILDER.) Mr. Gilder, I've tried for twenty years to land that crook, but he managed to slip through my fingers every time. Just ring for your man, will you, please, Mr. Gilder? (GILDER *presses call button under table edge and flash-light from Metropolitan tower floods the room with a white light for a few minutes.* BURKE *with some surprise.*) What's that?

GILDER. That's the flashlight from the Metropolitan tower. (BURKE *turns and crosses up C. facing door L.* GILDER *goes to the portieres and during the remainder of the speech draws them over the bay window.*) The servants forgot to draw the curtains. It won't bother us again. (THOMAS *enters door L., closing the door after him.* GILDER *turns, facing* THOMAS *and* BURKE *and standing at the portieres.*)

BURKE. My man, I want you to go up on the roof and open the scuttle. You'll find three men up there. Bring them down here. (*A frightened start from* THOMAS.) Oh, they won't hurt you. They're police officers. Then you go to bed and stay there till morning, understand? (THOMAS *looks at* GILDER.)

GILDER. Do as the inspector tells you, Thomas.

THOMAS (*as he starts across the stage R*). Very good, sir. (BURKE *watches* THOMAS *as he crosses and exits at R. upper door, closing door after him.*)

GILDER (*as* BURKE *comes down C. and he crosses to* BURKE *at C.*). How do you know they are going to break into this house, or do you only think they are?

BURKE. I know they are. I fixed it.

GILDER. You did?

BURKE. Sure! Through a stool pigeon.

GILDER. Oh, an informer.

BURKE. Sure. The stool pigeon in this trick is a swell English crook named Griggs who went to Garson yesterday morning with a scheme to rob your house. Garson fell for it, and Griggs got word to me at once that it was coming off tonight —and that's how I know.

GILDER. But why have your men come down over the roof?

BURKE. It wasn't safe to bring them in the front way. It's a cinch this house is being watched. Just let me have your latchkey. (GILDER *hesitates.*) Oh, come on.

GILDER (*as he starts to take ring of keys from pocket*). What for?

BURKE. I want to come back and make this collar myself.

GILDER (*as he hands* BURKE *the key*). Why not stay now that you're here?

BURKE. Suppose someone saw me coming in? There'd be nothing doing until they saw me go out.

GILDER. I see. (BURKE *takes the stage down R.* GILDER *goes up C.; door up R. opens and* THOMAS *enters and stands to R. of the door, facing* GILDER. CASSIDY *enters after* THOMAS, *followed by* THOMPSON *and* WILLIAMS, *whom* CASSIDY *motions to each side of the door up R. and then* CASSIDY *comes to L. end of table at R.*) Go to bed. (THOMAS *exits door up R. and closes it after him.*)

BURKE. Where can these men stay until they're needed?

GILDER. There's an empty room on the next floor that——

BURKE (*interrupting him*). Won't do. (*Crosses up to door up R., opens it, and steps into next room and looks off L.*) What's that door leading from this room here?

GILDER (*taking a step down stage so that he can see* BURKE). That leads to the third floor——

BURKE. No, I don't mean that one. The one on the other side of the room.

GILDER. Oh, that? That opens into a hall which leads to a storeroom.

BURKE (*as he enters to lower end of couch*). Take a look at that room, Cassidy. (CASSIDY *exits through door up R. and disappears off L. To* GILDER.) These men came through number twenty-six on the other street, then round the block on the roof.

GILDER. I see. To avoid suspicion. (GILDER *crosses up stage just above upper end of couch.*)

BURKE. Sure. You can't be too careful in a case like this. (CASSIDY *enters at door up R. and comes down L. end of table at R. As* CASSIDY *enters.*) Well, Cassidy?

CASSIDY. It'll do. Now if the light is out in that room, we can leave the door of the room where we are open. Will that be all right, Inspector?

BURKE. How about it, Mr. Gilder? Anyone likely to be using that room?

GILDER. No one.

BURKE. That'll do then. (*Up to* GILDER.) Now, I'm going to give you the same tip I gave your man. Go to bed and stay there.

GILDER. I'm doing this because there seems to be no other way; but I don't like it.

BURKE. Believe me, it's the easiest and quickest for us all. (*Coming down C.*) Cassidy!

CASSIDY (*stepping forward to meet* BURKE). Yes sir?

BURKE. You're in charge here and I hold you responsible.

CASSIDY. Yes, chief.

BURKE. Now listen to this and get it! I'm coming back to get this bunch myself, and I'll call you when I want you. You'll wait in that storeroom out there and not make a move until you hear from me, unless by any chance things go wrong and you get a call from Griggs—you know who he is?

CASSIDY. Yes sir.

BURKE. He's got a whistle and he'll use it if necessary. Got that straight?

CASSIDY. Yes sir.

BURKE. On your way then. (CASSIDY *starts toward door up R.*) Just a minute. (CASSIDY *stops and comes down to* BURKE.) The minute you get in the room, jump for that window. (*Indicating window R.*) Understand?

CASSIDY. Yes sir.

BURKE. That's all. (CASSIDY *goes up toward door R., motions* THOMPSON *and* WILLIAMS *off, and follows them, closing door after him. As* BURKE *crosses up above couch to table, gets his hat, and turns to* GILDER.) Now then, Mr. Gilder, I'll have to ask a little help from you to delay things a little to give that Turner girl time to get here. Keep your lights burning until about half-past eleven. They won't try anything as long as a light can be seen. Then go to bed and stay there. (GILDER *sighs.*) Don't worry about the boy. We'll get him out all right.

GILDER. I hope so.

BURKE. Nothing to it. Good night. (BURKE *exits L. door, closing it after him.* GILDER *pauses a moment, looks around, then crosses to portieres and parts them and looks out.*)

CURTAIN

(*As the curtain touches the stage all lights out except the moonlight. Chimes as a distant town clock starts striking twelve o'clock.*)

ACT THREE

SCENE II

TIME—*Same night. Twelve o'clock.*
SCENE—*The same.*
LIGHTS—*Everything out but the moonlight. In this scene every time the chandeliers go up and down the amber foots work with them.*
AT RISE—*On the eleventh stroke of the chime the curtain rises on a dark stage. On the twelfth stroke the portieres part and* GARSON *steps into the room and closes them. All his movements are made without a sound but are not stealthy. On the contrary, he works in an extremely businesslike manner. He takes care, however, to walk on the balls of his feet with a peculiar catlike tread. He then lights a pocket flash and flashes it around the room. He crosses to door at up R.C. and listens, then crosses to door L. and quietly opens it and listens, then quietly closes it and flashes his lamp on the switch on the wall just below the door L. Then he crosses to the table down R., flashes his lamp up through the shade, then lights the table lamp. As soon as the table lamp is lit, he puts out his flash lamp, puts it in his pocket, and looks around the room. He then crosses up, takes the chair from in front of fireplace, and places it against the up R.C. door in such a way that anyone entering would stumble over it. Then, coming down to the back of the table at R.C., he takes up the phone in both hands and calls 999 Bryant. As he is waiting he again looks around the room as if watching the door, and then, setting down the phone with the receiver at his ear, picks up a penholder and turns to the phone as if he had an answer from his number. Then he taps out a message in Morse code on the mouthpiece with the penholder. A reply is heard in the Morse code and then he hangs up receiver. Looking around, he finds the bell box of the phone on the surbase below the bay window. He kneels down facing front and unscrews one bell and lays it on the floor, then removes the other one. Then, picking up both bells, he rises and sets them on the table under the lamp. Then, as he stands at the R. end of the table, he takes out his revolver and silencer. He is watching the doors all the time. Then, putting the revolver in his right side trouser pocket, he takes out his pocket flash from his inside coat pocket, turns out the table lamp, and, with his flash lamp showing ahead of him, crosses to door L. and exits, leaving the door open. The stage remains dark for a few moments, then the light from the pocket flash is seen on the ceiling and gradually comes down until it is shining directly across the stage on the door up R.C. Then enter at door L.* DACEY, *who crosses to the R. upper corner of the table at R.C.* DACEY *is followed by* GRIGGS, *who crosses around the upper end of the couch then down C. and stands facing up stage.* GRIGGS *is followed by* CHICAGO RED, *who crosses*

over to upper end of bay window. Each of the men passes in front of the light of the flash lamp as they enter. GARSON *then enters, putting out his flash lamp and closing the door quietly. Then he turns to switch on the wall below the door. All talking from here until* MARY *orders to turn up lights is carried on in monotone.*

GARSON. All right so far. Wait till I turn up the lights. (*Presses switch for chandelier lights. As chandelier lights,* DACEY *and* CHICAGO RED *turn to portieres.* GRIGGS *starts up toward portieres, and* GARSON, *as he speaks, crosses down below couch and over to portieres and is just at up R.C. as the phone buzzes.*) Is that what we want?

GRIGGS. Yes.

GARSON. We got to hurry and—— (*Phone buzzes.* GARSON *jumps quickly and picks up the phone and removes the receiver. The phone then stops buzzing.* GRIGGS *comes quickly down to* GARSON'S *L. shoulder.* CHICAGO RED *turns and leans over up R. corner of table and* DACEY *over back of* GARSON'S *chair.*) We got to take a chance. (*Then puts the receiver to his ear and a telegraph message is heard coming over the phone, and after it stops* GARSON *speaks.*) That's Mary's call.

GRIGGS, RED, *and* DACEY. Mary's? (*Telegraph message starts again.*)

GARSON. Yes, she's on. (*He holds receiver a few inches away from his ear and as the message comes over the phone he translates.*) Am—at corner—drug—store! Have—some-one—open—door—for—me—immediately. (*During the translation* GRIGGS *draws away up C. watching* GARSON.*)

GRIGGS. She's coming over?

GARSON. I'll stop her. (*Sets down phone and picks up penholder.*)

RED. Right! Stop her.

GARSON (GARSON *taps out a message on the mouthpiece—pause—but gets no answer*). She don't answer! (*Tries again, gets no answer, and then as he quickly hangs up receiver.*) She's gone.

GRIGGS. Probably on her way.

GARSON (*at the upper left corner of the table*). What's she coming here for? This is no place for her! If anything should go wrong now——

GRIGGS. Nothing can. (*As he quickly crosses to door L.*) I'll let her in.

GARSON (*as he advances to C. and sharply to* GRIGGS). Griggs! (GRIGGS *stops at door L. and turns to* GARSON.) Got a lamp?

GRIGGS. Sure. (*Exits at door L., leaving it open.*)

GARSON (*after a look at* GRIGGS, *then coming down L. corner of table at R.*). If anything should go wrong now! Oh! Why did she have to come? (MARY *enters hurriedly at L. door and crosses above couch and down to* GARSON. *As* MARY *enters.*) What do you want here? (GRIGGS *enters, removes his hat quietly, closes door, and drops down to table back of couch.*)

MARY. You lied to me. (*Amber light back of door up R., on.*)

GARSON. That can be settled later.

MARY (*turning up stage*). You're fools, all of you. This is burglary. How can I protect you if you're caught? Come, we must get away at once. (*Turning to* GARSON.) Joe, make them go.

GARSON. We're here now and we can't leave.

MARY. Joe, for my sake.

GARSON. I can't leave till we've got what we're after.

MARY. But there are reasons—I can't have you rob this house! (*Turning up stage.*) Boys, let's get away— please—please. (*To* GARSON.) Joe, for God's sake.

GARSON (*as he crosses L. in front of* MARY *and to the middle of the front of the couch and facing up stage*). I'm going to see this thing through.

MARY. Joe!

GARSON. It's settled.

MARY. Then—— (*starts to go toward door L.*).

GARSON (*as he takes a step up stage*). You can't go.

MARY. Why?

GARSON. You might be caught.

MARY. And if I were—do you think I'd tell?

GARSON. Of course not. You'd go for a lifer first.

MARY. Rather than——

GARSON. Just the same, we can't take any chances. We'll all get away in a minute and you'll come with us. Tom, get to that light switch. (DACEY *crosses to switch L. and places his L. hand on it as* GARSON *continues.*) If you hear me snap my fingers, turn 'em off. Understand?

MARY. Joe, don't do this.

GARSON. You can't stop it now, and you're only making it dangerous for us all. (*To* RED.) Red, you get to that door. (RED, *who is at R., goes quickly up, takes chair away from door up R., puts it at R. side of the fireplace, and returns to the door as* GARSON *continues.*) If anyone comes in, get him and get him quick— don't give a chance to cry out.

RED (*as he holds up his R. hand*). Not a chance with dis to cover his mug. (RED *turns then with his ear to the jamb of the door, listening.*)

GARSON (*with his face still up stage. To* GRIGGS). Now let's get to work. (GRIGGS *quickly goes up, puts his hat on the chair L. of the fireplace, returns, and stands at the up stage side of the table back of the couch.*)

MARY. Listen to me, Joe: if you do this, I'm through with you—I quit.

GARSON. If this goes through we'll all quit. That's why I'm doing it. (*To the others.*) Come, boys, push that table. (*Indicating table back of the couch.*) Against the wall so I can stand on it. (GRIGGS *bends down as if to pick up table;* GARSON *starts up stage and over toward portieres. MARY tries to stop* GARSON *as he passes her, then crosses around lower end of couch as if to hold table.)*

MARY. No, Joe! NO! NO! NO!

RED *(makes a hissing sound and everybody stops just where he is.* GARSON *is up C., facing* RED. MARY *is at the lower end of the table back of couch.* DACEY *is at the light switch L.* GRIGGS *is above the table back of the couch in the act of lifting it, and* RED *has his ear at the door up R. There is a short pause, and* RED *again gives the warning hiss).* I hear something. *(Pause.)* It's comin' this way!

GARSON *(as he snaps his fingers).* Lights! *(The lights go out, and in the pause of darkness before* DICK *enters at up R. door,* GARSON *first crosses back of couch to left side of table just above* MARY *with his pocket flash ready.* GRIGGS *then crosses up C.* DACEY *follows* GRIGGS *and stands at his left, and* CHICAGO RED *steps well back into the corner between the door up R. and the bay window.* DICK *opens up R. door, stands for a moment in the light, and then steps into the room, drawing the door closed after him. Just before the door closes* RED'S *right hand grabs* DICK'S *wrist and forces* DICK'S *hand over his own mouth. The door then closes, and in the darkness* RED *grabs* DICK'S *other wrist and they struggle down to the lower end of the front of the couch;* DICK *is then forced down on his knee. As* DICK *goes to his knee* RED *speaks.)*

RED. I've got him. *(*GARSON *flashes pocket flash on* DICK'S *face. As* DICK'S *face is seen* MARY *speaks.)*

MARY. It's Dick.

GARSON *(as he takes flash off* DICK'S *face and returns it to his pocket and crosses up around the upper end of the couch and to the front of it).* Get away, Red. *(*RED *lets go of* DICK *and goes up stage quickly between* GRIGGS *and* DACEY. *As soon as* DICK *is released he rises and, kneeling on couch, leans over and lights the lamp on the table back of the couch. As he lights the lamp both baby spots come on, trained on* DICK'S *and* MARY'S *faces.* DICK *is kneeling on the couch and* MARY *is back of it, and then they are face to face.* MARY'S *hand is on the back of the couch.)*

DICK *(as he places his hand over* MARY'S).* Good God! You.

MARY *(warningly).* Hush! You don't understand.

DICK. I understand this—whether you ever did before or not, this time you have broken the law. You're in my hands now, and these men as well—and unless you do as I say, I'll jail every one of them.

MARY. You can't. I'm the only one you've seen.

DICK. That's soon remedied. *(Starts to turn away.)*

MARY *(as she grabs* DICK'S *left arm with her left hand).* Don't turn, Dick. It isn't safe.

DICK. I'm not afraid.

RED. Who is this?

DICK. Her husband. Who are you?

MARY. Don't speak, any of you. Don't let him hear your voices.

DICK (*to* MARY). You're fighting me like a coward. You're taking advantage of my love—you think because of it I can't make a move against these men. Now you listen to me.

MARY. I won't. There's nothing to listen about. There never can be anything between you and me. (*Turns away to L. and attempts to go up stage.*)

DICK (*as he draws* MARY *back to him*). There can be and there will be. (*To the men and half turning to them.*) You men back there, if I give you my word to let every one of you go free and pledge myself never to recognize one of you again, will you make Mary listen to me? Give me a few moments to state my case, and whether I win or lose, you men go free and I forget everything that has happened here tonight. (RED *laughs derisively. To* MARY.) Tell them I can be trusted.

GARSON. I know that.

DICK (*to* MARY). You must listen! Your very safety depends on me. Suppose I call for help.

GARSON (*as he comes quickly down to* DICK's *side* GRIGGS *comes quickly down to C. and* DACEY *and* RED *each step forward*). You'd only call once.

DICK (*as he turns and looks at* GARSON). Perhaps once would be enough.

GARSON (*short pause*). You win. (GARSON *turns and faces up stage,*

then to RED). Red, you go into that hall. (*Indicating door L.* RED *crosses quickly to the door,* GRIGGS *goes up stage, and* DACEY *returns to his former position.* RED *pauses at the door L. as* GARSON *continues.*) Don't take any chances with a whistle—come in and tell us if you hear anything. If we're rushed and have to make a quick getaway, see that Mary has the first chance.

RED. Right. (RED *exits at L. door, closing it after him.*)

GARSON (*to* DICK). Make it quick, remember. (*Then* GARSON *goes up stage to the others.*)

DICK (*turning to* MARY *and putting his left arm around her waist*). Don't you care for me at all?

MARY. No, no.

DICK. I know you do, a little, anyway—if you'll only give me half a chance. Oh, Mary, can't you see you're throwing away everything that makes life worth while? (*Pause.*) Why don't you answer me?

MARY. That wasn't in our bargain.

DICK. Mary, Mary, you've got to change—don't be so hard—give the woman in you a chance.

MARY (*sharply—to hide her feelings*). I am what I am and I can't change—keep your promise now and let's get out of this. (MARY *tries to get away and turns up stage to her R.*)

DICK (DICK *draws her back and around the corner of the couch*). You can change. After all, you've married me, and it's up to you to give me a chance to make good. I need you and you need me—come away with me.

MARY (*as she turns to* DICK *and puts her hands on his shoulders*). No. No. I married you, not because I loved you, but to repay your father. I wouldn't even let myself think of you—then suddenly I realized I had spoiled your life.

DICK. Spoiled it?

MARY. Absolutely. If I understood I really cared I wouldn't have married you for anything in the world.

DICK. But now, dear?

MARY. Can't you see, I'm a jailbird? Nothing can alter that.

DICK (*putting both his arms around* MARY *and drawing her close to him*). But you do love me, and nothing else matters. Don't you know you can't beat the law? Suppose you were caught here tonight with a gang of burglars, where would you get off? Why didn't you protect yourself? Why didn't you go to Chicago as you had planned?

MARY (*quietly, as if she didn't understand*). What?

DICK. Why didn't you go to Chicago as you had planned? (GRIGGS *starts quietly to draw away from the others at up C. and crosses down to L. end of table at R.C., listening intently.*)

MARY (*a little more interested and disengaging herself*). Arranged with whom?

DICK. With Burke.

MARY (*suspiciously*). Burke?

DICK. Yes.

MARY. Who told you I had arranged it?

DICK. Burke did.

MARY (*now thoroughly alert*). When?

DICK. Less than an hour ago.

MARY. Where?

DICK. In this room.

MARY. Burke was here?

DICK. Yes.

MARY. What was he doing?

DICK. Talking to my father. (GRIGGS *turns and rushes up to bay window, parts the portieres, and looks out.*)

MARY (*to* GARSON *as she crosses below the couch to C. facing up stage*). Joe! Turn up those lights. (GARSON *crosses to switch on the wall left.*) I want to see the face of every man in this room. (*Chandelier lights up and* GARSON *quietly comes down back to the couch and to the front lower end of it.* GRIGGS, *at the chandelier lighting, jumps away from the portieres and backs up into the corner between the door up R. and the bay window, breathing heavily and scared, with his eyes on* MARY. MARY *keeps her eyes on* GRIGGS *as she speaks.* DICK *gets off couch and crosses to the upper front corner of it, watching* MARY.) Dick, how much are those tapestries worth?

DICK. Oh, two or three hundred dollars. Why?

MARY. Never mind that. How long have you had them?

DICK. Ever since I can remember.

MARY. Then they're not the famous masterpieces your father bought recently?

DICK. I should say not.

MARY. It's a trick. (*Turning to* GARSON, *and as* MARY *takes her eyes off* GRIGGS *to turn to* GARSON, GRIGGS *jumps for the up R. door.*) Burke's done it. (*The noise of the lock turns* MARY'S *attention back to* GRIGGS.) Griggs!

GRIGGS (*turning and facing* MARY *and coming a little to C. and with fear in his voice*). He's lying to you. They're worth half a million.

MARY. You stool pigeon, you did this for Burke.

GRIGGS. I swear I didn't.

MARY. You came to me yesterday with this plan from him.

GRIGGS. I swear I was on the level.

GARSON (*at the front lower end of couch*). It's a frame-up.

GRIGGS (*defiantly*). Well, what of it?

GARSON (*as he draws his revolver*). I'll get you for this. (GRIGGS *puts police whistle to his mouth.*) Drop that whistle. (GARSON *rushes up C. as he fires at* GRIGGS. *No sound is heard. As* GRIGGS *drops straight down stage, so that his head is at the end of the table and his feet up stage,* MARY *gives a little scream and, with her eyes on* GRIGGS, *backs*

quickly to the couch. DICK *steps down, puts his left hand under* GARSON'S *wrist and then his right over* GARSON'S *wrist, and turns* GARSON'S *arm over. This forces* GARSON *around in front of and to* DICK'S *right side, and facing front with his arm turned over so that it forces him to drop the revolver.*)

GARSON (*as he drops the revolver*). Give me that gun.

RED (*as he enters door L. hurriedly and stands at it and closes it after him*). Somebody's opening the front door! (*There is a pause, then* GARSON *and* DICK *break.* GARSON *quickly steps over* GRIGGS'S *body, crosses to bay window, throws the down stage portiere back and looks out. As* GARSON *starts for the bay window,* DACEY, *who is up L.C., and* RED, *who is at the door L., quickly follow* GARSON *across right to bay window and stand above him; and as he turns back into the room,* DACEY, *who is front, throws the up stage portiere back and they both hurriedly exit through bay window. As* GARSON *leaves* DICK *he bends down and picks up the revolver and puts it in his pocket, then quickly runs to door L. and looks out, then closes it and stands listening at the doorjamb.*)

GARSON (*at the bay window*). The street's empty. We've got to jump for it. (*Turns and crosses quickly back toward* MARY, *passing between the chair and the table at R. as far as the body of* GRIGGS; *then, as he leans over the body of* GRIGGS *with his hand out to* MARY.) Come on, Mary.

DICK (*at door L.*). She can't make it.

GARSON. But if she's caught?

DICK. She won't be.

GARSON. If she is, I'll get you, so look out. (DICK *is urging in dumb motion, from the door L., to get out as he is watching through the crack of the door.* GARSON *looks down into* GRIGGS's *face. To* GRIGGS.) You stool pigeon, now tell that to Burke. (GARSON *turns and quickly exits through bay window.* MARY, *who has been perfectly still, her eyes riveted on* GRIGGS, *now starts slowly to move the body.*)

(*The spot from the Metropolitan tower light is lit with the blinder on.*)

DICK (*moving quickly toward* MARY *with his eyes on the door L. and speaking as he comes*). Mary! (*Then as he grabs* MARY *by both shoulders.*) Mary! (*Mary gives a start.*)

MARY (*in a semihysterical way*). I never saw a man killed before. (DICK *now half carries* MARY *and half pushes her down toward lower end of couch, where he throws her at the end of her line and she falls with her face buried in the down stage arm.*) He was standing there a moment ago and now—— (*As* MARY *falls on the couch* DICK *hurries up around the upper end of couch to the switch below the door L. and presses it. The chandelier goes out, and as* DICK *watches the door L. he quickly comes to the back of the couch above the table and takes a cigarette and match from the table, then sits on the back of the couch, leans over, gently shaking* MARY *by the shoulder, speaks in a whisper.*)

DICK. Talk to me! Talk to me! And above everything keep your head. (*Turns to the door and in his natural voice.*) It was bully of you to come and see me. (*In a whisper to* MARY.) Talk to me! Talk to me! Pretend you've come to see me. (*Naturally.*) I've been trying to see you all day. (*Prepares to light cigarette.*) I know that my father will eventually—— (*Strikes match and about to light cigarette.*)

BURKE (*as he quickly opens door with revolver in his right hand aimed into the room and quickly steps halfway into the room*). Hands up! All of you! (MARY *comes up quickly to a sitting position facing down stage.*)

DICK (*with lighted match in his hand showing his nervousness*). Why, what are you doing in this house at this time of night? Don't you know there are limits even to what you can do?

BURKE (*sharply and indicating* MARY *with the revolver*). What's she doing here?

DICK. You forget yourself, Inspector: this is my wife.

MARY (*in a semihysterical way*). Why shouldn't I be here?

BURKE (*sharply*). Where's your father?

DICK. In bed, I suppose. (*Shakes out watch.*) Again I ask you what you are doing here at this time of night?

BURKE (*as he puts revolver in his pocket—impatiently*). Oh, call your father. (MARY *starts to turn toward the body and slides up to the middle of the couch.*)

DICK. It's too late and I'd rather not disturb him. Oh, I see, Inspector, I'll have to tell you the truth. My wife has decided to give up. (DICK *puts his right hand back and puts it on* MARY's *right shoulder and draws her back so that her face is directly under the lamp. He then lets go of her as he continues, and* MARY *starts again moving toward the body and sliding up stage on the couch.*) We're going away together, but you see we had to talk things over. Now if you could come back in the morning?

BURKE. Oh, so that's it?

DICK. Why, yes, what did you think?

BURKE. I didn't know. You see, I had some business here and—— (*Metropolitan tower light flashes around and lights up the room, disclosing the body of* GRIGGS. MARY *screams and half rises.* DICK *quickly gets off the back of the couch and paces around the upper end of it and takes* MARY *in his arms and seats her again on the couch as the white light discloses the body of* GRIGGS.) What's that? (*Presses switch on the wall which lights the chandelier and calls.*) Cassidy! (*As he runs across the stage towards door up R. At C.*) Cassidy! (*As he throws open door up R.*) Cassidy!!! (*Quickly turns as he is crossing the body.*) Right where you are, both of you. (*Kneels at L. of the body and feels the breast.*)

CASSIDY (*as he rushes in door up R. and down to L. of the body,* followed by WILLIAMS *and* THOMPSON, *who stand one each side of the door up R.*) What is it, chief?

BURKE. They've got Griggs.

CASSIDY. Got Griggs?

BURKE. Yes, I'll break you for this. Why didn't you come in when you heard the shot?

CASSIDY. There wasn't any shot. We didn't hear a sound.

BURKE (*as he rises and faces* DICK *and* MARY). Why, you could drive a hearse through the hole they've made in him. (*To* DICK *and* MARY. *Quietly.*) So now it's murder? Where's the gun? Hand it over. (*Pause.*) Search him.

CASSIDY (*as he just crosses body toward* DICK). Yes sir. (GILDER *enters up R. door and comes down to table at R. of the body.*)

DICK (*as he takes revolver from his pocket and offers it to* BURKE). Here it is.

GILDER. What's this?

BURKE (*to* GILDER). You wait. (*As he crosses down R. in front of table examining revolver.*) So you did it, eh? Cassidy, you and Thompson take 'em both downtown. (CASSIDY *motions with his hand and* THOMPSON *crosses from L. of door up R. to upper corner of the couch.*)

DICK. Not her, you don't want her. It's all wrong.

MARY (*as she takes* DICK's *hand in both hers and lays her cheek against it and facing front.)* Don't talk, Dick—don't talk.

BURKE *(turns facing* DICK*).* What did you expect? Either you killed Griggs or she did. Did she kill him?

DICK. Good God, no!

BURKE. Then it's you.

MARY. It isn't. It isn't.

BURKE. Now one of you killed Griggs. Did she do it?

DICK. I told you no.

BURKE. Did he kill him? *(Stepping to C. and indicating* MARY *with the revolver which is in his right hand.)* You, I'm talking to you. Did he kill him?

MARY *(showing that she has an idea).* Yes.

DICK *(as he draws back from* MARY*).* Mary!

GILDER. So that's your revenge?

MARY. I don't want revenge.

GILDER. But they'll try my boy for murder.

MARY. They can't. They can't.

BURKE. What's the reason we can't?

MARY *(turning to* BURKE*).* Because you can't convict him.

BURKE. Can't, eh? *(Indicating body with revolver.)* There's the body. *(Showing the revolver.)* The gun was found on him. And you'll swear he killed him?

MARY *(as she rises).* Quite true. *(Stepping forward to* BURKE*.)* But that man was a burglar, and he shot him in defense of his home. *(*MARY *starts to sink.* DICK *steps down to her quickly and they are in each other's arms as the curtain falls.)*

CURTAIN

ACT FOUR

TIME—*The next morning.*
SCENE—*Office of* INSPECTOR BURKE. *The interior part of the set runs back to two. There is a door L. which leads to the hall leading to the stand. At R. a door leading into the interior of the building. At R.C. is a flat-top desk set so that* INSPECTOR BURKE, *who sits at it, faces the audience and there is just passageway between his chair and the windows back of it. At each side of the desk is an office chair, each placed so that there is walking space between them and the desk. There is an office chair down L., below door L. At the back of the office are four large windows with practical shades. Through the windows can be seen four cells. There is a passageway between*

the cells and the windows. At the opening of the act the shades are up and the doors of the cells are open except the one at the extreme L., which is closed.

LIGHTS—*The office is well lighted with white foots and white first border. There is no light behind the windows.*

AT RISE—BURKE *is in dress uniform, standing back of his desk.* WILLIAMS *is standing above door R. which is open.* CHICAGO RED *is at lower R. corner of desk and facing* BURKE. DACEY *is at left side of desk facing* BURKE. *Door is closed.*

BURKE. Come across now, Red.

RED. I don't know nothin'. Ain't I been tellin' you that for over an hour? (*As* BURKE *turns and looks to* DACEY, RED *takes stage R.*)

BURKE (*taking hold of* DACEY'S *coat lapels, pushes him around to the front of the desk and, as he comes to a standstill at the lower L. corner of the desk, gives* DACEY *a final push and lets go of him*). Dacey, how long you been out?

DACEY (*facing* BURKE). 'Bout a week.

BURKE. Want to go back for another stretch?

DACEY. God, no.

BURKE. Who shot Griggs?

DACEY (*as he advances to* BURKE). I don't know, honest I don't. (BURKE *suddenly hits* DACEY *alongside the jaw and* DACEY *goes to the floor.* DACEY *scrambles to his feet and backs away from* BURKE *as far as the door R.*)

BURKE (*as* DACEY *goes down*). Now get up and talk.

CASSIDY (*entering door L. and closing it after him and standing at the door*). The district attorney's here.

BURKE (*with his eyes on* DACEY). Oh, he is, eh? Well, send him in. (CASSIDY *exits door L., closing it after him.*)

BURKE (*as he goes up to his chair back of desk*). I'll attend to you two later. Williams, take 'em back. (RED *and* DACEY *exit R.,* WILLIAMS *about to follow.*) And, Williams!

WILLIAMS (*stopping and turning to* BURKE). Yes sir.

BURKE. Don't be rough with them. (WILLIAMS *exits and* BURKE *sits.*) Dan! (DAN *enters R.*) Just pull down those shades, will you, please? (DAN *crosses first to the far shades and pulls them all down and exits R.* DEMAREST *enters L.*) Thanks for coming so soon.

DEMAREST (*as he crosses brings chair L. of desk close to the desk and sits facing* BURKE). I came as soon as I got your message. I've sent for Mr. Gilder——

BURKE. Yes, he phoned me he was on his way.

DEMAREST (*taking cigar from his pocket and lighting it*). Now then, Burke, let me have it quickly.

BURKE. Well, Joe Garson, Chicago Red, Tom Dacey, and Eddie Griggs broke into Edward Gilder's house last night. I knew it was coming off and planted Cassidy and a couple of men just outside the room and went away, coming back in about an hour to make the arrests myself. When I broke into the room I found young Gilder and the Turner woman talking together.

DEMAREST. No trace of the others?

BURKE. I found Griggs lying dead on the floor. The Turner girl says young Gilder shot Griggs because he broke into the house.

DEMAREST. What does the boy say?

BURKE. Nothin'. (*Pause.*) She told him not to talk.

DEMAREST. What does she say?

BURKE. Refuses to talk until she sees a lawyer.

DEMAREST. Anything else?

BURKE. We've got Chicago Red and Dacey. And we'll have Garson before the day is over. Oh yes, they've just picked up a young girl at the Turner woman's flat. I don't know who she is, but I'm going to talk to her in a minute.

DEMAREST. What else have you got?

BURKE. Well, for once luck's with the police. We've got a real clue. Never saw a gun like that before, did you? (*Takes revolver with silencer out from under newspaper at R. end of desk and hands it to* DEMAREST.)

DEMAREST (*as he takes revolver and examines it*). No, not exactly like that.

BURKE. I'll bet you didn't. That thing on the end is a Maxim Silencer. There are thousands of them in use on rifles but——

DEMAREST (*as he hands revolver to* BURKE). But what?

BURKE. But they've never been able to use one on a revolver before. That's a specially made gun, that's absolutely noiseless. (*Puts revolver in his pocket.*) It'll be the easiest thing in the world to trace it. (CASSIDY *enters at door L., closes it after him, and comes a few steps into the room.*) Well, Cassidy, did you get anything? (DEMAREST *turns in his chair so that he can see* CASSIDY.)

CASSIDY. Yes, I had the factory at Hartford on the phone and they gave me Mr. Maxim.

BURKE. Good! Now we're getting to it. Well, what did he say?

CASSIDY. He said it was a specially constructed gun made for the use of Henry Sylvester, one of the professors at Yale. They've never been put on the market and never will be.

BURKE. Get hold of this man Sylvester.

CASSIDY. I just had him on the phone. He says his house was robbed about eight weeks ago and the silencer was stolen among other things. He adds the startling information that the New Haven police have not been able to recover any of his property. (*As he crosses to door R.*) Gee, them rube cops are immense.

DEMAREST (*on his first move,* CASSIDY *stops at door R. With a laugh*).

The New York police always recover stolen property.

CASSIDY (*as he exits hurriedly at door R.*) Good night.

DEMAREST (*to* BURKE). Is there any chance that young Gilder did shoot Griggs?

BURKE. You can search me. My men who were just outside the door of that room didn't hear a sound. Of course I know that all the gang were in the house.

DEMAREST. How do you know? Did you see them go in?

BURKE. No. But Griggs said——

DEMAREST. Griggs is dead. Burke, you're up against it; you can't prove that Garson or Chicago Red or Dacey ever entered that house.

BURKE. But Griggs said they were going to——

DEMAREST. I know, but Griggs is dead. (*Pause as* BURKE *turns away.*) You can't repeat what he told you. It isn't evidence.

BURKE. Then I'll charge young Gilder with that murder and call the Turner woman as a witness.

DEMAREST. You can't call her; you can't make a wife testify against her husband. And you can't arrest her and put him on the witness stand. Burke, your only chance of getting the murderer of Griggs is by a confession. (DEMAREST *rises but still faces* BURKE.)

BURKE (*as he rises, facing* DEMAREST). Then I'll charge 'em both

with that murder, and by God they'll both go to trial unless someone comes through. If it's my last act on earth, I'm going to land the man who shot Eddie Griggs.

DEMAREST. Burke, I don't believe for a minute that young Gilder killed this pet stool of yours, and understand I want him to go free.

BURKE. He'll go free when he tells me what he knows, and not before. (*Pause as* BURKE *turns away from* DEMAREST *and prepares to sit.*) Perhaps the old gentleman can make him talk. I can't. (*Sits.*) On account of his being his father's son, when it comes to young Gilder, I'm a little cramped in my style.

DEMAREST. Then you think that young Gilder knows——

BURKE. I don't think anything—yet. I know that Eddie Griggs, the most valuable crook that ever worked for me, has been murdered. And someone—man or woman—has got to pay for it.

DEMAREST. Woman?

BURKE. Mary Turner.

DEMAREST (*as he takes stage· L.*). But she's not that sort! (*Turns to* BURKE.)

BURKE. Oh! She ain't? She's made a monkey out of the Police Department; and first, last, and all the time, I'm a copper. Now, if you'll wait for Mr. Gilder in the room outside, I'll get busy with the girl they've just brought in. (BURKE *presses buzzer button on the right end of his desk.*)

DEMAREST. Very well. (*As he crosses to door L.*) I'll wait for him. (*Exits door L., closing it after him.*)

(BURKE *turns around so that he is facing door R. Door opens R. and* DAN *enters and stands above door.* AGGIE *follows. She is beautifully dressed and uses her best and most ladylike manner. She is making the bluff of her young life and pretends to be very indignant. She comes slowly inside the door and crosses to the back of the chair which is right of* BURKE'S *desk.*)

BURKE (*after* AGGIE *gets back of chair. Very bluff*). Now then my girl, I want to know——

AGNES (*blazing with wrath*). How dare you?

BURKE. What?

AGNES. What do you mean by this outrage? I demand my instant release.

BURKE. Wait a minute—wait a minute. Sit down. (*Motions to chair R. of desk.*)

AGNES. I shall do nothing of the kind. I have been arrested, and by a common policeman!

BURKE. Excuse me—a detective sergeant.

AGNES. You wait—just wait till my papa hears of this.

BURKE (*puzzled*). Who is your papa?

AGNES. I shan't tell you. You'd probably give my name to the re-porters, and if it ever got into the newspapers, my family would die of shame.

BURKE. Now the easiest way out for both of us is for you to tell me just who you are. You see, you were found in the house of a notorious crook.

AGNES. How perfectly absurd. I was calling on Miss Mary Turner!

BURKE (*quick and sharp*). How'd you meet her?

AGNES. I was introduced by Mr. Richard Gilder. He's the son of the owner of The Emporium.

BURKE. I know all about him.

AGNES. Then you must see at once that you are entirely mistaken in this whole matter. (*A pause as* AGNES *crosses to* BURKE *and leaning a little toward him.*) Don't you see it?

BURKE. Well, no, not exactly.

AGNES (*as she turns sharply away and crosses down between the chair and the desk to the front of the chair, looking front*). Sir!

BURKE. Not yet! Not yet! The fact is, even if you were introduced by Mr. Gilder, Mary Turner is an ex-convict who has just been arrested for—(*pause*)—murder.

AGNES (*shows start of surprise on her face, then with a smile as she turns to* BURKE). Murder?

BURKE. Yes, and if there's a mistake about you, we don't want it to go any further; that's one of the reasons I must know who you are. You see that, don't you?

AGNES. Oh yes. You should have told me that in the first place (*with an air*). My name is Helen—Travers —West. (*Sits in chair.*)

BURKE (*in surprise*). Not the daughter of the railway president?

AGNES. Yes. (*As she turns in her chair.*) Oh, please don't tell anyone. Surely you must see now why it mustn't be known that I have been brought to this dreadful place. Please let me go home. (*Turns front and starts to sob.*)

BURKE. That's all right, little lady. Don't you be worried. Just tell me all you know about this Turner woman—did you see her yesterday?

AGNES (*as she turns to* BURKE). Will you let me go home as soon as I've told you what little I know?

BURKE. Yes, no one's goin' to hurt you.

AGNES (*turns front*). Well, you see —it was this way—Mr. Gilder was calling on me one afternoon, and he said he knew a charming young woman, who—who—— (*Apparently breaks down and takes out handkerchief and starts wiping her eyes.*) Oh, this is dreadful.

BURKE (*soothingly*). That's all right, little lady—that's all right—no one's goin' to hurt you!

AGNES (*through her tears*). Oh dear! Oh dear!

BURKE. Isn't there something else you can tell me about this woman?

AGNES. I'm so frightened.

BURKE. Now there's nothing for you to be frightened about.

AGNES. I'm afraid you'll put me in a c-c-cell.

BURKE. No one could think of a cell and you at the same time.

AGNES (*as she dries her tears and turns and gives* BURKE *a smile*). Oh, thank you, sir.

BURKE (*as he leans forward in his chair*). Are you sure you've told me all you know about this woman?

AGNES (*turning to* BURKE). Oh, yes, I've only seen her two or three times. Oh, please, won't you let me go home—Commissioner?

BURKE (*shows he is flattered by swelling up and leaning way back in his chair—graciously*). If I let you go now, will you promise to let me know if you can think of anything else about this woman?

AGNES (*as she rises and pushes the chair close to the desk*). I will, indeed I will.

BURKE. Now you see, no one's hurt you. You can run right home to your mother.

AGNES (*as she crosses quickly toward door L.*). I'll go just as fast as I can. (*Stops and turns to* BURKE *on his first word.*)

BURKE. Give my compliments to your father, and tell him I'm sorry I frightened you.

AGNES. I will, Commissioner. (*Starts toward* BURKE.) Father will be so grateful to you. (AGNES *is just below chair L. of desk and has just put out her hand and* BURKE *is about to shake hands as* CASSIDY *enters.*)

CASSSIDY (*entering door R. and as he steps in and drops a little below door, closing the door after him*). Hello, Aggie.

AGNES (AGNES *stops short, gives* CASSIDY *a look, then* BURKE *a look, then as she sits in chair with her back front*). Ain't that the damnedest luck? (*Watches* BURKE *out of the corner of her eye.*)

BURKE (*gives* CASSIDY *a quick look, then, while watching* AGNES, *slowly rises and crosses to* CASSIDY. *To* CASSIDY). Do you know this girl?

CASSIDY. Sure. She's little Aggie Lynch—con woman from Buffalo—two years for blackmail.

BURKE (*as he puts his hand to his chair*). Oh! (*He then crosses the stage to L. of* AGNES, *watching her all the time, then with a laugh*). I certainly got to hand it to you, kid—you're a beaut.

AGNES (*to* CASSIDY). Just as I had him goin', too.

BURKE. Have we a picture of this young woman?

CASSIDY (*as he crosses to lower R. corner of desk*). Not in our gallery.

BURKE (*in society manner*). I'd dearly love to have a photograph of you, Miss Helen—Travers—West.

CASSIDY. Helen—Travers—West?

BURKE. That's what she pulled!

CASSIDY. No?

BURKE. Had me winging too. (CASSIDY *laughs.*) Oh, I admit it. (*To* AGNES.) You're immense, little one, immense. (*In society manner as he takes the stage down L.*) When may I have the pleasure of escorting you to our gallery?

AGNES (*rising and crossing to* BURKE *and in* AGGIE'S *natural way*). Oh, can that stuff. Let's you and me get down to cases.

BURKE. Now you're talkin'.

AGNES. You can't do anything to me. Why, I'll be sprung inside an hour. Why, habeas corpus is my lawyer's middle name.

BURKE. On the level now, when did you see Mary Turner last?

AGNES (*with an air of perfect truth*). Early this morning. We slept together last night because I had the willies—she blew the joint about half-past eight.

BURKE. Now what's the good of you lyin' to me?

AGNES. What, me? Oh, I wouldn't do a thing like that. On the level, what'd be the use, I couldn't fool you. (BURKE *puts his R. hand to his jaw as if he had been hit as he takes the stage a little to L.* AGNES *follows him.*) So help me, Inspector, Mary never left the house all night. I'd swear that's the truth on a pile of bibles a mile high.

BURKE. Have to be higher than that. She was arrested just after midnight.

(*Sharply.*) Young woman, you better tell all you know.

AGNES (*as she faces front*). I don't know a thing.

BURKE (*as he quickly produces revolver from his pocket, leans forward, and holds it in front of* AGNES—*sharply*). How long has she owned this gun?

AGNES (*glancing at revolver*). She didn't own it.

BURKE. Then it's Garson's, eh?

AGNES. I don't know whose it is. I never laid eyes on it till now.

BURKE. English Eddie was killed with this last night. Now, who did it? Come on, now, who did it?

AGNES. How should I know? Say, what do you think I am, a mind-reader?

BURKE (*straightening up and dropping revolver to his side. Quietly*). You'd better come through, and if you're the wise kid I think you are, you will.

AGNES. I tell you I don't know anything. (*About to cry.*) Say, what are you trying to hand me, anyway?

BURKE (*as he puts revolver back in his pocket and in a quiet, coaxing tone*). Now, it won't do, I tell you. I'm wise. Now listen to me—you tell me what you know and I'll see that you make a clean getaway and slip you a nice little piece of money, too.

AGNES (*turning to* BURKE). Say, let me get this straight.

BURKE. Sure.

AGNES. If I tell you what I know about Mary Turner and Joe Garson, I get away?

BURKE. Clean.

AGNES. And you'll slip me some money too?

BURKE. That's it! Now what do you say?

AGNES. I say, you're a great big stiff.

BURKE. What?

AGNES. What do you think I am? (*As she crosses to lower L. corner of desk. To* CASSIDY.) Say, take me out and lock me up. I'd rather be in the cooler than here with him.

BURKE (*threateningly*). You'll tell or you'll go up the river for a stretch.

AGNES (*to* BURKE). I don't know anything, and if I did I wouldn't tell in a million years. Now then, send me up if you can.

BURKE (*to* CASSIDY. *Hard and sharp*). Take her away. (CASSIDY *goes up to door R., throws it open, and stands above it.*)

AGNES (*as she crosses to R. lower corner of desk*). Do, Cassidy, and do it in a hurry. Bein' in the room with him makes me sick. (*A start toward door R., stops, and turns to* BURKE.) Thought I'd squeal, did yer? Yes, I would—(*as she crosses to door R.*)—like hell! (*Exits door R. followed by* CASSIDY, *who closes door.*)

(BURKE *appears nonplused. Kisses his hand and blows it after* AGNES, *then crosses to his desk and sits and puts revolver under newspaper at R. end of desk. As he sits* GILDER *and* DEMAREST *enter L.*)

BURKE. How do you do, Mr. Gilder? (*Presses call buzzer on his desk.*)

GILDER (*as he crosses in front of* BURKE'S *desk turns chair at R. of it and sits placing his hat on the desk, and* DEMAREST *stands L. of* BURKE'S *desk*). Inspector—— (DAN *enters L.*)

BURKE. Dan, have Mr. Gilder's son brought up. (DAN *exits R. closing door. To* GILDER.) Bad business, sir —very bad business.

GILDER. What does he say?

BURKE. Nothing. That's why I sent for you. Mr. Demarest has made the situation plain?

GILDER. Perfectly. It's a terrible position for my boy. You'll release him at once, won't you?

BURKE. I can't. You oughtn't to expect it.

GILDER. But you know very well he didn't——

BURKE. I don't know anything about it—yet.

GILDER. Inspector, you don't mean ——

BURKE. I mean we've got to make him talk. (DAN *enters door R. and stands above door. The sound of the door opening causes* GILDER *to turn and rise.*) That's what I want you to do for all our sakes. (DICK *enters door R.* DAN *exits door R., closing door after him.*)

GILDER. Dick, my boy—(*crossing to* DICK *and putting his R. hand on* DICK'S *L. shoulder and taking* DICK'S *L. hand in his L. hand and leads* DICK *down stage*)—the inspector tells me you have refused to answer his questions. (DICK *is looking straight ahead of him and nods.*)

GILDER. That wasn't wise under the circumstances. However, Demarest and I are here now to protect your interests and you can talk freely.

BURKE. He's got to talk freely.

GILDER. Now, who killed that man? We must know. Tell me!

BURKE (*as he half rises.*) Where did you get——

DEMAREST (*interrupting him*). Wait, please wait. (*As he crosses to* DICK *and* GILDER *steps back, he comes down to* DICK'S *right.*) Give the boy a chance. (*As he places his hand on* DICK'S *shoulder.*) Dick, I don't want to frighten you, but your position is really a dangerous one. Your only chance is to speak with perfect frankness. I pledge you my word I am speaking the truth. Dick, let me forget that I'm the district attorney and remember only that I'm an old friend of yours and your father's who is trying very hard to help you. Surely you can trust me? (*Hand off shoulder.*) Tell me—who shot Griggs?

DICK (*after a pause*). I did.

DEMAREST. Why?

DICK. Because I thought he was a burglar.

DEMAREST. Oh, I see. Now, let's go back a little. Burke says you told him last night that you had persuaded your wife to come over to the house and join you. Is that true?

DICK. Yes.

DEMAREST. And while you were talking—tell me, Dick, just what did happen? (*A pause as* DICK *does not answer.*) Did this burglar come into the room?

DICK. Yes.

DEMAREST. And he attacked you?

DICK. Yes!

DEMAREST. And there was a struggle?

DICK. Yes.

DEMAREST. And you shot him?

DICK. Yes.

DEMAREST (*very quietly*). Then where did you get the revolver?

DICK (*as he turns to* DEMAREST). Why, I grabbed—— (*Suddenly realizing that he was about to tell the truth.*) So you're trying to trap me too? (*As he crosses to* L.C. *and stands facing* L.) You and your talk of friendship——

DEMAREST (*crossing up to* R. *corner of desk*). I am your friend.

BURKE (*rising*). Yes, and you don't want to take us for fools either. If you shot Griggs in mistake for a burglar, why did you try to hide the fact? Why did you pretend that you and your wife were alone in the room? Why didn't you call for help —for the police, as any honest man would under the circumstances?

GILDER (*crossing to chair* R. *of desk*). We are trying to save you.

BURKE (*as he gets revolver and holds it out toward* DICK). Where did you get this gun?

DICK (*crosses to desk and throws chair* L. *of it up out of his way and looks squarely into* BURKE'S *face*). I won't talk any more until I've seen my wife. I want to know what you've done to her.

BURKE. Did she kill Griggs?

DICK. No, no!

BURKE. Then who did? Who did?

DICK. I won't speak again until I've seen a lawyer I can trust.

GILDER. Dick, if you know who killed this man you must speak to protect yourself.

BURKE. The gun was found in your pocket. Don't forget that.

GILDER. You don't seem to realize the position you are in—nor the position I am in. (*Pleadingly.*) If you won't speak for your own sake, do it for mine.

DICK. I'm sorry, Dad, but I can't. (*A look of despair between* GILDER *and* DEMAREST.)

BURKE (*with sudden change to his quiet manner and putting revolver under newspaper again*). I'm going to give him time to think things over. (*Sits.*) Perhaps he'll understand the importance of what we've been saying. Now, young man, you want to do a lot of quick thinking and honest thinking—(*presses call buzzer*)—and when you get ready to tell me the truth let me know. (DAN *enters R., leaves the door open, and stands above the door.*) Dan, have one of the other men take him back. You wait outside.

DICK. I want to know about my wife. Where is she?

BURKE (*to* DAN). He's not to speak to anyone. (*To* DICK.) You'll know all about your wife, young man, when you've made up your mind to tell me the truth. (DICK *gives* BURKE *a look of defiance, then crosses in front of desk and is going to go right on out between the chairs and* GILDER *when* GILDER *speaks.*)

GILDER (*as* DICK *is about to pass him*). Dick!

DICK. I'm sorry, Dad. (DICK *then goes up to door R. and exits followed by* DAN, *who closes the door.*)

BURKE (*who has been watching* DICK, *speaks at the closing of the door*). Well, you see what we're up against. I can't let him go.

GILDER (*as he picks up his hat from the desk and crosses to L.C.*). He's thinking of that woman—he's trying to shield her.

BURKE. He's a loyal kid, I'll say that much for him. (*As he presses call buzzer.*) And now I'll show you the difference. (DAN *enters R., leav-ing door open.*) Dan, have that Turner woman brought up. (DAN *exits and closes door.*) I'll have to try a different game with her. She's a clever little dame.

GILDER (*crossing to* BURKE's *desk*). Do you think she could have done it?

BURKE. If she didn't she knows who did. Someone has got to pay for killing Griggs. I don't have to explain to Mr. Demarest. (DEMAREST *slowly walks around back of* BURKE's *chair and over to window at up L.C.*) But, Mr. Gilder, the very foundation of the work done by this department rests on the use of crooks who are willing to betray their pals for coin. If the murderer of Griggs goes unpunished, it will put the fear of God into the hearts of every stool pigeon we employ.

GILDER. I see.

BURKE. If we'd only caught GARSON it wouldn't be such hard sleddin'. (GILDER *up to the L. of* DEMAREST. BURKE *rises and, going up to L. of extreme R. window, raises shade and calls.*) Williams!

WILLIAMS (*off stage R.*). Yes sir.

BURKE. Bring your notebook and pencil. (*Pause.*) And hurry up. (WILLIAMS *enters from R. back of window with notebook and pencil.*) Now I want you to take down everything that's said in here, until I give you the notice to stop. Understand?

WILLIAMS. Yes sir.

BURKE (*as he pulls down shade*). Now don't make any mistake. (WIL-

LIAMS *gets chair and sits back of shade. As* BURKE *crosses down below desk and to the back of the chair L. and faces the door R.*) Now this time I'll do the talking. No matter what you hear me say don't be surprised. Remember when you deal with crooks you have to use crooked ways.

(*Enter* DAN *at R., step above the door, and* MARY *follows dressed as in* ACT III. *She pauses in doorway a moment, then slowly crosses down to lower R. corner of desk. As soon as she passes* DAN *he exits and closes the door after him.*)

BURKE (*as* MARY *comes to a standstill*). I just sent for you to tell you that you're free.

MARY. Then I can go?

BURKE (*as he goes up to* GILDER *and* DEMAREST *and stands facing up stage.*) Sure you can go.

(MARY *looks at them a moment, then looks back of her, then at* BURKE, *and then starts toward door L. slowly —then makes up her mind to go and starts quickly toward door L. Just as she is about back of chair L.,* BURKE *crosses to the lower end of his desk quickly and, as he watches* MARY, *speaks.*)

BURKE. Garson has confessed.

MARY (*stops short and answers quickly*). Oh no, he hasn't.

BURKE. What's the reason he hasn't?

MARY (*turning to* BURKE). Because he didn't do it.

BURKE. Well, he says that he did.

MARY. But how could he when he went to——

BURKE (*eagerly*). Where did he go?

MARY (*as she comes down to back of chair at L.*). You ought to know that if you've arrested him.

BURKE (*quietly*). Who shot Griggs?

MARY. My husband shot a burglar— was his name Griggs?

BURKE. Oh, we know better than that. You see, we've traced that Maxim Silencer. Garson bought it himself at Hartford.

MARY (*interrupting him, and nearly trapped*). But he told me——

BURKE (*eagerly*). What did he tell you?

MARY (*recovering herself*). He told me that he'd never seen one. We were talking about one the other day. Surely if he had anything of the sort he'd have shown it to me then.

BURKE (*coaxingly*). Now see here, I can make it a lot easier for you if you'll talk. Come on now, who shot Griggs?

MARY. That's for you to find out. (BURKE *shows he's mad, crosses up to his desk as he calls.*)

BURKE. Dan—(DAN *enters R.—leaves door open and stands above door. As* BURKE *sits at his desk looking straight front*)—take her back.

MARY (*pause—as* MARY *crosses R. and just as she gets to R. corner of the desk she stops and turns to* BURKE). I suppose it's no use for me to stand on my constitutional rights and demand to see a lawyer?

BURKE. You guessed it right the first time.

MARY. That is my constitutional right, isn't it, Mr. Demarest?

DEMAREST. It is.

MARY. Well, Inspector?

BURKE. The Constitution don't go here. (*A look between* DEMAREST *and* GILDER. MARY *turns and starts for door R.*)

CASSIDY (*entering in a hurry, door L.*). Say, chief, we've got Garson. (MARY *turns quickly and stands at door R., leaning against the jamb.*)

BURKE (*rising*). Fine.

CASSIDY (*as he crosses quickly to* BURKE). And here's a letter that's just been delivered at that woman's flat. (*Hands letter to* BURKE *and returns to door L. and stands above it. There is a pause as* BURKE *opens letter, reads it, then gives* MARY *a look and turns to* CASSIDY.)

BURKE. Cassidy, you go stay with Garson. I'll send for him when I want him.

CASSIDY (*as he exits L., closing door after him*). Yes sir.

BURKE. Mr. Demarest, I'll have to ask you to take Mr. Gilder outside for a little while. I'll send word later. (*Indicating letter.*) I'm going to get action on this right now. (MARY

starts to exit.) Don't go, young woman, I want you.

GILDER (*crossing to* BURKE). But, Inspector——

DEMAREST. Better let Burk have his way, Mr. Gilder. (GILDER *crosses to door L. and exits, and* DEMAREST *follows as he speaks.*) I'll expect a report from you, Inspector.

BURKE. You'll get it all right. (DEMAREST *exits L., closing door after him.*) That's all, Dan. (DAN *exits R., closing door after him.*) Sit down. (MARY *crosses to chair R. of* BURKE's *desk and sits facing directly front.* BURKE *sits at the same time as* MARY.) I want to talk to you. (*On the R. end of* BURKE's *desk is a paperweight with a looking-glass back, and during the following scene she fixes her hair in it and also exposes the looking-glass side to the audience.*)

BURKE. Now I'm going to be your friend.

MARY. Are you?

BURKE. Yes. Give up the truth about young Gilder. I know he shot Griggs, but I'm not taking any stock in that burglar story, and no court would either. What was back of the killing? Was he jealous of Griggs? He was always a worthless young cub—a rotten trick like this would be just about his gait. Why did he shoot Eddie Griggs?

MARY (*with an outburst of feeling*). He didn't kill him—he didn't kill him. He's the most wonderful man in the world. I'll fight you today and tomorrow and to the end of my life for Dick Gilder.

BURKE. That's just what I thought. Who did shoot Griggs? We've got every one of that gang! They're all crooks. Why don't you start afresh— I'll give you every chance in the world. I'm on the dead level with you this time.

MARY (*scornfully*). Hah. (*Picks up paperweight and during the following speech exposes the looking-glass side to audience.*)

BURKE. Oh, I'll prove it. (*Picks up letter from desk.*) Here's a letter that came for you. (MARY *reaches for letter—*BURKE *draws it away.*) No, I'll read it. (*He reads.*) "I can't go away without tellin' you how sorry I am. There won't never be a time I won't remember that it was me that got you sent up; that you done time in my place. I don't know how you could have gave me all that money after I told you what I done. Please don't hate me. I ain't goin' to forgive myself ever. And I swear I'm goin' straight always. Your true friend— Helen Morris." (*Pause.* BURKE *looks at* MARY.) You knew this?

MARY. Two days ago.

BURKE (*eagerly*). Did you tell old Gilder?

MARY. What would be the use? I had no proof—no one would believe me.

BURKE (*holding out letter*). They'd believe this. This letter sets you square. Why, this wipes out everything. If old Gilder saw this letter there's nothing he wouldn't do to make amends. (*There is a pause as* MARY *fixes her hair in the paperweight.*) Say, I'll tell you what I'll

do. (MARY *is all attention.*) You tell me who shot Griggs and I'll see that old Gilder gets the letter. (MARY *returns to fixing hair.*) Now listen, I give you my word of honor— (BURKE, *while continuing speech, leans back in his chair, pulls the shade aside to look for* WILLIAMS, *and* MARY *gets the reflection of what he is doing in the paperweight*)— that anything you say in here is just between you and me. Just tip me off to the truth and I'll get the evidence in my own way. There's nobody here but just you and me.

MARY (*laying down paperweight and in a low tone after a quick glance around the office*). Are you sure no one will ever know?

BURKE. No one but you and me.

MARY (*with a laugh* MARY *rises quickly, crosses up to R. side of shade on extreme R. window, pulls it up, disclosing* WILLIAMS, *who quickly picks up his chair and exits R.* MARY *then crosses down to* BURKE). Did you get it all?

WILLIAMS (*from back of shade*). No ma'am, not quite.

BURKE (*looking straight ahead*). Oh hell!

MARY. Right on the level with me, aren't you, Burke?

BURKE. Dan! (*Dan enters R., stands above door, leaving it open.*) Take her back. (MARY *turns and exits R. followed by* DAN, *who closes door.*)

BURKE (BURKE *sits a moment, then gets a new idea*). Cassidy! (*Rises, crosses to* CASSIDY, *as he enters from*

L., closing door after him, and crosses to L.C., eagerly.) Does Garson know that we've arrested the Turner woman and young Gilder?

CASSIDY. No sir.

BURKE. Or that we've got Chicago Red or Dacey here?

CASSIDY. No. He hasn't been spoken to since we made the collar. He seems worried.

BURKE. Well, he'll be more worried before I get through with him. Remember the third degree Inspector Rymes worked on McGloin? (*CASSIDY nods.*) That's what I'm going to do to Garson.

CASSIDY. Great!

BURKE. He's got imagination, that crook. The things he don't know are the things he's afraid of. After he gets in here I want you to take his pals one after the other and lock them up there (*indicating the cells back of windows*). Then when you get the buzzer from me, have young Gilder and the Turner woman sent in. The last time you get the buzzer come in yourself and tell me that the gang has squealed. I'll do the rest. Now don't bring in Garson till you get the signal.

CASSIDY. Yes sir. (*Crosses and exits L., closing door after him.*)

BURKE. Dan! (*DAN enters R., leaving door open.*) Just take those chairs out of here for a few minutes. (*As BURKE goes up and pulls up the shade at extreme L., DAN crosses the stage to chair down L. and is about to pick it up.*) No, don't touch that one. (*DAN then picks up chair each*

side of desk and exits L., closing door after him as BURKE pulls up the remaining shades. BURKE then starts humming, "Every little movement has a meaning all its own," looks around the office, crosses down to chair down L., takes it by the back, turns it so that a person sitting in it is half facing desk and half facing the cells. He then walks around the chair, sits in it, looks around the office, then rises and quickly crosses to his desk and sits. He then opens the right-hand top drawer of desk, takes out cigar, bites the end off, lights it, then stops humming. Picking up a pad of paper from L. end of the desk, puts it on top of the ledger in front of him, picks up the special quill pen, gives a glance at the door L. as he presses the buzzer on his desk, and starts to write. There is a pause, and only the scratching of the pen is heard.*)

CASSIDY (*enters door L. and steps above it*). Here's Garson, chief. (*GARSON follows CASSIDY and crosses to L.C.*)

BURKE (*without looking up*). Hello, Joe.

GARSON. Hello. (*Turns and looks at CASSIDY. CASSIDY then exits L., closing the door after him, and passes around to L. entrance of passage back of the windows then crosses to R. side of the stage.*)

BURKE (*very quiet and affable*). Sit down a minute, won't you?

GARSON (*after a quick look around the office crosses over to BURKE's desk. BURKE goes on with his writing*). Say, what am I arrested for? I haven't done anything.

BURKE (*carelessly*). Who told you you were arrested?

GARSON. I don't have to be told; but when a cop grabs me and brings me down here, I've got sense enough to know I'm pinched.

BURKE (*without looking up*). Is that what they did to you, Joe? I'll have to speak to Cassidy about that. (BURKE *reaches over and presses dead buzz button on his desk.*) Sit down, won't you, Joe? I just want to talk to you. I'll be through here in a second.

GARSON (*there is a silence as* GARSON *looks around the office, then to* BURKE). Say, I'd like to send for a lawyer.

BURKE (*as if calming a nervous child*). What's the matter with you, Joe? There's no use your hollerin' till you're hurt. You know you're not arrested—maybe you never will be. Now for the love of Mike keep still and let me finish this letter. (BURKE *goes on with his writing.* GARSON *looks a moment at* BURKE, *then makes up his mind to do as* BURKE *says and crosses to chair down L. and sits in chair facing cells and* BURKE. *As he is seated* CASSIDY *enters from R. end of passage back of windows, with* DACEY *on his R., and marches to third cell from R., motions to* DACEY *to go in, closes the door, locks it from a bunch of keys he carries, and then turns and exits R. end of passage. At their first appearance* GARSON *gets a start then watches the whole business intently until* CASSIDY'S *exit then turning to* BURKE.)

GARSON. Say, Inspector, if you've got any charge against me, I'd like to know what it is.

BURKE (*assuming a puzzled manner*). What's the matter with you, Joe? I told you I wanted to ask you a few questions, that's all. (GARSON *half rises.*) Now, sit down—(GARSON *sits*)—and keep still and let me get through with this job.

GARSON. Say, Inspector—— (*He stops suddenly and leans forward in his chair as* CASSIDY *enters.* CASSIDY *does same business as before, this time with* CHICAGO RED, *and puts him into the next cell to R.*)

GARSON (*showing more nervousness at* CASSIDY'S *exit, rises and crossing rapidly to desk as he speaks*). Say, Inspector, if you have anything against me, why——

BURKE (*sharply*). Who said there was? (*Quietly.*) What's the matter with you today, Joe? You seem nervous.

GARSON (*stepping back from the desk. Eagerly*). No, I ain't nervous. Why? What made you think that? This ain't exactly what I'd pick out as a pleasant place to spend the morning. (*Pause, then* GARSON *crosses to L. side of desk and leans over it.*) Could I ask you a question?

BURKE (*sharply*). What is it?

GARSON. I was going to say if——

BURKE (*sharply*). If what?

GARSON. I was goin' to say—that is—well, if it's anything about Mary Turner—(BURKE *without another move stops writing*)—I don't know a thing. (*As he turns from* BURKE.) Not a thing.

BURKE (*resumes writing*). What made you think I wanted to know anything about her? (*Presses dead buzzer.*)

GARSON (*hastily*). I don't know, you were up to her house. (*Crosses to* BURKE'S *desk and leans over it to* BURKE.) Don't you see? (CASSIDY *brings in another man.* GARSON *sees the business over* BURKE'S *shoulder.* CASSIDY, *after locking door, crosses* L. *and exits.* GARSON *watches him as long as he can without moving his body, then turns and as he backs up stage gives* BURKE *a quick look, then crosses to chair down* L. *and sits with his back to cells.*)

GARSON (*as he sits*). God!

BURKE (*quietly*). I did want to see her, that's a fact, but she wasn't at her flat. I guess she must have taken my advice and skipped out. Clever girl that, Joe.

GARSON. Yes. I was thinkin' of goin' west myself.

BURKE. Were you? (*He quietly lays down his pen, takes revolver in his right hand from under newspaper, folds his arms so that revolver is under his left arm, turns in his chair so that he is facing* GARSON, *and leans toward him then speaks quietly.*) Why did you kill Eddie Griggs?

GARSON (*pause, then quietly through a nervous laugh*). I didn't kill him. (*Turning in his chair to face* BURKE.) I didn't kill him.

BURKE (*quietly but hard and sharp*). You did—you killed him last night with this (*points revolver at* GARSON). Why, come on now, why?

GARSON (*slowly rising with persistence*). I didn't, I tell you. (*Slowly crossing to* C. *during* BURKE'S *speech.*)

BURKE (*sharp and quick and louder*). You did, I tell you—you did.

GARSON (*as he rushes over to* BURKE *and stares him straight in the eye, and as* BURKE *has not moved the revolver is against* GARSON'S *chest. Strong*). I tell you, I didn't. (*There is a pause without a move, then* BURKE *sees his trick has failed, with his eye on* GARSON *drops the revolver back on the* R. *end of desk and sits in his chair and speaks quietly.*)

BURKE. Well, I didn't think you did. (*Picks up his pen and starts writing again.*) But I wasn't sure, so I had to take a chance. (*Turns quickly and looks at* GARSON.) You understand, don't you? (BURKE *starts writing again.*)

GARSON (*straightening up and moving a little to left*). Yes, sure.

BURKE (*lightly*). We've got the right party all safe enough.

GARSON (*a quick look at* BURKE). You have?

BURKE. You can bet we have.

GARSON (*as he starts toward door* L.). If you don't want me—— (*Stops short at* BURKE'S *first word.*)

BURKE (*lightly*). What's that?

GARSON (*as he starts again toward door* L. *and just reaches door with his hand on the knob as* BURKE *speaks, which makes him stop short again*). I say if you don't want me I'll get along.

BURKE (*stops writing and lays cigar on ash tray—lightly*). What's your hurry? (BURKE *lays down pen, presses dead buzzer, and as he rises and crosses to L.C. speaks casually.*) Where did you say Mary Turner was last night?

GARSON (*as he turns and with almost a scream*). I don't know where she was, I—— (*Realizes he has made a mistake and correcting himself and controlling his voice.*) She was home. She never left the house last night.

BURKE (*looking sharply at* GARSON *and crossing to him and speaking sharply*). Know anything about where young Gilder is?

GARSON (*looking right at* BURKE *and with an air of truth*). Not a thing. (BURKE *watches* GARSON *closely. Door L. opens.* DAN *enters, stands above it, and* MARY *follows, sees* GARSON, *and a look passes between them, and* MARY *quickly crosses toward* GARSON *below desk.* BURKE *turns, crosses down, and meets* MARY *at lower L. corner of desk, takes her R. arm in his L. hand, places her at the upper L. corner of desk, then, without taking his eyes off* MARY, *steps up against the windows just midway between* MARY *and* GARSON. *As* MARY *comes to a standstill at the upper end of the desk* DICK *enters and quickly crosses to down R.C. As* DICK *is well on* CASSIDY *enters quickly door L. and speaks sharply from just below door.*)

CASSIDY (*all give a start and look at* CASSIDY. BURKE *turns and watches* GARSON. *There is a pause, then in a tone of apology*). Oh, I beg your pardon, I didn't know you were busy. (*Looks straight at* GARSON. GARSON *is looking at* CASSIDY *and feels* BURKE *watching him. He slowly turns and looks* BURKE *in the eye, then slowly draws himself up and throws his shoulders back defiantly.*)

BURKE (*after* GARSON'S *business and looking at* GARSON). Squealed, eh? (*Pause as he turns and looks at* DICK.) They tell the same story?

CASSIDY. Yes sir.

BURKE (*looking at* CASSIDY). I was right then all the time?

CASSIDY. Sure.

BURKE. Good enough. (*Turns quickly to* MARY *and speaking hard and rapidly.*) Mary Turner, I want you for the murder of——

GARSON (*as he springs to* BURKE). That's a damn lie. (*Coming down C.*) I did it.

MARY (*crossing quickly to* GARSON'S R.). NO, JOE, NO. Don't—talk—don't talk.

BURKE (*as he crosses to his chair back of desk*). Joe has talked.

MARY. He did it to protect me.

BURKE. Dan! Send Williams here to take Garson's confession! (DAN *exits R. and closes door.*)

MARY. He's not going to confess.

BURKE. Oh yes, he is. (*Perfunctorily*). You are all cautioned that anything you say will be used against you. (*As he sits.*) Come,

Joe. (*Picks up cigar and starts smoking.* WILLIAMS *enters door R. with notebook and pencil, closes door, and crosses to* BURKE'S *R., and stands ready to take dictation.* CASSIDY *moves up above door L. and stands.*)

MARY (*to* GARSON). Don't speak until we can get a lawyer for you.

BURKE (*impatiently*). It's no use, my girl. I told you I'd get you. I'm going to try you and Garson and the whole gang for murder—every one of you. Gilder, you'll go to the house of detention as a witness. Come on, Joe.

GARSON (*pause as* GARSON *starts to cross to* BURKE. MARY *attempts to stop him, and he in action tells her to leave it to him. He then crosses in front of* MARY *to* BURKE.) If I come through, will you let them two go? (*Indicating* MARY *and* DICK.)

MARY (*crossing up to* GARSON). We'll spend every dollar we can raise.

BURKE (*impatiently*). Now, it's no use. He said he did it. Now that we're sure he's our man, he hasn't got a chance in the world.

GARSON. Well, how about them? Do they go clear?

MARY. We'll get the best lawyers in the country. We'll save you, Joe, we'll save you.

GARSON. You can't. They've got it on me. My time's come, Mary, and I can save you a lot of trouble.

BURKE. He's right. We've got him cold. What's the use of dragging you two into it?

GARSON. They go clear? They ain't even called as witnesses?

BURKE. You're on. (*Sits back in his chair smoking.*)

GARSON (*as he straightens up*). Then here goes.

MARY (*backing away from* GARSON *and starting for chair down L.* DICK *crosses to* MARY *and helps her to chair.*)

GARSON. There's no other way. (*After* DICK *passes him.*) I'm going through with it. (MARY *watches by* GARSON. *Pause until* MARY *is seated in chair facing front with her head bowed and resting on the back of the chair and* DICK *standing above her with his hands on her shoulders.* WILLIAMS *takes the confession in shorthand notes in his notebook.*)

GARSON (*facing front in mechanical tone*). My name's Joe Garson.

BURKE. Alias?

GARSON (*to* BURKE). Alias nothin'. Garson's my moniker. (*To the front.*) I shot English Eddie Griggs because he was a skunk and a stool pigeon, and he got just what's comin' to him.

BURKE. Oh, we can't take a confession like that.

GARSON (*to* BURKE, *doggedly*). Because he was a skunk and a stool pigeon. (*To* WILLIAMS.) Have you got it? (WILLIAMS *nods—facing front.*) I croaked him just as he was goin' to call the bulls with a police whistle. I used a gun with smokeless powder and a Maxim Silencer, so it

didn't make any noise. (*To* BURKE.)
Say, I'll bet it's the first time a guy
was ever croaked with one of them
things—ain't it?

BURKE. That's right, Joe.

GARSON (*to* BURKE—*proudly*). Some
class to that, eh? (*Facing front.*) I
got the gun and the Maxim thing
from a fence in Boston. (*To*
BURKE.) Say, them things cost sixty
dollars, and they're worth the
money, too. They'll remember me
as the first to spring one of them,
won't they?

BURKE. They sure will, Joe.

GARSON (*facing front*). Nobody
knew I had it. (MARY *starts to speak.
With meaning.*) Nobody knew I
had it. Nobody. And nobody had
anything to do with the killin' but
me. (MARY *again bows her head on
the back of the chair.*)

BURKE. Was there any bad feeling
between you and Griggs?

GARSON (*facing front*). He was a
stool pigeon and I hated his guts—
that's all.

BURKE. Have you anything else to
say?

GARSON. NO, NOTHIN'. I croaked
him, and I'm glad I done it. He was
a skunk. And this is all true, so help
me God.

BURKE. That's all, Williams. He'll
sign it just as soon as you've tran-
scribed the notes. (WILLIAMS *exits
R., closing door after him. To*
MARY.) Young woman, it's just like
I told you, you can't beat the law.

Garson thought he could, and
now——

GARSON (*interrupting and crossing
to* MARY). That's right, Mary, you
can't beat the law. And this same
old law says, "A frail must stick to
her man." (MARY *doesn't answer.*)
It's the best thing to do. (*With real
sincerity.*) And say, you want to cut
out that worryin' about me. I ain't
worryin'. Why, it's somethin' new
I've pulled off. I'll bet there'll be a
lot of stuff in the newspapers and
my pictures in most of them. (*Turns
and, crossing to* BURKE, *eagerly.*)
Say, if the reporters want any pictures of me, could I have some new
ones taken—the one you've got of
me in the gallery's over ten years old
—I've took off my beard since then—
could I have some new ones?

BURKE. Sure you can, Joe. I'll send
you right up to the gallery now.

GARSON (*to* BURKE). Immense.
(*Crosses down and gives* DICK's *right
shoulder a slap, and* DICK *turns and
offers his hand—as* GARSON *takes*
DICK's *hand to shake hands.*) Well,
so long, young feller. (*Looks at*
MARY *and starts to cross R. as he
speaks.*) Good-by, Mary.

MARY (*as she rises and follows* GAR-
SON). Joe, Joe!

GARSON (*he turns, and* GARSON *takes*
MARY *in his arms*). That's all right.
That's all right. He'll look after you.
Gee, I'd like to see you two with
three or four kids playin' around the
house. (*To* DICK.) Take good care
of her, won't yer? (DICK *comes down
stage back of* MARY, *and* GARSON
turns MARY *over to him, and* DICK
puts his arms around MARY *and she*

buries her face on his L. shoulder.)
Well—*(as he crosses stage R.)*—so
long. *(Exits door R. There is a
pause.* BURKE *rises with cigar in his
mouth, looks at* MARY *and* DICK,
picks up the HELEN MORRIS *letter.)*

BURKE *(quietly).* Cassidy—*(*CASSIDY
crosses to BURKE*)*—Mr. Gilder out
there?

CASSIDY. Yes sir.

BURKE *(handing letter to* CASSIDY*).*
Give him this letter and tell him to
read it at once. *(*CASSIDY *nods,
smiles, crosses to door L., and exits
as* BURKE *crosses to door R.* BURKE
stops in doorway R. and comes a
little down R. To DICK *and* MARY—
*removing cigar from his mouth—
sternly.)* Just one thing more. When
I get back I don't want to find anyone here, not anyone. *(Lightly with
a smile.)* Get me? *(Up to door R.
and exits smoking.* MARY *disen-
gages herself from* DICK'S *arms and,
crying, crosses to R. end of* BURKE'S
desk, looking off toward where GAR-
SON *made his exit.* DICK *waits until
she is standing still, then starts for
door L., changes his mind and,
crossing over after* MARY, *puts his R.
hand on her L. shoulder and turns
her around to face him and steps
back. She looks up and with a cry of
gladness comes to* DICK *with her
arms outstretched. They embrace.)*

CURTAIN

Seven Keys To Baldpate

A Mysterious Melodramatic Farce By

GEORGE M. COHAN

Based on the Novel, "Seven Keys to Baldpate," by Earl
Derr Biggers, published and duly copyrighted by
The Bobbs-Merrill Company, 1913

CHARACTERS

(In the order of their appearance)

ELIJAH QUIMBY, *the caretaker of Baldpate Inn.*
MRS. QUIMBY, *the caretaker's wife.*
WILLIAM HALLOWELL MAGEE, *the novelist.*
JOHN BLAND, *the millionaire's right hand man.*
MARY NORTON, *the newspaper reporter.*
MRS. RHODES, *the charming widow.*
PETERS, *the Hermit of Baldpate.*
MYRA THORNHILL, *the blackmailer.*
LOU MAX, *the Mayor's man "Friday."*
JIM CARGAN, *the crooked mayor of Reuton.*
THOMAS HAYDEN, *the president of the R. and E. Suburban R.R.*
JIGGS KENNEDY, *Chief of Police of Asquewan Falls.*
THE OWNER OF BALDPATE.

The scene is laid in the office of Baldpate Inn.

Time: The present.

SEVEN KEYS TO BALDPATE

ACT ONE

At rise of curtain the stage is bare. No lights on the stage except the rays of the moon shining through glass door and the sky above. The wind is heard howling outside. The effect is that of a terrific storm taking place. Everything within the scene proves that it is a deserted, desolate spot; in fact, an inn, a summer resort on the mountains closed for the winter.

After thirty seconds ELIJAH QUIMBY *appears at glass door upstage and is seen swinging a lantern. He does this as if guiding someone who is following; a sort of signal to* MRS. QUIMBY, *who presently appears trudging behind him. He hands her the lantern while he fumbles with a bunch of keys he has taken from his pocket. She gives him a light from the lantern while he finds the right key and unlocks the door. As the door swings open the wind is heard howling unmercifully. He holds the door open for her to enter, then follows her in, closing the door. They both stamp their feet to get them warm.* MRS. QUIMBY *goes down R.C., holding up lantern and peering around room, then goes up R. and to C. and down to table L., on which she places the lantern.* QUIMBY, *after locking the door, goes slowly down L. to table, meanwhile stamping feet, removing ear muffs and placing cap and mittens on table.* MRS. QUIMBY *removes her mittens, and they both stand rubbing their hands and ears. All this business is done without a word being spoken. The reason for it is to prove to the audience that the night is bitterly cold and that the two people are half frozen after their climb up the mountain.*

QUIMBY (*at table L., right of Mrs. QUIMBY, shivering*). You know, Mother, I think it's colder in here than it is outside.

MRS. QUIMBY (*shivering*). I was going to say the same thing, Elijah.

QUIMBY. Maybe we'd better open the door and let in some warm air.

MRS. QUIMBY. You'd better not; the snow'll blow all over the place. See if there's any logs over there and we'll build a fire. (*Indicates fireplace with a nod of her head.*)

QUIMBY (*starts R., stops and stamps his feet*). You know, Mother, I think my feet are froze. I can't feel 'em when I walk. (*Knocks hands together.*)

MRS. QUIMBY. I don't wonder, after that climb up the mountain. Lord, I'll never forget this night! I'm about perished. (*She straightens chairs, et cetera, while* QUIMBY *is looking for logs.*) Any logs there?

QUIMBY. Yep, plenty of 'em. I got this thing all ready, anyway. I was goin' to build a fire when I was up here last week. I'll have 'em blazin' in a minute if I can find them darned matches. (*Searches through his pockets.*) I can swear I put a box of 'em in my pocket before I left the house! (*Finds them.*) Yep, here they are!

MRS. QUIMBY. You'd better light a lamp first, so's you can see what you're doin'.

QUIMBY. That's a good idea.

(*Clock in distance strikes eleven while he is scratching match and lighting lamp over fireplace R. Note. —Footlights up slightly when lamp is turned up.*)

MRS. QUIMBY (*standing at foot of stairs*). Eleven o'clock.

QUIMBY. Yep, that's what it is— eleven o'clock. (*Goes upstage and looks through glass door.*) That train's been in over twenty minutes already. I suppose it's the storm that delays him. 'Tain't over a ten-minute walk up the mountain from the depot. (*Comes down R.C.*)

MRS. QUIMBY (*goes to R., near desk*). Maybe the train's late on account of the storm.

QUIMBY. No; I heard it signal the crossing at Asquewan Junction a half hour ago. That feller'll be here before we know it. (*Hands her matches.*) Light the other lamp, will you, Mother, while I get at this fire?

(MRS. QUIMBY *takes matches and lights lamp up L., near stairway. He builds fire in fireplace. Both are busily engaged in fixing room, heating and lighting it during following conversation:*)

MRS. QUIMBY. Maybe we should have gone to the depot to meet him?

QUIMBY (*going C.*). No; we shouldn't have done nothin' of the kind. The telegram just said to come here and to open up the place and have it ready for him. Them's the instructions, and them's the only things I foller—is instructions. (*Starts toward R.*)

MRS. QUIMBY (*going C.*). But what do you suppose anybody wants to be doin' in a summer hotel on the top of a mountain in the dead of winter?

QUIMBY. Mother, you know I can't figger out nothin'. (*Goes up to door, peers out, then comes down to* MRS. QUIMBY.) If I could I'd 'a' been a multi-millionaire years ago, instead of an old fool caretaker. (*Goes nearer to* MRS. QUIMBY.) Dust up a bit there, will you, Mother, and make the place look a little respectable? (*Goes toward fireplace.*) She'll be goin' all right in a minute now.

MRS. QUIMBY (*dusting with cloth she has taken from foot of stairs*). What's his name again?

QUIMBY. Magee, I think the telegram says. (*Meets* MRS. QUIMBY *at C.*)

MRS. QUIMBY. Magee?

QUIMBY. Wait a minute, I'll make sure. (*Takes telegram from his pocket.*)

MRS. QUIMBY (*takes telegram from him and goes L.*). Give it to me; I want to read it myself. The whole thing's very mysterious to me. (*Goes to table and sits, reading by light of lantern.*)

QUIMBY (*goes toward* MRS. QUIMBY—*fire begins to blaze up*). Of course it's mysterious, but it's none of our business. Mr. Bentley is the owner of Baldpate Inn. If Mr. Bentley wants to permit some darn fool to come to this place to be froze to death by stale air and to be frightened to death by spooks, it's his concern and not ours. (*Turns and looks at fire, which is blazing.*) Ah, there she goes; she's blazing up fine. That'll warm it up a little. (*Goes L.C. to* MRS. QUIMBY *during next speech.*)

MRS. QUIMBY (*reading message slowly*). "My friend, William Hallowell Magee, will arrive in Asquewan Falls tonight on the ten-forty. He will occupy Baldpate Inn, so be prepared to receive him there, and turn the key over to him and do whatever you can to make him comfortable. He has important work to do, and has chosen Baldpate for his workshop. Follow instructions. Ask no questions. Hal Bentley."

QUIMBY (*has been listening attentively*). Sounds like them Black Hand notes they send to rich men, don't it?

MRS. QUIMBY. I can't understand it for the life of me. (*Hands telegram back to* QUIMBY.)

QUIMBY. Mother!

MRS. QUIMBY (*over to* QUIMBY *C.*). Yes?

QUIMBY (*R. of C.*). Maybe the feller's committed some crime and is comin' here to hide.

MRS. QUIMBY. Do you think so, Elijah?

QUIMBY. I don't know; I say—mebbe.

MRS. QUIMBY. Well, if that's so, why should Mr. Bentley be interested in such a man?

QUIMBY (*thinks*). I never thought of that. (*Thinks.*) Well, whatever it is, it's none of our business, and we mustn't mix in other people's affairs. (*Goes R.*)

MRS. QUIMBY (*thinks a moment, then comes down near* QUIMBY). Elijah!

QUIMBY (*looks up*). What?

MRS. QUIMBY. Do you think I'd better fix up one of them rooms?

QUIMBY. Sure; he'll have to have a place to sleep. Here—(*gives her key*)—that opens the linen closet. You'd better fix up that first room to the left. (*Points to room on balcony R.*) That's the one Mr. Bentley always takes when he comes.

MRS. QUIMBY (*as she goes toward stairs, taking lantern from table*). And you'd better put another log on the fire. (QUIMBY *goes toward fireplace.*) He'll probably be chilled to the bone by the time he climbs that mountain. Do you think he'll find his way alone? (*Goes upstairs during speech.*)

QUIMBY. Oh, he'll find his way all right. The station agent will most likely direct him. (*Puts log on fire, which blazes up.*)

MRS. QUIMBY (*going up the stairs*). Occupying a summer hotel in the dead of winter! It beats all what some people will do! (*Exits door L., leaving door open.*)

QUIMBY (*takes out his pipe and sits thinking near fire*). Humph! It's pretty darned mysterious, all right. (*Lights pipe and smokes.*) I'll be jiggered if I can figger it out.

(MRS. QUIMBY *remains inside room four counts after cue, then comes from room carrying linen and bed coverings in her arms. She crosses balcony to room R. of balcony and exits, closing door.* QUIMBY *sits smoking and thinking.* MAGEE *appears at door upstage and peers through. He is carrying a suit and typewriter case. He puts them down and knocks on window.* QUIMBY *doesn't move at first, but sits listening, to make sure he has heard a sound.* MAGEE *repeats the knocking.* QUIMBY *shifts around in his chair, looks up toward the window, sees a form there, then gets up and sneaks along downstage until he gets to foot of stairs, then calls in suppressed tones to* MRS. QUIMBY.)

QUIMBY. Mother, Mother! (*No answer from* MRS. QUIMBY. *He runs halfway upstairs and calls a bit louder.*) Mother!

MRS. QUIMBY (*appears on balcony, peers over and sees* QUIMBY). Did you call me, Elijah?

QUIMBY. Hush! Don't talk so loud! (*Warns her to be quiet.*)

MRS. QUIMBY (*lowering her voice*). What's the matter? (*They both listen for a second.* MAGEE's *third rap comes.*) Good Lord, what's that?

QUIMBY (*on stairs*). It's him—he's here! (*He points to door upstage.*)

MRS. QUIMBY. Who?

QUIMBY. The telegram—I mean the man.

MRS. QUIMBY (*starts down the stairs*). Where?

QUIMBY. At the door.

(MAGEE *again raps impatiently.*)

MRS. QUIMBY (*urging* QUIMBY *down the stairs*). Why don't you let him in?

QUIMBY (*both come downstairs*). Do you think I'd better?

MRS. QUIMBY. Well, ain't that what the telegram said?

QUIMBY. Why, yes, of course, but——

MRS. QUIMBY (*shoving* QUIMBY toward door). You got your instructions. Go on and do as you're told.

(MAGEE *knocks again and rattles the doorknob.*)

QUIMBY (*in a loud voice as he goes up toward door*). Yes, yes; jest a minute, jest a minute!

(*As* QUIMBY *goes up to door,* MRS. QUIMBY *comes down L.* QUIMBY *unlocks door and swings it open. The wind howls.* MAGEE, *carrying the two cases, enters and comes to C. and stands bowing, first to* MRS. QUIMBY *and then to* QUIMBY, *then drops the cases in the middle of the stage. Looks around the room for a moment, wild-eyed, then sees fire burning and goes over to it as fast as his half-frozen legs will allow him. He pulls chair in front of fire and sits warming himself.* QUIMBYS *stand C., watching him in amazement. As soon as* MAGEE *has entered* QUIMBY *has locked the door and come down*

R. As MAGEE *sits*, QUIMBY *goes to* MRS. QUIMBY *at L.C.*)

MRS. QUIMBY (*aside to* QUIMBY). The poor thing's half froze.

QUIMBY (*approaches* MAGEE, MRS. QUIMBY *following him to fireplace*). What's the matter, young fellow, are you cold?

MAGEE (*smiles a sickly smile, shakes his head, laughs half-heartedly, then replies*). Humph! Am I cold! I feel pretty rocky, but I've got to laugh at that one.

MRS. QUIMBY (*aside to* QUIMBY). Better give him a drink of whisky.

QUIMBY. Yes, I guess so. (*Takes flask from his pocket and hands it to* MAGEE.) Here, young fellow, try a little of this.

MAGEE (*looks up, sees flask, and grabs it*). Thanks! (*Takes a long drink.* QUIMBY *goes C. to* MRS. QUIMBY.)

MRS. QUIMBY (*aside to* QUIMBY). Do you suppose it's him?

QUIMBY (*aside*). How do I know?

MRS. QUIMBY (*aside*). Well, ask him and find out.

MAGEE (*offers flask to* QUIMBY). Thanks again, a thousand thanks.

QUIMBY. Oh, you just put that in your pocket; you might need it later on.

MAGEE. Thanks.

(MRS. QUIMBY *picks up cases from floor and takes them to table L.*)

QUIMBY. You're Mr. Magee, ain't you?

MAGEE. Right! What's left of me is still Magee. You expected me, of course.

QUIMBY. Oh, yes; we got Mr. Bentley's telegram all right. My name's Quimby.

MAGEE. So I surmised.

QUIMBY. This lady is my wife, Mrs. Quimby. (*Points to* MRS. QUIMBY, *who crosses to* MAGEE *at fireplace.*)

MAGEE. I thought as much. Delighted, Mrs. Quimby. (*Bows to* MRS. QUIMBY *without rising.*)

MRS. QUIMBY. Glad to meet you, Mr. Magee.

MAGEE. You'll pardon me for not rising, but really I'm terribly cold.

MRS. QUIMBY (*goes to* QUIMBY *during following speech*). That's all right. You sit there and get het up. We've been living here in the mountains so long we don't mind the cold as much as strangers do, but even we felt it tonight, didn't we, Elijah?

QUIMBY. That's right, Mother; this is an uncommon cold night.

MAGEE (*rises, removes overcoat, muffler, and hat, and places them on chair*). That little trip from the railroad station to the top of the mountain has taught me to firmly believe everything Jack London ever wrote about and everything old Dr. Cook ever lied about. (*Crosses to L.C., looking at everything, very much interested, and rubbing his hands.*) So this is Baldpate, is it? Well, well, well!

MRS. QUIMBY (R.C., *aside to* QUIMBY). Don't he talk funny?

QUIMBY (L. *of* MRS. QUIMBY— *aside*). Yes. Acts funny, too. Something's the matter with him, sure. (*Both watch* MAGEE *closely*.)

MAGEE (*coming* C.). You say you received Mr. Bentley's telegram saying I would be here?

QUIMBY. Yes; it only came about an hour ago, so we didn't have much time to prepare.

MAGEE. I didn't decide to come here until four o'clock this afternoon.

MRS. QUIMBY. We was scared most to death gettin' a telegram in the middle of the night.

MAGEE. I'm very sorry to have taken you out on a night like this, but it was altogether necessary in order that I accomplish what I've set out to do. Let me see—the rooms above are equipped with fireplaces, I believe? (*Looks up at rooms on balcony*.)

MRS. QUIMBY (*crosses* C. *to* MAGEE). Yes; I'm just fixin' up one of the rooms. I'll start the fire, too. I'll have it all ready for you inside of five minutes. (*Crosses to* R., *gets wood from box, and comes to* R. *of* QUIMBY.)

MAGEE. I wish you would. (*Looks around room*.) Yes; this would be too big a barn to work in. (QUIMBYS *look at each other*.) I'll no doubt be more comfortable up there. (*Continues to take in surroundings*.)

QUIMBY (*aside to* MRS. QUIMBY). He says he's goin' to work. I wonder what he means.

MRS. QUIMBY (*aside, crossing to* L. *of* QUIMBY). Pump him. Try to find out. (*Aloud*.) Give me the matches.

QUIMBY. Here you are. (*He hands her a box of matches*. MRS. QUIMBY, *with wood in her arms, starts for stairs and goes up on balcony*.)

MAGEE. This, I presume, is the hotel office.

QUIMBY. That's right.

MAGEE (*strolls around stage looking at everything carefully*. QUIMBY *watching him closely*). Well, well! This certainly is old John H. Seclusion himself.

MR. *and* MRS. QUIMBY (*together*). Good Lord, where did those lights come from? Good Lord, what's happened? (*As lights go up*, QUIMBY *darts behind desk* R. MRS. QUIMBY *is leaning over balcony* C. *Both are frightened*.)

MAGEE (*laughs*). Don't be alarmed, Mrs. Quimby; it's all right. I think I can explain this thing. Mr. Bentley has probably had the power turned on. He knew I'd have to have some real light for this kind of work. (MRS. QUIMBY *exits into room* R. *on balcony, closing the door*. MAGEE *goes to* QUIMBY *up* R.) I suppose you're wondering what the devil I'm doing here.

QUIMBY. That's just what I was wondering, young fellow.

MAGEE. Well, I'll try to explain, although I'm not sure you'll understand. Sit down, Mr. Quimby. (QUIMBY *hesitates.*) It's all right, sit down. (QUIMBY *gets chair and places it R.C., then sits.*) Now, you are not, I take it, the sort of man to follow closely the light and frivolous literature of the day.

QUIMBY. How's that?

MAGEE. You don't read the sort of novels that are sold by the pound in the department stores.

QUIMBY. Nope.

MAGEE. Well, I write those novels.

QUIMBY. The dickens you do!

MAGEE. Wild, thrilling tales for the tired businessman's tired wife; shots in the night; chases after fortunes; Cupid busy with his arrows all over the place. It's good fun—I like to do it, and—there's money in it.

QUIMBY. You don't mean to tell me!

MAGEE. Oh, yes, considerable. Of course they say I'm a cheap melodramatic ranter. They say my thinking process is a scream. Perhaps they're right. (*Moves chair out and sits L.C.*)

QUIMBY. Perhaps.

MAGEE. Did you ever read *The Scarlet Satchel?*

QUIMBY. Never.

MAGEE. That's one of mine.

QUIMBY. Is it?

MAGEE. I've come here to Baldpate to think; to get away from melo-

drama, if possible; to do a novel so fine and literary that Henry Cabot Lodge will come to me with tears in his eyes and beg me to join his bunch of self-made immortals. And I'm going to do all this right here in this inn, sitting on this mountain, looking down on this little old world as Jove looked down from Olympus. What do you think of that?

QUIMBY (*shakes his head, affecting an air of understanding*). Maybe it's all for the best.

MAGEE. Of late I've been running short of material. (*Rises, moves chair to R. of table and goes to* QUIMBY.) I've needed inspiration. A title gave me that—"The lonesomest spot on earth," suggested by my very dear friend and your employer, Mr. Hal Bentley. "What and where is the lonesomest spot on earth?" I asked. "A summer resort in winter," said he. He told me of Baldpate—dared me to come. I took the dare—and here I am.

QUIMBY (*rising and going to* MAGEE *at C.*). You mean you're goin' to write a book?

MAGEE. That's just exactly what I'm going to do. I'm going to novelize Baldpate. I'm here to get atmosphere.

QUIMBY (*laughs*). Lord, you'll get plenty of that, all right! When are you goin' to start in?

MAGEE. Just as soon as I absorb my surroundings and make a few mental notes. You see, I do most of my work in the dead of night. I find I concentrate more readily from midnight on. But I must have absolute solitude. The crackle of the fire, the roar of the wind, and the ticking of my watch will alone bear me company at Baldpate Inn. This all sounds very strange and weird to you, I suppose.

QUIMBY. How's that?

MAGEE. I say, you can't quite fathom me.

QUIMBY. Well, you're here of your own accord, I take it.

MAGEE. My dear Mr. Quimby, I'm here on a bet.

QUIMBY. On a bet!

MAGEE. Exactly. I have here an explanation of the thing in Bentley's handwriting. (*Takes paper from his pocket.*) Do you care to look it over yourself, or would you rather I'd read it to you?

QUIMBY. Yes, go on and read it—I like to hear you talk. (*Sits R.C.*)

MAGEE (*smiles*). Ah, then my personality has wormed its way into your good graces.

QUIMBY. How's that?

MAGEE. I mean to say, I evidently appeal to you.

QUIMBY. Well, I don't know as you particularly appeal to me, but——

MAGEE. But what?

QUIMBY (*laughs, confused*). Oh, I guess I better not say it.

MAGEE. Come on, what's on your mind? Tell me.

QUIMBY. Well, to be honest with you, I can't figger out whether you're a smart man or a damn fool.

MAGEE (*laughs*). Would you believe it, my dear sir, I've been stalled between those two opinions of myself for years? My publishers say I'm a smart man; my critics call me a damn fool. However, that's neither here nor there. This—(*indicating paper*)—will perhaps clear away the cloud of mystery to some extent. Oh, perhaps Mrs. Quimby would be interested enough to hear this also. Will you call her, please?

QUIMBY. Sure! (*Rises and calls.*) Mother! Oh, Mother!

MRS. QUIMBY (*appears at door R. on balcony and comes to C. of it*). Yes, I'm all through. Everything's ready up here. (*Leans over balcony C.*) You'd better come up, mister, and see if it satisfies you before we go.

MAGEE. It's all right, Mrs. Quimby. I'll take your word for it that everything's all right.

QUIMBY. Come on down here, Mother; Mr. Magee wants to read something to you. (*Places chair for her R.C., next his own.*)

MRS. QUIMBY. Is that so? (*Starts downstairs.*) I started the fire, so I guess the room'll be comfortable enough to sleep in by the time you get ready to go to bed. (*Is downstairs by now.*)

QUIMBY. Sit down, Mother.

MRS. QUIMBY. What!

QUIMBY. Go on. See, I'm sittin. (MRS. QUIMBY *goes toward*

QUIMBY.) Mr. Magee's goin' to tell us why he's here.

MRS. QUIMBY (*sits L. of* QUIMBY). Is that so? Lord, I'd love to know!

MAGEE. I have just explained to your husband that I am an author. I do popular novels, and I'm here to write a story—a story of Baldpate Mountain, laid in this very hotel, perhaps in this identical room. I am to complete this task within twenty-four hours, starting at midnight tonight.

QUIMBY. Understand, Mother? He's goin' to write a book.

MRS. QUIMBY (*to* MAGEE). Goin' to write a book in twenty-four hours!

MAGEE. That is the wager that has been made between Mr. Bentley and myself. He claimed it couldn't be done. I claimed it could. Five thousand dollars' worth of his sporting blood boiled, and he dug for his fountain pen and checkbook. I covered the bet, and we posted the checks at the Forty-fourth Street club. He was to choose the godforsaken spot. (*Looks around room.*) He succeeded. I ran to my apartment, placed some manuscript paper, a dozen sandwiches, and my slippers in a suitcase, grabbed my faithful typewriting machine, just made the train, and here you see me, ready to win or lose the wager, as the case may be.

QUIMBY. What do you think of that, Mother?

MRS. QUIMBY (*to* MAGEE). I never heard of such a thing!

MAGEE. Here is a copy of the agreement, in which you will notice your name is mentioned, Mr. Quimby. Listen. (*Reads.*) "You are to leave New York City on the four fifty-five for Asquewan Falls, arriving at ten-forty, and go direct to Baldpate Inn, atop the Baldpate Mountain, where you will be met by my caretaker, Mr. Elijah Quimby, who, after making you comfortable, will turn over to you the key to the inn, the only key in existence." (*To* QUIMBY.) Is that correct?

QUIMBY. It's the only key I know of.

MRS. QUIMBY. There ain't no other key; I can swear to that.

MAGEE. Good! (*Continues reading.*) "This will insure you against interruption, and give you the solitude necessary for concentration. You are to begin work at twelve o'clock Tuesday night, and turn over to Mr. Elijah Quimby the completed manuscript of a ten-thousand-word story of Baldpate no later than twelve o'clock Wednesday night." (*To* QUIMBY.) You understand?

QUIMBY. You're to turn it over to me?

MAGEE. Precisely.

QUIMBY. What do you think of that, Mother?

MRS. QUIMBY. I never heard of such a thing!

MAGEE. You know Bentley's handwriting; there's his signature—see for yourself. (*Hands paper to* MRS. QUIMBY. QUIMBYS *get up and read it together.* MAGEE *takes stage.*)

QUIMBY. It's his writin', ain't it, Mother?

MRS. QUIMBY (*doubtfully*). Looks like it, but—— (*Looks at* MAGEE *suspiciously.*)

QUIMBY (*aside*). But what?

MRS. QUIMBY (*aside*). The whole thing don't sound right to me.

QUIMBY (*aside*). Me neither. We'd better watch this cuss.

MRS. QUIMBY (*aside*). I think so, too.

(QUIMBY *puts chair up R.* MRS. QUIMBY *goes toward table L. Phone rings.* MRS. QUIMBY *runs to foot of stairs, screaming.* QUIMBY *hugs the desk, frightened.*)

MRS. QUIMBY. Good Lord!

QUIMBY (*over to* MAGEE, *up C.*). Did you hear that?

MAGEE. You mean the telephone?

MRS. QUIMBY (*runs to* MAGEE— QUIMBY *grabs* MAGEE *by the arms*). Spooks!

QUIMBY. Why, that thing's been out of commission all winter!

(*Phone continues ringing.* MAGEE *laughs.*)

MRS. QUIMBY. Let's get out of here, Lije.

MAGEE (*laughs*). Don't be alarmed, Mrs. Quimby; I think I can explain. Bentley has just about had the service renewed. He probably wants to find out if I've arrived. Excuse me just a moment. (*Goes to phone and stops buzzer.* QUIMBYS *stand C., watching.*) Hello, hello! . . . Yes. Yes, right on time. . . . Almost

twenty minutes ago. . . . Half frozen, thank you. . . . Yes, he's here now, also Mrs. Quimby. . . . Oh, we understand each other perfectly well. . . . It's everything you said it was. . . . The lonesomest spot on earth is right. (*Laughs.*) You still feel that way about it, eh? Well, your opinion is going to cost you five thousand, old man. (*Laughs.*) All right, we'll see. . . . You want to talk to him. . . . Just a second. (*To* QUIMBY.) He wants to talk to you, Mr. Quimby.

QUIMBY (*goes over to phone*). Is it Mr. Bentley?

MAGEE. Yes, here you are. Sit right down. (*He hands* QUIMBY *receiver and goes L.C., taking notes.* MRS. QUIMBY *goes up R. and listens to phone conversation while watching* MAGEE.)

QUIMBY (*in phone*). Hello! (*Smiles as he recognizes* BENTLEY'S *voice.*) Hello, Mr. Bentley. . . . Yes, sir; yes, sir. . . . I understand, sir. . . . At twelve o'clock? . . . Yes, sir. . . . Oh, I'll be right here waiting. . . . Fine, thank you, sir; we're both fine. . . . All right, sir. . . . Wait a minute. I'll ask him. (*To* MAGEE, *who is on first landing of stairs.*) He wants to know if there's anything more you want to say?

MAGEE (*on stairs, taking notes*). No; just give him my regards, and tell him I'm spending his money already.

QUIMBY (*in phone*). He says there's nothing else, sir. . . . Yes, sir, I understand. . . . Good-by, sir. (*Hangs up receiver and crosses to* MAGEE.)

He wants me to be here at twelve o'clock tomorrow night to talk to him on the telephone again.

MAGEE (*laughs as he goes to phone and severs connection*). And it's very sad news you'll impart to him, Mr. Quimby. I'm going to win this wager! (*R., below phone.*) You know this whole thing wouldn't make a bad story in itself. (*Crossing to L.*) I'm thinking seriously of using it for the ground plot. (*Points to door L.*) Oh, this leads to where? (*Goes to door of dining room L. and opens it.*)

MRS. QUIMBY (*going over toward door*). That's the dining room—leads through to the kitchen. That door to the left goes to the cellar. (*Goes back to table L. QUIMBY looks at his watch.*)

MAGEE. Ah, ha, I see! (*Goes toward QUIMBY, R.C.*) Have you the exact time, Mr. Quimby?

QUIMBY. Mine says half-past eleven.

MAGEE. Thirty minutes to get my bearings and frame up a character or two for a start. (*Crosses C. to R.C.*)

MRS. QUIMBY (*picks up suitcase and machine case from table L.*). Will I put these in your room?

MAGEE. No, no; you needn't bother.

MRS. QUIMBY. Oh, it's no bother at all. (*Starts for the stairs.*) I'm only too glad to do anything for any friend of Mr. Bentley. (*Climbs stairs with cases and exits into room R.*)

MAGEE (*up to QUIMBY, L.C.*) Now you're quite sure I won't be disturbed while I am writing?

QUIMBY (*L.C.*). Who's goin' to disturb you here? No one ever comes within a mile of this place till around the first of April, except myself, and I only come up about once a week this kind of weather.

MAGEE. You don't suppose any of Bentley's Asquewan friends, hearing of the wager, would take it upon themselves to interrupt the progress of my work?

QUIMBY. Nobody knows you're here except me and the missus, and we ain't goin' to tell no one.

MAGEE. I have your word for that? (*Offers his hand to QUIMBY.*)

QUIMBY (*takes MAGEE's hand*). I never broke my word in my life. Guess that's why I'm a poor man. (*MAGEE crosses to R.C.*) The only other time I remember of anybody comin' here in the winter was the time of the reform wave at Reuton. The reformers got after a lot of crooked politicians, and they broke in here in the middle of the night and hid a lot of graft money in that safe over there. (*Points to safe. MAGEE goes up to safe, opens the door, then comes down to QUIMBY, after closing safe door.*)

MAGEE. You mean to tell me the reformers hid money in that safe?

QUIMBY. No, the politicians. Reformers never have any money.

MAGEE (*laughs as he goes R.*) Splendid!

QUIMBY. What are you laughing at?

MAGEE (*turning back to QUIMBY*). Nothing; it's all right. Go on, tell me about the hidden graft.

QUIMBY (MRS. QUIMBY *starts downstairs, bringing lantern and placing it on table L.*). Oh, there's nothing much to tell. Some fellers up and gave 'em away, and the police come the next morning and found it here. Nobody claimed it, so of course they never got the gang. They threw a lot of fellers out of office, I believe. I didn't read much about it. But that's over four years ago. You needn't be afraid; you won't be disturbed here. (*Goes L. to table and gets his mittens and cap.* MRS. QUIMBY *is at table putting on mittens, et cetera.*)

MAGEE (*going slightly R.*). Grafting politicians—reformers—hidden money! Sounds like a good seller.

MRS. QUIMBY (*goes to* MAGEE *at C.* —QUIMBY *takes lantern and goes back of table*). Is there anything more we can do for you, Mr. Magee?

MAGEE. No, nothing I can think of, thank you. I'll be quite—— (*Crossing to* QUIMBY *at table*—MRS. QUIMBY *to R.C.*) Oh, yes, of course. You've forgotten something, Mr. Quimby.

QUIMBY. Forgot what?

MAGEE. The key.

QUIMBY. Oh, Lord! Yes, the key! Here it is. (*Hands* MAGEE *the key.*)

MAGEE. You're positively certain that this key is the only key to Baldpate in existence?

QUIMBY. Yes, sir; I'm sure.

MRS. QUIMBY. I can swear to it.

MAGEE. Good!

MRS. QUIMBY. What are you going to do, lock yourself in?

MAGEE. Precisely.

QUIMBY. I don't mind staying here and keepin' watch for you if you want me to.

MAGEE. No, thanks; I much prefer to be alone.

MRS. QUIMBY. I'd rather it would be you than me. Lord, I should think you'd be afraid of ghosts.

QUIMBY (*crosses to* MRS. QUIMBY). Mother, I've told you twenty times there ain't no such a thing. (MAGEE *goes up L.*)

MRS. QUIMBY. Well, they've been seen here, just the same.

MAGEE (*goes L.C. to* QUIMBYS). Ghosts!

QUIMBY. Oh, don't mind her, Mr. Magee. We think we know what the ghost is. There's an old feller up here in the mountain by the name of Peters—he's a hermit.

MAGEE. A hermit!

QUIMBY. Yes; he's one of them fellers that's been disappointed in love. His wife run off with a traveling man. He come here about ten years ago—lives in a little shack about a mile and a half north of here; calls it the Hermit's Cave. All the summer boarders buy picture post cards from him. We figger he's the feller that's been frightening the people down in the valley by wavin' a lantern from the mountainside with a white sheet wrapped around him.

MRS. QUIMBY. But no one ever proved it was him.

QUIMBY. Well, who else could it be? There ain't no such a thing as ghosts, is there, Mr. Magee?

MAGEE. Well, I hope not. (*Muses. Byplay between the* QUIMBYS.) Ghosts—hermits—not bad at all!

QUIMBY. Well, come along, Mother; I guess maybe Mr. Magee is anxious to get to work. I'll say good night, sir. (*Offers hand to* MAGEE.)

MAGEE (*shakes* QUIMBY's *hand*). Good night. And remember, twelve o'clock sharp for Mr. Bentley's phone call tomorrow night.

QUIMBY. I'll be here on the minute. (*Goes up C.*)

MRS. QUIMBY (*shaking hands with* MAGEE). And I'm comin' to see if you're still alive. Lord, I should think you'd be scared to death.

QUIMBY (*comes down L. of* MAGEE). Mother, he will be if you keep on like that. Well, good night, sir, and good luck. (*Goes up toward door, followed by* MRS. QUIMBY.)

MAGEE (*goes up to door and unlocks it*). Good night. I don't envy you your trip down the mountain on a night like this. (*Opens door. Wind effect.*)

MRS. QUIMBY. Good night, sir. (*Starts through door, followed by* QUIMBY, *carrying lantern.*)

MAGEE. Good night, Mrs. Quimby. Keep a sharp lookout for ghosts and hermits. (*Laughs.*)

MRS. QUIMBY (*outside*). Lord, don't remind me, please!

MAGEE (*Slams door quickly, locks it, waves his hand to the* QUIMBYS, *then stands looking at key in his hand*). The only one, eh? Humph, we'll see! (*Puts key in his pocket, looks around room, thinks, then claps his hands as if decided on something; grabs his coat and hat from chair near fire, extinguishes lamps and bracket lights, takes a last look around room, and then exits upstairs into room R. on balcony.*)

(*Black drop down for ten seconds. End of Prologue. Drop up for Act I. The clock strikes twelve. The sound of a typewriter is heard clicking from the room occupied by* MAGEE. *A short pause of absolute silence, then* BLAND *appears at door, peering into room.*)

BLAND (*opens door, enters, locks door, then comes down to C. and looks about, rubbing his hands and blowing on them to warm them. Sees safe, goes up to it, tries the door, opens it, and goes down R. As he starts for phone he sees fire burning, and stops dead*). A log fire! Who the devil built that? (*Thinks, snaps fingers, goes to phone and puts in plugs.*) 2875 West. Hurry it along, sister. (MAGEE *enters from room and stands on balcony listening, leaving door of room open. In phone.*) Hello, is that you, Andy? . . . This is Bland. . . . Yes, Baldpate. . . . Yes, damn near frozen. . . . Oh, awful! It's like Napoleon's tomb. . . . I thought you said Mayor Cargan would meet me here? . . . No, no, I can't stay here all night; I'd go mad. . . . Listen, I'll hide the money here in the safe, and meet him at nine o'clock in the morning and turn it over to him then. . . . There isn't a chance in the world of anything happening. . . . The money's safer here than any spot on earth. . . . I'll lock the safe as soon as I put the package in. . . . Mayor Cargan knows the combination. . . . My advice is to let it lay here a week. It's the last place they'll look for it. Besides, how could they get in? My key to Baldpate is the only one in existence. (MAGEE, *on balcony, takes out his key and looks at it.*) They don't figure we'd take the chance after the other exposure. I tell you I know best. . . . I'll be back in town by one o'clock. . . . I've got the president's machine waiting at the foot of the mountain. . . . All right; good-by. (*Hangs up receiver, goes C., takes package of money from his pocket, looks at it and around room, then goes to safe and deposits the money therein.* MAGEE *starts slowly and stealthily downstairs.* BLAND *closes door of safe, turns the handle, tries doors to see if they are locked securely, then comes down to fireplace and warms himself. As he turns his back to the fire, he comes face to face with* MA-GEE, *who by this time is standing R.* BLAND's *hand goes to his pocket for his gun as he comes slowly C. to* MAGEE.)

MAGEE (*cool and collected*). Good evening—or perhaps I should say good morning.

BLAND (*keeping his hand on gun as he advances toward* MAGEE). Who are you?

MAGEE. I was just about to put that question to you.

BLAND. What are you doing here?

MAGEE. I rather think I'm the one entitled to an explanation.

BLAND. Did you follow me up that mountain?

MAGEE. Oh, no; I was here an hour ahead of you.

BLAND. How'd you get in here?

MAGEE (*points*). Through that door.

BLAND. You lie! There's only one key to that door, and I have it right here in my pocket.

MAGEE. My dear sir, I was laboring under that same impression until a moment ago; but as your key fits the lock, and my key fits the lock, there are evidently two keys to Baldpate instead of one. (*He shows* BLAND *his key.*) See?

BLAND. You mean to tell me that's a key to Baldpate?

MAGEE. Yes. That's why I became so interested in your arrival here. I heard you telephone your friend just now and declare that your key was the only one in existence. (*Laughs.*) It sort of handed me a laugh.

BLAND. You heard what I said over the telephone?

MAGEE. Every word.

BLAND (*pulls pistol*). You don't think you're going to live to tell it, do you?

MAGEE. Have no fear on that score. I'm not a tattletale, nor do I intend to pry into affairs that do not concern me. But I should like your answering me one question. Where did you get your key to Baldpate?

BLAND. None of your damned business! I didn't come here to tell you the story of my life!

MAGEE. Well, you might at least relate that portion of it that has led you to trespassing on a gentleman seeking seclusion.

BLAND. Trespassing, eh? Who's trespassing, you or I?

MAGEE. My right here is indisputable.

BLAND. Who gave you that key?

MAGEE. None of your damned business! If I remember rightly, that's the answer you gave me.

BLAND (goes slightly nearer MAGEE). You've got a pretty good nerve to talk like that with a gun in front of your face.

MAGEE. Oh, that doesn't disturb me in the least. While I have never experienced this sort of thing in real life before, I've written so much of this melodramatic stuff and collected such splendid royalties from it all, that it rather amuses me to discover that the so-called literary trash is the real thing, after all. You may not believe it, but, really, old chap, I've written you over and over again! (Laughs heartily and slaps BLAND on the shoulder. The latter backs away after second slap. MAGEE sits at table, still laughing heartily.)

BLAND (up close to MAGEE). Say, I killed a man once for laughing at me.

MAGEE. That's my line—I used it in The Lost Limousine. Four hundred thousand copies. I'll bet you've read it.

BLAND (pointing gun). If you don't tell me who you are and what you're doing here, I'll kill you as dead as a doornail. Come on, I mean business—who are you?

MAGEE. Well, a name doesn't mean so much, so you may call me Mr. Smith.

BLAND. What are you?

MAGEE. A writer of popular novels.

BLAND. What are you doing here?

MAGEE. Trying to win a bet by completing a story of Baldpate in twenty-four hours. (Gets up.) A few more interruptions of this sort, however, and it's plain to be seen I'll pay the winner. (Up close to BLAND.) You can do me a big favor, old man, by leaving me this place to myself for the night. I give you my word of honor that whatever I've seen or heard shall remain absolutely sacred.

BLAND (sneeringly). You must think I'm an awful fool to swallow that kind of talk!

MAGEE. Very well, if you don't believe I'm who I say I am, and you doubt that I'm here for the reason I gave, go upstairs into that room with the open door—(points to room R. on balcony. BLAND looks up and backs away)—and you'll find a typewriting machine, several pages of manuscript scattered about the floor, and a letter on the dresser from the owner of this inn to the caretaker, proving conclusively that all I've told you is the truth and nothing but the truth, and there you are.

BLAND (*up close to* MAGEE). And you're not in with the police?

MAGEE. No. I wish I were, if the graft is as good as they say it is.

BLAND. You say you have a letter from the owner of the inn?

MAGEE. Yes. Wait a minute, and I'll get it for you. (*Starts upstairs, but is stopped by* BLAND *as he is about halfway up.*)

BLAND (*shouts*). Come back!

MAGEE (*comes down and goes to* L.C.). What's the matter?

BLAND (*going L.C. to* MAGEE). I've been doublecrossed before, young fellow. I'll find it if it's there.

MAGEE. Oh, very well. If you prefer to get it yourself, why, go right along. (*He turns from* BLAND. *As he does so,* BLAND *fans him for a gun.* MAGEE *turns, surprised; then, as he understands, he laughs.*) You needn't be alarmed; I never carried a gun in my life.

BLAND. But you keep one in your room, eh?

MAGEE. If you think so, search the room.

BLAND. That's just what I'm going to do. I guess I'll keep you in sight, though. Go on; I'll let you show me the way.

MAGEE. All right. (*Starts toward stairs.*) If that's the way you feel

about it, why, certainly. (*Goes upstairs leisurely, followed by* BLAND, *who keeps him covered.* MAGEE *starts to exit into room.* BLAND *stops him.*)

BLAND (*C. of balcony*). Wait a minute; I'll peek around that room alone first. You don't look good to me; you're too damned willing. (*Goes to door of room R.* MAGEE *steps out to R. of door.*) You wait out here. I'll call you when I've satisfied myself you're not trying to spring something.

MAGEE. Very well. If you don't trust me, go ahead.

(BLAND *exits into room, keeping his eyes fixed on* MAGEE. *The latter stands thinking for a moment, then turns and slams door quickly, locks it, and runs downstairs to phone. When he is halfway down* BLAND *starts hammering on door.*)

BLAND (*yelling and hammering on door*). Open this door! (*Hammers.*) Damn you, I'll get you for this!

MAGEE (*at phone*). Hello, I want to talk to the Asquewan police headquarters. . . . That's what I said, police headquarters.

(BLAND *pounds on door. As* MAGEE *sits waiting for connection,* MARY NORTON *appears at door. She unlocks it and enters, closing door. The cold blast of wind attracts* MAGEE, *who jumps up and yells.*)

MAGEE. Who's there? What do you want?

MARY. Don't shoot; it's all right. I'm harmless.

MAGEE. How did you open that door?

MARY (*slightly down toward MAGEE*). Unlocked it with a key, of course.

MAGEE (*half aside*). My God!

MARY (*comes toward MAGEE*). If you will allow me to bring my chaperon inside, I will explain in a moment who I am and why we're here.

MAGEE. Your chaperon!

MARY (*going up to door*). Yes; another perfectly harmless female who has been kind enough to accompany me on this wild adventure. (*Turns to MAGEE.*) I have your permission?

MAGEE (*looks up at room R., then back at MARY, puzzled*). Say, what the deuce is this all about?

MARY. You'll soon know. (*Opens door and calls.*) All right, Mrs. Rhodes.

(MRS. RHODES *screams off stage, then enters and runs past MARY to above table L., terribly frightened.*)

MAGEE. What's the matter? What's happened?

MRS. RHODES (*shouting to MARY*). Lock the door! Lock the door!

(MARY *hurriedly locks door.*)

MAGEE (*crosses to MRS. RHODES, speaking hurriedly*). Tell me, please, what is it?

MARY (*runs down L. to MRS. RHODES*). What frightened you, Mrs. Rhodes?

MRS. RHODES (*almost hysterical*). A man!

MAGEE. A man?

MARY. What man?

MRS. RHODES. I don't know. He appeared at the window above, flourishing a revolver, and then he jumped to the ground and started running down the mountainside.

MAGEE. Are you sure?

MRS. RHODES. Of course I'm sure.

MAGEE. Just a moment. (*Turns and darts upstairs, taking key from his pocket as he goes.*)

MARY (*going R.C. with MRS. RHODES*). Is there anything wrong?

MAGEE. I'm beginning to think I am. (*Opens door R. on balcony and exits.*)

MRS. RHODES (*still hysterical*). Why did you ever come here?

MARY (*coolly*). It's all right. Don't get excited.

MAGEE (*enters from room R. and comes to C. of balcony*). The bird has flown, but he forgot this when he took the jump. (*Points gun at women.* MRS. RHODES *runs R., screaming;* MARY *screams and runs L.*) Don't be alarmed; I'm not going to shoot—at least, not yet. (*Is on landing of stairs as he speaks next lines.*) Now might I ask why I'm so honored by this midnight visit? (*Snaps on bracket lights and comes down C.*)

MARY (*goes L.C. to MAGEE*). I can explain in a very few words.

MAGEE. That will suit me immensely. My time is valuable. I'm losing thousands of dollars, perhaps, through even this waste of time. (*Looks at* MARY *intently.*) Be as brief as possible, please. I—— (*Stares at her.*)

MARY. Why do you stare at me so?

MAGEE. Do you believe in love at first sight?

(MRS. RHODES *takes a step toward them, surprised.*)

MARY. What do you mean?

MAGEE. You know, I've written about it a great many times, but I never believed in it before. It's really remarkable! (*Looks from* MARY *to* MRS. RHODES, *puzzled; then laughs in an embarrassed manner.*) Oh, pardon me, you were about to explain your visit here.

MARY. Well, to begin with, I—— (*Phone rings. All turn and look at it.*)

MAGEE (*goes to phone, stops buzzer, then backs upstage C.* MRS. RHODES *is R.C. To* MARY). Will you be kind enough to answer that phone? I don't care to turn my back on anything but a bolted door tonight. (*As* MARY *looks surprised.*) If you please.

MARY. Certainly. (*Goes to phone.* MRS. RHODES *goes R.C. above* MARY.) Hello! . . . What's that? . . . Hold the wire, please, I'll see. (*Turns to* MAGEE.) Did you wish to talk to police headquarters?

MRS. RHODES (*goes to* MAGEE C., *frightened*). Police headquarters!

MAGEE (*crossing* MRS. RHODES, *who goes over to R. of table L.*). Yes. (*Starts, then stops and looks up at room R. on balcony.*) But, no; just say they must have made a mistake. (*Backs upstage C.*)

MARY (*in phone*). Hello! . . . No, no such call put in from here. Must be some mistake. That's all right. (*Stands up receiver and goes L.* MAGEE *goes to phone, severs connection, then comes down C.* MARY *up to him.*) Then you did call police headquarters?

MAGEE. I did.

MRS. RHODES (*goes to C.*) Why did you call police headquarters?

MARY. Yes, why did you call police headquarters?

MAGEE (*looks at both, puzzled, then laughs*). You know, these are the most remarkable lot of happenings. No sooner do I get rid of one best seller, then along comes another dyed-in-the-wool "to-be-continued-in-our-next." (*To* MARY.) You know there's no particular reason for my saying this, but I really believe I'd do anything in the world for you.

MARY. I don't understand.

MAGEE. But you promised to explain your presence here.

MARY. Which I fully intend to do; but first of all I should like to ask you one question.

MAGEE. Proceed.

MARY. How did you get in here without this key? (*Shows him her key.*)

MAGEE (*laughs*). Oh, no, no! (*Laughs.*) You know, I'm beginning to think this whole thing is a frame-up.

MARY. What do you mean?

MAGEE (*points to her key*). You have the only key to Baldpate in existence, I suppose?

MARY. So I understood.

MAGEE. Well, if it's any news to you, ladies, believe me, there are more keys to Baldpate than you'll find in a Steinway piano.

MARY. Then he lied!

MAGEE. Who lied?

MRS. RHODES (*quickly*). Remember your promise, Mary! (*Crosses to chair in front of fire and sits.*)

MAGEE (*follows* MRS. RHODES *with his eyes, making complete turn*). Well?

MARY. I can't tell you his name.

MAGEE. Well, at least tell me your name.

MARY. My name is Mary Norton. I do special stories for the *Reuton Star.*

MAGEE (*surprised*). In the newspaper game?

MARY. That's it. And this lady— (*pointing to* MRS. RHODES, *who is now removing her rubbers*)—is Mrs. Rhodes, with whom I live in Reuton, and who is the only other person who knows I'm here to do this story.

MAGEE. What story?

MARY. The story of the five-thousand-dollar wager you have made with a certain gentleman that you would write a complete novel inside of twenty-four hours.

MAGEE. Who told you this?

MRS. RHODES. Remember your promise, Mary.

MAGEE (*crosses to R.C.* MARY *goes L.C.* MAGEE *looks at* MRS. RHODES *and then at* MARY). You've made many a promise, haven't you, Mary? I should certainly like to know who gave you this information.

MARY (*goes to* MAGEE *R.C.*). I can tell you only that when the wager was made at the Forty-fourth Street club this afternoon, a certain someone dispatched the news to me at once. Believing that I had the only key to Baldpate, I hurried here to let you in, and lo and behold— (*takes stage L.,* MAGEE *following her*)—I find you already at work, and as snug and cozy as you would be in a New York apartment. (*Comes down R. of table,* MAGEE *following her.*) Now that you know my story, I am going to throw myself on your mercy and ask you to allow me to stay here and get the beat. I promise you we shall not disturb you in the least. Have you any objections?

MAGEE. And you won't tell me who gave you the story?

MARY. I can't.

MAGEE. Nor where you got the key?

MRS. RHODES. Remember your promise, Mary.

MAGEE (*turns and looks at* MRS. RHODES *and then at* MARY). You know, I wish you hadn't brought her with you.

MRS. RHODES. What! (*Gets up and starts L. toward* MAGEE.)

MAGEE (*goes toward her as she starts up*). No offense, Mrs. Rhodes. Of course I understand that Mary is a very promising young woman, but why continually remind her of the fact? (*Laughs apologetically.*) That's just my little joke. Excuse me. (*Goes to* MARY C. MRS. RHODES *goes to window, looking out.*) Let me get this clear. Your idea is to stop here and write the story of my twenty-four-hour task?

MARY. With your permission.

MAGEE. Well, I'll tell you. Had you put such a proposition up to me— (MRS. RHODES *comes downstage to R.C.*)—half an hour ago, I should have said emphatically, no; but since my little experience with the gun-flourishing, window-jumping gentleman, I'm inclined to entertain the idea of a companion or two.

MRS. RHODES (*R. of* MAGEE). Who was the man with the gun?

MARY. Why did he jump from the window?

MAGEE. You might as well ask me why he placed a package of money in that safe. (MARY *and* MRS. RHODES *go up toward safe.*) Or why he telephoned the fact to someone else, who was to pass the word along to Mayor Cargan.

MRS. RHODES (*turns to* MAGEE, *amazed*). Mayor Cargan!

MAGEE. What seems to be the trouble?

MARY (*to* MAGEE, C.). Mrs. Rhodes is a widow; Mayor Cargan a widower. Perhaps you will understand why the name startled her when I tell you that Mrs. Rhodes is to become Mrs. Cargan next Sunday morning.

MAGEE. Oh, indeed! (MARY *goes up C., then down again during next speech.* MAGEE *crosses to* MRS. RHODES.) Well, congratulations, Mrs. Rhodes. And again I say I did not mean to offend. I am not accusing Mayor Cargan of any transaction, dishonest or otherwise. I was merely trying to point out to you ladies that it has been a night of wild occurrences up to now. However, if you care to take the risk, stay here. It won't disturb me in the least, and may possibly benefit this young lady in her business. (*Goes toward* MARY. *Looks at his watch and whistles.*) I've lost half an hour already, and as every minute means money to me right now, I'll have to work fast to make up for the time I've lost. (*To* MRS. RHODES—MARY *comes down L.C.*) Again I apologize for any mistake I may have made, Mrs. Rhodes.

MRS. RHODES. I assure you a more honest man than Jim Cargan never lived.

MAGEE. I sincerely trust you're right, especially for your own sake. (MRS. RHODES *sits in front of fire.* MAGEE *goes to* MARY *and takes her hand.*) I hope the story proves a whale. I wish——

MARY. What do you wish?

MAGEE. Oh, nothing—I was just thinking of Sunday morning. Good night.

MARY. Good night.

MAGEE (*as he goes up the stairs*). I'd gladly offer you ladies my room, but it's the only one cleaned and heated, and I must have some comfort for this kind of work. (*On balcony R.*) Good night, ladies.

MARY *and* MRS. RHODES. Good night.

MAGEE (*leaning over balcony*). Mary—that's the sweetest name in the world.

MARY (*looking up at him*). Thank you.

MAGEE. Good night.

MARY. Good night.

MAGEE (*a long look at* MARY *and then at* MRS. RHODES). I still wish you hadn't brought her with you. Good night.

MARY. Good night.

(MAGEE *exits into room R. on balcony, closing door.*)

MRS. RHODES (*over to* MARY, *R.C.*). You don't believe Jim Cargan guilty of any treachery? Tell me you don't, Mary.

MARY. I don't know, Mrs. Rhodes. I told you of the Suburban bribe story we got last night, but I certainly hope the name of Cargan is kept clean, for both your sakes.

MRS. RHODES. I can't believe he's wrong! I won't believe it! (*Crosses to L.C.*)

MARY (*following* MRS. RHODES). But if he is wrong, it's best you should know it now. The fates may have brought us here tonight to protect you; who knows?

MRS. RHODES (*going toward safe*). Money hidden in that safe, he said.

MARY. Yes, and that dovetails with the Suburban bribe story. (*Both come down stage a trifle.*) I came down here to do a special. I may get two sweeps with the one broom. Wouldn't that be wonderful? I'd be made!

MRS. RHODES (*turns upstage, looks toward door, and sees* PETERS). Great Heavens, Mary, look!

MARY. What is it? (*Looks up at door, sees* PETERS, *screams and runs L. behind banister.* MRS. RHODES *screams and runs R. and hides behind chair.* MAGEE *enters on balcony after second scream.*)

MAGEE (*looking down at women*). What's wrong down there?

MRS. RHODES. A ghost!

MAGEE. What!

MARY. A ghost! A ghost!

MAGEE (*laughing*). I'll bet you four dollars that's the fellow whose wife ran away with a traveling man! (*Starts to come downstairs.*)

MARY *and* MRS. RHODES (*they wave* MAGEE *back*). Ssh!

(MAGEE *snaps out lights.* PETERS *unlocks the door, enters, locks door, then throws the sheet over his arm and comes downstage, looking from* MARY *to* MRS. RHODES, *who both come forward a trifle.* MAGEE *comes to L. of* PETERS *at C.*)

MAGEE. I beg your pardon; but have you any idea just how many keys there are to this flat?

PETERS (*ignores question*). What are these women doing here?

MAGEE. How's that?

PETERS. I don't like women.

(MRS. RHODES *and* MARY *scream and run to foot of stairs.*)

MAGEE. It's all right, ladies; he's not a regular ghost. I know all about him. He's in the picture post card business.

PETERS (*gruffly*). What!

MAGEE (*to* PETERS). Just a minute, Bosco. (*To ladies.*) If you ladies will kindly step upstairs into my room, I'll either kill it or cure it. (*Ladies go up and stand on balcony.*)

PETERS (*gruffly*). What?

MAGEE (*to* PETERS). See here, that's the second time you've barked at me. Now don't do it again, do you hear? (*To ladies.*) Go right in, ladies. (*They exit into room R., closing door.* MAGEE *down to* PETERS.) So you're the ghost of Baldpate, are you?

PETERS. How'd you people get in here?

MAGEE (*laughs*). You're not going to pull that "only-key-in-existence" speech on me, are you?

PETERS. What?

MAGEE. You know there are other keys besides yours.

PETERS. They're all imitations. Mine's the real key. The old man gave it to me the day before he died.

MAGEE. What old man?

PETERS. The father of that young scamp who wastes his time around those New York clubs. You know who I mean.

MAGEE. Then you're not particularly fond of the present owner of Baldpate?

PETERS. I hate him and all his men friends.

MAGEE. You don't like women either, you say.

PETERS. I despise them!

MAGEE. How do little girls and boys strike you?

PETERS. Bah!

MAGEE (*laughs*). I can understand your wife now—anything in preference to you, even a traveling man!

PETERS. Don't mention my wife's name, or I'll—— (*Raises lantern to strike* MAGEE.)

MAGEE (*pulls lantern out of* PETERS's *hand*). Now, see here, old man, if you make any more bluffs at me I'll take that white sheet away from you and put you right out of the ghost business. Haven't you any better sense than to go about frightening little children this way? Why don't you stick to your own line of work? You're a hermit by trade, if I'm rightly informed.

PETERS. Yes, I'm a hermit, and proud of it.

MAGEE. Then why don't you cut out this ghost stuff and be a regular hermit?

PETERS. I play the ghost because I love to see the cowards run.

MAGEE. Oh, they're all cowards—is that it?

PETERS. Cowards, yes! (*Laughs gruffly.*)

MAGEE. And you're a brave man, I suppose?

PETERS. A cave man is always a brave man.

(*Pistol shots heard outside, then a woman's scream.* PETERS *laughs and dances up to door and peers through.*)

PETERS. Ha, ha! They're shooting again! They're shooting again!

(MARY *and* MRS. RHODES *have come out on balcony at shots.*)

MAGEE (*up to door and peers through*). What's that?

MARY. What's happened?

MRS. RHODES. Is someone hurt? (*Both lean over balcony, looking down.*)

MAGEE. Did you hear a woman scream?

MARY (*frightened*). Distinctly.

MRS. RHODES (*frightened*). And a pistol shot!

PETERS (*dramatically, as he goes toward door L. slowly*). A woman in white—a woman in white! They shot at her as they shoot at me when I play the ghost. (*Laughs.*) They thought it was the ghost. (*Almost whispers.*) Thought it was the ghost. (*Laughs viciously and exits door L.*)

(MYRA THORNHILL *appears at door C. and is seen unlocking it.*)

MAGEE (*runs to foot of stairs and calls up to women*). My God, another key!

MARY *and* MRS. RHODES. What?

MAGEE. Ssh! It's a woman! (*He waves them back.*) Ssh!

(MARY *and* MRS. RHODES *go back into room R.* MAGEE *crouches behind banister, unseen by* MYRA *until he speaks.* MYRA *enters, locks door, then tiptoes cautiously to dead C. She takes a sweeping glance around, then goes to fire and warms herself; comes to C. again, and on making sure that no one is in the room, she goes to safe and starts working combination, first picking up lantern from desk and holding it in her left hand, while working combination with her right.*)

MAGEE (*snapping on bracket lights*). I thought I'd give you a little more light so you could work faster.

(MYRA *puts lantern on desk and throws up her hands.*) You needn't throw up your hands; I'll take a chance on that quick stuff. Come on out here, please. (*Laughs as* MYRA *comes around desk R. to C. slowly.*) I didn't think they did that sort of thing outside of melodrama and popular novels, but I see I was wrong, or I should say right, when I wrote it. (MYRA *continues to advance to him slowly.*) Really, you're the most attractive burglar I've ever seen. That is, if you are a burglar. Are you?

MYRA (*coolly*). Are you one of the Cargan crowd, or do you represent the Reuton Suburban people?

(MARY *and* MRS. RHODES *enter on balcony and listen.*)

MAGEE. No, I'm just an ordinary man trying to win a bet; but up to now the chances have been dead against me. Perhaps you'd like to tell me who you are.

MYRA. I will, if you'll answer me one question.

MAGEE (*laughs*). Of course, of course. I'll answer that one before you ask it. A friend of mine gave it to me. Of course you thought you had the only one in existence, but he lied to you. I have a cute little key of my own. Oh, there are keys and keys, but I love my little key best of all. (*Shows her his key, kissing it.*) See?

MYRA. I can't understand it at all.

MAGEE. You haven't anything on me. And just about two more keys, and I'll pack up my paraphernalia,

go back to New York, and never make another bet as long as I live!

MYRA (*up close to him*). Will you please tell me your name?

MAGEE. Well, a name doesn't mean so much, so you may call me Mr. Jones. And yours?

MYRA. My name is—— (*Hesitates.* MARY *and* MRS. RHODES *lean over balcony, listening.*) Listen! (*Brings* MAGEE *downstage.*) My husband is the president of the Asquewan-Reuton Suburban Railway Company. He has agreed to pay a vast amount of money for a certain city franchise—a franchise that the political crowd at Reuton has no power to grant. They are going to cheat him out of this money and use it for campaign funds to fight the opposition party at the next election. If he sues for his money back, they are going to expose him for entering into an agreement he knows to be nothing short of bribery. The present mayor is at the bottom of it all. (MARY *and* MRS. RHODES *start at mention of mayor's name.*) I ran to my husband tonight and begged him not to enter into this deal. I warned him that he was being cheated. He wouldn't believe me, but I know it's true. He's being cheated, and will be charged with bribery besides. That's why I risked the mountain on a night like this. I must have been followed, for I was shot at as I reached the top of Baldpate. Oh, I don't know who you are, but you're a man and you can help me. (*Puts her hands on his shoulders, pleadingly.*) You will help me, won't you?

MAGEE (*interested*). Yes. What do you want me to do?

MYRA (*looks at* MAGEE *for a moment without speaking, then goes up to safe and back to* MAGEE). In that safe there is a package containing two hundred thousand dollars.

MAGEE (*goes up toward safe*). Two hundred thousand dollars!

(MARY *and* MRS. RHODES *start downstairs very slowly.*)

MYRA (*following* MAGEE *up* R.). That's the amount. It must be there. A man named Bland was to bring it here and deposit it at midnight. Cargan was to follow later, and was to find it here.

MAGEE (*coming downstage*). Cargan coming here!

MYRA. So they've planned it. I must have that money out of there before he arrives. You'll help me, won't you? Don't you understand? My husband is being cheated, tricked, robbed, probably ruined.

MAGEE. But I don't know the combination.

MYRA (*wringing her hands*). Oh, there must be something we can do! Please, please—— (*She kneels at his feet and puts up her hands imploringly.*) For the sake of my children, help me, please! (MAGEE *sees women on stairs, and warns* MYRA *with a look as he helps her to her feet. She turns and faces* MARY *and* MRS. RHODES, *then turns abruptly to* MAGEE.) Who are these women? What are they doing here? (*She has changed from hysteria to dignified coldness.*)

MAGEE. Oh, of course, pardon me! (*Goes to women at foot of stairs.*

MYRA *crosses to* R.) May I introduce Miss——

MYRA (*cuts him off sharply*). Please don't! (*Turns to women.*) Will you pardon me for a moment, ladies?

MARY *and* MRS. RHODES. Certainly. (*They step off stairs and remain* L., *keeping their eyes fixed on* MYRA *and* MAGEE. MAGEE *goes* R. *to* MYRA.)

MYRA (*aside to* MAGEE). For God's sake, don't tell them who I am. My husband will kill me if he ever learns that I've been here on such an errand.

MAGEE (*aside*). I understand; you may trust me. I sympathize with you very deeply, madam, and I promise you that no one shall take that money away from here tonight unless it be yourself. And I'll get it out of that safe if I have to blow the thing to smithereens!

MYRA. You give me your word as a gentleman?

MAGEE (*offers his hand*). My word as a gentleman.

MYRA (*takes his hand*). Thank you.

MAGEE (*pulls down his vest and goes up to* MARY *and* MRS. RHODES). Ladies, I wish to present a girl schoolmate of mine, Miss Brown, who has become interested enough in my career to find her way to Baldpate to witness my endeavor to break all records as a speedy story-writer.

MARY *and* MRS. RHODES. Miss Brown. (*Both bow.* MYRA *returns the bow.*)

MAGEE (*takes out his watch and looks at it*). Up to now I'm almost an hour behind myself. However, I expect to catch up with myself before the night is over. That is, of course, provided there aren't over three hundred more keys to the old front door.

MARY (*goes up to* MAGEE *C.*). Now, might I have a word wtih you alone?

MAGEE. I'd be delighted. I'd like to be alone with you forever.

MARY (*to* MYRA). Will you pardon me for a moment?

MYRA. Certainly.

MAGEE. Go right upstairs, Miss Brown, and make yourself quite at home. (*Starts toward stairs with* MYRA.) Oh, Mrs. Rhodes, will you be good enough to show her to the room? (MARY *crosses C. to R.*) I'm sure she needs a little drop of something after that bitter cold trip up the mountain. You'll find a flask on the table.

MRS. RHODES (*starts up the stairs*). Come right along, Miss. I know where it is; I've already tried it. (*Exits room R.*)

MYRA (*following* MRS. RHODES *upstairs*). Well, really, I don't know what to say to all this kindness. I—— (*Stops C. on balcony, looks down and warns* MAGEE *to silence with finger on her lips. He reassures her, then goes C.*)

MRS. RHODES (*appearing at door*). Right in here, Miss.

MYRA. Thanks, awfully. (*Exits into room, followed by* MRS. RHODES, *who closes door.*)

MARY (*goes quickly to* MAGEE *at C.*). Who did that woman claim to be?

MAGEE. That's a secret I've promised never to reveal.

MARY. But I overheard everything she said.

MAGEE. Then you know.

MARY. I know she lied.

MAGEE. She lied!

MARY. She claimed to be the wife of Thomas Hayden, president of the Suburban Railway. She lied, I tell you. Why, I've known Mrs. Hayden all my life; was brought up and went to school with her daughters. Mrs. Hayden is a woman in her fifties. You can see for yourself that she is nothing more than a slip of a girl. There's a mystery here of some kind—someone's playing a desperate game. (*Goes upstage excitedly, looking up at door R.*)

MAGEE. Yes, and it's costing me five thousand dollars. I'll never get my work done tonight, I can see that right now. (*Looks at watch.* MARY *comes down C.*) But what do I care? I've met you!

MARY. You're going to give this money over to that woman?

(PETERS *enters from L. and hides behind banisters.*)

MAGEE. Not if she lied.

MARY. Well, you believe me, don't you?

MAGEE (*takes her hand*). Believe you! Let me tell you something, little girl. I've written a lot of those Romeo speeches in my novels, though I never really felt this way before, but here goes: The moment you walked through that door to-night and I laid eyes on you, I made up my mind that you were the one woman in the world for me. Why, there's nothing I wouldn't do for you. Try me.

MARY. Very well, I shall. Get me that package of money out of that safe before Cargan comes to steal it. Help me to reach Reuton without being molested, and I'll annihilate the graft machine with tomorrow's edition of the *Star*. With that money to turn over to the proper authorities as proof of the deal, I'll wipe out the street-car trust and the Cargan crowd with one swing of the pen. And just think, I'll save Mrs. Rhodes from an alliance with a thief! I know Cargan's crooked, always has been; but I must prove it before she'll break off the engagement. Great Scott! what a story I'll write! Think what it will mean to me and to the city of Reuton itself! (*Puts her hands on his shoulders pleadingly.*) You will do this for me, won't you? Please, please!

MAGEE. Yes. What do you want me to do?

MARY. Come, we must hurry! Can't you think of some way to open that safe? (*Goes up toward safe, MAGEE following. He comes down C.*)

MAGEE. What are we going to do? We don't know the combination, and I haven't any dynamite. But we must have that $200,000.

(*PETERS moves chair just enough to betray his presence.*)

MARY (*comes down to MAGEE, frightened, placing her hand on his arm*). What was that?

MAGEE. Oh, that was nothing. It was just the wind creeping through the cracks, I fancy. (*Aside.*) Go up-stairs; there's someone hiding in this room. (*Aloud.*) Good night, Miss Norton.

MARY. Good night. (*She hurries up-stairs and exits into room R.*)

(*MAGEE looks around room for a moment, reaches over banisters and snaps out lights; starts whistling, and then goes upstairs to L. room on balcony, opens door, slams it loudly, and then comes out and sits behind banisters, watching PETERS. PETERS makes sure no one is in sight, then goes quickly over to safe and starts working combination quietly, but hurriedly, MAGEE watching him from stairs. CARGAN and MAX appear outside, peering through into room. As the safe door flies open, they enter quickly, CARGAN opening the door. MAX enters and goes quickly up C. and covers PETERS with gun. CARGAN closes door and goes quickly to PETERS.*)

MAX. Get away from that safe! (*PETERS jumps away.*) Put up your hands! (*PETERS's hands go up.*)

CARGAN (*recognizes him as he goes toward safe*). Oh, it's you, is it? (*To MAX.*) The ghost came near walking that time, for fair! (*To PETERS.*) Come out of there! (*PETERS comes in front of desk.*) How did you know the combination of that safe?

(*No reply from* PETERS.) Who told you there was money in there? (*No reply from* PETERS.) Get out of here, you vagabond! (*Throws* PETERS *toward L.*) What do you mean by breaking into a man's safe in the middle of the night? Throw him in the cellar, Max.

MAX. Come on, hurry up! Get out! (*Throws* PETERS *L.*)

PETERS (*at door L.*). Damn you, Cargan, I hate you!

CARGAN. Get out! (*Goes up and locks door.*)

MAX. Go on, get out!

(PETERS *exits L. door.* MAX *follows him off and returns almost immediately.*)

CARGAN (*goes to safe and gets package of money.* MAX *enters*). By gad, we weren't any too soon! (*Goes to table L.*) Another moment, and he'd have had it sure. It would be good-by to the hermit if he ever got hold of a roll like this! (*Flips bills in his hands.*) Two hundred one-thousand-dollar bills.

MAX. Is it all there?

CARGAN. I don't know; I'll see. (MAGEE *comes downstairs and goes behind desk while* MAX *and* CARGAN *are counting money.*) You seem surprised that I found the money here.

MAX. What do you mean—surprised?

CARGAN (*rises, puts money in his pocket, then comes in front of table.* MAX *comes forward and stands L.*

of CARGAN, *below table*). I'm going to tell you something, Max. I didn't trust you all day, and I didn't trust you tonight.

MAX. What do you mean—you didn't trust me?

CARGAN. I'll be truthful with you. I thought you were going to double-cross me. I thought you were going to beat me to the bank roll through this woman Thornhill.

MAX. Myra Thornhill?

CARGAN. Yes, Myra Thornhill. Oh, don't play dead; you knew she was around. You've had secret meetings with her during the last forty-eight hours. I know every move you've made—I've had you watched. You've worked with her before. (*As* MAX *makes a motion of protest.*) You've told me so. I had my mind made up to kill you, Max, if this money had been gone, and that's just what I'm going to do if you ever double-cross me, do you understand?

MAX (*in a hangdog tone*). Yes, I understand.

(MAGEE, *who has been crouching between safe and desk, now stands up, takes aim, and fires at L. wall, then rushes over and turns on bracket lights. At the sound of the shot the women come out on balcony, frightened, and stand looking down at men.*)

CARGAN (*as* MAGEE *shoots*). My God, I'm shot! (*Reels against table.* MAX *draws back L.*)

MAGEE (*comes down R.C.*). No, you're not. I just put a bullet into the wall, and I'll put one in you if you don't toss that package of money over here! Come on, hurry up! I mean business! (CARGAN *hesitates, then throws money to* MAGEE *R.C. The latter picks it up and puts it in his pocket.*) You see, being a writer of sensational novels, I'm well up in this melodramatic stuff.

MRS. RHODES (*on balcony, watching* CARGAN). Jim Cargan!

CARGAN (*he and* MAX *look up and see women on balcony*). What are you doing here? (MRS. RHODES *doesn't reply, but continues staring at him.*)

MYRA (*looking down at* MAX). Max, Max, are you hurt?

MAX. No; I'm all right.

CARGAN (*turning slowly to* MAX). Myra Thornhill, eh? So you were trying to cross me, you snake! (*Chokes* MAX. *Women scream.*)

MAGEE. I must insist upon orderly conduct, gentlemen. No roughhouse, please. (*To* MAX.) Young man, be good enough to put that gun of yours on the table. (MAX *hesitates.*) Hurry now. (MAX *does as directed.*) Now kindly remove that gun from Mr. Cargan's pocket—I'm sure he has one—and put it on the table also. He might want to take a shot at you, and I'm giving you the necessary protection. Hurry, please.

(MAX *takes* CARGAN's *gun and places it on table.*)

MAGEE. Now, Mrs. Rhodes, will you kindly ask the street-car president's wife to step back into that room, then lock the door and remove the

key? (MYRA *goes slowly to room R.* MRS. RHODES *follows her, locks the door, then comes to C. of balcony.*) Thank you. And now, Miss Norton, will you kindly step down here— (MARY *starts downstairs and hangs muff on chair L.*)—and take those two revolvers from the table and place them in the hotel safe, and then close the safe and turn the combination? (MARY *places guns in safe, turns combination, and remains up near desk.*) Thank you very much. (*To men.*) Now, gentlemen, I must insist that you step upstairs to the room on the right of the balcony. And, Mrs. Rhodes, will you please step over there and lock the door when these gentlemen are on the other side? (MRS. RHODES *crosses balcony, goes to room L., unlocks door, and stands aside for the men to pass in.*) I shan't keep you there long, gentlemen; I'll release you as soon as I've transacted some important business with this young lady. Lively now, gentlemen! Lively! (*As men start upstairs slowly.*) That's it! Now to your right. Correct! Now straight ahead. (MAX *exits into room.* CARGAN *stops as he gets to door, and turns and looks appealingly at* MRS. RHODES, *who ignores his outstretched hands.*) Now right in. (CARGAN *exits into room L.*) Lock the door, Mrs. Rhodes, and bring the keys down to me. (MRS. RHODES *locks door and brings keys to* MAGEE *at C.*) That's the ticket! Thanks very much. (MARY *comes to C.*) Well, how's my work? Some roundup, wasn't it? (*To* MRS. RHODES.) I'm awfully sorry about this, for your sake, Mrs. Rhodes.

MARY (*to* MAGEE, R. *of him*). It's best she should know. (*To* MRS.

RHODES, *extending her hand.*) Isn't it, dear?

MRS. RHODES (*going R.C., after taking* MARY's *hand*). I suppose so, dear, I suppose so.

MAGEE. Well, come on, little girl! You've got to work fast. Here's the graft money. (*Takes money from his pocket and gives it to* MARY.) Now what?

MARY. I've everything planned. I know just what I'm going to do. What's the time?

MAGEE (*looking at watch*). One-thirty. But you can't get a train out of Asquewan until five.

(MARY *crosses to L., gets muff, and places money in it.*)

MRS. RHODES. We can't sit around the station for three hours, dear. (MARY *returns L.C. to* MAGEE.)

MAGEE. Try to get a taxi, or whatever sort of conveyance they have in the darned town; but whatever you do, get out of Asquewan as soon as you can.

MARY. You leave it to me; I'll find a way. Are you going to stay here?

MAGEE (*looks up at room R. and L.*). I'll have to. I want to keep guard on this crowd of lady and gentleman bandits until I'm sure you're well on your way. I'll keep them here until you phone and tell me you're out of danger, even though it's all night tonight and all day tomorrow.

MARY. But your work?

MAGEE. Never mind the work; I can write a novel any old time. So far as the bet is concerned, I can lose that and still be repaid a million times over—I've met you. (*Takes her hand, then crosses to* MRS. RHODES. MARY *goes up* C.) Good night, Mrs. Rhodes, and God bless you both!

MRS. RHODES. Good night. (*Shakes hands with* MAGEE, *then starts for door and stands looking up at door L. on balcony.*)

MAGEE (*to* MARY, *near door*). I wonder if we'll ever meet again?

MARY. I live in Reuton—good night. (*Turns up near foot of stairs and looks up at door L.* MRS. RHODES *exits.*)

MAGEE. Good night. (MARY *comes to door* MAGEE *is holding open. She pauses for a moment, looks at him intently, then down at floor, then exits quickly.* MAGEE *locks door, stands peering out at them for a moment, looks up at door L., then comes downstage and stands thinking.*) Crooked politicians—adventuress—safe robbed—love at first sight! (*Points to different rooms and at safe.*) And I wanted to get away from melodrama! (*Hears* HAYDEN *at door, and backs away to foot of stairs.*) And still they come!

(HAYDEN *enters, locks door, puts key in his pocket, takes off gloves, rubs his hands and nose trying to warm them, then comes down to fireplace and stands with his back to the fire. As he turns he comes face to face with* MAGEE, *who has come to* C. *He goes to* MAGEE *slowly.*)

HAYDEN. I beg pardon, but who are you?

MAGEE (C.). I'm Mayor Cargan's butler.

HAYDEN. Mayor Cargan!

MAGEE. Yes, he's here. Do you wish to see him?

HAYDEN (importantly). Yes. Say to him that Mr. Hayden of the Reuton-Asquewan Suburban Road is calling.

MAGEE. Oh, I see! Are you the president of that road, sir?

HAYDEN (pompously). I most certainly am, sir.

MAGEE (looks at HAYDEN, and then up at room R. and laughs). Your wife's here.

HAYDEN. What!

MAGEE. Yes; locked in that room up there. (MAGEE points to room R. on balcony. HAYDEN turns and looks up. As he turns, MAGEE fans him for gun. HAYDEN turns to MAGEE quickly, sputtering.) Pardon me, I just wanted to see if you had a gun on you. Just a minute; I'll tell the mayor the president has arrived. (Starts upstairs, laughing.)

HAYDEN (when MAGEE is on first landing). Are you a crazy man, sir?

MAGEE. That's what the critics say, but I'm beginning to think they are all wrong. Sit down, Mr. Hayden. I'll tell the boys you're here. (Unlocks door L. and steps aside.)

HAYDEN. The boys!

MAGEE. Come on, boys; everything's all right; the president's here. (As men come down, HAYDEN steps forward toward stairs.) Watch your step. Easy, that's it; one at a time, please. Lead on, boys. I'll walk a little behind.

(CARGAN and MAX come downstairs, followed by MAGEE, who covers them with gun. As men get to foot of stairs, HAYDEN backs away, thunderstruck. MAX goes to table L. MAGEE goes over R. CARGAN comes down to HAYDEN C.)

CARGAN (gruffly). Hello, Hayden.

HAYDEN. What is the meaning of this, Cargan?

CARGAN. I don't know. Ask him. (Nods toward MAGEE.)

HAYDEN (to CARGAN). Who is he?

CARGAN. I don't know, and I don't care a damn! I'm disgusted with the whole works. We're nailed, that's all I know. (Sits R. of table L. PETERS enters from door L. On seeing crowd of men, he starts to back out, but is stopped by MAGEE.)

MAGEE. No, you don't! Come back here. I'll keep my eye on you, too. You'd better sit down and join the boys, Hermy. (PETERS sits L. of table.)

HAYDEN (up to MAGEE, who is R.C.). I'd very much like to know the reason for such strange actions, young man?

MAGEE. Your wife will be down in a minute; she'll probably tell you all about it.

HAYDEN. Confound it, sir, my wife is home in bed!

MAGEE. That's what you think. (*Laughs.*) You're not the first fellow that's been fooled, you know. (HAYDEN *backs away from* MAGEE. MAGEE *throws key to* PETERS.) Here, Hermy; take that key and open the first door to the left on the balcony, and tell Mrs. Hayden that her husband wants to see her downstairs right away. (*As* PETERS *hesitates.*) Hurry along, that's a good ghost—go on. (PETERS, *mad all through, does as he is told, picking up the key from floor and going upstairs.*) Better sit down, boys, and make yourselves comfortable. We're liable to have quite a wait.

(MAX *sits L. of table.* MAGEE *goes up R.*)

HAYDEN. Well, I'll be running along.

MAGEE (*stops* HAYDEN *as he starts for door*). Better stay a while, Mr. Hayden; I'd like to have your wife meet you. I don't think she's ever had the pleasure.

(MYRA *and* PETERS *enter on balcony and start downstairs.*)

HAYDEN (*down to* CARGAN, R. *of table*). What the devil sort of a man is this?

(BLAND *knocks on door. All jump and look upstage.*)

MAGEE. Well, here's a novelty at last—a man without a key.

HAYDEN. It's Bland. I have his key; I'll let him in. (*Starts for door.*)

MAGEE. Don't bother. I have a dandy little key of my own; I'll let

him in. (*Opens door, keeping all covered.* HAYDEN *goes over R.*)

BLAND (*Enters as* MAGEE *unlocks door, the latter keeping him covered.* BLAND *comes down R. to* HAYDEN. *Men all sit as* BLAND *enters.* BLAND *to* HAYDEN.) What's the matter, guv'nor?

HAYDEN. I don't know.

BLAND (*goes to* MAGEE, L.C., *as he recognizes him*). That's him, the man I told you about. He locked me in!

MAGEE. Oh, hello! Are you back again? I thought you jumped out of town.

BLAND (*over to* CARGAN *at table—* MAGEE *goes over R.C.*). Did you get it all right?

CARGAN. No; he's got it.

BLAND. What? (*Rushes over to* MAGEE.) Give me that money!

MAGEE (*covering* BLAND *with gun*). Say, I killed a man once for hollering at me. (BLAND *backs away to L.* PETERS *comes downstairs to L. above table. To* MYRA, *as she advances slowly to C.*) Ah, here we are! Mr. Hayden, although I think you are getting a shade the best of it, this young lady claims to be your wife.

HAYDEN. What! (*Over to* MYRA, C.) You claim what?

MYRA. Go on, holler your head off, Grandpa! (*As she strolls languidly over R. to fireplace.*) It's music to my ears to hear an old guy squawk. (*Sits in chair in front of fire.* HAYDEN *goes to* BLAND, L.C.)

BLAND (*waves* HAYDEN *away.* HAYDEN *goes upstage.* BLAND *crosses to* MAGEE, *R.C.*). What are you going to do with that money?

MAGEE (*goes up around* BLAND *and up R.C., keeping all covered*). I haven't got the money. (*All turn and look at him in amazement.*) It's on its way to Reuton. Miss Norton will see that it is placed in safe and proper hands directly she arrives at the office of the Reuton *Daily Star*.

CARGAN. The *Daily Star!* We're gone! (*To* MAGEE.) Where did Mrs. Rhodes go?

MAGEE. Out of your life forever, Cargan; she's got your number. (CARGAN *lowers his head without speaking. Pause, then* MAGEE *gets chair for* BLAND *and places it R.C.*) Sit down there. (BLAND *pays no attention.*) Did you hear me? Sit! (BLAND *sits slowly and sulkily.*) Sit down, Hermy. Come on, that's a nice ghost, go on. (PETERS *sits above table.* MAGEE *places chair for* HAYDEN.) Sit down, Hayden.

HAYDEN. I don't care to sit down, sir.

MAGEE. Do as you're told; sit down.

HAYDEN. Confound it, sir, do you know that I'm the president of the Reuton-Asquewan Railway Company?

MAGEE. I wouldn't care if you were president of the National League. Sit down! (HAYDEN *sits, indignant.*

MAGEE *sits in chair, front of switch board, facing all and covering them with gun.*) Now we're all going to stay right here till that phone bell rings and I get word that Miss Norton is safe and sound in Reuton. That may mean three hours or it may mean six hours; but we're all going to stay right here together, no matter how long it takes; so get comfortable and sit as easy as you can. (*All move uneasily.*)

CARGAN (*to* MAX, *after a pause*). So you tried to cross me, eh? The chances are I'll kill you for this.

BLAND (*after a pause, looking at* HAYDEN). I'm afraid I made a mistake in bringing you up here, guv'nor.

HAYDEN (*after a slight pause*). You're always making mistakes, you damned blockheaded fool!

MAX (*after a pause*). I'm sorry I got you into this, Myra. (*No reply from her.*) Oh, Myra, I say I'm sorry I got you into this.

MYRA (*turns and looks at* MAX). Oh, go to hell!

PETERS (*after a slight pause*). I hope to God you're all sent to prison for life!

MAGEE (*after a pause*). This is going to be a nice, pleasant little party; I can see that right now. (*After three counts, ring curtain.*)

SLOW CURTAIN

ACT TWO

The curtain rises on the same situation. After curtain is up, there is silence for about six seconds, then the clock is heard striking two.

HAYDEN *takes out his watch and looks at it. All squirm and look at each other impatiently.*

MAGEE. Two o'clock. We've been sitting here over twenty minutes already. Say, Hermy, you'd better put another log on the fire. (PETERS *crosses to fireplace, puts a log on the fire, looks closely at* MYRA *in front of fireplace, then goes back to former position and sits.*) I think someone ought to say something. Come on, let's start a conversation. Things are getting awfully dull.

HAYDEN (*gets up after a short pause and goes toward* MAGEE). This is all damned nonsense! I refuse to stay here another minute.

MAGEE (*coolly, and without moving*). Sit down, Hayden. I'm very sorry to inconvenience you in this way, but it's necessary that you should stay here and keep us company; so sit down before I shoot you down! That's a good little president. (HAYDEN *sits sulkily.*) That's it. Now, let me see, what can we talk about to kill the monotony and keep things sort of lively? I have it! Let's all tell each other where we got our keys to Baldpate. (*All move uneasily.*) What do you think of the idea? (*No reply.*) No? Well, I'll start the ball rolling, then perhaps we'll all 'fess up. I brought a letter from the man who owns the inn to the caretaker, giving him instruc-tions to turn the key over to me. That's how I got mine. Next? (*Pause. No one speaks.*) No? Big secrets, eh? (*Laughs.*) By George! that's funny. Let's see, how many keys are there? I had the first, Bland the second, Miss Norton the third, our friend the ghost the fourth, this young lady had the fifth, and, if I'm not mistaken, you had the sixth key, Mr. Cargan. Hayden doesn't count —he had Bland's key. Six keys to Baldpate so far. I wonder if there are any more.

PETERS (*after a pause*). There are seven keys to Baldpate. (*All turn and look at* PETERS *in surprise.*)

MAGEE. Seven! How do you know?

PETERS. The old man told me the day before he died. Mine's the original—all the others are imitations. (*All turn from him in disgust.*)

MAGEE. Seven keys, eh? *More* company expected. More melodrama, I suppose. Where did you get your key, Bland?

BLAND *and* MAGEE (*together*). None of your damned business!

MAGEE (*laughs*). I knew you were going to say that. How about you,

Mr. Cargan? Perhaps you'll be good enough to throw some light on the key subject. Where did you get yours?

CARGAN. I wouldn't tell you if my life was at stake.

MAGEE. Well, perhaps the young lady will be good enough to inform me where her key came from? (*All turn and look at* MYRA.)

MYRA (*turns and faces men*). I've no objections.

MAX (*pleadingly*). Myra, please!

MYRA (*pointing to* MAX). He gave the key to me. (*All turn and look at* MAX.)

CARGAN (*to* MAX). Where did you get a key to Baldpate?

MAX. I can't tell you, Mr. Mayor; I've sworn never to tell.

CARGAN (*to* MYRA). I suppose he also gave you the combination to the safe.

MYRA. He did.

MAX (*pleadingly*). Myra!

MYRA. Oh, shut up! You never were anything but a cry baby! You've got me into a pretty mess! Do you think I'm going to sit here like a fool and not pay you back when I've got the chance to do it? (*Gets up and faces men. They all stare at her.*) I'll tell you the whole scheme. I was to come here and make off with the package, and Cargan was to follow and find it gone. We were to meet tomorrow and divide the money equally.

CARGAN (*turns on* MAX). You rat! (MAX *turns from* CARGAN *in hang-dog fashion.*)

MYRA. His excuse to Cargan for the disappearance of the money was going to be to accuse Bland of never having put it there. (*Points to* BLAND *at mention of his name.*)

BLAND. What! (*Starts toward L.*)

MAGEE. Sit down, Bland. (BLAND *hesitates, then sits.*)

BLAND (*turning to* HAYDEN). Do you hear that, guv'nor? He was going to accuse me of stealing the money.

CARGAN (*to* MAX). You mark my words, I'm going to kill you for this!

BLAND (*to* CARGAN). Where did you get a key to Baldpate, Cargan? You told me you couldn't get in here unless I met you and unlocked the door.

(CARGAN *looks embarrassed, but does not reply.*)

MYRA. I can explain that. (*All look toward her.*) He was to meet you here tomorrow morning at nine o'clock. Am I right?

BLAND. That's right; I made the appointment over the phone.

MYRA. Well, the plan was to steal in here in the dead of night and take the money. He fully intended to keep his appointment here tomorrow morning, however, and appear just as much surprised as you would have been when you discovered the safe empty and the package gone. In other words, he was going to cross not only you, but Hayden and everyone else connected with the bribe. He tried to cross you—(*points to* BLAND)—and Lou Max tried to double-cross him. (*Points to* CARGAN. *Laughs and sits.*) If I hadn't been interrupted by our friend here —(*nods her head in* MAGEE's *direction*)—I'd have gotten the money and *triple* crossed the whole outfit!

BLAND *and* HAYDEN. What!

MYRA. Yes, that was my intention. Scruples are a joke when one is dealing with crooks.

CARGAN (*starts up*). Who's a crook?

MAGEE. Sit down, Cargan.

CARGAN (*infuriated*). Do you think I'll stand to be——

MAGEE (*sternly*). Sit down, I tell you! I'm the schoolteacher here. Be a good little mayor and sit down. (CARGAN *sits.*)

MYRA (*sneeringly, after a slight pause*). Why, you're not even clever crooks. You trusted Max, and Max trusted me. (*Laughs.*) A fine chance either one of you had if ever I had gotten hold of that money!

HAYDEN (*to* BLAND, *after thinking a moment*). Who is this woman?

BLAND. I don't know.

CARGAN (*turns to* HAYDEN). Her name is Thornhill. Don't believe a word she says, Hayden; her oath isn't worth a nickel. She's a professional blackmailer, pure and simple.

HAYDEN (*to* MYRA). Is this true?

MYRA. I never heard of a pure and simple blackmailer, did you? (*Laughs.*) So far as my word is concerned, I fancy it will carry as much weight as the word of a crooked politician or the word of his man "Friday," whom he knows to be an ex-convict.

MAX (*starts up*). What!

MAGEE. Sit down, Maxy; it's just getting good. (MAX *slinks into his chair.*)

HAYDEN (*to* BLAND, *who looks at him*). Fine people you've introduced me to, you lunk-headed idiot!

BLAND. Well, what are you blaming me for? You wanted the deal put through, didn't you? After this you can do your own crooked work. I'm not anxious to get mixed up in a thing of this kind. You've got a fine nerve to go after me.

HAYDEN (*gets up*). How dare you talk to your employer in such a manner!

BLAND. Oh, sit down! (HAYDEN *sits.*) What do you think I care for this job? I told you to stay out of the deal—that it was wrong. You know well enough that it's only cheating the city of Reuton out of its rights. If this thing ever comes to light, we're all lucky if we don't spend five or six years in a stoneyard! I tell you right now, if it comes to a show-down, I'm going to make a clean breast of the whole affair. I don't care who I send away, so long as I can save myself. You needn't think you can get me in a fix like this and have me keep my mouth shut. No, sir; I'm going to tell the truth, and I don't care a damn who suffers, so long as I get away.

MYRA (*laughs*). One of our best little squealers!

BLAND (*to* MYRA). Well, you squealed, didn't you?

MYRA. Sure, I'm with you, Cutey! I'm going to scream my head off all over the place. (*All show alarm.*)

CARGAN (*to* MAX, *after a pause*). So you tried to cross me, eh?

MAX. Certainly I tried to cross you. Why shouldn't I? You're around crossing everybody, ain't you? (*Rises.*) I've stood for your loud talk long enough, Cargan. I've been wanting to call you for the last two years. You're a great big bluff, that's all you are, and I'm going to get even for that punch you took at me, do you hear? Now you shoot any more of that killing stuff at me, and I'll go after you like a wild bear! You're never going to kill anybody, you haven't got the nerve; but I have, and the next bluff you make at me will be your last! (*Sits.*) It's your fault I'm mixed up in this affair, and the best thing you can do is to get me away clean, do you understand? (*Smashes table with fist. Pause, then looks at* HAYDEN.) You didn't think you were going to get that franchise for two hundred thousand, did you, Hayden? Why, this man would have bled you for half a million before the bill went through, and then held you up for hush money besides. I know what I'm talking about. He was going to rob you, Hayden, and I dare him to call me a liar! (*All look at* CARGAN,

who swallows the insult in fear of MAX's attitude.)

HAYDEN (*after a pause*). Cargan, is it true that you were going to rob me of this money?

CARGAN (*turns to* HAYDEN, *after a slight pause*). Well, if you want to know—yes, that's what I was going to do, rob you; just what you deserve. You were trying to rob the city, weren't you? You're just as much a thief as I am. If I'm a crook, it's your kind that has made me so— you, with your rotten money, tempting men to lie and steal! (*Settles back in his chair.*) Big corporations such as yours are the cause of corrupt politics in this country, and you're just the kind of a sneak that helps build prisons that are filled with the poor devils that do your dirty work. You're worse than a crook—you're a maker of crooks. (*Turns to* HAYDEN, *leans forward and points at him.*) But I promise you, Hayden, that if I go up for this, you'll go with me! It's your fault that I entered into this thing, and, by Gad! I'll get even if I have to lie over a Bible and swear your life away! (*Turns, facing audience.*) Rob you! Humph! You've got a hell of a gall to yell about being robbed, you have!

PETERS (*after slight pause*). I hope the prison catches fire and you're all burned to a crisp!

MAGEE (*laughs*). You know, my suggestion was to start a conversation, not a rough house.

HAYDEN (*after a slight pause*). This woman who took the money—who is she?

MYRA. A newspaper reporter.

BLAND. On the *Daily Star*.

CARGAN. The sheet that has fought me ever since I've been in office. They've got me this time, sure!

MAX (*after a pause, looking nervously at* MAGEE). How much longer are you going to keep us here?

MAGEE. That's for the telephone to say. I'll release you as soon as I'm sure Miss. Norton is safe and sound in Reuton. (*All turn toward* MAGEE, *surprised.*)

BLAND. Then you're not going to turn us over to the police?

MAGEE. Certainly not. Why should I? (*Movement of relief from all.*)

PETERS (*gets up*). Because they're a lot of crooks. (*All turn toward* PETERS.) Oh, how I'd love to be on the jury!

MAGEE. Sit down, Hermy. I need a little target practice, and remember, there's no law against killing ghosts! (PETERS *sits.*)

HAYDEN. There's no train to Reuton till five o'clock. That means we must stay here till six, eh?

MAGEE. I'm afraid so, unless they make it by automobile from Asquewan. It means several hours at the best, so you might as well be patient; you've got a long wait. (*All move uneasily.*)

MYRA (*cuddling up in her chair*). Me for my beauty sleep! Good night. (*Short pause, then phone rings. All start and stare at it.* MAGEE *gets up and stops buzzer.*)

MAX. She couldn't have made it as quick as that. It's over an hour by automobile.

MAGEE (*keeps them all covered with gun*). Answer that phone, please, Miss Thornhill. (MYRA *gets up and goes to phone.* MAGEE *backs upstage.*) I'm going to keep looking straight ahead of me tonight. Hurry, please. Give me the message as you get it. I'll tell you what to say if it requires an answer.

MYRA (*at phone, in a bored tone*). Hello! . . . Yes, Baldpate Inn. . . . Yes, I know who you mean. Just a moment. (*To* MAGEE.) Someone wants to talk to you.

MAGEE. Get the name.

MYRA (*in phone*). Hello! who is this, please? . . . Oh, yes. . . . Very well, I'll tell him. (*Turns to* MAGEE.) Miss Norton.

MAGEE. Say that it is impossible for me to turn my back long enough to come to the phone, and that you will take the message and repeat it to me as you get it.

MYRA (*in phone.* MAGEE *backs up R.C.*). It is impossible for him to turn his back long enough to come to the phone. You are to give me the message and I am to repeat it to him as I get it. . . . You're talking from the Commercial House in Asquewan. . . . You missed the package of money five minutes ago . . . (*All turn.*) You either dropped it in the inn before you left, or else lost it while hurrying down the mountain. . . . Search the inn thoroughly. (*Pause, while all look around room.*) Ask him whether or not you should notify the police. (*All show fear.*) You're nearly crazy, and don't know which way to turn. . . . Just a moment. (*Turns and looks at* MAGEE.) Well, what shall I say?

MAGEE (*looks around at all, then answers, after a pause*). Say to hold the wire.

MYRA (*in phone*). Hold the wire, please. (*Gets up and goes toward chair R.*)

HAYDEN. The money lost!

CARGAN. Thank God, there goes their evidence!

MAX. Who ever heard of losing two hundred thousand dollars!

BLAND. Can't be done outside of Wall Street. Surest thing you know, she's holding out.

MAGEE (*smiles*). You're a quick thinker, Miss Thornhill.

MYRA (*turns to* MAGEE). What do you mean?

MAGEE. That I don't believe you got that message at all.

MYRA (*shrugs her shoulders indifferently*). Very well; she's on the wire—see for yourself. (*Sits in chair in front of fire.*)

MAGEE. Come here, Hermy.

PETERS. My name's not Henry; my name's Peters.

MAGEE. Well, whatever it is, come here. (PETERS *goes up to* MAGEE, *up R.*) I know you don't like anybody in this room any better than I do, so I'm going to take a chance on you. Take this gun and guard that door until I get this message, and you kill the first man or woman that makes a move, do you understand?

PETERS (*vindictively*). I'd like to kill them all!

MAGEE. Don't shoot unless you have to. (*He hands* PETERS *the gun and goes to phone.*) Hello!

PETERS. Damn you, Cargan, I've got you at last!

(PETERS *goes toward* CARGAN *and is grabbed by* HAYDEN. MYRA *screams and jumps up.* BLAND *springs on* MAGEE *and struggles with him.* MAX *rushes over to* R., *and the two overpower* MAGEE *at phone. When* HAYDEN *grabs* PETERS, CARGAN *rushes over and struggles with* PETERS, *wresting gun from him.*)

MAX (*to* MAGEE). Take it easy, young fellow; you haven't got a chance.

BLAND. We've got him!

CARGAN (*after wrenching gun from* PETERS, *he hits him a blow, knocking him down*). What do you think of that? (BLAND *and* MAX *are* R., *each holding* MAGEE *by the arms.* PETERS *is on the floor* C., CARGAN *standing over him, with gun.* HAYDEN *is* L., *looking on.* CARGAN *to* PETERS.) So you wanted to take a shot at me, eh? (*Kicks* PETERS.) Get up! (PETERS *gets up in fear.* CARGAN *backs upstage slightly.*) Put them both up in the room where he put us, and lock the door.

BLAND. They can make a getaway from the window, Cargan; I did it myself.

CARGAN. There's no window in that room; it's a linen closet. Put them up there. (*He backs upstage, gun in hand.* PETERS *starts upstairs.*)

MAGEE (*to* CARGAN, *as he comes to C. on way to stairs*). What's the idea, Cargan?

CARGAN (*backing up C. and pointing gun*). Go on, I'm the school-teacher now—do as you're told. (HAYDEN *goes to extreme L. as* PETERS *and* MAGEE *go upstairs, followed by* MAX. BLAND *goes R., below phone.* CARGAN *speaks next lines to* MYRA *with his back to her.*) Get on that phone, Miss Thornhill, and tell that woman not to notify the police. Say that she is to return here at once, and see what she says.

(MYRA *goes to phone.* MAGEE *and* MAX *are now on landing.* PETERS *is standing at door of room L. on balcony.*)

MYRA (*in phone*). Hello! . . . Yes. . . . Why, the message is that you are not to notify the police of the loss. Say nothing to anyone, but return here at once. . . . That is the message. . . . Yes, good-by. (*Hangs up receiver.*)

CARGAN (*to* MYRA, *still watching* MAGEE). All right.

MYRA (*rising from switchboard*). As quick as she can get here, she says. (*Goes down R. to chair.*)

MAGEE (*stops on landing as he hears phone conversation*). What are you going to do, Cargan?

CARGAN. Never mind; I'm running things now. Get in there! (PETERS *exits into room L. on balcony.*)

MAGEE. You harm that girl, and I'll get you if it's the last act of my life!

CARGAN. I've read that kind of talk in books.

MAGEE. I write books of that kind, but I'm talking real talk now!

MAX (*to* MAGEE). Go on, get in there.

(MAGEE *goes upstairs and exits into room L.* MAX *locks door and comes to foot of stairs.* BLAND *has gone L.* CARGAN *puts gun in his pocket and comes down C.*)

HAYDEN (*over to* CARGAN *at C.*). Now what's the move, Cargan?

CARGAN. We're going to get that money if she's got it on her.

BLAND. You don't think she's fool enough to bring it back with her if she's trying to get away with it, do you?

HAYDEN. What are you going to do with it if you find it on her, Cargan?

CARGAN. Keep it, of course.

HAYDEN. It's my money.

CARGAN. Our agreement holds good. You people will get the franchise. Don't worry.

HAYDEN. Why, you've just openly declared that you were going to rob me of the money.

CARGAN. Oh, because I was mad clean through. Wasn't I being accused right and left? I didn't mean a word I said, Hayden. I don't even know now what I said. (*Pats* HAYDEN *ingratiatingly on the shoulders, then goes up* C., *looking up at room* L.)

HAYDEN (*goes to* BLAND, *who is below table* L.). What do you think, Bland?

(CARGAN *and* MAX *come downstage to* C.)

BLAND. Don't ask me; you bawled me out once tonight; that's enough!

CARGAN. I haven't forgotten what you said to me, Mr. Max.

MAX. I don't want you to forget it. I want you to remember it all your life. (*As* CARGAN *reaches for gun.*) I wouldn't care if you had six guns on you. Cut out that wild talk; I ain't going to listen to it any more. Why, you're nothing but a cheap coward, Cargan! (CARGAN *looks at* MAX *a moment, then turns upstage, cowed.* MAX *crosses to* MYRA, R.) So you tried to double-cross me, eh?

MYRA (*turns and faces* MAX). Why, certainly! Who are you?

MAX. Why, damn you, I—— (*Raises his hand to strike* MYRA, *who shrinks away.*)

BLAND (*crossing quickly to* C.). Here, wait a minute, Max; nothing like that while I'm around.

MAX (*turns to* BLAND). Maybe you want some of it? Why, I—— (*Raises his hand to strike* BLAND.)

BLAND (*grabs* MAX's *arm and throws it back*). Now behave yourself. The same speech you just made to Cargan goes for me. I want you to cut out this wild talk. I'm not going to listen to any more of it. I'll put you on your back if you make another bluff at me!

HAYDEN (*goes toward* MAX *and* BLAND C.). Gentlemen, gentlemen, please! (MAX *and* BLAND *look each other in the eye for a moment, then* MAX *goes up* R., *near safe.*)

BLAND (*turns to* HAYDEN *after* MAX *has gone up* R.). You keep out of this, Hayden; you'll get all you're looking for if you don't. (*Raises his hand to* HAYDEN *as if to strike.*)

HAYDEN. Put it down! Put it down, do you hear me? What do you mean by raising your hand to me? Why, damn me, for two pins I'd take and wipe up the floor with you! I can whip a whole army of cowards like you! Now get away from me! Get away from me before I knock you down! (BLAND, *surprised at* HAYDEN's *attitude, goes up to* C. *door, after staring at* HAYDEN *a moment.* HAYDEN *goes to* MYRA R. MAX *goes to safe and begins working combination.*) Now, madam, what do you mean by claiming to be my wife? I demand an explanation.

MYRA (*turns quickly and angrily on* HAYDEN). Now let me tell you something, old man. You can scare these three little boys, but I don't want you to annoy me, because I've got a nasty temper; so go on, get away before I lose it!

(HAYDEN *stares at* MYRA, *dumfounded, then goes quickly to* L.

MYRA *seats herself in chair after* HAYDEN *turns from her.* MAX, *by this time, has worked combination of safe, and at this point the door flies open. He grabs a gun from safe and slams door shut.* CARGAN, *who has been standing at foot of stairs looking up at room L., turns quickly as he hears the door slam and crosses quickly to R.C., catching* MAX *at safe door.* BLAND *crosses* CARGAN *to L.C.*)

CARGAN (*pulling his gun*). Get away from that safe! What are you doing there?

MAX (*flashes revolver.* MYRA *rises and stands L. of chair and below it*). Oh, you needn't be afraid. I ain't going to do anything, only I—— (MAX *has come in front of desk while speaking above lines, and now takes deliberate aim at* MYRA *and shoots. She screams and drops into chair.*)

BLAND (*runs to* MYRA). God!

CARGAN (*crosses to L. of* MAX). What's the matter, Max? Have you gone crazy? (*Puts gun in his pocket.*)

HAYDEN (*over to R. of* MAX, *looking toward* MYRA). Now we're in for it. Is she hurt?

MAX (*down L. of* HAYDEN). I couldn't help it; it was an accident! I didn't mean it, I tell you!

(MAGEE *raps on door upstairs. All look up.*)

MAGEE (*from upstairs*). What's wrong down there? (*Raps again.*) What's happened? (*All stand rigid, staring.*)

BLAND (*in a low voice*). Put out the lights.

(CARGAN *tiptoes upstage and turns out bracket lights, leaving only the reflection of burning logs on* MYRA's *face, then tiptoes back to C.*)

HAYDEN. Anything serious, Bland?

BLAND. You're a damn good shot, Max; you got her, all right! (*Feeling* MYRA's *pulse.*)

CARGAN. Don't say that! (*Backs away to L.C.*)

HAYDEN. It can't be possible!

BLAND. It's all over—she's gone! (*Drops her hand, then turns her chair around to R.*)

MAX (R.C., *wild-eyed*). But I didn't mean it, I tell you—it was an accident!

BLAND. You lie!

CARGAN. I saw you take aim.

HAYDEN. So did I.

MAX (*pleadingly*). No, no, don't say that! It isn't so! Before Heaven, I swear it was an accident!

(MAGEE *pounds on door upstairs.*)

HAYDEN, CARGAN, *and* BLAND (*to* MAX. HAYDEN *is L. of* MAX). Ssh! (*All look up in direction of door.*)

MAGEE (*from room R.*). Tell me what the matter is down there.

CARGAN (*goes to foot of stairs and calls up*). Everything's all right— nothing wrong.

MAGEE. I know better! Open this door! (*Pounds on door.*)

BLAND. Give me a hand, Cargan, and we'll get her out of here. (MAX *and* HAYDEN *go up C.*)

CARGAN (*over to* BLAND). Where do you mean?

BLAND (*pointing to room R. on balcony*). Up in that room. Come on, hurry up! (CARGAN *assists* BLAND *in lifting* MYRA *to the latter's shoulders.* BLAND *starts for stairs, carrying* MYRA; CARGAN *following with her wraps, et cetera.*)

MAX (*R.C. as* BLAND *passes with* MYRA). I didn't mean it, I tell you! I'm innocent! Why, I wouldn't harm a fly!

HAYDEN (*goes R.C. to* MAX *and silences him roughly*). Keep quiet, you damn fool! Do you want the world to hear you?

(MAGEE *resumes pounding on the door. Just as* BLAND *and* CARGAN *get to first landing,* MAGEE *kicks the door open from the inside, and in the breakaway the lock falls to the floor.* MAGEE *enters on balcony as the door flies open,* PETERS *following him out.* MAGEE *comes to first landing and follows* BLAND *and* CARGAN *up opposite stairs a few steps.* PETERS *remains outside door R.* BLAND *and* CARGAN *stop only a second on first landing, and then continue on up the stairs during following lines.*)

MAGEE. What's happened?

CARGAN. She's fainted, that's all.

MAGEE. Where are you taking her?

CARGAN. You'll keep out of this, young fellow, if you know what's good for you! (BLAND *and* CARGAN *exit into room R.,* CARGAN *closing door.*)

MAGEE (*has followed them on balcony. Watches them exit with* MYRA, *then rushes downstairs to* HAYDEN *C.*). Who fired that pistol shot?

MAX (*R.—blurts out*). It was an accident!

HAYDEN (*quickly to* MAX, *R.C.*). Shut up!

MAGEE. See here, Hayden, if there's anything wrong here, you can't afford to mix up in it; you're too big a man.

MAX (*hysterically*). I didn't mean to kill her. I'm not responsible! It was an accident.

MAGEE (*R.C.*). Oh, we have a murder case on our hands—is that the idea?

HAYDEN (*R. of* MAGEE). I don't know; but whatever it is, we're all in this thing together. We must frame a story and stick to it, do you understand?

MAGEE. No, I don't understand.

HAYDEN. We must claim suicide.

MAX (*going toward C.—*HAYDEN *goes up C.*). That's it! She killed herself! I was an eyewitness—she killed herself!

MAGEE. Do you think I'd enter into such a dastardly scheme? (BLAND *and* CARGAN *enter and stand on bal-*

cony C., listening.) No! If it's murder, there's the murderer—(*points to* MAX, *crosses to him R., then back to L.C.*)—self-confessed. But you're all as guilty as this man—every one of you. It's the outcome and result of rotten politics and greed. I'll swear to every word that's been uttered here tonight. I've had my ear against the crack of that door for the last five minutes. I overheard every word that passed between you. I'll tell the story straight from the shoulder. You can't crawl out of it, gentlemen, with your suicide alibi. It's murder in the first degree, and I'm going to help make you pay the penalty!

(HAYDEN *and* MAX *stand staring at him.* HAYDEN *goes up R., near desk.* CARGAN *and* BLAND, *after a bit of pantomime, come downstairs,* CARGAN *goes to L. of* MAGEE *and* BLAND *to R. of him.* MAX *is R.*)

CARGAN (*after a pause—L. of* MAGEE). I'm afraid you're in wrong here, young fellow.

(PETERS *sneaks across balcony to R. of it and stands listening to next few speeches, hidden behind post R.*)

CARGAN. I'm sorry for you. From the bottom of my heart I pity you. (*Takes stage a little L.* MAGEE *does not reply; simply looks at* CARGAN, *then at* BLAND.)

BLAND (*after a pause*). She's dead—you killed her, all right!

(MAGEE *looks* BLAND *in the eye, then at* CARGAN. *The latter turns upstage after a pause, then crosses down to back of chair L.* MAGEE *crosses to* HAYDEN, *who comes down C.*)

HAYDEN (*comes down C. to R. of* MAGEE). Better plead insanity, old man; it's the only chance you've got.

(MAGEE *stares at* HAYDEN, *then crosses over to R. and looks* MAX *straight in the eye.* MAX *stares back at him.*)

MAX (*after a pause*). Bad business, this carrying guns. Who was the woman—your wife?

(PETERS *exits into room on balcony R., closing door.* BLAND *is L.C.*)

MAGEE (*turns, sees the three staring at him, smiles and comes C.*). No, no, gentlemen! You can't get away with it! It's good melodrama, but it's old stuff. I know every trick of the trade. I've written it by the yard. You can't intimidate me. I won't be third-degreed. You work very well together, but it's rough work, and it isn't going to get you anything. Besides, you forget I have a witness in Peters, the hermit. (*All turn and look up at room L.*)

CARGAN (*front of table L.—looks up at room, then says to* BLAND). Get him. Bring him down. (*Goes to foot of stairs as* BLAND *goes upstairs.*)

BLAND (*runs up and looks into room L., then comes out on balcony*). He's gone!

(HAYDEN *looks at* MAX, *then back to* BLAND.)

CARGAN. Gone! Where?

BLAND (*comes quickly down the stairs*). He probably found a way; he knows the place better than we do. (*Goes R. of* MAGEE.)

CARGAN (*comes down to* MAGEE, *R.C.*). I saw you when you fired; you shot to kill.

BLAND (*R. of* MAGEE). I tried to knock the gun from your hand, but I was too late. (*Goes upstage.*)

HAYDEN (*R. of* BLAND). I didn't witness the shooting myself, but I turned just in time to grab you before you got away.

MAX (*R.*). But you shouldn't have choked her; that was the brutal part of it.

MAGEE (*starts for* MAX, *who backs away to fireplace, frightened*). Why, you dog, I——

(CHIEF KENNEDY *appears outside door and pounds on it three times. All on stage stop abruptly and look toward door, holding the picture for a repeat of the pounding.*)

CARGAN (*loudly*). Who's there?

KENNEDY (*yells through door from outside*). Open this door in the name of the law!

MAX. The police!

HAYDEN (*quickly to* MAX). Keep quiet! (*Gets behind desk.*)

BLAND (*to* CARGAN). You'd better let them in, Cargan.

MAGEE (*starts for door*). I'll unlock the door.

CARGAN. No, you don't; I'll attend to it! (*Crosses* MAGEE, *goes up to door and unlocks it.* KENNEDY *steps in, watching* CARGAN *as the latter locks*

the door. As CARGAN *is about to put key in his pocket,* KENNEDY *speaks.* BLAND *has gone L., above table, when* CARGAN *goes up to door.*)

KENNEDY (*up L.C., just inside door*). Here, wait a minute! I'll take that key. I'll take that gun I saw you stick in your pocket, too.

BLAND (*takes a couple of steps toward* KENNEDY *up L.*). What authority have you?

KENNEDY (*comes down L.C. to* BLAND). Close your trap! I'm Chief Kennedy of the Asquewan Falls Police Headquarters—that's my authority!

CARGAN (*down to Kennedy, pointing to* BLAND). It's all right, Chief; he's all right.

KENNEDY. Where's the light switch?

MAGEE. Up there to your left.

KENNEDY (*goes up L. of door and turns on lights, then comes downstage L. of* CARGAN, *recognizing him*). Hello, Mr. Mayor! What are you doing here?

CARGAN. I can explain all that.

MAGEE (*pointing to* MAX). That man has a gun on him also. (HAYDEN *moves over toward L. slowly.*)

KENNEDY (*goes over R.C. and looks* MAGEE *over carefully*). Who are you? (CARGAN *crosses to L.C.*)

MAGEE. I'll tell you who I am at the proper time and place. You'd better get on your job quick here, Chief; there's something doing. Two of these men are carrying weapons, and two of them also have keys to that door. I'm telling you this to prevent a getaway.

KENNEDY. What are you trying to do, run the police department?

MAGEE. This is an important case, Chief. Thousands of dollars are involved, and a crime committed besides. I advise placing every man in this room under arrest immediately.

KENNEDY (*to* CARGAN). What's this all about, Mr. Mayor? (*All appear anxious.*)

CARGAN. He's four-flushing, Chief. He's stalling for a chance to break away.

KENNEDY. Don't be afraid; I've got men outside; nobody'll get away. (*Crosses* MAGEE *to* MAX *R., and looks at him closely.*) Lou Max, eh? Quite a crowd of celebrities. (*To* MAX.) You got a gun? (MAX *hands him his gun.*) What are you totin' this for? (*No reply from* MAX. *Chief turns and fans* MAGEE.) He's clean. (*Turns* MAGEE *upstage and crosses to* CARGAN.) I'm sorry to trouble you, Mr. Mayor, but I'll have to relieve you of that hardware. (CARGAN *hands* CHIEF *his gun.*) And the key, too, please. (CARGAN *hands* CHIEF *his key.*) I've come here to investigate, and I've got to do my duty. (*Crosses* CARGAN *over to* BLAND *L.C.*)

BLAND (*holding up his hands as* CHIEF *approaches him*). There's nothing on me.

KENNEDY (*fans* BLAND). Who's got the other key? He said there were two.

BLAND (*points to* HAYDEN). This gentleman.

KENNEDY (*goes to* HAYDEN *L., who hands the* CHIEF *his key*). Hello! Mr. Hayden. Humph! This is a real highbrow affair, isn't it? Well—— (*Smiles, goes up C. to R. of* CARGAN *and looks them all over.*) Come on. somebody open up. What's the big gathering all about?

MAX (*pointing to* MAGEE). He's got a key. Make him give it up.

KENNEDY (*to* MAGEE). Come on. (MAGEE *hands* CHIEF *his key.*) You got anything more to say?

MAGEE. I prefer to tell my story in the presence of witnesses. I insist upon the immediate arrest of everyone here, myself included.

HAYDEN. Don't mind him, Chief; he's a madman.

KENNEDY. Well, somebody telephoned police headquarters from here about two hours ago, and when we got on the wire Central said they'd hung up. We got a new connection, and asked if they'd called, and some woman said, "No, it was a mistake." We got to thinking it over at headquarters, and it didn't listen good, so we looked it up and found out that the call had been put in from Baldpate Inn; so I made up my mind to come here and investigate. Now, when I started up the mountain ten minutes ago the lights were on full blast, and all of a sudden they went out, and there was a pistol shot, too. Every one of my men heard the report, and we all agree it came from this direction. Now, what's it all about?

MAGEE. 'Twas I who called up police headquarters. (*All look at* MAGEE.)

KENNEDY. You! The sergeant said it was a woman's voice on the wire.

MAGEE. That was the second time when you called up, but I tried to get you first.

KENNEDY. What for?

MAGEE. I don't intend to tell my story until I'm under oath. I want every word I say to go on the court records. I charge these men with conspiracy and murder!

KENNEDY. What is this, Cargan?

CARGAN. The poor devil's gone mad, I guess. He shot and killed a woman a few minutes ago, and he's accused every man here of the crime.

KENNEDY. Murder, eh?

HAYDEN. Yes, cold-blooded murder.

KENNEDY (*to* MAGEE). Who was the woman you shot?

MAGEE. Don't let these men get away with this, Chief. I can prove my innocence. (*Pointing to* MAX.) There's the real murderer. These men know it as well as I do. They're accusing me in an attempt to save their own necks. They're afraid to tell the truth because this man is a squealer, and they know that a confession from him of a scheme to steal the right of way for a street-car franchise in Reuton will send them all to the state penitentiary. I can prove why I'm here tonight. Ask these men their reason for being here, and let's hear what they have to say.

(KENNEDY *looks from one to the other without speaking.*)

CARGAN. He's been raving like that for the last ten minutes, Chief.

KENNEDY (*to* MAGEE). What is your reason for being here?

MAGEE. I came here to write a book.

KENNEDY (*to* CARGAN). You're right; he's a lunatic, sure. (*To* CARGAN.) Who was the woman that telephoned to headquarters?

MAGEE. Miss Norton, of the Reuton *Star*.

KENNEDY. The Reuton *Star*, eh? (*To* CARGAN.) Is she the woman that was killed?

CARGAN. No; her name is Thornhill.

KENNEDY. Where is she?

CARGAN. In one of the rooms upstairs.

KENNEDY. Was there anybody else here besides you people?

MAGEE. Yes; Peters, the hermit.

KENNEDY. Another crazy man, eh?

BLAND. But he's disappeared.

KENNEDY. Well, he won't go far. (*Goes upstage and looks out of door.*) I've got the house surrounded. (*Coming downstage.*) I'll look the ground over before I send for the coroner. He won't be here till seven or eight o'clock. You people will have to stay here till he comes. (CARGAN, BLAND, *and* HAYDEN *sit near table* L. MAX *sits* R.) What room is she in? (*Looking up at balcony.*)

CARGAN (*gets up from table*). I'll show you, Chief. (*Starts toward stairs, leading the way, followed by the* CHIEF, HAYDEN, BLAND, *and* MAX *in order named. All look back at* MAGEE *as they go upstairs.*)

KENNEDY (*to* MAGEE, *when he gets on balcony*). Take my tip and don't try to get away, young fellow. One of those cops outside will blow your head off if you do.

MAGEE (*goes* L. *near foot of stairs as men go up*). You needn't be afraid. I'm going to stay right here, and I'm going to make sure these other men do until we're all taken into custody.

HAYDEN. It's a sad case, Chief.

KENNEDY. We're used to that. They generally go out of their minds after they shoot. Where is she?

CARGAN (*goes to door of room* R.). In here, Chief.

(CHIEF *exits into room, followed by* HAYDEN, BLAND, MAX, *and* CARGAN, *the latter closing the door. During the last few speeches* PETERS *has been peering through glass in dining-room door* L. *He now enters and goes quickly to* MAGEE C.)

PETERS. I carried the body from that room through the secret passage to the cellar.

MAGEE (*amazed*). What!

PETERS. I heard them accuse you of the crime. (*Backs toward door* L. *slowly.*) They'll never find the secret passage—(*laughs*)—and they'll never find the body! (*Laughs viciously.*)

MAGEE. What did you do that for, you damn fool? (*Door opens on balcony* R.)

PETERS. Hist! (*He points up at door* R. *on balcony.* MAGEE *looks up.* PETERS *exits hurriedly through door* L.)

(CARGAN *enters, wild-eyed, from room, runs downstairs and comes to* L.C. MAX *follows him down and goes to* R. HAYDEN *follows* MAX, *and comes down to* L.C. BLAND *follows* HAYDEN, *and comes to* R. *All the men show extreme fear.* MAGEE, *standing* C., *watches them.* KENNEDY *comes out on balcony, looks at people downstairs, then back at room for a moment, then out again at cue.*)

HAYDEN (*to* CARGAN, *who is front of table* L.). What do you make of this, Cargan?

CARGAN. The damn place is haunted!

MAX. She must have escaped by the window.

BLAND. How could a dead woman jump from the window? Besides, the windows are closed.

(*They all stand staring up at balcony.* KENNEDY *appears from room* R. *and closes door.*)

KENNEDY (*comes to* C. *of balcony and stands looking down at men*).

Say, what are you fellows trying to do, string me? (*Starts downstairs.*) You know I was born and brought up in New York City, even if I do live in Asquewan Falls. (*Comes down to C. and looks them all over.*)

HAYDEN. I can't understand it at all.

CARGAN. She was in that room ten minutes ago, Chief.

BLAND. I'll take a solemn oath on that.

MAX. My God, I'm going insane! (*Grabs chair to steady himself.*)

KENNEDY. Say, what the devil is this all about? (*Looks from one to the other.*) If you people think you can make a joke out of me, you're mistaken. I won't stand for it. Now come on, what's the answer?

MAGEE. It's no joke, Chief; there has been a murder committed here.

KENNEDY. Then where's the victim?

MAGEE. In the cellar.

BLAND, CARGAN, HAYDEN, *and* MAX. What!

KENNEDY. In the cellar?

MAGEE. If I'm not mistaken, that's where she was taken after the murder.

HAYDEN. You lie!

CARGAN. You know she was taken to that room. (*Points to room R. on balcony.*)

BLAND. You saw us carry her there.

MAX. Of course he did.

KENNEDY (*to* MAGEE). What are you trying to do, trap me in the cellar?

MAGEE. I tell you, Chief, you'll find the victim in the cellar. Then you can judge for yourself if I'm as crazy as these men claim me to be, or whether they've suddenly gone mad themselves.

KENNEDY (*blows his whistle*). I'll get at the bottom of this thing pretty quick! (*Rushes up to door, unlocks and opens it. Two cops enter, come to L. of stage up C. and await orders.* KENNEDY *locks door and goes to cops.*) Search the cellar of this place, and report to me here what you find—every nook and corner. And don't leave a thing unturned, understand? (*Cops salute.* MARY *appears outside door.*) Hurry up, then! (*Cops exit through door L.* KENNEDY *comes down C.*) If this thing is a practical joke, you'll all land in jail for it. I'm not going to be made the laughing stock of Asquewan Falls, I'll tell you that right now. (MARY, *who has been peering through door, opens it during this speech and enters.* KENNEDY *turns as door opens and goes upstage.*) Hello! Who's this?

MAGEE (*goes L. as* MARY *enters*). Miss Norton! (MARY *locks door and starts down L.C.*)

KENNEDY (*to* MARY). I'll take that key, please.

MARY (*hands* CHIEF *the key and goes to* MAGEE *L.C.*). Why are the police here?

(KENNEDY *goes down R.C. to* BLAND.)

MAGEE (*reassuring* MARY). It's all right.

KENNEDY (*to* BLAND). Who is this woman?

BLAND. She claims to be a newspaper reporter.

MAX. She's a thief; she stole a package of money!

KENNEDY. Whose money?

HAYDEN. My money.

CARGAN (L., *in front of table*). No, my money.

MAGEE. It's bribe money, Chief.

KENNEDY. Where is the money?

MARY (*turns and faces* CHIEF). The money's been lost.

BLAND, HAYDEN, MAX, *and* CARGAN. What!

KENNEDY. Say, what the hell are you people trying to do to me, anyway?

MAGEE (*to* MARY). Where did you lose it?

MARY (*to* MAGEE—KENNEDY *goes over, listening*). I don't know—somewhere between here and Asquewan. I searched every inch of the way from the bottom of the mountain to the top. It's gone, I'm afraid.

MAGEE. Where is Mrs. Rhodes?

MARY. She became too hysterical to return. I left her at the Commercial House in Asquewan.

KENNEDY. How much money was it?

MAGEE. Two hundred thousand dollars.

KENNEDY (*looks from one to the other*). Come on, cut out the kidding stuff! How much was it?

HAYDEN (L., *near table*). That's the exact amount the package contained, Chief—two hundred thousand dollars.

KENNEDY (*to* MARY). Where'd you get this money?

MAGEE. I gave it to her.

KENNEDY. Where did you get it?

MAGEE. From Mayor Cargan.

KENNEDY. Where did you get the money, Cargan? (*No reply from* CARGAN.)

MAGEE (*after a pause*). He took the money from that safe.

KENNEDY (*goes upstage a couple of steps, looks at safe, then comes back to C.*). How'd you open the safe, Cargan?

CARGAN. I didn't open the safe.

KENNEDY. Who did?

MAGEE. Peters, the hermit.

KENNEDY. Who put the money in the safe?

MAGEE. Bland. (*Points to* BLAND.) That man to your right.

KENNEDY (*over to* BLAND, R.C.). Where'd you get the money to put in the safe?

BLAND. From Mr. Hayden.

KENNEDY (*looks at* HAYDEN, *L.*). Is this true, Mr. Hayden?

HAYDEN. I refuse to answer for fear of incriminating myself.

KENNEDY (*over to* MAX, *R.*). What do you know about this, Max?

MAX. Don't ask me; I don't know. My brain's on fire—I'm going mad! (*Tugs at his collar, breathing hard.*)

KENNEDY (*comes to C. and looks them all over*). Huh! Hayden gave the money to Bland; Bland put the money in the safe; Peters opened the safe; Cargan took the money from Peters; this fellow took the money from Cargan and gave it to the newspaper reporter; she loses the money in the mountains; then somebody killed a woman and the corpse got up and walked away. And you expect me to believe this bunk, do you?

MARY (*to* MAGEE). What does he mean by saying that somebody killed a woman?

MAGEE. Don't worry; it's all right. (MARY *and* MAGEE *go up L., near foot of stairs.*)

COP (*off stage*). Come on, come on! Go on, get in there! (*He opens door L. and throws* PETERS *to C. of stage. The other* COP *follows them on.*) That's all we could find in the cellar, Chief.

KENNEDY. No dead bodies or packages of money?

COP. Nothing else, Chief. (*Goes up L. near door.*)

KENNEDY (*looks at* PETERS *and laughs*). Oh, it's you, is it, Peters? So that's where you hide, eh? In the cellar of Baldpate? Well, you'll have a nice room in the county jail to-morrow.

PETERS. Damn the police; I hate them!

KENNEDY (*throws* PETERS *to R.*). Go on, get over there! (*To* COPS *as he goes up to door.*) Guard the outside. (*As he goes up to door,* MARY *and* MAGEE *come down to L.C.* CHIEF *unlocks door. To* COPS.) And question anybody who passes up or down the mountain. (*Opens door.* COPS *exit.* CHIEF *locks door and comes downstage to* MARY.) You'll have to step upstairs, Miss. I've got a lot to say to these men here, and I'm not particular about my language when I'm on a case; so come on, step upstairs.

HAYDEN (*extreme L., near table*). I don't believe this girl lost the money, Chief.

KENNEDY. Well, I'll get the matron of the jail here and have her searched. If she's got anything on her we'll get it. (MARY *starts for stairs,* CHIEF *following her up.*) Go in one of those rooms till I call you. (MARY *is now on balcony C.* CHIEF *comes downstage to C.*) Who is the woman this girl says she left at the Commercial House?

CARGAN. Mrs. Rhodes. She's all right.

BLAND (*goes slightly toward* CARGAN). How do we know? Maybe they're working together.

CARGAN. That's enough, Bland.

KENNEDY (*as he goes toward phone all back up and watch him*). I'll call up the Commercial House and see if she's there. (*In phone.*) Hello! Get me 35, Central, quick. (MARY *exits into room R. on balcony.*) Ring me when you get it. (*Hangs up receiver and comes down to C.*) What's her name again?

MAGEE. Mrs. Rhodes. (MARY *screams off stage and rushes from room to balcony.*) What's the matter?

MARY (*screaming*). She's dead! Someone's killed her!

ALL. Who?

MARY (*hysterically*). That woman there in that room! This is terrible!

(KENNEDY *looks at* MAGEE. MAGEE *looks at* CARGAN. *All stand rigid, staring at each other for a moment; then* KENNEDY, CARGAN, BLAND, HAYDEN, *and* MAX *rush upstairs on balcony and cross to room R. As they pass in front of* MARY, *she backs up against windows and stands with arms outstretched against them.* PETERS *is standing R., laughing.*)

MAGEE (*goes over R. to* PETERS *quickly*). What did you do, bring her back to that room?

PETERS. Isn't that what you wanted me to do?

MAGEE. No, you blithering idiot! (*Turns and takes* MARY *in his arms as she runs to him.*)

MARY. Tell me who did this? How did it happen?

MAGEE. It's all right; take it easy.

(MAX, BLAND, CARGAN, *and* HAYDEN *enter from room R. in this rotation, all wild-eyed. They line up on balcony and keep their eyes glued to door of room.* KENNEDY *enters on balcony, also keeping his eyes fixed on room. He looks at men on balcony and then down at* MAGEE *and* MARY, *who stare up at him; then at* PETERS, *who is over R.*)

KENNEDY. Say, what are you people trying to do to me? (*To men on balcony, who are still staring at door.*) Go on, get downstairs where you belong. (*Four men come downstairs and go to former positions. Telephone rings.* KENNEDY *runs downstairs.*) Don't touch that phone! I'll answer it! (*Looks from one to the other suspiciously.*) Is this dump haunted, or is the joke on me? (*No one replies. The phone still rings.*) I'll soon find out! (*Goes to phone. All back up and watch him.*) Hello! . . . Yes, I called you. Say, listen, Charlie. This is Chief Kennedy talking. Is there a woman there by the name of Rhodes? She was. . . . She did, eh? How long ago? . . . I see. . . . What's that? . . . She asked you to mind a package for her till she got back? (*All look at one another, startled.*) Where have you got it? . . . In the safe? . . . Say, listen, Charlie. Call headquarters right away and get a man over there. Give him that package, and tell him to bring it up to Baldpate Inn as quick as he can. Understand? . . . Never mind, you do as I tell you. And listen. Tell them to guard the garage and the depot, and put all strangers under arrest, men and women. . . . I know what I'm doing, Charlie. You take orders from me. And listen. Get the coroner on the phone and tell him to get up here to Baldpate Inn in a rush. This is a case for him. . . . Don't lose any time now. Keep your mouth shut and get busy. (*Hangs up receiver and comes to C. All come forward.*) She left the hotel a quarter of an hour ago. She put the package in the hotel safe before she went. (*He looks them all over. They stand staring at each other.*) Humph! Somebody kills a woman—the victim disappears and then comes back! That's pretty good stuff!

MAGEE (*aside to* MARY, *R.C.*). How do you account for this?

MARY (*aside to* MAGEE). She must have stolen the money from me as we were running down the mountain. (*Whistle is heard outside door. All turn and look toward door.*)

KENNEDY. They've got somebody! (*Rushes up to door and unlocks it.* COP *enters.* CHIEF *locks door.*) What is it?

COP. A woman.

KENNEDY. Shoot her in. (*Unlocks door, opens it, and closes it as* COP *exits.*) Here comes the bird, I guess, that tried to fly away with the coin. (*Opens the door as* MRS. RHODES *appears. She enters and watches* KENNEDY *as he locks door.*)

MRS. RHODES (*turns, takes in situation, then to* CHIEF). What is the meaning of this?

KENNEDY (*up near door*). That's what I'm trying to find out.

MRS. RHODES (*goes to* MARY, *R.C.*). Is there any trace of the money?

(MARY *turns from her without replying.* MRS. RHODES *then turns and looks at men, who all give her a contemptuous look.* KENNEDY *comes downstage C., standing back of her.*)

HAYDEN (*crosses to L.C., between* CARGAN *and* KENNEDY). Are you going to have these women searched, Chief?

KENNEDY (*down L. of* MRS. RHODES). Maybe it won't be necessary. (*Looks intently at* MRS. RHODES *over her L. shoulder.*) We'll wait until we see what's in the package she left at the Commercial House. (MRS. RHODES *starts, regains her composure, then seeing all watching her, she turns and makes a dash for the door.* CHIEF *speaks as he follows her up.* HAYDEN *crosses back to L.*) No, you don't! Nobody leaves here until this whole thing has been cleared up and I find out who killed that woman.

MRS. RHODES (*turns, startled*). Killed a woman! (*Over to* CARGAN.) What does he mean? (CARGAN *turns from her without speaking. She goes to* MARY.)

MARY (*to* MRS. RHODES). You stole the money from me, didn't you? (MRS. RHODES *goes to* CARGAN *without replying to* MARY.)

CARGAN (*looks* MRS. RHODES *straight in the eye*). I'll never trust another woman as long as I live!

PETERS (*R.*). They're no good—they never were.

KENNEDY (*to* PETERS). Shut up! (*Comes to* MRS. RHODES *at C.*). Well, what have you got to say, missus?

MRS. RHODES (*after a pause*). Yes, I did steal the money.

(MARY *looks at* MAGEE; *others look at* MRS. RHODES.)

MRS. RHODES (*over to* CARGAN, *L.*). But I did it for you, Jim Cargan. I knew that if the story was ever made public you would be a ruined man. I knew the package of money was the evidence that would convict you. I intended to return it to Mr. Hayden and try to kill off the bribe and save you from disgrace. I did all this because I thought you cared, and what is my reward? You stand there ready to turn against me—to condemn me. Very well, now I'll turn! (*Turns to* KENNEDY.) Officer, these men have bargained to cheat the city of Reuton. I demand their arrest on the charge of conspiracy!

HAYDEN. It's a lie!

MAGEE. It's the truth, Chief, the absolute truth. This young lady and I will testify against these men and prove them guilty of conspiracy and murder.

MRS. RHODES. Murder!

KENNEDY. What have you got to say to this, Mr. Cargan?

CARGAN. Nothing at all—I'm through. (*Sits at table L.* BLAND *goes upstage, then crosses to above table L.*)

MAX. So am I. I can't stand this any longer; I'm going mad! (*Goes to* CHIEF. PETERS *takes chair* MAX *vacates. During following speech* MA-GEE *takes* MARY *up R.*) I want you to know the real truth. 'Twas I who killed that woman upstairs. I shot her down like a dog. I know that I haven't got a chance, but I don't want to be sent to the chair. I'll confess, I'll tell the truth, I'll turn state's evidence, anything—but, for God's sake, don't let them kill me! (*Kneels at* KENNEDY'S *feet.*)

KENNEDY (*to* MAX). Get up. (MAX *rises.* CHIEF *takes handcuffs from his pocket.*) Come on. You'll have to wear these, young fellow. (*Puts handcuffs on* MAX. MRS. RHODES *goes to foot of stairs.*)

BLAND (*throwing up hands*). There we go!

HAYDEN (*to* CARGAN). What are we going to do, Cargan?

CARGAN. No less than ten years, I'm afraid.

KENNEDY (*to* MAX). Go on, get over there. (*Pushes* MAX *over R., then goes upstage R. and down in circle.* MAX *takes* PETERS'S *chair.*)

MRS. RHODES (*goes to* MARY, *R.C.*). Can you ever forgive me?

MARY (*giving* MRS. RHODES *her hand*). I didn't understand—I do now. (*Both go to foot of stairs, crossing in front of* CHIEF.)

KENNEDY (*down to* MAGEE, *R.C.*). And you came here to write a book, eh?

MAGEE. That was the original idea.

KENNEDY. You know, I don't know yet whether you people are kidding me or not. (*All turn toward door as police whistle is heard.*) They've got somebody. (*Rushes up to door and unlocks it.* COP *enters. He closes door.*) Well, what now?

COP (*hands package to* CHIEF). A package brought to you by the police messenger. He says it's from the Commercial House. (*All start.*)

KENNEDY. Tell the messenger to hurry back and to tell the coroner to hurry up. (*Opens door.* COP *exits.* CHIEF *locks door and comes downstage a bit, a sickly smile on his face.*) Say, before I open this thing, I want to tell you something. If this turns out to be a bunch of cigar coupons, I'm going to smash somebody, sure. I won't stand to be strung, even if I am a small-town cop. (*Opens package and sees bills.*) Great Scott, it's the real thing! How much did you say was here?

MAGEE. Two hundred thousand dollars.

HAYDEN (*goes to* KENNEDY, C.). I'll take that money, please; it belongs to me.

CARGAN (*goes to* KENNEDY C.). No, it doesn't; it belongs to me.

MAGEE. You hold that money, Chief; it's the only real evidence of bribery we've got.

KENNEDY. Go away! (HAYDEN *goes upstage;* CARGAN *goes R. of chair at table;* MAGEE *goes C.*) You needn't tell me what to do; I know my business. (HAYDEN *crosses to L. of table.* KENNEDY *puts money in his pocket and goes to phone. As he does so, all on stage back up and watch him. In phone.*) Hello! Get me 13, Central. (*Wait.*) Hello! Is that you, Jane? . . . This is the Chief. I want to talk to my wife. (*Wait.*) Hello! Hello! Betty? . . . Listen, Betty; get this clear. Get some things together and get the children ready and take that five o'clock train to New York. . . . Never mind now, listen. When you get there, look up the railroads, and get on the first and quickest train that goes to Montreal. . . . Montreal. I'll be there waiting for you Thursday morning. . . . Don't ask a lot of questions; do as I tell you. . . . What are we going to do there? We're going to l i v e there. . . . Montreal. . . . I don't know. (*Turns to* MAGEE.) How the hell do you spell Montreal? (*No one replies.*) Listen; go to Canada—any part of it. I'll find you. . . . What? . . . Never mind the furniture; we're going to live in a palace. . . . Canada, that's all. . . . You do as I tell you. (*Gets up from phone and goes C., looking at the money. As he sees everyone staring at him, he puts it in his pocket.*)

MAGEE. What do you think you're going to do?

KENNEDY. You heard me, didn't you? I'm going to Canada.

PETERS. Canada! I hope to God you freeze to death!

MAGEE. You mean you're going to steal that money?

KENNEDY. Why shouldn't I steal it from a gang of crooks like this? It's one chance in a lifetime to get this much money. You don't suppose I'm going to pass it up when I've got it right here in my kick, do you? Not me! I'm going to have one hell of a time for the rest of my life and send my two boys to college!

BLAND (*over to* KENNEDY). Do you imagine we're going to stand by and let you get away with it?

KENNEDY (*whips out his gun and backs upstage a trifle. All but* BLAND *and* MAGEE *back away from him*). That's just what you're going to do, and I'm going to have my men keep you here all night until I get a damn good start!

(BLAND *knocks the gun from the* CHIEF's *hand.* MAGEE *grabs his arms and pins them behind him.* BLAND *gets a hold on his legs. Women scream and run halfway upstairs.*)

MAGEE. I've got him! Get that money!

PETERS (*rushes toward* KENNEDY, *yelling*). I'll get it! I'll get it!

KENNEDY (*yelling from the time he is grabbed*). Let me go, do you hear! Let me go!

PETERS (*grabs money from* CHIEF's *pocket*). I've got it!

CARGAN (*starts for* PETERS). Give me that money!

HAYDEN (*starts for* CARGAN *and grabs him by the arm when the latter is* C.). No, you don't, Cargan; that's my money.

MAGEE. Don't let them get it, Peters!

PETERS. Let them try to get it! (BLAND *and* MAGEE *release the* CHIEF.) Now let me see you get it! (*Throws money in fire, laughing viciously. All stare into fire, watching the money burn.*) Watch the rotten stuff burn!

MAGEE (*comes down* C.). What have you done!

BLAND. He's burned the money!

CARGAN. A fortune!

HAYDEN. Good God!

KENNEDY. I'll have my men here and shoot you down like a pack of hounds! (*Starts up* C. *as two pistol shots are heard outside.* BLAND *goes* L., *near women.* MAGEE *goes up* R.; CARGAN *to table* L. MAX *goes* R. KENNEDY *goes up toward door.*)

MAGEE. What's that? (*All turn and stare toward door.*)

MAX (*looks up on balcony and yells*). Look, look! (*All look up on balcony as he points to* MYRA, *who is walking from room to room* R.)

PETERS. A ghost! A real ghost!

(MARY *screams and grabs* MAGEE; MRS. RHODES *screams and grabs* CARGAN; HAYDEN *crouches* L.; BLAND *jumps behind desk;* MAX *huddles up in chair near fire;* PETERS *is on his knees.*)

MAX. Take her away! I didn't mean to kill her! Take her away!

KENNEDY (*yells*). Let me out of this place! It's a graveyard! (*Starts for door. Door flies open and the* OWNER *enters. All stare at him.*)

HAYDEN (*after a pause*). The seventh key!

BLAND. The seventh key!

(MARY *runs to* MRS. RHODES, R. MAGEE *goes up center.*)

KENNEDY (*to* OWNER). Who are you?

OWNER (*standing at door*). I'm the owner of Baldpate Inn. Two policemen refused to allow me to pass, and I shot them dead.

(MAGEE *comes down to C.*)

ALL. What!

MAGEE. This isn't true! It can't be true! I'm a raving maniac!

OWNER (*comes downstage to R. of* MAGEE). I just arrived, Billy. I motored from New York. I expected to find you alone. (*Looks around at people, circles up R. and back to C.*) Who are these people? How did they get in here? Have they disturbed you in your work? How are you getting on with the story?

MAGEE. How am I getting on? Great heavens! man, to what sort of a place did you send me? Nothing but crooks, murderers, ghosts, pistol shots, policemen, and dead people walking about the halls. Hundreds of thousands of dollars, and keys and keys and keys! You win—I lose. Twenty-four hours! Why, I couldn't write a book in twenty-four years in a place like this! My God, what a night this has been!

(OWNER *starts laughing, then all join in, laughing and talking ad lib.* MAGEE *stands looking at them in utter amazement.*)

OWNER. I'm not going to hold you to the wager, Billy. I just want you to know it isn't real.

MAGEE. What isn't real?

MRS. RHODES (*steps toward* MAGEE, *smiling*). I'm not a real widow.

(*Crosses to foot of stairs.* MARY *comes down C. The* OWNER *goes up to desk, laughing.*)

CARGAN (*comes to* MAGEE). I'm not a real politician. (*Goes upstage.*)

KENNEDY (*down to* MAGEE). I'm not a real policeman. (*Backs upstage.*)

PETERS (*comes downstage to* MAGEE). This isn't real hair. (*Takes off wig and goes upstage R.*)

HAYDEN (*goes to* MAGEE *C.*). These are not real whiskers. (*Takes off whiskers and goes upstage L.*)

BLAND. That wasn't real money that was burned. (*Goes upstage R.*)

MAX (*over to* MAGEE *C.*). These are not real handcuffs—see? (*Breaks handcuffs and goes upstage R.*)

MYRA (*appears on balcony R.*). I'm not a real dead one. (*Hearty laugh from all.*)

MAGEE (*to* MARY, *after looking around in amazement. Goes to her, L.C.*). Are you real?

(OWNER *comes downstage to C.*)

MARY. Not a real newspaper reporter.

MAGEE. I mean a real girl.

MARY (*smiles*). That's for you to say.

MAGEE (*turns to* OWNER). Well, for heaven's sake, don't keep me in the dark. Explain; tell me what it all means.

OWNER. It means, old boy, that I wanted to prove to you how perfectly improbable and terrible those awful stories you've been writing would seem if such things really and truly happened. I left New York an hour ahead of you today. I got to Reuton at nine o'clock tonight; went directly to the Empire Theater; told the manager of our bet; framed the whole plan; engaged the entire stock company; hired half-a-dozen autos; shot over to Asquewan after the performance, and we arrived at the top of the mountain at exactly twelve o'clock. Since then you know what's happened. I've been watching the proceedings from the outside, and if it were not for the fact that I'm nearly frozen stiff, I'd call it a wonderful night. (*All laugh heartily.*)

MAGEE. You did this to me?

OWNER (*laughs*). You're not mad, are you? Of course, if you want to go through with the bet, why——

MAGEE. No, thanks; the bet's off. I've had enough of Baldpate. Me for the Commercial House until the train is ready to start. (*Over to* MARY, *L.C.*). Is your real name Mary? (*She nods affirmatively.*) Well, Mary, the shots in the night, the chases after fortunes, and all the rest of the melodrama may be all wrong, but will you help me prove to this man that there is really such a thing as love at first sight? (*All show interest.*)

MARY. How can I do that?

MAGEE. Don't you know?

MARY. Well, you don't want me to say it, do you?

MAGEE (*whispers in her ear—she nods affirmation*). Now remember your promise, Mary. (*Hearty laugh from all as he kisses her.*)

(*Lights go out and black drop falls for about thirty seconds.*)

END OF ACT II

EPILOGUE

(*Curtain goes up again. Fire is out and lock replaced on door. The stage is bare. Typewriter is heard clicking from room R. on balcony. The clock strikes twelve.* ELIJAH QUIMBY *is seen outside waving a lantern as he did in the first act.* MRS. QUIMBY *appears, et cetera. Same business, except that instead of unlocking the door, he raps on it. When* MAGEE *enters from room R. and gets to C. of balcony,* QUIMBY *raps again.* MAGEE *comes out on* balcony with hat and coat on, and carrying the suit and typewriter case and a manuscript under his arm. He stops on stairs, and as he hears Quimby's rap he comes down the stairs, puts the cases on the table L. and then goes up to door and unlocks it.*)

MAGEE (*as he opens door*). Come right in, folks. You're right on time. I see. (*Closes door and locks it.*)

QUIMBY (*comes down R.C.*). We've been out there ten minutes waiting for the clock to strike.

MRS. QUIMBY (*comes down R.C.*). Lord, I didn't think we'd find you alive!

MAGEE (*comes down C.*). The only difference between me and a real live one is that I'm tired, hungry, and half dead.

QUIMBY (*L. of* MRS. QUIMBY). How'd you come out?

MRS. QUIMBY. Did you finish your book?

MAGEE (*handing* MRS. QUIMBY *the manuscript*). Allow me.

QUIMBY. What do you think of that, Mother?

MRS. QUIMBY. Lord! Wrote all that in twenty-four hours!

MAGEE. Just made it. Finished work a couple of minutes ago.

QUIMBY. Were you disturbed at all?

MAGEE. Never heard a sound. (*Sits at table L.*)

MRS. QUIMBY. No ghosts?

MAGEE. Nary a ghost, Mrs. Quimby, except those concealed in the manuscript. (*Rises.*) How about the Asquewan hotels? I'd like to get a bath and a bite to eat before I take that train.

QUIMBY. There's the Commercial House.

MAGEE. The Commercial House! That's strange! I guessed the name.

MRS. QUIMBY. How?

MAGEE. I've got it in the story.

MRS. QUIMBY (*aside to* QUIMBY). What's he mean, Lije?

QUIMBY (*aside*). Darned if I know. (*To* MAGEE.) The missus has got a fine breakfast waiting for you up at our house.

MRS. QUIMBY. And a nice feather bed for you to take a nap in. The train don't go till five.

QUIMBY. And the drummers all say the hotel's rotten.

MAGEE. Lord, I'm tired! (*Sits at table L.*) Me for the breakfast and the feather bed. Some wild and woolly scenes have been enacted in this room since you left last night, Mrs. Quimby.

MRS. QUIMBY. What happened?

MAGEE. Nothing, really—just in the story.

MRS. QUIMBY. What's he mean, Lije?

QUIMBY. How do I know? (*Telephone rings.* QUIMBYS *start and look toward it.*)

MAGEE (*goes to phone, stops buzzer, and then goes L.*). There's Bentley—he's pretty near on time.

QUIMBY. Will I talk to him?

MAGEE. Of course. That's the idea, isn't it?

QUIMBY (*goes to phone*—MRS. QUIMBY *stands C., watching him*).

Hello! hello! Mr. Bentley. . . . Yes, sir, I've got it right here, sir. Two minutes ago, sir. . . . I'll have to find that out. Wait a minute. (*To* MAGEE.) What's the name of the story?

MAGEE. It's typewritten on the cover.

MRS. QUIMBY (*holds up script and reads by light of lantern*). Seven Keys to Baldpate.

QUIMBY (*in phone*). Seven Keys to Baldpate. (*To* MAGEE.) He's laughin'. (*Pause, then to* MAGEE.) He says there's only one. (*In phone.*) Hello! . . . What, sir? . . . Wait, I'll see. (*To* MAGEE.) You want to talk to him?

MAGEE. No. Yes, just a minute. (*Goes to phone.* QUIMBYS *go R.C.*

and stand listening.) Hello! hello! Hal. I'm going to collect that five thousand from you, old pal. . . . Yes, some title, isn't it? And, say, some story. Wild, terrible, horrible melodrama as usual, the kind of stuff you always roast me about. Treated as a joke, however, this time. And say, Hal, listen; I've got you in the story. . . . Yes, really. . . . Oh, I didn't mention your name or anything. . . . And, say, I'm in the story, too. . . . Oh, I'm the hero. . . . Say, Hal, this thing's going to sell over a million copies. . . . The what? The critics? (*Laughs.*) I don't care a darn about the critics. This is the stuff the public wants. . . . Yes, I'll meet you at the Forty-fourth Street club at two-thirty tomorrow. (*Ad lib. as the curtain falls.*)

SLOW CURTAIN

On Trial

A Dramatic Composition in Four Acts By

ELMER RICE

CAUTION

On Trial, *at the* Candler Theatre, New York City, August 19, 1914.
Presented by Cohan & Harris (by arrangement with Arthur Hopkins),
under the direction of Sam Forrest.

ON TRIAL

THE FIRST DAY OF THE TRIAL

PROLOGUE: THE COURTROOM

ACT ONE

Scene I: The library in the home of Gerald Trask, June 24, 1913,
               9:30 P.M.
Scene II: The courtroom.

ACT TWO

Scene I: The courtroom.
Scene II: The sitting room in the home of Robert Strickland, June
               24, 1913, 7:30 P.M.
Scene III: The courtroom.

THE SECOND DAY OF THE TRIAL

ACT THREE

Scene I: The courtroom.
Scene II: A room in a hotel on Long Island, thirteen years earlier.
Scene III: The courtroom.

EPILOGUE

Scene I: The jury room.
Scene II: The courtroom.

ORIGINAL CAST OF CHARACTERS

THE DEFENDANT	Frederick Perry
HIS DAUGHTER	Constance Wolf
HIS WIFE	Mary Ryan
HER FATHER (Deceased)	Thomas Findlay
THE DEAD MAN	Frederick Truesdell
HIS WIDOW	Helene Lackaye
HIS SECRETARY	Hans Robert
A NEWS AGENT	J. Wallace Clinton
A HOTEL PROPRIETOR	Lawrence Eddinger
A PHYSICIAN	George Barr
A MAID	Florence Walcott
A WAITER	John Adams
THE JUDGE	Frank Young
THE DISTRICT ATTORNEY	William Walcott
THE DEFENDANT'S COUNSEL	Gardner Crane
THE CLERK	John Klendon
THE COURT STENOGRAPHER	J. M. Brooks
THE COURT ATTENDANTS	James Herbert and Charles Walt

THE JURY

Foreman, Howard Wall

R. A. Thayer
Edmund Purdy
Arthur Tovell
Samuel Richner
Anson Adams

Robert Dudley
Harry Friend
Nat Leavitt
J. H. Mathews
Joseph McKenn

George Spivins

ON TRIAL

PROLOGUE

SCENE: *Courtroom.* JUDGE *on bench, et cetera. Twelve men in the jury box.*

CLERK. Mr. Summers, take the vacant place in the jury box. (*Shuffling of feet.*)

GRAY. What's your name?

SUMMERS. John Summers.

GRAY. Mr. Summers, what is your occupation?

SUMMERS. Electrical engineer.

GRAY. Are you in business for yourself?

SUMMERS. Yes, sir, at 1 Madison Avenue.

GRAY. Mr. Summers, are you opposed to capital punishment?

SUMMERS. No.

GRAY. Do you know Robert Strickland, the defendant in this case? Stand up, Strickland.

(STRICKLAND *rises, right arm in sling.*)

SUMMERS. No.

(STRICKLAND *resumes his seat.*)

GRAY. Do you know anyone related to him?

SUMMERS. No.

GRAY. Did you know Gerald Trask, for whose murder Strickland is on trial?

SUMMERS. No. I've often read the gentleman's name in the papers, but I never met him.

GRAY. Do you know Mrs. Trask, the widow of the murdered man?

SUMMERS. No.

GRAY. Do you know Stanley Glover, who was Mr. Trask's private secretary at the time of his death?

SUMMERS (*uncertain*). Glover? I'm not sure.

GRAY. Call Mr. Glover.

ATTENDANT (*opens door L.*). Stanley Glover.

(GLOVER *enters left.*)

GRAY. This is Mr. Glover.

SUMMERS. No; I don't know him.

GRAY. You may retire, Mr. Glover.

(GLOVER *exits left.*)

GRAY. Do you know anyone associated with the District Attorney's office, or Mr. Arbuckle, the defendant's attorney?

SUMMERS. No.

GRAY. Are you familiar with the facts in this case?

SUMMERS. Very slightly. I don't read details of murder cases!

GRAY. Have you formed any opinion which would prevent you from rendering a fair and impartial verdict?

SUMMERS. No, sir; I have not.

GRAY. That's all. Any questions, Mr. Arbuckle?

ARBUCKLE (*Has been seated L. of table, rises*). Mr. Summers, are you a married man?

SUMMERS. Yes, sir; I am.

ARBUCKLE. How many years have you been married?

SUMMERS. Fifteen, next March.

ARBUCKLE. Have you any family?

SUMMERS. I have. Two boys and a girl.

ARBUCKLE. The jury is satisfactory, Your Honor. (*Sits.*)

DINSMORE. Satisfactory to you, Mr. Gray?

GRAY. Yes, Your Honor.

DINSMORE (*to the* CLERK). Swear them.

CLERK (*to the* JURORS). Rise, gentlemen, and raise your right hands. (*They do so.*) You and each of you

do solemnly swear in the presence of the ever-living God, that you will well and truly try the indictment found by the people of the state of New York against Robert Strickland, and a true verdict rendered therein, according to the evidence, so help you God!

DINSMORE. Proceed, Mr. Gray.

GRAY (*addressing the jury*). May it please the Court: Gentlemen of the Jury, this case is a very simple one. The facts, as they have appeared from time to time in the newspapers, are no doubt familiar to all of you. In order to refresh your recollections, however, I shall outline very briefly the circumstances which we shall put into evidence. Mr. Gerald Trask, as you know, was a prominent banker of this city. He was a distinguished member of the community, and occupied important places in the social and financial worlds. Among Mr. Trask's acquaintances was Robert Strickland, the defendant. At the time they became acquainted Strickland was a rather prosperous businessman, and he and Mr. Trask met frequently. Some months ago Strickland began to have business troubles. The cause of these difficulties does not concern us. But what does interest us, gentlemen, is that Strickland, becoming more and more involved, found it necessary to go to his friend, Gerald Trask, for financial assistance. Mr. Trask responded with his habitual generosity, and promptly loaned Strickland ten thousand dollars, taking the latter's note as security. But Strickland's business didn't improve, and he decided to migrate to the West. The note was payable on the 22d of June, two days before the murder. When the 22d arrived, Strickland was in Cleveland, Ohio, making arrangements for himself and family. He returned, however, on the 24th, the night of the murder, sent for Mr. Trask, and took up the note. I call your attention to the fact, gentlemen, that Strickland paid the debt in cash. He was a businessman. (ARBUCKLE *whispers to* STRICKLAND.) He did not pay it in check or draft, but cash! Ten thousand dollars in cash! Mr. Trask had offered to let the loan stand until Strickland was on his feet again, but Strickland wouldn't hear of it. You will understand his eagerness to cancel the debt in a moment, gentlemen; it was because he had evolved a little plan whereby he could wipe out the obligation without it costing him a cent. The scheme was simple enough, gentlemen. He knew that Mr. Trask would have to keep the ten thousand in his house overnight, and that he would almost certainly lock it up in the safe in the library. And what is more, gentlemen, he knew the combination to Mr. Trask's safe. Bear in mind that only two people knew the combination to that safe —Mr. Trask and Strickland. But Strickland hadn't the nerve to do the job alone, so he called in an assistant. Accordingly, he and his accomplice entered Mr. Trask's house a few hours after Strickland had paid over the money. The accomplice went to work on the safe and Strickland stood guard. The burglar succeeded without much difficulty in opening the safe and extracting the ten thousand dollars, while Strickland superintended the job. Before they could escape, however, they were interrupted, first by Mrs. Trask, and then by her hus-

band. The accomplice made a hasty exit, taking the plunder with him. That was the last that was heard of the accomplice, gentlemen. Who he is or where he went we have been unable to learn. But Mr. Strickland was caught red-handed, and knowing that dead men tell no tales, he shot and killed Mr. Trask in cold blood. There you have the story, gentlemen. Mrs. Trask, the widow of the murdered man, will tell it to you in detail. Her testimony will be corroborated by Mr. Glover, Mr. Trask's secretary, thanks to whose bravery the assassin was disarmed and captured, and who gave us material assistance in linking up the chain of evidence against him. Not one of the acts is disputed. Strickland, realizing the futility of interposing a defense, has refused——

ARBUCKLE. I object to that. (*Rises.*)

DINSMORE. Counsel will not interrupt.

(ARBUCKLE *sits.*)

GRAY. Strickland, I say, has refused to make any effort to defend himself. When he was arraigned——

ARBUCKLE. I object to that. (*Rises.*)

DINSMORE. Counsel will not interrupt.

(ARBUCKLE *sits.*)

GRAY. When he was arraigned, he pleaded guilty to the indictment of murder in the first degree; perhaps, gentlemen, you ask, if this is so, why are we here? Why is the County put to the expense of the trial? An expense which we taxpayers must meet in the end? Why must you businessmen be taken from your occupations; be compelled to lose valuable time? Why is not the penalty allotted to murderers inflicted upon the defendant? And in answer to that I say to you, because, gentlemen, the State is jealous of the lives of her citizens. To her the existence of an individual is sacred, no matter if he be depraved, degenerate, possessed of criminal instincts, dangerous to society. She will not allow even a self-confessed murderer to be put to death until twelve of his fellow-citizens, sitting in solemn judgment, calmly, dispassionately hearing and weighing the facts, have decreed that that man shall suffer the consequences of his crime. That is why we are here today, gentlemen. That is why His Honor has assigned such distinguished counsel to defend Strickland; and that is why, before we ask you to visit upon this defendant the punishment he merits, we shall, by the unimpeachable testimony of eye-witnesses, convince you of his guilt, beyond the peradventure of a doubt. Unfortunately, his partner in crime has made good his escape. But the greater criminal is in our hands, gentlemen. We shall make him pay the penalty of the law. I shall take up no more of your time. The facts will speak for themselves. (*Looks* JURY *over. He takes his seat, R. of table.*)

ARBUCKLE (*rising and addressing the* JURY *and standing along table*). If the Court pleases: Gentlemen of the Jury, when His Honor assigned me to the defense of this case, it seemed to me that the prosecution's theory was untenable. I knew Mr. Strickland by reputation, and I scouted the burglary hypothesis. This belief strengthened as I became better acquainted with Mr. Strickland. A man of superlative honor and integrity, equipped with a splendid mentality and an excellent reputation, not addicted to bad habits or expensive luxuries, devotedly attached to his wife and child—that is not the sort of man who breaks into his friend's house for the purpose of theft. The case seemed to me to be not nearly so clear and simple as my friend, Mr. Gray, makes it out to be. But, despite my certainty that there lurked a mystery in this grim affair, I could learn nothing that would aid me in substantiating my belief. As my friend has told you, Mr. Strickland has maintained throughout an obstinate, unbreakable silence. In all my years at the bar, gentlemen, I have never encountered anyone who has declined so resolutely to yield to persuasion. Threats, entreaties, and logic alike have left him indifferent. At last I reached the conclusion that Strickland was shielding someone, most likely the unknown accomplice who assaulted Mrs. Trask and broke open the safe. In the hope of learning the identity of this man, and, if possible, Strickland's motive in shielding him, I endeavored to locate the members of Strickland's family. Judge of my surprise, gentlemen, when I learned that the defendant's wife had disappeared from home on the night of the tragedy and has not since been heard from. All my attempts to find her have been fruitless. I have been forced to believe—(*pause—looks at* STRICKLAND)—that she took her life. I did succeed in finding Doris, the little daughter of the defendant. When you have heard her story, gentlemen, you will agree with me that to send Strickland to his death would be a gross miscarriage of justice. That is all for the present, gentlemen. (*He takes his seat.*)

STRICKLAND (*has been seated at lower end of table L. Rising*). Your Honor, I won't have it. I won't have my little girl dragged into this case. I've pleaded guilty. I'm willing to suffer the consequences.

(ARBUCKLE *entreats* STRICKLAND *to sit.*)

DINSMORE. Your case is in the hands of your counsel.

STRICKLAND. I don't want counsel. I have no defense. Why don't you sentence me? Why——?

DINSMORE. Proceed, Mr. Gray.

STRICKLAND. Your Honor——

DINSMORE. Silence!

(STRICKLAND *takes his seat.*)

GRAY. Call Mrs. Trask. (ATTENDANT *opens door L., exits, and calls* MRS. TRASK. *She enters, left.*) Mrs. Trask, will you kindly take the witness chair, please?

CLERK. Raise your right hand, please. Do you solemnly swear that the testimony you are about to give will be the truth, the whole truth, and nothing but the truth, so help you God? (*She nods yes.*) What's your name?

MRS. TRASK. Joan Trask.

GRAY. Mrs. Trask, are you the widow of Gerald Trask?

MRS. TRASK. Yes, sir.

GRAY. How long were you married to Mr. Trask?

MRS. TRASK. Almost fifteen years.

GRAY. Do you remember the night of June 24th?

MRS. TRASK. Indeed I do.

GRAY. Where were you on that evening?

MRS. TRASK. I had been dining out with friends.

GRAY. What time did you arrive home?

MRS. TRASK. About half-past nine.

GRAY. Now, Mrs. Trask, I want you to tell to the court and jury everything that occurred after you arrived home.

MRS. TRASK. Just as I entered my home the telephone in the library rang.

LIGHTS OUT—CURTAIN.

ACT ONE

SCENE: TRASK's *library. Entrance door right; door to* TRASK's *room right; door to* MRS. TRASK's *room left; french window in rear; safe right.*

At rise of curtain, telephone rings. MRS. TRASK *enters upper left, and goes to phone.*

MRS. TRASK (*goes to phone R.*). Hello! Yes—yes—this is 182 River. No, Mr. Trask is not in. Who is this, please? I'm his wife. Who are you? What do you want to talk to him about? Well, I'm his wife. Oh, very well. I don't know when he will be in. I don't know. All right. Good-by. (*Turns away from phone in evident distress.*)

GLOVER (*enters at right center; starts for phone*). I thought I heard the telephone bell.

MRS. TRASK. Yes; I answered it. (*Crosses L.*)

GLOVER. Oh, it was for you?

MRS. TRASK. No; for my husband.

GLOVER. Who was it?

MRS. TRASK (*at door L.*). A woman, as usual.

GLOVER. Oh! (*Sits right at table.*)

MRS. TRASK (*crosses L.C.—suspiciously*). Do you know who she is?

GLOVER. Why, no!

MRS. TRASK. No, I suppose my husband doesn't take his secretary into his confidence to that extent, although he doesn't make any great attempt to keep things secret. He hasn't. even a sense of shame.

GLOVER. You must excuse me——

MRS. TRASK. Yes, of course. I don't ordinarily discuss these things; but even my endurance has its limits. (*Down L., puts cloak on sofa.*)

GLOVER. Really, Mrs. Trask——

MRS. TRASK. I've put up with this for fifteen years now. Oh, what a fool I am to stand for it.

GLOVER. My dear Mrs. Trask, you understand my position. (*Crosses to her.*)

MRS. TRASK (*sits on sofa L.*). Yes; forgive me. It was wrong of me to talk about it to you.

GLOVER. Not at all; but——

MRS. TRASK. Sometimes I lose patience. Well, we won't say anything more about it. Is Mr. Trask coming home tonight?

GLOVER (*crosses R., looks at watch*). Yes; he telephoned this morning. He's coming on the nine-twelve from Long Branch. It's half-past nine now. He should have been here by this time. (*Sits R. of table.*)

MRS. TRASK. I can't imagine what he's doing down there these two days.

GLOVER. Golfing and fishing, I suppose.

MRS. TRASK. He might have waited until next week. We'll be there all summer. By the way, I'd like you to go over my tradesmen's accounts for me before we leave the city.

GLOVER. I'll do it at once. Where are the books?

MRS. TRASK. In the safe.

GLOVER (*going to safe and trying it*). It's locked; do you know the combination?

MRS. TRASK. No; not to the new safe. Don't you know it?

GLOVER. No; I never have any occasion to open the safe when Mr. Trask is away.

MRS. TRASK. I must have him give me the combination. (*Up L.C.*)

(TRASK *enters, left C.*)

TRASK. Hello, Joan! (MRS. TRASK *turns her back to him and goes down L.*) Hello, Glover!

GLOVER. Good evening, Mr. Trask.

(MRS. TRASK *does not answer.*)

TRASK (*to* MRS. TRASK). What's wrong with you again? (*Down L.C.*)

MRS. TRASK. Nothing. (*Sits on sofa.*)

TRASK. Oh, is that all?

GLOVER (*rises*). Allow me.—(*Takes hat and coat from* TRASK; *puts them on chair upper right.*)

TRASK. Anything new, Glover?

GLOVER (*down to table R., where he sits*). No, sir.

MRS. TRASK. A woman called you up.

TRASK. Oh, that's it. Who was it?

MRS. TRASK. I suppose you know well enough.

TRASK. If I knew I wouldn't ask you. Who was it?

MRS. TRASK. I don't know.

TRASK. Didn't you ask her to give you her name?

MRS. TRASK. You don't suppose she'd tell me her name, do you?

TRASK. Did she say she'd call again?

MRS. TRASK. I don't know.

GLOVER (*hastily rising*). Do you mind opening the safe, Mr. Trask? I want to get Mrs. Trask's account books.

TRASK. All right. (*Feels in his pockets.*) What did I do with that?

GLOVER. Lost something?

TRASK (*still searching*). Yes; I had a card with the combination written on it. That's a funny thing.

GLOVER. Look in your inside pocket.

TRASK (*searching there*). No; it's not there. Where the devil did I put the thing?

MRS. TRASK. Maybe it's in some other suit.

TRASK (*irritably*). No, no; I had it right in this pocket.

GLOVER. When did you have it last?

TRASK. Yesterday morning before I left; I opened the safe to get my checkbook.

MRS. TRASK. Perhaps you left it down at Long Branch?

TRASK. That's ridiculous. Why would I leave the combination to the safe at Long Branch?

GLOVER. You may have pulled it out with something else.

TRASK. No; there's nothing else in my pocket. (*Turns up, then stops.*) Oh, I know what I did with it.

GLOVER. What?

TRASK. I gave it to Strickland.

GLOVER. To Strickland?

TRASK. Yes. I've just come from there. I invited him down to Long Branch to spend Sunday, and wrote the address on the card.

GLOVER. Are you sure the combination was on that card?

TRASK. Yes. I never stopped to look at the other side—damn careless. You'll have to wait until tomorrow for your books. (*Goes up L., crosses to R.C.*)

GLOVER. Well, there's no hurry about it.

TRASK (*thinking*). Wait a minute: I believe I can get that combination. (*Goes to safe and manipulates the disk.*) No, that's not it.

GLOVER. Well, I guess it can wait until morning.

TRASK. Say, you know if you're going to talk I never can remember these numbers. I've got it; there you are. (*Opens safe.*) Help yourself. (*Crosses L., business with humidor on bookcase.*)

GLOVER. Thanks! (*Goes to safe and takes books.*) Do you want to do any work tonight? (*Sits R. of table.*)

TRASK. No, I don't think so. I want to turn in early. I've been golfing all day, and I'm tired.

MRS. TRASK. Seems to me you might have waited until we all went down to Long Branch.

TRASK. When are you going? (*Down L.C.*)

MRS. TRASK. Monday. Aren't you coming with us?

TRASK. I'm going down Saturday night.

MRS. TRASK. Why?

TRASK. I've got up a fishing party for Sunday morning. Like to join me, Glover?

GLOVER. Thanks; I'll be glad to.

TRASK. Strickland's coming with us.

GLOVER. When did he get back from the West?

TRASK. Tonight. He wired me to meet him at his home.

GLOVER. What are you going to do about that note of his? It was due on the 22d, you know.

TRASK. He paid it. (*Sits L. of table.*)

GLOVER. He did?

TRASK. Yes; I have the ten thousand here. (*Takes money from his pocket and counts it.*)

GLOVER. I'm surprised. I thought he would fall down.

TRASK. He got it from those business connections of his in Cleveland. When I got to his house tonight, he had the ten thousand. I didn't want to take it; I told him I knew he was hard pressed, and that I didn't mind holding off for a while.

GLOVER. What did he say?

TRASK. He wouldn't hear of it. Wants to begin with a clean slate, he says.

GLOVER. That's like Strickland—straight clean through.

TRASK. Yes.

GLOVER. He's a fine chap. Too bad he couldn't make things go.

TRASK. Well, that's business. Somebody's got to go to the wall.

GLOVER. Strickland takes it pretty hard. On account of his wife, I guess. He's awfully fond of her.

MRS. TRASK. Is she a nice woman?

TRASK (*yawning*). Couldn't say. Never met her. (*Hands* GLOVER *money.*) You better put that ten thousand—(MRS. TRASK *goes up to french window*)—in the safe, Glover.

GLOVER. Why the cash? (*Rises.*)

TRASK. Well, he said it had been so darned hard for him to get it, that he wanted the pleasure of handing it to me in ten one-thousand-dollar bills. Be sure to deposit it in the morning.

GLOVER. All right, sir. (*Goes to sofa. At safe.*) Shall I lock it? (*He covers the safe with his body while he turns the disk.*)

TRASK. Yes. (*Goes up L. Business with book on case.*)

GLOVER (*rising*). Anything else?

TRASK. I don't think so.

GLOVER. I'll go to my room then. (*Takes books.*) I'll have these ready in the morning, Mrs. Trask.

MRS. TRASK. Thank you very much, Mr. Glover. Good night. (*Down L. Sits on sofa.*)

GLOVER. Good night!

TRASK. Good night. (*Down L.*)

MRS. TRASK. Good night!

(GLOVER *goes out right.*)

TRASK (*calling after him*). Oh, Glover.

GLOVER. Yes, sir!

TRASK. Better remind me to get that card from Strickland tomorrow.

GLOVER. All right.

TRASK (*looks at* MRS. TRASK, *yawning*). I'm going to turn in. (*Gets hat and coat and starts R.*)

MRS. TRASK (*rises*). Gerald, who is this woman? (*Crosses C.*)

TRASK. What woman?

MRS. TRASK. The one who called up a while ago.

ΓRASK. Aren't you done with that yet? I told you I don't know.

MRS. TRASK. You do know.

TRASK (*moving right*). Good night!

MRS. TRASK. No—I want to know who she is.

TRASK. What's the good of ragging me like this? I tell you I don't know who it is. I suppose it is some business matter.

MRS. TRASK. Nobody would call you up at this time of night on business. You know very well it's not business.

TRASK. Well, what's your theory? (*Puts hat and coat back on chair R. Sits R. of table.*)

MRS. TRASK. Aren't you ever going to change? (*Sits L. of table.*)

TRASK. Am I never going to have a minute's peace? You're as jealous as a schoolgirl!

MRS. TRASK. Jealous!

TRASK. Yes; you're forever raising a racket about nothing.

MRS. TRASK. Oh, it's nothing, is it?

TRASK. If I look at a woman, or a woman talks to me, you're ready to fly at her throat.

MRS. TRASK. Don't you think you give me cause, the way you conduct yourself? You seem to forget that you have a wife.

TRASK. You never give me a chance to forget it. Every time we're alone, it's the same thing.

MRS. TRASK. Then why don't you treat me as your wife?

TRASK. I don't see what you're complaining about. I don't beat you, do I? You get everything you want. You go where you please and when you please. I allow you more money than you can possibly spend, and your time is all your own. Do you think there are many women who can say the same?

MRS. TRASK. Do you think that's all I care about? Don't you suppose marriage means something more to me than spending money and amusing myself? What good is it if I haven't the companionship of my husband?

TRASK. My God! are you going to get sentimental?

MRS. TRASK (*crosses L.*). I've never known what it meant to be really married. For six years I hid myself away because I didn't happen to suit your family.

TRASK. Well, you didn't lose by it. If my father had cut me off, you wouldn't be living in luxury today.

MRS. TRASK. You seem to think that money is all that one needs. It's been that way ever since we were married. I didn't want to keep our marriage secret. But you thought a great deal more of your inheritance than you did of me.

TRASK. You'd have sung a different tune if he'd left me penniless.

MRS. TRASK. All your money hasn't brought me happiness. No other woman would have borne what I have for fifteen years. If you had a spark of manhood in you, you'd lead a decent life—if not for my sake, then for your children's.

TRASK. Oh, now we're around to the children again!

MRS. TRASK (sits on sofa). You never consider them. They'll soon be old enough to understand.

TRASK (slams table, rising). Well, what of it? They've got everything they want, too. (Crosses to her.) They're getting a good education and a liberal allowance. That's all they have a right to expect of me.

MRS. TRASK. You're sending them out into the world with a stigma——

TRASK. Oh, stigma be hanged! I lead a pretty straight life.

MRS. TRASK. Gerald!

TRASK. Yes, I do. You don't expect me to sit home by the fireside twirling my thumbs, do you? I've got time for that thirty years from now. When that time comes, the children won't regulate their lives to suit me, will they?

MRS. TRASK. You've promised me a dozen times to change.

TRASK. Well, that's the only way I can get any peace. (Sits L. of table.)

MRS. TRASK. I won't stand it any longer.

TRASK. What are you going to do about it?

MRS. TRASK. I'll get a divorce. (Crosses to him.)

TRASK. Well, go ahead; I won't attempt to prevent you.

MRS. TRASK. No; you'll be glad, I suppose. (Up L.C., crossing R.)

TRASK. I won't be sorry, you can wager on that.

MRS. TRASK. To think I've lived with you all these years!

TRASK. Well, why have you?

MRS. TRASK (R. of table). You know why—to keep up appearances on account of the children. To give them a good name.

TRASK. And because I took pretty good care of you.

MRS. TRASK. You talk as though you had been bribing me to throw away my self-respect. I won't stand any more of it. (Crosses R.)

TRASK. Do as you please about it.

MRS. TRASK. I will. I'll bring suit against you tomorrow.

TRASK. As soon as you like.

MRS. TRASK. I should have done it years ago.

TRASK. Why didn't you?

MRS. TRASK (*crosses to him*). Because I always took your word. I always deluded myself into the belief that you were going to change. I've waited just thirteen years too long. I might have known, after that affair at Great Neck——

TRASK. Now, see here.

MRS. TRASK. Oh, I haven't forgotten it, though it is thirteen years ago. That little Miss Deane, that innocent child—and to think that I have lived with you after that. (*Crosses L.*)

TRASK. Never mind digging up the past. (*Crosses to her.*)

MRS. TRASK. I will dig up the past. I'll tell the whole story.

TRASK. Look here, Joan, what's the use of kicking up a row? That divorce idea is all nonsense. There's no reason why we can't go on together. (*Tries to take her hand.*)

MRS. TRASK. No; I'm through with you. (*Sits L.*) I've forgiven you a dozen times, and it's been the same thing over again.

TRASK (*sits above her on sofa*). Make this the last time. What do you want me to do?

MRS. TRASK (*turns to him*). I want you—— No, it's no use; it'll be just the same as ever.

TRASK. I tell you it won't. What more do you want? I give you my word.

MRS. TRASK. You've broken it before.

TRASK. But this time I'm in earnest.

MRS. TRASK. You always say that.

TRASK. Well, give me a chance to convince you. I'm on the dead level this time. What'll you gain by dragging me through the divorce court? You'll be the sufferer—you and the children. There'll be newspaper notoriety and all that. Let's try to make it go once more.

MRS. TRASK. Gerald, if I do it's the last time.

TRASK (*taking her hand*). Good! We'll begin all over again?

MRS. TRASK. Yes.

TRASK. We'll drop the past?

MRS. TRASK. Yes——

TRASK (*kissing her. Rises, crosses R., gets hat and coat and starts for door R.*). All right; that's over.

MRS. TRASK. Gerald, you'll keep your word? (*Rises, crosses C.*)

TRASK. I've said so.

MRS. TRASK. Promise me that you'll break off with this woman, then.

TRASK. What woman?

MRS. TRASK. The one who called up.

TRASK (*crossing to her*). Oh, you're wrong about that. You've misjudged me this time.

MRS. TRASK. On your word?

TRASK. Yes.

MRS. TRASK. Forgive me, then. (*Puts her hands on his shoulders.*)

TRASK. It's all right.

MRS. TRASK. We'll try to make it go right this time. (*They kiss.*)

TRASK. Good! I'm going to turn in now; I'm dog tired. Good night. (*Goes R.*) Want those lights?

MRS. TRASK. No. Good night! (*Crosses L.*)

TRASK (*switching off light*). Good night, then. (*Stage dark. Enters his bedroom.*)

MRS. TRASK. Good night.

LIGHTS OUT.

(MRS. TRASK *goes L. to her bedroom. The stage is dark.* GLOVER *enters L.C.; goes to safe, opens it, takes money out of cash box—drops box.* MRS. TRASK *rattles doorknob, and enters L.*)

MRS. TRASK. Who is it? Is there someone here? (*Instantly* GLOVER *forces her to the sofa. As he is struggling with her,* STRICKLAND *appears, entering the window at back. The man hears him and looks up.* STRICKLAND *enters the room, and the man disappears into the darkness at the L. side of the room.* STRICKLAND *goes to* MRS. TRASK *and looks at her, puzzled. The telephone rings.* TRASK *stumbles in from his bedroom and switches on the light. Lights up.* MRS. TRASK *is on the floor;* STRICKLAND *is crouched beside her, covering her with his revolver.*)

TRASK (*at phone*). Hello! Yes, this is Trask. Is that you, May?

STRICKLAND. You—you—— (*Fires, and misses. At the same moment* MRS. TRASK *screams.* TRASK *drops the receiver and turns.* STRICKLAND *fires again, and* TRASK *falls dead.* GLOVER *rushes in at R. with a heavy stick, and dashes at* STRICKLAND. *He raises the stick above his head.* STRICKLAND *raises his arm instinctively. The stick falls with a crashing blow on* STRICKLAND's *forearm. The revolver falls from his grasp, and his arm drops limply to his side. He utters a groan and sinks to the floor.*)

MRS. TRASK (*crosses C.*). My God, he's killed Gerald!

GLOVER. Telephone for the doctor. (*Ring bell.*)

MRS. TRASK. Gerald! Gerald!

LIGHTS OUT—CURTAIN.

SCENE II: The courtroom.

GRAY. Yes, and then——?

MRS. TRASK. A few minutes later the police arrived.

GRAY. And your husband was dead by that time?

MRS. TRASK. Yes; he died instantly, the doctor said.

GRAY. Now, Mrs. Trask, did you observe the safe before the police arrived?

MRS. TRASK. Yes; the safe was opened.

GRAY. Did you notice if any of the contents was missing?

MRS. TRASK. Yes, sir; the ten thousand dollars was gone.

GRAY. That's all, Mrs. Trask. (*Takes his seat.*) You may cross-examine the witness, Mr. Arbuckle.

ARBUCKLE (*rising*). Mrs. Trask, did you recognize your assailant—the man who opened the safe?

MRS. TRASK. No. He came upon me so quickly. And the room was in total darkness.

ARBUCKLE. Are you sure that no one but Mr. Trask knew the combination of the safe?

MRS. TRASK. Mr. Strickland knew it.

ARBUCKLE. I move to strike out the answer as not responsive.

GRAY (*springing to his feet*). I——? Your Honor.

DINSMORE. The motion is denied.

ARBUCKLE. I respectfully except. Mrs. Trask, did any words pass between Strickland and your assailant?

MRS. TRASK. I can't be sure. There was a ringing in my ears. He almost strangled me.

ARBUCKLE. But, to the best of your knowledge, they did not speak to each other?

MRS. TRASK. I can't say one way or the other.

ARBUCKLE. Mrs. Trask, do you know who "May" is?

MRS. TRASK. *No, sir, I do not.*

ARBUCKLE. I have no further questions, Your Honor.

GRAY. That's all, Mrs. Trask. (*She steps down, goes L., pauses, looks at* STRICKLAND, *and exits L.*) Is Dr. Morgan in the witness room?

ATTENDANT (*opens door and exits*). Dr. Morgan! (*There is no answer.*)

GRAY (*waits until* MRS. TRASK *is off. To* JUDGE DINSMORE). Dr. Morgan is the physician who examined Mr. Trask's body, Your Honor. He told me that he might be detained.

(ATTENDANT *enters.*)

ATTENDANT. Dr. Morgan is not here.

GRAY. With Your Honor's permission, I'll call Mr. Glover, in order not to delay the trial.

DINSMORE. Yes.

GRAY. Call Mr. Stanley Glover!

ATTENDANT (*opens door left and calls off*). Stanley Glover.

(GLOVER *enters L.*)

GRAY. Mr. Glover. Will you take the witness stand, please?

(GLOVER *takes the stand.*)

CLERK. Raise your right hand, please. Do you solemnly swear that the testimony you are about to give will be the truth, the whole truth, and nothing but the truth, so help you God? What's your name?

GLOVER. Stanley Glover.

GRAY (*down stage*). Mr. Glover, you were Mr. Trask's private secretary.

GLOVER. Yes, sir.

GRAY. On the night of June the 24th, after you left the library with Mrs. Trask's books, what did you do?

GLOVER. I went directly to my room.

GRAY. Describe what occurred then.

GLOVER. I began going over the books. About half an hour later I heard a shot, then I heard Mrs. Trask scream, and another shot fired. I picked up a heavy cane I had in my room and rushed downstairs to the library. Mr. Trask's body was on the floor, and Strickland was standing at the other side of the room, with a revolver in his hand.

GRAY. What did you do?

GLOVER. I dashed at Strickland with the cane and struck his arm. He dropped the revolver and fell to the floor.

GRAY. When you entered the room, did you see any sign of the other man?

GLOVER. No, sir; the french windows at the back were open, and he must have escaped that way.

GRAY. What happened then?

GLOVER. While Mrs. Trask was telephoning for the police I kept watch on Strickland. Then I happened to remember what Mr. Trask had said about giving Strickland the card with the combination to the safe on it, and I thought he might have it on him—(ARBUCKLE *interrupts*)—and that if he did it would prove of value to the police.

ARBUCKLE. I object to the witness stating what he thought.

DINSMORE. Yes; strike out that part of the answer.

(*Stenographer does so.*)

GRAY (*up stage*). Just tell what you did and saw, Mr. Glover.

GLOVER. Well, I began to search Strickland's pockets.

GRAY. Was that before the police arrived?

GLOVER. Yes; I was afraid he might destroy the card.

ARBUCKLE (*springing to his feet*). Your Honor, I ask that the witness be instructed to answer the questions and no more.

DINSMORE. Yes; strike out the answer. (*To* GLOVER.) You must confine your answers to the questions which are put to you. You are not to volunteer anything, and you are not to tell what passed through your mind. Is that clear?

GLOVER. Yes, Your Honor.

DINSMORE. Proceed, Mr. Gray.

GRAY. Mr. Glover, did you take the card from Strickland's pocket? (*Gets card from book on table L.*)

GLOVER. Yes, sir.

GRAY. Is this it? (*Passes card to* GLOVER.)

GLOVER (*examining it*). Yes.

GRAY (*takes card from* GLOVER). I offer it in evidence, Your Honor. (*Gives card to stenographer who marks it and gives it back to* GRAY.)

GRAY (*crossing L.C.—to the jury*). This People's Exhibit A is a visiting card. On the face is engraved in old English type the name of "Mr. Gerald Trask." Below that is written in pencil, "206 Henderson Place, Long Branch." On the other side is written in words and figures: "14 right 2, 27 left 3." Is there any question about the handwriting, Mr. Arbuckle?

ARBUCKLE. You'd better prove it.

GRAY (*down stage*). Mr. Glover, are you familiar with Mr. Trask's handwriting?

GLOVER. Yes; I know it perfectly.

GRAY. You've seen it often on letters and documents?

GLOVER. Hundreds of times.

GRAY (*gives card to* GLOVER). I show you this card and ask you whether the address, "206 Henderson Place, Long Branch," is in Mr. Trask's writing.

GLOVER. It is.

GRAY. Now turn the card, please. Are the words and figures, "14 right 2, 27 left 3," also in Mr. Trask's writing?

GLOVER. They are.

GRAY. There's no doubt in your mind about it? (*Takes card.*)

GLOVER. Absolutely none.

GRAY. Do you know the significance of these figures, "14 right 2, 27 left 3"?

GLOVER. Yes, sir. It's the combination to Mr. Trask's safe.

GRAY. How do you know?

GLOVER. When the police arrived I gave them this card. They locked the safe and opened it with this combination.

GRAY. Now, Mr. Glover, I call your attention to the fact that the card is torn almost in half. Can you explain how that *occurred?*

(*Ring slow curtain.*)

GLOVER. Yes, sir. As I took the card from Strickland's pocket, he snatched it out of my hand and started to tear it in half. Before he had torn it all the way, I managed to get hold of it again.

GRAY. Yes! and what happened then?

(*Note:* GRAY's *line is spoken after curtain is down.*)

ACT TWO

SCENE: *Courtroom.*

GRAY. Dr. Morgan, in what condition did you find Mr. Trask's body?

MORGAN (*on witness stand*). I found two bullet wounds.

GRAY. Describe them, please.

MORGAN. One was a slight wound on the right shoulder caused by a grazing bullet.

GRAY. And the other?

MORGAN. The other bullet entered the body just above the left breast and lodged in the heart.

GRAY. That's all, Dr. Morgan.

ARBUCKLE. I have no cross-examination, Your Honor.

(MORGAN *steps down—crosses L.*)

GRAY. That's the case for the prosecution, Your Honor.

DINSMORE. Proceed with the defense, Mr. Arbuckle.

ARBUCKLE. I shall call Miss Doris Strickland.

(ATTENDANT *goes out L., calling* "Doris Strickland.")

STRICKLAND (*springing to his feet*). No, Your Honor—don't let her testify; she's my little girl. She's all I've got left. Don't let her testify.

DINSMORE. You must leave your case in the hands of your counsel. He will protect your interests.

(ARBUCKLE *tries to force* STRICK-LAND *to sit.*)

STRICKLAND. I don't want to be protected; protect my little girl. Don't bring her in here. (*Sits.*)

(DORIS *enters L., walks to* STRICK-LAND, *puts arms around him.*)

ARBUCKLE. Come, Strickland, this won't do. Come, Doris, sit up in that chair there.

STRICKLAND (*rising*). No, no; take her out of here. She's all I have left to me.

ARBUCKLE. Up there, Doris. (*Takes* DORIS *to stand.*)

STRICKLAND. Your Honor, I want to keep her out of this; it's the only request I've made. You're a man, Your Honor, a father, perhaps——

DINSMORE. I am powerless to help you. I am merely an instrument of the law which will mete out justice to you. The law must be permitted to take its course. Proceed, Mr. Arbuckle.

(STRICKLAND *sinks into his chair and buries his face in his arms.* AR-BUCKLE *crosses left to table.*)

GRAY (*rises*). Your Honor, I respectfully ask that the competency of this child to testify be determined.

ARBUCKLE. By all means, Your Honor.

(GRAY *sits.*)

DINSMORE. How old are you, Doris?

DORIS. I'm going to be nine years old on the 6th of November.

DINSMORE. And do you·go to school?

DORIS. Yes, sir. I was promoted; I'm in the grammar school now.

DINSMORE. Did you ever go to Sunday school?

DORIS. Yes, sir. I went every Sunday before Mamma went away. But now Aunt Helen won't let me go, because all the children talk about me and make me cry.

DINSMORE. Did you learn in Sunday school that you must always tell the truth?

DORIS. Yes, sir; that's one of the Ten Commandments, "Thou shalt not bear false witness against thy neighbor." That means that you should never tell a lie. Miss Weston told me that.

DINSMORE. Who is Miss Weston?

DORIS. She's my Sunday-school teacher. She taught me all the Ten Commandments. Shall I say them for you?

DINSMORE. Not now. (*To* GRAY.) I think she may testify. Proceed, Mr. Arbuckle.

ARBUCKLE. Doris, what is your full name? (*Crosses to her.*)

DORIS. Doris Helen Strickland.

ARBUCKLE. Who is your father?

DORIS. That's my daddy there. (*She starts down—*ARBUCKLE *stops her.*)

ARBUCKLE. Robert Strickland is your father?

DORIS. Yes, sir.

ARBUCKLE. Doris, do you remember the night on which Mr. Trask was shot?

DORIS. Yes, sir. (*Pause.*)

ARBUCKLE. Your father had been away from home?

DORIS. Yes, sir. He was in Cleveland buying a house for us to live in.

ARBUCKLE. And he came back that evening?

DORIS. Yes, sir.

ARBUCKLE. Now, just before he came home, where were you?

DORIS. I was in the sitting room.

ARBUCKLE. That was about half-past seven, wasn't it?

DORIS. Yes, sir.

ARBUCKLE. What were you doing?

DORIS. I was waiting for my daddy.

ARBUCKLE. Yes, I know; but were you reading or playing or sitting still?

DORIS. I was practicing my piano lesson.

(*The stage is dark; piano is heard, in orchestra. The lights go up in library of* STRICKLAND'S *home. Entrance door near R. Door to* DORIS'S *room rear L.* DORIS *playing piano. Crosses R. to little stool back of sofa and plays with dolls.* MAY *enters R., goes to phone, looks up number on card she brings on.*)

MAY (*at telephone; her back to sofa*). Hello! give me 4000 Jersey City, please. . . . Hello! is this the Jersey railroad? . . . Give me the lost articles clerk, please. . . . Hello! this is Mrs. Robert Strickland, of New York City. . . . That's right. Have you found a purse belonging to me? . . . Are you sure? . . . Why, I don't know. I came in from Long Branch yesterday afternoon, and when I got off the train I noticed that my handbag was open. The purse must have fallen out. . . . Yes, I've telephoned to the stationmaster at Long Branch several times. . . . No, it hasn't. . . . He re-

ferred me to you. . . . (DORIS *sits on sofa.*) The four-seventeen from Long Branch, yesterday. . . . A small black velvet purse. . . . About forty dollars in bills, some visiting cards with my name and address on them, and some very important memoranda. . . . I wish you would. . . . Very well. Good-by. (*She hangs up receiver, turns and sees* DORIS, *who has emerged from the sofa.*) Doris! Where did you come from?

DORIS. I was sitting behind the sofa.

MAY (*sits R. of table*). Whatever were you doing there?

DORIS. I was playing with my dolls. (*Crosses to* MAY.) Mamma, was it that nice, soft black little purse you lost?

MAY. Listen to me, Doris. When Daddy comes, I don't want you to say anything to him about the purse.

DORIS. Why not? (*Kneels beside her.*)

MAY. Because he'll be angry if he knows it's lost, and then he'll worry about it. You don't want to worry Daddy, do you?

DORIS. No; but, Mamma, weren't you shopping yesterday?

MAY. Of course, dear.

DORIS. But you told the man you were at Long Branch.

MAY. It was a friend of mine who was there. I loaned her the purse, and she lost it.

DORIS. Who was it?

MAY. You don't know her.

DORIS. Why did you lend her your purse?

MAY. Because she hadn't any money of her own.

DORIS. But, Mamma, wasn't it fibbing to tell the man——?

MAY. No; I'll explain some other time. Promise Mamma you won't say anything. (*Door slams off R.*)

DORIS. I promise.

STRICKLAND (*off stage*). Hello, Bertha, how are you?

BERTHA. How are you, Mr. Strickland?

STRICKLAND. Everybody all right?

DORIS. It's Daddy, Mamma! It's Daddy! (*Runs off.*)

(MAY *puts card in bosom of her dress, places doll on stool. Goes up R.C.*)

STRICKLAND (*calling*). Yes, it's your old daddy. Hello, sweetheart!

DORIS. Hello, Daddy dear! What have you got for me?

STRICKLAND. Something wonderful. Give me another kiss. Are you glad to see your daddy?

DORIS. Oh, Mamma and I have been so lonesome.

STRICKLAND. Where is Mamma?

DORIS. In here. (DORIS *and* STRICKLAND *enter. Business of* MAY *waiting.*)

STRICKLAND. Hello, May, sweetheart!

(DORIS *puts bag on table, then crosses R. behind them.*)

MAY (*runs to him; hysterical business*). Robert, dear! I'm so glad you're back.

STRICKLAND. It's good to be back. By Jove! I was homesick.

MAY. Those few days seemed like ages. Didn't it seem a long time, Doris?

DORIS. Oh, an awfully long time.

STRICKLAND. Did you miss your daddy?

DORIS. Yes, I cried every night; didn't I, Mamma?

MAY. Yes, you did.

DORIS. And whenever the clock struck today, I wished it was time for you to be here. Didn't I, Mamma?

STRICKLAND. Well, next time we will all go together.

MAY. Everything's all right, then?

STRICKLAND. Yes; just as I wrote you.

MAY. I'm so glad.

(DORIS, *up stage.*)

STRICKLAND. Yes, I feel easier, too.

MAY. Have you had your dinner, Robert?

STRICKLAND. No; I was so anxious to get home that I didn't stop.

MAY. You poor boy, you must be famished.

STRICKLAND. I *could* eat something.

MAY. I'll have Bertha get it ready for you. It won't take long.

STRICKLAND. Thanks, dear. (*To* DORIS.) Come here, to Daddy! (*Goes to R. of table and sits.*)

MAY. I'm leaving you in good hands.

STRICKLAND (DORIS *sits on his knee*). Yes, Doris and I have lots and lots of things to tell each other.

(MAY *goes out R.*)

STRICKLAND. Now, young lady, tell your daddy, who hasn't seen you for four whole days, exactly what you've been doing with every minute of your time.

DORIS (*vaguely*). Oh, lots of things.

STRICKLAND. Well, let's begin at the beginning. Monday you went to school.

DORIS. Yes; and then Mamma took me to Aunt Helen's for supper.

STRICKLAND. And Tuesday you went to school?

DORIS. Yes; Tuesday was the last day. Oh, Daddy, I was promoted!

STRICKLAND. Of course you were promoted. I didn't expect anything else. You're in the grammar school now?

DORIS (*proudly*). Yes.

STRICKLAND. Oh, dear, oh, dear, at this rate you'll soon be through college.

DORIS. I don't want to go to college. I want to be a cook, with a big white apron and lots of shiny pans.

STRICKLAND. Why do you want to be a cook?

DORIS. So that I can make cookies and pies and bread and give them to the heathens.

STRICKLAND. To the heathens!

DORIS. Yes, I'm learning to cook, Daddy.

STRICKLAND. Are you?

DORIS. Yes; I helped Aunt Helen yesterday.

STRICKLAND. Were you at Aunt Helen's yesterday?

DORIS. Yes, all day. Because Mamma was downtown shopping.

STRICKLAND. And what did you do today?

DORIS. Today I stayed home and played house. We were going to the park, but Mamma wanted to lie down, so we didn't go.

STRICKLAND. Isn't Mamma well?

DORIS. She has a headache.

STRICKLAND. Has she had it long?

DORIS. No, only today. Did you get a house, Daddy?

STRICKLAND. Yes; a nice white house, with a large garden.

DORIS (*clapping her hands*). And cows?

STRICKLAND. No, no cows; but lots of flowers and a dog.

DORIS. Oh! A big dog?

STRICKLAND. Yes; and now let me show you what Daddy brought you.

DORIS. Something for me? (*Crosses to L. of table.*)

STRICKLAND. Yes, something for you.

BERTHA (*enters R.*). Mr. Trask is here.

STRICKLAND. Oh! yes, show him in.

(BERTHA *exits R.*)

DORIS. Oh, Daddy, what's that shiny thing? (*Takes revolver from bag.*)

STRICKLAND (*takes doll from bag*). That's a revolver, and don't you ever dare touch it. (*Puts it in bag. Unwrapping doll.*) There, what do you think of that?

DORIS. Oh, Daddy, isn't he beautiful? What shall we call him?

STRICKLAND. Well, as he came from Germany suppose we call him Herman.

TRASK (*enters upper R.*). Hello, Bob!

(TRASK *and* STRICKLAND *shake hands.*)

STRICKLAND. Hello, Jerry, how are you?

TRASK. Fine. Just get back?

(DORIS *comes between them.*)

STRICKLAND. Yes; about fifteen minutes ago.

TRASK. Everything arranged?

STRICKLAND. Yes. Oh, you haven't met Doris, have you? Doris. shake hands with Mr. Trask.

TRASK. So you're Doris, are you?

DORIS (*shyly*). Yes, sir.

TRASK. Who is this?

DORIS. This is Herman.

TRASK. How do you do, Herman? How do you like America? You're quite a girl, aren't you?

STRICKLAND. Yes, indeed; she's in the grammar school now.

TRASK. That's great.

STRICKLAND. Oh! here, Jerry, sit down, down.

(TRASK *sits R. of table.* DORIS *sits up R.C.*)

TRASK. So everything's all right, Bob?

STRICKLAND. Yes; I made very favorable terms with the Briggs people.

TRASK. When do you begin?

STRICKLAND. In a few weeks. I got a crackerjack house. (*Puts bag on piano bench.*)

TRASK. You'll leave soon, then?

STRICKLAND. Yes; you got my wire, of course. (*Down to table.*)

TRASK. Yes.

STRICKLAND. I want to take up that note.

TRASK. Can you make it? If you can't spare it——

STRICKLAND. Thanks all the same; but I want to pay it.

TRASK. I don't mind holding off for a few months. That ten thousand won't put me out of business.

STRICKLAND. No; I don't want to leave any debts behind me. I thought I might have to ask for an extension, but I managed to scrape it together. The Briggs people helped me out.

TRASK. Well, you may need it anyhow. I'll wait till you get on your feet.

STRICKLAND. Thanks, Jerry, but I want to wipe it out. I'll feel easier. (*Back of table.*)

TRASK. All right, just as you like. Here's the note. (*Gives note to* STRICKLAND. *Business.*)

STRICKLAND. And here's the money. (*Takes money from wallet and gives it to* TRASK.)

TRASK. Why the bills?

STRICKLAND. Well, I'll tell you. It was so darn hard to get, that I just wanted the pleasure of handing you ten one-thousand-dollar bills. You'd better count it.

TRASK. Did you count it?

STRICKLAND. Yes.

TRASK. Well, that's good enough for us.

STRICKLAND. You gave me a big lift, old boy. (*Pats* TRASK *on back.*) I got lots to thank you for.

TRASK. Any time you need help—— (*Rises—crosses L. of table, sits.*)

STRICKLAND. Yes, I know you've been a good pal, Jerry, but I hope things will run smoothly now.

TRASK. I'm sorry to see you go, but I think it will be a big thing for you.

STRICKLAND (*sits on front of table*). Should have gone long ago. May has been urging me for over a year.

TRASK. She must have guessed what was coming.

STRICKLAND. Yes; women have instincts about those things. I tell you, Jerry, she's one woman in a million. She's stuck to me like a major through all this business. Never whimpered a minute; never a complaint or an angry word. Ah, she's an ace.

TRASK. She must be.

STRICKLAND. You know it's too bad you never met May; I want you to know her. (*Up R.C.*) Doris, dear, run and tell Mamma that Mr. Trask is here.

TRASK. Some other time, Bob, I've got to hurry away. By the bye, I'd like to have you come down to my place at Long Branch Sunday. I'm getting up a fishing party, six or eight of us. The bass are running well now.

STRICKLAND. I'll be glad to come. (*Down C.*)

TRASK. I'll give you the address. (*Takes card from his pocket and writes on it.*) It's on Henderson Place—three blocks from the railroad station. First house on the left.

(STRICKLAND *pockets card.*)

STRICKLAND. Thanks.

TRASK. Better come down Saturday night, as we want to leave by five Sunday morning.

STRICKLAND. All right, I will.

TRASK. Well, I've got to run along. (*Crosses to R.C. above table, turns up C.*)

(MAY *enters at R. and sees* TRASK, *and is about to withdraw; but* STRICKLAND *has seen her.*)

STRICKLAND. Come in, dear. (MAY *enters R.*) I want you to meet Mr. Trask, May. Jerry, my wife.

TRASK (*bowing*). Delighted, Mrs. Strickland. (MAY *bows in silence.*) I've often heard Bob speak of you.

STRICKLAND (*laughing*). Yes, dear; Jerry has heard a lot about you.

TRASK. Well, I've got to hurry away. (*Starts for door R.*)

STRICKLAND (*up R.C.*). Oh, wait just a few minutes. Good Heavens! I want May to know you.

TRASK. Sorry, but I can't. Some other time. Good night, Mrs. Strickland.

MAY (*in a low voice*). Good night!

TRASK. I hope to have the pleasure again, Mrs. Strickland. Good night! Good night, Doris! (*Goes out, followed by* STRICKLAND.)

DORIS. Oh! Mamma, look what Daddy brought me. (MAY *crosses C.*) But, Mamma, look.

MAY (*brings* DORIS *to table. To* DORIS). Doris, dear, was he—Mr. Trask—here long?

DORIS. Yes; they were talking an awfully long time. Daddy's going fishing at Long Branch.

MAY. What do you mean, child?

DORIS. Mr. Trask lives at Long Branch, and Daddy's going fishing with him Sunday. Wouldn't it be funny if Mr. Trask found your purse, Mamma?

MAY. Be quiet, Doris.

STRICKLAND (*entering upper R.*). Isn't he a corker? Well, you weren't very talkative, dear.

MAY. I was rather taken aback. I didn't expect to find a stranger here.

STRICKLAND. I am glad you two met at last. It's too bad you didn't get to know each other sooner.

(DORIS *goes to piano above table.*)

MAY. What brought him here?

STRICKLAND. I wired him to come. I took up that note.

MAY. The note?

STRICKLAND. Yes; the ten thousand dollars I owed him.

MAY. You mean you paid it?

STRICKLAND. Yes. Why, what's the matter?

MAY. Nothing. But I thought—I'm glad you're able to.

STRICKLAND. Yes, I feel better too. Although Jerry would have given me as much time as I wanted. He's a big-hearted chap.

MAY. Yes.

STRICKLAND. He invited me to go fishing with him to Long Branch on Sunday.

MAY. Oh, I think Helen will expect us for dinner.

STRICKLAND. By George! I never thought of that. All right, I won't go then.

MAY. No, don't. Besides, I dislike the idea of your being out in a boat.

STRICKLAND. All right; I'll phone Jerry in the morning. (*Gets cigarette from tray on piano—lights it. Hums all the while. Then crosses down R.*)

MAY. Yes, do. (*Crosses L. to* DORIS.) Doris dear, run off to bed now.

DORIS. Oh, Mamma, please——

MAY. No; you should have been there long ago.

DORIS. Just five minutes.

MAY. No, not a second. Run away, dear.

DORIS. But I want to talk to Dad.

MAY. You can talk to Daddy in the morning. He's tired too. Now kiss Daddy good night.

DORIS (*crosses right*). Good night, Daddy.

STRICKLAND. Good night, sweetheart. (*Kissing her.*) Sleep soundly. Oh, hang this up for Daddy. (*Gives her his vest. Sits on sofa R.*)

DORIS (*kissing* MAY). Good night, Mamma.

MAY. Good night, my little girl. Now, in you go.

DORIS. Come on, Herman. (*Carrying doll. Exits L.*)

MAY. Mamma will look in at you later.

DORIS. Leave the door open.

MAY. All right, sweetheart. (*Crosses R.*) Oh, Robert, I've read your letter a dozen times; I feel as though I knew every nook and corner of the house. I'm so anxious to go; I wish we were there already. (*Crosses to sofa and sits.*)

STRICKLAND. We'll be there soon.

MAY. How soon?

STRICKLAND. Why, as soon as we can get ready; say two weeks.

MAY. Oh, as long as that?

STRICKLAND. Well, ten days, if you like.

MAY. Let's go next week. I have grown to detest New York.

STRICKLAND. But we've waited so long; a few days more or less——

MAY. That's just it; we've waited so long that it's gotten on my nerves.

STRICKLAND. Aren't you well, dear?

MAY. Yes, certainly; why do you ask?

STRICKLAND. Doris says you aren't feeling well today.

MAY. That child gets such queer notions in her little head. I was a trifle excited about your homecoming; that was all. It's the first time we've been separated.

STRICKLAND. Yes, and the last, let us hope.

MAY. We'll go next week, then?

STRICKLAND. Why, it's scarcely time. There'll be some things to buy.

MAY. We can get almost everything we need when we arrive.

STRICKLAND. Still, when you're breaking up housekeeping there are always odds and ends.

MAY. That won't take long—a day or two.

STRICKLAND. You'll need a traveling dress.

MAY. I'll buy one ready-made.

STRICKLAND. I know you've been looking already; Doris said you were shopping yesterday.

MAY. Yes, I was looking for a traveling dress, but I couldn't get anything to suit me.

STRICKLAND. Well, wait a minute; I've been doing a little shopping myself. (Gets box from bag.)

MAY. For me? (Crosses to him.)

STRICKLAND. Yes, for you.

MAY. Oh, Robert, I'll be so happy to get away; I'll start packing tomorrow.

(BERTHA enters upper R.)

BERTHA. There's a Mr. Burke here to see you, Mrs. Strickland.

STRICKLAND (above table to MAY). Who's Mr. Burke?

MAY. Why, I don't know.

STRICKLAND. Tell him to come in, Bertha.

BERTHA. Will you come in, please?

(BURKE enters; BERTHA exits.)

MAY. Mr. Burke.

BURKE. Yes, ma'am. Are you Mrs. Robert Strickland, mum?

MAY. Yes.

BURKE. I don't like to bother you, ma'am——

STRICKLAND. Sit down, Mr. Burke.

BURKE (seating himself on sofa—R.). Thank you, sir. I found a purse that belongs to you, mum, I think.

MAY. Robert, dear, your dinner will be ready now; you'd better go in before it gets cold.

STRICKLAND. I can wait a few minutes.

MAY. Perhaps Mr. Burke will excuse you.

BURKE. I'll only take a minute, mum; I've come all the way from Long Branch.

STRICKLAND. Have you lost a purse, May? (*Takes string from box.*)

MAY. Why, no; I don't think so. (*Down C.*)

BURKE. Are you sure, mum?

MAY. Positive.

STRICKLAND. Where did you find the purse, Mr. Burke?

BURKE. On the platform of a railroad station at Long Branch last night. I'm the news agent there.

STRICKLAND. Long Branch? Then it can't be yours, May?

MAY. Certainly not. Mr. Burke has evidently made a mistake.

BURKE. There are a half-a-dozen cards in it, with your name and address on them.

STRICKLAND. That seems strange.

MAY. Perhaps one of my friends.

STRICKLAND. What kind of a purse is it, Mr. Burke?

BURKE. Well, if you haven't lost one? (*Rises and goes up a step.*)

STRICKLAND (*crosses R.*). It's just possible that you've made a mistake, May. Let Mrs. Strickland look at it?

BURKE. I'd rather have you describe it first.

STRICKLAND. Oh, yes, of course. You haven't more than two or three purses, May; describe them to Mr. Burke.

MAY. But I haven't lost a purse.

STRICKLAND (*crosses L., unwraps box*). I know; but it would only take a moment to describe them.

MAY (*crosses R.C.*). Well, there's my mesh bag, with the oxidized silver purse.

BURKE. No, that's not it.

MAY. Oh! Robert, there's that green leather bag you gave me for my birthday——

BURKE (*rising*). I guess this isn't yours. (*Goes up C.*)

MAY. No, I knew it wasn't. (*Down C.*)

STRICKLAND (*crosses R.C.*). Wait a moment; you've forgotten that Frenchy black velvet affair you usually carry.

BURKE. What kind?

STRICKLAND. Black velvet with a gold clasp.

BURKE (*comes down R. and takes purse from pocket. Holding up purse*). This it?

STRICKLAND. Why, yes, of course; isn't it, May? (*Takes purse.*)

MAY (*faintly*). Yes, it looks like it. I——

STRICKLAND. You see, you were so positive——

MAY. I don't understand.

BURKE. How much was in it, mum?

MAY. About forty dollars, I think.

BURKE. That's right. Thirty-eight dollars and seventy-five cents; count it, sir.

STRICKLAND (counting money). That's the amount that's here? Is that correct, May?

MAY. Why, yes, I think so.

STRICKLAND (puts money back in purse and closes it). You say you found this at Long Branch, Mr. Burke?

BURKE. Yes, sir. On the platform last night. There was a slip of paper in it, with a Long Branch address written on it—206 Henderson Place. I didn't get a chance to go around there until this evening, as it's a good bit out of my way. There was nobody home but an old housekeeper. She said she didn't know anyone named Strickland, but there'd been a lady there yesterday; so I thought I'd come to the address on the card.

STRICKLAND. I see. Well, we're greatly obliged to you, Mr. Burke.

(BURKE starts to exit.)

STRICKLAND. Hold on, wait a minute. You're entitled to some compensation for your trouble. (Gives him some bills.)

BURKE (pleased). Thank you very much, sir.

STRICKLAND. Not at all; we're indebted to you.

BURKE. Well, I always say that honesty is the best policy.

STRICKLAND. Quite right.

BURKE. Yes, I found it so. Well, good night, mum. Good night, sir.

STRICKLAND. Let me show you to the door. (Crosses R.)

BURKE. Thank you, sir. (He goes out, followed by STRICKLAND.)

(DORIS enters L.)

DORIS. Oh, Mamma, you found your purse, didn't you?

MAY. Yes, darling; now run away to bed.

DORIS. But I can't sleep.

MAY. But you must sleep, dear. Try, try, dear, just a little while. There's a good little girl. (Takes her L. DORIS enters door, L.)

(STRICKLAND re-enters; puts purse on table.)

STRICKLAND. It's strange you didn't know you lost your purse. You almost drove the man away. What made you so insistent?

MAY. I didn't want you to think I'd been careless.

STRICKLAND (surprised). Oh, then you knew you'd lost your purse.

MAY. Why, I——

STRICKLAND. Did you know?

MAY. Yes; I missed it last night. (*Facing him.*)

STRICKLAND. But why did you pretend you didn't know?

MAY. I thought you'd be angry if you knew I'd lost the purse.

STRICKLAND. But why on earth——

MAY. It was careless of me to lose it.

STRICKLAND. But, my dear girl——

MAY. I just didn't want to worry you.

STRICKLAND. Well, I wouldn't be likely to worry about a recovered purse, would I? (*Crosses R. of table.*)

MAY. It was foolish.

STRICKLAND. How did the purse get to Long Branch? You weren't there yesterday. (MAY *does not answer.*) Were you?

MAY. Yes.

STRICKLAND. But you said before that you'd been shopping.

MAY. That was on account of Doris. (*Comes to table.*)

STRICKLAND. On account of Doris?

MAY. Yes; she wanted to know where I was going. (*Sits L. of table.*) If I had told her I was going to the seashore, she would have teased me to take her along.

STRICKLAND. But you told me the same thing after Doris had gone to bed.

MAY. Did I? I couldn't have been thinking of what I was saying.

STRICKLAND. Yes, you even mentioned that you were looking for a traveling dress.

MAY. Queer, isn't it? My thoughts must be wandering tonight. The excitement of your homecoming and all that. (*Rises.*)

STRICKLAND. What took you to Long Branch?

(BERTHA *enters.*)

MAY. What is it, Bertha?

BERTHA. Mr. Strickland's dinner is ready.

STRICKLAND. All right, Bertha; I'll be there in a moment.

(BERTHA *exits upper R.*)

MAY. You'd better go in, Robert; everything will get cold. (*Up behind table.*)

STRICKLAND. In a moment.

MAY. But you must eat, dear; you'll be ill if you don't.

STRICKLAND. Just tell me about Long Branch. I don't quite understand it.

MAY. I'll tell you some other time. I'm tired now, and your dinner is waiting.

STRICKLAND. Won't you tell me why you went down there? (*She goes L. a step.*) You didn't write that you were going. Why are you acting so strangely, dear? (*Takes her in his arms.*)

MAY. I'm not acting strangely. Of course I'll tell you why I went down. I went down to see a friend.

STRICKLAND. I didn't know you had friends at Long Branch.

MAY. You don't know her.

STRICKLAND. Who is she?

MAY. Ruth Green is her name.

STRICKLAND. Who's Ruth Green?

MAY. An old school friend of mine.

STRICKLAND. Have I ever met her?

MAY. No; and I haven't seen her for years.

STRICKLAND. Then how did you happen to go down to see her yesterday?

MAY. She wrote, asking me to come down.

STRICKLAND (R., a few steps). You haven't met her for years, then she suddenly asks you to come down to Long Branch to see her. Why didn't she come to see you?

MAY. She's critically ill, and she wanted to see me again. So she had me looked up. We used to be quite intimate in school.

STRICKLAND. How did she manage to write, if she's so ill?

MAY. Someone wrote for her.

STRICKLAND. From what is she suffering? (Crosses to her.)

MAY. Why—pneumonia.

STRICKLAND. Oh, she's dangerously ill then?

MAY. Oh, yes.

STRICKLAND. But Burke said there was no one there.

MAY. Burke?

STRICKLAND. Yes—at the Henderson Place address. The house he went to. He said he found only an old housekeeper.

MAY. Oh, yes, I remember; they said they were going to remove her to a hospital today.

STRICKLAND. With pneumonia?

MAY. Yes—there are serious complications.

STRICKLAND. I see. (Crosses R. and sits on sofa.)

MAY. Your dinner won't be fit to eat, Robert.

STRICKLAND. Never mind about it; I'm not hungry. Just be patient with me for a few minutes more. (Sits on sofa, R.)

MAY. What are you thinking about, Robert? (Sits L. of table.)

STRICKLAND. (crosses C.). I'd like to see that letter from Miss Green.

MAY. I can't show it to you.

STRICKLAND. Why not?

MAY. Because it contains some personal matters that she wouldn't want anyone but me to know about.

STRICKLAND. But she didn't write the letter herself.

MAY. No—her mother wrote it for her.

STRICKLAND. Oh, she has a mother?

MAY. Certainly she has a mother.

STRICKLAND (*sits on edge of table*). In other words, your friend whom you haven't seen for years chooses a moment when she is critically ill to get her mother to write to you concerning matters which your husband daren't know anything about? Is that correct?

MAY. Yes; but there's nothing strange about it.

STRICKLAND. Perhaps not. (*Crosses R.C.*) Still, I'd like to see the letter. I don't want to read it. I only want to look at it.

MAY. Why do you want to see it?

STRICKLAND (*Sits R. of table*). I want to know why, if you had a letter containing your friend's address, you went to the trouble of copying it on another piece of paper.

MAY. Who said I copied it on another piece of paper?

STRICKLAND. Burke. He said the purse contained the Henderson Place address on a piece of paper.

MAY. Oh, that was because—I did that to—— (*Rises and goes L. a step.*)

STRICKLAND (*Goes to her with hands on her shoulders*). May, you're keeping something from me.

MAY. Don't say that, Robert. Why should I keep anything from you?

STRICKLAND. I don't know; but you are, nevertheless. What is it, May?

MAY. There is nothing.

STRICKLAND. There is. I've never seen you like this before. Won't you tell me?

MAY. There's nothing, dear—nothing! (*Down L.*)

STRICKLAND. Well, then I can't see why you have any great objection to showing me the letter?

MAY. I can't show it to you.

STRICKLAND. You can't?

MAY. No; I destroyed it.

STRICKLAND. Oh, you destroyed it?

MAY. Yes.

STRICKLAND. Why?

MAY. I never keep letters.

STRICKLAND. Why didn't you say so in the first place?

MAY. Say what in the first place?

STRICKLAND. That you destroyed the letter.

MAY. Because you're cross-examining me as though I were a criminal. My head's whirling like a top. I can't stand it much longer. (*Up L.*)

STRICKLAND (*up to table*). May, dear, I don't want to hurt you.

Won't you tell me what's troubling you? We've never before had secrets from each other.

MAY. But there's nothing to tell—there's nothing to tell.

STRICKLAND. I'll have to find out for myself, then. (*Sits in chair R. of table.*) I didn't look for this kind of a homecoming. (*He relapses into silence.*)

MAY (*above table. Pause*). What are you thinking about now? (*He does not answer.*) I wish you'd eat your dinner instead of exciting yourself about nothing.

STRICKLAND. Henderson Place. Where is that card Trask gave me? (*Searches in his pockets.*)

MAY (*L. of table*). What are you talking about?

STRICKLAND (*finding card*). Here it is! What's this? "14 right, 2, 27—" No, that's not it. Yes—206 Henderson Place. Two hundred and six! (*Rises.*) That's the very number Burke mentioned, isn't it?

MAY. I don't know; I don't know.

STRICKLAND (*crosses R.C.*) Is it, or isn't it?

MAY. I don't know.

STRICKLAND. I'll soon find out. (*He reaches for purse on table, which MAY seizes first.*) Let me have that purse.

MAY. What do you want it for?

STRICKLAND. I want to see that address.

MAY. There's no address there.

STRICKLAND. Give me that purse.

MAY. No, Robert!

STRICKLAND. I want that purse; do you hear me?

MAY. Robert!

STRICKLAND. Will you give it to me, or not?

MAY. Please—Robert.

(*He snatches the purse from her; she gives a little scream; STRICKLAND opens the purse; scatters the contents on the table; he searches through them until he finds what he is looking for.*)

STRICKLAND. This is it. Two hundred and six Henderson Place. (*R. of table.*) Trask's address. So that's where you were? Well, what have you got to say?

MAY (*down L. Desperately*). I'll tell you.

STRICKLAND. Wait a moment. It was Trask's house you went to, wasn't it?

MAY. Yes.

STRICKLAND. Then your friend—then her mother—and the letter you destroyed were all lies, weren't they?

MAY. Yes, but listen to me.

STRICKLAND. Go ahead, I'm listening. (*Sits R. of table.*) I want to know why you went to Trask's house.

MAY. I'm going to tell you, if you'll only be patient.

STRICKLAND. Go on.

MAY. I'd heard you say that Mr. Trask had a home at Long Branch.

STRICKLAND. Well?

MAY. When you wrote to me about the house——

STRICKLAND. Well—why are you stopping?

MAY. You frighten me.

STRICKLAND. Go on.

MAY. Well, I don't know much about house planning, and I wanted to see a well-planned house. So I went down to Long Branch to look through Mr. Trask's house.

STRICKLAND. With him?

MAY. No, alone; the housekeeper showed me through.

STRICKLAND. So that's why you went down—to look at the house?

MAY. Yes.

STRICKLAND. Then why have you been lying to me?

MAY. I thought you might not like it.

STRICKLAND. Why did you think that?

MAY. I don't know; it was a foolish thing to do—going to a stranger's house; and your manner seemed so suspicious—you forced me into it. (Down L. a step.)

STRICKLAND. When I introduced you tonight you pretended you'd never met each other?

MAY. We hadn't.

STRICKLAND. How did you know his address then?

MAY. I called him up.

STRICKLAND. You called him up?

MAY. Yes, of course; I couldn't go without asking his permission.

STRICKLAND. So you called him up to ask permission to visit his house —a man you'd never met.

MAY. He's a friend of yours—I didn't see any harm.

STRICKLAND. What did he say?

MAY. He said he didn't mind at all.

STRICKLAND. And he gave you his address?

MAY. Yes.

STRICKLAND. Over the phone?

MAY. Yes.

STRICKLAND (half mad). That's the last lie you'll tell me. (Rises and goes up R.)

MAY. What do you mean?

STRICKLAND. I mean that this address is in Trask's handwriting (Crosses to her.)

(MAY with a cry sits L. of table.)

STRICKLAND. I want the truth now. You met Trask before tonight?

MAY. Yes.

STRICKLAND. He came here.

MAY. Yes.

STRICKLAND. When?

MAY. Night before last.

STRICKLAND. And you arranged to go down there yesterday? He was there? You went down there to meet him. My God! (*Up R.C.*)

MAY. Robert, dear.

STRICKLAND. May, why did you go down there? I'm waiting.

MAY. Because—— No, no, I can't tell you; I can't tell you. (*Crosses R.*)

STRICKLAND. May, if you love me—if you ever loved me——

MAY. I can't—I can't!

STRICKLAND. You can't tell me? You mean—— No! Say it's not true! (*She does not answer.*) Won't you answer? Is it true?

MAY. Robert, dear, you mustn't ask me any more questions, because I can't answer them. There is something I can't tell you. You must trust me Robert. We've loved each other all these years. Believed in each other. You're everything that life means to me—you and Doris. We're going away now, to begin a new life. Perhaps someday when we are in our new home I'll tell you, but not now. You've always believed in me; believe in me now.

STRICKLAND. I do—I do! But there's one thing you must tell me. What have you been to Trask? (MAY *drops on sofa, sobbing.* STRICKLAND *starts C., looks at door L., buries his face in his hands—groans—starts for door R., stops—rushes to bag, gets revolver and rushes off R. Door slams.*)

MAY (*sobbing on sofa. Gets up. Goes up C.*). Robert! Robert! He's gone! He's gone! If he finds him, he'll kill him. His whole life will be ruined. Robert, my husband, my husband. (*Rushes to phone.*) Hello, hello! give me 182 River——

DORIS (*rushes from left*). Oh, Mamma, I'm afraid—I'm afraid.

MAY (*takes her in her arms*). Oh, my darling! My baby! (*Takes* DORIS *in her arms.*) My little girl! HELLO! HELLO!——

CURTAIN

SCENE III

DORIS *heard sobbing.*

DORIS. I'm afraid, I'm afraid.

(*Lights go up on courtroom scene.*)

DORIS (*sobbing*). I'm afraid; I'm afraid. (*On witness stand.*)

ARBUCKLE. Don't cry, Doris. I won't be much longer. Whom did your mother call up?

DORIS. Mr. Trask; but he wasn't there.

ARBUCKLE. How do you know he wasn't there?

DORIS. Because Mamma said, "I will call again."

ARBUCKLE. Then what did she do?

DORIS. She cried and walked up and down the room and said lots of terrible things.

ARBUCKLE. What did she say?

DORIS. Why didn't I tell him? Why didn't I tell him?

ARBUCKLE. What then?

DORIS. Then I cried, too, because I was afraid. I wanted to talk to her, but she wouldn't. I was awfully afraid. I'm afraid now. (*She cries.*)

ARBUCKLE. Don't cry, Doris. It will only be a few minutes longer; then we'll be through with you.

DORIS (*crying*). I want my mamma.

ARBUCKLE. Try not to cry. Just a little while longer. (*Takes her hand from her face.*) That's a good girl. Are you listening to me?

DORIS (*choking back a sob*). Yes, sir.

ARBUCKLE. Did your mother call up again?

DORIS. Yes, sir; and she said: "Is that you, Gerald Trask?" I don't want to talk any more. My head hurts, and I'm afraid.

ARBUCKLE. Don't be afraid. We'll be finished in a moment. Your mother said: "Is that you, Gerald Trask——"

DORIS. Yes, sir.

ARBUCKLE. What happened then?

DORIS. Then—then—— Oh, I don't know.

ARBUCKLE. Yes, you do, Doris. Just try to think. You've told me about it a great many times.

DORIS. I don't remember.

ARBUCKLE. Try to think a moment. Be a brave girl. Did you hear a noise through the telephone?

DORIS. Yes, sir.

GRAY (*rises*). If the Court please; I must again insist that my friend refrain from leading the witness.

ARBUCKLE. I submit, Your Honor, that the child is laboring under a terrific strain, and that I must be allowed some latitude.

DINSMORE. Try not to lead the witness.

(GRAY *sits*.)

ARBUCKLE. You say you heard a noise, Doris?

DORIS. Yes, sir.

ARBUCKLE. What kind of a noise was it?

DORIS. I don't know—a funny noise —like a little firecracker.

ARBUCKLE. And what did your mother do when she heard the noise?

DORIS. She screamed and said: "My God, he's killed him!" Please let me go. I don't want to talk any more——

ARBUCKLE. Just one more question, and you'll be all through.

DORIS. I don't want to.

ARBUCKLE. What did your mother do after she said, "My God, he's killed him"?   •

DORIS. She took me in her arms and kissed me and said, "Good-by," and I cried because it hurt when she kissed me.

ARBUCKLE. Did she go away then?

DORIS. Yes.

ARBUCKLE. And have you seen your mother since that night?

DORIS (*sobbing*). No, no; I want to see her.

ARBUCKLE. Do you know where she is?

DORIS (*sobbing*). No, no—please tell me. I want to see her. I want to see her. Daddy dear—(*ring. She starts down steps of stand*—ARBUCKLE *catches her in his arms*)—why did you make Mamma cry and run away from me?

ARBUCKLE (*catches her in his arms*). That's the child's story, Your Honor.

STRICKLAND. For God's sake, you're torturing my little baby.

GRAY. I move that the child's testimony be stricken out.

DINSMORE (*raps once*). Silence.

STRICKLAND (*rises*). You're torturing my little girl.

CURTAIN

ACT THREE

SCENE I

SCENE: The Courtroom.

DINSMORE. Mr. Gray, have you seen Mr. Arbuckle this morning?

GRAY. No, Your Honor, I have not.

DINSMORE (looking at his watch. As JUDGE looks at his watch several of the jury look at their watches). It's twenty minutes after ten. Mr. Daniels!

CLERK (rises). Yes, Your Honor.

DINSMORE. Just call up Mr. Arbuckle's office and find out what's detaining him.

CLERK. Yes, Your Honor. (Goes right. ARBUCKLE enters, breathless, with bag—puts bag on table L.) Here's Mr. Arbuckle, Your Honor.

DINSMORE (sharply). This court convenes at ten o'clock, Mr. Arbuckle.

ARBUCKLE (crosses C.). I must ask Your Honor to excuse me. I have been working all night on this case. There has been an unexpected development over night. Last evening Mrs. Strickland, the wife of the defendant, came to my house. It seems that she became dangerously ill after the catastrophe, and it is only the realization of the importance of her testimony that has enabled her to be in condition to take the witness stand. She has told me a story, Your Honor, which puts an entirely different aspect upon this case.

GRAY. I object to counsel commenting upon the testimony of a witness who has not yet been called.

ARBUCKLE. Very well, Your Honor. I shall call Mrs. Strickland at once. Her testimony will require no comment. Call Mrs. Strickland, please. (Talks to JUDGE. ATTENDANT opens door left and calls.)

ATTENDANT. Mrs. Strickland.

(MAY enters left. Stands below table L.)

ARBUCKLE (crosses to her—takes her hand—helps her to stand). Kindly take the stand, please.

(MAY does so.)

CLERK. Raise your right hand, please. Do you solemnly swear that the testimony you are about to give will be the truth, the whole truth, and nothing but the truth, so help you God? What's your name?

MAY. May Deane Strickland.

ARBUCKLE. Now, Mrs. Strickland, you are the wife of Robert Strickland, the defendant?

MAY. Yes, sir.

ARBUCKLE. When were you married?

MAY. July 15, 1903.

ARBUCKLE. Did you know Gerald Trask?

MAY. Yes, sir, I did.

ARBUCKLE. When did you first meet Mr. Trask?

MAY. In March 1900.

ARBUCKLE. That was before you knew Mr. Strickland?

MAY. Yes, sir; more than two years before.

ARBUCKLE. How old were you at that time?

MAY. Just seventeen.

ARBUCKLE. Where did you meet Mr. Trask?

MAY. At Lakewood.

ARBUCKLE. Now, Mrs. Strickland, describe your relations with Mr. Trask at that time.

MAY. He was very attentive to me and took me about a good deal. About ten days after I met him I returned to the city, and he came back too. He kept sending me things and

taking me out. Then one day he asked me to marry him.

ARBUCKLE. When was that?

MAY. In April 1900.

ARBUCKLE. Did you accept him?

MAY. Not the first time. I asked him to wait.

ARBUCKLE. What did he say?

MAY. He said he would wait as long as I wanted him to. But every time he saw me he spoke to me about it —telling me how much he loved me and how much I meant to him. He seemed so earnest and sincere that I believed everything he said. At last I yielded and consented to marry him.

ARBUCKLE. When was that?

MAY. On the 19th of May. He said he wanted to be married next day. But on account of his family he couldn't let it be known for a while, so we'd have to be married secretly. Next day he called for me in his automobile and said we were going to a hotel in Great Neck, Long Island, to meet a clergyman with whom he had made arrangements. We got to Great Neck at about seven o'clock that evening.

ARBUCKLE (pause). Yes?

MAY. The next morning we were to have breakfast in our rooms.

RING. LIGHTS GO OUT. CURTAIN.

SCENE II

(*Knocking heard off right. Curtain rises. Lights go up. Enter* MAY *from left.*)

MAY. Just a minute, just a minute, please. (*Opens door right.*) Come in.

WAITER (*enters with breakfast*). It's the breakfast, ma'am.

MAY. Put it right there.

WAITER. Shall I set the table, ma'am?

MAY. No—no.

(RUSSELL *enters with bunch of flowers.* WAITER *exits R.*)

RUSSELL. Good morning, Mrs. Trask.

MAY. Oh, good morning, Mr. Russell.

RUSSELL. I just came in to supervise the laying of the breakfast. I want it to be a function.

MAY (*laughing*). Yes, considering it's the first.

RUSSELL. I told the chef to make the effort of his life.

MAY. That's darling in you, Mr. Russell.

(WAITER *goes off left.*)

RUSSELL (*presenting the flowers*). And here's the bridal bouquet. I wish you both lots of happiness.

MAY. Thank you ever so much, Mr. Russell. They're beautiful.

RUSSELL. From our own garden. Permit me to lay the table.

MAY. Oh, no; please let me.

RUSSELL. Well, I hope you enjoy your breakfast.

MAY. I'm sure we shall. Thank you again. (*Holding out flowers.*)

TRASK. Hello, Russell! (*Enters R.*)

RUSSELL (*at door*). Good morning, Mr. Trask. (*Goes out R.*)

MAY. Gerald, look at the beautiful flowers Mr. Russell brought me. Aren't they lovely?

TRASK. Fine.

MAY. He's awfully nice.

TRASK. He can't help being nice to you.

MAY. You deserve a flower for that.

(*Business of adjusting flower on his coat.*)

TRASK. That breakfast smells very interesting.

MAY. Before you can have a mouthful to eat, you must tell me where you've been all the while.

TRASK. I've been fixing up the car.

MAY. You were gone ages and ages.

TRASK. Only fifteen minutes.

MAY. Only fifteen minutes! Why, that's a lifetime. I thought you were never coming back.

TRASK (*laughing*). Did you?

MAY. Yes. That would have been a nice state of affairs, wouldn't it—on our first day?

TRASK. Yes. Parted at the altar, eh?

MAY. I think you deserve a scolding for running off for so long. (*Puts flowers in vase.*)

TRASK. Don't scold me. I hate to be scolded on an empty stomach. (*Gets tablecloth.*)

MAY. Will you promise never to do it again?

TRASK. Yes, I promise.

MAY. Oh, that isn't enough. You must say, "I'll never, never, never leave you again, as long as I live." Say that.

TRASK. I'll never, never, never leave you—how does it go? (*Both lay tablecloth.*)

MAY. "—again, as long as I live."

TRASK. Again, as long as I live. Is that right?

MAY. Yes. And now you must ask me to forgive you.

TRASK. Forgive me.

MAY. May, dear.

TRASK. May, dear. (*Kisses her. They stand each side of the table.*)

MAY. Ooh! You taste of gasoline.

(*Business of breakfast throughout.*)

TRASK. Yes; I've been tanking up the car. (*Crosses R.*)

MAY. Why? (*Crosses R.*)

TRASK. We're going away this afternoon. (*Puts grapefruit on table.*)

MAY. Going away? Where to?

TRASK. Anywhere you like.

MAY. Why leave here?

TRASK. Oh, there's no fun here. This place is dead.

MAY. But I love this place. It will always be sacred to me—our wedding place. It's the greatest happiness we'll ever know. (*Gets knives, forks, napkins, and toast. Crosses to L. of table. Sets table.*)

TRASK. Of course there's a lot in that. Still, it's not very lively. (*Gets omelet.*)

MAY. Every once in a while, Gerald, years from now, we'll slip down here quietly—just you and. I alone, and live this day again, won't we.

TRASK. Yes; that will be bully. (*Gets cups, saucers, plates, then cream and coffee.*)

MAY. Isn't it strange! Yesterday this place was only a queer name to me, and now it's the dearest spot on earth. I'm so happy, Gerald dear.

Must we keep it quiet long? (*They embrace.*)

TRASK. ·Yes, quite a while, I'm afraid.

MAY. It seems so wrong for families to interfere in these things. If people love each other, I don't see why they must consult anyone else about it. (*Puts vase on table.*)

TRASK. You can't get everybody to see that. (*Gets sugar, salt, and pepper.*)

MAY. I wish we could tell. (*Sits L. of table.*) I'm just longing to go about telling everybody how happy I am.

TRASK. Don't say a word to anyone.

MAY. No, I won't—I've promised. But the clergyman may tell someone, Gerald. Clergymen are sometimes gossipy, you know.

TRASK. I'll see that he doesn't tell. (*Gets butter plates.*)

MAY. What's his name?

TRASK. The clergyman? (*Sits R. of table.*)

MAY. Yes.

TRASK. Oh—Smith. Walter Smith.

MAY. Is he nice? (*Pours coffee, sugar, and cream.*)

TRASK. Yes; fine chap.

MAY. You're very good friends, aren't you?

TRASK. Oh, yes; we were classmates at college.

MAY. I'm glad of that.

TRASK. Why?

MAY. Well, it will be so much nicer than having a stranger. Don't you think so?

TRASK. Yes, of course. That was why I asked him.

MAY. Do you think he'll be here soon?

TRASK. Sometime during the morning, he said.

MAY. It's strange, he didn't receive your first message last night, isn't it?

TRASK. There's nothing strange about it. His maid forgot to deliver it, that's all.

MAY. Of course, it was too late for him to come down after you telephoned from here.

TRASK. Yes, of course, it was almost midnight. I couldn't have asked it of him.

MAY. I wish he had come last night.

TRASK. Yes; it's too bad he didn't.

MAY. I feel uncomfortable about it.

TRASK. I don't see why. A few hours sooner or later—what difference does it make?

MAY. Well, I guess it doesn't make any difference. I wish, though, you had gotten someone in the neighborhood.

TRASK. I told you I tried. The only clergyman who could have married us is out of town attending a convention. But if I had thought you were going to be cut up about it——

MAY. You aren't angry, are you, dear. (*Rises, goes to back of table.*)

TRASK. No, certainly not. I understand how you feel about it; but it's only a matter of form, after all, you know.

MAY. Of course it is. I'm a silly girl, and you're so patient with me. Do you know, Gerald, I'm almost afraid of you sometimes.

TRASK. Nonsense! Why? (*Puts omelet on plates.*)

MAY. You know so many things. (*Sits L. of table.*)

TRASK. That's no reason you should be afraid of me. (*Hands plate to* MAY.)

MAY. I know it isn't. Gerald, dear, you're sure you never cared for any other girl?

TRASK. My dear child, I've told you a hundred times. Don't you believe me?

MAY. Of course I do. But it seems so strange that you should fall in love with me. You've met so many other girls.

TRASK. Yes; but I've never met anyone like you.

MAY. You do care a great deal, don't you? (*Takes his hand.*)

TRASK. I've told you.

MAY. And you'll be very good to me.

TRASK. As good as I know how.

MAY. And you'll always love me?

TRASK. As long as I live. Haven't I said so?

(*Both drink, looking at each other.*)

MAY (*pauses—goes to window L.*). I do wish Mr. Smith would come.

TRASK. I can't imagine what's keeping him.

MAY. Don't you think you'd better telephone?

TRASK. No. Let's be patient a little while longer.

MAY. What will we do if he doesn't come?

TRASK. Well, you see we must leave here this afternoon at any rate.

MAY. But we can't leave without being married.

TRASK. Why not?

MAY. Why not! Surely, Gerald, you wouldn't want to.

TRASK. I thought we had agreed about that.

MAY. I know, but——

TRASK. I don't see what you're worried about. It's only a matter of ceremony—a formality.

MAY. I know; but a girl looks at these things differently.

TRASK. Well, if my man doesn't come, it would be impossible to be married here anyhow.

MAY. Couldn't you find someone——
(*Sits L. of table.*)

TRASK. Impossible! There's no one available. Besides, we couldn't get a ring down here.

MAY. Oh, haven't you a ring?

TRASK. No, I forgot it. It's all right, though. I told Wallace to bring one down with him.

MAY. Wallace? I thought you said his name was Walter?

TRASK. So it is. Wallace is a nick-name I gave him because he's so proud of his Scotch ancestry.

MAY. Oh! Gerald, I've got a plain gold ring. I'll get it. (*Exits left. Pause. Knock at door R.*)

TRASK. Come in. (RUSSELL *enters, with open telegram in his hand.*) Hello, Russell, what have you got there? Dispatches from the front?

(MAY *enters left.*)

MAY. Gerald, look; will this do? (*Down L.C.*)

RUSSELL. I'd like an explanation of this. (*Reads telegram.*) "Detain May Deane until I arrive. She is with Gerald Trask.—Henry Deane."

MAY. From Father!

TRASK (*angrily to* MAY). What is this?

MAY. I don't know, Gerald. I don't understand it.

TRASK. Didn't I tell you——?

MAY. I didn't tell him.

RUSSELL. Well, Mr. Trask?

TRASK. Well, what?

RUSSELL. Is this young lady your wife, or isn't she?

TRASK. What difference does that make to you?

RUSSELL. It makes a great deal of difference to me. You registered here as man and wife.

TRASK. Well, then, what are you worrying about?

MAY. But explain to Mr. Russell, Gerald. (TRASK *crosses L. up to window. Looks out window.*) We're going to be married this morning, Mr. Russell. We were going to be married last night, but there was no clergyman.

TRASK. Keep quiet, May!

RUSSELL. Quite so. There probably aren't more than about a dozen clergymen within a mile of this place.

MAY. What do you mean! GER-ALD—— (*Comes down R. to* RUSSELL.)

TRASK. Keep quiet, I tell you, and let me .nanage this. What do you want, Russell?

RUSSELL. I want you to get out at once.

TRASK. We're planning to leave this afternoon.

RUSSELL. That won't do; you must leave immediately. It's eleven o'clock now—I want you out by noon.

TRASK. I'll go when I get ready.

RUSSELL. No, you won't; you'll go now. I won't have any questionable characters in my house.

MAY. How can you let him talk like that!

TRASK. Will you be quiet!

RUSSELL. I've been years building up a reputation for this place, and I don't intend risking it for you or anyone else.

TRASK. You're damned independent, old man. This isn't the only road-house on Long Island, you know.

RUSSELL. I guess I can stand the loss of your business. I don't care for your sort, anyhow.

TRASK. You've said enough, Russell. You'd better clear out. (Crosses L. and up stage.)

RUSSELL (up to door R.). Yes; but I want you out by noon, understand that. Young lady, for your sake, I hope your father gets here before then.

TRASK. If you don't get out of this room I'll kick you out.

RUSSELL. If you're not out by noon I'll send for the police. (Exits R.)

(TRASK crosses R.—locks door, followed by MAY.)

MAY. Gerald, why did he talk like that? Why didn't you explain?

TRASK. This is a nice mess we're in.

MAY. But, Gerald, if you had only explained——

TRASK. Didn't I tell you not to let your father know where we were.

MAY. But I didn't.

TRASK. What!

MAY. I didn't, I tell you. I would have if you hadn't told me not to.

TRASK. I told you fifty times that I didn't want anyone to know. (Down L.)

MAY. But I didn't—I didn't!

TRASK. How else could he have found out?

MAY. I don't know—but not from me.

TRASK. The very thing I wanted to avoid has happened. (Crosses R.)

MAY. But it's not my fault——

TRASK. He'll come down here and make a scene.

MAY. Not when he finds it's all right. But I wonder how he knew we weren't married yet.

TRASK. Don't waste time now. Get ready. (Crosses L.)

MAY. Ready for what?

TRASK. To go. We've got to clear out before the old man gets here.

MAY. Oh, no, Gerald; let's——

TRASK. I'm managing this. Get ready. (Up to door L. Knock at door.)

MAY. Oh, that must be Mr. Smith.

TRASK. Damn it! That's your father, I'll bet. There'll be a devil of a row——

MAY. Shall I tell him to come in?

TRASK. Wait a minute. If it's your father, I don't want to see him.

MAY. But, Gerald——

TRASK. Listen to me. I'm going into the other room. I'll wait in there while you talk to the old man. If he asks for me, tell him I'm out. Get rid of him as quickly as you can. Do you understand?

MAY. Yes; but if it's Mr. Smith——

TRASK. Do as I tell you, do you hear me? (*Knock at door. He goes into bedroom.* MAY *pauses irresolutely. Crosses R. and unlocks door.*)

MAY. Father! (*Retreats R.C.*)

DEANE. Where's Trask?

MAY. Why did you come, Father?

DEANE. Where is he? (*Crosses C. below table.*)

MAY. He—he's out.

DEANE. Where did he go?

MAY. Why—I don't know—he didn't say. But, Father——

DEANE. When is he coming back?

MAY. Why—not for quite a while. (*Pause.*) How did you know we were here, Father?

DEANE. Never mind now. Get your things, May. (*Looks at breakfast.*)

MAY. My things? Why?

DEANE. We're going home.

MAY. But, Father, Gerald and I are going to be married this morning.

DEANE. Get your things, May.

MAY. But, Father, you don't seem to understand. Gerald and I are going to be married this morning; we're waiting for the clergyman. (*Goes to him.*)

DEANE. He can't marry you. (*Puts arms around her.*)

MAY. He can't! What do you mean?

DEANE. He is a married man. (*Turning away.*)

MAY (*inarticulately*). Married?

DEANE. His wife telephoned to me this morning. She's been having him watched.

MAY. No! I don't believe it! I don't believe it!

DEANE. Come, May.

MAY (*with her back to the door*). Father, don't you understand? We're to be married this morning. There's a clergyman coming down. (MRS. TRASK *enters.*) He was to have come last night. Don't you understand? (MAY *turns and sees her. Pause.*) Who are you? What do you want? Who is she?

DEANE. This is Mrs. Trask.

MRS. TRASK. You'd better go home with your father.

(MAY *stands dazed, looking from one to the other.*)

DEANE (*crosses to her*). Come, May, come.

(MAY *then rushes to the bedroom door, which she flings open.*)

MAY. Gerald! Gerald! (*Goes in room; comes out; stands at door.* DEANE *rushes out door L. Count five then auto effect; she rushes to window.* DEANE *enters the bedroom.*) Gerald! Gerald! (*Screams and faints.* DEANE *enters*)

DEANE. May!

LIGHTS OUT. CURTAIN.

SCENE III

CURTAIN. LIGHTS UP.

MAY (*discovered on witness stand*). I don't know what happened then—(*ring up*)—I must have fainted. But the sound of that automobile went through my head for weeks. Soon after, Father died. Then I met Robert—my husband. When I saw that he loved me, I tried to tell him about—about that terrible experience, but I was afraid of destroying his happiness. He would not have understood. Men *don't* understand, and I loved him so. He seemed to need me and to need his belief in me. I came to realize I must never tell him. He was all that life meant to me. I wanted to devote my every thought to shielding him from the slightest unhappiness. Even though he was a strong man, he seemed to need my protection. Two years later we were married. I had begun to think of that awful experience only as a terrible dream. Then my baby —Doris—came. And I had two to watch over; their happiness was my one aim in life. For nine years we three were so happy together. Then one day about a year ago Robert

mentioned that man's name; he had met him somewhere. I hoped that their acquaintance was only passing; but they became more friendly. Robert spoke several times of having us meet, but for a year I avoided that meeting. Meanwhile Robert's business troubles had begun. He—that man—lent him money and helped him in other ways. With their growing friendship I dreaded the wrecking of all our happiness. Then a business opportunity arose, which would take us from New York. I urged Robert to accept this, and he finally decided to. It seemed as if some power were guarding the happiness of my husband and baby. It was a Monday when Robert left for Cleveland. Tuesday night *he* came. It was about the note which was due then. He recognized me, and threatened to tell Robert everything. He taunted me, saying that Robert would believe anything against me because of my long silence. He demanded that I come to his house at Long Branch the next day. I begged for mercy. I went down on my knees to him. I begged, and begged, and begged. He wouldn't even listen to me. He said he would ruin Robert and make a pauper of him. I was mad with fear. I didn't care for myself, I only thought of Robert and my baby. Their happiness was in my hands. I would have paid any price to shield them. If by dying I could have saved them, I would have died willingly. It would have been much easier than—— But there was only one way, and I *had* to save them. Then Robert found out, and all my years of planning were shattered. Last evening, as I lay half-conscious in the hospital, I heard the nurses discussing the testimony of a little girl. I learned it was my little girl, and that my husband was on trial for murder and burglary. They didn't want to let me go, but I made them understand that my husband might be put to death unless the truth were known. I've *told* you the truth. Can't you understand? He didn't go there to rob; he didn't take the money. Robert's not a thief. I am to blame. The fault is all mine. I've ruined the lives of my husband and baby. God forgive me! (*Ring curtain.*) God forgive me! God forgive me.

CURTAIN

ACT FOUR

The Jury Room

FOREMAN. Mr. Mathews.

MATHEWS. Not guilty.

FOREMAN. Mr. Adams.

ADAMS. Not guilty.

FOREMAN. Mr. Richner.

RICHNER. Not guilty.

FOREMAN. Mr. Leavitt.

LEAVITT. Not guilty.

FOREMAN. Mr. Oton.

OTON. Not guilty.

FOREMAN. Mr. Summers.

SUMMERS. Not guilty.

(*Ring up.*)

FOREMAN. Mr. Tovell.

TOVELL. Not guilty.

FOREMAN. Mr. Elliott.

ELLIOTT. Not guilty.

FOREMAN. Mr. Friend.

FRIEND. Not guilty.

FOREMAN. Mr. Leeds.

LEEDS. Not guilty.

FOREMAN. Mr. Moore.

MOORE (*rises down R. after hesitating*). Not guilty.

JUROR LEEDS. Good!

JUROR FRIEND. That's the stuff!

JUROR ELLIOTT. At last!

JUROR TOVELL. Good for you!

JUROR MOORE. Wait a moment. Mr. Trumbull hasn't voted. How do you vote, Trumbull?

FOREMAN. Gentlemen, we stand eleven for acquittal and one for conviction.

JUROR LEEDS. Oh, I say, Trumbull! Don't hold out now! (*Crosses R. down stage.*)

JUROR FRIEND. What's the good of being pigheaded? (*Rises.*)

JUROR TOVELL. Make it acquittal, and let's get it over with.

FOREMAN (*quietly*). I've voted, gentlemen.

JUROR SUMMERS. Look here, Trumbull, will you listen to reason? (*Crosses R.C.*)

FOREMAN (*pushes back chair and puts one foot on table*). Go ahead.

SIXTH JUROR. What's the good of sending Strickland to the chair? You don't bring Trask back to life, do you? All you do is kill off a good, clean, straightforward chap who's a valuable asset to the community. And who suffers most? Strickland?

Not he! His wife and his little girl —they're the sufferers. You throw a sensitive woman out on the world and give a little girl a blot upon her name that she'll never be able to wipe out. What's your idea? Why do you want to convict him?

FOREMAN. I don't want to convict him. I don't want to be instrumental in sending any man to his death. I guess I've got as much humanity in me as the rest of you. To hear you talk, a person would think I'm thirsting for Strickland's blood.

(SUMMERS *crosses to* FRIEND.)

JUROR MATHEWS. Well, why are you holding out?

JUROR LEAVITT. Why don't you vote for acquittal?

JUROR TOVELL. Your attitude doesn't bear out your words.

MATHEWS (*sits on table in front of* FOREMAN). Come on, Trumbull, be reasonable!

(LEEDS *goes up R.*)

FOREMAN. There's one thing you gentlemen seem to overlook. We're citizens as well as men. We've sworn to do our duty as jurors—to render a fair verdict. We mustn't be swayed by personal sentiments. We must govern ourselves by the evidence. (TOVELL *rises—sits.*) That's what we're here for—to render justice.

(MATHEWS *goes L., gets a drink of water at cooler—sits L.*)

JUROR SUMMERS. Now listen to me, Trumbull; you're a reasonable man.

(LEEDS *crosses to* R.C.) Just let's get away from strict logic for a moment. You say you want to render justice. Well, so do I. So do we all.

JUROR LEEDS. Yes, of course!

JUROR FRIEND. Certainly.

JUROR TOVELL. That's what we're here for!

JUROR LEAVITT. Of course we do.

JUROR SUMMERS. But rendering justice means something more than applying hard-and-fast rules of law. I'll grant you that the letter of the law declares that if one man kills another, the penalty must be death. But we've got to get beneath the letter—we must get at the spirit. We're not machines, you know. There's more to this case than a mechanical application of the penal law. We've got to attack this from the human standpoint. We must try to put ourselves in Strickland's place. Just consider that for a moment. (*Down* R.) Suppose that Mrs. Strickland had been your wife —and Trask had been the other party. What would you have done?

JUROR FRIEND. Yes, he's right.

JUROR LEEDS. That's the way to look at it.

JUROR TOVELL. You'd have done the same. (*Rises—sits on table, facing* FOREMAN.) Shooting was too good for Trask!

JUROR MATHEWS. Yes, there's an unwritten law that—— (*Rises.*)

JUROR SUMMERS (*interrupting*). I don't agree with you there. Ordi-

narily I don't believe that there's any justification for taking a human life. But this case is one in a thousand. This man Trask deliberately invaded his friend's home—and wrecked it! The woman was helpless, and he played on her helplessness. That's why I'm for acquittal. And that's why you should be for acquittal too. Trumbull, you have a wife. Just consider——

JUROR MOORE (*down* R. *followed by* LEEDS—*interrupting*). I think that you gentlemen are going off at a tangent. Unless I'm greatly mistaken, Trumbull agrees with you that Strickland had ample justification for killing Trask.

(SUMMERS *goes up* R.C.)

JUROR LEEDS. Then why's he holding out?

JUROR TOVELL. What's keeping him back? Let's hear from you, Trumbull.

FOREMAN. Mr. Moore is right. I do think that Strickland had cause for killing Trask. If I had been placed in similar circumstances, I probably would have done the same thing.

JUROR SUMMERS. But still you vote for conviction.

FOREMAN. Yes, because I'm not sure that Strickland went to Trask's house solely because of his wife. I'm inclined to think he also went there to rob the safe.

JUROR LEEDS. That's nonsense. (*Goes to chair and sits.*)

JUROR FRIEND. Absurd!

JUROR TOVELL. Strickland's no burglar. (*Up stage R.*)

JUROR SUMMERS (SUMMERS *sits on edge of table facing* TRUMBULL). You don't really believe that, Trumbull. One look at Strickland ought to convince you that he's not a safe cracker. Of course I don't know him personally, but I've known him by reputation for a number of years. He's as straight as a die. Ask anyone in the business world.

JUROR FRIEND. Why, of course!

JUROR LEEDS. Everybody knows that!

JUROR TOVELL. Does he look like a burglar?

FOREMAN (*rises and stands R.*). I grant you all that, gentlemen; but you can't dodge the facts. There's a chain of circumstances woven around Strickland that, to my mind, would damn the Angel Gabriel. Just consider the facts. Strickland was hard pressed. He paid Trask the ten thousand dollars in cash. Why didn't he pay it by check like a businessman? He was the only one besides Trask who knew the combination of the safe. And he was on the spot when the safe was opened. Looks pretty bad, don't you think?

JUROR SUMMERS (*up a step*). Of course it looks bad; but it's all been explained. We know why Strickland went there.

JUROR LEEDS. Of course we do.

JUROR FRIEND. Certainly!

JUROR TOVELL. That's all been cleared up! (*Rises.*)

FOREMAN. Well, if it's all been explained, as you say it has, there are two things I'd like you to explain to me. (TOVELL *sits.*) Firstly, how did the burglar open the safe?

JUROR SUMMERS. He tampered with it. (*Starts L.*)

FOREMAN. No, he didn't. The police officer testified that the tumblers were in perfect order. No, gentlemen, he opened the safe with the combination. And the only source from which he could learn the combination was Strickland.

JUROR MOORE. It does look pretty bad, I'll admit that.

JUROR ELLIOTT. Oh, I don't know!

JUROR LEAVITT (*sits on edge of table*). I don't believe in circumstantial evidence!

JUROR MATHEWS. Neither do I.

JUROR TOVELL. You can't convince me that Strickland's a burglar!

FOREMAN. That's not all, gentlemen. There's something else you'll have to explain to my satisfaction before I vote for acquittal.

JUROR SUMMERS. What's that?

FOREMAN. Strickland had that combination on a card. The card was the only really incriminating evidence against him. If he's innocent of the burglary, as you say he is, why did he attempt to destroy the card?

JUROR LEAVITT. Who says he did?

JUROR TOVELL. How do you know he did?

FOREMAN. Why, here's the card! (MOORE *crosses to* TRUMBULL.) Don't you see that it's torn almost in two? And didn't Glover testify that it was Strickland who tore it?

JUROR LEAVITT. No!

JUROR ELLIOTT. Yes!

JUROR LEEDS. That's right!

JUROR FRIEND. I don't remember it!

JUROR TOVELL. He did not!

FOREMAN. Well, gentlemen, it seems to me it's rather an important point.

JUROR MOORE. Yes, it is. I'm glad you raised it. I'm inclined to agree with you about it.

FOREMAN. There's only one reason why Strickland should attempt to destroy that card, gentlemen, and that is to wipe out the evidence that would be bound to convict him.

JUROR SUMMERS. I don't believe he did attempt to destroy the card.

JUROR LEAVITT. Yes, he did!

JUROR LEEDS. No!

JUROR TOVELL. I don't think Glover said so!

JUROR MOORE. Wait a minute, I seem to remember Glover saying so.

JUROR LEEDS. He didn't.

JUROR MATHEWS. I don't know if he did or not.

FOREMAN. We don't seem to agree about it. We ought to find out, I think.

JUROR SUMMERS. Let's send for Glover and ask him. (*Crosses L.*)

JUROR MOORE. We can't do that. We'll have to get permission to have his testimony read to us.

FOREMAN. All right; I'll send a note to the judge. (*Sits, writes.*)

JUROR SUMMERS. Ring for an attendant. (*Drinks at cooler. Moore pushes buzzer.*)

LIGHTS OUT. CURTAIN. *Effect of buzzing call button during change.*

EPILOGUE

(*Buzzer is heard as lights go up in courtroom. The* CLERK, *the* STENOGRAPHER, *and the two* ATTENDANTS *talking together.* GRAY *and* DR. MORGAN *are sitting on the table. An* ATTENDANT *hurries to the jury room, re-enters a moment later with a note, crosses right, enters* JUDGE's *room.*)

GRAY. There's something doing.

DR. MORGAN (*sitting on edge of table*). An agreement, do you think?

GRAY (*crosses R.*). Most likely.

DR. MORGAN. How long have they been out?

GRAY (*crosses L.*). Almost five hours.

DR. MORGAN. Well, what do you think?

GRAY. I don't know what to think, Dr. Morgan. This is an unusual case.

(ATTENDANT *enters right.*)

ATTENDANT. His Honor is coming, gentlemen. (*To the other* ATTENDANT.) Notify counsel to bring in the prisoner.

(SECOND ATTENDANT *goes off left—* FIRST ATTENDANT *opens the door of the jury room, crosses up L.*)

FIRST ATTENDANT. All right, gentlemen.

(DOCTOR *goes back of table.* JURORS *file in, take their places.* JUDGE *enters right.*)

CLERK. Justice of the Court.

(JUDGE *takes his place, sits;* JURORS, *et cetera, sit.* ARBUCKLE, MAY, DORIS, *and* STRICKLAND *enter left and sit at table left.* STRICKLAND *enters first followed by* ATTENDANT, *then* MAY *and* DORIS. MAY *sits upper chair L. of table with* DORIS *on her lap.* ARBUCKLE *enters last, stands above table.*)

DINSMORE (*to* GRAY *and* ARBUCKLE). Gentlemen, I have received a note from the jury, in which they request that a portion of Glover's testimony be read to them. (*To the* STENOGRAPHER.) Turn to Glover's testimony, please. Now read that portion which pertains to the tearing of the card. People's Exhibit A.

STENOGRAPHER (*reading*). Question, by Mr. Gray: "Now, Mr. Glover, I call your attention to the fact that the card is torn almost in half; can you explain how that occurred?" ANSWER: "Yes; as I took the card from Strickland's pocket, he snatched it out of my hand and started to tear it in half; before he had torn it all the way I managed to get it back again." Question——

(ARBUCKLE *crosses L. and whispers to* DOCTOR *then to* GRAY.)

FOREMAN. That's enough. (*He turns to the other jurors, and there begins what is apparently a heated discussion. Meanwhile* DR. MORGAN *is whispering in an animated fashion to* GRAY *and* ARBUCKLE.)

DINSMORE. Is that all, gentlemen?

FOREMAN. One moment, if Your Honor pleases. (*Discussion is resumed between* FOREMAN *and* SUMMERS.)

FOREMAN. Your Honor, the jury would like permission to ask Mr. Strickland a few questions.

DINSMORE (*to* ARBUCKLE *and* GRAY). Do you consent to the case being reopened, gentlemen?

GRAY. Yes, Your Honor.

DINSMORE. Mr. Arbuckle——

ARBUCKLE (*looks at* STRICKLAND. *Pause*). Yes, Your Honor.

DINSMORE. Mr. Strickland! (STRICKLAND *rises.*) Are you willing to take the stand?

STRICKLAND. Yes, Your Honor. (*Goes to stand.*)

CLERK. Do you solemnly swear that the testimony you are about to give will be the truth, the whole truth, and nothing but the truth, so help you God? What's your name?

STRICKLAND. Robert Strickland.

FOREMAN. Mr. Strickland, the jury would like to know why you attempted to destroy this card with the combination to the safe on it?

DINSMORE. You need not answer that question unless you want to.

STRICKLAND (to the jury). I didn't attempt to destroy it.

(Sensation in the jury.)

FOREMAN. You mean that you didn't tear the card?

STRICKLAND. I did not.

FOREMAN. Do you know who did?

STRICKLAND. No, sir.

FOREMAN. Did you know the card contained the combination to the safe?

STRICKLAND. Not until I heard it yesterday in court. I saw some figures on the card, but they had no significance to me. I never thought of the card from the time I looked at the address on it until I saw it here in court.

(DOCTOR in pantomime tells ARBUCKLE to let him go on the stand again.)

FOREMAN. Do you mean that you didn't see or feel Mr. Glover take it from your pocket?

STRICKLAND. No, sir, I did not. I was almost blind with pain at that time.

FOREMAN. That's all.

(STRICKLAND steps down. The JURORS whisper excitedly.)

ARBUCKLE (crosses C.). With Your Honor's permission, I will recall Dr. Morgan.

DINSMORE. Any objection, Mr. Gray?

GRAY. No, Your Honor.

ARBUCKLE. Dr. Morgan.

(DR. MORGAN takes the stand.)

ARBUCKLE. Dr. Morgan, on the night of the shooting, did you examine the defendant?

MORGAN. Yes, sir. When I found that it was too late to do anything for Mr. Trask, I turned my attention to Mr. Strickland.

ARBUCKLE. In what condition did you find him?

MORGAN. He was lying on his back on the floor in a semi-conscious state, moaning with pain.

ARBUCKLE. Did you examine his arm?

MORGAN. Yes, sir; I examined it very carefully while Mr. Glover and the police officers were testing the safe.

ARBUCKLE. Will you describe the condition of the arm, please.

MORGAN. The arm had been struck a terrific blow with a heavy cane.

The blow fell squarely on the wrist, dislocating the wrist joint. Both bones of the forearm—the radius and the ulna—were badly fractured. It was one of the worst fractures I have ever seen.

ARBUCKLE. Now, Dr. Morgan, in your opinion, could the defendant have torn this card, as you see it here, between the time his arm was broken and the time you arrived?

DR. MORGAN. He could not.

ARBUCKLE. You are sure of that?

MORGAN. Yes! The hand was entirely paralyzed. It would have been a physical impossibility, assuming even that his mental state would have permitted it. The bones haven't knit yet. At that time he couldn't have moved the arm or the hand a fraction of an inch.

ARBUCKLE. Thank you. That's all, Dr. Morgan. (MORGAN *steps down. Goes back of table L.*) Do you know where Glover is, Mr. Gray?

GRAY. The last time I saw him he was in my office reading.

ARBUCKLE (*to* ATTENDANT). See if you can find Mr. Glover, please. (ATTENDANT *goes off left.* ARBUCKLE *talks to* STENOGRAPHER. *Tense waiting.* ATTENDANT *returns with* GLOVER. ATTENDANT *crosses R., closes door R.*) Will you be good enough to take the stand, Mr. Glover? (GLOVER *takes the stand.*) I'm sorry to trouble you again, but there's one little point upon which we're not quite clear.

GLOVER. I'll be glad to do anything in my power——

ARBUCKLE. Thank you. You remember, Mr. Glover, that while you were waiting for the police to arrive, you happened to think of this card which you thought might help the police.

GLOVER. Yes, and I was right too.

ARBUCKLE. Indeed you were. Now, Mr. Glover, you will recall that you proceeded to search Mr. Strickland's pockets in the hope of finding the card.

GLOVER. Yes; and I did find it.

ARBUCKLE. Precisely. It was in his coat pocket you found it, I believe?

GLOVER. Yes; side pocket.

ARBUCKLE (*down stage*). Now, if you don't mind, I'd just like to have you describe that scene in detail. Where was Mr. Strickland?

GLOVER. He was on the floor, lying on his back.

ARBUCKLE. And you were standing over him?

GLOVER. Yes.

ARBUCKLE. On which side of him?

GLOVER. The right side.

ARBUCKLE. And as you bent over him and went through his pockets, did he make any attempt to prevent you?

GLOVER. Oh, yes; he tried to push me away.

ARBUCKLE. I see. He kept warding you off like this, huh? (*Indicating*

*with right arm as if pushing some-
one away.)*

GLOVER. Yes.

ARBUCKLE. Finally, however, you
succeeded in getting the card?

GLOVER. Yes.

ARBUCKLE. Let's see. It was in the
left side pocket of the coat, wasn't
it?

GLOVER. Left? (*Pause.*) Yes.

ARBUCKLE. Now as you straightened
up you held the card in your right
hand, didn't you?

GLOVER. That's correct.

ARBUCKLE. But before you had a
chance to get the card out of reach,
Strickland raised himself on his
right elbow, and with his left hand
snatched the card out of your hand.
That's all right so far, isn't it?

GLOVER. Yes.

ARBUCKLE (*up stage*). Now, if I'm
wrong in any of these details, I
want you to set me right. My memory fails me sometimes.

GLOVER. All right; I'll let you know
when you make a mistake.

ARBUCKLE. Thank you, that's very
good of you. Now there was something else. I must ask you to be
just a little patient with me.

GLOVER. Certainly.

ARBUCKLE (*down stage*). Oh, yes!
Strickland snatched the card, then
he tore it. Now, how did he tear it?

GLOVER. How? What do you mean?

ARBUCKLE. Well, I mean, did he
tear it quickly or slowly or——

GLOVER. Well, rather quickly, because I snatched it out of his hand
almost instantly.

ARBUCKLE. Oh! I see. Now let's get
that straight. Strickland had the
card in his left hand—like this.
Right?

GLOVER. Yes.

ARBUCKLE. And he was supporting
himself on his right elbow—like this.
Yes?

GLOVER. Yes.

ARBUCKLE. Then he made a quick
backward movement—like this—
tearing the card almost in half.
That's right, isn't it?

GLOVER. That's right.

ARBUCKLE. I see. And then you
snatched the card away from him?

GLOVER. Yes.

ARBUCKLE. And he threatened you,
didn't he, as you took the card?

GLOVER. Yes. He swore at me and
said he'd fix me.

ARBUCKLE. And if I remember correctly, you said that he made a
quick pass for the revolver—like this?
Yes?

GLOVER. Yes; but it was out of his
reach.

ARBUCKLE (*up to witness stand*).
That explains it beautifully. You've

cleared up the point for us, Mr. Glover. We're greatly indebted to you.

GLOVER. Not at all. Is there anything else!

ARBUCKLE. No, I think that's all. (GLOVER *is about to leave the stand.*) Oh, just one moment.

GLOVER. Certainly.

ARBUCKLE. Mr. Stenographer, will you read the latter part of Dr. Morgan's testimony to Mr. Glover?

STENOGRAPHER. Question, by Mr. Arbuckle: "Now, Dr. Morgan, in your opinion, could the defendant have torn this card as you see it here, between the time his arm was broken and the time you arrived?" Answer: "He could not." Question: "You are sure of this?" Answer: "Yes; the hand was entirely paralyzed. It would have been a physical impossibility, assuming even that his mental state would have permitted it. The bones haven't knit yet. At that time he couldn't have moved the arm or hand a fraction of an inch."

ARBUCKLE (*to* GLOVER). Glover, what did you do with that ten thousand dollars?

GLOVER (*panic-stricken*). What are you talking about? What do you mean? What ten thousand dollars?

GRAY (*rises and goes down L.*). Your Honor, I ask for a warrant for the arrest of this man as an accomplice to the murder of Gerald Trask.

GLOVER (*springing to his feet*). No, no, Your Honor, it isn't true! I didn't kill him! I took the money,

but I didn't kill him! I'll tell you where the money is. I don't want it. I don't want it! I'll plead guilty—I'll go to jail, but don't arrest me for the murder. I'll tell you how it happened—I'll tell everything. I didn't know Strickland was coming. I planned the robbery that night. When Trask gave me the money, I put it in the safe, but I didn't lock the safe. I left it open—he didn't notice it. Then I came back to get the money. I didn't know about Strickland—it's God's truth! Mrs. Trask heard me come in, and I choked her! But she's all right —she's not hurt. That's not murder! I got the money, then I saw Strickland come in. I didn't know he was coming. I didn't. I swear I didn't! I'm innocent! I'm innocent, I tell you! I left the room. Then I heard the shot and came in. It was the first I knew of it. I'm innocent, I tell you! Send me to jail—give me twenty years—I don't care, but don't try me for murder. (GRAY *goes up stage.*) I tore the card so they'd think Strickland planned the burglary. We weren't working together. Ask him! He'll tell you we weren't. I didn't know he was coming. Ask him; he'll tell you. (*He crosses left, hammers on table.*) Strickland, tell them, tell them we weren't working together.

DINSMORE. Remove the man.

(*Two officers seize him and drag him off left.*)

GLOVER. My God, Your Honor, I didn't kill him, I took the money, but I didn't kill him. Don't take me away. My God, I'm not a murderer, I took the money, et cetera, et cetera.

(ATTENDANT *slams door as the three are off.*)

DINSMORE. You may resume your deliberations, gentlemen.

FOREMAN. Your Honor, we have agreed already.

CLERK. Robert Strickland! (STRICKLAND *rises, advances to center.*) Prisoner, look upon the jury; jury, look upon the prisoner. Gentlemen of the jury, have you agreed upon a verdict?

FOREMAN. We have.

CLERK. And how do you find, gentlemen?

FOREMAN. We find the defendant Not guilty!

MAY. Robert! (*Falls into his arms.*)

CURTAIN

Under Cover

A Melodrama In Four Acts By

ROI COOPER MEGRUE

CAUTION

UNDER COVER *was first produced by Selwyn & Company*
At Court Theatre, New York, October 26, 1914

THE CHARACTERS
(In the order of their first appearance.)

JAMES DUNCAN, *Assistant to Daniel Taylor*	Harry Crosby
HARRY GIBBS, *a Custom Inspector*	Earle Mitchell
PETER, *a door-keeper at the Customs*	George Stevens
DANIEL TAYLOR, *a deputy in the Customs*	De Witt C. Jennings
SARAH PEABODY	Rae Selwyn
ETHEL CARTWRIGHT	Lilly Cahill
AMY CARTWRIGHT	Phoebe Foster
MICHAEL HARRINGTON	Wilfred Draycott
LAMBERT, *butler at the Harringtons'*	John May
NORA RUTLEDGE	Lola Fisher
ALICE HARRINGTON	Lucile Watson
MONTY VAUGHN	Ralph Morgan
STEVEN DENBY	William Courtenay

SYNOPSIS OF SCENES

Act One: The Office of a deputy surveyor of the Port of New York in the Customs House, New York City.

Act Two: At the Harringtons', Long Island. (During Act Two the curtain will be lowered for thirty seconds to indicate the lapse of two hours.)

Act Three: Denby's room at the Harringtons'.

Act Four: Same as Act Two.

(The action of the fourth act is supposed to begin at a time five minutes before the curtain falls on the third act.)

The play takes place during the afternoon and evening of a day in August.

UNDER COVER

ACT ONE

SCENE—*Office of a deputy surveyor of the Port of New York in the Customs House, New York City. It is a plain businesslike interior. There is a door L.C., one down R. and another down L. There is a desk at up R., behind which is a large bay window, showing a view of tall buildings and the distant river. There is another desk at L.C.*

TIME—*It is four o'clock on a Friday afternoon in August.*

DISCOVERED—*At rise,* DUNCAN *is seated at his desk L. He is a miniature* DANIEL TAYLOR *and as an actor, must have authority and ability to get lines over as the telling of most of the early plot depends on him. He is dressed in the uniform of a customs inspector. As the curtain rises,* DUNCAN *is in the middle of a telephone conversation.*

DUNCAN (*continuing speech impressively*). Yes! Yes! Yes! And say, be right on the job. The minute the *Mauretania* gets to quarantine, go through the declarations and phone me here whether Steven Denby declares a necklace or not. No—D-e-n-b-y—it's valued at two hundred thousand dollars. You bet it's a big case. No; I can't tell you who's handling it. Never mind whether R. J. is at work on it or not; your job is to telephone me as soon as you get a peek at those declarations. Bye-bye.

(GIBBS *enters C. door as* DUNCAN *hangs up receiver.* GIBBS *is a fat man, full of interest in any gossip that comes his way. He is dressed in the uniform of a customs inspector.*)

GIBBS. Hello, Jim.

DUNCAN. Hello, Harry, thought you were searching tourists over on the *Olympic* this afternoon.

GIBBS. Oh, I was with two thousand crazy women, all of 'em swearing they hadn't brought in a thing. Gosh, women is liars.

DUNCAN. What're you doing here?

GIBBS. I brought along a dame they want your boss Taylor to look over. It needs a smart guy like him to land her. (*Comes down R. to right of desk.*)

DUNCAN. The old man is down with the surveyor now—he'll be back soon.

GIBBS. I'll be tickled to death to wait here all day. I'm sick of searching trunks that's got nothin' in 'em but clothes. It ain't like the good old days. In them days if you treated a tourist right he'd hand you his business card and when you showed up at his office the next day he'd come across without a squeal.

DUNCAN. That's true. Why, when I was inspector, if you had any luck picking out your passenger you'd find twenty dollars lyin' right on the top tray of the first trunk he opened for you.

GIBBS. And believe me, when that happened I never opened any more of his trunks. (*Taking stage to C.*) I just labeled the whole bunch. But now—why, since the new administration got in, I'm so honest it's pitiful.

DUNCAN. It's a hell of a thing when a government official has to live on his salary.

GIBBS (*reflectively*). Ain't it funny why it's always women who smuggle? They'll look you right in the eye and lie like the very devil—and if you do land 'em they ain't ashamed, they're only sore.

DUNCAN. I guess men are honester than women.

GIBBS. They are above smuggling. Why, we grabbed one of these here rich society women this morning and we pulled out about forty yards of old lace—and say, where do you think she had it stowed?

DUNCAN (*grinning*). In a petticoat?

GIBBS. No, in a hot-water bottle. That was a new one on me. Well, when we'd pinched her she just turned to me and said, cool as you please, "You've got me now, but damn you, I've fooled you lots of times before."

DUNCAN (*who has been glancing over some papers*). Say, here's another new one. Declaration from a college professor who paid duty on spending seventy-five cents to have his shoes half soled in Paris.

GIBBS. That's nothing. A gink this morning declared a gold tooth. I didn't know how to classify it so I just told him nobody'd know if he'd keep his mouth shut. He did slip me a cigar, but women who are smugglin' seem to think it ain't honest to give an inspector any kind of a tip.

DUNCAN. Say, you'd better keep your own eyes peeled. Old man Taylor's been raising the deuce around here about reports that some of you fellows still take tips.

GIBBS (*airily*). Oh, that's just the annual August holler.

DUNCAN. No, it isn't. It's because the collector and the Secretary of the Treasury have started an investigation about who's getting the rake-off for allowing stuff to slip through. I heard the Secretary was coming over here today.

GIBBS. Well, if times don't change, I'm goin' into the police department. (*Crosses up to bay window and looks out.*)

(PETERS *enters C. He is a uniformed attendant at the Customs.*)

PETERS. Mr. Duncan, Miss Ethel Cartwright just telephoned that she was on her way and would be here in fifteen minutes.

DUNCAN (*a bit excited*). She did, eh? All right. (PETERS *exits up C. In phone*). Hello, give me the Surveyor's office. Hello—I'd like to speak to the Deputy Surveyor, Mr. Taylor. It's Duncan in his office. (*He holds the wire.*)

GIBBS. Got a cigar, Jim? (*Coming down to C.*)

DUNCAN (*taking cigar from pocket*). Yes.

GIBBS (*crossing to* DUNCAN *and reaching for it*). Thanks.

DUNCAN. And I'm going to smoke it myself. (*Puts cigar in his pocket.*)

GIBBS (*taking cigar from his own pocket*). All right, then. I'll smoke one of my own. (*Goes over to desk R. and, getting match, lights cigar.*)

DUNCAN (*in phone*). Hello, hello, Chief. Miss Ethel Cartwright just phoned she'd be here in fifteen minutes—— Yes, sir—I'll have her wait. (*He hangs up receiver.*) Well, what do you think of her falling for a bum stall like that?

GIBBS. Who? What? Which stall?

DUNCAN. Why, Miss Cartwright did.

GIBBS (*crossing to* DUNCAN). What is she? A smuggler?

DUNCAN. No, she's a swell society girl.

GIBBS (*crossing to C.*). If she ain't a smuggler, what's she down here for?

DUNCAN. The chief wants to use her in the Denby case, so he had me write her a letter saying we'd received a package from Paris containing dutiable goods, a diamond ring —and would she kindly call here this afternoon to straighten out the matter—and she fell for a fake like that——

GIBBS. I get you—but what does he want her for?

DUNCAN. For the Denby case.

GIBBS. What's that?

DUNCAN. The biggest smuggling job Taylor has ever handled.

GIBBS. You don't say so? Why, nobody's told me anything about it.

DUNCAN. Can you keep your mouth shut?

GIBBS. Sure. I ain't married. (*Sits on stool R. of desk L.*) Now, what is all this about?

DUNCAN (*very confidential*). Last week the chief got a cable from Harlow, a salesman in Cartier's.

GIBBS. Cartier's—what's that?

DUNCAN. The biggest jewelry shop in Paris. Harlow's our secret agent there. His cable said that an American named Steven Denby has bought a pearl necklace there for two hundred thousand dollars.

GIBBS (*greatly impressed*). Two hundred thousand dollars? Gee! But who's Steven Denby? A millionaire? I never heard of him.

DUNCAN. Neither did I, and what's more, we can't find out a thing about him. That's what makes it so suspicious. You ought to be able to get the dope on a man who can throw away two hundred thousand dollars on a bunch of pearls.

GIBBS. Did he slip the necklace by the Customs?

DUNCAN. No, he hasn't landed yet. He's on the *Mauretania*.

GIBBS. On the *Mauretania*? Why, she gets in this afternoon.

DUNCAN (*more confidential than ever*). Yes. He and a fellow named Monty Vaughn are traveling with Mrs. Michael Harrington.

GIBBS. You mean the Mrs. Michael Harrington?

DUNCAN. Sure. There's only one.

GIBBS (*rising, crossing to C.*). Well, if he's a friend of Mrs. Harrington, he's no smuggler. He'll declare the necklace.

DUNCAN. The chief has a hunch that he won't. (*Rises and crosses to* GIBBS *L.*) He thinks that Denby may be a slick confidence guy who has wormed his way into the Harringtons' friendship so he won't be suspected.

GIBBS. But maybe he ain't traveling in their party at all, but just picked 'em up on the boat?

DUNCAN. No, he's a friend, all right. Mrs. Harrington's taking Denby and Vaughn down to her country place on Long Island direct from the dock. The head steward, he's our agent on the *Mauretania*, sent us a copy of her wireless to old man Harrington.

GIBBS. He sounds like a sort of a smart-set Raffles, doesn't he?

DUNCAN (*as he crosses to desk at L.C.*). That's just the idea.

GIBBS. What's Taylor going to do?

DUNCAN. I don't know; he's kind of up against it. If Denby's on the level and he's pinched on the dock and searched and nothing's found on him—(*crossing* GIBBS *at* C.)—think of the roar that Michael Harrington —worth ninety billion dollars—will put up at Washington because we bothered his friends! Why, he'd go and kick to his pals down there and we'd all get fired. (*Crosses to down corner of desk R. and picks up papers.*)

GIBBS. But where does this girl out there—Miss Cartwright—come in on this job?

DUNCAN. I don't know, except that she's going down to the Harringtons' this afternoon, too, and Taylor's got some scheme. He's a pretty smart boy.

GIBBS. You bet he is, and maybe he's smarter than you know. Ever hear of R. J.?

DUNCAN. R. J.? (*Crosses to* GIBBS *with papers.*) You mean that secret service agent?

GIBBS. Yes—they say he's a pal of the President's.

DUNCAN. Well, what's he got to do with this?

GIBBS. Don't you know who he is?

DUNCAN. No—(*crosses to desk L.*)— and neither does anybody else. No one but the President and the Secretary of the Treasury know who he really is.

GIBBS. Well, I know, too.

DUNCAN (*contemptuously*). Yes, you do, just the same as I do—that he's the biggest man in the secret service, that's all.

GIBBS (*crosses to desk L.*). Ain't it funny that you, right here in the office, don't know?

DUNCAN. Don't know what?

GIBBS. Why, your boss Taylor is R. J.

DUNCAN (*laughing*). Taylor? You're crazy—— (*Sits.*)

GIBBS (*chestily*). Am I? Do you remember the Stuyvesant case?

DUNCAN (*impressed*). By George, that's so.

GIBBS. Why, all the boys are on.

DUNCAN. Say, I wouldn't be surprised if you were right.

GIBBS. I know I am.

(*Door slams and* TAYLOR'S *voice is heard off R.*)

DUNCAN. That's the boss now.

(GIBBS *nervously fumbles with his cigar and goes up stage to left of door up C.* DUNCAN *also gets busy with papers.* TAYLOR *enters door R. hurriedly and crosses to chair at desk R. He is an incisive, smart, bulldoggy sort of man, typical of the surliness of a certain well-known kind of government official. He is a bully, catering to his superiors and ragging his inferiors. He must have much authority, force and menace.*)

TAYLOR (*to* DUNCAN). Has Miss Cartwright got here yet?

DUNCAN. No, sir.

(TAYLOR *pushes buzzer on desk. There is a brief pause.*)

TAYLOR (*looking up*). Want to see me, Gibbs?

GIBBS. Yes, sir——

(PETER *enters door up C. and stands at the right of open door.*)

TAYLOR. Well, wait outside—come back in five minutes.

GIBBS. Five minutes. Yes, sir. (*He exits door up C.*)

TAYLOR (*as he presses buzzer*). Peter, let me know the instant Miss Cartwright arrives——

PETER. Yes, sir. (*Starts to exit at door up C.*)

TAYLOR. Now don't forget—it's very important. That's all. (PETER *exits door up C.* TAYLOR *crosses below desk at R. to* DUNCAN.) Duncan, did Bronson from the New York Burglar Insurance Company send over some papers to me relating to the theft of Miss Cartwright's jewels?

DUNCAN. Yes, sir; they're here. (*Gives them to* TAYLOR.)

TAYLOR. Good. (*He reads them.*) Ah! By George, I was right. I knew it was a cinch there was something queer about her ·diamonds being stolen.

DUNCAN (*puzzled*). What diamonds do you mean? The case wasn't in our office, was it?

TAYLOR (*still reading papers*). No, this is a little outside job my friend Bronson's mixed up in, but it may help us. (*He is still reading the papers.*) I'm sure it was a frame-up, that she wasn't robbed, that she collected from the company on a false claim.

DUNCAN. But I can't see——

TAYLOR. No, if you could, you'd have my job. (*As he crosses to desk R., puts his hat down on hat tree and sits, starts looking through papers.*) Has the *Mauretania* got to quarantine yet?

DUNCAN. No, sir.

TAYLOR. Telephone Brown to notify you the minute she does—tell him we've got to know as soon as possible whether Denby declares that necklace—everything depends on that!

DUNCAN. And if he does declare it?

TAYLOR. Then, of course, we haven't a case; but, somehow, I don't think there's going to be a declaration.

DUNCAN (*nodding his head and crossing to C.*). Well, I'm holding Ford and Hammet to search Denby at the dock.

TAYLOR. Well, keep them here until I let you know. I'm not sure whether I want Denby searched.

DUNCAN (*as he crosses to upper end of desk R.*). But, Chief, if he doesn't declare the necklace, it'll prove he's smuggling it.

TAYLOR. I know, I know, but we've got to be pretty careful about offending any friend of Michael Harrington's. He's mighty rich and very influential. We've got to be absolutely sure we have the goods on Denby.

DUNCAN (*watching* TAYLOR *and feeling his way*). Well, I guess it won't take R. J. long to land him.

TAYLOR. R. J.? (*Pauses as he looks at* DUNCAN.) What's he got to do with this?

DUNCAN (*insinuatingly*). I thought you might be able to get him interested in the case.

TAYLOR (*after another pause, as he returns to his work*). I don't know anything about him.

DUNCAN (*skeptically, and looking to where* GIBBS *has made his exit*). Oh, don't you? (*Changing the subject.*) Well, if we don't search him at the dock, what are we going to do?

TAYLOR (*looking up at* DUNCAN *and leaning back in his chair*). If we let him slide through and think he's fooled us, it might be easier to get him after he's down at the Harringtons' and is off his guard.

DUNCAN (*eagerly*). Have you got one of the Harrington servants to spy for us?

TAYLOR. No, but don't you know that Miss Ethel Cartwright is leaving this afternoon to spend the week end with the Harringtons? (*Presses buzzer.*)

DUNCAN. You mean you're going to get her to work for us down there?

TAYLOR. Well, that wouldn't be a bad idea, would it, Jim?

DUNCAN. But how can you?

TAYLOR. That's what I am going to find out as soon as Miss Cartwright comes.

(GIBBS *pokes his head in at door C.*)

GIBBS. Can I see you now, Chief?

TAYLOR. What is it?

GIBBS (*coming in*). There's a deaf-and-dumb chicken out here.

TAYLOR. A what?

GIBBS. A girl that can't hear or speak or write. They say she smuggled in a bracelet, but they've searched her eight times and can't get a trace of it, so they sent her to you.

TAYLOR. Well, they don't expect me to search her?

GIBBS. No, but they thought you might want to hand her the third degree.

TAYLOR. Well, bring her in.

GIBBS. Yes, sir. (*He exits at door up C.*)

TAYLOR (*significantly*). She's probably bluffing. Put that chair over there. (*Indicates down R. of C. DUNCAN moves chair from L. of desk and returns to upper end of desk.*) We'll try the gun gag on her. There's a revolver in this drawer (*indicating upper left drawer of his desk*). When I say "go," you shoot. Got it?

DUNCAN (*by drawer*). Yes, sir.

(GIBBS *enters C. bringing* SARAH PEABODY *after him by her left hand. He puts her in front of chair.* SARAH PEABODY, *if she were not deaf and dumb, would be a slangy young woman with a temper. Anyhow, she ought to be pretty.* GIBBS *steps to L.C.*)

TAYLOR. Well, where's the rest of her?

GIBBS. That's enough.

TAYLOR (*sizes her up in a second*). Well, tell her to sit down.

GIBBS (*crosses to her and motions*). Sit down—— (*She pays no attention to him.*) Hey, squattez vous—— (*Same business.*) Setzen Sie—— (*Turns away from her to L.C.*) I'm done. That's all the languages I know. I used to think it was a terrible thing that women could talk, but I guess the Almighty knowed more than I did.

DUNCAN. Hey you, sit down there. (*He grabs her roughly from behind and pushes her in chair. He then returns to upper end of desk R. and gets revolver from drawer and holds it behind his back.*)

TAYLOR (*rises and comes around in front of desk*). She's not shamming?

GIBBS. She ain't spoke all day, and no woman could keep from talking that long.

TAYLOR. Women do a lot for diamonds.

GIBBS. None of 'em ever do me for none.

TAYLOR (*crosses to her quickly and talks roughly*). If you're acting, you'd better give it up now, because I'm sure to find out, and if I do, I'll send you up to jail. (*Stands back to R. regarding her keenly.* SARAH *stares straight ahead.*) So you won't answer me, eh? Going to force my hand, are you? (*Raises hand and signals* DUNCAN *by snapping his fingers.*) Go. (DUNCAN *fires pistol.* SARAH *does not wince or move.* TAYLOR *and* GIBBS *bend over and look her in the eye.*) She's deaf all right, that's a cinch. Now, Gibbs, what is all this?

(TAYLOR *at lower end of desk R.* GIBBS *crosses to her.* DUNCAN *crosses down L. of* GIBBS, *after replacing revolver in drawer.*)

GIBBS. She's got a bracelet chuck-full of diamonds, and we can't find it.

TAYLOR (*sits on edge of desk*). How do you know she's got it?

GIBBS. She showed it to the woman who was in the same cabin with her. (*Turns to* DUNCAN.) She was the one who tipped us off.

SARAH (*rises suddenly and speaking at the same time*). Why, the dirty hussy.

GIBBS (*looks at her, then at* DUNCAN, *then at* TAYLOR *in great amazement*). For the love of Mike!

(*All three men in great surprise—* TAYLOR *quickly off desk.*)

SARAH. You know why she told about me? (*To* GIBBS.) She wanted to alibi herself, make you think she was an honest, God-fearing lady that would never smuggle—and she had four times what I had.

TAYLOR. Ah, ha! (*Quickly crosses to* SARAH. SARAH *turns to* TAYLOR.)

SARAH. Why, it was her who put me up to smuggling—she even taught me to be deaf and dumb—— Gee, I'd like to meet her again some time.

TAYLOR. Well, when we arrest her we'll need you to testify against her.

SARAH. You can bet your life I won't be dumb then.

TAYLOR. Now, where's your bracelet?

SARAH. Wait a minute—what's going to happen to me?

TAYLOR. Produce the bracelet, pay duty on it, and we'll let you go free for the tip.

SARAH. You're on. (*Parasol in R. hand.*) This is it—(*showing it to* TAYLOR). The ring handle of my parasol. (*Turns to* GIBBS.) I just painted it, that's all.

GIBBS (*grabbing it from her*). Well, can you approach that? (*Takes bracelet over and shows it to* DUNCAN. SARAH *takes out powder puff and glass, starts powdering.*)

PETER (*enters C.*). Miss Ethel Cartwright is here, sir.

TAYLOR. Bring her in in just a minute. (PETER *exits C.* TAYLOR *calls the attention of* GIBBS *and* DUNCAN *to* SARAH, *as he goes up to his desk.*) Send this girl down to Ford, Gibbs. He can handle her from now on.

GIBBS. All right. (*Crosses to* SARAH *and takes her left arm.*)

SARAH (*crosses up to desk R.*). I'll be glad to have someone else on the job. I've been trottin' around with this fat guy till I'm sick of the sight of him.

GIBBS (*injured*). Say now——

TAYLOR. Take her along. (*Crosses up to window.*)

SARAH (*to* TAYLOR). Ta-ta, old sport. I certainly fooled you when you shot that gun off. (*To* GIBBS *as they go toward door L.*) And I could have kept it up if it hadn't made me sore——

GIBBS. Ah, come on.

SARAH. —her putting one over on me like that. And she was so blamed nice to me. But when one woman's nice to another you can bet your B. V. D's she means mischief. (*They exit L.*)

DUNCAN (*a bit excited, crosses and replaces chair at left of desk R. and stands above desk*). You really think you can get Miss Cartwright to help us on the Denby case?

TAYLOR (*crosses to lower end of desk*). I shouldn't be a bit surprised.

(PETER *opens door C.*)

PETER. Miss Ethel Cartwright.

(MISS CARTWRIGHT *enters and comes down C.* PETER *exits.* ETHEL CARTWRIGHT *is a tall, very pretty woman of twenty-seven, and while her manner is one of extreme poise that comes from perfect breeding, and the almost unconscious knowledge that she is what she is, none the less she is, underneath, very much of a girl. She has a great deal of charm and a decided sense of humor; she is loyal and plucky. Physically she is the sort of woman who, when she enters a room, other people say "Who is that?" and mentally she is the kind that men love and women criticize; and the one's love and the other's criticism, are alike a matter of indifference to her.*)

TAYLOR (*rises, stands behind desk*). Sorry if I have kept you waiting, Miss Cartwright.

ETHEL. It doesn't matter in the least. I've never been down at the Customs before. I've found it quite interesting.

TAYLOR. Won't you sit down, Miss Cartwright? My name is Taylor— I'm a deputy surveyor.

(ETHEL *crosses and sits front of desk.*)

ETHEL. I believe, Mr. Taylor, you wanted to see me about a ring.

TAYLOR. Yes, the intention evidently was to smuggle it through the Customs.

ETHEL. Do you really think so? Of course I haven't the least idea who could have sent it to me.

TAYLOR. Of course you haven't. It's probably some mistake. Perhaps, however, the record will shed some light on the matter. Duncan, go and get those papers relating to Miss Cartwright.

DUNCAN (*blankly*). What papers?

TAYLOR (*significantly*). About the package that was sent to her from Paris.

DUNCAN. Oh, those papers. Yes, sir—— (*Crosses back of* ETHEL *to door L. and exits.*)

ETHEL. You know, I feel quite excited at being here. Almost like a smuggler myself.

TAYLOR (*sits*). Speaking of smuggling, Miss Cartwright, while we're waiting I'd like to have a little business chat with you if I may.

ETHEL. With me?

TAYLOR. Yes. As perhaps you may know, there has lately been a great deal of smuggling by those prominent in New York society. It is often difficult to detect because of the influence and position of the participants. They move in a world where neither I nor any of my operatives could enter—frankly, we couldn't pass muster for a moment. You follow me? (*Looks at her sharply.*)

ETHEL (*doubtfully*). Yes, but——

TAYLOR. We are looking for someone who belongs in society, someone who is clever enough to provide us with information and yet never be suspected. We would prefer that someone to be a woman—above suspicion—like you, for instance.

ETHEL. Really, Mr. Taylor—— (*Turning away.*)

TAYLOR. Miss Cartwright, I have reason to know that you and your family have been in financial difficulties—(*a look from* ETHEL. *He breaks in*)—since your father died. The position I describe could be made very profitable. (*Pauses and looks at her.*) How would you like to enter the secret service of the United States Customs?

ETHEL. Really, that's quite too preposterous. You must be joking.

TAYLOR. No, I'm quite in earnest.

ETHEL. The whole idea is too absurd. I must ask you for the papers regarding the ring.

TAYLOR. They'll be here any moment. I'm sorry you don't care to

entertain my proposition, but that, of course, is up to you—— (*Rises.*) Miss Cartwright, as it happens there's another little matter I'd like to discuss with you. Do you recall a George Bronson, the claim agent of the New York Burglar Insurance Company—the company which insured your jewels that were stolen? (*Looks at papers.*)

ETHEL. I think I do—but——

TAYLOR. Well, that company has had a great deal of trouble with society women who have got money by pawning their jewels, then putting in a claim that they had been stolen, and then recovering from the company on the alleged loss.

ETHEL. Are you trying to insinuate that——? (*Rises.*)

TAYLOR. Certainly not. I'm merely explaining that that was Bronson's first idea—but of course, on investigation he realized as I do now how absurd that was.

ETHEL. Naturally. (*Faces front.*)

TAYLOR. And yet there were certain things that he could not quite understand.

ETHEL (*turning to* TAYLOR). May I ask what Mr. Bronson's inability to understand has to do with you?

TAYLOR. Simply that he happens to be a very good friend of mine. He often consults me about cases that puzzle him. The theft of your jewels puzzled him greatly.

ETHEL. Puzzled him? It was perfectly simple.

TAYLOR. Perhaps you will be good enough to tell me the circumstances of the case.

ETHEL. I really don't see how this concerns the Customs.

TAYLOR. It doesn't, except that I am acting as Bronson's friend, and if you will answer my questions, I may be able to recover your jewels for you.

ETHEL. Oh, I see. (*Sits.*) That would be splendid. Of course, I'll tell you anything I know.

TAYLOR (*sits*). Well, the first feature that impressed Bronson—and me—was that the theft seemed to be an inside job.

ETHEL. I don't believe I quite understand.

TAYLOR. Well, there was no evidence to indicate that a thief had broken into your home.

ETHEL. But, that could be the only explanation——

TAYLOR. Why?

ETHEL. Our family consists of just my mother, my sister and myself, and two old servants who've lived with us for years. And, of course, it wasn't any of us.

TAYLOR. Naturally not, but—how did you come to discover the loss of your diamonds?

ETHEL. Oh, I didn't discover it. I was at Bar Harbor.

TAYLOR. Oh, you were away—I didn't know that. Who did find out your jewels were gone?

ETHEL. My sister. She missed them——

TAYLOR (*significantly*). Oh, your sister? I see. Your sister missed them. (*Writes on paper.*)

ETHEL. So, naturally it must have been some thief from the outside.

TAYLOR (*thoughtfully*). Of course, of course—I wonder if you'd mind telephoning your sister to come down here now——

ETHEL (*rises*). Why, she came with me—she's outside.

TAYLOR (*pleased*). Oh, that makes it much easier. (*Pushing buzzer.*) Perhaps we can have a little chat with her.

ETHEL. Of course if you wish, but I'm sure she knows even less about the matter than I do.

TAYLOR (*smoothly*). Undoubtedly, but possibly there may be certain facts that she could tell us that, while unimportant to you, would be significant to me.

(PETER *enters up* C.)

ETHEL. I'm sure Amy will tell you all she can.

TAYLOR. Ask Miss Amy Cartwright —she's in the waiting room—to step in a moment. Just say her sister wants to speak to her.

PETER. Yes, sir. (*He exits up* C. *and leaves door open.*)

ETHEL. It must be quite wonderful to be a detective and piece together little unimportant facts into an important whole.

TAYLOR (*dryly*). Oh, quite wonderful.

(DUNCAN *enters, stands at door L. He is followed by* AMY CARTWRIGHT. *She is a pretty young girl of eighteen, weak, sweet, and dependent. She is the opposite of her sister* ETHEL, *upon whom she relies absolutely.*)

PETER. Miss Amy Cartwright.

AMY. You wanted me, Ethel?

ETHEL (*rises, meets* AMY *and hugs her*). Yes, dear. (*Crosses over to* TAYLOR's *desk, passing* AMY *in front of her.* AMY *sits.*) Amy, this is Mr. Taylor—my sister.

TAYLOR (*rising*). How do you do?

ETHEL. Mr. Taylor seems to think he may be able to help me recover my diamonds.

AMY (*startled—*ETHEL *is standing at her side*). Your diamonds!

TAYLOR. Your sister has been kind enough to give me some information in reference to the theft—I thought you might be able to add to the facts we have.

AMY. I?

ETHEL. Yes, so you must answer Mr. Taylor's questions.

AMY. Of course.

TAYLOR (*to* AMY). How did you discover your sister's jewels were stolen?

AMY (*nervously*). Why, I—I went to her dressing table one morning and they weren't there.

TAYLOR (*meaningly*). Oh, they weren't there—then what did you do?

AMY. Why—I telephoned the company.

TAYLOR. Without consulting your sister?

ETHEL. But she couldn't do that. I told you I was out of town.

AMY (*relieved*). Yes, she was out of town——

TAYLOR (*to* AMY). But how did you know your sister hadn't taken her diamonds with her?

AMY (*hesitating*). Why, I think she must have told me before she left.

TAYLOR. Oh, you think so——!

AMY (*to* ETHEL). Didn't you tell me, Ethel?

ETHEL (*reflecting*). Perhaps I did ——

TAYLOR (*to* AMY). But you didn't telegraph your sister to make sure?

AMY (*frightened and confused*). Why, no—no.

TAYLOR (*with complete change to genial manner*). Well, as it happens, that didn't make any real difference—(*sits*)—as long as the jewels were stolen—and not just mislaid.

AMY. Yes!

TAYLOR (*to* ETHEL). Now, one other point—regarding the money you recovered from the company —please don't think me impertinent —but you still have it—of course?

ETHEL. Only part—I gave half of it to Amy.

TAYLOR. I rather thought perhaps you'd done that. Of course you realize that if I do find your diamonds the money in full must be returned to the company—(*looking at* AMY) —*from you both*——

AMY (*quickly*). But, I couldn't do that— -

ETHEL (*surprised*). But, Amy, why not?

AMY. I haven't got all of it now——

ETHEL. But what did you do with it?

TAYLOR (*leaning back in chair*). Yes, that's quite an interesting question, Miss Cartwright. What did you do with the money?

AMY. I—I paid a lot of bills——

ETHEL (*amazed*). You paid a lot of bills? But, Amy, you told me——

TAYLOR (*interrupting* ETHEL). Just a moment, Miss Cartwright—— (*Sharply to* AMY.) What sort of bills?

AMY. Why, dressmakers, and hats and things.

TAYLOR. Of course you have receipts for the money?

AMY. Why, why, I don't remember.

TAYLOR. Oh—you—don't—remember! But you do remember whom you paid the money to?

ETHEL. Of course you do. Think— Amy.

AMY. Why, yes.

(DUNCAN *enters door L.*)

TAYLOR. Who was it?

DUNCAN. The collector and the Secretary want to see you right away, Chief.

TAYLOR (*annoyed*). I can't leave now.

DUNCAN (*apologetic*). I explained you were busy, but they said they must see you immediately about those Amsterdam diamond frauds. The Secretary's got to go right back to Washington.

TAYLOR (*annoyed—rises and crosses back of desk, to* DUNCAN). Oh, very well. (*To* AMY *and* ETHEL.) I shall have to ask you ladies to wait five minutes for me.

ETHEL. Certainly.

TAYLOR (*speaks in pantomime to* DUNCAN *at* L.) Understand?

(DUNCAN *nods his head.* TAYLOR *exits* L. *and* DUNCAN *up* C. ETHEL *turns and looks after* TAYLOR *as he exits.*)

AMY (*hysterically as she turns to* ETHEL, *rising*). Oh, Ethel—they know—they know!

ETHEL. Know what?

AMY. That man suspects—I know he does—the way he spoke to me.

(NOTE: *This scene must be played in undertones to indicate the fear of being overheard.*)

ETHEL. What are you talking about —suspects what?

AMY. Oh, Ethel, don't let them take me away—oh, don't—don't——

ETHEL (*sharply—draws a step away from her in amazement*). What are you saying?

AMY. Your jewels weren't stolen— (*pauses*)—I took them—I pawned them.

ETHEL. Amy!

AMY. I took them. I had to have money. A woman told me I could get it by pretending to the company the things were stolen and they'd pay; and I did—I did it.

ETHEL (*stunned, horrified—not believing*). Amy, you swindled the company!

AMY. Yes, but I couldn't help it. I didn't mean to—I didn't——

ETHEL.   Why—why—why—please, tell me, why?

AMY (*turns her head away*). Oh, I lost a lot of money gambling—playing bridge.

ETHEL. Playing with whom?

AMY (*avoiding* ETHEL's *gaze; turns, faces R.*). Oh, they're people you don't know—and one night—we'd

all had dinner together at Claremont —and they wanted to play bridge —I said no at first, but they insisted—I got excited—I didn't realize how much I was losing—I kept on trying to get even but I couldn't—I lost a thousand dollars.

ETHEL (*looking around frightened*). Ssh—— Ssh——

AMY. Oh, I didn't mean to—— (*Turns to* ETHEL.) Ethel, believe me, I didn't—I didn't——

ETHEL. What happened then?

AMY. I couldn't pay, of course, and the other women said they'd expose me and tell you and mother—and put me in jail. (*Turns away to R.*) I didn't know what to do. I went out of my head, I think; a man there, Philip Sloane, offered to lend me the money.

ETHEL (*horrified*). You didn't borrow from that man?

AMY. I did—what else *could* I do? You weren't here and I had to do something right away.

ETHEL. But what about the jewels?

AMY. Then he loaned me the money—— (*A step away to R.*) Oh, I can't tell even you, Ethel, what he said—I never knew there could be men like that. When I wouldn't —wouldn't go away with him and do as he wanted, oh, he threatened all sorts of things. I had only one idea then, to pay him back, no matter what happened. I got half the money from the pawnshop and the rest from you, when the company settled. I paid him—then I knew he couldn't say anything—do anything—Oh, Ethel. (*She sinks into chair L. of desk, crying.*)

ETHEL (*crosses to* AMY *slowly, puts her arms around her*). My poor sister—my little Amy—I'm so—so sorry for you. Why—why didn't you tell me so I could help you?

AMY (*looking up into her face*). I was afraid to. I meant to tell you next month, when we got the money from father's estate. I thought we could pay the company then, so I wouldn't be a thief any more. Oh, I'm glad I've told you. I've been so frightened.

ETHEL (*soothing her*). There—there—there——

AMY. And this man knows. Can't you see he suspects—can't you?

ETHEL (*looking toward door L.*). Yes, yes, that's what he's been leading up to. (*Turns to* AMY.) But, he can't be sure or he'd have accused you direct. Oh, thank God, you've told me!

AMY (*quickly*). Oh, Ethel, don't let them take me away—don't let them put me in prison! I'd die. Don't, please—don't let them.

ETHEL (*comforting her*). Ssh—ssh—you've got to keep control of yourself. He doesn't know anything. If you'll just do as I say, I'll save you—I promise—you believe me, don't you?

AMY. Yes, Ethel, I believe you.

ETHEL (*standing up*). Now, talk of something else—anything——

AMY. Oh, I'm afraid I'll break down. Can't I go home now? (*Rises.*)

ETHEL (*turns up C.*, AMY *with her*). Yes, that'd be best; quick, before he comes back. (*Opens door.* DUNCAN *is standing there.*)

DUNCAN. Sorry, miss, but you can't leave.

ETHEL. I'm not leaving—it's my sister—she's not well—she must go home.

DUNCAN. Neither of you can go— - (*He shuts door. They come down C.*)

AMY. You see, they're going to keep me here.

ETHEL. When he comes back—let me do all the talking. If we can just get home, now, today, we'll think of something. There must be a way out.

AMY. Oh, Ethel, I didn't mean to steal—I didn't—I didn't.

ETHEL. Ssh. I'll invent a story to fool him. He won't be able to find out now if it's true or not—so he'll have to let us go. Then I'm sure everything will be all right.

AMY. Oh, Ethel, you're wonderful.

ETHEL. Now, sit there. (AMY *sits in chair L. of desk at R.* ETHEL *hears click of the doorknob L. She quickly crosses to down C. and stands facing* AMY.) Yes, Amy, just think, I read somewhere that they often take in a million dollars a day at the Customs House.

TAYLOR (*entering, coming over to R. of desk at L. and below it*). Sorry

I had to leave, just as matters were getting rather interesting——

ETHEL (*crosses to C.*). Nevertheless, I fail to see what all that cross-questioning of my sister has to do with——

TAYLOR. You will see, Miss Cartwright, very soon.

ETHEL. Meanwhile, I'm afraid I can't wait any longer for the papers about the ring.

TAYLOR. There isn't any ring.

ETHEL. What?

TAYLOR. That was merely a pretext —I was afraid the truth would not serve to bring you.

ETHEL. You asked me to come here because you thought I'd swindled the company.

TAYLOR. Well, we all make mistakes.

ETHEL. Oh, you admit it's a mistake?

TAYLOR. I'm quite sure of *your* innocence, because—(*looking at* AMY) —well, I have the thief now.

AMY (*startled—rises*). You have the thief?

TAYLOR. Yes, I've arrested the man who robbed your sister!

AMY. The man?

TAYLOR. Yes. Poor devil, he has a wife and children. He swears they'll starve; but he's guilty and he's got to go to jail.

AMY. Are you sure he's guilty?

TAYLOR (*leaning forward*). Yes, why? Have you any reason to think he's not?

AMY. No, no——

ETHEL. But I have every reason to believe he is innocent——

(AMY *gasps.*)

TAYLOR. *You* have?

ETHEL. Yes. I know who stole my jewels—it was my maid——

TAYLOR (*genuinely surprised*). Your maid? Why didn't you tell the company that?

ETHEL. Well, it was not till after the claim had been paid that she disappeared. Then I got a note from her—from Canada, confessing.

TAYLOR. Whereabouts in Canada?

ETHEL. I don't quite recall.

TAYLOR. Oh, what was your maid's name?

ETHEL. Marie Garnier.

TAYLOR (*crosses to desk L. and sits. Writing*). Marie Garnier. (*He pushes buzzer.*) Why didn't you say all this before?

ETHEL. What was the good? I was fond of Marie—she was really almost one of the family—I didn't want to brand her as a thief—and when I learned she'd got away to Canada where the law couldn't reach her——

DUNCAN (*entering at C.*). Yes, sir.

TAYLOR (*handing him paper*). Attend to this at once and telephone me the answer.

DUNCAN. Yes, sir. (*He exits L.*)

TAYLOR (*rises and crosses to* ETHEL). May I ask why you make this admission about your maid to me now?

ETHEL (*promptly*). Because I don't want to see an innocent man go to prison.

TAYLOR. Oh—did your sister know all this, too?

ETHEL (*quickly*). No——

TAYLOR. Why hadn't you told her?

ETHEL (*innocently*). I didn't think it made any difference.

TAYLOR (*annoyed*). Your behavior is most extraordinary.

ETHEL (*apologetically*). I know so little about the law and insurance and those things.

TAYLOR. Well, you must know you owed it to the company to give them all the information in your possession.

ETHEL. I really never thought of it in that way.

TAYLOR. There seems to be a lot you young ladies haven't thought of —and don't remember.

ETHEL. I suppose there's no use our waiting any longer. (AMY *crosses to* ETHEL's *L. as they go to door up C.*) Come, Amy.

(*The phone rings.*)

TAYLOR. Just a moment, Miss Cartwright. (*They pause and turn. In phone.*) Hello—— Oh, she hasn't —— Good-by. (*He rings off and crosses to* AMY *and* ETHEL.) Miss Cartwright—when you didn't know what town in Canada your maid's note came from I felt you were lying. Now, I know you were. I just had my assistant telephone your mother. You haven't had a maid for over a year and your last maid's name was Susan. You put the blame on a woman who doesn't exist because it was your sister who stole your jewels.

ETHEL. She didn't—she didn't——

TAYLOR (*to* AMY). You swindled that company.

AMY (*weakly*). No, no—— (*Crosses around in front of* ETHEL *and to her R.*)

ETHEL. How dare you make such an accusation, when neither you nor the company has any proof?

TAYLOR. Quite true now—but when we get the proof——

ETHEL. You can't, because there isn't any——

TAYLOR (*to* ETHEL). Now, see here, you're just trying to protect your sister; that's very natural, but it'll go easier with you both if you'll tell the truth. (AMY *starts to speak—* ETHEL *stops her.*) You won't answer, either of you? Well, of course the stuff's pawned someplace. That's what they all do—Bronson only searched the pawnshops in New York. He didn't give you credit for pawning 'em out of town, but I do.

Now we'll see where your sister did go—— (*Going to phone at desk L.* AMY *slowly to desk R.*) Hello, give me Ford—— That you, Bill? Go over to Bronson at the New York, get a description of the jewels *reported* stolen from a Miss Ethel Cartwright and have all the pawnshops searched in—(ETHEL *gives* AMY *a quick look. He pauses after naming each town, eying* AMY)—Trenton—Boston—Washington—Providence—Baltimore—Albany—Philadelphia—— (AMY *gives a gasp. To* AMY, *triumphantly, as he hangs up receiver and crosses to* ETHEL.) So you pawned them in Philadelphia.

ETHEL (*frantic*). No, no, I did it——

TAYLOR. No, you didn't. You're only trying to shield your sister. (*To* AMY.) You're the thief.

AMY (*breaking in*). Yes, yes, I did it—I did it.

ETHEL. Amy, don't speak, don't—don't.

AMY. But, I didn't mean to—I didn't—— Oh, don't put me in prison.

TAYLOR (*to* AMY). Young woman, you're under arrest.

ETHEL (*turning to* TAYLOR). No, no, don't take her—take me. She's only a child; don't spoil her life. I'll go. I'll do whatever you like; it doesn't matter about me. For God's sake, don't do anything to my sister.

TAYLOR. She's guilty, and the law——

ETHEL. Please don't send her to prison. If someone pays, what dif-

ference does it make to you? If you'll just let her go, I'll do anything. Isn't there anything I can do?

TAYLOR (*after a pause*). Yes, there is. You can accept my proposition to enter the secret service of the United States Customs.

ETHEL. Oh, yes, yes, anything.

TAYLOR. Now, you're talking. Then we won't send your sister to prison.

AMY. Oh! (*She breaks down, sobbing.*)

ETHEL. You won't tell Bronson?

TAYLOR. No.

ETHEL. Ah!

TAYLOR. Now that I realize the situation, I am very sorry for you both, so suppose we leave that little episode of the jewels as between your sister and her conscience, so long as you do what I ask. I'll let you know when I need you. It may be tonight, it may be in a month, but when I want you——

ETHEL. I shall be ready.

(AMY *crosses up to door C., and stands quietly crying.*)

DUNCAN (*entering L., crosses to lower end of desk*). Say, Chief——

TAYLOR. Get out. I'm busy——

DUNCAN. I thought you'd want to know the *Mauretania's* coming up the bay now.

TAYLOR. She is!—Wait a minute. Now good afternoon, Miss Cart

wright. Remember what's at stake
—your future—your sister's happiness, my silence, depend on your
not failing me.

ETHEL (*with a break in her voice*).
I shall not fail you. (*She takes* AMY
out C.)

(TAYLOR *goes up and closes door.*)

TAYLOR. (*Crosses down R.C.*) Did
Brown phone you from quarantine?

DUNCAN. Yes, sir, Steven Denby did
not declare the necklace.

TAYLOR. Ah, then I was right—
Denby is trying to smuggle it——

DUNCAN. I've got Ford and Hammet all ready to meet him at the
dock.

TAYLOR. Don't send 'em—there's to
be no search.

DUNCAN. No search?

TAYLOR. Let 'em slide through with
the ordinary examination. Trail 'em
to Long Island, to be sure they don't
slip it to someone on the way—but
no fuss, no arrests. Meanwhile get
up a warrant, a fake warrant, for
the arrest of Miss Amy Cartwright.
It may come in handy.

DUNCAN. Yes, sir.

TAYLOR (*crosses up to hat tree*).
Now change your clothes. Bring
Gibbs with you; meet me at the
Pennsylvania station at six o'clock.

DUNCAN. Where are we going?

TAYLOR (*turning at door C.*). To
Long Island to call on Miss Ethel
Cartwright.

DUNCAN (*excited—starts up a step*).
Then you can use her to land
Denby?

TAYLOR. Use her? (*With grim
humor.*) Say, Jim, she doesn't know
it, but she's going to get that necklace for me tonight! (*He exits hurriedly C. door.*)

CURTAIN

ACT TWO

SCENE I

SCENE—*The scene is the large hall or living room of the* HARRINGTON *country home on Long Island. The furnishings and atmosphere should be charming and, while simple, indicate the good taste and the wealth of the owners.
There are two french windows R.C., leading out to the lawn, and double
doors R., to the dining room, and one at up L. to the library; an alcove at up
L.C. in which are the first half dozen steps and the landing of a flight of
stairs leading to the floor above. There is a table at L.C., chairs around it,*

and a fireplace at L. with a club fender and a half-folded screen. The back-drop indicates a lawn and distant trees.

AT RISE—MICHAEL HARRINGTON *in armchair L. of table L., reading a paper and sipping a scotch highball. On the table is a bottle of scotch, a siphon, and also a pint bottle of champagne.* HARRINGTON *is a man of fifty-five or sixty, genial, charming, and with a sense of humor. He is in love with his wife, although he is always by way of poking fun at her and she at him. His desire for highballs is more of a hobby because his wife forbids his drinking rather than a real keenness for alcohol. He is conscious of his own frailty. There is a toot of a motor horn heard in the distance.*

LAMBERT (*Enters R. and crossing to C.* LAMBERT *is a smart English butler*). Please, sir, the car is just coming up the drive. Mrs. Harrington is in it.

MICHAEL (*rising hastily and crossing to up C.*). Good—my wife! The boat must have docked early. (*Crosses R. toward door R.*)

LAMBERT. Yes, sir.

MICHAEL. Get rid of these. (*Indicating bottles.* LAMBERT *crosses to table and gathers up bottles, glasses, etc.*) And not a word, Lambert, not a word.

LAMBERT (*as he backs to L.*). Certainly not, sir—I quite understand. I was valet to an English lord for seven years. You can rely on me, sir. (*He exits up L. with the tray. The motor horn is heard full blast off R.* NORA RUTLEDGE *is heard calling off R.*)

(NORA *is a clever young ingenue of twenty-two or twenty-three, with a tendency toward pert remarks, whose pertness must be removed by the charm of her own personality.*)

NORA (*excitedly off stage*). Mr. Harrington! Mr. Harrington! Alice is here—(*enters door R., comes R. of table C.*)—Alice is here, and Monty Vaughn is with her.

MICHAEL. Fine, fine. How is she—have they had a good voyage? (ALICE HARRINGTON *enters door R. and rushes into* MICHAEL'S *arms.*) By George, I'm glad to see you. (*He leads her down to front of table down L.*)

(ALICE HARRINGTON *is a delightful woman of thirty-four, in love with her husband, aware of his foibles, humoring them and yet maintaining a maternal watchfulness over him. She is very smart. She has an ingenuous realization of her own sarcasm and irony that takes the sting out of her remarks. She is never bitter, merely humorous.*)

ALICE (*in his arms, patting him on back*). You dear old thing.

NORA (R. *of table as* MONTY VAUGHN *enters.* MONTY *is a good-looking young man of twenty-five or twenty-six years, with a slight mustache which he is continually fussing with. He is* DENBY'S *opposite—timid, high strung, nervous, but basically not really a coward*). Hello, Monty.

MONTY (*shaking her hand enthusiastically*). It's bully to find you here, I nearly hugged you.

NORA. Well, why didn't you?

MONTY (*stretching out arms*). I've half a mind to.

NORA. No, not now. It's cold. Hugs must be spontaneous.

ALICE (*to* NORA). Where's Ethel?

NORA. We didn't expect you for another half-hour—she's upstairs, changing, she'll be down in a minute.

MONTY (*over to C.*). I say, old man, why weren't you down at the dock?

MICHAEL. Wife's orders.

ALICE (*crosses to* MICHAEL). I should say so. I know of no greater nuisance than having people meet you at the pier. (*To* MICHAEL.) You were very obedient.

MONTY. The perfect husband.

ALICE (*Smiling*). Well, I shouldn't say that.

MONTY (*to* ALICE *as he looks at his hands*). If you don't mind, I'll go up and wash up. (*Crosses to door R., to* NORA.) I've got almost all of Long Island in my eyes.

(ALICE *and* HARRINGTON *move L. so that* ALICE *can sit in armchair.*)

NORA. Go ahead—perhaps you'll be able to see me better then.

MONTY. I couldn't see you better if I tried. I'll meet you in the pagoda in five minutes. (*As he goes.*) It's mighty nice to see a pretty girl again who talks American.

NORA. As if men cared what girls say—it's the way they look that counts.

(MONTY *exits door R.*)

MICHAEL (*to* ALICE). Did you have a good trip?

ALICE (*sits in chair L. of table*). Bully. Steven Denby's most attractive and mysterious.

(NORA *goes slowly to chair L. of table, and kneels on it.*)

MICHAEL (*L. to* ALICE—*back to fire*). Denby? Oh, yes, I'd quite forgotten he was coming. Where is he?

ALICE. The limousine was so full of Monty and me and bags and things, we put him in the big car. They had a blowout five miles from here, but he'll be along presently.

NORA. What Mr. Denby is he?

MICHAEL. Yes. I never heard of him. Who is he?

ALICE. Perhaps that's what makes him so mysterious. I haven't the least idea.

MICHAEL. Then why on earth have him down here?

ALICE. Because Monty suggested it. They went to school or college or something together—and because even if I am married—(*smiling at* MICHAEL)—love has not made me blind to other charming men. (*Light laugh.*)

NORA. Will I like him?

ALICE. I did the minute I met him. He has a sort of "come hither" in his eyes and the kind of hair I always want to run my hand through. You will too, Nora.

NORA. But you see I'm not a married woman, so I haven't your privileges.

ALICE. Don't be absurd. I haven't done it—but I may.

MICHAEL. I don't in the least doubt it.

ALICE. He has such an air—sort of secret and wicked. He might be a murderer or something fascinating.

MICHAEL. Splendid fellow for a week end.

ALICE (looks at her watch. Rises and is going toward stairs). Heavens! I ought to dress.

NORA (comes round R. of table and up L. to stairs). Come on, I can't imagine what's keeping Ethel.

MICHAEL (as ALICE moves toward stairs). Oh, just a minute, Alice.

ALICE. Run along, Nora, I'll be right up.

NORA. I'll go wait for Monty—I think you're going to be lectured. (She exits at french window to R.)

ALICE. What is it?

MICHAEL (brings her down to L. of table—she is on his R.). I just wanted to tell you how mighty glad I am to see you.

ALICE. And Mikey dear—I'm mighty glad to see you.

MICHAEL. Are you really? You're not missing Paris?

ALICE. Oh, Paris be hanged! I'm in love with a man—not a town.

MICHAEL. It's still me?

ALICE. Always you! One big reason I like to go abroad is because it makes me so darned glad to get back to you. (She sits on arm of chair L. of table.)

MICHAEL (playfully reproving). See here, now, every time I want a little trot around the country and suggest leaving you, you begin——

ALICE. Oh, that's very different. When we do separate I always want to be the one to leave, not to be left.

MICHAEL (nodding his head). It is much easier to go than to stay. I've been pretty lonely here these last six weeks.

ALICE. Even with all the scotch you wanted?

MICHAEL (crossing to ALICE). 'Tisn't nearly as much fun to drink when you're away. It takes the sport out of it not to be stopped.

ALICE. Fibber!

MICHAEL (crossing to L.). Well, most of the sport. Do you know, I sometimes wonder whatever made you marry me.

ALICE. Sometimes I wonder, too. (Rises, crosses to HARRINGTON.) But not often. I really think we're the ideal married couple.

MICHAEL. Do you honestly? (*Holding her off at arm's length.*)

ALICE. Yes. We're sentimental when we're alone and critical when we've guests.

MICHAEL. That's true—most people hate each other in private and love each other in public. (*He takes hold of her hand.*)

ALICE. You're a dear old thing.

MICHAEL. Do you know, I don't feel a bit married? I just feel in love.

ALICE. That's the nicest thing you ever said to me. (*She kisses him.*) But I must find Ethel. (*Crosses up to stairs.*)

MICHAEL. You know, you've made me fairly dizzy. I need a drink to sober up.

ALICE (*crossing to him*). I believe you've been trying to get around me just for that.

MICHAEL. Oh, no, you don't.

ALICE. No, I don't, Mikey. (*Crosses up on first platform.*)

(MONTY *and* NORA *enter at french window.*)

NORA (*L. of* MONTY *by window*). Heavens, still lecturing, you two?

MONTY (*as* MONTY *and* NORA *cross down C.*). You do look rather henpecked, Mr. Harrington.

MICHAEL. Yes, we've been having a dreadful row.

ALICE. Now, I am going upstairs to see Ethel. (*She exits.* MICHAEL *waits till she has gone upstairs, then crosses to table.*)

MICHAEL. I think I'll go for my one solitary cocktail—(*crosses back of them and turns.* NORA *crosses to table*)—in my own private bar, but keep that confidential. (*He exits R. There is a slight pause.*)

MONTY (*going toward french windows*). I wonder where the deuce Steve is? A blowout oughtn't to keep him all this time.

NORA (*in front of table*). What's the matter with you, Monty?

MONTY. Me? (*Turns to her.*) Nothing. (*Suddenly.*) What's that?

NORA. What?

MONTY. Oh, nothing.

NORA (*crosses toward couch*). You never used to have a nerve in your body—now—you jump at everything.

MONTY (*coming down to her L.*). Why, I guess I'm a bit nervous. Steve and I are in a big deal together—and it's got me sort of anxious.

NORA. You don't mean to say you've gone into business?

MONTY. Well, it's not exactly business—it's something secret.

NORA. Well, if it frightens you so, why go in it?

MONTY. Well, everything was sort of tepid in Paris.

NORA. Tepid—in Paris?

MONTY. Well, even Paris can get like that when you live there. I wanted excitement, and when Steve told me about the scheme——

NORA (*she kneels at L. end*). Oh, if it's exciting, tell me about it.

MONTY (*sits on L. arm*). I wish I could but I promised Steve. We're pretty old friends.

NORA. I know, I know. You and he went to college together and sang a "stein on the table" and went on sprees together and made love to the same girls, and played on the same teams. I know all that college stuff.

MONTY. But we didn't go to college together.

NORA. But Alice said you did.

MONTY (*anxiously*). Oh, did she?

NORA. Well, anyhow, don't be reminiscent, Monty. I hate reminiscences. They make me so darned envious. I wish I'd been a man.

MONTY (*smiling*). I don't.

NORA. Don't try to flirt with me.

MONTY. Why not?

NORA. You don't know how.

MONTY. Teach me.

NORA. It can't be taught. It's got to be born in you. (*Sits on couch. Pauses, looks down.*) Well, go on.

MONTY (*rises, crosses down L.C. Reflectively*). I wonder where Steve is.

NORA (*exasperated*). You're hopeless. I don't know where Steve is and frankly I don't care. I hope he's under the car with gasoline dripping in his eyes.

MONTY (*coming to her suddenly*). Do you know, Nora—(*kneeling on couch*)—for the last year there's been something trembling on my lips.

NORA (*ecstatically*). Oh, Monty, don't shave it off—I love it. (*MONTY down C., then up to french window.*)

(ALICE *and* ETHEL *come downstairs in order named.* MICHAEL *enters from R. at the same time, wiping mustache—works back to L. of* ETHEL.)

NORA (*rising*). Here's Ethel.

ALICE. Monty, I want you to know my very best friend, Miss Cartwright, Mr. Vaughn.

(MONTY *goes to* ETHEL *at back of table.*)

ETHEL (*offering hand*). How do you do?

MONTY (*at back of table. Shakes her hand.* ALICE *to stool R. of table, sits*). How do you do?

MICHAEL (*at fireplace*). Be kind to him, Ethel; he's a nice boy.

NORA (*sitting on couch*). And an awful flirt.

MONTY. Oh, I say.

ALICE (*sitting on stool*). Are you a flirt?

MONTY. No.

ALICE. Of course, he never flirts with me. That's the penalty of age. I've known him a disgracefully long time —ever since the Palisades were that high.

(NORA *sits on couch.* MONTY *to couch back.*)

ETHEL (*down to armchair L. of table*). I'm sorry I couldn't get down to the dock to meet you, Alice.

ALICE. Thank heaven you didn't.

ETHEL. But I had some business——

MICHAEL. Business in August—I say, you do look a bit fagged—no bad news, I hope.

ETHEL (*nervously*). I was afraid it might be, but it came out better than I hoped.

ALICE. How's Amy?

ETHEL (*nervously*). Oh, she's all right.

MICHAEL. We ought to have had her down here.

ALICE. No, we shouldn't. I didn't intend it to be a big party, and anyhow young men are scarce in August.

MONTY. I wonder where the deuce Steve is?

ALICE. I hope he hasn't gone over the cliff.

MICHAEL. So do I. It was a mighty good car, almost new.

ETHEL. Is someone else coming?

(MONTY *crosses to back of couch.*)

ALICE. A perfectly charming man— Steven Denby.

ETHEL (*her face lighting up*). Steven Denby?

ALICE. Yes, do you know him?

ETHEL. Indeed, I do.

(NORA *rises.*)

MONTY (*surprised*). You know Steve? (*Crosses to table.*)

NORA (*crosses to* ALICE. *Over beside* ALICE). Tell us about him.

MICHAEL. Who is he?

(MONTY *drops down R.*)

ALICE. Isn't he fascinating?

ETHEL. I know him, and that's really all I can tell you. I met him in Paris a year ago.

ALICE. Didn't you like him?

ETHEL. Yes, I did, very much.

NORA. Well, he's evidently yours for the week end.

ETHEL. Oh, I dare say he won't even remember me.

NORA. Oh, I bet he will and I'll just have to stick around with Monty. (*Turns to him, and crosses to him.*)

MONTY (*crosses to* NORA *and grandly*). Oh, I don't particularly mind.

(*Dressing bell rings off stage.*)

MICHAEL. Time to dress, good people.

ALICE (*turning at stairs*). Come, Nora; come, Monty. (MONTY *quickly to stairs and up.*) You'll have to amuse yourself, Ethel; you can't depend on Michael.

(MONTY *exits upstairs.*)

MICHAEL. Quite right, my dear.

NORA. I think I'll strum a bit. (*She exits door R.*)

MICHAEL (*crosses door R.*). I'm going for my one solitary cocktail.

ALICE (*at stairs*). And only one!

MICHAEL (*at C.*). My dear, you know me.

ALICE. That's why I said only one. And wait for Mr. Denby. Tell him we'll be down in a minute.

MICHAEL. I'll send him in to Ethel.

(ALICE *exits upstairs.*)

ETHEL. Yes, do.

(MICHAEL *exits door R. Motor horn is heard in distance.* ETHEL *crosses in front of table, goes up and looks out of french window. Motor horn is heard in short, full blasts.* ETHEL *goes down to back of couch and arranges herself in anticipation of* DENBY'S *arrival. Confused murmur heard off, of* MICHAEL *welcoming* DENBY. STEVEN DENBY *enters R.* DENBY *is a young man of thirty or thirty-one, charming, good-looking, with, as* MRS. HARRINGTON *says, a "come hither" in his eye. He is cool, self-possessed, quiet. Nothing ruffles*

him. *He takes adventures as they come, and lets them come often. He is the kind that women pursue and yet men respect. He is a man's man and yet a woman's lover. He crosses toward stairs.*)

DENBY (*most enthusiastically, crosses to her at C. offering his hand*). Why, how do you do, Miss Cartwright?

ETHEL (*at C., graciously shaking hands*). How do you do, Mr. Denby?

DENBY. Mr. Harrington said there was a surprise in here for me, but I had no idea it would be so delightful—how are you?

ETHEL (*gaily*). Splendid—and you?

DENBY. Grateful to be here——

ETHEL. I didn't think you'd remember me——

DENBY. Remember you? Why, it was only the day before yesterday we were in Paris.

ETHEL (*crosses to couch*). What are you doing in America?

DENBY (*crosses to C.*). Oh, I thought I needed a run over to see if New York was finished yet.

(*Piano off stage starts playing: "I loved you a thousand years ago."*)

ETHEL. Are you still doing—nothing?

DENBY. Still—nothing.

ETHEL. And I did have hopes of you. (*Sits on R. end of couch.*)

DENBY (*meaningly*). And I of you.

ETHEL (*changing the subject*). I'm afraid I don't admire idlers. Why don't you do something?

DENBY. It's so difficult to get a thrill out of business.

ETHEL. And you must have thrills?

DENBY (*sits on L. arm of couch*). Yes, it's such a dull old world nowadays.

ETHEL. Why don't you take to crime?

DENBY (*mockingly*). Ah, the stake's too high—a thrill against prison.

ETHEL. Oh, you want little thrills?

DENBY. No, a big one—life or death —but not prison—— (*Piano stops.*) And you? You are still doing nothing, too?

ETHEL. Nothing.

DENBY. Still Miss Cartwright?

ETHEL. Only Miss Cartwright.

DENBY (*rises, leaning toward her*). Good! (*Embarrassed as she looks quickly at him.*) By George, it doesn't seem a week since that week in Paris. (*Backs away to C.*)

ETHEL. No, it doesn't.

DENBY. What made you disappear just as we were having such bully times?

ETHEL. I had to come back to America suddenly; I had only an hour to catch that boat—didn't you get my note?

DENBY. Of course I didn't. I thought you'd dropped me. I tell you I hit with an awful crash.

ETHEL (*encouragingly*). No, I hadn't dropped you. (DENBY *crosses to L. end of couch.*) In fact I thought it was just the other way.

DENBY. I should say not! I did try to see you when I was over here six months ago, but you were at Palm Beach. (*Whimsically.*) I can't tell you how often I've sent you telepathic messages—ever get any of 'em?

ETHEL. Some of them, I think. And now we meet on Long Island. It's a far cry to Paris.

DENBY. Oh, it's people who make places. (*Crosses to end of couch.*) The places themselves don't matter —you and I are here.

ETHEL (*sighing*). Still Paris is Paris.

DENBY (*sighing*). Rather! Do you remember that afternoon in front of the Café de la Paix? We had Vin Gris and watched the Frenchman with the funny dog and the boys calling La Presse—(*piano starts "Un Peu d'Amour"*)—and the old woman with her newsstand.

ETHEL (*romantically*). And there was a hole in the tablecloth.

DENBY (*smiling*). And wasn't it a dirty tablecloth? (*Romantic.*) And we had tea in the Bois at the Cascade, and the Hungarian Band played "Un Peu—(*he hears piano playing "Un Peu d'Amour" and marks the coincidence)*—"Un Peu d'Amour."

(They listen to it for a second; she hums. When piano finishes chorus, it stops.)

ETHEL *(romantically)*. And the poor skinny horse in our fiacre fell down and we walked all the way home out of pity.

DENBY. You were tenderhearted.

ETHEL. Do you remember dinner at Vian's that ˙night—— *(Pauses.)* Wasn't the soup awful?

DENBY *(smiling)*. Ah, but the string beans!

ETHEL. The string beans were an event.

DENBY *(around to back of couch, leaning over)*. And afterward I can remember a moon over the Bois as we sat under the trees, can you?

ETHEL *(softly)*. Yes.

(Piano finishes chorus about here.)

DENBY *(leaning over her)*. And the day we went through the whole Louvre—*(pauses)*—in an hour—and the loveliest picture I saw was you——

(Pause. He sighs. She sighs. Pause. LAMBERT interrupts the picture. He comes from up L. and crosses.)

LAMBERT. Pardon me. *(DENBY coughs, embarrassed, and walks away down L.)* There is a gentleman to see you, Miss Cartwright.

(He hands her card on tray. Crosses to C.)

ETHEL *(rises, crosses to LAMBERT)*. To see me? *(She takes card, looks at it, startled.)* Ask him to come in. *(Turns to DENBY.)* Will you forgive me?

DENBY *(going and removing auto coat)*. Surely—I must dress anyhow.

LAMBERT. Your room is at the head of the stairs, sir. *(LAMBERT exits L.)*

DENBY *(crosses to stairs)*. Till dinner?

ETHEL. Till dinner.

(DENBY exits upstairs. ETHEL shows great anxiety. In a moment TAYLOR enters.)

TAYLOR *(crosses down L., then to ETHEL. Enters door L. genially)*. Good evening, Miss Cartwright.

ETHEL *(trembling)*. My sister? Nothing's happened?

TAYLOR. Sure, sure—I haven't bothered her—the little lady's all right.

ETHEL *(alarmed)*. What are you doing here?

TAYLOR. I thought I'd drop in in reference to our little chat this afternoon. *(He crosses R. ETHEL up to stair looking off. He looks about.)* Ah, nice place here.

ETHEL. Yes, but——

TAYLOR. I suppose you remember our conversation?

ETHEL *(coming down C.)*. Of course, of course.

TAYLOR. You said when I needed you, you would be ready. (*During this scene he glances around apprehensively.*) Well, I need you now.

ETHEL. But I don't understand.

TAYLOR. A man smuggled a two-hundred-thousand-dollar necklace through the Customs today. For various reasons we allowed him to slip through, thinking he'd fooled us. Now that he believes himself safe, it ought to be easy to get that necklace. In fact, we've got to get it —through you.

ETHEL. Through me? But I wouldn't know how to act—what to do.

TAYLOR. You're too modest, Miss Cartwright. I'm quite sure you'll be very successful.

ETHEL. But, I'm spending Sunday here—I couldn't very well make an excuse to leave now.

TAYLOR. You don't have to leave.

ETHEL. What?

TAYLOR. The man who smuggled that necklace is staying here—his name is Steven Denby.

ETHEL (*startled*). Steven Denby? You must be mad—he isn't a smuggler.

TAYLOR. Why isn't he?

ETHEL. I know him.

TAYLOR. You do? Where did you meet him?

ETHEL. In Paris.

TAYLOR. How long have you known him?

ETHEL. A year.

TAYLOR. What do you know about him? What's his business? What does he do?

ETHEL. Why—nothing.

TAYLOR. Nothing, eh? Well, that hardly proves he's not a smuggler.

ETHEL. I'm sure you're wrong. He's my friend.

TAYLOR. Your friend! (*Changes to insinuating tone.*) Well, that ought to make it much easier for you to get him.

ETHEL. I'm certain he's absolutely innocent.

TAYLOR. This is your chance to prove it.

ETHEL. But, I couldn't spy on a friend.

TAYLOR. If he's innocent it can't make any difference, he'd never know. If he's guilty—he deserves punishment—you've no right to try and protect him. You would merely be doing your duty in helping to detect a criminal.

ETHEL. No, no, I can't do it. (*Crosses to front of table at L.*)

TAYLOR. You're going back on your agreement, eh? Suppose I go back on mine?

ETHEL. You wouldn't do that?

TAYLOR. It's give and take in this world.

ETHEL. But, I couldn't be so contemptible.

TAYLOR (*meaningly*). Now, you'd better think it over, Miss Cartwright; I would if I were you.

ETHEL. But, suppose you're wrong—suppose Mr. Denby has no necklace—then——

TAYLOR. Don't you worry about that. Our information is positive. We got a telegram late this afternoon from a pal of his who's squealed giving us the tip about the necklace. Well, what do you say?

ETHEL. Oh, I can't—I can't.

TAYLOR (*with menace*). It's Steven Denby or your sister. Which are you going to choose?

ETHEL (*pauses, then quietly turns away*). Then I have no choice. (*To* TAYLOR.) What do you want me to do?

TAYLOR. Good! (*Crosses up C., looks upstairs, then crosses to* ETHEL.) Denby has that necklace concealed in a tobacco pouch, a brown leather tobacco pouch which he always carries in his pocket. You must get that pouch.

ETHEL. Sssh! How can I?

TAYLOR. I'll leave that to you.

ETHEL (*pleadingly*). But why ask me—can't you do it?

TAYLOR. It may be a bluff, some clever scheme to throw me off the track. I'm not going to risk a mix-up with the Harringtons, or tip my hand until I'm absolutely sure. Denby's your friend—you can easily find out. If you discover the necklace is in that tobacco pouch, get Denby to go for a walk in the garden, say you want to look at the moon, say anything, but get him in the garden and we'll grab him there.

ETHEL. But he might go there alone.

TAYLOR. If he comes alone we won't touch him. But if he comes with you we'll know.

ETHEL. But, if I can't get him to go into the garden?

TAYLOR. If you're sure he has it on him—or if you make certain just where he has concealed it—(*looks around thinking for a second or two*) —pull down one of those window shades. My men and I can see those windows from the pagoda. When we get that signal we'll come in and arrest him—you understand?

ETHEL. Pull down the curtain shade.

TAYLOR. Yes, but be careful. Don't bring him out in the garden, and don't signal, unless you are absolutely positive.

ETHEL. Yes, yes.

TAYLOR. And under no circumstances must you mention my name.

ETHEL. But——

TAYLOR. There's no "but" about it. It is most important to the United States Government and to me that my identity be in no way disclosed.

ETHEL. But it may be necessary.

TAYLOR. It cannot be necessary. If you tell Denby I'm after him—if it comes to a showdown—I'll not only swear I never saw you before—but I'll put your sister in prison.

DENBY (*heard off stage*). Thanks very much, Lambert.

TAYLOR (*hurriedly going up to french window*). Good evening, Miss Cartwright. Don't forget to get Denby tonight.

(*She collapses R. of table L. He exits.* ETHEL *is left wretched and miserable. Dinner chimes ring off stage.* DENBY *comes downstairs.*)

DENBY (*crosses down C.*). Ah, dinner. (ETHEL *rises.*) Come, I wish it were Paris, with the hole in the tablecloth, and the eventful string beans, and the gay old moon, but, after all, what do they matter? It's a great world—you're here, and I'm hungry. Are you hungry?

(*They are walking off R. as the curtain falls.*)

CURTAIN

(*Curtain remains down thirty seconds to indicate a lapse of two hours until after dinner.*)

SCENE II

SCENE—*Curtain rises on a dark stage.* LAMBERT *enters from R., turns up lights and exits L.U. During this,* NORA, ALICE, *and* ETHEL *are heard talking. At* LAMBERT'S *exit they enter and* ETHEL *enters last, crosses around table and sits in front.*

NORA (*crosses down C. to couch*). What I can't see is why we didn't stay and have our cigarettes with the men.

ALICE (*crosses to R. of table*). Oh, I always leave the men together. That's the way I always get all the newest naughty stories. Michael tells 'em to me later.

NORA. Alice!

ALICE (*at R. of table C.*). Oh, I like 'em when they're really funny; so does everybody else. Besides, nowadays it's improper to be proper. Cigarette, Ethel?

ETHEL (*who has crossed to mantel now crosses to table and sits in front of it*). You know I don't smoke.

NORA. That's so old-fashioned. I'd rather die than be that—— (*She coughs slightly.*) I do wish, though, I enjoyed smoking.

ALICE (*sits stool R. of table*). Nora, what do you think of our new friend, Mr. Denby?

NORA. I like him in spite of the fact that he didn't notice me. He couldn't take his eyes off Ethel.

ALICE. I saw that myself. You know, Ethel, I meant him to take you in to dinner, but Nora insisted that she sit next to him. She's such a man hunter.

NORA. You bet I am—that's the only way you can get 'em. (*Crosses down R.*)

ALICE. Didn't you and Mr. Denby have a tiny, tiny row? You hardly spoke to him all through dinner.

ETHEL. Didn't I? I've a bit of a headache.

NORA (*crosses to R.C.*). I'll bet they had a lover's quarrel before dinner.

ALICE (*smilingly interested*). A lover's quarrel?

NORA. Certainly, I'm sure Ethel's in love with him.

ETHEL (*embarrassed*). How perfectly ridiculous. Nora, don't be silly. I met him for a week in Paris. That's all. I did find him interesting. He had big talk as well as small, but as for love, please don't be idiotic. (*Crosses to fender seat and stands.*)

ALICE. Methinks the lady doth protest too much.

NORA (*crosses to ALICE*). Well, I don't blame you. If he'd give me a chance I'd fall for him in a minute, but attractive men never bother about me. The best I can draw is Monty. I'm beginning to dislike the whole sex. (*Steps to R.* ETHEL *sits on lower end of club fender, facing front.*)

ALICE. Theoretically you are quite right, my dear. Men are awful things—God bless 'em—but practically—well—someday—you'll explode like a bottle of champagne and bubble out all over some man.

NORA (*steps to ALICE*). I wish I had another of Michael's purple drinks.

ALICE. Do tell him that. The surest way to Michael's heart is through his buffet. He's taken to mixing cocktails now in a graduated chemist's glass. He should have been a bartender.

NORA. Is he drinking as much as ever?

ALICE. When I'm at home? I should say not. Nothing after 1 A.M. If he goes to bed, then he's all right. If he doesn't he sits up till five going the pace that fills. (*Laughs.*) I wouldn't mind if it made him amusing—but it doesn't—it merely makes him sleepy. For heaven's sake, Nora, do sit down.

NORA (*crosses to front of table*). I can't. I always stand up for twenty minutes after each meal. It keeps you thin.

ALICE (*crosses down stage and to R.C. Eagerly*). Does it? (*Rising.*) Does it, really? (*Comfortably.*) Still I lost nine pounds abroad.

NORA. Goodness! How?

ALICE. Buttermilk.

NORA. I walked four miles this morning in a rubber suit and three sweaters and gained half a pound. (*Crosses to L.C. and up around table to back.*)

ALICE. I do wish hips would come in again. (ALICE *to R. end of couch.*

MICHAEL *crosses to R., up.* MONTY *to back of couch and* DENBY *to L.C., to* NORA *at back of table.*)

(*Heard speaking off. Enter R.*)

DENBY. It's a delicious liqueur.

(ALICE *has crossed over to couch and* NORA *behind table meets* DENBY.)

MICHAEL. I used to think so, too, before my wife stopped my drinking.

(DENBY *comes to* ETHEL.)

MONTY (*back of couch R.*). Fine stuff. I could still feel it warming up all the little nooks and crannies.

DENBY. Purple, but pleasing.

ALICE. Michael—did they tell you any stories—purple stories?

DENBY (*standing behind table C.*). We don't know any new stories; we've been in England.

(*All laugh.*)

ALICE (*to couch and sits*). Do sit down, all of you. We've been standing up to get thin.

MICHAEL. Come on. If they're going to discuss getting thin—let's get out.

MONTY. Woman's favorite topic.

NORA (*coming round front of table to L. of table.* HARRINGTON *comes to R., and* DENBY *to L. below table and between* ETHEL *and chair L. of table*). But you mustn't sit down yet; it isn't twenty minutes.

ALICE. Well, I think it's twenty minutes, and if it isn't I don't give a damn.

(DENBY *crosses to upper end of fender.*)

MICHAEL. Women are so self-denying! (*Crosses and sits R. of table.*)

ALICE. By the way, Nora, there was a girl on the boat who lost twelve pounds.

MICHAEL. Twelve pounds! Why, that's sixty dollars. How women gamble.

ALICE. Pounds of flesh. She was on a diet. She didn't eat for four days.

(DENBY *crosses to chair L. of table.*)

NORA. Oh, that's a fine idea. I must try it sometime—when I'm not hungry. (NORA *sits front of table C.*)

ETHEL (*suddenly coming into the conversation*). Speaking of the boat, Alice, what did you smuggle in?

(*During this talk about smuggling,* MONTY *looks anxiously at* DENBY *and foot by foot, watching him, moves till he is behind table C.*)

ALICE. Not a thing this time. I declared every solitary stitch——

MICHAEL. I'd like to believe you— but knowing you as I do——

ALICE. I paid seven hundred dollars duty——

NORA. Disgusting.

MICHAEL. What mental revolution was responsible for your deciding that smuggling is wrong?

ALICE. I don't think it's wrong—you men seem to—but I'd swindle the government any day.

NORA. Then, for heaven sakes, why——

ALICE. Behold my reformer, Mr. Denby.

ETHEL (*suspicious and nervous. Speaks quickly*). Mr. Denby?

NORA (*turns to* DENBY). What did he have to do with it?

(ETHEL *has little part in the following conversation, but is most keen, alert, and watchful.*)

ALICE. He frightened me.

MICHAEL. I want to have a good look at the man who can do that.

DENBY. I'm afraid Mrs. Harrington is exaggerating. I merely explained that things lately had been in rather a muddle at the Customs.

ALICE. They didn't give us the least bother at the dock.

DENBY. That sometimes means the greatest possible trouble afterwards.

NORA. How can it?

DENBY. Well, according to some articles in *McClure's* a few months ago—by Burns—— (*Turning to* ETHEL.)

NORA. Oh, was it in dialect? I love Scotch stories.

DENBY (*to* NORA). I'm afraid you're thinking of the wrong Burns; this wasn't Bobby, the poet. It was Bill, the detective.

ETHEL. What did he have to say about it?

DENBY. It seems that very often a dishonest official will let a prominent woman, like Mrs. Harrington, slip through the lines without the least difficulty—even if she is smuggling—only afterward to come to her home, threaten exposure and a heavy fine. Usually the woman or her husband—(*look between* HARRINGTON *and* ALICE)—will pay largely to hush things up. That's why I advised Mrs. Harrington to declare everything.

ALICE. Even so, I'd never have listened to it if you hadn't scared me half to death with that talk about R. J.

ETHEL. What's R. J.?

MICHAEL. Sounds like a collar, or a corset.

ALICE. He's one of those frightfully clever detectives who get you "if you don't watch out."

NORA. Oh, I'll bet he's fun. I adore detectives. Do tell us about him, Mr. Denby.

DENBY. I know very little. Just that he's supposed to be one of those impossible secret-service agents, traveling incognito, all over the place. He's known only by his initials—R. J. The stormy petrel—some people call him—always in the wake of trouble. Where there is intrigue, diplomatic tangles—if the Japs steal a fortification plan or send a cross-country airplane to drop a bomb on the Singer Building, R. J.'s supposed to be there—and catch the bomb.

NORA. What an awfully unpleasant position!

DENBY. You see, I thought I ought to tell Mrs. Harrington about him, because we heard in Paris that he was busy over here now—with the Customs.

MICHAEL. But what I can't see is—suppose Alice had smuggled and she came through without any fuss, as she did, how on earth, without a search, could they know she had anything dutiable, and if they didn't know, how could they blackmail her?

DENBY. Oh, that's the simplest part of it. The clerk in Paris who sells you a set of sables or some rare bit of lace is most of the time a government spy, unofficially and directly after he has assured you: "It is simple to smuggle, one can hide things so easily," he is cabling the Customs here of your purchase.

MICHAEL. They do that? I never did trust foreigners.

ETHEL (*rises, crosses to* DENBY, *leaning forward coquettishly to* DENBY). Tell me truly, Mr. Denby, didn't you smuggle something—just one tiny little scarf pin?

(MONTY *to* C., *then slowly to back of table.*)

DENBY (*turning to her*). Truly, nothing. Not even one tiny little scarf. What makes you think I did?

ETHEL. It seemed to me that your protection of Mrs. Harrington was so very insistent you must have been afraid that she—less clever than you—would be caught.

DENBY. But how could that affect me?

ETHEL. If she were found out, that might direct suspicion to you.

MICHAEL. That sounds plausible—come on, Denby, 'fess up, what did you bring?

DENBY. Only myself and Monty—but you see he isn't dutiable.

(MONTY *goes up to window, and in a moment strolls back to table.*)

ETHEL. Well, I'm not convinced, Mr. Denby, that it wasn't one thought for Alice and two for yourself.

MICHAEL (*rising*). Come on, Denby —tell us.

NORA (*rising and coming to* DENBY). Oh, do—it'd be so nice if your picture was in the Rogues' Gallery.

ALICE (*rises, crosses to* C.). Yes, do tell us, Mr. Denby.

MICHAEL. We'll keep mum, we won't turn you over to the Police.

(MONTY *to table. Crosses to* ALICE *at* C.)

ETHEL. You're safe with us.

DENBY. Oh, I'm sure of that—so sure that if I had anything to tell, I'd tell it.

NORA. That's always the way—every time I meet a man who seems exciting, he turns out to be just a nice man—I hate nice men. (*Goes and stands by* MONTY *behind table.*)

ETHEL. Yes, you are a disappointment. Couldn't you think of any new way to smuggle?

DENBY. Oh, it wasn't lack of ingenuity—just respect for the law.

MICHAEL. I didn't know we had that in America any more.

ETHEL (*takes cigarette box from mantel, crossing L. to* MONTY, *then to* MICHAEL). Cigarettes, gentlemen?

MONTY (*taking cigarette*). Thank you very much, Miss Cartwright.

MICHAEL. No, I want something I can get my teeth in. (*Turns to* ALICE *at* C.)

ETHEL (*crossing back to* L. *of* DENBY). You, Mr. Denby?

DENBY. Thanks, no, I'll roll my own —if you don't mind. (*He has taken pouch from pocket and puts pouch on table.* ETHEL *starts as she sees the pouch, and shuts the cigarette box with a click. Crosses to mantel and puts cigarette box on mantel.*)

NORA. Oh, can't you do it with one hand—like the cowboys do in books?

DENBY (*smiling*). I'm sorry to disappoint you again, but I find two hands barely enough.

ETHEL (*crosses to* DENBY). Sometime you must roll me one, will you?

DENBY. With pleasure. (*He finishes the rolling and lights the cigarette.*)

ALICE. But you don't smoke.

ETHEL. Ah, but I've been tempted.

NORA. The only thing that makes my life worth living is yielding to temptation.

MICHAEL. Well, I'm thirsty—who'll split a pint?

ALICE. That's your last drink tonight.

MICHAEL. I'm not likely to forget it. You know my wife thinks I'm a restaurant. She closes me up at one sharp.

ALICE. Shall we have some bridge, Ethel?

ETHEL. Thanks, no, I've given it up.

NORA (*surprised*). Why, you used to love it.

ETHEL. I've come to think that all gambling is horrible.

MICHAEL. Me too, unless stocks go up or the Democratic party goes down I'll be broke soon. (*Crosses to back of couch.*) How about a game of pool? (*Crosses to door* R.)

NORA (*enthusiastically*). I've never played, but I'd like to learn.

MONTY. That'll make it a nice game. (*Steps back as* ALICE *crosses to* NORA *at* C.)

ALICE (*up to french window*). I suppose there's nothing else to do but turkey trot. (*Down to* NORA.) Come, Nora.

MICHAEL. Well, I'll play pool or bridge or poker—I'll sit or talk and sing—but I'll be hanged if I turkey trot.

ALICE. Oh, if you were only light-footed instead of lightheaded.

(ALICE *and* MICHAEL *exit* R.)

NORA. Coming, Monty? (*She follows* MICHAEL *and* ALICE *off R.*)

MONTY. Sure, but I'd much rather tango. (*He starts to go off R.*)

DENBY (*crosses to back of table at L.C. Detaining him*). Oh, Monty.

ETHEL. Aren't you playing, Mr. Denby?

DENBY. In just a moment. There's something I want to say to you, Monty.

ETHEL (*crossing up between the men toward door R. to upper R.C.*). I know, man's god—business.

MONTY. We have rather a big deal on.

DENBY. Yes, a two-hundred-thousand-dollar proposition—so we're a bit anxious.

ETHEL (*a look on the mention of the amount*). I should think anyone would be—in your place—but don't be too long, I shall want that cigarette presently. (*She goes out door R.* DENBY *looking after her.*)

DENBY. Bully, bully girl.

MONTY (*anxiously at L. of couch R.*). Anything wrong, Steve?

DENBY (*coming out of his trance and down to* MONTY *at L. end of couch*). I don't understand why they haven't done anything. I'm certain we were followed from the dock.

MONTY. Why, you're crazy. If they'd had the least idea about the necklace, they'd have pinched you at the pier.

DENBY. That's just what makes me suspicious—they let us slide through too easily.

MONTY. They were mighty casual.

DENBY. And Cartier's must have tipped off some of the Customs crowd that I got the necklace there. It all looks too fishy. They're up to some dodge.

MONTY. You're too fidgety. (*Crosses down R.*)

DENBY. You don't know the game as I do. (*He goes around table to L. of light switch up on C. wall by window.*) Get over by that window. (MONTY *starts hurriedly for the window.*) Easy, easy. (DENBY *has got to light switch and quickly turns it— the lights go out—leaving stage in darkness except for the moonlight coming through the french window.*)

MONTY (*excitedly*). What the dev——

DENBY. Is anyone there on the lawn?

MONTY. No—— (*Quick and mysterious, looks to L.*) By Jove, yes, there is. There's a man over by the big oak.

DENBY. What's he doing?

MONTY. Just standing, looking over this way.

DENBY. He's watching the house. Anybody with him?

MONTY. No.

DENBY. Come away, Monty. (MONTY *crosses back of table and down L.*

He switches light on.) Now, do you believe they've followed us?

(DENBY *comes down C.*)

MONTY. The chills are running up and down my spine. Gee, I hope we don't have a fight.

DENBY. Don't be nervous, old man, they won't touch you. They're after me.

MONTY. Huh—those fellows are likely to shoot first and then ask which is you?

DENBY (*quoting* MONTY's *previous speech*). Nonsense, you're too fidgety.

MONTY. Why the deuce don't they come in?

DENBY. I think they'll stay out to keep us in.

MONTY. I hope they do.

DENBY. They must have someone here on the inside—working under cover to try and get the necklace. (*Crosses up to french windows, looks out to L., using door as screen.*)

MONTY. Who can it be? (*Crosses to table.*)

DENBY (*up at window*). That's what we've got to find out, and then, Monty, then we'll have some sport.

MONTY (*disgustedly*). Then we'll have some shooting. Say, where's the necklace now?

DENBY (*up at french window looking out to L.* MONTY *back to audi-*

ence). Still in my tobacco pouch. (ETHEL *opens R. door very quietly and stands listening. Turns away to L.*) I know they mean business. This is going to be a fight, Monty, a fight to the finish.

(MONTY *turns and, seeing* ETHEL, *interrupts* DENBY *sharply.*)

MONTY. Will you have a cigarette, Dick?

(DENBY *wheels about quickly. Picture.* ETHEL, *seeing she is discovered, comes down smiling to R. of table.*)

ETHEL (*as she crosses down C.*) Still talking business? I left my fan here somewhere.

DENBY. Girls are always doing that, aren't they? (*As he crosses down L.*) We'll help you find it, eh, Monty.

MONTY (*nervously crosses to sofa*). Sure, Steve, sure.

ETHEL. Steve? (*Turns to* MONTY). But as I came in I thought I heard you call him Dick.

MONTY (*embarrassed*). Who? Me? Why?

DENBY (*promptly crossing to* ETHEL *at table*). Oh, that was a signal in our private code.

ETHEL. It sounds mysterious.

DENBY. It's only commonplace. My favorite parlor trick is making breaks, and good old Monty has invented a signal to warn me when I'm on dangerous ground. "Will you have a cigarette, Dick?" he says.

(ETHEL *turns to* MONTY.)

MONTY (*relieved*). Yes, that's it.

ETHEL (*to* MONTY). But why, Dick?

DENBY (ETHEL *turns to* STEVE). Oh, that's the signal—if he said Steve I mightn't notice it—so he always says Dick, don't you, Monty?

MONTY. Always, Steve.

ETHEL (*gaily*). Were you about to make a break when I came in?

DENBY. I'm afraid I was.

ETHEL (*crosses to* DENBY). What was it? Do tell me.

DENBY. Ah, if I told you, then it would indeed be a break.

ETHEL. Discreet man! You must have been talking about me.

DENBY. You are imaginative—(*as he takes stage L., looking around on the ceiling*)—even about your fan—there doesn't seem to be a sign of it here.

ETHEL (*going toward stairs*). I dare say it must be in my room. May I have that promised cigarette now to cheer me on my way? (*Crosses to* DENBY.)

DENBY. Surely. (*He takes pouch from pocket and rolls cigarette.*)

MONTY (*crossing to* C.). Can't I get your fan for you?

ETHEL. No; you'd have to rummage, and that's a privilege I reserve only for myself.

(MONTY *crosses down to* R.C. *slowly.*)

ETHEL (*taking cigarette, licks it, and puts it in mouth*). You are expert. Thanks.

DENBY. Thanks. (*He lights her cigarette. She takes one puff amateurishly, gives slight cough.*)

ETHEL. What a delicious cigarette! (DENBY *turns away up stage to toss away match at fireplace and smiles, with pouch in left hand. She holds out hand and touches pouch, showing she wishes to get hold of it.*) What sort of tobacco is it?

DENBY (*turning to* ETHEL *and not giving her the pouch and returning it to his pocket*). Without fire.

ETHEL. Without fire?

DENBY. Yes. You see no smoke without fire. (*He puts pouch in his pocket.*)

ETHEL. You don't believe in that old phrase?

DENBY. Not a bit—do you?

ETHEL (*as she goes backing up the stage*). Do make another break sometime. (*On first platform and leaning over balustrade.*) Won't you, Dick?

DENBY (*crossing to table and C. and R. of stairs.*) I probably will—unless Monty or you warn me?

ETHEL (*on first landing of stairs, leaning over balustrade*). I'd never do that—I'd rather like to see you put your foot in it. You seem so very sure of yourself—Steve! (*She laughs and exits upstairs.*)

MONTY (*crosses to C.*). Say, who is that girl?

DENBY (*looking after her*). Ethel Cartwright.

MONTY. Yes, yes, but what do you know about her?

DENBY (*he crosses toward* MONTY *down stage*). Nothing, except that she's a corker.

MONTY. You met her in Paris, didn't you?

DENBY. Yes.

MONTY. What was she doing there?

DENBY (*turning and coming to him*). What on earth are you driving at?

MONTY. She was behind that door trying to listen to us.

DENBY (*quickly*). You thought that too?

MONTY (*triumphantly*). Ah! Then you do suspect her of being the one they've got on the inside?

DENBY. It can't be possible—that girl—— (*Looks upstairs.*) No, I won't believe it.

MONTY (*suddenly*). Say, Steve, you're not sweet on her?

DENBY (*overdoing his denial. Looks at* MONTY). No—(*looks upstairs*)—no, no, no. I know you're wrong—it's impossible.

MONTY. But you have the same idea I have.

DENBY (*slowly to front*). I know, I know. (*Reluctantly.*) She did seem mighty interested in my tobacco pouch.

MONTY. But how could she know the necklace was there?

DENBY (*faces front*). They've had a tip, and if she's one of 'em she'd know. Wouldn't it be just my rotten luck to have that girl, of all girls I've ever known, mixed up in this? (*Looks upstairs.*)

MONTY. I believe you're in love with her.

DENBY (*looks toward stairs, speaks slowly*). I know I am.

MONTY (*coming back to* DENBY). Oughtn't we to find out if she is the one who's after you or not?

DENBY. No, we oughtn't. I'm sure now. I won't insult her by trying to trap her.

MONTY. Flub dub. I suspect her. Isn't it only fair to her to clear her of that suspicion? If she's all right, I'll be darned glad of it; if she isn't, wouldn't you rather know?

DENBY. But, old man, I don't want to fight her.

MONTY. I understand, but you can't quit now—you've got to get through.

DENBY. I suppose you're right.

MONTY. Of course I am.

DENBY. Understand, Monty, I'm only doing this to prove how absolutely wrong you are.

MONTY. Sure, Steve, sure.

DENBY. Go in there and keep the rest of the people from coming back. (*Crossing L. in front of table and facing up stage.*)

MONTY. How can I do that?

DENBY. Oh, recite, make faces, do imitations, play Going to Jerusalem.

MONTY (*goes to door R., turns*). And say, old man, whatever turns up, don't take it too hard. Just remember what happened to Samson and Antony and Adam. (*MONTY exits R. As soon as he has done so, DENBY looks around, drops pouch in front of chair, looks upstairs; sees door L., crosses to door, looks off L., leaves door open, stands in doorway, determines to change position of pouch. Crosses to pouch, looks around room, picks up pouch, places it on table; pushes plant away, moves chair a little, looks around, crosses to door L., exits, drawing door to until almost closed—but audience can see him. After a second's pause ETHEL speaks, coming downstairs.*)

ETHEL. Oh, Mr. Denby, my fan was in my room. (*She pauses at foot of the long flight of stairs, as she sees he isn't there. She looks around the room and comes down to above table and sees the pouch. She starts for it, pauses, suspecting a trap. Steps back, goes over to french window, looks out, comes back, goes for pouch, and sees that door L. is slightly ajar, then pauses. She is now absolutely aware of his trap. She moves nervously toward servant's bell, down L., passing back*) of the table at L.C. Then, as she gets within range of the door, changes to a determined walk, goes to bell over mantel, and rings for servant without ever looking at the door. She stands facing the audience. LAMBERT enters R. to C.*) Lambert, please find Mr. Denby, and say that I am here.

LAMBERT. Yes, miss. (*Starts right.*)

ETHEL (*coming toward table*). Oh, here's Mr. Denby's tobacco pouch —he must have forgotten it—— (*LAMBERT comes and picks up pouch with his left hand.*) No, I'll give it to him.

LAMBERT. Yes, madam.

(*She pretends to try to take it from his hand and pulls it open. It falls to the floor, scattering the tobacco*).

ETHEL. How careless of you, Lambert. (*She looks keenly at spilt tobacco and sees no necklace has dropped from it.*)

LAMBERT. I beg pardon, miss. (*He picks up pouch.*)

ETHEL. Did you spill all the tobacco?

LAMBERT (*opens pouch*). Yes, miss, the pouch is quite empty. (*He hands it to her. She gives sigh of relief. He starts R.*)

ETHEL (*nodding her head to L. door*). No, I think Mr. Denby went to the library.

LAMBERT. Yes, miss. (*He goes to door; but DENBY, realizing he must not be seen there, has gone. LAMBERT opens door.*) No, miss, Mr. Denby is not in the library. (*LAMBERT exits L.U.E.*)

ETHEL (*under her breath*). Thank God. (ETHEL, *first making sure no one is watching or listening, goes quickly to french window and lowers the curtain as a signal. Crosses to stage C. and stands breathlessly happy that there is no necklace. She has pouch in her hand, standing at C. In a moment* TAYLOR *enters.*)

TAYLOR. Well, you've got him? Where is he? Where is the necklace?

ETHEL. You were wrong—there is no necklace.

TAYLOR. You're crazy.

ETHEL. You said it was in the tobacco pouch—I've searched, it isn't there.

TAYLOR. You're trying to protect him—you're stuck on him—you can't lie to me.

ETHEL. No, no, no—look, here's the pouch. There's no necklace in it.

TAYLOR. How did you get hold of it? (*As he takes pouch and looks in it.*)

ETHEL. He left it lying there on the table.

TAYLOR. He did, eh? Well, of course the necklace isn't in it. He suspects you. He's trying to bluff you. (*Hands pouch to* ETHEL.)

ETHEL. No, no, he hasn't got it.

TAYLOR. I know he has and you've got to find out tonight where it is. You may have to search his room.

ETHEL (*steps down*). I couldn't. I couldn't.

TAYLOR. Yes, you could, and you will. If you land him, use the same signal—pull down the shade in his room—we'll be watching. I can get in through the balcony.

ETHEL. I can't! I've done what you asked. I won't try to trap an innocent man.

TAYLOR (*snarling*). Oh, you won't, eh? Well, you will; I've been pretty nice to you, but I'm sick of it. You'll go through for me and you'll go through right. I've had your sister followed—see, look at this—(*he opens paper*)—it's a warrant for her arrest—unless you land that necklace tonight, she'll be in the Tombs in the morning.

ETHEL (*turning away, crosses to side of table. Covering her face*). Oh, not that—not that. (*Comes down a few steps.*)

TAYLOR. It's up to you.

ETHEL (*piteously*). But what can I do? What can I do?

TAYLOR (*crossing to* ETHEL). I'll tell you what you can do. You're a good-looking girl, make use of your good looks, get around him, jolly him, get him stuck on you—make him take you into his confidence—he'll fall for you—those guys always do.

ETHEL (*bracing up*). I know he's innocent—so I—I will get around him; I will get his confidence. I'll prove it to you and I'll save him.

TAYLOR. Yes, but don't give him your confidence. Don't give him the least tip-off—understand? If you can get him out in the garden, I'll take a chance he has the necklace on him. We'll nail him there. And don't forget I've got that warrant. (*He exits and puts pouch on table. She comes down to front of table and stands there, thinking. He exits through french window and to L.*)

DENBY (*entering from stairs and going to R. of* ETHEL). Oh, hello!

(ETHEL *bracing up.* ETHEL's *note during this scene is "I must get his confidence and prove his innocence."*)

ETHEL. Oh, hello, I've been looking for you.

DENBY (*starting R.*). Shall we join the others?

ETHEL (*sharply*). No. No. (DENBY *turns quickly, looks at her, as she goes on covering her embarrassment*). I want to talk to you. (*She sits L. of table.*)

DENBY (*crosses to R. of table*). I am flattered——

ETHEL (*sits*). Curious, isn't it? When you like people you may not see them for a year?

DENBY. Exactly. But when you do, you begin where you left off.

ETHEL (*flirting*). Where did we leave off?

DENBY. Why, in Paris——

ETHEL. But you've changed a lot since Paris.

DENBY. For better?

ETHEL. For worse.

DENBY. Oh, come now.

ETHEL. In Paris, you used to trust me.

DENBY. And you think I don't now.

ETHEL. I'm sure you don't.

DENBY. Why? (*Sits R. at table.*)

ETHEL (*lightly*). When I asked you why you were in America you put me off with some playful excuse that you were just an idler. Tell me, didn't you come over on some important mission?

DENBY (*slowly, beginning to suspect her*). And if I did, why do you want to know?

ETHEL. Shall we say feminine curiosity?

DENBY (*seriously*). I think not. You must have some more vital reason for asking than a mere whim.

ETHEL (*leaning forward*). I have— I want to be friends, good friends —I regard frankness as a test of friendship—why won't you tell me?

DENBY. Shall we say man's intuition? (*A move from* ETHEL.) Oh, I know it's not supposed to be as good as woman's—but sometimes it's much more accurate.

ETHEL. So you won't trust me after all? (*Serious.*)

DENBY. Can I?

ETHEL. Don't you think you can?

DENBY (*meaningly*). If you do——

ETHEL. But aren't we friends? (*Faces front.*) Pledged that night under the moon in the Bois—— (*Turns to* DENBY.) You see, I have memories of Paris, too.

DENBY. You put it as a test of friendship?

ETHEL. Yes.

DENBY (*suddenly about to put her to the test. Rises*). Then so do I. Miss Cartwright, you were right. I did not come to America idly. I came to smuggle a necklace through the Customs. I did it today.

ETHEL (*rising, horror-stricken*). You didn't—you didn't.

DENBY (*a quick look around*). Sh, sh, I did.

ETHEL (*turning toward fireplace*). Oh, I'm sorry, I'm sorry.

DENBY (*eying her keenly and crossing in front of table to* ETHEL). But I fooled 'em.

ETHEL (*afraid for him*). Oh, but perhaps you didn't.

DENBY. What makes you think that?

ETHEL (*nervously*). How can you be sure they didn't suspect?

DENBY. Here I am and there are no detectives after me. And if there were, they'd never guess I carry the necklace in my tobacco pouch.

ETHEL (*quickly*). But your pouch was empty.

DENBY (*keenly*). How did you know that?

ETHEL (*hastily*). I—I was here when Lambert spilt it.

DENBY (*looks at spot where pouch was dropped*). Oh, to be sure. But —I have another pouch—— (*Takes it from his pocket.*)

ETHEL (*aghast*). Two pouches?

DENBY. One would have done. They never suspected me at all.

ETHEL. But you can't be certain. If they found out they'd put you in prison.

DENBY. Would you care?

ETHEL (*turning to front*). Of course I would—aren't we friends?

DENBY (*pauses*). Are we?

ETHEL (*not looking at him*). Of course, of course. (*Turns to* DENBY.) But what are you going to do?

DENBY (*straight to her*). I've made my plans—I shan't be caught. Whoever is after me, I won't give in. No matter what it costs or whom it hurts—I've got to win.

ETHEL (*crosses to club fender, distressed and frightened*). Oh!

DENBY. What is it?

ETHEL (*nervously and looking at* DENBY). Oh, nothing. (*Pauses, crossing to above table.*) Isn't it warm in here? (*Pauses.*) Won't you take me in the garden and show me the moon? (*Not looking at moon.*) It's gorgeous.

DENBY (*turns to* ETHEL). Surely, come.

(ETHEL *steps back, waits for* DENBY. *They start for french window, get halfway there.*)

ETHEL (DENBY *up to* ETHEL). No, no, after all don't let's go. (*Turning back to R. of table.* DENBY *at window watching out in garden.*)

DENBY. Why not?

ETHEL (*shaking*). I don't know, but let's stay here. I'm just nervous.

DENBY. Nonsense. The moon will take your nerves away—he's so soothing—that old chap—— (*Pauses,* ETHEL *is R. of table. He takes step to her.* ETHEL *sighs, facing front.*) What is it? You're miles away.

ETHEL (*slowly*). I'm thinking of my sister.

DENBY. Eh? Come, let's go. (*They start up toward french window.*) Surely there are many things I can tell you.

(NORA *enters. A shrill scream off R.* ETHEL *backs to R. back of table, then slowly to club fender, and faces front. A slight pause and* MONTY *rushes on through french window from R.*)

MONTY (*sharply*). Look out, Steve. (*Enters R. to step at window.*) Don't go out there!

DENBY. What's the matter?

ETHEL (*nervously*). What is it?

MONTY (*crossing to R.C.*). Nora and I went for a walk in the garden and suddenly two men jumped from behind the pagoda—— (DENBY *gives* ETHEL *a look. Frightened, she stares straight ahead at the silence and crosses to fireplace.*) They started for us and one man said: "No, we're wrong!" And Nora screamed and they turned and ran like the very devil.

(DENBY *watches* ETHEL *and crosses slowly to R. table at L.C.* NORA, ALICE, *and* MICHAEL *enter R.* NORA *at C.,* ALICE *back of R. end of couch, and* MICHAEL *L. end of couch, talking excitedly, and so they play the following.*)

NORA. Wasn't it awful—has Monty told you?

ALICE. What's happened?

MICHAEL. Won't somebody explain?

NORA. Oh, it was perfectly frightful.

MONTY. Let me tell it.

NORA. You'll get it all wrong—I wasn't half as scared as you were.

MONTY. I was talking to Nora—and suddenly from the bushes——

NORA. Somebody stepped right out ——

MICHAEL. Wait—wait, one at a time.

NORA. Why, you see, Monty and I went for a walk in the garden——

MONTY. And the two men jumped out and started for us.

MICHAEL. Great Scott!

ALICE. What did you do?

NORA. I screamed—and they ran away. Wasn't it exciting? (*Taking a deep breath.*) Just like a book.

ALICE. They might have killed you.

MICHAEL. You want a drink—I'll ring for some brandy.

(NORA *beckons* MR. *and* MRS. HARRINGTON *to french window.*)

MONTY. I'd be all right if I could just get one long, deep breath——

(MICHAEL *in the middle,* ALICE *to R., and* NORA *L. of* MICHAEL *go up to window.*)

DENBY. You do look a bit shaken, old man. What you need is a comforting smoke—there's a pipe in my suitcase.

MONTY. But——

DENBY. Here's my tobacco—— (*Hands pouch to* MONTY.)

MONTY. Gee, I don't want that.

DENBY (*looking at* ETHEL). That's all right, I've smoked enough for tonight, anyhow. Only when you're through with it just drop it in the drawer in the desk in my room, so I'll have it for coffee in the morning.

MONTY. Sure, Steve, sure. I'll leave the pouch in the drawer. (*Exits upstairs.*)

ALICE (ALICE *first, then* MICHAEL, *and* NORA *coming down R.C.*). But suppose those men are robbers and try to break in here tonight?

DENBY. I'm sure they were only a couple of tramps.

ALICE. Oughtn't we to do something?

MICHAEL (*weakly*). Do you want me to look for them?

ALICE. Certainly not. I can imagine nothing more useless than a dead husband.

MICHAEL. I absolutely agree with you.

ALICE. Go telephone for the police.

(ETHEL *turns to* MRS. HARRINGTON.)

MICHAEL. I'll do that with great pleasure. (*He exits R.*)

NORA (*going toward stairs*). Goodness! I left my rings on my dressing table.

ALICE. Heavens! Let's get them. (*She crosses towards stairs.* NORA *runs upstairs and off.*) Ethel, you look frightened to death. (*Goes to upper end of fireplace.*)

ETHEL (*on fender seat*). Oh, no, no.

ALICE. You needn't worry after all. We've two men here and Michael. (ALICE *exits upstairs.*)

(ETHEL *turns away.*)

DENBY (*crosses down to table*). Now, shall we look at the moon?

ETHEL. But those men out there——

DENBY. I'm sure they weren't after me. They wouldn't wait in the garden. And even if they are detectives, the necklace is safe. Now come. (*Moves to go.*)

ETHEL. No, no, I'm nervous. I'm afraid. It's been rather an upsetting evening—I'd prefer to stay here.

MONTY (*coming downstairs nervously to back of table*). I thought I'd rather be down here with you, Steve.

DENBY (*smiling*). All right, old man. Did you leave the pouch in my desk?

MONTY. Yes. To make sure you'd find it in the morning I locked it up. Here's the key.

DENBY (*taking key*). Good!

ETHEL (*registering this talk of pouch*). Good night, Mr. Denby. (*Goes to stairs.*)

(MONTY *crosses to D.R.C.*)

DENBY (*following her to stairs*). You're not leaving?

ETHEL. Yes, I'm quite tired. I think I'll go to my room. (*Going up the stairs.*) ·

MONTY. Oh, I guess everything's all right now.

DENBY. Let's hope so. Still, the night isn't over yet. Pleasant dreams.

ETHEL (*on stairs, halfway to top landing*). I'm afraid they won't be quite—that. (*Exits upstairs.* DENBY *at bottom of stairs looking after her.*)

MONTY (*crossing to* DENBY). Say, Steve, she's gone now to get into your room.

DENBY. No, no, she hasn't.

MONTY. Why, she never made a move to leave till she knew I'd put the pouch in the drawer.

DENBY. I tell you you're wrong.

MONTY. I tell you I'm right—if she gets that necklace it's all up with us.

DENBY. But she won't get it.

MONTY. What's going to stop her?

DENBY. The necklace isn't up there.

MONTY. What! (DENBY *draws the necklace from a false pocket under the right lapel of his coat. Relieved.*) Gee, then everything's all right.

DENBY. But everything's all wrong.

MONTY. But, Steve, the necklace.

DENBY. Oh, damn the necklace! (*He turns and looks after the girl.*)

CURTAIN

ACT THREE

SCENE—*The scene is* DENBY'S *room at the* HARRINGTONS'. *An attractive, daintily furnished guest chamber. There is an entrance door up L.C.; a door at L. to another room; an alcove up R.C. with a bed and appropriate furniture in it. A french window down R. with a balcony off. A table desk at R.C.; a couch down L. with a small table above it. Other furnishings as necessary.*

AT RISE—*When the curtain rises the stage is in complete darkness, save for the moonlight which streams through the window. There is a slight pause. A key is heard rattling in lock of door L.* ETHEL *opens door and goes cautiously across stage to the table. She turns on lamp on table. After a quick survey of table, she takes paper knife and tries to open drawer. She hears footsteps in hall, stops, listens, and runs up to C. door and listens; runs back to table and turns off lamp, and in doing so accidentally brushes paper knife on the floor. She runs off stage at door L.*
After a slight pause DENBY *enters at door C. with noisy assurance. He stops just inside the door and utters a stifled yawn as he switches on lights. He goes over to table, looks out at window, then takes necklace from lapel and looks at it and puts it on the table. Then he goes to alcove and changes his evening coat for a dinner jacket. He comes out, takes cigarette from pocket, and is in the act of lighting it at C. when he spies paper knife on floor. He throws cigarette and match away and hurries to pick up knife, strikes match, and examines desk drawer, then goes to door at L. and stands listening. Steps are heard in hall up L. He hurriedly goes to table and gets necklace, puts it in his pocket, comes back to couch. A knock at U.L.C. door. Pause as he takes book from small table and sits on couch, reading.*

DENBY. Who is it?

MONTY (*outside*). Me.

DENBY. Come in, Monty.

MONTY (*enters up L.C., comes down quickly to* DENBY, *nervously*). Is everything all right?

DENBY (*laughing*). Yes, yes.

MONTY (*crossing to C.*). Thank the Lord. That's the first time I've been able to swallow comfortably in an hour. I thought my heart was permanently dislocated.

DENBY. What's happening downstairs?

MONTY. Nothing. And it's the limit to have nothing happen.

DENBY. Did you search the garden again?

MONTY. Yes, they haven't come back.

DENBY. That's queer—you're sure?

MONTY. Lambert and I've been over the whole place—garden—shrubbery, even the cornfield—not a trace of 'em.

DENBY. Well, they will be back——

MONTY. I'll bet they will—with the militia!

DENBY (*rises and crosses to* MONTY). Don't lose your nerve, Monty.

MONTY. I wish I would. This certainly is getting on it—and all the time I've got that creepy feeling that they're coming closer to us.

DENBY. But that's real sport, Monty.

MONTY. Sport be damned. You don't think the fox enjoys the hunt, do you? And, at that, he's got it on us. He knows who's chasing him.

DENBY. We'll find out tonight.

MONTY. Yes, when they shoot us full of holes. (*Crosses to table R.*)

DENBY. You're not afraid?

MONTY. I'm scared to death. I thought I wanted excitement—but hereafter give me life on a farm. (*Crosses to window.*)

DENBY. You can always clear out—I'll understand.

MONTY (*as he crosses to* DENBY). And leave you to face it alone—you ought to know me better than that, Steve. (*Crosses to R.C. in front of chair L. of table.*) But oughtn't we do something before they come back and search this room?

DENBY. Somebody's done that already.

MONTY. Who was it—the girl?

DENBY. I think not. Her room is in the other wing. She'd hardly dare risk being seen over here till everybody'd gone to bed.

MONTY. Then who could it be? (*Knock at C. door by* HARRINGTON. DENBY *to couch, sits, takes cigarette.* MONTY *dropping in chair L. of table and putting hand over mouth.*) Pinched!

DENBY. Come in.

(HARRINGTON, *carrying two highballs, enters smilingly.*)

HARRINGTON. Hello, boys.

MONTY (*relieved, laughs*). Oh, it's you. (*He jumps up and crosses to window.*)

(DENBY *lights cigarette.*)

DENBY. Come in, Harrington.

HARRINGTON (*crosses to table, puts tray with highball glasses on it*). Brought up a couple of highballs—you said after dinner you might want a scotch later.

DENBY. Thanks—I don't believe I do, after all.

HARRINGTON. Good! Luck's with me. (*He drains the entire glass with great satisfaction.*) Ah-h! How about you, Monty?

MONTY (*laughing*). No, thanks.

HARRINGTON. Splendid fellow. I'll take the encore in a minute. You know, now that my wife's home—she allows me one light one for dinner—mostly vermouth—and one drink afterward—— 'Tain't fair.

MONTY. Aren't you master in your own house?

MICHAEL. You bet your life I'm not.

DENBY. In union there is strength. Have the other.

MICHAEL. I'm about to. (*Slowly crosses to C.,* MONTY *to table and sits on it.*) Say, by the way, if you should change your mind and want a drink any time during the night, just ring for Lambert. He's used to it.

DENBY (*smiling*). Thanks.

MICHAEL. I hope you will want one. I hate to think of Lambert's having a good night's rest for the first time in six weeks. (*He turns up.*) But, mind you, don't get up half asleep and push that red thing over there. (*He points to alarm on the wall right of L.C. door.*)

MONTY (*off table*). What on earth is that? It looks like a hotel fire alarm—"Break the glass in case of fire."

MICHAEL. It's a burglar alarm that rouses the whole house.

MONTY. What!

DENBY (*laughing*). In spite of our visitors of this evening, you don't really fear burglars?

MICHAEL (*sitting L. of table R.*). I know it's funny, but I'm vice-president of the New York Burglar Insurance Company—and I've got to have one of all of their beastly patents in my house to show they're good.

DENBY. I'll keep away from it.

MICHAEL. The last guest who had this room accidentally knocked against it at 4 A.M. The blamed thing went off and Mrs. Harrington made me get up and search the whole house. At that I was glad it was a false alarm. (*He takes up second highball and is drinking when voices are heard off stage.*) Good lord, my wife—here, quick. (*Hands* MONTY *empty glass, then crosses to* DENBY *with half-filled one.* ALICE *knocks on door C.*) Boys, I count on you.

(DENBY *rises and crosses to lower end of couch.* MONTY *smiles and nods.* HARRINGTON *crosses to back of table.*)

DENBY. Come in.

(ALICE *and* NORA *enter.* ALICE *to C.* NORA *to L. C.*)

ALICE (*pauses till she gets to C.*). Do we intrude?

DENBY. Rather no. Delightfully welcome.

NORA. We thought you'd still be up —Michael said he was bringing you some highballs.

MONTY. Great stuff, too—best whisky I ever tasted.

(ALICE *glances at* MICHAEL, *who is innocently looking at the ceiling.*)

DENBY. Your husband is a noble abstainer with temptation right before him.

ALICE. Is he? How unusual—put temptation before Michael and he's just like old Adam—only Michael's weakness is for grapes—(*crosses to chair L. of table and sits*)—not apples.

NORA (*to* DENBY). Alice and I aren't the least bit sleepy—we thought perhaps one of you'd make a fourth at bridge.

DENBY (*at lower end of couch*). Among my other deficiencies I don't play.

ALICE. You, Monty?

MONTY (*nervously*). Surely—— (DENBY *shakes his head at him.* MONTY *continues awkwardly.*) That is, if you don't mind waiting fifteen or twenty minutes. Steve and I are talking over a deal about a—a gold mine.

ALICE. Are you interested in a mine?

DENBY (*smiling*). Something like that.

NORA (*half turkey trotting*). I'd rather dance than bridge it. (*She hums a late turkey trot, and as she dances,* DENBY *goes to small table head of couch L. and places highball on it.*)

ALICE (*rises*). Heavens, be quiet—you'll disturb Ethel.

DENBY (*quickly*). Has Miss Cartwright gone to bed? (*He crosses back of couch down L.*)

ALICE. Yes, she felt rather tired.

NORA (*humming and dancing at C.*). It's wrong to go to bed so early. It can't be much after two. (*Singing.*) Oh, this is the life.

ALICE (*crossing to* NORA). Hush, hush, hush, Nora—Ethel has the next room.

(DENBY *at bookcase L. drops cigarette in vase and turns quickly.*)

NORA. I thought you weren't using it this summer?

ALICE. Ethel insisted on it——

MICHAEL (DENBY *crosses to door L., listening*). And why the devil she was so persistent about it I can't see.

ALICE. Oh, Michael, I told you those tramps scared her and she wanted to be down here near the men.

MICHAEL. I know, I know, but why make me look through forty-seven bunches of keys to get one to fit that door? (MONTY *and* DENBY *exchange looks.*) Seemed positively afraid of you, Denby, thought you were a tough customer.

ALICE. You're not drinking your highball, Mr. Denby.

DENBY (*crosses up, picks up drink, and stands at table*). I'm saving it.

NORA. That's a hint.

DENBY. No, really——

NORA. Come on, Alice. (*She goes to door humming, and exits.*)

ALICE. Coming, Michael?

MICHAEL. In just a moment. I've got one more old wheeze I want to spring on Denby—he's a great audience for old ones——

ALICE. When you've told it, you come directly downstairs and play bridge.

MICHAEL. Certainly, my dear.

ALICE. And, Michael—don't think you've fooled me.

MICHAEL (*innocently*). Fooled you? Why, my dear, I'd never dream of even trying to.

ALICE (*looks at* MICHAEL, *then goes over and takes highball from* DENBY's *hand and, returning, hands it to* MICHAEL). Here's the rest of your drink. (*She exits L.C. door.* MICHAEL *drinks and goes up to door.*)

(DENBY *to* D.L.)

MICHAEL. My wife's a damned clever woman. (*He obediently trots out.*)

DENBY (*quickly goes to door to make sure* MICHAEL *has gone—then turns to* MONTY). By George, it was that girl.

MONTY (*crosses to* DENBY). Are you sure?

DENBY (*coming down* C.). She tried to pry open that drawer with this paper knife. You can see the marks. (MONTY *goes to drawer.*) I found the knife on the floor where she dropped it, when she heard me coming down the hall, and hurried back to her own room.

MONTY. Gee! That's pretty tough, old man.

DENBY. It's hard to believe she's the sort of woman who'd try to take advantage of my friendship to turn me over to the police, but that's just what she tried to do.

MONTY (*crosses to* DENBY). I'm sorry, old man—mighty sorry.

DENBY. But I don't want to fight her.

MONTY. What are you going to do?

DENBY. I don't know. (*Pauses. Crosses to front of table.*) If she'll tell me who it is that sent her here —the man who's after me—I'll fight him and leave her out of it.

MONTY. But if she won't tell you?

DENBY. Then I'll play her own game —only this time she follows my rules. (*Crosses to R. end of table.*)

(*Both suddenly start and then turn toward door L., with their backs to audience.*)

MONTY (*in a whisper*). What's that?

DENBY. Ssh—— (*He tiptoes to door L. back of table and listens.*)

MONTY (*crosses to* C.). Is she there?

DENBY (*puts fingers over lip and then crosses to small table*). Yes.

MONTY. Has she heard us?

DENBY (*coming to* MONTY, C., *quietly*). No. I heard her close the window and then she came over to the door. She's listening now. (*He crosses to desk quickly and starts writing.*)

(MONTY *at C., scared to death. Pauses.*)

MONTY. What are you doing?

DENBY (*writes and hands paper to* MONTY). Sh, sh. Here's my plan. Read it. (*As* MONTY *reads,* DENBY *goes up to door C., reaches out in hall—turns off light switch, leaving hall in darkness. He comes back as* MONTY *looks up from paper. During the reading of the paper* MONTY *has slowly crossed to back of table at right.*)

MONTY (*in whisper, reading*). Jumping Jupiter!

DENBY (*low*). Do you understand?

MONTY. Perfectly.

DENBY (*goes over to* ETHEL'S *door, speaks loudly for her benefit*). It's a pity Miss Cartwright's gone to bed. I might have risked trying to learn bridge if she'd been a player. She's a bully girl. (DENBY *beckons* MONTY *to come nearer and speak louder.*)

MONTY (*crossing up C.—speaking loudly*). Don't talk so loud—in these dictagraph days the walls have ears. We can't tell who may be listening. Let's go out on the lawn where we're surely safe.

DENBY. Good idea. (*He leaves* ETHEL'S *door and goes to door C. beside which is light switch.* DENBY *switches out light as he speaks loudly.*) Well, Monty—what's your scheme? (*The door closes, the room is in darkness. Audience thinks* DENBY *has left room but he hasn't. He is standing with his face to the door up L.C. The footsteps fade away.* MONTY'S *voice is heard as he goes down the hall. There is silence for five seconds, then the sound of a key turning in lock of* ETHEL'S *door.* ETHEL *enters; she hurries to desk and gives one pull at drawer.* DENBY *pushes wall switch and the lights go up.* ETHEL *gives exclamation and turns.* DENBY *is standing inside door C. Coming down C.*) So, you've come for the necklace! Why do you want it?

ETHEL (*crosses to back of chair L. of table*). I am employed by the government. I was sent here to get it.

DENBY. What? The charming Miss Cartwright a secret-service agent? Why, it's incredible.

ETHEL. But, it's true.

DENBY. Who employed you?

ETHEL. I can't tell you.

DENBY. Then I must refuse to believe you.

ETHEL. But it's the truth.

DENBY. Was it John H. Bangs of the secret service who engaged you?

ETHEL. Yes—yes——

DENBY (*bitingly*). You lie, Miss Cartwright, you lie.

ETHEL. Mr. Denby.

DENBY. I've no time for politeness now. There is no Bangs in the secret service.

ETHEL. How do you know?

DENBY. It's my business to know my —opponents.

ETHEL. I can't tell you who it was— (crosses to DENBY)—but if you'll just give me the necklace——

DENBY. And if I refuse, you'll call those men out there and have me arrested.

ETHEL. I don't know—what else can I do? I can't fail.

DENBY. Nor can I. Do you know what this means to me? Prison— (ETHEL looks front)—gray walls and iron bars—solitude—to be caged like some beast. Do you know what that means? I do—I've seen it—I've feared it—I've gone sick at the thought of it. No, Miss Cartwright, you are not going to send me to prison.

ETHEL (turns to DENBY). But I don't want to. I don't want to do that to any man——

DENBY. Then there is a way out of it for both of us.

ETHEL (eagerly). What?

DENBY. Tell them you've failed— that you couldn't get the necklace and I'll give you ten thousand dollars.

ETHEL. No—no——

DENBY. Twenty thousand—no one but you and me would know——

ETHEL. No——

DENBY. Twenty thousand's all I can afford.

ETHEL. I can't accept. I've got to get that necklace. It means more than any money to me.

DENBY. Ah, they have some hold on you.

ETHEL. No, no—— (Crosses to chair L. of table.)

DENBY. Then why should you be in the secret service, unless it's for money, or you've been forced into it?

ETHEL. I can't explain. What difference does it make to you who sent me here?

DENBY. Because I don't want to fight a woman—any woman—I'll fight the man behind you—I'll trick him—I'll beat him. (DENBY crosses to ETHEL.) Will you tell me who he is?

ETHEL. No.

DENBY. You're going to make me fight you?

ETHEL (turns to DENBY). I've got to fight——

DENBY. Very well. (Going to door L., he opens it, takes key from other side, closes door and locks it, and puts key in his pocket.)

ETHEL. What do you mean?

DENBY. I'm going to keep you here. (ETHEL tries to open up C. door but it is locked; then she turns and faces DENBY.) I feared we might be interrupted——

ETHEL (*turning to him, and crossing to back of small table above couch*). Open that door——

DENBY (*crosses to* ETHEL). You don't leave until I am ready to let you go.

ETHEL. You wouldn't do that——

DENBY (*crosses to her*). I regret the necessity of using such methods—on you of all people—but you leave me no choice.

ETHEL. But I don't understand——

DENBY (*to R.C.*). Only that you are a beautiful woman and I am a man. (*She shrinks away.*) It's nearly three—you are in my room after asking that your apartment adjoin mine—your insistence that a key be found is only incriminating—you are frankly *en négligé* and very charming. Inevitably you must be found here—I'm afraid there can be only one construction put upon it.

(ETHEL *at* R.C.)

ETHEL (*with bitter contempt*). I thought at least *you* were a man!

DENBY. I am—and you are a woman —that's the point.

ETHEL. I thought you were my *friend*.

DENBY. You dare talk of friendship! You knew I liked you—liked you very much—and because you knew it you tried to wheedle me into betraying myself. You smiled, and lied, and pledged our friendship, until I'd told you the truth—and all the time you were only trying to trap me—hunt me down—send me to prison.

ETHEL. I wasn't—I wasn't——

DENBY. And when I'd told you the truth, you asked me to go in the garden, knowing that those men out there were waiting for me.

ETHEL. I couldn't help it.

DENBY. When you thought I was sending the necklace here you trumped up a flimsy excuse to leave so you might sneak in here to get it—is that freindship?

ETHEL (*turns to him*). I wasn't trying to trap you—I thought you were innocent—I wanted to make sure so I could convince them——

DENBY. Yes, you proved that. When you found out I was guilty you still tried to save me, I suppose, by asking me to walk into their trap?

ETHEL (*faces him, trying to defend herself*). After all, you had broken the law—you were guilty——

DENBY (*comes to her*). If you had only played fair, but you didn't—you used a woman's last weapon—her sex. Well, I can play your game, too —I can use your methods—and I will. You stay here until morning.

ETHEL (*frightened*). You don't dare——

DENBY (*easily*). Oh, yes, I do.

ETHEL (*turns and crosses to front of table R., then turns back. After a pause—with bravado*). And you think the possible loss of my reputation is going to frighten me into letting you go?

DENBY. I do.

ETHEL. Well, you're wrong. I have only to tell them the truth about the necklace and what I'm doing here——

DENBY. But the truth is so seldom believed—especially when there is no evidence to support it.

ETHEL. All the evidence I need is there, in that locked drawer. (*Turning and pointing to drawer.*)

DENBY. Quite so. I'd forgotten—(*he goes around to back of desk.* ETHEL *crosses to C.—keeping her eyes on* DENBY)—only it's not in the drawer! (*He takes it from his pocket and shows it.* ETHEL *gasps.*) It's a beauty, isn't it? (*He writes quickly.*)

ETHEL (*at center*). What are you doing?

DENBY. Manufacturing evidence.

ETHEL. Meanwhile I propose to leave this room.

DENBY. How, may I ask?

ETHEL. If you believe you've frightened me, you're quite mistaken. (*She moves toward bell, on wall, L. of C. door.*)

DENBY. And what are you going to do?

ETHEL (*pushes bell violently*). I've rung for the servants. (*Triumphantly.*) Now, Mr. Denby.

(DENBY *looks up.*)

DENBY. What a pity you did that—you'll regret it so very soon.

ETHEL. Oh, shall I? When the servants come I shall send for Mr. and Mrs. Harrington and tell them exactly who you are and I shall take that necklace from the room with me.

(DENBY *wraps necklace in note he has written; crosses to window, signals with curtain; whistle is heard off stage.*)

DENBY (*throws necklace wrapped in note he has just written out of window*). But, you see, the necklace won't be here.

ETHEL (*runs down by desk, as if almost to stop him, but the necklace is gone. She stops at L. side of desk and above it*). I shall tell them it's on the lawn where you just threw it.

DENBY. Wrong again. If you'll stand here, you may see that my friend Monty was waiting below—he has it.

ETHEL. But your friend Monty can't get away from those men out there.

DENBY. Perhaps you heard a whistle. That was Monty's signal telling me the coast was clear. For the moment your friends of the secret service have gone.

ETHEL. But I'll tell the Harringtons about Monty, too; that he's your accomplice.

DENBY (*crosses to* ETHEL). And who would believe Monty Vaughn, of the Washington Vaughns, the accomplice of a smuggler?

ETHEL (*beaten*). Oh! (*Backs to C.*)

DENBY. You see? And since you forced me I've had to play my last card, and a very low one—(*crosses to* ETHEL)—I'm sorry to say. That note I wrote that I threw to Monty he'll leave on the floor of the living room—it was a note to you.

ETHEL (*amazed*). To me?

DENBY. It contained the suggestion that you try to get the room next to mine—that you come to me here to-night—it was the invitation—of a lover!

ETHEL (*flaming. Backs away to L.C.*). You beast! You coward!

DENBY (*at C.*). It's certain to be found where you apparently dropped it—its evidence is conclusive. They all know we are not new friends. If you are still in this room in the morning—as you will be—what other explanation can you offer? (*She doesn't answer.*) I think the episode of the necklace remains as between just you and me. (DENBY *crosses to back of table-desk, looking out the window.*)

ETHEL (*turning away*). You cad!

DENBY (*pauses—crosses R. behind desk*). The servants seem to be sleeping soundly—I fear they are not coming.

ETHEL (*a step down stage*). But they will—they will.

DENBY. If they don't, may I suggest that you ring that burglar alarm? (*Crosses to* ETHEL.) It will serve your purpose even better—it will wake up everybody. (*He speaks urgingly. She faces front; he is close beside her.*) Why don't you ring it? I dare you! (*Knock on door C. She shudders and looks out front. He whispers to her.*) Well, why don't you answer? (ETHEL *pauses.*

Shrinks.) Ah—— (*Backs up to door up L.C. and watches* ETHEL. *Aloud.*) Who is it?

LAMBERT (*off stage*). You rang, sir?

DENBY. Yes, I forgot to tell you that Miss Cartwright wishes to be called at seven.

LAMBERT. Very good. Anything else, sir?

DENBY. Call me at the same time. That's all. Good night.

LAMBERT. Good night, sir. (*He is heard departing down the hall—* DENBY *listening at door.*)

DENBY (*mockingly; he comes down to her*). So you didn't dare denounce me, after all?

ETHEL (*turning to* DENBY, *trying to laugh*). Oh, I knew it was all a joke —that you couldn't be so contemptible.

DENBY (*grimly*). A joke, eh?

ETHEL. Yes, if you'd meant what you said you'd have called in Lambert just then. That would have answered your purpose—I knew you wouldn't—that you couldn't.

DENBY. I'm not ready yet.

ETHEL (*hardly daring to believe him*). You really mean to keep me here?

DENBY. I've no other course.

ETHEL. But you can't do it. (*Clock off stage strikes three.* DENBY *looks at watch.*)

DENBY (*crosses to back of table-desk. Serenely*). It's four hours till the maid goes to call you and finds the room empty, so meanwhile won't you sit down, Miss Cartwright? (*Indicating chair L. of table-desk.* DENBY *looks out of window.*)

ETHEL (*crosses to desk and as she sinks into chair speaks hysterically; dropping her head on her arm on the table*). Oh, I can't face it—I can't—I learned that just now, the disgrace—the humiliation—I can't face it!

DENBY (*turns up stage. Grimly*). You've got to face it.

ETHEL. I tell you I can't—it's unfair—it's horrible—if you'll just let me go—I'll promise I won't betray you.

DENBY. You don't dare keep silent about me—how can I let you go?

ETHEL. I'm telling you the truth.

DENBY (*leaning over table to her*). Then tell me who sent you here. (ETHEL *turns head away.*) If you don't, it means prison for me and dishonor for you—if you do tell, it means your safety—perhaps mine—now choose. (DENBY *crosses quickly around to her R., then she rises.*)

ETHEL (*pauses, sobbing*). I can't—I can't—oh, please, please—— (*She turns face front.*)

DENBY (*takes her by both wrists, grasps her in his arms*). I'll make you tell.

ETHEL. Don't touch me—let me go—don't—don't——

DENBY. Who sent .you here? (*He fairly shakes her.*)

ETHEL. I'm afraid—I'm afraid.

DENBY. Who sent you here?

ETHEL. I hate you; I hate you! Let me go, let me go—don't——

DENBY (*takes her in his arms*). Who sent you here?

ETHEL. Oh, I'll tell. Oh, I'll tell. (*Backing away from him as he releases her. She sinks into chair—pathetic—broken.*) I can't go through with it—you've beaten me—— (*Looking at* DENBY.) Oh, I've tried so hard, so hard, but you've won. I can't go on—oh, it's too unfair when it's not my fault—it's not—— Oh, you don't understand—you can't or you wouldn't spoil my whole life like this—you wouldn't! It is not only me—it's my mother—my sister Amy—— (*She pauses. Looks up.*) Amy! (*She rises.*) No, I won't quit —no matter what happens to me— I'll expose you—I'll tell them everything—I'll let them decide between us—whether they'll believe you or me—it's you or my sister. I'll save her.

DENBY (*amazed*). Your sister?

ETHEL. They shan't send her to prison.

DENBY (*hoping against hope*). You're doing all this to keep your sister from prison?

ETHEL. Yes, yes, I love her—they shan't take her.

DENBY. Then you haven't done it because you wanted to?

ETHEL. No, no—what else could I do? She's my sister—she comes first.

DENBY. Then you weren't just lying to me—trying to trick me for money?

ETHEL. No, no. (DENBY *backs away to C.*) Don't you see, I wanted to save you, too—I wanted you to get away—I told them you were innocent—but they wouldn't believe me—they said I had to go on—(*slowly crosses to* DENBY)—if I didn't they'd send Amy to prison. That's why I'm here. (*Pathetically.*) Oh, let me go—let me go!

DENBY (*looking her squarely in the eyes*). Are you telling me the truth?

ETHEL. Oh, yes, yes—can't you see I am? Please, please believe me.

DENBY (*looking straight in her eyes, takes her by her arms. After a moment he is convinced, as he goes to door L. and unlocks it*). It may spoil everything I've built on, but I've got to take the chance. You can go, Miss Cartwright. (*Goes to small table by couch.*)

ETHEL (*coming to him with her hands together*). Oh, you are a man after all.

(DENBY *has her hands and is about to put arm around her. Police whistle off R. They both pause, staring front, with their heads together.*)

DENBY (*hurriedly crosses to window R., pulls chair in up R. corner out of his way and, half hiding behind up-stage curtain, looks out*). The devil!

ETHEL. What is it?

DENBY. Your friends of the secret service have come back—they mustn't see us together. (*He lowers shade on window R.*)

ETHEL (*with a scream*). What have you done? That was the signal that I'd trapped you—that was the signal to bring Taylor here——

DENBY (*triumphantly, crossing to lower end of table-desk*). Ah, then it's Taylor who's after me?

ETHEL (*frightened at having told*). Oh, I didn't mean to tell—I didn't—I didn't.

DENBY (*crossing to her in front of table*). Now it'll be a fight to a finish!

ETHEL. Go, go, before he comes!

DENBY. And leave you to face him alone? (*A pause—he bends his head and touches his lips to her hand.*) No—I love you.

ETHEL. Please—please—while there's time—he mustn't take you—he mustn't—— Oh, I couldn't bear it—I couldn't——

DENBY (*realizing*). Ethel!

ETHEL (*in his arms, tenderly*). I love you—— Oh, my dear—I love you.

DENBY (*triumphantly*). I can fight the whole world now, and win.

ETHEL. No, no, for my sake go—let me see him first—let me try to get you out of it.

DENBY. No, I stay here. When he comes, say that you've caught me.

ETHEL. No, no, I can't send you to prison, either.

DENBY. I won't go to prison. I'm not done for yet, but Taylor mustn't think you've failed him; do you understand?

ETHEL. But then he'll take you away.

DENBY. Do as I say; tell him the necklace is here somewhere.

ETHEL. No, no——

DENBY. It's for your sister. We're going to save her. (*Sounds of* TAYLOR'S *approach off stage.*) He's coming. (DENBY *starts to door C. Turning L.*)

TAYLOR (*coming in at window with revolver in hand, crosses to U.R.C.*). Hands up, Denby! (DENBY'S *hands go up at U.C.*) Well, congratulations, Miss Cartwright, you landed him—I thought you would.

DENBY. What's the meaning of this! Who are you?

TAYLOR. Oh, can that bunk. (*To* ETHEL.) Where's the necklace?

ETHEL. I don't know.

TAYLOR. You don't know?

ETHEL. I haven't been able to find it, but it's here somewhere.

TAYLOR. He's probably got it on him.

DENBY. All this is preposterous.

TAYLOR. Hand it over.

DENBY. I have no necklace.

TAYLOR. I'll have to search you. (*Comes to* DENBY, *gun in hand, and searches him.*)

DENBY. I'll make you pay for this.

TAYLOR. Will you give it to me—or have I got to search this place?

DENBY. Oh, well, if you'll let me take my hands down I'll get it for you.

TAYLOR. Well, you haven't got a gun on you—take 'em down.

DENBY. It's right here. (*He grabs match safe from bookcase and smashes burglar alarm, alarm starts—switches off lights, stage is entirely dark. Voices start off stage.* TAYLOR *utters an ejaculation—there is a steady murmur of a deep gong off stage; they struggle in the dark.* ETHEL, *in dark, goes up to light switch R. of C. door. The revolver is fired in struggle.* ETHEL *screams.*) Turn on the lights.

(ETHEL *switches on lights and comes down to lower end of couch.* DENBY *is seen in possession of revolver, just thrusting* TAYLOR *away from him and covering him with the revolver.*)

TAYLOR. Damn you!

DENBY (*to* TAYLOR). Sit down! Sit down!

(TAYLOR *sits chair L. of desk, as knocking and clamor of voices at door C. begin.* DENBY, *keeping* TAYLOR *covered, backs up to door, fishing in his pocket for key, reaches behind him and unlocks and opens it. Alarm stops.* MICHAEL, *to C.* ALICE, *to L.C., and* LAMBERT *enters, crosses to back of desk.*)

MICHAEL. What's the matter? ⎫
                              ⎬ *Together.*
ALICE. Good heavens, what's happened? ⎭

DENBY. That man tried to break in here—he's a burglar—I caught him.

MICHAEL. Good lord! ⎫
ALICE. How splendid ⎬ *Together.*
of you.   ⎭

(MICHAEL *and* ALICE *are* L. *of*
DENBY. *As they enter they come
down* C. LAMBERT *has gone behind
desk.*)

TAYLOR. The man's crazy—don't believe him—he's a crook. I'm an agent
of the United States Customs—I
came here to get Denby.

DENBY. That's a pretty poor bluff.
This is one of the men who were in
the garden tonight.

ALICE. I told you they'd break in.

MICHAEL. Good work, Denby.

TAYLOR. I tell you I came to arrest
him.

ALICE. Arrest that charming man?
Why, that's absurd.

TAYLOR. Absurd, eh? You won't
think so when you learn who I am.
That girl can tell you.

ALICE. Ethel can tell us?

(*They all turn to look at her.*)

MICHAEL. Ethel!

ETHEL (*facing front, after a second*).
I never saw the man before.

TAYLOR. You didn't, eh? I guess
you'll remember me when I serve a

warrant for your sister's arrest.
(ETHEL *sits on couch.*) I've got it in
my pocket and papers proving that
I'm working for the United States
Government. (*He reaches hand
toward inside coat pocket to get
them.*)

DENBY (*poking gun under his nose*).
No, you don't! (DENBY *moves his
hand toward* TAYLOR's *pocket to get
them.*)

TAYLOR (*snarling*). Here, don't you
touch 'em!

DENBY (*smoothly*). Certainly not—
Mr. Harrington will get them.

(MICHAEL *crosses to* TAYLOR; *starts
to look at them.*)

DENBY (*grabbing papers from* HAR-
RINGTON's *hand*). Keep out of range,
Harrington. (HARRINGTON *backs up
above* TAYLOR. DENBY *backs to door
C., hastily glancing at papers.*) It's
all right, Miss Cartwright—it's all
right. (*Exits door C.*)

(ETHEL *rises and up to* C. *door last.*)

TAYLOR. Grab him. I tell you, he's a
crook! (*Ad lib. He blows whistle.*)
Don't let him get away. (*He runs
off* C. MICHAEL, ALICE, *and* LAM-
BERT *after him screaming down hall.*
ETHEL *goes up to door* C. *and looks
anxiously down hall.* DENBY, *having
fooled them and disappeared, runs
on from door* L., *locks it, and motions* ETHEL *to follow others.* ETHEL
exits C. *as the voices and whistle
keep up off stage.*)

THE CURTAIN FALLS

(*Picture:* DENBY, *gun in hand at door* C. *slightly open, looking off. Pande-
monium reigns in hallway.*)

ACT FOUR

SCENE—*The scene is the same as that of Act Two. The action is supposed to begin five minutes before the conclusion of Act Three. When the curtain rises,* ALICE, R. *of table,* NORA, *lower side of table with her back to audience, and* MICHAEL, *at upper side of table, are discovered playing bridge.* MICHAEL *is fast asleep.* ALICE *is counting on score sheet.*

ALICE (*seated R. of table. Looking up*). What on earth is keeping Monty?

NORA (*seated at table*). Oh, I don't know.

ALICE. He must have an awful headache to stay out in the garden all this time.

NORA. Goodness, he's been gone twenty minutes. (*Rising and going to windows at up R.C.*)

ALICE. And look at Michael, fast asleep——

NORA. It's those highballs he just had upstairs in Mr. Denby's room.

ALICE. I told you they always made him sleepy. Michael! (*She leans over as if to wake him.*)

NORA (*coming back of* ALICE *to* R.). Before you wake him, do tell me what happened in Jane's divorce case.

ALICE. Although the judge was a man—she won it.

NORA. I wonder why she married him.

ALICE. My dear, don't go into that. Why anybody ever marries anybody is never apparent to anybody else.

NORA. Marriage *is* funny.

(MONTY'S *whistle heard off stage.*)

ALICE. If there weren't so many awful things against it, I'd be tremendously in favor of trial marriage.

NORA. Wouldn't it be wonderful? I get so bored going around with one man.

ALICE. That's the difficulty—so does every other woman.

NORA. Still, I do like Monty—but he's such a coward about proposing.

ALICE. Why don't you make him?

NORA. Oh, I will—yet. (MONTY *enters from garden from* L., *nervously stuffing into his breast pocket the package containing the necklace that* DENBY *threw him from the window in Act Three.*) Oh, hello! (*To seat.*)

MONTY (*nervously*). How do you do. Hope I haven't delayed the game too long.

NORA. We never missed you.

ALICE. How's your headache?

MONTY. My headache? What headache? (*Remembering.*) Oh, it's all gone. Well, shall we play? (*He picks up cards as he sits at L. of table.*)

NORA. Yes, let's—Michael dealt, before he went to sleep.

ALICE (*tapping* MICHAEL). Michael! You're not at the opera—you're playing cards.

MICHAEL (*after a pause—drowsily*). Who opened it?

ALICE. We're playing bridge, dear—. bridge, bridge, bridge.

(*The clock strikes three. In Act Three, five minutes before the curtain, a clock also struck the same hour.*)

NORA. I make it no trumps.

ALICE. It isn't your bid. What do you say, Michael?

MICHAEL. What'd the dealer draw?

ALICE. We're not playing poker.

MICHAEL. Oh, yes, sure, what's trumps?

ALICE. Oh, stop it! It's your bid.

MICHAEL. I go one spade.

MONTY. One—no trump.

NORA. Two royals.

ALICE. Pass.

MICHAEL. Give me three cards.

(*Everybody disgusted.*)

ALICE. Michael, if you're so sleepy, you'd better go to bed.

MICHAEL. I never broke up a poker game in my life. It's only the shank of the evening. (*To* NORA.) What's happened, partner?

NORA. I went two royals.

MICHAEL (*looking at his hand*). Three aces—I'd like to open it for two dollars—as it is, I pass.

MONTY. Two no trump.

NORA. Pass.

ALICE. Pass.

MICHAEL. It's by me.

MONTY. Your lead, Nora——

(ALICE *lays down dummy.*)

MONTY. Fine little partner, just what I wanted!

NORA. Wish I had luck like that. (NORA *plays, then* MONTY *plays from dummy.*)

MICHAEL (*playing*). There——

NORA (*to* MICHAEL). What did you play that for?

MICHAEL (*withdrawing card*). I do beg your pardon. What's trumps?

ALICE. No trumps!

MICHAEL. Well, I haven't got one. (*He plays another card.*)

NORA. Oh, Michael, can't you see the king is in the dummy?

MICHAEL. Well, why put it there? This game makes me sick. Nothing but reproaches.

NORA. I wish Mr. Denby were playing, instead of poor Michael.

MONTY. Steve's got the right idea—he's in bed asleep.

MICHAEL. Great man, Denby—he knows you can't sit up all night unless you drink.

ALICE. Oh, let's play one more rubber and stop. Remember, Michael, it's not poker.

MICHAEL. I wish it were—no partners—no reproaches in poker. If you make a fool of yourself you lose your own money and everybody else is glad of it.

ALICE. After this, one round of jacks then, to please Michael.

MONTY. And then quit.

MICHAEL. I'm for that. (*Yawning.*) But don't think it's because I'm sleepy. I'm not. I'm thirsty.

(*The burglar alarm rings. All rise. NORA down R., MONTY down L., ALICE and MICHAEL over to bay window. Amazed—look at each other and then toward stairs.*)

NORA. Good heavens!

ALICE. What'll we do?

MONTY. Nonsense—the alarm's probably gone off by accident. (*Sound of shot off stage.*)

ALICE. Somebody's killed. (*Crossing to R.*)

NORA (*crossing to ALICE R.C.*). Isn't it awful?

(MONTY *has gone to L. of table.*)

MICHAEL (ALICE *and* MICHAEL *down C. in front of table*). Go on, Monty, find out what's the matter.

(MONTY *turns away to fender with scared expression. Sound of alarm stops.*)

ALICE (*crossing to* MICHAEL). You go, Michael. Are you afraid?

MICHAEL. Certainly not, but of course the beggar's armed.

LAMBERT (*entering L.U.*). The burglar alarm, sir! The indicator shows it's Mr. Denby's room.

MICHAEL. Good old Lambert. Go ahead—we'll follow.

LAMBERT. I brought a revolver for you, sir. (*Proffers pistol—ALICE and NORA shriek and back away.*)

MICHAEL. Keep it, keep it—you may need it yourself. (LAMBERT *starts, followed by* MICHAEL. *As* MICHAEL *gets to stairs,* ALICE *crosses to him.*)

ALICE. Mikey! (*He stops, she is at his left.*) Michael, if you're going to be killed, I want to be killed, too.

(*The three exit upstairs.*)

NORA (*C., blankly*). I don't want to be killed.

MONTY (*crossing to L. of her*). Neither do I. Great Scott! I wish I'd never gone into this.

NORA. Gone into what?

MONTY (*crosses to* C., *teeth almost chattering*). Nora, I may get shot any minute.

NORA. What?

MONTY. This may be my last five minutes on earth.

NORA. Monty, what have you done? (*Then ecstatically crossing to him.*) Murder?

MONTY. If I come out of this alive— will you marry me?

NORA. Oh, Monty—— (*She goes limply into his arms.*) Why didn't you ask me last year?

MONTY. I didn't need to be protected then and, anyhow, it takes a crisis like this to make me say what I really feel.

NORA. I love you, anyway.

MONTY. Gee, if I don't get shot, I'm the happiest man in the world.

NORA (*backs away from him and taps the package in his breast pocket*). What on earth have you got in your pocket?

MONTY. That's my heart.

NORA. On that side?

MONTY. Oh, that? I've almost forgotten—it belongs to Steve. (*There is a sound of a police whistle off R.*) The police!

NORA. Don't let them arrest you!

MONTY. Here, quick, hide behind this door.

(*They exit R. talking ad lib.* DUNCAN *and* GIBBS *enter R.U.*)

DUNCAN (*hastily surveys room and crosses to stairs*). Come on, Harry. He's upstairs.

GIBBS. The chief's got him, sure.

(*They exit upstairs.* MONTY *and* NORA *come on* R., *cross as far as french window, then to back of sofa.*)

MONTY. This is awful. Nora, in case of trouble you'd better go into the next room.

NORA. What are you going to do?

MONTY. I'll just wait for Steve— please go——

NORA. I'm not afraid.

MONTY. But I am.

NORA. What?

MONTY. For you! For you! I'd rather face them alone.

NORA. Don't get shot, Monty dear.

MONTY. Believe me, I'll try not to. (*Kiss. Pause.* NORA *keeps hold of him and keeps looking at him.*) Now, please go. Please——

NORA (*backing to door*). All right, but I hate to miss anything. (*She exits.*)

(MONTY *attempts to hide necklace first over* R. *on mantel, then under pillow on couch at* L. *He gives up in disgust as he can't find a satisfactory place; sees bottle on table up* C., *pours drink and is in the act of drinking it when voices are heard off L.U. He puts drink down and exits R. with annoyance.* DUNCAN, GIBBS, TAYLOR, *to C.;* MICHAEL, ALICE, *at* MICHAEL'S *L., come trooping downstairs, followed by* ETHEL *D.L., a silent nervous figure.* GIBBS *and* DUNCAN *go to windows,* TAYLOR *at C.,* MICHAEL *and* ALICE *L.C.*)

TAYLOR. Ford and Hammet are outside?

DUNCAN. Yes, sir.

TAYLOR. It's moonlight—Denby can't have gotten away—they'd have seen him——

GIBBS. Maybe he's somewhere in the bushes.

TAYLOR. Get out and search there—both of you—I'll whistle if I need you.

(GIBBS *and* DUNCAN *exit through french window.*)

MICHAEL (*coming to* TAYLOR *nervously*). I want to beg your pardon, Mr. Taylor, it was a very natural mistake to think you were a burglar.

TAYLOR. I suppose so—lucky for me I had my men here to prove my identity.

MICHAEL (*nervously*). Surely, surely.

ALICE. We had no idea Mr. Denby was a smuggler.

TAYLOR. No, of course you hadn't.

MICHAEL. He seemed a mighty nice chap.

ALICE. But I always did say he might be a murderer.

MONTY (*coming in from library followed by* NORA, *who goes down R. Airily*). Hello, did you get the burglar?

ALICE. Why, you see, there wasn't any burglar.

MICHAEL. It's your friend who caused all the trouble.

TAYLOR. Don't explain. (*To* MONTY.) Have you seen Steven Denby in the last ten minutes?

(NORA *to front of couch.*)

MONTY (*coolly*). No, isn't he in bed?

TAYLOR. No! You know he isn't—maybe you're his pal—in on the job with him—come here——

(MONTY *crosses to him at C.*)

ALICE. Why, that's too absurd—I've known Monty for years.

MONTY. Who is this man?

TAYLOR. Never mind who I am. (*Starts to search* MONTY.)

NORA (*rushing to* MONTY *and taking him in her arms*). Oh, Monty, don't strike him!

MONTY. It's all right, Nora. (TAYLOR *is searching him. He finishes and finds nothing.* MONTY *continues with bravado.*) My room's three doors down from the landing, if you want to search there.

TAYLOR. That'll be enough from you. I guess you're not smart enough to be Denby's pal—clear out!

(NORA *makes a face at* TAYLOR.)

MICHAEL. Do you want us any longer?

TAYLOR. No, leave me alone to talk with this girl. (*Indicating* ETHEL.)

ALICE. But——

MICHAEL. Please keep her out of it. I'm quite sure she's absolutely innocent in the matter.

TAYLOR. Are you? Well, I'd like to talk with her alone.

ETHEL (*crosses to table facing up stage*). It's all right. There's just some misunderstanding. Please go.

MICHAEL. You really want us to?

ETHEL. Yes, yes.

(LAMBERT *enters downstairs R., coming to* MICHAEL.)

MICHAEL. Come, Alice. (*As they go.*) I really need a drink.

ALICE. My dear, under these circumstances you may have an all-night license.

(LAMBERT *moves toward* MICHAEL.)

LAMBERT. Beg pardon, Mr. Harrington, can I speak to you privately?

MICHAEL (*stops, crosses to* LAMBERT *at C.* ALICE *goes and waits by door R.*). What is it? (LAMBERT *whispers to him.*) What!

TAYLOR. Say, what is all this?

MICHAEL. A long-distance from my partner—mighty important—excuse

me. Alice, I'll use the upstairs phone. (*He hurries upstairs.* LAMBERT *exits R.*)

MONTY. Do you want me any longer?

TAYLOR. I told you to get out.

MONTY. With pleasure. Come, Nora.

(NORA *and* MONTY *go with* ALICE.)

NORA (*crosses to* MONTY). Oh, you are perfectly splendid. I had no idea you could be so brave. (*Crosses to* ALICE *above couch.*)

MONTY. Neither had I!

ALICE. Don't you think we all need some champagne? I do.

MONTY. Sure. But on a night like this, what's a quart among three?

(*All three exit right. All laugh.*)

TAYLOR (*turning to* ETHEL *vindictively*). What did you mean by telling them upstairs you'd never seen me before?

ETHEL (*beside the table*). You said under no circumstances must I mention your name.

TAYLOR (*C.—discomfited*). Yes, but——

ETHEL. That it was imperative your identity should not be disclosed. Didn't you?

TAYLOR. I suppose that's true, but when you saw me wanting to prove who I was——

ETHEL. I didn't understand. I was afraid to do anything but follow your instructions.

TAYLOR. Um—how did you find Denby had the necklace?

ETHEL. I got into his room and caught him—he had it in his hand.

TAYLOR. Yes, yes.

ETHEL. Then he suddenly turned out the lights and in the dark he hid it. I couldn't see where.

TAYLOR. Do you realize what all this means to you—to your sister if you're lying?

ETHEL. Oh, yes, yes, that's why you can believe me.

DUNCAN (*coming hurriedly through french window*). Say, Chief, Denby's back in his room.

(ETHEL *gasps.* TAYLOR *turns a step from table.*)

TAYLOR. What—how do you know?

DUNCAN. Gibbs got up on the pagoda—he can see into the room from there.

TAYLOR (*starting toward windows*). Now, we've got him.

DUNCAN. And Mr. Harrington's with him.

TAYLOR. What!

DUNCAN. Yes, Gibbs said they were talking together.

TAYLOR. I was right then; Denby is smuggling the necklace for the Harringtons—Harrington didn't go to the phone—he got a message from Denby. Jim, this is a big job—get out there to make sure he don't escape by the balcony.

DUNCAN. Yes, sir. (*Starts to go.*)

TAYLOR. Wait a minute. Give me your gun. (DUNCAN *hands him gun and exits through french window and to R. with a grin.*) Now, he's done for sure.

ETHEL (*advances to R. lower end of table*). No, no, you mustn't—you mustn't.

TAYLOR (*suddenly*). You knew all the time that he'd got back to his room; you've been trying to fool me.

ETHEL. No, no, you're wrong.

TAYLOR. Am I? I'll give you a chance to prove it. Send for Denby, ask him what he did with the necklace—where it is now; tell him that I suspect you—that he's got to tell you the truth—that you won't turn him over to me. Talk to him as if you two were alone—but I'll be there—(*looks around, pointing*)—behind that screen watching and listening, and if you tip him off, give him the slightest warning, or signal, I'll arrest you both anyhow. (ETHEL's *hands touch cigarette box on table.*) Wrong, am I? We'll see—and if you try to fool me again—you and your sister will have plenty of time to think it over in Auburn. (*Pauses as* TAYLOR *crosses to screen.*) Now send for him. (*He gets screen and places it up in corner above door and gets behind it. During foregoing speech* ETHEL *has been very frightened, breathing fast, but as she talks her hand nervously touches box of cigarettes on table. She sees a way out. She musters up all her bravado and courage.*)

ETHEL. Of course I'll send for him. You'll see you've been all wrong about me. (*She goes up stage and rings bell and returns to front of table and picks up cigarette box.*)

TAYLOR (*snarling*). I guess not. (*He adjusts screen so as to see better between the folds.*)

LAMBERT (*enters*). Yes, miss?

ETHEL. Mr. Denby's in his room, say that I'm here alone and must speak to him at once.

LAMBERT. Yes, miss. (*He exits upstairs and is heard knocking at a door. Coming downstairs.*) Mr. Denby is coming now, miss. (*He exits R. After a two seconds' pause DENBY enters quickly and comes down to foot of stairs.*)

DENBY. Yes, what's happened? Where is—— (*Crosses to french window and looks out.*)

ETHEL (*quickly interrupting*). Will you have a cigarette, Dick?

DENBY (*realizing her signal, eyes her keenly*). Thanks, yes, Miss Cartwright. (*He takes cigarette from box she holds out to him. He shows to audience he suspects someone is listening, by looking around the room sharply. He spots screen, suspects that TAYLOR is there. He does this as he lights cigarette.*)

ETHEL. Now that we're alone and you've beaten me, I want you to tell me the truth about the necklace. What did you do with it?

DENBY (*calmly*). Are you still persisting in that strange delusion? I never had a necklace.

ETHEL. But I know you did.

DENBY. Really, this is most extraordinary. We went over all that in my room—I thought I'd convinced you.

ETHEL. That agent of the secret service has been here—he suspects that I am defending you for some reason—he won't believe what I say. If you tell me the truth, I'll make him let you go.

DENBY. Are you quite mad? (*Crosses to ETHEL.*) I haven't any necklace. Really, Miss Cartwright, I don't care to prolong this absurd conversation.

(*LAMBERT enters R., crosses to DENBY at C.*)

LAMBERT. Pardon me, sir, but Mr. Vaughn asked me to take this to your room.

DENBY. What is it?

LAMBERT. Mr. Vaughn didn't say—except that it was very important that you get it at once. (*LAMBERT hands DENBY a package and exits L.*)

DENBY. Curious! What on earth can Monty be sending me at this time of night—it must be important—forgive me if I open it? (*He does so and lets necklace fall to floor, apparently unintentionally. He gives exclamation, hastily picks it up, and puts it back in his left-hand coat pocket. He is in front of lounge at right.*)

(*ETHEL sinks on stool R. of table, sobbing. TAYLOR knocks down screen, blows whistle, and comes down L. of table with leveled gun.*)

TAYLOR. Hands up, Denby! I don't know how you tipped him off, but you two are damned smart, ain't you? (GIBBS *and* DUNCAN *rush in from french windows.*) But I've got you both. You're under arrest. Boys, take her into that room—they can talk without speaking. (DUNCAN *comes down and gets her.* GIBBS *crosses to door L. and holds it open.*) I'll question 'em separately—I'll call you when I want you. (DUNCAN, ETHEL, *and* GIBBS *exit L.* ETHEL *is sobbing.*) Well, this time I've got you. (*He comes over with leveled gun.*) Where's the necklace? (DENBY *starts to drop hand to his right-hand pocket.*) No, you don't! (*He puts hand in* DENBY's *right pocket and takes out gun; he smiles at* DENBY; *then* DENBY *lowers hand and produces necklace from left-hand pocket. As he looks at it.*) It's a pippin, all right—two hundred thousand dollars for that? How much did you pay the girl to square yourself?

DENBY. Not a cent; you're all wrong there.

TAYLOR. Then why did she tip you off just now?

DENBY. She didn't tip me off.

TAYLOR. Can it—can it—why did she?

DENBY. Well, I guess she didn't want to see me go to prison.

TAYLOR. Oh, you pulled the soft stuff, eh? Well, she tried to double-cross me, and that don't pay, Denby, it don't pay. She'll find it out all right.

DENBY. As long as she did the decent thing by me, I'd like to see her out of it. You've got me—let her go.

TAYLOR. No, you'll both have a nice little trip South to Atlanta for about five years. (*Necklace in L. pocket.*)

DENBY. I guess we're up against it.

TAYLOR. You are, son—right up against it.

DENBY. Take it out on me—ease up on her—she's a woman. After all, it isn't as if she were a grafter. Why, I offered her twenty thousand dollars to square it.

TAYLOR. Tried to bribe a government official, eh? That don't make it any better for you.

DENBY. Well, you can't prove it against me.

TAYLOR (*curiously*). Twenty thousand? So you were trying to smuggle it for the Harringtons, eh?

DENBY. Suppose we don't mention any names.

TAYLOR. They'll come out in the court—twenty thousand! It meant a lot to you—or somebody—to get this through.

DENBY. Yes, but I'd rather pay than go to jail—see?

TAYLOR. Say, what the hell are you trying to do—bribe me?

DENBY. What an imagination you have—you couldn't be bribed.

TAYLOR. Not on your life.

DENBY (*meaningly*). What a pity I didn't meet a businessman instead of you.

TAYLOR. You couldn't square it even with a businessman for twenty thousand dollars.

DENBY (*slowly*). But I'd give thirty thousand dollars.

TAYLOR. You would, eh?

DENBY (*slowly*). I would—cash. (*He fishes down behind his collar and produces three bills.*) Three ten-thousand-dollar bills—beauties, aren't they?

TAYLOR (*hypnotized as he looks at them*). I didn't know they made 'em so big!

DENBY. Taylor, this talk about my having bought a necklace in Paris is absurd—I haven't been in Paris for two years.

TAYLOR (*slowly*). You haven't!

DENBY. In case of a comeback I have witnesses to prove an alibi.

TAYLOR (*slowly*). You have!

DENBY. How much does the government pay you?

TAYLOR (*looking at money, fascinated*). Three thousand a year.

DENBY. Ten years' salary! And these witnesses of mine—they're reliable witnesses.

TAYLOR (*slowly*). They are?

DENBY (*eye to eye*). Well?

TAYLOR (*slowly*). Well?

DENBY. Ten years' salary. (*He crackles bills. A look of understanding between them.*)

TAYLOR (*removes his hat and his whole manner changes to one of great geniality as he backs to C.*). Too bad a mistake like this should happen.

DENBY. Just a little inconvenient, sometimes.

TAYLOR. Sorry to have bothered you, Mr. Denby—but you're all right. I figured from the first that you'd be a businessman—that's why I let you slide through.

DENBY. You're pretty smart, Mr. Taylor. (*Holding out money.*) I think these belong to you.

TAYLOR (*crosses quickly to* DENBY, *reaching for money*). Yes, I think they do.

DENBY (*holding money away*). Wait a minute. How do I know you won't take the money and then double-cross me?

TAYLOR (*eagerly*). I'll give you my word.

DENBY. Your word! That security isn't good enough—those two men of yours—are they in on it?

TAYLOR. Not on your life. I haven't split with anybody for five years. This is a one-man job, Mr. Denby.

DENBY. How can you square them? They saw you pinch me.

TAYLOR. I'll say it's all a mistake—that I've got to call it off.

DENBY. You're sure you can get away with it?

TAYLOR. I always have.

DENBY. Now see here. This R. J. of the secret service isn't onto you, is he?

TAYLOR (*quickly*). R. J.? What you know about him?

DENBY. Nothing, only we heard in Paris he was busy over here, investigating this bribery business in the Customs.

TAYLOR. Well, don't you worry about him—I'm the guy on this job.

DENBY. But I don't want to give up thirty thousand, lose the necklace, and get pinched as well.

TAYLOR (*eagerly*). Say, if you're afraid I'm going to ball things up, I don't mind admitting to you who R. J. really is—in confidence.

DENBY. Who is he?

TAYLOR. Well, he isn't a thousand miles from *here*.

DENBY. What?

TAYLOR. Get me?

DENBY (*laughing*). That's funny.

TAYLOR. What's funny about it?

DENBY. Why, R. J.'s supposed to be after the grafters, isn't he, and you're a grafter yourself.

TAYLOR. I'm not a grafter—I'm a businessman.

DENBY. Well, I guess I'll take the chance.

TAYLOR (*reaching for money*). That's the idea.

DENBY (*withholding it again*). Provided you'll let me talk to your men. They've got to understand I'm innocent. They've got to back you up in squaring me with the Harringtons. I'm in rather an awkward fix here just now.

TAYLOR. Why, sure—talk your head off to 'em.

DENBY. You'll leave the girl out of it?

TAYLOR (*grinning*). I'll do more than that—I'll leave the girl to you.

DENBY. Well, here's your money.

TAYLOR (*as he takes money and puts it in his pocket*). Much obliged —and anyhow, I've got no evidence that you ever had a necklace. (*He returns necklace.* TAYLOR *holds out his hand which* DENBY *shakes.*) Have a cigar, Mr. Denby——

DENBY (*taking it*). Thanks; now call 'em in.

TAYLOR. Certainly. (*Going to C., then returning.*) And say, glad to have met you. Next time you're landing in New York and I can be of use—you know—(*calling*)—Duncan! Gibbs! (GIBBS, *to above table, enters.* ETHEL *enters—crosses to L. of table.* DUNCAN *enters, crosses to above table—*TAYLOR *to C.*) Say, boys, it's all a mistake.

DUNCAN *and* GIBBS (*together*). What!

ETHEL (*under her breath*). Thank God.

TAYLOR. Our dope was phony. We were in all wrong, but he's been very nice about it—very nice indeed. It's just a case of mistaken identity —but he's all right. Let the lady go, boys.

(ETHEL *goes down* L. *to fender,* GIBBS *crosses to* R.U., *and* DUNCAN *to* U.L. *of table.*)

DENBY (*crossing up* C.). Now, I don't want any comeback to all this —I want you all to understand the facts, if you don't mind waiting, Miss Cartwright.

ETHEL. Of course I'll wait. (*Sits on fender.*)

TAYLOR. Listen to him, boys—you see, he's anxious to straighten things out. So tell him anything he wants to know. (*To* DENBY.) Fire ahead. (*Behind lounge* R.)

DENBY (*to* DUNCAN). Well, you got a tip from Harlow that a Steven Denby had bought a necklace at Cartier's——

DUNCAN. Yes, sir.

DENBY (*to* GIBBS). Then you got a wireless that Denby had sailed with a Mrs. Harrington, which threw suspicion on her as a possible smuggler.

GIBBS. That's right, too.

DENBY. And yet you fellows let Denby slip through the lines at the pier today without a search—why was that?

TAYLOR (*worried*). We didn't have any absolute evidence to arrest him on.

DENBY. But after he got through— you received an anonymous telegram late this afternoon that Denby carried the necklace in a tobacco pouch, didn't you?

TAYLOR (*crossing to* DENBY *quickly*). How did you know that?

DENBY. Oh, I found it out tonight.

TAYLOR (*coming to him*). What is all this, anyhow?

DENBY. You don't object to your men answering my questions? (*Meaningly.*) I was pretty nice to you, Mr. Taylor.

TAYLOR (*embarrassed, remembering the money*). No, that's all right—go ahead. (*He returns behind couch.*)

DENBY (*to* GIBBS). You knew about that tip in the telegram?

GIBBS. No, this is the first we've heard of·it.

DENBY (*to* TAYLOR). Oh, you didn't tell them?

TAYLOR. That was my own business.

DENBY. Did it ever occur to you boys that it was rather peculiar that this supposed smuggler wasn't searched—that he got through without the slightest trouble?

GIBBS. Why, the Chief didn't want to get in any mix-up with the Harringtons, in case he was wrong about Denby.

DENBY. Oh, that's what he told you.

DUNCAN. It sure was.

DENBY. Don't you boys know the whole job looks very much as if the scheme was to let Denby slip through and then blackmail him?

DUNCAN. I never thought of that.

GIBBS. Me neither.

TAYLOR (*nervously, crossing to* DENBY). What's all this got to do with you? I admit it was a mistake and we're sorry about it. That's all —come on, you fellows. (*Starts toward door R.*)

DENBY. Just a moment. (*To* DUNCAN *and* GIBBS. TAYLOR *slowly drops down R.*). Don't you realize that it's rather a dangerous thing to monkey with the United States Government?

GIBBS. I haven't been monkeyin' with the government!

DUNCAN. Neither have I.

TAYLOR. But it's all settled, now that we know you never had a necklace.

DENBY. That's clearly understood?

TAYLOR. What I say is right.

DENBY. But you see, boys, he's wrong. I did smuggle a necklace through the Customs today. (*He shows it.* ETHEL *rises.*)

DUNCAN, GIBBS, *and* TAYLOR. What?

TAYLOR (*quickly crossing to* DENBY). Then you're under arrest.

DENBY. No, I'm not. (*To others.*) He caught me with the goods and I paid him thirty thousand dollars to square it.

TAYLOR (*threateningly, with upraised fist*). Why—you, I'll——

DENBY (*pulling down his hand*). You won't do anything—you're only a bully—you couldn't graft on your own—you had to drag a girl into it —you made me do some pretty rotten things tonight to land you. I've had to make that girl suffer, but now you're going to pay for it. I've got you—you're under arrest.

TAYLOR. Aw, quit your bluffin'—you can't arrest me, Denby.

DENBY. I'm not Denby—my name is Jones.

TAYLOR. Well, who the hell is he?

DENBY. Oh, yes, you and the boys don't know who I am—here's my commission. (*Handing* GIBBS *parchment.*) That's my photograph—a fairly good likeness, isn't it?

DUNCAN (*who has crossed to* GIBBS L., *leans over his shoulder*). Yes.

GIBBS (*looking at paper*). Sure. Why, this thing's made out to Richard Jones.

DENBY. Well, do you get the initials, boys?

DUNCAN (*reading initials without realizing their significance*). R. J.

DENBY. That's me—R. J. of the United States Secret Service. (*Turns and looks at* TAYLOR *smilingly.* TAY-

LOR *gives an amazed gasp and backs a step or two away.* ETHEL *crosses part way to table and stands facing up stage.*)

GIBBS (*shaking hands with* DENBY). Are you really R. J.?

DENBY (*smiling and shaking hands*). I'm afraid I am.

TAYLOR. It's a lie.

DENBY (*pointing to paper*). You can't get away from that signature —it's signed by the President of the United States.

TAYLOR. I tell you it's a fake.

DENBY. They don't seem to think so.

DUNCAN. This is on the level all right.

(GIBBS, *looking at it and him, takes it.*)

DENBY. Taylor, for three years the government has been trying to land the big blackmailer in the Customs. We set a trap for him with a necklace as bait. The whole thing was a plant from Harlow's tip to my dropping the necklace here just now— and you walked into it.

TAYLOR (*coming to him threateningly*). Say, you can't get away with this.

DENBY. Wait a minute. You've been in the service long enough to know that the rough stuff won't go—you'll only get the worst of it—so take it easy. (*To* DUNCAN *and* GIBBS *and taking commission from* GIBBS.) Take him along, boys. I was mighty glad to find out just now that you fellows weren't in on it. Keep the necklace for me. Exhibit A—it's a fake. (*Comes down to front of table.*)

GIBBS. And I've been working for a crook for two years and never knew it! (GIBBS *and* DUNCAN *cross over near windows.*)

TAYLOR (*goes down to* DENBY *furiously*). Damn you, you've got me all right, but I'll send that girl and her sister up the river. I'll get even —you're stuck on her and she goes with me.

DENBY. Oh, I think not. You forget that Mr. Harrington's vice-president of the New York Burglar Insurance Company and a very good friend of Miss Cartwright's. I saw him upstairs.

ETHEL (*under her breath*). Thank God.

TAYLOR. Oh, get me out of this. (*As he goes up to french window.*)

DENBY. Oh, just a minute, I'll trouble you for that thirty thousand.

TAYLOR (*turning to him*). You think of everything, don't you?

DENBY (*to* ETHEL). You see, I borrowed it from Monty—he's been a great help as an amateur partner. (*Crosses to* TAYLOR.) He'll be glad you're out of the way, Taylor. You quite frightened him.

TAYLOR (*going to him*). There's your thirty thousand.

DENBY. Thanks. There's your cigar.

TAYLOR (*sticking cigar in his pocket —then with bravado*). Well, it took the biggest man in the secret service to land me, Mr. R. J. But I've got some mighty good pals in some mighty good places who'll come across for me. After all, you're not the jury and all the smart lawyers aren't dead yet.

GIBBS. Aw, come on, you dirty grafter.

(*The three exit at french window.*)

DENBY (*to* ETHEL). I'm sorry I had to leave you alone as I did, but I wanted to arrange matters with Mr. Harrington about your sister, so Taylor would have no comeback.

ETHEL (*crosses to R. end of table*). And you are really R. J.!

DENBY. I really am. I did want to tell you before, but I couldn't be sure you weren't Taylor's accomplice until you told me about your sister. I had my job to do for the United States—I'm only a soldier—I was under orders, but I wish I hadn't had to make you suffer.

ETHEL (*crosses toward* DENBY *a step*). And everything's all right now? (DENBY *backs toward doors R. as far as C.* ETHEL *crosses to* DENBY *and above him.*)

DENBY. Yes, and I'll tell you all about R. J.

ETHEL. How silly of me to think that you were a criminal.

DENBY. But you see you've caught me!

ETHEL. But have I really—(*pauses*) —got you, Steve? (*She goes in his arms.*)

CURTAIN FALLS

The Thirteenth Chair

A Play in Three Acts By

BAYARD VEILLER

The *Thirteenth Chair* was produced by William Harris, Jr., at the 48th Street Theatre, New York, on November 20, 1916, with the following cast:

HELEN O'NEILL	Katherine La Salle
WILL CROSBY	Calvin Thomas
MRS. CROSBY	Martha Mayo
ROSCOE CROSBY	Gardner Crane
EDWARD WALES	S. K. Walker
MARY EASTWOOD	Eva Condon
HELEN TRENT	Sarah Whitford
GRACE STANDISH	Rose Aiken
BRADDISH TRENT	Charles Lait
HOWARD STANDISH	Walter Lewis
PHILIP MASON	George Graham
ELIZABETH ERSKINE	Alice Claire Elliott
POLLOCK	A. J. Hendon
ROSALIE LA GRANGE	Margaret Wycherly
TIM DONOHUE	Harrison Hunter
SERGEANT DUNN	Walter Young
DOOLAN	Wm. Scott

THE CAST

HELEN O'NEILL
WILL CROSBY
MRS. CROSBY
ROSCOE CROSBY
EDWARD WALES
MARY EASTWOOD
HELEN TRENT
BRADDISH TRENT
HOWARD STANDISH
PHILIP MASON
ELIZABETH ERSKINE
GRACE STANDISH
POLLOCK
MADAME ROSALIE LA GRANGE
TIM DONOHUE
SERGEANT DUNN
DOOLAN

Act One: The Italian room in Roscoe Crosby's House. Time: Evening.
Act Two: Same scene. Ten minutes later.
Act Three: Same scene. A half hour later.

THE THIRTEENTH CHAIR

ACT ONE

Scene—*Italian room in* ROSCOE CROSBY's *home. A handsomely furnished square room, door opening on stage down L. Door opening on stage at back L.C. Large fireplace C. at back. Door opening on stage R.C.*

NOTE: *Fireplace—antique firedogs—must be large enough for men to make entrance coming down through chimney. Large window over R. in arch. Platform one step high running full length of window, which is three sashes long. Trick blind on C. pane. Curtains on pole on C. windows to work on cue. Up C. in front of fireplace, facing up stage, large Chesterfield sofa two feet wide. Facing audience another large Chesterfield sofa, C., sofas sitting back to back. At each end of sofas small console table. Console table at R. end of sofa is the trick table which* ROSALIE *lifts. R. of the door, R.C., large antique Italian chest. L. of door, L.C., large antique chest. Vases on chests. On flat over L., large tapestry. Against wall over L., running up and down stage, long ornate Italian chest. At either end of this chest Italian lamps, seven feet high, standing on floor. On console tables at either end of sofa, table lamps. On console table L. end of sofa, fancy cigarettes, box with cigarettes and matchbox and ash tray, and below door down L., on flat, an antique clock. Below door down L., armchair. L. side of fireplace chair with cushion seat. On mantel two large antique vases. R. side of fireplace with cushion seat. L. side below console table, large armchair. Over R. is a large library table sitting diagonally up and down stage. On table: bookrack with four books, desk pad, stationery holder with stationery, pens, pencils, ink box, magazines, armchair back of table, chair below table, chair above table. On platform in window arch, long seat. Below window arch large armchair. Large wall lanterns, on up stage and down stage end of window arch. Plush valance or drapery for windows. Rugs on ground cloth. On flat R. of doors up R.C. small-sized, painted image of the Virgin. Interior backing for door down L., up L.C., and R.C. Fireplace backing. Exterior backing for window over R. Off stage down L., run on floor, large Italian table with two bronze vases, and a shrine of the Virgin on it. Off stage R.C. are eight small chairs, to be brought on stage on cue during first act. In ceiling, directly over table R., is a double slot to hold knives. During first act, after* WILL *puts out table lamp, after* MISS EASTWOOD's *scream, the knife, in down-stage slot, is let down in sight of audience. Seen with point sticking in ceiling. Between second and third acts, the knife that falls on cue, during third act, is placed up stage slot in ceiling, with point downward. Setting the knife down in view of audience in first act, as well as releasing the second knife so that it falls, and sticks in table during third act, is worked by strings off stage R.*

(*As the curtain rises* MISS HELEN O'NEILL *and* WILLIAM CROSBY *are discovered standing R.C. They are in each other's arms, and the rising curtain discloses them as they kiss. Windowshade down.*)

HELEN. I love you so.

WILLIAM. You are the most wonderful thing in all the world. (*She gives a little laugh and moves away from him a step R.*)

HELEN. I can't believe it.

WILL. That I love you?

HELEN. Oh, no, I'm sure of that.

WILL. If there's any doubt in your mind, I'll prove it again.

HELEN. They'll see us. (*He takes her in his arms again and kisses her. She laughs happily. And then, turning a little, stands with her cheek pressed against his.*) Oh, my dear, my dear.

(MRS. CROSBY, *a fashionably dressed and extremely attractive woman, enters from door down left; closes door. She stops for a moment, and watches the lovers and then with a little laugh comes toward them.* MRS. CROSBY *is fifty-five and looks ten years younger. She has charm, beauty, and kindliness, and is as far removed from the typical stage mother as it is possible for the management to picture.*)

MRS. CROSBY (*coming to C. a step.* WILL *breaks a step*). Don't move, you look so comfortable! (*They start apart.*) Well, are you happy? (*To R.C.* WILL *pats* MRS. CROSBY *on arm.*)

WILL. Oh, Mother!

HELEN. Happy!

(MRS. CROSBY *crosses to* HELEN, *pats her hand, and stands between* WILL *and* HELEN, *R.C.*)

WILL. Shall we tell 'em all?

MRS. CROSBY. Tell them? (*She laughs.*) What do you think they are? Blind and deaf? It's been a perfectly wonderful dinner. You were so blind to everything but each other. Oh, Billy, I thought your father would have a fit.

HELEN. I thought he had an awful cold; he was coughing terribly.

MRS. CROSBY. Coughing? He nearly strangled, to keep from laughing. I told him I'd send him from the table if he laughed at you.

WILL. Why, you never spoke to him once.

MRS. CROSBY (*between* HELEN *and* WILL, *C.*). Child, explain to him that wives don't have to—— Oh, I forget you haven't learned that yet. You know, Billy, I can talk to your father very effectively without words. (*Cross below table R.*)

HELEN (*turning to* MRS. CROSBY). Mrs. Crosby——

WILL. Mother, Nell's all fussed up because we've got money. She thinks you'll think—I'm—what in novels they call marrying beneath me. (*He and* MRS. CROSBY *laugh.* NELL *looks a little hurt.*)

HELEN. Well, he is.

MRS. CROSBY. Nonsense, child, don't be silly. (*Sits down stage end of table.*)

HELEN (*to* MRS. CROSBY *a step*). It's not silly, Mrs. Crosby. Everyone will say it, and they'll be right.

WILL. Let's settle this thing now once and for all, then. In the first place, it's all nonsense and in the second it isn't true——

HELEN. Oh, yes, it is.

MRS. CROSBY. Oh, the first row! I'll settle this one. Nelly!

WILL. Now then, Nell, out with it, get it all out of your system.

HELEN (*crosses to table R. a step*). In the first place; it's the money.

MRS. CROSBY (*seated below table R.*). Yes, but—Helen——

HELEN. Please, let me say it all. You have social position, great wealth, charming friends, everything that makes life worth—— Oh, what's the use? You know as well as I do the great difference between us, and——

MRS. CROSBY. My dear child, suppose we admit all that, what then?

HELEN. But don't you see——

WILL (*embracing her in front of table R.*). You little idiot! I don't see anything but you.

MRS. CROSBY. That's the whole of it, children. You love each other, suppose you listen to an old woman.

WILL. Old! Huh!

MRS. CROSBY (*seated at table R.*). Well, old enough. Well, if Billy was the usual rich man's son, it might be different. There might be something in what you say. But, thank God, he isn't. Mind you, I don't say he wasn't like most of them when he was younger. I dare say he was. I know he went to supper with a chorus girl once.

WILL. Twice.

HELEN. What was she like?

WILL. Like a chorus girl.

MRS. CROSBY. The trouble with you, my dear, is that you've been reading novels. When Billy's father married me, I was a schoolteacher and he was a clerk. We didn't have any money, but we were awfully in love —we still rather like each other. Now, just for the sake of argument, suppose we should have acted like stern parents, what would be the use? Billy's in business for himself, he's making his own money, he can marry when he wants to and as he wants to, and if you want my real opinion, I don't mind confessing that I think he's pretty lucky to get you.

WILL. There!

HELEN (*in front of table R.*). But you know so little about me.

WILL. Oh, rot.

MRS. CROSBY. Thank you, Billy, I was trying to think of an effective word. (*To* WILL. *To* HELEN.) You've been my private secretary for over a year, and no matter how much my looks belie it, I'm not a bit of a fool. I know a great deal about you.

HELEN. My family——

WILL (C.). I'm not marrying your family!

HELEN. I'm afraid you are.

WILL. Oh!

HELEN. There's only Mother.

MRS. CROSBY (contritely, rises to HELEN in front of table R.). Oh, my dear, forgive me. Your mother should have been here tonight.

HELEN. No, my mother—Mrs. Crosby—Mother doesn't go out—she'd be unhappy here, and you'd be uncomfortable if she came. You'll find her trying sometimes; you'll think she's common. Oh, don't misunderstand me. She's the most wonderful mother in the world. And she's——

MRS. CROSBY. Suppose, my dear, that we take your mother for granted—— (Crosses between WILL and HELEN.) Take us as you find us and we will try to be happy. (Enter CROSBY from door L. He is a fine-looking man of about sixty, with a pleasant personality, a good deal of charm, and that masterful self-possession which sometimes marks the man of affairs. It is always evident that the most delightful intimacy exists between himself and his wife.) Well, Roscoe?

CROSBY (crosses to L.C.—takes HELEN, who crosses to CROSBY, in his arms). Welcome, my dear.

HELEN. Oh, Mr. Crosby—I——

CROSBY (placing HELEN L. of him with arms still around her—reaching his other hand to WILL). Bill, shake! (Father and son shake hands. CROSBY looks at his wife and they laugh gently.) Shall I tell 'em?

MRS. CROSBY (standing in front of table over R.). I would.

WILL (R.C.). Tell us what?

CROSBY (C.). You did this just in time. Tomorrow I was going to forbid you to have anything more to do with this young woman.

HELEN (L. of CROSBY). You see!

WILL. What for?

CROSBY. Your mother and I felt that you were pretty slow with your love-making.

WILL. Oh, Mother!

CROSBY (continuing). And I know darned well that if I interfered, you'd take the girl out and marry her.

HELEN. Oh!

WILL. You old schemer.

CROSBY (crossing over R.C. below MRS. CROSBY). I bet it would have worked.

WILL (as CROSBY crosses right, WILL slaps him on the back). It would. (Crosses back of HELEN to L.C.)

(Door down L. opens and EDWARD WALES enters.)

WALES. I came ahead of the others to tell you——

CROSBY. Why, Ned, old man, you came just in time to congratulate them. (*He points toward* WILL *and* HELEN.)

WALES. On what? (*L.C.*)

MRS. CROSBY. They're going to be married; isn't it fine?

WALES. Oh! (*There is a long pause.*)

WILL. You haven't congratulated us, Mr. Wales.

WALES. No, Will, I haven't. I'm not sure that I can. (*Down stage a step.*)

CROSBY. Why, Ned!

WILL. I'm afraid that calls for an explanation, sir.

WALES. Yes, I expect that it does. (*There is a long pause.*)

WILL. Well?

WALES. I'm sorry, but I can't explain anything until tomorrow.

MRS. CROSBY. But really, Mr. Wales, don't you think——

WALES. I think my action is almost indefensible. I'm admitting that. But I have very good reasons for what I am doing. (*He turns to* CROSBY.) Roscoe, I've been your close friend for a great many years. You've trusted me, believed in me. I'm going to ask you to wait. After all, twenty-four hours can't make any difference, and it may save you all a great deal of unhappiness.

WILL (*coming to* WALES *a step*). Why, this is intolerable.

CROSBY. Ned, I can't understand——

WILL. Father, this is my affair.

WALES. I'm sorry.

WILL. Sorry? I should think you would be.

HELEN. Billy, I told you what would happen. Mr. Wales, I don't know what you have discovered, but it's nothing of which I am ashamed, nothing.

WILL. Dear, you mustn't mind what he says.

HELEN (*in front of* WILL—*crosses to* WALES *a few steps*). Oh, but I do. I can't bear it. Why, my mother is the most wonderful woman in the world. I won't have her attacked. Do you know what she did? When I was ten years old she sent me away from her. I was the one thing she had in the world to love and she gave me up because she thought—because she thought it was the best thing she could do for me. I was sent to a fine school, then to college, and then when I was nineteen, quite by accident I found out that she wasn't dead, as they'd always told me, and when I went to her all she said was, "Well, my dear, I wanted to make a lady of you." (*Crosses to* WILL—*C. He takes her in his arms, then* HELEN *crosses to R. of him.*)

MRS. CROSBY (*in front of table R.*). I think she succeeded, my child.

WALES (*L.C.*). Miss O'Neill, I didn't even know that you had a mother.

WILL (C.). Then you'd better tell us now what your objection is.

WALES. I can tell you nothing until tomorrow. (*He turns to* WILL.) Billy, I'd rather be shot than do what I'm doing. If I'm wrong I'll come to you gladly and eat dirt. I'll beg this young lady's pardon on my knees if she likes. (*Voices and laughter heard down L.*) Now that's all I'm going to say about it until then. (*Crosses up L.*)

(*The door at L. opens.* MISS EASTWOOD, HELEN TRENT, MISS ERSKINE, MISS STANDISH, STANDISH *and* MASON *enter laughing and talking.*)

MISS EASTWOOD (*at L.C. To crowd in doorway*). And he said whose wife? (*All laugh.*)

WILL (C.—HELEN *in front of table R.*). Quiet, quiet, everybody, I've got a surprise for you. (*People at door ad lib., laugh, and buzz.*) Nellie and I are going to be married.

(GIRLS *rush up C. and congratulate* HELEN. MEN *and* WILL *go to L.C. ad lib., business congratulating him.*)

MISS EASTWOOD (*coming to* WILL, *C.*). If you hadn't been engaged to her, she could have you arrested for the way you made eyes at her at dinner, Billy. But, of course, if people will marry—why—— (*She turns away R. from them.*) I hope you will be awfully happy. (*Crosses to* MR. *and* MRS. CROSBY *down R.*)

MISS ERSKINE (*coming to* WILL). Isn't it beautiful? (*Crosses to L.—to settee.*)

MRS. TRENT (*crosses to* WILL, *kissing him*). I'm glad, Billy, glad. (*Crosses to* STANDISH, *comes down L.* TRENT *over L.* MISS STANDISH *crosses to front of table R.* WILL *and* HELEN *look around—see that no one is paying attention to them.* WILL *sneaks up to door R.C.—opens it—he and* HELEN *exit door R.C. quickly.* MRS. CROSBY, MR. CROSBY, MISS EASTWOOD, *in front of table over R.* TRENT, STANDISH, MRS. TRENT, MASON *talking together over L.* WALES *up L. Ad lib. conversation until* MISS EASTWOOD *speaks.*)

MISS EASTWOOD (*to* MRS. CROSBY). Marriage is such an awful gamble. I know a girl who tried it four times. Billy, I hope you—— (*Turning to C.*) Why, they are gone.

(*Ad lib. laughter of buzz and conversation.* MISS EASTWOOD *runs up to door R.C., opens it, looks in dining room, gives a scream, closes door quickly, comes down to R. end of settee.* TRENT, *to console table L. of settee, gets cigarette, lights it. Crosses to C. back of settee in front of fireplace.* STANDISH *and* MRS. TRENT *to table L. of settee.* WALES *and* MISS ERSKINE *sit on settee facing audience up C.* MRS. CROSBY, *at upper end of table R.* CROSBY *seated R. end of settee, facing audience up C.* MASON *L. end of settee, faces audience C. Enter* BUTLER *from down L.*)

BUTLER. Mrs. Crosby, the person you sent the car for has arrived.

(ALL *turn eagerly toward the door L.*)

WALES (*rises—goes to front of armchair L.C.*). Can we see her now, Mrs. Crosby?

MRS. CROSBY. Certainly—Pollock, ask Madame La Grange if she will come in, please.

BUTLER. Yes, madame. (*He exits and closes the door after him.*)

MISS EASTWOOD (*coming between table and settee R.C.*). I'm perfectly thrilled. Do you suppose she expects to be taken seriously?

MISS ERSKINE. Of course.

MISS EASTWOOD (*at table R.*). How funny! If you don't laugh at her, we can have no end of fun. I'll guy her terribly and she'll never know it in the world.

MRS. CROSBY (*at table R.*). Oh, I wouldn't do that, Mary. She may be quite in earnest.

MISS EASTWOOD. Oh, I can't believe that. Madame La Grange! I can see her now. Tall, black-haired creature, regular adventuress, see if she isn't. Isn't she, Mr. Wales?

WALES (*in front of settee*). She's the most remarkable woman I have ever known.

(*Enter* BUTLER *from door L., coming well on stage.*)

BUTLER. Madame La Grange.

(*Enter* MADAME ROSALIE LA GRANGE. *She is a little Irish woman of about fifty, but old for her age. She is dressed quaintly. As she comes well on stage she stands and drops a little curtsey.*)

ROSALIE. Good evenin', all av yez.

(MEN *all rise.*)

MRS. CROSBY. How do you do, Madame La Grange?

ROSALIE. I'm well, thank ye, ma'am.

MRS. CROSBY. Won't you come in?

ROSALIE. I will, ma'am. (*She sees* WALES L.C. *and goes to him.*) Good evenin' to ye, Misther Wales. Sure it was a grand hack ye sent for me.

WALES. We all wanted you to be comfortable.

ROSALIE. Sure, an' I was. (*She laughs and turns to* MRS. CROSBY R.C.*) Do ye know, ma'am, when the gintleman in uniform come for me, I thought at first it was th' police.

MRS. CROSBY. I hope you weren't frightened.

ROSALIE (C. CROSBY R. *end of settee* C. MRS. TRENT *and* STANDISH *move down* L., TRENT *comes to* L. *of armchair.* MISS ERSKINE *seated on settee up* C. MRS. CROSBY *at table* R. WALES L.C. TRENT *and* MASON L.C.*). Divil a bit. Sure I'd like to see the cop that could frighten me. They're nice boys, thim cops, and most of thim good Catholics.

MISS EASTWOOD (*to R. side of* ROSALIE). Mr. Wales tells us you are wonderful.

ROSALIE. I am that. Anny woman is.

MISS EASTWOOD (*with a meaning glance at the* OTHERS). So you tell fortunes?

ROSALIE. No, miss, I do not. I get messages from thim that have passed

on. I don't hold at all wid the cards
nor tea leaves nor any of thim tricks.
(ALL *laugh*—MISS EASTWOOD *loudest.*) Wance in a while I give advice. (*She turns to* MISS EASTWOOD.)
If I was you, Miss, I wouldn't meet
Jimmy at the Ritz at three tomorrow. (ALL *laugh.* MISS STANDISH
crosses to settee C. Sits. MISS ERSKINE *rises, crosses to table R., and
sits in armchair.* MASON *crosses—sits
on up stage settee.* TRENT *to L. end
of settee.* MISS EASTWOOD *in front
of table R.* ROSALIE *goes to* WALES
L.C., CROSBY *seats* MRS. CROSBY
*down stage end of table R., then
crosses back of* MISS ERSKINE *to upper end of table.*) Well, sor, and
how are ye?

WALES. We're expecting great things
from you tonight, Madame La
Grange.

ROSALIE. Are ye now? Well, I hope
ye won't be disappointed.

CROSBY (*above table R., coming C.
a step*). I suppose there are a lot
of tricks that——

ROSALIE (*interrupting him*). You
said it, sor. But I suppose mine is
the only trade in the world there's
anny tricks in.

MISS EASTWOOD (*coming to* ROSALIE, *who is C.*). Why shouldn't I
meet Jimmy at the Ritz tomorrow?

ROSALIE. If you do, sure, something
awful is liable to happen to him.

MISS EASTWOOD. What?

ROSALIE. Sure if you keep meeting
the man he is liable to marry ye.
(EASTWOOD *up stage a step.*)

CROSBY (*upper end of table R.*).
Would you mind telling me how
you know this young lady was going
to meet Jimmy at the Ritz tomorrow afternoon?

ROSALIE. I would not. Sure she left
his letter in her bag in the hall, and
while I was waitin' I read it.

MISS EASTWOOD. How did you know
it was my bag? (C.)

ROSALIE. Sure, the stuff on the bag
matches the stuff on your dress.

MRS. CROSBY (*seated below table
R.*). Then it is all trickery?

ROSALIE. It is, ma'am, and it ain't.
I tell ye, ma'am, most of the time
it's tricks, with even the best of us.
But there's been times in my life
when—well, ma'am, thim times it
wasn't tricks. There's been things I
couldn't understand myself, messages
from thim that's passed on. There
is a power—a wonderful—power—
that comes to us. But the divil of it
is ye never can tell when it's comin'.
Sure, if ye waited for it ye'd starve
to death. So when it ain't there we
use tricks.

MRS. CROSBY (*seated at lower end
of table at R.*). I think I understand.

ROSALIE. Do ye now, ma'am? Well,
do you know, maybe I thought ye
would. (*Puts handbag on table R.*)

(MRS. TRENT *seated below door
down L.* WALES *crosses down L.
and joins* MRS. TRENT *at door L.*
CROSBY *above table R.C.*)

MISS EASTWOOD (*coming down to
R.C.*). Don't you think all this is
dishonest?

ROSALIE (*in front of table R. Turning to her*). What's dishonest?

MISS EASTWOOD. Tricking a lot of poor, ignorant people.

(MASON *back of settee C.*)

ROSALIE. It's all in the way ye look at it. A widdy woman came to me this mornin' wid a breaking heart for the man that was gone. I went into a trance and Laughing Eyes, me spirit control, came with a message from him. Sure, she said he was in Heaven wid the angels, and there was no cold nor hunger; and the streets was paved with gold, and there was music and happiness everywhere. She told her he was thinkin' of her every day and every hour and watchin' and waitin' fer the day she'd come to him. Sure, wasn't that worth fifty cents of any woman's money? The man may have been in hell for all I know.

TRENT (*by armchair L.C.*). What I can't understand is why you are telling us all this.

(MISS EASTWOOD *to settee C.* ROSALIE *to armchair L.C.*)

MRS. TRENT (*seated over L. by door*). If we know you are fooling——

ROSALIE. Didn't Mr. Wales tell ye?

WALES (*L.C.*) I've told them nothing.

(MASON *drops down R. of settee.* STANDISH *down L.* CROSBY *is R. end of settee C.*)

ROSALIE (*C.*) Well, tell thim now, plaze sur. (*Sits upper end of table*

—*takes off gloves, takes out glasses from bag.*)

WALES (*down L.*). As I told you some time ago, Madame La Grange has done a lot of things that we can't explain. When I asked her to come here tonight, she said she would under certain conditions.

MASON (*between settee and table*). You mean test conditions?

WALES. Not exactly. What she said was that no money should pass between us, and that whatever she did, she would be honest.

MASON (*very eagerly*). You mean that you won't play any tricks?

ROSALIE (*whisper.* MASON *comes to her, upper end of table R.*). Av I do I'll tell ye.

MISS EASTWOOD (*seated on settee C.*). Of course we understand all about spirit rappings.

ROSALIE. Do ye now?

STANDISH (*down L.*). Well, rather.

ROSALIE (CROSBY *sits R. end of settee*). Well, well, what do ye think av that?

MISS EASTWOOD. You have to be near a table or something like that and——

ROSALIE. Maybe a chair or a desk would do?

MISS EASTWOOD. And then in the dark——

ROSALIE. Av course in the dark. And ye got wan rap for yes and two for no. (*There is a short pause.* ROSALIE *comes down C.—stands and says.*) Are those spirits near? (ALL *laugh.*)

STANDISH. Oh, no, don't.

(*One rap is heard—from back of fireplace. Little laugh.*)

MISS EASTWOOD. But—— (*Rises, comes down L.C. a step.*)

MASON. Oh, please keep still—— (ALL *gather a little closer around* ROSALIE.)

ROSALIE. Is it Laughing Eyes? (*One rap is heard—still louder.*) And ye can't talk to me in the light? (*One rap.*) Are ye happy? (MRS. TRENT *rises. Two raps again.*) Is there someone here ye don't like? (*One rap.*) A gentleman? (*Two raps.*) Dear, dear, a lady. (*One rap. She points to* MISS EASTWOOD.) Is it that one? (*One rap.*) Laughing Eyes don't like you. (*General laugh.*)

MASON (*R.C.*). That's the most wonderful thing I ever heard.

STANDISH (*down L.*). Oh, I don't think——

MASON. It couldn't be a trick. She just stood there. I watched her hands every minute.

ROSALIE. Sure, ye watched the wrong end of me. I have a wooden sole in me shoe. (*She lifts her skirt and shows that she has taken one foot from her slipper.*) Ye do it with yer foot. Like this. (TRENT *goes up to armchair L.C. Laughingly.*) Sure, it's a trick.

(MISS EASTWOOD *goes to* WALES *L.C.* MRS. TRENT *crosses up to armchair*

L.C. STANDISH *crosses up to L. end of settee,* CROSBY *C.* MRS. CROSBY *seated at table R.* STANDISH *crosses back of settee to R.C.*)

MASON. Then if we get any messages—— (*R.C.*)

ROSALIE. If ye get any messages. Well, sur, I'm tellin' ye the truth now. Most of the time it's fake. With me, or that dago Palladino, and it was with Slade, and all the rest of the trance mediums. But to-night there'll be no fakin'. (*Rises.*) I'm a stranger to all of yez except Mr. Wales. I don't know who lives in this house, I don't know the name of any one of ye. Mr. Wales told me he wanted me to come here, he said he'd be sendin' for me. He ain't told me one word about any of ye. (*Goes to R. end of settee.*)

WALES. That is quite true. (*Over L.*)

TRENT (*by armchair L.C.*). You haven't given her a hint of any sort?

WALES (*L.*). On my word of honor.

MASON (*above table R.*). Madame La Grange?

ROSALIE. Sor?

MASON. I know a man who saw this woman Palladino lift a table just by putting her hands on it.

(ROSALIE *points to a small console table R. end of settee. It has a lamp on it.* MISS EASTWOOD *L. end of settee.*)

ROSALIE (*putting handbag on chair above table R.*). Will someone please take the lamp off that table? And will you bring it here to me? (MISS STANDISH *crosses R. to upper end of table R., takes lamp and holds it.* MASON *brings console table to* ROS- ALIE *down C.—wide side to audience.* ROSALIE *puts her hands on table with her thumbs under its edge and lifts the table and turns R. and L.*) You mean like that?

MASON. Yes, I suppose that was it.

ROSALIE. In the dark ye wouldn't hardly notice my thumbs. (ALL *laugh.* MISS ERSKINE *seated back of table over R.*) But it can be done, it can be done. I don't say I can do it in the light, but if ye want I'll try.

ALL. Oh, yes, yes, of course, please do, yes, yes.

MASON. You mean without any trickery?

ROSALIE (*getting back of console table. Turning table around—narrow side to entrance*). I mean like this. (*She places the tips of the fingers of both hands on the C. of the table and stands rigid for a few moments. No one speaks.* ALL *watch her with breathless interest. Slowly the table tips a little to one side, and then tips in the opposite direction. Then it slowly rises about a foot from the floor, and then drops suddenly and falls over. There is a long pause.*)

MASON (*R. of small table*). Good God.

WALES (*L.C. Quietly*). What did I tell you?

(*There is a long pause,* ALL *turn toward* ROSALIE *to see what she will do next.* MASON *takes console table back to its place R. end of settee.* TRENT, MRS. TRENT, *over L.* STANDISH *and* CROSBY *C.*)

ROSALIE (*C.*). Now ye all know what I can do, but I can trick ye too; so ye'll have to take my word for it that I won't. I'm not makin' you any promises. I'll go into a trance for ye, and it will be a real trance and no fake. My spirit controls a little girl named Laughing Eyes.

CROSBY (*coming C.*). Are you asking us to believe that the spirit of a dead child——

ROSALIE (*C.*). To them that believes there is no death. Glory be to God, your own religion teaches ye that.

CROSBY. But not that the spirits of the dead can come back to earth.

ROSALIE (*goes to chair upper end of table.* CROSBY *crosses to end of settee*). Man, go read your Bible. (STANDISH *crosses to back of table R.*) Sure, I'm not going to argue with any of you. I didn't come here for argument. Most of you don't believe, you're all of little faith; sure, it's hard to get messages then. Perhaps I'd better go about me business? (*Crosses to L.C.*)

MRS. CROSBY (*at table R.*). Oh, no, please stay.

ROSALIE. Sure, ma'am, I'll be glad to.

(WILL *and* HELEN *enter R.C. Cross down R.C.*)

TRENT (*down L. of armchair*). And you're willing to submit to our conditions?

ROSALIE. Of course, anything in reason—I——

HELEN. Why! (*Coming down R.C.*)

(ROSALIE, *at the sound of a new voice, turns. She gives a little start, and then moves quickly to* HELEN *C.*)

ROSALIE. Wait, something's coming to me. Don't anyone speak. (ALL *laugh. She goes close to* HELEN *and looks at her. Crosses down C.*) It's a message—give me your hand, Miss. (HELEN, *in a good deal of confusion, gives* ROSALIE *her hand.* ROSALIE *stands and holds, her eyes are closed.*) Lady, there's nothin' but happiness comin' to you. The spirits tell me you're the favorite child av fortune. (WILL *comes to R.C.*) You'll have wealth, and prosperity, and happiness. You'll marry the man you love, and ye'll be happy all your life long. (WALES *goes up L.* TRENT *comes to* ROSALIE *a step.* ROSALIE *turns to others.*) There's something I got to tell her, just fer herself it is. Sure, a young girl like, it's her modesty I'm sparin'.

(MRS. TRENT *goes up L.* TRENT, MISS EASTWOOD, *and* WALES *go up L.C.* ROSALIE *brings* HELEN *down L.* WILL *joins* CROSBY *and* MRS. CROSBY *R.* MISS ERSKINE *and* STANDISH *back of table R.*)

HELEN. Mother!

ROSALIE. Sure, darlin', I didn't know, they just brought me here. Ye know I wouldn't have come fer anythin' in the world. (HELEN *starts to break away.*) Don't tell them, dear, don't have me shame you before all your fine friends. I'll go in a minute—I'll get away the minute I can.

HELEN. But, Mother, there's no shame. I'm proud—

ROSALIE. Tell them afterward av ye must, but let me get away first. (*Aloud.*) Remember now, miss, all the love in the world is hangin' over ye and prayin' for your happiness. Don't let it go. (*Buzz.* ROSALIE *turns to* WALES *L.* NELLIE *stands looking after her.* WILL *comes to her R.C.*)

WILL. What did she tell you?

HELEN. You heard most of it. I'll tell you the rest later. (WILL *and* HELEN *go up R.C.*)

ROSALIE. I'm afraid I'd better go.

(MISS EASTWOOD *and* TRENT *come down L.*)

WALES (*to the* OTHERS). What do you think? Madame La Grange wants to call off the séance.

MISS EASTWOOD (*down L.*). I thought she might.

ROSALIE (MASON *above table R.*). Did ye, now?

MRS. CROSBY. Oh, won't you please stay?

(WILL *and* HELEN *R.C.* MISS ERSKINE *above table R.*)

ROSALIE (*comes C.*). I'm afraid I can't, ma'am. I'm not feeling right. I ain't just meself.

WALES (*L.C.*). Really, Madame La Grange. I'm afraid under the circumstances.

ROSALIE (*getting handbag from chair*). I'm sorry but I got to go.

MISS EASTWOOD (*down L. of ROS-ALIE*). I think it's a shame to bother her. And I think she's quite right to go. Her sort of tricks aren't for people of intelligence.

HELEN. Oh, won't you please stay? (*To ROSALIE C.*)

ROSALIE. I mustn't.

HELEN. Won't you as a great favor to me?

ROSALIE. Well, miss, since you ask it. I will stay.

(MISS EASTWOOD *laughs. She and* TRENT *go up L.* CROSBY *by settee C.* MASON *below table R.* MRS. CROSBY *seated lower end of table.* MRS. TRENT *comes down to armchair L.C., sits.*)

MRS. CROSBY. I'm very glad. Really, I'm greatly interested.

ROSALIE (*crosses R.*). Are ye now, ma'am?

CROSBY (*to C.*). I think after what we've seen that we must ask Madame La Grange to submit to certain conditions.

ROSALIE. Anythin' at all, sur, anythin' at all.

MASON (*down R.*). I agree with you. Frankly, this woman impresses me. I think this test should be taken seriously.

(MISS EASTWOOD *laughs. Crosses to L. end of settee.*)

WALES (*L.C.*). Just what I was going to say.

CROSBY (*R.C.*). If you will submit to the conditions we impose, Madame La Grange, and then show us any manifestations, I will never scoff at anything again.

ROSALIE. Sure, our scoffin's the easiest thing any one can do. (CROSBY *crosses down R. below table.*) If I could stop that even in one person, it would be a good job. What is it you want?

CROSBY. I want the window fastened.

MASON. That's the idea.

CROSBY (*coming in front of table R.*). Then we will have the doors locked. Will that be all right?

ROSALIE. It will.

MISS EASTWOOD (*coming down L.C.*). At the risk of seeming unnecessarily skeptical, I'm going to suggest that we search Madame La Grange—that is, of course, if she's willing.

(MISS ERSKINE *and* MISS STANDISH *back of table R.*)

ROSALIE (*C.*). Why not? There's no holes in my stockings. (ALL *laugh.*)

MASON (*down R.*). I suppose it's going to be difficult for you to get results if we are all so antagonistic, Madame La Grange.

(MISS EASTWOOD *goes up L.C.*)

ROSALIE. Well, sur, it's up to them. If there's any who wants to communicate with any here, maybe they can reach us. I don't know. I don't understand ye. Sure, I showed ye all the tricks; would I have done that, if I wanted to fool ye? I would not. Then why won't ye give me credit for bein' honest?

WALES (*down L. Ad lib. buzz*). I'm sure Madame La Grange is perfectly honest. We've made certain stipulations to which she has agreed. I think we've discussed matters enough already. We're ready if you are, Madame La Grange.

ROSALIE. I'm ready.

(CROSBY *looks at window fastenings.*)

MRS. CROSBY (*seated at table over R.*). Do you know, I don't believe it will be necessary to subject Madame La Grange to being searched. I'm quite sure we can spare her that indignity.

ROSALIE. Sure, I don't mind if you fine ladies won't be shocked at seeing plain, hand-sewed underwear.

(WALES *up L. Ad lib. laugh.* MISS ERSKINE *joining* WILL *and* HELEN, *R.C.*)

MRS. CROSBY (*crossing to L. of ROS-ALIE C.*). Come with me then, please. I'm sure we won't be shocked. (*Aside to* ROSALIE.) I wear that kind myself.

ROSALIE. Do ye now, ma'am? (*They go to door at L.*)

MRS. CROSBY (*at door L.*). We shan't be long.

ROSALIE (*at door L.*). Ma'am, would ye mind if all the ladies came? Then

they'll all be sure I ain't concealing nothing.

(*The ladies all talk together and exit L., following* MRS. CROSBY. WALES *closes door down L.* CROSBY *comes to back of table R.*)

WILL (*by table R.*). Do you really want that window fastened?

(STANDISH *back of chair below table R.*)

WALES (*L.C.* CROSBY *and* TRENT *sit on settee corner*). I don't care.

MASON (*at table R.*). I'd like to make the test that way. I've a queer feeling about that woman. I believe she really has power of some sort. I know it seems funny, but—well, you all saw her lift that table. I watched her carefully. There was no trick about it at all. I'm sure of it.

CROSBY. All right, then. You fasten the window. Billy, you and Brad go and get some chairs out of the dining room; we'll need a lot. (WALES *walks up and down L. stage.* WILL *and* TRENT *exit door R.C.*) You put them in a circle, don't you? (*Begins to place chairs that are already in the room in a circle C.—armchair first L. of fireplace.*) What are you going to do, Wales? Ask her a lot of questions?

WALES (*over L.*). I'm going to try to find out who killed Spencer Lee.

CROSBY. Still harping on the murder of Spencer Lee?

(STANDISH *places chairs above and below table in circle, then chair R. side of fireplace in circle.*)

WALES. Yes.

MASON (*over R., opening window curtains and raising windowshade*). Who was Spencer Lee?

WALES. The best friend I ever had.

(TRENT *and* WILL *enter door R.C., each carrying two chairs, bring them down R.C. and exit R.C.*)

STANDISH (*placing chairs C. with backs to audience*). We all knew Lee pretty well. And I know he was no good.

WALES (*crosses to L.C. outside of circle*). You can't talk that way about him, Standish!

CROSBY (*in circle, comes down C.*). The man's dead, why not let him rest in peace.

(STANDISH *outside of circle, L.C. seat.*)

STANDISH. I didn't bring up the matter, you know, and I don't want to hurt Ned's feelings, but I know that the police found a lot of compromising letters and rotten things of that sort.

(WILL *and* TRENT *re-enter from R.C.* WILL *crosses and places two chairs R. side of circle. Closes door.*)

WALES (*L.C.*). I don't care what they found, or what anyone thinks of Lee, he was my best friend, and if I can find out who killed him I'm going to do it. It was a damned brutal murder, stabbed in the back, poor chap, with never a chance to fight for his life. (*Crosses over L.*)

MASON (*by table R.*). I don't seem to remember anything about the case.

WALES. It happened before you got back from France—no, by Jove, it didn't either. It was a day or two after. I remember you and I had lunch together the day you got home, and I had dinner that night with Spencer. Funny you don't remember anything about it.

(WILL *sitting R. in circle.*)

MASON. Well, of course I must have seen it in the papers, but I don't go in much for crimes, and not knowing the man I wasn't interested.

STANDISH (*sitting in circle L.C.*). It was a good deal of sensation. The man knew a lot of nice people. Came here a good deal, didn't he, Mr. Crosby?

CROSBY (*sitting in circle up C.*). At one time. But after Helen married he rather dropped out of it. Fact is until Trent here appeared on the scene, he was always hanging around.

(TRENT *comes down and sits in R. side of circle.*)

STANDISH. Funny they never found out who killed him.

WALES (*standing outside of circle, L. side*). They may yet. They haven't stopped trying.

MASON (*seated on table R.*). Oh, are the police still interested?

WALES. Yes, they're interested. As a matter of fact, there's a reward of five thousand dollars for the discovery of the murderers.

STANDISH. Are you sure of that?

WALES. I offered it.

TRENT. You?

WALES. Yes. What sort of a man do you think I am? Do you expect me to sit still and let the murderers of Spencer Lee go free? Why, I'd known the man all his life. We were the closest kind of friends.

WILL. But if he was the kind of a man that Standish says——

WALES. I don't give a damn what he was. He was my friend, and I'm never going to rest till I find out who killed him.

TRENT. But——

WALES. I wouldn't care so much if they'd given the poor devil half a chance for his life, but they stabbed him in the back.

MASON. Wasn't there any indications—— (Sitting on table R.)

WALES (standing upper L. side—outside of circle). There wasn't a thing to show who did it or how it was done. A knife wound between the shoulder blades and no knife ever found. Nothing stolen, nothing disturbed. The police have found out that a young woman called to see him that afternoon, two or three hours before his body was discovered. That's all that we know.

TRENT (with a laugh—still seated in circle). And now you're going to try spiritualism?

WALES. Why not? (There is a pause.) Do any of you object?

TRENT. Certainly not. I'm rather for it.

MASON (rises. Still at L. table). You are doing this seriously? This is not a joke?

WALES. Quite seriously. (There is a pause.) Well, why don't somebody laugh?

CROSBY. My dear fellow, why should anyone laugh? This queer old woman may have powers of which we know nothing at all. Personally, I haven't much belief in that sort of thing, but I'm not going to laugh at it. (Rises.) Neither am I going to have any trickery, or if there is any I'm going to expose it.

WALES (over L.). That's perfectly fair.

CROSBY. You've been at her séances or whatever they call them before?

WALES. Yes.

CROSBY. In the dark?

WALES. Invariably.

CROSBY. I may want light. (He turns to his son.) Billy, if I call for lights you give them to me. Don't wait for anything, understand?

WILL. Perfectly, Dad. (WILL goes up to small table R. of settee. Brings table with lamp on it down to between chair and his chair in circle.)

CROSBY. That's all right, then. (Still in circle. Door opens at L. MRS. CROSBY enters, followed by MADAME LA GRANGE and other ladies. WALES crosses to R.C. outside circle. STANDISH crosses to upper end of table R. TRENT crosses to L. side of circle.)

MRS. CROSBY. I think it wasn't fair of us.

ROSALIE. Sure, ma'am, I didn't mind.

(MRS. CROSBY *crosses back of settee to up R.C.*)

MISS EASTWOOD (*coming down L.*). I can assure you there isn't anything up her sleeve.

ROSALIE. Well, what did you expect, burglar's tools?

(MISS EASTWOOD *goes up L. end of settee.* HELEN *and* MRS. TRENT *up L.* MRS. TRENT *closes door down L.*)

WALES (*over R.*). Madame La Grange, we've fastened the windows.

(MISS STANDISH, MRS. TRENT, HELEN, *over L.* TRENT, STANDISH, MISS ERSKINE *by console table L. of settee.*)

ROSALIE. Have ye now?

CROSBY. And now if you don't mind I'm going to lock the doors and keep the keys in my pocket.

ROSALIE. Anything at all, sir. Sure, it's all one to me. (*Goes inside circle and sits down C. in circle.*)

MASON. May I see that it's done, Mr. Crosby? (*R.C.*)

CROSBY (*L.C. With a laugh*). Can't you trust me?

MASON. It isn't that—I—well, I just want to be sure. To see for myself.

CROSBY. Lock that one yourself, then. (*Indicating door R.C.* CROSBY *goes to door at L.C., locks it, takes out the key and puts it in his*

pocket.) Better try it, Mason. (MASON *crosses to door L.C.—shows it is locked.*) Now we'll do this one. (*He starts to door down L., then stops suddenly.*) No, I've got a better way than this. My dear, will you ring for Pollock?

MRS. CROSBY (*upper end of table R.*). What are you going to do now?

CROSBY. Wait and see. (*To* ROSALIE.) You don't object to this?

ROSALIE. I do not.

(BUTLER *enters from door L.—comes well on stage.*)

CROSBY. Oh, Pollock, I want you to put these keys in your pocket. (*Hands them to him.* POLLOCK *puts them in his waistcoat pocket.* MRS. TRENT *and* HELEN *down L.*)

POLLOCK. Yes, sir.

CROSBY (*L.C.*). Now, then, I want you to take the key out of that door, and lock it on the outside, understand?

POLLOCK. Perfectly, sir.

CROSBY. Then take the key from the lock and put that one in your pocket also, after that you are to stand outside that door, and you are not to unlock it until I tell you to. Understand?

POLLOCK. Yes, sir, I'm to lock this door on the outside, keep the key in my pocket, and then stay just outside, and not open it for anyone until you tell me.

CROSBY. Exactly. (*Ad lib. buzz of conversation,* POLLOCK *goes to door*

L., takes out key, exits, closing the door after him. The key is heard turning in the lock.) Now then, Mason, you'd better try that door too. (MASON *goes over and tries the door L.* CROSBY *follows him. Speaking through the door L.)* Are you there, Pollock?

POLLOCK (*outside*). Yes, sir.

CROSBY. And the keys are in your pocket?

POLLOCK. Quite so, sir.

CROSBY. Now we're ready, Madame La Grange.

ROSALIE. Then if ye'll all sit in a circle and hold hands.

MISS ERSKINE. Hold hands? I'm going to love this. (ALL *laugh.*)

MASON (*down to chair L. of circle*). How shall we sit? I mean do you want us in any particular order?

ROSALIE. Any way at all.

MISS EASTWOOD (*L. to* MISS ERSKINE, MRS. TRENT). And he said whose wife.

WILL. I'll sit here. (*Takes chair and sits in reach of lamp on table R.C.)*

ROSALIE. Any way will do.

(HELEN *and* MRS. TRENT *come down L. The* OTHERS *sit in a circle in the following order:* ROSALIE, *C.;* CROSBY *L. of* ROSALIE; MISS ERSKINE, MISS STANDISH, TRENT, MISS EASTWOOD, MASON, HELEN, MRS. TRENT, STANDISH *and* MRS. CROSBY. *This brings* WALES *sitting at C. with his back to the audience,* ROSALIE *di-*

rectly opposite up stage, facing him. As they are being seated ad lib. buzz of conversation.)

MISS ERSKINE. I'm to sit next to you, Mr. Crosby.

CROSBY. I've always wanted to hold your hands, my dear. (*Sitting in circle.)*

MRS. CROSBY. Don't trust him, Daisy. (*At R. of circle—sits in circle R. side.)*

MISS ERSKINE. I won't, Mrs. Crosby.

(*Sits in circle.)*

MISS STANDISH. I'll chaperon them. (*Sits in circle between* TRENT *and* MISS ERSKINE.)

MASON (*to* HELEN). Will you sit by me? (*They sit in circle.)*

TRENT. I'll take this place, then. (*He sits in circle L. side.)*

MISS EASTWOOD (*as she sits in circle*). I'm really getting quite a thrill. (ROSALIE *laughs.*) What's the joke, Madame La Grange?

(MRS. TRENT *crosses outside of circle to R.C. and sits in circle.)*

ROSALIE. I didn't know anything could thrill you.

MISS EASTWOOD. You don't like me, do you, Madame La Grange?

ROSALIE. Sure, miss, I'm crazy about you.

WALES (*standing below circle R.C.*). I think we're all ready. (*The* OTHERS *sit.* WALES *is about to sit.)*

MISS ERSKINE. There are thirteen of us. Oh, don't sit there, Mr. Wales. (*Counting hurriedly. She sits L. side of circle.*)

WALES. Oh, I don't mind those little superstitions. (*Sits down-stage side of circle.*)

MRS. CROSBY. What do we do now?

ROSALIE. I'd like for ye to join hands, and then sit' quiet. Don't try to think of anything.

TRENT. By Jove, that'll be easy for me. (*The* OTHERS *laugh.*)

WALES. We can't get any results if you treat this as a joke. (ALL *laugh.*)

STANDISH. Oh, let's be serious.

MISS ERSKINE. Why, Howard!

STANDISH. Well, there might be something in it. Anyhow, it's only fair to do what Madame La Grange wants. I suppose you'd like the lights out? I've always understood that was necessary.

ROSALIE. We'll get better results that way.

CROSBY. All right, then. (*He rises— goes to door L., pushes light switch below door L. This leaves only the two table lamps R. and L. of settee C. still lit. All other lights on scene out. Crosses back to his chair—turns out table lamp L.*) Will, you turn out that light as soon as we are ready.

WILL. Right you are, Dad.

ROSALIE. That's all, then. Sure, you're not to be frightened if I cry or moan when I go into a trance. I'm not in pain or anything like that. I don't even know that I do such things, but I've been told that it sometimes happens. Me spirit control is a sweet little child named Laughing Eyes. When she begins to talk ye can ask her anything you want. If she don't answer ye, she don't want to talk to ye. Then whoever's speaking had better let someone else try it. That's all. (*She settles back in her chair.*) Now, thin, sir, ye can put out that light.

(WILL *turns off the light, and the stage is in darkness, all but spots on ceiling. House lights are all out too.*)

CROSBY. That won't do. Billy, pull down the blind, that light on the ceiling is too strong.

(WILL *turns on lights. Crosses, pulls blind down, closes curtains, resumes his seat, and puts light out.* ROSALIE *rises, crosses back of circle to back of* MISS EASTWOOD'S *chair. There is a pause. Suddenly* MISS EASTWOOD *screams shrilly.*)

MISS EASTWOOD. There's a hand on my face, there's a hand on my face!

CROSBY. Lights, son!

(*The light on the table goes up, showing* WILL *leaning back in his chair with one hand on the switch, the other tightly clasped in his father's hand.* ROSALIE *is seen standing back of* MISS EASTWOOD, *with her hand resting on* MISS EASTWOOD'S *cheek. All start to speak.*)

MRS. TRENT. It's a trick.

ROSALIE. Sure, it is a trick. (*They stop and stare at her. Her manner is commanding and a little stern.*) I was going to ask ye to tie me hands to the arms of the chair, but I thought I'd show ye this first.

MASON. I don't see how you did it—even now.

ROSALIE (*standing outside of circle L.*). Things happen in the dark. The sense of touch isn't much developed except ye're blind. When this young gentleman let go my hand to turn out the light, I took my other hand away from Mr. Crosby and when we joined hands again the two gentlemen were holding hands as comfortable as you please. And I was free. It's an old trick. All the mediums use it. Anyone can do it. (*Back to her chair and sits.*) Now, if someone will tie me in, we'll go on.

MASON. How do we know that you can't get free even then?

ROSALIE. Tie me so I can't.

CROSBY (*rising*). I'll see to that. I want something strong.

MASON. Take handkerchiefs, they are strong enough. (*Takes handkerchief.*)

CROSBY. They'll do very well. (*Takes out his own.*) I want three more.

WILL. Here's mine. (*Hands his handkerchief to his father.* MASON *and* TRENT *give* CROSBY *theirs.*)

CROSBY. Now, Madame La Grange, if you don't mind. (*He goes, ties her hands to the arms of the chair.*) I don't see why you did that just now.

ROSALIE. I told you I wanted to be sure.

CROSBY. Why?

ROSALIE. Because I think something's going to happen. I think there will be manifestations. I wanted you to know I wasn't faking.

MISS EASTWOOD. Why should we think that you were?

ROSALIE. Sure, ye thought nothing else since I came into the room.

CROSBY. Mason, see if she can get free from that now.

(MASON *comes over, inspects the knot,* CROSBY *tying the other hand.*)

MASON. That seems pretty secure—someone else look at it.

(WILL *and* TRENT *rise and go to* ROSALIE'S *chair.*)

CROSBY. I'm going to fasten your ankles now, Madame La Grange.

ROSALIE. That's right.

(CROSBY *ties* ROSALIE'S *ankles to leg of chair. The other two men look on.*)

WALES. I don't believe all this is necessary.

ROSALIE. Why not, if they want it?

CROSBY. Now I'm sure she can't get away. (MASON *inspects knot.*)

MASON. So am I. (*The men resume their places.*)

ROSALIE. Well now, if ye'll all sit down, please—(*pause*)—ye'll have to reach over and take my hands this time—are ye all satisfied now? Is there anything more ye want me to do? (*There is no answer*). Then, if ye'll all sit quiet, just keep yer minds free, that's all ye have to do. Now, sir, ye can turn out the lights.

(*There is a long pause.* ROSALIE *moans and whispers as if in pain.*)

HELEN. I can't stand this, I——

WALES. Please keep still—she asked us to keep still.

(ROSALIE *moans again. After a short pause she gives a choking sob. Another pause. Finally she speaks with frequent pauses, using the voice of a little child.*)

ROSALIE. Laughing Eyes is sad, very sad. I'm a long way off—a long way. (*Pause.*) Bad people, bad people, unhappy—he's unhappy—— (*Pause. Knife is set down in sight of audience, seen sticking in ceiling.*) Spencer wants to tell Ned—— (*She moans heavily.*) It hurts—terribly—like a knife—it burns—burns, in the back—— (MAN'S *voice from settee, facing fireplace.*)

VOICE. Ned, I want Ned—why in *hell* don't Ned answer?

ROSALIE (*in child's voice*). He wants to talk to Ned. Is Ned here?

STANDISH. Ned who? Who is it? Who does he want to speak to?

ROSALIE (*in child's voice*). Tell Ned it's Spencer—Spencer wants to tell Ned about the letters and the pain in the back—in the back.

STANDISH. What was in the back? (*There is no answer.*) Ask him what was in the back!

ROSALIE (*still using child's voice*). The knife—Ned—he wants Ned.

WALES. What do you want?

ROSALIE. A swimming pool—don't forget the swimming pool. Don't ever forget——

WALES. You mean the time he went in after me when I was drowning? When we were little boys? Is that what he wants me to remember?

ROSALIE. Spencer says he can't rest—he wants to tell you it's hard to reach —too far away—you promised——

WALES. Promised what? When did I promise?

ROSALIE. Your life saved——

WALES. Now I know—I told him I'd do anything in the world for him. Spencer, of course, I remember—what do you want me to do?

ROSALIE. Find—find——

WALES. Do you want me to find the letters?

ROSALIE. In the back—someone came —someone came.

WALES. You're trying to tell who killed you?

ROSALIE. Ask—ask—ask.

WALES. You want me to ask questions? Is that it? You mean you can't talk much?

ROSALIE. Too far away.

CROSBY. You know who killed you? (*There is a pause, but no answer.*)

ROSALIE. He says, Ned, he wants Ned.

WALES. You want me to ask?

ROSALIE. He wants Ned to ask.

WALES. Do you know who killed you?

MRS. TRENT (*hysterically*). Oh, my God!

CROSBY. Keep still, daughter.

WALES. Can you tell the name? (ROSALIE *suddenly gives a long moan.*) Quick, the name, the name. Spencer, tell me who killed you—she's coming out of her trance. I want the name. (ROSALIE *moans again. Her cry is overtopped by a shriek from* WALES.) Oh, my God. My back! Oh! (*Then there is a dead silence that lasts as long as it will hold.*)

CROSBY. Wales, is anything the matter?

MRS. TRENT. Father, he's pulling at my hand.

CROSBY. Lights, son.

(WILL *suddenly turns on the light at table.* WALES *is discovered leaning forward. The circle is unbroken.*)

MRS. TRENT. Look at him! Father! Look at him!

(CROSBY *drops* ROSALIE's *hand and springs forward toward* WALES. *At the same instant* WALES *falls forward on his face to the floor. The others all rise, chairs are knocked over in the confusion which follows.*)

CROSBY. Stand back, please. (*The* OTHERS *move back a little—*CROSBY *leans over* WALES.) Why, he—why —it's impossible.

MRS. CROSBY. Roscoe, look at your hand.

(CROSBY *looks at his hand, takes out his handkerchief and wipes it hurriedly. He crosses suddenly to the door at L.* ROSALIE *has come out of her trance and sits staring at* WALES *as he lies on the floor in front of her. The two figures are thrown out from the shadows of the room by the light on the table back of* MADAME LA GRANGE. *The rest of the room is in semi-darkness.*)

CROSBY (TRENT *kneels by* WALES's *body*). Pollock! Pollock!

POLLOCK (*outside*). Yes, Mr. Crosby. (TRENT *turns* WALES's *body over on back.*)

CROSBY. Get on the phone at once and call up Police Headquarters. Get Inspector Donohue if you can. Tell him to come to the house at once.

POLLOCK. Very good, sir.

(CROSBY *turns away from the door, and faces the* OTHERS, *who have followed him over.*)

WILL. Father, what do you suppose it is? Are you sure that——

MRS. TRENT. It can't be. He was talking and——

MRS. CROSBY. Roscoe, are you sure? Hadn't we better send for Doctor Griggs?

(TRENT *is leaning over* WALES's *body on floor.*)

TRENT. It's no use. He's dead.

CROSBY. Murdered.

TRENT (*rises*). What?

CROSBY. Mr. Wales was stabbed in the back, just as Spencer Lee was stabbed in the back.

STANDISH. Just as he was asking— just when he was trying to find out who——

(*There is a knock on the door down L.*)

CROSBY. What is it?

POLLOCK (*outside of door*). Inspector Donohue was at the Fifty-first Street Station, sir. He's on his way here. (*There is a pause.*) Shall I unlock the door, sir?

CROSBY. No—not until the inspector tells you.

CURTAIN

ACT TWO

SCENE—*Same as Act One.*

TIME—*Ten minutes later.*

DISCOVERED—CROSBY *is standing by door L.* ROSALIE *is still tied in chair. Dummy supposed to represent* WALES'S *body covered by a piece of drapery, has been placed on settee facing fireplace up C.*

MRS. TRENT *seated below console table L. end of settee.*

MISS EASTWOOD *seated next to* ROSALIE *at R. end of console table R. of settee.*

STANDISH *over R. by table.*

HELEN *and* WILL—*standing above table R.*

MRS. CROSBY *seated L., next to* ROSALIE. MISS ERSKINE *seated next to* MRS. CROSBY. MASON *in front of fireplace C., looking at* WALES'S *body.*

TRENT *walking up stage L. as curtain rises. All lamps on stage lit. Rose foots up full. Amber foots one quarter up. No border light.*

Arrangement of chairs for Second Act. Big armchair up C., facing audience. Single chair R. of armchair. Chair upper end of table R. Armchair back of table R. Chair lower end of table R. Small chair in front of table R. Small chairs down C., with space between; these two chairs turn sideways to audience. Chair down L. Armchair against flat below door L. Chair up L. Chair with upholstered seat L. of ROSALIE'S *chair. Small chair R. corner of console table, L. of settee. Small chair L. side, a little below console table L. end of settee. Book on table R. end of settee. Console table moved up stage to R. end of settee.* STANDISH *teetering chair below table R.,* MISS ERSKINE *tapping chair,* MISS EASTWOOD *rattling book leaves.* MASON *takes book away from her.* MISS STANDISH *sitting L.C. between* MRS. CROSBY *and* MRS. TRENT.

As curtain rises, MRS. TRENT *rises, goes to* CROSBY *L.* TRENT *walks up stage L. at rise.*

MRS. TRENT (*rises, goes L. to* CROSBY). Father, please let me go to my room.

CROSBY. It is impossible, my dear.

TRENT. But, Mr. Crosby—— (*Goes to* CROSBY L.)

CROSBY (*interrupting him*). It's quite impossible.

(MRS. TRENT *sits in chair up L., followed by* TRENT, *who stands R. side of* MRS. TRENT. STANDISH *is standing by table over R.*)

STANDISH (*below table over R.*). Mr. Crosby, I must——

CROSBY (WILL *sits back of table R.* HELEN *sits above table R.*). Mr. Standish, I just refused to let my own daughter leave the room. (*Slight pause.*)

STANDISH. But don't you see, sir——

CROSBY. My dear Standish, poor Wales was killed by someone in this room. We are all of us under suspicion. Every one of us. (*Slight movement from* ALL.) It's an awful thing to say—some one of us in this room has killed Wales. Which one of us?

(*Knock on door down L.*)

CROSBY. Yes.

POLLOCK (*outside*). The police are here, sir.

CROSBY. Who is it?

DONOHUE (*outside at door down L.*). Inspector Donohue.

CROSBY (WILL *rises*). Pollock, you will give Inspector Donohue all the keys.

POLLOCK. Yes, Mr. Crosby. (*There is a pause.*)

DONOHUE (*still outside the door*). What is all this?

POLLOCK (*outside door down L.*). I don't know, I'm sure. I was told to lock the door. I don't know what's been going on inside. Then I was told to call you. This is the right key for that door.

(*The noise of the key being put into the lock can be heard, then the click as it is turned in the lock, then the door is opened, and* INSPECTOR DONOHUE, *in citizen's dress, comes well on stage L.* SERGEANT DUNN *enters, drops below door L. He is seen to be a clean-cut, intelligent-looking man of fifty. It later develops that he is reserved and extremely quiet in manner. He speaks like a gentleman and acts like one. He is as little like the traditional stage police inspector as it is possible to induce a tradition-bound manager to permit.*)

DONOHUE. Oh, Wales! Where's Mr. Wales?

CROSBY (L.C.). How did you know that Wales——

DONOHUE (L. *of* CROSBY. *Interrupting him*). I don't know anything. I was thinking of something else. I was told that I was wanted here in a hurry.

CROSBY. Queer your asking for Wales. Mr. Wales is dead; that's why I sent for you.

DONOHUE. Wales is what?

CROSBY. Wales is dead.

MISS EASTWOOD (*still seated R.C.*). Yes, and if you ask me——

DONOHUE. Just a minute, please, miss. (*He turns to* CROSBY.) It must have been very sudden. Why, only this afternoon I—— Did he ask you to send for me?

CROSBY (*L.C.*). Inspector, you don't seem to understand. Mr. Wales was murdered in this room not fifteen minutes ago.

(*Other characters keep positions as at rise of curtain.*)

DONOHUE ·(*his manner changing abruptly*). Mike! That door! (SERGEANT DUNN *closes door L. and stands in front of it.*) Where have you taken him?

CROSBY (*pointing to the sofa C.*). There.

(DONOHUE *goes up L. end of settee C., stands looking down on the body. There is a long pause and then, slowly raising his head, looks with terrible deliberation at each person in the room.* MASON *goes to R. end of settee.*)

DONOHUE. Who did this?

CROSBY. We don't know.

DONOHUE (*very quietly*). Then I expect we'll have to find out. (*He comes down R. end of settee, stops when he sees* ROSALIE. *He gives a short laugh as he sees how she is tied to the chair.*) What's this? (*R.C.*)

MRS. CROSBY (*rises*). Good heavens, we forgot to untie her. I'm so sorry.

ROSALIE. Thank ye, ma'am, I'm quite comfortable as it is. I'll stay as I am if ye don't mind.

MRS. CROSBY. But——

DONOHUE. I think we'll leave things as they are for the present.

(MRS. CROSBY *resumes same seat as before.*)

ROSALIE. Bless me soul, a cop with brains!

DONOHUE (*goes to* CROSBY *down L., standing R. side of* CROSBY). Let's see if he can't use them then. Now, Mr. Crosby, tell me exactly what happened.

CROSBY (*L.C.*). I know it sounds foolish, but we were having a spiritualistic séance. Madame La Grange is a medium.

DONOHUE. I see.

CROSBY. We were sitting in the dark, in a circle, you know, holding hands. Suddenly Wales cried out. I called to my son to turn on the light. He did so. Wales was leaning forward in his chair. His hands were in those of the people he sat between, and all the rest of us were sitting around.

DONOHUE· (*R. of* CROSBY). All of you?

CROSBY. Yes.

DONOHUE. I thought you told your son to turn on the lights. (*L.C.*)

CROSBY. If you're implying that——

DONOHUE. I'm not implying anything, and please answer my questions.

WILL (*rises and stands back of table R.*). Why, Inspector, I was sitting there, and simply made a move to turn on the light. I had chosen the seat purposely. We wanted to expose trickery, if we found any.

DONOHUE. I understand. Go on, Mr. Crosby. (*He turns again to* CROSBY.)

CROSBY (*L.C.*). In a moment poor Wales fell to the floor. I ran to him and found that he had been stabbed in the back. Before we could call for aid, he was dead.

DONOHUE. Did he say anything?

CROSBY. No. I think that he was dead before we got to him.

DONOHUE. What happened then?

CROSBY. As soon as I realized what had happened, I sent for you.

DONOHUE. Why for *me?* Why not simply notify the police? I mean, was there any special reason for wanting *me?*

CROSBY. There was, but I wasn't conscious of it at the time. We'd been talking about the killing of Spencer Lee earlier in the evening, and I suppose that subconsciously I remembered that you were handling that case, which brought yours as the first name to my mind. That's all.

DONOHUE. I see. (*Goes to C. a few steps.*) Now, then, who's been in or out of this room since? Of course you know you had no right to move Mr. Wales.

CROSBY (*L.C.*). Yes, I know, but I couldn't let him lie there on the floor. It was a little too much. You see, we were all locked in here and——

DONOHUE. Locked in? You mean as I found you when I came?

CROSBY. Exactly. We had all of the windows fastened and all doors locked for the séance. Pollock had the keys. I refused to let him open the door until you came.

DONOHUE. Mr. Crosby, you are forgiven for breaking the coroner's rules. As I understand, then, you were sitting in this room with the doors and windows locked; you were in the dark, Wales was stabbed in the back, the lights were turned on, and no one has left the room or entered since?

CROSBY. No one but you.

DONOHUE. I didn't kill him. (*Crosses C. There is a long pause, then he turns with a sweeping gesture.*) Which one of you did? (*Slight movement from* OTHERS—*who are still seated. There is a long pause. No one speaks. Very quietly down R.C. Below table R.*) Now, I'm not going to employ the usual police methods. There is to be no bulldozing or threatening or badgering. But you all can see that there can be no escape for the guilty person. I realize that this is a terrible situation for all of you, but the only way to relieve it is for the murderer of Mr. Wales to confess. (*Another pause.*) It will save a long and I assure you a very trying police investigation. Let me say also that there will be no recriminations, no unpleasant scenes. I realize that this seems a very weak plea for a confession. But I am counting on the intelligence of the people now in this room. (*He takes out his watch, and holds it face upward in his hand.*) I have unlimited time. But not a great deal of patience. Well? (*There is another long pause. He finally replaces his watch with a little gesture of finality. He turns suddenly to* MISS EASTWOOD, *who is still seated up R.C.*) Very well, then. What is your name?

MISS EASTWOOD. Mary Eastwood.

DONOHUE. A moment ago, Miss Eastwood, you started to tell me something. You said "if you ask me." Now I am asking you. What was it you wanted to tell me?

MISS EASTWOOD (*seated R. of console table R.*). I don't want to especially. But I think I ought to tell you this. No one else seems to have thought of it. When the séance started we were all sitting in a circle holding each other's hands. As I understand it——

DONOHUE. We can take it for granted that I know how that is done. Go on, please.

MISS EASTWOOD. The medium got out of the circle without our knowing it, and then showed us how she did the trick.

DONOHUE. I see.

MISS EASTWOOD. Why couldn't she have done it again? Of course,

that's what someone did, isn't it? And if she could get out of the circle without our knowing it she could get back in again, couldn't she? (*With an air of triumph—* HELEN *rises.*) That's what I wanted to tell you.

ROSALIE. If any one of ye or all of ye can get me out of this chair without untying me or cutting me loose, I'll say I done that murder.

(HELEN *sits above table R.*)

DONOHUE. Thank you, Miss Eastwood. It's only fair to tell you that there isn't a trick or an effect that these people do that the police do not understand perfectly.

ROSALIE. Is that so?

(DONOHUE *goes over and examines the way in which* ROSALIE *is tied to the chair.*)

DONOHUE. Why was she tied up?

CROSBY (*down L.C.*). At her own request. As Miss Eastwood says, she showed us how she broke out of the circle and then suggested that we tie her into that chair to make sure she didn't do it again.

DONOHUE (*R. of* ROSALIE'S *chair*). It's lucky for her that she did. Even if she had gotten out of those knots, there's no way in the world that she could get back in.

ROSALIE. I said the cop had brains. (DONOHUE *turns away from her.*) Get me loose, Inspector, dear, me foot's asleep.

(DONOHUE *turns back, unties handkerchiefs with which she is tied. She gets up and stands in front of arm-chair C.)*

DONOHUE. Thank you very much, Miss Eastwood, that eliminates one.

ROSALIE. Then I can go? *(Starting for door L.)*

DONOHUE. You cannot. *(ROSALIE goes R. of armchair and sits R. end of settee C.)* Anyone else have anything they want to tell me? No? Mike, you'd better phone the coroner and ask him to come up here. Tell him I do not want the case reported yet. And suggest that he hurries.

DUNN. Yes, Inspector. *(He turns and exits L., leaving the door open behind him.* STANDISH *starts to door L.)*

DONOHUE *(turning to* STANDISH *and* TRENT—*who start to go L.).* That open door does not mean freedom for any of you yet.

TRENT *(coming to* DONOHUE *C.).* I'm awfully sorry, Inspector, but I've an important business engagement at ten o'clock. My father-in-law here will——

DONOHUE. That's quite impossible.

*(*TRENT *goes up L. again and stands L. side of* MRS. TRENT.*)*

STANDISH *(crosses L.C.).* This is all very well, Inspector, but you know you can't keep us in this room forever. If you want to take the consequences of accusing me of murder, well, that's your affair. But my patience is exhausted and I haven't the slightest intention of remaining

here much longer. Unless, of course, you are planning to arrest me.

DONOHUE. I see. *(C.)* By the way, who are you?

STANDISH *(L.C.).* Howard Standish, of Standish, Giles & Updegraff, 120 Broadway. My brother is Judge Standish of the Supreme Court.

DONOHUE. And you refuse to remain here any longer? *(C.)*

STANDISH. I do. *(L.C.)*

DONOHUE. Very well, Mr. Standish, of Standish, Giles & Updegraff. You are arrested as a material witness in this case. As soon as Sergeant Dunn returns, he will call a patrol wagon and take you down to the House of Detention. *(Turns—crosses R.)* Are there any others who insist on leaving this room?

STANDISH *(L.C.).* I beg your pardon, Inspector. I acted like a fool. *(*MASON *R. of settee C.)*

DONOHUE. Not at all, sir, your actions are entirely natural.

*(*STANDISH *goes up L.* DUNN'S *voice is heard outside.)*

DUNN. Hello! Hello! No, sir. But Inspector Donohue wants you to come here at once. We're at Mr. Roscoe Crosby's house. No, sir— *(*DONOHUE *crosses and closes the door L.)*—he doesn't want the case reported yet.

DONOHUE. We needn't be bothered with that, anyway. *(Crosses to R.C. There is a pause.)* Well, I'm afraid we'll have to begin work. *(He goes over to table R. and sits down stage end of table. Takes paper, gets pen-*

cil.) With the exception of Mr. Crosby, who is known to nearly everyone, and Mr. Standish, who has so pleasantly introduced himself to me, I know none of you. So I'll have to ask—— (*He stops suddenly and rises, facing them all. He points slowly to the sofa, facing fireplace up C.*) That's rather a gruesome thing there. I think we'll move it into another room. Will some of you gentlemen carry Mr. Wales' body into the other room? (*There is a pause. The* MEN *all hesitate. Finally* MASON *starts to settee C. down stage R.C.*) Thank you very much, we'll—— (*Coming to C.*)

(DUNN *enters from L.*)

DUNN. Dr. Bernstein himself is on the way here, Inspector.

DONOHUE. Good. Mike, get one of the servants to help you to carry this sofa into another room. (DUNN *turns and exits L. without speaking.*) I won't have to trouble you after all, sir. (MASON *drops to console table R. of settee. He gives a little laugh.*) Funny how these old superstitions cling to us. One of the first tests for guilt invented·by detectives was to ask a supposed murderer to touch the body of his victim. (*Slight pause.*) The test didn't work very well, did it? Certainly you four gentlemen can't all be guilty. (*Slight pause.*) Well, we'll have to try something else. (*Very impressively.*) Because you know I really am going to arrest the· murderer of Edward Wales tonight. (DUNN *enters from L., followed by* POLLOCK.) Carry the sofa into another room, please.

CROSBY (*down L.*). Into that room, please. (*Indicating door L.C.*)

(DUNN *goes up to door L.C., turns knob—discovers door is locked.* POLLOCK *crosses to R. end of sofa, facing fireplace on which dummy has been placed between first and second acts. Dummy is covered with a drapery.*)

DUNN (*at door L.C., the door is locked*). The door is locked.

DONOHUE (*C.*). Oh, yes, try these keys.

(DUNN *comes down L.C., gets keys, goes up and unlocks door. He and* POLLOCK *pick up settee—*POLLOCK *taking his end of settee through door L.C. first.*)

DONOHUE. And Mike—— (DUNN *turns his head.*)

DUNN. Yes, sir.

DONOHUE. Make as quick an examination as you can and report to me here. (*The* MEN *exit, carrying sofa into room L.C.* DONOHUE *crosses to chair below table R.—sits.* MISS STANDISH *sits in circle between* MISS ERSKINE *and* TRENT. TRENT *places chair L.C.*) If you will all come a little closer, please. (WILL *back of table R.—*HELEN O'NEILL *seated above table,* MISS EASTWOOD *seated below console table R. end of settee,* ROSALIE *seated C. settee,* MRS. CROSBY *seated in armchair up C.,* MASON *standing upper end of table R.,* MISS ERSKINE *seated up L.C.* MRS. TRENT *seated,* STANDISH *L. of armchair, and* TRENT *seated L.C.* CROSBY *down L.C.*) Now I can see you all quite comfortably. (*Seated lower end of table R.* POLLOCK *enters door L.C., closes door—crosses to door L. Exits, closing door.*) As I started to say a moment ago, I shall have to find out something about each of you. You, Madame? (*He turns to* MRS. CROSBY.)

MRS. CROSBY (*seated in armchair C.*). I'm Alicia Crosby. Mrs. Roscoe Crosby. (*He makes notes with pencil on paper in front of him.*)

DONOHUE. I'm sorry to trouble you, Miss—— (*He points his pencil at* MISS ERSKINE, L.C.)

MISS ERSKINE. Elizabeth Erskine. I'm——

DONOHUE. It's not necessary to tell your age.

MISS ERSKINE. I wasn't going to. I'm the daughter of Edward Erskine. My father is the banker. (*Sits L.C.*)

DONOHUE. I know him. Thank you. You are then merely a guest here?

MISS ERSKINE. A friend.

DONOHUE. Miss Eastwood I already know. And you, Miss?

MISS STANDISH. Grace Standish.

STANDISH. My sister.

DONOHUE. Oh! And this young lady?

CROSBY (*he puts his hand on* MRS. TRENT's *shoulder, L.C.*). My daughter, Mrs. Trent. She and Trent, here, live with us.

DONOHUE. And you, sir?

MASON (*there is a pause*). Philip Mason. (*At upper end of table R.*)

DONOHUE. That doesn't tell me very much.

MASON (*with a laugh*). There isn't much to tell. I'm just a friend of the family's. We've known each other for years. I've lived in Paris for the last two or three years. I'm a painter.

DONOHUE. You mean an artist?

MASON. Well, I don't paint houses or fences, but I'd hardly call myself an artist—yet.

DONOHUE. Poor, I suppose? I know you'll pardon that question, won't you?

MASON. Quite all right, I assure you. No, I'm not poor.

DONOHUE (*he turns toward* WILL *who is standing back of* HELEN's *chair above table R.*). Thank you. And you?

WILL. I'm young Crosby.

DONOHUE. I see. Live home, I suppose?

WILL. Certainly. Where else should I live?

DONOHUE. I thought perhaps you might be married.

CROSBY (*L.C.*). He's not, but if he were he'd live with us, and——

WILL. No, Father. When I marry I've got to have my own home, and——

CROSBY. Nonsense. Don't talk like a fool. You'd live here with me and your mother—and your wife, of course.

DONOHUE. I think perhaps we'd better defer that discussion, gentlemen. (*He turns toward* HELEN.) And this young lady?

WILL. My fiancée, Miss O'Neill.

DONOHUE. Well, that finishes that. (*Rises—stands below table R.*)

MISS EASTWOOD. But, Inspector, you haven't asked anything about the medium.

DONOHUE. Perhaps I don't consider that necessary, Miss Eastwood.

MISS EASTWOOD. But——

DONOHUE. And I'm terribly set on conducting this investigation in my own way, if you don't mind.

(*Enter* DUNN *from L.C.*)

DUNN. Inspector.

DONOHUE. Well?

DUNN (*at door L.C.*). I can't tell for sure, but I guess the knife went clean into the heart. He must have died instantly.

DONOHUE. All right. Let me know when the coroner arrives. (DUNN *turns and starts toward door down L.*) And Dunn!

DUNN. Yes, sir.

DONOHUE (*going C.*). You'd better let me have a look at that knife.

(DUNN *turns sharply and looks at him.*)

DUNN (*down L.*). The knife?

DONOHUE. Yes, the knife.

DUNN. I haven't seen any knife. I thought you had it.

DONOHUE. No. I haven't seen it. (*There is a long pause. R. of* CROSBY.) Mr. Crosby?

CROSBY (*still L.C.*). We didn't find it.

DONOHUE. Look carefully?

CROSBY. Everywhere. While we were waiting for you.

DONOHUE. Who moved Mr. Wales' body? (*C.*)

CROSBY (*C.*). I did.

DONOHUE. No one else touched him?

CROSBY (*L.C.*). No one.

DONOHUE. What did you do, after you had carried him to the sofa?

CROSBY. I saw that he had been stabbed. I looked for the knife.

DONOHUE. Where?

CROSBY. On the floor, under the chairs, everywhere I could think of.

DONOHUE. No trace of it?

CROSBY. None.

DONOHUE. What did you do then?

CROSBY. Nothing. I waited for you.

DONOHUE. How long after you found that Mr. Wales was killed did you turn on the lights?

CROSBY. Why, I told you; we turned on the light before we found what had happened.

DONOHUE. Would it have been possible for the murderer to have hidden it about the room?

CROSBY. I doubt it very much.

DONOHUE. Why?

CROSBY. I don't think there would have been time. I don't see how anyone could have done it at all. It's all a mystery to me. I told you the circle was intact. You remember?

DONOHUE (*there is a pause*). Yes, I remember. Then if the knife was hidden it's probably on the person of the man or woman who used it.

CROSBY. I think so, undoubtedly.

DONOHUE. Mike, phone over to the station house and have them send a matron over here. (DUNN *exits L. and closes the door after him.*) Now about that light. There was just one lamp turned on, as I remember.

CROSBY. Someone turned on the rest of the lights almost immediately.

DONOHUE. Could the knife have been hidden about the room since that time?

CROSBY. It's extremely unlikely. We have all been here together. A thing of that sort would have been seen.

DONOHUE. Then I expect we'll find it without much trouble. (*There is a pause, as he looks slowly at each person individually in the room.* WILL *puts arm on* HELEN'S *shoulders as* DONOHUE *looks at him.*) In the meantime, I think we'll let it remain where it is. (*Crosses down R. He turns with a gesture which takes them all in.*) You see how inevitably the guilty person must be discovered. Don't you think it would be much simpler to confess? (*Pause.*) No? Then I suppose we will have to continue. (*Crosses up L., gets chair, places it L. side of circle, then gets chair down L., places that in lower left-hand side of circle.* CROSBY *crosses to C.*) I'd like to visualize the scene a little more clearly. (TRENT *paces chair L. side of circle.*) Let's form that circle again—— (*Turns two single chairs down C., around with backs to audience. Crosses and gets chair in front of table—places it lower right-hand side of circle.* MRS. CROSBY, MISS ERSKINE, MRS. TRENT, TRENT *and* MISS STANDISH *rise, cross to L. of circle.*) Of course this time without Mr. Wales. (MISS EASTWOOD *rises, stands at R. end of settee. During these last few speeches of* DONOHUE, TRENT *and* CROSBY *have placed the remainder of chairs of the left-hand side in circle.*) Won't you all sit as you were sitting at the séance?

(*By this time circle is formed completely with chairs. There is a general movement of those on the stage.* STANDISH *crosses R. to above table R. The minute this suggestion is made* ROSALIE *comes down, nearer to* DONOHUE, *and looks at him anxiously. Something in his suggestion greatly disturbs her.*)

CROSBY (*in upper L. side of circle*). Will, you were there by the lamp, and Madame La Grange was next to you, and I was next to her——

DONOHUE. Then how did they sit? (*Down R.*)

CROSBY (*next to* ROSALIE *L.C.*). I'm trying to remember. It's queer what a jumbled memory one has. If anyone had asked me about it, I would have said I could have told how we were sitting with great accuracy. But I can't somehow.

MISS ERSKINE. I was next to you, Mr. Crosby. (*Upper L. side of circle. She turns to* MRS. CROSBY, *who is standing over L.*) Don't you remember, Mrs. Crosby, he said he'd always wanted to hold my hand, and we joked about it. (*Sits in her original chair.*)

MRS. CROSBY (*L.—outside of circle*) Yes. I remember.

DONOHUE (HELEN *starts L.*). That's all right, then. Who came next? (*Down R. They all hesitate.*)

ROSALIE (*eagerly*). Inspector, I can place them all for you.

MASON (*over end of table R.*). But you said you didn't care how we sat.

(HELEN *R.C. in circle.*)

ROSALIE. Nor did I, sorr. But I was mighty careful to know where ye were sittin'. Shall I show ye, Inspector?

DONOHUE (*after a pause*). If you will be so kind.

ROSALIE (MISS STANDISH *sits in circle*). The young lady was here. Well, this gentleman was here. (*Indicating* TRENT'S *chair.*)

TRENT (*from L.—outside of circle*). By George, I couldn't have told you, but she's right. This is exactly where I was sitting. (*Sits in circle.*)

ROSALIE (*taking* HELEN *hastily by the shoulder and putting her in the next seat*). And this young lady was here. (HELEN *looks at her for a moment and then sinks back in her chair.* ROSALIE *points at* MASON.) He came next.

MASON (*over R.*). No, you're wrong there. I—you're right. I remember perfectly. I was next to Miss O'Neill. (*Crosses L. and sits L. side of circle.*) I know just how her hand felt in the dark.

(WILL *looks at him quickly.* HELEN *turns and looks at him in wonder.*)

HELEN (*seated L. side in circle*). Well, really, Mr. Mason.

MASON. Oh, I don't mean it that way at all. I assure you I don't.

WILL. Then why did you say it? (*Seated R.C.*)

MASON. My dear fellow, I've apologized. You are misunderstanding me.

MRS. CROSBY. I think we're all pretty frazzled. (*L. outside of circle.*) Inspector Donohue, must we go through all this again?

DONOHUE. I'm afraid so, Mrs. Crosby.

CROSBY. Then let's get it over as quickly as possible. (*Sits C. in circle.*)

DONOHUE. Mr. Crosby, you seem to forget that this is a police investigation, and must be conducted as I see fit. Who sat next to Mr. Mason?

ROSALIE (*pointing to* MISS EAST-WOOD). This young lady.

MISS EASTWOOD. I was next to Mr. Mason, wasn't I, Philip? (*Crossing inside of circle—to chair lower L. side of circle.*)

MASON. Yes.

DONOHUE. Now then, who occupied this seat?

MRS. TRENT (*L.C. outside of circle*). Mr. Wales. I know because I sat *there*, and I was *next* to him. Shall I sit there now?

DONOHUE. If you will be so good.

(MRS. TRENT *crosses to R. and sits in circle.*)

STANDISH. I was next to Mrs. Trent. (*Upper end of table R. He sits.*)

MRS. CROSBY. And I was here between Mr. Standish and Billy. (*She sits.* DONOHUE *moves off a step down R. and stands looking at them as they sit.* ROSALIE *moves over and takes her place in armchair.*)

DONOHUE. You are all sure that's where you were sitting?

MISS EASTWOOD (ROSALIE *rises.*). There's some mix-up here. I know. I wasn't next to Mr. Wales.

HELEN (*rises*). Of course you weren't. I don't see what I could have been thinking of. *I* sat where Miss Eastwood is.

MISS EASTWOOD. Yes, and I was next to Mr. Trent, between Philip and Mr. Trent. I felt sure I was in the wrong seat. (*Rises.*)

DONOHUE (*quite casually*). Then if you ladies will exchange places. (ROSALIE *gives a little sigh of relief when she sees that* DONOHUE *attaches no importance to the substitution she has made.* HELEN *and* MISS EASTWOOD *change seats—* HELEN *crosses outside of circle.*) Now, we're all right, aren't we? (*Slight buzz of conversation.*) You are quite sure that you are all in the places you occupied during the séance?

CROSBY. Yes. I think so.

DONOHUE (*he puts his hand on the empty chair*). We'll pretend that Mr. Wales is still sitting here. (*Slight movement from* ALL.) Now, Mr. Crosby, I'll ask you to tell me what happened after the séance began. But first I'll ask you this question: Was there any special arrangement about the seats?

ROSALIE (*hurriedly—rises*). There was not, sorr. I towld them that they could sit anywhere they liked for all of me. Young Mr. Crosby must have sat by the light on purpose. And I'm sorry I made that mistake about the young ladies. I don't know how I came to make a mistake like that.

DONOHUE. Oh, well, if they couldn't remember where they sat, I don't see how I can expect you to be entirely accurate. (ROSALIE *sits in armchair up C.*) However, we're all right now. Now, Mr. Crosby. (*Down R.*)

CROSBY. Well, after Madame La Grange had shown how she broke out of——

(ALL *look at* DONOHUE.)

DONOHUE. We'll start with the séance. I know how mediums break the circle and all that. And you needn't describe how she went into that trance of hers.

MASON (*seated in circle*). Inspector, I don't think you're fair to this woman. I think there's something pretty important that you haven't been told.

(ALL *look at* MASON.)

DONOHUE. Then you'd better tell me now.

MASON. In order that there should be no deception, we had Madame La Grange searched.

DONOHUE. I see.

MASON. And while she was out of the room——

DONOHUE. Oh, she left the room?

(ALL *look at* DONOHUE.)

MASON. Yes, and all of the ladies went with her. Then someone suggested that we ask Madame La Grange about some special thing, and Mr. Wales said he was going to ask her to get in communication with Spencer Lee and see if we couldn't find out who killed him.

STANDISH. Most ridiculous thing——

MASON. As soon as she went into her trance, or whatever it was, Spencer Lee's spirit tried to talk to us.

DONOHUE. She began to give you messages from Spencer Lee without knowing that this was what you were trying to get?

MASON (*in triumph*). Exactly. And there's no use in trying to tell me that there's nothing in spiritualism, because now I know better.

DONOHUE. Thank you very much, Mr. Mason. What you've told me is extremely important. I'm anxious to know what was said, because I'm a good deal interested in the Spencer Lee case myself.

(MRS. TRENT *turns and faces door, still sitting in her chair.*)

MASON. Then you think there's something in this spiritualism? I never did until today, but, by Jove, you know you can't explain this any other way.

DONOHUE. Madame La Grange went into a trance. We'll grant that much, anyway. What happened then?

CROSBY. After a few minutes she began talking to us in the voice of a little child.

ROSALIE. That was Laughing Eyes, me spirit control.

DONOHUE. Just what did Laughing Eyes say?

CROSBY. It was all mixed up; none of it very clear. But she seemed to be trying to talk for someone to someone. She kept calling for Ned. Then suddenly she spoke deeply, in a man's voice.

DONOHUE. Did the man's message have any importance? I mean, did it seem to make sense?

CROSBY. It was perfectly coherent, at any rate. I can't give you the exact words, but——

MASON (*interrupting*). I can. He said, "Ned, I want Ned. Why in *hell* don't Ned answer me?"

DONOHUE (ALL *seated in circle except* DONOHUE, *who is standing at lower end of table* R.). And did anyone answer?

CROSBY. Eventually Wales replied.

DONOHUE. I want you all to be extremely careful in what you tell me. I don't want any surmises. In the first place, did the message come for anyone but Mr. Wales?

CROSBY. There was at no time the mention of Wales' name. The calls were always for "Ned."

DONOHUE. I see. Did anyone else answer the calls?

STANDISH. I asked two or three questions, but no attention was paid to them.

DONOHUE. What did Mr. Wales say to all this?

CROSBY. I don't think Mr. Wales spoke at all until the message about saving his life came.

DONOHUE. And after that?

MISS EASTWOOD. There was a regular conversation between them.

CROSBY (MRS. TRENT *puts handkerchief on lips*). Then there was some mention about some letters. I remember, too, that Mr. Wales said, "Are you trying to tell me who killed you?"

DONOHUE. What was the reply to that?

MRS. CROSBY. All we got were the words, "ASK—ask—ask."

CROSBY. And then I said, "Do you know who killed you?"

DONOHUE. Did you get an answer?

CROSBY. Not directly. The message was another cry for "Ned."

DONOHUE. What happened then?

CROSBY. Then Mr. Wales said, "Do you know who killed you?"

DONOHUE (*eagerly*). What answer did he get?

CROSBY. None. The medium began to moan and cry. Then Mr. Wales asked her again and again for the name. He kept crying, "Tell me who killed you. I want the name." He must have asked her two or three times. Then he cried out that he was hurt.

DONOHUE. And then?

CROSBY. That's all.

(*Enter* DUNN *from door* L.)

DUNN. The matron is here now, sir.

DONOHUE. Just a minute. Just one more question, Mr. Crosby. Did you get the impression that if Mr. Wales had not been killed, his question would have been answered?

CROSBY. If you grant that the séance was real, it would be impossible to arrive at any other conclusion.

DONOHUE. It was well established in your mind that Wales was the only person able to get a message?

CROSBY. Yes.

DONOHUE. It follows then that he was killed in order to prevent his question being answered.

CROSBY. That's the impression I got.

DONOHUE. This leads to the conclusion that whoever killed Wales knew who had killed Spencer Lee.

CROSBY (*still seated in circle*). I should think so.

DONOHUE (*front of table R.*). And it is not difficult to surmise that the person who killed Wales was actuated by the strongest of all motives —self-protection. So in all human probability the murderer of Wales was also the murderer of Spencer Lee. You see, ladies and gentlemen, that by the use of a little patience we have come a long way in our investigation. (*There is a long pause.*) I don't wish to put you all through the humiliation of a search. I should like to end this inquiry here and now. (*Breaks a step R. There is another pause.*) No? Then we'll have to go on. (*Moves briskly —below table R.*) There is a police matron in the other room who will search the ladies of the party. Sergeant Dunn will perform a similar duty with the men. Mike, you will take them one at a time. It makes no difference to me in what order they go.

MASON. Well, I've got nothing to conceal. (*He rises and places chair up L., then to door L.*)

ROSALIE. Me neither. (*She rises and crosses down C.*)

DONOHUE. I'd rather you waited for a few minutes, Madame La Grange. (ROSALIE *looks at him sharply.*) Any of the other ladies will do.

MRS. CROSBY. Suppose I set the others a good example? (*Rises.*)

DONOHUE. Thank you very much. (*He looks at the* OTHERS, *where they are still seated.*) And thank you for the great help you've given me. You need not sit there any longer—(MRS. CROSBY *comes down C., then crosses to door L.*)—unless you wish.

(MISS STANDISH *crosses R. back of table R.* MRS. CROSBY, MASON, *and* SERGEANT DUNN *exit L.* DUNN *closes door on his exit.* HELEN *goes up C.* —TRENT *crosses one chair up L. of door L.C., then one chair R. of door L.C., right back of settee C.* MISS ERSKINE *crosses to back of table R.* MRS. TRENT *seated R.C.* WILL *in front of settee C.*)

MISS EASTWOOD (*crossing to* DONOHUE *R.*). Inspector, I think you're perfectly wonderful.

DONOHUE. Oh, we haven't done very much yet, Miss Eastwood. Give the police a little time. (*He turns and crosses to L.C. L. with an abrupt change of tone.*) Madame La Grange, there's a question I wish to ask you.

ROSALIE (*coming down to L.C.*). Anythin' at all, sor.

DONOHUE (*L.C.*). When Mr. Wales asked you for the name, why didn't you answer him?

ROSALIE. I don't know, sor. I was in a trance. (*Down L.*)

DONOHUE. Then you didn't hear the question?

ROSALIE. How could I?

DONOHUE. I didn't ask you that. I want to know why you didn't answer him.

ROSALIE. I've already told you, I was in a trance. I didn't know what was going on.

DONOHUE. Why didn't you tell the name that you had agreed with Wales you would tell?

ROSALIE (*L.C., astonished*). Agreed?

DONOHUE. You heard what I said. (*There is a pause.*) Well, why didn't you carry out your part of the bargain? (CROSBY *crosses back of settee to C., front of settee.*) Why didn't you give him the name as you'd planned?

ROSALIE. I don't know what ye mean.

DONOHUE. My words are perfectly plain. I asked you why you didn't carry out your part of the bargain?

ROSALIE. There wasn't any bargain!

DONOHUE. Your whole séance was a fake. (*Slight movement from* OTHERS.) It was not only planned but rehearsed between you and Wales. He thought that a woman had killed his friend. He told you about it, and asked your help to discover the murderer.

ROSALIE. Sure, I don't know what ye're talking about at all.

DONOHUE (*ignoring her reply*). Every detail of this séance was planned. When he asked you the name you were to tell him the name of a woman.

(MRS. TRENT *crosses up R. and joins* TRENT *and* MISS ERSKINE *at table R.*)

ROSALIE. So help me, Inspector, I never heard a word of this before.

DONOHUE. Not a word?

ROSALIE. So help me, not a word.

DONOHUE (*L.C. Taking paper out of the inside pocket of his coat, and reading aloud*). "What do you want? Answer. Don't forget the swimming pool. Don't ever forget the swimming pool. Do you mean the time he went in after me when we were little boys? Spencer Lee says he can't rest." And so on and so on, down to—"Do you know who killed you?" (*He turns to the* OTHERS.) The answer to that should have been "yes." What did she say?

CROSBY (*in front of table R.*). She didn't answer that question.

DONOHUE (*he looks at paper again. L.C.*). The next question is, "Can you tell the name?" And then she was to have told that woman's name. Just the first name. Mr. Crosby, what did she reply to that question?

CROSBY. She moaned and cried.

DONOHUE. What did she say after that?

CROSBY. Nothing. She moaned again and came out of so-called trance.

DONOHUE. Why didn't you do as you agreed?

ROSALIE (*down L.C.L. side of* DONOHUE. *Stonily*). I don't know what you're talking about.

DONOHUE. The police know that some woman killed Spencer Lee. Something was taken from the inside pocket of his vest. We think it was a package of letters. This woman left traces. We have her fingerprints—many of them. Eventually we'll find her. For three or four weeks Mr. Wales has been working among the people who knew Lee. His theory was that this woman wanted to get back her letters—in fact, did get them back. He felt reasonably sure that he had found the woman. That one of you ladies here tonight is probably the woman we are hunting. He thought that he could play on her superstitious fears, and that when her name seemingly came from the spirit of the dead man she would confess. He told Madame La Grange the name, explained to her just what he wanted, and together he and I worked out the exact wording of the messages that were supposed to come from Spencer Lee's spirit. (*He turns suddenly to* ROSALIE, *who is down L.C.*) You agreed to all this; why didn't you speak the name?

ROSALIE. I don't know anything about it. He—he must have forgotten to tell it to me.

DONOHUE. Oh, no, he didn't.

(MISS EASTWOOD *down in front of table R.*)

ROSALIE (*with great decision*). There was no name. He didn't tell me any name.

DONOHUE. My good woman, you mustn't take me for a fool. You agreed to use a certain name; you came here for that purpose, and then after you got here something happened to make you change your plans. Something unexpected happened. (*He stops for a moment—turns to* MISS EASTWOOD.) Miss Eastwood, what did you say was your first name?

MISS EASTWOOD. Mary.

DONOHUE (*to* MISS ERSKINE). And yours?

MISS ERSKINE (*back of table R.*). Elizabeth.

DONOHUE. Yours?

MISS STANDISH. Grace.

DONOHUE. Mr. Crosby, your wife's given name is——

CROSBY. Alicia.

DONOHUE. Mrs. Trent?

MRS. TRENT (*R.C.*). Helen.

DONOHUE. Miss O'Neill?

HELEN (*up C.*). Helen. (*There is a long pause.*)

DONOHUE (L.C. WILL *comes to* HELEN C.). Helen, I see. So there are two Helens. Two Helens. (*He *stands looking first at one and then at the other of the two women.*) Mr. Crosby, when Madame La Grange first came tonight did she show any surprise at seeing any of the people here?

CROSBY (*R.C.*). Not that I noticed.

MISS EASTWOOD (*below table R.*). Oh, yes, she did. Miss O'Neill wasn't in the room when she arrived. Later, when she came in, the old woman seemed upset. She said something to her that none of us could hear. Then I remember she argued with Mr. Wales and said she didn't feel like having a séance.

DONOHUE. Now we're getting it. (WILL *stands R. of* MISS O'NEILL *up C.*) Everything was going along smoothly until Miss O'Neill came in. The extra Helen. (*He turns to* CROSBY.) Mr. Crosby, your daughter was in the room when Madame La Grange came in?

CROSBY. Yes.

DONOHUE. You noticed nothing unusual in this woman's manner?

CROSBY. I'd never seen her before.

DONOHUE. I mean she did nothing to attract your attention; the fact that Helen Trent was in the room made no impression on her?

CROSBY. Seemingly not.

DONOHUE. Then Helen O'Neill came in. (*Goes up to* HELEN C., *then crosses to* ROSALIE L. *He turns sharply to* ROSALIE *down L.*) Rosalie La Grange, what's that girl to you?

ROSALIE. Nothin' at all.

DONOHUE (*C.*). Nothing at all! Then why did you try to deceive me as to where she sat? Why did you place her so that I would not know she was sitting next to Mr. Wales when he was stabbed?

ROSALIE. It was just a mistake. I didn't go for to do it.

DONOHUE. I'm afraid that won't do. It's perfectly apparent that the name you were to speak was—Helen. (*He turns to* ROSALIE L.) What's the use of lying to me? You've tried your best to shield this girl. I want to know why.

ROSALIE. There's no reason. I never saw the young lady before in all my life.

DONOHUE. What's that girl to you?

ROSALIE. Nothin', nothin' at all——

DONOHUE (*starts to* ROSALIE). *Damn you*, you old harridan, you come across——

MISS O'NEILL (*springing forward from up R.C. down to L., throwing* DONOHUE *up stage*). Let my mother alone, let my mother alone! (*Then she goes to* ROSALIE, *puts arms around her. Pause.* ROSALIE WEEPS.)

DONOHUE (*very quietly*). I thought perhaps I'd get it that way.

HELEN O'NEILL (*getting L. side of* ROSALIE). There, there, dear, it's all right, it's all right.

DONOHUE (*with a grim smile, coming down C.*). Of course it's all right! We've got the fingerprints and——

WILL (*interrupting him—crosses down to C.*). If you think for one minute I'm going to let you——

CROSBY. My son, wait—(*grabbing him and pinning down his arms to sides C.*)—think what——

WILL. Think nothing. (*He shakes himself free and goes to* DONOHUE *L.C.*) That's the girl I love, and I'll be *damned* if I let you take her fingerprints.

DONOHUE. Young man, don't be a fool. I'm sorry, but it's too clear.

ROSALIE (*breaking away from her daughter to* DONOHUE *C. of L.C.*). Clear! Glory be to God, how can it be clear? Inspector, you're never goin' to accuse me little girl of a thing like that?

DONOHUE (*C.*). She was next to him; she had only to free one hand, and strike and then take his hand again!

ROSALIE. There was something else she had to do before she could ever do that. She had to have murder in her heart.

DONOHUE (*C.*). Well?

ROSALIE (*turns suddenly, seizes her daughter, who is L. of* DONOHUE, *by the hand, turns her to him.* ROSALIE *stays between* DONOHUE *and* HELEN). Look at her. Look in the eyes of her, at the face of her. Is there murder there? Man, man, haven't ye got eyes in yer head?

(DUNN *enters from L.*)

DUNN. It's not on either of them.

DONOHUE. I know where it is. Tell the matron she'll find the knife on this girl.

ROSALIE (*to* DONOHUE *C.*). Inspector, for Gawd's sake, don't do it! I'll tell you anything I know, only keep your hands off me little girl. I did come here like you say, and whin I seen me own child I lost me head. I'm a poor old woman that ain't got any sense. I tried to save her and I only made matters worse. You've looked at her, the poor young thing that wouldn't harm a fly, and you think she could do a thing like that?

DONOHUE. Yes.

ROSALIE (*still crying bitterly*). Thin Tim Donohue, you're a damn fool, and God helpin' me, I'll prove ut.

CURTAIN

ACT THREE

SCENE—*The eight small chairs that were brought on in the first act are taken off stage. The big armchair that* ROSALIE *sat in has been taken up the left corner of set. Table has been moved up and on stage about a foot. The knife that is to fall on given cue has been placed in slot in ceiling. The window blind is pulled down; the curtains on window are opened. Armchair back of table R. Chair below table R. Chair above table R. Settee has been moved down stage C. about a foot. Shelf back of settee has been fixed for* WALES *to lie on. Console table back in its original position, right end of settee C. Chair with upholstered seat put back to L. side of fireplace. Line hung off stage back of fireplace for policeman's entrance. Bright amber lights in entrance down L. Lamps with blue mediums at window lit. Spot outside of window R. ready for cue. Lights on set out. Door down L. which is open.*
Be sure to clear table R.C. for knife.
DISCOVERED—ROSALIE *by table over R.*

ROSALIE. Father in Heaven, help me. Me Nelly's in trouble, terrible trouble, and there ain't anywan to help her but me. She's a good girl. You know all things, you know she's a good girl. Show me the way. Sure, I been a fakir all my life. I've tricked 'em and fooled 'em, but honest, I never meant to harm a soul, I never knowingly done harm to anywan. And there is a power. It's come to me before, a way of knowin', that I couldn't understand. I felt it, and I showed it. Oh, God, give it to me again. Do this for my little girl, for the sake of your Son. Amen.

(*Turns and goes up stage to the window at R. She pulls up the shade and raises the window. The light comes up from the street lamp, throwing out her figure in strong silhouette and showing a square patch of light on the ceiling. In the center of this patch, sticking*

point up in the heavy wooden paneling, can be seen the knife. ROSALIE *stands for a few moments looking out at the night.* DONOHUE *enters down L. As he does so, he turns on the lights from the switch below the door down L. Lights in room on. Spot outside of window—out.*)

DONOHUE (*crosses to L.C.*). Who turned off the lights?

ROSALIE (*at window R.*). I did, sor

DONOHUE. Why?

ROSALIE. I was prayin'. (*Coming to above table R.*)

DONOHUE. Praying? What for?

ROSALIE. Guidance.

DONOHUE (*with a laugh*). I hope you get it.

ROSALIE (*with conviction*). I will, sor, I will. (*She starts toward the* door L.) I'll be joinin' the others now.

DONOHUE. I think you'd better wait. (*Calls off L.*) Mike. (ROSALIE C.)

(DUNN *enters from L.*)

DUNN. Yes, Inspector?

DONOHUE. Did Madame La Grange see you as she came in here?

DUNN (*down L.*). No, sir. I followed your instructions and kept out of sight.

DONOHUE. How long has she been here? (L.C.)

DUNN. About ten minutes.

DONOHUE. Time enough for her to find what we couldn't.

DUNN. I'll bet she's got it.

DONOHUE. Take her to Mrs. Mac-Pherson. She's not to go near anyone or speak to anyone. Tell Mrs. Mac to search her. (*He turns to* ROSALIE, *who is C.*) Unless, of course, you want to give up that knife now.

ROSALIE. I've got no knife, and I've been searched once.

DONOHUE (L.C.). Exactly, and then you were allowed to come back into this room. We're rather anxious to see what you've found while you were in here. Well?

ROSALIE. I found nothing that ud be any good to you.

DONOHUE. I'm the best judge of that. What was it you found?

ROSALIE. A sort of comfort, sor. A feelin' that the innocent would come to no harm.

DONOHUE (*dryly*). Take her to Mrs. MacPherson. Come back as soon as you turn her over to the matron.

DUNN. Yes, Inspector. Come on—come on, you.

ROSALIE (*crossing L.*). I'm coming!

(*They exit. He stands looking after them for count of five when* DUNN *re-enters.*)

DUNN (*above door L.*). Mrs. Mac's got her.

DONOHUE (*to* DUNN). She turned out that light. I wonder why? What did she want in the dark?

(*He goes over toward the light switch at L. and puts out his hand. He stops suddenly as his attention is attracted by a policeman coming feet foremost down the chimney.* DONO-HUE *gives a little start and then comes L.C. The policeman jumps down all the way in fireplace, and comes into the room to console table L. end of settee. His uniform is covered with soot, and so are his face and hands.* DUNN *goes down L. below door.*)

DUNN. I sent him to see if they'd hidden that knife up there.

DONOHUE. Good. (*To* POLICEMAN.) Find anything?

POLICEMAN. Nothing but dirt. Who pays for this uniform?

DONOHUE. You don't, anyway. Could you hear anything while you were up there?

POLICEMAN. Not a thing.

DONOHUE. You are sure?

POLICEMAN. Certain.

DONOHUE. Go take a bath.

POLICEMAN. 'Tain't Saturday. (*He exits at* L. DONOHUE *crosses* R. *Pause.*)

DUNN (*down* L. *After a pause*). Don't it beat *hell?*

DONOHUE. Why?

DUNN. That knife couldn't have flew away.

DONOHUE (*coming* C.). We'll find it eventually. It's in this room somewhere.

DUNN. No, sir, it ain't.

DONOHUE. Where have you looked?

DUNN. Everywhere.

DONOHUE. Not hidden in the furniture?

DUNN. I'll gamble it ain't. Took up all the rugs, shook 'em. Dug through the upholstery in the furniture, looked back of mat on the wall. It's not in the bric-a-brac or whatever these swells call their jugs.

(DONOHUE *crosses to table* R.)

DONOHUE (R.C.). Unless we find it on the old woman, it's still in this room.

DUNN. I suppose you noticed that she opened the window?

DONOHUE (*upper end of table* R.). Yes, I noticed that. Mike, you've the makings of a great detective.

DUNN. I'm a darned good detective now.

(DONOHUE *goes to window at* R. *and calls out.*)

DONOHUE. Say, Doolan! See anything?

DOOLAN (*outside window* R.). An old woman put up the window just now. She stood there a while looking up in the air—(*pause*)—watching the stars, I guess.

DONOHUE. Have anything in her hand?

DOOLAN. No, sir. The light from this lamp was shinin' right on her. I could see everything.

DONOHUE. Throw anything out of the window?

DOOLAN. No, Inspector.

DONOHUE. All right. You're to arrest anyone leaving the house.

DOOLAN. I gotcha.

(DONOHUE *comes below table* R., *turns to* DUNN. *Crosses to* L.C.)

DONOHUE. We'll find the knife eventually. We've got to. Get me Mr. Crosby and the O'Neill girl— that's the order I want to see them in here.

(DUNN *exits* L. DONOHUE *crosses up* R. *end of settee to chest up* R., *starts to cross* L. *below settee.* CROSBY

closes door, enters down L. DONO-
HUE *comes down to C.—R. end of
settee.*)

CROSBY (*to L.C.*). Your man told
me to come here.

DONOHUE. Yes. Sorry to have to give
orders in your house. If you don't
like it I can take everyone down to
Police Headquarters. You know
what will happen—what the newspapers will do if I take all these
ladies and gentlemen downtown. In
the end this way will be the best
for you and your friends. Well, how
about it?

CROSBY (*L.C.*). Thank you. I think
you'd better regard this house as
your own for the present.

DONOHUE (*C.*). All right. If you
don't mind I'll use this room as a
headquarters for the present.

CROSBY. I have already told you to
use this house as your own.

DONOHUE. Thank you. Good evening.

CROSBY (*with a laugh*). I'm dismissed?

DONOHUE. You're dismissed. (CROSBY
walks toward door L.) Why did
Wales object to the engagement of
your son and Helen O'Neill?

CROSBY (*turns to* DONOHUE). Who
told you that? (*R. a few steps.*)

DONOHUE. It doesn't matter. I know
that he did. Why?

CROSBY. I can't talk about it. (*Turns
front.*)

DONOHUE (*C.*). All right. You're the
best judge of that. Only I'm attach-
ing a great deal of importance to
this fact. If I'm unduly emphasizing
its value, don't you think you'd better set me straight about it?

CROSBY. What possible bearing can
it have on——

DONOHUE. Motive, my dear sir, motive.

CROSBY. Come, now—you can't
think that this girl killed Wales because she heard him ask us to wait
before we sanctioned her engagement to my son.

DONOHUE. She did hear Mr. Wales
make that objection? That's just
what I wanted to know.

CROSBY (*L.*). I think I'd better send
for my lawyer.

DONOHUE (*C.*). Well, you can do as
you like about that. Frankly, I don't
understand your attitude at all. I
can appreciate your desire to spare
your son all the unhappiness that
you can. But if this young woman
killed Wales and Lee, the sooner we
find it out the better for you and
your family.

CROSBY. Oddly enough, I was thinking only of Miss O'Neill at the moment.

DONOHUE. You'd better think of
yourself and your family first.
(*Crosses R. a few steps.*)

CROSBY. That's for me to decide, sir.
I certainly am not going to allow
that child to be bullied and badgered
in the usual police fashion. (*Crosses
R. a step.*)

DONOHUE. You're going to do as you are told, sir. If you warn that girl, if you caution her in any way, I'll drag every one of you downtown. You and your wife and your son and the girl and all your friends. Be reasonable, Mr. Crosby. If the girl is innocent, telling me the truth won't hurt her. If she's guilty, and I think she is, by God, I'm going to drag the truth out of her and her mother. (*Knock on the door down L.*) Come in.

HELEN (*enters L.*). You wanted me?

DONOHUE. Yes, come in. Sit down, please. (*Indicating table below R.* HELEN *sits.* CROSBY *starts R.*)

CROSBY. Helen.

DONOHUE. What you are planning to do, Mr. Crosby, will only make matters worse, I promise you that. (*After a moment's pause* CROSBY *exits at L. and leaves door open.* DONOHUE *turns, closes door and turns sharply to* HELEN—*crosses to table R.*) Now then, young woman, let's hear what you've got to say.

HELEN. Nothing.

DONOHUE (*C.*). Nothing. I don't suppose it's necessary for me to tell you that you're under grave suspicion.

HELEN. No, I realize that.

DONOHUE. Now the best way to help yourself if you're innocent is to be quite frank with me. (*She simply looks at him, but does not speak.*) Well?

HELEN. I've already told you that there is nothing that I can say.

DONOHUE. Someone has advised you not to answer me. Who was it? (*There is a pause.*) You'd better tell me. (*Crosses R.C.*)

HELEN. I am not going to answer any of your questions.

DONOHUE. I told you that if you were innocent, nothing that you could say would hurt you. If you're guilty—well, that's a different matter.

HELEN. You know that I didn't do it.

DONOHUE (*in front of table R.*). Well, there you are. Why not answer my questions, then? The sooner we find out who is guilty the sooner you'll be freed from suspicion. You see that, don't you?

HELEN. Yes.

DONOHUE (*brings chair and sits in front of table R.*). Now we're getting along. How well did you know Spencer Lee? (HELEN *does not answer him—looking front.*) You'd better make up your mind to talk. Do you hear? (HELEN *does not speak. Losing his temper.*) Why, you little fool, do you think you can fight me? (*He turns sharply to face her, turning his back on the door at L.*) You were the last person to see Spencer Lee alive. Yes, and you saw him dead too. You heard Wales threaten to tell these fine people what he knew about you; you knew he'd prevent your marriage to this young millionaire, and then—(ROSALIE *enters quietly from L. and stands for a moment watching them*)—when your chance came in the dark, you killed him. Now then, you come across with the truth.

ROSALIE. She'll come across with nothin'. (*Crosses R. to table.* DONOHUE *rises and stands by table R.C.* HELEN *rises.*) Ye said she was the wan that did ut and ye'd find the knife on her. Well, ye didn't, did ye? Ye think she's the wan that killed Spencer Lee?

DONOHUE. Yes.

ROSALIE. Well, she ain't. Ye say ye got the fingerprints of the girl that was in his rooms—now take Nelly's, then. Take hers and put 'em alongside of the others, bad cess to you, and then ye'll see. I dare ye to do that.

HELEN (*with a cry*). Mother! (*She stops suddenly.*)

DONOHUE. What were you going to say?

HELEN. Nothing. (*She creeps over to R. side of her mother.* ROSALIE *puts her arms about the girl.*)

(DUNN *enters with box and envelope.*)

DONOHUE. That's very wise of you.

DUNN. Got it, Inspector. (*Crosses to C.*)

DONOHUE (*down R.*). Do they compare?

DUNN. To a T.

(ROSALIE *C.,* HELEN *down R.* DONOHUE *in front of table between* HELEN *and* ROSALIE.)

DONOHUE. All right. Let me have 'em. Now ask Mr. Crosby and his son to come here at once. (DUNN *turns and exits at L.* DONOHUE *up C., crosses to back of table R.*) I already have your daughter's finger prints, Madame La Grange.

ROSALIE. Have ye, now? It's smart ye are.

(HELEN *crosses to* ROSALIE *R.C.* ROSALIE *swings* HELEN *L. of her. When* DONOHUE *opens box back of table,* CROSBY *and* WILL *enter from L., accompanied by* DUNN.)

DONOHUE. That's all, Mike. (DUNN *exits at L., closes door down L.* CROSBY *L. of* HELEN. WILL *L. of* CROSBY.) Mr. Crosby, I told you that I'd settle this case in a few minutes. The end has come sooner than I thought. I am now ready to make an arrest. I have sent for you and your son because—— (*He suddenly turns toward* HELEN.) This is the woman we have been hunting.

ROSALIE. That's a lie! (*R. end of settee—*WILL *to* HELEN.)

DONOHUE (*picking up cup and holding it out toward them*). Here is the cup—(CROSBY *crosses down R. to below table—moves chair over R.*)—which we took from Spencer Lee's rooms. These are the fingerprints of the woman who used it. (*Ignoring* CROSBY *for the moment.*) Here is the saucer that she used. More fingerprints. A few minutes ago I sent this young woman a note. The man who gave it to her wore gloves. So did I when I addressed the envelope. Hers are the only naked hands that have touched it. (*He picks up the envelope gingerly by one corner, and holds it outward to them.*) They are unquestionably Helen

O'Neill's fingerprints. (HELEN *in* WILL'S *arms.* DONOHUE *puts down the envelope. Then he picks up the cup and points to the fingermarks on it.*) And so, Mr. Crosby, are these. There can be no doubt about it. There is never any doubt about this method of identification. In twenty years there has never been one mistake. We now have what we've been hunting for. The woman who went to Spencer Lee's rooms. (DONOHUE *steps back with a little gesture of triumph.* CROSBY *stands staring at the girl.* ROSALIE *comes to R. of* HELEN, *turns to her.*)

ROSALIE (*C.*). Look at me, me dear. Look at your old mother. (*She takes* HELEN'S *face in her hands and looks at her closely. Then, with a little cry of contentment, stands R. of* HELEN. ROSALIE *and* HELEN *back up to settee.*) Now, me-dear, ye mustn't be frightened. Look up, child. Why don't ye say somethin'?

HELEN. I can't. (*Sits on settee.*)

(DONOHUE *gives a short laugh.*)

DONOHUE. What can she say?

WILL (*going to her*). Dear, tell him it's a lie.

CROSBY (*crosses to* HELEN, *at settee*). Wait. Let me talk to her. (CROSBY *comes over to* HELEN *and sits beside her on the sofa, R. side.* WILL *at settee L. end.*) My dear, you understand that none of us believe—what the inspector wants us to believe. We know that you have never done anything—that you are no more guilty of this atrocious crime than I am. We all want to help you. You understand that, don't you?

HELEN. Yes.

WILL. I won't have this.

CROSBY. I'm afraid you must, son. (*He turns again to* HELEN.) We want to help you, so, my dear, you must be perfectly frank with us. Inspector Donohue says he can prove that you went to that man's rooms. Is that true?

HELEN (*slowly and reluctantly*). Yes.

(DONOHUE *gives short laugh. Sits back of table R.*)

ROSALIE. An' what if she did? She had a good errant. What did ye go for, darlin'?

HELEN. I can't tell you.

WILL. Dear, you must tell us. (*She looks at him suddenly. He comes over and kneels beside her and talks to her as if to a little child.*) My dear, it isn't that we don't trust you. Surely you know how we all love you. But we must know the truth— (*strong*)—because we have to show *him* how wrong he is.

DONOHUE (*seated back of table R.*). Yes, and I'm waiting to be shown.

WILL (*kneeling L. of* HELEN *by settee*). Why did you go to Spencer Lee?

HELEN (*sitting on settee*). You mustn't ask me that. I can't tell you.

CROSBY (*still on settee*). But if you don't tell us, how can we help you?

HELEN. I didn't do anything. I didn't do anything.

CROSBY. We know that, my child. But why did you go? (HELEN *does not answer.*) Did you know Spencer Lee?

WILL. Of course she didn't.

DONOHUE (*seated back of table R.*). Why don't she speak for herself?

WILL. Because I'll speak for her.

CROSBY. Can't you answer even that question?

(HELEN *shakes her head and makes a despairing gesture.*)

WILL. But, dear, don't you see what they'll think? Helen, you must tell me.

HELEN. Could I speak to Mother alone? (*Rises.*)

DONOHUE. You cannot.

(CROSBY *and* WILL *rise, cross to C.* CROSBY *crosses to L. end of settee.*)

ROSALIE (*R. end of settee*). Where's the harm in that? Sure, a child's the right to talk to her own mother any time she wants.

DONOHUE. Anything you wish to say, you can say in front of me.

ROSALIE (*coming to* HELEN *C.*). Sure, darlin', ye needn't mind the nice inspector. Don't I well know that there was never anything in your mind that ye couldn't say before all the world? (*There is a pause.*) Tell yer old mother, me dear.

(CROSBY *C.* WILL *standing below him C.*)

HELEN (*beginning to cry*). I can't. I can't.

ROSALIE (*C.*). Stop! There's been cryin' enough. I lost me head through that and me fears. Stop cryin' or I'll give ye what for. (*She, too, begins to cry and takes her daughter in her arms again.*) There, there, me dear. Sure, yer old mother ain't going to let anyone hurt ye. Not anyone at all. (*They cry together for a moment and then* ROSALIE *gets her self-control back. She blows her nose vigorously.*) We'll both be the better for that. Now then, tell me.

HELEN. Mother, I can't.

ROSALIE (*R.C.*). Who did ye promise ye wouldn't?

HELEN (*surprised*). Why, how did you——

ROSALIE. She's shieldin' someone.

HELEN. No. No.

ROSALIE. And that's the first lie ye ever told, and I know it. I want to know who ye're shieldin'? (HELEN *does not answer.* ROSALIE *suddenly turns to* WILL.) Is she your girl?

WILL. Yes. (*L.C.*)

ROSALIE. Then make her tell.

WILL (*to* HELEN *C.*). Nell, dear, you must——

HELEN. Billy, I can't.

CROSBY (*drops down L. of group*). My dear, even if you're protecting someone else, I think you ought to tell us.

HELEN (*with a sudden outburst*). Why are you all against me? Why are you all trying to make me break my—— (*To R. end of settee.* WILL *comes to her.* CROSBY *L.C.*)

ROSALIE (*interrupting* HELEN, *coming to R.C.*). Break yer word, is ut? Ye should not. Sure, there never was an O'Neill in the world that was an informer. Ye needn't tell. Sure, I know it meself now. 'Tis blind I've been. (*She turns suddenly on the inspector—to down table R. above him.*) Ye're the one that found out there was two Helens. The extra Helen, says you. Well, send for the other Helen and ask her.

HELEN. Mother, stop!

ROSALIE. Stop, is ut? Sure, I will not.

CROSBY (*C.*). Wait, please. Is it my daughter you're protecting? (HELEN *does not answer.*) Because if it is— much as we love her, my dear, we can't accept that sacrifice from you. I'm her father, and you must tell me the truth. Did my daughter send you? (*There is a long pause.*) Did you go for my daughter?

HELEN (*slowly*). Yes.

ROSALIE. I knew ut. (*Above table R.*)

CROSBY. My daughter sent you. What for?

HELEN (*R.C.*). Some letters.

WILL (*in front of settee C.*). Why didn't she go herself?

HELEN. She was afraid.

DONOHUE (*still seated back of table R.*). Well, go on. (HELEN *does not speak.*)

WILL (*R.C.*). Tell him, dear, it's all right.

HELEN. I don't know what to say.

DONOHUE. Why not tell the truth? (*Rises to chair below table R.*)

ROSALIE. Tell the inspector what happened, dearie. (*Putting* HELEN *in chair front of table R.*)

HELEN. Nothing happened. That's the funny part of it. The minute Mr. Lee understood that I knew about the letters, everything was changed. I said that unless he gave them to me I'd tell Mr. Crosby about them. He seemed terribly upset. He said he hadn't meant to frighten Helen. That he loved her, and was desperate. I thought it was a funny kind of love, but I didn't tell him that. Then he gave me the letters.

DONOHUE. Was this before or after you had tea with him?

HELEN. Before.

DONOHUE. Go on. He gave you the letters.

HELEN (*seated in front of table R.*). Yes. And he seemed terribly unhappy. He begged me to stay and talk to him for a few minutes, and I did. He asked me to have some tea with him, and I did that too.

DONOHUE. How charming! What did you do after tea?

(ROSALIE *back of chair, front of table.*)

HELEN. I came home and gave Helen her letters.

DONOHUE. And that's all?

HELEN. That's all. (*Saucy.*)

DONOHUE. Why did you do this?

HELEN (*seated front of table R.*). She's Billy's sister.

DONOHUE. My compliments, young woman. That was beautifully done. And she looks so innocent too.

WILL. You don't believe—— (*C.*)

DONOHUE. Not a word of it. Not one word. (*Rises.*)

ROSALIE. And why not?

DONOHUE. That I *don't* is sufficient. Her story is preposterous. Your daughter's——

WILL. It's the truth.

DONOHUE. Do you expect me to believe for a minute that a man like Lee would threaten your daughter, and then when a total stranger comes to him and asks for the letters, give them up without a word? Why, no jury in the world would believe your story.

WILL. Jury? You're not going to arrest her?

DONOHUE. She is arrested.

ROSALIE. Ye got no proof.

DONOHUE (*below table R.*). All the proof that I need. If she was innocent, why didn't she tell me all this when I first questioned her? Why did she wait until she knew that I had proof—that she had been in Spencer Lee's rooms?

WILL. She was protecting my sister.

DONOHUE. Women don't hang together like that.

ROSALIE (*upper end of table R.*). Sure they do. The poor creatures.

DONOHUE (*down R.*). They do not. I know them. (*He turns to* WILL.) She wasn't protecting your sister. She was protecting herself. She went for the letters, of course; and they had tea before she asked for them, not afterward.

CROSBY (*R.C. to L. of* WILL). How do you know that?

DONOHUE. She couldn't take tea with a man she's just killed.

WILL. Why, *damn* you—— (*Starts R.*)

CROSBY (*grabbing* WILL *by shoulders*). Billy!

WILL (*breaks up stage a few steps, then down stage again*). I'm sorry. I didn't mean to lose my temper. I suppose we've got to take this thing calmly. Inspector, you honestly believe that Nelly killed this man?

DONOHUE. Yes.

WILL. Why should she?

DONOHUE. She was engaged to you— he had compromising letters she had written to him—he was threatening her with exposure—she went to get her letters. They had tea together—she's admitted that, after we proved it, and then when he wouldn't give up her letters, she killed him. So much for the first murder. (*Turns away.*) Now for the second: she was sitting next to Wales; he had already threatened her with exposure; in another minute the medium would have told her name as that of the person who had been at Spencer Lee's rooms. She pulled her hand away from his, struck, and took his hand again. (*There is a pause.*) Young man, you'll have a hard time tearing apart that chain of evidence.

ROSALIE. Barrin' the fact that she niver wrote the man a letter in her loife, 'tis a grand case ye got.

WILL (*down C. a step.* CROSBY *goes above* WILL *C.*). Of course. Dad, we've lost our brains. She didn't go for her own letters. (WILL *turns to the* INSPECTOR.) You were talking of juries. Do you think any jury will believe that a young girl would kill a man to get back another woman's letters for her? (*He starts toward door L.*)

CROSBY. Where are you going?

WILL. To get my sister.

DONOHUE. Wait. (WILL *stops.*) I'll send for Mrs. Trent.

WILL (*crosses L.C.*). But I want to ask her——

DONOHUE (*interrupts him*). I'll ask my own questions. If you want to help this investigation, you might call Sergeant Dunn for me.

(WILL *opens door at L.*)

WILL (*crosses to C.*). Sergeant Dunn, the inspector wants you. (*He turns back to the girl and* DUNN *enters L.*)

DONOHUE. Ask Mrs. Trent to come here. (DUNN *exits at L.* ROSALIE *R. end of settee.* HELEN *in chair in front of table R.* WILL *C.* CROSBY *walks up L., then back to L.C.* DONOHUE *below the table, looking at them with a grim smile. After a pause of ten counts* MRS. TRENT *and* TRENT *enter from L., followed by* DUNN, *who stands below the door.*) I sent for Mrs. Trent.

TRENT. I know that. What do you want to see her about? (*L.C.*)

DONOHUE. Mrs. Trent, did you ask this girl to go to Spencer Lee's rooms to get letters you had written to him?

TRENT (*L. of* MRS. TRENT). Did she what?

DONOHUE. Did you, Mrs. Trent?

MRS. TRENT (*L.C.*). Certainly not.

HELEN. Why—— (*Rises from chair in front of table R.*)

DONOHUE (*sternly*). Keep still, you. (*To* MRS. TRENT.) Are you sure?

TRENT (*L. of* MRS. TRENT). Of course she's sure.

DONOHUE. Mr. Trent, you must stop these interruptions. (*To* MRS. TRENT.) Will you please answer my question?

MRS. TRENT. I never wrote a letter to Spencer Lee in my life. (*She sud-*

denly turns to HELEN.) How dare you say I sent you there?

HELEN. You did! You did! (*Front of table.*)

MRS. TRENT (*down L.C.*). I don't know what she's told you, Inspector, but——

DONOHUE. Never mind what she told me. I want to be very sure of this. You did not ask this girl to go to Spencer Lee's rooms?

MRS. TRENT. No.

DONOHUE (*down R.*). He had no letters of yours?

MRS. TRENT (*L.C.*). No.

DONOHUE. Do you know whether this girl had written to him?

MRS. TRENT. I don't know anything about it.

WILL (*coming L. of* MRS. TRENT. CROSBY *to* C.). But Nell didn't know Lee, and Helen, you did.

DONOHUE (*still down R.*). How about that, Mrs. Trent?

MRS. TRENT. I hadn't seen Mr. Lee in two or three years. He used to come here a good deal. He wanted to marry me, but I didn't like him. And I certainly never wrote him letters of any sort. That is all I can tell you.

DONOHUE. Thank you very much. That is all that I want to know.

WILL (*turning on his sister*). You're lying to save yourself. You've got to tell the truth.

TRENT. She is telling you the truth.

WILL. She's not.

CROSBY (*after a pause, putting his hand on his son's shoulder*). I'm sorry, Billy.

(WILL *goes up to settee C., sits.* CROSBY *looks coldly at* HELEN *and turns to his daughter.*)

MRS. TRENT. Father, you know that——

CROSBY. Yes, dear—I know. Inspector, do you want us any more?

DONOHUE. Not any more, thank you——

CROSBY. Come then, children—— (*He exits with* MR. *and* MRS. TRENT *down L.* HELEN *still in front of table R.*)

DONOHUE (*as the door closes. Crosses L. to L.C.*). Mike, take her downtown.

ROSALIE (*C.*). I wouldn't if I was you. Inspector, I know who done it. (WILL *rises.*)

DONOHUE (*turning to* ROSALIE C.). You know—— Who was it?

ROSALIE. I can't tell you yet. (DONOHUE *laughs.* WILL R.C. *crosses to* HELEN.) But I will. I will!

DONOHUE. Tellin's not enough. There's just one thing that will convince me that she didn't kill Spencer Lee.

WILL (*down R.*). What, Inspector. what?

DONOHUE. The confession of the one who did. (*He turns to* ROSALIE.) Bring me that and I'll set your daughter free.

ROSALIE (*C.*). Inspector, give me a chance. Don't arrest me little girl. Give me time. I know who done it and I'll get ye what ye want.

DONOHUE (*L.C.*). Nonsense.

ROSALIE (*crosses L. to* INSPECTOR). Give me an hour, sor, keep them all here an hour more.

(WILL *crosses down R. to* HELEN.)

DONOHUE. No.

WILL (WILL *and* HELEN *in front of table R.*). Give her a chance. We're all here—no one will get away. What difference will a few minutes make?

(*There is a pause.* DONOHUE *takes out his watch and looks at it.*)

DONOHUE. I'll give her ten minutes, Mike. Tell Doolan again to arrest anyone trying to leave the house and get on the front door yourself and stay there until I tell you. (DUNN *turns and exits at L.*) You've got just ten minutes. (*He follows* DUNN *off L.*)

ROSALIE. Ten minutes. Ten minutes. (WILL *crosses to door L. and closes door.*)

WILL (*L.C.*). Why didn't you *tell* who did it?

ROSALIE (*C.*). How could I? Sure, I got no idea in the world. But I'm goin' to find out. I'm goin' to find out.

HELEN (*R.C.*). But how, Mother, how? (HELEN *starts L.*)

ROSALIE. Call them back. Make them all come, too. I want them all. (HELEN *runs off L.*) Sir, run down in the hall. Do you know which is Mr. Wales's overcoat?

WILL. Yes, I think so.

ROSALIE. See if you can find me a glove or something of his—and hurry. (WILL *runs off L.* ROSALIE *stands in thought for a moment—puts chair C. facing up stage.* WILL *runs on again and hands her a glove.*) Did you get it?

WILL (*L.C.*). What are you going to do?

ROSALIE (*L.C.*). Trick 'em. Lie to 'em. It's for Nelly. Do you blame me?

WILL. What can I do to help?

ROSALIE. Glory be! It's a man after me own heart. I'm going to do something to put the fear of God into the heart of that murderer. Don't pay no attention to me. Watch them. Don't look at me, don't take your eyes off them. I'm looking for one of them to do something that will show us the way. It's our only chance.

(HELEN *runs in at L.*)

HELEN. They're coming.

ROSALIE. Leave the door open so we can hear 'em. (HELEN *does so and returns to her mother, standing L. of* ROSALIE.) Child, kiss me fer luck. (*They kiss.*) It'll do no harm to kiss him too. (*They kiss.*) Now, son, can ye lie?

WILL. *Can I!*

ROSALIE (*C.*). Here's the talk you're to make when they come in. I'm goin' in a trance. You'll tell 'em that I asked fer Mr. Wales' glove and the minute I got it in my hand, I went off like they see me. Tell 'em ye thought maybe there might be some reason for it. And then leave the rest to me.

WILL. I understand.

ROSALIE. You stand here back of me. I want them all in front of me. (WILL *crosses back of* ROSALIE *to R. side of* ROSALIE'S *chair.* HELEN *crosses R. of* ROSALIE *above her.*) Nelly, stand close by me. Go further back. (HELEN *moves to R. of* ROSALIE.) That's right. Now don't you move from there. This'll be the realest trance ye ever saw, and the grandest fake. When I come out, make 'em go away, tell 'em you're afraid it'll kill me to see anyone, just then.

(*She suddenly stiffens in her chair. Lying rigid with her head thrown back on the headrest, and the hand in which she is holding* WALES'S *glove stretched out straight in front of her. Enter down L.* CROSBY, MISS EASTWOOD, STANDISH, TRENT, MRS. CROSBY, MRS. TRENT, MISS ERSKINE *and* MISS STANDISH.)

CROSBY (*crossing to up L.C.*). What is it, Billy?

(MISS EASTWOOD *L. side of* ROSALIE'S *chair,* MRS. TRENT *and* MRS. CROSBY *L. of settee C.;* TRENT, MISS ERSKINE, *and* STANDISH *lower L. end of settee.*)

STANDISH. What's happened?

WILL (*R. side of* ROSALIE'S *chair*). I don't know, exactly. We were talking about this awful thing. She knew, of course, that her daughter couldn't have done it, and she asked me to get her something that had belonged to poor Wales. I got a glove out of Wales' overcoat pocket and handed it to her, and then all of a sudden she went stiff like that. I don't know what it means.

(*The* OTHERS *draw closer to* ROSALIE. WILL *and* HELEN *on the R. side of* ROSALIE'S *chair.* MISS EASTWOOD *comes to* ROSALIE *and lays her hand on her forehead.*)

MISS EASTWOOD. She's like ice, she's not—— (*Breaking up C. a few steps.*)

HELEN. Oh, no, it's a trance.

(MASON *enters L. down L.*)

MASON. I wouldn't touch her if I were you.

ROSALIE (*sitting in chair R.C. Speaking as Laughing Eyes*). Hello, everybody. What you all so solemn about, anyway? I've got a message from a new friend. He don't want me to send it—he wants to talk; ha, ha, ha, he thinks he can talk, and he's only been here a little while. (*Still speaking as Laughing Eyes.*) He says you're all fools. It's so plain, so plain. He's looking right at the one who did it, right straight at the one who did it. (WALES'S *voice.*)

WALES'S VOICE. I'm coming to you until you tell. I can't speak names. You've got to tell. I'm coming, again and again and again, until you tell. Find the knife. You must find the knife. The marks will show. The marks will show.

(MISS EASTWOOD *shrieks and faints on L. end of settee.* MASON *is below end of settee looking at her.* WILL *is standing R. side and back of* ROSALIE, *looking eagerly about him.* HELEN *turns and looks at* MISS EASTWOOD. MRS. CROSBY *goes to* MISS EASTWOOD *on settee.*)

MASON. This has got to stop. (*Starts to* ROSALIE's *chair—L. side of it.*)

HELEN (*R. side of* ROSALIE's *chair*). You mustn't touch her.

MASON. It's all right as far as the men are concerned, but look at that girl. (*He points to* MISS EASTWOOD *on the settee.*) They'll all be fainting if this isn't stopped. (TRENT *goes to* ROSALIE.)

WALES'S VOICE. Trent, let the medium alone. Do you understand? Let the medium alone.

TRENT. That's Wales' voice—and Wales is dead.

(MASON *crosses slowly to* ROSALIE's *chair.* TRENT *crosses L. above* MASON *to* STANDISH—ROSALIE *begins to mutter and moan. Suddenly she brings her hands together, and then throws her arms wide apart.* WALES'S *glove sails out of her hand and strikes* MASON *on the face. It falls to the floor.* STANDISH *exits very quietly door down L.* MASON *picks glove up—holding it in his hand—looks at it—suddenly drops it to the floor—turns to* MRS. CROSBY.)

MASON. Mrs. Crosby, shall I take Miss Eastwood to your room for you?

MRS. CROSBY. Yes, please, Philip.

(MISS ERSKINE *crosses to door L.* MASON *assists* MISS EASTWOOD *near seat and helps her from the room, exiting door down L.* MRS. CROSBY *exits door L.* TRENT *wipes his hands with handkerchief.* ROSALIE *stirs uneasily and moans.*)

HELEN (*standing R. side of* ROSALIE's *chair*). Please leave her to me. I'm afraid seeing you all here will trouble her. I'm afraid she'll—— Oh, won't you please go? (*The* OTHERS *turn and go to door down L.—exit.*)

CROSBY (*below L. end of settee*). Let me know if there's anything I can do.

HELEN (ROSALIE *moans again*). Yes, yes. Only please go now.

(CROSBY *exits door L.* WILL *runs quickly to the door at L. and closes it and turns to* ROSALIE, *who is sitting up in her chair.*)

ROSALIE (*rises and crosses a step R.*). Well?

HELEN (*R.C.*). It was the Eastwood girl. Her face was terrible. I was glad when she fainted.

WILL (*L.C.*). I think you're wrong. Standish ran away. He couldn't bear it.

ROSALIE. And that's all ye saw? I told ye to use the brains that was back of yer eyes.

WILL. Well, of course there was Trent. You can't mean Trent? Why, he's the kindest man in the world. (*There is a pause.*) The letters. If he's known the truth about the letters—— (*Breaks L. a step.*)

HELEN (*coming down to L. of ROS-ALIE's chair and picking up glove*). Mother, why did you throw that glove at Mason?

ROSALIE. Did it hit him? Well, well, well. Anyhow it was a good séance.

(WILL *takes chair up L.* ROSALIE *crosses down R.C.*)

HELEN (L. *side of* ROSALIE). Mother, you know—you've found out?

(WILL *takes* ROSALIE'S *chair up to door R.C. and comes down to L. of* ROSALIE.)

ROSALIE. Sure, it's wan thing to know and another to prove.

HELEN (L. *of* ROSALIE). Mother, who was it?

ROSALIE. Child, child, do ye think it's a game we're playin'? I got two or three minutes. What I've got to do I've got to do quickly.

HELEN. But what, Mother, what?

ROSALIE. I don't know, I don't know. Child, if you don't get away from me you'll drive me mad.

WILL. But can't we——

ROSALIE. This is no work for children. Leave me be and leave me think. (WILL *and* HELEN *run off door L.—closing door.*) He'll never break in the world. Never in all this world. (L.C. *Half in thought.*) Sure, Laughing Eyes, you're no good

to me in the world. We've faked all our lives, and now when I want the real thing I get nothing at all. If I could find the knife, sure, there'd be marks av a hand on that. But it's gone. It's gone. I can't let him get away with it. I want a sign. I want a sign. Laughing Eyes, are we goin' to be beaten by a schemin', cold-hearted murderer? (*Knock twice on table outside door down L., then count of five, rap twice more. Ready lights.* ROSALIE *starts, looks hastily around the room.*) I didn't do that. I didn't do that. (*She lifts her skirt and sees that her feet are still in her shoes.*) It's come! After all the years, a real message. A real message. I'll take it in the dark, believin' and trustin' that I'm to be shown. (*Lights out. Crosses down to door L.—pushes light switch. All lights in room out. The spot from the window shines on the ceiling, is brilliantly illuminating the knife.* ROSALIE *crosses to chair C.*) Laughing Eyes, have you a message for me? (*She looks up at knife in ceiling.*) Look at it! Glory be to God. The knife!

(*The door at L. opens.* POLLOCK *stands in the doorway. He sees that the lights are out and turns them on. Then he sees* ROSALIE, *who is standing C., facing front as in a trance.*)

POLLOCK. Excuse me, Madam. I knocked twice, but you didn't hear me.

ROSALIE. I heard ye. It was a message just the same.

POLLOCK. The inspector says have you got anything you want to tell him? (ROSALIE *stands lost in thought.* POLLOCK *looks at her for a moment and then nervously begins to set the chair below table up R. corner of set. He notices that the window blind is up, goes over and pulls it down and draws the curtains. He then comes back to* ROSALIE *above table R.*) The inspector says have you got anything you want to tell him?

(ROSALIE *crosses down R. in front of table.* DONOHUE *enters from L.*)

DONOHUE (*crosses to C.*). Time's about up. (*He laughs.*) Well?

ROSALIE (*below table R.*). I want them all here. All of them. Every one.

DONOHUE. What for?

ROSALIE. You're going to hear the murderer confess.

DONOHUE. Pollock, ask Mr. Crosby to bring everyone here. (*Crosses R. to above table.*)

POLLOCK. Very good, sir. (*He exits L.* DONOHUE *takes out his watch and stands with it in his hand, watching* ROSALIE. *She stands lost in her dreams.* DUNN *enters with* HELEN O'NEILL *down L.*)

DUNN. Here she is, Inspector.

DONOHUE. Come here, miss. (HELEN *crosses to* DONOHUE. *To* DUNN.) Go get a taxi.

(DUNN *turns and exits L. The* OTHERS *enter and stand crowding in the doorway.* WILL *pushes through and crosses and stands by* HELEN *up R.C. right end of settee.*)

CROSBY (*up L.C.*). What is it? You sent for us.

DONOHUE (*between table and settee C.*). She says her daughter's not guilty. I gave her ten minutes to find out who is. The time's up. (*He puts his watch back in his pocket. He turns to* ROSALIE.) Well?

(ROSALIE *stands rigid. There is a long pause.*)

ROSALIE (*below table R.*). You that's hidin', come out.

DONOHUE. Come on. (*He takes* HELEN *by the hand. They go up R. above table.*)

ROSALIE (*lower end of table R.*). You that's skulkin', come out! The message has come. I call on the spirit of Edward Wales. I call on the spirit of Edward Wales. Now you that's killed two men, look!

(*The door at L. of fireplace slowly swings open.* MASON, *with a cry of horror, pushes through the crowd at the doorway, which parts to let him through. He follows the spirit he sees moving across the stage until he is at C. and a little above the table.* MRS. TRENT, MISS ERSKINE, *and* STANDISH *below door down L.* TRENT, MRS. CROSBY, MISS EASTWOOD C. *above door L. All watch* MASON. *Suddenly the window curtains are thrown back, the shade runs up noisily, and the lights go down. The street light strikes the knife in the ceiling as it begins to fall.* MASON's *eye follows the light. He sees the knife and gives a cry of horror as it strikes the table and sticks in front of him.* MASON *rushes up stage end of table R.*)

MASON (*with a cry*). I can't fight the dead! I can't fight the dead!

(*Slowly* ROSALIE *points at him. The* OTHERS *stand and stare.*)

ROSALIE. Go on, tell it. (*Lower R. side of table R.*)

MASON. I had to do it. I was afraid Mr. Wales would know.

ROSALIE. You killed them both?

MASON. Yes.

ROSALIE. Mr. Wales to prevent his finding out about Spencer Lee?

MASON. Yes.

ROSALIE. And Spencer Lee?

(WILL *up R.C. above settee C.*)

MASON. He ought to have been killed. I'd been waiting for years to kill him.

ROSALIE. Why?

MASON. That's between him and me. He smashed my life, and, by God, I got him. He knows why I killed him, I told him I would, I'm glad I did. I only wish I could have done it over and over again. That's all.

ROSALIE. Why did you kill Spencer Lee?

MASON. He took her away from me. She was the one thing in the world and he took her away from me. I went to Paris to forget and all I could do was to remember. Then she died, and I made up my mind that he must die too.

DONOHUE. How did you get the knife in the ceiling?

MASON. I threw it. Just as I threw a knife into Spencer Lee's back. I stood in the doorway of his room and told him I'd come to kill him, and he ran for his revolver, and as he ran I threw the knife into his back. Then I picked up my knife and walked away. No one saw me. I was quite safe. Quite safe until she came. And unseen hands pushed me forward. Unseen hands have pointed the way. She's not human. Lee's message came through her—you all heard Wales speak; out of her lips we heard Wales' voice. He said he'd come back again and again and again. And then he came! I saw him as he came through the door! God Almighty, you can't fight the dead! (*He turns suddenly and walks to door L. As he opens it* SERGEANT DUNN *steps into the room.*)

DONOHUE. That's your man, Sergeant.

DUNN (*putting his hand on* MASON'S *arm*). You got him?

DONOHUE. Yes, I got him.

DUNN. Great work, Chief, great work. (*He takes* MASON *off down L.*)

(HELEN *crosses down to lower end of table R.*)

ROSALIE (*as they disappear from view*). The poor young fella, the poor young fella.

DONOHUE. Ladies and gentlemen, you are all quite at liberty. (*He goes toward door L.*)

CROSBY. Thank you, Inspector, for your consideration.

DONOHUE. Not at all; it was the best way out of it.

ROSALIE. Inspector. (*Coming below table R. to R.C.*)

DONOHUE (*half turning*). Yes?

ROSALIE. My congratulations.

(*He looks at her for a moment, then turns back and shakes hands with her.*)

DONOHUE. You were quite right about me. I was a damn fool. (*He exits at L.*)

(HELEN *coming below table R.*)

MRS. TRENT (*turning to her father up L. C., with a cry*). Oh, Daddy, Daddy! I lied about her. I lied about her. .

(CROSBY *takes her in his arms up L.* HELEN *crosses to* ROSALIE *from below table R.*)

ROSALIE (C.). There's nothing but happiness comin' to ye. The spirits tell me ye're the favorite child af fortune. You'll have wealth and prosperity and happiness. You'll marry the man ye love, and ye'll be happy——

CURTAIN

The Cat and the Canary

A Melodrama in Three Acts By

JOHN WILLARD

The Cat and the Canary was first presented by Kilbourn Gordon, Inc., at the National Theatre, New York, February 7, 1922.

CAST OF CHARACTERS

ROGER CROSBY	Percy Moore
"MAMMY" PLEASANT	Blanche Friderici
HARRY BLYTHE	John Willard
SUSAN SILLSBY	Beth Franklin
CICILY YOUNG	Jane Warrington
CHARLIE WILDER	Ryder Keane
PAUL JONES	Henry Hull
ANNABELLE WEST	Florence Eldredge
HENDRICKS	Edmund Elton
PATTERSON	Harry D. Southard

THE PEOPLE IN THE PLAY

(In the order in which they speak.)

ROGER CROSBY, *the lawyer*
MAMMY PLEASANT, *old negress*
HARRY BLYTHE
CICILY YOUNG
SUSAN SILLSBY
CHARLIE WILDER
PAUL JONES
ANNABELLE WEST
HENDRICKS, *guard at asylum*
PATTERSON

SYNOPSIS

The action takes place at Glencliff Manor on the Hudson—is practically continuous.

Act One: *Library. Eleven-thirty. Night.*
Act Two: *The next room. A few minutes later.*
Act Three: *Library. A few minutes later.*

THE CAT AND THE CANARY

ACT ONE

SCENE—*Library at Glencliff Manor.*
TIME—*About eleven-thirty in the evening.*
A large, old-fashioned room, full of dark corners and shadows. Door L. High-backed couch R.; bookcases line the walls at back.
AT RISE—MAMMY *enters—followed by* CROSBY. *Lights stage R. are on.*

CROSBY (*an old family lawyer. He looks at his watch*). A little more light, Mammy, please. (MAMMY *lights lamp table L.* CROSBY *looking around.*) That's better. Well, the old place looks just the same.

MAMMY (*closes door*). Yes sir—nothing's been changed here in twenty years.

CROSBY. You've been faithful to your trust, Mammy.

MAMMY. I certainly has. I stuck right here guarding the old place all the time.

CROSBY. Haven't you been lonely—living here by yourself?

MAMMY. No sir. I've got my friends.

CROSBY. Friends!

MAMMY. Yes, my friends from the shadow world!

CROSBY (*cynically*). Oh! *You* believe in spirits, eh?

MAMMY. I don't believe. I know. They are with me all the time. (*She makes a mysterious gesture in the air.*)

CROSBY (*amused*). You never really saw one, did you, Mammy?

MAMMY (*coming to him, her eyes bright with feverish excitement*). Yes sir—I see 'em! And they done warn me there's a evil spirit working around this house.

CROSBY (*amused*). Ever see it?

MAMMY. No sir—but I felt it—pass me in the dark—on the stairs——

CROSBY (*at safe*). Nonsense, your nerves are upset—it's living alone—here all this time——

MAMMY. No sir!

CROSBY (*working combination at safe*). Never mind, cheer up! In a few minutes the house will be full of people, and all your spooks will vanish.

MAMMY. How many heirs coming?

CROSBY. Six! All the surviving relatives. By the way—Mammy—your job as guardian of this house is up tonight. What are you going to do? (*Opens safe and takes out will.*)

MAMMY. It all depends. If I like the new heirs—I stay here. If I don't—I goes back to the West Indies.

(CROSBY *closes safe in wall and moves to front of sofa.*)

CROSBY. There's the will. It's been in that safe, undisturbed, for the last twenty years, think of that. (*In front of sofa.*)

MAMMY (*looking at him sardonically*). I'se thinking.

CROSBY (*opens portfolio and takes out three large sealed envelopes.*) There you are, just as your master sealed them and locked them in that safe—marked one, two, three—hello. (*As he is looking at them he shows excitement. He examines each seal intently.*) These envelopes have been opened—every one of them! The seals have been cut away and very cleverly glued back again. Someone has opened that safe and read this will.

MAMMY. How could they? Nobody knows how to open the safe but you.

CROSBY (*with anger*). Well, I didn't do it.

MAMMY. I ain't suspecting nobody —I'd just like to know—why they opened 'em. (*Grins at him venomously.*) What you expect they'd want to do, change the will?

CROSBY (*looking at her keenly*). Perhaps. But if it *has* been changed, it won't do them any good. I drew up duplicate wills, according to Mr. West's instructions. One copy is here —the other is in the vault of the Empire Trust Company, and if this one *has* been tampered with, I'll know it—and I'll know who did it. (*Doorbell rings.*)

MAMMY. You don't think that I——

CROSBY. See who that is, Mammy And mind—say nothing about this

(MAMMY *gives him a poisonous look and exits.* CROSBY *starts looking for a secret spring near bookcase up R. and stops as he hears* MAMMY *at door.* MAMMY *opens door, admits* HARRY BLYTHE, *a tall, dark man about thirty-five years of age. A quiet, cynical, bored man, but dangerous. He is of the gentleman heavy type.*)

HARRY (*enters, shakes hands with* CROSBY). How are you, Mr. Crosby?

CROSBY. Hello, Harry! Did you come up on the train?

HARRY. No. Some friends of mine motored me over from Tarrytown. The train had just pulled in as I passed the station. Am I the first of the pack?

CROSBY. Yes. I guess the others will be right up.

HARRY. How many heirs besides myself?

CROSBY. Five.

HARRY. Five, eh? Well, I'm fortunate. I only know two of them, and I wish to heaven I only knew one.

CROSBY (*slowly*). Why do you dislike Charlie Wilder?

HARRY. In the first place because he is my cousin, in the second place because he's a poet, and—— (*Lights cigarette.*)

CROSBY (*grins*). And in the third place, because Annabelle is very fond of him!

HARRY. You've said it! (*Looks at him, then turns away and changes subject.*) So this is the old man's library?

CROSBY. Yes. Haven't you ever been here before?

HARRY. No. Why did you ask?

CROSBY (*glancing at will in his hand*). Well, someone has.

HARRY (*quickly*). Just what do you mean by that?

CROSBY (*turning away*). Oh, nothing.

HARRY (*sees* MAMMY *in doorway*). I beg your pardon, would you mind parking yourself in the kitchen for a while?

(MAMMY *glares at him venomously but, at a nod from* CROSBY, *exits.*)

CROSBY. You've offended her. Do you know who she is?

HARRY (*coming C.*). No.

CROSBY. She's Mr. West's old and trusted servant.

HARRY. That's possibly all very true —but it's not interesting. What are you getting at?

CROSBY. You mustn't treat her like an ordinary servant. She's a West Indian—a voodoo woman.

HARRY (*smiles*). My dear fellow—I don't care what she is. Is that the will?

CROSBY (*offended by his manner*). Yes, but it can't be read until all the heirs are assembled in this room. (*Crosses to safe and closes panel.*)

HARRY (*seated on arm of chair*). All right. Oh, Mr. Crosby. You knew old man West—was he all there?

CROSBY. *All* there?

HARRY. Wasn't he a little bit off? You know, a little coo-coo. Didn't he collect things—in the West Indies?

CROSBY (*sternly*). Have you no respect for a dead relative?

HARRY (*cheerfully*). None whatever—unless, of course, he has made me the sole heir. (*Laughs and sits down to read a book.*) Come on, Mr. Crosby—you'll admit he was a nut.

CROSBY (*slowly*). He was a little eccentric.

HARRY. Eccentric! He was fantastic! Why did he want a twenty-year-old will read to his heirs—at midnight in this old house? Why not in the daytime at your office? Why drag us out here?

CROSBY (*coming in front of sofa*). Mr. West stipulated—that this will should be read—in this very room —at the very hour of his death— one of his whims. (*Crosses C. to back of table L.*)

HARRY. Whim—— (*Rises.*) It's going to make me miss the last train to New York and I'll have to sleep here.

CROSBY. That's all been taken care of. (*Goes to* HARRY *R.C.*) Mammy will see that you're made comfortable, and you'll have company—the others will have to sleep here too. (MAMMY *opens door and admits two more heirs,* CICILY YOUNG, *a pretty blonde girl, and* SUSAN SILLSBY, *a female with an acid temper. Seeing* SUSAN.) How do you do!

SUSAN. How do you do!

CROSBY (*shakes hands with* CICILY). You two know each other?

SUSAN. Oh yes, yes—we met after we got off the train. My, what a small world it is.

CICILY. I overheard Miss Sillsby asking for a taxi to take her to Glencliff, so we rode up together.

SUSAN. What was I saying? Oh yes —I was telling Cicily——

CROSBY. Excuse me, Miss Sillsby— let me introduce Mr. Harry Blythe. Miss Susan 'Sillsby and Miss Cicily Young——

HARRY. Ladies, delighted!

SUSAN (*gushes over to* HARRY). So you are Harry Blythe! Well! Well! Well! My, what a small world it is.

HARRY. Yes, isn't it?

SUSAN (*taking* HARRY *by the arm to front of sofa*). Now, you must tell me all about yourself. We must find out just how we're connected! Did you know my great-aunt Eleanor ——

HARRY (*interrupting*). No, Miss Sillsby, I did not know your great-aunt Eleanor.

SUSAN. Well, she's——

HARRY. I'm not anxious to hear about her—so why delve into ancient history?

SUSAN. But I——

HARRY. Aunt Eleanor and I are related—aren't we?

SUSAN. Yes.

HARRY. It can't be helped.

SUSAN. No!

HARRY. So let it go at that. (*Crosses R. of table R.*)

SUSAN (*bounces back to* CICILY). Why—he's the rudest man I ever met—he's positively insulting!

CICILY. Don't pay any attention to him. He doesn't know any better probably. Anyway, I like him better than I do this house. (*Looks around.*) It's such a spooky old place!

SUSAN. You know, my dear—I've had the queerest feeling ever since we came in the house. I feel as if someone were—peering at me—— Oh! (*Suddenly sees* MAMMY *looking fixedly at her.*) This house is haunted. I know it.

MAMMY (*keeping her eyes on* SUSAN, *speaks in a deep sepulchral voice*). Lady, there is someone in the other world trying to tell you something. You is mediumistic—(*cry from* SUSAN)—a spiritist—I knew it when you came in that door. There are spirits all around you.

SUSAN (*sits chair C.*). I knew it—I knew it.

CROSBY (*sternly*). What are you trying to do, Mammy? Frighten her to death?

HARRY (*laughs*). Nonsense. (*To end of sofa.*) No one was ever frightened to death.

CROSBY. It has happened, and you know it. Lots of women have lost their minds—sometimes their lives —through—fright. The asylums are full of such cases. (MAMMY *exits.*)

HARRY (CROSBY *walks down L. in front of table*). I don't believe it.

SUSAN (*rises*). Oh, I wish I hadn't come—you heard what she said! It's terrible—I want to go home. (CICILY *takes her over to sofa.*)

HARRY. Come and sit down.

SUSAN. I don't want to sit down. (*Sits on sofa.*)

(MAMMY *opens door and admits* CHARLIE WILDER. CHARLIE *is a tall, handsome, leading-man type. He is full of charm—smiles all the time, and has a magnetic personality.* CHARLIE *down to* CROSBY.)

CHARLIE (*holding out his hand to* CROSBY). How are you, Mr. Crosby? Hope I'm not late. (*Looks toward the ladies.*)

CROSBY. Hello, Charlie! Miss Susan Sillsby and Miss Cicily Young— this is Charlie Wilder, another distant relative.

CHARLIE (*smiles and shakes hands with them*). It's a pleasure to discover that I have such charming relatives.

SUSAN. Oh!

CROSBY. Oh, Harry, you know Charlie, of course.

HARRY (*coming C.—stands, staring at* CHARLIE). Oh yes, I know him!

CROSBY. Now, boys, forget this foolish quarrel of yours. This is a family reunion—stop acting like children and shake hands.

CHARLIE. I'd like to. Come on, old man. Let's bury the hatchet. Shake! (*Offers hand to* HARRY. HARRY *shakes hands reluctantly. Drops his hand, turns to* CROSBY.) When are you going to read the will, Mr. Crosby?

CROSBY. As soon as the other two heirs arrive. (*Phone.*) Excuse me. (*Sits L. of table. Answers telephone.*) Hello—yes—yes, this is Mr. Crosby. (*Listens.*) Oh, all right—yes, we're waiting for you. (*Hangs up phone.*) That's one of them now. She's on her way from the station. She had trouble getting a taxi.

CHARLIE (*back of table*). I left the other downstairs. Chap by the name of Jones.

CROSBY. What's he doing down there?

CHARLIE. Arguing with the driver of the taxi we came up in.

(MAMMY *admits* PAUL JONES.)

CROSBY (*holds out his hand*). Come in, Paul. Glad to see you. My, my, but you're looking fit!

PAUL (*shaking hands with him doubtfully*). Well, I may look all right—but I don't feel so good.

CROSBY. No.

PAUL. I have felt better—but on the other hand, I *have* felt worse.

CROSBY. Here are some cousins you ought to know. Miss Cicily Young. Mr. Paul Jones.

CICILY (*seated L. of sofa. Smiles*). So you're Cousin Paul.

PAUL. Yep! That's who it is.

CICILY. Isn't it a wonderful night?

PAUL. Well, the sky didn't look any too good when I came in, but of course on the other hand it may be all right by tomorrow.

CROSBY. Miss Sillsby, Mr. Jones.

SUSAN (*crosses to* PAUL, *gushing*). Well! Well! Paul Jones?

PAUL. Yep!

SUSAN. Isn't the world a small place?

PAUL. Yep, it certainly is, but not too small.

SUSAN. I quite agree with you. You're a professional man, aren't you?

PAUL. Yes, ma'am, *I'm* a horse doctor.

(SUSAN *crosses to sofa and sits.*)

CHARLIE (*coming around the R. of* PAUL). Horse doctor!

CROSBY. Oh, Paul, your cousin Charlie Wilder.

CHARLIE. How do you do!

CROSBY. And Harry Blythe.

PAUL. Mr. Blythe!

CHARLIE. I thought you were in the automobile business.

PAUL. Well, when I graduated from college as a first-class vet, I went back home to practice and found I was sunk. The farmers had quit using horses and were all driving cars, so I naturally began doctoring them—there isn't much difference, is there—and I want to tell you I've got about the snappiest garage in Wickford.

MAMMY (*who has been in the door all this time, suddenly speaks*). I hear a taxi comin' down the drive—the sixth heir. (MAMMY *looks at them with a malicious smile and exits.*)

CICILY (*shows fear*). Ugh! She gives me the creeps.

CHARLIE (*up to door*). She is rather weird. I don't hear any taxi.

SUSAN. This house is haunted.

PAUL (*with a start*). Eh!

SUSAN. I know it!

CROSBY. Rubbish! (*Turns to* SUSAN.) You'll be seeing ghosts the first thing you know.

PAUL (*nervously*). Well, personally, I've never seen a ghost—however, on the other hand, that doesn't prove that there aren't any. I've felt kinda queer ever since I've been in this house.

HARRY. What will you do with it if you inherit it?

PAUL. I don't expect to inherit it. I never—(*crossing to* HARRY L.)—inherit anything—but on the other hand, you never can tell, I might.

(MAMMY *opens door and* ANNABELLE WEST *enters.* ANNABELLE *is a vigorous, beautiful girl, frank and fearless and very modern.*)

ANNABELLE. Sorry I'm late, Mr. Crosby.

CROSBY (*greets her*). Well, Annabelle, you did get here. Miss Cicily Young—Miss Annabelle West.

(ANNABELLE *smiles and shakes hands with them.*)

CICILY. Annabelle West, the illustrator?

ANNA. I suppose so!

CROSBY. Miss Sillsby, Miss West.

HARRY (*to C.*). Hello, Annabelle!

(*As* ANNABELLE *turns and sees* HARRY, *she gasps in amazement.*)

ANNA. Harry!

CHARLIE (*coming down C.*). Annabelle!

(*Then, seeing* CHARLIE, ANNABELLE *gasps in great amazement.*)

ANNA. Charlie Wilder! Why didn't I see you on the train?

CHARLIE. I was in the smoker.

HARRY. I motored up. Now you can go ahead, Mr. Crosby.

(ANNABELLE *is speechless for a moment.*)

CROSBY (*L. of table*). If you'll all sit down, I'll begin.

CHARLIE. Annabelle! (CHARLIE *offers chair at R. of table which* ANNABELLE *takes. At the same time* HARRY *pushes armchair for* ANNABELLE *to sit in and* PAUL *takes it.*)

ANNA (*as she sits down she sees* PAUL *staring at her with open mouth*). Well, Cousin Paul?

PAUL (*who has been staring at her, fascinated, with his mouth wide open, chokes and stammers*). Yes, that's right. Little Annabelle West —all growed up an' everything.

ANNA (*smiles and takes his hand.*) When did you leave Wickford?

PAUL. This morning, I think—yes, as a matter of fact I——

CROSBY (*is seated*). Now I'm going to be brief.

HARRY (*flippantly*). Good!

(PAUL *gives him a look.*)

CROSBY (*glares at him*). Cyrus Canby West died in this house twenty years ago tonight. He made me executor of his estate. Mr. West was a very eccentric man—and hated all his living relatives.

HARRY (*sotto voce*). I don't blame him.

CROSBY. Not wishing his near relatives to enjoy his fortune, Mr. West invested it in government bonds to mature in twenty years. At the end of that time I was to assemble all his surviving relatives and read his will. Now you understand why I've kept track of you all. You six people are the last living descendants of Cyrus Canby West.

HARRY. I thought you were going to make this brief.

CROSBY. Please! (*Holds up the three envelopes.*) Here is the will in these three envelopes. (*At this moment a muffled, weird gong sounds somewhere in the house. It tolls seven and stops.*) I will now read instructions on envelope marked 1. (*Everyone looks at each other with a certain amount of nervousness.*)

MAMMY (*in trance*). Oh, tell me— Oh, tell me!

(*Everyone turns and looks at* MAMMY.)

CROSBY (*annoyed, because in spite of himself he is chilled by the unearthly gong, turns to* MAMMY). Mammy—Mammy Pleasant!

MAMMY (*who has been standing near the door, has her eyes closed and is rocking her body to and fro, muttering incantations to herself*). Yes—I hear you—Eliza——

CROSBY. Mammy!

MAMMY. Eliza, what are you trying to tell me about—about——

CROSBY (*sharply*). Mammy! Stop that and answer me.

MAMMY. Tell me—tell me the name ——

CROSBY (*sharply*). Mammy!

MAMMY (*opening eyes*). What?

CROSBY. What was that noise—like a gong?

MAMMY (*in a deep voice surcharged with malice*). That is the warning of death. The master heard it just before *he* died.

(*All look at each other, impressed in spite of themselves.* PAUL *stands up and mops his brow with his handkerchief and runs his hand around his collar, which has suddenly grown too tight.*)

PAUL. I've been thinking that there isn't any use of my staying round here; besides, I don't feel so good —and it looks like rain, so if it's all the same to you, I think I'll run to the station. (*Starts for the door.* MAMMY *moves in front of him.*)

ANNA (*stops him and begins to laugh*). Nonsense, Paul, it isn't going to rain—and I want you here to—to—— You don't believe in ghosts, do you?

PAUL. No! No! Of course not! But then on the other hand, that gong and——

CROSBY. It's nothing.

ANNA. An old grandfather's clock in one of the rooms.

MAMMY. There is no clock running in this house.

PAUL. You see!

MAMMY. The toll says seven may live. There is eight persons in this room. One must die before morning.

SUSAN. Oh! I feel faint.

PAUL. Say, listen, honest to goodness, it's too hot in here. I want some air. (PAUL *starts for door.* HARRY *grabs* PAUL *and forces him in chair.*)

HARRY. Quit your kidding and sit down.

PAUL (*as he sits down*). But I'm not kidding.

HARRY. Crosby, go on with the will.

CROSBY (*clears his throat and reads instructions on envelope* 1). "At midnight, September 27, 1921, you will open this envelope and read its contents to such of my relatives— (*movement of everybody*)—as are assembled in my library at Glencliff Manor." (*He opens the envelope, takes out sheet of paper, and reads.*) "First, let my executor ask the prospective heirs assembled this night if they are willing to take what fortune offers them and not question my judgment in the manner in which I shall dispose of my fortune." (*He looks up inquiringly.*) Is that clear? Any objections?

SUSAN. No, that's all right, go ahead.

(*All nod satisfaction.*)

CROSBY. "If they are willing——"

PAUL. Just a minute, I don't know about that. Maybe his judgment isn't good. Mind you, I don't say that it isn't, but then on the other hand it might not be.

CROSBY. Are you satisfied or not?

PAUL. Well, it seems to me under the circumstances——

CHARLIE. Sure he is—go on.

CROSBY. Are you?

PAUL. I didn't say I wasn't. I merely started to say that it seemed to me under the circumstances——

HARRY. Will you dry up?

CROSBY (*continues reading*). "If they are willing to take what fortune offers, then let my executor open envelope number two and read my will." (*He puts down the paper, opens the envelope marked* 2. *All show their anxiety and lean forward to hear as he reads.*) "I, Cyrus Canby West, being of sound mind and body, do hereby declare as the sole heir to all my money, bonds, securities, estate, real and otherwise, my descendant, man or woman, who bears the surname of West. If more than one bear the surname of West, then my estate shall be equally divided among them. Cyrus Canby West. Witnesses: Mammy Pleasant, Roger Crosby." (CROSBY *looks up and pauses.* PAUL *stands up to congratulate* ANNABELLE.) There is, however, a codicil. (PAUL *coughs and sits.* CROSBY *continues to read.*) "In the event of the death of the beneficiary, or if he or she be proved of unsound mind, or if it be proved in a court of law that the said beneficiary is not competent to properly handle the estate, then my executor will open envelope marked 3 and declare the next heir." (CROSBY *puts down paper, looks at them and speaks.*) Therefore— (*rises*)—in accordance with the will, I now declare Miss Annabelle West as sole heiress of the West estate and the mistress of Glencliff Manor. Annabelle, I congratulate you. (*Offers his hand.* PAUL *rises—moves chair back.*) And as there is no doubt as to the good health and sanity of Miss West—I trust this envelope shall never be opened. (*Puts envelope in his pocket.*)

CHARLIE (*over table*). It's wonderful, Annabelle, I'm glad.

HARRY. I congratulate you with all my heart. (*Crosses to back of chair C.*)

ANNA (*dazed by her good fortune*). I—I can't realize it yet—all I can say is—that Glencliff is open to you all—and everything I have is—— (*Almost breaks down.*)

SUSAN (*on sofa*). I knew there was a catch in it.

CICILY (*rises, crosses, and shakes hands*). I confess I'm disappointed, but I congratulate you.

ANNA. Thanks.

(*CICILY crosses up to L. of HARRY.*)

SUSAN (*with an acid smile*). I suppose there's nothing else to do but to wish you many happy returns.

ANNA. It is so—so unexpected—I can hardly—— (*Turns to CROSBY*). I can't believe it yet. (*To PAUL.*) Isn't it wonderful?

PAUL (*L. of sofa*). Well, of course money doesn't always bring happiness—but then again, on the other hand, sometimes it does.

SUSAN. I quite agree with you, money is the root of all evil.

PAUL. It is, it certainly is! When you haven't got any! (*Goes up stage.*)

ANNA (*to CROSBY*). Mr. Crosby, one thing puzzles me about the will.

CROSBY. What is it?

ANNA. What did he mean when it said if the heir is proved to be unsound in mind?

CROSBY. Mr. West believed that there was a streak of insanity in the family. That clause was put there in case that failing should reappear in the heir. In that event, the estate would go to the heir named in envelope three.

(*ANNABELLE sits R. of table. CROSBY sits L. of table.*)

PAUL. I wonder who that is?

HARRY. I wonder.

ANNA. I didn't know there was any insanity in our family.

HARRY. Neither did I until I heard that will.

CROSBY. But it is legal—absolutely!

HARRY. I don't dispute that—I'm only saying that the old man was dotty.

CROSBY. He was peculiar, yes, but as sane as any man living.

MAMMY (*comes to R. of ANNABELLE and offers her a ring full of keys*). Here are the keys to the house, Miss West.

ANNA. Won't you remain as my housekeeper?

MAMMY (*puts keys in pocket of apron. She takes out a sealed enve-*

lope, hands it to ANNABELLE). When Mr. West died he gave me this letter to give to the heir after the will was read. (MAMMY *backs up to door again.*)

ANNA (*reads what is written on the outside of the envelope*). "You will open this envelope tonight, in my room, where you are to sleep." (*Looks at* CROSBY, *then puts the letter in her pocket.*) Where is the room, Mammy?

MAMMY (*points*). There. Across the hall.

CICILY (*to* HARRY). I agree with you. Mr. West was certainly insane. Imagine trusting that woman to deliver a letter twenty years after his death.

CROSBY (*blankly*). It's all news to me. Mammy, when did he give you that letter?

MAMMY. Just before he died, when you and the doctor were talking in a corner of the room. (*Glaring at* CICILY.)

SUSAN. I'm afraid that cousin Cyrus *was* a little out of his mind.

PAUL (*to* SUSAN). I wonder what's in that letter.

CROSBY. It may refer to the lost necklace.

HARRY. Necklace?

CICILY (*coming down C. To* HARRY). Oh, I remember my mother telling me she saw it once and said it was the most gorgeous thing imaginable. All sapphires and rubies.

ANNA. Seems to me I heard something about it. (*To* CROSBY.) Wasn't it a family heirloom?

CICILY. Yes. Mother told me it had been in the family for—oh, generations. But she said it was lost or stolen—after it came into Mr. West's possession.

CROSBY. It did disappear—but I don't think it was lost or stolen. I believe Mr. West hid it—somewhere in this house.

CHARLIE. Why should he do that?

CROSBY. Another of his whims.

SUSAN. Did you ever see it?

CROSBY. Once. It was magnificent. The stones alone are worth a fortune. Annabelle, I congratulate you again.

SUSAN (PAUL *goes up R.*). Gracious —some people have all the luck.

CICILY. You know the old saying— "Them that has—gets."

ANNA (*excited*). Before I go to bed— (*rises*)—I'll open this letter. Perhaps in the morning I will show you the necklace. This is going to be a wonderful evening. Mammy, how about some supper?

MAMMY. I'll put it on the table in the dining room.

ANNA. While you're doing that, we'll explore the place—and you two can pick out your rooms.

CICILY. I'd like one next to Susan. I'm afraid to sleep alone in this ghostly old house.

SUSAN (*crosses to* CICILY). I know I won't sleep a wink.

ANNA. Nonsense. There is nothing to fear.

CICILY. Aren't you afraid to sleep in the room where he died?

ANNA. Certainly not, why should I be?

SUSAN (*exaggerated*). This house is haunted; she—(*points to* MAMMY) —has seen them—spirits!

ANNA. Suppose she has? She has been living here a long time—and they haven't hurt you, have they?

MAMMY (*at door*). But there is an evil spirit in this house now.

ANNA (*just a trifle nervous*). I don't believe it—nothing can frighten me.

CHARLIE (*seeing that* ANNABELLE *is growing nervous*). Keep still! Don't you see—you are making Miss West nervous.

(MAMMY *gives a venomous look and goes out.*)

ANNA (*starting after* MAMMY—L. *of door*). Come on, Susan and Cicily ——

SUSAN. I won't budge without a man.

ANNA. Come on, Paul, you'll protect us, won't you?

PAUL (*going toward door*). Well, I don't know as I'd be much use to you—but then again, on the other hand, you never can tell—maybe I might. (*Exits with* ANNABELLE.)

(SUSAN *moves up stage.*)

CICILY (R.C., *speaking at* CROSBY). I haven't much confidence in Paul —I wish Mr. Crosby would come!

CROSBY. Me?—I—of course I'll come —delighted.

SUSAN. The more the merrier.

(*Exeunt* CICILY *and* SUSAN.)

CROSBY (*at door. To* HARRY *and* CHARLIE). Why don't you boys make it up! (*Exits and closes door.*)

CHARLIE (*as soon as they are alone, he grins at* HARRY *and crosses to* C.). Here we are again!

HARRY (*coming over to* CHARLIE). But it won't be for long. One of us will be gone before morning.

CHARLIE. Meaning me?

HARRY. You!

CHARLIE. Until *Annabelle* tells me I'm not wanted, I'm going to stick right here.

HARRY. You won't stick here and you won't get her—except—— Well, just try it!

CHARLIE. Now that she's the heiress, you've decided that you're in love with her.

HARRY. I've decided that she needs my protection—(ANNABELLE *re-enters*)—and she's going to have it. —So you keep out of my way—or I'll—— (HARRY *makes a threatening move.*)

ANNA. Well—what's it all about?

HARRY. Nothing! (*Turns away to back of sofa.* CHARLIE *moves over to table L.*)

CHARLIE. Sorry to disappoint you, Annabelle. Where did you put me?

ANNA. At the end of the hall. Mammy will show you. Harry, you are to sleep in the first room at the head of the stairs.

CHARLIE. Find any spirits in the house?

ANNA. The sideboard is full of scotch whisky. Run along—make yourself a highball!

CHARLIE (*going to door*). All right, I will, but I'd like to see you later, Annabelle.

ANNA. Come back when you've had your scotch.

CHARLIE. I will. And I'll bring you some. (CHARLIE *exits, closes door.*)

ANNA (*to sofa*). Harry, what's all this nonsense between you and Charlie?

HARRY. It isn't nonsense, Annabelle. It's serious. You know how I—think about you, and it exasperates me the way you smile on that rotter.

ANNA. See here, Harry, don't talk that way about Charlie—he's one of my dearest friends.

HARRY. If he's a sample of your dearest friends, God help you!

ANNA. I used to think you were one of them, but when I see you with such an ugly look in your eyes—— (*Sits.*)

HARRY. You're shocked, are you?

ANNA. No! I've *always* thought there was a good deal of the brute in you.

HARRY. And is that why you told me to run along and find some other girl?

ANNA. Not exactly. I didn't mind the brute in you—I was only afraid you mightn't be able to control it —and it looks as though I were right.

HARRY. How can a man control himself when he sees the woman he loves is being swept off her feet by a romantic milksop?

ANNA (*rises*). If you mean Charlie——

HARRY. I do. (*She goes L. He follows.*) Charlie's a dreamer—a visionary. He'll never amount to a row of pins. Don't throw yourself away on him!

ANNA. Do you suggest that I throw myself away on you?

HARRY. You'd better!

ANNA. Is that a threat?

HARRY. Whatever it is, Annabelle— it comes straight from my heart.

ANNA. Just for a moment—the old trust in you—comes back to me.

HARRY. And if you'll give me the chance I'll make you trust me forever.

ANNA. It's too late.

HARRY. You love him.

ANNA (*crosses in front of table*). Please!

HARRY. All right, but I know a cure for it!

ANNA. A cure?

HARRY. Yes! Just marry him! . . . And you can take my word for it, you'll be sorry as long as you live.

ANNA (*lightly*). What are you doing—putting a curse on me?

HARRY. What do you want me to do—give you my blessing?

ANNA. You can give me one thing —a promise—(*crosses to* HARRY. *Holds out her hand*)—that you'll always be my friend.

HARRY (*taking her hand*). That goes! You'll need me, Annabelle, and when you do, I'll come a-running.

ANNA. I've a mind to give you a kiss for that!

HARRY. No, thanks—I want all or none.

(*Enter* CROSBY, *followed by* CHARLIE, *who brings on tray, whisky bottle, and glasses.*)

CROSBY. Annabelle, as hostess, I think you might hurry along the supper.

ANNA (*starting for door*). Mammy may not like my interfering, but I'll see what I can do. (*Exits.*)

CROSBY (*to* CHARLIE). That was a great highball! Charlie! Just like old times.

CHARLIE. I'll say the old man knew scotch.

HARRY. I'll say he didn't know much about wills.

(SUSAN *enters in trance—she stands staring into space.* PAUL *re-enters.*)

SUSAN. I know it—I know it, I know it. (*In front of chair R. of table.*)

PAUL (*uneasy—to* CROSBY). What's —what's the matter with her?

CROSBY (*to* SUSAN). Anything wrong, Miss Sillsby?

SUSAN. I know it, just as sure as I'm standing on this spot.

PAUL. What do you know?

SUSAN. That something is going to happen. Something terrible. (HARRY *laughs.*) Don't you laugh at me, Harry Blythe. Don't you know Aunt Eleanor is trying to warn me?

PAUL. What's she trying to warn you about?

SUSAN. Some danger. (PAUL *crosses to sofa.*)

HARRY (*coming down L. of sofa*). Miss Sillsby, aren't you stretching your imagination—just a little?

CHARLIE (*back of table*). You're not a medium, are you?

SUSAN. Yes. I've always thought I was a psychic, and now I know it. Didn't you hear Mammy Pleasant say a spirit was trying to warn me? Aunt Eleanor!

CROSBY (*indulgently*). You mustn't believe everything that Mammy tells you, Miss Sillsby.

SUSAN. But I do. I felt it in my bones, the moment I entered this house, that something terrible was going to happen. (*Crosses to L. of sofa.*)

PAUL (*on sofa*). And I suppose if nothing terrible happens—you'll be disappointed?

(MAMMY *starts to open door.*)

SUSAN (*acidly*). Mr. Jones! Really!

PAUL. Sorry—no offense.

MAMMY (*opens door*). There's a man outside. He says he wants to see the boss of this house.

CROSBY. Who is he?

MAMMY. He's from the sanitarium at Fairview.

CROSBY. You mean—the asylum?

MAMMY. Yes sir.

CROSBY. What does he want?

MAMMY. I don't know.

(CROSBY *looks at the others, perplexed.*)

HARRY. Why not see him, and find out?

CROSBY. Send him in, Mammy.

(MAMMY *exits and closes door.* SUSAN *sits chair C.*)

CHARLIE (*lights cigarette*). Could he be after some——

HARRY. Where is this asylum, Mr. Crosby?

CROSBY. Up past the village. (*Looks at all of them.*) What do you suppose he wants?

PAUL. Maybe he wants to take one of us back with him.

(MAMMY *admits* HENDRICKS, *a typical guard—rough and brutal, with a dangerous manner. He carries a strait jacket.*)

MAMMY. This is the man.

HENDRICKS (*looks at* CHARLIE, *then* HARRY, *then* MAMMY, *who exits and closes door. He then comes C. to* CROSBY). Are you the boss?

CROSBY. I represent the owner of this house. Who are you?

HENDRICKS. My name's Hendricks. I'm the head guard up at Fairview.

CROSBY. Yes, I know. What are you doing down here?

HENDRICKS. We're looking for a patient who got away this afternoon. (*Crosses to window below table.*)

CHARLIE. A patient!

HARRY. You mean you're looking for an escaped lunatic?

HENDRICKS (*looks at* HARRY). Yes.

HARRY. Why didn't you come right out with it?

HENDRICKS (*gruffly*). Because I didn't want to scare you.

CROSBY (*quickly*). Is there any cause for alarm?

HENDRICKS. Yes.

CROSBY. And this—this patient is dangerous?

HENDRICKS (*crosses to* CROSBY). Dangerous! (*Pauses.*) He's a killer. A homicidal maniac!

CHARLIE (*sharply*). What makes you think he's here?

HENDRICKS (*in a surly tone to* CHARLIE). I didn't say he was here. I'm asking at all the houses and thought I was doing a favor in warning you, that's all.

CROSBY (*placating him*). Just a minute. No offense was intended.

HENDRICKS (*stops and turns*). Well?

CROSBY. Have you any reason to believe he might be around here?

HENDRICKS (*comes down a step*). Well, he might be in any of these houses. You see, he always gets in a house when he escapes, and hides until everyone goes to bed—then he prowls around like——

HARRY. He's escaped before?

HENDRICKS. Yes. He got away from us about a year ago and hid in a house in the village, and—well, I got there just in time.

HARRY. What does he look like?

HENDRICKS. When he escaped he had on a black slouch hat and a long coat. He's an old guy with a bald head, sharp teeth and fingernails—like claws. He crawls around on all fours like a——

CROSBY. An animal?

HENDRICKS. Yeh, a cat!

HARRY. A cat!

HENDRICKS. Yes, and I'm the only one up there that can handle him. (*Grins at them brutally.*) He's afraid of me.

CHARLIE (*with irony*). I suppose you control him through kindness.

HENDRICKS (*with a savage laugh*). Control him through kindness! Yes, I do—not. I control him with a club, a chair, an iron bar—anything I can get my hands on. (*To others.*) We have to keep him strapped down most of the time in this strait jacket! (*Shows it.*)

CHARLIE. That's the cruelest thing I ever heard of. Think of being strapped down in that—it's enough to make anyone violent.

HENDRICKS (*sneeringly*). You don't say so. Hah!

CHARLIE. Yes, and I dare say, because of his treatment up there, this old man thinks everyone is against him. He's probably just a poor old nut.

HENDRICKS (*to* CHARLIE *with a truculent air*). Poor old nut! Say, young feller, let me tell you, this poor old nut could rip you wide open—just like a cat rips open a bird. Don't make any mistake about him. (*To others.*) The last time I got him he had his hands—— (*Indicates strangling.*) Well, it took three of us to get him away. (*Looks at all of them and then sneers at*

CHARLIE.) Poor old nut! Say, young feller, you take my tip, if you see him—you—you run like hell!

SUSAN (*gasps with terror*). Oh!

HENDRICKS. Sorry, ma'am, I forgot you was there. (*Crosses to window in front of table.*)

SUSAN. Do you think——

HENDRICKS. Now don't get excited. It ain't likely he's around here. (*Comes back to C.*)

CROSBY. Where are the rest of your men?

HENDRICKS. Looking over the estate —next to this one. (*Goes to door.*) Well, I guess I'll be going.

CROSBY. But suppose——

HENDRICKS (*coming down*). Don't get nervous; he ain't liable to ever get in this house. 'Tain't likely he's even around here.

CROSBY (*relieved*). You think so?

HENDRICKS. Sure. He may be prowling around the neighborhood, waiting for a chance to sneak in somewhere, so just to play safe, none of you had better go out before morning. (*Pauses a moment and speaks seriously.*) But—be sure to lock all the outside doors and windows. I'll be around here, and if we get him, I'll drop in and let you know—good night. (*Exits.*)

CROSBY (*pauses—turning to them all*). What do you think we ought to do?

CHARLIE (*to everyone*). We'd better not say anything about this to Anna-

belle or Cicily. It would only throw them into a panic.

HARRY (*insolently*). You're wrong. Both these girls should be told. If there *is* any danger they ought to know it.

CHARLIE. What do you think, Mr. Crosby?

CROSBY. I agree with *you*. It would throw them into a panic. I don't believe there is any danger, so there is no use alarming them. Harry, you won't tell them, will you?

HARRY. I don't know about that. (*Turns to* PAUL.) What do you think, Paul?

PAUL. I think I'd better go down and lock all the cellar windows.

SUSAN. Yes! Yes! Do, do!

(HARRY *touches* PAUL *on shoulder.* PAUL *jumps with exclamation.*)

PAUL. Oh!

HARRY. I mean about telling the girls.

PAUL (*doubtfully*). Well, I don't know. Maybe they ought to be told, and on the other hand maybe they oughtn't.

HARRY (*back of sofa*). You're a lot of help to me! (*To* CROSBY.) You win. I shall say nothing.

CROSBY (*to* PAUL). You'll keep quiet, Paul?

PAUL (*doubtfully*). Well, I don't know—it seems to me under the circumstances——

CROSBY (*exasperated*). Will you answer me?

PAUL. What I started to say was—it seems to me under the circumstances——

CROSBY. Will you or won't you?

PAUL (*rises*). Well, you don't give me a chance to talk. (*Rises.*) Of course I won't say anything. (*Goes back of sofa to bookcase.*)

CROSBY. Now, Susan, promise not to mention this to the girls!

SUSAN. Of course I won't. Good heavens, do you think I'm the kind who can't keep a secret? (*Rises.*) Let me tell you, Mr. Crosby, that we girls don't talk half as much as you men. (CROSBY *goes to window.* SUSAN *changes her voice to a moan.*) Oh dear—oh dear—I just know we'll all be murdered in our beds. (*Crosses to sofa.*)

HARRY (*grins*). Cheer up—the worst is yet to come. (*Cautions silence as* CICILY *enters and leaves door open.*)

CICILY. Annabelle wants you to come to supper!

CROSBY. We'll be right along.

CICILY (*goes to* SUSAN *on couch*). Why, Cousin Sue—what is it?

SUSAN (*getting up*). Oh, it's nothing —nothing! Come, Cicily, I must have a strong cup of tea! (*The men have their backs to them, and as she walks to door with* CICILY *she says rapidly.*) My dear—I've something to tell you about a terrible old maniac—who is loose in this house—

he thinks he's a cat!—Oh, I wish there was a train back to New York. (SUSAN *and* CICILY *exit.*)

CROSBY (*continuing his conversation*). Now I don't—think there is any danger, but it is just as well to be prepared. (HARRY *starts to go.*) Where are you going, Harry?

HARRY (*at door*). Out in the garden for a little air. (PAUL *goes, sits on sofa.*)

CROSBY (*alarmed*). But—suppose you run across this madman?

HARRY. You mean the cat—if I do— I'll bark at him and chase him up a tree! (*Grins at them in a peculiar manner.*) I—I won't see you again, Mr. Crosby—I'm leaving early in the morning. Good-by! (*Exits.*)

CROSBY. Good-by! (*To* CHARLIE.) We had better go down and see that all the windows and doors are bolted.

CHARLIE. I'll be right along—I want to speak to Annabelle.

CROSBY. Come on, Paul.

PAUL (*in reverie*). Eh!

CROSBY. Come on. (*Exits.*)

PAUL. Well, I don't know that I'll be much use to you—but then again, I'm always nervous before going into action. (*Meets* ANNABELLE *at door.* CHARLIE *is looking out of window L.*)

ANNA. Paul, are you coming back?

PAUL. I hope so. (*Exits.*)

ANNA (*seeing* CHARLIE). Charlie, don't you want anything to eat?

CHARLIE. I'd rather talk to you while I have the chance. (*Closes door.*)

ANNA (*sits R. of table*). Go ahead!

CHARLIE. I don't know just how to begin!

ANNA (*smiles at him*). Then let's begin by asking you a few questions.

CHARLIE (C.). All right!

ANNA (*looks at him intently*). What's the trouble between you and Harry?

CHARLIE. You.

ANNA. Oh, I thought it was something deeper than that—more important, you know.

CHARLIE. There's nothing in the world quite so important as you, Annabelle.

ANNA. That isn't so awfully good, Charlie.

CHARLIE. My dear, I'm not trying to flatter you. I was only speaking the truth. Our quarrel was about you. Of course I don't exactly blame him —he's jealous.

ANNA. Just jealousy doesn't explain this deadly hate that's sprung up between you and Harry—and I don't like it.

CHARLIE. The hate's all on his side —I've tried to make it up. But I'm afraid that's Harry's nature—he broods over the fact that I've cut him out.

ANNA. With me?

CHARLIE. Of course—I didn't tell him about it—he just sort of sensed it.

ANNA. Still you must have been quite sure that you had cut him out. (*Faces front.*)

CHARLIE. Why, I thought I had some reason to feel that—well—it *is* all right, isn't it? (*Crosses back of her and sits on table.*)

ANNA. It's all right to feel anything you choose, but isn't it taking a great deal for granted to think that I'm in love with you?

CHARLIE. Perhaps it is—but when you chased Harry off—and encouraged me——

ANNA. And I don't mind owning up that for a while I was a *wee* bit foolish about you——

CHARLIE. Thanks.

ANNA. And it might have got worse —you know, you have a way of making yourself rather attractive—and you did seem to be so fearfully sincere. Then—suddenly you changed. I couldn't make out what it was. You seemed worried about something. I thought it must be one of two things—another girl or money. But it couldn't be money—you're too successful.

CHARLIE. No, just successful enough —to get what I go after.

ANNA. That's just it—what you go after. But you sort of let up going after me.

CHARLIE. You're mistaken, I never——

ANNA (*rises and crosses to C.*). It was the other girl—(*leaves envelope that* MAMMY *gave her on table. Turns*)—or girls—how many were there?

CHARLIE. None.

ANNA. That's such an old one. Charlie! (*Crosses R.*)

CHARLIE. It doesn't make it any the less true.

ANNA. All right—I'll take your word for that part—(*sits on sofa*)—but the rest—I know—when it came—your growing coldness——

CHARLIE (*going to her*). There was no such thing.

ANNA. Then call it distraction—whatever you like.

CHARLIE. But that passed and I came back—more in love with you than ever.

ANNA. Yes, and I welcomed you—I tried to warm up the old affection. And only today I ′realized that it couldn't be done.

CHARLIE. You can't really mean——(ANNABELLE *looks and turns head away.*) Isn't there the slightest hope —ever?

ANNA. No! Fate has taken the matter out of my hands!

CHARLIE. You—you—really—love him?

ANNA. I can't help it, Charlie.

CHARLIE. Then I guess this is my finish. (*Moving L.*)

ANNA. Not unless you wish it.

CHARLIE. You think after this—we could be just friends?

ANNA. I wish you'd try.

CHARLIE. Very well, I'll try. Good night, Annabelle.

ANNA. Good night, Charlie. See you in the morning. (CHARLIE *exits.* ANNABELLE *puts out light R., crosses to table L. for envelope, sees book, opens book. Starts at what she sees.*) Fear! Eh! (*She reads, sits R. of table, very much interested.* CROSBY *enters and starts up R. before he sees her.*) Paul. Oh, Mr. Crosby.

CROSBY (*pausing R.C.*). You here alone, Annabelle? I don't want to worry you, but there's something you ought to know.

ANNA. Won't it keep till morning, Mr. Crosby? (ANNABELLE *reading.*)

CROSBY. No—tomorrow may be too late. Annabelle! (ANNABELLE *looks at him.* ANNABELLE *smiles and continues to read.*) You know Mr. West was a very eccentric man—I have just made a discovery—it has convinced me it would be dangerous for you to be left here alone. (*Over to bookcase R. and feels along case for spring.*)

ANNA (*looking over her shoulder at him and laughing*). Mr. Crosby.

CROSBY. Don't laugh, Annabelle! (*Examining R.U. corner of bookcase.*) I know what I'm talking about, believe me. I'm alarmed—and I want you to take me seriously. (*Panel opens;* CROSBY's *back is to it. He half turns toward* ANNABELLE.) Annabelle, you're in danger—great danger—but, thank God, I can tell you who they——

(*Hand comes through panel and drags* CROSBY *off by throat.* CROSBY *disappears into panel, which closes after him.*)

ANNA (*does not see what has happened but is interested in book. Finally, in vague sort of way, she becomes aware that* CROSBY *has stopped talking so she turns to answer him*). But, Mr. Crosby, I've heard so much about ghosts and spirits tonight that in spite of myself I'm growing nervous. And so that's why I'd rather not hear——— (ANNABELLE *looks up and finds herself alone. She is startled and rises.*) Mr. Crosby! Mr. Crosby! (*She goes to door and opens it.* MAMMY *is standing in door looking at* ANNABELLE *with a peculiar look.*) Where did Mr. Crosby go?

MAMMY (*enters and crosses R. of door*). I ain't seen him.

ANNA (*startled*). You haven't seen him? You must have passed him in the hall.

MAMMY. No, Miss West, I passed no one in the hall, and I ain't seen Mr. Crosby. Are you sure he was in this room?

ANNA (*crosses R. of door. She is shaken*). Yes—yes—I was talking with him just a moment ago. (*Goes to hall, calls.*) Susan, Cicily, Paul! Why do you look at me like this?

(CICILY *enters with* SUSAN. *She sees something has happened. She goes to* ANNABELLE.)

SUSAN. What is it, Annabelle?

ANNA. Was Mr. Crosby with you in the dining room?

CICILY. No. Only Charlie and Paul. (PAUL *and* CHARLIE *enter. Boys enter, cross to back of table.* PAUL R. CHARLIE L.) Mr. Blythe is outside in the garden. (*Looks at her keenly.*) What's wrong, Annabelle?

ANNA (*trying to speak calmly*). An extraordinary thing has happened. A few moments ago I was sitting there—(*points to chair R. of table*)—and Mr. Crosby was there—(*points up stage and continues*)—talking to me—when suddenly he—vanished. (*All look at each other.*)

CICILY (*exchanges an alarmed look with* SUSAN). Vanished! (SUSAN *sits chair R. of table.*)

CHARLIE (*puzzled*). Mr. Crosby vanished?

(PAUL *moves to back of* ANNA.)

ANNA. Yes, he melted into the air. I ran and opened the door. Mammy was standing there. (*All look at* MAMMY.) And she said that no one had left the room.

MAMMY (*with a malicious look*). I didn't see anyone leave this room.

ANNA (*wildly*). But you must have heard him talking to me when you came down the hall.

MAMMY. I only heard you—talking to yourself.

(ANNABELLE *down R.* MAMMY *exits, leaving door open.*)

SUSAN (*sitting R. of table. To* CICILY). I'm afraid Cyrus West wasn't the only lunatic in our family. (*Looks at* ANNABELLE.) When a woman begins to talk to herself and to see people vanish right in front of her—it is curious.

CHARLIE. Are you trying to insinuate that Annabelle is losing her mind?

SUSAN (*faintly*). Oh dear, oh dear.

ANNA (*crosses to L. of sofa*). You—you mean you don't believe me?

CHARLIE (*to* CICILY). Certainly we do.

PAUL. Certainly.

ANNA (*at sofa*). But you do think that I imagined Mr. Crosby disappeared in front of me. If that's imagination—where is Mr. Crosby?

SUSAN (*crosses to* ANNABELLE). Probably out with Harry Blythe in the garden. My dear, you are upset and nervous—I didn't mean to say you were crazy—I was only trying to—— Come, Cicily, let us go to our room and pile the furniture in front of the door. What with a dozen lunatics in the house, it will be a mercy if we're not all murdered in our beds. (*Exit with* CICILY.)

CHARLIE (*crosses to* ANNABELLE. PAUL *crosses up to panel, takes book, and opens it as if to read*). Is there anything I can do?

ANNA. Yes—yes—please find Mr. Crosby!

CHARLIE. Where—was he standing—when he vanished?

ANNA (*points to the exact spot where* PAUL *is standing looking at them*). There. (PAUL *closes book with a slam and dashes madly round sofa R. and sits.*) Please try to find him.

CHARLIE. I'll do my best, Annabelle! (*Exits, giving them a curious look, closes door.*)

ANNA (*crosses to front of table L.*). Paul! You don't think I'm mad, do you?

PAUL (*rising—doubtfully*). Well, I guess I'd get goldarned mad if some old chatterbox said I was crazy—but then again, if I really was crazy, I wouldn't have sense enough to get mad.

ANNA (*sighs*). You're such a help to me! Good night!

PAUL (*crosses to* ANNABELLE). But I want to talk to you. I haven't had a chance.

ANNA. Your chance will come later—it's almost one o'clock.

PAUL. But I've got an idea.

ANNA. Keep it until morning.

PAUL. But it may not keep until morning.

ANNA. Run along now, and see if Mr. Crosby has returned. Good night, Paul. (ANNABELLE *goes to chair at window.*)

PAUL. Annabelle, I really do think under the circumstances, honest to goodness—— Good night! (*Goes up*

to door. Turns at door.) I only
wanted to say that now I am here
and you're here, too, how awfully
glad I was—glad I am—I mean that
we both am—*was*— Good night.
(PAUL *exits.*)

(*As soon as* ANNABELLE *is alone she
goes to the bookcase where* CROSBY
*was standing when he vanished. She
looks along the rows of books, then
she turns front, shrugs her shoulders, and comes down C.* MAMMY
enters.)

MAMMY. Mr. Crosby ain't come in
yet.

ANNA (*in front of chair C.*). Where
can he be?

MAMMY. I know. It's got him—the
demon in this house. *It's* here.

ANNA (*nervous*). Oh, don't—don't,
please!

MAMMY (*crosses R.*). All right.
Your room is ready and remember
you've got to open that letter.

ANNA (*looks at letter*). Oh yes! Un-
pack my bag, Mammy—I'll be right
in.

(MAMMY *gives her a mysterious look
and goes out, closing door in.* ANNA-
BELLE *crosses to table, looking at envelope, then* ANNABELLE, *sensing
danger, reaches up and turns off the
light, leaving herself in the dark
with the maniac. She rushes to the
door through the moonlight from
the windows, opens it and dashes
out, slamming the door. The monster's head appears above armchair
C. as the*

CURTAIN DROPS

ACT TWO

SCENE—*Bedroom next to library.*
TIME—*A few moments later.*
*A gloomy room with a four-poster bed up stage, L.C. Fireplace L. Door R.C.
Usual tables and chairs.*
DISCOVERED—MAMMY *is taking* ANNABELLE'S *slippers out of suitcase on
chair near window.* MAMMY *crosses to bed and puts slippers under bed, mut-
tering: "Rhonda! Rhonda! Spirit of Evil!" Door opens and* ANNABELLE *enters
from library, holding book in her hand. She shows a certain amount of ap-
prehensive terror—or fear. Something that frightened her—in the other room.
She closes door quickly and then her fear leaves her as she sees the fire and*
MAMMY.

MAMMY (*at bed—as she enters, looks
inquiringly at* ANNABELLE). Why!
what is it?

ANNA (*smiles and shakes her head*).
It's nothing. (*Looks all around.*)
Mammy, that fire is an inspiration.

You have no idea what a difference it makes. (*Over R.*)

MAMMY (*fixing covers on bed—and looking at* ANNABELLE *impassively*). It does make the room more cheerful.

ANNA (*C. Crosses to fireplace L.*). But wait until I redecorate it—I'm going to have a real boudoir here. Mammy, this is—the most wonderful night of my life. I can't realize that I've inherited this house and this estate and everything.

MAMMY. I hope you'll be happy here.

ANNA (*sees a large grandfather's clock in corner up R.*). What a darling old clock. (*Crosses R. to clock.*) Why, it isn't running!

MAMMY. That clock stopped—twenty years ago tonight—just as Mr. West died.

ANNA (*sets it with her wrist watch and it starts ticking*). Let's see if it will go—I guess that's about right. Hear it—isn't that lovely? (*Listens to the tick-tock a minute.*) Hear it? It makes the room cozier than ever. (*Looks around.*) This house has character—(*C.*)—Mammy——

MAMMY. Yeh! (*Crossing to chair R.C.*)

ANNA. —and I'm beginning to love it—more and more every minute—(*crosses L. and changes her tone.* MAMMY *walks over to bag on chair R.C.*)—in spite of—of—what the others said and in spite of what—just happened.

MAMMY. What was that?

ANNA. Nothing really—(*over to* MAMMY *R.C.*)—but—well, just a moment ago—when I turned off the light in the library—I felt—or rather sensed the approach of something—evil.

MAMMY. Evil?

ANNA. For a moment I felt trapped. (*Shudders.*) It was the same horrible feeling I had when I was a little girl—hurrying up the stairs in the dark—afraid something was going to catch me—— Mammy, do you think there could be anything in the house?

MAMMY. Yes, spirits! But there is two kinds. The good ones that help you and the others—like the one that was—behind you in the dark. That was the demon that's got into this house.

ANNA. Oh!

MAMMY. As long as you ain't afraid—it can't get you.

ANNA (*stoutly—crosses L.*). I'm not afraid—of anything. (MAMMY *business with suitcase.*)

MAMMY (*with a sarcastic smile that only the audience sees. Finishes unpacking grip, closes it, and puts it on floor of window R.*) Don't forget that letter—miss.

ANNA (*takes it, with animation*). Oh yes—— (*Sits in armchair. Looks at it.*) Uncle Cyrus gave this to you twenty years ago!

MAMMY (*few steps C. In a peculiar voice, watching her narrowly*). Twenty years ago tonight—just before he died on that—bed!

ANNA (*rises. As she realizes she must sleep on that bed, she shivers and shows fear*). Oh!

MAMMY (*quickly. Few steps nearer* ANNABELLE). You is still a-scared——

ANNA. No—I'm not—in the library just before you called, I picked up this book without knowing what it was—it seemed to open itself at this chapter—called "Fear."

MAMMY. Fear!

ANNA. Listen. (ANNABELLE *sits in armchair L.*) "Fear is a delusion—Fear, or the belief in fear, can be controlled and eliminated by understanding."

MAMMY. You believe that? (*Coming C.*)

ANNA (*reads*). Yes, I do! "Only the ignorant suffer through fear." (*Skips a couple of pages and reads.*) "Take a bird—a canary in its cage—put it on a table—then let a cat jump up and walk around the cage, glaring at the canary. What happens? The canary, seeing its enemy so close to it, is frightened almost to death. But if it had understanding, it would know that the cat couldn't reach it while it had the protection of the cage. Not knowing this, it suffers a thousand deaths—through fear."

MAMMY. But you ain't in no cage.

ANNA. Yes, I am. I am surrounded and protected by my faith and philosophy and my friends. I am not afraid.

MAMMY. But you *is* afraid for Mr. Crosby!

ANNA (*looks at* MAMMY *with a startled expression*). Why—why—I'd forgotten for a moment. Could he have—no—if he had—you would have seen him. (MAMMY *nods. With a note of entreaty in her voice,* ANNABELLE *continues.*) Are you—sure—you didn't see him go out? He must have gone—somewhere—but where? Mammy—(*rises*)—I couldn't have imagined—that he was in the room with me, could I? (*Crosses C.*)

MAMMY (MAMMY *shakes her head doubtfully*). No!

ANNA. He *was* there—(*crosses R. of* MAMMY)—and—yet he's not in the house—but he couldn't have——(*Desperately.*) Mammy, I tell you he was there!

MAMMY. I believe you, miss.

ANNA (*looks at her sharply*). Well, if he *was* there—and you didn't see him go out—where is he?

MAMMY. I tell you—*it*—got him.

ANNA (*angrily—crosses L.*). Rubbish—how could a—spirit—if there was one there—take a man like Mr. Crosby—and—and—disappear with him? No spirit could do a thing like that.

MAMMY. How do you know it couldn't?

ANNA. Well—I just know—that's all.

MAMMY. Huh! What was Mr. Crosby telling you—when he was taken away?

ANNA (*slowly—looking at* MAMMY *with frightened eyes*). He was telling me about—about some danger that was near me—oh!

MAMMY (*with a sinister look of triumph*). You see! He was trying to warn you about—*it*—when *it*—got him.

ANNA. No—no. Impossible. (*Puts book and envelope on mantel.*) Absurd!

(*Three slow knocks at door. First knock,* ANNABELLE *wheels around, looking at door. Second knock,* MAMMY *looks at* ANNABELLE. MAMMY *looks front. Third knock,* MAMMY *looks at door and takes two steps toward door, when it opens and* HARRY *appears and speaks.*)

HARRY. Annabelle—may I come in?

ANNA (HARRY *comes down R.C.* ANNABELLE *looking at* HARRY *keenly*). Yes! Yes! Where have you been?

HARRY. Out in the garden. What is this about Crosby——

ANNA. He was talking to me in the library. I was sitting with my back to him so I couldn't see exactly what happened, but when he stopped talking—I looked around and he'd gone! Could—could—anything have taken him?

HARRY. Of course not. You don't believe in ghosts, do you, Annabelle?

ANNA (*uncertainly*). No—no! But I thought I'd ask you.

HARRY (*gives her a curious look*). As soon as I heard about it, I went to the library and looked around.

There's no place he could hide—no closets or anything. I don't understand it. Are you sure he was in the room with you?

ANNA. Yes, of course I am. Why does everybody keep asking me that? (*Crosses L. to fireplace.*) It's all perfectly exasperating.

HARRY. Annabelle, you're just working yourself up needlessly. Crosby's an able-bodied man—he can take care of himself. Don't worry, it's all right.

ANNA. I hope so. What were you doing in the garden, Harry?

HARRY. Just looking around. Better lock your door tonight, Annabelle.

ANNA. Why should I?

HARRY. Just to be on the safe side. Perhaps I had better sleep in the library.

ANNA (*excitedly*). Why should you?

HARRY. Er—in case you needed me.

ANNA (*more excited*). Why should I need you?

HARRY. I don't know—you might get nervous or something.

ANNA (*almost hysterically*). What about?

HARRY. Oh Lord, I don't know—well, anyway—(*goes to door*)—if you want me—call.

ANNA. Yes, I will. What time do you leave in the morning?

HARRY. Early.—May I say good-by to you before I go?

ANNA (*at corner of bed*). Yes, I wish you would.

HARRY (*looks at her*). Good night, Annabelle.

ANNA. Good night.

HARRY. Don't worry, it's all right. (*Exits with look at* MAMMY *as he closes door.*)

ANNA (*to* MAMMY). He wanted to tell me something—but he didn't dare. I wonder what it was? Heavens, everyone seems to be acting so strangely, I begin to think I must be losing my mind. (*Crosses to fireplace.*)

(MAMMY *looks fixedly at her without speaking.* MAMMY *is on her way to bed with* ANNABELLE'S *negligee when knock is heard; she puts negligee on bed and opens door.* SUSAN *and* CICILY *enter clad in their negligees.*)

SUSAN. Oh, Annabelle!

ANNA (*coming C.*). Just a minute! Mammy, won't you please go and see if Mr. Crosby has returned—look in his room. (MAMMY *exits.*) What is it—anything happened?

SUSAN (*taking* ANNA *to stool L.*). My dear—I simply couldn't sleep. I just had to tell you—that Charlie absolutely misunderstood me—he put the wrong construction on a most innocent remark. I never meant to say that you were really crazy—I only thought that you were upset—my, my dear, please say you understand!

ANNA (*kindly, but with double meaning—to stool*). Yes—I understand—perfectly. (*Indicates for them to sit down.*) Won't you sit down?

SUSAN (*sits in armchair.* ANNABELLE *sits on stool.* CICILY *sits on chair near foot of bed*). Annabelle—I feel it's my duty to tell you something——

CICILY (*stops her—speaks quickly in low voice*). Cousin Sue—you promised you wouldn't.

ANNA (*turns around*). What was that, Cicily?

CICILY (*confused*). Why—why—nothing of importance—Annabelle.

SUSAN. I feel it's my duty to——

CICILY (*interrupts her. Rises*). Oh, your duty!—It would be a lot better, Cousin Sue, if once in a while you would think of other people's feelings—instead of your duty. (*Goes R.C.*)

SUSAN. Heavens! Hear the child rave. You'd think I'd done something terrible. Cicily, where's your respect for me?

CICILY (*tearfully*). I do respect you—(*coming to* SUSAN)—but—but—I've felt so nervous ever since I've been here—and you pick on me because it's your duty—and, oh dear, no one understands me! (*Sits chair at foot of bed.*)

ANNA (*pets her*). Come, come—Cicily—what's it all about?

CICILY. Something—happened—that would make you nervous—if you knew——

ANNA. Anything serious?

CICILY. No—just something that was told me—about the——

SUSAN. I am in duty bound to tell——

CICILY. No, now, Susan——

ANNA. And I don't want to hear it. (*Rises.*) I don't want to hear it! If it will make me any more nervous than I am now. (*Over to window.*) I've had enough for tonight—Susan, you may tell me in the morning.

SUSAN (*asks abruptly*). Are you quite all right now—my dear?

ANNA (*looks at her puzzled*). Why, yes—of course—why do you ask?

SUSAN. I was anxious about you—you know you were—were a little—hysterical in there!

ANNA (*sees what she is driving at and smiles*). I'm all right, thank you.

SUSAN. Your health always been good—my dear?

ANNA (*brings chair down R.C.*). Splendid. I need good health to work the way I do—at my painting and dancing.

SUSAN. I suppose you've led a feverish life—down there in the village with those—those artistic folk?

ANNA (*smiles*). No—never had money enough for that. (*Sits.*)

SUSAN. Ever have black spots in front of your eyes?

ANNA (*smiles*). No——

SUSAN. Ever feel dizzy? (ANNABELLE *shakes her head.*) Pains in the back of your head?

(ANNABELLE *looks at* CICILY.)

ANNA. No.

SUSAN. But you have terrible dreams —don't you?

ANNA (*laughs*). Only—when I sleep on my back.

SUSAN. Do you suffer much from hallucinations?—Come on, tell me!

ANNA (*seriously*). No—but I have— I don't know what you would call them—but they're——

SUSAN (*eagerly*). Symptoms!

ANNA (*intensely*). That's it! I have them every morning—and every evening.

SUSAN. That's the dangerous time, my dear——

CICILY. What are they?

ANNA. Every morning—as soon as I wake up—I have the queerest feeling, it's some feeling——

SUSAN (*her eyes popping out in excitement*). Yes—you—I knew it—I knew it—where——

ANNA (*points to her stomach*). Here —and the funny part of it is—it disappears—as soon as I've had my breakfast. (*Laughs and winks at* CICILY.) I was just fooling, Susan. I'm just an ordinary—healthy, normal girl. If I weren't so normal I'd probably be a better artist. Anything else you'd like to know?

SUSAN. I hope you're not offended at my questions, my dear? It's only because I take such an interest in you, *now that you're the heiress!* And I've been wondering if there really is anything in hereditary insanity. It's in our family, you know.

ANNA (*rises—laughing*). I'm afraid it's missed our side entirely, eh, Cicily? (*Placing chair near window.*)

CICILY. I don't know anything about that—but it certainly missed *our* side. (CICILY *looks at* SUSAN.)

SUSAN. Well—let us hope so. Another thing, my dear—now that *you are* the heiress, men will suddenly find that you are very attractive. Beware of them, my dear—all of them.

ANNA (*laughing*). All of them?

SUSAN. All of them! Every man who tells you he loves you—is only in love with your money—they're all alike—there isn't a decent man in the world.

CICILY. Oh, Cousin Sue—don't say that! There are lots of nice men in the world. Who could be nicer than those—three men?

SUSAN (*loftily*). Dumbbells—**my** dear—all of them—dumbbells.

(ANNABELLE *goes to the window.*)

CICILY (*firing up*). I don't think so at all—I think Charlie is awfully sweet.

SUSAN. An overgrown ribbon clerk—a bluff—and as cold as a dead fish.

CICILY. You can't say that about Paul. (*Interest from* ANNABELLE.)

He's real cute—and he has such expressive feet.

SUSAN. Paul! He! He don't know anything—not even his own mind. And he's as timid as a rabbit, my dear. Never trust a man with wiggly feet—they're treacherous.

ANNA (*laughing—goes C.*). Let's get them all in. What about Harry?

SUSAN. He's the biggest fool of the lot. Every time he looks at me he begins to laugh.

ANNA (*with mock gravity*). Really? You know men—don't you?

SUSAN. I do—and that's why I'm warning you about these fourth- and fifth-rate cousins of yours. (*Rises. Crosses to* ANNABELLE.) Take my advice and get rid of them as soon as you can. Good night, dear—(CICILY *rises*)—and I hope you won't have any more—more—— (*Goes to door, turns, and speaks firmly.*) Annabelle, I feel it's my duty to tell you something——

(CICILY *interrupts* SUSAN.)

CICILY. Susan——

SUSAN. Don't you dare to interrupt me! Annabelle, they made me promise that I wouldn't tell you about the dreadful maniac—who's prowling around the house.

(ANNABELLE *aghast—the scene switches to the serious.*)

ANNA. What are you saying—a maniac—in this house?

CICILY. Yes—and the guard——

SUSAN (*comes to her*). The guard from the asylum was here; he had traced him to this house. He's a terrible old person. He thinks he's a cat—and goes around ripping people wide open. They made me promise I wouldn't tell you, but I felt it my duty to warn you—because if we are all going to be murdered in our beds —I think we ought to know about it.

CICILY. If there's anything in anticipation, Cousin Sue—you've been murdered a dozen times.

ANNA. So that's why Harry was so mysterious—that's what he wanted to tell me.

CICILY. Harry wanted to warn us, but Mr. Crosby and Charlie wouldn't let him.

ANNA (*almost to herself*). I wonder if that was what Mr. Crosby was trying to tell me when——

SUSAN (*with terror*). Perhaps—perhaps—he got Mr. Crosby——

ANNA (*gasps*). Then he *must* be in the house.

SUSAN. He must be. (*Whispers.*) He must be sneaking around the hall—now—waiting to jump on us— I could scream——

ANNA (*white but calm*). Yes—if he got Mr. Crosby—then—he *must* be in the house.

SUSAN (*hysterically*). Maybe he's out there now—*waiting* for us.

(*Door bangs and* PAUL *enters. At bang a scream from the three girls as they fly over L.* SUSAN L. *corner,* CICILY L. *of* SUSAN, *and* ANNABELLE *down extreme L.*)

PAUL (*dashes in, slams door after him—white with terror and hair standing on end, he stammers in his fright. Points at door*). Out in the hall, out in the hall—something passed me—I couldn't see it—but I felt it, it touched me—I heard it breathe——

SUSAN. You did. (*Doorknob rattles.*)

PAUL. Look out. (*All scream.*)

MAMMY (*enters and fixes her eye on* PAUL). Why did you run away from me?

PAUL. You! Was it you—that passed me in the hall?

MAMMY. Yes sir! (PAUL *falls in* chair. MAMMY *to others.*) I was coming from Mr. Crosby's room— Mr. Paul saw me in the hall and he turned and ran like a mouse.

SUSAN (*with triumph*). You were scared!

PAUL (*rises*). Well, I don't know that I was exactly scared—I may have been a trifle nervous—you see, I was just coming——

MAMMY. No sir, you was going!

PAUL (*few steps R.*). Well—maybe I was——

ANNA. You see, Paul, you were frightened by an idea—a delusion. You thought Mammy was a ghost and she frightened you. Your fear was nothing but imagination.

SUSAN (*exchanges knowing look with* CICILY *and says soothingly*). Yes—yes, my dear, no doubt—you're right. But all the same, if I were you I'd lock the door tonight and look under the bed. That's what I'm going to do.

ANNA. Really! (*Begins to laugh.*)

SUSAN. Don't laugh, my dear. I've never gone to sleep in my life without first looking under the bed.

PAUL (*going to her*). What do you expect to find there?

SUSAN. Why, a man, of course.

PAUL (*smiling*). Wouldn't that be terrible for the man?

SUSAN. Mr. Jones!

PAUL. And then on the other hand maybe it wouldn't. I don't know!

SUSAN (*glares at him, takes* CICILY'S *arm, and goes to door*). Come, Cicily, let us go to bed—we'll feel safer there. (*Exits.*)

CICILY (*wails*). I'm afraid to go upstairs—in the dark.

ANNA. Mammy—go along with them —good night.

(CICILY *and* MAMMY *exit. Close door.*)

PAUL (*looks at* ANNABELLE, *suddenly embarrassed*). I wonder if— well, I guess it's all right, but on the other hand——

ANNA. What's all right?

PAUL. My being here alone with you. (*Looks at her negligee and gulps.*)

ANNA (*crosses L.*). Of course it's all right. This isn't an ordinary occasion, and besides, we're cousins, aren't we? (*Sits in armchair L.*)

PAUL. Yes, we're fifth or sixth cousins. But somehow you seem like a perfect stranger to me. (*Crosses L. to* ANNABELLE.)

ANNA. Is that why you acted so queerly when we met in the other room?

PAUL. Yes. It didn't seem possible that you—were Annabelle West, my little—(ANNABELLE *looks at him. Gulps*)—the little girl I used to know in Wickford—so long ago.

ANNA (*looking front*). It must have been all of five years.

PAUL. Five years and eleven months —(ANNABELLE *looks at* PAUL)—yes, five years and eleven months—since you left Wickford and went to New York to study art. Remember, you always wanted to be a great artist or a trained nurse.

ANNA (*smiles and nods*). And you were going to be a *great surgeon*— and so——

PAUL. I went to college and became a horse doctor. The folks never did think I'd amount to much—no—but on the other hand, well, I've got ideas. I've got one now. (*Crosses to stool L. and sits.*)

ANNA. I'm sure you have! But—isn't —it strange for us to meet like this— after five years?

PAUL. Well, maybe it is strange— but I think it's wonderful. I used to think about you a lot.

ANNA (*pleased*). You did! Really! How nice!

PAUL (*embarrassed*). Yes—oh yes—no doubt of it—now that I remember—I did think of you—often.

ANNA (*smiles*). You don't seem to be quite certain about it. Are you ever sure about anything?

PAUL (*seriously—swinging stool around*). There's one thing—I'm dead sure about!

ANNA (*amazed*). You mean that you're really positive about something? (*Looking front.*)

PAUL (*intense*). Yes, Annabelle—I—I—— (ANNABELLE *looks at* PAUL. *Stops and gulps.*) But on the other hand—you probably wouldn't believe me.

ANNA. How do you know? You've never been really serious with me. Why don't you try?

PAUL (*floundering*). I am trying—but I don't seem to get anywhere. I've been trying to ask you something for the last five minutes.

ANNA. Then for heaven's sake, stop rambling around and ask me.

PAUL. I'm going to—just as soon as I get myself wound up.

ANNA. Paul—about how long does it take you to wind yourself up?

PAUL. I don't know—exactly.

ANNA. Evidently it's quite an operation.

PAUL. Well—this time—it's taken me five years—and eleven months—and I don't know if I'm wound up yet—but I'm getting set—to—— (*Gulp.*)

ANNA (*exasperated*). Paul—*what*—are you trying to tell me?

PAUL. Listen—Annabelle—I—— (*Gulps.*) You know I'm only a vet. (ANNABELLE *nods.*) But from doctoring horses and mules—I've learned a great deal about women—I mean that all three of them do a lot of things they shouldn't do and without any reason.

ANNA. Yes.

PAUL. Yes.

ANNA. What *are* you trying to tell me?

PAUL. This—Annabelle—— (*Gulps.*) Did Cousin Susie tell you about something that's going on around the house tonight?

ANNA. You mean about spirits?

PAUL (*nervously*). Well—not altogether about spirits. You know, Annabelle, I'm not exactly afraid of spirits—but on the other hand you can't see them—and—— (*Looks around as if expecting to see spirits.*)

ANNA. You mean about the crazy man?

PAUL. That's it. *I* couldn't tell you—but from my knowledge of women I guessed that Cousin Susie'd tell you because she had promised she wouldn't.

ANNA. Yes—she told me—and it hasn't cheered me up any. I wonder if he really is around the house, Paul?

PAUL. I—I don't know—I don't know—but what I want to tell you is that *I'll protect you.* I've handled wild horses and wilder mules, and there isn't a spook or a maniac living that I'm afraid of—— (*Gong is heard tolling the half hour.* PAUL'S *knees are knocking together.* PAUL *rises and crosses* L.) Good Lord—that gong again.

ANNA. It's only the clock, Paul, see?

PAUL (*mops his brow, crosses* C.). Lord—I thought it was that other gong. The one Mammy said was tolling for someone's death tonight!

ANNA (*shudders*). Don't, Paul—please don't talk about it.

PAUL (*crossing to her*). I'm awfully sorry——

ANNA (*smiles*). You were saying that——

PAUL. I was saying that I wasn't afraid—— (*Breaks off and grins at her.*) You know I'm lying, don't you? I'm scared stiff—but I'm always like that—I always get nervous when I go into action. Every time we went over the top I was paralyzed—but I had to go—scared or not. So scared or not—if that maniac is in your house, I'm going to get him.

ANNA. You always did fight for me, didn't you, Paul? Even away back there in Wickford when you used to carry my books to school!

PAUL (*sits on arm of chair*). I'll never forget those days.

ANNA. Remember the time big Jim Daly pulled my hair? (PAUL *nods.*) Remember how you flew at him? (*She doubles up her fists.*) And what a *terrible beating*——

PAUL. *He* gave me. Yes—I'll never forget it. Seems I always got licked fighting for you. Well, I hope I have better luck—(*a few steps* C.)—with the lunatic—if I find him. Listen, Annabelle! If you hear a rumpus or anything, don't come out—just sit tight and yell like hell!

ANNA. I feel safe now, knowing *you* are protecting me. Good night, Paul.

PAUL (*taking her hand*). Good night.

ANNA. —And good luck if you find him.

PAUL (*up to door*). Thanks! I'll probably need it, if he finds me.

ANNA. Good night, Paul.

PAUL. Good-by!

ANNA. Good-by? Won't I see you in the morning?

PAUL. God knows——

(*Door opens;* PAUL *gives a startled "Ah!" and flies out the door.* MAMMY *enters and goes to dresser with glass of water.*)

ANNA (*seated in armchair*). There's a *man*, Mammy! He's just naturally frightened to death, but he conquers his fear!

(MAMMY *looks at her intently.*)

MAMMY. Don't forget that letter.

ANNA. Oh yes! (*Starts for mantel. There's a knock—it stops her.* MAMMY *opens the door.*)

CHARLIE (*stands in doorway*). Did I interrupt you, Annabelle?

ANNA. Come in.

CHARLIE. You don't mind? (*Coming down L.C.* MAMMY *closes door and crosses to window.*)

ANNA. No, I'm glad you came. I wanted to see you. Charlie, what do you think has become of Mr. Crosby?

CHARLIE. I haven't any definite theory—I've been trying to figure it out. It's very puzzling—but I think he'll turn up all right. You are the one—I am worried about.

ANNA. That's very sweet of you—but why worry about me?

CHARLIE. Just the natural feeling a man has for the woman he—— (*Looks at her sincerely.*) Annabelle —you know how I feel—toward you. (*Reaches for her hand.*)

ANNA (*turns away*). Please, Charlie.

CHARLIE. This is a queer old house— and if—well, if you need me—just call. My room is at the end of the hall, you know.

ANNA. Thanks, Charlie, I know I can count on you. I guess I'll be safe with all the men guarding me. Harry just told me the same thing.

CHARLIE (*bitterly*). So he was here? Leave it to him to get anywhere first.

ANNA. And, Charlie—I know all about that crazy man.

CHARLIE. So you know—about that?

ANNA. Yes.

CHARLIE. And—*he* told you?

ANNA. I'm not telling you who told me. (*Smiles.*) You ought to be able to guess.

CHARLIE. All right. Now—I'll be ready if you need me—because I'm not going to—I'm going to sleep with my shoes on. (*A few steps R.*) Annabelle—don't you think you could ever feel—a little—a little—— (*Over to* ANNABELLE.)

ANNA. Please, Charlie—I'm very fond of you—I'm awfully sorry.

CHARLIE (*looks at her sadly*). Good night—Annabelle. (*Exits—closes door.*)

(ANNABELLE *goes up to bed and picks up negligee.*)

MAMMY. Don't forget that letter, miss.

ANNA. Oh yes. (*Crosses to mantel— takes letter from back of mantel.* ANNABELLE *starts to open letter.* MAMMY *starts to go out.*) Don't go— I want you to help me—just the negligee! It's so late I'm not really going to bed—just lie down. (*Opening envelope, reading.* MAMMY *gets negligee from bed.*) "To my heir— man or woman—as you read—pause and reflect that this is the twentieth anniversary of the hour that my spirit left my body——" (*Looks up, impressed.*) "I could take no earthly possessions with me—I was compelled to leave them to you—my unknown heir—your hour will come and you will follow me." (ANNA-BELLE *becomes uneasy, gives a sickly laugh, then continues reading.)* "In your brief ·span of life, enjoy the glittering symbols of the world which I have renounced." *(Looks up.)* Oh—it gives me the creeps. *(Looks at letter.)* Here's a verse. It's a little more cheerful. *(Reads verse.)*

"Find the number beneath the vine;
The sparkling gems forthwith are thine.
Find the number; its rhyme is 'mine'!"

(Looks up.) What a silly little verse; but it's the key to the necklace—it must be. Come along, Mammy— help me. *(Crosses to mantel, puts letter there.)* "Find the number beneath the vine"? And then—what number rhymes with mine?

MAMMY. Nine!

ANNA *(thinking it over. Crosses to* MAMMY *and unhooking dress as she goes).* Of course. Nine rhymes with "mine." And the date—today is the twenty-seventh—two and seven— make nine—and—September—is the —ninth month; nine *must* be the number.

MAMMY *(putting negligee on her).* But you have two nines now.

ANNA *(crestfallen).* True. *(MAMMY picks up dress and folds it over her arm.)* But two nines make eighteen —and eight and one make nine. It must be nine. Now I wonder where the vine is? *(Business of looking around room. Sees where MAMMY is looking.* MAMMY *looks at mantel.)* There, Mammy?

MAMMY. Nine! *(Pointing to mantel.* ANNABELLE *crosses to mantel.*

MAMMY *puts dress on chair at dresser and goes to door.)* Need me any more, miss?

ANNA. Not now, Mammy—if I want you I'll call—beneath the vine—— *(MAMMY goes to door and turns the knob and opens door. Nervously.)* Oh, Mammy, put the key in this side of the door, will you?

(MAMMY changes the key from the outside of the door to the inside, so ANNABELLE *can look at it.)*

MAMMY. Good night, miss!

ANNA. Good night, Mammy! *(Crosses to door and locks it, then goes to mantel and looks at scrollwork, thinking.)* Beneath the vine —the vine—the—— *(ANNABELLE'S eye notices on the carven scrollwork of the fireplace a vine. With growing excitement she stands up and examines it, then she counts the little carven knobs from the edge of the mantel.)* One—two—three— four — five — six — seven — eight — nine. *(The ninth is directly under the vine. She presses it; a secret recess opens and, reaching in, she pulls 'out a blazing necklace. She gazes at its beauty and stands in front of fire to examine it; she kneels and puts it round her neck. The doorknob is seen to turn slowly. She jumps to her feet, crosses to door, unlocks it—opens it quickly but there is no one there—she calls.)* Who's there? *(There is no answer but the echo of her own voice. The house is deathly quiet. Taken with a sudden terror, she quickly closes door and locks it. She starts back to fire, gets her slippers from under the bed. She sits in front of fire and begins to put on slippers. When she gets first slipper on, there are heard three dull taps on door.* ANNABELLE *looks quickly at door but thinks it's her imagination. At second slipper, a scratching is heard on door.* ANNABELLE *rises, picks up book on mantel to reassure herself that there is nothing to fear. Then she starts to electric switch at L. of door but no one is there; she smiles and says:*) How silly. (*Then she kicks off slipper at lower end of bed, arranges the pillows. Then she puts out lights and gets into bed. After wriggling around for a moment to get comfortable, she takes off necklace and slips it under pillow—gives a sigh and relaxes into sleep. Then a long arm with a clawlike hand is thrust from the panel. With crooked fingers it reaches slowly, cautiously toward* ANNABELLE'S *throat as if to strangle her. As it touches her, she jumps up in bed. The arm disappears—the panel closes and she screams.*) Oh! Help! Help! (*She jumps from bed to the door. She tries to get out; when she finds she can't, she pounds on door in a frenzy and calls.*) I can't get out—the key is gone! Paul, Charlie, Harry! Paul, Paul! (ANNABELLE *faints.*)

(*There is a slight pause, then* HARRY *is heard running down the hall. He raps on the door saying:*)

HARRY. Annabelle, Annabelle, did you call?

PAUL. Harry, I heard Annabelle call.

SUSAN. What is it, Annabelle?

CICILY. What's happened?

(*All this time* HARRY *is pounding on door trying to open it.*)

CHARLIE. Try the door, break it down!

(*Door is broken in and* HARRY, *with flashlight, followed by* PAUL, CHARLIE, SUSAN, *and* CICILY *dashes in.* HARRY *comes down L. of* ANNABELLE *with flashlight on her.* PAUL *to her.*)

PAUL (*seeing* ANNABELLE). Annabelle!

CHARLIE. What is it?

PAUL. She's fainted. (PAUL *and* HARRY *lift her and* PAUL *places her in armchair L.*)

CHARLIE. What's happened?

HARRY (*turns on lights and looks at door*). I don't know. (*Flashing light on* MAMMY, *who is entering door.*)

(CICILY *crosses to* PAUL *with smelling salts, then she puts on* ANNABELLE'S *slippers.* SUSAN *down stage R., looking out of window.*)

CHARLIE (*crosses and looks under side of bed*). I heard her scream for help.

HARRY. She's had a shock.

CHARLIE. How did she get it?

HARRY (*looking around stage R.*). I don't know. There's no one here! It couldn't be her imagination.

CHARLIE (*coming down C. Has been glaring at* HARRY *all this time, now speaks with a cold fury*). It must be her imagination.

HARRY (*turning to* CHARLIE. *Startled*). What do you mean——

CHARLIE. That you told her——

HARRY. Told her what?

CHARLIE. Told her about the maniac after we'd all agreed to keep silent.

HARRY (*hotly*). I didn't——

CHARLIE (*cuts him off*). Don't lie—you were here—you told her.

HARRY. You're crazy. I didn't tell her a thing.

CHARLIE (*violently*). You're a liar.

(HARRY, *furious, starts for him with clenched fists*.)

CICILY (*turning to them*). Charlie, you're wrong. Cousin Sue told her.

CHARLIE (*crossing to* SUSAN R. *Furiously to* SUSAN). So you're the one?

SUSAN. Yes, I'm the one. I told her because it was my duty, and I'd do it again.

CHARLIE. You ought to be gagged for the rest of your life. (*To* HARRY.) I was mistaken—I'm sorry——

HARRY (*with menace*). Save your breath—you'll need it later!

CHARLIE (*sneers*). Will I—really?

HARRY. Yes. You called me a liar. You'll have to make good for that.

PAUL. Sh! Quiet—Annabelle!

(*All stand and watch* ANNABELLE.)

CICILY. She's coming to.

ANNA (*comes out of her faint, sobs, and holds* PAUL *with a convulsive grip*). Oh! Oh!

PAUL (*soothes her*). There! There! Annabelle, what was it?

ANNA (*still dazed, looks wonderingly at them*). It came from the dark—it—it touched me. (*Points to throat.*) Here! (*Feels for necklace.*) It's gone!

SUSAN. What's gone—my dear?

ANNA. My necklace—the—the hand took it.

HARRY. What hand?

ANNA (*looks at him with frightened eyes and gasps*). I don't know—just —a hand.

SUSAN (*with incredulity*). Just a hand! My dear Annabelle, you're raving again. It's nothing but your imagination.

CHARLIE (*to* SUSAN). Sh!

ANNA. No—I saw it—it was here—it touched me——

CICILY (R. *of* ANNABELLE). But, Annabelle—if there was anything here—where is it now?

ANNA (*vaguely*). It *was* here—it—it took my necklace.

CHARLIE. There was no one in here —when we broke in, Annabelle.

PAUL. If Annabelle says that something was here in the room—something was in the room! Now, the question is, what was it?

HARRY (*cynically*). Why not the maniac?

SUSAN (*R.*). Ha! Even if he had been here—which he wasn't—what possible use would he have for a necklace? (*Few steps up stage.*)

CICILY (*with pity—crosses to* SUSAN. PAUL *crosses to dresser for glass of water, gives some to* ANNABELLE, *and puts it on mantel, then comes back to her*). Oh, the poor dear—isn't it a shame? What do you think, Charlie?

CHARLIE (*at window*). I don't think she saw anything.

HARRY (*crosses to* CICILY). Well, I do. (*Doggedly.*) She must have seen something—terrible to make her faint like that. Her imagination couldn't do it.

SUSAN (*coming down between* CICILY *and* HARRY). No! But an unsound mind could! (*Looks at them in triumph.*)

CICILY (*sadly*). What!

SUSAN. Ha—I've known all along that Annabelle was as crazy as a March hare.

(PAUL *looks at them.*)

CHARLIE. That's absurd.

SUSAN. It's true. Didn't she say that Mr. Crosby vanished right in front of her? (*Looks at them.*) And now she says that a hand reached out and took her necklace. Rubbish! If anything was here—where did it go? People don't disappear in the air—even if she says they do. Annabelle is unbalanced. (PAUL *looks.*) And I for one am going to see that she is examined by a specialist!

HARRY. You ought to be ashamed.

CICILY. Oh, Cousin Sue!

SUSAN. Don't Cousin Sue me! All of you—every one of you—think just the same as I do—that Annabelle is crazy. (PAUL *moves C.*) Only none of you are honest enough to come right out with it.

(HARRY *goes up to dresser and puts flashlight on it.*)

ANNA (*who has been listening to all this, suddenly stands up*). So that's it—you all think I am mad.

PAUL. I don't.

ANNA. I know you don't. (*Crosses to C.* PAUL *works over to L. of bed.* HARRY *and* CHARLIE *start to say something.* ANNABELLE *silences them with a gesture.*) You've had your say about me—now I'll have mine. I've been through enough tonight to drive anyone mad—and a few moments ago I was hysterical—but now I can think clearly. I'm going to tell you exactly what happened to me in this room and you're going to believe it. (*Pauses and looks at them. They all stand motionless, watching her.*) I found the necklace there—(*points to fireplace*)—then—I felt something watching me. The doorknob turned when I opened the door—there was no one there—something was either trying to frighten me—or my nerves were getting jumpy. I looked under the bed—nothing there—then I was certain it was my nerves. I turned out the light—and went to bed—and then—just as I was falling asleep

—I felt an icy breath sweep over me —I opened my eyes and out of the darkness a long clawlike hand reached toward me—it came—nearer —and nearer—I was like a person in a dream—I couldn't move—it touched my throat—(*her voice gradually gets higher in pitch as she hits her climax*)—I jumped up—the hand disappeared with my necklace —I ran to the door—I couldn't open it—I screamed—and that's all I—— (SUSAN *gives* CICILY *a look and smiles.* ANNABELLE *sees this.*). You don't believe me—some of you think that—(*glancing at* SUSAN)—I'm mad. I'm not—I'm as sane as anyone in this room. You must believe me— because what I've told you is the truth—so help me God. (*She waits a moment. No one speaks—but all look at each other with a certain amount of guilt. Then* ANNABELLE *resumes, with a new note in her voice—a note of triumph—a note of*

truth.) And I'm going to prove it to you. The hand that took my necklace—(*turns and points toward bed*) —came out of that wall. (*Slowly she turns and goes to wall. Others watch her without moving. There is something about* ANNABELLE'S *personality that awes them to silence. She feels along the wall near the bed; her nervous fingers press here and there, trying to find the spring that will open the panel. After a moment's search she accidentally touches the spring, and as the panel starts to open she steps aside with a cry of:*) There! (*Which is cut short by a gasp of horror as a dead body slowly falls forward into the room as the panel opens. All stand without moving, horror-struck at the discovery of the murder.*)

HARRY (*crosses to body, looks at the body's face, and gasps in a low voice*). Crosby! Dead!

CURTAIN

ACT THREE

SCENE—*Same as* ACT I.
TIME—*A few moments later.*
DISCOVERED—MAMMY *opening door, allowing* PAUL *to enter, carrying* ANNABELLE, *who has fainted again. Then* MAMMY *goes down to table L. and turns on lamp.*
CICILY, CHARLES, SUSAN, *and* HARRY *follow.*
HARRY *closes door.* CICILY *goes to table R. and turns on lamp.* CHARLIE, *at table L., pours out whisky.* SUSAN *sits R. of table L.* HARRY *at door looking off L.*

PAUL (*puts* ANNABELLE *on couch and motions to* CHARLIE *on knees in front of sofa*). Give me that—over there.

(CICILY *offers him smelling salts. Points at bottle of whisky on small table.* CHARLIE *comes over with glass of whisky which* PAUL *refuses.*

CICILY *takes glass and puts it on table L. All the others act in an abnormally quiet manner. They have just been through an abnormal scene* [CROSBY *murder*], *and they are trying to keep calm at the same time. They carry a terrifically tense atmosphere.* MAMMY, *alone, is impassive. She is like a sphinx.* HARRY *walks up and down the room;* CHARLIE *stands there—trying to think;* SUSAN *is almost out; she is sunk.*)

CICILY (*back of sofa*). Oh, isn't it terrible! Poor Mr. Crosby——

(PAUL *takes salts from* CICILY.)

HARRY (*silences her with a gesture. At door.* MAMMY *above table L.*) Yes—yes——

CHARLIE (*goes to* PAUL). Is she all right?

PAUL (*shakes his head*). Hasn't come out of it yet.

CHARLIE. God!—what she has been through!

CICILY (*wailing*). What are we going to do!

HARRY (C.). Wait a moment. (*Closes door.*) I'm trying to figure it out. (*Goes up to* PAUL *and looks at* ANNABELLE, *then turns to others.*) When Annabelle recovers—no talk about—that—in there—(*points to other room.* MAMMY *moves to front of small table R. of door*)—understand? (*All nod.*)

PAUL. That's right—not a word to remind her about it—she's been through enough to drive anyone mad. Harry, what do you think we ought to do?

HARRY (*speaking in a low tone*). Listen, all of you—there's no doubt about our having company in the house—Crosby's death proves that—and Annabelle has been in terrible peril. But how did he—or whatever it was—get in there? (*Looking at* MAMMY.)

PAUL. God knows. Crosby and I locked every window and door. Then after you started for bed, I went through the house but didn't see or hear a thing.

CHARLIE (L. *of sofa*). Of course you didn't. The maniac—or whatever killed Crosby—was hiding behind that panel.

HARRY. That's just what I'm coming to—that panel. I'm wondering if it would be best to explore it now —or to wait for the police? (*Opens door.*)

CICILY. Don't go in there and leave us alone.

HARRY. There's probably no one in it—now—and yet—there may be something we don't ever dream of—— (*Opens door and looks across hall.*)

SUSAN (*wails*). Close the door.

(HARRY *closes the door, stands R. of it, looking off L.*)

PAUL. I know what I'm going to do just as soon as Annabelle recovers.

CICILY. Oh, is she all right?

PAUL. Well, she's breathing regularly—and her color's coming back.

CHARLIE. What *are* you going to do?

PAUL. I'm going through that panel, and I'm not going to wait for anybody—not even the police.

HARRY (*slams door and comes down C.*). Just a moment—now think it over, according to the law—no one is supposed to enter a room where a murder has been committed until the police arrive. You probably wouldn't find anything there—anyhow—and you might disturb some valuable clues.

CHARLIE (*turns to* HARRY). For once I agree with you; whoever killed Crosby probably beat it. It isn't natural to believe that the murderer would wait behind that panel to be caught.

HARRY. Even if we found him there —we'd probably have to kill him——

SUSAN. Oh!

HARRY (*continuing*)—defending ourselves, Miss Sillsby. No, we'd better wait. (*Opens door and looks off L.*)

SUSAN (*moaning to herself*). Oh, oh, what a terrible night.

CHARLIE (PAUL *crosses R. to back of sofa, and* CICILY *comes round to front of sofa, sitting L. of* ANNABELLE. *Crosses to* SUSAN—*sternly to* SUSAN). Miss Sillsby—look at me! Look at me! Are you now convinced that Annabelle really saw everything she said she did? Answer me.

SUSAN. Yes—yes——

CHARLIE. Then don't you ever open your mouth again about her being unbalanced—do you hear me?

SUSAN. Yes—yes——

CHARLIE. Now the first thing to do is to get the police and a doctor. (*Goes to telephone back of table.*)

SUSAN (*rises*). The police! And I'm in a negligee!

HARRY (*opening door wide and standing L. of it*). Well, you have plenty of time to change.

SUSAN (*up to door*). Yes, of course!

CICILY (*rises and takes a few steps toward door*). But I'm afraid to go upstairs.

MAMMY. I'll go with you, miss.

SUSAN. Come on, Cicily. Let's pack up and get out of this terrible house. (SUSAN *exits.*)

CICILY. Mammy, you go first.

(MAMMY *and* CICILY *exit.* HARRY *closes door a little, looking off L.*)

CHARLIE. Are we all agreed that it's better to keep out of there— until they come? (HARRY *nods.* CHARLIE *takes phone.*) Hello! Hello! Must be out of order.

HARRY. Probably cut.

CHARLIE. It's all right now.

HARRY. Outside. (*Closes door.*) Paul! (*Comes down C.*) Did you and Crosby fasten all the cellar doors when you were downstairs?

PAUL. There was only one door. It has a bolt on the inside and I bolted it.

(*Suddenly a noise is heard downstairs like the banging of a shutter in the wind—all listen. Two slams of door.*)

HARRY (*cautions silence and they listen*). Hear? That! (*Door slams again—one slam.*)

PAUL. Sounds like a door swinging against the house in the wind.

HARRY. Listen! I think our—guest —has left us—without closing the door. You locked the door, Paul—it couldn't have opened unless *he* went out. He probably escaped while we were talking here. I'm going to see. (*Starts for door.* PAUL *goes back of sofa to* ANNABELLE.)

CHARLIE. I'll go with you.

HARRY. No, you stay here and watch that door—in case—I'm mistaken.

CHARLIE. But—I want——

HARRY (*insolently*). Do as you're told.

CHARLIE (*furiously*). Why should I take orders from you?

HARRY. Because I'm giving them to you.

CHARLIE (*begins to smile*). Oh, I see. Now that you believe it's safe —you're going to be a hero in front of Annabelle.

HARRY (*white with anger*). Go down and do it yourself.

CHARLIE (*taunting him*). Oh, I couldn't rob you of that—honor.

HARRY. Just—just come along with me—will you—I want to—talk with you—alone.

CHARLIE. Yes, and I want to——

PAUL (*rushes over between them*). Here, cut it out! Maybe I'd better give the orders from now on—you fellows don't seem to be able to do anything—except snarl at each other. I'm not much of a hero—but at that—I reckon I'm as good as either of you. You fellows look after Annabelle. I'll go and see about that door.

(*Two men watch him as he exits.*)

ANNA (*coming out of a faint*). Oh! Oh!

HARRY (*crosses to back of sofa*). Annabelle!

CHARLIE. Annabelle! (*Crosses to L. of sofa.*)

ANNA (*opens her eyes and looks at them. She smiles bravely at them*). Where's Paul?

(HARRY *back of sofa .R.* CHARLIE *down L. of sofa.*)

HARRY (*fixing cushions*). He'll be back in a moment.

CHARLIE. Are you all right, Annabelle?

ANNA (*calm*). I feel very weak. Did I faint again?

(MAMMY *opens door slowly as though she were listening, then stands in door.*)

CHARLIE (*nods*). Yes. Just after Mr. Cr——

HARRY (*silences him*). Sh!

ANNA. Is he—still there?

HARRY (*nods*). Yes—and no one must go in there until the police come.

ANNA. Did you telephone for them?

CHARLIE. The wires have been cut.

ANNA. The wires are cut?

CHARLIE. Yes—but I'm going after the police myself—as soon as Paul comes back.

HARRY. I think the most important thing to do is to get a doctor. (*Looks at* MAMMY.) Mammy, can you tell me where the nearest doctor lives?

(CHARLIE, *in front of sofa, helps* ANNABELLE *to sitting posture. Very attentive to her.*)

MAMMY. I could tell you—but you'd never find it—I'll go if Miss West wants me to. (*Starts to go.*)

HARRY. But, Mammy, aren't you afraid?

MAMMY (*with a peculiar smile*). Afraid! Me what's lived alone in this house for twenty years! (*Starts to exit.*)

CHARLIE (*stops her*). Wait a minute, I'll go with you. (HARRY *stands behind chair C.* CHARLIE *up to R. of door.*) Is the doctor's house near the police station?

MAMMY (*to L. of door*). No—you go to the village—I go the other way. If you'll come with me—I'll show you the road.

(PAUL *enters, goes to* ANNABELLE. CHARLIE *down C.*)

PAUL (*down to* ANNABELLE). Are you all right, Annabelle?

ANNA. Yes. Mammy is just going for a doctor.

HARRY (*coming down C.*). Paul! What did you find?

PAUL (*few steps over to* HARRY). You were right. The door was open. It must have been opened from this side, because I'm positive I bolted it myself when I was down there. Mr.——

HARRY. Sh!

PAUL. Never mind.

ANNA. What is it?

PAUL (*explains to* ANNABELLE). We heard a door swinging against the house. The one I locked tonight. I went down and found it open— so I locked it again, that's all.

HARRY (*crosses to back of table L.*). I don't think there's any doubt now but that our guest—has left us—I think we are all pretty safe now— eh, Paul?

PAUL (*doubtfully*). Well, maybe we are—but then on the other hand —you never can tell.

ANNA (*shudders*). I'll never feel right again—until Mr. Crosby—— (*Looks toward the other room.* PAUL *sits L. of* ANNABELLE, *comforting her.*)

CHARLIE. The police will attend to all that, Annabelle. I'll be back as soon as possible. Come, Mammy. (*Up to door.* HARRY *above table.* MAMMY *exits.* PAUL *takes* ANNA-BELLE'S *hand.* CHARLIE *speaks to* HARRY *in a low voice.*) I don't want any more words with you than I can help—but while I'm gone—you just look after Annabelle.

HARRY (*smiles*). There's no more danger——

CHARLIE. How do you know? The maniac may be in the house now. The open door doesn't prove that he's gone.

HARRY (*loses his smile and he looks at* CHARLIE). You're right—he may still be here.

CHARLIE. And do you realize that another shock like she just had—might kill her—or *drive her insane?*

HARRY (*nods*). Yes—another shock might kill her or she might be——

CHARLIE. Yes, she might—or *someone else might.* Until the police get here—look out for that room and don't believe yourself too safe. (*Starts for door.*)

HARRY. I know—you don't have to tell me. (*Looking front.*)

CHARLIE (*coming down to* HARRY. *Angrily but keeping his voice down*). I'm not telling you—because I'm worried about *you.* (*Exits*).

ANNA (*to* HARRY). Has Susan gone?

HARRY (*coming down L. to front of table*). No, but she's threatening to go. I believe she's packing up.

ANNA. Oh, I hope she goes. (*Rises.*) You can't imagine how nervous she makes me.

PAUL (*rising*). Oh yes, I can—she makes me nervous. *I can't make her stop talking.*

HARRY. Suppose she won't go? It's still dark.

ANNA (*crosses to* HARRY). You must make her go.

HARRY. What!

ANNA. I'll feel so much better when she's out of the house—Paul!

PAUL (*suddenly*). Harry, I've got an idea. If she stalls about being afraid to go to the station before daylight—*you* take her.

ANNA (*with animation*). Splendid —that gives her no excuse for not going.

HARRY. Great Scott! Have you people got a grudge against me?

ANNA. You'll do it for me, won't you?

HARRY (*sighs*). Yes, if you really want me to. (*Looks at her keenly.*) Sure you won't be nervous—staying here alone?

ANNA. Alone! You forget—I have Paul.

HARRY (*looks at* PAUL *with a curious expression and replies in a peculiar voice*). Oh yes.

SUSAN (*enters, dressed for the street, followed by* CICILY. *To* ANNA-

BELLE. *At door*). Have the police come? (ANNABELLE *crosses R. in front of sofa—*PAUL *L. end of sofa.* HARRY *moves L. to back of table.*) Oh dear! What a night! (*Coming down R.C. There is silence for a moment, then she starts again.*) I just know it—I felt it in my bones— the minute I entered this terrible house—that something would happen. And just to think it had to be poor Mr. Crosby—(*turns L.*)— and it might just as well have been— (*looks at* HARRY)—you! (PAUL, *growing uncomfortable, tries to stop her talking by glaring at her.* HARRY *stands listening with a cynical smile.* CICILY *nervous.* ANNABELLE *very nervous.* CICILY *up stage C.*) It's a wonder we weren't *all* murdered.

CICILY. Poor Mr. Crosby!

SUSAN. And I'll never forget to my dying day—how he pitched out of that panel—nearly into your arms, Annabelle!

(ANNABELLE *gives a nervous start.*)

PAUL (*firmly*). Miss Sillsby—stop talking.

SUSAN (*flaring up*). Mr. Jones—to whom are you speaking?

PAUL. To you. I'm the boss around here and I command you to—to—to dry up. (*To back of sofa.*)

SUSAN (*glares at both of them*). Well, I never! In all my born days I never—— (*She is speechless for a moment, then turns to* CICILY.) Come, Cicily—now we're packed up, let's get out of this terrible house. (*Few steps toward door—then turns*

down to ANNABELLE.) I'm so sorry to leave you, dear.

ANNA (*smiles at her*). That's nice of you—but I'll be all right.

SUSAN. Perhaps I had better stay here after all.

(HARRY *and* PAUL *exchange looks of dismay.*)

ANNA. Don't stay on my account. The doctor will be here soon.

SUSAN. But I wonder if there'll be any trains—it isn't dawn yet.

HARRY (*back of table at R. end of it. Smoothly*). If you hurry you've got just about time to catch the milk train.

SUSAN. Milk—train! I never rode on a milk train in my life!

PAUL. You ought to try anything once!

CICILY. But I'm afraid to go, and now—it's still dark.

HARRY. Miss Sillsby—if you're really anxious to go—I'll be only too happy to see you and Miss Young to the station!

CICILY. Oh! Will you—really? (*Crosses to* HARRY *and takes his arm.*)

SUSAN (*scornfully*). Young man— I'll allow you to come with us on one condition. You may talk with Cicily if she will let you—but—I'll have nothing to say to you.

HARRY (*huskily*). Can I depend on that?

(SUSAN, *with a sniff, turns away.* CICILY *goes up to* R. *of door and* HARRY *to* L.)

SUSAN (*marches to* ANNABELLE). Well, Annabelle—I am glad you are all right because I was afraid the next time I saw you—you'd be non compos mentis. Good-by, my dear. I hope you'll soon be well again—but I'm afraid you won't. (SUSAN *exits.*)

CICILY. Good-by, Annabelle! (CICILY *exits, followed by* HARRY, *who closes door.*)

PAUL (L. *of sofa at back*). She's just a nice little pal!

ANNA. I don't think she's half—as—malicious as she seems to be, do you?

PAUL. Well, I don't know. *Maybe* she's only one half—but—on the other hand, I think she's one hundred per cent poison.

(*Pause while they look at each other and gradually realize they are quite alone in the house.*)

ANNA. It's rather nice to be alone—isn't it, Paul?

PAUL. Yes sir, it certainly is. (*Shivers.*) But it's kinda quiet, though.

ANNA. This is the first time we've been really alone tonight.

PAUL (*smiles*). It's the first time —we've been really alone since you left Wickford.

ANNA. What was it you—wanted to tell me?

PAUL. When?

ANNA. Tonight—don't you remember, you said you had an idea.

PAUL (*crosses his brows trying to remember*). That's right—I did have an idea then—but it's gone now.

ANNA. That's nothing—you'll get another.

PAUL. I'm not so sure about that—ideas are scarce with me.

ANNA (*smiles*). Really.

PAUL (*soberly*). Yes. Up at college —they used to say I only got one idea a week, but let me tell you right now when I *do* get one—it's a bear.

ANNA. What was this last idea about? (*Moving over to* R. *of sofa and indicates for* PAUL *to sit down.*)

PAUL. It was about you. (*Sits beside her on sofa.*)

ANNA. Me! (*Looking at* PAUL. PAUL *moves away from her.*)

PAUL. Yes—now wait a minute. (*Thinks a moment, then the silence gets oppressive. Whistles.*) Gosh! It's quiet in here—I never knew a house could get so quiet. (*Looks all around, and as he looks at door he gives a nervous start and quickly looks at* ANNABELLE, *who is watching him.*)

ANNA (*seems as if she were listening for something—speaks in a low tone*). Was that—that door really open—downstairs?

PAUL. Yes—and I closed it and bolted it. (*Chokes a little. Rises, back a few steps.*) You didn't—want me to —to—go down and see again?

ANNA. No—no—— (*Pause.*)

PAUL (*looks at whisky*). Thanks—I mean much obliged. I think I need a drink. Do you mind? (*Crosses to back of table.* ANNABELLE *shakes her head—still listening. Fills glass and drinks half.* PAUL *coughs and chokes—but it has an almost immediate effect on him—as shown in his bearing and in the tone of his voice.*)

ANNA (*crosses to chair R. of table L.*). Paul, do you really think that —it—is out of the house?

PAUL. Now, Annabelle—you mustn't think about it.

ANNA. Tell me, Paul—are we—are we safe?

PAUL (*with confidence*). Of course —now doesn't it stand to reason that —the door couldn't open itself? Of course it's gone—don't think about it.

ANNA. But suppose it *didn't* go out. (*Sits in great excitement.*)

PAUL. Annabelle, you're getting nervous. (PAUL *drinks half of what's left in glass. Business of putting stopper in decanter—then the stimulating effect to drink.*) You know it's wonderful—wonderful how all my ideas are coming back to me. (*Stopple business.* PAUL *thinks a moment, then snaps his fingers.*) I've got one——

ANNA. Tell me.

PAUL (*leans forward in his excitement. Looking front*). The *whole*

thing *just struck me as being darned queer.*

ANNA. What?

PAUL. Everything. Right straight through from the start to finish.

ANNA. You mean——

PAUL. From the time the will was read tonight—until now.

ANNA (*interested*). Yes.

PAUL. Remember when you were declared the heiress? (*Seated on back of table, facing* ANNABELLE.)

ANNA. Yes.

PAUL. Remember the codicil? (AN-NABELLE *nods.*) That if anything happened to you—or you were to lose your mind or anything—the estate was to go to the next heir?

ANNA. Yes, yes, I remember.

PAUL. And his or her name was in the third envelope.

ANNA. You mean the one that Mr. Crosby put in his pocket when he said, "I trust that this shall never be opened!"

PAUL. Exactly. And from that moment on things began to happen to you.

ANNA. And to Mr. Crosby.

PAUL (*sitting on edge of table*). Because he was the one who drew up the will—and he was the *only* one—who *knew* the name of the next heir—unless—(*rises*)—maybe—

(*crosses* R.C.)—and then again maybe not.

ANNA (*turning in chair to face* PAUL). Paul Jones—what are you saying?

PAUL (*silences her with a wave of his hand*). Didn't I tell you that while my ideas are scarce—when I do get one it's a humdinger?

ANNA. Heavens—you don't mean——

PAUL. I'm liable to mean anything. Listen. This is just an idea of mine, but you never can tell—it may lead us somewhere. All right! Things began to happen to you in this house tonight, what for? To scare you.

ANNA. You mean someone was—— Oh!

PAUL. Just a minute. Crosby got on to this plot—he tried to tell you—before he finished, something happened to him—then gradually all of them—I don't say they did it intentionally—but they started to think and to say that you—were unbalanced.

ANNA. And you mean—that all this was a plot to frighten me——

PAUL. I don't know—I don't know. (*Goes R.*) I'm just trying to figure it out. Just seeing where my idea will carry me.

ANNA. Yes, yes, go on.

PAUL. Now, just suppose that someone—call it the next heir—thinks that you—might possibly have inherited—the family——

ANNA. You mean—the family failing.

PAUL. Exactly—and they—that is he —she—it—well, someone starts to frighten you—hoping to shock you into—or worse—then—it discovers that Crosby is on to the plot—so it —kills Crosby.

ANNA (*rises*). No! No! Impossible!

PAUL. Why is it impossible? The doorknob turning—locking you in your room—the panel—the hand—— (ANNABELLE *gives a little cry of terror.*) I'm awfully sorry, but don't you see—it *is* possible? The whole thing might have been arranged 'to frighten you into——

ANNA. No, no. How can you explain about that bell—and Mammy's warning of Mr. Crosby's death?

PAUL. They might have all been planted. (*Crosses to R.C. Thinking.*) They might have all been planted—they—— (*Pause.*) Give Mammy Pleasant a thought.

ANNA. Mammy Pleasant! Why, she's not the next heir?

PAUL. How do you know she's not? She might be—besides, your necklace alone is worth a fortune. She might be the next heir.

ANNA (*silent a moment, thinking. A few steps to* PAUL). But—that old man who had escaped from the asylum—how did——

PAUL. He might have been brought here to frighten you—*now suppose —just suppose that*—(ANNABELLE *gives a little cry*)—now don't get nervous—but just suppose that Crosby had brought him in the house——

ANNA (*stops him. Crosses R. in front of* PAUL *to front of sofa*). No —no—don't, Paul——

PAUL (*turning to her*). Now don't get so excited. I'm just supposing, that's all. Suppose Crosby had brought him into the house, then the maniac suddenly grew violent—turned on Crosby—and *killed him*——

ANNA. Oh no!

PAUL (*long pause. Crosses to chair R. of table L.*). On the other hand —suppose *I* were the next heir.

ANNA (*smiles at him. Sits on sofa L.*). Now, I *know* you're joking.

PAUL (*crosses to table L.*). Well— I can tell you right now it's not me —now who's left? (*Sitting at table L.*) Susan! Charlie! Cicily! Harry! Take your choice.

ANNA. It's fantastic—absurd.

PAUL. Well—maybe it is—but then again maybe it isn't. But there's one thing I'm dead sure of. Your brain is one hundred per cent normal. If there's any insanity in this family— it's not in you. But the more I think of it—— (*Thinks a moment, then snaps his fingers.*) I've got another idea. (ANNABELLE, *in alarm, leans forward.* PAUL *crosses to sofa.*) But I'm not going to tell you about this until I'm sure of it. But—part of my idea is this—*law or no law*, I'm going in there—and get that envelope out of Crosby's pocket and find out who *is* the next heir. (*Starts for door.*)

ANNA (*rises and holds* PAUL). No— no—don't leave me.

PAUL (*brings her to couch*). I won't be gone a minute. I'll leave both doors open and nothing can possibly happen—but, mind you, nobody must know that I've been in there, especially the police—understand? Now don't tell a soul. I'll be right back! (*As he opens door.*) See, I'll leave both doors open; I'll be right back.

(*Sees him cross the hall and go into the other room.* ANNABELLE *sitting on sofa. Waits for him, looking at door, then she turns her head away a moment. As* ANNABELLE *turns her eyes from the door a tall man* [DOCTOR PATTERSON] *in black clothes, wearing a black hat, glides into the room without making any noise and stands looking at her.* ANNABELLE *turns and sees this man —she shrinks in terror.*)

PATTERSON (*coming down C.*). Miss Annabelle West?

ANNA (*whispers*). Who are you?

PATTERSON. I'm Doctor Patterson— your maid just brought me over. (*Putting hat on chair C. Comes over and looks at her with a professional eye.*) She told me you were here—so I walked in. Did I frighten you?

ANNA (*trying to conceal her fears for* PAUL). Yes—no—I thought it was——

PATTERSON. I see—your condition is more serious than I thought. (*Looks in her eyes a moment.*) You've been under a nervous strain! (AN-NABELLE *stares at him, petrified by fear.*) Humm! (*Takes a small pocket flash and holds it near her eyes. Flashes it in her eye and watches the pupil dilate and recede.*) H'mm!— Your eyes hurt you. (*Takes her pulse.*) Very quick action. (MAMMY *enters with glass of water.*) Were you excited?

ANNA (*shakes her head*). No.

MAMMY. Feeling better, Miss West?

ANNA (*relieved at sight of* MAMMY). Yes—yes——

PATTERSON. I'll take that. (*Crosses to* MAMMY *and takes glass. Indicates with nod to* MAMMY *to get out.* MAMMY *exits, closing door.*) H'mmm! Very strange. (*Crosses back of sofa, puts glass on small table R. Works down round table R. to front of sofa.*)

ANNA. Strange?

PATTERSON. Yes—your actions— your eyes suggested a terrible worry —or anticipation—you act as if you recently had a shock. (*Putting pill in water.*)

ANNA. Didn't—Mammy tell you about me—about the—the——

PATTERSON. Miss West, I never discuss my patients with their servants. Besides, your maid told me nothing. I think she's dumb. As I was saying, your physical condition is normal—but your mental—— Tell me about yourself.

ANNA (*hysterically—crosses C. to front of chair R. of table*). Oh, I can't stand it any longer. Why doesn't he come out? He went there. (*Points.*)

PATTERSON (*watching her keenly —crosses to* ANNABELLE). He? Who? And where—is—there?

ANNA. Paul—went in there—that room where—where—Mr. Crosby was murdered. Charlie went for the police. Don't tell them.

PATTERSON (*observing her narrowly*). I won't—murder—police— yes—he is in there—with the dead body—what for?

ANNA. To get the envelope.

PATTERSON. Yes—the letter.

ANNA. No—the will.

PATTERSON. All right—and you're afraid? Of something in that room?

ANNA (*down L.*). Don't ask me any more questions. Go—Paul! (PATTERSON *gives her another look and goes toward the other room.* ANNABELLE *waits; as* PATTERSON *reaches door, he turns and looks at* ANNABELLE.) Hurry!

(PATTERSON *exits.*)

PATTERSON (*returns, carrying unconscious body of* PAUL). He was lying on the floor. (ANNABELLE *helps put* PAUL *on couch. Examines* PAUL'S *head.*) Nasty bruise. (*Gets out bandages.*) He must have tripped, and as he fell he probably struck his head on the corner of the table. (*Bandage business.*)

ANNA (*back of sofa. Cannot restrain herself any longer*). Was he lying near—near——

PATTERSON. Near what? (*Cutting bandage but not looking at her.*)

ANNA. The—body.

PATTERSON. What body?

ANNA (*shrilly*). Mr. Crosby—he was murdered there tonight.

PATTERSON. Drink this—it's merely a sedative. (ANNABELLE *obeys him.* ANNABELLE *sits L. of* PAUL.) Miss West—your nerves are completely upset. There was no one in that room but this young man. (*Sticks adhesive tape on* PAUL's *forehead. Smells* PAUL's *breath.*) Did you have some? (*To* ANNABELLE. ANNABELLE *shakes head.* PATTERSON *grins.*) The young man probably had too much. He'll come round in a minute.

(PAUL, *after a moment, opens his eyes, looks blankly at them and asks.*)

PAUL. What time did the eclipse take place?

PATTERSON. How do you feel now?

PAUL. Did you hit me?

PATTERSON. No—you must have hurt yourself on the table.

PAUL. Nothing of the kind! Nothing of the kind! (*To* ANNABELLE.) Somebody hit me from behind when I went in to get that envelope from Crosby's body.

PATTERSON (*startled*). Well—you got 'em too.

ANNA. Was the body there, Paul?

PAUL. No—it was not. While I was looking for it—someone slugged me.

PATTERSON. What's all this about?

ANNA. I told you—but you wouldn't believe me.

PATTERSON. Yes, I believe anything *you* say.

ANNA. But I—— (MAMMY *enters.*)

PATTERSON. You're all right now—Miss West. Young man, *you'd* better not drink any more. (PAUL *sees* MAMMY *and crosses to her. Then he asks her a question.* MAMMY *nods—and points to the north.* PAUL *nods satisfaction and tells her something.* MAMMY *exits.*) I'll look in tomorrow. Everything will be all right then. Both of you have been seeing things. (*Goes to* ANNABELLE *and feels her pulse.*) Just to check up!

PAUL (*returns to* ANNABELLE *and* PATTERSON—*crosses to* ANNABELLE). Pulse normal, Doctor?

PATTERSON. No—take care of yourself, Miss West. I'll drop in tomorrow.

ANNA. But Paul's head——

PATTERSON. He's all right. Does it hurt you?

(PAUL *puts his hand to his head.*)

PAUL. No.

PATTERSON (*looks at bottle*). It never does. Good morning. (*Exits, closing door.*)

ANNA. You say that—it wasn't there.

PAUL. No—but someone else was. Who could it have been? (*Crossing L.*) Who the dickens could it have been? (*Groans a little.*) Oh, my head begins to hurt now.

ANNA (*soothes him—rises and crosses C.*). There—there—don't try to think. (*Leading* PAUL *to sofa.*)

PAUL (*looks at her—owlishly from the blow—and the booze—he is just a trifle stunned.* ANNABELLE *brings him over to sofa and sits him down*). I've just got to think, I've just got to think. I've just got to think! Just as I had the dol-gone thing figured out —now it goes and gets itself all balled up again—we saw Crosby fall on the floor—didn't we? (PAUL *on sofa—*ANNABELLE R. *and* PAUL L.)

ANNA. Yes.

PAUL. He was dead—wasn't he?

ANNA. Yes. (*Looks at him.*)

PAUL. Ha! Ha!

ANNA. What is it, Paul—what is it?

PAUL. How do we *know*—he was dead?

ANNA. Why—why wasn't he?

PAUL. I don't know. I suppose he was—but that doesn't prove it. I couldn't swear he was dead—neither could you.

ANNA. No.

PAUL. I got an idea—maybe the whole thing was only a plant—that he was shamming all the time to frighten you and waiting in there to wallop *me*?

ANNA (*shakes her head*). Oh no!

PAUL (*rises—unsteadily*). You don't think much of that one.

ANNA. No!

PAUL. Well, neither do I. (*Crossing to table.*) Guess my ideas aren't coming as good as they might—since I got hit on the bean, but at that, I've had worse.

ANNA. Where's Mammy?

PAUL. She's out. I sent her on a personal errand of my own.

ANNA. I wish she were here.

PAUL (*crosses to sofa*). Now don't worry about Mammy. (*Sits.*) I'll take care of you. You know I'll take care of you, don't you?

ANNA. Yes.

PAUL. All right. Now where was I? Oh, I know, Mammy. I sent her for a——

ANNA (*in sudden terror, thinks she hears something—cautions silence*). Sh! (*She and* PAUL *listen for a moment, then he looks at her.*)

PAUL. Think you—heard something? (ANNABELLE *and* PAUL *listen for a moment then:*) Oh, yes, I know. (*He looks at her.*)

ANNA (*trembling*). I thought I heard—a footstep.

PAUL (*listens*). Guess you're mistaken. I don't hear any—where was I—oh yes, my garage.

ANNA. Your garage. You didn't tell me about that.

PAUL. Didn't I! Well—I meant to—I've got the nicest garage in Wickford. Most of the cars in it are flivvers—but it's a good garage. One that any girl would be proud of. It's got a—— (*As* PAUL *looks at her, he shows all his love for her in his eyes, but on account of* ANNABELLE *being the heiress, he rambles around trying to tell her.* ANNABELLE *tries to help him. She shows audience she loves him.*)

ANNA (*softly*). Paul, did you miss me—when I left Wickford?

(*Door opens, showing hand.*)

PAUL (*fervently*). Did I miss you?—Did I miss you! (*Suddenly embarrassed.*) Sure I did—and when you went away—you didn't think—that someday I'd own a garage, did you?

ANNA. I hadn't the slightest idea. (*Door closes.*) I'm glad you missed me, Paul, but why didn't you write to me?

PAUL. I didn't think you wanted to hear from me. Besides, I didn't have my garage then.

ANNA. Well, you have it now.

PAUL. Y-e-s! But you can't ask a girl to marry you just because you've got a garage.

ANNA. Why can't you? Does having a garage make you tongue-tied?

PAUL. S-see—here, Annabelle, are you making fun of me?

(*Open panel slowly.*)

ANNA. No—indeed—I'm only trying to help you.

PAUL. You could have helped me more if you hadn't turned out to be the heiress.

ANNA. I'm awfully sorry, but I don't see why you should keep me from helping you—with your garage.

PAUL. But I don't need a mechanic. What I need is a wi—oh—oh—well—you wouldn't understand anyway. You've been living so long in Greenwich Village, with all those artists, you'd never be content to settle in the country, in a little cottage with a little garden around it and·a——

ANNA. Don't be too sure—I could live anywhere—anywhere with the man I loved.

PAUL. Could you—could you—honest?

ANNA. Of course I could—so could any woman—if she loved a man.

PAUL (*after a gulp*). Annabelle, could you—could you?

ANNA. Yes? You want to tell me——

PAUL (*rises and stands L. of sofa*). I want to tell you—about a new idea of mine—I've got an idea for a twelve-cylinder car—all twelve cylinders all in a row. That would give the crank shaft thirteen main bearings. Think of the power and flexibility.

ANNA. Very interesting—but what about your idea of getting someone to keep the little cottage for you?

PAUL (*with determination, but hesitating*). Annabelle—would—would you—— (*Sits beside her.*)

(*Noise like body being dragged along floor.* PAUL *alert in a moment, remains quiet and they listen. After a moment a curious shuffling noise is heard—like dragging footsteps.*)

ANNA (*white—clings to* PAUL). There—hear that?

PAUL (*with his eyes popping out— listens a moment*). Sounds like someone dragging something across the floor. (*Noise. Repeat.*) It's all right, dear. (*They both listen.* PAUL *shakes and quivers and whispers.*) It's—upstairs. (*Points up.* ANNA- BELLE *gasps.*) I suppose I ought—to go up there, but I hate to leave you alone. (*Looks at her, showing he doesn't want to leave her alone. Pause.*)

ANNA. I'm not afraid.

PAUL. No! Neither am I. (*Rises.*) Here, you'd better take this in case anything happens—wait a minute, I'll cock it for you. (*Gives her re- volver.*) Now all you got to do if you see something is just point this at it—and pull the trigger. (*Starts for door.*)

ANNA (*nods*). Yes—but you——

PAUL (*he takes the mold of a hero*). Never mind about me! If that's the guy that beaned me a while ago— may God help him. (*Opens door, turns, sees drink on table L., takes drink.*) I'll be back in a minute. (*Glides out without a sound. Clos- ing door.*)

(ANNABELLE *sits on couch looking at closed door, then looks front. All is deathly quiet.* ANNABELLE *jumps up and goes to door, opens it and* looks off L. a second. The panel opens very slowly. ANNABELLE crosses to window, then backs away a few steps, turns toward panel, and gives a little shriek.*)

ANNA (*with a trembling hand, points gun at panel. Her voice fails her, and she speaks like a person in a dream*). I—I—don't know why you are trying to frighten me, but if you don't go away—I'll—— (ANNABELLE *is about to fire the gun to summon help.* HENDRICKS *rushes into the room, catches her, and speaks gently.*)

HENDRICKS. What is it, miss—any- thing wrong?

ANNA (*clings to him frantically, sobs her relief, and points to dark corner, where monster is crouching*). There! There!

HENDRICKS (*shows his astonishment as he sees him*). Gee—just in time— I knew he was around here. (*Takes gun.*) Close call, miss. Don't worry —he can't get you now—he knows me—he's afraid of me. (*Crosses over R. between chair and sofa.* HEN- DRICKS *goes toward monster and speaks soothingly.*) Come on—old- timer—I've got you—and you and me are going home—come on—come on—I won't hurt you. Sure! He knows me all right—and he won't try no monkey tricks.

ANNA. Oh!

HENDRICKS. Now, miss, everything is all right—and I'll just take him along to the asylum. (*Panel opens wider and monster comes out slowly. To monster.*) Come on, you—and no funny business. (*Monster starts for door.*) Come on! Move along faster, can't you? That's it, go on.

(*Monster is R. of door now.*)

ANNA (*as monster is gliding toward the door—she sees it for the first time—out of the shadow. She darts forward, and with a quick movement, before* HENDRICKS *can stop her, she pulls the Benda mask off the head of the monster—revealing the face of* CHARLIE WILDER. *She gasps*). Charlie!

(CHARLIE, *snarling like a trapped ghost, grabs her by left arm.* HENDRICKS *claps his hand across her mouth, shutting off her screams, and then the two men slam her down on the couch and hold her there.*)

CHARLIE (*C.*). How did she get wise?

HENDRICKS (*holding her down L. of sofa—he is back of sofa*). How do I know? I got her—just as she was going to blow the gat.

CHARLIE. Sure, she did a dance with them down in Greenwich Village. What did you do with Crosby?

HENDRICKS. Rolled him under the bed. (ANNABELLE *tries to scream.*) Oh, shut up! Another yip out of you and I'll——

CHARLIE (*starts for door*). I'll get him if it's the last thing I——

HENDRICKS. No, no more killing. I did everything you told me. I planted the gong—made 'em think I was from the asylum and locked her in the room, and while I was doing that, you got one of your crazy spells and croaked the old man.

CHARLIE. What!

HENDRICKS. And—if we're caught—I don't go to the chair with you—oh no, I'll squeal—and save my own neck. (ANNABELLE *tries to scream.*) Shut up. What's the matter with you? What are we going to do with her?

CHARLIE (*suddenly shows a venomous, unnatural hate for* ANNABELLE). I'd like to——

HENDRICKS. No—I won't stand for it—do you hear—I won't have it—we'll tie and gag her and put her up there. (*Nods toward bookcase.*) I knew you couldn't drive this girl mad! From now on it's fifty-fifty—I want half of that necklace—and then I go my way—and you go yours. I'm through with you—do you get me? (ANNABELLE *tries to scream.*) Aw, shut up, will you!

CHARLIE (*pays no attention to* HENDRICKS, *but is staring at* ANNABELLE *with the grin of hate on his face*). I'll make you scream, damn you! You cheated me out of my inheritance. You didn't know that I used to play around this house when I was a kid, did you? Well, I was the old man's favorite—he showed me the secret passage—and I should have been his heir, too—I *am* the next heir—see, there's my name—my name—— (*Pulls out* CROSBY'S *envelope and shows it to her. Voice gradually works up to a hysterical pitch.*)

HENDRICKS. Can it! You're getting one of your spells.

(*Here* CHARLIE *suggests that he might be the one in the family who is really unbalanced.*)

CHARLIE. When I opened that safe and read the will—I found out you had robbed me—yes, robbed me. You thought I went for the police—ha, ha! Well, I didn't, and here's your necklace! (*Shows necklace.*)

HENDRICKS. I want my half now.

CHARLIE. Try to get it.

HENDRICKS. Oh! Double-cross, eh? Well,' I'll take it all. Come on, kick in! (*Pointing revolver.*)

(CHARLIE *drops necklace and* HENDRICKS *stoops down for it and* CHARLIE *grabs his gun arm and makes him drop it.* HARRY *enters.* ANNABELLE *sees him and shouts.*)

ANNA. Harry! (*Rushes into his arms.*)

(CHARLIE *makes rush to door and meets* HARRY, *who covers him with gun.* PAUL *comes through panel and makes a leap at* HENDRICKS, *lands on his shoulders, and pins arms.* MAMMY *enters.*)

PAUL (*to* HARRY). Thank God you're here—I'm scared to death.

HARRY. Scared?

PAUL. Maybe.

HENDRICKS. I'didn't kill him. He did it. He's been getting crazier and crazier. Just now he had one of his spells and tried to kill me.

HARRY. Tell that to the judge. Come on, you fellows, the police are wait-ing—remember—I'll shoot! Now move!

PAUL (*to* HARRY). Teamwork.

(CHARLIE *and* HENDRICKS, *still holding up their hands, exit, followed closely by* HARRY.)

MAMMY. It's all right, Mr. Paul. (MAMMY *exits.*)

ANNA (*to* MAMMY). What's all right? (*Turns to* PAUL.) What's all right, Paul?

PAUL. You see, that was just another little idea of mine. I thought—that is, I got to thinking, after what you'd been through tonight, that maybe you wouldn't be so nervous if you were to wake up suddenly and found me your husband.

ANNA. What?

PAUL. I mean found me by your side.

ANNA. *What?*

PAUL. I mean in the same room.

ANNA. *Oh!*

PAUL. I mean in the next room.

ANNA. Oh! (*Relieved.*)

PAUL. I *thought* that maybe you wouldn't be so nervous, so I sent Mammy. *I sent Mammy* for a minister.

ANNA. Oh, Paul, you did have an idea, didn't you? (*They embrace.*)

CURTAIN

The Bat

A Play of Mystery in Three Acts By

MARY ROBERTS RINEHART

and

AVERY HOPWOOD

The Bat was presented at the Morosco Theatre, New York, August 23, 1920, with the following principals:

LIZZIE	May Vokes
MISS CORNELIA VAN GORDER	Effie Ellsler
BILLY	Harry Morvil
BROOKS	Stuart Sage
MISS DALE OGDEN	Anne Morrison
DR. WELLS	Edward Ellis
ANDERSON	Harrison Hunter
RICHARD FLEMING	Richard Barrows
REGINALD BERESFORD	Kenneth Hunter
AN UNKNOWN MAN	Robert Vaughan

SYNOPSIS

Act One: Living room in Miss Van Gorder's Long Island house.

Act Two: The same.

Act Three: The garret of the same house.

THE BAT

SCENE—*A combined living room and library of a country house. Open book shelves (four) in the set. Single door to the left of the audience leads to front door; dining room. Double doors leading to alcove, small staircase and terrace door, and exit below the stairs and off to the library up in the back to the left. All along the back of set are french windows. Six small frames in these windows. Double doors in the C. of window to open on stage. On the right, a single door leads to billiard room and a fireplace.*

The six small windows in french window effect are fitted with long narrow shades. Light in color. Shades remain down throughout Acts One and Two.

Beyond the double doors a small and supplementary staircase, showing stair rail, two steps, newel post (supposed to be newly varnished). Platform and steps carry off to the left. Terrace door in the alcove at right angle to the french windows. Thus one enters the house from the terrace past the french windows and the terrace door opens directly on foot of small staircase.

DISCOVERED—CORNELIA VAN GORDER *and* LIZZIE. CORNELIA *is knitting by the light of the lamp on center table. She is seated in armchair by the table.* LIZZIE *is at the city telephone. When curtain is well up,* LIZZIE *sets down the phone, with angry snap; hangs up the receiver.*

LIZZIE. He says the reason they turned the lights off last night was because there was a storm threatening. He says it burns out their fuses. (*Low rumble of thunder in the distance.*) There! They'll be going off again tonight! (*Scared.*)

CORNELIA. Humph! I hope it will be a dry summer. Ask Billy to bring some candles and have them ready.

LIZZIE (*frightened, moves down to back of table*). You're not going to ask me to go out into that hall alone?

CORNELIA (*putting down knitting*). What's the matter with you, anyhow, Lizzie Allen?

LIZZIE (*pleadingly, and shivering with terror*). Oh, Miss Neillie, I don't like it! I want to go back to the city.

CORNELIA (*firmly*). I have rented this house for four months, and I am going to stay.

LIZZIE (*clutching at* CORNELIA'S *arm*). There's somebody on the terrace!

CORNELIA (*also nervous and looking over her shoulder*). Don't do that!

LIZZIE (*relieved*). I guess it was the wind.

CORNELIA. *You* were born on a brick pavement. You get nervous out here at night when the crickets begin to sing, or scrape their legs together, or whatever it is they do.

LIZZIE. Oh, it's more than that, Miss Neillie, I——

CORNELIA (*turning to her fiercely*). What did you really see last night?

LIZZIE. I was standing right at the top of that there staircase with your switch in my hand—then I looked down and I saw a gleaming eye. It looked at me and *winked*. I tell you, this house is haunted!

CORNELIA (*skeptically*). A flirtatious ghost? Humph! Why didn't you yell?

LIZZIE. I was too scared to yell. And I'm not the only one. Why do you think the servants left all of a sudden? Did you really believe that the housemaid had a pain in her side? Or that the cook's sister had twins? (*Moves slowly up and back of table*.) I bet a cent the cook never had any sister—and her sister never had any twins. No, Miss Neillie, they couldn't put it over on me like that. They were scared away. (*Impressively*.) They saw—*it*.

CORNELIA. Fiddlesticks! What time is it?

LIZZIE (*looks at mantel clock*). Half past ten.

CORNELIA (*yawns*). Miss Dale won't be home for half an hour. Now you forget that superstitious nonsense! There's nothing in that sort of thing. (*Rolls up her knitting and puts in bag*.) Where's that Ouija Board? (*Rises and turns armchair*.)

LIZZIE (*shuddering; indicating; points*). It's up there—with a prayer book on it—to keep it quiet.

CORNELIA. Bring it here.

LIZZIE (*hesitates; shuddering; protesting in every movement, brings the Ouija Board, places it in COR-NELIA's lap*). You can do it yourself.

CORNELIA. It takes two people, and you know it, Lizzie Allen.

LIZZIE (*gets small chair*). I've been working for you for twenty years. I've been your goat for twenty years, and I've got a right to speak my mind.

CORNELIA. You haven't got a mind. Sit down. (LIZZIE *sits*.) Now make your mind a blank.

LIZZIE (*frightfully; she and* COR-NELIA *put their fingers on Ouija Board*). You just said I haven't got any mind.

CORNELIA. Well, make what you haven't got a blank.

LIZZIE (*mumbles*). I've stood by you through thick and thin—I stood by you when you were a Vegetarian—I stood by you when you were a Theosophist—and I seen you through Socialism, Fletcherism and Rheumatism—but when it comes to carrying on with ghosts——

CORNELIA. Be still! Nothing will come if you keep chattering.

LIZZIE. That's *why* I'm chattering! My teeth are, too. I can hardly keep my upper set in. (*She starts*.) I've got a queer feeling in my fingers all the way up my arms. (*Wiggles arms*.)

CORNELIA. Hush! (*Pause*.) Now, Ouija, is Lizzie Allen right about this house—or is it all stuff and nonsense?

LIZZIE. My Gawd! It's *moving*.

CORNELIA. You shoved it!

LIZZIE. I did not—cross my heart, Miss Neillie, I——

CORNELIA. Keep quiet! (*A moment's pause. Ouija wildly writes, then stops;* CORNELIA *calls off the letters.*) B—M—C—X—P—R—S—K—I.

LIZZIE (*breathlessly*). Russian! (*Ouija Board continues to move. Pause.*)

CORNELIA. B—A—T—Bat! (*Pause. Ouija stops.* CORNELIA *takes her hands off board.*) That's queer.

LIZZIE (*turns round, to front*). Bats are unlucky—everybody knows it. There's been a bat flying around inside this house all evening. (*Rises. Steps back.*) Oh, Miss Neillie, please let me sleep in your room tonight. It's only when my jaw drops that I snore. I can tie it up with a handkerchief.

CORNELIA (*who is evidently revolving a thought in her mind*). I wish you'd tie it up with a handkerchief now. (*Still thinking. Rises. Puts board on table.*) B—A—T—Bat! Give me the evening paper and my glasses. (*Straightens the armchair to face front, then crosses front of table and sits by table.*)

LIZZIE (*turns, looks around, then sees newspaper on settee. Brings it to* CORNELIA. *Then over to fireplace, feels mantel over fireplace*). I don't see your glasses here. You'll hurt your eyes reading without 'em. (*Returns to table.*)

CORNELIA (*seated, holding newspaper at arm's length. Testily*). My eyes are all right—but my arms aren't long enough. (*She reads.*)

"Police again baffled by the Bat!" (LIZZIE *stands, scared.*) "This unique criminal, known to the underworld as 'The Bat,' has long baffled the Police. The record of his crimes shows him to be endowed with almost diabolical ingenuity. So far there is no clue to his identity—but Anderson, City Detective, today said—'We must cease combing the criminal world for The Bat and look higher. He may be a merchant—a lawyer—a doctor, honored in his community by day—and at night a bloodthirsty assassin.'"

LIZZIE. I'm going to take the butcher knife to bed with me!

CORNELIA (*puts hand on Ouija Board*). That thing certainly spelled Bat! (*Sits facing front; glances at paper.*) I wish I were a man! I'd like to see any doctor, lawyer, or merchant of my acquaintance lead a double life without my suspecting it! (*Lays down paper on table.*)

LIZZIE (*over to chair she brought down earlier*). A man takes to a double life like a woman does to a kimono—it rests him! (LIZZIE *takes up chair; puts it back below billiard-room door.*)

CORNELIA (*knits*). If I had the clues the Police have about that man, I could get him. If I were a detective——

LIZZIE (*overcome*). Now it's Detective-ism!

(*Enter* BILLY. *He is an impassive Jap. Carries tray with small glass pitcher of water, and two glasses. Places tray on table. He starts to exit.* CORNELIA *calls him. He stops.*)

CORNELIA. Billy. What's all this about the cook's sister not having twins—did she? (LIZZIE, *scared watching Jap, moves to top of table; pours out two glasses of water; places one for* CORNELIA.)

BILLY (*has come down, facing* CORNELIA). Maybe she have twins—— It happen sometime.

CORNELIA. Do you think there was any other reason for her leaving?

BILLY. Maybe!

CORNELIA (*knits*). What *was* the reason?

BILLY. All say same thing—house haunted!

CORNELIA (*slight laugh*). You know better than that, don't you?

BILLY (*shrugs shoulders*). Funny house—find window open—nobody there—door slam—nobody there! (*Door slam.* LIZZIE *gives a little jump and squeal. All three look off stage.*)

CORNELIA (*irritably*). Stop that! It was the wind.

BILLY (*impassively*). I think not wind.

CORNELIA (*look of slight uneasiness. Knitting rapidly*). How long have you lived in this house?

BILLY. Since Mr. Fleming built.

CORNELIA. And this is the first time you have been disturbed?

BILLY. Last two days only. (LIZZIE *scared.*)

CORNELIA. What about the face you saw last night at the window?

BILLY. Just face—that's all!

CORNELIA. A man's face!

BILLY. Don't know—maybe! It there! It gone!

CORNELIA. Did you go out after it?

BILLY (*shakes head*). No, thanks!

LIZZIE. Oh, Miss Neillie—last night when the lights went out I had a token. My oil lamp was full of oil, but do what I would to keep it going, the minute I shut my eyes, out that lamp would go. There ain't a surer token of death! The Bible says, "Let your light shine——" When a hand you can't see puts your lights out—good night! (*There is a moment's silence. Even* CORNELIA *is uncomfortable.*)

CORNELIA. Well, now that you have cheered us up—— (*Distant roll of thunder.* CORNELIA *rises. Pause.*) Bring some candles, Billy, the lights may be going out any moment. (BILLY *starts off.*) And, Billy—— (BILLY *stops.*) There's a gentleman arriving on the last train. After he comes you may go to bed. I shall wait up for Miss Dale. (BILLY *starts off.*) Oh, and, Billy. (BILLY *stops.*) See that all the outer doors on this floor are locked and bring the keys here. (*Exit* BILLY.)

LIZZIE. I know what all this means! I tell you, there's going to be a death sure!

CORNELIA. There certainly will be if you don't keep quiet. Lock the billiard-room windows and go to bed. (*Sits by table. Knits.*)

LIZZIE (*angry*). I am not going to bed. I am going to pack up and to-morrow I'm going to leave. (*Pause; look.*) I asked you on my bended knees not to take this place, two miles from a railroad. For mercy's sake, Miss Neillie, let's go back to the city.

CORNELIA. I am not going. You can make up your mind to that. I'm going to find out what's wrong about this place, if it takes all summer. I came out to the country for a rest, and I'm going to stay and *get* it.

LIZZIE (*grimly*). You'll get your Heavenly rest.

CORNELIA (*puts knitting away*). Be-sides—I might as well tell you, Liz-zie, I'm having a detective sent down tonight from Police Head-quarters, in the city.

LIZZIE (*startled*). A detective? Miss Neillie, you're keeping something from me! You know something I don't know.

CORNELIA. I hope so. I don't know that I need him—but it will be in-teresting to watch a good detective's methods. (*She picks up newspaper off table. Reads.*) "His last crime was a particularly atrocious one. The body of the murdered man——"

LIZZIE (*with a wail—quickly to bil-liard-room door*). Why don't you read the funny page once in a while? (*Exits quickly, closing door behind her.*)

(*Lightning flashes across french win-dows.* CORNELIA *reads on to herself,* then thinks she hears something; goes into alcove; bolts terrace door; then comes into room and pushes light button. Lights all out. Thun-der, distant flashes lightning. While lights are out, CORNELIA crosses over to french windows, slowly pulls one shade aside and looks out. Then she goes back to switch button; pushes it. Lights full up.*)

BILLY (*enters with three candles and box of parlor matches. He crosses to small table, puts them on table*). New gardener come! (*Puts water glasses on tray, at large table.*)

CORNELIA. Nice hour for him to get here! What's his name? (*Takes out knitting.*)

BILLY. Say name Brook.

CORNELIA. Ask him to come in—and, Billy—where are the keys?

BILLY (*takes two keys out of pocket; places on table center. Then crosses to left with tray, pitcher, and glasses. As* BILLY *crosses* CORNELIA, *he turns around and faces her and points up at terrace door*). Door up there—spring lock. (*Exits.*)

CORNELIA. I know, spring lock.

LIZZIE (*enters from billiard room as if she had been shot out of a gun; leaves door partly open as she enters. Loud whisper. To* CORNELIA). I heard somebody yell out in the grounds. Away down by the gate!

CORNELIA. What did they yell?

LIZZIE. Just yelled a yell!

CORNELIA (*crosses front of table and sits chair. Knits*). You take a liver pill and go to bed. (BILLY *opens hall door. Unseen.* BROOKS *enters.* BROOKS *is a handsome young fellow, shabbily dressed, but very neat, and carries a cap in his hand.* BILLY *closes the door behind him.* BROOKS *is smooth shaven.*) You are Brooks, the new gardener?

BROOKS. Yes, madam. The butler said you wanted to speak to me.

CORNELIA (*pause. Looks at him*). Come in. (BROOKS *comes forward two steps. Faces* CORNELIA.) You're the man my niece engaged in the city, this afternoon?

BROOKS. Yes, madam.

CORNELIA (*knitting*). I could not verify your references, as the Brays are in Canada.

BROOKS. I am sure, if Mrs. Bray *were* here——

CORNELIA (*turns in chair; looks at* BROOKS). Were here? (*She eyes him with quick suspicion.*) Are you a professional gardener?

BROOKS (*doubtful*). Yes.

CORNELIA. Know anything about hardy perennials?

BROOKS. Yes, they—they're the ones that keep their leaves during the winter—aren't they?

CORNELIA. Come over here. (BROOKS *steps over to* R.C. CORNELIA *scrutinizes him carefully*). Have you had any experience with rubeola?

BROOKS. Oh, yes—yes—indeed! (LIZZIE *stands; watches* BROOKS.)

CORNELIA. And—alopecia?

BROOKS. The dry weather is very hard on alopecia.

CORNELIA. What do you think is the best treatment for urticaria?

BROOKS. Urticaria frequently needs —er—thinning.

CORNELIA (*rises. Faces him across table*). Needs scratching, you mean. Young man, urticaria is hives, rubeola is measles, and alopecia is baldness. (*Slight pause. She crosses front of table to* BROOKS. *Suspiciously.*) Why did you tell me that you were a professional gardener? Why have you come here at this hour of the night, pretending to be something you are not?

BROOKS (*suddenly smiles at her, boyishly*). I know I shouldn't have done it. You'd have found me out anyhow. I don't know *anything* about gardening. The truth is, I was desperate! I *had* to have *work*.

CORNELIA. That's *all*, is it?

BROOKS. That's enough, when you're down and out! (*Turns to front.*)

CORNELIA (*somewhat melted*). How do I know you won't steal the spoons?

BROOKS (*turns to* CORNELIA. *Lighten up*). Are they *nice* spoons?

CORNELIA. Beautiful spoons.

BROOKS (*again engagingly boyish*). Spoons are always a great temptation to me, Miss Van Gorder, but if you'll take me, I'll promise to leave them alone.

CORNELIA (*with grim humor*). That's *extremely kind* of you. (*She goes to bell and pushes button.*)

LIZZIE (*quickly over and up to CORNELIA*). I don't trust him! He's too smooth! (*CORNELIA to window, LIZZIE following her, their backs to BROOKS.*)

CORNELIA. I haven't asked for your opinion, Lizzie.

LIZZIE. You're just as bad as all the rest of 'em. A good-looking man comes in the door and your brains fly out the window. (*During this, BROOKS has a chance to make a stealthy survey of the room. He does this in such a way that from that time on it is perfectly plain to the audience that his interest in the house is not that of a gardener only. BROOKS quickly runs up to alcove, looks off and quickly back, so that when CORNELIA turns to him, he is where she saw him last.*)

CORNELIA. Have you had anything to eat lately?

BROOKS. Not since this morning.

(*BILLY enters from the left.*)

CORNELIA. Billy, give this man something to eat, and then show him where he is to sleep. (*To BROOKS, holding out candle and matches. He takes a step up to her.*) Take a candle and a box of matches to your room with you. The local light company crawls under its bed every time there is a thunderstorm. Good night, Brooks.

BROOKS. Good night, ma'am. (*Over to door.*) You're being mighty good to me. (*CORNELIA smiles at him as BROOKS exits. BILLY exits, closing door.*)

LIZZIE. Haven't you any sense, taking strange men into the house? How do you know that isn't the Bat? (*Distant thunder, lights blink.*) There go the lights.

CORNELIA (*crosses front of table to right*). We'll put the detective in the blue room when he comes. You'd better go up and see if it's all ready. (*LIZZIE lifts newspaper off Ouija, gets board off table, puts prayer book on Ouija and on small table, starts for alcove doors.*) Lizzie! (*LIZZIE stops; looks at CORNELIA.*) You know that stair rail's just been varnished—use the other stairs—(*LIZZIE starts for hall door*)—and Lizzie——

LIZZIE. Yes'm.

CORNELIA. No one is to know that he is a detective—not even Billy.

LIZZIE. What'll I *say* he is?

CORNELIA (*sits at table*). It's nobody's business.

(*Doorbell off stage.*)

LIZZIE. A detective! Tiptoeing around with his eyes to all the keyholes. A body won't be safe in the bathtub—— (*Exits. Pause.*)

(*Enter BILLY from left.*)

BILLY (*as he comes and goes to table for key*). Front-door key, please.

CORNELIA. Find out who it is before you unlock the door. (*BILLY gets key off table and exits, leaving door*) *open.* CORNELIA *rises; looks toward door.*)

DALE (*off stage*). Won't you come in for a few minutes?

DOCTOR (*off stage*). Oh, thank you. (CORNELIA *sits with knitting.*)

(*Enter* DALE OGDEN. *She is a beautiful young girl of twenty-five. She wears a pale-colored charming evening frock and evening wrap. She enters quietly and without animation.*)

CORNELIA. Aren't you back early, Dale?

DALE (*throws off her wrap*). I was tired——

CORNELIA. Not worried about anything?

DALE (*comes down to chair by table. Sits. Unconvincingly*). No, but I've come out here to be company for you, and I don't want to run away all the time.

DOCTOR (*off stage*). How have you been, Billy?

BILLY (*off stage*). Very well, thanks.

CORNELIA. Who's out there, Dale?

DALE. Dr. Wells—he brought me over from the club. I asked him to come in for a few minutes—Billy's just taking his coat.

CORNELIA. Your trunks have come.

DALE (*listlessly*). That's good. (*Rises and turns; goes up back of table.*)

CORNELIA. I hope this country ai, will pick you up. I promised your mother before she sailed that I'd take good care of you. (DALE *leans over; kisses* CORNELIA. *Then* DALE *goes and sits on settee, which is up and down stage to the right. Faces fireplace.*)

(DR. WELLS *enters. He is in dinner clothes; good-looking man in his early forties—with a shrewd, rather aquiline face.* BILLY *enters, goes to table, puts key on table, then exits; closes door.*)

DOCTOR (*crosses to table; shakes hands with* CORNELIA). Well, how are we this evening, Miss Van Gorder?

CORNELIA. Very well, thank you, Doctor. Well, many people at the Country Club?

DOCTOR. Not very many. This failure of the Union Bank has knocked a good many of the club members sky high.

CORNELIA. Just how did it happen?

DOCTOR. Oh, the usual thing. The cashier, a young chap named Bailey, looted the bank to the tune of over a million. (CORNELIA *surprised.*)

DALE (*visibly agitated*). How do you *know* the cashier did it?

DOCTOR. Well, he's run away, for one thing. The Bank Examiner found the deficit this morning. Bailey, the cashier, went out for lunch and didn't come back. The method was simple—blank paper substituted for securities.

DALE. Couldn't somebody else have done it? (CORNELIA *looks at* DALE, *then at* DOCTOR.)

DOCTOR. Of course the President of the bank had access to the vaults. But as you know, Mr. Courtleigh Fleming, the late President, was buried last Monday.

CORNELIA. Dale dear, did you know this young Bailey?

DALE (*controlling herself with an effort*). Yes—slightly.

CORNELIA. What with bank robberies and Bolshevism and the Income Tax, the only way to keep your money these days is to spend it.

DOCTOR (*sits at table*). Or *not* to have any! Like myself!

CORNELIA. You know, Dale, this is Courtleigh Fleming's house. I rented it from his nephew only last week.

DOCTOR. As a matter of fact, Dick Fleming had no right to rent you this property before the estate was settled. He must have done it the moment he received my telegram announcing his uncle's death.

CORNELIA. Were you with him when he died?

DOCTOR. Yes—— In Colorado—— It was very sudden.

CORNELIA (*knitting and in an innocent tone*). I suppose there is no suspicion that Courtleigh Fleming robbed his own bank?

DOCTOR. Well, if he did—I can testify he didn't have the loot with him. No, he had his faults—but not that.

CORNELIA. Doctor, I think I ought to tell you something. Last night and the night before, attempts were made to enter this house. Once an intruder actually got in, and was frightened away by Lizzie, at the top of that staircase. (*Indicating rear.*) And twice I have received anonymous communications threatening my life if I did not leave this house.

DALE (*startled*). I didn't know that, Auntie. How dreadful!

CORNELIA. Don't tell Lizzie. She'd yell like a siren. It's the only .thing she can do like a siren, but she does it superbly. (*At this moment, pane of one of the french windows is smashed in, and a stone with a note tied to it with a piece of string is thrown into the room.* ALL *rise quickly and look up at windows.*)

DALE. What's that?

CORNELIA. Somebody smashed a window pane.

DALE. And threw in a stone.

DOCTOR. Wait a minute. I'll—— (*He hurries up to alcove and terrace door.*)

CORNELIA (*follows up a few steps*). It's bolted at the top. (DOCTOR *unbolts door leading to terrace, and goes out. Meanwhile,* DALE *has picked up stone; unties string off stone, hands note to* CORNELIA *after she has closed terrace door.* DALE *drops stone on settee.* CORNELIA *to top of table, unfolds the note and reads it.*) "Take warning. Leave this house at once! It is threatened with disaster, which will involve you if you remain."

DALE. Who do you think wrote it?

CORNELIA. A fool, that's who! If anything was calculated to make me remain here, this sort of thing would do it. (*Slaps paper.*)

DALE. But—something may happen.

CORNELIA. I hope so! That's the reason I——

(*Doorbell rings off stage.*)

DALE. (*startled*). Oh, don't let anyone in. (*Down a step below* CORNELIA.)

BILLY (*enters. Crosses to table, gets key before he speaks*). Key front door, please; bell ring.

CORNELIA (*crosses front of table*). See that the chain is on the door. And get the visitor's name before you admit him. (*Crosses to* BILLY.) If he gives the name Anderson, let him in and take him to the library. (BILLY *exits; closes door.*)

DALE. Anderson—— Who is——

CORNELIA (*pause; thinks*). Dale dear —perhaps you had better go back to the city.

DALE (*surprised*). Tonight?

CORNELIA (*impassively*). There is something *behind* all this disturbance —something I don't understand. But I mean to. (*Looks to see if* DOCTOR'S *returning, then moves close to* DALE.

Lowers voice.) The man in the library is a detective from Police Headquarters.

DALE (*unaccountably aghast*). Not— the Police.

CORNELIA. Sh—— Be careful. It's not necessary to tell the *doctor*. I think *he's* a sort of perambulating bedside gossip. (*Slight pause.*) If it's *known* that the Police are here, we'll *never* catch the criminals.

(DOCTOR *enters terrace door, trifle out of breath. Takes out handkerchief; shakes off rain.*)

DOCTOR. He got away in the shrubbery.

CORNELIA (*steps from front of table to* DOCTOR; *hands him note*). Read this. (DALE *sits settee, stares front, clearly terrified.*)

DOCTOR (*reads, pauses, then looks at* CORNELIA). Were the others like this?

CORNELIA. Practically.

DOCTOR. Miss Van Gorder, may I speak frankly?

CORNELIA. Generally speaking, I detest frankness.

DOCTOR. I think you *ought* to leave this house.

CORNELIA (*takes it lightly*). Because of that letter?

DOCTOR (*seriously*). There is some deviltry afoot. You are not safe here.

CORNELIA. I have been safe in all kinds of houses for sixty years. It's time I had a bit of a change. Besides, this house is as nearly impregnable as I can make it. (*She faces the french windows.*) The window locks are sound—the doors are locked and the keys are here. (*Steps to back of table; points to keys on table.*) On that door to the terrace—(*looks*)—I had Billy today place an extra bolt. By the way, did you bolt that door again? (*She is about to go up to terrace door.* DOCTOR *takes a step up to stop her.*)

DOCTOR. Yes, I did. (CORNELIA *stops.*) Miss Van Gorder, I confess I'm very anxious for you. This letter is ominous. Have you any enemies?

CORNELIA. Don't insult me! Of course I have. Enemies are an indication of character.

DOCTOR. Why not accept my hospitality in the village tonight? It's a little house, but I'll make you comfortable. Or, if you won't come, let *me* stay *here.*

CORNELIA. Thank you, no, Doctor, I'm not easily frightened. (DOCTOR *looks at letter.*) And tomorrow I intend to equip this entire house with burglar alarms on doors and windows. (*She goes up into alcove and to terrace door; pushes bolt.*) I knew it. (*Triumphantly.*) Doctor, you *didn't* fasten that bolt!

DOCTOR (*facing up stage*). Oh, I'm sorry——

CORNELIA. You pushed it only part of the way. (*Sees door is bolted.*) The only thing that worries me now is that broken window. Anyone can reach a hand through it and open the latch. (*She goes to settee.* DALE

rises to see what CORNELIA *intends to do.*) Please, Doctor!

DOCTOR. What do you mean to do?

CORNELIA. I'm going to barricade that window. (DOCTOR *and* DALE *push up settee until it is against french windows.*)

DOCTOR. It would take a furniture mover to get in there now.

CORNELIA. Well, Doctor, now I'll say good night—and thank you very much. (*Faces* DOCTOR.) Don't keep this young lady up too late—she looks tired.

DOCTOR. I'll only smoke a cigarette. You won't change your mind?

CORNELIA (*smiles*). I've got a great deal of mind. It takes a long time to change it. (*She exits; closes door.*)

DOCTOR (*rather nettled*). It may be mind—but—forgive me if I say I think it is foolhardy stubbornness.

DALE. Then you think there is really danger?

DOCTOR. Well, those letters—(*he has placed it on table*)—mean *something* —— Here you are—isolated—the village two miles away—and enough shrubbery around the place to hide a dozen assassins.

DALE. But what enemies can she have?

DOCTOR (*takes cigarette from case*). Any man will tell you what I do. This is no place for two women, practically alone. (DALE *walks away to fireplace; back to* DOCTOR. *Unseen by her, he steps down right of table, takes match box off match holder and slips it into his side pocket. Then with assumed carelessness.*) I don't seem to see any matches. (*Looks up at stand.*)

DALE (*turns; faces him*). Oh, aren't there any? I'll get you some. (DALE *quickly crosses front of table and exits R.; closes door.* DOCTOR *watches her off, then swiftly he runs up into alcove and unfastens bolt on terrace door. He quickly comes back to same position, picks up a book and opens it. Enter* DALE *with matches. She crosses to him; gives him matches.*)

DOCTOR. I'm so sorry to trouble you —but tobacco is the one drug every doctor forbids his patients and prescribes for himself. (DALE *smiles at his little joke.* DOCTOR *lights cigarette.*) By the way, has Miss Van Gorder a revolver?

DALE (*turns; faces him*). Yes, she fired it off this evening to see if it would work.

DOCTOR. If she tries to shoot at anything, for goodness sake stand behind her. Oh, I must be going. (*Starts to go; looks at wrist watch.*)

DALE. If anything happens, I shall *telephone* you at once.

DOCTOR (*stops on word "telephone," hesitates; then*). I'll be home shortly after midnight. I'm stopping at the Johnsons'. One of the children is ill. (*Faces* DALE.) Take a parting word of advice. The thing to do with a midnight prowler is—let him alone. Lock your bedroom doors, and don't let anything bring you out until morning. (*Goes to door.*)

DALE. Thank you. Billy will let you out. He has the key.

DOCTOR (*at door*). By Jove, *you're* careful, aren't you? (*Looks around.*) The place is like a fortress! Well, good night, Miss Dale.

DALE. Good night. (*Exit* DOCTOR. *Pause. Door slam off stage.* DALE *is left alone. Stands motionless, takes out handkerchief, dabs eyes. She is distressed for some unknown reason. Crosses to fireplace.* BILLY *enters, puts door key on table.* DALE *picks up book.*) Billy, has the new gardener come?

BILLY. He here—name Brook. (*Exit* BILLY, *leaving door open. Stands in sight while they enter.* CORNELIA *sweeps in, followed by* ANDERSON. *He is a man of probably fifty, an aggressive person with a loud voice. Not at all the typical stage detective.*)

CORNELIA. Dale dear, this is Mr. Anderson.

DETECTIVE. How do you do? (DALE *bows; does not speak.*)

CORNELIA. This is the room I spoke of. All the disturbances have taken place around that door. (*Indicating terrace door.*)

DETECTIVE (*up to alcove*). This is not the main staircase?

CORNELIA. No, the main staircase is out there. (*Indicating.*)

DETECTIVE (*looking over at french windows*). I think there must be a conspiracy between architects and the House Breakers Union these days. Look at all that glass. All a burglar needs is a piece of putty and a diamond cutter to break in.

CORNELIA. But the curious thing is that whoever got into the house evidently had a key to that door. (*Indicating terrace door.*)

DETECTIVE. Hello—what's that? (*Sees broken glass on floor in front of settee. He crosses up and over to window.* CORNELIA *comes down to table, watching* DETECTIVE. DETECTIVE *picks up piece of glass off floor front of settee. Places glass on settee.*)

DALE. It was broken from the outside, a few minutes ago. (DETECTIVE *pulls aside one of the blinds; looks out.*)

DETECTIVE. The outside?

DALE. And then that letter was thrown in. (*Points to table.* DETECTIVE *comes down to top of table C.* CORNELIA *hands him the note that was thrown in.* DETECTIVE *pauses; looks at letter.*)

DETECTIVE (*calm; self-assured*). Um! Coy, isn't it? Somebody wants you *out* of here, all right!

CORNELIA (*facing him across table*). There are some things I haven't told you *yet*. This house belonged to the late Courtleigh Fleming.

DETECTIVE (*with interest*). The Union Bank?

CORNELIA. Yes. I rented it for the summer and moved in last Monday. I have not had a really quiet night since I came. The very first night I saw a man with an electric flashlight

making his way through that shrubbery. (*Points.* DETECTIVE *is looking up at window.*)

DALE. You poor dear! And you were here alone!

CORNELIA. Well, I had Lizzie—(*she opens drawer in side of table. Takes out a small revolver*)—and I had a revolver. I know so little about these things that if I didn't hit a burglar I'd certainly hit *somebody* or something. (*Looks into the barrel; then waves it about carelessly.*)

DETECTIVE· (*turns; faces* CORNELIA. *Sees revolver. Starts*). Would you mind putting that away? I like to get in the papers as much as anybody, but I don't want to have them say "omit flowers." (CORNELIA *replaces revolver in drawer; closes it.* DETECTIVE *goes up, facing alcove doors.*) Now, you say, you don't think anybody has got upstairs yet?

CORNELIA. I think not. I'm a very light sleeper, especially since the papers have been so full of the exploits of this criminal they call "The Bat." I was just reading your statement about him in the evening paper. (*Sits beside table.*)

DETECTIVE (*comes down, professional manner*). Yes. He's contrived to surround himself with such an air of mystery that it verges on the supernatural.

CORNELIA. I confess I have thought of him in *this* connection. (DETECTIVE *laughs.*) Nevertheless, somebody has been trying to get into this house—night after night.

DETECTIVE (*looks around. Seriously*). Any liquor stored here?

CORNELIA. Yes.

DETECTIVE (*interested*). What?

CORNELIA (*with pride; knits*). Eleven bottles of homemade elderberry wine.

DETECTIVE. You're safe. (*Moves to table; looks newspaper. Shakes head.*) You can always tell when The Bat has anything to do with a crime. When he's through he signs his name to it. (*Sits; plays with box of matches.*)

CORNELIA. His name? I thought nobody knew his name.

DETECTIVE. That was a figure of speech. The newspapers named him "The Bat" because he moved with incredible rapidity—always at night —and he seemed to be able to see in the dark.

CORNELIA. I wish I could. These country lights are always going out.

DETECTIVE. Within the last six months he's taken up the name himself—pure bravado.—— Sometimes he draws the outline of a bat, at the scene of the crime. Once, in some way, he got hold of a real bat and nailed it to the wall. (*Shudder from* DALE *and* CORNELIA.) He seems to have imagination. (*Slaps knee, rises, takes step determinedly.*) I've got imagination, too. (*Stands second, then with effort brings himself back to present situation.*) How many people in this house, Miss Van Gorder? (DALE *starts to cross to table. She does this slowly.*)

CORNELIA. My niece and myself; Lizzie Allen, who has been my personal maid for twenty years—the Japanese butler and the gardener. The cook, parlormaid, and housemaid left yesterday—frightened away. (*Smiles.* DALE *picks up her wrap from chair and exits.* DETECTIVE *just glances at her as she goes.*)

DETECTIVE. Well, you can have a good night's sleep tonight. I'll stay right here in the dark and watch.

CORNELIA. Would you like some coffee to keep you awake?

DETECTIVE. Thank you. Do the servants know who I am?

CORNELIA. Only Lizzie—my maid.

DETECTIVE. I wouldn't tell anyone that I am remaining up all night.

CORNELIA. You don't suspect my household?

DETECTIVE. I'm not taking any chances.

LIZZIE (*enters; stands at door*). The gentleman's room is ready.

CORNELIA (*knitting at table*). The maid will show you your room now, and you can make yourself *comfortable* for the night.

DETECTIVE (*facing up stage*). My toilet is made for an occasion like this when I've got my gun loaded. (LIZZIE *gives a start. His hand on hip pocket,* DETECTIVE *stares at* LIZZIE, *and goes over to her.*) This is the maid you referred to? (LIZZIE *stiffens.*) What's your name?

LIZZIE. Elizabeth Allen.

DETECTIVE. How old are you? (LIZZIE *looks across at* CORNELIA.)

LIZZIE. Have I got to answer that? (CORNELIA *nods her head. Cute-like.*) Thirty-two.

CORNELIA. She's forty. (LIZZIE *gives a start.*)

DETECTIVE. Now, Lizzie, do you ever walk in your sleep?

LIZZIE. I do not.

DETECTIVE. Don't care for the country, I suppose?

LIZZIE. I do not.

DETECTIVE (*facetiously*). Or detectives?

LIZZIE. *I do not.*

DETECTIVE. All right, Lizzie. Be calm! I can stand it! (*He goes to table, picks up note that was thrown through window, crosses back beside* LIZZIE, *holds out note so* LIZZIE *can read it. Quick.*) Ever see this before?

LIZZIE (*reads it; is horrified. Makes gesture with arm, nearly hitting* DE-TECTIVE *in face.*) Mercy on us!

DETECTIVE (*watching her*). Didn't write it yourself, did you?

LIZZIE (*angrily*). I did *not!*

DETECTIVE. You're sure you don't walk in your sleep?

LIZZIE (*strong*). When I get into bed in this house I wouldn't put my feet out for a million dollars.

DETECTIVE. Well, that's more money than I'm worth.

LIZZIE. Well, I'll say it is. (*She flounces out; slams door behind her.* CORNELIA *laughs.*)

DETECTIVE (*turns and goes to table; puts note back on table*). Now, what about the *butler?*

CORNELIA. Nothing about him—except that he was Courtleigh Fleming's servant.

DETECTIVE. Do you consider that significant?

(DALE *enters from below stair alcove. Stands watching and listening to* DE-TECTIVE.)

CORNELIA. Is it not possible that there is a connection between this colossal theft at the Union Bank and *these* disturbances?

DETECTIVE (*looks at* DALE. *Pause*). Just what do you mean? (DALE *slowly moves to table.*)

CORNELIA. Suppose Courtleigh Fleming took that money from his own bank and concealed it in this house?

DETECTIVE. That's the theory you gave Headquarters, isn't it? But I'll tell you how Headquarters figures it out. In the first place, the cashier is missing. In the second place, if Courtleigh Fleming did it, and got as far as Colorado, he'd have had it with him. In the third place, suppose he had hidden the money in or around this house. Why did he rent it to you?

CORNELIA. But he didn't. I leased this house from his nephew—his heir.

DETECTIVE. Well, I wouldn't struggle like that for a theory. The cashier's *missing*—that's the answer.

CORNELIA (*resents with pride*). I've read a great deal on the detection of crime, and——

DETECTIVE (*interrupting her*). Huh! I suppose so—there are a lot of amateur detectives crawling around over the country today, measuring footprints with a tape measure. Much as your life's worth to leave a thumbprint on a soda-water glass. The only real detectives outside the profession are married women.

CORNELIA. Then *you* don't think there's a chance that the money from the Union Bank is in this house? (*Puts knitting away.*)

DETECTIVE. Very unlikely!

CORNELIA (*rises*). If you come with me, I'll show you to your room. (*She crosses front of table.* DETECTIVE *follows her toward door.*)

DETECTIVE. Well, I suppose I might as well see where I park my toothbrush.

(CORNELIA *exits, followed by* DETECTIVE. DALE *is now seen to be in a state of violent excitement. She goes to hall door; then to alcove door; quick to center of stage. Alcove door opens cautiously.* BROOKS *enters.*)

DALE. Sh! Sh! Be careful! That man's a detective! (BROOKS *looks quickly off stage, then closes door, and goes to table.* DALE *follows him over.*)

BROOKS. Then they've traced me here?

DALE. I don't think so.

BROOKS. I couldn't get back to my rooms. If they've searched them—

(*pause*)—as they're sure to—they'll find your letters to me. (*Pause.*) Your aunt doesn't suspect anything?

DALE. No, I told her I'd engaged a gardener—and that's all there was about it.

BROOKS. Dale! (*Turns and faces* DALE.) You *know* I didn't take that money.

DALE. Of course! I believe in you absolutely.

BROOKS (*he catches her in his arms, kisses her, then breaks*). But—the Police here—what does that mean?

DALE. Aunt Cornelia says people have been trying to break into this house for a week—at night.

BROOKS (*sharply*). What sort of people? (*Steps back.*)

DALE. She doesn't know.

BROOKS. That proves exactly what I have contended right along. (*Turns; looks at* DALE.) Courtleigh Fleming took that money and put it here. And somebody knows that he did.

DALE. The detective thinks you're guilty because you ran away.

BROOKS. Ran away? (*Turns front; smiles.*) The only chance I had was a few hours to myself, to try to prove what actually happened.

DALE. Why don't you tell the detective what you think? That Courtleigh Fleming took the money, and that it's still here?

BROOKS. He'd take me into custody at once—and I'd have no chance to search.

DALE. Why are you so *sure* it is here?

BROOKS (*crosses to* DALE). You must remember, Fleming was no ordinary defaulter—and *he* had no intention of being exiled to a foreign country. He wanted to come back here and take his place in the community while I was in the Pen.

DALE. But even then——

BROOKS (*interrupting*). Listen, dear. The architect who built this house was an old friend of mine. We were together in France and you know the way fellows get to talking when they're far away. Just an hour or two before a shell got him, he told me he had built a *hidden room* in this house.

DALE (*pauses; then speaks*). Where?

BROOKS. I don't know. We never got to finish that conversation. But I remember what he said. He said, "You watch old Fleming. If I get mine over here, it won't break his heart." He didn't want any living being to know about that room.

DALE (*excitedly; whisper*). Then you think the money is in this hidden room?

BROOKS. I do. I don't think Fleming took it West with him. He knew the minute this thing blew up he'd be under suspicion. (*Looks off stage.*) Only if he left the money here, why did he rent this house?

DALE. He didn't. His *nephew* rented it to us. (*Pause. She takes a step, looks, and then crosses to* BROOKS.) Jack, could it be the nephew who's trying to break in?

BROOKS. He wouldn't *have* to break in. He could make an excuse and come at any time. (*Looks around.*) If I could only get hold of a blueprint of this place.

DALE. (BROOKS *crosses to fireplace.*) Oh, Jack, I'm so confused and worried!

BROOKS (*he stops her; hands on shoulders in effort to cheer her. Pause*). Now, listen—this isn't as hard as it sounds. I've got a clear night to work in—and as true as I'm standing here, that money's in the house. Now listen, honey, it's like this. (*Pantomime action of house on floor.*) Here's the house that Courtleigh Fleming built—here, somewhere, is the Hidden Room in the house that Courtleigh Fleming built —and here, somewhere—pray Heaven —is the money, in the Hidden Room, in the house that Courtleigh Fleming built! When you're low in your mind, just say that over!

DALE (*smiles faintly*). I've forgotten it already!

BROOKS (*still trying to cheer her*). Why, look here! (*Hands on her shoulders, turns her around*). It's a sort of game, dearest—"Money, money, who's got the money?" You know. (*Looks around room.*) For that matter, the Hidden Room may be behind these very walls. (BROOKS *sees golf sticks in bag leaning against small table; quickly up and gets one club. Comes down to fireplace.* DALE *watches him.* BROOKS *taps wall above fireplace. Roll of thunder. Lights blink. Lightning.*)

DALE. The lights are going out again.

BROOKS. Let them go. The less light the better for me. The only thing to do is to go over this house room by room. (*Indicates billiard-room door.*) What's in there?

DALE. The billiard room. (BROOKS *starts toward billiard-room door.*) Jack! Perhaps Courtleigh Fleming's nephew would know where the blueprints are!

BROOKS. It's a chance, but not a very good one. (*Exit* BROOKS *and* DALE *into billiard room, leaving door open.*)

(BROOKS *raps with golf club off stage. Pause, then raps again. Enter* LIZZIE *with white table napkin. As soon as she gets inside, thunder. Lightning.* LIZZIE *looks nervously about. She shows she is scared; to table with napkin; spreads it on upper end of table.* BROOKS *repeats raps.* LIZZIE *starts off stage, looking back.*)

LIZZIE. Spirits! (*Over to door*). Go back to Hell, where you started from. (*Exits. Lights out. Lightning and thunder stop. Enter* BROOKS *and* DALE.)

BROOKS. Well, here we are, back where we started from.

DALE. There's a candle on the table, if I can find the table. Here it is. (*Finds candle on table.*)

BROOKS. I have matches. (*He lights candle. Places candle on table.*) It's pretty nearly hopeless. If all the walls are paneled like that. (*Rappings heard overhead—four dull raps.*)

DALE (*suddenly interrupting*). What's that?

BROOKS (*in tense voice and looking up at ceiling*). Someone else is looking for the Hidden Room. (*Four dull raps heard again.*)

DALE (*looking up at ceiling*). Upstairs!

BROOKS. Who's in this house besides ourselves?

DALE. Only the detective—Aunt Cornelia—Lizzie and Billy.

BROOKS. Billy's the Jap?

DALE. Yes.

BROOKS. Belong to your aunt? .

DALE. No, he was Courtleigh Fleming's butler. (*Four raps upstairs.*)

BROOKS (*looks up at ceiling*). He was, eh? (*Quickly puts down candle; crosses to alcove doors and into alcove.*) It may be the Jap. (*Four more raps upstairs.*) If it is, I'll get him. (BROOKS *exits quickly but quietly. Closes door behind him.* DALE, *left alone, stands thinking. Her distress and anxiety are evident. At last she forms a resolution. Goes up to city phone.*)

DALE (*at phone*). One-two-four. (*She looks around before calling number, her voice is cautious.*) Is that the Country Club? Is Mr. Richard Fleming there? Yes—I'll hold the wire. (*Moment's pause. She looks around nervously.*) Hello—— Is this Mr. Fleming?—This is Miss Ogden. —Do you remember my aunt has rented your house, Cedarcrest? I know it's rather odd my calling you so late, but—I wonder if you could come over here for a few minutes.

Yes—tonight. I wouldn't trouble you but—it's awfully important. Hold the wire a moment. (*She puts the receiver down; glances up the stairs; goes, listens at door, then back again to phone.*) Hello. I shall wait outside the house on the drive. It—it's a confidential matter.—Thank you so much. (*She hangs up phone. A moment's pause, then* DETECTIVE *enters with unlighted candle in his hand.*)

DETECTIVE. Spooky sort of place in the dark, isn't it?

DALE. Yes—rather!

DETECTIVE. Left me upstairs without a match. I found my way down by walking part of the way and falling the rest. I don't suppose I'll ever find the room I left my toothbrush in! (*Lights his candle from the lighted candle on table.*)

DALE. You're not going to stay up all night, are you?

DETECTIVE (*takes cigar out*). Oh, I may doze a bit. What's your opinion of these intrusions your aunt complains of?

DALE. I don't know. I only came today.

DETECTIVE. Is she a pretty nervous temperament usually? Imagines she sees things and all that?

DALE. I don't think so.

DETECTIVE. Know the Flemings?

DALE. I've met Mr. Richard Fleming once or twice.

DETECTIVE (*turns to table*). Know the cashier of the Union Bank?

DALE (*after a barely perceptible pause*). No. (*Moves to fireplace.*)

DETECTIVE. Fellow of good family, I understand—very popular. That's what's behind most of these bank embezzlements. Men getting into society and spending more than they make. (*Phone rings.* DETECTIVE *starts for house phone.*)

DALE. No, the other one; that's the house phone.

DETECTIVE (*looking at house phone*). No connection with the outside, eh?

DALE. No, just from room to room, in the house.

DETECTIVE (*goes to city phone*). Hello! Hello! (*Pause. Hangs up phone.*) This line sounds dead.

DALE. It was all right a few minutes ago.

DETECTIVE. You were using it a few minutes ago?

DALE (*hesitates, then*). Yes. (*Phone rings again.*)

DETECTIVE (*picks up phone*). Yes, yes—this is Anderson—go ahead—— (*Rather impatiently.*) You're sure of that—are you?—I see—— All right! 'By! (*Hangs up phone; turns and looks at* DALE *intently.*) Did I understand you to say that you are not acquainted with the cashier of the Union Bank? (*Pause.* DALE *stares ahead; does not reply.*) That was Headquarters, Miss Ogden. They have found some letters in Bailey's room which seem to indicate that you were not telling the entire truth just now.

DALE. What letters?

DETECTIVE. From you to Jack Bailey—showing that you had recently become engaged to him.

DALE. Very well. That's true.

DETECTIVE. Why didn't you say so before?

DALE (*frankly*). It's been a secret. I haven't even told my aunt yet. (*Rises.*) How can the Police be so stupid as to accuse Jack Bailey—a young man about to be married? Do you think he would wreck his future like that?

DETECTIVE. Well, some folks wouldn't call it wrecking a future to lay away a million dollars. (*Speaks slowly and ominously.*) Do you know *where* he is now?

DALE. No.

DETECTIVE. Miss Ogden, in the last minute or so the Union Bank case and certain things in this house begin to tie up pretty close together. (*Steps a little nearer to her.*) Bailey disappeared at three o'clock this afternoon. Have you heard from him since then?

DALE. No.

DETECTIVE. You used the telephone a few minutes ago. Did you *call* him?

DALE. No.

DETECTIVE. I'll ask you to bring Miss Van Gorder here.

DALE. Why do you want her?

DETECTIVE. Because this case is taking on a new phase.

DALE. You don't think I know anything about that money?

DETECTIVE. No, but you know—somebody who does.

(DALE *hesitates, about to reply, finding none. Taking a lighted candle with her, exits.* DETECTIVE, *left alone, reflects for a moment, then he picks up lighted candle from table; proceeds to make a systematic examination of walls.* MAN *appears outside windows. His shadow shows on shades. He then disappears to terrace door. At same time* LIZZIE *appears at hall door with tray of dishes and food, Parker House rolls, chop, plate, cup, and saucer. She walks slowly, with her head turned to look behind her. The faint light of a candle from the hall gives her enough light to advance. As she gets to table, she hears key turn in terrace door. Registers fright. She has tray poised over the table.* MAN *who passed the windows now enters terrace door. He closes the door, reaches out his left arm, as if feeling his way to stairs. On his wrist he has a wrist watch with luminous face. It glows in darkness.* LIZZIE *stands galvanized with fright.* MAN *about to go up staircase.* LIZZIE *drops the tray on top of the table with a crash. She makes three attempts to scream before her voice responds. Then she shrieks. The* MAN *quickly runs up the stairs and off stage.* CORNELIA *runs on from the left. She is carrying a lighted candle.* CORNELIA *also carries a coffeepot, half filled with burnt sugar and water (coffee) and spills it at every step. At same time* DETECTIVE *enters with candle lighted.*)

CORNELIA. For the love of Heaven, what's wrong? (CORNELIA *holding the coffeepot inclined, the coffee pours out of the spout on* LIZZIE'S *foot.*)

LIZZIE (*screams*). Oh, my foot! My foot!

CORNELIA. My patience! Did you yell like that because you stubbed your toe?

LIZZIE (*wildly*). You scalded it! It went up the staircase.

CORNELIA. Your toe went up the staircase?

LIZZIE (*stands on one foot*). No, no! An eye—as big as a saucer! It ran righ: up that staircase—— (CORNELIA *puts pot and candle on table.*)

DETECTIVE (*sternly*). Now, see here. Stop this chicken-on-one-leg business, and tell me what you saw.

LIZZIE (*still holding up one leg*). A ghost! It came right through that door and went up the stairs! (DALE *and* BROOKS, *with lighted candle, come on, followed by* BILLY.)

DALE. Who screamed?

LIZZIE. I did. I saw a ghost. (*Then to* CORNELIA.) I begged you not to come here. I begged you on my bended knees. There's a graveyard not a quarter of a mile away.

CORNELIA. Yes, and one more scare like that, Lizzie Allen, and you'll have me lying in it.

LIZZIE (*holding foot*). Oh, my foot! If anything tries to get me now, I won't even be able to run away. (BROOKS *up with candle.* CORNELIA *goes up to terrace door in alcove.*)

DETECTIVE (*sore*). Now, Lizzie— what did you really see?

LIZZIE. I told you what I saw.

DETECTIVE (*rather threateningly*). You're not trying to frighten Miss Van Gorder into leaving this house and going back to the city?

LIZZIE (*grimly*). Well, if I am, I'm giving myself a good scare too, ain't I?

CORNELIA (*coming down from terrace door; annoyed*). Somebody who had a key could have got in here, Mr. Anderson. That door's been unbolted from the inside.

LIZZIE (*hysterically*). I *told* you so! I *knew* something was going to happen tonight. I heard rappings all over the house today, and the Ouija Board spelled "Bat"!

DETECTIVE. I think I see the answer to your puzzle, Miss Van Gorder! An hysterical and not very reliable woman—(LIZZIE *glares at him*)— anxious to go back to the city, and terrified over and over by the shutting off of the electric light.

CORNELIA. I wonder!

DETECTIVE. A good night's sleep and——

LIZZIE (*interrupting, aghast*). My God! We're not going to bed, are we?

DETECTIVE (*kindly to* LIZZIE). You'll feel better in the morning. Lock your door and say your prayers and leave the rest to me.

CORNELIA. That's very good advice. You take her, Dale. (CORNELIA *puts arm around* LIZZIE. DALE *comes down R. of* CORNELIA. LIZZIE *is passed along by* CORNELIA *to* DALE, *who puts arm around her shoulder, leads her toward door.*)

LIZZIE (*does not want to go, but does*). I'm not going to bed. Do you think I'm going to wake up in the morning with my throat cut? (DALE *and* LIZZIE *exit.*)

DETECTIVE (*speaking to* CORNELIA). There are certain things I want to discuss with you, Miss Van Gorder, but they can wait till tomorrow morning.

CORNELIA (*looks off stage*). Do you think all this pure imagination?

DETECTIVE (*close to table*). Don't you?

CORNELIA. I'm not sure.

DETECTIVE (*laughs a little*). I'll tell you what I'll do. (*Puts candle down.*) You go upstairs and go to bed comfortably. I'll make a careful search of the house before I settle down.

CORNELIA (*turns; looks at* DETECTIVE; *picks up coffeepot off table*). I'm afraid Lizzie has *absorbed* most of your coffee. Billy shall make you some more. (*She turns to* BILLY. *He steps forward and takes pot. Registers it is hot. He bows and exits with coffeepot.*) Well, I hope we're at the end of our troubles. (*She crosses to table.* DETECTIVE *hands her candle.*)

DETECTIVE. Sure you are. Now you go upstairs. (CORNELIA *starts off with candle.*) Get your beauty sleep. I'm sure you need it. (*Earnestly, without intention, then realizing what he said.*)

CORNELIA (*has reached door, turns, smiles caustically at him*). I begin to understand why The Bat has so long eluded you! (*Exits majestically.*)

DETECTIVE (*takes out handkerchief; mops his face*). Whew! (*Then looks at* BROOKS. BROOKS *about to exit, when* DETECTIVE *speaks.*) So you're the gardener, are you?

BROOKS (*lightly*). Yes.

DETECTIVE. Well, I don't need any gardening done just now—you can —— (*Looks attentively at* BROOKS.) I've seen you somewhere—and I'll place you before long. (*There is a little threat in his voice.*) Not in the portrait gallery at Headquarters, are you?

BROOKS (*resentfully*). Not yet.

DETECTIVE. Well, we slip up now and then. All right, Brooks. If you're needed during the night you'll be called.

BROOKS. Very well, sir. (BROOKS *exits. Closes door.*)

(DETECTIVE *watches him off with expression of suspicion. With noiseless step,* DETECTIVE *goes to hall door; listens. Opens door suddenly. Then closes door. Takes out revolver. To table; picks up candle;* DETECTIVE *proceeds to make a careful search of the entry, floor, walls, stair, and stair rail. He looks up staircase. Then bolts terrace door; comes back into room.* DETECTIVE *draws revolver from hip pocket; examines it; then exits with candle. Wind, thunder, lightning. Pause.* DALE *comes down the stairs holding a lighted candle high. She carries a rubber slicker and a pair of rubbers. She is cautious. She unbolts the terrace door; comes into the room from alcove. She places the candle on table and sits by table; places coat on back of chair. She is about to put on her rubbers when she hears a knock on terrace door. She starts at the sound, terrified, as she opens drawer right side of the table, takes out revolver. Steps up back of table with revolver pointed up at alcove. Noise as of opening terrace door with key.*)

DICK (*DICK FLEMING enters terrace door; closes it. He steps into room from alcove; stands there a moment. He is a man of perhaps thirty, rather dissipated as to face, foppish in dress, with collar of his dinner coat turned up against the rain*). Did I frighten you?

DALE. Oh, Mr. Fleming—yes! (*She puts revolver on table. She goes toward him.*)

DICK. I rapped—but as nobody heard me, I used my key.

DALE. You're wet through.

DICK. Oh, no! (*Takes off cap and raincoat; places them on back of chair.*) Reggie Beresford brought me over in his car. He's waiting down the drive.

DALE (*closes double door*). Mr. Fleming, I'm in dreadful trouble!

DICK (*over a few steps to her*). I say! That's too bad.

DALE. You know the Union Bank closed today.

DICK. Yes, I know it! I didn't have anything in it—or in *any* bank, for that matter—but I hate to see the old thing go to smash.

DALE. Well, even if *you* haven't lost anything by this failure, a lot of your friends have, surely?

DICK. I'll say so! Beresford is sitting down the road in his Rolls-Royce now—writhing with pain!

DALE (*pause*). Lots of awfully poor people are going to suffer, too.

DICK (*rather heartlessly*). Oh, well, the poor are always in trouble. They specialize in suffering. (*Takes out cigarette case and cigarette; moves closer to table.*) But look here—you didn't send for me to discuss the poor depositor, did you? Mind if I smoke?

DALE. No! (*DICK takes up candle from table; lights cigarette; slight pause.*) Mr. Fleming, I'm going to say something rather brutal. Please don't mind. I'm merely desperate. You see, I happen to be engaged to the cashier—Jack Bailey.

DICK (*whistles and sits on edge of table*). I see! And he's beat it!

DALE. He has not! I'm going to tell you something—he's here now, in this house. My aunt thinks he's a new gardener. He is here, Mr. Fleming, because he knows he didn't take the money, and the only person who could have done it—was—your uncle. (*DICK drops cigarette on tray. Pause. Turns; faces her.*)

DICK. That's a pretty strong indictment to bring against a dead man.

DALE. It is true.

DICK. All right. (*Smiles.*) Suppose it's true? Where do I come in? (*Steps toward her.*) You don't think I know where the money is?

DALE. No, but I think you might help to find it. (*She turns to make*

sure no one is listening, then faces
FLEMING.) If anybody comes in—
you've just come to get something of
yours. (*Comes close to him.*) Do you
know anything about a Hidden
Room in this house?

DICK. A Hidden Room—that's good.
(*Laughs.*) Never heard of it. Now,
let me get this straight. The idea is—
a Hidden Room—and the money is
in it—is that it?

DALE (*nods "yes"*). The architect
who built this house told Jack Bailey
he had built a Hidden Room in it.
(DICK's *expression has changed. A
slowly growing look of avarice and
calculation has taken the place of
his smile. He no longer looks at
DALE. His eyes are shifty and uncertain. They open and close as though
already he has them on the treasure.*)
Do you know where there are any
blueprints of the house?

DICK (*starts; restrains himself*). Blueprints? (*It is evident to the audience
that he does know.*) Why, there may
be some—— (*He formulates; one can
see almost the plot growing in his
mind.*) Have you looked in that old
secretary in the morning room? My
uncle used to keep all sorts of papers
there.

DALE. Why, don't you remember, you
locked it when we took the house?

DICK (*gets out his key ring and
selects the key*). So I did. Suppose
you go and look. Don't you think
I'd better stay here? (DALE *takes
key.*)

DALE (*cheerful; grateful*). Yes——
Oh, I can hardly thank you enough!
(*She quickly crosses and exits; closes
door.*)

(DICK *quickly looks around room,
then goes around room from bookcase to bookcase. Turns; looks around
room again. Pause. Decides to try the
bookcase above fireplace. All these
moves are quick. He takes out the
books in top shelf and puts them
quickly on mantel at fireplace;
reaches behind books on shelf and
pulls out a roll of three blueprints.
He leans over to see what they are at
fireplace. Then over to table. Holds
blueprints close to candle on table.
Looking carefully at each blueprint,
finds the third one is the one he
wants. He tears off a corner of it.*)

DALE (*enters; closes door behind her.
Quickly over to him, rejoiced*). Oh,
you found it! (*Gives him the key.*)
Please let me have it. I *know* that's
it.

DICK (*his manner changed*). Just a
moment. (*He steps away from her.
Picking up candle and looking at the
piece of blueprint in his hand; then
turns; looks at* DALE.) Do you suppose, if that money is actually here,
that I can simply turn this over to
you—and let you give it to Bailey?
Every man has his price. How do I
know that Bailey's isn't a million
dollars? (*He inspects piece of blueprint closely.*)

DALE. What do you mean to do,
then?

DICK (*turning over blueprint in his
hand. Pause*). I don't know. (*Puts
candle down on table. Looks at*
DALE.) What is it you want me to
do?

DALE. Aren't you going to give it to
me?

DICK. I'll have to think about that.
So the missing cashier is in the house
posing as a gardener?

DALE. If you won't give it to me—there's a detective in the house. (*She makes a turn as if to call him. Then to* DICK.) Give it to him—let him search.

DICK (*quickly, facing her, startled*). A detective? What's a detective doing here?

DALE. People have been trying to break in.

DICK. What people?

DALE. I don't know.

DICK (*to himself, looking out front*). Then it *is* here. (*At this one of the alcove doors opens noiselessly just an inch or so. Evidently someone is listening.*) I'm not going to give it to the detective. (DICK *picks up the roll of blueprints; quickly goes to fireplace; throws in the roll of blueprints.* DICK *takes the small piece of blueprint from pocket; watches papers burn.* DALE *has followed him over to fireplace.*)

DALE (*as she follows* DICK). What do you mean? What are you going to do?

DICK (*turns and faces* DALE, *near fireplace*). Let us suppose a few things, Miss Ogden. Suppose my price is a million dollars—suppose I need money very badly—and my uncle has left me a house containing that amount in cash—suppose I choose to consider that that money is mine—then it wouldn't be hard to suppose, would it, that I'd make a pretty sincere attempt to get it?

DALE (*close up to him*). If you go out of this room with that paper, I'll scream for help.

DICK. To carry on our little game of supposing—suppose there is a detective in this house—and that if I were cornered I should tell him where to lay his hands on Jack Bailey, do you suppose you would scream? (DALE *stands helpless. He quickly crosses and stops by table, looks up at alcove doors a moment, then he hurries up and opens them; makes for stairs in alcove.*)

DALE (*follows him over to table. When he starts to move off, she picks up revolver off table and hurries up after him. Speaks as she goes. Suddenly desperate*). No! No! Give it to me! Give it to me! (DALE *up to* DICK *at foot of stairs in alcove. He turns and waits for her. He snatches the revolver from her. A very short scuffle in the darkness of the entry in effort to secure the revolver. He unguards the piece of blueprint, which she tears from him, leaving only a corner of it in his grasp.*)

(*A light flashes on from the top of stairs and covers* DICK *at foot of stairs. Supposed to be a pocket flash, held by an invisible hand. Light shows him poised ready to come down after the girl, his face shown distorted with fury. Shot off stage.* DICK *falls forward, dead. The revolver* DALE *carried falls between them.* DICK *lies with head just inside the double doors into the room proper, face downward.*)

DALE (*backs away into room; hides the blueprint in dress. With a little whimpering cry of horror*). Oh, no, no! (*The storm dies out. Pause. Voices off stage heard ad lib.*)

VOICES. The noise came from this room—I think it is in here.

(General entrance. (1) DETECTIVE. *Sees body. (2)* BROOKS. *(3)* BILLY, *the Jap. (4)* CORNELIA. LIZZIE *enters last and stands in doorway. They all perceive* DALE *and the body. A tense silence.)*

DALE *(stepping back until she is almost to door).* Oh! I didn't do it! I didn't do it!

DETECTIVE *(goes to body; examines it; takes plenty of time).* He's dead. *(Pause. Picks up revolver, looks at it, then turns, and looks at* DALE *curiously.)* Who is he?

DALE *(hysterically).* Richard Fleming—— Somebody shot him!

DETECTIVE *(takes a step toward her).* What do you mean by somebody? *(*CORNELIA *sinks into chair.)*

DALE. Oh, I don't know. *(Hysterically.)* Somebody on the staircase.

DETECTIVE. Did you see anybody?

DALE. No—there was a light from somewhere—like a pocket flash.

LIZZIE *(in doorway, hysterically points up at stairs).* I told you I saw a man go up that staircase. *(Pause.* DETECTIVE *has turned from facing* DALE. *He looks at* LIZZIE *and* CORNELIA.*)*

CORNELIA. That's the only explanation, Mr. Anderson.

DETECTIVE. I've been all over the house. There's nobody there. *(House phone rings.)*

CORNELIA *(rises. Slight pause).* The house phone—— *(Looks at the other characters.)* But we're all here. *(They* ALL *stand, pause, aghast. Then* CORNELIA *goes up to phone.)* Hello! Hello! *(*ALL *stand, listening rigidly. She gasps. An expression of horror comes over her face.)*

CURTAIN SLOWLY FALLS

ACT TWO

SCENE—*Same as Act One.*

DISCOVERED: ALL CHARACTERS *as at end of Act One. The action being continuous. They are staring aghast at* CORNELIA, *who still stands clutching the phone.*

CORNELIA *(gasps).* Somebody groaning! It's horrible! *(*DETECTIVE *crosses to* CORNELIA. *She gives him the phone. She steps down to table.)*

DETECTIVE *(listens in phone).* I don't hear anything. *(Slight pause.)*

CORNELIA. I heard it! I couldn't *imagine* such a dreadful sound! I tell you somebody in this house is in terrible distress.

DETECTIVE. Where does this phone connect?

CORNELIA. Practically every room in the house.

DETECTIVE (*puts receiver to ear again*). Just what did you hear?

CORNELIA. Dreadful groans, and what seemed to be an inarticulate effort to speak.

LIZZIE (*trembling violently*). I'd go somewhere, if I had somewhere to go! (*Rises.*)

CORNELIA (*faces up to* DETECTIVE). Won't you send these men to investigate? Or go yourself?

DETECTIVE. My place is here—you two men. (*To* BROOKS *and* BILLY.) Take another look through the house. (BILLY *opens door.*) Don't leave the building—I'll want you pretty soon.

BROOKS. If you'll give me that revolver—— (*Indicating* CORNELIA'S *revolver, which* DETECTIVE *still holds in his hand.*)

DETECTIVE. This revolver will stay where it is. (*Exit* BILLY, *followed by* BROOKS. *Close door. As* BROOKS *goes reluctantly, puzzled and anxious glance at* DALE, DETECTIVE *looks at body, then turns quickly on* DALE.) Now I want the real story. You lied before.

CORNELIA (*indignantly*). That is no tone to use! You'll only terrify her.

DETECTIVE (*turns; looks at* COR-NELIA). Where were you when this happened? (DALE *moves down a little.*)

CORNELIA. Upstairs in my room.

DETECTIVE (*to* LIZZIE). And you?

LIZZIE. In *my* room, brushing Miss Cornelia's hair.

DETECTIVE (*goes to table; breaks revolver and looks at it*). One shot has been fired from this revolver.

CORNELIA (*looking over shoulder*). I fired it myself, this afternoon.

DETECTIVE. You're a quick thinker. (*Places revolver on table.*)

CORNELIA. I demand that you get the Coroner here.

LIZZIE. Dr. Wells is the Coroner.

DETECTIVE (*to* DALE). I'm going to ask you some questions.

CORNELIA. Do you mind covering that body first? (DETECTIVE *eyes her in a rather ugly fashion, then gets* FLEMING'S *raincoat on chair. Goes up to body. Throws coat over it.*) Shall I telephone for the Coroner?

DETECTIVE (*goes to phone*). I'll do it. What's his number?

DALE. He's not at his office—he's at the Johnsons'.

CORNELIA (*up to phone*). I'll get the Johnsons, Mr. Anderson. (DETEC-TIVE *relinquishes phone to* COR-NELIA; *gives her a look.*)

DETECTIVE (*to* DALE). Now what was Fleming doing here? (DALE *down to fireplace.*)

DALE. I don't know.

DETECTIVE. Well, I'll ask that question another way. How did he get into the house?

CORNELIA (*at phone*). One—four——

DALE. He had a key. He used to live here.

DETECTIVE. A key to what door?

DALE. To that door over there. (*Indicating terrace door.*)

CORNELIA (*at phone*). Hello—is that Mr. Johnson's residence? Is Dr. Wells there? No? (DETECTIVE *turns during this; watches* CORNELIA. CORNELIA *pauses; listens in on phone.*) All right, thank you. Good night! (*Hangs up phone, puzzled. She comes down table center. Same time* DETECTIVE *registers, sees ashes of blueprints in fireplace.*)

DETECTIVE (*to* DALE). When did you take that revolver out of the table drawer?

DALE. When I heard him outside, on the terrace, I was frightened.

LIZZIE (*tiptoes over to* CORNELIA). You wanted a detective! I hope you're happy now you've got one! (CORNELIA *gives* LIZZIE *a look.*)

DETECTIVE (*to* DALE). When he came in, what did he say to you? (CORNELIA *sits by table.*)

DALE. Just—something about the weather.

DETECTIVE. You didn't have any quarrel with him?

DALE (*after hesitation*). No.

DETECTIVE. He just came in that door—said something about the weather—and was shot from that staircase? Is that it?

DALE (*after moment's hesitation*). Yes.

CORNELIA. Are all these questions necessary? You can't for a moment believe that Miss Ogden shot that man? (DALE *sits at fireplace.*)

DETECTIVE (*looks at* DALE). I think she knows more than she's telling. She's concealing something. The nephew of the President of the Union Bank shot in his own house on the day the bank has failed—that's queer enough. (*He turns; looks at* CORNELIA.) But when the only person present at his murder is the girl who is engaged to the guilty cashier—— (*Looks at* DALE.) I want to know more about it! (*Picks up cigarette* DICK *put on ash tray Act One.*)

CORNELIA (*rises*). Is that true, Dale?

DALE. Yes.

CORNELIA. What has *that* got to do with it? (*To* DETECTIVE.)

DETECTIVE (*turning to* CORNELIA). I'm not accusing this girl, but behind every crime there is a motive. When we've found the motive for *this* crime we'll have found the criminal.

(DALE'S *hand instinctively goes to her bosom where she has concealed the blueprint. Her expression shows that she realizes that her having the blueprint is damaging evidence against her.*)

DETECTIVE (*who has been facing* CORNELIA, *now turns on* DALE).

What papers did he burn in that grate? (*Slight pause.*)

DALE. Papers!

DETECTIVE. Papers! The ashes are still there.

CORNELIA. Miss Ogden has said he didn't come into this room.

DETECTIVE. I hold in my hand proof that he was in this room for some time. (*Holding up half-burnt cigarette.* CORNELIA *sits.*) His cigarette with his monogram on it. (*He goes to fireplace and picks up small piece of blueprint from the fender; looks at* DALE.) A fragment of what is technically known as a blueprint. What were you and Richard Fleming doing with a blueprint? (DALE *hesitates.*) Now think it over! The truth will come out sooner or later! Better be frank *now!*

BROOKS (*runs on, followed by* BILLY. BROOKS, *a trifle breathlessly*). Nothing in the house, sir.

BILLY. Me go all over house. Nobody. (BOTH *start off as if to continue search.*)

DETECTIVE. You men stay here! I want to ask you some questions. (*Then to* DALE.) Now, what about this blueprint?

DALE (*still seated*). I'll tell you just what happened. I sent for Richard Fleming, and when he came I asked him if he knew where there were any blueprints of the house.

DETECTIVE. *Why* did you want blueprints?

DALE. Because I believed old Mr. Fleming took the money himself, from the Union Bank, and *hid* it here.

DETECTIVE. Where did you get that idea?

DALE. I won't tell you.

DETECTIVE. What had the blueprints to do with it?

DALE. I'd heard there was a Hidden Room built in the house.

DETECTIVE (*leans forward*). Did you locate that room?

DALE (*hesitates*). No.

DETECTIVE. Then why did you burn the blueprints?

DALE. *He* burned them. I don't *know* why.

DETECTIVE. Then you didn't locate this Hidden Room?

DALE. No.

DETECTIVE. Did he?

CORNELIA. What's that? (DALE *rises.*)

DETECTIVE. What's what?

CORNELIA. I heard something.

(THEY ALL *turn and look up stage at windows.* BROOKS *is near windows,* BILLY *beside him.* CORNELIA *at table. Suddenly from outside a circle of brilliant white light is thrown on the window shades up stage. In the C. of the light area is seen a vivid black shadow resembling a gigantic black bat. For an instant it glows there, traveling across, and disappears.*)

LIZZIE (*wails*). Oh, my God—it's The Bat! That's his sign. (BROOKS *starts for terrace door.*)

CORNELIA. Wait, Brooks! (*Then to* DETECTIVE.) Mr. Anderson, you are familiar with the sign of The Bat. Did that look like it?

DETECTIVE (*puzzled and evidently disturbed*). Well—it looked like the shadow of a bat—I'll say that. (*Doorbell rings.* ALL *look at hall door.*)

BROOKS. I'll answer that!

CORNELIA (*gives him key off table*). Don't admit anyone till you know who it is.

(BROOKS *exits.* ALL *stand and wait.* CORNELIA, *hand over her revolver on table where* DETECTIVE *had laid it.* BROOKS' *and* WELLS' *voices heard off stage, raised in angry dispute. Some evidence of a light scuffle. Ad lib.* "What do I know about a flashlight?" "I haven't got a pocket flash." "Take your hands off me." *Then* WELLS *enters, cap on, followed by* BROOKS. *He comes down and faces* CORNELIA. *He is ruffled and enraged.* BROOKS *close behind him, vigilant and watchful.* CORNELIA, *relieved, quickly drops revolver.*)

DOCTOR. My dear Miss Van Gorder! Won't you instruct your servants that, even if I do make a late call, I am not to be received with violence. (*Takes off cap; bag on chair by table.*)

BROOKS (*strongly*). I asked you if you had a pocket flash about you. If

you call a question like that violence——

CORNELIA. It's all right, Brooks. (BROOKS *places key on table.*) You see, Dr. Wells, just a moment before you rang the doorbell a circle of white light was thrown on those window shades.

DOCTOR. Why—that was probably the searchlight from my car—I noticed as I drove up that it fell directly on that window.

LIZZIE (*with deep suspicion*). "He may be a merchant, a lawyer, a doctor——"

CORNELIA (*suspiciously watching the* DOCTOR. *Lift scene*). In the center of this ring of light there was an almost perfect silhouette of a bat.

DOCTOR. A bat? Ah—I see—the symbol of the criminal of that name. (*Laughs.*) I think I can explain what you saw—quite often my lamps collect insects at night. A large moth spread on the glass would give precisely the effect you speak of. Just to satisfy you—I'll go out and take a look. (*He turns and is about to go when he sees body on floor. At same time* CORNELIA *turns and faces* DOCTOR.) Why—— (*Startled, stares at covered body. Then he glances from covered body on floor to the faces of the* OTHERS.)

CORNELIA (*at table, facing* DOCTOR). We have had a very sad occurrence here, Doctor.

DOCTOR (*turns; looks at* CORNELIA). Who?

CORNELIA. Richard Fleming.

DOCTOR (*pauses. Horrified*). Richard Fleming! (*Bends over body; turns raincoat back.*)

CORNELIA. Shot and killed, from that staircase.

DETECTIVE. Shot and killed, anyhow.

DOCTOR (*on knees, beside body. He has been blithe and gay up to that moment; seems almost instantly to become aged. His face is stricken. He repeats*). From that stairway. (*Rises. Straightens up and glances up the stairs, then.*) What was Richard Fleming doing in this house at this hour?

DETECTIVE. That's what I'm trying to find out. (*DOCTOR looks over at DETECTIVE. DOCTOR is puzzled.*)

CORNELIA. Doctor—this is Mr. Anderson. (*DOCTOR crosses to DETECTIVE. They shake hands.*)

DETECTIVE (*to DOCTOR*). Headquarters!

LIZZIE (*loud whisper to CORNELIA*). Don't you let him fool you with any of that moth business. He's The Bat! (*She sits by table.*)

CORNELIA (*to DOCTOR*). I didn't tell you, Doctor, I sent for a detective this afternoon. (*Then suspiciously.*) You happened in very opportunely.

DOCTOR (*pulling himself together*). After I left the Johnsons' I felt very uneasy. I determined to make one more effort to get you away from this house. As this shows, my fears were justified. (*CORNELIA sits. DOCTOR takes off muffler; puts it in* pocket of overcoat. Takes off overcoat; throws it up stage on settee, front of french windows. He takes out handkerchief, mops face and neck as though under great mental excitement. Looks over at body, then looks at CORNELIA.*) Died instantly, I suppose. (*Looks at DETECTIVE.*) Didn't have time to say anything?

DETECTIVE (*looking at DALE*). Ask the young lady. She was here when it happened. (*DOCTOR looks at DALE.*)

DALE (*pitifully*). He just fell over.

DOCTOR (*there is no question but that the DOCTOR is relieved. He draws a long breath. Looking at body. Speaks as he crosses above table*). Poor Dick has proved my case for me better than I expected. (*Stops. Turns; looks at DETECTIVE, who stands up.*) Mr. Anderson, I ask you to use your influence to see that these two ladies find some safer spot than this for the night.

LIZZIE (*half rises*). Two? If you *know* any safe spot, lead *me* to it! (*DOCTOR up to body.*)

CORNELIA. I have a strange feeling that I'm being watched by unfriendly eyes.

(*BILLY up to window, scared, pulls shade aside, looks out; sees something outside when he looks out window. Moves down while the OTHERS are not looking at him. Pretending to straighten the tray which LIZZIE brought on in Act One, he gets possession of front-door key from table, and exits. LIZZIE speaks on word cue; does not wait for BILLY's business.*)

LIZZIE (*clutching at* CORNELIA, *across table*). I wish the lights would go out again. (CORNELIA *slaps* LIZZIE.) No, I don't neither! (LIZZIE *crosses to door; stands there.*)

DETECTIVE (*steps to table. To* DOCTOR). You say, Doctor, you came back to take these women away from the house. Why?

DOCTOR. Miss Van Gorder has explained.

CORNELIA (*at table. To* DOCTOR). Mr. Anderson has already formed a theory of the crime.

DETECTIVE. I haven't said that. (*House phone rings.* ALL *are startled. Turn; look at phone.* CORNELIA *and* DALE *rise.*)

DALE. The house telephone—again! (CORNELIA *makes movement as if to answer it.*)

DETECTIVE (*going to phone. Takes up phone*). I'll answer that! Hello! Hello! (*The* DOCTOR's *face is a study in fear. He clutches the back of chair by table to steady himself.*) There's nobody there! (*Hangs up phone.*) Where's that Jap? (*Looking at door.* DALE, *relieved, sits down.* LIZZIE *sits.*)

CORNELIA. He just went out.

DETECTIVE (*to* DOCTOR). That Jap rang that phone. Miss Van Gorder believes that this murder is the culmination of the series of mysterious happenings which caused her to send for me. I do not.

CORNELIA. Then what is the significance of the anonymous letters? Of the man Lizzie saw going up the stairs, of the attempt to break into the house? Of the ringing of that telephone bell?

DETECTIVE (*deliberately*). Terrorization.

DOCTOR (*moistening his dry lips*). By whom?

DETECTIVE (*with cold deliberation*). I imagine by Miss Van Gorder's own servants. By that woman—(*points at* LIZZIE. LIZZIE *rises*)—who probably writes the letters—by the gardener, who may have been the man Lizzie saw slipping up the stairs—by the Jap, who goes out and rings the telephone.

CORNELIA. With what object?

DETECTIVE. That's what I'm going to find out.

CORNELIA. Absurd—the butler was in this room when the telephone rang the first time.

(*Ad lib. noise between* BERESFORD *and* BILLY *off stage. Violent scuffle.* ALL *turn to hall door. Door opens and* REGINALD BERESFORD *is catapulted into the room by* BILLY. BERESFORD *falls to floor.* BILLY *stands in doorway, arms folded; he is impassive.* BERESFORD *speaks as he picks himself up; brushes clothes off. He is in dinner clothes; carries straw hat.*)

BERESFORD (*turning on* BILLY). Damn you! What do you mean by this?

BILLY (*impassively, in doorway*). Jujitsu. Pretty good stuff. Found on terrace with searchlight.

DETECTIVE. With searchlight!

BERESFORD. Well, why shouldn't I be on the terrace with a searchlight? (CORNELIA *crosses to side of table.*)

DETECTIVE. Who *are* you?

BERESFORD. Who are you? (DETECTIVE *flashes his police badge, which is on inside of lapel of coat, right side.* BERESFORD *looks at it.*) H'm! (*Takes out gold cigarette case.*) Very pretty—nice, neat design—very chaste! (*He takes a swift glance around room; sees* DALE; *suddenly senses the situation without suspecting a tragedy.*)

DETECTIVE. If you've finished admiring my badge, I'd like to know what you were doing on that terrace?

BERESFORD (*hesitates, glances at* DALE, *then*). I've had some trouble with my car down the road. (*Looks again at* DALE.) I came to ask if I might telephone.

CORNELIA. Did it require a searchlight to find the house?

BERESFORD. Look here—why are you asking me all these questions?

CORNELIA (*stepping toward* BERESFORD). Do you mind letting me see that flashlight? (BERESFORD *hands it to her. She examines it.* DETECTIVE *takes it from her; examines lens, then down R. of* BERESFORD. CORNELIA *gives way for* DETECTIVE. *She is now at table.*)

DETECTIVE (*to* BERESFORD). Now— what's your name? (*Hands flash back to* BERESFORD.)

BERESFORD (*sulkily*). Beresford— Reginald Beresford—if you doubt it —I've probably got a card somewhere. (*Goes through his pockets.*)

DETECTIVE. What's your business?

BERESFORD. What's my business here?

DETECTIVE (*sharply*). How do you earn your living?

BERESFORD (*flippantly*). I don't. I'm a *lawyer.*

LIZZIE (*sepulchrally, quoting from newspaper*). "He may be a lawyer."

DETECTIVE (*to* BERESFORD). And you came here to telephone about your car?

DALE. Oh, don't you see—he's trying to protect me—— It's no use, Mr. Beresford. (CORNELIA *turns, and steps beyond chair by table.* DALE *comes over to L. of table.* CORNELIA *places* DALE *in chair by table, placing her hand on* DALE's *shoulder.*)

BERESFORD. I see. Well, the plain truth is—I didn't know the situation—and I thought I'd play safe, for Miss Ogden's sake.

DALE (*to* DETECTIVE). He doesn't know anything about—(*pause*)— this. He brought Mr. Fleming here in his car—that's all.

DETECTIVE (*to* BERESFORD). Is that true?

BERESFORD. Yes—I got tired waiting and so I——

DETECTIVE (*breaks in curtly*). All right—— (*Turns.*) Now, Doctor. (*Nods toward body.* BERESFORD *turns, follows* DETECTIVE's *glance, stands rigid.*)

BERESFORD (*tensely*). What's that? (DOCTOR *uncovers body and kneels beside it.* BERESFORD, *thickly.*) That's not—Fleming—is it? (*Looks at* DETECTIVE. DETECTIVE *nods head.*)

DOCTOR. If you've looked over the ground—— (*To* DETECTIVE.) I'll move the body to where I can have a better light.

BERESFORD (*takes another step up and says, with force*). Do you mean to say that Dick Fleming—— (DOCTOR *takes paper from* DICK's *hand; throws cigarette to floor as he starts up.*)

DETECTIVE (*interrupting, eyes on* DOCTOR, *silences* BERESFORD *with an uplifted hand. Then, menacingly, to* DOCTOR). What have you got there, Doctor?

DOCTOR (*on knees beside body*). What do you mean?

DETECTIVE. You took something just then, out of Fleming's hand.

DOCTOR. I took nothing out of his hand.

DETECTIVE. I warn you not to obstruct the course of Justice. Give it here.

DOCTOR (*gets up, and hands* DETECTIVE *small piece of blueprint he took out of* FLEMING's *hand*). Why, it's a scrap of paper—— Nothing at all. (DOCTOR *crosses around body.*)

DETECTIVE (*with blueprint, down to table, eyes the* DOCTOR). Scraps of paper are sometimes very important. (*Looks at* DALE.)

BERESFORD (*angry. Crosses few steps over and up to* DETECTIVE). Look here—I've got a right to know about this thing. I brought Fleming over here—and I want to know what happened to him.

LIZZIE (*overcome*). You don't have to be a mind reader to know that!

BERESFORD (*to* DETECTIVE). Who killed him? That's what *I* want to know.

DETECTIVE. Well, you're not alone in that.

DOCTOR (*nervously*). As the Coroner—if Mr. Anderson is satisfied—I suggest that the body be taken where I can make a thorough examination. (DETECTIVE *up to body; turns body half over, then lets it fall back on face. Same as before.* DETECTIVE *steps back; glances from blueprint in his hand to* DOCTOR. DETECTIVE *takes off the overcoat from body.*)

DETECTIVE. All right.

CORNELIA. Into the library, please. (CORNELIA *goes over to fireplace while body is being moved.* DALE *watches* DETECTIVE. DOCTOR, *in alcove, takes hold of body by legs.* BERESFORD, *right side, hands* BILLY *his hat, takes body under arm.* BROOKS, *left side, under arm.* DOCTOR *going off first.* DETECTIVE *follows body off. As body disappears,* LIZZIE *up to double doors. Then* BILLY *picks up the rug where* DETECTIVE *dropped it.* BILLY *exits with rug.* DALE *gets piece of blue-*

print from front of dress and gets roll from floor, front of table. She puts blueprint in the roll, replaces roll on floor. BILLY *returns from door. Enters; goes to table; picks up tray. Sees roll on floor; places it on tray.* DETECTIVE *comes back on as* BILLY *enters.*)

CORNELIA. Take that tray out to the dining room.

DETECTIVE (*steps down in front of* BILLY). Wait, I'll look at that tray. (*Makes a thorough search of the tray; even examines the napkin, lifts the dishes, etc.* DALE *sits, tensely apprehensive.* DETECTIVE *fails to find anything.*) All right, take it away. (BILLY *exits with tray.*)

CORNELIA. Lizzie, go out in the kitchen and make some fresh coffee. I'm sure we'll all need it.

LIZZIE. Go out in that kitchen—alone?

CORNELIA (*sits*). Billy's there.

LIZZIE. That Jap and his jujitsu! One twist, and I'd be folded up like a pretzel! (*Exits.*)

DETECTIVE (*to back of table. Looks at piece of blueprint in his hand, and then at* DALE). Now, Miss Ogden—I have here a scrap of blueprint which was in Dick Fleming's hand when he was killed. I'll trouble you for the rest of it.

DALE (*is seated by table*). The rest of·it?

DETECTIVE. Don't tell me that he started to go out of this house holding a blank scrap of blue paper in

his hand. He didn't start to go out at all!

DALE (*rises*). Why do you say that?

DETECTIVE. His cap's there on that table.

CORNELIA (*is seated at table. Disturbed*). If you're keeping anything back, Dale, tell him.

DETECTIVE. She's keeping something back, all right. She's told part of the truth but not all. You and Fleming located that room by means of a blueprint of the house. He started—not to go out, but probably to go up that staircase. And he had in his hand the rest of this. (*He holds out the scrap of blueprint.*)

DALE (*slight pause, then, rather pitifully*). He was going to take the money and go away with it.

CORNELIA (*alarmed*). Dale!

DALE. He changed the minute he heard about it. He was all kindness before that, but afterward—— (*She closes her eyes.*)

DETECTIVE (*turns triumphantly to* CORNELIA). She started in to find the money—and save Bailey, but to do it she had to take Fleming into her confidence, and he turned yellow. Rather than let him get away with it—she—— (*He makes expressive gesture, hand on hip pocket.* DALE *registers. He indicates revolver. Then to* DALE.) Is that true?

DALE. I didn't kill him.

DETECTIVE. Why didn't you call for help? You—you knew I was here?

DALE (*hesitates*). I couldn't. (*Steps toward him.*)

CORNELIA (*agitated*). Dale! Be careful what you say!

DETECTIVE (*advances step to* DALE). Now I mean to find out two things —*why* you didn't call for help, and *what* you have done with the blueprint.

DALE. Suppose I could find that piece of blueprint for you? Would that establish Jack Bailey's innocence?

DETECTIVE. If the money's there—yes.

CORNELIA (*rises, crosses to* DALE; *turns on* DETECTIVE). But her own guilt! No, Mr. Anderson—granting that she knows where that paper is—and she has not said that she does, I shall want more time, and much legal advice, before I allow her to turn it over to you.

(*Enter from below the stairs,* DOCTOR, BERESFORD, *and* BROOKS *silently.*)

DETECTIVE (*turns and looks up at them*). Well, Doctor?

DOCTOR. Well, poor fellow—straight through the heart!

CORNELIA. Were there any powder marks?

DOCTOR. No—and the clothing was not burned. He was apparently shot from some little distance—and I should say, from above.

DETECTIVE. Beresford, did Fleming tell you why he came here tonight?

BERESFORD. No. He seemed to be in a great hurry; said Miss Ogden had telephoned for him, and asked me to drive him over.

DETECTIVE. Why did you come up to the house?

BERESFORD. Well—— (*Looks over at* DALE). I thought it was putting rather a premium on friendship to keep me sitting out in the rain all night, so I came up the drive, and by the way—(*suddenly remembering*)—I picked this up, about a hundred feet from the house. (*Pulls out a man's battered open-face silver watch from pocket; holds it out on his hand.*) A man's watch. It was partly crushed into the ground, and you see it's stopped running.

DETECTIVE (*taking it, and examining it*). Yes! (*Thoughtfully.*) At ten-thirty——

BERESFORD. I was using my pocket flash to find my way, and what first attracted my attention was the ground torn up. Anyone here recognize the watch? (DETECTIVE *shows watch, holding it up so* ALL *can see it. No one replies.*) You didn't hear any evidence of a struggle, did you?

CORNELIA. Just about ten-thirty Lizzie heard somebody cry out, in the grounds. (DETECTIVE *looks* BERESFORD *over.*)

BERESFORD. I don't suppose it has any bearing on this case, but it's interesting. (DETECTIVE, *having finished his examination of the watch, slips it into his pocket.*)

CORNELIA (*suspiciously*). Do you always carry a flashlight, Mr. Beresford?

BERESFORD. Always at night in the car.

DETECTIVE. This is all you found?

BERESFORD. Yes.

CORNELIA (sits by table). Someday I hope to meet the real estate agent who promised me that I would sleep here as I never slept before. He's right. I've slept with my clothes on every night since I came.

BILLY (enters hurriedly. He carries a butcher knife in one hand, his face is excited; comes over to CORNELIA). Key, kitchen door, please.

CORNELIA. Key? What for?

BILLY. Somebody outside try to get in. I see knob turn so—(illustrating turning hand)—and so—three times. (They are all startled.)

DETECTIVE (quickly puts hand to revolver in pocket). You're sure of that, are you? (Roughly to BILLY.)

BILLY. Sure I sure!

DETECTIVE (looks at CORNELIA). Where's that hysterical woman, Lizzie? She may get a bullet in her if she's not careful. (DALE sits fireplace.)

BILLY. She see too. She shut in closet. Say prayers maybe.

DETECTIVE. Doctor, have you a revolver?

DOCTOR. No.

DETECTIVE. How about you, Beresford?

BERESFORD (hesitates). Yes. Always carry one at night in the country. (CORNELIA registers this.)

DETECTIVE. Beresford, will you go with this Jap to the kitchen? (Exit BILLY, leaving door open.) If anyone's working at the knob, shoot through the door. I'm going round to take a look outside. (Starts up for doors.)

BERESFORD (going to hall door, turns, looks up at DETECTIVE. DETECTIVE stops, looks at BERESFORD as he speaks). I advise you not to turn the doorknob yourself, then.

DETECTIVE. Much obliged. (Exit DETECTIVE terrace door. Closes door. At same time BERESFORD exits to hall.)

BROOKS (to BERESFORD). I'll go with you if you don't mind. (Exit BROOKS, closing door. DOCTOR crosses up to below staircase.)

CORNELIA (at table, to DOCTOR). Doctor.

DOCTOR. Yes?

CORNELIA. Have you any theory about this occurrence tonight? (Watching him closely.)

DOCTOR. None whatever—it's beyond me.

CORNELIA. And yet you warned me to leave the house. (Stops knitting.) You didn't have any reason to believe that the situation was even as serious as it has proved to be?

DOCTOR. I did the perfectly obvious thing when I warned you. Those letters made a distinct threat.

CORNELIA (*pauses*). You said he'd probably been shot from above.

DOCTOR. Yes, apparently.

CORNELIA (*suddenly*). Have you a pocket flash, Doctor?

DOCTOR (*hesitates*). Why—yes—a flashlight is more important to a country doctor than castor oil.

CORNELIA (*turns to* DALE). Dale, you said you saw a white light shining down from above?

DALE. Yes.

CORNELIA (*crosses to* DOCTOR). May I borrow your flashlight? (DOCTOR *gives her his pocket flash.*) Now that I've got that fool detective out of the way, I want to do something. Doctor, I shall ask you to stand at the foot of the small staircase, facing up.

DOCTOR. Now?

CORNELIA. Now, please. (DOCTOR *walks up and takes position foot of stairs.* CORNELIA *turns, looks at* DALE.) And, Dale—when I give the word, put out the lights here, and then tell me when I have reached the point on the staircase from which the flashlight seemed to come. All ready. (DALE *moves up toward door, ready to turn out stand lamp.* CORNELIA *at door.*) I shall go up this way and down the other. (*Exit* CORNELIA, *closing door.* DOCTOR, *looking up staircase. His face changes, showing surprise and apprehension. He glances back into room to see if* DALE *can see him. She cannot. To somebody, evidently at top of stairs, he makes an insistent gesture, "Go back,*

go back." DALE *turns out stand lamp.* DALE *then walks by the french windows to electric button. Stands with finger on button.* THE UNKNOWN *reaches hand in through the broken pane in french window, turns knob on window, unlocking the window door. Then the window door is pushed inward, evidently to admit a crouching figure. When* UNKNOWN *is in and behind couch, which he pushes down to make room for his body, he closes the door in window. Only his hand seen during this business. When* UNKNOWN *is on stage, back of settee, window closes.*) All right! Put out the lights! (DALE *pushes button on wall. Lights out.* DALE *steps just inside alcove, looks up and off stairs. She leans heavily against the double door.* CORNELIA *off.*) Was it here? (*Spot focuses on* DOCTOR'S *face.* DOCTOR *stands at foot of stairs, looking up.*)

DALE. Come down a little.

DOCTOR (*to* CORNELIA *with an attempt at jocularity*).. I hope you have no weapon.

CORNELIA (*off*). How's this?

DALE. That's about right.

CORNELIA (*off*). Lights, please. (DALE *pushes the wall button. Lights up.* CORNELIA *has evidently left the staircase.* DALE *back into room. She goes down to table.* DOCTOR *backs into room.*)

DALE (*by table; sits*). Doctor, I'm so frightened!

DOCTOR (*down to her*). Why, my dear child, because you happened to be in the room when a crime is committed?

DALE. But he has a perfect case against me.

DOCTOR. That's absurd!

DALE. No.

DOCTOR. *You don't mean?*

DALE (*horrified*). I didn't kill him, but you know the piece of blueprint you found in his hand?

DOCTOR (*tensely*). Yes?

DALE. There was another piece—a large piece—I tore it from him just before——

DOCTOR (*trying to control his excitement*). Why did you do such a thing?

DALE. Oh, I'll explain that later. It's not safe where it is—Billy may throw it out, or burn it without knowing——

DOCTOR. Let me understand this. The butler has that paper now?

DALE. He doesn't know he has it. It was in one of the rolls that went out on the tray.

DOCTOR (*slight pause*). Now don't you worry about it. I'll get it. (*He starts, stops, turns to* DALE.) But you oughtn't to have it in your possession. (*Comes a step toward her.*) Why not let it be burned?

DALE (*startled*). Oh, no! It's important—it's vital!

DOCTOR. The tray is in the dining room?

DALE. Yes.

(DOCTOR *exits to hall, closing door.* UNKNOWN *back of settee raises himself, just for a second. Audience just sees top of his head. Moves settee slightly.* DALE *crosses slowly to fireplace. Enter* BROOKS *from hall; closes door behind him. He carries two logs of wood for fire.* DALE *turns; sees him.*)

DALE (*as soon as* BROOKS *is on*). Oh! Things have gone awfully wrong, haven't they?

BROOKS. Be careful! (*Turns, looks around room.*) I don't trust even the furniture in this house tonight. (*Moves to* DALE, *kisses her, then crosses back of her to fireplace. Raises his voice very formally.*) Miss Van Gorder wishes the fire kept up! (*Drops the wood, turns back to* DALE, *speaks in undertone.*) Play up!

DALE (*distinctly*). Put some logs on the fire, please. (*Then, in undertone, facing away from him.*) Jack, I'm nearly distracted! (BROOKS *drops the wood at fireplace, and quickly comes up behind her; puts his arms around her.*)

BROOKS. Dale, pull yourself together. We've got a fight ahead of us. (*As he releases her and starts back to fireplace.*) These old-fashioned fireplaces eat up a lot of wood. (*Drops on , knees; places wood inside fender.*)

DALE (*turns and goes toward him; leans on arms of armchair, which is between them*). You know why I sent for Richard Fleming, don't you?

BROOKS (*on knees, turns and faces her*). Yes—but who in God's name killed him?

DALE. You don't think it was Billy?

BROOKS (*half rises*). More likely the man Lizzie saw going upstairs. I've been all over the upper floors.

DALE. And nothing?

BROOKS. Nothing. (*Leaning over armchair toward* DALE.) Dale, do you think that——

DALE (*is conscious that someone is coming. To* BROOKS). Be careful! (BROOKS *turns to fireplace; works with logs.* CORNELIA *enters from hall; closes door behind her. She carries her black bag. She sees* BROOKS *at fireplace as soon as she enters. Coming to table.*)

CORNELIA. Well, Mr. Alopecia—Urticaria, Rubeola—otherwise Bailey. (BROOKS *rises with a start; faces her. Stares at her. Look between* DALE *and* BROOKS.) I wish you young people would remember that even if hair and teeth have fallen out at sixty the mind still functions. (*She reaches into her black knitting bag and brings out a cabinet photograph of* BROOKS.) His photograph—sitting on your dresser! (DALE *crosses to table, across from* CORNELIA. *To* DALE, *as* CORNELIA *holds out the photo toward her.*) And that detective with as many eyes as a potato, Burn it and be quick about it!

DALE (*takes photo, but continues to stand facing* CORNELIA. *Then glances at* BROOKS, *and back at* CORNELIA). Then—you knew?

CORNELIA (*sitting by table*). My dear child, I have employed many gardeners in my time and never before had one who manicured his fingernails, who wore silk socks, who talked like Harvard condescending to Yale—(BROOKS *registers this by looking down*)—and who regards baldness as a plant instead of a calamity. (DALE *crosses to fireplace; throws photo in fire.*)

BROOKS (*facing* CORNELIA). Do you know why I'm here?

CORNELIA. I do—and a pretty mess you've put me in by coming here. If that detective was as smart as he thinks he is, he'd have had you an hour ago. (*She rises, crosses toward* DALE; *then* DALE *becomes very grave.*) Now, I want to ask *you* something. Was there a blueprint and did you get it from Richard Fleming?

DALE. Yes.

BROOKS (*facing* CORNELIA *and* DALE). Dale! Don't you see where this places you? If you had it, why didn't you give it to Anderson when he asked for it?

CORNELIA. Because she had sense enough to see that Mr. Anderson considered that piece of paper the final link in the evidence against her!

BROOKS. But she could have no *motive.*

CORNELIA. Couldn't she? The detective thinks she could—to save you!

BROOKS (*takes step back; slight pause*). Good God!

CORNELIA (*close to* DALE). Where is the paper now?

DALE. The doctor is getting it for me.

CORNELIA. *What!*

DALE. It was on the tray Billy took out.

CORNELIA (*puts hands up, depressed*). Well, I'm afraid everything's over. (*She crosses to front of table.*)

DALE (*plaintively*). I didn't know what else to do.

CORNELIA (*looks at hall door*). One of two things will happen now. Either the doctor's an honest man, in which case, as Coroner, he will hand that paper to the detective, or he is *not* an honest man, and he will keep it for himself. *I* don't think he's an honest man.

DALE (*goes, meets* CORNELIA *back of table*). Then you think the doctor may give the paper to Mr. Anderson?

CORNELIA. He may, or he may not. (*Enter* BILLY. CORNELIA *takes a step toward* BILLY.) I want to know the moment *anybody goes upstairs.* I want to know—immediately. (BILLY *is about to go.*) Oh, Billy—— (*She looks up stairs, then.*) Where is the doctor?

BILLY. In dining room, having cup coffee.

CORNELIA. And Mr. Beresford?

BILLY. Sit on kitchen floor, inside door, with gun. (CORNELIA *motions* BILLY *to go. Exit* BILLY.)

CORNELIA (*to* DALE). Dale, watch that door. (*Indicating hall door.* DALE *crosses to door.*) And warn me

if anyone is coming. (CORNELIA *gets* DOCTOR'S *bag, carries it to table, places on table, turns to* BROOKS.) Get some soot.

BROOKS. Soot?

CORNELIA. Yes, soot, from the back of that fireplace. (BROOKS *takes envelope from pocket, goes to fireplace, reaches far in, scrapes back of fireplace; envelope blackened. At same time* CORNELIA *steps up to stand, gets piece of writing paper, places it with lead pencil on table.*)

BROOKS (*to table*). Is this all right?

CORNELIA. Yes. Now rub it onto the handle of that bag. (*Indicating* DOCTOR'S *bag.* BROOKS *blackens the handle.*)

DALE. Somebody's coming! (BROOKS *quickly to fireplace; pretends to work at fireplace.*)

CORNELIA (*pretending to carry on conversation and carries bag back to chair. She does not touch the handle of bag*). We all need sleep and I think—— (*Motions to others.*)

BILLY (*enters just inside of hall door*). Doctor just go upstairs. (*Exits, leaving door open.*)

CORNELIA (*steps to door; looks off; calls*). Oh, Doctor! Doctor!

DOCTOR (*off stage. Apparently from stairway*). Yes? (*A moment's pause.* DOCTOR *enters; he takes a furtive glance around the room. Faces* CORNELIA; *just about to speak.*) Your maid insists that a man went up that staircase before the crime. I was going to take a look around.

CORNELIA (*pleasantly*). The gardener has just made a thorough search.

DALE (*coming down to* DOCTOR). Doctor, did you? (DETECTIVE *knocks on terrace door. On the knock* DOCTOR *half turns, looks up.*)

DETECTIVE (*outside on terrace; muffled voice*). It's Anderson.

BROOKS (*crosses up to terrace door*). The detective. (*Unbolts door for* DETECTIVE.)

DALE (*following* DOCTOR). Did you get it?

DOCTOR (*turns; looks at* DALE). My dear child, are you sure you put it there?

DALE (*dismayed*). Why, yes, I—— (*She looks at him; suddenly distrusts him.* DALE *turns; exchanges looks with* CORNELIA. BROOKS *stands near window.* DETECTIVE *comes in terrace door, slams it behind him.*)

DETECTIVE (*stays up in doorway; irritably*). I couldn't find anybody. I think that Jap's crazy.

DOCTOR (*getting coat from settee*). Well, I think I've fulfilled all the legal requirements. I must be going.

DETECTIVE (*turns and faces* DOCTOR). Doctor, did you ever hear Courtleigh Fleming mention a Hidden Room in this house?

DOCTOR (*does not look directly at* DETECTIVE). No—and I knew him rather well.

DETECTIVE. You don't think, then, that such a room and the money in it could be the motive of this crime?

DOCTOR. I don't believe Courtleigh Fleming robbed his own bank. If that's what you mean. (DOCTOR *crosses to get his bag.* DOCTOR, *to* CORNELIA.) Well, I can't wish you a comfortable night, but I can hope it will be a quiet one. (DOCTOR *gets bag in right hand, cap in left.*)

CORNELIA (*crosses to* DOCTOR). We're naturally upset. Perhaps you will write a prescription. Some sleeping medicine.

DOCTOR. Why, certainly. (*He comes toward table.* CORNELIA *hands him paper and pencil. He is about to write on paper, using the bag as a pad.*)

CORNELIA. I hoped you would. Here is paper and pencil.

DOCTOR (*taking the paper in right hand*). I don't generally advise these drugs, but—— (*Then stopping short.*) What time is it?

CORNELIA (*looks at clock on mantel*). Half-past eleven.

DOCTOR. Then I'd better bring you the powders. The pharmacy closes at eleven. (*She takes the paper from* DOCTOR; *puts it down on table without looking at it. From the blackened handle of the bag his thumb has made a clear impression on the paper. He is quite unconscious of this.* CORNELIA *picks up the paper, with apparent carelessness, glances at it, and lays it with the print down. She picks up a key off table.* DOCTOR *goes toward door.*)

CORNELIA. Dale will let you out, Doctor. (DALE *gets key from* CORNELIA.)

DOCTOR (*stops, turns, smiles at* COR-NELIA). That's right. Keep things locked up. Discretion is the better part of valor. (DALE *waits just in hall doorway for* DOCTOR.)

CORNELIA. I've been discreet for sixty years, and sometimes I think it was a mistake. (DALE *exits R.* DOCTOR *follows her off.*)

DETECTIVE (*looks with angry eye on* BROOKS). I guess we can do without you!

BROOKS. All right, sir. (*Exits. Closes door.*)

DETECTIVE (*comes over to table. To* CORNELIA). Now, I want a few words with you! (*His tone is surly.*)

CORNELIA (*beside table*). Which means that you mean to do all the talking. Very well! But first I want to show you something. Will you come here, please? (*She starts up to alcove.*)

DETECTIVE. I've examined that staircase.

CORNELIA. Not with me! I have something to show you. (DETECTIVE *follows her up. They exit up the staircase. The room is now empty.*)

(LIZZIE *enters, carrying hot-water bottle and a large butcher knife.* UNKNOWN *opens the door in french windows. He is getting out of the room by the window, unseen.* LIZZIE, *after closing door, sees the french window move. It closes. She gives a wild screech; drops the water bag on chair by stand.* CORNELIA *and* DETECTIVE *run down the stairs. When* LIZZIE *sees them she points at window.* DALE *enters from hall.*)

LIZZIE (*wildly*). That window! It closed—w i t h o u t human hands! (CORNELIA *goes up to window; looks out.* DETECTIVE *stands in alcove door; looks at* LIZZIE.)

DETECTIVE (*speaks to* CORNELIA, *but looking at* LIZZIE). I wish you'd put this screech owl to bed!

LIZZIE (*agitatedly*). You'd screech owl yourself if you saw what I saw! (LIZZIE *collapses into chair; sits on water bottle. She gives a scream, jumps up and points to water bottle on chair.*) I'm scalded again! I can't walk and now I can't sit. (DETECTIVE *takes her by the shoulder and pushes her. They exit. Close door.*)

DALE (*starting over cautiously to* CORNELIA). It isn't there. The doctor says he didn't see it and I've looked. It's gone.

CORNELIA. Then the doctor—— (*She stops; hears doorknob move to left.* DALE *sits chair. Enter* DETECTIVE; *closes door.*)

DETECTIVE (*to* CORNELIA). Now, your point about that thumbprint on the stair rail is very interesting. But just what does it prove?

CORNELIA. It points down——

DETECTIVE. It does—and what then?

CORNELIA. It shows that somebody stood there, for some time, listening to my niece and Richard Fleming, in this room below.

DETECTIVE. All right, I'll grant that to save argument, but the moment that shot was fired the lights came on. If somebody on that staircase shot him, and then came down and took the blueprint, Miss Ogden would have seen him. (*He turns to* DALE.) Did you?

DALE. No, nobody came down.

CORNELIA. Now, Mr. Anderson——

DETECTIVE. Now, I'm not hounding this girl. I haven't said yet that she committed the murder, but she took that blueprint, and I want it.

CORNELIA. You want it to connect her with the murder.

DETECTIVE (*savagely*). It's rather reasonable to suppose that I might want to return the funds to the Union Bank, isn't it? Provided they're here.

CORNELIA. I see. Well, I'll tell you this much, Mr. Anderson, and I'll ask you to believe me as a gentlewoman, granting that at one time my niece knew something of that blueprint, at this moment we do not know where it is or who has it.

DETECTIVE. Damnation—— (*Mutters.*) That's the truth, is it?

CORNELIA. That's the truth. (*She sits by table C.; takes out knitting; knits. Pause. To* DETECTIVE.) Did you ever try knitting when you wanted to think?

DETECTIVE. No. (*He crosses over to table, takes out cigar, lights it. Matches on table.*)

CORNELIA. You should some time! I find it very helpful!

DETECTIVE. I don't need knitting to think straight!

CORNELIA. I wonder! You seem to have so much evidence left over. (DETECTIVE *turns; looks at her.*) Did you ever hear of the man who took a clock apart, and when he put it together again he had enough left over to make another clock? (DETECTIVE *comes down, looking at* DALE.)

DETECTIVE (*ignoring* CORNELIA. *To* DALE.) What do you mean by saying that paper isn't where you put it?

CORNELIA (*quickly*). She hasn't said that. (DETECTIVE *walks up, impatient movement.*) Do you believe in circumstantial evidence?

DETECTIVE. It's my business.

CORNELIA. While you have been investigating, I too have not been idle. (DETECTIVE *gives a mean laugh.*) To me it is perfectly obvious that one *intelligence*—(DETECTIVE *stops; looks at* CORNELIA)—has been at work, behind many of the things that have occurred in this house.

DETECTIVE. Who?

CORNELIA. I'll ask you that! Some one person who, knowing Courtleigh Fleming well, probably knows of the existence of a Hidden Room in this house—and who; finding us in occupation of the house, has tried to get rid of me in two ways: first by frightening me with anonymous threats, and second, by urging me to leave. Someone who very possibly entered this house tonight, shortly before the murder, and slipped up that staircase.

DETECTIVE (*startled*). The doctor? (*Step down.*)

CORNELIA (*still knitting*). When Dr. Wells said he was leaving here earlier in the evening for the Johnsons', he did not go there. He was not expected to go there. I found that out when I telephoned.

DETECTIVE (*moves head, eyes narrowing*). The doctor!

CORNELIA. As you know, I had a supplementary bolt placed on that door. (*Refers to terrace door.*) Earlier this evening Dr. Wells said that he had bolted it when he had left it open, purposely as I now realize, in order that later he might return. You may recall that Dr. Wells took a scrap of paper from Richard Fleming's hand and tried to conceal it. Why did he do *that*? (*Slight pause; changes tone.*) May I ask you to look at this? (*She picks up from the table the paper containing* DR. WELLS' *thumbprint.*)

DETECTIVE (*over to table; takes the paper*). A thumbprint—— (*Looks at it.*) Whose is it?

CORNELIA. Dr. Wells'. (*She picks up reading glass and offers it to* DETECTIVE. *He takes it; looks through it at paper.*) They say thumbprints never lie.

DETECTIVE (*slight pause, looking at paper. Sarcastically*). You don't really think you *need* a detective, do you?

CORNELIA (*quietly ironical*). I am a humble follower in your footsteps.

DETECTIVE (*ironically bows to her; then she bows*). Well, I'll bite! Anything to help a sister in the profession!

CORNELIA (*calmly*). You'll find that the same hand that made that left the imprint on the staircase. (*DETECTIVE looks at* CORNELIA, *then up; goes up to foot of staircase. He turns and surveys the two women, then he goes slowly up the staircase and off.* DALE *half rises, as if to speak to* CORNELIA. CORNELIA *makes a warning gesture.* DALE *sinks back into chair.*)

BERESFORD (*enters. Closes door. Comes over and faces* CORNELIA). Miss Van Gorder, may I ask you to make an excuse and call your gardener here? (*DALE starts violently.* CORNELIA *betrays no emotion, save that she knits a trifle more rapidly.*)

CORNELIA. The gardener? Certainly —if you'll touch that bell. (*BERESFORD pushes button on wall; stands there.* DALE *is in an agony of suspense.*)

DETECTIVE (*comes quietly down the stairs into the room*). It's no good, Miss Van Gorder. The prints are not the same.

CORNELIA. Not the same!

DETECTIVE (*smoking cigar; lays down the reading glass and paper on table*). If you think I'm mistaken, I'll leave it to any unprejudiced person or your own eyesight. Thumbprints never lie. Did you ever try a good cigar when you wanted to think?

CORNELIA. I still believe it was the doctor.

DETECTIVE. And yet the doctor was in this room tonight, according to your own statement, when the anonymous letter came through the window. (*BILLY enters.*)

BERESFORD (*steps down a little; to* BILLY). Tell the gardener Miss Van Gorder wants him—and don't say we're all here. (BILLY *exits.*)

DETECTIVE (*to* BERESFORD, *rather grimly*). I seem to have plenty of *help* in this case!

DALE (*rises; to* BERESFORD). Why have you sent for the gardener?

BERESFORD (*grimly*). I'll tell you that in a moment. (*Enter* BROOKS; *takes a swift survey of the room; closes door. Slight pause.*)

BROOKS (*to* CORNELIA). You sent for me?

BERESFORD (*with eye on* BROOKS *speaks to* CORNELIA *brusquely*). How long has this man been in your employ?

CORNELIA (*still seated*). Why does that interest you?

BROOKS. I came this evening.

BERESFORD. Exactly. (*To* DETECTIVE.) I've been trying to recall this man's face ever since I came tonight —I know now who it is.

DETECTIVE. Who is he?

BROOKS (*straightening*). It's all right, Beresford. I know you think you're doing your duty, but I wish to God you could have *restrained* your sense of duty for about three hours more.

BERESFORD. To let you get away?

BROOKS. No—to let me finish what I came here to do.

BERESFORD. Don't you think you've done enough? (*Turns to* DETECTIVE.) This man has imposed on the credulity of these women. I am quite sure, without their knowledge. His name is Bailey, of the Union Bank.

DETECTIVE (*puts cigar on ash tray. To* BROOKS). That's the truth, is it?

BROOKS. It's true, all right.

BERESFORD. I accuse him not only of the thing he is wanted for but of the murder of Richard Fleming.

BROOKS (*fiercely to* BERESFORD). You lie!

DETECTIVE (*turns; goes down a step toward* DALE). You knew this? (*Turns to* CORNELIA.) Did you?

CORNELIA. Yes.

DETECTIVE. Then it's a conspiracy, is it? All this case against the doctor! (*Wheels on* BROOKS.) What did you mean by that—"three hours more"?

BROOKS. I could have cleared myself in three hours. (*Doorbell rings off stage.*)

CORNELIA. Probably the doctor. He was to come back with some sleeping powders. (*Enter* BILLY. *He goes to table, upper end; gets key.*)

DETECTIVE (*to* BILLY). If that's the doctor, admit him. If it's anybody else, call me. (BILLY *exits; leaves door open. To* BROOKS.) Have you got a gun on you?

BROOKS. No.

DETECTIVE. I'll just make sure of that. (*Crosses to* BROOKS. DETECTIVE

frisks BROOKS; *then takes pair hand-*
cuffs out of pocket and puts them
on table.)

DALE (*at sight of handcuffs*). Oh,
no! I can't bear it! I'll tell you everything. (ALL THE CHARACTERS *turn*
and face DALE. DOCTOR *enters from*
hall, leaving the door open behind
him. In the intensity of the scene
the DOCTOR'S *entrance is ignored.*
DALE *continues.*) He got to the foot
of the staircase—Richard Fleming,
I mean. (*To* DETECTIVE.) And he
had the blueprint you've been talking about. I had told him Jack Bailey
was here as the gardener, and he
said if I screamed he would tell that.
I was desperate—I threatened him
with the revolver, but he took it
from me. Then I tore the blueprint
from him—he was shot—from the
stairs.

BERESFORD. By Bailey!

BROOKS (*strongly*). I didn't even
know he was in the house.

DETECTIVE. What did you do with
the blueprint? (DOCTOR *is listening*
intently.)

DALE. I put it first in the neck of my
·dress—then, when I found you were
watching me, I hid it, somewhere
else. (*She glances over at the* DOC-
TOR. *He is apprehensive and anx-*
ious. It is evident that he would
make his escape, but BILLY *at that*
moment enters with key.)

BILLY. Key—front door. (*He crosses*
in front of DOCTOR *and behind the*
OTHER CHARACTERS *to table, upper*
end; places key there, and exits.)

DALE (*does not wait for this busi-*
ness). I put it—somewhere else.
(*Again she glances at* DOCTOR.)

DETECTIVE. Did you give it to Bailey?

DALE. No—I hid it, and then I told
where it was—to the doctor (ALL
turn in surprise to DOCTOR, *who is*
at hall door. CORNELIA *rises.*)

DOCTOR (*smiles grimly, then slowly*
comes down into scene). That's
rather inaccurate. You told me
where you had placed it, but when
I went to look for it it was gone.

CORNELIA (*strongly*). Are you quite
sure of that?

DOCTOR (*gaining courage*). Absolutely. (*Then to* DETECTIVE.) She
said she had hidden it inside one of
the rolls that were on the tray. (*He*
crosses to table, front of the OTHERS,
takes out a box of powders from
overcoat pocket, and places them on
table.) On that table. She was in
such distress that I finally agreed to
look for it—it wasn't there.

DETECTIVE (*has come down behind*
the DOCTOR. *To* DOCTOR). Did you
realize the significance of this paper?

DOCTOR (*turns to* DETECTIVE).
Nothing beyond the fact that Miss
Ogden was afraid it linked her with
the crime.

DETECTIVE (*considers a moment,*
then to CORNELIA). I'd like to have
a few minutes with the doctor alone.

(CORNELIA *and* DALE *cross front of*
table toward hall door. CORNELIA
with arm around DALE. BROOKS
stands by hall door. As DALE *passes*
him she puts out her hand to him.
BROOKS *grasps* DALE'S *hand. Exit*
CORNELIA *and* DALE.)

DETECTIVE (*as* CORNELIA *and* DALE *are crossing to right*). Beresford, take Bailey to the library and see that he stays there.

(DOCTOR *has crossed to left; takes off his overcoat and places it on settee.* BROOKS *and* BERESFORD *exit.* BERESFORD *closes the door behind them.* DETECTIVE *up to alcove doors; closes them; then he comes down a few steps, facing the* DOCTOR.)

DETECTIVE. Now, Doctor, I'll have that blueprint.

DOCTOR (*eying him warily*). I've just made the statement that I didn't find that blueprint.

DETECTIVE (*dryly*). I heard you! Now, this situation is between you and me, Dr. Wells—it has nothing to do with that poor fool of a cashier. He didn't take that money and you know it. It's in this house, and you know that too.

DOCTOR. In this house?

DETECTIVE. In this house! Tonight when you claimed to be making a professional call, you were in this house—and I think you were on that staircase when Richard Fleming was killed!

DOCTOR. No, Anderson, I'll swear I was not.

DETECTIVE. I'll tell you something. Miss Van Gorder very cleverly got a thumbprint of yours tonight. Does that mean anything to you?

DOCTOR. Nothing. I have not been upstairs in this house in three months. (*Up to this point he is obviously telling the truth.* DETECTIVE *is puzzled.*)

DETECTIVE. Before Courtleigh Fleming died, did he tell you anything about a Hidden Room—in this house?

DOCTOR (*his air of honesty lessens; he becomes furtive*). No.

DETECTIVE. You haven't been trying to frighten those women out of here with anonymous letters so you could get in?

DOCTOR. No—certainly not. (*Slight pause.* DETECTIVE *walks toward* DOCTOR.)

DETECTIVE. Let me see your key ring.

(DOCTOR *unwillingly produces key ring.* DOCTOR *hands out keys to* DETECTIVE, *who takes them.* DETECTIVE, *with revolver in hand, goes up into alcove, unlocks terrace door, goes out, leaving terrace door open.* DOCTOR *glances up stage to see if* DETECTIVE *is out of sight. He gets piece of blueprint out of his pocket and tiptoes to the fireplace with it. He throws paper toward grate, but it falls on floor outside of grate. A flash of lightning reveals through the broken pane in window* DETECTIVE, *who is on terrace, and has drawn the shade aside. Slight rumble of thunder, lightning, while* DETECTIVE *on terrace looking through window.*)

DETECTIVE (*sees* DOCTOR *throw the paper to floor; with noiseless swiftness the* DETECTIVE *is back in the room, and has the* DOCTOR *covered*

with revolver). Pick that up. (DOC-
TOR *does pick it up.*) And put it on
the table. (DOCTOR *slowly to· table
with paper.*) Now—stand away from
the table—— (DOCTOR *backs away.
A low rumble of thunder. Lightning.* DETECTIVE *lowers revolver,
puts keys on table and stands back
of table, looking at the blueprint.
Lays the revolver on table. Looks
up at* DOCTOR *with a half-sardonic
smile, then examining blueprint.*)
Behind a fireplace, eh? What fireplace? In what room?

DOCTOR (*sullenly*). I won't tell you!

DETECTIVE (*by table*). All right. I'll
find it, you know. (*Consulting blueprint again, leaning over table.*)

(DOCTOR *maintains a furious silence.
Slight pause. Then with a leap the*
DOCTOR *is on top of the* DETECTIVE.
*There follows a silent, furious strug-
gle.* DOCTOR *pins* DETECTIVE'S *arms
behind him.* DETECTIVE *bends down;
gets his right arm free; gets revolver
off table, but he drops it to floor.
Then* DOCTOR *gets* DETECTIVE'S
*both arms pinned behind him, and
reaches back to stand up C. and gets
hold of the telephone.* DOCTOR *hits
the* DETECTIVE *over the head with
base of phone, rendering* DETECTIVE
*insensible. T h u n d e r, lightning,
wind.* DETECTIVE *falls.* DOCTOR
*straightens up; listens tensely. There
is no sound from the rest of the
house. Only the thunder and lightning.* DOCTOR *picks up the revolver,
puts in pocket, gets the blueprint,
puts in pocket. Now gets down on
his knees beside* DETECTIVE. *Rapidly gags him with handkerchief.*
DOCTOR *then takes his own muffler
and wraps it around head of* DETEC-
TIVE. *After the gag is on,* DOCTOR

*listens and looks around, then he
gets the handcuffs off the table, left
there in scene with* BROOKS. DOCTOR
now locks the handcuffs on DETEC-
TIVE'S *wrists; not behind his back,
but in front of him. Then he puts
arms under* DETECTIVE'S *arms and
drags* DETECTIVE *off into billiard
room. Comes into the room again.
Closes and locks door. And then
cautiously starts to go up into alcove. He makes a dash for the staircase. There is a knock on terrace
door behind him. He backs down
quickly, looks at door where the
knocks come from. Backs into room.
Then he is about to start up into alcove again when* BERESFORD *enters
from below staircase. Goes to terrace door.* BERESFORD *looks at* DOC-
TOR. DOCTOR *points at door, and
backs into room.*)

BERESFORD (*four knocks. Speaking
through the door*). Who's that? (*No
answer.* BERESFORD *draws revolver
from pocket.* THE UNKNOWN, *outside terrace door, repeats knocks on
terrace door.* ALL THE OTHER CHAR-
ACTERS *now enter from hall.* COR-
NELIA, LIZZIE, DALE, BROOKS, *and*
BILLY. BILLY *closes door behind
him.*)

CORNELIA (*as she enters and goes
up toward alcove doors; sees* BERES-
FORD). What was that noise?

DOCTOR. Someone at that door.

BERESFORD (*still in alcove at door*).
Sh! Sh! Shall I open it? (*Thunder,
wind, lightning throughout this
scene.* CORNELIA, *up to double doors;
stands.*)

LIZZIE (*with a low wail*). If it ain't
human, it's dead! If it *is* human,

we're dead! (*Four knocks repeated by* UNKNOWN.)

CORNELIA. Be careful, Mr. Beresford.

LIZZIE (*moans*). It's The Bat!

(BERESFORD *very cautiously opens the terrace door. As he does so—clap of thunder, wind, lightning, lights blink. At the same moment* UNKNOWN, *who has been leaning against the terrace door, falls into* BERESFORD'S *arms.* BERESFORD *drops his revolver and catches the man so he does not fall to floor in alcove.* UNKNOWN *straightens up himself, achieves a certain measure of action, and balances himself; staggers into room.* UNKNOWN *is rather good-looking. It is seen that there is dried blood on his forehead. His feet and hands have been tied, and pieces of rope still dangle from his wrists and ankles.* UNKNOWN *staggers to table.* DOCTOR *beside him.* BERESFORD *on his other side. When clear of the table,* UNKNOWN *gives a couple of steps forward and falls prone on his face.*)

BERESFORD (*beneath his breath*). Good God!

CORNELIA (*comes down toward* DOCTOR. *General movement when* UNKNOWN *fell*). Doctor!

(*Thunder and lightning and wind die out.* DOCTOR *stoops down over prostrate man, turns him over, puts hand over heart.*)

DOCTOR. He's fainted! Struck on the head, too.

CORNELIA. Who is it?

DOCTOR. I never saw him before. Does anyone recognize him? (ALL *look at* UNKNOWN. *Slight pause. No one recognizes him.*)

CORNELIA. Is he badly hurt?

DOCTOR. It's hard to say. I think not. (UNKNOWN *moves, and makes effort to sit up.* BERESFORD *and* DOCTOR *assist him. He gets to his feet. He sways.*) A chair—— (BROOKS *quickly steps forward from table and places the chair for* UNKNOWN, *who collapses into it.*) You're all right now, my friend. (*In professional, cheerful voice*). Dizzy a bit, aren't you?

UNKNOWN (*makes no answer, stretches his arms, rubs his wrists*). Water!

CORNELIA (*to* BILLY). Bring some water. (BILLY *crosses right*).

DOCTOR. Whisky would be better.

CORNELIA. Billy! (BILLY *stops and turns.*) There's whisky in my room.

BILLY (*brightening*). Yes—hid in closet—I know. (CORNELIA *stares at him. He exits through alcove and goes up and off by stairs.*)

DOCTOR (*to* UNKNOWN). Now, my man, you're in the hands of friends. Brace up.

BERESFORD.   Where's   Anderson? (UNKNOWN *starts, then controls himself. From this point on it is evident to the audience that the* UNKNOWN *is not as dazed as he seems to be.*) This is a police matter. (*Makes a movement as if to go.*)

DOCTOR (*raises hand to stop* BERESFORD). He was here a moment ago.

He'll be back presently. (*Gives* UN-KNOWN *a little shake*). Rouse yourself, man! What has happened to you?

UNKNOWN (*slowly and apparently with difficulty*). I'm dazed—I don't remember!

CORNELIA. What a night! (*Front of table; turns to* DALE.) Richard Fleming murdered in this house—and now—this! (UNKNOWN *is sitting so that his face is visible to the audience but not to those on the stage. He gives a swift, stealthy glance at* CORNELIA, *then his eyes fall again.*)

DALE. Why doesn't somebody ask him his name? (BROOKS *over to* UN-KNOWN.)

BERESFORD. Where the devil is that detective? (*He rushes off through hall door. Leaves door open.*)

BROOKS (*to* UNKNOWN). What's your name? (UNKNOWN *makes no reply.*)

CORNELIA. Look at his papers. (BROOKS *and* DOCTOR *look in his pockets. Trousers only. He has no coat or vest on. Slight pause.*)

BROOKS. Not a paper on him.

(*Glass crash off stage, apparently at head of stairs.* BERESFORD *rushes on and* ALL *turn up; look at the alcove doors, except the* UNKNOWN, *who half rises in his chair. Tense and alert.* BILLY, *terrified, backs down the small staircase and into the room. He stands with his back to the audience, a rigid little figure, with horror in every outline.*)

CORNELIA (*sharply*). Billy!

DALE. Billy! What is it?

BILLY (*moistens his dry lips with his tongue*). It—nothing. (UN-KNOWN *sinks back into· his chair, and resumes his pose of immobility.*)

BERESFORD (*crosses and catches* BILLY *by the shoulders; swings* BILLY *round to face him*). Now, see here! You've seen something! What was it?

BILLY (*trembling*). Ghost! Ghost!

CORNELIA. He's concealing something. Look at him!

BILLY. No! No! No! (BERESFORD *releases* BILLY *and steps back.*)

CORNELIA (*to* BROOKS). Brooks, close that door. (*Points up at terrace door in alcove.* BROOKS *quickly up into alcove. Terrace door is slammed shut in his face. At same time lights out. All dark.*)

BROOKS (*in alcove*). This door's locked—the key's gone. (*To* BERES-FORD.) Where's your revolver, Beresford? (*Goes over to table.*)

BERESFORD. I dropped it, in the alcove.

CORNELIA. I have one. Quick, there's a candle on the table. Light it, somebody!

BERESFORD (*over to table, quickly*). Righto! (*He tricks light in his wrist watch on.* LIZZIE *sees wrist watch light; points at it.*)

LIZZIE. The eye! The eye! (*Meanwhile* BERESFORD *has struck match and lighted candle.*)

(LIZZIE *and* BILLY *back away toward hall door to get out.* BROOKS *has come down to door.*)

BROOKS. This door's locked.

CORNELIA (*taking the candle and revolver off table*). I know there's somebody upstairs. We'll go this way. (*She starts up to alcove doors.*

OTHERS *all turn and take a step toward doors.* BROOKS *up to doors. Doors are closed and locked.*)

BROOKS. Locked!

CORNELIA (*holds up the lighted candle*). A bat!

(*Black paper bat is tacked to the door R.C. The* UNKNOWN *rises and stands looking up at alcove doors.* ALL THE CHARACTERS *are facing up toward doors.*)

CURTAIN

ACT THREE

SCENE—*The trunk room on the third floor.*

The walls of room, except fireplace up C., window to the right of the audience and a door to the left, are lined with high closets, with practical doors in each. At the rear, a wooden fireplace (mantel).

Instead of the grate, there is an iron fireplate fastened in, making the mantel, when it moves, as solid as a door. Mantelpiece swings open on concealed hinges, revealing behind it a room, perhaps 6 feet by 6, in which is a tall iron safe. Next to the mantel is a row of drawers. The mantel is opened by pushing aside a panel in the drawers, revealing a knob which, when turned, swings the mantel out like a door.

To the left is a large wicker hamper. Beside this two small old battered trunks. Set up and down stage, one on top of the other. Next to hamper, a kitchen chair without back.

To the right a kitchen chair with back. Two old boxes behind door. Some paper bundles up on high shelf above closets at the left. Old sewing machine against wall. A box pin-hinged to set below the casement window, for characters to step on, getting in and out of window. Two old dress-suit cases, to dress scene. Important: Woman's satchel, on floor, front of hamper; matches on top of trunk.

AT RISE—*Stage dark.*

DISCOVERED—MASKED MAN (DETECTIVE) *at safe, up stage, C., back of the open mantelpiece. He is working at the knob of safe. After a moment* MASKED MAN *swings open the safe. He takes out the money bag, shuts safe, blows out the candle on floor beside safe, shuts off his pocket flash, and closes the mantel.*

Remote hammering heard off stage. MASKED MAN *to door, about to open door. Crash of splintering wood heard off stage. Ad lib.*

BERESFORD (*off stage*). You go this way. I'll go that.

BROOKS (*off stage*). Have your revolver ready.

(*During this ad lib.* MASKED MAN *darts back, drops the money bag into hamper, and closes lid of hamper. He runs to window. Gets out of window; goes up ladder below window, up onto the roof. Footsteps heard coming upstairs. Door flung open;* BROOKS *rushes on, stands a second, then runs to window.*)

CORNELIA (*suddenly enters with revolver and dead candle*). Hands up —or I'll shoot!

BROOKS (*is seen silhouetted against window. He turns, faces* CORNELIA, *throws up his hands*). Don't shoot! It's Bailey!

CORNELIA (*to front of trunk*). What brought you up here? (*She lights candle.*)

BROOKS. The others will search downstairs. But, Miss Van Gorder, you mustn't run over the house by yourself. Don't you realize that the man who locked us in was probably The Bat?

CORNELIA (*crosses room*). That's why I'm running! Anyway, where would a body *be* safe? When eight of us could be locked up together in one room and have to break out, it's a pretty kettle of fish!

BROOKS. That window's open.

CORNELIA. It's a good forty feet to the ground.

BROOKS (*looks around room*). Well, he isn't here. I'll take a look over the rest of this floor. (*He gets to door.*)

CORNELIA (*suddenly looks at floor and sees candle grease, near window*). Candle grease! (BROOKS *stops, turns, and looks at* CORNELIA. CORNELIA *touches the grease on floor with finger.*) Fresh candle grease! Now, who do you suppose did that? Do you remember how Mr. Gillette, in Sherlock Holmes—when he—— (*Voice trails off; she stoops down, follows the candle grease marks to fireplace.*) It leads straight to the fireplace. (*She stands erect and surveys the mantel.*) It's been going through my mind for half an hour that no chimney flue runs up this side of the house.

BROOKS. Then why the fireplace?

CORNELIA. That's what I'm going to find out.

DALE (*off stage*). Jack! Jack! (*Cautiously.*)

(CORNELIA *raps on mantel.*)

BROOKS (*beckons* DALE, *who enters*). Come in—— Lock the door behind you. (DALE *closes and locks door.*) Where are the others?

DALE. They're searching the house. There's no sign of anybody.

BROOKS. Where's Anderson?

DALE. I haven't seen him.

CORNELIA (up at mantel; raps on wall above mantel with her revolver). Hollow as Lizzie's head. (She carefully examines the painted small drawers left of mantel.) Some of these ought to slide or push or something. (She works small drawer. It slides slowly open' [panel], revealing a white doorknob behind the panel.) Merciful powers! It's moving! (DALE backs away.)

BROOKS (up to CORNELIA). Give me the revolver, and stand back. (BROOKS and CORNELIA back away. Pause. BROOKS up to the open panel; turns the knob. It opens slowly, swinging back against wall. BROOKS faces mantel as it moves.)

DALE. Look! (The black aperture of room beyond revealed. BROOKS takes candle from CORNELIA and revolver; goes up.)

DALE. Jack! Be careful!

BROOKS (goes in. A pause). Nobody home! (Then triumphantly.) Money! money! We've got the money. (Stoops, turns lever, and opens safe. Stands a moment. Comes out of safe with candle.)

CORNELIA. Well!

BROOKS. The safe's empty—— (For a moment no one speaks, their disappointment is so great.) The money's gone. Well, that settles me! (With forced laugh.)

CORNELIA (over to him. She takes candle from him). Nonsense! The location of this room—the presence of that safe—is enough to establish the facts.

DALE. Jack, get Mr. Anderson and show him. (Violent hammering on door and a loud scream from LIZZIE off stage.)

LIZZIE (hysterically). Let me in! For the love of Heaven, let me in! (BROOKS runs over, unlocks and opens the door. LIZZIE staggers in, her candle hanging down in her hand. Almost immediately she gives a cry, and candle goes out. Candlelight burns her. Her movement puts it out.)

CORNELIA. Good Heavens, what's the matter?

LIZZIE (in front of hamper; hysterically). I saw him! I saw The Bat! He dropped through that skylight out there—(points)—and run along the hall. He was eight feet tall and he had a face like a demon.

BROOKS. Did you see his face?

LIZZIE. No, he didn't have any face. He was all black where his face ought to be.

DALE. A mask!

LIZZIE (crosses over toward DALE; volubly). Yes'm, that's what it was, a mask! (BROOKS, followed by CORNELIA, has started for the door. He carries CORNELIA's revolver. CORNELIA carries the lighted candle. LIZZIE turns; sees CORNELIA going toward door; steps quickly after CORNELIA.) Where are you going, Miss Neillie? (BROOKS stands at open door, waiting for CORNELIA.)

CORNELIA (turns to LIZZIE). Keep quiet and don't stick to me like a porous plaster.

LIZZIE. It's not you I'm sticking to, it's the candle!

CORNELIA (*to* LIZZIE, *as* CORNELIA *starts for door*). Go back and stay with Miss Dale. (CORNELIA *and* BROOKS *exit with lighted candle. Room in darkness.*)

DALE. Lizzie, give me your candle and the matches. (LIZZIE *crosses over to* DALE; *gives her the candle and matches.*)

LIZZIE (*terrified*). I won't stay here and be murdered in the dark. (*Starts for door.*) If I've got to die, I want to see myself do it! (*She bolts out; closes door after her.*)

(DALE *tries to light candle, striking matches on box. They do not light. Slight pause.* DALE *looks around the room, then door very slowly opens about an inch. At first a thread of light from flashlight gradually widening, then it is extinguished.* DALE *sees this. She is frightened. She darts up to Hidden Room, goes in and closes the two iron doors noiselessly. All dark.* MASKED MAN, *overcoat on, large flash, opens door very slowly; backs in; flash off. Sweeps room with flashlight. It is the man who was discovered at safe, opening of the Act. He locks the door. Goes to hamper; puts flash for a moment on satchel, front of hamper; picks satchel up; empties its contents into the hamper (old clothes and two paper-backed novels); thrusts the bag of money into satchel; uses flash; works with feverish haste; closes the grip; turns to go to door; hears footsteps off stage. He uses flash sparingly. With satchel in hand, he starts for the window. As he nears the window, extensión ladder comes up and leans against the* window. *He drops the satchel up stage above window. He is plainly trapped. He darts for the mantel room; closes the mantel behind him. There is absolute silence. Pause. Then the ladder moves as someone climbs it. Stealthily a man's silhouette* (DOCTOR) *is seen outside. The figure on the ladder, as he is about to step through the window into the room, is heard to hiss cautiously.*)

DOCTOR. Sssssst! (*Receiving no reply, with infinite caution he crawls in through window. Then he starts for mantel; uses flash—off—on.*) Ssst! (*Doorknob heard turning.* DOCTOR *starts.*)

BROOKS (*off*). Dale!

CORNELIA (*off stage*). Dale! Dale! The door's locked——

BROOKS (*off stage*). Dale! (BROOKS *rattles the knob; pounds on door; tries to break in.*)

DOCTOR (*after a moment*). Wait a moment! (*He goes to door; unlocks it.* BROOKS *hurls himself into room. He is followed by* CORNELIA *with candle.* LIZZIE *stands in doorway.*)

BROOKS (*turns on* DOCTOR). Why did you lock that door? (BROOKS *takes a look around the room, and realizes the amazing fact that* DALE *is not there.*)

DOCTOR. But I didn't.

BROOKS (*turns on* DOCTOR). You— you—— Where is Miss Ogden? What have you done with her?

DOCTOR. Done with her! I don't know what you're talking about. I haven't seen her.

BROOKS (*threateningly*). You didn't lock that door?

DOCTOR. Absolutely not. I was coming through the window when I heard your voice at the door.

LIZZIE (*in doorway, in shaking tones*). In at the window, just like a bat! (CORNELIA *places candle and revolver on hamper.*)

DOCTOR. I saw lights up here from outside, and I thought——

CORNELIA (*interrupting*). That mantel's closed.

DOCTOR (*starts as he discovers their knowledge of the Hidden Room*). Damn!

BROOKS (*to* DOCTOR). Did you close it?

DOCTOR. No!

BROOKS (*as he starts up to mantel*). I'll see whether you closed it or not. (*Leans against mantel; speaks loudly.*) Dale! Dale!

(DOCTOR *turns front of hamper, back to audience. Picks up the candle from hamper where* CORNELIA *placed it.* BROOKS *starts to open mantel. As it begins to swing out,* DOCTOR *deliberately extinguishes candle. Dark stage.* DOCTOR *drops the candle to floor, front of hamper.* MASKED MAN *rushes out of Hidden Room, back of hamper, to door. Bumps* LIZZIE *in doorway. She falls to stage, as* MASKED MAN *exits.*)

CORNELIA (*as the lights go out*). Doctor, why did you put out that candle?

DOCTOR. I didn't—I——

CORNELIA. You did—I saw you do it. (*Door slams.*)

BROOKS. What was that?

LIZZIE (*on floor at doorway*). Oh! Oh! Somebody knocked me down and tramped on me.

CORNELIA (*beside hamper*). Matches —quick! Where's the candle?

DOCTOR (*front of hamper*). Awfully sorry. I assure you it dropped out of the holder. (*Stoops down; gets candle.*) Here it is! (BROOKS *to* DOCTOR; *strikes match; lights candle as* DOCTOR *holds it.*)

(CORNELIA *takes the candle after* BROOKS *lights it.* BROOKS *up to Hidden Room.* DALE *is seen on floor in Hidden Room, in front of the safe.* BROOKS *carries* DALE *down to chair.* DALE'S *eyes closed.*)

BROOKS (*as he comes out of Hidden Room with* DALE). Doctor! (DOCTOR *crosses to chair; feels* DALE'S *pulse.* CORNELIA *holds up candle.*)

CORNELIA. Lizzie, get some whisky.

LIZZIE (*as she gets up off floor*). Oh, Miss Neillie, I can't stand any more of this. My spine's driven clean up through my brains.

CORNELIA (*going with candle*). You haven't got any spine and you haven't got any brains! Get that whisky. (LIZZIE *turns to go out door; sees* DETECTIVE *in doorway.* DETECTIVE *a grim and menacing figure. He carries a lighted candle.*)

LIZZIE (*facing* DETECTIVE *in doorway*). That's right! Come in when everything's over. (DETECTIVE *steps in, and* LIZZIE *exits.*)

DOCTOR (*with back turned toward* DETECTIVE, *looking at* DALE). She'll be all right in a moment.

DETECTIVE (*to* DOCTOR). You took my revolver from me downstairs. (*Places lighted candle on trunk, beside hamper.* DOCTOR *turns and faces him.*) I'll trouble you for it. (*The* OTHERS *are startled.* DOCTOR *sullenly gives up revolver to* DETECTIVE, *who examines and puts it in his hip pocket.*) I've something to settle with you, pretty soon, and I'll settle good and proper. (*Crosses over to* DALE.) Now what's this? (*Indicating* DALE. *Meanwhile* DOCTOR *walks slowly and quietly toward door.*)

CORNELIA. She's coming to. We found her shut in there, Mr. Anderson. (*Indicating Hidden Room.* DETECTIVE *goes over and looks at open Hidden Room. As* DOCTOR *is about to exit,* DETECTIVE *turns; sees* DOCTOR.)

DETECTIVE. Wells! (CORNELIA *and* BROOKS *work over* DALE. BROOKS *rubs her hands.* CORNELIA *beside* DALE. DOCTOR *stops and turns; faces* DETECTIVE.) Where were you when she was locked in this room? (*Points up at Hidden Room.*)

DOCTOR (*front of hamper*). I didn't shut her in—if that's what you mean! There was someone shut in there— (*points up at Hidden Room*)—with her. Ask these people here. (*Indicating* CORNELIA *and* BROOKS.)

CORNELIA (*angry*). The fact remains, Doctor, that we left her here alone. When we came back you were here. That door was locked. (*Indicates door to Hidden Room.*) And she was in that room. (DETECTIVE *goes in Hidden Room. Pause.* CORNELIA *up with candle.*) Unconscious! As we opened that door—(*indicates mantel*)—the doctor deliberately extinguished the candle.

DETECTIVE (*wheeling on* DOCTOR. CORNELIA *comes down*). Do you know who was in that room?

DOCTOR (*sullenly*). No—I didn't put out the candle. It fell. And I didn't lock that door. (*Indicates door.*) I found it locked. (DALE *opens her eyes and sits up. She looks around; suddenly realizes where she is and what is happening. She looks over her shoulder; sees open Hidden Room.* DALE *shudders; half rises.*)

DALE. Please close that awful door. I don't want to see it again. (DETECTIVE *goes up; closes the iron doors to Hidden Room.*)

BROOKS (*gets down on his knees beside* DALE). What happened to you? Can you remember?

DALE. I was here alone in the dark —then that door opened—(*indicates door*)—and I saw a man come in. I hid in there. (*Indicates Hidden Room.*) It was the only thing I could think of.

DETECTIVE (*facing* DALE). And then——

DALE. He came in, too, and closed the door, and I think he heard me gasp, for he turned a flashlight on me and said, "If you make a sound I'll kill you!" That's all I remember.

DETECTIVE (*looks at* DOCTOR, *then looks at* DALE; *suspiciously*). Do you know who that man was?

DALE. No. (DETECTIVE *looks at* DOCTOR.)

CORNELIA. But I do—it was The Bat!

DETECTIVE (*turns on her rather sardonically*). Ha! Still harping back to The Bat!

CORNELIA. I have every reason to believe The Bat is in this house.

DETECTIVE (*jeeringly*). And that he took the Union Bank money out of that safe, I suppose? No, Miss Van Gorder! (*Turns; faces* DOCTOR.) Ask the doctor who took the Union Bank money out of that safe. Ask the doctor who attacked *me* downstairs in the drawing room; knocked *me* senseless, and locked *me* in the billiard room! (*To* DOCTOR. *Pause.*) The next time you put handcuffs on a man, be sure to take the key out of his vest pocket! (*An astounded pause, then* CORNELIA *speaks.*)

CORNELIA. Perhaps I am an obstinate old woman, but the doctor and all the rest of us were locked in the drawing room not ten minutes ago.

DETECTIVE (*sneeringly*). By The Bat, I suppose!

CORNELIA (*obstinately*). By The Bat! (DETECTIVE *looks at* DOCTOR.) He went to the trouble to leave his visiting card fastened to the door!

DETECTIVE. The Bat, eh? (*Confronts the* DOCTOR.) You knew about this room, Wells?

DOCTOR (*looking up at* DETECTIVE). Yes.

DETECTIVE. And you knew the money was in the room?

DOCTOR. Well, I was wrong, wasn't I?

DETECTIVE. You were up in this room earlier tonight.

DOCTOR. No. I couldn't *get* up.

DETECTIVE. You know where that money is, Wells, and I'm going to find out!

DOCTOR (*goaded beyond endurance*). Good God! Do you suppose if I knew where it is I'd be here? I've had plenty of chances to get away. No, you can't pin anything on me, Anderson. It isn't criminal to have known that room is here.

DETECTIVE. Don't be so damned virtuous. Maybe you haven't been upstairs, but unless I miss my guess, you know who was. (DOCTOR's *face changes. Crosses to* DOCTOR.) What about Richard Fleming?

DOCTOR (*impressively*). I never killed him! I don't even own a revolver!

DETECTIVE (*crosses down stage and front of* DOCTOR. *As he goes*). You come with me, Wells. This time I'll do the locking up. (DETECTIVE *stands by door; looks at* CORNELIA. *He takes lighted candle off trunk.*) Better get the young lady down to bed. I think that I can promise you a quiet night from now on.

CORNELIA (*sardonically*). I'm glad you think so, Mr. Anderson! (DOCTOR *crosses past* DETECTIVE; *exits.* DETECTIVE *follows* DOCTOR.)

(CORNELIA *swiftly crosses over to door; closes it. Then she turns and faces* DALE *and* BROOKS.)

DALE (*with force*). I can't believe the doctor killed Richard Fleming. (CORNELIA *crosses back to center with lighted candle.*)

CORNELIA (*swiftly moves to C.*). Of course he didn't. He's just guilty enough to look more guilty than he is. (*She stands for a moment, then says to* DALE.) But the man who was shut in the mantel room with you was the man who *killed* Richard Fleming and took the money. But what brought him back? (*Pause. She looks at door, then down at floor.*) It's clear as a pikestaff. In some way he heard me coming—got out on the roof—(*points*)—through the skylight —(*points*)—and back here again. (*To verify her theory about the roof, she goes up to window; looks out.* BROOKS *follows and stands watching her. She then faces into room again; stands looking around.*) But what brought him back? (*Pause, while* CORNELIA, *candle in hand, moves quickly, now stooping to examine floor. Now straightens, looks about her. She also makes a careful search of the Hidden Room. As she comes out of Hidden Room she partly closes the two iron doors.*)

BROOKS (*watching her*). Is this something else you saw Mr. Gillette do?

CORNELIA (*over to hamper*). I'm using my wits! I never saw *any* man do that. (*At last, with an air of great satisfaction, she sets candle on hamper. Evidently she has made some important discovery.*) I know very little about bank currency. Could such a sum be carried away in a man's pocket?

BROOKS. Even in bills of large denomination it would make a pretty sizable bundle.

(*Enter* LIZZIE *with tumbler of wine in one hand and a lighted candle in the other.* CORNELIA *pursues her search of the room up.*)

LIZZIE (*front of hamper*). That Jap broke the whisky, but here's some of that elderberry wine. It's kind of comforting. Say, that assault and battery case is wandering all over the second floor. Think he's out of his head. I ran into him in the dark. I thought all my goose-flesh was standing on end before, but I raised a whole new crop. (*She goes back to door; kicks it shut with her foot.* CORNELIA *crosses with candle to front of hamper.* LIZZIE *toward* DALE, *who is still seated.*) I think there's a whole gang of crooks in this house. That Beresford—the Jap—and that assault and battery case—— Everybody pretending to be somebody he isn't! (*Starts.*) Oh! (*She offers the wine to* DALE, *who shakes her head in refusal.*)

BROOKS (*beside* DALE, *with his arm about her*). Take it, sweetheart.

LIZZIE (*stares, astounded; looks over at* CORNELIA). The gardener's calling her "sweetheart."

CORNELIA. Oh, be still! He's *not* a gardener.

LIZZIE. My God! Another one! (*Then she raises wine to her lips; drinks it.* CORNELIA, *with the lighted candle, looking around room near hamper. As she gets near door, she hears something. She makes gesture to others. The others stand and watch. The door is suddenly thrown open and* BERESFORD *stands in the doorway, crouching, ready to spring. Sees them. His attitude relaxes. He looks rather sheepish.*)

BERESFORD (*smiles—in doorway*). Oh —it's you?

CORNELIA (*suspiciously*). Who did you *think* it was?

BERESFORD (*relieved*). I've been making a rather hectic search for the man who locked us in. But I didn't find a sign. (*He shuts the door. His eyes travel to* BROOKS. *He crosses over to him. In ugly tone.*) Oh, still at large, Bailey?

BROOKS (*up close to him*). I am, but the doctor is not. Now, see here, Beresford, the situation has changed in the last few minutes—— (COR-NELIA *puts candle on hamper.*) Dr. Wells is under arrest! I didn't mind your recognition of me—that was your duty—but I do object to the implication in your tone that I am a criminal. You've done your damnedest—now cut it. (*Doorknob turns.* COR-NELIA *lifts up candle.*)

CORNELIA (*faces door*). That doorknob's moving. (ALL *turn and look at door.*)

BERESFORD (*in whisper to* COR-NELIA). I'll open it. (*He crosses front of* CORNELIA *to door. Jerks open door.* BILLY, *who has hold of the off-stage side of doorknob, is jerked into room. Pause.*)

BILLY (*evidently very nervous, turns, steps back to door; looks off, then turns, faces others in room*). I come in, please? I not like to stay in dark.

CORNELIA. Come in. What is it, Billy? (*Steps forward a step or two.*)

BILLY (*nervously*). Man with sore head.

CORNELIA. What about him?

BILLY. Act very strange.

BERESFORD (*near door*). The man who fell into the room, downstairs?

BILLY. Yes—on second floor, walking around.

BERESFORD (*to* CORNELIA). I was watching that fellow downstairs that fell in the room. I didn't think he was as dazed as he pretended to be.

CORNELIA (*to* BILLY, *brightly*). Bring him up, Billy. (BILLY *starts to go, then turns back; faces* CORNELIA.)

BILLY (*nervously—over to* COR-NELIA). You give candle, please? Don't like dark.

CORNELIA (*hands lighted candle to trembling* BILLY). Billy, what did you see when you came running down the stairs, before we were locked in?

BILLY (*candle shakes in his hand, nervously*). Nothing! (BROOKS *now stands between* CORNELIA *and* LIZ-ZIE.)

LIZZIE (*feeling the wine somewhat*). It must have been some nothing to make him drop a bottle of whisky.

BILLY. Ghost walk in house! (*Backs away toward door.*)

LIZZIE (*leaning close to* BROOKS, *shivering*). Ghosts! It makes my very switch stand on end! (*She puts the bottom of the glass on the flame of candle. Candle out. Almost at same time* BILLY *disappears through door with lighted candle. Stage dark.*)

BERESFORD. Can't we have a light?

BROOKS. Wait, I'll——

(*Strange flapping sound is heard, first in one part of the room and then the other. Hits near ceiling.*)

CORNELIA (*sharply, after a moment*). What's that?

LIZZIE (*plaintively*). If you hear anything, it's my teeth chattering.

CORNELIA. Take them out and put them in your pocket. (*Flapping sound again.*)

BERESFORD (*after a moment*). That's odd! There *is* something moving around the room. (*Flapping sound again.*)

BROOKS. It's up near the ceiling.

LIZZIE (*slow wail*). Oh—h—h—— (*Flapping sound again.*)

BERESFORD. Good God! It hit me in the face. (*He slaps hands together.*)

LIZZIE. I'm going! I don't know where, but I'm going. (*She quickly crosses to hamper. Flapping sound again. She screams.*) It's in my hair! It's in my hair!

BROOKS (*voice in the dark, crosses right, then back to left*). I've got it! It's a bat! (*Scream from LIZZIE. He goes up quickly to window, throws something out. There is a pause.*)

CORNELIA (*facing up stage*). Lizzie—— (*Pause.*) Lizzie, where are you?

LIZZIE (*on her knees back of hamper —voice out of the gloom*). Trying to

crawl under the floor. I'd go down a rathole if there was one. (*Door slowly opens and* BILLY, *leading the* UNKNOWN MAN, *enters.* LIZZIE *gets rid of her glass and dead candle as she kneels behind hamper. She places them on floor behind hamper.*)

BERESFORD. Come in. (*Steps to end of hamper; gets the chair without back; places it.*) Sit down. (BERESFORD *steps back and stands above* UNKNOWN.)

CORNELIA (*to* UNKNOWN, *who sits down*). Are you better now?

UNKNOWN (*slowly*). Somewhat.

CORNELIA. Lizzie, give him some wine.

LIZZIE (*back of hamper, head just in sight*). Somebody drank it.

CORNELIA (*speaks to* BILLY). Billy, you can go.

BILLY (*turns to* CORNELIA. *His tone is fairly pitiful*). I stay, please.

BROOKS (*by* CORNELIA. *Watches* BILLY *suspiciously, then to* CORNELIA). Anderson intimated that the doctor had an accomplice in the house. (*Crosses to* BILLY, *front of the* OTHER CHARACTERS. BROOKS *close up to* BILLY.) Why isn't this the man? (*Takes the candle from* BILLY.)

BILLY (*cringing*). Please, no.

BROOKS (*puts candle on hamper, catches* BILLY *by the shoulders, and half turns him to look up at the Hidden Room*). Did you know that room was there?

BILLY. No.

CORNELIA. He couldn't have locked us in. He was *with* us.

BROOKS. He may *know* who did it. (*To* BILLY.) Do you? (BILLY *shivers.*) Who did you see at the head of the small staircase? (BROOKS *swings* BILLY *in half circle around.*) Now we're through with nonsense. I want the truth.

BILLY. See face. That's all.

BROOKS (*strong*). Whose face?

BILLY (*evidently lying*). Don't know. (*Looks down.*)

CORNELIA. Never mind Billy—— (*Looks at* UNKNOWN MAN.) Solve the mystery of *this* man and we may get at the facts. (BERESFORD *holds lighted candle above* UNKNOWN. BROOKS *has turned when* CORNELIA *speaks. Takes eyes off* BILLY, *who has started on tiptoes for door. Just as he gets to door,* BROOKS *turns and sees* BILLY *trying to get away.*)

BROOKS (*takes a step or two toward* BILLY). You stay here. (BILLY *stops; stands by door.*)

BERESFORD. This chap—(*indicating* UNKNOWN)—claims to have lost his memory. I suppose a blow on the head might do that. I don't know.

LIZZIE (*back of hamper*). I wish somebody would knock *me* on the head. I'*d* like to forget a few things.

CORNELIA (*to* UNKNOWN). Don't you remember even your name?

UNKNOWN (*shakes head*). Not—yet.

CORNELIA. Or where you came from? (UNKNOWN *shakes his head.*) Do you remember how you got into this house?

UNKNOWN (*with difficulty*). Yes, I remember that, all right. (*He puts hand to his head.*) My head aches— to beat the band.

CORNELIA. How did you happen to come to this house?

UNKNOWN (*slowly*). Saw the lights.

BROOKS (*quickly*). Where were you when you saw the lights?

UNKNOWN. I broke out of the garage.

BERESFORD. How did you get there?

UNKNOWN. I don't know.

BROOKS (*with keen suspicion*). Had you been robbed?

UNKNOWN. Everything gone—out of my pockets.

BROOKS (*stepping closer to* UN-KNOWN). Including your watch?

UNKNOWN. If I had a watch, it's gone. All my papers—are—gone.

CORNELIA (*suspiciously*). How do *you* know you *had* papers?

UNKNOWN (*looks front; haltingly*). Most men—carry papers, don't they? I'm dazed, but my mind's all right. If you ask me—I think I'm d-d-damned funny. (BROOKS *and* BERESFORD *exchange glances.*)

CORNELIA. Did you ring the house phone? (BROOKS *and* BERESFORD *change places.*)

UNKNOWN. Yes. (*A start from* COR-NELIA *and* BROOKS.) I leaned against the button in the garage—then, I think maybe I fainted. That's not clear. (DALE *rises*.)

DALE (*leaning over, and looking at* UNKNOWN; *brightly*). You don't remember how you were hurt?

UNKNOWN. No. The first thing I remember I was in the garage, tied. I was gagged, too—that's what's the matter with my tongue now. Then I got myself free—and got out of a window.

BERESFORD. Just a moment, Miss Van Gorder—Anderson ought to be here for this. (*On word "Anderson,"* DALE *sits again*.)

(BERESFORD *starts for door.* DETECTIVE *enters. Closes the door after him. On word "Anderson,"* UNKNOWN'S *face shows intense alertness. The* UNKNOWN *gets to his feet.* DETECTIVE *has closed the door before he catches sight of the* UNKNOWN. *He stands rigid, his hand still on the knob of the door. It is to be remembered the* DETECTIVE *has not yet seen or heard of the* UNKNOWN.)

CORNELIA (*raises voice, watching* ANDERSON). A new element in our mystery, Mr. Anderson. (*Slight pause.* DETECTIVE *and* UNKNOWN *look at each other for a moment. The* UNKNOWN'S *face is blank and expressionless.*) Quite dazed, poor fellow! (UNKNOWN *sways.*)

DETECTIVE (*slowly*). How did *he* get into the house?

CORNELIA. He came through the terrace door some time ago, just before we were locked in.

DETECTIVE (*dryly*). Doesn't remember anything, eh? (*Crosses to* UNKNOWN. BERESFORD *crosses over same time with candle.* DETECTIVE *speaks roughly and puts hand under* UNKNOWN'S *chin; jerks* UNKNOWN'S *head up.*) Look up here! (UNKNOWN *looks up at* DETECTIVE *with a blank face.*) Look up, you—— (*Same business.*) This losing your memory stuff doesn't go down with me!

UNKNOWN (*weakly*). It doesn't go down very well with me, either!

DETECTIVE. Did you ever see me before? (BERESFORD *holds the candle a little nearer* DETECTIVE'S *face.*)

UNKNOWN (*looks at* DETECTIVE; *slight pause, haltingly*). You're the doctor I saw downstairs, aren't you?

DETECTIVE (*takes the watch of Act Two from his pocket; holds it out toward* UNKNOWN). Does this watch belong to you? (*Looks suspiciously at* UNKNOWN.)

UNKNOWN (*looks at watch*). Maybe —— (*Falls back against* BROOKS.) I don't know.

CORNELIA. He has evidently been attacked. He claims to have recovered consciousness in the garage, where he was tied, hand and foot.

DETECTIVE. He does, eh? If you'll give me five minutes alone with him, I'll get the *truth* out of him!

CORNELIA (*half turning back to* DETECTIVE). Do you believe that money is irrevocably gone?

DETECTIVE. There's no such word as "irrevocable" in my vocabulary, but I believe it's out of the house, if that's what you mean.

CORNELIA. Suppose I tell you that there are certain facts that you have overlooked?

DETECTIVE (*sardonically, to* COR-NELIA, *but looks at* UNKNOWN). Still on the trail!

CORNELIA. I was right about the doctor, wasn't I? (*Goes to door.*)

DETECTIVE. Just fifty per cent right, and the doctor didn't turn the trick alone. Now, if you'll all go out and close that door—— (CORNELIA *looks off stage. Takes candle from* BROOKS.)

CORNELIA (*starts out*). Quick! A man just went through that skylight and out onto the roof.

DETECTIVE. Out onto the roof!

BROOKS. Come on, Beresford!

(CORNELIA *exits.* BROOKS (2), DE-TECTIVE (3), BERESFORD (4), BILLY (5), *and closes door behind him. Ad lib. from the men as they run off,* "A man on the roof," *etc. Talking and excitement and noise of running. As the* DETECTIVE *goes off he draws his revolver.*)

BERESFORD. Righto—— (DALE, LIZ-ZIE, *and* UNKNOWN *remain in room. In the dark, except for the light from doorway.*)

LIZZIE (*goes over to* DALE). I'd run if my legs would!

DALE. Hush!

LIZZIE (*wails*). How do we know this fellow right here isn't The Bat? (*Indicating the* UNKNOWN, *who has half risen, back into chair.* CORNELIA *re-enters with lighted candle.* COR-NELIA *comes in very cautiously, looks over her shoulder, and quietly closes the door.*)

DALE. What did you see?

CORNELIA (*calmly*). I didn't see anything! I had to get rid of that dratted detective before I assassinated him.

DALE. Nobody went through the skylight?

CORNELIA. They have now—the whole outfit.

DALE. Then why did you——

CORNELIA (*interrupting*). Because that money's in this room. If the man who took it out of the safe had got away with it, why did he come back and hide there? (*Indicates Hidden Room. They look up at Hidden Room.*) He got it out of the safe, and that's as far as he *did* get it! There's a *hat* behind that safe—a man's soft felt hat.

LIZZIE. Oh, I wish he'd take his hat and go home. (UNKNOWN *listens intently.*)

CORNELIA (*disregarding* LIZZIE; *goes over in front of the closets, back of the hamper. On floor she picks up a half-burned candle*). A half-burned candle. Another thing the detective overlooked. (*She steps back; looks from candle to closet. Suddenly at the window* BROOKS *quickly lowers himself in from the roof ladder on down-stage side of window.*)

LIZZIE (*horrified*). Oh, my God, another one! (CORNELIA *gets her re-*

volver *from top of hamper; points at the figure of* BROOKS.)

DALE (*recognizes* BROOKS; *puts her hand up so* CORNELIA *won't shoot*). It's Jack! (DALE *moves over to* BROOKS *as he comes in window.* COR-NELIA, *on seeing that it is* BROOKS, *lays her revolver on top of hamper.* UNKNOWN *sees her do this.*)

BROOKS (*up at window*). The man Lizzie saw drop from the skylight probably reached the roof from this window—easiest thing in the world.

CORNELIA (*looks at the closets*). Never mind the window! When that detective comes back I may have a *surprise party* for him! (DALE *crosses toward* CORNELIA.)

LIZZIE. No more surprises for me. I've been surprised pretty near to death all night.

DALE (*up to* BROOKS). Aunt Cornelia thinks the money's still here. (LIZZIE *sits in chair.*)

CORNELIA (*over to closets; opens three, one after another*). I *know* it's here. (BROOKS *crosses to* CORNELIA.)

(LIZZIE *sits still, her eyes riveted on the* UNKNOWN, *who is looking at re-volver on hamper.* DALE *looks at* LIZZIE, *then steps down to* LIZZIE.)

DALE (*nervously*). Lizzie—— What are you looking at?

(UNKNOWN *is again sunk in apathy.* CORNELIA *resumes trying of the closet doors. She is now at one of the closets.*)

CORNELIA. This one is locked, and the key gone.

LIZZIE (*seated; crying*). If there's anything locked up in that closet, you'd better let it stay. There's enough running around loose in this house as it is. (*There is no question about the interest in the* UNKNOWN's *face.* BROOKS *up and stands back of* CORNELIA. CORNELIA *hands* BROOKS *the candle.*)

CORNELIA. Lizzie, did you ever take that key?

LIZZIE (*seated*). No'm.

CORNELIA. It may be locked from the inside. (DALE *up beside* BROOKS; *watches* CORNELIA *at closet.*) I'll soon find out. (CORNELIA *takes from her hair a wire hairpin and runs it through the keyhole.*) There's no key inside. (BROOKS *shakes the door of closet, but it does not yield.*) I want to see the inside of that closet.

LIZZIE. If you could see *my* insides, you wouldn't recognize them.

CORNELIA. Bring me the other closet keys. (DALE, *with the candle, goes from closet to closet; then down to closet below the window. Gets key.* LIZZIE *follows* DALE *and the candle.*)

(DALE *up to* CORNELIA *and gives her key.* LIZZIE *follows her. Meanwhile* BROOKS *goes to closets against back wall, gets keys. During above busi-ness,* UNKNOWN, *with infinite cau-tion, moves his chair over toward re-volver* CORNELIA *has left on top of hamper. He reaches out, gets revolver, moves back chair, and sits same as before, revolver partly covered.*)

CORNELIA. There! That unlocked it!

BROOKS. I'd keep *back* a little. You don't know *what* may be inside. (CORNELIA *and* DALE *draw back.*)

LIZZIE *´ivering, speaks as she crosses front of* UNKNOWN, *over to front of hamper*). Mercy sakes, who wants to know! (LIZZIE *sits on the hamper.* BROOKS *takes the candle, and slowly and cautiously opens the door of the closet. He stands for a moment and stares, appalled, at something on the floor of the closet.*)

(BROOKS *looks into closet. Pause.*)

DALE (*aghast*). What is it? What did you see? (*Staring at* BROOKS.)

BROOKS (*does not answer; then pulling himself together*). Miss Cornelia, I think we have found the ghost the Jap butler saw. How are your nerves?

CORNELIA (*holds out her hand*). Give me the candle. (*He does.* BROOKS *crosses over to* DALE. *They stand and watch* CORNELIA.)

(CORNELIA *opens closet door.* CORNELIA *closes door of closet and comes down again.* UNKNOWN *half turns and watches the others out of the corner of his eye. A tense pause.*)

CORNELIA. It is Courtleigh Fleming.

BROOKS. It *was* Courtleigh Fleming.

DALE (*with hand on back of chair*). Then he did not die in the West.

BROOKS. He died in this house—within the last hour. The body is still warm, and Dr. Wells killed him.

CORNELIA. I wonder! (*Then to* BROOKS *as she crosses to* DALE.) Please look and see if Courtleigh

Fleming wore a wrist watch with a luminous dial. (BROOKS *up to closet; opens down-stage door; gets on his knees; puts arm in closet. Time for brief examination. Rises; closes closet door.*)

BROOKS. Yes.

CORNELIA (*to* DALE). The *eye* Lizzie saw was the wrist watch. (*The* UNKNOWN *sinks down in chair, but listens intensely.*)

BROOKS. Isn't it clear, Miss Van Gorder? The doctor and old Mr. Fleming formed a conspiracy—Fleming to rob the bank and hide the money here. Wells to issue a false death certificate in the West, and bury a substitute body, secured God knows how. It was easy—it kept clear the name of the President of the Union Bank—and it put the blame on me. (*Turns quickly and looks up at* CORNELIA.) Only they slipped up in one place. Dick Fleming leased the house to you, and they couldn't get it back.

CORNELIA (*quickly*). Then you think that tonight Courtleigh Fleming broke in, with the doctor's assistance, and that he killed Dick, his own nephew, from the staircase?

BROOKS. Don't you?

CORNELIA. No.

BROOKS (*facing* CORNELIA). It's as clear as crystal. Wells tried to get out of the house tonight with that blueprint. *Why?* He knew the minute we got it we'd come up here, and Fleming was here.

CORNELIA. Perfectly true, and then?

BROOKS. Old Fleming killed Dick, and Wells killed Fleming. (*Crossing over to* DALE.) *You can't get away from it!*

CORNELIA. No—no, the doctor is not a murderer. He's as puzzled as we are about ˙some things. He and Courtleigh Fleming were working together, but remember this—Dr. Wells was locked in the drawing room with us. He's been trying all evening to get up the stairs and failed.

BROOKS. He was here ten minutes ago, locked in this room.

CORNELIA. I grant you that—but at the same time an unknown masked man was locked in that mantel room with Dale. The doctor put out the candle when you opened that Hidden Room. *Why?* Because he *thought Courtleigh Fleming was hiding there.* But at this moment he believes that Fleming has made his escape. No—we haven't solved the mystery yet—— There's another element—an *unknown* element—and that element is—The *Bat!*

DALE (*half hysterically*). Oh, call the detective. Let's get through with this thing. I can't *bear* any more.

CORNELIA. Wait. Not yet. Nobody can help Courtleigh Fleming, and I'm not through.

LIZZIE (*seated on hamper*). Well, I'm through, all right!

CORNELIA (*looks and sees hamper*). Open the lid of that hamper. (*Indicates hamper which* LIZZIE *is sitting on.*) And see what's inside. (BROOKS *crosses over to hamper; opens lid; looks inside.*)

BROOKS. Nothing here but some clothes and books.

CORNELIA (*beside* BROOKS). Books? I left no books in that hamper.

BROOKS (*reading title of cheap paper novel*). *Little Rosebud's Lovers, or a Cruel Revenge*, by Laura Jean——

LIZZIE (*beside hamper*). That's mine! Oh, Miss Neillie, I tell you this house is haunted. I left that book in my satchel, along with *Wedded but No Wife* and—— (BROOKS *closes lid.*)

CORNELIA. Where's your satchel?

LIZZIE (*looks around front of hamper and leans over hamper; looks behind it and around on the floor of hamper*). Where's my satchel? My satchel—— My satchel's gone. (*Over hamper at end.* CORNELIA *holds candle high.*)

CORNELIA (*at last sees satchel, by window on floor, where* MASKED MAN *left it when he darted into the Hidden Room earlier in Act. Indicating it*). Isn't that your satchel, Lizzie? (LIZZIE *quickly over to* CORNELIA, *then crosses to above window; looks scared; then looks at* CORNELIA.)

LIZZIE. Yes, ma'm.

CORNELIA (*points to chair*). Put it there. (LIZZIE *stalls, scared.* CORNELIA *continues to point at chair.*)

LIZZIE. I'm scared to touch it. It may have a bomb in it! (*She reluctantly gets the satchel; carries it very slowly between thumb and forefinger as she might carry a loaded gun.*)

CORNELIA. Do as I tell you—put it on that chair. (LIZZIE *deposits the satchel on chair and backs away up near window.* CORNELIA *starting up stage, looking at* BROOKS *and* DALE. DALE, *behind hamper.* BROOKS *beside her. To* BROOKS.) You open it. If the money's there, you're the one who ought to find it.

(BROOKS *looks at* DALE, *then with a smile crosses front of* CORNELIA. DALE *follows him.* CORNELIA, *with candle, follows them.* BROOKS *fumbles at catch of satchel on chair,* DALE *beside him. While they are occupied with this business,* UNKNOWN *rises and quickly gets to door; faces the others, his back to door. With hand behind him, he locks the door, takes the key out, and puts it in his pocket. Meanwhile* BROOKS *has succeeded in opening the satchel.* BROOKS *and* DALE *show they are delighted as they see the canvas bag with the packages of money in it.*)

BROOKS. The money is here.

DALE. Oh, thank God!

(*Red glow starts faintly outside window, increases and goes up and down. Flame effect. Crackling of burning wood heard off stage.* ALL *stand; watch window as red glare fills room.*)

LIZZIE. Fire!

BERESFORD (*off stage*). The garage is burning!

(*Sound of men's voices and running of feet on tin, supposed to be the roof.* CORNELIA, BROOKS, DALE, *and* LIZZIE *all turn toward door. Suddenly their attention is riveted on the* UNKNOWN, *who is standing in front of door. His back to door, facing the* OTHER CHARACTERS, *he has the revolver in his hand.*)

UNKNOWN (*savage tone*). This door is locked and the key is in my pocket—— (LIZZIE *opens her mouth to scream. He looks at her and in an ominous tone.*) Not a sound out of you. (*To* BROOKS.) Close that bag—(*referring to satchel*)—and put it back where you found it.

BROOKS (*starts toward him a step*). You!

DALE. Jack!

CORNELIA (*to* BROOKS). Do what he tells you! (BROOKS *closes bag, and puts it up by window.*)

LIZZIE (*horrified whisper*). It's The Bat!

UNKNOWN (*at door*). Blow out that candle! (CORNELIA, *after a moment's hesitation, blows out candle. Only light in room now is the flicker from fire outside window.*)

LIZZIE (*hysterically*). I'm going to scream! I can't keep it back.

UNKNOWN (*over at door; savagely*). Put that woman in that mantel room —(*points*)—and shut her up. (BROOKS *pushes* LIZZIE *up to mantel.*)

LIZZIE (*as she goes*). Don't shove! I'm damn glad to go. (*She goes in Hidden Room.* BROOKS *closes the iron doors behind her.*)

UNKNOWN (*unlocks the door; opens it a little; listens; closes it without locking it*). Not a sound, if you value your lives. (*Pause.*) In a moment or two a man will come into this room, either through the door or by that window. (*Steps toward window.*) The man who started the fire to draw you out of this house.

BROOKS (*steps toward* UNKNOWN). For God's sake don't keep these women here!

UNKNOWN. Keep them here where we can watch them! Don't you understand? There's a *killer* loose!

(*The red glow dies out.*)

CORNELIA (*to* UNKNOWN). I have understood very clearly for the last hour. The man who struck you down and tied you in the garage, the man who killed Dick Fleming and stabbed that poor wretch in the closet, the man who locked us in downstairs and removed the money from the safe—the man who started that fire outside is——

UNKNOWN (*as if hearing someone outside window, puts up his hand*). Sh! (*He runs quickly over to door, locks it, and hurries back.*) Stand back out of the light. The ladder!

(DALE *and* CORNELIA *stand back.* BROOKS *up stage by window.* UNKNOWN *flattens his body against wall beside* BROOKS. *The ladder is seen to shake, outside the window. A breathless pause, then outside on the ladder* THE BAT *is faintly outlined coming up ladder, in cap and black silk handkerchief disguise. He steps in window, and backs up to get the grip. As he does this,* UNKNOWN *and* BROOKS *grab him, just as* BAT *focuses flashlight on the satchel. There is a struggle in the dark.* BROOKS *and* UNKNOWN *overpower* THE BAT.)

UNKNOWN (*to* BROOKS). Get his gun. (*Pause.*) Got it?

BROOKS. Yes.

UNKNOWN. Hold out your hands, Bat, while I put on the bracelets! (*Puts handcuffs on* BAT'S *wrists.*) Sometimes even the *cleverest* Bat comes through a window at night and is caught! Double murder—burglary, and arson—— That's a good night's work even for you, Bat! (UNKNOWN *turns flashlight on* THE BAT'S *face.*) Take off that handkerchief. (BROOKS *does this business, revealing* ANDERSON, *the detective.* UNKNOWN *above* ANDERSON, BROOKS *below him.* DETECTIVE *is covered with two revolvers. The storm being over, the lights flash on.*)

DALE (*with* CORNELIA). It's Mr. Anderson!

UNKNOWN (*without taking his eyes off* THE BAT). I'm Anderson. This man has been impersonating me. You're a good actor, Bat, for a fellow that's such a *bad* actor! How did you get your dope on this case? Did you tap the wires to Headquarters?

THE BAT (*with sardonic smile*). I'll tell you that when I—— (*With swift movement, though handcuffed, he jerks the revolver by the barrel from the real* ANDERSON, *wheels on* BROOKS *with lightning rapidity, brings down the butt of revolver on* BROOKS' *wrist.* BROOKS' *revolver drops to floor.* THE BAT *swings around, keeping the characters covered with gun. Speaks as he moves or backs away.*) Hands up, everybody! (CORNELIA *has not raised her hands.*) Hands up—you! (*Savagely to* CORNELIA.)

CORNELIA. Why, I took the bullets out of that revolver two hours ago.

(THE BAT *throws the revolver toward her. It drops in front of her on floor. As soon as* THE BAT *drops revolver, the* UNKNOWN *picks up the other gun, and runs back of* CORNELIA *and blocks* THE BAT's *getaway.* UNKNOWN *covers* BAT *with gun.*)

UNKNOWN (*to* BAT). Don't move! (CORNELIA *picks up her gun from the floor.*) You see, you never know what a woman will do! (*Tauntingly to* BAT, *who turns and growls at* UNKNOWN.)

CORNELIA (*breaks the revolver and the loaded shells fall to floor.* THE BAT *wheels and looks at her, and bullets on floor.*) As it happened, I didn't. The first lie of an otherwise stainless life!

CURTAIN FALLS

On SECOND CURTAIN, LIZZIE *sticks her head out of Hidden Room, scared, and disappears into Hidden Room again.*

Broadway

A Play in Three Acts By

PHILIP DUNNING

and

GEORGE ABBOTT

CAUTION

Professionals and amateurs are hereby warned that *Broadway*, being fully protected under the Copyright Laws of the United States of America, the British Empire, including the Dominion of Canada, and all other countries of the Copyright Union, is subject to a royalty. All rights, including professional, amateur, motion pictures, recitation, public reading, radio broadcasting, and the rights of translation into foreign languages, are strictly reserved. Amateurs may produce this play upon payment of a royalty of twenty-five dollars for each performance, payable one week before the play is to be given to Samuel French, at 25 West 45th St., New York, N. Y., or 811 West 7th St., Los Angeles, Cal., or if in Canada, to Samuel French (Canada) Ltd., at 480 University Ave., Toronto.

The following is a copy of program of the first performance of "BROAD-WAY," presented by JED HARRIS at the Broadhurst Theatre, New York, N.Y., September 16, 1926:

Staged by the Authors

THE CAST

(In the order of their appearance.)

NICK VERDIS	Paul Porcasi
ROY LANE	Lee Tracy
LIL RICE	Clare Woodbury
KATIE	Ann Preston
JOE	Joseph Spurin-Calleia
MAZIE SMITH	Mildred Wall
RUBY	Edith Van Cleve
PEARL	Eloise Stream
GRACE	Molly Ricardel
ANN	Constance Brown
BILLIE MOORE	Sylvia Field
STEVE CRANDALL	Robert Gleckler
DOLPH	Henry Sherwood
PORKY THOMPSON	William Foran
SCAR EDWARDS	John Wray
DAN McCORN	Thomas Jackson
BENNIE	Frank Verigun
LARRY	Millard Mitchell
MIKE	Roy R. Lloyd

GANGSTERS, WAITERS

The action takes place in the private party room of the Paradise Night Club, New York City.

Act One: A spring evening, just before the first show.
Act Two: Half an hour later.
Act Three: The next night.

DESCRIPTION OF CHARACTERS

NICK VERDIS: *A middle-aged Greek; mercenary and hard. Talks with a dialect.*

LIL RICE: *Prima-donna type. Heavy and middle-aged with a certain amount of good looks, which, however, have long since lost their bloom.*

ROY LANE: *A slender, agile young man of the typical small-time song-and-dance variety, magnetic and lovable.*

MAZIE, GRACE, RUBY, PEARL, and ANN *are young chorus girls of contrasting types.*

JOE: *Ordinary Italian waiter who speaks in dialect.*

BILLIE MOORE: *A beautiful little chorus girl, more refined and unsophisticated than the others.*

STEVE CRANDALL: *Tall man; handsome in a hard, sophisticated way. Wears evening clothes.*

DOLPH: *A dark, wiry little man. Evening clothes.*

PORKY: *A stout, bald-headed, placid type; in evening clothes.*

SCAR EDWARDS: *A slight, tense man. Rather short in stature and slightly overdressed. Scar on face.*

DAN McCORN: *Well-built, rather well-dressed young detective. Quite matter-of-fact and with a sense of humor.*

BENNIE, LARRY, and MIKE: *Contrasting types of Chicago gunmen. All in evening dress.*

KATIE: *A typical hard-boiled cloakroom girl.*

CAST

(In the order of appearance)

NICK VERDIS
ROY LANE
LIL RICE
KATIE
JOE
MAZIE SMITH
RUBY
PEARL
GRACE
ANN
BILLIE MOORE
STEVE CRANDALL
DOLPH
PORKY THOMPSON
SCAR EDWARDS
DAN McCORN
BENNIE
LARRY
MIKE
GANGSTERS
WAITERS

BROADWAY

ACT ONE

SCENE—*The private party room of the Paradise Night Club, New York City. There is a carpeted stairway at R., a heavy oak door with a grated slide peekhole in it just below the stairs; at the back double doors, now closed, lead to a private party room; on L. double doors open into a hallway running at right angles—the hall is three feet wide and across it swinging doors lead into the cabaret proper.* NICK's *office is at the extreme L.*

There is a piano, poker machine, wall phone, and a number of red chairs.

BEFORE RISE—*The thump of the piano and the chorus girls singing can be heard. Also the voice of* NICK VERDIS *giving directions to the chorus girls, who are rehearsing a Charleston number.*

AT RISE—*Slow curtain. Five chorus girls are in line, singing and dancing one of the numbers from the revue. The rehearsal is under the direction of* NICK, *a middle-aged Greek, mercenary and hard.*

LIL, *the prima donna of the cabaret, at the piano. A heavy, middle-aged woman with a certain amount of good looks, which, however, have long since lost their bloom. She rolls her own and removes tight slippers from swollen feet whenever occasion permits.*

ROY LANE, *a typical song-and-dance man, with his coat off, sleeves rolled up, is leading the number C. The chorus girls,* ANN, RUBY, *and* ROY, *in front line, and* GRACE, PEARL, *and* MAZIE *behind.*

Some of the girls are in street clothes, others in practice clothes. GRACE, PEARL, *and* MAZIE *in rompers,* ANN *in red practice clothes,* RUBY *in thin dress.*

JOE, *waiter with an eccentric walk, enters party room with hatrack.*

NICK (*as they dance*). Hey, straighten your line—you—(*to* ANN, *who gets in line*)—straighten it up. Now listen, don't forget to smile, Pearl—some pep. (*Girls continue to dance in straightened line.* NICK *sings.*) Shake it, shake it. (*Shouts at first step of kangaroo step.*) No, no! Stop! (JOE *exits to hall with pinwheel. Light effect. They all stop guiltily.*) Pearl, watch what you're doing.

PEARL (*turns up*). Go fry an egg.

ROY (*crosses to* PEARL *and back*). You went into that step on the off-beat, girlie.

NICK (*to the dancers*). For heaven's sake, think what you're doing, will you? Now once again, the finish.

LIL. Where from?

(*Music No. 1.*)

ROY (*singing the cue music*). Ta da-ta-tadada-ta-ta.

(*They finish the dance and break up L. After break,* ROY *down R.,* ANN *down R.,* MAZIE *up C.,* RUBY *up C.,* PEARL *up R.C.,* NICK *watching coldly.*)

NICK (*as they stand waiting for a decision. Cross up C.*). No good.

Nothing like it. It ain't only ya dance with your feet, ya gotta smile —show the teets. (*He illustrates by showing his teeth. Cross L.*) Last night—oh—hoo. (PEARL *and* RUBY *are talking up C. Makes a noise of disgust.*) Rotten. Will you pay attention? (PEARL *looks guilty. Cross L. of* PEARL.) I say smile. Show the teets. Like this. (*Shows teeth.*)

ROY (*down R.*). I guess ya got it now, ain't ya, girls? (*Ad lib. He motions them to say yes and winks at them.*)

MAZIE. Sure, we have.

NICK (*up C., left of* RUBY). Last night a gentleman gets up in the middle of the first number. He says to me, "Outside your place it says: 'Paradise Club—Best Cabaret in New York'—that's what it *says*"— (*cross down L.*)—and then he walks out.

LIL. Wisecrackin' rounder.

RUBY. Had to be smart.

NICK (*cross L. of* RUBY). He was right. This show ain't bad, it's lousy. Say, look—I pay you—and I can't even look at it. The show's too tame. (PEARL *sits up R.,* ANN *armchair,* GRACE *up L.,* RUBY *up C.,* MAZIE *up C. Cross down L.*) I have to undress you. Live it up—— Gee, I don't know.

ROY. The show is good, what there is of it, boss, but you ought to get in more people.

NICK. Yeh?·

ROY (*crosses to* NICK). Sure. *Variety* says the Golden Slipper is doing a nifty biz, but they got fourteen weenies and six performers. Now, if you ask me——

NICK (MAZIE *cross to stairs.* NICK *brushes hair*). Well, I don't ask you —I don't ask nobody, y'understand?

ROY. Well, if you don't want good advice, that's your loss.

RUBY (*R.C.*). Anyhow, I should think you might save some of your raspberries for the one that caused the whole trouble. (*Ad lib.*)

PEARL. That's what I say.

GRACE *and* ANN. Yeah. That's what I say.

MAZIE. Hey, easy.

ROY (*to them*). Nix, nix.

RUBY (*step down*). How can we get it right if Miss Billie Moore don't take the trouble to come to rehearsals?

ROY (*under his breath. Pushes* RUBY L. *and crosses to* NICK, *who sits down L.*) Hey, don't be a kibitzer.

RUBY. Who the hell does she think she is—keep us waiting for her?

ROY. Well, I tell you, Mr. Verdis, I don't think she knew there was a rehearsal.

RUBY (*step R. of* ROY). She was standing right alongside me in the dressing room last night when you called it.

ROY. No, she had gone.

MAZIE. Certainly she had.

ANN. No, she heard it—she was in the room.

GRACE. Sure. I saw her.

MAZIE. You're crazy—I say she was gone.

(*Stop No. 1.*)

LIL. Oh, for God's sake—listen. You poor bunch of baby saps—if you spent half your time minding your own business instead of watching other people——

ROY. So says I.

LIL. When I was your age, before I got fat—(RUBY's *razz*)—yeh, fat—I kin say it myself—I was so busy tryin' to get somewhere, trying to get out of the chorus, I didn't know whether anybody was in the dressing room or not. If you're going to rehearse this, do it. If you ain't, tell me, 'cause I ain't supposed to sit here and pound this music box—I sing here and I am just doing this for Nick.

RUBY. You ain't so fat you can't talk —are you?

LIL (*starts to get up*). Say, listen, Owl. I'll pull all the sawdust out of you if you ain't nice. (*Movement and ad lib.*)

NICK (*pushes* RUBY *up C.*). Here, here, here! What is this? Lil is right —gals today ain't nothin' but a lot of jumpin' jacks. Come on—we'll do it again.

GRACE. Oh, please—I'm tired.

NICK (*cross down L.*) You're tired! My God, I got better girls in a dump once.

ROY. Aw, quit ridin' 'em, will ya, Mr. Verdis?

NICK (*cross to* ROY). Ah, shut your face. I run this place.

ROY. They been rehearsin' since eight-thirty tonight.

RUBY. Yeh, and don't forget we can't get this right till Billie gets here.

ANN. That's what I say.

PEARL. Why make us the goat?

GRACE. How am I gonna give a performance?

NICK. Quit it. I don't need no advice what to do with girls that come late.

ROY. Listen, Mr. Verdis, Billie's only been in this game a short while——

NICK. And she won't be in it a hell of a while longer. (JOE *enters from hall with drink which* NICK *takes.*) As soon as she comes in, she goes out. (LIL *plays "How Dry I Am."*) Joe, get Lil a drink.

(*The girls lounge about the room, smoking, using nail files, etc.* JOE *exits to hall.*)

ROY (*goes to* NICK). Gee, Mr. Verdis, it's not like Billie to fall down on the job. Why, that kid is one of the best lookers and neatest workers you got. (NICK *puts glass on table up L.*) You'll make one big mistake if you let her out. (*Cross to* NICK.) She's a mighty nifty little trick.

NICK (*step down*). Why all the talk? You don't work for her—you work for me.

ROY. God knows I know that.

NICK. Whadda ya mean?

ROY. Well—— (*Step R.*) Not to pin any bouquets on myself, but where could you get a guy to do what I'm doing for the coffee and cake money you're paying me?

RUBY. He's off again.

ROY. You see, it ain't only I can dance, but I got personality.

MAZIE. Huh!

ROY. Personality plus. (*Step down L.*)

MAZIE (*cross to* GRACE *up L. and sits*). Ain't he a darb?

GRACE. He hates himself.

NICK. Somethin' else ya got is a terrible swell head.

ROY. Who, me? Nothin' swell-headed about me, boss. I could-a been that way long ago, if I'd wanted to.

(*Music No. 2.*)

(KATIE *enters down hall; cross L. of* NICK.)

NICK. Aw, cut out the bellyachin' and quit any time you want.

KATIE. Mr. Verdis——

NICK. Don't bother me. Can't you see I'm busy?

RUBY. In conference.

NICK. What? (RUBY *looks around innocently to see who said it.* NICK *looks at* ANN. *To* KATIE.) Well, why don't you go?

KATIE. It's for Mr. Crandall.

NICK (*manner changes*). Oh—well —he ain't here yet. Who is it? Who wants him?

KATIE. Them two same gentlemen that was in last night.

NICK. All right. I'm coming out. Tell 'em I'm coming. (KATIE *exits to hall.*) Don't go to your dressing rooms till I come back—we ain't done rehearsing yet. (*Exit down hall.*)

ANN. Gee, it's about time.

GRACE. He's a slave driver.

MAZIE. Thank God!

PEARL. Don't he ever get tired?

ROY (*cross up C.*). Lay dead.

GRACE. Oh gee, I can't rehearse any more.

ANN (*cross L. of* GRACE). Well, you're gonna have to, whether you can or not, so don't start squawking about it.

RUBY. Ah, I think I'll quit this dump, anyhow. (MAZIE *rise.*)

PEARL (*rise*). I'm gonna buy everybody a drink.

ANN. Bighearted.

LIL. My God, it can talk.

PEARL. What?

LIL. That's the first time I heard you speak since you been working here—I always supposed you was a deaf-and-dumb girl up to now.

PEARL. I worked in night clubs before—it don't pay to talk too much.

ROY (*up C.*) Like to see anybody stop me talking.

MAZIE (*gets phone book, sits up L.*) So would I.

GRACE. Say, what about this drink?

PEARL. Does he let you have the waiter come in here?

ANN. Sure—Joe can go anywhere.

GRACE. Come on, girls. Let's go down the hall to the bar.

RUBY (*cross to machine.* PEARL *cross to hall*). Wait a minute—maybe Pearl doesn't have to pay for mine. Four to one—a dollar or nothing. (*Plays poker machine.* ANN *and* GRACE *watch.*) That's what I thought. (ANN, GRACE, RUBY, *and* PEARL *start out hall.*)

PEARL (*to* LIL *at hall.* ROY *gets shoes up L.*). Ain't you coming? (ROY *waves her aside.*)

LIL. They're bringing mine.

MAZIE (*sits up L.*). I gotta phone. (*The girls exeunt.*)

LIL (*turns up*). Where the hell is Joe with my drink? He must be down in the laundry making it. Say, listen, Personality. I'll tell you one thing: If your girl friend gets late to another rehearsal like this, she's gonna get a piece of my mind.

ROY. They must be some good reason why Billie ain't here. Listen—(*cross to armchair*)—Lil, don't put it into Nick's head to give her the air, will you? 'Cause she needs the do-ray-me pretty bad—she's got a mother and sister over in Trenton.

LIL. I never knew a jane in this business that didn't have.

ROY. On the level. I met 'em.

MAZIE. I room with her and I happen to know she's a good kid.

ROY. And believe me, it pays to be good.

MAZIE. Sure, but not much.

(*Stop No. 2.*)

LIL. So you met the family, eh?

ROY (*working on shoes*). Yeh, I went out there one Sunday. You see, I take a sort of brotherly interest in that kid.

LIL. Brotherly?

ROY. You heard me. Anyhow, I and her are fixing up a little vaudeville act together.

LIL. Say, sweetheart, why don't you get hip to yourself?

ROY. What do you mean?

LIL. Ain't you wise that she's given you the bum's rush? Why, that guy's got her so dizzy she don't know you're alive.

ROY. Who? Crandall? No—no—not at all. She'll get over that. She ain't used to going to such swell places, that's all. She's got more sense than to care a thing about Crandall himself personally—it's just the buggy ride. I seen it happen lots of times—young kids get taken out by a rich guy—everything swell; music, lights—they get baffled. You know what I mean, dazzled—and then suddenly they get wise to themselves that the whole works is a lot of boloney and they realize where the real guys in this world is at.

(MAZIE *crosses to phone.*)

LIL. Hoofing in cabarets.

ROY. Yeah. That's no kid, neither. Billie's ambitious to get ahead in this game. I guess she'd want to stick with somebody could learn her something, huh? (*Sits armchair.* MAZIE *puts coin in phone.*)

MAZIE. Pennslyvania 5000.

ROY. Her and me ain't long in this joint, anyhow. I'm going to make her something besides a chorus girl.

LIL. What's coming off?

ROY. As soon as I get Billie ready, we're all set for a lot of nice booking on the big time.

LIL (*puts out cigarette*). Soon as you get Billie ready? Are you—all ready? (MAZIE *gets chair.*)

ROY. Who—me? Well, that's a funny question—you're lookin' at me every night. You can see. I don't belong here.

MAZIE. Pennsylvania 5000. (*She sits.*)

(JOE *enters from hall with drink which* LIL *takes.*)

JOE. I couldn't find Pete and he had the keys—that's what kept me.

LIL. That's all right. The longer it stands, the better it is. It was only made this afternoon.

JOE (*exits*). Not this stuff. That's last week's.

MAZIE (*rise*). Operator, I want Pennsylvania 5—— What? I did give you my nickel. Wonder if we could get Pullman service with this phone. (*Placated. Sits back of chair.*) Pennsylvania 5000.

LIL (*offering glass*). Want a piece of this?

ROY. No—I can't drink and do what I do.

LIL (*drinking*). I see. You ain't never played any of the big time yourself, have you, Personality?

ROY. No—but then, I've been waiting—but you know as well as I do —it's just the breaks. Look at all the loafers in this man's town—getting by—— Getting by big. Have they got anything on me? I ask you, have they? This big Greek Nick is always —cracking about Jack Donahue— there ain't a thing that guy's doin' that I can't do—yeh—and mebbe I done some of those steps first—but Jack got the breaks and mine ain't here yet.

MAZIE. Pennsylvania 5000.

ROY. Listen, when I was out on the Gus Sun time, couple years ago— the manager in McKeesport comes back to my dressing room and tells me—that never did anybody do the stuff I was doing. (*Step L.*) And the road show of the Follies was only there the week before. But the act with Billie is a sure thing. And then you'll see the old names—with a big ad in *Variety*, telling 'em—look who's here. God, I dreamed about it years. (*Cross up C.*)

MAZIE (*gets off chair*). Pennsylvania Hotel? Listen, I want to speak to Mr. Manuel Tellazar——

LIL. My God, you can't find a guy with a name like that in a hotel—he's in Ellis Island.

(*Music No. 3.*)

MAZIE. Oh, for God's sake—— (*Hangs up.*)

(BILLIE *enters back door—cross C.*)

LIL. Here she is now.

MAZIE (*cross L.C.*). Where you been, kid?

ROY (*step down*). Gee whiz, Billie——

BILLIE. Is Mr. Verdis sore?

LIL. Oh no, nobody's sore—we're just curious.

ROY. He was kinda sore till I talked him out of it. He may say a little something, but don't pay no attention to him. Where the hell you been?

BILLIE. Mr. Crandall said he'll keep track of the time.

LIL. Hah!

ROY. Oh, him.

MAZIE (*cross to* BILLIE). You been out with Steve?

BILLIE. I didn't think there was anything wrong.

MAZIE. There ain't.

ROY (*points to flowers; steps up*). Did Crandall give you them dandylions?

MAZIE. Listen, Billie, if you was out with Steve, you got nothing to worry about, 'cause Nick won't dare say a word to you.

BILLIE. I didn't mean to be late, honest I didn't—but it was just so wonderful and the orchestra was playing special numbers that he asked 'em to play just for me—and I just seemed like I was in a dream or something.

LIL. And ain't it hell when you wake up?

BILLIE (MAZIE *cross L.*). I just don't know where the time went, that's all. Roy, here's some more coupons.

MAZIE. I wonder if that banana gave me a phony name.

BILLIE. When Mr. Crandall asked me to go to dinner with him, I told him I had a rehearsal and he promised to get me here.

ROY. Where's the big stiff?

BILLIE (*turns R.*). He's outside parking the car.

ROY (*stops her*). I guess maybe it's time I give you a piece of advice, Billie—lay off these sugar daddies—

I seen a lot of these big cabaret spenders—they're only after one thing. Don't let your head get turned by a lot of soft gab—bowing you out of a taxi like you was Texas Guinan or somebody, don't think that—— Say, where do you s'pose he got his money, anyhow?

BILLIE. In Florida real estate.

LIL. Listen, Personality—what difference does it make in this man's town where you get the sugar so long's you got it?

(RUBY, ANN, *and* GRACE *enter from up hall.*)

RUBY (*cross to property table up R.*). Oh, so you finally showed up, eh? Say, you got a nerve.

ANN. That's what I say.

GRACE. What'd you think we are?

(NICK *enters from down hall.*)

BILLIE. I'm awfully sorry.

(PEARL *enters from up hall.*)

NICK. Well—so—you did come. What you got to say for yourself—no, don't say it. Of all the damn nerve——

(STEVE *appears in back door.*)

STEVE (*cross R. of* BILLIE). Evening, Nick.

NICK. Well, look who's here! Good evening, Mr. Crandall. Glad to see you.

STEVE. Hello, girls.

GIRLS. Hello.

STEVE. Hello, Lil.

LIL. Hello.

STEVE. Hope I didn't keep Billie from rehearsal, Nick.

NICK. I was just gonna ask her where she was.

STEVE. Guess it didn't put you out much, did it?

NICK. No, no, it didn't make so much difference.

RUBY (*above piano. Bitterly*). I should say not.

NICK (*to* RUBY). What?

RUBY (*step L.*). I didn't say anything.

BILLIE (*to girls*). Well, gee, I'm awfully sorry.

NICK. You and me can talk about that later.

LIL. Well, are we going to rehearse some more or ain't we? I been sitting here for three hours and my feet hurt like hell.

NICK. Billie can rehearse separate with Jack Donahue here.

ROY (*up C.*). No trouble at all.

NICK (BILLIE *up R., PEARL to steps, rest close in*). So that's all for the rest of you.

RUBY. Thank God!

STEVE (*step C.*). Oh, by the way, I'm tossing a little party tonight, and I'd like to have you all stay.

MAZIE. That's us.

(*Stop No. 3.*)

ANN. Sure we will.

GRACE. You tell 'em.

RUBY. Yes, we'll come.

STEVE (BILLIE *cross below arm-chair*). How about it, Pearl?

PEARL (*at steps*). I don't think I can, Mr. Crandall.

STEVE (*step R.*). You old cross-patch, I got some Chicago friends just dying to meet you.

NICK. She'll be there.

PEARL. Sure, I'll be there.

STEVE (*step L.*). Fine. I can get the party room, can't I, Nick?

NICK. Anything you say, Mr. Crandall.

STEVE (*takes hat off, kisses* BILLIE'S *hand*). Bye, bye, little one, and thank you again for a very pleasant evening.

(ROY *makes derisive sound known as "the bird." Girls snicker.* STEVE *looks around, not quite sensing what happened.*)

NICK. Come on, now. Get made up, girls. (STEVE *cross L. to* NICK.) Dolph and Porky are outside waiting for you.

GRACE (*starting upstairs.* ANN *exits*). Gawd, I'm all in. I'm going to hit the hay tonight——

RUBY (*gets key, cross to stairs*). Well, if you was a rich man's darling, you wouldn't have to rehearse.

MAZIE (*at foot of stairs.* BILLIE *gets keys, gives* MAZIE *one*). The trouble with you is you're jealous 'cause he don't take you out no more.

RUBY (*pausing foot of stairs*). Say, where do you get off to jump me?

MAZIE. If you don't stop passing remarks about Billie, I'll jump you, all right—I'll knock your block off.

RUBY. You and who else?

LIL. Shut up. (*Pushes* RUBY *up.*) Why don't you two hire a hall? (LIL *and* RUBY *exeunt upstairs.* BILLIE *cross to* MAZIE.)

STEVE. Tell 'em I'll wait for 'em here. (NICK *exits down hall.*)

MAZIE. I'm going to bust everything God gave her some night—all but her teeth. I'll take them out and give them back to her dentist.

(MAZIE *and* BILLIE *exeunt upstairs.*)

ROY (*cross R. of Steve down L. with shoes under arm*). Have a nice ride this afternoon?

STEVE. Lovely. Sorry you weren't along.

(*Pause.*)

ROY. Say, tell me something, will you?

STEVE. Shoot.

ROY. I been knocking around cabarets, dance clubs, vaudeville, everything for a long time, and what I can't get through my head is this— why is it that all the guys like you are never satisfied with the hundreds of janes that will do anything you want—all the rummies and bums you can have, and by God—you'll quit 'em all to go after one girl that you know is good—why is that, huh?

STEVE. Do you know some that are good?

ROY. I know one that's good.

STEVE. Who is that?

ROY. That's Billie.

STEVE. You're sure she's good?

ROY. I'll give you odds she is.

STEVE. Where the hell do you get the idea that no one can speak to this Moore girl but you? Who are you? What can you do for her?

ROY (*pitifully*). I can do a lot for her, Mr. Crandall. I can put her in the Palace Theatre—inside six months.

STEVE. Doing what?

ROY. Doing a swell dancing act. Now there's my cards on the table, Mr. Crandall, that's what I'm going to do for her. We can't lose. She's got looks, a shape, and with my personality——

(*Music No. 4.*)

STEVE. Your personality. Oh, I see, that's what you're going to sell. Well, kid, that's a great idea—just an idea. By the way—(ROY *cross C.*)

—I guess I'll have you do a little clowning for a few minutes for my friends tonight. I'm not inviting you to remain on the party, understand, because there won't be dames enough to go around. I'll give you a ten-spot.

ROY. Sure I'll do some stuff I ain't done here, seeing how you want some laughs. (*Cross to stairs.*)

(NICK, DOLPH, *and* PORKY *enter down hall.*)

DOLPH (*down R.*). Hello, Steve.

STEVE. Hello, boys. Get Joe in here, Nick. Let's have a drink. (NICK *goes up hall.*)

DOLPH. Well, if it ain't old Fred Stone himself.

ROY (*stops on stairs*). That ain't no insult neither. For his own kind of stuff, he's a hundred-percenter, that guy. We can all learn something from him, believe me, even the best of us.

PORKY (*C.*). Yeh, but I like your stuff much better.

ROY (*cross to top of stairs*). That's all right. Just keep your eye on me. Pretty soon you'll see my name in lights. It's in the boy. I can't lose. (*Exit upstairs.*)

STEVE. Never leave any strychnine around. This guy is just dying to commit suicide. The poor nut.

DOLPH (*cross C.*). I got the bracelet, Steve.

STEVE. Good. I'll look at it later.

PORKY. Let's sell this load of stuff to Nick, and then——

STEVE (*warningly*). All right. (PORKY *stops abruptly.* NICK *enters up hall. Cross R.*) Say, Nick, where's all your chairs?

DOLPH (*gets armchair, places R.C.*). Here you are, Steve.

NICK. We moved them back for re-hearsing. (*Brings down a chair, places L.C.* PORKY *places his C.*) It's all your fault, too, keeping that gal out all day.

STEVE. Ain't sore, are you, baby?

NICK (STEVE *sits armchair*). A lot good it would do me. (*They all laugh.*)

PORKY (*sits C.* DOLPH *L. of* PORKY). Had a lucky break last night, Nick.

NICK (*sits*). Yeh, you fellas is always lucky.

PORKY. I'll say so.

DOLPH (*L. of* PORKY). Got hold of some great stuff.

NICK. Yeh?

DOLPH. You bet, fresh from the boat.

NICK. Didn't know you had any boat coming.

PORKY. We didn't.

DOLPH. But Scar Edwards did. (*They laugh.*)

NICK. This hijacking is no good.

DOLPH. But it's luck for you just the same, eh, kid?

NICK. I don't know. (JOE *enters with drinks which he passes around.*) Someday you get in trouble.

PORKY. Let Steve do the worrying about that.

DOLPH. Ah, here we are. (PORKY *holds nose and drinks.* NICK *lights cigar. Step R. of* NICK.) If Steve wasn't a bighearted guy, he'd never sell you this stuff at the same price.

NICK. Good, eh?

DOLPH. It's the real thing, Nick, no kid.

NICK (*puts glass on floor*). No, I got quite a lot on hand. (JOE *exits.*)

STEVE. You got nothin' but cut stuff. You better get in on this—White Horse in the clear—not white mule, neither. You can get twenty bucks a quart for it.

NICK. No, they drank bum stuff so long they don't know when it's good. Anyhow, if I take booze you hi-jacked off Scar Edwards, he'll come down here and raise hell.

STEVE (*puts glass on floor.* DOLPH *puts glass on poker machine*). I'll take care of Scar.

NICK. If you fight with his mob—then I'll get it in the neck. Of course they won't make no trouble if you keep below 125th Street.

STEVE. Roll over—trade is where you find it.

(*Stop No. 4.*)

DOLPH. You tell 'em.

STEVE. My connections are better than any man in this town.

DOLPH. You bet you.

STEVE. In that same we got people on our list with streets named after them.

PORKY. That's no lie either.

STEVE. You don't think I am going to let a greasy lot of Polish second-story men tell me where to head in, do you? I'm telling you that I want to clean up this order quick, and I think I got a right to count on you.

DOLPH. Sure. Where would you be today if it wasn't for Steve?

PORKY. Yeah—a waiter.

STEVE. Never mind that—where would *you* be, as far as that goes?

DOLPH. Ain't that what I'm sayin'?

STEVE. It ain't what you was—it's what you are. I cleaned spittoons in my time, fella, and I'm proud of it —that's when Porky tried to make a box fighter out of me. Eh, Porky?

PORKY. I always said you had stuff in you—and now I'm workin' for you.

STEVE. Say, boys, this business of peddling booze is the second largest industry in the United States right now. Give me a year more at it and we'll all retire.

NICK. Listen, Steve, I'm on your side.

STEVE. Well, good God! Would I be sitting here talking to you if I thought you wasn't?

NICK. But the Edwards gang might shoot things up.

STEVE. They ain't got a monopoly on it, have they?

PORKY. Oh, Nick—— (*Waves him laughingly away.*)

NICK. You're too quick with the gun, Steve. Sometime you might get in trouble. Anyhow, it's no good. A lot of murders—very bad for business. Scar might get me raided again.

STEVE. Listen, Nick—you never got poor taking my tips yet.

PORKY. Damn right he didn't.

STEVE. And I wouldn't advise you to change right now.

NICK. Oh no. (*Deprecating the idea vehemently.*)

STEVE. Listen, Nick, if my trade is going to grow, I got to crush a little competition now and then. I'm taking Scar's booze when I can lay my hands on it, and I'm taking his territory. It's just business, that's all. Are you with me or not? You gotta declare yourself in or out.

NICK. All right—send me what you want. I'll pay for it.

(JOE *enters hall, gets glasses, exits.*)

PORKY. Now you got sense.

DOLPH (*step D.*). Sure.

STEVE (*takes hat off*). Now, Nick, this party I'm giving is for the Chicago gang that hits town tonight. They're all itching to show what they can do, and if Edwards starts anything they'll be very handy—see.

NICK. Well, I'm counting on you.

STEVE. Sure, you can count on me, 'cause I got everything fixed. Now, Porky, you go to the hotel, and as soon as the gorillas land, get 'em dressed up and bring 'em around.

PORKY (*puts chair up L.*) Sure.

STEVE. I want all the girls to stay. Make it right, and tell Joe champagne, flowers, and all the rest of it.

DOLPH. Hot dog!

NICK. Anything you say, Steve.

STEVE. Now go down the cellar and check up your stuff and see if you can't make this order a record. Eh, old-timer?

NICK (*crosses to cabaret door*). Anything that's for you, I want to do it. Come on, Porky. (*Peek through doors.*) Not so good for Friday night. (PORKY *and* NICK *exeunt to hall.*)

DOLPH (*step R.*). That's the way to handle him, all right. He's got a nerve to argue after all you've done for him.

STEVE. Well, we'll spend a lot of money tonight, anyhow—make Nick feel good. Let's see the bracelet. (DOLPH *passes it and stands watching.*) Who owned it?

DOLPH. The fence wouldn't tell me. But he says it was lifted off one of the classiest mammas in this town.

STEVE. How much?

DOLPH. Five yards. He wanted a grand at first. I beat him down.

STEVE. All right—we'll keep it. It'll look nice on the kid—eh, Dolph?

DOLPH (*cross to poker machine*). You tell 'em. You certainly have fell for that baby, ain't you? I never seen you waste so much time on a jane, Steve. (*Plays machine.*)

STEVE (*coolly. Puts bracelet in silk handkerchief*). Don't see too much.

DOLPH (*apologetically*). You know me, boss.

STEVE. Got to handle each one different. Wouldn't want me to show my technique first thing, would you?

DOLPH. Not if you mean what I think you mean.

STEVE. This gal is a nice kid.

DOLPH. She won't be after she knows you long.

STEVE. That's all right, too. (*Plays the machine.*) But you gotta use your head.

DOLPH. Gee! This machine is crooked.

(SCAR *enters back door. Stops above piano.*)

STEVE. You see, she don't belong in this cage at all—consequently you got to treat her different.

DOLPH (*turning and seeing* SCAR). Well, for God's sake.

STEVE. Hello, sweetheart.

SCAR (*step down L. of piano*). How
are you? (DOLPH *closes cabaret
door.*) I thought this is where I'd
find you.

STEVE. What made you think that?

SCAR. Do you think Steve Crandall
is the only bird in town that's got
ways of findin' things?

STEVE. Well, I'll tell you, Scar, I
wouldn't advise you to do it often.

SCAR. No?

STEVE. No. In fact, I think you got
a hell of a nerve to come bustin' in
this way.

SCAR. Not much busting about it.

STEVE. Next time, knock—see.

SCAR. You don't always knock when
you come to visit me.

STEVE. I don't visit you, Scar.

SCAR. You visit in my neighborhood
sometimes, don't you, Steve?

STEVE. Do you own it?

SCAR. All depends on how you look
at it.

STEVE. I'm just telling you for your
own good, Scar. Come gumshoeing
in the back way of a strange place
—you know, somebody might take
you for a burglar.

SCAR (*steps down R.C.* DOLPH *steps
in*). I ain't scared of you guys. I
come down here to have a showdown—alone—with no gun. (*Pats
pocket to show he is unarmed.*) So
let's talk turkey.

STEVE. All right, Edwards, but listen
to what I tell you—next time you
better let us know when you're coming or you may wish you'd brought
your gun.

SCAR. You don't let me know when
you're coming.

STEVE. Meaning what?

·SCAR. I s'pose you don't know.

STEVE. You heard me ask you.

SCAR. Aw, you know god-damn well
what I mean—you been poaching
on me, Steve—you been cutting in
on my territory and it's got to stop.

DOLPH (*steps up above* STEVE). Will
you listen to that——

STEVE. You own everything above
125th Street, do you?

SCAR. We stocked that territory and
we got a right to it. My mob worked
for four years to get things the way
we got 'em—and *nobody*—get that
—nobody is goin' to cut in from
down here and spoil a nickel's
worth of it. You hijacked another
truckload—(STEVE *rises*)—last night.
Yes, and you been spillin' more jack
round for protection than we can
afford. We ain't never come down
here to horn in on your Broadway
trade, but you're ruinin' our game
up there and I'm here to tell you
that you can't get away with it.

STEVE. If you knew me a little better, you'd know that yelling wouldn't
get you much.

DOLPH. That's just what I was goin'
to say.

(*Bugle call and battle. Music No. 5.*)

SCAR. Peddle your papers, will you? (DOLPH *crosses up R. To* STEVE.) I'm talking to the boss now. I come here for a showdown with you guys, see.

STEVE. All right. I don't mind a little showdown myself once in a while. You're looking for trouble, is that it?

SCAR. No, I ain't lookin' for trouble. Nothin' like that. Not that my friends ain't capable of holding up their end, if it comes to that. But I say they's plenty of business for everybody and them what works up the trade should be the ones to get it.

STEVE. And supposing I say that I'll sell any damn place I can get away with it?

SCAR. Then I'm warning you that it's dangerous for you to do business in Harlem, 'cause from now on 125th Street is the dead line. Get me?

STEVE. Yeah?

SCAR. Yeah.

STEVE. Well, that's just dandy, Scar. Thanks for the tip-off. Now if you've spoke your piece you can take the air. I don't care about having a public fight with the likes of you, because everybody in this place don't know my business yet, and I don't care to have you stand around and broadcast it.

(*Band plays "Over There" with revolver shots for battle effect.*)

SCAR. There's a lot of things I can broadcast, if I have to.

DOLPH (*steps down R.*). You heard what the boss said, didn't you?

SCAR (*to* DOLPH). You too—the both of you—since you're looking for tips, I'll give you another one. (*To* STEVE.) I happen to be the guy who can clean up a few murder mysteries in this town. I suppose you don't know who knocked O'Connell off!

(*Shots off.*)

DOLPH. What are you talking about?

SCAR. And who dumped his body up in Harlem so my mob would get blamed for it.

STEVE. What the hell are you driving it?

SCAR. This is what I'm driving at.

DOLPH. Wait a minute.

SCAR (*to* DOLPH). I've waited long enough. (*To* STEVE.) Now get this —you guys stay down here in your own territory and you leave my trucks alone. See—cause I got the dope on you, Steve—you croaked O'Connell.

(*Shots off.*)

DOLPH. Look here—— (*Grabs* SCAR).

SCAR (*turns to* DOLPH). Take your hands off me or I'll bust your goddamn face. You guys can't put me out of business. (*Step R.*)

(SCAR *is facing* DOLPH. STEVE *is in back of* SCAR. STEVE *quickly pulls out his gun, presses it against* SCAR'S *back, and fires once.* SCAR *pitches forward.* DOLPH *catches him in his arms.* SCAR'S *hat falls off. Sound of shot smothered by noise of battle music.*)

DOLPH. My God, Steve, what have you done?

STEVE (*remaining cool*). Get hold of him under the arms. Quick—walk him out of here. (*Orchestra still playing battle number.* DOLPH *on one side of* SCAR *and* STEVE *on the other hold him up as they would a drunken man.*) Wait a minute. (*Gets* SCAR'S *hat and puts it on* SCAR'S *head.*)

(*As* STEVE *and* DOLPH *are walking the dead man toward back door under stairs,* ROY *and* BILLIE *come downstairs from dressing room.*)

ROY (*to* BILLIE). Come on. I'll run through the number with you—we got time. (BILLIE *in smock and* ROY *in tuxedo look over railing and see* STEVE *and* DOLPH *with* SCAR *between them.*) Who's the drunk?

STEVE (*as* DOLPH *helps him walk* SCAR *out back door*). Just one of the boys we're helping home.

(*Trumpets and shots off.*)

(SCAR, DOLPH, *and* STEVE *exit back door, closing it after them.*)

ROY (*cross to chair L.C.*). It's powerful stuff Nick dishes out.

PEARL (*appears at top of stairs in silk kimono*). Billie, was there a shot?

ROY (*laughs*). That's the band.

BILLIE. They're doing the battle number.

(*Orchestra just finishing battle number.*)

PEARL. I'm nervous as hell tonight. (*Exits to dressing room.*)

ROY (*to* BILLIE). Come on, now. Ready—let's do it together. One—two—three—— (*They dance.*)

(NICK *enters from hall and stands watching* BILLIE *and* ROY. ROY *cross up.*)

BILLIE (*seeing* NICK *watching them*). You didn't want to see me, did you, Mr. Verdis?

NICK (*unlocks door of office*). I did—but now I don't. All the same, you shouldn't miss that rehearsal.

BILLIE. I'm awfully sorry.

NICK. Don't let this happen some more.

BILLIE. I won't—thank you, Mr. Verdis.

NICK. See if you can dance better tonight.

(*Stop No. 5.*)

BILLIE. Yes sir.

ROY (*puts coat on chair L.C., no sleeves on shirt*). She will. I just came down to skate over it with her. (*He shows Charleston steps.*) One—two—three—four—— (NICK *exits to office.*)

BILLIE. Wasn't he nice to me, though?

ROY. Sure, he was afraid he'd lose me if he gave you the gate. The last step where you went into the side kick is where it got muddled last night, Billie. (*He hums the tune and they both dance as he counts —one—two—three—four.* BILLIE *gets mixed up on one of her kicks.*) No —no—— (*Cross L. and back.*) That's where you went wrong last night. Second time you do it with the left foot. Ready again—go—— (*They do the dance again—this time correctly.*) You can't wish a number on—you got to rehearse 'em. (*She does the dance alone while he hums and counts.*) Fine. That's it. You just keep picking up a little each day and improving and you'll be going fine before long—you'll be as good as I am soon. (*She demurs.*) Honest. Then we'll tie the merry old can to this saloon, eh, kid?

BILLIE. I s'pose so. (*Cross to piano.*)

ROY. What do you mean—I s'pose so?

BILLIE. Well, that's what I mean— only Mazie says not to count on it, that's all. She says—well, I s'pose she's just kiddin'—but she says it's a pipe dream.

ROY. Yeh, no wonder she never gets anywhere with that kind of a out- look, huh? (*She limbers up by put- ting her foot on piano and bending down.* ROY *takes her by back of the neck and helps her.*) That's right. Don't forget what I told you. The act is just as good as booked and you'll make a great partner, too. We'll soon be copping three hun- dred a week—one hundred for you and two hundred for me. You could send fifty or so home to your old lady every week instead of ten. (*Gets coat.*)

BILLIE (*starts for stairs*). I hope it comes true.

ROY (*puts coat on*). Come true? It's just as good as if I was handing you the money right now. (*She starts for stairway.*) Is that all you're going to do? Say, Billie, you're still strong for the act, ain't you?

BILLIE. Sure, why not?

ROY. Well, you been wasting quite a lot of time lately.

BILLIE. Oh, I don't know.

ROY. We used to get in early and have a special rehearsal. Now you been staying out to dinner with some guy or other.

BILLIE (*step L.*). Well, I don't mean to do what's not right. I'll rehearse —only a person ought not to miss wonderful opportunities. I mean, I ought not to miss a chance to go out with Mr. Crandall.

ROY. You ought not to miss a chance to go out with me neither.

BILLIE. Well, of course, you're dif- ferent.

ROY. I'll say I am. (*Cross L. to chair and back C. Imitates* STEVE.) Bye, bye, little one. Thank you for a very pleasant evening—huh! That's the parrot's cracker—that stuff. (*Cross down L.*)

BILLIE (*cross to armchair*). Mr. Crandall has been very nice to me —(ROY *grunts*)—well, he has, Roy.

And I don't like you making fun of him.

ROY. Well, I don't like him interfering with our act.

BILLIE. He isn't. I'll rehearse any time you say.

ROY. It ain't only a matter of rehearsing—you gotta keep your mind on your work. Don't be thinking about hotels and things like that. Be thinking about your partner.

BILLIE (sits arm of chair). Well, I do.

ROY (cross R. to BILLIE). Do you? Say, Billie, suppose we go out after, tie on the feed bag, and talk over the act, huh?

BILLIE. Tonight?

ROY. Oh, I remember, this is the night you go home to see your old lady, ain't it?

BILLIE. Well, this is the night I usually do.

ROY. Give her and your sister my love. By the way, Maloney Brothers are breaking in their new act over in Trenton, the last half. If you see 'em around, tell 'em I was asking for 'em.

BILLIE. Well, I don't know as I'll go.

ROY. (turn L.). Oh!

BILLIE. I thought maybe I ought to stay to Mr. Crandall's party.

ROY (step up). Can't they get soused without you?

BILLIE. Mr. Crandall asked me first one of all—he said it would be just flat and stale without me.

ROY (step down; laughs up sleeve). That would be tough. Pardon me while I laugh—ha-ha. I'm tellin' you to go home. Suppose anything ever happened like your old lady kicking the bucket?

BILLIE (walking away R.). You would!

ROY. Listen, Billie, tell me something straight, will you?

BILLIE. Sure.

ROY (step R.). Are you falling for this guy?

BILLIE. I never thought of such a thing.

ROY. Are you falling for anybody?

BILLIE. Mr. Crandall never thinks of me that way at all. He just considers me like a friend or just a kind of pal.

ROY. I suppose he's going to adopt you. (Cross to BILLIE.) You wait a couple of days and I'll give you the low-down on him. I'm gonna do a little detective work myself. Florida real estate—hah!

BILLIE. Now, Roy.

ROY. I'm thinking of your career, that's all.

BILLIE (flirting. At steps). Is that all? I thought you might perhaps be thinking about me.

ROY. I take a personal interest in you too. After all, we're going to be partners, ain't we?

BILLIE. Sure, on the stage.

ROY (BILLIE *and* ROY *start upstairs*). Sure. And I know what's best for you. Just think of your career. Here you got the opportunity to hook up with me in the act—we mustn't let nothing get in the way. You got talent, kid, when I bring it out. We're likely to be the sensation of vaudeville—everybody talking about us. Why, I can see our names in lights now—Roy Lane and Company. (*At top of stairs. Exit upstairs.*)

(*Music No. 6.*)

(STEVE *enters back door quietly— stands with back to door, looks around.* DOLPH *follows, very nervous, cross up* C. STEVE *closes the door—puts hat on piano, gets cigarette out of case, R. of* DOLPH.)

STEVE (*nodding head toward cabaret, lights cigarette*). You better go in there for a while.

DOLPH. What'll I do?

STEVE. Why, get yourself something to eat, kid.

DOLPH. You sure everything's all right.

STEVE (*smiles, faintly scornful*). Ain't got any appetite, huh? (*Jovially.*) You yellow bum, I didn't think a little thing like that would bother you.

DOLPH. Say, nothing bothers me if I know what's coming. (*Cross L.*) Gee, I never seen nothing like this before.

STEVE (*step down*). That's why it's good. I've often thought it would be a nice thing if Scar—was out of the way. And look at the way it broke for us. Ever see anything prettier in your life? Now if Scar's mob has got any sense, I'll hook up the two gangs and run this town right—all the protection in the world, plenty of profits for everybody.

(PORKY *enters from down hall.*)

PORKY (C.). Well, I got the Chicago boys out there.

DOLPH (*jumps at voice*). Oh, that you, Porky?

PORKY. All yelling for ringside seats, so they could see the dimples.

DOLPH. Well, I guess I'll have a drink.

(DOLPH *exits to hall.* PORKY *watches him, puzzled.*)

PORKY. What's the matter, Steve? (STEVE *blows out flame of lighter he has just lighted for his cigarette.*)

STEVE. Not a thing in the ·world, Porky.

PORKY. You act kind of——

STEVE. Kinda what?

PORKY. I don't know.

STEVE. Neither do I. (LIL *enters on stairs in silk kimono.*) I'll go ask Nick if he knows. (*Cross L.*)

PORKY (*looking at* LIL). Well, I guess I'll stay out here.

STEVE. Go to it. (*Starts out.*) Lil, have you met my friend, Mr. Thompson?

LIL (*at foot of stairs; cross to prop table up R.*). I don't know as I have. How are you?

PORKY. Pleasure. (*Nods.*)

STEVE. Great admirer of yours. (*Exit to office.*)

PORKY (*cross L. of* LIL). I've seen you before, Miss Rice.

(*Stop No. 6.*)

LIL (*buffer business*). That so?

PORKY. Yes, from out in the audience—out in front, I guess they calls it. You might have noticed me last night after your last song—I was applauding and——

LIL. They was two of you.

PORKY. I mean, you know, extra loud—and yelling, too—I yelled, Bravo! Bravo!

LIL. Was that what you yelled? If I'd known that, I'd-a done an encore.

PORKY. I hadn't been in to see Nick since you joined the troupe. Steve— that is, Mr. Crandall—my business associate—he's in here quite a lot— and I dropped in and I thought your stuff was extremely good.

LIL (*looks in drawer of prop table, gets atomizer*). Well, I certainly am flattered, Mr. Thompson. Who the hell's been monkeying with my props?

PORKY. Very interesting, the life back stage.

LIL. All depends on how you look at it. Of course it's nicer here than in a regular theater, 'cause here there's nobody can drop scenery on you—all we got to dodge is the stuff out front. (*Cross to steps with atomizer.*)

PORKY. Well, I'm going to be out in front looking at you.

LIL. Don't look at me—just listen to me. I guess when that squab scenery comes out, you won't pay much attention to the old-timers. (*On stairs.*)

PORKY (*cross to below piano*). Whadda you mean, old-timers? I'm an old-timer myself. Me. I'm allus strong for the guy that's been somewhere and seen something.

LIL. That takes me in—I've seen a lot.

PORKY. Here too.

(DOLPH *enters down hall, crosses to office door, and knocks for* STEVE.)

LIL. There's your boy friend. I'll take the elevator. (*On stairs.*)

PORKY. Well, Miss Rice, I'd like to see some more of you, sometime.

LIL. Stick around. (*Exits upstairs.* DOLPH *crosses to chair L.C.*)

PORKY (*cross C.*). Hey, listen, there's a gal I could fall for. No skinny-legged, slat-sided baby pigeons like you guys pick. Me, I like a dame that can sit in a Morris chair and fill it.

DOLPH (*L. of* PORKY). Say, Porky, you know Dan McCorn?

PORKY. I speak to him—I ain't never been arrested by him.

DOLPH. Cut the comedy. He's out here. Keep an eye on him for a second till I come back, will you?

PORKY (*impressed*). Sure. (*Exit down hall.*)

(STEVE *enters from office, closing door.*)

DOLPH. There's a bull out there.

STEVE (*at door*). What of it?

DOLPH. Maybe there's something up.

STEVE. Go home and go to bed.

DOLPH. There might be.

STEVE. Do you know him?

DOLPH. Sure. Dan McCorn.

STEVE (*taking a little interest*). Homicide Squad. What's he doing?

DOLPH. Sitting there reading a newspaper.

STEVE (*impressed*). That don't look so good.

(JOE *enters from hall and goes toward office.*)

STEVE (*stops him*). Joe.

JOE. Yes sir.

STEVE. Just run upstairs and ask Miss Moore—Billie Moore—to step down here.

JOE. Sure, Mr. Crandall. (*Exits upstairs.*)

STEVE (*cross C. below chair*). You better go out and cool off.

DOLPH (*step R.*). Don't think I'm shaky, but——

STEVE. Go on, now. Keep out of sight for a while.

(JOE *appears at head of stairs.*)

JOE. She ain't changed yet.

STEVE. Tell her it's important. (JOE *disappears.*)

DOLPH (*cross to* STEVE). Listen, you better fix the hoofer, too.

STEVE (*impatient*). Keep away from him or you will get me in trouble—I know how to handle this.

DOLPH. Listen, you still got that rod on you—let me get rid of it.

STEVE. Oh, for God's sake, don't have a panic. Who do you think I am, Johnnie the Dope? Should I have my pockets' sewed up or something because a bull's in the next room? (JOE *comes downstairs, followed by* BILLIE *in red costume, who pauses at the top of stairs. To* DOLPH.) Beat it. (DOLPH *goes out down hall.* JOE *goes up hall.*)

BILLIE. I haven't quite dressed yet. (*She comes down steps hooking dress.*)

STEVE. I won't keep you a minute. Just a little something I want to ask you. (*She crosses to him.*) Listen, cute fella, I want to ask you a favor.

BILLIE. Why, Mr. Crandall, of course.

STEVE. 'Tisn't so much. I want you to forget you saw Dolph and me helping that drunken fellow out of here a while ago.

BILLIE. What drunken fellow? Oh, I know—out there—(*indicates back door*)—I remember.

STEVE. Well, I want you to be a good kid and promise to forget to remember.

BILLIE. All right.

STEVE. You see, he's a big politician —if it got out it might cause a lot of trouble—just thought I'd warn you so that—you know—if you happened to talk you might get yourself in a bad jam.

BILLIE. Oh, I wouldn't say anything.

STEVE. I can count on you, then.

BILLIE (*back R.*). Positively.

STEVE. Oh, by the way, here's something else I just happened to think of. (*Takes out handkerchief with bracelet.*) Guess what?

BILLIE. Why, Mr. Crandall—how should I know?

STEVE. Birthday present for you.

BILLIE. But, Mr. Crandall, I had my birthday.

STEVE (*gives her bracelet, she puts it on*). Be smart and have two of them.

BILLIE. Oh, Steve—oh, I never *saw* anything—— Oh, Mr. Crandall— why, it's beautiful!

STEVE. I'm glad you like it.

BILLIE. But I couldn't take it.

STEVE. Now, listen, don't give me any of that silly talk—why, it's just a little trinket that doesn't amount to anything.

(*Buzzer sounds and lights flash.*)

BILLIE. Oh, my goodness, there's the opening.

(MAZIE *enters on stairs, with* BILLIE's *ruff, followed by* ROY *in tuxedo and girls in red costume, carrying ruffs, which they put on the prop table.*)

MAZIE. Hey, kid, you forgot part of your props.

BILLIE (*they come down. She crosses to prop table up R.*). Oh, did I? Thanks, Mazie.

ROY (*heard*). Come on, girls. There's the opening. Make it snappy, now.

ANN. Gimme a drag on that weed before you kill it.

RUBY (*to* GRACE). Say, Grace, you better remember what I told you about cutting in front of me in this number.

GRACE (*at L. prop table*). I will.

RUBY. See that you don't.

MAZIE. Aw, tie it outside.

RUBY. Who's talking to you?

ROY. Get your places. (*Pulls* BILLIE *away from* STEVE. NICK *enters from office.*) Every night a first night. They all paid for their seats. Heavy cover. We got to be good.

NICK. Now, girls, tonight some pep, and for God's sake, remember, smile at the men.

RUBY (*open doors*). Smile at 'em—it's all we can do to *keep from laughing* at 'em.

("*I Love My Baby*"—*Music No. 7. Loud.*)

(ROY *and girls exeunt to cabaret.* (1) RUBY, (2) MAZIE, (3) GRACE, (4) PEARL, (5) BILLIE, (6) ANN, (7) ROY. "*I Love My Baby*." *Charleston exit. Girls sing. Applause in cabaret.*)

NICK (*sits C.*). According to my bookkeeping, I owe myself money—I don't know.

STEVE. Well, I've heard that before. How much, Nick? (DAN MCCORN *enters from hall.*) Well, good old Dan McCorn. (NICK *rises.*)

DAN. Hello, boys.

NICK. What you want in here?

DAN. Oh, just dropped in.

STEVE. You're unusually sociable, ain't you?

DAN (*cross down L.*). Well, mebbe—I paid the rent today and two grocery bills—that always makes me feel good.

NICK (*sits*). Grocery bills shouldn't worry you if you would listen.

STEVE. A square dick, huh?

DAN (*cross L. of NICK*). Figure it out yourself. (JOE *comes from hall* with two drinks—sees MCCORN *and quickly exits.*) Well, Nick, how's business?

NICK. Can't complain.

DAN. How's your business, Steve?

(*Stop No. 7.*)

STEVE. So-so.

DAN. Extending your trade a little, ain't you?

STEVE. How do you mean?

DAN (*step up C.*). Kinda moving uptown.

STEVE. Where do you get that idea?

DAN (*cross R. of NICK*). Oh, I hear everybody's troubles.

NICK. And they got a lot of 'em, I bet you.

STEVE (*deliberately*). Say, Dan, you don't suppose for a minute——

DAN. That you can't peddle it where you please? No, I ain't sayin' that, only ain't it likely to cause trouble?

STEVE. Trouble?

DAN. That's a bad bunch up there. Some of 'em two-term men.

NICK. Some of them gorillas of Steve's ain't such a sweet bunch either.

DAN. That's what I say—that's why it looks like fireworks. (STEVE *glares at* NICK.)

NICK. Wouldn't you think, with all the trouble it is to get it, they wouldn't fight over who sells it?

STEVE. Well, some people ain't never satisfied.

DAN. By the way, seen Scar Edwards lately?

STEVE. Speaking to me?

DAN. Well, not exactly. Have you?

STEVE. About two weeks ago I saw him—at the races.

DAN. Spéaking to him?

STEVE. Sure—why not? I gave him a tip that paid twenty to one.

DAN. Yeah? You didn't see him, then, when he was here tonight?

NICK. Huh?

STEVE. Here? Who?

DAN. You didn't, Steve? Huh?

STEVE (long pause). Your arm is swelling, Dan. What did you put in it?

DAN. Scar Edwards was here, wasn't he?

STEVE. Listen, Dan. Scar Edwards and me are personal friends, but we don't do business together.

DAN. Maybe that's why he came.

STEVE. Don't be silly.

DAN. I'm not.

NICK. He wouldn't come to my place.

DAN. Well, he was in this neighborhood, anyway—anyway—that much I know, 'cause I saw him myself.

STEVE. You saw him? Where?

DAN. Under a blanket in a Westcott Express truck, just a block and a half from here—lying on his face with a slug in his back.

NICK. For God's sake!

STEVE. So they got him, eh? That's too bad—Scar wasn't a bad sort when you knew him.

DAN. I hope to tell you.

STEVE. Well, that's a tough break—I'm sorry to hear it.

DAN. Now that I don't sound so silly—who pulled that off?

STEVE. How the hell should I know?

DAN. Funny part of it all is, he didn't have a rod on him.

NICK. You find him?

DAN. No, the Westcott driver found him, when he came out of the lunch room. I got there shortly after.

STEVE. Can you imagine that driver.

DAN. Yeh, lucky thing he found him so soon, still warm when I got there.

STEVE. What time was it?

DAN. Must have been—say—twenty minutes or half-past ten.

STEVE. Well, I've been here all evening, haven't I, Nick?

DAN. I didn't ask you for an alibi, but since you mention it—let's have it—who was with you?

STEVE. Why, Porky Thompson and Nick here part of the time. Billie Moore—one of the girls—most anybody could tell you they all saw me.

(PORKY *comes down hall cross to above chair L.C.*)

PORKY (*to* DAN, *surprised*). Oh, you're here—I was looking at the show and—yeah—how are you?

DAN. Thompson, what time were you here with Steve and Nick tonight?

PORKY (*hesitatingly.* STEVE *motions with his hands five after ten*). I came in—about—five after nine—(STEVE *signals again*)—yes sir—five minutes after ten.

(STEVE *walks away with satisfied expression.*)

DAN. Why so positive?

STEVE. I happened to ask him for the correct time when he came in.

DAN. You didn't have a watch?

STEVE. Sure. But I wanted to see if I was right.

DAN. When he told you—then you knew you were right—is that it?

STEVE. Where do you get off to sweat me?

PORKY. What's the matter—what's up?

NICK. Someone killed Scar Edwards.

PORKY (*smiles*). Well, well——(*Sees* DAN's *look—changes mood.*) Gee, that's too bad.

(*Music No. 8. Loud.*)

DAN. You guys ain't thinking of goin' in mourning, are you?

(*Open doors.*)

(ROY *and girls come back in line—reverse order of exit, doing "falling off a log" step.* LIL *enters on stairs.*)

(*Stop No. 8.*)

ROY. Holy gee, but the orchestra put that number on the fritz—a bunch of plumbers—they're off the beat like a night watchman.

LIL. Why ain't you guys out there giving the kids a hand?

ROY (*at cabaret door*). All set, Lil. I'm going to announce you.

LIL (*cross to cabaret*). Anybody out there?

ROY. Not yet. They don't come in as a rule till just before my big number. (*Open doors. Exit to cabaret followed by* LIL. *Roll of drums.*) Miss Lillian Rice.

(*Music No. 9 off.*)

(*The girls change into the other costumes, take off red dresses, and put on ruffs.* NICK *crosses L. to* DAN.)

DAN (*crosses below chair L.C.*). Nice-looking bunch, Nick.

NICK. You got your eyes open, eh, Dan? Would you like to know one of 'em?

DAN. That redheaded one sort of appeals to me.

(NICK *crosses to* PEARL.)

STEVE. Don't introduce him to Billie. I'm taking no chances.

BILLIE (*hears her name*). What?

STEVE. Don't have anything to do with these handsome cops.

NICK (*brings* PEARL *down, between them*). Pearl, I want you to be nice to my old friend, Dan McCorn, here.

PEARL (*they shake*). How are you?

DAN. I was thinking I'd seen you somewhere before.

PEARL. That's an old one.

DAN. On the level. You used to be dancing at—the Golden Bowl, didn't you?

PEARL (*cross up L.—*NICK *turns up*). No sir, not me.

DAN (*shakes with* NICK. STEVE *and* PORKY *cross to* DAN *up L.*). Well, boys, I guess there's nothing else I can talk about just now—sorry to have took so much of your time.

STEVE (*shakes with* DAN. PORKY *business*). Hell, Dan, glad to give you all the time we got—only wish I could help you. I know you got your job same as I got mine.

NICK. Sure, it's best everybody get along.

DAN. Well, so long.

NICK (ANN *sits at piano*). So long, Dan.

STEVE. Come again, Dan.

DAN. Sure. (*Exits to cabaret.*)

STEVE. Porky, take a stroll out. (PORKY *follows* DAN.)

MAZIE (*seeing bracelet on* BILLIE *up R.*). Hey, will you look at that.

(ALL GIRLS *crowd around.*)

ANN (*rise,* BILLIE *and* GIRLS *come down R.*). Let's see. Where'd you get it?

RUBY. Where'd you s'pose she got it?

MAZIE. Oh gee, the Knickerbocker Ice Company. Gee, you got him *going strong.*

(*Doors open.*)

(*Stop No. 9.*)

ROY (*enters from cabaret*). Well, boss, they're eating it up out there. (*Ad lib.*)

RUBY (*up C.*). Well, hoofer, I guess you'll be looking for a new partner.

ROY (*cross to* BILLIE). What?

PEARL. Oh boy, when'd he give it to you?

GRACE. Some rocks!

ROY (*L. of* BILLIE). What you got there?

ANN. Steve gave it to her.

ROY. You ain't gonna keep it?

MAZIE. Certainly she is.

ROY. Give it back to him.

BILLIE. Now, Roy——

ROY. Listen, Billie, don't be a fool. You know what everybody'll be saying about you.

BILLIE. Don't tell me what to do!

ROY. I tell you, give it back to him.

BILLIE (NICK cross R. of BILLIE). Listen, General Pershing. (Buzzer sounds.)

ROY. You do what I say.

BILLIE. Mind your own business.

ROY. Please, Billie, I'm telling you something straight from the heart.

NICK (pushes BILLIE L.). Hey, hey, what you gonna do—have some heart talks instead of doing your number?

ROY. No sir, Mr. Verdis. I'm right here waiting to do my stuff. Nobody can say I don't give the customers one hundred per cent every per-

formance. The night my old man died, I went out at the Regent Theatre in Danbury and give as good a performance as I ever done in my life—(turns L.)—and even if a jane I'd put my hope and trust in was going to hell, I could still go out and give 'em my best. (Cross up.) Line up, kids. (They take their places.)

(PORKY enters from hall.)

PORKY. Dan McCorn is sittin' out there waitin'. What to hell's—(doors open)—the matter?

(Buzzer. "Valencia." Music No. 10 loud.)

ROY. There's the cue. Give it to 'em. Cut 'em deep and let 'em bleed. Here we go. Here we go. Let's mop up. (Exeunt to cabaret with girls, same order as first number, holding each other's hips. ROY puts on paper hat.)

(Ring after first three notes of vamp.)

(Medium—fast.)

CURTAIN

(Music No. 1 loud.)

(Slow Curtain.)

ACT TWO

Back door bolted. Hatrack with ROY's *checked outfit and blue coat up C. Also his white derby, brown derby, shirt front, etc., white hat, flower, and prop cigar on chair and table. Move chair down L. away from telephone. Girls' costumes as at end of Act One. Party C. room set.*

Half an hour later.

Music off in cabaret heard until doors L.C. are closed.

PORKY *sits picking his teeth—shakes his head pessimistically. He tosses a coin —is dissatisfied with the result.*

STEVE *enters from hall, closes doors to cabaret.*

(Stop No. 1.)

STEVE *(cross R.C.).* Good thing I went out there and calmed down them Chicago gorillas. If they kept on talking shop so loud, I'd lose my reputation as a butter-and-egg man from Florida.

PORKY. Dan McCorn still out there?

STEVE. He's talking to one of the pickups.

PORKY. Wish to God he'd go for good.

STEVE. I don't know—he seems to be having a good time. (*L. of chair R.C.*)

PORKY. I seen 'em act that way before. Believe me, I think he's getting all set to make a pinch.

STEVE. Cut that out. Don't be so jumpy. What makes you so jumpy every time somebody gets bumped off?

PORKY. Well, I was thinkin', maybe he's got a lot of bulls hanging around the block, for all we know. (*Cross to* STEVE. STEVE *lights a cigarette.*) Say, Steve, tell me on the square, you know who done it, don't you?

STEVE *(with emphasis).* I haven't the faintest idea.

PORKY. Well, you know it ain't healthy for you to hang around here after Scar's been killed, don't you?

STEVE. Are you talking to me?

PORKY. Sure thing I am.

STEVE (*stops him with look—then speaks casually*). A gang shooting is no novelty in this burg. The cops will be glad he's out of the deck.

PORKY. But, Steve, you done it, didn't you?

STEVE. I don't know a thing about it. Me and the deceased was great friends. We'll spare no expense in giving him a swell funeral. Flowers —all kinds—we'll make it the biggest event of the season—a great success —and tell the boys I want 'em all to turn out for it.

PORKY. Say, you talk like it was his wedding.

STEVE. Not much different, at that.

(*Knock on back door. Pause.* STEVE *gestures to* PORKY. PORKY, *fearful but obedient, peeks through shutters.*)

PORKY. It's Dolph. (*Opens door.* STEVE *crosses up* C. DOLPH *comes in and* PORKY *locks door behind him.* PORKY *R.,* DOLPH *C.,* STEVE *L.*) What's the matter?

STEVE. I thought I sent you out for air.

DOLPH (*pulls "News" and "Mirror" with headlines from under coat*). The morning papers just came out.

STEVE. Yeah?

DOLPH. A lot of stuff about Scar Edwards' bump-off.

PORKY (*takes paper*). What's it say?

STEVE (*takes paper*). Let's see.

PORKY (*reading*). "Gang leader murdered. Story on Page 4."

STEVE. Pictures and everything. Say, that's quick work, ain't it? Dan McCorn himself only knew it about two hours ago. Wonderful what they do nowadays. We should be very thankful for these modern inventions, boys—keeps us posted on the underworld.

DOLPH. Believe me, all that stuff ain't gonna be so good for somebody —all this talkin' and chewin' about it.

PORKY. "Harlem Gang Leader's Body Found in Roaring Forties. Old Gang Feud Likely to Break Out."

STEVE. Read to yourself.

DOLPH. It says the cops have got some hot tips.

STEVE. Sure they have. Here's the real dope, though. Now listen—this is good, see. (*Read.*) "It is learned from confidential sources that the police suspect one of Edwards' own gang who is said to have nursed a grudge against his leader. An arrest is expected within twenty-four hours."

DOLPH. What do you know about that?

STEVE (*fold paper*). Smart boys, them cops. Yes sir, Porky, you want to be very careful how you conduct yourself in the future, because them fellows don't let nothing get by.

DOLPH (*takes* STEVE's *paper; he and* PORKY *read*). It says they suspect one of Scar's own crowd, huh?

STEVE. That's what it says. Well, that's my theory. It's a good hunch, don't you think so, Dolph?

DOLPH (*back up*). Sure.

PORKY. But even if the cops don't bother us—they's something in that gang-war talk all right.

STEVE. What do I care? I got you two boys to protect me.

DOLPH. Listen, Steve, this ain't as sweet as it looks.

PORKY (*step L.*). Dolph is right.

STEVE. Oh, shut up. (*Quietly.*) I certainly get a lot of co-operation out of you two. For the love of Mike, pull yourselves together.

PORKY. We're together.

STEVE. Anybody'd think you was a couple of Staten Island hicks trying to find the subways.

DOLPH. Well, what's the matter? I was just tipping you what was going on.

PORKY. He was just thinking about your safety, Steve. (DOLPH *crosses to door under stairs, peeks out.*) Wish I knew who done it—I'm worried.

STEVE (*cross to* PORKY). Will you shut up, or will I crown you with a gun butt?

PORKY. I'm shut. (STEVE *strolls away L.*) But I'm worried, just the same. What if the Edwards' outfit bump me off?

DOLPH. Me too. (*Cross down.*)

STEVE (C.). Well, what of it? (PORKY *steps L.*) You only have to die once. You got nothing to worry about—I'll bury you right—I may get a special professional rate from Campbell's if they get the both of you. (*Laughs.*) Say, quit worryin'. I wish they *would* start something. We'll go up to Harlem in a couple fast cars and let these Chicago boys show off some of their machine-gun stuff.

DOLPH. No, Steve, on the dead, whyn't you go out of town till this blows over?

STEVE (*sits L.C.*). I got something here that interests me.

PORKY. Take her with you.

DOLPH. I hate to see this chorus amitshure playing you for a sucker. Why don't you take her for a ride and then stop off at Little Ed's roadhouse?

PORKY. Sure, we might all get in trouble if you stay here.

(*Music No. 2. Loud applause.*)

STEVE. Say, have you both lost all your sense? If I wanted to get myself accused of the murder of Scar Edwards, the surest way to do it would be to blow town. No, I'm staying here because *I am innocent.*

(*Doors open. Girls enter from cabaret, pick up their dresses, talking as they go.*)

(*Stop No. 2.*)

(KATIE *enters, gives* PEARL *note, who reads it R. of armchair.*)

STEVE. That's intermission. (PORKY *cross to* STEVE. *Rise.*) You go out now and keep the visitors from coming back here, and don't be rubbering at McCorn—act unconcerned.

PORKY. Sure.

STEVE (*gestures for him to go*). You too, Dolph.

PEARL. Tell him I'll come as soon as I've changed. (*This to* KATIE *as* PEARL *goes upstairs and* KATIE *exits hall L.C.*)

(BILLIE *cross to below piano, with* MAZIE, *who takes her dress.* PORKY *and* DOLPH *go to cabaret.* STEVE *cross to* BILLIE.)

STEVE. Billie, I've been waiting here for half an hour trying to get a word with you. In fact, ever since I was out in front looking at you and saw that something was missing. Didn't you like the bracelet?

BILLIE. Oh, of course I did—awfully —I thought it was lovely.

STEVE. Then why don't you wear it?

BILLIE. Well—I—Mr. Crandall, I'll explain about it a little later when we've got time.

STEVE. We've got time now. This is the intermission, isn't it?

BILLIE. Yes, but I—I mean——

STEVE (*takes her hand*). No, really, I want to know. I'm proud of you, little fella—so I thought it would be nice for you to wear my bracelet.

BILLIE. I did wear it for a while.

STEVE. If you don't like it, I'll take it back to Tiffany's and change it.

BILLIE. Oh, I'm just crazy about it.

STEVE. Then why'd you take it off?

BILLIE. Well, Ruby began making some dirty cracks about it—and then I got wise to what it really meant.

STEVE. What does it mean?

BILLIE. I guess you know.

STEVE. No, tell me. I just thought it was a good-looking bracelet and you were a good-looking kid, and the two of you looked awfully well together.

BILLIE. It's a slave bracelet, isn't it?

STEVE. I guess that's what it's called.

BILLIE. That's what they said—and they said if a rich man gives you one and you wear it, then that's a sign that you belong to him.

STEVE. I don't mind if they say that.

BILLIE (*step R.*). Well, I do.

STEVE. You like me, don't you? I know you like me—I can tell.

BILLIE. Yes.

STEVE (*takes her arms*). And I sure like you—and—I want to be able to do things for you and——

BILLIE. It isn't fair to you—that—I mean I can't take this bracelet off you because it wouldn't be fair.

STEVE. Don't you think I'd treat you right?

BILLIE. I s'pose I shouldn't have let you take me out at all, Mr. Crandall, because I knows it sounds silly, but I'm not that kind of a girl, that's all.

STEVE. Maybe that's why I like you.

BILLIE. I know there's nothing wonderful about being the way I am—I mean being virtuous, I s'pose you call it—I know lots of the best-hearted girls in the world that aren't, so it isn't that; but I mean it isn't fair for me to keep your bracelet because that's the way I am.

STEVE (*takes her hand*). Well, listen, baby, have I ever tried to pull any rough stuff?

BILLIE. No, you haven't, and that's what I always say——

STEVE. Then why haven't I got as much right to hang around you as some of these other yaps?

BILLIE. Well, you're married, of course, and——

STEVE. No, I'm not.

BILLIE. They said you was.

STEVE. No, I'm divorced—I'm all right—I'm divorced—twice. Just because you're here in the show, don't think I regard you in a light way—no indeed—I'm no fly-by-night—I'm a very sincere sort of person, baby, and I want you to understand how I feel about you. I'm crazy about you. Honest, no foolin'. (*Draws her to him a little.* ROY *enters on stairs, in frock coat, white spats.*) Don't listen to nobody but me, kiddie—'cause I'll treat you right.

ROY (*on steps*). Mazie wants to see you right away, Billie.

BILLIE. Oh, does she? All right—excuse me. (*She goes up.* ROY *comes down to platform.*)

STEVE. Say, listen, actor—(ROY *stops*)—did anyone ever hit you right on the nose? (*Pause.*)

ROY. Yeh, once—come to think of it —twice. Why?

STEVE. I was wondering if you'd like to have it happen again.

ROY. What did I ever do to you?

STEVE (*cross L.*). Nothing—you couldn't. I was a sucker to get sore. Forget it. (*He exits down hall.*)

(MAZIE *and* BILLIE *enter at top stairs.*)

MAZIE (*on stairs*). Hey, oilcan, what is this?

BILLIE. She never said she wanted me at all. You had no right to say that, Roy.

ROY (*cross C.*). What I done was for the best—I had to get you out of hearing so I could chase that twenty-five-cent guy out of here.

MAZIE (*cross downstairs to R.C.*). Listen to what's a yapping about twenty-five-cent guys.

ROY (*cross L. of chair R.C.*). He ain't a fit companion for Billie, and from now on I'm making it my business to see that he don't have nothing to do with her.

MAZIE. Where's your wings?

BILLIE (*cross downstairs to second step*). Well, Roy, it seems to me you're taking an awful lot for granted without consulting anybody.

MAZIE. And picked out an exciting job for himself, too.

ROY. In the first place, you ain't going to stay to his party tonight.

MAZIE. She certainly is.

ROY. It's no place for a nice girl like Billie.

MAZIE (*cross to* ROY). Oh, I see. But it's perfectly all right for me, though, eh?

ROY. Well, maybe you know how to handle gorillas—you know your goolash. She don't.

MAZIE. Billie'll be all right. Steve's a fine fellow and he's just out for some innocent fun.

ROY. Says you.

MAZIE. Says I.

ROY. This staying up all night, running wild, drinking poison, don't get you a thing. I'm no prude. I'm for light wines and beer—(MAZIE *step* R.)—but if a girl wants to get ahead in this racket, she shouldn't start out her career partying with roughnecks. In the second place—you're going to give back that bracelet.

MAZIE. Give it back—— Ha! Ha! I'll tell one. Why, she could get five hundred for it in hock. Listen— (*cross to* ROY)—small time, this little novice has got a great chance to grab off a millionaire if she works her points. Are you going to stand around and try to gum it?

ROY. I certainly am.

MAZIE. Then you ain't the gentleman I thought you was. (*Step R.*) He might marry her. Did you see that cracked ice? When Steve gives up like that, he's gone, hook, line, and sinker.

ROY. Marry!

MAZIE. I'm telling you—hand-embroidered nightgowns and everything.

BILLIE (*cross to R. of* MAZIE). Now, if you're all done discussing me, perhaps I could say a word myself.

ROY. Well, if there's any thought of his trying to get away with that marriage stuff, it's time for me to do something definite.

MAZIE (*cross R. to piano*). Sure it is—bow yourself out of the picture.

ROY. Is that the way you feel about it, Billie?

BILLIE. No.

ROY. All right. Then I'd like to speak to you about something very private. (*To* MAZIE.) Would you kindly leave us?

MAZIE. Go to it. I got to get in some work on a sandwich, anyhow. Don't believe a word he says, Billie. (*Exit upstairs.*)

BILLIE (*cross to chair R.C.*). Roy, I wish you wouldn't keep acting that way.

ROY. What way is that?

BILLIE. Just going around arguing with everybody and making trouble.

ROY. I'm going to save you from getting into a lot of trouble.

BILLIE. I didn't ask you to.

ROY. I know you didn't. And take it from me, I ain't achin' to play— (BILLIE *sits armchair*)—the hero in this picture myself, but there's nothing else to do. Now first I'm going to put a plain proposition to you. (*Cross to her.*) I guess you know pretty well that I'm very strong for you, but I ain't said nothing about matrimony on account of my old man has just recently died. But since this big fourflusher is talking about a wedding ring, I'll play my own ace. Listen, honey, how about getting hitched up?

BILLIE (*faintly*). Roy, I don't know.

ROY. It would be better for the act, wouldn't it?

BILLIE. I never thought much about it.

ROY. I s'pose I should of tipped you off how I felt before, but anyhow there it is in black and white.

BILLIE. Gee, I don't know what to say.

ROY. Take your time. I know it's kind of sudden. But I sort of thought you was wise to how I felt anyhow.

BILLIE. Well, I did think you liked me—I mean I hoped you liked me.

ROY. Well, now that you know how much I like you, what do you think about the idea?

BILLIE (*rise*). I don't know what to say.

ROY. I always thought, way down in our insides, we knew we was for each other. (*Step R.*) God knows I'm for you, Billie girl, so just say the word that you're for me and I won't let out no yells or nothing, but I sure would feel just like doing that little thing. (BILLIE *turns front.*) What do you say?

BILLIE. Well, Roy, of course I'd have to think a thing like this over and——

ROY. Nothing doing. Just as easy to say it now as some other time.

BILLIE. How can I say it, when I don't know for sure whether I'm in love with you or not?

ROY. Well, we certainly get on well together.

BILLIE. Oh, I know we do, just wonderful.

ROY. Well, when you see me coming to say hello to you in the morning, don't your heart never beat no faster?

BILLIE (*looking down*). Yes, it does.

ROY. Well, that's it. That's what they call love at first sight, kid. It's wonderful. I'm the same way.

BILLIE. But I don't know if we ought to talk about marrying when we're so poor.

ROY (*hurt, turns L.*). Oh—— (*Pause.*) You want a rich guy.

BILLIE. I didn't say that.

(*Ready coin return.*)

ROY (*contemptuously*). A gold digger.

BILLIE (*step R.*). I'm not. I'm not. But I don't want to be foolish and say something that I'll be sorry for afterwards. All I say is that I ought to think about a thing like this.

ROY. Aw, you want to think.

BILLIE. Yes.

ROY. All right, my duty's plain. Go on upstairs and think.

BILLIE. Well, don't talk to me that way or I never will marry you.

ROY (*dismissing her*). Sure. Talk it over with you next week. (*She bites her lip to keep back the tears and runs upstairs.* ROY *watches her until she's off, then goes to phone and drops a nickel in slot.*) Hello—I want long distance. (*Gets returned nickel.*) Long distance? I want to get Trenton, New Jersey. I want the Capitol Hotel there and I want to speak to one of the Maloney Brothers. No, not Baloney—Maloney—Maloney— M-a-l-o-n-e-y—Maloney. "M" as in matrimony. Yes, that's right. Maloney—there's two of them in the act and any one of them will do. Make it snappy, girlie, will you, 'cause this is a very important call. How much will this set me back? What? Gee—— Well, all right. This is Roy Lane. Circle 5440. (*During the latter part of his speech* BILLIE *enters from dressing room and comes downstairs hesitatingly.*) Now do me a favor, sister, and put this call through right quick, will you, please?

BILLIE. Roy—— (ROY *hangs up.*)

ROY. What do you want?

BILLIE (*on stairs*). I ought to explain.

(*Ready phone bell.*)

ROY (*cross to below piano*). Now, listen. I told you where I stood. All you got to do is say yes or no.

BILLIE. First you ought to give me a chance to explain.

ROY. Hey, you've got your make-up all streaked. You been crying.

(*Ready lights and buzzer.*)

BILLIE. Yes, I have.

ROY. One of the first things every artist should learn is, never cry during a performance.

BILLIE. I cried because of the way you talked to me.

ROY. Forget it, forget it. I'm wise now to how you feel—that's what I wanted to know. I got my duty, that's all.

BILLIE. But you don't know how I feel. You never gave me a chance——

ROY. I got the idea, and just now I'm expecting a phone call, so——

BILLIE. You make me feel terrible. I don't want a rich man, but I know that it's just awful to be poor.

ROY. Well, tomorrow——

BILLIE. All my life everybody I've known has been poor, and my mother always says, whatever you do, don't marry a poor fellow——

(*Phone bell.*)

ROY (*step R.*). Well, for God's sake, haven't I told you what they get on the big-time vaudeville and productions? (*Phone rings.*) All right. Now get out of here, willya? This is a business call. (*She exits upstairs. ROY at phone.*) Hello.—Yes, I'm trying to get Trenton. All right. (*Drops two quarters in slot.*) There you are, sister. Hello—hello—this one of the Maloney Brothers? Jack? Oh, Babe —Babe, this is Roy—— How's the act going? Yeah. Got you opening the show, eh? Well, don't worry, Babe. I'll take a peek at it—I'll probably make some suggestions that will fix it O.K. That's duck soup for me, you know. What? Oh, nothing's wrong with me. Everything's O.K. But listen, Babe——

(*Light; buzzer.*)

(*Lights flash. Buzzer sounds, warning for next number. RUBY, GRACE, and MAZIE, in schoolgirl costume, enter from dressing rooms, come downstairs talking.*)

ROY (*lowers voice*). Listen, can you hear me? I want you to do me a big favor—listen—— Have you got a pencil? (*Continues talking—speaking low.*)

RUBY. Sure, we'll have to stay for Steve's party. Who's yowling about it?

GRACE. Oh, Billie.

(*GRACE gets schoolbook props. PEARL appears stairs in pirate costume, sits armchair.*)

RUBY. That one. Guess one party won't spoil her.

MAZIE. How many did it take to spoil you?

RUBY. You ought to know—I saw you at the first.

(*GRACE gives MAZIE and RUBY books and slates.*)

ROY (*at phone—turns to them*). Hey, take it easy.

MAZIE. Steve's passed you up like a white chip, ain't he, dearie?

RUBY. Say, want me to haul off and knock you down?

MAZIE. If you do, I'll bounce up and *separate your ideas—(doors open)—* from *your habits!*

(*GRACE sees door open for cue and harshly pushes MAZIE into line.*)

GRACE. There's the cue. (*The three girls exit to cabaret, singing "Mississippi." Continue singing off.*)

ROY (*at phone*). You're a lifesaver—do as much for you sometime. So long. (*To PEARL.*) Want the phone?

PEARL. No, I gotta meet a john.

ROY. I got a john I'm going to meet pretty soon and bust him right square in the beak. (*Cross up L. Grabs hat and book and eyeglasses and listens for cue, but finds he has more time.*)

PEARL. Say, Roy.

ROY (*step down to her*). Yeah?

PEARL. You been extra sweet to me since I been around here, and let me tip you off to something. Don't monkey with the Crandall fellow. You might get hurt.

ROY. Him? I'll have him in Sing Sing before I get through. (*Cross to cabaret.*) You know what I think he really is? (*Cross to her.*)

PEARL. What?

ROY (*listens for cue*). A bootlegger!

PEARL. No? You don't say so.

ROY. *Wait and see.* (*Doors open. Exit to cabaret.*)

(PEARL, *finding herself alone, goes to phone, drops coin in slot.* DAN *enters from up hall.* PEARL *quickly hangs up receiver, turns from phone.*)

DAN. Hello.

PEARL. Oh!

DAN (*cross C.*). You got my note all right, did you?

PEARL. Sure.

DAN. Was you going to telephone?

PEARL. No, nothing important.

DAN. Positive?

PEARL. Didn't I tell you? (*Waits, then adds, impatient to be away from him.*) I gotta get ready for my number in a minute. (*Cross R.*)

DAN. I won't keep you long. (PEARL *stops, back towards* DAN. *Pause.*) Seen Scar Edwards lately?

PEARL (*stalling, turns*). What?

DAN (*ignoring her bluff*). Have you?

PEARL. What's the idea?

DAN. You know who I am?

PEARL. Sure, you're a cop.

DAN. Well, I know who you are, too. You're the girl I seen palling around with Scar Edwards when you were dancing up in the Golden Bowl.

PEARL (*turns away*). You never saw *me*.

DAN (*cross R. Turns her to face him*). Oh—yes—I—did—didn't I?

PEARL. Well, that's no crime, is it?

DAN. Not exactly, but why are you working down here?

PEARL (*dropping bravado*). You ain't going to give me away to Nick, are you?

DAN. Not a bit. What I'm asking you is for my own information, see. It don't go any further. Are you on the outs with Scar?

PEARL (*looking front*). No, and if it's all the same, would you mind calling him Jim?

DAN (*step R.* PEARL *turns R.*) Excuse me. (*Looks at her steadily.*) You're keeping tabs on this bunch for Scar?—I mean Jim. Is that right?

PEARL. He didn't want to put somebody down here he couldn't absolutely trust, for fear they'd double-cross him—a lot of dirty skunks. They wouldn't stop at nothing.

DAN. But Jim Edwards trusts you, eh?

PEARL. Sure—we're gonna be married as soon as he gets his final papers.

DAN (*turn L.*). That's too bad.

PEARL. What is? (*Pause.*) Has he done something you want him for?

DAN. No, I haven't a thing on him, lady.

PEARL. Well, tell me straight—has something happened? You act so kind of funny.

DAN. You gotta finish this show tonight? Sing and everything?

PEARL. Sure, I go on again.

DAN. Well, I won't take up any more of your time, then. I just wanted to know if you'd seen Edwards tonight.

PEARL. No, I ain't seen him since breakfast, but—I don't know why I shouldn't tell you—he told me he was coming down here tonight to have a showdown with Steve.

DAN. Oh, oh, he told you—— Well, I'll be going along about my business. Thanks, Mrs. Edwards.

PEARL (*pleased*). In three weeks.

(*Music No. 3.*)

DAN. You just keep this under your hat, won't you?

PEARL. Will I? (ROY *enters, followed by girls. Girls singing "Farmer in the Dell."*) If I want to get out of here with all my neck, I will.

(*Stop No. 3. Applause.*)

DAN. Pleased to—(*doors open*) —have met you. (*Strolls out cab-*aret arch, then turns to his L. and goes down hall. PEARL is puzzled—depressed—tries to shake off her fear —walks to stairs and exits. ROY grabs up a prop.*)

(*Music No. 4.*)

ROY. After this, a little more room, girls—(*doors open*)—when I make that side kick. (*Exits cabaret.*)

GRACE. All right.

RUBY (*cross upstairs*). In your hat— which one of you tarts got on my slipper, huh?

MAZIE (*on stairs*). These must be yours, dearie. They're a mile too big for me.

(*Girls go upstairs to dressing room. NICK and PORKY enter from hall.*)

PORKY (*up R.*) I can't look at that hoofer no longer—a different suit, but the same old dance.

(BILLIE *comes downstairs with telegraph blank and goes L.*)

NICK (*L.C.*). It's the best I can do for the money. (*To BILLIE.*) Where you going?

BILLIE (*up L.*). I'll be back in time for my number.

NICK. That ain't what I asked you.

BILLIE (*at cabaret door*). I want to give this telegram to the doorman to send my mother. If I'm going to stay to the party, I have to tell her. (NICK *gestures to go ahead. She exits up hall.*)

PORKY (*R.C.*). Is that the one that Steve is nuts about?

NICK (*shrugs, L. of armchair*). Yeh, I don't know why—but that's it. He says she got best-looking legs in New York——

(LIL *enters on stairs, coming down, at foot of steps below piano, in green dress, with fan and headdress.*)

PORKY. Legs—ain't all one size— some is lean—some is fat. (*Sees* LIL. NICK *sees* LIL *and he exits to office.*)

(*Ready buzzer.*)

LIL (*at foot of steps*). And how do you like 'em, Mr. Thompson?

PORKY (*surprised. Step R.*). Me? If a woman's got sense, I never see her legs.

LIL (*cross to piano, puts box on it*). Ain't you a comfort.

PORKY. Well, my friends say they liked your act very well.

LIL (*step down*). Yeah? Did you like it?

PORKY. Sure I did. Didn't you see me out there?

LIL. Yeah—but I was a little bit dis- couraged when I looked down and seen you was asleep.

PORKY. What? Oh, my God, lady— no. No, that's the way I get—you know—carried away—I shut my eyes when I'm terribly interested.

LIL (*cross R.C.*). I guess you didn't shut your eyes when the weenies was out there.

PORKY (*cross R. of* LIL). No. I wasn't interested. They wasn't nothing

worth listening to, so the least I could do was to look at 'em. But your singin' was—well, I can't ex- press it—it's like I says to a friend of mine sittin' next to me—I says, "I consider that she's got one of the finest voices of her sex," I says.

LIL. Well, I'm generally in key.

PORKY. Sure you are, and that is more than a lot of these opera singers can say, too. Listen, I want you to tell me how you do that singin' sometime—a long personal talk, if you know what I mean. You're stayin' to Steve's party to- night, ain't you?

LIL. I will—(*smiles*)—if you do.

PORKY. Sure.

LIL. Only don't ask me to sing, 'cause I don't know a single dirty song—that is, not dirty enough for that bunch.

PORKY. This ain't no singing party. That bunch all lost their voices ask- ing for bail.

(*Buzzer.*)

LIL (*starts out*). Well, there goes the whistle. I gotta step out now and hit a couple of high ones.

PORKY. I'm coming too.

LIL. Sit where I can see you. (*Doors open.*)

(ROY *enters from cabaret and goes to prop table.*)

(*Stop No. 4.*)

PORKY. Sure—I'll be right at your feet.

(LIL *exits to cabaret, followed by* PORKY *down hall.*)

(*Music No. 5.*)

(ROY *stands looking after them. Cross up* C. BILLIE *enters from hall* L. *He turns away from her, goes to hatrack table, and begins to undress.* BILLIE *starts upstairs, expecting him to speak, but he doesn't. She pauses.* ROY'S *back to audience. Takes off coat, collar, tie, and vest.*)

BILLIE. All I've got to say is, if you always treated me like you have tonight, you'd make a terrible husband.

ROY. Oh, that's all you got to say, huh?

BILLIE. I should think that would be enough.

ROY. Not for me. (*She starts up.*) Come here a minute!

BILLIE. If you have anything to say, you know where to find me.

ROY. I gotta make a quick change, you know that.

BILLIE (*comes to him*). What is it?

ROY. Was you out there taking a drink?

BILLIE. No.

ROY. I'm glad to hear that, anyways.

BILLIE. I was sending a telegram to my mother.

ROY. What?

BILLIE. You tried to boss me so much, I just thought I'd find out if I had a mind of my own. So I just went and telegraphed that I wouldn't be home tonight 'cause I'm going to the party.

ROY. Well, I'm sorry you done that. (*Takes off trousers and puts them over arm.*) Listen to me, kiddie, if it's just to spite me you're doing this, why, I'll eat mud.

BILLIE. It's not only that—it's because I have an obligation.

ROY (*cross to* BILLIE, *trousers over arm*). Listen, partner. I've been your pal, anyhow, and I got some right to talk to you. Who have you got the greatest obligation to in this world, huh—a big rounder like Steve Crandall, who's got no respect for pure womanhood, or your poor old gray-haired mother who is sitting at home alone waiting for you?

BILLIE. But she's not alone—my sister's with her.

ROY. Oh. (*In disgust he throws his trousers on chair.*)

BILLIE. If you don't think I got enough character to be decent at a party, you better look for somebody you got confidence in.

(PORKY *enters from down hall.*)

PORKY. Your shirttail's hanging out. (*Exit to office.*)

ROY (*paying no attention to him*). That ain't the life for you. (*Getting on trousers while he pleads earnestly.*) You don't want to be pegged with them bags, do you? They think they're wiser than Almighty God, the guy that wrote the book—but when they're hittin' the home stretch for Potter's Field, they'll be wiser still. For God's sake, think of all the plans we made, Billie. Don't be a dumbbell.

(*Ready buzzer.*)

BILLIE. I'm not.

ROY (*puts on collar and shirt front*). You're giving a good imitation of one.

BILLIE. I'd go, if for nothing else, just to show you good and proper that I don't belong to you.

ROY. If you did, I'd spank you.

(*Stop music No. 5.*)

BILLIE. Oh, you would—would you?

ROY. You bet I would—and if I catch you inhaling any of that poison, I'll spank you before the whole mob.

BILLIE. Then I *would* be finished with you.

ROY (*takes off silk hat, puts on coat*). I don't care if you never spoke to me again. I gotta do my duty by my partner—first the artist, that's me—and second, the human bein'. (*Buzzer.*) I done everything I could to appeal to your better instincts. I pulled every wire I knowed to keep you decent—and we ain't heard from all the precincts yet. (*Tries out comedy hat.*)

(*Start music No. 6.*)

ROY. I told you just what my feelings for you is. Nothing up the sleeve, so far as I'm concerned, so

if you want to be sore, I guess that's how it'll have to be, that's all. (*Doors open. Dances into cabaret in comic position, with trick cigar in mouth.*)

(PORKY *comes in from office—stops a second in door, talking into office.*)

PORKY. Sure you're right. Sure you are. (PORKY *sees* BILLIE, *who has started upstairs, shuts door, and crosses C.*) Say, little girl, did you see . . . ? (*The party doors C. open and* DAN *appears.*) Ah, yeah—well, never mind. I'll talk to you about it some other time. (DAN *cross* PORKY. BILLIE *looks over railing to see who it is, then exits.*) Well, hello, Dan. What you doin' in here? I thought you was out with one of the frails.

DAN (*coming down*). Well, I'm broad-minded. I go in for everything. Got a light?

PORKY (*lights match, lights* DAN'S *cigarette*). Sure. (PORKY'S *hand shakes.*)

DAN. What are you shaking about?

PORKY. I'm not shaking.

DAN (*laughs*). Sure you are. Look. (*He holds* PORKY'S *wrist.* PORKY'S *hand shakes.*)

PORKY. That's the way I always get.

DAN. When a cop's around?

(*Light in party room.*)

PORKY. No, when I'm in love.

(DOLPH *enters from hall. Stops, alarmed at seeing* PORKY *and* DAN *together, then hurries down hall.*)

DAN. Ever been accused of murder?

PORKY (*inarticulate with fear*). Me? Listen, Dan. Don't get me wrong —that stuff ain't in my line.

DAN. Oh no, no—I didn't mean that —I was thinking about a fella I knew—it's tough, that's all—it's tough.

PORKY. Oh, very tough.

DAN. The fella would-a been all right if he'd told what he knew in the first place—but he tried to hold out.

PORKY. Oh gee, what a mistake— always come clean, that's me—always come clean.

DAN. He was mixed up with kind of a sour crowd and——

PORKY. That's another thing. Bad company, that's something we all should avoid, Dan—eh? Ain't that right? (DAN *smokes.* PORKY *steps* L.) Listen, Dan . . . (STEVE *enters from down hall,* L. *of* DAN, *followed by* DOLPH, *who hovers in the background up* R.) I didn't have nothing to do with this thing—I——

(*Stop No. 6.*)

STEVE. What the hell you trying to do, Mac, crab my party?

DAN. No, I am waiting for someone who saw Scar Edwards when he was here.

STEVE. Well, we've all told you he wasn't here.

DAN. You might be mistaken.

STEVE. No one around here has got any reasons for holding out on you. If I saw him, I'd say so—why not?

DAN. You might forget.

STEVE (*cross* R.). Bushwah.

PORKY (*cross to* DAN). I think some of his own crowd done it that got jealous.

DAN. I figger different. You see, he didn't have a gun on him and he was shot in the back, which looks to me like he come peaceful to have a showdown—and just for that one reason he didn't carry his cannon.

PORKY. Well, I said once—and I'm willin' to repeat it—I didn't know him.

DAN (*sharply*). How do you know you didn't see him since you don't know him?

PORKY. Well—I—there wasn't anyone here when I came in.

DAN (*slowly*). No one?

STEVE. Well, I was—but I was in the office.

DAN (*without looking around*). Oh, and you were where, Dolph?

DOLPH (*step down,* R. *of armchair*). I was out riding with a couple of janes—and if you want me to bring 'em into court and tell about it, I'll be glad to oblige you—— Why? What's happened?

DAN. No matter what it is, you got your alibi all fixed now, eh?

DOLPH (*step* L.). What do you mean?

STEVE (*restraining him*). Dan don't mean a thing, Dolph. Treat him civil even if he is a dick.

DAN. When did you get here tonight, Dolph?

DOLPH. Early, then I left Steve here and went out for the ride.

DAN. You left Steve alone?

STEVE. No, Porky was here.

DAN (*to* DOLPH). When you left?

DOLPH. No, I was——

PORKY. I was just coming in when he was going out.

DAN (*slowly*). Oh, now I got it— Steve was here when Porky comes in, but Porky didn't see him 'cause Steve was in the office. (*To* PORKY.) Well, how did you know Steve was in the office if you didn't see him?

PORKY. Why——

STEVE (*quickly. Cross to* DAN). He could hear me talking—the door was open. Say, for God's sake, Dan, you been all over this once. Now listen, if you think any of us here had anything to do with it, 'why, go ahead and make the pinch, let's get some bail fixed and get it over with. But don't stand around here and make a coroner's inquest out of the place. I got a party on here tonight.

DAN. Well, now listen, sweetheart, why get excited? You know it's my business to ask questions, ain't it? I know you guys didn't have anything to do with it, but I got to make a report and I'm workin' at this from a couple of angles.

PORKY. Sure, Dan—that's right.

DAN. Trouble with you, Steve, is that you've had so much business with a lot of half-baked federal dicks, you ain't used to talking to just a plain old New York cop any more.

STEVE. Well, maybe you're right.

DAN. I ain't always—— (*Steps up— they turn up.*) I been wrong lots of times, but this case of Edwards interests me—terribly. You see whether a guy shoots square or not —according to the law—ain't always it—but no matter what he's done, to me, he should have a break, and somebody shot this guy in the back. (*Start out—hall L.C.*)

(BENNIE, *a thug in a dress suit, enters from hall L.C. as* DAN *turns slowly to exit.*)

BENNIE. Hey—fellows——

(*Ready buzzer.*)

(DAN *looks him over.*)

DAN. Well, Bennie, you're out in Chicago now, eh?

BENNIE (*above* PORKY). Huh? What's the idea?

(DAN *exits down hall.*)

DOLPH (*cross to doors L.C.*). The son of a gun——

BENNIE. Who's that guy? (*Cross to* STEVE.)

PORKY. Dan McCorn.

STEVE. What you doing back here, Bennie? We ain't ready for you yet.

(*Buzzer.*)

BENNIE. The boys want to be with the lingerie. (*To* STEVE.) The nerve of that big stiff looking at me that way! (GIRLS *start coming downstairs, dressed in pirate costumes, carrying flags.* GRACE *and* BILLIE *cross to piano, then* PEARL, *then* ANN, RUBY *and* MAZIE *enter steps.*) What's the idea, anyhow?

STEVE. Nothing that concerns you, Bennie.

RUBY (*off*). Ready, Pearl?

PEARL. Sure, I'm ready.

STEVE. A local nuisance by the name of Scar Edwards got bumped off tonight, that's all.

(PEARL *screams and faints on third step and rolls downstairs.*)

GRACE. What—what's the matter? My God.

MAZIE (*hurrying to see.* GIRLS *all crowd around and help her up*). Pearl.

STEVE. What happened?

(PEARL *starts up.*)

RUBY. What the hell happened?

ANN. What happened; what's the matter?

BILLIE. Pearl! But, dearie, you must of——

PEARL. I'm all right.

MAZIE. What is it, Pearl?

PEARL. I tell you I'm all right.

MAZIE. Gee Christmas, kid——

STEVE. What'd you do?

PEARL (*gets up*). I tripped on the stairs. That's all.

RUBY. I thought you fainted.

PEARL. Fainted? Fer what? Twisted my ankle, that's all.

(BILLIE *helps* PEARL.)

STEVE. Sure you're all right?

PEARL. Sure I am.

MAZIE. She'll be all right.

STEVE (*cross C. To* BENNIE). All right, Bennie. Bring your bunch back. Pretty near time, anyhow. Go ahead, Dolph. (*Exit* DOLPH *and* BENNIE *down hall.* GIRLS *cross to prop table.* PEARL *sits up L.*) Come on, girls. I want to buy you a drink. What say?

MAZIE. We can't now, Steve. We're on for this flash, you know.

STEVE. Well, I'll have a flock of them waiting for you as soon as you come off. All ready for a big night?

MAZIE. Try us.

STEVE. I am going to. Now here you are—girls—see these hundred-dollar certificates? Well, you each get one of them. (*They crowd around, except* PEARL.)

GIRLS. One for each?

GRACE. Atta boy.

PEARL. You tell 'em.

ANN. Me for you.

RUBY. Go to it.

STEVE. Wait a minute—this is the way we do it. I'll tear 'em in half and give each one of you your bit. Now if you're all good babies, when the party is over I'll tack the other half on. Fair? (*Business of tearing them and passing each girl half.* GIRLS *putting half of bills away.*)

MAZIE. Sure it's fair.

GRACE. Three cheers for Steve.

ANN. This sure looks like a good start.

RUBY. Everything is hotzy-totzy.

STEVE. Just be yourselves with these friends of mine and the sky is the limit. This party will be nobody's business. Here, Pearl, if you make good you get the other half.

PEARL (*rise*). Don't worry. I'll make good.

STEVE. Atta baby. Here, Billie. (*Doors open.* BILLIE *won't take hers.* STEVE *laughs.*) I'll keep it for you.

(ROY *enters from cabaret.*)

ROY. Come on, girls. Give 'em your best. This is a short one. I just got a flash at a guy standin' in the back that I thought was Al Jolson. (*Changes to blue coat, dagger and mustache, and felt hat.*)

GIRLS. Oh!

(*Music No. 7. Loud.*)

ROY. On your toes—alley oop. (*Doors open. They exit, with daggers in mouths.*)

PORKY (*cross to* STEVE). Did I say the right things?

STEVE (R. *of chairs*). What do you mean?

PORKY. To Dan McCorn.

STEVE. Sure, don't worry about him. Forget it.

PORKY. I do, but——

(JOE *opens doors up* C.)

STEVE (*calling to party room*). Joe, fix up some highballs and make mine a strong one. (BENNIE *and* DOLPH *come in from hall* L.C. *with Chicago mob.* STEVE *crosses to piano.* PORKY *does comedy lockstep.* BENNIE *kicks* PORKY *in fun.*) Come on in, boys. What do you think of it, huh?

MIKE. Class, all right.

(*Stop No. 7.*)

STEVE. Nothing like this in the Loop.

LARRY. This is get-together week in old Manhattan.

(*Music No. 8.*)

BENNIE. The place you got to go through to get to Chicago.

DOLPH. Wait till you're here awhile.

BENNIE. It looks like a big night.

LARRY. How long before we meet the dames?

STEVE. They'll be here in a minute. (*Cheers.*) Now remember, boys, no shoptalk tonight. Everybody here don't know our racket.

DOLPH. Steve, you better be the one to serve out the introductions.

PORKY. And don't let anyone sing the "Prisoner's Song" or we'll all be in tears. (*Laugh.*)

(*Doors open. Down R.* GIRLS *come in from cabaret.*)

DOLPH. Here they come. Come on, boys. Step up. Don't be bashful.

STEVE. Here we are. Now how about the drinks?

(*Applause. Stop music No. 8.*)

MAZIE. Not yet, Steve. This is the quick change for the finale.

RUBY (*putting on flags and taking spears out of basket*). The parade of the nations.

DOLPH. Step up, fellows. Don't be bashful. (GIRLS *up L.C.*)

(*The Chicago mob get an eyeful.* GIRLS *keep right on with their change. They now change to flag costume and take spears. Gang and* DOLPH *R.C.*)

STEVE (*up*). Sure. Let me present you fellas. Boys, this is Miss Billie Moore—and this is Mazie.

MAZIE. Just Mazie? I got another name.

STEVE. Excuse me—Miss Mazie Smyth.

MAZIE. *Smith*—ordinary Smith.

STEVE. Excuse me again—common, ordinary Smith.

MAZIE. Ordinary, but not common. (*All men laugh.*)

STEVE. And here's Ruby—Pearl— Grace. (*To* ANN.) What's your name, baby?

ANN (BENNIE *shakes hands with her. Weakly*). Ann. (*All laugh.*)

STEVE. Sure—Ann it be. Girls, my friends from Chicago.

RUBY. My Gawd, from way out there in Montana?

LARRY. Illinois.

PORKY. She's kiddin'.

(MIKE *cross to* GRACE, DUKE *to* BIL-LIE. NICK *enters from office.*)

STEVE. And here's the old chief himself, boys. This is Nick Verdis, a regular. He's paid so many fines, he owns stock in the White House. (GIRLS *bunch L.*)

LARRY. Glad to get in wid youse.

BENNIE (*shakes with* NICK; *cross to* BILLIE). Ya got some swell frills— yes sir.

DOLPH. I could use one right now.

LARRY (*shakes with* DOLPH). Split one with you.

DUKE. I heard of you, fellow.

NICK. Any friends of Steve's is K.O. with me. Come on in here, and we can set down. (GIRLS *line up flags.*)

BENNIE (*with* ANN). Sit down and leave all this lingerie? Am I crazy?

STEVE. They got to finish the show yet. We'll see 'em all afterwards.

MAZIE (*getting positive*). Well, I hope to tell you.

DOLPH. Me for you.

MAZIE. Be generous—your friends may like me.

(*Music No. 9.*)

(*Doors open. Parade starts.* RUBY, GRACE, PEARL, BILLIE, ANN, *and* MAZIE.)

ROY (*rushes in from cabaret, out of breath, changes to Uncle Sam blue coat and white hat with whiskers*). Ready to unravel the last one, kids?

STEVE (*in doorway*). And fellows, this is Roy Lane, better known as Personality.

ROY (*cross L.*) In person—not a moving picture.

STEVE. Possibly the greatest living song-and-dance artist who never played the Palace. (*Crowd laugh.*)

ROY. There's a lot of time, wisenheimer. I ain't worryin' about my future. (*He exits to cabaret.*)

NICK. Don't get him started now.

STEVE (*going in*). He's a character. I'm going to have him stay for a little while. He'll hand you a million laughs.

NICK. Come on, Chicagoes. (*Center doors open.*) I'll buy the first one.

(LIL *enters from cabaret.* NICK *leads way to party room.*)

LARRY. We ain't exactly what you call broke ourselves, you know. (*They all laugh and start drinking.*)

(*Warn light.*)

PORKY (*sees* LIL). Wait a minute, gang. Here's one you ain't met yet. This is Lil, the silver-toned songbird.

LIL (*goes to party room. Kidding*). Give the little girl a big hand. (*They applaud.*)

PORKY. Maybe we can get her to wobble something—— (*Business of passing drinks, etc.*)

DOLPH. How about "Silver Threads Amongst the Gold"?

BENNIE. Nix—nix——

PORKY. One of these guys knows you, Lil—says he heard you sing at Jim Tomasso's joint in Chicago seven years ago.

BENNIE (*yells*). I said seventeen years ago.

LIL. What do you mean? That was my mother.

(*The girls and* ROY, *after finishing finale, enter from cabaret, take off hats and flags. Everyone laughs.* DOLPH *hands* LIL *a drink. The Chicago mob kid* PORKY *and* STEVE *ad lib while drinking and eating off in party room C.*)

(*Applause. Music No. 9 stops.*)

MAZIE. Well, that's over.

GRACE. Now for the big feed.

RUBY. And my Gawd, how I could use a drink.

(ROY *comes in from cabaret—go toward stairs—with his quick-change costumes and props.*)

MAZIE. One of them guys is kinda good-lookin'.

RUBY. What great eyesight you got.

ANN (*dancing down R.*). She saw his pocketbook.

MAZIE. Oh, you're waking up too.

DOLPH (*steps out, cross R.*). Come on, girls—let's have fun. In here, everybody. (PEARL *sits L.C., overcome for the moment.*) Hey, young fellow, have a drink.

ROY (*at top of stairs*). No, thanks. I just had my hair cut. (*Exits.*)

(*Music, piano, in party room.*)

NICK (*suddenly*). What's the matter with you?

PEARL (*recovering herself—tough*). I'm waiting for someone to bring me a drink.

(BENNIE *and* LARRY *rush for* PEARL.)

LARRY. I saw you first, redhead. (*Carries her into C. room.*)

PORKY. This way, everybody. We'll get Lil to sing. (*Crowd make noise.*)

(*Dim lights.*)

NICK (*turns off most of light in room—party room is lighted brightly*).

Not so much noise. (*Going out L.C. as he closes the doors after him.* DOLPH *exits to party room.* STEVE *is on stage.* BENNIE *chases* BILLIE *from party room.*)

BENNIE. Come on. Jazz it up, blue eyes.

(BILLIE, *frightened, runs toward* STEVE. STEVE *pushes* BENNIE *back.*)

STEVE (*throws* BENNIE *back*). Bennie, cut it. Get to hell in there——

BILLIE. Oh, Steve!

(BENNIE *joins* ANN. *They go off into party room and* DOLPH *closes the doors.*)

(*Piano very soft.*)

STEVE (*down L.*). It's all right, Billie. Don't be scared. Everything's all right.

BILLIE. Oh, Steve, what'll I do?

STEVE (*holding her in his arms*). I won't let anybody bother you. (*He looks at her tenderly. Is suddenly overcome by his passion.*) I love you —kid. (*Holds her close to him.*) God, I love you. I'd do murder for you. (*He kisses her passionately. She tries to break.*)

BILLIE (*sits L.C.*). Steve, please don't.

STEVE. All right—I'm sorry. Listen —(*kneels*)—Billie, just to show you that I appreciate what a real nice girl you are, you don't need to stay to the party. You can go home if you'd be happier about it.

BILLIE. No, I ought to stay because I owe that much to you, and anyhow—(*looking upstairs*)—I said I'd stay and I'm going to.

STEVE. But you're such a little peach I want to make you happy—see. Listen, tomorrow night, after the show, let's get in the car—go for a ride and have a good talk. Will you? (BILLIE *nods. He puts arms around her.*) All right, that's a date. We'll stop at Ed's place and get a nice little supper, and I've got something important to tell you. (*He fondles her.*)

BILLIE. Make your hands behave, Steve.

STEVE (*rise*). All right. I'm just as meek as a lamb, see! Whatever you say.

(*The door opens from party room and* MAZIE *chases* RUBY *out. Others follow with great clamor.*)

MAZIE (*after* RUBY. MIKE *and* DOLPH *hold her back.* NICK *enters hall*). I'll make your shirt roll up your back like a window shade.

RUBY (*R.C. Drunk.* NICK *holds her as she kicks*). I'll step on you. I'll spit in your eye——

(*Stop music party room.*)

DOLPH. Cut it out. (*Separates them. Ad lib.*)

NICK. Hey, hey! Quiet! Quiet! Shut up that noise. (*Others separate them.*)

MAZIE. No phony blonde with store teeth can pull that on me and live.

NICK. Shut it. Shut it. Take 'em back.

STEVE (MIKE *drags* RUBY *off, dances with her. Cross R.*). All right. I'll handle this.

LIL (*to* PORKY). Andrew, dance for mama.

(*Music loud in party room.*)

(PORKY *dances Charleston in party room. They · dance into room—* MAZIE, DOLPH, ANN, BENNIE, LARRY, GRACE.)

STEVE. Inside. It's all right, Nick. I'll pay for the noise, too, so keep your shirt on.

GRACE. Where's my boy friend?

NICK (*to* STEVE). McCorn is sitting just outside there. (STEVE *motions quiet and herds them back.*)

STEVE. Listen, folks. The party is on the inside—nobody is to come out here without a permit from the Chief—that's me. (MAZIE *crosses to* BILLIE. ANN *jumps on* STEVE. *They exit, party room.*)

ANN. Hail the Chief. (*Cheer from party.*)

(JOE *enters from hall with more drinks.*)

JOE. I never seen such a thirsty gang. (*Exits party room.*)

STEVE. Excuse me a minute, Billie. (*He shuts doors to party room, leaving only the two girls and* NICK *outside.*)

(*Music soft party room.*)

NICK (*going down hall*). What do they think this is, Ike Bloom's?

MAZIE (*going to* BILLIE, *who sits armchair*). Ain't you having a good time?

BILLIE. I'm all right.

MAZIE. Come on, have some fun. You're only going to live once.

BILLIE (*cross R.C.—sits*). You go ahead—don't pay any attention to me.

MAZIE. Don't be afraid. Nothin'll happen to you. Listen, Billie, crack wise. It ain't so serious. Just kid 'em along, that's all, kid 'em along. It ain't so bad as it looks. I wouldn't give you a bum steer, kid, honest I wouldn't—but you don't always want to pay too much attention to what people say. Take me, for instance, you think I'm a pretty tough character. Sure I am, in a way—(KATIE *enters from hall*)—but I seldom give up—(*step up*)—very seldom.

KATIE. Say, Miss Moore, here's a telegram for you.

BILLIE (*taking it*). Me?

KATIE. The hostess told me to bring it in.

BILLIE. Thanks.

KATIE (MAZIE *cross to* BILLIE). 'S all right. (*Exit to cabaret.*)

BILLIE (*to* MAZIE). Gee whiz. I'm scared of telegrams. Ain't it crazy?

MAZIE. Once I got an offer of a job that way.

BILLIE. Yeah?

MAZIE. Sure. And it can't talk, so you gotta read it. (BILLIE *tears it open—reads—looks at* MAZIE, *terrified.*) What's the matter, kid? It ain't bad news? (BILLIE *nods, bites her lip, and begins to weep.*) What is it?

BILLIE (*passes her the wire, trying not to sob*). It's Mamma.

MAZIE (*reads. Steps L.*). "Mother very low—come at once. Mary."

BILLIE (*rises*). Oh, Mazie, and to think I'm acting like this and she's maybe dying.

MAZIE (*takes her around*). Now, Billie, maybe it ain't nothing at all. Now you get hold of yourself, Billie. (ROY *enters on stairs, in street clothes.*) Roy, Billie's got some bad news.

ROY. What is it? (*Foot of steps.*)

MAZIE. Her mother.

BILLIE (*going to him impulsively*). Oh, Roy—she must of had a stroke or something. She was all right last week—a telegram from Mary—maybe she's dying. Oh dear! Oh, how could I have acted this way!

MAZIE (*turns around* BILLIE). You didn't do anything, darling.

ROY (*takes her in his arms*). It's all right, kid. Everything's all right now. You're among friends. We'll take care of you. (*She weeps more uncontrollably.*) There. There.

MAZIE. Gee, I can't stand seein' her like that.

ROY. It'll come out all right. Take it from me. Everything's goin' to be all right, Billie.

BILLIE. I want to go home.

ROY. Of course you do, and I'm right here to take you, too, honey. The sooner the better, so stop your crying now. Just leave it to me. Come on, let's get out of here fast.

BILLIE. You're so good to me.

ROY. You bet I'm good to you. Why wouldn't I be? Ain't we pals through thick and thin? That's us, kid. Now you hurry and jump into your traps, honey, and we'll be on the train for Trenton in twenty-five minutes.

(*Swell music.*)

(STEVE *enters from party room. Inside they are singing and dancing.*)

MAZIE (*step L.*). Oh, Steve, Billie's got to go home—her mother's sick.

BILLIE (*to* STEVE). I'm awfully sorry. Mazie, have you got a handkerchief? (*Handkerchief business.* MAZIE *shakes her head, calling attention to her undress.* ROY *dries her eyes.*)

STEVE (*cross to* BILLIE). Well, that's tough luck, but we'll see what we can do. To hell with the party. I gotta get you home. Hurry up now. The car's out back. I'll have you out there in no time.

(KATIE *enters from down hall.*)

ROY. You don't need to bother, Mr. Crandall. Everything is already arranged, see?

KATIE. Here's another one, Miss Moore.

BILLIE. What? (STEVE *takes it and opens it.*)

KATIE. Almost like an opening night, or something. (*Exit to hall.*)

STEVE (*reads to himself, then grunts*). Huh.

BILLIE. What's it say? She's not——

STEVE (*reads*). "Your wire received. Stay to party and have good time. Mother." (*They all look at each other.*)

ROY. She must-a got better.

MAZIE. Ain't that peculiar?

BILLIE (*takes telegram*). I don't see.

ROY. Sometimes those things gets mixed.

MAZIE. I'll say they do.

STEVE. Well, everything's all right, anyhow, isn't it? See? All that worry for nothing. So dry up those tears and powder the little nose and join the bunch.

ROY. I think, as long as we planned to go, Billie, the best thing would be to—start out now and see for sure if everything's all right. I'll take you home. (STEVE *and* ROY *both pull* BILLIE.)

STEVE. Of course she ain't going home.

ROY. It seems to me it's the wisest thing to do.

STEVE (*pushes* BILLIE *L.*). No, she's going to stay. Come along, Billie. You come on too, Lane. Do your clowning.

ROY. I'm particular what kind of society I'm seen with——

STEVE. Wait a minute.

(NICK *enters hall, cross C.*)

ROY. I don't know as I will.

STEVE. What do you mean?

ROY. I mean Billie ought to get out of here—and as for me, I wouldn't stay and entertain your gang of goofers if you kissed my foot in Macy's window at high noon.

STEVE. Why, you dancing tramp!

ROY. I know all about you. It's guys like you give New York a bad name.

STEVE. You waxed-floor bum!

NICK. Steve, easy.

STEVE (*controlling himself*). Tell him to get.

NICK (*to* ROY, L. *of* MAZIE). Get!

MAZIE (*grabs* STEVE, *looking at telegram.* BILLIE L. *of* ROY). Say, I just thought of something. This last wire is an answer to Billie's. Now, the other one is an answer to something else. I'll bet my winter hat the boy scout framed it himself.

ROY. You're full of chestnuts.

STEVE. What?

NICK. Framed what?

MAZIE. He was telephoning long distance. Billie, you told me yourself.

ROY. Maloney Brothers, that's all.

(*Swell stop.*)

(*Ad-lib party enters,* DOLPH *and* RUBY *enter,* ANN *calls rest of party.* NICK *motions them quiet.*)

MAZIE. He got the Maloney Brothers to send the wire.

RUBY. What is it?

PEARL. What's going on?

GRACE. What's the riot?

ANN. They got drinks out here?

BILLIE. Roy, you didn't?

ROY. Certainly I didn't.

MAZIE. You certainly did.

STEVE. So you framed a wire on her? That's the kind of tricks you're up to, eh?

BILLIE. Roy, you wouldn't scare me like that.

ROY. Don't pay any attention to any of 'em. (*Wavering.*) Anything I done, I guess I'd know if I done it.

BILLIE (*seeing the truth in his eyes*). You did. (*Hurt.*) That's the dirtiest trick anybody could ever do. Oh, Roy, making me think—— (*Turns L.*)

ROY. Now, Billie, listen——

BILLIE. I don't want to listen—I don't want anything to do with you —you big sap. (*Cross L. Walks away. Movement of party into room C.*)

ROY (*half angry, almost ready to cry*). Suppose I did do it? I did it for you, didn't I? I know these kind of guys, and you can't be right if

you run with guys like Steve Crandall—he's just out to grab you—and
he don't care what means he uses.
I'm tellin' you he's just plain no
good, and I don't give a damn who
knows it! (ROY *shouts the last.*
STEVE *says something to* PORKY.)

(*Music loud.*)

(*Ad lib. Men cross to* ROY. NICK
holds them back. MAZIE *and* BILLIE
exit party room.)

DOLPH. Hey, wait a minute.

PORKY. What'll we do to him?

RUBY. What do you think of that?

MAZIE. You're going fine.

GRACE. Look who's here.

NICK (*getting between them*). No
more. Nobody. Get back in the
room. There's still peoples out there.

PORKY (*downstage, pushes girls into
party room*). Come on, girls. I want
to tell you a bedtime story. Come
on, now. All the girls in with me.
Come on, Billie. (*Exits with girls to
party room.*)

(*Stop music.*)

(JOE *enters, closes party-room doors,
and stands there.*)

STEVE. Now, you lousy little bum,
I got you where I want you. (*Hits
him and knocks him down.*)

ROY. Thanks. (*Getting up.*) Ain't
you a brave guy, though. That's all
right, but look out for this one.

(ROY *rushes at* STEVE. STEVE *pulls
his gun.*)

STEVE. And look out for this one!

DOLPH. Don't shoot. They'll hear
you.

JOE. Cheese it.

DOLPH. Look out, the dick!

(DOLPH *grabs his arms, struggles.*
STEVE *drops gun.* ROY *takes gun.*
MCCORN *enters hall. They all be-
come quiet.*)

DAN. What's the matter, boys?

STEVE. Little argument, that's all.

DAN. *Little* argument? (*Goes to
ROY.*) So little you pull this? (*Takes
gun from* ROY *before he knows it—
C. of group.*)

ROY. That ain't mine.

DAN. No? Whose is it, then?

STEVE. It's his, all right—he pulled
it on me just now.

ROY. You big liar!

NICK. Liar yourself, Lane. We all
saw you do it. (*Ad lib.*)

(NICK *closes cabaret doors.* JOE *at
party doors.*)

GANG. Yes, sure—we saw him.

DAN (*to* ROY). You got a permit to
carry this?

ROY. No, of course not.

DAN. Oh, you're the boy that——

ROY. I'm the chief performer here,
mister, Roy Lane.

DAN. Oh yes.

ROY. Singing and dancing specialties; this is just a filler-in.

DAN. Ever hear of the Sullivan Act?

ROY. What time is it playing?

DAN. This Sullivan Act is a law—it gives you plenty of time for carrying one of these.

LARRY. You said it. . . . (*The gang laughs.*)

ROY. I tell you it ain't mine.

DAN. No—then I'll keep it till I find out who owns it. You better come along with me now. (*Pulls* ROY *up, puts gun in his pocket.*)

DOLPH (*to* STEVE). He's just stallin' about the hoofer. He wants the gun.

STEVE. Shut up.

LARRY (*grabs* DAN). Who the hell is this guy, Steve?

STEVE. He's a dick.

BENNIE. The one I was telling you about. (*Ad lib. Surround* DAN.)

LARRY. Well, what the hell——

BENNIE. What's the idea hornin' in —what's the idea——

STEVE. Give him back his rod, Dan —I can settle my own arguments with him. (*Ad lib.*)

LARRY. I'll say we can.

DOLPH. You tell him.

BENNIE. You bet you can.

DAN. So these are your friends from Chicago?

STEVE (*pushes* BENNIE *aside*). Listen, Mac. What the hell are you tryin' to do? You been gumshoeing around here all night. For what? Now you come buttin' in here around my party. Understand, *mine*. . . . You ain't got a warrant to go tearing around here as you like. This room is private. Now I'll thank you to run along and call it a day—and give the kid back his cap pistol. I can settle my own arguments with him. (*DAN stands surrounded.*)

DAN. I said I'd keep the gun. (*Ad lib.*)

LARRY. You said what?

BENNIE. Not if Steve says to give it back—you won't. (*Ad lib.* DOLPH *closes in R.—rest close in.*)

DOLPH (*cross to* DAN). Yeah—you bet you won't.

LARRY. Not while we're here. (NICK *at chair L.C.*)

STEVE. Better give it up, Dan, while you're able, and take the ozone.

DAN (*sees he's in tight place, uses his head*). Well, Steve, you're a damn fine ungrateful guy for the finish—I'll say that. So I been gumshoeing around here all night, have I?

STEVE. I'll say you have.

DAN (*intense*). Shall I tell you why? You know Scar Edwards was bumped off tonight. (ROY *becomes interested.*) You know, the minute his mob heard it, they got together, didn't they? And where would they head for? Right here. And who would they be looking for? Why, for you. So I phoned over to the house and gets seven of the boys to lay around outside in case that mob of Scar's show up.

STEVE (*break*). You did? You did that, Dan?

DAN. Just to protect you. There's three of my men wasting good time out there in back now.

STEVE. Dan, I didn't know that.

DAN. Besides, maybe I saved you from getting shot up by this Indian. (*Indicates* ROY.) And you yelling your head off about me buttin' in.

STEVE. But you been hangin' around all night, asking questions and acting like you really thought I might have had something to do with Scar's bump-off.

DAN. Well, I gotta ask questions, Steve, but that don't say I suspect you.

ROY. Well, I suspect him.

NICK (*cross C.*). Oh, shut up!

ROY. And I got a good reason, too. (*Points to* DOLPH.) I saw this guy and Steve helping a fellow with a scar on his face—out the back door there—tonight.

DOLPH. Who, me?

STEVE (*starts for* ROY). You're a liar! (*The mob step forward toward* ROY).

(*Warn curtain.*)

DAN (*holds arm up—keeps* STEVE *from hitting* ROY). Wait! Wait a minute, Steve—take it easy. (*Pause* —*to* ROY.) What time did you see Steve with Scar?

ROY. Before the show—about ten o'clock.

STEVE. He's lying, Dan.

DOLPH. Sure he is.

DAN (*to* ROY). Would you know this guy with the scar if you saw him again?

ROY. Sure I would. I saw them, and Billie Moore saw them too. They were taking him out that door. I asked, "Who's the drunk?" and Steve said, "One of the boys we're helping home." If you don't believe me, ask Billie—she'd never tell nothing but the truth—ask her.

STEVE. Dan, this kid is sore at me— he's jealous—he made up that rotten lie to get me in bad.

DOLPH. Sure. Dan can see through him.

DAN. Verdis, call in the Moore girl.

(NICK *glances at* STEVE. STEVE *makes sign, so* NICK *goes up, opens door of party room.*)

DOLPH (*during above, speaks to* DAN *confidentially, R. of* DAN). Don't believe nothin' this hoofer says. I tell you, he's nuts.

DAN (*impressed*). Yeah?

NICK. Billie—hey, Billie—come— want to see you a minute.

DOLPH. Sure—ask anybody—he's an awful liar.

(BILLIE *comes in from party room.* JOE *exits C. Some of the girls come to doorway ad lib and drift down C.* BILLIE *below armchair.*)

BILLIE. What do you want me for?

GRACE. What's the matter?

MAZIE. Why ain't you guys paying us attention?

RUBY. Shut up. Look what's going on.

DAN (*to* BILLIE). Miss Moore—— (*They become quiet.*) Miss Moore, about ten o'clock tonight, before the show started, when you came down here to rehearse with the dancer here, did you see Steve and this gentleman—(*points to* DOLPH)— helping a drunken man out the back door?

BILLIE (*pauses—glances at* STEVE— *he stares at her*). Why——

ROY. Tell the truth, Billie.

DAN. Did you? (*She is trying to think.*) A man with a scar on his face?

BILLIE (*pause*). No. (STEVE *shrugs as though to say, "I told you."*)

DOLPH. I told you that kid was nuts.

DAN (*to girls*). Did any of you see Scar here tonight?

CIRLS. Nô. (PEARL *steps forward, starts to speak, then turns up to piano.*)

ANN (*starts down.* MAZIE *pulls her back*). Who? Somebody else coming?

NICK. I'm here all the time. I didn't see him.

STEVE. Now are you satisfied?

DAN. Yes.

MAZIE (*to* DAN). Say, copper, will you do me a favor? Take Personality with you before he tries to make any more trouble here. (*Exits with* BILLIE, *party room.*)

STEVE. Is that all you want, Dan?

DAN. That's all for now. (*Pulls* ROY *up R. by the arm.*) Come on, Lane. I'll tell you some more about the Sullivan Act.

ROY (*struggling*). You can't take me like this, Officer. Who's going to look after Billie? She don't know what kind he is—— (*Crowd start for party room.*)

DAN. Come on——

ROY. No. Wait a minute. For God's sake, give me a chance. She's only a kid. She don't know what she's up against. Mazie, tell him. This Crandall guy is out to grab her——

STEVE (*below chair R.C.*). Take him along.

ROY. I'll fix you! (*Breaks away, rushes at* STEVE. BENNIE *grabs him, then* DAN. PORKY *starts crowd back.*) I'll kill you if you touch her—I will, damn you. . . . (DAN *grabs* ROY, *drags him up.*) Lil—somebody—why don't you say something? I don't care what you do to me—— Oh God, Billie! (DAN *drags* ROY *off back door.*)

(*Music loud.*)

FAST CURTAIN

(Slow curtain on "Yanks Are Coming.")

(Music very loud. No. 1.)

ACT THREE

SCENE—*Same as Act One. Chair L.C. off.* DOLPH *enters down hall.*

(Music soft after curtain.)

DOLPH (JOE *is asleep on two chairs up C.).* What's the idea? (*Kicks* JOE'S *foot.*)

JOE. I'm resting.

(NICK *enters on stairs.*)

NICK. What's the matter?

DOLPH. I come in here and find this guy asleep.

JOE. The show didn't start yet.

NICK (*R.C.*). That's enough—Joe. (JOE *exits, muttering, hall.*)

DOLPH (*cross L. of* NICK). Now, listen, Nick, I gotta get out of here fast. Steve phoned me to drop in and tell you that the stuff will be here at three o'clock.

NICK. What's the rush? I wasn't expecting it tonight. Where's Steve, anyway?

DOLPH. I don't know where he is just now, Nick. He might be goin' out of town for a couple of days. He phoned me to tell you about the truck.

(Stop No. 1.)

NICK. Some trouble come up?

DOLPH. No, no, everything's all right.

NICK. Listen, Dolph, you shouldn't hold out on me. Now, tell me straight, what is it? If Steve is in trouble, then I should be the one to know as much as anybody.

DOLPH. Everything is all right, Nick —everything is perfectly all right.

NICK. That hoofer done some pretty wild talking last night and——

DOLPH. Hey, don't pay no attention to him. He was sore at Steve, that's all—even McCorn could see that.

NICK. Yeh, but he might tell a lot of lies. They got him in jail—and——

DOLPH. No, they ain't.

NICK. No?

DOLPH. They turned him loose. They give him the air a couple of hours ago.

NICK. Yeh?

DOLPH. Sure—they could see he didn't have no sense—he was just a false alarm, so they threw him out. (*Step L.*)

NICK. Then why don't he come back to work? I gotta give a show tonight. Half my actors didn't turn up.

DOLPH. I don't know anything about that. I just wanted to tell you about the truck, that's all. (RUBY *appears on stairs in kimono.*) Hello, baby. (*Starts for hall.*) Well, Nick—three bells it is, remember. So long. (*Exit down hall.*)

RUBY. Got any news yet? (*He looks up—shrugs shoulders.*) Well, what do'y say? (NICK *steps up. She comes down and sits armchair.*) Looks like we get a night off, then—huh?

NICK (*looks at watch*). Where the hell do you think they is?

RUBY. Sleeping it off.

(JOE *enters from up hall, leans against door, with a slip of paper.*)

JOE. Want to O.K. this?

NICK. Don't bother me—got to think someways to give some kind of a show tonight—Pearl not here, Billie not here, Lil not here, the hoofer not here—every other time he's around so much I don't want to see the sight of him—tonight when I need him, where is he? Go on, let me alone. (JOE *exits to hall again.*)

RUBY. Steve's party sure busted up the show for fair. That Chicago spendthrift I drew must've been born in Scotland. (ROY *enters back door in street clothes. He expects*

to *be ordered out—stands just inside the door.*) Here's God's little gift to the night clubs now. (NICK *looks at him, waiting for explanation.*)

NICK. Gee whiz, you're late.

ROY (*cross up C.*). Late for what?

NICK. For work.

ROY. Ease off, Greek, you didn't think I came back to this bucket of blood to work, did you?

NICK. Why not?

ROY. After what you slipped me last night?

NICK. I don't know what you're talking about.

ROY. You thought we parted good friends, did you?

NICK. Oh, a little thing like that—we forget—it's just like I says to Steve last night—I says, don't be mad at the hoofer, he can't help it —he's just a little nutty. Now here it is pretty near time for show to go on—I need you, you need me——

ROY. No, I don't need you—all I need is what dough I got coming and a chance to pick up my traps and get out of here. After the raw deal I got last night—me keep on working in this shooting gallery? (*Takes paper hat and silk hat.*)

NICK. Listen, Lane—you gotta work —just tonight——

ROY. What a chance.

NICK (*cross to* ROY). It ain't for me I ask you to stay—I can get another hoofer—but it's because of the peoples that come here especially to see you, see?

ROY. What?

NICK. Already big party come in—they ask me how long before that young fella comes on with that wonderful personality—they say——

ROY. Well, wait a minute—you say that—what kind of looking people?

NICK. I don't know who they was—very important people—I say, Mr. Lane, he's not in yet, but he's sure to come because he don't never disappoint his public.

ROY. I never disappointed my public yet.

NICK. That's what I said—I told 'em about that time in Danbury, Massachusetts. I told 'em what I always said, that you're a real artist and, that no matter what happens, I could always count on you, for the very best that's in you.

ROY. Listen, I'll go on tonight.

NICK. Good.

ROY. But I'm leaving at the end of the week—and the doorman can tell anybody that's interested where to find me. (*Puts props back.*)

RUBY. Mills Hotel.

NICK. I knew I could count on you, Lane. Now I'll go out in front and see what I can do. Use the big brain figgerin' how to give a show—— Lil not here—nor Billie—nor Pearl—I'll be back. (*Exit down hall.*)

ROY (*hat on rack. Step L.*) They ain't showed up yet, huh?

RUBY. That's how I heard it.

ROY. I wouldn't go back in this dump, neither, if I didn't think it was my duty. (RUBY *gives him the bird.*) My big chance will come; I figure I might as well be eating while I'm waiting for it. Billie's usually on time—wonder what's keeping her tonight? (*Step L.*)

RUBY. The same guy that kept her last night.

ROY. Now I ask you, is that nice?

RUBY. You going to worry about her after the royal raspberry she slipped you? She's got you goin' around like a top.

ROY. I'm thinkin' about the good of the show, that's all. Didn't Nick call up the agents to get a gal to shout in Lil's place?

RUBY. Sure, he called 'em, but the agents are no damn good when you want 'em.

ROY. It's me that knows that, sister.

RUBY. Well, how was the dear old jail?

ROY. That's all right.

RUBY. Come on, spill it, how'd your act go in the night court?

ROY. Aw, that don't concern you.

RUBY. A mysterious guy. Yeah, if Nick hadn't got you off——

ROY. The big baloney never had nothing to do with it. I got myself off.

RUBY. What'd you say to 'em?

ROY. I told 'em a few things.

RUBY. Didn't you even get a fine?

ROY. No, I wouldn't stand for it. I give 'em a little spiel.

RUBY. I bet you made quite an impression.

ROY. I told 'em who I was—there was a guy there had seen me play on the Poli time, and of course that was in my favor. I gave 'em a rough idea what I thought of Steve, too. (*Steps R.*) And that cop that was here—I and him got to be very good friends. He was wise from the start that that wasn't my gun—just a stall to get me out.

RUBY (*drawing him out.*) Go on.

ROY. Sure. And it was a stall about them other bulls laying outside, too. He's a smart cop, that fella; he knows his oats. (*Cross C.*)

RUBY. And then they just turned you loose?

ROY. Well, listen—— (*Cross R. of RUBY.*) McCorn told me to keep this under my hat, but I guess it wouldn't get no further with an old-time trouper like you.

RUBY. No.

ROY. Listen, they took me to the morgue to identify the other guy.

RUBY. Yeah?

ROY. Gee, the way these gangsters pop each other off. Well, I guess it's nothing but a lucky break kept me from occupying the slab right next to him.

(BILLIE *enters back door. She and* ROY *face each other; he crosses up.* NICK *enters down hall.*)

BILLIE. Ruby.

RUBY. So you decided to come.

NICK (*cross to* BILLIE). All right—I won't say anything—go on—get made up.

BILLIE (*L. of chair*). I'm terribly sorry—the Trenton train had a breakdown.

RUBY. Hah! (*To stairs.*) She wants to have us believe she's been out to see her mother. God, if ever I seen a professional virgin, she's it. (BILLIE *step R.*)

NICK. Don't start nothing now—things is worse 'nough.

RUBY (*on stairs*). All right, sweetheart, but Faith, Hope, and Charity is waiting here for news—do we give a show tonight or don't we?

NICK. Sure we give a show—we gotta.

RUBY. All right, I'll go up and tell the other inmates. (*To* BILLIE.) Come on, Purity. (NICK *exits office.* RUBY *exits upstairs.* ROY *crosses to stairs.*)

BILLIE. Roy. (*He stops. She crosses to him.*) Roy, I'm terribly glad to find out you didn't get hurt or anything.

ROY (*back to* BILLIE). Sure. See you again sometime.

BILLIE. I don't think that's a very nice way to act—all I says was I'm glad you didn't get hurt.

ROY. It's no thanks to you I didn't.

BILLIE. Everything would have been all right if you hadn't tried to boss me.

ROY (turn L.). Well, I'm done trying to boss you now. Course I feel kinda sorry on account of the act.

BILLIE. What do you mean?

ROY. On account of its being busted up, I mean.

BILLIE. Is it busted?

ROY. Sure.

BILLIE. Oh.

ROY. Of course, when a fella's worked like I have to get together the best dancing act in the business, and gets all ready for bookings, he hates to see it go blooey just because a big stiff that's rancid with coin comes along and cops his partner.

BILLIE. What right have you got to say that he's copped me?

ROY. Last night you lied to save him and against me.

BILLIE. Yes, but I didn't know—you got no right talking that way—all the girls around here are always saying I'm too good—(crosses C.)—and you're saying I'm too bad. I hate this damn place.

ROY. And another thing—last night you called me a sap in the presence of several witnesses.

BILLIE (almost in tears). Oh, shut up. That's what you are.

NICK (enter from office). All right—all right—get made up.

(BILLIE starts upstairs, so agitated that she scarcely senses NICK's presence. She pauses and leans over the banister.)

BILLIE (vehemently). And I'll tell you something else, and it's most likely the last thing I'll ever tell you —the reason I went to my mother's was to ask her, if a girl was terribly in love with a person, so much it was like regular love at first sight, was it all right to marry 'em even if they was poor—that's what. Now, how'd you like to go to hell? (Exits upstairs.)

(Music No. 2.)

ROY. (ROY looks after her, then at NICK. Step L.). They pick up that language quick around this honky-tonk.

NICK. She's right. Don't be interfering with her.

ROY. Well, they's a lot of personal things mixed up here you don't understand. (Sits arm of chair.) But I'll tip you off to one thing— my next partner is going to be a man.

NICK. Fine. Now, I want to tell you about something. (Sits down L.) If Steve comes, don't start yowling at him.

ROY (gives NICK a look of mild surprise). I wouldn't.

NICK. You done it last night.

ROY (*below chair C.*). I got wise to a lot of things since then—I didn't know those guys would shoot you right out in public.

NICK. Well, don't argue with him.

ROY. I ain't going to. I don't carry any gatlin' gun. The Sullivan Act is O.K. with me—and for one thing—(*crosses L. to* NICK)—I wouldn't think it was fair to you for me to get in any argument with him, 'cause if he put a hole in me, your show'd be out in the alley. Of course, if Mr. Crandall cares to meet me over in the Y.M.C.A. gym, I'd just as leave tell him what I think about him.

NICK. He's all right, Lane. Good customer. Look—last night the party alone cost him two thousand dollars, you understand?

ROY. I wasn't saying nothing to Steve anyhow—I was showing Billie the truth about him. He had a fall out of every girl in the place. Why couldn't he leave her alone?

NICK. 'Cause all men like what's hard to get.

ROY. She had the chance of a lifetime if she'd only have stuck. It's pretty tough after I had a swell double act framed. (*Crosses C.*) Oh well—nobody never got their name in lights by getting discouraged. (*Step R., stops.*) Say, what I want to ask you, boss, what we gonna do for a solo in Lil's spot tonight?

NICK (*crosses to* ROY). That's what I want to ask you. You sing it.

ROY. I might fake up a mammy song at that.

NICK. Sure. (*Slaps his back.*) You'll be the whole show tonight.

ROY. I am every night. If you don't think so, you're crazy. On the level, boss, I don't know what you'd do without me. (*Step up C.*)

(PORKY *and* LIL *enter back door, drunk and dignified.*)

LIL (*silly.* PORKY *closes back door*). Hello.

PORKY (*closes door; comes down to armchair*). I told you this was the place.

ROY. We been looking for you, Lil.

LIL. I was looking for you, too. (*Cross to* NICK *C.*) Shake hands, Nick, and guess who I am. (*Shakes.*)

NICK. Minnie Stew, that's who you are. What I ought to do is slap a good stiff fine onto you. (PORKY *bristling.*)

PORKY. Slap? (LIL *forces him in chair C.*)

LIL. Don't pay any attention to Nick, baby, he don't mean anything —it is just the way these foreigners talk. (*Pats his face, puts his hat in his lap.*)

NICK. Now you are here, would you hurry a little—*please?*

LIL. We been hurrying, Nick—we hurried and hurried. We been the longest time getting here, haven't we, Andrew?

PORKY. That's right, dearie.

NICK. For God's sake, where you been? What's happened to you?

LIL. Almost everything—we're married. (PORKY goes asleep.)

ROY. Holy gee.

NICK. What?

LIL. That's the reason we're so proud.

ROY. Oh, is *that* what you are!

LIL. The joke's on you. You'll all have to give us presents and everything. (*Laughs.*)

NICK. Well, going to work tonight?

LIL. Did I return for these purposes?

NICK (*helping her R.*). Then go up and lie down. I'll send up some coffee—and we'll find a place in the office for Porky.

LIL. Andrew—if you please——

NICK. All right, Andrew. (*Motions to ROY to take LIL.*) Go ahead, Lane.

ROY (*down R.*). Come on, Lil, I'll fix you a couch. (*Whispers to LIL.*) You ain't got anything on your hip, have you?

LIL. Only a birthmark, and you're the first guy that's asked me about it.

(ROY *pushes her upstairs.* NICK *shakes* PORKY. *He wakes suddenly, rising as* NICK *walks him to office.*)

PORKY. I think I'm married.

(NICK *pushes* PORKY *into office.* PORKY *exits;* NICK *exits hall.*)

ROY. Come on, Lil—I'll help you. (*She drops pocketbook and gloves on stairs.*)

LIL. I feel so damn foolish. (*Pushes him.*)

ROY. Cut it out—lemme help you.

LIL. Sure. You help me and I'll help you. (*Nearly knocks him downstairs.*)

ROY. Behave yourself, will you? You wouldn't want to have anybody say you missed a performance. Come on, now, Lil; this is serious business. (LIL *exits, singing.* ROY *comes back for her gloves.* DOLPH *comes in back door.*)

DOLPH (*to* ROY). Hello, nut—where's Nick?

ROY (*at head of stairs*). Find out, wise guy—I dance here. I ain't a waiter. (*Exits.*)

(DOLPH *motions to* STEVE, *who follows him in, very nervous; stands in doorway.*)

STEVE (*up C.*). All right. (JOE *enters from hall with coffee, crosses to stairs.*)

JOE. Good evening, Mr. Crandall.

STEVE. Hello, Joe. (*To* DOLPH.) Get outside and do as I told you. (DOLPH *exits.* JOE *L. of* STEVE *at stairs.*) Listen, Joe—I'm not here to anyone tonight. Get that. And tip me if McCorn or any dick blows in. (JOE *starts to leave. Crosses R. of*

STEVE.) Wait a second. Don't be in such a hurry. Here—— (*He hands* JOE *a bill.*)

JOE. Thanks, Mr. Crandall.

STEVE. And tell the doorman to turn away anybody he don't know, and give him this. (*Hands* JOE *another bill.*) Some of Scar Edwards' playmates might try to crash in, looking for trouble. (NICK *comes from down hall.*) I got my own lookout men planted, but I'm taking no chances. (*Crosses to back door and looks through peephole.*)

NICK. Hurry along with that, Joe. (JOE *starts.*) Hello, Steve. (JOE *exits upstairs.*) What's the matter? You look sick.

(*Stop No. 2.*)

STEVE (*crosses C.*). I ain't feeling as well as I could.

NICK (*puzzled—L. of* STEVE). No?

STEVE (*takes off his hat*). Look at that lid. (*Shows hat.*)

NICK. Huh?

STEVE. Look at that hole!

NICK. Sure, I see it. Cigarette?

STEVE. No—bullet.

NICK (*impressed*). For God's sake!

STEVE. Just a minute ago. I'm standing down here in the middle of the block—in front of the Midtown Garage—talking to Dolph, when buzz—(*puts hat on*)—it goes through my hat.

NICK. Mmm! Who done it?

STEVE. That's the hell of it. I don't know.

NICK. I mean, where'd it come from?

STEVE. That's what I'm telling you —there wasn't a sound—whoever took a crack at me must of had a silencer on his gat.

NICK (*guttural exclamation*). Ohoo!

STEVE. There wasn't anyone on the street—that is, anyone but what seemed to be walking along minding his own business—but just as the shot went through my lid, a taxicab across the street started up and went toward Sixth Avenue like a bat out of hell—but there was only a woman in it.

NICK. A woman?

STEVE. Yeh—it couldn't been her—I don't think—it must have come from some of those windows on the second floor—Scar Edwards' mob, I guess—they use silencers.

NICK. Whoo—that's bad, Steve—extra bad.

STEVE. An inch lower and it would have been a lot worse. It's good—I planned to get out of here when I did.

NICK. You goin' tonight?

(*Music No. 3.*)

STEVE. Yeh. (*Cross to back door.*) Get me a drink, will you? (NICK *exits office.* JOE *comes downstairs and goes to hall.*)

STEVE. Joe—don't forget to give that bill to the doorman.

JOE. No sir. (*Exits down hall.*)

(NICK *enters from office with bottle and glass.*)

NICK. And—a—where you going? (*At office door.*)

STEVE (*crosses to* NICK—*takes drink*). I'll lay in with some friends up in Montreal for the time being.

(PEARL *enters back door with black purse under arm. She is in street clothes.*)

NICK. About time!

STEVE. Hello, Pearl.

NICK. Hurry up, you're late; don't waste any time. (PEARL *exits stairs.*)

NICK. If you didn't croak Scar Edwards, what you blowin' for?

STEVE (*crosses R.*). I can make my plans without your help, Nick.

NICK. Sure. You taking Billie with you?

STEVE (*crosses R.—bolts back doors*). That's some more of your business.

NICK. I want to know if I gotta get a new gal, that's all.

STEVE (*crosses to* NICK, *who pours him a drink*). Well, I'm taking her, all right, but she don't know it yet, so you don't need to advertise. I prefer to get 'em without being rough— but I'm pressed for time, so I'll have to try Dolph's stuff this crack.

(*Drinks.*) Now—I gotta get hold of Porky. (*Step C.*)

NICK. He's here.

STEVE. He is?

NICK. In there. Drunker than hell— he got married.

STEVE. He got what?

NICK. Sure, to Lil. They both come in while ago stewed to gills.

STEVE. To Lil? Gee! Well, will you tell me why he fell for that big horse?

NICK. Maybe she ain't your kind— but them big broads that's been all through the war sometimes make pretty women at home.

STEVE. Oh, I ain't boosting for Porky —at that I think Lil got the worst of it. Let's take a lamp at him. I want to see what he looks like married.

(*Stop No. 3.*)

(BILLIE *comes downstairs.*)

STEVE. Wait a minute. Hello, beautiful. (NICK *exits office.*) Well, you look sweet as sugar. How's tricks?

BILLIE (*R. of armchair*). All right. I came in late and then I hurried so— that I'm about the first one ready.

STEVE. Found the folks all right, did you?

BILLIE. Oh, fine.

STEVE. That's good. That gives me a great deal of pleasure. Of course we missed not having you stay for the finish of the party last night.

BILLIE. Well, you were awfully nice about letting me go home, Mr. Crandall.

STEVE. Well, I'll tell you, Billie girl, any time I'm not nice, you remind me and I'll get nice, 'cause as far as you're concerned, that's the way I want to be, see?

BILLIE. Of course. I don't understand about the detective and everything.

STEVE. Of course you don't, girlie, but I'll explain it to you. It's just politics . . . that's all. I'll tell you all about it after the show tonight. It'll be very interesting. You're going for a ride with me tonight, you know. (*Takes her hand.*)

BILLIE (*step R. away from him again*). Well, I don't know.

STEVE. You haven't forgotten. That was a promise—you wouldn't try to go back on that.

BILLIE. Well——

(*Buzzer sounds and lights flash.*)

STEVE (*quite frantic*). You did promise—don't forget that.

BILLIE. I wouldn't go back on my promise.

(MAZIE *enters on stairs.*)

MAZIE. Hello, Steve.

STEVE. Hello, Mazie. (*Touches BILLIE's arm.*) Don't forget now. (*Exits to office.*)

MAZIE (*comes downstairs*). I see he's still friends.

(RUBY *enters stairs.* ROY *and* GIRLS, *except* PEARL, *come downstairs. Red costume No. 1.*)

RUBY. Yeh, she promised to come early and shave my neck.

(NICK *enters office.*)

MAZIE (*up L.*). Well, here we are for the merry-merry.

NICK. Now, remember, some pep tonight.

MAZIE. I'm full of pep and no control.

ROY (*starts to cabaret*). Save your pep, kid—*you may need it.* (*Cabaret doors open.*) Good evening, folks. (*Exit. Doors close.*)

RUBY (*up R.*). If that's pep, I never smelled gin.

MAZIE. Listen, Dizzy—you won't smell anything again—'cause I'm going to *bust your smeller.* (*Doors open. She starts.* ROY *enters.*)

BILLIE. Mazie, behave yourself.

GRACE. What is this, Grand Street?

ANN. My head aches.

RUBY (*steps C.*). Wait till the show's over—I'll show you.

(BILLIE *pulls* MAZIE. GRACE *pulls* RUBY.)

MAZIE. Why wait?

ROY (*ad lib.* ROY *pushing* MAZIE L.). That's enough of that. You can't go out there scrapping like that. I don't want my stuff spoiled. I got friends out there—agents and managers—looking me over every night.

MAZIE (*crosses L.*). Oh, I forgot—I ain't used to working with these headline acts. (PEARL *enters.*)

ROY (*up R.*). Well, there's lots worse than me headlining, sister.

MAZIE. Well, for Gawd's sake, what did I say?

(*Buzzer is heard again, this time imperatively.*)

ROY. Come on—quit it—line up. Let's unravel our daily dozen. *Every night's a first night.*

(*Music No. 4.*)

(*Cabaret doors open.*)

ROY. Give 'em your best.

(STEVE *enters from office.* ROY *thumbs nose as he exits. Dance, etc., same as No. 1 in Act One.*)

STEVE (*up to cabaret door*). You'd think last night would-a took all the freshness out of that hoofer, wouldn't you?

NICK (*R. of chair*). Hu—forget it. I'm going to fire him.

STEVE. You don't need to bother—I'll tend to him myself when I get the time. I don't want to have it happen too quick after his visit with McCorn. (*Crosses to down R.*) He hasn't been around tonight, has he?

NICK. Who?

STEVE. McCorn.

NICK. No. Why? You want to see him?

STEVE. That's just what I don't want to do. I thought he might come snoopin' around again.

NICK. You afraid of him—Dan McCorn?

STEVE. Me? What for? He ain't got nothing on me—not a thing.

NICK. Sure he ain't—so why get excited?

STEVE. Well, I'll tell you, Nicholas—a guy like McCorn gets on my nerves—he don't say anything—he don't make any accusations, but that damn rotten slow way of talking he's got and that dirty smile—you know—sorta gets me ragged. Now what the hell did he want to take my gun for last night?

NICK. Well, after all, Steve, none of us ain't got no right to carry—a gat.

LIL (*comes from dressing room, starts downstairs*). Where's my husband?

(STEVE *looks her over and shakes his head and exits to office.*)

NICK. He's all right, Lil.

LIL. Tell him his little wife—— No, I'll tell him myself. (*She finds that coming downstairs backward is lots easier.*)

(*Stop No. 4.*)

NICK. Feel better now, Lil? All ready for going on?

LIL (*cross R.C. to* NICK). Say, Nick, please can I cut my first number? I can do it, if I have to, but I ain't just set.

NICK (*resigned*). All right—go on out—sit down, drink some more black coffee, and see the show.

LIL. Thanks, old-timer—you're a true friend. That's just what I said to Andrew—I says, if ever your little Lillie had a true friend—it's that greasy Greek, Nick Verdis. (PORKY *enters from office.* LIL *crosses to* PORKY.) I'm going out and see the show, darling.

PORKY. I'll go with you, dearie.

LIL. Take my arm, sweetheart, and keep the *hell off my feet.*

(*Music No. 5.*)

(*They exeunt down hall.* GIRLS *and* ROY *come in from cabaret.* MAZIE *and* BILLIE *are chatting together;* PEARL *sits up L.*)

(*Music Stop No. 5.*)

ROY. Well, we ruined 'em, boss.

NICK. Listen, Lane, Lil ain't able to work—— Listen, I gotta find something to fill that spot.

ROY. Better give 'em an orchestra specialty.

NICK. They'll get sick of that, too, before the night's over. Listen, I been thinking—I'll take a chance—how'd you like to break in your act with Billie—huh? (GIRLS *get interested.*)

ROY (MAZIE *pokes* BILLIE; GIRLS *show interest*). What?

NICK. You can do it for the next number.

ROY (*crosses L.*). No—the act is split —it's off—all busted up.

NICK. Listen, you been talkin' about it—rehearsin' and everythin'—now I give you a chance.

ROY. I'd like to do it for you, boss, but I ain't got my partner, I——

NICK (*to* BILLIE *up C.*)..What's the matter? You won't work?

BILLIE. I didn't say I wouldn't. He don't want me any more.

(*Start music loud.*)

NICK. Go on. (*To* BILLIE, *who exits upstairs.*) Just because I need the two of you, you're busted up. Come on, I ask it for special favor. There's a orchestra number first, so you got lots of time. This is a chance for you. I'll give the agent a good report no matter how rotten it is.

ROY. As long as Miss Moore wants to do it, I'm willing to, just to keep the show going.

NICK. Fine. (*To others.*) We'll do the Hawaiian number after that. Go on now, get ready. (*They start.*)

ANN. The Hawaiian number next.

ROY (C.). We didn't rehearse today. (ROY *starts going through steps.*)

MAZIE. Can we go out to the tables and watch, Mr. Verdis? (RUBY *and* PEARL *start for stairs.*)

NICK. Sure, go ahead.

RUBY (*as she exits upstairs*). They'll die standing up.

MAZIE (*as* PEARL *starts upstairs*). Come on, Pearl, and watch 'em, why don't you?

PEARL. I'll change first and be right out.

ROY (*cross to* MAZIE *up L.*). Mazie, tell Brophy to play my introduction music when this orchestra number is over—he'll know what you mean.

MAZIE. Sure.

(*Exeunt* MAZIE, GRACE, *and* ANN *to hall.* NICK *cross C., starts figuring program on card.*)

ROY (*practices steps*). Boss, there's gotta be a better understanding—(*cross to* NICK)—about the money in the future——

NICK. Maybe after you do this act you have no future. (*Laughs.*)

ROY. Razzin' me, eh? All right, after tonight you gotta struggle along without me. How do you like them grapes? (*Step L.*)

NICK (*cross to* ROY). Aw, you can't take a joke. You and me, Lane, we're friends. Go on, now, like a good fellow. Maybe I'll have a sign fixed with your name in lights.

ROY. Well, how big a sign?

NICK. I'll tell you after I see the act. (*Exits to hall.* ROY *rosins shoes.* BILLIE *enters stairs in special dance costume.*)

BILLIE (*C.*). We might as well go on and try it, now that we rehearsed it so much, even if you don't like me any more.

ROY (*he hooks her dress*). It ain't a question of liking you. But when I get a throwdown like last night, I get wise to myself.

BILLIE. Well, when I get a throwdown like I just got today, I'm wise to myself, too. But lots of people that don't like each other, they still work together. I mean, if you still think we'd make a good team, then it's just a business proposition. A couple can be in the same act without being crazy about each other.

ROY. Well, I used to think we'd make about the best combo I could imagine—but I'm the kind of a guy I don't want to butt in where I ain't wanted. You want to run over a few of them steps? (BILLIE *nods.*) Just remember your routine, that's all you got to do.

BILLIE. Let's try the finish—that's where we got mixed up at the last rehearsal.

ROY. All you gotta do is follow me. Watch me out the corner of your eye and you can't go wrong. (*Takes place to do steps. She puts her arms around his neck, pulling their cheeks together. He puts her hand down to his waist.*) Down here.

BILLIE. The last time we did it this way.

ROY. Well, that was the last time. We'll do it now the old way. (*Stops acting and looks away from her.*) You see, it's kinda spoiled it for me, thinkin' you might have had your arms around Steve that way.

BILLIE. I haven't. (*Pause.*) And when I lied last night about the drunken man, it was because I had promised Steve to say that, and I didn't know a thing about that you'd said the opposite. And I went home alone last night.

ROY (*after thinking it over*). We'll do the finish the new way—like this. (*Puts her arm around his neck.*) Billie, you know that, what you asked your mother when you went home today—about marryin' a poor fellow?

BILLIE. Yeah.

ROY. Well——

(*Stop No. 6.*)

(*Buzzer. They jump apart.*)

ROY. Never mind. You can tell me later. We gotta think of our work now. On your toes, baby—don't get nervous. (*At door.* BILLIE *at armchair.*) Listen, Mr. Verdis is makin' an announcement—sensational newcomers—Roy Lane and Company. Oh boy, don't that make you feel proud?

(*Music No. 7.*)

BILLIE (*overcome with sudden panic*). Roy—I'm scared.

ROY (*cross to her*). Don't be scared —remember, I'm right beside you. It'll all be over 'fore you know it.

BILLIE. Roy, I don't believe I can go on. Can't we wait till tomorrow till we have a chance to rehearse?

ROY. Pull yourself together. We can't have no stage fright gummin'

our act. I'll give you a sock in a minute. There's our music. We'll finish in a blaze of glory. Lots of snap now. We'll show 'em. (*Pulls her to entrance—blesses himself— doors open. They exit to cabaret.*)

(DAN MCCORN *enters down hall— looks around.* JOE *follows on.*)

JOE. No strangers allowed back here —mister.

DAN. That's all right, Aloysius. I'm no stranger.

JOE. Well, you can't——

(NICK *enters from up hall!.*)

DAN. Oh yes, I can—evening, Nick.

NICK. Joe. (JOE *exits hall.*) What you doin' back here?

DAN. Just thought I'd drop in and say hello. Steve around?

(*Stop No. 7.*)

NICK. Nope, I ain't seen him all day.

DAN. He'll be in later, though, won't he?

NICK (*cross down L.*). No—he won't come tonight. He had such big night last night—y'understand. You want to see him?

DAN (*step down C.*). Nothing in particular. They'll be lots of other chances. Have a good time last night?

NICK (*sits down C.*). No, them kinda things make me sick. You gotta do it, understand, but it ain't no fun. When I get drunk for pleasure, that's one thing—but when I get drunk for business, daugh! No—no.

DAN. Sure. All the girls stay?

NICK. Yes, I guess so. I don't know. I got cockeyed awful soon. I ain't sure of nothing last night.

DAN. Well, guess I'll blow. My partner's waiting for me outside.

NICK. Is he waiting like them other bulls you told Steve about last night?

DAN (smiles). No, he's waiting.

NICK. You're a pretty slick guy, Mac—you put it over on me, too.

DAN (still smiling). Oh, you're all wrong, Nick—they were there.

NICK (puts chair back, cross to DAN). Yeah, like hell—well, it's all right with me—put me in awful bad—them Chicagoes started everything.

DAN. That's a bad buncha bail hoppers, Nick, on the level. I coulda grabbed a couple of 'em—but it wouldn't get me anything. We don't want 'em here in New York.

NICK. Steve tells me they're goin' back to Chicago in a couple of days.

DAN (pause). I thought you said you didn't see Steve all day?

NICK (pause—caught). I didn't—he called me on the phone—he told me——

DAN. Oh! (Pause.) Well, see you later. (Start up L.)

NICK. You ain't coming round again?

DAN. Oh, I don't mean tonight.

NICK. Well, that's good. You're a fine fellow, Mac, but every time you come in my cabaret, 'bout twenty people goes out.

DAN. You got nothing to fear from me, Nick.

(RUBY and PEARL enter from dressing rooms. They have changed to hula costume. They come down the stairs.)

NICK. I know that, but it looks bad when you're round so much.

RUBY. My Gawd, this place is getting like Headquarters—every time you come into a room around here, you fall over a badge.

NICK. Mac's just visiting. Beside, you shut up.

RUBY (going toward hall). Is that act out there so bad you can't look at it? (Exits to down hall.)

DAN (as PEARL crosses toward cabaret). Hello, there.

PEARL. Hello. (Exits down hall.)

DAN. She's still around, huh?

NICK. Why not?

DAN. I thought that party last night would be too much for her.

NICK. These kids I got are tanks—they can drink any ten men under.

DAN. Well, be good. I'll take a peek at this new act of yours. (Exits to hall.)

(NICK *peeks out to be sure* DAN *is not coming back, turns to office.* STEVE *opens door and comes out, almost twitching with nervousness, leaves office door ajar.*)

STEVE (*cross C.*). Damn him, what does he want?

NICK. Nothing important, he says. Just asked for you. I said you wasn't here, like you told me.

STEVE (*guilty conscience*). He's got nothing on me. Not a thing. (*Sits armchair.*)

NICK. Say, listen, what the hell's the matter with you? (PEARL *passes up hall.*) Soon as somebody mentions this dick, McCorn, you go—up in the air. What's the reason for this?

STEVE. I'm all shot, I tell you. Too much booze last night, I guess, and —oh, a lot of things—— (*There is a noise of someone trying back door under stairs, then a loud knock. Rises and sits. Pause.*) Take a look first!

NICK (*peeks out*). It's Dolph. (NICK *unbolts the door, opens it.* DOLPH *enters.* STEVE *crosses up.*)

STEVE. What's the matter?

DOLPH (*frightened*). Why—I—a——

STEVE. What the hell is it?

DOLPH. There's a guy out there been walking up and down—passed by a dozen times—makes me all nervous.

STEVE. A dick?

DOLPH. Either that or one of Scar Edwards' bunch—nobody I seen before.

NICK (*step down*). There's a lot of people walk up and down—it's a free country almost. What's to be afraid of? You guys ain't done nothing.

DOLPH (*cross to* STEVE). Ain't there some way to get out of here, Steve —now—before——

STEVE. No, I'm not ready yet. I'll break cover in an hour. Go on, wait out there.

DOLPH. But it ain't safe out there. One of the Edwards crowd might take a shot at me, with a silencer.

STEVE. Go on out—stick by that back entrance, like I told you to. You're my right-hand man, ain't you? (*Slaps him on back. Pushes him out.*)

DOLPH. Sure; all right. (*Exits out back door.* STEVE *closes door and bolts it, closes cabaret doors.*)

NICK (*C.*). I don't get this business, Steve.

STEVE (*L. of* NICK). Listen, Nick, you and I been best kind of pals for a long time. I'd shoot the works for you and I hope you would for me.

NICK. Sure I would. What you want?

STEVE. I am going to blow tonight. I don't want to have any slips. This damn bull McCorn is getting too curious. He thinks some of my mob got Edwards.

NICK. Did they?

STEVE. No, they didn't. Now, listen, I want you to get Joe or someone you can trust to beat it over to Charlie's and tell him to bring his car, *not mine,* they know mine—and leave it at the back entrance for me.

NICK. You can phone him.

STEVE. No, these dicks might have the wires tapped. Sending Joe is safer. After the show I'll take Billie and a couple of these broads and pile in the car. Looks like we're going for a joy ride, savvy? Then if they trail us, when I get 'em out on the Post Road, I can lose 'em, see, but they won't think I'm going to blow, so long as I got the girls with me. I can get rid of the ones I don't want later on.

NICK. You go to lots of trouble just 'cause a bull's asking questions. My Gawd, Steve, where is your guts?

STEVE. You think I'm yellow, huh? I don't want no man thinking that. Listen, Nick. (*They look at each other intently. Grabs* NICK's *arm.*) I did that job myself. (NICK *motions quiet with both hands.*) Now, they can't get me for it—they got nothing on me but that gun—but it's getting on my nerves—I'm getting ragged and I want to get out of here. Now, have you got it?

NICK. Sure, I understand. But don't bump anybody else off in here.

STEVE. You won't get in trouble—I'll fix that. Now send for the car.

NICK. Sure, right away—you wait in the office, Steve. (*He hurries down hall.*)

(*Music No. 8.*)

(STEVE *goes to big door under stairs, peeks out cautiously through peep-hole, then crosses to cabaret doors. Closes them.*)

(*Stop No. 8.*)

(*As the C. doors open,* PEARL *appears. She steps into room with silencer pistol and purse.*)

PEARL (*soft*). Turn around, rat! (STEVE *turns around.*) I don't want to give it to you like you did him—in the back.

STEVE (*he can't move*). For God's sake, don't.

PEARL (*step L.*). I'm giving you more chance than you gave him—I'm looking at you—and the last thing you see before you go straight to hell is Jim Edwards' woman, who swore to God she'd get you.

(*Music No. 9.*)

STEVE (*back away*). Don't—don't kill me—don't——

PEARL. Whine, you rat—— (*She fires the silencer. There is just a pish as the gun goes off, a slight curl of smoke.* STEVE *runs toward office. He lurches into open door of office and falls in, clutching door and closing it.*) I knew you would. (*She runs upstairs.*)

RUBY (*opens sliding doors*). A total loss. My God, *what a bloomer.* (*Doors open.*)

(*The* GIRLS *enter from the cabaret.* BILLIE *and* ROY *rush in,* BILLIE *on* ROY's *shoulders.*)

MAZIE. Them guys don't know a good act when they see it.

(GRACE *and* ANN *enter hall.*)

ROY (*he drops her*). Come, Billie, it's good for a bow. (BILLIE *and* ROY *run back.*)

RUBY. And they even steal a bow.

ANN. And they rehearsed it.

(BILLIE *and* ROY *enter ad lib.*)

BILLIE. How do you think it went?

GRACE. That bunch are full of novocain.

RUBY. You'd be a riot in the Palace.

(*Stop No. 9.*)

ROY. We could have grabbed another. That detective and Nick crabbed our act with their argument. How could we get attention, everybody watching them? Gee, what a rotten break. Well, go on up, kids; make your change. (*They exit.*) I'll give the leader a buzz—see how they like it. (*He exits down hall.*)

BILLIE (*as they exit stairs*). I did my best.

MAZIE. Sure you did, kid; cheer up. I don't think it's as bad as they say it is.

(NICK *and* DAN *enter down hall.*)

NICK (*L. of chair*). Dan, you're getting me sore, y'understand—I gotta right to send any of my waiters any place I want—without any advice from you.

DAN (*down R. of* NICK—*pulling him around*). Now, listen to me, Greek—

I been pretty nice to you in a lotta ways—now, you get this—you don't want to be accused of helping some guy that's wanted for murder, do you?

NICK. No, but I——

DAN. Then listen to me; before you do any more for Steve Crandall I want to have a talk with him—and after that you can do as you please. I been waiting around here until your show was over before I started something—as I didn't want to give your dump any worse name than it's got. So keep out of my business and you won't have to sit in a witness chair. Now, I happen to know Steve's here; come on, where is he? Where is he? (NICK *motions toward office.*) Tell him I want to see him. (NICK *opens door to office. He stops abruptly and gasps.*) What's the matter? (*Joins him—pushes him inside and enters.*) Come in. Shut the door.

(RUBY *enters, half dressed, followed by* MAZIE, *who catches her on stairs and chokes her—bending her over the banisters.*)

MAZIE. Now you're going to eat mud.

RUBY. Quit.

MAZIE. Now what am I the son of?

RUBY. You're an angel.

MAZIE. Say uncle.

RUBY. Uncle.

MAZIE (*releases her*). Now, get back. I'd drop you over if I wasn't feeling so good-natured.

(RUBY *exits.* MAZIE *dusts off her hands as* ROY *enters with a rush. He has supper card in his hand.*)

ROY (*on stairs*). Look, Mazie—look at this—I got this from Mike Shea— he just caught our act.

MAZIE. Who's he?

ROY (*above* MAZIE). He's one of the biggest booking agents in New York —he wrote me on this supper card——

MAZIE. Mike Shea—never heard of him.

ROY (*at top of stairs*). Listen, what he wrote. At last I got a break. I got to show it to Billie. "I can offer you and partner Chambersburgh and Pottsville next week"—— Billie, Billie! (*Exits stairs.*)

MAZIE (*laughs*). That's one for the book—is that the big time? (*Exits stairs.*)

(DAN *enters office, followed by* NICK.)

DAN. He's dead, all right. (NICK *mutters, edging away from the room.*) Right through the old pump.

NICK (*suddenly*). Lane, the hoofer. He's the one. He killed Steve. I'll betcha. He was out to get him. (*Crosses R. to* DAN.)

DAN. The actor, you mean?

(PEARL *enters stairs.*)

NICK. Sure, he's been tryin' to get him. He's been lyin' about him.

DAN. No, it wasn't Lane—it was suicide.

(PEARL *starts downstairs, with back to wall.*)

NICK. Suicide?

DAN. Sure—here's Steve's own gun —with one chamber empty.

(*Warn curtain.*)

NICK. I thought you had that?

DAN. I gave it back to Steve today.

NICK. But Steve said——

DAN. I said I gave it back to him today. He knew I was going to pinch him, so he took the shortest way out. I'm calling up headquarters to report it suicide—so that's what it is.

NICK. All right—all right—whatever you say.

DAN. Give me the key to this door. (PEARL *sits at piano.* NICK *gives him key to the office door.* DAN *locks it.*) I want to keep everyone out of there till the coroner gets here. I'll wait for him out back. (*Cross to back door. Speaks out of corner of his mouth as he passes* PEARL.) Pull yourself together, kid. (*Exits back door.*)

(ROY *and* BILLIE, *followed by the other* GIRLS *except* PEARL, *come from dressing rooms in hula costume. They are laughing and joking.*)

MAZIE. Pottsville and Chambersburgh. Gawd, Billie, you must love this guy.

BILLIE. I certainly do.

ROY. I been so busy gettin' the act framed, I ain't had time to show you how much I love you. But here goes.

(ROY *and* BILLIE *embrace and he kisses her.* GIRLS *crowd around and ad lib.*)

ANN. My Gawd, in front of everybody——

GRACE. When do you two play the matrimonial circuit?

MAZIE. Break—time——

RUBY. Look at 'em.

(GIRLS *laughing and pulling* BILLIE *and* ROY *apart.*)

NICK (*standing with back to office door—nervously*). Cut out this noise—I—er—we gotta cut it out, y'understand.

(*Buzzer.*)

ROY (*gets ukulele from piano.* GIRLS *take places*). There goes the gong again—all ready, girls? Come on, Pearl. Gee, I'm happy. Our names will be in bright lights soon, *Roy Lane and Co.* (*Doors open.*) Remember you're all artists. Here we go—here we go——

(*They dance into cabaret singing as* NICK *crosses himself and prays, leaning against the door as though half fainting.*)

(*Music No. 10, loud.*)

(*Ring at end of vamp.*)

SLOW CURTAIN

Payment Deferred

*A Play in a Prologue,
Three Acts, and an Epilogue by*

JEFFREY DELL

From the novel by C. S. Forester

THE CAST

As produced by Gilbert Miller at the Lyceum Theatre, New York, under the direction of H. K. Ayliff

A PROSPECTIVE TENANT	Horace Sinclair
WILLIAM MARBLE	Charles Laughton
ANNIE MARBLE	Cicely Oates
WINNIE MARBLE	Elsa Lanchester
JIM MEDLAND	Paul Longuet
CHARLIE HAMMOND	S. Victor Stanley
MADAME COLLINS	Dorice Fordred
DOCTOR ATKINSON	Lionel Pape
HARRY GENTLE	Stanley Harrison
BERT BRICKETTS	Malcom Soltan

SYNOPSIS OF SCENES

The entire action of the play passes in the living room at 53 Malcolm Road, Dulwich, and is spread over a period of two years.

PROLOGUE and EPILOGUE.—A short while ago.

ACT ONE

Scene I: A night in March about two years earlier.
Scene II: The next afternoon.
Scene III: About a week later.

ACT TWO

Scene I: Two months later.
Scene II: An evening in August.

ACT THREE

Scene I: A year later.
Scene II: About three weeks later.

PAYMENT DEFERRED

PROLOGUE

SCENE—*The living room at 53 Malcolm Road, Dulwich.*

In the center of the right wall is the fireplace into which some rubbish has been thrown; also a dusty umbrella. In the left wall is a window overlooking the back garden. Outside the door C. is a passage leading from the front door on the R., past the staircase to the kitchen on the L. The wallpaper (which should be of bold and hideous design) and the decorations generally are in a shabby condition.

When the curtain rises the room is quite empty—the door is shut. There is the sound of someone coming downstairs and voices are heard. The door is opened, and HAMMOND, *a house agent's clerk, comes in, followed by a* GENTLEMAN *to whom he hopes to sell the house.* HAMMOND *is a red, stoutish, usually rather loud-mannered man of thirty-five. The* PROSPECTIVE TENANT *is about fifty: tall, stooping, slightly shortsighted, wearing a high collar and glasses.*

HAMMOND (*as they enter*). Well, you've got the genuine article here all right.

PROSPECTIVE TENANT (*to L.C., looking at the window, then to R.*). Yes. You know, it's really quite a . . . a momentous occasion. You see, it's the first time I've actually been inside a house where there's been a murder committed. I've seen the outside of a good many, but that's not the same.

HAMMOND. No. Not everyone gets the chance.

PROSPECTIVE TENANT. I've half a mind to take it. (*He takes a step away to L.*) It has a kind of attraction for me.

HAMMOND (*R.C.*). If you're quick it's yours for the asking. If you take my tip you'll put down the deposit when we get back. There's been talk of putting up the price a bit since the appeal was dismissed. (*Going toward the fireplace.*) Marble was pretty famous for a few weeks. (*Looking at the fireplace.*) Hullo! Hullo! What have we here? (*He picks up the umbrella out of the grate.*) Blimey . . . that's a bit of luck, if you like.

PROSPECTIVE TENANT. What is it? (*He peers at it.*)

HAMMOND (*coming to R.C.*). Why, that's Marble's umbrella. I'd know it anywhere. Ought to make a nice little bit, eh?

PROSPECTIVE TENANT. How do you mean?

HAMMOND. Good Lord! People'd do anything to get something of Marble's like this. If it doesn't fetch ten quid, then my name's not Charlie Hammond. Money for jam!

PROSPECTIVE TENANT. And you knew him?

HAMMOND. Known him for years. I gave evidence, you know.

PROSPECTIVE TENANT. Yes, I read about it, I think.

HAMMOND. Must have if you read the case at all. I was one of the principal witnesses for the Crown . . . seeing I was the only one who knew the family before it happened.

PROSPECTIVE TENANT. I should very much like to hear about them.

HAMMOND (crossing L.). Well, if you take this place . . . I'm next door. (Points through the window.)

PROSPECTIVE TENANT (goes to the window). Of course, there are always certain things which don't get made public . . .

HAMMOND. Ah, you're right there. (Taps side of the window with the umbrella.)

PROSPECTIVE TENANT (going R.C.). Oh, by the way . . . that cupboard they talked about in the case . . . a glass-fronted one.

HAMMOND. Well?

PROSPECTIVE TENANT. Where exactly was it?

HAMMOND (pointing through the doorway). Why, just there. You can see the marks, look, against the banisters.

PROSPECTIVE TENANT (goes up C.). And that's where the bottle of cyanide was, eh?

HAMMOND. That's it . . . along with his photographic stuff.

PROSPECTIVE TENANT (C.). So this is the very room where he is supposed to have sat for hours at a time . . .

HAMMOND. There's no supposed about it. He did. Seen him myself dozens of times . . . over there by the window generally.

PROSPECTIVE TENANT. Ah . . . (Turns to the window.) In this room . . . One can imagine the idea creeping into his brain . . . his mind gradually becoming fascinated . . . (Turns toward the door.) That little bottle only just outside the door there—calling to him, becoming insistent—maddening. He would fight against it and then find himself drawn irresistibly toward the cupboard.

HAMMOND. I don't think it was—like that.

PROSPECTIVE TENANT. It's interesting to reconstruct. (Steps toward HAMMOND.) I've sat through a great many trials for murder. Their feelings are difficult to imagine. For instance, in cases where they're not found out for a very long time—I wonder if it gets less . . . the fear, I mean . . . whether at times they ever forget it altogether.

HAMMOND. Don't know, I'm sure. (He crosses R.)

PROSPECTIVE TENANT. Of course, there's one thing I always find myself thinking in cases like this man Marble's. Imagine what he'd go through if he hadn't done it at all.

HAMMOND (*coming C.*). Done it? Are you suggesting Marble didn't do it?

PROSPECTIVE TENANT. No, only . . . well, apart from experts . . .

HAMMOND. Experts! Ah, no getting round them. Only got to look at a body, and they can tell whether it could have got up and downstairs when it was alive. Wonderful, I call it.

PROSPECTIVE TENANT. I suppose there's no doubt really.

HAMMOND. No one round here ever had any doubt. I said he was guilty right from the start, and I was his best friend. Why, the papers all said it was one of the clumsiest murders on record, and I reckon they just about hit it on the head. The whole thing is as clear as daylight.

PROSPECTIVE TENANT. I dare say . . .

HAMMOND. Look here—I knew him and I knew her.

PROSPECTIVE TENANT. His wife, you mean?

HAMMOND. Yes, and if you ask me what was at the bottom of it, I'd say it was her. Nagging at him till he didn't rightly know what he was doing. I know what women are.

PROSPECTIVE TENANT. I suppose you heard her?

HAMMOND. Didn't exactly hear her, no. But one can put two and two together, can't they? And I'll take my oath she drove him to it. I should say it all started about two years ago or more. They were on their beam ends . . . owing money all over the place—and she used to keep on at him to give her more a week than he could manage; at least that's my idea and a good many agree with me. There wasn't a shop round here would give 'em any more credit, and what with her always at him . . . well, you know how one thing leads to another. Anyone round this part would tell you the same as I do, that it was her fault. At him morning to night. You know—(*tapping on the floor with the umbrella*)—nag-nag-nag . . .

(*Start to check down lights.*)

(*A barrel organ commences to play outside and continues until after black-out.*)

If it had been my old woman I wouldn't have stuck it as long as he did . . . not me . . . not likely. (*Laughs.*) Wonderful what some chaps'll put up with . . .

BLACK-OUT

ACT ONE

SCENE I

SCENE—*The same—about two years earlier.*

It is eight o'clock on a very wet night in March and the rain beats frequently on the window. A fire is burning, and on the mantelpiece above it are a cheap clock and some vases of the seaside souvenir type. There is a sideboard to the left of the doorway, through which one can see part of a glassfronted cupboard in the passage. On the wall there are two wedding groups and a few bad prints. Dining table L.C., armchair by fire; a few bentwood chairs; two aspidistras in massive green jars on occasional table by the window and on the sideboard.

When the curtain rises, WILLIAM MARBLE *is sitting R. of the table biting the end of a pencil and staring at a sheet of figures which lies on a heap of bills. He is a worried-looking man of forty, wearing shabby black city clothes with black woolen socks wrinkled about his ankles.* ANNIE, *his wife, a rather dowdily dressed but pleasant-featured woman, a year or two his senior, is seated on the edge of the armchair, darning clothes.* WINNIE, *their daughter, a pretty child of nearly sixteen, is sitting opposite her father at the table, which she kicks rhythmically with one foot. She is so engrossed in her homework that she does not notice her father's gesture of impatience, and continues to beat time on the table leg, tap, tap, tap.*

MARBLE (*in chair R. of the table—sharply.*) For Heaven's sake, Winnie, keep those feet still, can't you? Lord knows it's hard enough to think without that.

WINNIE (*in chair L. of table*). Sorry, Father.

(*A pause.* MARBLE *runs his fingers through his hair.* ANNIE *watches him anxiously.*)

ANNIE (*in chair at the fireplace R., putting down her work*). Is it very bad, Will?

MARBLE. I don't know what you call bad. This lot alone comes to eighty-five quid.

ANNIE (*astounded*). Eighty-five? But, dear, it can't!

MARBLE. I tell you it does! You can add it up for yourself, if you want to. . . . (*Holds out a sheet of figures.*) Eighty-five, fourteen, ten. There's bound to be some more, too, that I haven't got down. I can't remember everything.

ANNIE. But . . . Oh, Will, it's awful!

MARBLE. I know that, don't I? I don't need any telling.

(*A pause.*)

ANNIE. Will . . . what are we going to do?

MARBLE. God knows! What can we do?

ANNIE. But, dear, we must do *something*.

MARBLE. I know that, but what? Here's Colvin . . . five pounds! Now, how on earth, Annie, do you manage to run up a bill like that—just for milk?

ANNIE. Well, since you've given me less for the house, dear, I've had to put things down; I always paid cash before.

MARBLE. Just because I used to give you two-ten a week doesn't mean that I can always afford to do it. You've never had less than thirty-five bob, Annie. That ought to be ample.

ANNIE. You don't know, dear. Thirty-five shillings goes no way nowadays. It isn't enough for three of us, really it isn't. Mrs. Hammond was saying only this morning over the wall—and she's only got two of them to feed, mind—she said *she* can't make do on two pounds, even with Charlie doing the gas.

MARBLE. That's not the point. The point is what we can afford, and it's pretty clear from these bills that if you'd had two pounds we'd still be in the soup. So it's not much use talking about what Mrs. Hammond says.

ANNIE. I don't think that's quite fair, Will. I don't, really.

MARBLE. It's true, isn't it?

ANNIE. No, I don't think it is. (*Rises, goes above* MARBLE *to the sideboard up* L.C.) There's a lot of things there I've never ordered.

MARBLE. I don't know what you mean. If they're down here you've ordered them, haven't you?

ANNIE. No, dear, a lot of them are yours.

MARBLE. Oh! Meaning?

ANNIE. Well, all those photography things, for instance.

MARBLE. Why, I haven't done any since the summer.

ANNIE. I know. But if you look at the chemist's bill there are a whole lot of things down for August. Films and hypo and cyny-ide-of-something. I can't have ordered that! I don't even know what it is.

WINNIE. Oh, Mum—that's his photograph stuff with the red label. It's poison!

MARBLE. Cyanide? (*Thoughtfully.*) Yes, I'd forgotten. . . . Looks as if it might come in useful. . . .

(WINNIE *looks up.*)

ANNIE (*turns to him*). Will! What do you mean?

MARBLE. What I say. It looks as if we may need a drop before we're through with this. It's soon over, so I've heard.

ANNIE. Oh, how can you say things like that, dear? Before Winnie, too!

MARBLE. Well, it may come to it yet. It's getting too much for me,

Annie. I can't get away from it all for a single second. I lay awake at night . . . thinking and thinking . . .

ANNIE (*gently*). Yes, dear, I know.

(*He covers his face with his hands.* ANNIE, *meeting* WINNIE'S *eyes, motions her to get on with her work, then gets the scissors out of the workbox which is in the cupboard of the sideboard.*)

MARBLE (*suddenly*). I suppose you didn't remember to ask about my whisky?

ANNIE. Yes—(*returning to the chair at the fireplace R.*)—but it wasn't any use, Will. Mr. Evans was really quite rude.

MARBLE. How? What did he say?

ANNIE. It would only make you cross, dear. I——

MARBLE. Never mind . . . I want to know what he said.

ANNIE (*sits*). Well, he—he said something about—being tired of standing you drinks.

MARBLE (*through his teeth*). Oh, he did, did he? I'll be even with Master Evans for that, one of these days. When a chap's down he's got to take that sort of thing from a dirty little grocer. I always hated that fellow, anyway. He's chapel, of course. By the way, Annie, if Charlie Hammond comes in tonight, don't you go asking him to have one.

ANNIE. No, Will.

MARBLE. I've only got enough for two small ones left. I need those myself, if ever a man did.

ANNIE. Yes, dear.

MARBLE. It's pretty hard when you're half out of your mind with worry and want of sleep, not to have even a few drinks. I suppose you told Evans we'd settle his account at the end of the month?

ANNIE. He wouldn't listen, Will. He said we'd had long enough and he was . . . (*She hesitates.*)

MARBLE. What?

ANNIE (*breathlessly*). Will, he said he was putting in the brokers.

MARBLE. The brokers? Oh, my God! It only needed that! If the Bank get to hear of this it's all U-P, that's a dead certainty.

ANNIE. Perhaps he only said it to try and frighten us, dear.

MARBLE. Oh, no, he didn't. He meant it. I know his sort. That's just like Evans. I don't know why he should be such a swine about his account, all the same. Several of the other bills here are as big as his. Bigger!

ANNIE. If we could only let him have part of it. . . .

MARBLE (*rises, and crosses to the fireplace*). Oh, what's the use of talking like that, Annie? With nothing coming in till the end of the month and today only the third! Let alone having to live in the meantime. Just when I had the chance to make a bit . . . chance of a lifetime, too . . .

ANNIE. Why, how, Will?

MARBLE. Francs. They're going to rise. Got a line on it this morning—on the quiet. And here am I without a bean. Ugh! It's just my cursed luck.

(A pause.)

ANNIE. I wonder if any of the men in the office could do anything for you, dear?

MARBLE. They have . . . most of them. (Pause. Returns to R. of the table and sits.) That's what worries me most. One of them has only got to talk and out I go as sure as I'm here.

ANNIE. And if——

MARBLE. You don't understand, Annie. Bank clerks can't behave like human beings. Oh, it's all so damned unfair!

ANNIE. Surely, dear, after twenty years' service——

MARBLE. A fat lot of difference that would make! Why, if the Bank had any idea of the mess we're in, twenty years' service would be worth—(flicks finger and thumb)—that! I know 'em! (Pause.) It means the workhouse.

ANNIE. Oh, my dear, it can't! It mustn't! Think what Mrs. Hammond and them would say. The whole street would think——

MARBLE. You talk as if I wanted to go in the workhouse! Damn the

street! They'll be glad to see us in a mess. They've always hated us—just because I wear a bowler hat and dress respectable!

ANNIE. I'm so sorry, Will. I——

MARBLE. That's all very well, you know, Annie. Being sorry, and all that. But if you'd begun a bit sooner and kept those bills down . . .

WINNIE. Oh, Father, it's awfully difficult. Really it is! When mother was ill——

MARBLE (loudly). And who's talking to you? You keep your mouth shut. . . . When I want your opinion I'll ask for it. See?

WINNIE. Yes, Father, but you don't know——

MARBLE. Look here, my girl, if you're going to answer back when you're spoken to, the best place for you is bed.

WINNIE. But I haven't done my homework yet.

MARBLE. You should have thought of that before. Answering your father like that! Is that what they teach you at school? Here am I scraping and saving to be able to send you to a decent school, and this is all the return I get for it. . . .

WINNIE (humbly). I did get a scholarship. . . .

MARBLE. Yes, and if you hadn't you'd still be at the Council School and I shouldn't be paying for music lessons and things like that. And we'd probably not be in the mess we're in today. The sooner you realize that, young lady, the better. A little gratitude never yet did anyone any harm.

WINNIE (*almost in tears*). Oh, I am grateful. Really I am.

MARBLE. Well, stop that sniveling, then. God! This house is enough to drive anyone crazy. Next time you

— —

ANNIE. Oh, let the child alone, Will, do. She didn't mean it. (*To WINNIE.*) Perhaps you'd better go out in the kitchen for a bit, dear, while Father is talking business. It's quite warm out there. . . . You can light the gas.

WINNIE. Oh, Mum—need I?

MARBLE. Run along now, and do as your mother says. How many times do you want telling?

(WINNIE *rises and gathers her books very reluctantly. A loud knock on the front door startles all three into immobility. Then* MARBLE *looks at the clock.*)

MARBLE (*almost whispering*). Half-past eight!

ANNIE. Perhaps it's Charlie Hammond.

MARBLE. No. That's not his knock. (*Pause.*) My God! They've come! Evans hasn't wasted much time.

ANNIE (*frightened*). Oh, Will . . . (*Rises.*)

(*Another knock.* MARBLE *gets up as if to go.*)

MARBLE (*to* WINNIE; *moves below the table to* L.C.). You'd better see.

(WINNIE *goes out* C. *to* R. *Shuts the door.*)

(MARBLE *and* ANNIE *listen intently. A masculine voice asks for "Mr. Marble."*)

JIM (*off*). Mr. Marble?

WINNIE (*off*). Yes—come in.

(MARBLE *closes his eyes.* ANNIE *crosses to him and puts her hand in his.* WINNIE *returns.*)

WINNIE (*in door* C.). Someone for you, Father.

(MARBLE *grips the table.* ANNIE *squeezes his hand.* JIM MEDLAND, *a good-looking, sun-tanned boy of twenty, appears. He is very well dressed. Seeing their frightened expressions, he stops. Then he laughs.* WINNIE *closes the door.*)

JIM. Oh! Good evening! Sorry if I scared you. You look as if you'd seen a ghost! Mr. Marble, isn't it?

MARBLE. Yes.

JIM. Good! (*Comes down* R.C.) Found you first shot. I don't expect you know me.

MARBLE. No . . . I . . . I don't think so.

JIM. Well, it's some time since you saw me last. I was about four, I think. . . . My name's Medland.

MARBLE. Medland?

JIM. Yes, Jim Medland. My mother was your sister, wasn't she?

MARBLE (*realizing he is reprieved*). Not . . . not Win's boy? ·Good Lord! (*Goes to* JIM, *shakes hands*). You must excuse me. Gave me a bit of a turn, you coming in sudden like that. Here, let me introduce you. This is Annie—your aunt, I mean.

JIM (*shaking hands*). How do you do?

ANNIE. Nicely, thank you. This is a surprise!

JIM. Yes. I'm sorry to burst in on you like that without letting. you know, but I've only just landed.

ANNIE. I'm sure we're very pleased.

MARBLE. Winnie, here's a new cousin for you. (*To* JIM.) This is our girl.

JIM *and* WINNIE (*together, awkwardly, shaking hands*). How do you do?

MARBLE. We named her after your mother, you know.

JIM. Oh, yes?

MARBLE (*awkwardly*). Well . . . you must sit down for a bit and tell us all the news.

JIM. Yes, rather. I'll just go and get rid of my taxi.

MARBLE. Taxi?

JIM. Yes. He's waiting. I wasn't sure I'd got the right place.

MARBLE. Oh, I see.

JIM. Shan't be a moment. (*He goes out* C. *to* R.)

(MARBLE *follows up to* C., *then back to the table*. MARBLE *and* ANNIE *look at each other*.)

MARBLE. Taxi, eh?

ANNIE. Oh, Will! He . . . he might be able to help us!

MARBLE (*quickly*). I know. I know. Did you see that coat? Worth a tenner if it's worth a penny. Besides, you can't get over here from Australia unless you've got a bit. (*Excitedly*.) Did I say fifty to one against us? You wait. You leave this to me. My God, what a bit of luck, eh?

ANNIE. What about the whisky, dear? You'll have to offer.

MARBLE. No fear. I shan't. I'm not wasting that on a mere boy, don't you think it. He probably doesn't drink it, anyway. Look out! (*Goes out* C.)

(ANNIE *hurriedly hides the bills and tidies the room*. JIM *appears and looks through the glass front of the hall cupboard*. MARBLE *follows him*.)

JIM. Oh, I say . . . you go in for photography?

MARBLE (*helping him off with his overcoat, which he hangs in the hall*). Yes. Why, do you?

JIM. Yes, I'm rather keen. (*In passage*.) I've just got a topping new camera . . . telephoto lens. You can do ultra-rapid stuff with it. I'd like to see some of your pictures.

MARBLE (R. *of* JIM). I'm afraid I haven't done much in that way. Not an expert, you know. Here, come and get warm. (*Indicates the armchair.* JIM *sits by the fire.*) You must be frozen. Never known such a night.

(MARBLE *sits R. of the table.* ANNIE *drags chair L. of the table down a little and sits.* WINNIE *sits on the lower end of the club fender.*)

JIM. It's pretty awful, isn't it? Does it always rain like this in England?

MARBLE. I suppose this is about the worst we've had this winter. Where have you just come from?

JIM. Oh, Euston. I just dumped my kit there.

MARBLE. Euston? Why, that must have cost you a pretty penny.

JIM. He charged me a pound. I don't call that bad at this time of night. It seemed a jolly long way.

MARBLE. Yes. (*A glance at* ANNIE.) Well, and how's your mother after all this time?

JIM. Mother died . . . six months ago.

MARBLE. I say! I'd no idea. That's terrible, that is.

JIM. She never really got better after the shock of Father's death.

MARBLE. Tom dead, too? You don't say that? Well, upon my soul! That is rough and no mistake.

ANNIE. Haven't you any brothers or sisters?

JIM. No, none. You didn't know about . . . Mother, then?

MARBLE. Not a word. It must be fifteen or sixteen years since we had any news of them. That was soon after they first went out to Australia. Your father had some job with a shipping firm at that time.

JIM. That's right. He started on his own soon afterward. About five years ago he bought up his old Company.

MARBLE (*more interested*). Is that so? He must have done pretty well for himself.

JIM. Oh, yes.

MARBLE. And you carry on the good work, I suppose?

JIM. No. When he died, Mother sold out. I was too young to take over then. I only left college last summer.

MARBLE. Really? So you're a young man of leisure, eh?

JIM. Well, yes . . . but only for the moment. I shall want something to do, of course. I thought I'd take a look round first.

ANNIE. How ever did you manage to find us?

JIM. It wasn't very difficult. Mother hunted up the address ages ago. She'd planned to come over with me. I know she meant to come and see you and . . . I thought I'd look you up right away.

MARBLE. Yes. Quite right, too! I'm afraid we can't put you in the spare room, because we haven't got one. (*Laughs.*)

JIM. Oh, I say . . . I hope it didn't seem as if I was asking to be——

ANNIE. But I'm sure we'd have been very pleased if we'd only got the room. I'm sorry we're so cramped.

JIM. Oh, really, it's quite all right. I simply came here first because I don't know the ropes over here and I thought you'd know the best hotel to stay at.

MARBLE (*judicially*). Well, that depends, of course. . . .

JIM. Someone on the boat said the Carlton wasn't bad.

MARBLE. The Carlton, eh? Yes, well, you might .do worse. A good deal worse. Of course, it isn't exactly what I should call cheap. But I suppose that doesn't matter much in your case.

JIM. Oh, I don't know about that. I'll give it a run for a day or so while I have a look round.

(MARBLE *and* ANNIE *exchange glances.* JIM *turns to find* WINNIE *gazing at him. He smiles.*)

WINNIE (*timidly*). Have you seen many kangaroos?

JIM. Kangaroos? Yes, rather! I've hunted them quite a bit.

WINNIE. Oh, I say!

MARBLE (*forcing a jocular tone*). Kangaroos! What will she be thinking of next? (JIM *laughs.*) Did you ever know such a kid? (*He scowls at* WINNIE *and jerks his head to indicate the door.* WINNIE *gets up, and* MARBLE *feigns surprise*). What? Not bedtime already, surely? (WINNIE *kisses her mother, gets her books,*

etc., off the table and is going. JIM *rises and goes up.*) Well? Haven't you got a kiss for your old father, then?

(WINNIE *looks at her mother, goes reluctantly and kisses him on the forehead.*)

JIM (*holding out his hand*). Good night, Winnie.

(*She shakes it.* JIM *opens the door, and she goes out quickly.* JIM *moves down R.C.*)

MARBLE. What a queer child it is! By the way, Annie, what about a bit of supper for our young friend here?

ANNIE. I'm afraid we haven't anything very——

JIM. Oh, please, don't worry about me. I had something before I came down. I'd like to smoke, though, if I may?

ANNIE. Why, of course.

MARBLE. Here, have one of these. (*Rises.*)

(*While he fumbles in his pocket,* JIM *produces a leather case containing cigarettes in one side and a thick wad of notes in the other.*)

JIM (*handing them*). You try one of mine.

(MARBLE *puts his case back in his pocket and stares at* JIM's *case, fascinated by so much wealth.*)

MARBLE (*taking cigarettes*). That's a nice case you've got.

JIM. Yes, birthday present. It's rather well made.

MARBLE (*holding the case*). Well lined, too!

JIM. They're only stinkers. (MARBLE *laughs.*) I'm afraid. (*Realizing.*) Oh! . . . The notes, you mean . . . ? (*He is embarrassed.*)

MARBLE (*hands back the case*). Well, it's rather a lot, isn't it, for a young man to be carrying about on him?

JIM (*coolly*). Oh, I don't know.

(*A pause.* MARBLE *goes to the fire-place, lights his cigarette; seems to be lost in thought.* ANNIE *nerves herself to entertain.* JIM *lights his own cigarette.*)

ANNIE. Did you have it very rough on your journey?

JIM. Yes. (*To chair R. of the table.*) It was pretty rough all last week.

(*A pause.*)

ANNIE. Are you a good sailor?

JIM. Oh, yes, quite.

(ANNIE *looks at* MARBLE *for help, but he does not notice.*)

ANNIE. Staying in London long?

JIM. Well, I haven't decided. I want to have a good look round. I've always been very keen on architecture. Perhaps you can save me—(*sits R. of the table*)—time by telling me the most interesting bits to see.

ANNIE. Well, let me see . . . there's . . . Madame Tussaud's.

JIM. But I thought . . . I mean, that's modern, isn't it?

ANNIE (*uncomfortably*). Yes, I suppose it is. I don't go out much. If you like old places, there's the Tower.

MARBLE (*suddenly waking up*). He isn't a schoolboy, Annie. I expect he knows how to amuse himself in a place like London: eh, Jim? (*Sits in the armchair.*)

JIM. As a matter of fact, the Tower was one of the buildings I particularly wanted to see.

MARBLE. Really? Well, with most of us, that's about as far as it ever gets! (MARBLE'S *mouth appears to be dry. He looks round at the sideboard, is about to get up, then thinks better of it and says:*) Don't you bother to sit up, Annie, if your head's bad. I expect Jim will excuse you if you feel you'd rather go on up.

(ANNIE *rises.*)

JIM (*rises*). I say, I'm awfully sorry. I didn't realize you were feeling rotten. I'll go——

ANNIE. No, no, please. . . . You stay and talk to Will for a bit. He so seldom gets anybody fresh to talk to. I'll just say good night now if you don't mind.

JIM (*shaking hands*). Of course not. Good night.

ANNIE. Good night. You'll be sure to come again soon, won't you?

JIM (*without conviction*). Oh, yes . . . thanks.

(JIM *to C., opens door.*)

ANNIE (*crosses to* MARBLE). I'll say good night, dear, in case I'm asleep when you come in. (*Kisses him and looks into his eyes for a moment.*)

MARBLE. If you are, I shan't disturb you. Sleep well!

ANNIE (*to* JIM). Good night.

JIM. Good night.

(ANNIE *goes out.*)

(JIM *shuts the door, returns to the chair R. of the table.*) I mustn't stop long. I——

MARBLE. That's all right. No need for hurry, is there . . . seeing you're a gay young bachelor? Tell me, what are your plans after you've had a look round London?

JIM (*sits*). Oh, nothing very definite. I want to get hold of a car and go and see some of the places Mother and Dad talked about: Stratford and Clovelly and Windermere.

MARBLE (*suspiciously*). Going to look up some of your father's people?

JIM. No; I don't think there are any. Not in England, at any rate. I think you are the only relatives I've got. (*His eyes wander over the room.*)

MARBLE (*eagerly*). Really?

JIM. Yes. Out there I knew no end of people, of course, but here . . . I don't know anyone at all . . . except you and Aunt Annie.

MARBLE (*deeply interested*). I see.

JIM. I was thinking that as I came along in the taxi just now. . . . It made me feel sort of . . . well, lonely. (*He laughs shyly.*) I say, I'm afraid this is awful rot.

MARBLE (*starting as if returning to the present*). Not at all. I understand exactly what you mean. Exactly.

JIM. That's why I'm glad to come here.

(MARBLE *is silent so long that* JIM *turns to look at him.* MARBLE *realizes he is being watched and starts slightly.*)

MARBLE (*turns to* JIM). Are you going to stay over here? For good, I mean?

JIM. Yes, provided I get a job which suits me. Why?

MARBLE. I was thinking you'll probably want to invest your capital, that's all. I don't know what arrangements you've made?

JIM. Oh, my money's nearly all tied up. I've nothing to worry about.

MARBLE (*leaning forward*). Did your mother ever tell you anything about my job, I wonder?

JIM. Yes, I think so. To do with a bank or something like that, isn't it?

MARBLE. Yes, that's right. The County National, foreign exchange department. Been in it all my life. Buying and selling money, you know.

JIM. I'm afraid I don't know much about that kind of thing.

MARBLE. No. Not many people do. But what I was going to say is, it's a bit of luck for you that you turned up when you did. You've chosen just the moment when I might be able to do you rather a good turn.

JIM. Me? Er . . . how do you mean?

MARBLE. Well, through my job I get bits of information that don't reach everybody. And, what's more, I get it red-hot, which is the only time it's any use.

JIM (puzzled). Well?

MARBLE. Well—(confidentially)—I got a bit today. From a chap in the Paris branch. He says that the French Government are going to take a hand in stabilizing the franc.

JIM. Oh? And what does that mean?

MARBLE. Well, it's just possible that it's only a rumor and doesn't mean anything at all. On the other hand, there are several indications that there is something in it, and if so, my boy, then the franc is going to rise. Rise like hell!

JIM. I'm afraid it's all rather like Greek to me.

MARBLE. It means simply this: that if I'm right, francs are going to be handy little things to have about the house. They closed tonight at one-twenty. Anyone who bought at that, or anywhere near it, would make a packet.

JIM. Oh!

MARBLE. If one knows the ropes one can buy on what's called a "mar-gin." That is, by only putting up ten per cent of the purchase money. It's money for jam! The sort of chance fellows in my job wait years for, this is. That's why I say you were lucky to turn up when you did.

JIM. But why? What's it got to do with me?

MARBLE (slightly menacing). Well, you've got the capital. And I've got the knowledge. It seems to me we ought to be a pretty strong combination.

JIM. Oh, I've really very little money that I can touch, and what's more, I don't think I——

MARBLE. But it only needs a little. You could probably find enough out of your income. (JIM fidgets, and MARBLE grows more dictatorial.) The whole thing's as simple as A B C. You open an account at the Threadneedle Street office. If the franc begins to move I'll let you know. Then all you have to do is to tell them you want to buy francs as a forward operation. Got that? Forward operation, see?

JIM. Yes, but I really don't want——

MARBLE. There's nothing else for you to worry about. They'll send you straight along to me and I'll manage the whole thing. You'll just ring me up once or twice during the rise to give me authority to shift the account about when necessary.

JIM. No, honestly, I . . . I'm not keen on it.

MARBLE (desperately). But, damn it all, you don't object to making money, do you? (*Rises.*) If the franc goes to sixty and you bought tonight, that would mean a hundred per cent on your money. But if you'd bought on a margin you'd make a thousand per cent, and if you'd sold out and bought again once or twice during the rise, then it's a whole lot more than that!

JIM. Well, you see, I've never had much to do with that sort of thing and——

MARBLE. But I'm telling you, you don't have to know anything about it.

JIM. No, perhaps not, but . . . well, the truth is, I don't much like the sound of it.

MARBLE (*snarling*). What do you mean? (*Crossing to L.C.*) Do you think I'm suggesting something that isn't straight, or what?

JIM (*nervously*). No, of course not, but——

MARBLE. Because if you do, I'll have nothing to do with it, see? After all, I couldn't pinch your money, could I? If that's what you are afraid of. It would be in your account and you don't suppose the Bank dish out current accounts of their customers to their clerks, do you? (*Goes up toward the sideboard.*)

JIM (*rather nettled*). Then what *do* you stand to gain by it?

MARBLE (*puts cigarette end in aspidistra pot on the sideboard, moves to the table*). Well, if it came off I should naturally expect a commission. I suppose you wouldn't grudge me ten per cent, would you?

JIM. Why don't you do the thing yourself and take the whole lot?

MARBLE (*behind the table, dropping bluster and becoming confidential*). Well, now, Jim, I'll be perfectly frank with you. One reason is that bank clerks aren't allowed to put through forward operations for themselves. It's a rule. But the more important reason is that one must have capital and, like the chap in the story, that's a thing which, just at the moment, I haven't got.

JIM. I see.

MARBLE (*hurriedly*). Of course, if you prefer to put up a little for me along with your own, I'm quite willing to stand in with you on a joint deal.

JIM. No, I'm sorry, I couldn't do that.

MARBLE. I expect I know the trouble. All this talk about exchanges and things . . . it's a bit frightening, isn't it, at first? Perhaps I haven't made it clear enough.

JIM. No, it isn't that. It's just that I don't want to have anything to do with it.

MARBLE (*frantically*). Look here! Don't you be a young fool! I know a hell of a lot more about this game than you do and I tell you it's the chance of a lifetime. I wouldn't let you go in until I was dead sure it was coming off. (*Pats him on the shoulder.*) You take my advice and think it over before you——

JIM (*firmly, looking at* MARBLE). It wouldn't be any use. I'm quite certain now.

MARBLE (*after a pause, very quietly —sits chair behind table*). I see. (*His failure seems to have tired him out.* JIM *moves the chair.* MARBLE *says in almost a whine:*) I say, you're not resenting what I said just now, are you?

JIM. Oh, let's forget it! (*Rises.*) I must be moving. (*Throws cigarette end in the fireplace.*)

MARBLE. You . . . you can't go like that. I mean, I shall feel you're fed up about what I've been saying.

JIM. Oh, please . . . don't let's talk about it any more.

MARBLE. But I *must* explain. I've had a bit of trouble lately over . . . well, I don't see why you shouldn't know . . . over money. (JIM *makes a gesture of impatience and turns away.* MARBLE *continues hurriedly. Rises.*) You see, I've got Annie and the kid to think of, and if I don't find a hundred pounds pretty quick it means the workhouse for the three of us. You're old enough to understand what that means to anyone who's always kept themselves respectable?

JIM (*greatly embarrassed*). Yes, I . . . I'm very sorry, but——

MARBLE (*to R. of the table—with great feeling*). I think the shame of it will kill me. I just don't know which way to turn, straight I don't . . . I wonder, if . . . if I might ask you a great favor. (*He looks at* JIM, *who turns away.*) There's no one else I can go to. Will you lend me . . . a hundred . . . just for . . . just till the end of the month? I swear I'll pay back every penny.

JIM. I'm sorry, I . . . I really haven't got it to spare. I think it's a pity I came down here. . . . (*He moves towards R.C., holds out hand.*) Good night.

MARBLE (*panicking*). You . . . you're not going?

JIM. Yes, I must.

MARBLE. But I can't let you go like that. I . . . I should never forgive myself. I should feel you wouldn't care to come here again.

JIM. Well, to be candid, I'm not very keen. Perhaps you'd better know it now. I came down here looking forward tremendously to seeing my own people . . . the only ones I've got . . . and from practically the first second I got inside this room you've done nothing else but try and get money out of me in one way and another. I'm sorry to have to talk to you like this. But . . . well, you rather asked for it, you know. (MARBLE *turns away.*) Surely you see . . . ?

(*Suddenly* MARBLE *opens his eyes and stares at* JIM. *He braces himself and lets go of the table.*)

MARBLE (*in a new, decisive tone, quietly*). Yes. You're quite justified. I've behaved very badly. (*He lowers his head.*)

JIM (*surprised*). I say. I'm awfully sorry. I——

MARBLE. No. You were quite right. It's not much use me apologizing. I do ask one thing, though. That you have a drink with me before you go. (*He looks up suddenly.*) Just to show there's no ill feeling, eh?

JIM. Well . . . thanks. It will have to be rather a quick one.

MARBLE. That's the way! (*Going toward the fireplace.*) Sit down for half a minute. (MARBLE *takes photo from the mantelpiece, gives it to* JIM.) Here, have a look at this. . . . D'you know anybody there? (*Goes to the sideboard.*)

JIM (*sits in the armchair*). Is this your wedding?

MARBLE. Yes; that's right. (*Pours out whisky and water into the glasses.*) What was that?

JIM (*turns his head*). I didn't hear anything.

MARBLE. Sounded like young Winnie calling out. Just a minute. (*Opens the door.*) I'd better just see. This storm, you know . . . she's a nervy kid. (*Takes one of the glasses he just filled out into the passage, and puts it on the cupboard. He then takes the cyanide bottle out of the cupboard and comes back, into the doorway, with it in his hand.*) You don't mind?

JIM (*without turning round*). No, of course. . . . Carry on.

(MARBLE *goes out; shuts the door. After a slight pause he returns, carrying the glass. Shuts the door after him.*)

MARBLE. False alarm! Must have been the storm. It's worse than ever. (*Goes to the sideboard, gets the second glass, and comes down L. of the table, carrying both glasses, and crosses to* JIM.)

JIM. Is Mother here?

MARBLE (*jerkily*). Yes, yes, I think so. On the left there, isn't she?

JIM. Oh, yes, I don't think I should ever have known her if you hadn't said. (*Rises.*) That must have been taken just before they went out to Melbourne? (*Puts photo on the mantelpiece.*)

MARBLE. Yes. (*Hands* JIM *his drink; then, as if with a great effort, he says:*) Well . . . drink up!

JIM. Cheero! (*He raises his glass.*)

(MARBLE *watches very intently.*)

CURTAIN

SCENE II

SCENE—*The same—about four o'clock the following afternoon.*

ANNIE *is watering the aspidistra at the window L. with a china jug. She dusts the leaves.* WINNIE *enters C. with* MARBLE'S *black clothes, which are crumpled and muddy, and comes to R. of the table.*

ANNIE. That storm has made a mess of the garden—it's like a marsh out there. Are they dry yet?

WINNIE. I think so. They feel all right.

(ANNIE *crosses to the table, takes them, and holds them up.*)

ANNIE (*L. of the table*). Goodness me, what a pickle! Get me the brush, dear, will you? (WINNIE *goes out for the brush.*) How I'm ever going to get them clean I don't know.

WINNIE (*handing the clothes brush*). Mum, how *did* he get them in that state?

ANNIE. I can't imagine. It reminds me of the time he used to play football.

WINNIE (*laughing incredulously*). Father play football?

ANNIE (*slightly indignant*). Well . . . and why not? When we were engaged he was considered a good player. He played every Saturday for years.

WINNIE. Yes, Mother, but . . . not in the middle of the night!

ANNIE. Don't be so silly, Winnie.

WINNIE. Well, what was he doing? Did he go out somewhere with Mr. Medland?

ANNIE. He didn't say anything. I thought he looked rather queer this morning.

WINNIE. And he didn't eat any breakfast.

ANNIE. Oh, he didn't do so bad. Two rashers——

WINNIE. Mum, he didn't eat them!

ANNIE. Didn't eat them!

WINNIE. No . . . I did.

ANNIE (*astonished*). You?

WINNIE. Yes. He told me to. After you'd gone out.

ANNIE. But . . . whatever for?

WINNIE. He said he couldn't eat and it would only worry you if you knew. He told me not to say anything.

ANNIE (*with conviction*). He's sickening for something! A good thing you told me. (*Reconsidering it.*) No. No, it isn't. You're a very naughty girl to tell me when your father said not.

WINNIE. Well, I thought you ought to know. He was ever so stiff, too. He could hardly get up from the table.

(WINNIE *goes up to the sideboard.*)

ANNIE. There! It's his lumbago again, I'll be bound. Well, it's not to be wondered at, getting sopped to the skin like this. (*Takes coat to the window and continues to brush it.*) Whyever couldn't he have told me about his things? I didn't find them till I was tidying up about eleven. He must have gone off in a damp vest, too, this morning! What *can* he have been doing to get in this state? These'll have to go to the cleaner's, I should think.

WINNIE. There isn't any whisky left. Perhaps that's it.

ANNIE (*comes back to the table and continues brushing*). Winnie! How dare you say such things? (*Revolving the possibility in her mind.*) There was hardly any left last night and—(*rejecting it*)—in any case, you've no call to talk like that about your father. I don't think Mr. Medland—— Well! Now that's funny!

WINNIE (*comes down R. of* ANNIE). What, Mum?

ANNIE. Why, the glasses! It's only just struck me. There weren't any. Of course, Mr. Medland may not have had anything. But . . . I wonder what Father did with his.

WINNIE. Perhaps he took it upstairs.

ANNIE. No, I should have seen it. I'll ask him when he comes in.

WINNIE (thoughtfully). Mum! (Kneels on chair R. of the table.)

ANNIE. Well?

WINNIE. Why did Father want me to kiss him last night? He never does in the ordinary way.

ANNIE. I don't know, dear. I expect he wanted to make it up. And that reminds me . . . you'd better do your homework out there another evening. It worries Father so when you fidget.

WINNIE. Well, I can't see why he wants to get so cross.

ANNIE. You don't understand, dear. He's had a lot of worry lately.

WINNIE. About Mr. Evans?

ANNIE. Yes, and . . . other things.

WINNIE. Mum, how awful if Mr. Evans puts in the brokers!

ANNIE. Well, there's no need to worry over that any more. Father gave me the money this morning and I went straight down and saw Mr. Evans and made it all right.

WINNIE. But I thought Father said last night he hadn't got any money.

ANNIE. He hadn't then, but . . . Mr. Medland did something for him, I think.

WINNIE. Oh! How lovely! (Sits on chair R. of the table.) I liked Mr. Medland awfully, Mum, didn't you?

ANNIE. Yes, I thought he was a very nice young man.

WINNIE. Will he come a lot, do you think?

ANNIE. I expect so. I don't think he knows anyone over here.

WINNIE. Did he stop late?

ANNIE. I think so. I didn't hear Father come up. Now I come to think of it, it must have been late because I remember waking up and looking at the clock, and he hadn't come to bed. The storm was making such a noise . . . like furniture being dragged about . . . I couldn't get off again for some time.

WINNIE. I didn't notice the storm at all. Mr. Medland's awfully good-looking, isn't he?

ANNIE. Yes. Your auntie was good-looking as a girl.

WINNIE. Mum, what's the Carlton?

ANNIE. Goodness me, child, what a lot of questions you do ask.

WINNIE. I only wanted to know.

ANNIE. I dare say, but I've got something else to do. Just run and put my iron on the gas, there's a good girl. I must try to do something with these. (WINNIE *rises.*) It's doing his best suit no good to be sitting about in it in the office. (*Sound of front door opening.*) There is Father, now.

(WINNIE *passes up C. to L.*)

(MARBLE *is wearing a blue serge suit, an overcoat, and bowler. A paper-wrapped bottle sticks out of one pocket. His face appears strained and white. His manner is very jerky, suggesting that his nerves are at high tension. Throughout the following he is continually glancing out of the window and is unable to keep still for two seconds.*)

ANNIE (*upward inflection*). Will.

MARBLE (*after a glance round the room and through the window*). Has . . . anyone been? (*He appears to be holding his breath to hear her answer.*)

ANNIE. No. Who did you mean, dear? (*Crosses R.*)

MARBLE. Anyone. You're sure?

ANNIE. Of course, dear. Why?

MARBLE. Oh . . . nothing. (*Goes to the window L., then up to the sideboard.*)

ANNIE. Is anything . . . the matter, Will?

MARBLE. No. Did you pay Evans? (*Puts bottle on the sideboard.*)

ANNIE. Yes. It will be quite all right, he said. He was very apologetic. . . .

MARBLE. I've no doubt . . . *now!* You won't go there again, Annie,

understand? I won't have a single thing from that fellow after this.

ANNIE. But I don't think he——

MARBLE. You heard what I said. You can get what you want from the Stores.

ANNIE (*after a glance of surprise*). Very well.

(MARBLE *goes up to the door.*)

MARBLE. Where's Winnie?

ANNIE. In the kitchen, dear.

MARBLE. Did she come straight back from school?

ANNIE. Yes, I think so.

MARBLE. Straight in here to you?

ANNIE. Yes. Why?

MARBLE. I wondered, that's all. (*He goes off, takes hat and coat out. In the passage.*) Did you settle with all the others?

ANNIE. All except Tanner's. I hadn't quite enough.

MARBLE (*returns to sideboard up L.C.*). I'll give it to you. I want them all settled up. We don't want anything more like that with Evans. (*Unwrapping the bottle.*)

ANNIE. It was very generous of that boy, dear, wasn't it?

MARBLE (*very quietly*). Yes. (*Busies himself with the cork.*)

ANNIE (*R. of the table, folding clothes*). It isn't every boy who would act like that . . . specially not knowing us very well.

MARBLE. No.

ANNIE. We must do everything we can to see that he's paid back, Will.

(MARBLE *gives a little shudder and pours a stiff whisky.*)

MARBLE. Of course . . . in time . . .

ANNIE (*seeing his drink*). Let me get you some tea, dear.

MARBLE. No, thanks . . . I don't want any.

ANNIE. Do. I've got a really nice tea for you today.

MARBLE. I say I don't want any! (*Gulps the whisky neat.*)

ANNIE. All right, dear. (*A pause.*) Whatever happened last night, Will?

MARBLE (*gasping*). What . . . what do you mean?

ANNIE. Your clothes . . . just look at them.

MARBLE. I . . . I fell down.

ANNIE (*genuinely concerned*). Oh, I'm sorry, Will. That's why you were stiff, then?

MARBLE (*jumping at it*). Yes. Yes, that's it. It shook me up, rather.

ANNIE. You're sure you're not hurt, Will? You look so white.

MARBLE. It's nothing.

ANNIE. These will have to go to the cleaner's, I think. How did you come to fall? (*Folding the clothes.*)

MARBLE (*improvising desperately*). I don't quite know . . . it was dark. I went with . . . with young Medland to find a taxi . . . We had to go right down to Goldstone Road. I . . . came in by the back way and . . . fell over the border. It was pouring . . .

ANNIE. Yes, it's taken all day to dry your things. If I'd known I'd never have let you go off in those wet underthings this morning. (*Puts the clothes on the fender, below the fire.*)

MARBLE. They weren't wet.

ANNIE. They must have been, with your suit like this. And Mr. Medland getting drenched, too . . . I hope neither of you take cold . . .

MARBLE. Oh, for goodness' sake, let's talk about something else, Annie. (*Turns up L.*)

ANNIE. I'm sorry, dear. Only, you know what you are with colds at this time of year and——

(MARBLE *starts violently and clutches the sideboard as a sharp knock is heard on the front door.*)

MARBLE. Who . . . who's that? (*He looks terrified.*)

ANNIE. I'll see. (*Noticing his expression.*) Why, whatever's the matter, Will?

MARBLE. I felt a bit queer. It's nothing. . . .

ANNIE. It's those wet things. (*She goes out C.*)

(MARBLE *stands trying to get a grip on himself, then goes and stands behind the door.* HAMMOND *enters, looks round—*MARBLE *comes from behind the door.*)

HAMMOND. Hullo, Will!

MARBLE (*with tremendous relief*). Oh, it's you?

HAMMOND. Who did you think it was—Betty Nuthall? Well, how goes it?

(ANNIE *re-enters.*)

MARBLE. Oh, all right, thanks.

HAMMOND (*to* ANNIE). And Mrs. M.?

ANNIE (*C.*). Very well, thank you. How is Mrs. Hammond?

HAMMOND (*L.C.*). Nicely. Will's looking a bit off color, isn't he?

ANNIE. He got very wet last night. We had a young——

MARBLE (*almost shouting her down—crosses over L.*). I wish you'd stop talking about me not being well. It's absolute nonsense.

HAMMOND (*a great success in the bar-parlor at this sort of thing*). Ought to be like me, my boy. Five miles every morning before breakfast. Nothing like it.

ANNIE (*politely*). Oh, Mr. Hammond.

HAMMOND (*C., laughing loudly*). Well, *if* I did it, I should enjoy it!

MARBLE (*unable to raise a smile*). You'd better have a drink. Annie, we shall want another glass. I broke one last night.

(HAMMOND *moves down to front of table—R. end.*)

ANNIE. I'll get you one. (*Goes out with the clothes.*)

HAMMOND (*front of the table*). Well . . . and how's the world been treating you?

MARBLE (*to L. of the table*). Oh, all right. (*Feeling he must say something.*) And you?

HAMMOND. Mustn't grumble. Sold two houses this week. One's a bargain . . . if it doesn't fall down. (*Laughs.*) Haven't seen you in the Crown lately.

MARBLE. No . . . I haven't been down lately.

HAMMOND. Nothing wrong, is there?

MARBLE. Of course not. What do you mean? (*Turns and looks out of the window.*)

HAMMOND. Nothing. Just wondered. (*Looking out of the window.*) Hullo! Started gardening at your time of life? (*Goes to window L.*)

MARBLE (*nearly dropping his glass*). What?

HAMMOND. Been digging a bit, haven't you? Those weeds . . .

MARBLE. I haven't touched them. I . . . It must be that dog of

Kingston's. It's always straying about.

HAMMOND. Better hire him. Clean the garden for you cheap! (*Laughs.*)

MARBLE (*with a ghastly smile*). Yes. . . . That's right. (*With great relief.*)

(ANNIE *enters with glass and jug of water.*)

MARBLE. Here you are. . . . There's only water.

(ANNIE *goes R. and sits up-stage end of the club fender.*)

HAMMOND (L.). That doesn't hurt us in small quantities. (MARBLE *pours it.*) Whoa! Thanks. Well, God bless the sergeant-major! (*Drinks. Goes C.*) Mrs. M.—my best respects. (*He drinks.*) By the way, while I think of it . . . have you ever thought of moving?

MARBLE. Moving? (*Puts glass on the sideboard.*)

HAMMOND. Out of here, I mean. There's a rumor these houses are going to be sold. We've got a little place on our books now . . . suit you both down to the ground. Dirt-cheap, too. Do you a treat.

MARBLE (*slowly*). We aren't moving.

HAMMOND. No harm in talking it over. (*To* ANNIE.) You'd like to get out in the country, wouldn't you?

ANNIE (*rises*). Oh, yes . . . if——

HAMMOND. Well, here's your chance. Lower rates. Not much longer to the City——

MARBLE. We aren't moving from here. . . . (*Looking out of the window.*) We'll never move from here.

HAMMOND. Never's a long time. Look here, Will, it's the——

MARBLE. I don't care what it is. I don't care if it's Buckingham Palace rent free. I tell you I don't want it. That's plain enough, isn't it?

HAMMOND. Well . . . I suppose you know your own mind. No accounting for tastes, is there? I shouldn't have thought this place was so lovely as all that.

MARBLE (*violently, nerves jangling*). What the hell is it to you where I live? You seem to find it pretty comfortable here. You're in often enough!

HAMMOND. Here! Here! What's up with you?

ANNIE. Will, really! Mr. Hammond was only trying to——

MARBLE. Yes, yes, I know. (*Sits L. of the table.*)

HAMMOND. No need to jump down a chap's throat just because he——

MARBLE. All right . . . I'm sorry, Charlie. Only for God's sake don't keep on about moving, because I don't want to hear it. We shall never leave here.

HAMMOND. No offense where none's meant, I'm sure. (*Finishes drink and puts the glass on the table. As* MARBLE *takes no notice,* HAMMOND *goes R.C. and says to* ANNIE:) Been in the new shop at the corner yet? You know—Modes-ay-robes. (*Makes gesture to indicate sign over shop.*)

ANNIE. No. They've got some very nice things.

HAMMOND. Yes. It's a Frenchwoman—Madame Collins.

ANNIE. Oh! It doesn't sound French, does it?

HAMMOND. That's because she married an Englishman—ex-officer. He's in a nursing home at present. We let the shop to her. She's French all right! You haven't seen her?

ANNIE. No, I don't think so.

HAMMOND. Built for speed if ever a girl was! Mouth the color of a pillar box, and can't she use it! You should have heard her beating the guv'nor down over the rent. Talk? I've never heard anything like it! And the scent . . . She must have had a bath in it.

ANNIE. I expect she dresses very well, doesn't she, being French?

(MARBLE *has been watching something in the garden very intently.*)

HAMMOND. Not half! You'll have to keep an eye on the old man. Eh, Will?

(*As he turns toward* MARBLE, *the latter suddenly jumps up and runs from the room without answering.*)

HAMMOND. Why, what's up?

ANNIE *and* HAMMOND (*together*). Will! What is it?

(*They look at each other blankly.*)

HAMMOND. Well, I'm blowed!

ANNIE. He's gone out in the garden! (*Crossing toward the window.*)

HAMMOND (*following*). What's the matter with him?

ANNIE (*looking out*). Why, it's Mrs. Smither's little boy come after his ball.

HAMMOND (*disappointedly*). Oh! I thought at least it was a fire or something decent! (*Excitedly.*) Gawd! Look at Will! He isn't half wild.

ANNIE (*fearfully*). Oh, he'll hurt the child, Mr. Hammond. . . . Go and stop him, do. What is he thinking of? Go on, quick!

HAMMOND. Not me. I'm not being dragged into it. Old Smither's going to have something to say about this, I'll bet.

ANNIE. There, he's taking him to the gate. I can't think why he wanted to be so rough. It's not like him.

HAMMOND. Darn shame, I call it. Kid's not doing any harm. It isn't as if there was anything in the border to hurt. Lot of old weeds.

ANNIE (*goes across to R.C.*). I'm worried about Will. He's so queer . . .

HAMMOND. Look at the way he bit my tongue off just now about moving. Anyone would think I'd said something terrible.

(POSTMAN'S *knock is heard.*)

ANNIE. That's the postman. (*Goes out C. to R.*)

(*Then* MARBLE *appears in the passage L. of the door, watching the front door.*)

(ANNIE *off, to* POSTMAN). Have you got a pencil?

(HAMMOND *goes across to the fireplace.*)

HAMMOND (*R., amazed at his own tact*). Evenings begin to draw out now, don't they? Summertime'll be here before we know where we are.

(*Voices from the passage.* MARBLE *listening,* HAMMOND *stealing glances at him.* ANNIE *returns with quarto registered envelope.*)

ANNIE. For you, dear. (*Hands it to* MARBLE.) I had to sign for it.

(MARBLE *comes behind the table, stares at it. Then opens it and pulls out a letter and enclosure. The others watch—a registered letter is not an everyday event in Malcolm Road.*)

MARBLE. What on earth . . . (*He reads it. Turns it over and back, his mouth open. He appears dazed.*)

ANNIE. What is it, Will?

(*A pause.*)

MARBLE. Notice to quit!

ANNIE. What?

HAMMOND. What do you mean?

MARBLE (*still facing the window*). Notice to quit. . . . To get out of here . . . in a month!

ANNIE. But, Will . . . why?

MARBLE (*same dead voice*). I don't know.

ANNIE (*R.C.*). But after all this time . . . it's . . . it's so funny.

HAMMOND (*R.—the opportunist*). Well, if the worst comes to the worst, there's that place I spoke about. I expect we'll be able to fit you up. . . .

MARBLE (*suddenly violently alive, shaking with excitement*). No, you won't! We're not leaving here. . . . I told you just now . . . we're stopping here if . . . if we have to buy the place! Buy it! See? (*He looks quite aggressive.*)

HAMMOND. Oh!

ANNIE. Will, how *can* you buy it? . . . Besides, do we want to? There must be lots of other places——

MARBLE (*the strain of the last half-hour and the two neat whiskies making him quite formidable*). I don't care if there are a thousand other places! I'm going to have *this* place!

ANNIE. But—— Will dear, how are you going to find the money?

MARBLE (*hysterically*). We'll find it, I tell you! We've *got* to!

(ANNIE *and* HAMMOND *exchange glances.* MARBLE *is breathing with difficulty.*)

CURTAIN

SCENE III

SCENE—*The same. It is six o'clock on an evening nearly a week later.*

At the rise of the curtain, MARBLE *is discovered pacing across the room reading* Medical Jurisprudence. *He throws the book onto the table, goes up, opens the door, listens, goes to the front door, opens it, pauses, shuts it, and comes back into the room. He picks up the book and continues to pace backward and forward, reading. The front door is heard to open.*

MARBLE (*calling*). That you, Annie? (*Goes to the door.*)

ANNIE (*from the passage*). Yes, dear.

MARBLE. Where have you been? It's after six.

(ANNIE *and* WINNIE *enter. They wear hats and coats.*)

ANNIE (*C.*). I know, but as you didn't come by the four-twenty, we——

MARBLE (*goes to the fireplace*). I *did* come by it. I stopped for a minute or two at the library, that's all.

ANNIE. Well, dear, we weren't to know. We walked along as far as the cleaner's, and called in for your black clothes . . . but they weren't ready. (*Taking off gloves.*)

MARBLE. Well, hurry up and get your things off. I've got something to tell you. . . . Yes, both of you. Buck up!

ANNIE (*going*). Come along, then, Winnie.

(*They go up toward the door.*)

MARBLE. No. Take them off here. Why can't you? I've been waiting about quite long enough.

WINNIE (*looking at the book on the table*). Medical Jurisprudence. What a funny name!

ANNIE. Hush, dear. Father's got something to tell us.

MARBLE (*as they sit down*). Take them off, for goodness' sake! I can't talk properly with people sitting about in hats and things.

ANNIE. Very well. (*They take off hats and coats. To* WINNIE.) Put them over there, dear. That's it. (WINNIE *puts them on the chair L. To* MARBLE.) What was it you wanted to say?

MARBLE. Sit down and I'll tell you. (ANNIE *sits C. and* WINNIE L. *of the table.*) It's all spoilt now, anyway. All this hanging about has about taken the edge off.

ANNIE. Well, I'm sorry, dear, but we weren't to know, were we?

MARBLE. Oh, all right, all right. It doesn't matter. (*Comes to above chair R. of the table. He assumes a very offhand tone.*) What I was going to tell you is nothing really to get excited about, I suppose. . . . It's only that . . . I've pulled off a little deal. . . . Merely a matter of finance, which, of course, wouldn't interest you.

ANNIE. But . . . Will, what is it? Have you made some money?

MARBLE. Yes, a little. Ha! Nothing much. Just enough to keep us all in luxury for the rest of our lives.

(*They gape at him.*)

MARBLE. Well? Lost your tongues?

ANNIE (*dazed*). I . . . I don't understand, Will. How much do you mean?

MARBLE (*recovering his spirits as he makes his impression*). Never mind. Quite a lot, Annie, anyway. (*Moving down below R. of the table.*) The right side of thirty thousand pounds, shall we say?

ANNIE (*staggered*). Thirty thousand . . . ?

WINNIE. Father!

(*A pause.*)

ANNIE. But . . . Will, how *can* you have made all that?

MARBLE. Perhaps because I'm not quite such a fool as you thought, Annie. (*He crosses over L., pleased with the sensation he has caused.*) You're not the only one who's had a surprise . . . not by a long chalk! (*Stopping.*) You don't believe me, eh?

ANNIE. Well, dear, I . . . I hardly know what to think. It's all so sudden . . . I can't understand . . .

MARBLE. That shouldn't be difficult. It means that instead of scraping and pinching and not knowing where the next bob's coming from, you'll have all you want for the house and your clothes and——

(ANNIE *and* WINNIE *notice whisky on the sideboard.*)

ANNIE. Oh! Will! It isn't a joke, is it?

(*They stare at* MARBLE.)

MARBLE. No! No! No! It's the *truth*.

ANNIE. Well! I can't get over it! Why . . . we could have those new curtains for the front!

MARBLE. Yes, and the back too, if you want 'em. And new carpets . . . and new furniture, and—— Stop a bit! I'll tell you what. You shall each choose what you'd like to have. Kind of celebration, see? You first, miss. What's your fancy, eh?

WINNIE. Oh, Father.

MARBLE. Well, come on, now! Give it a name!

WINNIE (*after deep thought, suddenly*). Green garters!

MARBLE (*highly amused*). Ho! And why green garters?

WINNIE. Gladys Brown's got some. She thinks she's everyone.

MARBLE. Ho! Ho! I see. And you want to take her down a peg, eh?

Well, I don't suppose they'll break us. (*Goes up.*) I think we might run to something a bit better than that. I've been thinking it over and I thought we might manage a college of some sort. Place for young ladies . . . abroad somewhere, perhaps. Parley-voo francy, eh, Winnie? What do you say to that?

WINNIE. Father! How marvelous! Gladys would be simply furious.

ANNIE. What are you thinking of, Will? Abroad——

MARBLE. Well, why not? The head cashier's girl went. (*Places his hand on her head.*) My daughter's as good as his, isn't she?

ANNIE. Yes, but——

MARBLE. There's no "but" about it. If she wants to go, she shall go. Wait a minute, though, we haven't had your choice yet, Annie. (*To* WINNIE.) If Mother's too greedy, Winnie, you won't be able to go, after all. Come on, Mother! What's it to be?

WINNIE. Yes, Mum, you say!

ANNIE. I can't, Will! I don't rightly understand yet what you were saying. I mean, I don't see how you came to make all that money.

MARBLE. I had a gamble in francs, and it happened to come off. Just a question of knowing the right time to buy and having the guts to chance it.

ANNIE. But . . . how could you buy anything? Where did you get the money?

MARBLE. Made some of 'em think a bit, I have. (*He chuckles.*)

ANNIE. Will . . . it won't mean that . . . that you'll lose your job, will it?

MARBLE. Oh, no. But the job's going to lose me!

ANNIE. My dear, but——

MARBLE. Twenty years of being ordered about like a blooming dog, Annie, is quite enough for yours truly, thank you. I'm independent now.

ANNIE. You . . . you don't mean you're not going to work, Will?

MARBLE. Not for the County National, Annie.

WINNIE. Oh, Mum, you still haven't said what you'd like to have. Do choose. It's so thrilling!

ANNIE. I can't, dear.

MARBLE. Why not? Of course you can. Anything you like within reason.

ANNIE (*more to humor him*). Well, you know what I've always wanted——

MARBLE. And what's that?

ANNIE. Why, a little house in the country.

(MARBLE *stops dead, facing the window.*)

WINNIE (*gaily*). Oh, yes, Father! Can we?

(MARBLE *remains quite still for a few minutes.*)

MARBLE (*rather hoarsely*). No! You can't.

ANNIE (*surprised*). Well, I'm sorry, dear, only . . . you did say *anything*.

MARBLE. I know I did and I meant anything . . . except *that!* (*Turns to her.*) Besides, as a matter of fact, I've fixed up this afternoon to buy this place.

ANNIE. Buy it?

MARBLE. Yes. So you'll have to choose something else. Go on. . . .

ANNIE. Well, if we're going to stay on here, the house wants doing up very badly.

MARBLE (*pretending to misunderstand*). You mean, you'd like some new furniture? All right, you shall have——

ANNIE. Not that so much, dear. I meant more the walls and ceilings, and the outside if we've got to see to it now.

MARBLE. That'd mean workmen all over the place.

ANNIE. But if we're so well off now, Will, couldn't we go for a holiday while they do it?

MARBLE. NO! At least . . . I'm not going. I'm not leaving a lot of strangers nosing about the place. I think I'd better choose for you, don't you?

ANNIE. Perhaps you'd better, dear.

MARBLE (*going behind the table toward the fireplace*). Well, what about you and I having a day up Tottenham Court Road, and getting a few things in place of all this muck? (*Kicks chair R. of the table as he passes.*) You'd like that, wouldn't you?

ANNIE. Yes. Thank you, Will.

MARBLE. You won't find me mean, Annie.

ANNIE. No, dear, I'm sure I shan't.

MARBLE (*with relief*). Well, then, that's settled. (*Filling pipe.*)

WINNIE. Mother, won't it be gorgeous going abroad?

ANNIE. I shouldn't set your mind on that, dear.

MARBLE. Why not, Annie? She'll be all right in a school. I mean, they'll look after her.

ANNIE. Yes, but——

WINNIE. And I expect I'll meet lots of awfully nice girls, don't you? Ladies, I mean. There's a girl at school and her mother used to teach music to a girl who was an Honorable. She used to go to school in Paris.

MARBLE. Oh, you'll be in with all the nobs, Winnie. Be looking down on your old father, likely enough, before long, eh?

WINNIE. Of course I wouldn't! Never! (*Rises.*) Oh, Mum, can I go up and look through my things?

ANNIE. Whatever for?

WINNIE. Well, I shall have to go through them. There'll be no end I'll want, won't there?

ANNIE. Good gracious me! Anyone would think you were off in the morning, to hear you talk.

WINNIE. Oh, Mother, *do* let me.

MARBLE. Let the kid go if she wants to, Annie. What harm is there? (*Lights pipe.*)

ANNIE (*to* WINNIE). Oh, very well.

(WINNIE *goes out and runs upstairs.*) Will—(*rises; puts chair under the table*)—do you think it's quite fair, dear, filling her head with ideas like that? She'll be terribly disappointed. She really thinks she's going.

MARBLE. Thinks? She *is* going.

ANNIE. That child? To . . . to Paris or somewhere?

MARBLE. Yes. Why not? Look here, Annie, you still don't seem to understand. I've made a lot of money . . . a hell of a lot. And . . . well, you want her to grow up a lady, I suppose?

ANNIE (*goes L., gets hats, etc.*). Well, naturally, dear, but——

MARBLE. Very well, then. With the money I'm prepared to spend we can make damn sure of it. A girl can't grow up a lady if she's only been to school in England. You know that as well as I do.

(*A pause.*)

ANNIE. Will. (*Crosses to C. below the table.*)

MARBLE. Yes?

ANNIE. I wish—— (*Hesitating, uncomfortable.*) I don't quite know how to . . . say it. . . .

MARBLE (*comes C.*). Well?

ANNIE (*making the plunge*). Will, couldn't you . . . tell me?

MARBLE. Tell you?

ANNIE. All about it, I mean.

MARBLE (*slightly uneasy*). About what? I don't know what you're talking about, Annie.

ANNIE. My dear, I'd never blame you . . . whatever you'd done, really I wouldn't.

MARBLE. How do you mean . . . whatever I'd done?

ANNIE. Will, can't you trust me? It frightens me not knowing. . . . I'd rather you told me . . . everything.

MARBLE (*getting really alarmed*). I . . . I don't know what you're driving at.

ANNIE (*feeling that he does*). I couldn't help guessing, dear. You've looked so worried and . . . that jumping so when anyone knocked . . . Oh, don't you see?

MARBLE (*trembling*). What have you guessed?

ANNIE. It won't make any difference between us, dear, I promise. I expect you think I'd say something

. . . but I wouldn't. I'd never say a word.

MARBLE. There isn't anything . . . for you to know. (*He avoids looking at her.*)

ANNIE. Oh, Will, you make it so difficult. . . . You know what I meant. . . . I suppose I do know . . . really.

MARBLE (*shrinking back, eyes starting—drops pipe*). You . . . know?

ANNIE (*puts her hand on his arm*). Dear . . . you've looked so queer and white . . . I couldn't help noticing. I tried to think that it wasn't that . . .

MARBLE (*whispering*). What?

ANNIE. I tried to pretend to myself that it was all my imagination, but all the time I . . . I knew. . . . (MARBLE *opens his mouth, but cannot speak.*) I didn't mean to worry you more, dear. I just thought if you *could* talk to me about it . . . it might . . . help. (MARBLE *is silent. He is shaking badly.*) There's one thing, Will . . . Does anyone suspect?

MARBLE. Annie——

ANNIE. All right, we won't talk about it. . . . I only felt that if the Bank sent anyone here when you weren't in, I shouldn't know what to——

MARBLE (*incredulously*). The Bank?

ANNIE. When they find the money's gone, I mean. (MARBLE *stares at her.*) Yes, dear, I guessed. I mean, a man in your position . . . Thousands of pounds like that . . . But I understand, Will. The temptation——

(MARBLE *finds an outlet in a burst of hysterical sounds, half laughing, half sobbing.* ANNIE *becomes frightened.*)

ANNIE. Dear, why do you look like that? I was bound to know sooner or later, wasn't I? I—— Will! Don't, dear! Don't! What is it? What have I—— What have I said?

MARBLE. You'll . . . be . . . the . . . death of me . . . Annie.

ANNIE. What do you mean, Will?

MARBLE (*laughing hysterically*). You really don't think I'm a thief, do you? (*Suddenly stops laughing.*) It's . . . so . . . damn . . . funny. . . .

CURTAIN

ACT TWO

SCENE I

SCENE—*The same, about two months later.*

The old paintwork and wallpaper look shabbier than ever by contrast with the over-gilded rococo and pseudo-Empire monstrosities which replace the old furniture.

When the curtain rises, MARBLE *is outside in the hall superintending the operations of remover's men.*

MARBLE (*entering*). In here—— (*He moves a chair, which is turned upside down on another, to above the fireplace.*)

(*Two men bring in a massive marble-topped table, richly encrusted with gilt cupids and bunches of fruit.*)

1ST WORKMAN. Where you goin' to 'ave 'er, guv'nor?

MARBLE (*to R.C., indicating*). Over here for now.

(*They carry table to position R.C.*)

1ST WORKMAN (*above the table*). Get your end round more, Bert. That'll do. (*Table is lowered.*) All right like that, guv'nor?

MARBLE. Yes, thank you. How much more is there to come in?

1ST WORKMAN (*looks round the room*). Nearly the lot, Bert, ain't it?

2ND WORKMAN. Yers, 'cept for the pictures. I'll fetch 'em in.

(*He goes out.*)

1ST WORKMAN. Only the pictures left, guv'nor.

MARBLE. Good. (*Crosses to R. of the table.*)

1ST WORKMAN (*dusts the top of the table with his cap*). Yes, it's a fine piece. If you was to ask me, I should say you was lucky to 'ave got 'old of it.

MARBLE. Yes. I think I was, rather. They said I might not see another like it for years.

1ST WORKMAN. That's a fact. (*Tapping carving.*) Nice bunch of fruit, you know. Must say I like a bit of carvin' on furniture.

MARBLE. What sort of furniture would you call it?

1ST WORKMAN. Eh! Oh! That's Looey Cans, that is. It's named after Looey Cans of France, same as some's named after Chippendale and some 'Epplewhite.

MARBLE. Well, he knew how to make furniture, whoever he was.

1ST WORKMAN. There now! Funny you should say that.

MARBLE. Oh?

1ST WORKMAN. Well, to tell you the truth, I shouldn't have known if it wasn't for the party outside.

MARBLE. Who do you mean?

1ST WORKMAN (*crosses to up C.*). Party been watching us get the stuff out of the van. She sez to me, "It's Looey Cans, ain't it?" "No," I sez. "It ain't—it's Mr. Marble's."

MARBLE (*comes down C. anxiously*). Who is she? What's she like?

1ST WORKMAN. Oh, young party. Very posh rig-out—wanted to look over the house. Told 'er there was people living here, of course.

MARBLE (*suspiciously*). She been trying to pump you? About me, I mean?

1ST WORKMAN. No, nothing except that about the furniture.

MARBLE (*slightly reassured*). Oh!

1ST WORKMAN (*with obvious financial interest*). Pretty keen she was to see the stuff. She lives in the neighborhood—got a shop round the corner. . . .

MARBLE. Oh!

1ST WORKMAN. Very nice, she seemed. (MARBLE *goes up*.) Bit of a looker, as you might say.

MARBLE (*goes up into the passage and looks off R.—daringly*). Yes—well—I don't see that it would matter. (*Comes down C.*) If she wants to see my furniture, I don't see why she shouldn't.

(2ND WORKMAN *appearing with two pictures*.)

2ND WORKMAN. 'Ullo!

1ST WORKMAN. That bit o' stuff still 'angin' about?

2ND WORKMAN. What, Mademoiselle from Armenteers?

1ST WORKMAN. Yers.

2ND WORKMAN (*R. of the door*). Yers . . . she's still outside. Just been tellin' me as how this stuff reminds 'er of the old shatoh! (*Dumps pictures against a leg of the table.*)

1ST WORKMAN (*to* MARBLE). What about it, guv'nor?

MARBLE. Well . . . I think so, yes. Say . . . say if she likes to look at the things no one won't object.

1ST WORKMAN. Right. You tell 'er, Bert.

2ND WORKMAN. Right you are. (*Goes out.*)

MARBLE (*to* 1ST WORKMAN). You might just put those up on the hangers. (*Pointing to the old picture hooks.*) Make the room look a bit brighter, eh?

(1ST WORKMAN *lifts massively framed reproduction of Landseer's most supercilious twelve-pointer.*)

1ST WORKMAN. Which way you goin' to 'ave 'em?

MARBLE (*indicating L. of doorway*). That one 'ud look all right there, I should think.

1ST WORKMAN. Right yer are. (*Starts to go up steps.*) Steps are a bit wonky, guv'nor. (MARBLE *goes up and holds steps. It is hung L. of the door.*) 'Ow's that?

MARBLE. That'll do. The other'll go the other side. (*Crossing to R. of the door.*) Over there.

(*The other, a framed reproduction of "True and Loyal," is duly hoisted.* MADAME COLLINS, *a striking-looking woman of thirty or so, appears in the doorway. She is smartly dressed and rather vividly made up and has a graceful figure. She speaks with a foreign accent and considerable gesticulation.*)

MADAME COLLINS. It is true, what they say? That I may come in?

MARBLE (*nervously*). Yes, that's right. I told them.

MADAME COLLINS. Ah, but you are very kind.

MARBLE. Not at all. Pleasure, I'm sure.

1ST WORKMAN (*on the steps*). Looks nice, don't they?

MARBLE. Yes, they'll do nicely like that. Thanks.

1ST WORKMAN. You're welcome.

(*Exit C.*)

MADAME COLLINS. I 'ave so much admired all your beautiful things. I say to the workmen that I must see 'oo it is that 'as such charming taste.

MARBLE (*smiling*). Oh, I don't know about that. Just a few odds and ends I've picked up, you know.

MADAME COLLINS. But they are delightful. That table I saw . . . (*turns R.*) there it is! So full of grace! So . . . dignified.

MARBLE. Glad you like it.

MADAME COLLINS. But I adore it. It is magnificent. And your fine English pictures, there! Always they tell a story, do they not? Tell me, now, 'oo is that nice little boy?

MARBLE. Can't say, I'm sure. Looks like little Lord Fauntleroy to me, but I don't rightly know. The wife chose that one.

MADAME COLLINS (*going across up L.*). And the other—that is what *you* like, eh?

MARBLE. Yes, that's it.

MADAME COLLINS. Well, that is quite right, I think. He is so . . . *mâle!*

MARBLE. I beg your pardon?

MADAME COLLINS. I mean, he is so what you call . . . 'ee-man!

MARBLE. Oh, I see.

(*They laugh.* 1ST WORKMAN *enters with another picture.*)

1ST WORKMAN. This is the last, guv'nor.

MARBLE. Right you are.

MADAME COLLINS. May I not see what it is? Another one—what is it now?

(1ST WORKMAN *holds it up, then puts it on the sideboard. It proves to be "September Morn."*)

MADAME COLLINS (*accusingly*). Oho! Can I guess 'oo choose this one?

MARBLE (*embarrassed*). Well . . . I don't remember exactly. (To 1ST WORKMAN.) We'll have that by the window there, I think. Yes, on that hook.

(MADAME COLLINS *works round behind* MARBLE *to the bookcase R.*)

1ST WORKMAN. That's the lot, guv'nor. (*Producing notebook.*) Just get you to sign for 'em, if you don't mind. (MARBLE *signs, gazing at* MADAME COLLINS *all the time.*) That's it, thankee. Anything you'd like us to do before we go?

MARBLE. I don't think there's anything.

(MADAME COLLINS *looks at book titles.*)

1ST WORKMAN (*goes down to the box*). There's that box. (*Pointing to the wooden box.*) Dunno if you wants it opened?

MARBLE. No. It's only some books. I have opened it.

(1ST WORKMAN *goes up C., front of the armchair.*)

1ST WORKMAN (C., *anxiously*). Nothing else, then?

MARBLE. No.

1ST WORKMAN. Oh!

MARBLE (*realizing his omission*). Oh, here . . . get yourself a drink. (*Handing coins.*)

1ST WORKMAN. Thank you, sir. Thank you. Good day to you.

MARBLE. Good day.

1ST WORKMAN. 'Afternoon, lady.

MADAME COLLINS. Good-by.

(1ST WORKMAN *goes out. Front door slams.* MARBLE *shudders.*)

MARBLE (*goes up*). Perhaps I'd better let the wife know you're here. She's upstairs getting things a bit straight.

MADAME COLLINS. But per'aps she will not be pleased to come now if she 'ave so-many things to do?

MARBLE (*catching her eye*). No. (*Shuts door.*) . . . Well, she'll be down directly, I dare say. Er . . . won't you sit down for a minute? (*Indicating the armchair L.C.*)

MADAME COLLINS. Well . . . per-haps. Just for one minute. (*She sits, carefully displaying her knee.*)

MARBLE (*looking quickly away. Goes to table at R.*). Er . . . do you live around here?

MADAME COLLINS. Why, yes! I 'ave the little shop, you know, at the cor-ner—Madame Collins.

MARBLE (*sits on the table R.—puts a foot on the chair*). Oh, so *you're* Madame Collins!

MADAME COLLINS. And why are you surprised?

MARBLE. I don't know. I didn't think of her quite . . . quite like you, somehow.

MADAME COLLINS. No? My 'usband, 'ee is a cripple. So, you see, I must work for both.

MARBLE. Just so. We're kind of neighbors, then, as you might say.

MADAME COLLINS. Yes, I 'ave 'eard already of the celebrated Mr. Marble. That is you, is it not?

MARBLE. Marble's right. I don't know so much about the celebrated.

MADAME COLLINS. There! You are too modest! The fortune that you 'ave made in francs is very well known. All my customers talk about it.

MARBLE. Do they, though?

MADAME COLLINS. Why, of course. They say how clever you are with affairs. My 'usband, 'ee understand nothing about affairs. Nothing! So I 'ave no one to advise.

MARBLE (rises, somewhat moved). Well . . . of course, if there's anything I can do, at any time . . . I shall be delighted.

MADAME COLLINS. I should like sometimes to talk with you.

MARBLE (gallantly). I should feel honored.

MADAME COLLINS. Thank you. You are very, very good.

MARBLE. Er . . . do you smoke?

MADAME COLLINS. Thank you, yes.

(He offers his gold case.)

MADAME COLLINS (admiring it). Ah! C'est ravissante! It is a present from a lady, I am sure?

MARBLE. Well, no . . . as a matter of fact, I bought it myself.

MADAME COLLINS. Oh! But I cannot listen to such stories.

MARBLE. No, really. It's the truth.

(He lights her cigarette—she blows out the match—he lights his cigarette from hers. They laugh.)

MADAME COLLINS. Tell me, why does your wife not come to my little shop, eh?

MARBLE (drags pouffe up close to her, and sits). Well, she's talked about it, I know. She'll come soon, I expect.

MADAME COLLINS. You must bring her.

MARBLE. You'd like me to?

MADAME COLLINS. Why, of course. (Smiles at him.)

MARBLE. Funny we haven't met before, isn't it? Living so close, I mean.

MADAME COLLINS. But I am glad that today we 'ave met. The people I meet 'ere are so dull. Oh! La, la! Lately I am getting bored.

MARBLE. Well, we shall expect to see something of you, now. The missus'd be glad if you'd come in sometimes of an evening, I know.

MADAME COLLINS. And you?

MARBLE. Bet your life!

MADAME COLLINS. If I come I must come alone. My 'usband is in a nursing 'ome.

MARBLE. Well, I could always see you home. That is . . . if you'd let me?

MADAME COLLINS. I think it would be very, very nice.

MARBLE. Same here. (*They laugh intimately. He glances round toward the door and starts to rise.*) I wonder if I ought to call Annie. . . .

MADAME COLLINS. Do you want to?

MARBLE. No.

MADAME COLLINS. Well, then . . .

(MARBLE *looks at her, obviously very attracted.*)

MARBLE (*moves closer to her*). I say, what's your name?

MADAME COLLINS. My name? Why, "Collins."

MARBLE. I mean . . . what else?

MADAME COLLINS. Marguerite. But my friends, they call me Rita.

MARBLE. Including me?

MADAME COLLINS (*smiling*). If you like. I think that your wife may be a little . . . surprised, eh?

MARBLE. Oh, I shouldn't call you that in front of her.

MADAME COLLINS. Oho! I think you are a very naughty man!

MARBLE. It's your fault, you know, if I am.

MADAME COLLINS (*affecting surprise*). *My* fault? And why, if you please?

MARBLE. You're so . . . I can't tell you here, can I?

MADAME COLLINS. Oh! And why not?

MARBLE (*leaning nearer to her*). Nice bit of lace, that.

MADAME COLLINS. You think so?

(*He kisses her.*)

MADAME COLLINS. Oh, you must not do that. It is very, very wrong for you to kiss me!

MARBLE. I'm sorry. I couldn't help it. (*Rises.*) You look so wonderful— I've never met anybody like you before. I'd like to have a talk sometime —somewhere where we shan't be interrupted. I wonder if we could fix it somehow.

(MADAME COLLINS *drops a handkerchief behind the cushion in the armchair.*)

MADAME COLLINS. Well . . . but that is for you to say—is it not?

MARBLE. Look here, I'll tell you what. . . . If I could manage to get away one evening . . . could you meet me, somewhere in town, and have a bit of supper?

MADAME COLLINS (*looking sideways at him*). Well——

MARBLE (*eagerly, kneels on pouffe*). You could manage it, couldn't you? You must! You'd like to come, wouldn't you?

MADAME COLLINS. I think that it would be delightful. I am very lonely sometimes.

MARBLE. Well, then, I'll let you know somehow. (*Looks round at the door.*) Are you alone in the shop in the daytime?

MADAME COLLINS. There is a young girl. She does not matter.

MARBLE. I'll call in as soon as I can fix it. Even if I can't manage it for a bit, it will be all right later on. They'll go away, I expect, this summer—I'll see they *do* go. Then it'll be easier.

MADAME COLLINS. What will be?

MARBLE. Well, I mean we can meet here without a lot of questions and that. . . . You know what people are.

(*She leans back and laughs.*)

MARBLE. What are you laughing at?

MADAME COLLINS. Oh, you amuse me so much, you great, big, strong men of affairs. No sooner 'ave you thought of something that you want and . . . *voilà, c'est arrangé!* (*Pretending indignation.*) And what about me? 'Ave I nothing to say in the matter?

MARBLE (*rather taken aback*). Yes, of course, but . . . well, I sort of thought you'd like to come. I mean —if you're so lonely and that.

MADAME COLLINS. What, to your 'ouse? When no one is 'ere but you?

MARBLE. Well, I'm sorry, madame, but I only meant—— (*Moves away.*)

MADAME COLLINS (*laughing again*). Oh, but I only tease you! (*Holding out her hands, leaning close to him, and speaking softly.*) Of course, I would like to come—send them away quickly and then . . .

(*He looks at her. She smiles. Sound of someone coming downstairs is heard.*)

MARBLE (*listening*). Look out! There's my wife. (*Louder as he crosses R.*) Well, I'm glad you like the table.

MADAME COLLINS. I think it is most charming. Ah——

(*She rises as* ANNIE *enters, and puts cigarette in fern pot.* ANNIE, *who wears an overall over her working clothes, stands in the doorway, staring.*)

ANNIE. Oh . . . I didn't know there was anyone here.

MARBLE. It's all right. Come along, Annie, and meet Madame Collins. You know . . .

ANNIE. Oh, how do you do? (*Shakes hands.*)

MADAME COLLINS. How do you do?

MARBLE. Madame Collins was admiring the furniture coming out of the van. I knew you wouldn't mind her having a look round.

ANNIE. Oh, not at all.

MADAME COLLINS. Your furniture reminds me of my 'ome in France. There were many pieces of this kind in the château of my father. I 'ave not seen such things in England. (Sits on pouffe.)

ANNIE. Really? (Rather coldly, sits on chair L. of the table.) You've got the shop on the corner, haven't you?

MADAME COLLINS. Oh, yes. We must all work now, since the terrible war. My father and my brothers have been killed and the château is sold. It is a tragedy, is it not?

ANNIE. Yes. I'm sorry.

MADAME COLLINS. So, you see, your beautiful things make me feel a little 'omesick.

ANNIE (looking at the table). Yes, I suppose they would. Your husband is a wounded officer, too, isn't he? Someone was telling me. . . .

MADAME COLLINS. That is so. They are so pathetic, these wounded ones. You must look after them like little boys.

ANNIE. It's very sad, I think. Where was he wounded?

MADAME COLLINS. Ah, that I cannot tell you. It is terrible! Sometime you must come to see my little shop and then I will tell you everything. I say to your husband that I 'ope you will come. Then we will 'ave tea and you shall see what nice things I

'ave. I 'ave now some new models from Paris which are made just for your style.

MARBLE (gaily). You mustn't go egging her on, you know. Father will have to pay.

MADAME COLLINS. Oh, they are so reasonable, my frocks. Very cheap, but very good. Your wife will look charming in what I shall choose for 'er. You shall see.

ANNIE. You must excuse me all untidy like this. I don't know what you must think, but we're just getting straight, you see.

MADAME COLLINS. But it is I 'oo must be excused . . . to come when you are so much engaged. I must not stop.

ANNIE. You'll take a cup of tea with us, won't you?

MADAME COLLINS. No, thank you. Sometime, per'aps. I 'ave to go back soon. It is nice to 'ave met you. The life 'ere is very dull after the life I 'ave in France. There we were never dull. Always there was riding and dancing and swimming, and I 'ave traveled so much. 'Ere I am tied to the little shop. . . . Oh, well! We must try to smile, eh? (Smiles bravely.)

ANNIE. You must find it a change.

MADAME COLLINS. Yes. But we talk only of me. Tell me, you 'ave children?

ANNIE. Yes. We've got one girl. She's fifteen.

MADAME COLLINS. No. (Laughs.) No, it isn't possible?

ANNIE. She's gone to school near Paris since Mr. Marble . . . did so well for himself.

MADAME COLLINS. Ah, and you will go to fetch 'er for the 'olidays? (*She catches* MARBLE'S *eye.*)

ANNIE. Oh, no. We shall meet her this side. There's several of them come over together. (*Rises.*)

MADAME COLLINS. Well—(*rises*)—I shall look forward to seeing 'er when she comes. And now I must say good-by. (*Shaking hands with* ANNIE.) When will you come to see me? Tomorrow, per'aps?

ANNIE. Well, I can't promise. I'll try. (*Opens the door.*)

MADAME COLLINS. That is good. (*To* MARBLE.) Au 'voir.

MARBLE. I'll just see you out. (*Follows her up.*)

(ANNIE *looks at him and he looks quickly away.*)

MADAME COLLINS. Thank you. (*She goes out.* MARBLE *follows.*)

(ANNIE *stands quite still for a moment, a puzzled expression on her face. Suddenly she sniffs, makes a grimace, goes to the window and opens it wide. Then she fidgets, with frequent glances at the door.* MARBLE *returns.*)

MARBLE (C., *not quite sure of his ground*). Well? What's the verdict? (*Filling pipe.*)

ANNIE (L.). What?

MARBLE. About her, I mean. What did you think of her?

ANNIE. Oh . . . I expect she's quite nice, dear . . . when you get to know her.

MARBLE (*defensively indignant*). Meaning you don't like her?

ANNIE. I didn't say so, Will.

MARBLE (C.). No, but you meant it all the same. Why? I can't see what you've got against her.

ANNIE. There isn't anything against her, Will. I . . . well, I just think it's rather soon to say, that's all. After all, I've only seen her for five minutes, haven't I?

MARBLE (*defiantly*). Well, I think it was very decent of her to come in like that. Matey, I call it. Especially after what she's been used to.

ANNIE. Yes, dear.

MARBLE (C.). Well, *isn't* it?

ANNIE. I don't know what she's been used to. (*Picks up the pouffe and carries it over to R. and puts it down below the fender.*)

MARBLE. Why . . . you heard her say, didn't you? Riding and living in a shatoh and that.

ANNIE. I heard her, yes.

MARBLE. Well, then. I can't make you out, Annie, upon my soul——

ANNIE. I'm sorry, dear.

MARBLE (*sits L. of the table R.*). I think she's done the decent thing, asking you down to her place, like that.

ANNIE. Yes. It was very kind of her.

MARBLE. I'm glad you think so. I'll give you some money in the morning and you can go down and get yourself something smart.

ANNIE. I've got some money, thank you, Will. That what you gave me before. (*Passing a duster over the table.*)

MARBLE. What, that twenty quid! I thought I told you to spend it.

ANNIE. I know, dear. But I simply couldn't spend all that. I got one or two things.

MARBLE. What?

ANNIE. Well, a new mop, for one thing.

MARBLE (*amused*). What else?

ANNIE. And some pie dishes.

MARBLE. But that's all for the house. What about yourself?

ANNIE. Oh, I got a new wing for my hat. Not the blue, the other. (*Arranging vases on the mantelpiece.*)

MARBLE (*laughing derisively*). Oh, my Lord! Twenty quid . . . and you buy a mop and some pie dishes!

ANNIE. But, Will, we needed them very badly.

MARBLE. Yes, I know. But I meant you to blow it on yourself, for once. A new rig-out, or something. You don't know how to spend money, I can see that. I shall have to show

you. How about if I come to Madame Collins' with you?

ANNIE. Yes. I'd much rather. (*Crosses to the window L.*) I don't want to go alone.

MARBLE. All right, then. We'll go down there tomorrow. You'll be wanting some things later on, when you go away.

ANNIE. Go away?

MARBLE. Well, you'll go to a decent place for your holidays this year. Make a nice change for you to stop in a hotel, won't it? Be waited on hand and foot, eh?

ANNIE. Oh, Will! (*Coming C.*) That would be wonderful. Can we manage it?

MARBLE. Of course we can. You need a good holiday, Annie. Winnie'd like a place like Bournemouth, wouldn't she? Where there's a pier and a band and what not.

ANNIE. I expect she'd love it, dear. But what about you? We want to go where you'll like it.

MARBLE. I shan't be going.

ANNIE. But . . . you need a change more than any of us, Will. Besides, we couldn't go away and leave you here alone. You need a holiday so badly, Will.

MARBLE. Who says so?

ANNIE. I do, dear. If you get away for a bit you'd probably get some sleep again. It can't do you any good to be sitting about in here all the time, even if it is by the window.

MARBLE. If I feel all right, I really don't see that you need worry so much.

ANNIE. I can't help it, Will, when you're so different.

MARBLE. What do you mean, different?

ANNIE. Well . . . so nervous and jumpy. You never used to be like that.

MARBLE. Well, I'm not going to argue with you about it, Annie. How can I leave my new billet just when they've taken me on? I'm not going away, and that's definite.

ANNIE. Oh—well, then I must get someone in to look after you.

MARBLE (*rises angrily*). You'll do nothing of the sort! How many times have I got to tell you that I don't like strangers nosing about the place? And what's more, I'm not going to have it, see?

(*A brief pause.* ANNIE *sighs.*)

MARBLE (*continues more gently*). You can take it from me that I can quite well take care of myself. I feel quite all right. . . . As a matter of fact, I feel better than I have for some time . . . and I want you and Winnie to go off somewhere and stay at a really slap-up hotel.

ANNIE (*completely deceived*). Oh, Will, it's so generous of you, I hate you to think I'm ungrateful. It is good of you, really it is——

(*She is about to embrace him; he avoids her, pretending not to notice.*)

MARBLE. That's all right, Annie. (*Going to the window* L.) What about a cup of tea? (*Takes the lid off the box.*)

ANNIE (*after looking at him rather sadly*). Yes, dear.

MARBLE (*coming to* L. *of her—stops by the armchair, picks up cushion, sees handkerchief, drops cushion*). We'll call it settled, then, about your holiday? We don't want all this argument over again. You'll go in Winnie's summer holidays, eh? Be away about three weeks?

ANNIE. Yes . . . if I could be sure you'll be all right.

MARBLE. Oh, I shall be all right.

(ANNIE *goes out. After* ANNIE *has gone out,* MARBLE *puts* MADAME COLLINS' *handkerchief in the left-hand pocket of his coat, takes a book out of the wooden box on the table down* L., *turns the armchair round to face the window—sits, and reads for a short time; then rises, throws book on the table, slams down the blind, moves to the armchair, takes the handkerchief out of his pocket, inhales the perfume, and sits on the arm of the chair.*)

CURTAIN

SCENE II

SCENE—*The same—a warm August evening.*

The room has not been cleaned for a fortnight. On the table L. is a bottle of whisky, a syphon of soda, two glasses, and a saucer filled with cigarette ends. A newspaper, and MARBLE's *Medical Jurisprudence lying open. On the table R. are two old trays on which are dirty plates, knives and forks, tumblers, a vegetable dish, teapot, and milk bottle. There is also a kettle on a newspaper on the table R. On the floor near the armchair L. are* MARBLE's *shoes.*

MARBLE *comes downstairs in a disheveled state. He has no coat or waistcoat on, and only socks on his feet. He comes down to the table L., pours himself out a whisky and soda, and is about to drink when the front door is heard to slam. He puts his glass down and goes out into the passage.*

HAMMOND (*off*). Hullo!

MARBLE (*off*). How the devil did you get in?

HAMMOND (*off*). Found the door on the jar.

MARBLE (*off*). On the jar? Must have been—— (*Checks himself.*) I mean——

HAMMOND (*coming in*). Not intruding, am I?

MARBLE (*following*). No . . . no, of course not.

HAMMOND (*up L. C.*). Still on your own, then?

MARBLE (*up C.*). Yes.

HAMMOND (*taking stock of the litter*). No one to do for you?

MARBLE (*C.*). I manage all right.

HAMMOND. And when do the family come back?

MARBLE (*C.*). Tomorrow, they said.

HAMMOND. Oh . . . (*Moves to the table L. He notices that there is whisky.*) Been pretty close, hasn't it? Shouldn't wonder if we're in for something before the night's out.

MARBLE (*C.*). Did you want to see me about anything?

HAMMOND (*going toward him*). Oh, yes, that's right . . . about those figures.

MARBLE (*with growing impatience*). What figures?

HAMMOND. You know, the apportionments on this place. I've got the Schedule A and the insurance adjusted and I——

MARBLE. Yes, well, sometime or other——

HAMMOND. I thought if you'd just agree the amounts——

MARBLE. Not now. I'll look at them later. It isn't as urgent as all that, is it?

HAMMOND. Not for a day or so, no. Expecting someone?

MARBLE. No . . . at least . . . no, I'm not. Why?

HAMMOND. I thought you seemed in a bit of a hurry.

MARBLE (*indignantly*). I'm not in any hurry. Not the least. (*To support this, reluctantly comes to the table L.*) You'd better have one before you go.

HAMMOND. Ah, that's the idea, certainly. (*Crosses to the table R.*) Today's been a hot 'un and no mistake.

(HAMMOND *spots the lady's handbag of black-and-white leather which lies on the table R. He looks round, sees that* MARBLE *is occupied, and examines the bag more closely.* MARBLE *crosses with the drink and meets* HAMMOND'S *eye. There is a moment's pause.*)

MARBLE. Here you are. (*Hands him the glass.*)

HAMMOND. Thanks. Not before I need it either, I don't mind saying. Cheero!

(*They drink.* MARBLE *steals a sidelong glance at* HAMMOND *and finds him doing the same. He looks quickly away.*)

HAMMOND (*hurriedly*). Heard from Mrs. M. lately?

MARBLE. I had a card Thursday.

HAMMOND. Enjoying themselves, I expect?

MARBLE. Seem to be.

HAMMOND. Got it hot the same as we have, very likely.

MARBLE. It's pretty general.

(*A pause.*)

HAMMOND (*who is terribly curious*). That's a nice bag.

MARBLE (*goes R., picks it up—puts it on the mantelpiece, after only a second's hesitation*). Yes. Gave it to the missus on her birthday.

HAMMOND. Really? Smart, I call it. that black and white.

MARBLE. Not bad, is it?

HAMMOND (*not wholly convinced*). Wonder she didn't take it down there with her . . . nice bag like that.

MARBLE (*with just a break*). She . . . she forgot it. She'd one with her and wrote that it didn't seem sense to risk spoiling the new one with salt water or anything. (*Puts the glass down and goes up to the door.*)

HAMMOND. Oh . . . quite. (*Finishes his drink and sits. Turns round and sees* MARBLE *holding the door open. He rises.*) Well, I must be toddling. . . . I'll leave these for you to look over. (*Handing a sheet of figures.*) I'll look in for 'em sometime tomorrow, probably.

MARBLE. All right. I'll see about them presently.

(*At the door* HAMMOND *takes a look round the room as if expecting to see*

*someone partly concealed, then goes
out.* MARBLE *follows, and, after seeing him out, tries the front door.*
MADAME COLLINS *comes downstairs.
She wears a light frock. Her hair is
untidy.*)

MADAME COLLINS (*coming downstairs*). 'Oo was that?

MARBLE (*coming into the room*).
That fellow Hammond from next
door.

MADAME COLLINS (*follows him in*).
'E know that I am 'ere?

MARBLE (*puts papers on the table,
picks up his glass, and goes to the
armchair L.*). I don't know how
much he guessed. What do you want
to leave your bag lying there for?

MADAME COLLINS. My bag? Why,
'ow am I to know that you will be
so imbecile to let a man come in?
(*Gets the bag from the mantelpiece.*)

MARBLE (*sits in armchair*). I didn't.
You must have left the door un-
latched. He spotted that bag, too. I
said it belonged to the wife. I had to
say something.

MADAME COLLINS. And he believed
you?

MARBLE. I think so. (*Encouraging
himself.*) I don't think he'll say anything, Rita. After all, he's got nothing
really to go on. . . .

(MADAME COLLINS *sits L. of the
table R., opens her bag and proceeds
to tidy herself. She combs her hair,
puts eye black on her eyelashes, and
hums a French song while doing so,*

MARBLE *occasionally coming in with
a word of the song.*)

MADAME COLLINS. Well . . . the
last evening, eh?

MARBLE (*gloomily*). Have to be . . .
for a bit, anyway. (*Putting on one
of the shoes he has left by the armchair.*)

MADAME COLLINS. You 'ave missed
them very much? (*Takes lipstick
out of her bag and makes up her
lips.*)

MARBLE. You know I haven't. It's
been . . . wonderful. Only, it's
gone so quick. . . . You've made all
the difference, Rita. You don't know
what it has meant, you coming in
like this. . . . At times I've almost
managed . . . to forget—— (*He
breaks off abruptly.*)

MADAME COLLINS (*rises, moves a
step up, and fastens R. suspender*).
That you 'ave a wife, eh?

MARBLE. No, not that . . . (*Puts
on his other shoe.*)

MADAME COLLINS (*turning a little
toward him, and fastening L. suspender*). What, then?

MARBLE. Oh, nothing. . . . Have a
drink, Rita?

MADAME COLLINS. No, but *you* shall
'ave one. (*Goes behind him to L. of
the table L.*) I want to talk with you.
. . . (*Mixes him a drink.*)

MARBLE. What about?

MADAME COLLINS. About my business.

MARBLE. Oh, Lord, won't it keep?

MADAME COLLINS (*comes round to R. of him with glass and sits on arm of his chair*). If they come back to-morrow, perhaps I will not see you soon. (*Puts her arm round his neck.*)

MARBLE (*anxiously*). You must! Do you understand, Rita? You've got to to go on seeing me. I . . . can't stand that . . . like it was before. It was driving me mad. You don't realize what it means. . . .

MADAME COLLINS. Oh, yes—I 'ave seen your wife.

MARBLE. No. Not that. Annie's all right. I know she's not your sort, but she's been pretty good all through these last few months.

MADAME COLLINS. It is easy to be pretty good if there is always money. (*Gives him his drink.*) What is difficult is to be good when there is none at all, I find.

MARBLE. You don't understand, Rita.

MADAME COLLINS. Don't I? So much you know about that! If you knew what I lose on my business and——

MARBLE. Lose? Do you mean to say that business of yours doesn't pay?

MADAME COLLINS. Pay? My God! It is I . . . I who pay. The rent, the rates, the wages, the stock, the advertisements. They tell me about the people 'ere 'oo 'ave money. Lies! No one 'ere 'ave money. They spend nothing on their clothes. They look like that, do they not?

MARBLE. They don't look much beside you, Rita, I'll admit.

MADAME COLLINS. Because they don't care 'ow they are looking, that's why. Since I come 'ere I sell not enough to pay for the rent. It is terrible. 'Ow can I go on like this? Well, I am asking you . . . 'ow can I?

MARBLE. I don't know.

MADAME COLLINS. But, darling, there is no one else. Of course, I come to you. And you will tell me what I must do, please?

MARBLE. Well, that's easier said than done.

MADAME COLLINS. The first time I see you, you say you will 'elp me with my affairs, so I come to you.

MARBLE. Yes, but I don't know anything about dress shops; I mean ——

MADAME COLLINS. Oh! Darling, do you not care what 'appen to me?

MARBLE. Of course I do. You ought to know that, Rita.

MADAME COLLINS. Then you will do for me something which I shall ask?

MARBLE. Well . . . that depends . . .

MADAME COLLINS. I must 'ave three 'undred pounds.

MARBLE. What? You don't want much, do you? Three hundred? Good Lord!

MADAME COLLINS. If I do not get it quickly I must be made bankrupt.

MARBLE. Yes, but three hundred! That's a lot of money, that is.

MADAME COLLINS. Not for you.

MARBLE. Oh, yes, it is. A dickens of a lot of money. I can't afford to go splashing it about like that. Not likely.

MADAME COLLINS. You can lend it until my business pays.

MARBLE. When your business pays might be never, according to what you said just now.

MADAME COLLINS. Ah, that is always the way. You say that you love me—you say that you are grateful. It is I who give everything, and you——

MARBLE. That's not fair, Rita. You talk as if I hadn't done anything for you. You had a tenner only yesterday.

MADAME COLLINS. And it go to the nursing 'ome to pay for my 'usband. I do not 'ave one penny.

MARBLE. And the twenty-five last Sunday? What about that?

MADAME COLLINS. That was to pay for the assistant. I tell you at the time.

MARBLE. And the other twenty just before that?

MADAME COLLINS (rising and going C.). Oh, la, la! What a fine lover! You will make out an account for what you give?

MARBLE. No, but sixty quid in three goes isn't so bad. And there was a lot more. That brooch.

MADAME COLLINS (C.). Per'aps you would like a receipt for the presents you give me?

MARBLE. I should never have brought them up if you hadn't said I did nothing for you. I don't think you've done too bad. You seem to think I'm made of money.

MADAME COLLINS. And you . . . you 'ave nothing from me?

MARBLE. Well . . . I wouldn't say that.

MADAME COLLINS (taking a step up —then down). Ah, this is charming! You say, "Give yourself to me." You give me presents. You make out the account and say to yourself, "Is she worth so much?" "Am I wasting my money?" Ho! And you English say that we are a mean people! My God, that is funny! (Goes up.)

MARBLE. There's no need to go on like this, Rita. I—— (Puts glass on the table.)

MADAME COLLINS. Go on? (Coming down to L. of the table.) And 'ow do you go on when you want love? Like a little dog 'oo beg! When I think 'ow you be'ave I feel sick! (Sits on the table, her back to him, pulls up her stockings, and at the same time humming a French song.)

MARBLE. Rita, Rita! Look here, Rita, I don't say but what I might be able to . . . well, I might manage a little toward it, anyhow. There's no sense in having a row about it.

MADAME COLLINS (blandly). 'Oo 'as a row? Mon Dieu! I don't 'ave a row.

MARBLE. No . . . well—— (Pulls her to him over the table.)

MADAME COLLINS (leaning back across the table). Well? (Her face beside his and says softly:) Darling, you are so kind always. What 'ave I done to make you feel you don't like me any more? (*Rubs her face against his cheek.*) Don't you love me a little tiny bit? And I love you so much.

MARBLE. Rita—— You know I do! When you come close to me I'd do anything you ask. Anything! It's a funny thing——

MADAME COLLINS. What is?

MARBLE. I mean, me giving in to you like this. Just because I'm afraid of losing you.

MADAME COLLINS. Then you still want me?

MARBLE. Want you? That first day . . . when I saw you walk across the room, I wanted you so much I——

MADAME COLLINS (*sits up and swings her legs round the front of the table*). That you would give three hundred pounds?

MARBLE (*laughing*). You're a knock-out, aren't you?

MADAME COLLINS. And you will give the money soon?

MARBLE. I suppose so.

MADAME COLLINS. Tonight?

MARBLE. Good heavens, no! I don't keep that amount in the house.

MADAME COLLINS. But you 'ave a check.

MARBLE. Yes . . . but checks——

MADAME COLLINS. Well, tomorrow morning, then?

MARBLE. I'll try. I can't promise.

MADAME COLLINS (*after considera-tion*). Ah, well, per'aps I, too, can-not promise to see you. . . . (*Gets down from the table—crosses him and goes up C.*)

MARBLE (*rises and goes to her*). Rita! I must see you. I couldn't stick it. Really I couldn't.

MADAME COLLINS. Well . . . (*Shrug-ging her shoulders.*)

(*They embrace.*)

MARBLE. Oh, all right, you shall have it. You know how to get round me, don't you?

(*She laughs, kisses him again, gets her bag from the table, and is going up to the door.*)

MARBLE. Where are you going?

MADAME COLLINS. To get my 'at. I must go now.

MARBLE. Not yet. It's not much after nine. Come and sit down and have a drink.

MADAME COLLINS. I cannot. I am sorry. I 'ave many things to do. (*Goes up a step.*)

MARBLE (*anxiously, up to her*). Rita, don't go. I—— It's awful here alone. Don't leave me alone, for God's sake.

MADAME COLLINS. But I must go. I 'ave been 'ere since four o'clock and——

MARBLE. I know you have, but I can't stand being left alone here. I get in a terrible state after you've gone.

MADAME COLLINS (*patting his cheek*). Why, you are like a baby that cannot be alone!

MARBLE. No, you don't understand, Rita.

(*She laughs.*)

MARBLE. It's no laughing matter. I get scared stiff. Just a few minutes can't make much difference . . . to you. To me they do. You don't know . . . (*Drops his head on her shoulder.*)

MADAME COLLINS. I don't know why you are like this, no. I cannot understand at all why you must be frightened.

MARBLE. I can't explain. I do, that's all. I get so that I don't know what I'm doing. I tell you I—— (*Embraces her.*) Look here, stay the night, Rita, why not?

MADAME COLLINS. No, I cannot do that.

MARBLE. Why not? I mean, where's the difference?

MADAME COLLINS. Why, it is mad! It will be observed and when your wife come back she will 'ear of it. They will fight to be the first one to tell 'er! No! I must go now. (*Goes up into the passage.*)

MARBLE (*pleading frantically*). No, Rita, no!

MADAME COLLINS (*going up the stairs*). Yes. I mean that. I will get my things.

(*She disappears.*)

MARBLE. Rita—— (*Goes into the passage.*) Rita—— (*Looks up on to landing toward R.*) Rita—— (*He staggers down to the window, leans on the fern stand for support, then suddenly his expression becomes brighter, a mixture of cunning and eagerness. He goes softly to the stairs and is going up, when there is a knock on the front door. He comes down a step and says, in a loud whisper, to* MADAME COLLINS, *who is apparently at the top of the stairs:*) No, stay where you are. Keep quiet. I'll get rid of whoever it is. (*He comes downstairs and goes to the door. Voices are heard. Off.*) I didn't know. . . . Why didn't you let me know? I——

WINNIE (*off—who has become a very assured young woman*). What does it matter? Aren't you pleased to see us?

MARBLE (*off*). What's Mother doing? Is she coming in?

(*WINNIE enters.*)

WINNIE (*laughing*). Of course! She's paying the taxi. You're not going to lock her out, are you? (*Puts down tennis racket, suitcase, and doll on chair R. of the table R.*)

MARBLE. Well . . . aren't you going to help her?

WINNIE. Oh, the taximan will bring in the things. What an awful mess! (*Surveys the room disgustedly.*)

MARBLE (*desperately*). I don't want Mother to pay. . . . Here! Take this out and settle up, there's a good girl. I can't go òut like this. (*As* WINNIE *looks at him questioningly.*) Go on. Don't stand staring at me!

(*She tosses her head and goes.* MADAME COLLINS *comes downstairs.*)

(MARBLE *goes up to the passage, beckons and says urgently:*) Quick! That way. . . . (*Pointing to the kitchen as* MADAME COLLINS *passes.*) Through the garden . . . gate at the end! Hurry, for God's sake!

(*He turns toward the front door and tries unsuccessfully to block* WINNIE'S *entrance to the room.*)

WINNIE. What's the matter? (*Goes toward the window.*) Who's that? Madame Collins?

MARBLE (*C.—with a great effort at calmness*). Who? . . . Oh, yes. . . . She . . . she came round touting for custom . . . wants Mother to get some things there. . . . She's not much good.

WINNIE (*turns to him*). How do you mean?

MARBLE. She's not . . . well, not a very nice woman, Winnie. I shouldn't say anything to Mother if I were you. It would only worry her. She might think she ought to go there for her things. . . . (*He breaks off and turns to greet* ANNIE, *who comes in wearing expensive but not very suitable clothes.*) Hullo—hullo! (*Kisses her.*)

ANNIE. Well, dear, there was a very good train this evening and we thought, tomorrow being Saturday—— (*Breaks off and goes into the passage as the* TAXIMAN *brings in the bags.*) Yes, there, please. That's it. Thank you very much.

(TAXIMAN *goes out.*)

ANNIE (*returns*). Well, have you really been getting on all right? I've wondered—— (*Noticing litter.*) Good gracious! Whatever——

MARBLE. If I'd known you were coming——

ANNIE (*above the table R.*). These marks won't ever come out, I'm sure. It's dreadful for you being like this. I knew I ought never to have gone!

(WINNIE *sits in armchair L.C. and picks up* Medical Jurisprudence.)

MARBLE. Nonsense, Annie. I've been all right.

ANNIE. Pity you didn't come, Will. You'd have enjoyed it down there.

MARBLE. Had a good time?

ANNIE. Yes, thank you, dear, lovely.

MARBLE. Hotel all right?

ANNIE. Oh, it was a beautiful place. You can't imagine. . . . And the meals, too, were ever so nice. Weren't they, Winnie?

WINNIE. Quite decent.

ANNIE. Oh, and Will—— (*Opening her bag.*)

MARBLE. What?

ANNIE. I suppose Mr. Medland hasn't been?

(MARBLE'S *jaw drops.*)

MARBLE (*with difficulty*). Medland? . . . No . . . Why?

ANNIE (*producing paper cutting*). Only I found this in the hotel this morning. I was sitting waiting for Winnie, and picked up the paper——

MARBLE (*interrupting feverishly*). Yes, yes, what is it?

ANNIE. An advertisement. Solicitors asking for information—(*consulting paper*)—as to the whereabouts of James Colville Medland. It's from an address in Australia and I thought it might be our Mr. Medland. . . .

MARBLE (*grabbing it*). Here, let me see! (*He reads it.*)

ANNIE. Do you think it's the one? It seemed so funny . . . the same name and from Australia. I thought if you knew where he was——

MARBLE. How should I know?

ANNIE. I only meant I thought if he had called while we've been away——

MARBLE. Well, he hasn't. It may not be the same one, anyway. There are probably any amount of Medlands. Besides, solicitors wouldn't want to advertise for . . . Jim. They could get him through his bank. He hasn't come to see us again and I don't see why you should bother with him. (*Throws cutting on the floor and goes to the door.*) I'll just go and tidy a bit. I'll hear all your news when I come down.

(*He goes upstairs.*)

ANNIE (*shuts the door*). I'm worried about Father . . . shaking like that. He'll be having a breakdown directly if he isn't careful. I'm sure it's only this sitting about all day, reading, instead of getting out in the air. Too much sitting about . . . (*Takes tray from the table R. and puts it on the sideboard.*)

WINNIE. And drinking.

ANNIE. Winnie!

WINNIE. Well, he does, Mother. It's no use pretending. (*Puts the book down.*)

ANNIE (*comes back to the table R.*). Not more than most men. It's wicked to say he makes himself ill with it. It's because he is ill that he feels he wants it.

WINNIE. I'm sorry.

ANNIE. I don't suppose he's had proper meals since we went. I knew I oughtn't to leave him here with no one to see to anything. (*Takes another tray from the table and puts it on the sideboard.*)

WINNIE. Oh, that's silly, Mother. You know he made you go. He practically forced you. And when you said you'd get someone in, he only got angry.

ANNIE (*takes the kettle off the table and puts it in the grate*). But all the same——

WINNIE. Mother! Do you think that he's . . . that he's all right? In the head, I mean.

ANNIE (*comes to L. of the table R.*) Winnie, really! I never heard——

WINNIE. Well, he never used to be like this.

ANNIE. Like what?

WINNIE. Why . . . going off the deep end and getting in violent tempers over the least little thing.

ANNIE (*a little impressed*). I haven't noticed that he does. (*Picks up the glasses from the table R.*)

WINNIE. Oh, Mother, you *must* have!

ANNIE. He gets a bit cross sometimes. We all do.

WINNIE. I know, but *he* does when there's nothing to get cross about. Like that cutting just now. He's always like that when you mention Mr. Medland. Why should he get so worked up about it?

ANNIE. Perhaps he's feeling it rather that Mr. Medland has never come again.

WINNIE. Well, I don't see any reason to have a heart attack over it. (*Picks up the book.*) And these books he reads——

ANNIE. Good gracious, if reading a book means a person's not right in the head . . . (*Goes up to the sideboard with the glasses.*)

WINNIE. But he doesn't read ordinary books, Mother. It's always such weird ones. This is the sort of thing. Listen . . . (*Reading.*) "Death is practically instantaneous, and after death——"

ANNIE (*interrupting*). Oh, don't, Winnie! Whatever book is it?

WINNIE. It's about being poisoned . . . by cyanide.

ANNIE. Cyanide? (*Goes and looks at the book.*)

WINNIE (*reads*). "After death the body often retains the appearance of life, the cheeks being red and the——" Why, it's enough to send anyone dotty reading stuff like that. Hark at this . . .

ANNIE. No! I don't want to hear it. (*Takes the book from* WINNIE.) I didn't know he was reading things like that.

WINNIE. He's always reading them. That's his favorite, by the look of the page. Thumb marks all over it.

ANNIE (*really worried*). What *can* he want to read that for?

WINNIE. That's just it. That was what I meant. I think you ought to stop him.

ANNIE. I can't understand . . . (*Firmly.*) No, it's nonsense talking like this. If he likes to read about poison or anything else it's no concern of ours. You run along and start getting your things unpacked, there's a dear. I'll be up soon.

WINNIE. Oh, all right. (*Picks up her things from the chair L. of the table R. She goes upstairs.*)

(ANNIE *stands thinking, a worried look on her face. She stands reading the book. She puts the book down on the arm of the chair, picks up the paper cutting—looks round at the cupboard in the passage where the bottle of cyanide is kept. Turns*

and picks up the book again and
continues reading. MARBLE enters,
sees her expression, stops, then seeing the book in her hand, he looks
to see what she has read and draws
in his breath sharply. ANNIE watches
his face, plainly terrified. Their eyes
meet. Then his go toward the win-

dow and she slowly turns and looks
out too. Quite suddenly she turns
back to him and whispers:) Will!
(He stares at her, motionless. She
backs away from him, crying in a
hoarse crescendo:) No! . . . No!

(MARBLE does not move.)

CURTAIN

ACT THREE

SCENE I

SCENE—The same—a year later.

ANNIE has finished her luncheon. MARBLE, seated on the opposite side
of the table, is gazing past her through the window. He appears shrunken
and feeble; his head rests on his hand. ANNIE looks at him anxiously. In
their conversation there is now a more intimate warmth noticeable, her tone
being one of maternal solicitude and protectiveness, and his rather wistful
and childlike timidity.

ANNIE (L. of table). Will.

MARBLE (R. of the table—starting).
Eh?

ANNIE. Isn't it nice, dear?

MARBLE. Yes . . . it's all right.

ANNIE. You've hardly had anything.

MARBLE. No . . . I don't feel I can
eat, Annie.

ANNIE. You must try, dear. It worries me.

MARBLE. I do try. It's no good.

ANNIE. If I get you some Brand's,
will you try that?

MARBLE. No, really. . . . Don't
bother about me.

ANNIE. I can't help it, Will, when
you don't keep up your appetite. It's
so important.

MARBLE. You're the one who ought
to eat more. You've always been
delicate. I'm pretty strong really.
Hullo! . . . (Leaning sideways.)
That gate's open again. The latch
must have gone. You shut it, didn't
you?

ANNIE (almost whispering). No.

MARBLE. I mean, after breakfast
. . . I told you.

ANNIE. I know.

MARBLE. Well . . .

ANNIE (*very agitated*). Will, I can't.

MARBLE. What?

ANNIE. I can't go out there any more!

MARBLE (*realizing*). Oh . . . all right. (*A pause. Fills his pipe.*) How much are you spending a week now, Annie?

ANNIE. Do you mean . . . altogether?

MARBLE. Yes.

ANNIE. Well, about three pounds, I suppose. It might be a little more. Why, dear?

MARBLE. I was only thinking . . . It's funny, isn't it, how badly we wanted money. We haven't got much out of it, have we? Fat lot of use it's been, really.

ANNIE. No, except it has given Winnie a good start.

MARBLE. I'm not even sure of that.

ANNIE. But, Will——

MARBLE. She's not the same girl.

ANNIE. She's growing up, dear. And going to a school like that and meeting people is bound to alter her a bit.

MARBLE. She's giving herself airs. These people she's gone to stay with . . . they're not our sort, Annie.

ANNIE. Oh, I don't think there's any harm. They give her a lovely time. We can't do much for her here.

MARBLE. She'll be looking down on us directly; you see if she doesn't. She's a bit inclined that way already. What time does she get here?

ANNIE. She ought to be here any minute.

MARBLE. Oh!

ANNIE. I'll leave the table a bit longer.

MARBLE (*after a short pause*). When does she go back?

ANNIE (*surprised*). Back?

MARBLE. To school.

ANNIE. How do you mean, dear? You know she's not going back.

MARBLE (*vacantly*). Isn't she?

ANNIE. Surely you remember, Will? She's going to take up this photography business with Mr. Gammans. I told you.

MARBLE. Did you? (*Lights his pipe.*)

ANNIE. Yes. Don't you remember I asked you if you minded? She was full of it before she went away. She's to start at two pounds. (*Rises.*)

MARBLE (*obviously not remembering*). Oh, yes. There was something about it. . . . She'll be here all the time then?

ANNIE (*going round to behind him*). Why, dear? Don't you want her here? You sound . . . disappointed. (*She puts a hand on his shoulder.*)

MARBLE. Yes . . . I can't help it. We get on all right alone, Annie;

this last three weeks since she's been away we've been all right, haven't we? We don't want anyone else——

ANNIE. Yes, but, Will . . . it's her home.

MARBLE. I know. All the same . . . Just lately it's been different . . . more like it used to be . . .

(MARBLE *squeezes her hand.* ANNIE *cries a little.*)

MARBLE (*turns to her*). What's the matter?

ANNIE. Oh, Will——

MARBLE. What is it?

ANNIE. Only after all this time. It's so wonderful. I'm almost glad that . . . that it happened!

MARBLE. You've been fine, Annie.

ANNIE. No.

MARBLE. Yes, you have, fine. I don't know how you've stuck it; must have been awful for you, all that. It was having it all to myself that made me like that. Oh, God! . . . You don't know——

ANNIE. I do *now*, Will.

MARBLE. It's been a sort of a help . . . you knowing. (*Quicker.*) I didn't mean you to, Annie. I did everything I could. But I couldn't help showing it sometimes. Things kept cropping up sudden and scaring me stiff. And when I felt I was showing it, it made me worse.

ANNIE. Yes.

MARBLE. And those books on poison trials, and that—I couldn't keep away from them, but they didn't help. . . . Ever since that night . . . Well, it's been different. Having someone else to share it with, even though we haven't talked about it . . . we ought to, really.

ANNIE. Oh, no, Will.

MARBLE. We ought . . . just in case . . .

ANNIE. What do you mean?

MARBLE. Well, suppose anything happened . . . suddenly . . .

ANNIE. No, no, it can't.

MARBLE. It might. We can't be sure. . . . The chances get less, of course, but we shall never be absolutely sure! Sometimes · I almost forget— for quite a long time—and then something happens suddenly—a knock on the door or something— and . . . I think they've come for me!

ANNIE. Oh, dear, don't.

MARBLE (*with more decision, having gone over it many times*). I'm sorry, Annie, but we must be ready. It would be mad not to. We must know what we're going to say. I've been wanting to talk to you about it for ages. If they came suddenly ——

ANNIE (*closing her eyes*). Oh, Will, don't talk like that! Please——

MARBLE. I must . . . so that you'd know what to do.

ANNIE. Will, I should never be able to do it. Really, I know I shouldn't.

Oh, don't let's talk any more about it. I——

(*There is a sound of the front door being opened. They listen.*)

ANNIE. There's Winnie.

(*She goes and opens the door.* WIN-NIE *enters, very smartly dressed and looking very pretty. She has achieved a mannequin walk and rather affected accent, with both of which she is obviously greatly pleased.*)

WINNIE. Oh, hullo, Mother! (*They kiss.*) Any lunch? (*Puts her hat on the armchair R.*)

ANNIE. We had ours, dear. We didn't know quite how long you'd be. (*Goes R.C.*)

WINNIE. Oh! (*Kisses* MARBLE.)

MARBLE. Enjoyed yourself?

WINNIE. Lovely time—(*goes below the table to L. of it*)—thanks. Hope there's a nice lot to eat.

ANNIE. Sit down straight away, dear. It's so late.

WINNIE (*inspecting the table*). Pig, eh? No salad?

ANNIE. I'm afraid there isn't, dear. We don't eat much. (*Sits on the arm of the armchair R.*)

WINNIE. Do you mean to say you two old dears have been solemnly munching pig without any salad?

ANNIE. I got that ham in case you came. I had something else.

WINNIE (*a little above the table; looking*). Bread and cheese? Quite

time I came home and took you both in hand, I can see.

MARBLE. You needn't worry about us.

WINNIE. But you don't know how to live. Now, I've got some really good tips for you. Paula's people live marvellously. (*Feeling the bread.*) I say, you haven't got a younger loaf than this, have you?

ANNIE. Why, what's the matter with it?

WINNIE. Well, it's only a bit tired, that's all.

MARBLE. *We're* not so particular.

WINNIE. Particular? Oh, well, never mind. I've had one lunch, anyway. (*Taking a cigarette case from her bag.*)

MARBLE. And what's *that*, may I ask?

WINNIE. This? Only my case. Why? (*Moves down L.*)

ANNIE (*R.C.*). Winnie! Do you smoke cigarettes?

WINNIE (*lighting a cigarette, rather defiantly*). Yes; cigars don't agree with me.

MARBLE. Now then, there's no need to be rude. Since when have you learnt to smoke, eh?

WINNIE. I really forget.

ANNIE. I think you're too young to start smoking, Winnie.

WINNIE. Oh, good Lord! Two to one again!

ANNIE. It isn't a question of two to one, dear, at all. It's a question of knowing what's good for you.

MARBLE. And while you're in this house you're to do what you're told.

WINNIE. Oh, all right. (*Throws cigarette at the fireplace and misses.*)

MARBLE. Mind! You'll burn something. . . .

(WINNIE *strolls R. with maddening slowness, stoops, throws it into the fireplace and sighs, then tidies her hair in front of the mirror.*)

ANNIE (*anxious to make peace*). Well . . . and what did you do all the time, dear?

(MARBLE *lights his pipe.*)

WINNIE (*pouting*). What *can* you do without clothes? I told you in my letter——

ANNIE. But . . . didn't you get the frock? I sent it off on the day after we got your first card.

WINNIE. I got it, yes. I'm afraid it wasn't exactly what I wanted.

ANNIE. How do you mean, dear?

WINNIE. Mother, do you really suppose people ride in flowered georgette?

ANNIE. Ride? Do you mean . . . horseback?

WINNIE. What did you think I meant, a push-bike? I said they were all going out for rides and I couldn't go and I asked you to send the money so that I could get a ready-made habit. I think it was jolly rotten of you not to. (*Sits in the armchair.*) As a matter of fact, I borrowed an old one of Paula's afterward, but everyone knew!

MARBLE. It wasn't your mother's fault. I didn't think it was necessary to go to all that expense just for a day or so. If you've got any complaints, you can make them to me, see?

WINNIE. It wasn't just for a day or so. I could have used it afterward.

MARBLE. Where?

WINNIE. Well, I don't see why I shouldn't ride sometimes. All the girls there do.

MARBLE. Girls of your class don't expect to ride.

WINNIE. Girls of my class, as you call it, haven't generally got fathers who are lousy with money!

ANNIE. Winnie! How dare you?

WINNIE. Well, it *was* stingy.

MARBLE. All right, my girl. (*Rises.*) Perhaps we'd better knock off your allowance, if you don't think it's worth having. Teach you a lesson to be more grateful. . . .

WINNIE. Oh, you don't understand.

MARBLE. What don't we understand?

WINNIE. Only that . . . it wasn't only the riding. It was everything.

MARBLE. How do you mean?

WINNIE. Well, their clothes. Whatever we were doing, they all had the right things. I just had two summer frocks that weren't really made for anything. I knew I looked a fright.

ANNIE. I think your blue is a very pretty dress.

WINNIE. Yes, but don't you see . . . people like that change for walking, and going on the river, and tennis and——

MARBLE. I don't see any necessity to keep changing your clothes all day. Your mother never has.

WINNIE. Mother? No, but——

MARBLE. Well? Let's have it.

WINNIE. Oh, nothing. (*Turns away.*)

MARBLE. I see. I should think the best thing you can do is not to go to these places if it makes you come back discontented like this. (*Crosses L.*)

WINNIE. I don't want to go again. I felt a perfect little fool. I shan't be asked, anyway, now.

ANNIE. Why not, Winnie?

WINNIE. Because they've seen this place. That's torn it.

MARBLE (*turns to her*). This place?

WINNIE. Yes. They drove me back. I tried to stop them, but they would come right up to the door, and . . . I could see what they thought. It was beastly.

MARBLE. Do you mean they . . . looked down on it?

WINNIE. Yes. I've never felt so awful.

MARBLE. Oh! So that's it? You're ashamed of us now, are you? We're not good enough for you, eh?

WINNIE. I don't say that. Only, when they saw the house they got a bit of a shock, naturally. Thank goodness they didn't come in.

MARBLE. What's that? You mean we aren't fit to meet them?

WINNIE. I don't mean you. I mean . . . oh, all this. (*Waving her hand to include the furniture.*)

MARBLE (*puzzled*). The furniture? Why, what's wrong with it?

WINNIE. Wrong? (*She laughs rather hysterically.*) My God!

MARBLE (*comes front of the table to R. end of it*). You stop that! Stop it, I tell you. I'll teach you to laugh at us, you stuck-up little snob!

ANNIE (*intervening*). Will! Winnie! Don't go on like this.

WINNIE. He doesn't want me here. He hasn't done for ages——

MARBLE (*at the same time*). I'm not going to be spoken to like that by a——

ANNIE. Will, sit down, do! Winnie, you'll say you're sorry at once. I can't think what's come over you.

WINNIE. All right then . . . I'm sorry. (*Rises, moves to the fireplace.*)

MARBLE. I should think you were.

WINNIE (*turns on him*). Well, I've said so.

MARBLE. Yes. (*Sits at R. of the table.*)

(*A pause. No one knows quite what to do.*)

WINNIE. Oh, by the way, that photography job with Gammans is off.

MARBLE. What?

WINNIE. I shan't be going.

ANNIE (*R.C.*). But . . . I thought you were so keen on it before you went away. I saw Mr. Gammans yesterday. He didn't say anything——

WINNIE. He doesn't know . . . yet.

ANNIE. I don't understand.

WINNIE. I can get something better to do—that's all.

ANNIE. Where?

WINNIE. Oh, I met someone . . . at Paula's.

ANNIE. What do you mean?

WINNIE. A man.

ANNIE. Oh!

WINNIE. He's got a friend who runs a ballroom in Regent Street, where they give lessons. He said he could get me a job.

MARBLE. What as?

WINNIE. As a dancing partner, at first. Afterward I might be taken on

as an instructress. He thinks it would be a pity for me to mess about with photography things. He rather liked the way I dance. He says I move well.

ANNIE (*very shocked*). Did he say that to you?

WINNIE (*R.C.*). Yes. He said I was a born dancer and he hated to think of me wasting my time down here.

ANNIE. Where did all this take place?

WINNIE (*wickedly*). In a wood.

(MARBLE *and* ANNIE *both start slightly.*)

ANNIE. Were you there alone with him?

WINNIE. Of course.

ANNIE. Did he——

WINNIE (*assisting*). Did he kiss me? Yes. Several times.

ANNIE (*moves behind the table to L. of it*). Well, I think Paula's mother might have had more sense.

WINNIE. I didn't expect you to approve. But I thought you'd better know before I start.

MARBLE. You're not going to start.

WINNIE. Oh, aren't I? (*To front of the chair R.*)

MARBLE. No. You can get it out of your head at once.

WINNIE. I knew you'd say that. Why must you treat me as if I was three? You didn't mind the idea of me spending days in a darkroom with Mr. Gammans.

ANNIE (*at L. end of the table*). That's different.

WINNIE. Why?

ANNIE. Well . . . Mr. Gammans isn't . . . a gentleman.

WINNIE. Oh!

ANNIE. I mean, we've known him a long time and——

MARBLE. We needn't bother about that. You're not going, and that's that. I know what ballrooms in Regent Street mean.

WINNIE (*violently, dropping back to the angry schoolgirl*). Then why do you send me to a place where I meet decent people if you don't want me to have anything to do with them? You're horrid and mean, both of you! You don't like gentlemen because you've never met any. You won't let me have anyone here. . . . (*Sits on the arm of the chair R. Picks up hat.*) Not that I'd want them to come. I'd be too ashamed. . . .

MARBLE. Here . . . you be careful what you're saying or——

WINNIE (*sobbing in fury*). I won't! You always do everything you can to stop me having any fun. It's always two to one.

MARBLE. Don't be ridiculous! All this just because you're told . . . you move well! . . . Move well! My God, by a fellow who——

WINNIE (*jumps up*). Don't you say anything about him. He's a jolly sight better than you are. . . .'

ANNIE. Winnie, Winnie!

WINNIE. Well, he is. And if you don't want me here I'll go to him

ANNIE. What *are* you saying?

WINNIE. I tell you, I'll go to his flat.

ANNIE. Oh, you wicked little girl!

WINNIE. He wanted me to last week and I wouldn't. I thought you wanted me. I don't want to stay where I'm not wanted. I'm no worse than Father, anyway. (*Puts her hat on in front of the mirror.*)

MARBLE. What's that?

WINNIE. I say, *you* can't talk . . . even if I do go.

ANNIE (*coming front of the table to C.*). Really, Winnie . . . your own father——

WINNIE. Ask him, then! Ask him about that Frenchwoman! Madame Collins . . .

MARBLE (*springing up*). Shut up! You little fool . . .

WINNIE. I won't! I won't shut up! She was here when we came back from Bournemouth. You know she was. I didn't realize then what it meant, but afterward—— (*Going up.*)

MARBLE (*shouting*). Stop that, I tell you!

WINNIE (*shouting too. To* ANNIE). She was upstairs, in the bedroom!

MARBLE (*shaking with rage*). Go up to your room, Winnie. By God, I'll teach you to——

ANNIE. Will! (*Holding him back.*)

WINNIE. You're afraid of Mother knowing. You're afraid! But she knows now what you're like, when her back's turned. . . .

MARBLE (*beside himself. Going to R.C.*). You young devil, you——

(WINNIE *goes out, slamming the door after her.* MARBLE *starts forward. Suddenly his hand goes to his heart and he almost falls.* ANNIE *lowers him into his chair at R. of the table.*)

ANNIE. Will! What is it? Your heart?

MARBLE (*panting*). Yes . . . I . . . I'll be all right . . . in a minute. Give me . . . some whisky.

(*She gets it from the sideboard and comes behind to R. of him.*)

ANNIE. There! (*Helping him.*) Is that better?

MARBLE. Yes.

ANNIE. Lean back, dear. Don't try to talk. (*Puts glass back on the table.*)

MARBLE. I'm better now. Where is she?

ANNIE. She's gone, dear. I expect she's gone up to her room. Keep still for a minute or two.

MARBLE. The young devil . . .

ANNIE. Don't think about it, dear. You must keep quiet.

MARBLE. Speaking to me like that!

ANNIE. She didn't mean it, Will. It's not like her, really. Is your heart still queer?

MARBLE. No; it's better now. (*Pause.*) It's funny how it's all changed. . . .

ANNIE. What, dear?

MARBLE. I was only thinking how one thing leads to another.

ANNIE. I'll just go and see what she's doing. (*She goes out C., runs upstairs, and calls up the stairs:*) Winnie! (*There is no reply.*) Will! Her bag's gone too! I'm sure it was in the passage. (*She goes to the front door and into the road. After a moment's pause she returns; comes down R.C. and says dully:*) Will, she's gone!

MARBLE. Gone?

ANNIE. Oh, Will!

MARBLE. She'll be back presently. Don't you fret.

ANNIE. But, Will . . . supposing she doesn't come back?

MARBLE. She will. She'll walk in presently and be damn sorry for herself. You see if she doesn't.

(*A pause.*)

ANNIE. Will . . . (*Goes C. and turns.*)

MARBLE. Yes?

ANNIE. What made her say that about . . . Madame Collins?

MARBLE (*nervously*). She . . . she didn't know what she was saying. She was talking wild. . . .

ANNIE. She said something about her being here . . . when we came back from Bournemouth. Will, she *wasn't* here, was she?

MARBLE. Of course not. She's off her head.

ANNIE. Whatever made her think of Madame Collins? She's been gone nearly a year now. I can't imagine what Winnie was thinking——

MARBLE. She'd say anything.

ANNIE. But she must have . . . had . . . some reason. . . .

MARBLE. Well, if she had, I don't know anything about it.

ANNIE. Will, she hasn't written to you, has she?

MARBLE. Written?

ANNIE. Madame Collins, I mean.

MARBLE. Whatever makes you ask that?

ANNIE. That letter . . . just before Christmas . . . with the foreign stamps . . . I couldn't help seeing the envelope.

MARBLE (*very uneasily*). I told you, Annie, I'd had a line from Parsons who used to be in the office. He's at the Paris branch now.

ANNIE. Oh!

MARBLE. I told you about the money, didn't I?

ANNIE. No.

MARBLE. Well, I meant to. He said he was down on his luck and might be fired if he didn't find three hundred pounds. Well, we don't spend much, so I thought I'd send it. He'll pay it back. (*Pause.*) Satisfied now?

ANNIE (*unconvincingly*). Yes.

MARBLE (*holds out his hands to* ANNIE. *Takes her hands*). You don't think I'd . . . let you down, Annie?

ANNIE. No, I know you wouldn't really, but—— Oh, Will, I couldn't bear to think that . . . that you'd been untrue to me. If I thought that . . . I don't think I could go on. I'd kill myself. . . .

MARBLE. Don't . . . Annie! There's never been anything . . . I swear!

ANNIE. Oh, I know, dear, really. (*Kisses him.*) I'm just silly. . . . (*Smiles.*) I trust you, Will . . . always. (*She goes out.*)

(MARBLE *sits quite still for a few seconds. Goes up and shuts the door. Then he is shaken by a terrible sobbing. He lifts his head up.*)

CURTAIN

SCENE II

Scene—*The same, about three weeks later.*

At the rise of the curtain the room is deserted. After a few seconds MARBLE *comes downstairs, carrying a tray, on which are a china bowl and plate, a spoon and a tumbler. He is also carrying a hot-water bottle. He is unshaven and wears carpet slippers. His shuffling walk suggests great fatigue. As he gets to the door of the room a knock on the front door is heard. He puts the tray and hot-water bottle down on the cupboard in the passage and goes to admit* HAMMOND, *who comes in with a great show of "keeping quiet."*

HAMMOND (*crosses down to above the chair R. In a sickroom whisper*). How is she?

MARBLE (*who sounds very tired but less antagonistic to* HAMMOND *than usual. He shuts the door and comes down to the chair R. of the table*). Oh, better, thanks. She had quite a good night.

HAMMOND. That's the way.

MARBLE. Have you just got back?

HAMMOND. Yes. . . . We were surprised to hear. The baker's chap told us. You *have* had a time!

MARBLE. Yes. She got wet through, you know—traipsing after our girl, that day. . . .

HAMMOND. What is it now, a fortnight?

MARBLE. Nearly three weeks. It was just after you went.

HAMMOND. Sure it's all right me coming in?

MARBLE. Yes. She'll have a nap now, I expect. I've just fetched her tray down.

HAMMOND. The missus was very anxious to know the latest. She thought there might be something she could do.

MARBLE. I don't think there's anything. Thanks all the same.

HAMMOND. Got all the help you need, I expect? I said you'd have got someone in.

MARBLE. No, I haven't got anyone, but I'm all right.

HAMMOND. Haven't got anyone? Who's doing the nursing, then? And the house and everything?

MARBLE. I am.

HAMMOND. What . . . cooking and all, for over a fortnight?

MARBLE. Yes.

HAMMOND. You don't mean you haven't had any help at all?

MARBLE. Yes. I've managed all right.

HAMMOND. Good Lord! No wonder you look about done in!

MARBLE. It's kept me busy. But I don't mind that. Less time to think.

HAMMOND. Don't know how you've done it. Look here, there's my missus just itching to come in. Why not let her give you a hand? Be only too pleased.

MARBLE. No, it's all right. I can manage. Annie's better. I'll soon have her well, now.

HAMMOND. Well, as you like, of course. Wonder the doctor didn't say you were to have help.

MARBLE. He did, at first. Wanted me to have a nurse in. I suppose he didn't think I could do it, but he said yesterday that he was very pleased with the way she'd been looked after. (*He appears rather to expect applause.*)

HAMMOND. Well, you're a marvel. That's what you are. Just fancy you doing all that alone.

MARBLE (*rather proudly*). She wanted me to. She didn't want to have anyone else.

HAMMOND. Must have kept you on the go.

MARBLE. I don't mind.

HAMMOND. Strain, though, I should think?

MARBLE. Not so much now. It was at first. She had fever, you know. Temperature a hundred and four for a few hours. (*Emotionally.*) My God, Charlie, it . . . it was awful! (*Sits in the chair R. of the table.*)

(HAMMOND *sits in the armchair.*)

MARBLE. At one time, about nine one night, I thought she was . . . going. (*He bites his lip hard, then continues as if giving himself courage.*) But she's better. Not well yet, of course, but better. There's no doubt about that.

HAMMOND. How does she seem in herself? Keeping up her spirits?

MARBLE (*with enthusiasm*). Yes . . . she's wonderful. Won't ever let me see she's down. She had a bit of pain this morning, but just now she was as bright as anything again.

HAMMOND. And how long before she'll be about again?

MARBLE. I'm afraid it will be some little time. You see, it's left her so weak. Can't move much without being helped. Still . . . she's really on the mend now.

HAMMOND. Well, that's the main thing.

MARBLE. It's *everything*!

HAMMOND. By the way, you've had your own grub, I suppose?

MARBLE. No, there's no hurry.

HAMMOND. Going to cook now?

MARBLE. No. I have enough of the kitchen without cooking stuff for myself. Bit of cheese or something does me.

HAMMOND. That's not much to keep going on. Don't know how you can miss your dinner middle day. I couldn't . . . whatever happened.

MARBLE. I don't worry much about food.

HAMMOND. Oh, I say, what about your kid? Heard anything?

MARBLE. No.

HAMMOND. Where is she? Don't you know?

MARBLE. No. We put it in the papers. We don't hear anything. It's that mostly that's keeping Annie back. It upsets her terribly. She never was strong and she's taken it hard.

HAMMOND. I bet. Well, that's a nice go, that is.

MARBLE. I think if Winnie came back it would do Annie more good than all her medicine.

HAMMOND. Ah, no doubt about that. (*Rises.* MARBLE *also rises.*) Well, I expect you've got plenty to do. I'll get back and report to the missus. She's dying to do something for Mrs. M.

MARBLE. You might thank her for the offer. It's very good of her, tell her.

HAMMOND. Right. (*Going up to the door C.*) And if there should be anything . . .

MARBLE. Thanks. If there is, I'll let you know.

HAMMOND. Don't bother to come. You have your grub. See you soon. Might look in after supper tonight.

MARBLE. Yes, that's right.

(HAMMOND *goes.* MARBLE *closes the door; takes the plate with oranges on*

and lemon squeezer from the sideboard, when he pauses, hearing voices in the passage. He listens.)

MADAME COLLINS (*off*). Is Mr. Marble in?

HAMMOND (*off*). Yes, he's in there now.

MADAME COLLINS (*off*). Thank you. I will go in.

(*The front door shuts.* MARBLE *puts down the plate, etc., and goes to the door and opens it.* MADAME COLLINS *appears. He falls back a step. She looks at him, a contemptuous smile on her face.*)

MARBLE (*in a hoarse whisper*). Rita!

MADAME COLLINS (*advancing into the room*). Well? And what 'ave you to say for yourself?

MARBLE (*shuts the door—shaking badly*). What are you doing here?

MADAME COLLINS. Mr. 'Ammond let me in.

MARBLE (*up C.*). What is it? Why have you come here?

MADAME COLLINS (*takes a step up to him*). Do you not guess? I come to find why you do not answer letters.

MARBLE. But you mustn't come here. You must go away, at once. My wife——

MADAME COLLINS. I am not afraid of your wife.

MARBLE. No, you don't understand. She's been ill. Terribly ill. She's upstairs now. . . .

MADAME COLLINS. Well?

MARBLE. Oh, don't you see? She'll hear you. She mustn't know you're here. It would upset her——

MADAME COLLINS. But I wish to talk to you.

MARBLE. No, not here. You can't.

MADAME COLLINS. But I 'ave come from France on purpose to talk to you.

MARBLE. Sh! Don't speak so loud. She'll hear you.

MADAME COLLINS (*moves down*). I don't care. (*She sits R. of the table.*)

MARBLE (*a step down R.C.*). Oh, God! (*He looks about him in desperation.*) Look here, Rita, it's no use your coming here. You've had all you're going to get from me.

MADAME COLLINS. That is what you think, eh?

MARBLE. I mean it. I won't keep on paying like this. You can clear out.

MADAME COLLINS. I shall not go until I am ready.

MARBLE. If you don't go, Rita, I'll—— (*He is uncertain what he can do.*)

MADAME COLLINS. What will you do? Listen, I will tell you something. If you will meet me somewhere this afternoon I will go now. But it must be very soon.

MARBLE. I can't. I can't leave her alone in the house.

MADAME COLLINS (*with sarcasm*). You are so fond of her now?

MARBLE. Yes, I am. (*Noticing her smile.*) I *am*, I tell you!

MADAME COLLINS (*surprised at his earnestness*). What, that old bundle of rags?

MARBLE (*with suppressed fury*). You keep your filthy mouth shut! You're not going to talk about her; you're not fit to. She's worth fifty of you any day.

MADAME COLLINS (*smoothly*). Oh, yes, I am sure.

MARBLE. Yes, she is! And if you've· got anything else to say about her——

MADAME COLLINS. No. What I wish to say is about you . . . and me.

MARBLE. Well, I'm not going to listen. (*Goes above her to L. of the table.*) I've finished with you. I wish to God I'd never set eyes on you! I might have guessed what you were. Well, it's going to stop now, anyway.

MADAME COLLINS. Listen to me! The last time you send anything was before Christmas——

MARBLE. No, it wasn't. It was two months ago.

MADAME COLLINS (*quickly*). I 'ave not received that. I write three letters to you which you do not answer. I tell you 'ow I am ill and cannot pay for the doctor——

MARBLE (*comes down to front of the table, L. end*). Yes, and I didn't believe it. I'm sick to death of the whole business. Being bled by a rotten——

MADAME COLLINS. Take care!

MARBLE. Why should I? That's what you are—(*crossing to the fireplace*) —a dirty little blackmailer! And you won't get another penny out of me, see?

MADAME COLLINS. No? Suppose I say to you that I must 'ave five 'undred pounds.

MARBLE. You can say it. You won't get it. . . .

MADAME COLLINS. Per'aps you think differently if I say I must tell some things to your wife?

MARBLE (*turns round—losing confidence*). What?

MADAME COLLINS. I might 'ave to tell 'er about three weeks when she was at Bournemouth——

MARBLE (*takes a step toward her*). You couldn't! She wouldn't believe you! Besides, she's ill, I tell you. If she had a shock like that, she——

MADAME COLLINS (*triumphantly*). So? She 'as never found out anything? Thank you, that is what I wish to know.

MARBLE (*sits on the arm of the armchair*). You . . . bitch!

MADAME COLLINS. Well, you see, when you do not answer my letters I think per'aps that she know something now. I was a little worried.

MARBLE (*without much confidence*). You wouldn't tell her. You . . . you're only trying to frighten me. You daren't really——

MADAME COLLINS. Oh, yes. Why, it is so simple. I tell 'er 'ow terrible I feel because we 'ave deceived 'er. I say that it worry me so much that I come to make a confession. And that I would come before, only *you* beg me not to.

MARBLE (*rises*). You . . . little . . . swine!

MADAME COLLINS. You call me names, but what will she think of you, eh? 'Er dear, faithful 'usband . . . so kind . . . so attentive, so fond of 'er——

MARBLE. You can sneer as much as you like. I *am* fond of her. I'm not ashamed——

MADAME COLLINS. Ach! I am not such a fool. . . . You are frightened of her, per'aps. That is something quite different.

MARBLE. You can't understand, because she's different from anything you've ever known. When I think that I could ever have wanted you, it makes me feel sick.

MADAME COLLINS. Well, that is enough, thank you. If you do not give me this money I shall tell 'er.

MARBLE. You won't—(*crosses to the window L.*)—even if I have to go to the police. (*Turns to her.*) I tell you, I *won't* have her upset.

MADAME COLLINS. If you go to the police, do you think that your wife will not 'ear something about it? (*Laughs ironically, then says briskly:*) Now, we 'ave wasted a long time. You will give me that money, please.

MARBLE (*goes up*). God, what a fool I've been!

MADAME COLLINS. Do you 'ear what I say to you?

MARBLE. Yes.

MADAME COLLINS. Then quickly, please.

MARBLE (*comes down to behind the table*). I can't do it! I—— (*Pitifully, all fight gone.*) Rita . . . you've had everything.

MADAME COLLINS (*tapping the table*). You will write for me a check.

MARBLE. No.

MADAME COLLINS (*taking a pen from her bag—rises*). 'Ere is a pen. Sit down!

MARBLE (*pleading*). Rita . . .

(*She points to the chair and he slowly shuffles to it. She puts the pen in his hand.*)

MADAME COLLINS. Where is your book? (*Takes checkbook from his coat pocket.*) Now . . . you will write a check for "Bearer" for five 'undred pounds.

MARBLE. It's impossible! . . . Besides, it wouldn't be met.

MADAME COLLINS. I will tell you about that. Tomorrow you will arrange for that with your bank. I shall send the check through the bank in France and the money *must* be there.

MARBLE. But——

MADAME COLLINS. If you do one thing to stop it . . . you know what will 'appen. If it is there, you will not 'ear from me again.

MARBLE. How could I be sure?

MADAME COLLINS. You must trust me.

MARBLE (*bitterly*). Trust you! Look at the last time!

MADAME COLLINS. You must do what I say. Will you write, please?

(*He looks at her. He is seated above the table with his back to the door.* MADAME COLLINS *looks over his shoulder. He writes the date, then looks up.*)

MARBLE. This can't go on, you know. Soon there won't be anything for you to get. Then I suppose you'll be satisfied?

MADAME COLLINS. You make a great fuss, but this will not hurt you. I know that you do not spend one 'alf of your income. I should ask for much more, only I remember 'ow much I love you once.

(*She puts her arm around his shoulder, and he shakes it off angrily.*)

MARBLE. Queer sort of love! You're hard as hell, aren't you?

MADAME COLLINS (*in a softer voice*). I wonder. You used to think so when I was 'ere?

MARBLE. That's finished . . . thank God! (*His head drops onto his arm.*)

MADAME COLLINS (*with a tender intonation, her head close to his*). Do you really think I can forget? (*As she is speaking, the door opens silently.* ANNIE *is seen supporting her-*

self by the upright. She wears a shawl round her shoulders. The other two hear nothing, and MAD-AME COLLINS *continues.*) I shall never forget. I think of the afternoons . . . just at this time . . . when you sit in that old chair waiting. And while you look out of the window I creep in and put my hands to cover your eyes. . . . (ANNIE'S *own eyes close. She stops herself falling by a great effort.*) Then you jump out of your chair and hold me in your arms—(ANNIE *closes the door silently*)—and give me a long, long kiss. Do you think I forget that . . . ?

MARBLE (*suddenly sitting up*). What was that?

MADAME COLLINS. What?

MARBLE. It sounded like the door.

MADAME COLLINS (*looking round*). No, it is shut. Does it make your 'eart beat to remember those things?

MARBLE. I'll write this check and then you can go. (*He writes it and tears it out.*)

MADAME COLLINS (*taking it*). Very good. You will not forget what you must do tomorrow? (*She puts the check in her bag.* MARBLE *does not answer.*) It will be wise for you to remember.

MARBLE. Yes, and you'd better remember that this is the last time.

MADAME COLLINS. I 'ave told you that it is the last time.

MARBLE. Yes.

MADAME COLLINS. I quite understand.

MARBLE (*rises*). Then, get out!

(*A knock is heard on the front door.*)

MARBLE. That's the doctor. He mustn't find you here. (*Pushes his chair under the table.*)

MADAME COLLINS. That is not polite . . . get out.

MARBLE. I must go to the door. You go the back way, and don't let anybody see you. (*Opens the door, goes down and draws her up toward the door.*) If they do, I'll stop the check —see?

MADAME COLLINS. I find it curious 'ow men change.

(*Another knock is heard.*)

MARBLE. Get out!

MADAME COLLINS. Well, I will go. And please remember what I 'ave told you about the bank. Good-by. (*Kisses him.*)

MARBLE. For God's sake, don't make a noise now.

(*She goes off to L.* MARBLE *goes off to R. and opens the front door.*)

DOCTOR (*off*). You didn't hear my first knock. (*Coming in to R.C.*) Well? Everything all right?

(MARBLE *follows him.*)

MARBLE. Yes, quite.

DOCTOR. I thought she was worse. You looked a bit flustered.

MARBLE. No. If anything, she's a bit brighter today.

DOCTOR. Had her lunch?

MARBLE. Yes. I fetched her tray about half an hour ago. She was going to have a doze.

DOCTOR. Did she like the fruit juice?

MARBLE. Yes, she did.

DOCTOR. Give her as much of that as she'll take.

MARBLE. I was just going to make some more. Oh, and the mixture . . . there's not much left.

DOCTOR. I'll let you have some more. Better keep on with it for another three or four days.

MARBLE. Very good, Doctor.

DOCTOR (looking him over). And what about you?

MARBLE. Me?

DOCTOR. Yes; you're not looking too good, you know. Been overdoing it rather, lately.

MARBLE. Oh, I'm all right, Doctor, thanks.

DOCTOR. Well . . . if you're not careful we'll be having you down too. Then you'll have to have that nurse, whether you want her or not.

MARBLE. No need to worry about me, Doctor.

DOCTOR. Did you take a chair out in the garden, as I said?

MARBLE. No . . . not yet, Doctor. I . . . I haven't had much time.

DOCTOR. Well, take half an hour sometimes. When she's sleeping would be a good time. You'd hear her out there, anyway, and while the weather's decent you're much better off outside.

MARBLE. Yes.

DOCTOR. I'll just take a look at her now I'm here. (Goes into the passage.)

MARBLE. All right, Doctor.

DOCTOR. You've stuck it pretty well. (Going upstairs.) You don't want to get crocked just as she's getting well, do you? Get out in the sun all you can.

MARBLE. Very well, Doctor.

(As MARBLE comes toward the window L., two knocks are heard on the bedroom door upstairs. MARBLE looks out at the garden and quickly turns away. He collects a knife, two oranges, and a lemon squeezer from the sideboard and brings them to the table. He halves the oranges and squeezes out the juice. The DOCTOR returns, carrying an empty tumbler which has been used. He looks at MARBLE.)

MARBLE (struck by his expression). Doctor . . . is anything the matter?

DOCTOR. Yes.

MARBLE. Is she . . . is she bad again?

(A pause. DOCTOR looks down at the glass.)

DOCTOR. She's dead. (He looks up quickly.)

MARBLE (he has to sit down L. of the table). How can she be . . . ? (He is terribly upset.)

DOCTOR. It can only just have happened . . . not more than a few minutes, I should say. It's . . . it's extraordinary.

MARBLE. Dead . . . Oh, my God! (*He breaks down.*)

(*The* DOCTOR *gives him time to recover a little.*)

DOCTOR. She appears to have been—poisoned.

MARBLE. What?

DOCTOR. Is there any poison in the house?

MARBLE. No . . . at least . . . not where she could get it.

DOCTOR. What is it? Cyanide of potassium or——

MARBLE. Cyanide, yes. I had it for photography. I've had it some time.

DOCTOR. Where?

MARBLE (*pointing*). Out there . . . in the cupboard. She couldn't have got it possibly.

DOCTOR. Wait a minute. (*He goes to the cupboard and opens it. He takes out an empty bottle and brings it down.*) Was this the one?

MARBLE. Yes. But . . . it was half full. (*Stretches out his hand for the bottle.*)

DOCTOR (*draws bottle away*). I see. (*He goes down to R. of the table, takes cork out of bottle, and sniffs.*) When did you give her the fruit juice?

MARBLE. About . . . three quarters of an hour ago. Why?

DOCTOR. Did you see her drink it?

MARBLE. Yes. There can't have been anything in that. I took it up and didn't leave her until I brought the glass down with the other things.

DOCTOR. Where is that glass?

MARBLE. On the tray. Out there on the cupboard. I put it down when someone came to the door. I'll show you.

(DOCTOR *goes up and stands in passage R. of the door.*)

MARBLE (*goes to the doorway and stops*). But . . . it was on the tray. I *know* it was! Did you take it? (*Backs to front of the armchair.*)

DOCTOR (*comes in and shuts the door*). I got this glass from beside her bed.

MARBLE. But . . . there was only one glass! I brought it down. It was there on the tray . . . (*A pause.*) Doctor . . . (DOCTOR *comes down to the chair R. of the table.*) She couldn't have got down alone.

DOCTOR. No.

MARBLE. Then . . . how did the glass . . . get upstairs?

DOCTOR. That's what I want to know.

(*They look at each other. Suddenly* MARBLE *falls back into the armchair and laughs hysterically.*)

LIGHTS FADE OUT

EPILOGUE

SCENE—*As in the Prologue.*

(*The conversation continues from the point at which it was broken off.*)

HAMMOND. What really made him do it in the end was the same thing as most other murders . . . he was having an affair with another woman and they wanted Mrs. M. out of the way.

PROSPECTIVE TENANT. I can't help thinking what a terrible thing it would be if a mistake was made.

HAMMOND. Mistake? Why, the judge said there couldn't have been a plainer case. The motive was there. They proved the stuff was in the cupboard. They proved she couldn't have got it alone. They proved that while she was ill he wouldn't have anyone in, and then to put the lid on it . . . all those books.

PROSPECTIVE TENANT. The books on crime?

HAMMOND. That's what really did him in, of course. That was one thing he hadn't got an answer for—and I don't wonder. (*Goes up to the door.*) Well, what about it?

PROSPECTIVE TENANT. Yes, I think I'll take it. I think it might suit me . . . temporarily anyway. (*Going toward the window.*) Oh, about the garden. It's in a pretty bad state, really a shocking state. I wonder if I might be allowed to come in sometimes just to start getting rid of some of those weeds? (*Turns to him.*) You know what weeds are once they get hold of a garden. (*Going up C.*) It means digging it right through from end to end.

HAMMOND. Yes, and if you ask me, I should say you'll probably have to dig very deep.

CURTAIN

Kind Lady

By

EDWARD CHODOROV

Adapted From a Story
By
Hugh Walpole

Kind Lady was first presented by H. C. Potter and George Haight at the Booth Theatre in New York City, Tuesday evening, April 23, 1935. The play was staged by Mr. Potter, the setting was designed by Jo Mielziner and the cast was as follows:

MR. FOSTER	Francis Compton
MARY HERRIES	Grace George
LUCY WESTON	Irby Marshal
ROSE	Marie Paxton
PHYLLIS GLENNING	Florence Britton
PETER SANTARD	Alan Bunce
HENRY ABBOTT	Henry Daniell
ADA	Justine Chase
DOCTOR	Alfred Rowe
MR. EDWARDS	Thomas Chalmers
MRS. EDWARDS	Elfrida Derwent
AGGIE EDWARDS	Barbara Shields
GUSTAV ROSENBERG	Jules Epailly

SCENES

PROLOGUE

An afternoon in spring.

ACT ONE

Scene I: Late Christmas Eve several years before.
Scene II: After dinner the following January.

ACT TWO

An afternoon later in January.

ACT THREE

An afternoon the following summer.

EPILOGUE

The action of the play takes place in.the living room of Mary Herries' home in Montague Square, London.

SCENE

The *downstairs living room in Mary Herries' house in Montague Square,
London.*

The *room proper is a large, comfortably furnished living room reflecting the
excellent taste and character of Mary Herries. Many of its furnishings, the
pictures in particular, are objets d'art. In the right wall are two large casement windows with fine lace curtains and heavy drapes. In the left wall is a
large fireplace (down stage) and a door (up stage) leading to the dining
room. Above the mantel is a large oil painting, a Whistler.*

Up *C. is a large arch. Going up stage through the arch one rises two steps
to a platform that extends off R. to the front hall and door, and off L. to the
rear of the house. Up stage of the platform two more steps lead to a bay window, and stair landing. Leading L. from this bay-window landing is a flight of
stairs to the upper part of the house.*

Between *the windows at R. is a desk and chair. A sofa with a coffee table in
front of it is at R. Against the R. section of the back wall is a chest and in the
up R. corner is a table with a lamp.*

In *front of the fireplace is a low upholstered fire seat. Two large overstuffed
chairs with a drum table between them occupy the L. side of the stage.*

Against *the L. side of the back wall is a chest and at its R. is a low table
with a lamp. On the wall above these are an El Greco and a Whistler. Above
the furniture at up R. on the back wall are two more Whistlers.*

Between *the windows in the bay window is a large chest. The windows
have drapes and curtains.*

A *chandelier hangs in the hall and there are wall brackets at R. and L. on
the pilasters framing the big C. arch.*

KIND LADY

PROLOGUE

SCENE—*There is a slight rearrangement of furniture on stage R. The sofa is between the windows R. with the coffee table below it. The desk is R. with a side chair behind it and another side chair at its L. On the R. and L. back walls and over the fireplace the "old masters" have been replaced by "modern."*

AT RISE—*Empty stage. It is raining outside. It is late afternoon. After the curtain rises the doorbell is heard ringing. After a moment it rings again. A* SERVANT *is seen crossing on the platform above the C. arch from the rear of the house (L.) toward the front door (R.). The doorbell rings again.*

MR. FOSTER (*off*). Mr. Abbott, please.

SERVANT (*off*). Mr. Abbott's out.

FOSTER (*entering to C. of platform. He is a small man. He carries an umbrella, hat, and brown paper envelope, and wears a coat*). I'm from the bank, Foster's the name. I had an appointment for four o'clock. (SERVANT *gestures him to sit down and wait.*) Then, if you don't mind, I'll take off my coat—it's damp.

(FOSTER *removes his coat, gives it, his hat, and umbrella to* SERVANT, *who exits R. and after leaving them crosses out L.* FOSTER *in the meantime has come down into the room proper. Gone to the L. end of the desk and left his envelope there. He then crosses R., glances out the window and then at the pictures. His attention is drawn to someone coming down the stairs. It is* MARY HERRIES. MARY HERRIES *comes down from upstairs uncertainly and rather furtively. She steps on the platform and looks off L. She turns and starts off R. on the platform.*)

FOSTER (*stopping her as she reaches the C. of the platform*). How do you do? (MARY *stops but doesn't answer.*) I am waiting for Mr. Abbott, if you please, madam. I'm from the bank. I have an appointment for four o'clock, but since he's not here, perhaps——

MARY. Mr. Abbott—is—not here?

FOSTER. No. Servant said he was out. Perhaps I should come back later.

MARY (*crossing on platform and looking off L.*). They—don't usually keep people waiting.

FOSTER. That's all right. I don't mind waiting. Only I hope I'm not in the way.

MARY (*crossing down C. of platform*). No. You're not in the way. Of course not—— From the bank?

FOSTER (*still at R. of desk*). Blakely's, madam.

MARY. Oh, yes. I know that bank very well. I used to do business with Blakely's Bank.

FOSTER (*crossing down R. to in front of desk*). Excuse me, madam. But is there any possibility that Mr. Abbott may not be here shortly? I'm to see another gentleman at five.

MARY. You've never been here before?

FOSTER. No, madam.

MARY. Then you've never seen me before. I don't see many people—from outside.

FOSTER. Oh.

MARY. Don't you think it odd that I never see anyone?

FOSTER. Why—I don't know, Mrs.——

MARY. Miss—Mary Herries.

FOSTER. Oh. (*Then suddenly.*) Herries? It seems to me I remember the name, madam. It's been on our books for years.

MARY. Yes—it has been. For years.

FOSTER. But I thought—I mean I took it for granted—that you were away. Abroad, or some place. For several years, I think?

MARY. No, I've been here—always. (MARY *crosses above to dining-room door and closes it. Then comes back to* FOSTER, *who has come to* C.) Don't you want to know why I never see anyone?

FOSTER. Uh—what is that, madam?

MARY. It's a very interesting reason. Very interesting. I think you might be very interested. You might be the very one.

(*During this last speech the lights have been slowly fading—and at the end of the speech the stage is in total darkness.*)

ACT ONE

SCENE I

The lights fade up very shortly and we find the stage is set as first described. LUCY WESTON is discovered sitting in the chair L. in front of the fireplace. In the chair L.C. is an open suitcase with wrapped Christmas packages in it. There are also some packages on the table L. and an envelope. It is late Christmas Eve, several years before the Prologue. A small Christmas tree is on the chest in the bay window.

ROSE (*entering immediately after the lights are up, with a piece of red ribbon and a tray containing a whisky decanter, siphon, and glasses*). This is all I could find, Mrs. Weston.

(ROSE *puts tray on chest upper L.* and crosses to table L. and ties up a Christmas package.)

LUCY. Fine! That will do nicely. Now let me see. Cynthia, Peter, John, Harold, Kitten, and Sybil. That's seven. Seven nieces and nephews. Rose, think of it. And I didn't have to go through a thing to have them! It is quite different when I have my own chickabiddies.

ROSE. Oh—Mrs. Weston!

LUCY. What's this? (*She notices a package which hasn't been put in suitcase.*) "Rose." Now who in heaven's name! Has my brother had another child? I mean his wife? Dear me, it's hard to keep track, Rose—— (*Looks at* ROSE.) Oh, my heavens! It's *you!* I nearly packed it with the others. Well, now the cat's out of the bag. (*Hands package to* ROSE.) Merry Christmas, Rose.

ROSE (*crossing in front of table*). Oh, thank you, Mrs. Weston. The same to you and many more.

LUCY. Well—we won't count how many more. And—(*takes envelope*)—this. For looking after me so nicely this visit.

ROSE (*takes envelope*). Oh, Mrs. Weston. This is too much!

LUCY. When you open it you won't say that. Well, things are going to get better someday. Those go in the bag to take with me tomorrow. Don't let me forget. Am I all packed?

ROSE (*putting packages in suitcase*). Yes, madam. Except for the blouse at the cleaner's. I'll send that on to you the moment it comes.

LUCY. That's fine. What time is it?

ROSE (*puts suitcase on floor above table*). After eleven o'clock, madam.

LUCY. What time are these operas usually over, Rose?

ROSE (*straightens L.C. chair*). It's hard to say, Mrs. Weston. But Miss Herries always leaves early when the weather's bad.

LUCY. There's one place I will not be found on Christmas Eve—and that is an opera house. Well—I have to leave in half an hour. Miss Herries is sure to be back by then, isn't she?

ROSE (*going upstairs*). That's hard to say, Mrs. Weston.

(*Front doorbell rings.* ROSE *puts suitcase on landing* R. *and goes to answer it.*)

PHYLLIS (*off stage*). Is Miss Herries in?

ROSE (*off stage*). No, miss, she's not back from the opera.

(PHYLLIS *enters and stops at* C. *on platform*).

PHYLLIS. Oh, dear, I was sure she'd be here. (*Sees* LUCY.) Mrs. Weston! Merry Christmas.

LUCY. Hello, Phyllis, Merry Christmas!

PHYLLIS. I'm doing the rounds of the relatives, bearing gifts. (ROSE *picks up suitcase and is crossing toward stairs.* PHYLLIS *turns toward off* R.) Peter! Come in—don't stand out there in the hall. (*To* ROSE.) Don't go, please. (ROSE *stops at foot of stairs.* PHYLLIS *calling off* R.) Peter!

PETER (*off*). Huh?

LUCY (*confidentially*). Is this——

PHYLLIS. I don't know yet, but I think so. (PETER *enters, carrying small package.*) Peter, this is Mrs. Weston. Mrs. Weston, Mr. Santard. (*Takes package.*)

PETER (*crosses to upper R.C.*). How do you do?

LUCY. How do you do?

PHYLLIS. Please put this—by the tree tomorrow morning. (*Gives* ROSE *package.*)

ROSE. Yes, miss. (*Exits upstairs.*)

PHYLLIS. Peter's an American.

PETER. You know——

(*Acknowledging this, Peter gives slight Indian war cry.*)

PHYLLIS. Now, Peter not *that* American!

PETER. Sorry.

PHYLLIS. Say something nice, Peter.

PETER (*to* MRS. WESTON). Are you Aunt Mary?

LUCY. No, I'm just—visiting—Phyllis' Aunt Mary.

PETER. I've heard a great deal about Aunt Mary and—(*brightly, for* PHYLLIS' *benefit*)—I've wanted to meet her! (*Nods to Phyllis with a "How's that?" expression.*)

PHYLLIS (*crossing off platform to upper C.*). You see—Peter and I—thought it would be a good idea to *bring* Aunt Mary her present—and now she isn't here! Peter!

PETER (*who has been looking around the room*). Oh! How do you like London, Mrs. Weston?

LUCY. Why—I should be asking that of you!

PETER. I know—that's why I asked you first.

PHYLLIS. Don't mind Peter, Mrs. Weston. No one in New York would dream of giving him a job, so his father sent him over here!

LUCY. I think he's very charming. Sit down, and tell me about—— (*Sees decanter.*) Oh, would you like a drink?

PETER. Yes, please—and *no* ice.

PHYLLIS. No, Peter. No time.

PETER (*bowing politely to* LUCY). Merry Christmas. (*Crosses up onto platform at R.*)

PHYLLIS. Sorry, Mrs. Weston. We have miles and miles of driving to do. (*Telephone.*) Good night.

LUCY. Good night. (*Crossing toward telephone on desk R.*)

PETER (*going off R.*) Good-by.

(ROSE *enters down the stairs.*)

PHYLLIS. Don't tell Aunt Mary we were here. Present—secret. Merry Christmas.

(*Exits R.—followed by* ROSE.)

LUCY. Merry Christmas, Phyllis. (*At telephone.*) Hello? Hello, Bunny! I'm on my way! Really I am—I thought I might induce Mary Herries to "step out" this once—What do you mean she's "no fun"?—Of course you don't know her—The car?—Oh, lovely—Yes—half an hour. Right you are. (*Hangs up*).

PHYLLIS (*off*). Merry Christmas.

ROSE (*off*). Merry Christmas, miss.

(ROSE *enters from R. Crosses and exits door L. to dining room.* LUCY *crosses above sofa toward C. as* ROSE *enters from dining room with a plate of sandwiches on a tray.*)

LUCY. Oh, those look good! (ROSE, *about to put sandwiches on table L., comes to* LUCY *at upper C. and offers them.*) Er—no. Not until I'm down ten more pounds. (*Turns away but looks back at sandwiches.*) Oh, well. Christmas comes but once a year. (*Takes a sandwich.*) Thank you. (*Crosses and sits L. end of sofa.*)

ROSE (*putting sandwiches on table L*). Is there anything else, madam?

LUCY. No—except my trunk. I'm sure I'll be in no mood tomorrow to worry about that.

ROSE (*takes whisky and siphon from chest upper L. and puts on table L.*). The baggage people promised to be here at seven sharp, they said.

LUCY. Well, if they're pretty and have curly hair you wake me up, Rose. Otherwise I'll leave their money on the dressing table.

ROSE (*laughs*). Yes, madam. (*Exits to dining room.*)

(*The door is heard to open and* MARY HERRIES *enters.*)

MARY (*in arch*). Hello! Head better, dear? (*Rings bell L. of arch for* ROSE.)

LUCY. Much.

MARY. Good! (*Speaking off R.*) Come in. (HENRY ABBOTT *appears and crosses to upper R.C. He is tall, handsome, emanates strength and charm immediately. Shabbily, miserably dressed.*) Here's a hungry young man we've got to feed, Lucy.

HENRY (*very quietly, half smiling*). Just a cup of tea, thanks.

MARY. Oh, nonsense. You've made me take you in here at this time of night. You'll have to justify it.

HENRY. I'm afraid I couldn't manage much more.

(ROSE *enters from dining room to above chair L.C.*)

MARY. Rose, would you make some tea, and let this gentleman have anything else he wants? (*To* HENRY.) If you feel better.

HENRY. Just some tea.

(*There is a moment's pause.*)

ROSE (*who has been eying him, crosses to platform L.*). This way, please. (*He turns and follows* ROSE *out L. past arch without any further sign.*)

MARY (*crossing L., puts purse on table L.*). Poor chap.

LUCY. Where did you find him?

MARY (*crosses to C.*). Just outside— I've never done this before! I never even give—(*crossing to desk R.*)— to beggars on the street. Anyway, all I had was a one-pound note. (*Reflects.*) There's something about him. Don't you think? (*Puts wrap on desk chair.*)

LUCY. Mmm.

MARY. Matter of fact. Made me feel awfully sorry for him. I just couldn't leave him standing there. But I'd never have brought him in if you weren't here. (*Laughs.*) Haven't I been trying to convince you that I'm getting sillier all the time! I really should apologize! (*Crosses C.*)

LUCY (*taking a cigarette*). What for?

MARY. After all, heaven knows *what* he is.

LUCY. What he looks like probably—a rather charming, hungry young man.

MARY. Isn't he? Striking, I mean.

LUCY. Very.

MARY. So unusual.

LUCY. Very. How was Covent Garden?

MARY (*above table L. taking off gloves*). Horrible, I thought. The place reeked of mackintoshes and galoshes. I could see the strings resenting it bitterly. I hate London at this time of year.

LUCY. In a few weeks I'll be home—in my garden—with an armful of the loveliest azaleas *you* ever saw.

MARY. What a persistent woman! Oh, I feel so stupid refusing.

LUCY. Well, now, why refuse? Now look here! Why shouldn't you give yourself a month of Riviera sun and warmth? What's keeping you here?

MARY. I don't know. It's simply——

LUCY. Simply rot.

MARY. Lucy, I'd love to go back with you.

LUCY. Then why not?

MARY. But I'm just comfortable here, I suppose——

LUCY. Why do you avoid everyone?

MARY (*not listening and looking off L.*). You know, Lucy, he didn't ask me for money.

LUCY. What? Ohh.

MARY. He simply stood there with the most disarming smile and said: "I wonder if I might have a cup of tea on Christmas Eve."

LUCY. Very touching. I asked you why you avoid everyone.

MARY (*crosses to L.C. chair and sits*). I? I don't do anything of the sort. I've just been busy—that's all.

LUCY. Don't tell me, Mary Herries. Won't you come with me tonight, just this once? Bunny would love to have you. (*Crosses C.*)

MARY. No, thank you, Lucy.

LUCY. Oh, ho! You're going to have a nice little chat with Tiny Tim.

MARY. Who?

LUCY. The striking young beggar you met in the fog—or snow—on Christmas Eve.

MARY. I am not! When he's had something to eat, Rose can let him out through the basement.

LUCY. Aren't you going to give him some money or something?

MARY. No, I am not.

LUCY. At least you must let him thank you.

MARY. Not necessarily.

LUCY. Well—if you want to sit all alone on Christmas Eve—I'll stay with you. I'll ring up Bunny. (*Starts R.*)

MARY (*rises and crosses to* LUCY). No, Lucy. I won't let you. Please go and have a good time.

(ROSE *enters from L. on platform.*)

ROSE. He's finished, madam.

MARY (*turns to* ROSE). What?

ROSE. He's had his tea.

MARY (*up C.*). Very well, Rose. You can show him out downstairs.

ROSE. But—— (*She pauses.*)

MARY. Yes?

ROSE. He says he wants to thank you.

LUCY (*R.C.*). There!

MARY. That's very nice of him. Tell him he's quite welcome.

LUCY. Mary!

ROSE. Yes, Miss Herries.

(*Turns to go—but* HENRY *enters from L. on platform, crosses to upper L.C.*)

HENRY (*half smiling; a peculiar somber smile*). I've had my tea. You're very kind.

MARY. I was happy to help you.

HENRY. I wanted to thank you, that's all.

MARY. Of course.

(*There is a pause.*)

HENRY (*sees sandwiches on table L.*). I—I wonder if I might take a few of those sandwiches.

LUCY (*ill at ease*). Please do!

MARY. Of course.

HENRY (*crosses to table L.*). I'll eat them outside.

(*Doorbell.* ROSE *goes R.*)

LUCY (*mischievously*). Eat them here!

(MARY *looks uncomfortably at* LUCY.)

HENRY. Thank you. I'm able to now, I think. (*Looks at whisky.*)

MARY (*weakly*). Have some whisky if you like.

HENRY. I will.

(ROSE *enters.* HENRY *crosses below table L. and mixes whisky and soda.*)

ROSE. The car's at the door for Mrs. Weston. (*Exits R.*)

LUCY. Oh, dear! Well—— (*Mischievously.*) Good night, Mary, and —a Merry Christmas.

MARY. Merry Christmas, Lucy. I'll see you in the morning.

LUCY. I hope so. (*She goes R.*)

HENRY (*looking at paintings*). You've a few nice things here. (MARY *smiles nervously—looking covertly back over her shoulder for* ROSE.) That's a good El Greco. (*Points to upper L. back wall.*)

MARY (*indicates immediately she is quite astonished*). It's not bad.

HENRY (*crossing up L.*). One of his early ones; they're not common.

MARY (*at upper C.*). No. There aren't two hundred people in London who'd know that! Are you an artist?

HENRY. Not really. One of many confused talents.

MARY. You talk as if you knew something about painting.

HENRY. I suppose I do. (*He starts toward sandwiches.*)

MARY. Look here—if you really want something to eat now—those stale sandwiches—— (*Paces to chair L. C.*)

HENRY. They're exactly right. Again, thanks. And again forgive me for disturbing you like this.

(ROSE *enters and gets* MARY's *wrap at desk.*)

MARY. You haven't. It isn't every day one bumps into an El Greco lover on the street.

(ROSE *exits L. on platform, a bit uneasy.*)

HENRY (*looking around again, crosses L.*). You collect seriously.

MARY (*amused*). How do you tell? Is this room that bad?

HENRY (*quickly—crossing up L. and pointing*). It's lovely of course. But it takes a collector to jam a Whistler, an El Greco, and a Ming horse all together, doesn't it?

MARY (*after a moment*). Well, whatever you are, you have an educated eye—no question about that! And you're right about the jam. (*Carries horse from upper L. chest and puts it on upper R. chest.*) There seems to be a difference between my maid and myself as to just where this bronze belongs!

HENRY. Your maid is a strong-minded woman.

MARY (*laughs—crossing down R.*). You've found that out? Rose is a good soul—and devoted to me. She won't go to bed now until she's quite sure you don't mean to murder me. (*Sits R. end of sofa.* HENRY *laughs and drinks.*) What do you do?

HENRY (*crossing to C.*). Nothing. Everything. The last year I've had odd jobs I shouldn't like to mention in this house. (*Crosses to sofa, puts glass on table below sofa.*)

MARY. But you certainly have a good eye—and knowledge. Collecting *is* my one interest.

HENRY. Mine, too, once—and not wasted. (*Sits L. end of couch.*) I find it very comforting to remember, standing in the line on the embankment.

MARY. The line?

HENRY. The bread line.

MARY. Oh.

HENRY. As a connoisseur of lines—I should say it was the best in London—and wonderfully philanthropic. I bothered you tonight because the two odd miles to the embankment seemed to stretch like eternity in the snow.

MARY. I'm glad you did.

HENRY. I, too.

MARY (pause). Are you alone?

HENRY. Alone, as they say, in the world?

MARY. Yes.

HENRY. Practically. I have a wife—and a child.

MARY. Oh—really?

HENRY. A nursing child.

MARY (very sympathetically). What do you do?

HENRY. We do rather nicely comparatively. Ada—my wife—is a delicate creature who scrubs floors occasionally, when she's lucky, in an office building in the City—a Fragonard charwoman.

MARY. A nursing child. That's dreadful.

HENRY. Not at all. What Ada makes pays the rent of our hovel in South Wharf Road—and buys approximately enough food for herself and the little brute, of course.

MARY. South Wharf Road. You live ——

HENRY. In the neighborhood. I've admired the outside of your house many times—from the drinking trough opposite. (Pointing off R.)

MARY (rises, crosses C.). And I'm going to send you back to your house right now.

HENRY (rises). Of course—I'm keeping you up.

MARY. That's an unkind remark, young man. I could sit here and tell you how I got that El Greco until you beg for mercy. But I won't—for a very good reason. (Starts up C.)

HENRY (stopping her). I should like to hear.

MARY. Oh, no. (Turns back to HENRY at C.) All my life the mistakes that I've made—and there have been plenty—have all arisen from the same thing—my heart swamping my good sense. (She looks at him. Paces to HENRY.) I'm telling you this because you're obviously a very unusual and intelligent young man—and you've just told me a terribly pathetic story.

HENRY (smiling). Thank you. I'm sorry.

MARY. I'm afraid of it—and you. I had a birthday a short time ago, and I thought at last I'm too old to be foolish any more. But here I am—helping an entirely unknown man into my house in the middle of the night and listening to a tale that's going to make me see white-faced babies in my dreams for a week.

HENRY. He's red as a herring—and looks like one.

MARY. Believe me—I don't care. Everything about you conspires to make me help you. Why—you even live around the corner! Well, I'm not going to help you. I'm a selfish old maid—and I never want to see you again—or hear anything more about that young girl you've presented with a baby. You're probably the worst sort of criminal. (*Turns and goes to upper C., as she finishes speech, then turns back quickly.*) Wait a minute. (*Goes upstairs and off.*)

(HENRY *looks after her quietly. Finishes whisky and puts glass on table below sofa. Then slowly crosses L. and easily he picks up a white jade cigarette case from table, examines it, takes out cigarette, taps it against the case, looks at case again, then puts it in his pocket in the most natural manner in the world—as if it had come from there. He lights his cigarette, crossing to below couch. As* MARY *comes down carrying a heavy cloth coat with a fur collar, over her arm,* HENRY *puts out cigarette.*)

MARY (*hands him coat*). Give this to your wife.

HENRY. That's good of you.

MARY (*going on as she gets her purse from table L.*). She'd better let a tailor do the alterations. Here.

(HENRY *crosses to her.*) And you'd better get some shoes.

HENRY (*without the slightest emotion*). You're saving our lives.

MARY. Nonsense. (*He looks at the money in his hand.*) It's all I have in the house—so you needn't bother holding me up now, you see?

HENRY. It *was* foolish of you to let a tramp in here at this time of night.

MARY. So I've been told. But an old woman like me—what's the difference?

HENRY. I could have cut your throat.

MARY. You might have—but you'd have been sorry.

HENRY. Oh, no. The ·police never catch anybody any more.

MARY (*going to arch R. and onto platform*). Don't let's worry about that.

HENRY. Not tonight. It would be ungrateful.

MARY. Good-by.

(HENRY *crosses to R. of* MARY *on platform—turns to her.*)

HENRY. Good night. (*Exits R.*)

MARY (*calling off*). Good luck. And —Merry Christmas!

(MARY *comes in. Hesitates in arch. Goes to above chair lower C., looks for cigarette case on table, then on chest up L. Then on mantel.*)

ROSE (*enters from L., stays on platform L.*). Is there anything you want, madam?

MARY (*looks for cigarette case*). No, Rose. You can go to bed.

ROSE. Yes, madam—good night. (*Starts to go L.*)

MARY. Rose. Have you seen my cigarette case?

ROSE (*comes to table L.*). The white jade, madam? (MARY *nods.*) It was layin' right there this evening.

MARY. I thought so. (*Pause as they both reflect about* HENRY.) Oh, well —never mind.

ROSE. I'd say he took it, madam.

MARY. Oh, no, Rose.

ROSE. Do you know where to find him, madam?

MARY. Mmmmm. It doesn't matter.

ROSE. Oh, dear—that's too bad. (*Puts stopper in decanter on table L.*)

MARY. No, Rose—he didn't take it— I remember now—I had it with me in the taxi.

ROSE. I didn't like him at all, madam. Too good-lookin'.

MARY (*sits chair L.*) He was good-looking, wasn't he?

ROSE. Too much so—I don't believe he was hungry at all. The way he sat in the kitchen! You're not hungry, I said to myself—you're too good-looking. And you're up to something. And sure enough. (*Picks up sandwich plate—crosses toward sofa.*)

MARY. No, Rose. (ROSE *stops and turns to* MARY.) I left it in the taxi, I'm sure.

ROSE (*shaking her head*). Yes, madam. (*Picks up glass from coffee table and goes to dining-room door.*) Good night. (*Exits.*)

(*Christmas chimes from a church ring out.* MARY *doesn't answer. Looks toward arch R. Turns front— shrugs shoulders.*)

CURTAIN

ACT ONE

SCENE II

Night. Two weeks later, January. PHYLLIS *sitting on couch reading.* PETER *standing in front of Troubetzkoi on table L. with glass.* PETER *looks at Troubetzkoi for a pause.* PETER *walks away about three steps R., half looking at Troubetzkoi, then stops, returns to statue, looks at it again.* PETER *puts glass down deliberately on table. Takes out match, strikes it and holds it to statue.*

PHYLLIS. Peter! Peter, put those matches away and sit down.

(PETER *hastily shakes out match and picks up brandy glass.*)

PETER (*indicates Troubetzkoi*). That —is a woman. Phyllis! We must get one of those.

PHYLLIS. Yes, dear.

(*Looking at her,* PETER *walks, imitating a tightrope walker, toward stage R. He stops in front of picture —looks at it for a pause—then suddenly—with extreme deliberation, he puts his glass down on chest upper R.*)

PHYLLIS. Peter, *please* don't set off any more matches!

(PETER *picks up glass and comes C.*)

PETER. Phyllis—who's that tall thin girl last night with the—(*makes series of adenoidal noises saying:*) "So pleased to meet you so very nice" —can't understand a word she says —who *is* that?

PHYLLIS. That, my dear—will be your cousin Elizabeth.

(PETER *looks at her for a moment.*)

PETER. That'll be nice. And *who*— was the fat gentleman with the— (*indicates fat stomach*)—and—the —(*indicates pompous look and monocle*).

PHYLLIS (*cuts in*). If you're attempting to describe Sir Arthur Verne— he's a *very* dear friend of Mother's —and happens to be a *very* distinguished man.

PETER (*agreeing quickly*). Yes— yes, indeed—I could see that. (*Suddenly gets a glint in his eyes and goes into the next speech as though he were tremendously puzzled.*) But who—*who*—was the little feller! (*He extends his hand about chest high.*)

PHYLLIS. Who?

PETER. You know—— (*Drops his hand about a foot.*) The *little* feller.

PHYLLIS. What are you talking about?

PETER (*drops his hand to about a foot from the floor—bending way over—and holding this stance. Speaks patiently*). The little feller!—with the—— (*Lifts his hand to pull at his chin.*)

PHYLLIS. With the *what*——

PETER. The goatee!

PHYLLIS. Peter—get *up!*

PETER (*straightens*). But who *is* he? Really!

PHYLLIS. There's no one like that in our family.

PETER. No? (*He shudders.*)

PHYLLIS. No.

PETER. Funny. I keep seeing him everywhere.

PHYLLIS. Peter, you simply mustn't drink brandy.

PETER. There's only *one* of your family that I really like.

PHYLLIS. Really?

PETER (*pointing wisely upstairs*). Aunt Mary.

PHYLLIS (*rises and crosses R. behind sofa*). We are rude, Peter, but we simply must dash off!

PETER (*sitting sofa L.*). Well, let's not! Let's stay here instead.

PHYLLIS (*with mock weariness, but real annoyance*). Darling—how can we?

PETER. I feel mellow and witty and dignified all at once for the first time in my life! I don't want to go out in the cold world!

PHYLLIS (*patronizingly crossing C.*). It has been awfully nice—but you have no sense of responsibility.

PETER. I like it here! This is what I call gracious living and it's the first dinner party I've enjoyed in a long while.

PHYLLIS. Much as you hate doing the rounds, you've simply *got* to. I don't like these continual introductions either. But do you make it any easier for me? No! You act as though I were whipping you through hoops or something!

PETER. Can't stand being introduced —wholesale.

PHYLLIS. You spend most of the time standing around and grinning foolishly at everyone.

PETER. I'm not grinning foolishly now. I like Miss Herries—and I'm crazy about this house—and I hope that—(*closes his eyes*)—the solidification—of our relationship will permit me to run in and out of here at frequent intervals. (*Both laugh.*) Furthermore, she has the best wine I ever tasted. (*He reaches for brandy decanter.*)

PHYLLIS (*taking his glass out of his hand and crossing and putting it table L.*). Don't imagine you can pop in and out of here whenever you please!

PETER (*lighting cigarette*). Why not?

PHYLLIS. Aunt Mary isn't a very sociably inclined lady.

PETER. She's damn nice.

PHYLLIS (*above table L.*). I know. We must see her more often, really. Most of the family don't, you know.

PETER. I'll see her without the family any time.

PHYLLIS. We've all neglected her shamefully.

PETER. Your dear mother.

PHYLLIS. Oh, no—it's not Mother. She couldn't keep me away. I don't know why—I'm so horribly busy.

PETER. Trotting me around to meet cousins and uncles.

PHYLLIS (*crosses to C.*). I hope she doesn't think this was that kind of a duty call. (*Crossing up C.*) Wonder what she's doing?

PETER. You hinted strongly enough that a wedding present would be acceptable.

PHYLLIS (*crossing down C.*). Now, Peter, that's not done.

PETER. Maybe she's gone to get us a present right now.

PHYLLIS. How many times must I tell you that I'm not showing you off to my relations just to get presents from them?

PETER. Then why visit the Howards tonight? Why not stay here awhile?

PHYLLIS. George Howard's not a relative. He's your best client. (*Crossing in front of sofa to R.*) Or will be now that he knows you're going to marry me.

PETER. I feel as if I were getting married for business reasons.

PHYLLIS. Marriage *is* a business.

PETER. Yeah!

PHYLLIS. Yes!

PETER. I suppose I'll go to the Howards' whether I want to or not. And all the other places. (*Rises and turns to* PHYLLIS.) "How do you do? Yes —I'm the lucky fellow! When! Oh, about the first of June. Yes! The first of June. What? Oh, I'm an American bond salesman. Do you want any nice bonds so I can get married?"

PHYLLIS. Oh! "I want you to meet Peter. I met him in New York, but he's over here now. (*Looks around.*) Oh, where has he gone? Peter, Peter, here, Peter! Oh, there you are! This is Aunt Evelyn. Oh, he's only joking, Aunt Evelyn. He's making believe he's shy. Say something to Aunt Evelyn, Peter."

PETER. "Hello, Aunt Evelyn."

PHYLLIS. There! (*Sits on sofa.*)

PETER. I wish your grandfather hadn't been so prolific.

(PETER *dresses up stage.* MARY *enters from stairs.*)

MARY (*coming C. between* PHYLLIS *and* PETER). I waited until the last second with this—because I just want to give it to you—and let that be the end of it. (*Hands* PHYLLIS *a small box.*) Don't open it now— your grandfather gave it to me— long time ago—to wear at *my* wed-

ding. (*Smiles brightly.*) It's very old
– but you'll love it.

(PETER *drifts L. looking at statue,
puts out cigarette on table L.*)

PHYLLIS. I know I shall, Aunt Mary.
But why so soon?

MARY. Oh—I don't know—I never
know where I'm liable to be when
people get married.

(PHYLLIS *and* MARY *are in front of
sofa.*)

PHYLLIS. Oh—— (*Very sweetly.*)
Thank you, Aunt Mary. I hope you
don't think we came here tonight
just to——

MARY. No, no. Even if it were I
wouldn't mind. And I know the
next time it will be because you
want to come.

PETER. Miss Herries, may I ask who
did that?

MARY (*crossing C.*). Which?

PETER. This one—the statue.

MARY. Troubetzkoi—Mr. Santard.

PETER. Troubetzkoi, eh? What's it
supposed to be?

MARY (*crossing to below table L.*).
I really don't know who she is. I
think it's listed in the catalogue as
"Figure" or something equally en-
lightening.

PETER (*crosses to* PHYLLIS *R.C.*).
I think it's grand. Phyllis, we must
get one of this fellow's things sometime.

PHYLLIS. Yes, yes—all right, darling.
That's the fourth time tonight you've
said that.

PETER. Is it? I must like it.

MARY (*crossing to chair L.C.*). Do
you like it very much, Mr. Santard?

PETER (*with mock sadness*). Please
call me "Peter."

MARY. All right, Peter. I'll tell you
what I'll do. I'll give it to you for
a wedding present.

PETER. What—really?

PHYLLIS (*crossing to her*). Oh, no,
Aunt Mary. I won't dream of it.
You simply mustn't!

MARY (*sits L.C.*). No—no. It's all
settled.

PHYLLIS. But you must be awfully
fond of it yourself.

MARY. I am. But I want you to have
it—if you like it too, Phyllis.

PHYLLIS. Oh—I like it. (*Gives a
look of disgust to* PETER.)

MARY. It's the best present I can
think of for me to give you.

PHYLLIS. Honestly, Aunt Mary—
after one drink of cold water, Peter
wouldn't know if Troubetzkoi or
Madame Tussaud did it. (*Crosses
L. above table.*)

PETER. What's the difference? And
anyway I know very well who did
it—Troubetzkoi. (*Snaps fingers and
returns to contemplating it.*)

MARY. Then that's that. (*She imitates his finger snap.*)

PETER. Have you any more Troubetzkois in the house?

(PHYLLIS *has crossed to in front of fireplace.*)

MARY. Oh, yes. Didn't you notice the one in the dining room?

PETER. Whereabouts?

MARY. On the sideboard.

PETER (*picking up brandy glass from table L.*). I'll have another look at it.

MARY. Do.

PETER (*as he passes into dining room, he salutes* PHYLLIS *with the glass*). Troubetzkoi!!

PHYLLIS (*silent for a moment, then very formal*). Look, Aunt Mary. We really *must* go. The Howards will be terribly offended and we can't afford that.

MARY. No, indeed!

PHYLLIS. I didn't mean it that way. Really, Aunt Mary——

MARY. That's all right.

PHYLLIS. *I* want to be friends with you—even if Mother insists on being an idiot!

MARY (*with a laugh*). The Howards are expecting you!

PHYLLIS (*looks for a moment at* MARY. *Shakes her head and goes to door up L.*). Peter!

PETER (*off in dining room*). Huh!

PHYLLIS. Say good-by to Aunt Mary.

PETER (*off*). Good-by, Aunt Mary.

(MARY *laughs.*)

PHYLLIS (*up L.*). Peter!

PETER (*enters from door upper L. to in front of fireplace*). Yes?

PHYLLIS. We're leaving!

PETER. Oh! Sorry! (*To* MARY, *crossing to down L. close to table.*) What did you say the name of that fellow was?

MARY. Troubetzkoi.

PETER. Oh, yes.

PHYLLIS (*crosses to above chair L. Quietly, shaking her head*). Oh, you *are* a fool!

PETER. What's the matter?

PHYLLIS (*pointing at* MARY). Here's someone with banks full of lovely money—and nothing to do with it except buy statues—and you go and get us a statue for a wedding present!

(*Doorbell rings.*)

PETER (*to* MARY). Don't you think she's a little commercial?

MARY (*rises*). No, Peter. Just frank. All our family is addicted to frankness.

PETER. Thanks for the tip. You must tell me all about the family.

PHYLLIS. Come on, Peter.

(ROSE *crosses on platform to door off R.*)

MARY. Come and see me in a few months and pick up the Troubetzkoi.

PETER. May I come sooner than that and look at it—and look at you?

MARY. Do that! And ·I'll see if I need any bonds.

PETER. Did she tell you you had to buy bonds, too?

PHYLLIS. Why not? She's always buying them from *somebody*.

PETER. My God!

(MARY *laughs.* ROSE *enters from R. on platform.*)

ROSE. Madam!

MARY (*crosses up C.*). What is it, Rose?

ROSE. It's——!

HENRY (*enters from R.*). I beg your pardon. I'll wait outside. (*He goes off R.*)

MARY (PETER *and* PHYLLIS *look at each other, a little embarrassed*). That's a young man whom I—never mind—you're in a hurry. It's all right, Rose. Get Miss Glenning's and Mr. Santard's things. (ROSE *exits R.* PHYLLIS *looks at* PETER *with a "What do you know."*) And now —run along, you two. Keep your "appointments." I hope I haven't made you too late.

PETER (*crossing up L. to join* PHYLLIS). Of course not. Please forget about it.

MARY (*as she reaches entrance to hall, speaks to* HENRY). Will you come in here?

HENRY (*as he passes*). I'm very sorry.

MARY. Please sit down.

(HENRY *crosses R. then down R.— then R.C. below sofa.* MARY *goes off R.* HENRY *sits.*)

PHYLLIS (*handing* PETER *box*). Put the box in your pocket, darling, and be very careful.

(PHYLLIS *and* PETER *exit R., glancing back at* HENRY.)

MARY (*off*). That's a lovely wrap, Phyllis.

PETER (*off*). I'll remember that hopping in and out business!

(ROSE *crosses past arch to L.*)

MARY (*off. Laughs*). Please do!

PHYLLIS (*off*). Good night, Aunt Mary. I'll ring you up. Honestly!

PETER (*off*). Good night—and permit an old man to bless you.

MARY (*off—laughing*). Good night. (*Door slams.* MARY *enters—crosses to down C.*)

HENRY (*rises, takes cigarette case from his pocket and holds it out*). I pawned it.

MARY (*takes it*). What a disgraceful thing to do. And what are you going to steal next?

HENRY. My wife made some money last week. That will see us through for a while.

MARY. Don't you ever do any work?

HENRY. I paint—but no one will touch my pictures. They're not modern enough.

MARY. You must show me some of your pictures sometime.

HENRY. I have some here. They're in the hall. (*Goes toward arch.*) You probably didn't notice. (*He goes out R. and returns immediately from the hall with two canvases, face to face—crosses to desk.*)

(MARY *puts cigarette case on table L.*)

MARY (*crosses up C. as* HENRY *re-enters*). Let's see what you have. (HENRY *places one picture on desk. He holds up another picture showing a cowherd playing his pipes to a group of cows. There is a pause while she looks at them.*) Oh, those are very bad.

HENRY (*crossing up R.C.*). I know they are. You must understand that my esthetic taste is very fine. I appreciate only the best things—like your cigarette case. But I can paint nothing but these. It's very exasperating.

MARY. It must be.

HENRY (*crosses to her a bit*). Won't you buy one?

(HENRY *is C.*—MARY *is L.C. by chair.*)

MARY. You don't mean it?

HENRY. Why not?

MARY. But what should I do with it? I'd have to hide it!

HENRY. Not necessarily. Bad as they are, they have something, I think. (*Puts cow picture on floor against sofa.*)

MARY. I don't see it—whatever it is. (*Crosses below chair L.C.*) I really don't want one.

HENRY (*two paces toward* MARY). Please buy one, anyway.

MARY (*retreating a pace*). No—but of course not.

HENRY (*comes closer to her*). Yes, please. (*She looks at him, disturbed by his peculiar insistence. At any rate there is something of the rabbit and the snake in this passing tableau.*) My wife is waiting in the street just opposite—waiting for me to call her.

MARY (*recovering herself*). What on earth for?

HENRY. She wanted to thank you. And I wanted her to see some of your lovely things.

MARY. How can you let her wait out in that deathly cold?

HENRY. I didn't like to bring her without your permission. And I don't like her to see me begging.

MARY. Well, you go straight out and take her home.

HENRY (*not moving*). Can't I possibly persuade you—— (*Then crosses up stage a bit.*) This one with the cows isn't so bad.

MARY (*shaking her head as she looks at it*). It's peculiar enough. What is it supposed to be?

HENRY. It's a Swiss scene. In Switzerland the cowherd pipes his cows from the pasture! He plays a traditional melody. "Ranz des Vaches" they call it. I read about it and I thought it was a rather nice macabre idea.

MARY. You've achieved a sinister quality in it, at any rate. How much is it?

HENRY. Five guineas. The other one is seven.

MARY (*laughing*). You're really amusing. And quite absurd. They're not worth anything at all.

HENRY. They may be one day. You never know with modern pictures.

MARY. I'm quite sure about those.

HENRY (*crosses to picture of cow, takes it to* MARY, *C.*). But I must sell one tonight—whatever you think of them. (*Holds out cow picture.*) Please buy it. (*But he is not pleading.*)

MARY (*after a pause*). I'm a perfect fool. (*She is crossing toward desk.* HENRY *puts picture behind L.C. chair, then crosses to desk for check.*) What's your name? (*Writing check at desk.*)

HENRY. Henry—Abbott. The baby's Henry, too.

MARY (*rises, hands him check*). Here—and please understand that I never want to see you again. Never. You will not be admitted. It's no use speaking to me in the street. If you bother me, I shall tell the police.

HENRY (*in spite of this he has not let go of her hand which he took when he reached for the check. He does so now, folding the check and putting it in pocket*). Hang that in the right light and it won't be bad. (*He crosses down a step.*)

MARY. You didn't get those shoes. Those are terrible.

HENRY. I'll be able to now.

MARY. The first thing you do is rescue that poor girl. You're a thorough brute, young man.

HENRY. She's used to it.

MARY. More shame to you!

HENRY. You can see her from here. (*He crosses to up-stage window.*) There she is.

MARY (*goes to down-stage window*). With the baby! Oh!! (*Gasps.*)

HENRY. Ada!!! My God!! (*He runs out R.*)

MARY (*running to arch*). Rose! Rose!

ROSE (*running from L. arch*). Yes, madam!

MARY. Run out and help him—the baby!!! (*As* ROSE *half turns to L.*) Never mind! Take my coat! Run! (*Almost pushing her.* ROSE *runs out R.* MARY *goes to window, thrusts shade aside. Watches.*) Oh. (*Suddenly goes quickly out to hall again. After a second* HENRY *enters, carrying* ADA. MARY *follows to arch.*) On the sofa!

(ROSE *enters with baby, crosses to below L.C. chair.* MARY *follows to*

L.C. HENRY *carries* ADA *to sofa and places her on it. Her head is stage R.* HENRY *is below sofa.* HENRY *has taken* ADA's *head in his hands, shaking it, drops it, grabs her hands, almost immediately lets go, pours drink of brandy from decanter on coffee table, puts it to her lips; it dribbles back.*)

HENRY. Ada! Ada! (*Again tries unsuccessfully to give her whisky. To* MARY.) What shall we do?

MARY (*quietly holding her heart—crosses to* ROSE). Isn't there any doctor near here—somewhere, Rose?

ROSE. Yes, madam. In the block of flats at the top of the street.

MARY. Get him! Get someone—the nurse—if there's no one there, call an ambulance.

ROSE. Yes, madam. (*Gives baby to* MARY. *Starts to go.*)

HENRY (*rises and meets* ROSE *at C. Holding* ROSE *with one hand*). I'll go. (*Rushes out R.*)

ROSE (*looks after* HENRY—*steps toward* ADA—*turns to* MARY). Miss Herries——

MARY (*almost simultaneously*). Get that bottle of smelling salts. . . .

ROSE. Yes, madam.

(ROSE *runs out upstairs.* MARY *tries to rub* ADA *and hold baby. She looks helplessly from* ADA *to the baby, puts baby in chair L.C., returns to* ADA, *crosses to window—then to baby R. of chair C. Takes baby.* ROSE *rushes in with smelling salts which she*

puts in front of ADA's *nose.* ADA *stiffens but does not come to.*)

MARY. It's all my fault—all my fault for letting him——

ROSE. What's the matter with her, madam? (*Crosses to* MARY.)

MARY. Go on, go on!

(ROSE *administers smelling salts, rubs* ADA *in a very inexperienced manner.* HENRY *and* DOCTOR *enter.*)

HENRY. Here! (*He does not take baby from* MARY, *but crosses to above sofa.* DOCTOR *crosses below sofa and looks at* ADA.) Ada! Ada!

ROSE. I'll take it, madam.

(*Crosses to* MARY. MARY *crosses up L.C.* MARY *gives baby to* ROSE. ROSE *goes above table L.*)

DOCTOR (*to* HENRY). Exposure. (*Picks up* ADA. *Crosses R.C.*) You'd better put her to bed at once.

MARY. Bed? She——

HENRY. You see, Doctor——

DOCTOR (*to* ROSE). Where's a bedroom?

MARY (*looks at* ROSE). Why——

DOCTOR. Upstairs? (*This to* ROSE *with the baby. He carries* ADA *out; as he goes.*) Don't worry. Nothing serious. Needs rest and nourishment. (*To* ROSE.) Some hot soup. Chicken broth.

(DOCTOR *exits upstairs, followed by* ROSE. MARY *goes up onto platform and turns back to* HENRY, *who is walking unconcernedly down R., lighting a cigarette.* MARY, *greatly agitated, hurries upstairs.* HENRY *calmly walks C., looking at room. Sees his painting of the cows. Picks it up. Looks about the room. Selects the mantel. Puts his picture there. Stands back, looking at it. Sits L.C. chair, admiring his picture. He is totally unconcerned about what has just happened.*)

CURTAIN

ACT TWO

Two weeks later—January.
The scene is the same. However, the desk is now behind the sofa at R. C. The coffee table is to the R. of the sofa. A side chair is behind the desk and another is between the windows.

HENRY *is at the desk. The doorbell rings—*HENRY *looks up from a paper he has been writing on—then resumes.* ROSE *comes from L. and crosses the room. She is dressed in street clothes. She walks, looks straight ahead, her hands folded before her.*

HENRY (*speaking just as she reaches C.—not looking up*). Rose. (ROSE *stops C., facing him but not looking at him. He looks up now.*) You're all dressed up, Rose. Why?

ROSE. I think you *know* why, Mr. Abbott.

HENRY. Leaving us?

ROSE. I think you know I *am*, Mr. Abbott.

(*She stands there as if anxious to continue the conversation—to get something off her chest. But after a moment, he looks down at his paper.*)

HENRY. Answer the bell.

(*She hesitates for a moment, then pressing her lips, walks off R.*)

MR. EDWARDS (*off stage*). Mr. Henry Abbott here?

ROSE (*she comes into room, and, not looking at* HENRY, *starts to cross L. toward dining room*). People outside.

HENRY. Who are they?

ROSE (*not stopping*). I don't know.

HENRY (*gently, as if admonishing a child*). Rose! Ask them to come in.

(*She stops, hesitates as though she were inwardly undergoing a struggle. Then turns and goes to L. arch.*)

ROSE (*standing in arch, C.*). Come in. (ROSE *exits off L. on platform.*)

(MR. EDWARDS *appears, followed by "his wife and daughter," AGGIE."* MR.

(EDWARDS *is a thick-set, reddish, and bulbous-faced man with a hearty hoarse voice.* MRS. EDWARDS *is short, black-clad, and eminently respectable-looking.* AGGIE *is a thin, sharp-faced girl whose eyes and hands are rarely still.* MR. EDWARDS *is carrying a portable gramophone.*)

MR. EDWARDS (*crosses to upper L.C.*). Hello, Henry.

(HENRY *gets up.*)

MRS. EDWARDS (*up C.*). How's Ada, Henry?

HENRY. Much better.

AGGIE (*up R.C.*). Hello, Henry.

(HENRY *nods.*)

MRS. EDWARDS. We brought Aggie with us.

MR. EDWARDS. We thought we'd better——

MRS. EDWARDS. How's the baby, Henry?

MR. EDWARDS. Doing well, Henry?

HENRY (*nods*). Ada will be glad to see you all.

MRS. EDWARDS. And we'll be awfully glad to see her—poor Ada.

MR. EDWARDS. I brought the gramophone. Thought she might like to hear some music.

MRS. EDWARDS. Layin' up in bed, you know.

HENRY. Sit down, and I'll call Miss Herries.

MRS. EDWARDS. Oh, Henry—the way I look.

(*Crosses and sits L.C. chair.*)

HENRY. I shall have to ask permission to bring you upstairs.

MR. EDWARDS. Sure, Henry—that's only right!

HENRY. Sit down. (*He goes upstairs.*)

MR. EDWARDS (*crosses down C.— looking over the room.* AGGIE *goes L. and picks up bronze on table upper L.*). Very nice layout. (*Crosses to down R., puts gramophone on coffee table and hat on L. end of desk.*)

MRS. EDWARDS. I should say it is. My—isn't it pretty!

MR. EDWARDS (*puts gramophone on coffee table*). Looks like a house I stayed in once—in Melbourne in Australia.

MRS. EDWARDS. Put that down, Aggie!

MR. EDWARDS (*crossing to upper C.*). Same layout. I'd be able to tell better if I saw the whole house. (*To* AGGIE, *who is touching things on mantel.*) Aggie! I wish you would talk to her, Mother. Nice thing if somebody saw her. (*Crosses down R. and sits in sofa.*)

MRS. EDWARDS. Father's right, Aggie. You ought to learn to behave yourself in a decent place.

(AGGIE *walks to arch up C. They watch her; she looks out and returns to rooms crossing to desk.*)

MR. EDWARDS (*after another moment*). You notice how nobody has pianos any more?

MRS. EDWARDS (*nodding*). If you lived in a house with a court you'd hear the children practicing, all day long.

MR. EDWARDS. It's the wireless that's spoiled it for pianos.

MRS. EDWARDS (*not looking at her*). Sit down, Aggie. Didn't you hear Henry say to sit down?

(AGGIE *crosses to R. end of sofa to fool with gramophone on coffee table.*)

MR. EDWARDS. Yep—now it's the wireless. But anything that's pushed out of a wire—sounds like it.

(AGGIE *is opening gramophone.*)

MRS. EDWARDS. Ts, ts. Oh, leave it be!

MR. EDWARDS (*has risen with surprising swiftness to* AGGIE *and stands over her*). Don't you realize there's somebody sick around here?

(AGGIE *looks frightened, stops playing with gramophone, and examines other objects on coffee table. After a moment* MR. EDWARDS *starts to arch C.*)

MRS. EDWARDS. I'll warrant we'll have to take you off your job, Aggie, and put you back in school, to learn some manners.

MR. EDWARDS (*looking upstairs in arch*). That staircase—just like this house in Melbourne—in Australia. A very good sign.

MRS. EDWARDS. I never *knew* you were in Australia, Father.

MR. EDWARDS. Sure—I must have told you. Been everywhere. (*Crosses down C. to* MRS. EDWARDS.)

MRS. EDWARDS (*shaking her head, puzzled*). Perhaps you did.

MR. EDWARDS (*crosses down C. level with* MRS. EDWARDS). Didn't I ever mention about staying in this house that used to belong to Lord—Greville? Something like that.

MRS. EDWARDS (*thinking*). I don't remember the name.

MR. EDWARDS. Fine feller—black sheep. (AGGIE *crosses up R.*) Came to Australia and made a pile of money.

MRS. EDWARDS. Never got married!

MR. EDWARDS. No—real black sheep. Lived all alone. Got peculiar in his old age with all that money. Used to keep it around the house, they said.

MRS. EDWARDS. Must have been a tough customer.

MR. EDWARDS (*nodding, lips pursed*). That's what they said.

MRS. EDWARDS. All that money around the house—ts, ts.

MR. EDWARDS. In gold—gold bars. (AGGIE *crosses to C., looks through arch.*) Some of 'em as long as your arm.

MRS. EDWARDS. Ts, ts. I suppose they found it all after he died?

MR. EDWARDS. No. I can't say they did. No. (*Laughs.*) Stop worryin' about it, Mother! (*Crosses to down R. below sofa.*)

MRS. EDWARDS. Well, it's interesting! My goodness!

MR. EDWARDS. I hope Ada ain't too sick to see us.

(AGGIE *crosses to painting up L.*)

MRS. EDWARDS. Henry said she was all right—she was much better, he said.

MR. EDWARDS. Yep—but you know Ada ain't a strong girl. If she's been layin' in bed for two weeks—there's something wrong with her.

MRS. EDWARDS. Very nice of this lady, isn't it, Father?

MR. EDWARDS. I should say. She sounds like a real fine woman.

MRS. EDWARDS (AGGIE *has wandered L. and is touching the things on table L.*). Keep your hands off, Aggie!

(HENRY *comes downstairs.*)

HENRY (*stops C., speaking from landing*). Miss Herries begs to be excused. She hopes to meet you all some other time.

MRS. EDWARDS (*rises*). I hope she ain't sick, Henry?

HENRY. No. (*Gestures them to go up.*)

MR. EDWARDS. Should I bring up the gramophone, Henry?

HENRY. I don't think so—no. (*Holding place R. of C. on platform.*)

MR. EDWARDS (*setting it at back of sofa*). I'll just set it here out of the way then.

MRS. EDWARDS (*crosses between L.C. chair and table toward stairs. AGGIE drifts behind her*). Oh—this is certainly a *beautiful* house, Henry!

MR. EDWARDS (*crosses below sofa—propelling AGGIE*). Go on, Aggie.

(*Doorbell rings when* MRS. EDWARDS *is at foot of stairs,* AGGIE *behind her on bay-window landing,* MR. EDWARDS *on hall platform,* HENRY R. *on hall platform. Bell rings second time. For some reason the four of them stop dead still. There is a pause.*)

HENRY (*indicates*). Two flights up—the little room at the head of the stairs.

(*Slowly they move up again.*)

MR. EDWARDS (*the last*). Lots of visitors today, Henry.

(*He is off.* HENRY *waits on the landing.* ROSE *enters and crosses. He watches her. She goes off R. A moment later.*)

LUCY (*off stage*). Hello, Rose. Is Miss Herries in?

ROSE (*off stage*). Yes, madam.

(LUCY *enters room, followed by* ROSE. *She stops on seeing* HENRY.)

HENRY. How do you do? (LUCY *nods in surprise.* LUCY *meets* HENRY *in arch.*) I'll tell Miss Herries, Rose. (*To* LUCY.) Excuse me. (*He goes upstairs.*)

LUCY (*crossing into room. Stopping* ROSE *as she starts off behind arch*). Rose! Isn't that the young man Miss Herries brought in here one night?

ROSE. Yes, madam—it is.

LUCY (*as if she knew something now*). Oh.

(ROSE *goes off L. on platform.* LUCY *crosses to desk to remove her gloves.*)

MARY (*coming down*). Lucy!

LUCY (*meets* MARY *C. below platform*). Mary, dear.

MARY. Not even a picture postcard! (*Kisses her.*)

LUCY. Didn't you get my letter?

MARY. No.

LUCY (*disturbed*). Oh, that's too bad!

MARY. Forget about it. Have a good time?

LUCY. That letter worries me.

MARY (*laughs*). Really? You probably addressed it wrong. (*Crosses to R. end of sofa and sits.*)

LUCY. No. Oh, well. (*Crosses to desk above couch, takes off gloves.*) How are you, Mary?

MARY. Oh, fairly well. *You* look splendid.

LUCY. Thanks. I feel as though I'd never get warm again!

MARY. Just an excuse to get back to the Riviera, isn't it?

LUCY. I'm leaving this afternoon. I'm flying to Paris. (*Crosses to L. end sofa—a bit away.*)

MARY. Oh, I'm sorry!

LUCY. That's what I wrote. I didn't think I'd have a chance to see you. Then I decided to come around for a minute anyway.

MARY. I'm glad you did!

LUCY. I just couldn't write you as I did and let it go at that. And when you didn't answer—I knew something was wrong.

MARY. What are you talking about?

LUCY. I'll tell you simply and to the point—if you'll tell me what's been going on here.

MARY. Going on? (*After a moment she sits back.*) Please say what you have to say, Lucy, before I go completely out of my mind.

LUCY. All right. Some days after we got to St. Moritz, a lady joined us. She had just arrived—and she had it on *excellent authority*—steady on— that you had taken a man to live with you——

MARY (*after a moment, as though this were the last straw, murmurs*). What?

LUCY. I laughed her down of course —told her she was a silly woman; I insulted her frightfully. (*Slowly.*) It didn't do much good.

MARY. But who would say a thing like that?

LUCY. She from whom all such blessings flow—your sister Emily.

MARY. Emily! It's incredible! How would she know?

LUCY. She didn't say.

MARY (*very puzzled—thinking*). Emily.

LUCY. Women like that make mountains out of blades of grass—you know that.

MARY. Oh! Ho!

LUCY. You've traced it!

MARY. No. My niece Phyllis—and her fiancé—were here one night. They saw him—but why would they—— Oh, no!

LUCY. Saw who?

MARY. Lucy—it's true.

LUCY. What?

MARY. I have taken a man in to live with me—and his wife and child.

LUCY. That one—you brought in here on Christmas Eve?

MARY. Hmmm. He came back with his wife. She fainted and I put her up for the night. She's been here ever since.

LUCY (*crosses to sofa and sits. After a pause*). Oh, Mary, Mary. My poor Mary!

MARY. That's only part of it. My cook left me last week—and Rose gave me notice. I've been on my knees to her in the kitchen. She insists on going.

LUCY. Who are those people?

MARY. I don't know. It's become nightmarish. What will I do without Rose? I'll never replace her.

LUCY (*dismissing this*). Rose! Throw those people out! How ill is she?

MARY. I don't know—I can't tell. I know *I've* been feeling badly the past few days. My heart has been raising red hell.

LUCY. Oh, Mary! (*Pause, then decisively.*) It's insane! You're being used in the most ridiculous and criminal manner.

MARY. Well, goodness knows, I begged for it!

LUCY. I know you! Throw them out! You've simply *got* to!

MARY. I suddenly feel very old and helpless. (*Doorbell.*)

LUCY (*quietly*). You fool, Mary—I haven't the heart to scream at you.

MARY. Now they've got friends upstairs—visiting. I don't know why that should bother me. But it does—intensely.

LUCY. Will you please get rid of them—and take a plane tomorrow with me? I'll wait on.

MARY. A plane?

LUCY. A train then.

(ROSE *crosses to door from L. to R. on platform.*)

MARY. I never felt more like it. I really want to.

LUCY. Fine!

MARY. Not tomorrow of course. I've got to clean up this mess. And if I go I'll close the house.

LUCY. Next week then——

MARY. Perhaps, in a week or so.

DOCTOR (*off stage*). Good afternoon.

ROSE (*off stage*). Good afternoon.

MARY. Now who? (*Rises, crosses to archway.*)

LUCY. You certainly have a busy house.

ROSE (*entering*). It's the doctor, madam.

MARY (*R. of archway*). Oh! Go straight up, Doctor.

(ROSE *starts to lead way, getting to C. of landing.*)

DOCTOR (*to* MARY). Thank you. (*To* ROSE.) That's quite all right. I know the way.

(DOCTOR *goes upstairs.* ROSE *goes off L. past arch on platform.*)

LUCY. I should go—but I'm not going to—(MARY *crosses down C.*)—until you promise to close this house and get out of here.

MARY. All right, I promise.

LUCY. Good. (*She rises and crosses C.*) I must rush. (*Crosses to desk and gets gloves.*) I expressed everything through the St. Moritz. But there's a coat I want—and some shoes.

MARY. Go on, then. (*Smiles wanly. Speaks simply.*) And thank you.

LUCY. Now remember—you've *promised!*

MARY. All right!

LUCY. Well—good-by—and God bless you. (*Starts off.*) Get rid of those strange leeches.

MARY. I will. (*As they go through the arch.*) Give my love to Phil and the children.

LUCY. Thank you, dear. (*From now on, off stage.*) When will I hear from you?

(ROSE *enters at R. and stands R.C.*)

MARY. I'll write.

LUCY. The minute you've decided— I wish you could come and tell me what you think of this coat. I'm spending far too much. Good-by.

MARY. Have a nice trip, Lucy. (*Door slams.*)

ROSE (*as* MARY *comes in*). Miss Herries——

MARY (*at C.—surprised as she looks at* ROSE'S *clothes*). Going already, Rose?

ROSE. Yes, madam. I was just waiting to say good-by.

MARY (*after a moment—as if tired of the whole thing. Crosses to desk*). Well—I suppose if you've made up your mind to leave, you'd better.

ROSE. Yes, madam. I'm sorry. I'd like to come back in a while.

MARY. Let me have your address?

ROSE (*crossing down C.*). It's on the bill hook—in the pantry.

MARY (*sees* EDWARDS' *hat on desk and distastefully puts it on chair between windows*). All right.

ROSE (*crosses down R.C.*). Good-by, Miss Herries.

MARY. Rose, I wish I really knew why you were leaving. Is it the work, Rose?

ROSE. I told you, madam.

MARY. What's the matter?

ROSE. Nothing, madam, I told you— I want to visit my sister in New-castle.

MARY. I don't believe that. You've never *mentioned* a sister all the time you've been with me. (*Crosses in front of sofa toward* ROSE.) Now look here, Rose, I didn't intend to plead with you to stay on. But I've decided to close the house. If you'll wait a week you can go where you like and I'll be glad to take you back in about three months.

ROSE (*with trace of eagerness*). You're closing the house, Miss Herries?

MARY. This week.

ROSE. But excuse me, madam—— What's happening to them?

MARY. The Abbotts? They're leaving, of course.

ROSE. They are?

MARY. Oh. So it *is* the Abbotts. Why didn't you say so?

ROSE. Miss Herries——! (ROSE *cannot speak.*)

MARY (*crosses to* ROSE). What is it? What are you crying for?

ROSE. Miss Herries—I don't want to go!

MARY. Then why?

ROSE. It isn't the work, madam, I don't mind that.

MARY (*close to* ROSE). What's wrong then? You must tell me!

ROSE. Are you sure they're leaving, madam?

MARY. Quite sure.

ROSE. Him, too?

MARY. Yes! What *is* it, Rose? (*Taking* ROSE'S *arm.* ROSE *pauses uncertainly.*) Has Mr. Abbott said anything to you?

ROSE. No, madam. (*Bursts out.*) It ain't what he says! I can't explain what I mean, Miss Herries! There's something about him! I'm afraid.

MARY. Afraid of what——?

ROSE. I don't know. I'm afraid to stay here.

MARY. What is it, Rose? Try to tell me.

ROSE. That Mrs. Abbott——

MARY. Yes.

ROSE. She's not ill, madam. She lays up there in that bed—lookin' like she's dyin'. But she ain't ill—and never was!

MARY. Never was?

ROSE. No, madam! There's some people always look that way—an' she's one of 'em. But I know she's not ill!

MARY. *How* do you know?

ROSE. I just do, madam. She's been putting it on all the time!

MARY. Putting it on?

ROSE. Yes. And the baby! Did **you** notice something funny about it?

MARY. No.

ROSE. Did you ever hear it cry?

MARY (*after quite a pause, as if she just realized*). No.

ROSE. Neither did I! Never! I never heard it make a sound. I think it *can't*, Miss Herries. It wants to—but it can't.

MARY (*a quick involuntary phrase*). Oh, no.

ROSE. Yes, madam—that's what I think. And something else—it don't look like her. It looks foreign—like an Italian baby. But it's not hers.

MARY. How can you tell—it's just an infant?

ROSE. No, it's not. Not as young as he said! Oh, I don't know, Miss Herries! I'm just scared to death! (*She cries again. There is a pause.*)

MARY. Rose, please stop crying.

ROSE. I'm sorry, madam.

MARY. I want you to pack up whatever belongs to the baby—at once.

ROSE. Yes, madam.

MARY. Then take a directory and see if you can find some private hospital which has an ambulance we can hire to call for Mrs. Abbott.

ROSE (*turns and crosses up C.*). Yes, madam?

MARY. Wait a minute. (ROSE *turns.* MARY *crosses to her.*) Tell them we don't want anyone taken to the hospital. We just want to hire the ambulance and an attendant for about an hour.

ROSE. I will, Miss Herries.

MARY. Tell them we'll ring up again —and let them know—will you, Rose?

ROSE. Yes, madam.

MARY (*ushers* ROSE *up C. onto platform*). Straight away. Now go on and don't be afraid of anything.

ROSE (*turning to* MARY). I don't want to be foolish, madam. As long as they're goin'——

MARY. It's all right. I'm sorry you didn't tell me all this before.

ROSE. I didn't want to interfere, Miss Herries. I thought perhaps you had some special reason.

MARY. I've just been very stupid, Rose. Now please go and do as I asked.

ROSE. Yes, madam.

(*Turns and goes off L. MARY watches her off—then suddenly goes to stairs, reaches landing, and is about to go up when she pauses as the sound of voices reaches her. She hesitates for a moment then returns to room, standing by fireplace. Lights dim from here to end of Act Two.*)

MRS. EDWARDS (*off*). Good-by. Aggie, say good-by to Ada.

AGGIE (*off*). Good-by, Ada.

MR. EDWARDS (*off*). That's a good girl.

MRS. EDWARDS (*off*). Mind your manners and you'll keep your friends. Ha! Ha!

MR. EDWARDS (*off*). Good-by, Ada. (*Door slams off L. Pause.*)

MRS. EDWARDS (*off stage*). We shouldn't have come, Father.

MR. EDWARDS (*off stage*). She's a pretty sick girl.

MRS. EDWARDS (*off stage*). Ts, ts. I hope we haven't done any harm.

MR. EDWARDS (*off*). Country air— that's what she needs.

MRS. EDWARDS (*off*). Leave that alone, Aggie!

MR. EDWARDS (*off*). There ain't an ounce of flesh on her. (*As he finishes he comes into view, crosses to upper L.C.*)

MRS. EDWARDS. You'd hardly know what was whiter—her or the sheets. I——

(*She, too, has come into view and stops up C., seeing MARY. Behind MRS. EDWARDS is AGGIE; from dining room comes HENRY, crossing to above L. table.*)

HENRY. Miss Herries, these are Ada's friends; Mr. and Mrs. Edwards and their daughter, Aggie.

(MARY *nods.*)

MR. EDWARDS. How do you do, ma'am?

MRS. EDWARDS. We've just been up to *see* Ada. My—she's a sight, isn't she?

HENRY (*crosses to C. to MRS. EDWARDS*). I'm afraid the excitement was too much.

(AGGIE *drifts to above desk.*)

MRS. EDWARDS. I hope we haven't done any harm.

MR. EDWARDS (*crosses to above table L.*). She's just all in! Not an ounce of flesh on her, ma'am.

HENRY (*paces down L.C.*). It occurred to me upstairs. We're looking for a cook. If I may take the liberty of recommending Mrs. Edwards——

MRS. EDWARDS. Now, Henry.

HENRY. I know she's worked in the very best homes.

MRS. EDWARDS (*crosses down R.C.*). As a cook only, ma'am.

HENRY. And with Aggie to help—if Rose insists on going—I thought we could struggle along for a while.

MARY. Thank you. I won't need anyone. I'm closing the house.

HENRY (*paces toward* MARY, *below L.C. chair*). Really, Miss Herries?

MARY (*below L. chair*). I'm not well, either. I need a rest.

HENRY. That's too bad.

MARY. I'm glad your friends are here. They can help move Ada. I'm hiring a private ambulance.

HENRY. You mean move her today?

MARY. Oh, yes!

HENRY. Where shall I take her?

MARY. Take her home!

HENRY. I would—willingly—but we have no home. (MARY *starts to speak.*) We were so far behind on the rent—we were dispossessed a week ago, I thought I told you.

MARY. I'm afraid your troubles can't concern me any longer. Take Ada any place you please.

MRS. EDWARDS. That's a pretty hard way to talk, Miss Herries.

MARY. You must understand, I don't want to seem brutal—but I think Mrs. Abbott is well enough to go now—and I wish you all good day.

MRS. EDWARDS. I'm sure you've been kindness itself, Miss Herries. Ada knows that, I'm sure. But to move her now would be to kill her, that's all. Any movement and she'll drop at your feet.

HENRY. Besides, we have no place to go—as I've told you.

MARY (*controlling herself*). But this lady——

MRS. EDWARDS. Oh, Lord, Miss Herries—we only have two rooms——

MR. EDWARDS. That's a good idea, ma'am! There ain't space now to swing a cat in!

AGGIE (*goes R. above desk*). Popper coughs all night, anyway.

MRS. EDWARDS. Keep still, Aggie.

MR. EDWARDS. And then there's the kid, mind you!

MARY (*to* HENRY). I don't care to discuss it! You will get Ada out of here today!

(HENRY *looks at her steadily.*)

MRS. EDWARDS. It might be life and death, you know. Do you think she ought——?

MARY. I told you I didn't care to discuss it! (MR. EDWARDS *crosses to fireplace.* MARY *crosses to* HENRY *on line. To* HENRY.) I believed your bad-luck stories—and I've done everything in my power to help you! I think it's pretty obvious that you've imposed on me in the crudest way!

HENRY. I'm sorry you think that.

MARY. You will please oblige me by getting out of here as quickly as possible.

HENRY. That's more easily said than done.

MARY. Why, you——! Leave at once, all of you!

(*They do not move.* MRS. EDWARDS *looks about her.*)

MRS. EDWARDS (*after pause. Crosses to desk*—AGGIE *drifts a pace R.*). Such a fine big house, ma'am. It's wonderful how clean it is with only one help.

MR. EDWARDS (*crosses to* MARY *one step*). Yep. I was telling Mother— that's my wife, Mrs. Edwards over here—how much it looks like a house I stayed in once in Melbourne, in Australia.

MARY (*to* HENRY). Will you please——!

MR. EDWARDS (HENRY *crosses up L. of arch.* EDWARDS *makes small movement toward* MARY). It's the staircase made me think of it—same layout. Used to be a private house. Turned into a lodging house later— when I stayed there.

MARY (*to* EDWARDS). Leave immediately, or I shall call the police!

MR. EDWARDS. Lady who ran it—she was a leftover from the old day. A real character, ma'am. I stayed on the top floor—(MARY *crosses up L.C. to ring bell.* MR. EDWARDS *follows to upper L.*)—that was the cheapest in those times.

(MARY *goes to the bell. Just before she reaches it,* HENRY *puts his hand out gently and covers it. They have somehow formed a semicircle about her.*)

MARY (*to* HENRY). How dare you!

(DOCTOR *comes downstairs and stands at upper C. below platform*

with the rest. MARY *sees him and reacts.*)

MRS. EDWARDS (*as* MARY *reacts to* DOCTOR'S *entrance*). Would you believe it, Miss Herries—he's never told me a 'word of this!

MR. EDWARDS. Well, the old lady used to start from the bottom floor in the morning. (MARY *turns to see* MR. EDWARDS *coming toward her.*) Knock, knock, knock—how do you like your ham and eggs this morning, sir? Thank you, sir. (MARY *starts backing down C.*) Second floor. Knock, knock, knock. How do you like your ham and eggs this morning, sir? (*As* MARY *has backed down C.,* HENRY, MRS. EDWARDS, *and* DOCTOR *have joined* MR. EDWARDS *in their slow walk forcing* MARY *down stage. They have her surrounded.* AGGIE *is down R.*) Thank you, sir. Third floor——

MARY (*with back to audience. To* HENRY, *who is upper C.*). This is monstrous. What do you want of me?

MR. EDWARDS (*down L.*). Well, ma'am, by the time she reached me —I was mighty glad to get myself a cup of tea! (*Laughs.*)

MRS. EDWARDS (*R.C.*). He was a one when I married him, Miss Herries!

MARY. What do you want?

HENRY (*comes to C.*). What about my pay for all these weeks?

MARY. Pay——?

HENRY. My pay.

MRS. EDWARDS. His pay.

MR. EDWARDS (*sings*):
"When the time comes to pay—
You must pay."

(MARY *staggers slightly. She looks around at them.*)

MARY (*starts to speak, but doesn't. She puts her hand to her heart— then looks around at the others. They are all watching her, quietly; starts to speak again—then bends over slightly as if in pain. Stands gasping*). Oh! (*Then groans and staggers to couch, moves toward desk with arm outstretched but suddenly sinks to couch—half lying.*) Oh, please! In the drawer—the green bottle——! (*Tries to point to the desk drawer.*) Oh, quickly, please! (*She is choking. Suddenly with a deep groan she collapses in the couch with head toward C. stage. They look at her.*)

MRS. EDWARDS. Ts, ts, ts—poor woman.

MR. EDWARDS. Luck——! The minute I laid eyes on that staircase I knew it!

(HENRY *snaps fingers to* DOCTOR, *who bends and touches her heart, who straightens and:*)

DOCTOR. Still going. (*Crosses to L. end desk.*)

HENRY. Take her upstairs. (*He gives* EDWARDS *the key.*)

MR. EDWARDS. Sure, Henry—you bet.

(*Bends to pick her up.* DOCTOR *helps.* AGGIE, *who has been standing*

over her, now kneels and claws at MARY'S *bracelet.*)

AGGIE. Gimme that!

MR. EDWARDS (*pushes her away*). Why don't you behave yourself?

MRS. EDWARDS. You're just like a little *animal*, Aggie!

MR. EDWARDS (*takes bracelet, looks at it, starts to pocket it*). It's a cheap one.

HENRY (*who has walked to C.*). Let me see. (*Looks and throws it to* AGGIE, *who is down R.*) There now, be quiet.

MR. EDWARDS (*pulls* MARY *to sitting position.* DOCTOR *takes her under arm,* EDWARDS *by feet*). Upsa-daisy!

MRS. EDWARDS. Don't hurt yourself, Father.

MR. EDWARDS (*as he goes up to landing carrying* MARY). Oh, you're not such a heavy old lady. Say good-by to everybody. (*As he goes up sings under his breath*):
"Where are the friends that—
that we used to know
Long long ago—long long ago?
Where are——"

HENRY (*crosses to bell L. of arch*). Sh, sh, sh, sh, sh.

(DOCTOR *and* MR. EDWARDS *go up carrying* MARY.)

MRS. EDWARDS (*crosses, sits sofa*). Came awful sudden, didn't it, Henry? Very unexpected. Saved a lot of trouble I should say.

HENRY (*rings bell. To* AGGIE, *who is examining necklace*). Put that away, please!

MRS. EDWARDS (*settling herself on the couch properly*). Sit down, Aggie.

(AGGIE *sits desk chair.* HENRY *takes bills from pocket and counts some off. Crosses to C. Holds bills in his hand.* ROSE *enters from up L. door, stops level with* HENRY *and looks around.*)

HENRY. Miss Herries asked me to give you this, Rose. Unless you changed your mind and stayed.

ROSE. Why—Miss Herries wanted me to stay on a week—she asked me to.

HENRY. I know—we thought of taking Mrs. Abbott home today—but that's impossible. (*Watches her face.*) I know you complained about us, Rose. Miss Herries told me; I convinced her that you were wrong. Well, which is it? Will you stay? If not—this lady is ready to take your place.

ROSE (*after a pause*). I'll go.

HENRY (*hands her money*). Here, then.

ROSE. I've *been* paid.

HENRY. I persuaded Miss Herries to give you this—in place of the extra week. (ROSE *takes the money.*) I'm not as bad as you think, Rose. But as long as you can't bear the sight of us—you'd *better* go. (ROSE *turns uncertainly and starts L.*). Did you order the ambulance?

ROSE (*stopping*). No.

HENRY. Whom did you call?

ROSE. St. Mary's Hospital——

HENRY. As long as you've spoken to them—would you call again before you leave and ask them not to come on—— Never mind, I'll call them myself. St. Mary's Hospital. Thank you, Rose.

(ROSE *does not leave immediately.*)

HENRY. Good-by.

(HENRY *watches* ROSE *off.* AGGIE *follows her to arch, stands looking after her.*)

MRS. EDWARDS. Very nicely done, Henry. Come away from there. Aggie!

(AGGIE *crosses to window.* DOCTOR *comes in from stairs. Stops up C.*)

HENRY (*taking money out—to* DOCTOR). The maid, Rose. (*To* MRS. EDWARDS.) Call St. Mary's Hospital, Paddington.

MRS. EDWARDS. Yes, Henry. (*Crosses to desk as she speaks next line to* DOCTOR.) The maid will be coming out of the basement.

HENRY (*gives · * DOCTOR *money*). Here.

DOCTOR. 'K you.

HENRY. Don't lose her.

(DOCTOR *goes off R.*)

MRS. EDWARDS (*looking in phone book*). Aggie, come away from that window.

HENRY. Sit down!

(AGGIE *sits · chair, scared.* HENRY *crosses to fireplace. Downstairs comes a strange white figure. It is* ADA *in a nightgown. She comes into the room, doing almost a little dance, at C. A sharp laugh from* ADA *draws* MRS. EDWARDS' *attention to her.*)

MRS. EDWARDS (*at phone*). Ada— you're going to catch your death of cold walking around here barefoot! Paddington 7831, please. Thank you. (ADA *really begins to dance, around C. of room. She takes a little springing side step around the room, holding the sides of her nightgown.*) Now that's enough, Ada—the floor is awfully draughty! (ADA *suddenly begins to laugh—a strange animalic laugh.*) Ada!

(ADA *dances toward* HENRY, *who has crossed to down L.C.*)

HENRY. Keep still!!

(HENRY *almost simultaneously has hit her across the mouth with the back of his hand. She gives a low cry, clasping both her hands to her mouth, and almost doubled up,* ADA *crosses to console up L., whimpering. She looks very much like an animal looking for a place to hide.* HENRY *has gone to* MRS. EDWARDS. *Down the stairs comes* MR. ED- WARDS, *heralding his approach by whistling "Long, Long Ago."* HENRY *crosses up foot of stairs, takes key from* EDWARDS.)

MR. EDWARDS (*crosses to window above desk and looks out*). Oh, that's fine. There goes Rose and there goes Doc. (*He leaves the window and crosses to gramophone.*

Picks it up and crosses above desk to table L.—where he places it on table, cranks it.)

HENRY. What's the matter, don't they answer? (*Crosses to* MRS. ED- WARDS.)

MRS. EDWARDS. Ringing. Hello? St. Mary's Hospital? This is the maid who called you a little while ago about an ambulance for an invalid. Montague Square? Yes.

HENRY. Never mind, they took her in a taxi.

MRS. EDWARDS. Well, please never mind—they took her in a taxi——

HENRY. To her own doctor.

(EDWARDS *puts gramophone on table. Takes crank out of pocket and winds.*)

MRS. EDWARDS. To her own doctor.

HENRY. Make sure the ambulance hasn't left.

MRS. EDWARDS. The ambulance hasn't left, has it? Thank you. (*Hangs up. To* HENRY.) No. They take their time.

MR. EDWARDS (*having placed the gramophone on table, winds it*). What's the matter, Ada?

HENRY (*going to* ADA, *who meets him up L.C.*). Never mind. (*Puts his arm around her. She responds but he quickly turns to business. To* MRS. EDWARDS.) Get the baby out of here. (*He crosses to window.*)

(ADA *crosses L.*)

MR. EDWARDS (*unlocking clasps on gramophone*). That's the trouble, Henry. Can't you just forget about it?

MRS. EDWARDS (*rises and crosses up C.*). No, Henry's right, Father. It's just a nuisance here, poor little thing.

MR. EDWARDS. What about Ada, Henry?

HENRY. Ada stays.

MRS. EDWARDS. What for, Henry? She's done her job.

MR. EDWARDS. Henry's right, Mother. You wouldn't want Ada roaming around the streets.

(MRS. EDWARDS *exits upstairs.*)

HENRY (*crosses to* MR. EDWARDS). See that the Italian woman gets the baby back tonight.

MR. EDWARDS. Whatever you say, Henry.

HENRY. Shutters nailed in her room?

MR. EDWARDS. Coming up, Henry. (*Lifting lid of gramophone as if it were covering a big surprise. And that's the way he talks.*) There you are, Henry! Ain't that nice?

(*Without replying* HENRY *takes a hammer and some nails out of record compartment in gramophone.*)

MR. EDWARDS (*taking a record from cover slot, puts it on the disk. Calls up the stairs*). I'm going to board over the window tomorrow anyway, Henry! (*Returns to gramophone, starts it going. It is an orchestra playing*—MR. EDWARDS *leans over, listening*—ADA *listens.*) I'm crazy about that record. Ain't it nice, Ada? (ADA, *who has been listening and moving her head to the rhythm, now starts to dance again.* MRS. EDWARDS *is heard coming down the stairs.*)

MRS. EDWARDS. Oh, he's a sweet little feller. Oh, he's a sweet little feller. (AGGIE *meets* MRS. EDWARDS *at C. trying to see baby.*) Go away, Aggie! Frightening the poor little chap. (MRS. EDWARDS *goes to sofa, sits, talking to baby.*)

MR. EDWARDS (*whistling, he goes to* MRS. EDWARDS). Cootchie—cootchie—coo. (*Tickles baby.*)

MRS. EDWARDS (*slapping* MR. EDWARDS' *hand*). Now, now, now! (AGGIE *is at up L. listening to music.* ADA *has come C., swaying to the music.* MR. EDWARDS *goes to* ADA. MRS. EDWARDS *continues her baby talk throughout.*) Oh, isn't he a sweet little baby? Whoooo. Sweet little feller. Whoooo—(et cetera, et cetera).

(ADA *and* MR. EDWARDS *start dancing*—ADA *breaks out into an exultant laugh.*)

CURTAIN

ACT THREE

SCENE—*The same room. The arrangement of the furniture is the same as in the Prologue. The only exception is that there are no "moderns" on the back R. wall. There is a solitary "old master" there.*

It is an afternoon during the following summer.

MRS. EDWARDS *is seated in chair L. of desk, peeling potatoes.*

MR. EDWARDS *is seated L. reading a newspaper.*

MARY HERRIES *sits in L.C. She is in a half daze, an unbelieving dream. The other two pay no attention to her as long as she keeps quiet. Finally, she attempts, slowly, to rise.* EDWARDS *notices this, pays no attention, lets her struggle and rise.* MRS. EDWARDS *rises.* MARY *looks at* MRS. EDWARDS *and sits. Then* MR. EDWARDS *resumes his reading.*

The doorbell rings, followed by two knocks on the door knocker. A trace of a glance passes between the EDWARDSES, *a ray of hope is visible in* MARY. MRS. EDWARDS *goes to the window and then goes to the door. There is a pause, then she returns with the mail.* MR. EDWARDS *has risen and crossed to U.C. to meet* MRS. EDWARDS.

MARY's *eyes follow the letters as they pass from* MRS. EDWARDS *to* MR. EDWARDS *and then back to the desk, in a neat pile.* MR. EDWARDS *returns to his newspaper at chair L. She looks for a time at the letters on the desk and finally at* EDWARDS, *who nods a solemn "No, no."* MRS. EDWARDS *takes her potatoes out L. That closes the incident and there is inaction until the door is heard to open.* MRS. EDWARDS *goes to door and meets* HENRY, *who enters.* HENRY *pays no attention to* MARY, *but questions* MRS. EDWARDS. *What they say is as much for* MARY's *benefit as for anyone else's.* HENRY *carries a portfolio. They both stand C. on platform.*

HENRY. Is Miss Herries in?

MRS. EDWARDS (*a pause, during which* MR. EDWARDS *slowly rises and looks at* MARY). Oh, no, sir—Miss Herries is traveling.

HENRY. Is that so? I had no idea.

MRS. EDWARDS (ADA *enters slowly and sits in front of fireplace*). Yes, sir. She left for America three weeks ago. From there she was going to South America—and from there to Australia.

HENRY (*looking about the room*). Really! Strange she didn't let us know.

MRS. EDWARDS (*very quietly and for* MARY's *ears*). Miss Herries had a bad nervous breakdown, sir. She wouldn't see anyone. She left very suddenly.

HENRY. Well! I'm sorry to hear it.

MRS. EDWARDS. Yes, sir. We're closing the house for the time being.

HENRY. You are the——?

MRS. EDWARDS. Housekeeper, sir.

HENRY. Thank you. Very good! (*Crosses to desk, puts portfolio on desk, looks at mail, never looking at* MARY. MRS. EDWARDS *crosses to upper R.C.* MR. EDWARDS *crosses to above table L.* MARY *looks at* HENRY *in the manner of a paralytic almost— an unwavering, dull stare, her head moving very slightly from side to side.* HENRY *crosses and addresses* MARY *as if she had just appeared, very much as if he were dealing with a child.*) Well! How do you feel, Miss Herries? (*She gives no sign she has heard.*) How do you feel?

MARY (*after a long time, very low*). Let me go!

HENRY. Let you go where, Miss Herries?

MARY (*after another long time*). What do you want?

HENRY. We want you to get well as soon as possible, Miss Herries. You know that. (*A slight pause, after which he looks up at* MRS. EDWARDS.) I'm afraid she's not much better, Mrs. Edwards.

MRS. EDWARDS (*crosses down R.C.*). No, sir, I'm afraid not.

HENRY (*to* MARY). The nurse tells me you haven't been eating well. (MARY *slowly looks at* MRS. EDWARDS, *then back to* HENRY.) You should, you know. It's very important.

MARY. What do you want?

MRS. EDWARDS. I do think she seems to be more herself, sir.

HENRY (*nods*). Do you understand what we are saying, Miss Herries?

(*After a pause,* MARY *slowly nods grimly. There is an immediate reaction on all of them.*)

MRS. EDWARDS. Well, that's fine!

MRS. EDWARDS. I knew it!

HENRY. I'm so glad. You're pulling through at last, Miss Herries. You'll be up and about in no time now.

MARY. Let me go! Let me go!! Let me go!!!

(HENRY *looks at* MRS. EDWARDS *and shakes his head.*)

HENRY (*takes pen and paper from pocket*). Will you sign this paper, Miss Herries? (*She looks at them uncomprehendingly.* MR. EDWARDS *crosses between L.C. chair and table with his newspaper. He places newspaper on* MARY'S *lap and stands at her L.*) Will you sign it now so your affairs can be taken care of? Here, please. (*Points out place.*)

MRS. EDWARDS (*crosses to* MARY, *takes pen from* HENRY, *who has moved R.*). I'll help, dear. (*Puts pen in her hand and holds the back of her fist.*) Go on.

(MARY *remains motionless; only her heavy breathing can be heard.*)

HENRY. Sign, Miss Herries. It's best.

MARY. Will you let me—go? I won't tell.

HENRY. Go on, Miss Herries.

MRS. EDWARDS. Here we go. "Mary," a nice "M" now.

MARY. No. No.

HENRY. You must, Miss Herries—do you hear?

MRS. EDWARDS. "Mary." (*Trying to guide pen.*)

MARY. No. No. (*Suddenly she gets up—screaming, spilling pen, paper, and newspaper on floor.*) No! (MRS. EDWARDS *grabs* MARY'S *shoulders and forces her to sit again.*)

MRS. EDWARDS. Stop it, you old——

(HENRY *almost hits* MRS. EDWARDS *for being so rough with* MARY. MRS. EDWARDS *goes above* MARY'S *chair.*)

MR. EDWARDS. Here we are now. (*Picking up pen, paper, newspaper from floor. He places them on* MARY'S *lap. Puts pen in her hand. Prompts.*) "Mary"——

MARY (*with every bit of resolution and finality but still in a dull, weak voice*). No. No.

(*There is a pause. All look at* HENRY *except* MARY.)

HENRY (*quietly*). Tomorrow, then. Or the day after. (*He takes pen, paper, and newspaper from* MARY. *To the others.*) Take her out. (*He goes to desk, puts pen and paper there.*)

MRS. EDWARDS. Don't be afraid, Miss Herries, I'll take care of you. I'm here.

(*They help her to rise and help her toward the stairs.*)

MR. EDWARDS. That's a good girl.

(*They are crossing up C.*)

MRS. EDWARDS. We'll have a nice little walk.

(MRS. EDWARDS *and* MARY *go upstairs.* MR. EDWARDS *stops on landing.* HENRY *returns to papers at desk.* ADA *lingers, crossing to C.* HENRY *looks up and talks to her in somewhat the same way he has talked to* MARY.)

HENRY. Hello, Ada. Everything all right?

ADA. Yes, Henry!

HENRY. You like it here?

ADA. Yes, Henry!

HENRY. So do I. (*Pause.*) Ada.

ADA. Yes, Henry?

HENRY (*crossing to* ADA *up C. As if he were suggesting a game*). Go upstairs and watch—and listen!

ADA. Yes, Henry! (*She goes, eager to do what he asks.*)

(HENRY *crosses to upper L., gets picture and places it in front of fireplace—then crosses to desk and sits.* EDWARDS *looks back up the stairs—turns to* HENRY—*shakes his head.*)

HENRY. Don't be impatient, Edwards.

MR. EDWARDS (*crossing down to L. of desk*). Whatever you say, Henry.

HENRY. Miss Herries is a very fine woman. She has character. She has strength——

MR. EDWARDS. That's true—but——

(HENRY *is reading the mail.*)

HENRY. Imagination—hope. She still has hope, Edwards.

MR. EDWARDS. Stubborn.

HENRY. *Time*, Edwards.

MR. EDWARDS. Perhaps.

HENRY. There is a dealer from Paris coming this afternoon to look at the Whistler. (*Gestures to the picture propped against the fireplace.*)

MR. EDWARDS. Here?

HENRY. He will also see Miss Herries—talk to her.

MR. EDWARDS. *Talk* to her, Henry!

HENRY. It would be comforting to have Miss Herries realize that if she ever should be in a position to appeal to anyone—no one would believe her.

MR. EDWARDS. Don't like it.

HENRY. Well, I'm going to try it. Edwards. (*Looks through letter.*) Ah! Lucy Weston is returning to London. (*This announcement worries* EDWARDS, *who crosses away a bit and turns back to* HENRY.) Dear Lucy. I shall look forward to seeing her again. (*He notices* EDWARDS' *worry.*) What is it, Edwards?

EDWARDS. It's about leaving this place.

HENRY. *You* may, if you want to.

EDWARDS. I didn't mean that. (*Pauses. Pulls chair L. of desk up a bit and sits.*) How was Paris?

HENRY. Very nice.

EDWARDS. Buy any pictures?

HENRY. Sold a few.

EDWARDS. Mind if I see the list?

HENRY. All right. (*Gives list to* EDWARDS.)

MR. EDWARDS (*he is impressed by list*). Quite right, Henry. There's a time to. After a while the odds keep stretching.

HENRY (*quietly and patiently*). We *live* here, Edwards. We are Miss Herries' best friends—her only friends—in London. The only ones who have cared for her since her—illness. I should think that idea would appeal to *you. Steady* employment. (*Doorbell.*) That should be the man from Bernstein et Fils.

MR. EDWARDS (*crossing up into bay window and calling upstairs*). Mother!

HENRY (*who has crossed to the window*). Wait! It isn't. It's Peter.

MR. EDWARDS. Peter!

(MRS. EDWARDS *comes down the stairs.*)

HENRY (*picks up portfolio and papers*). Show him in. (HENRY *exits to dining room L.* MR. EDWARDS *goes upstairs.* MRS. EDWARDS *waits until* MR. EDWARDS *is on the way, then goes to the hall. All this is done casually.*)

MRS. EDWARDS (*off*). Yes, sir?

PETER (*off*). I'm Mr. Santard.

MRS. EDWARDS (*off*). Oh, yes, sir. You rang up several weeks ago.

PETER (*off*). That's right.

MRS. EDWARDS (*off*). Will you come in, sir?

PETER (*off*). Thank you. (*He enters to C. of platform.* MRS. EDWARDS *follows.*) You are the——

MRS. EDWARDS. The housekeeper, sir. Mrs. Edwards.

PETER. I told *Mrs.* Santard, Miss Herries' niece, what you said and we all thought it would be a good idea for one of us to hop around sometime and get the details.

MRS. EDWARDS. Yes, sir.

PETER. America, you said?

MRS. EDWARDS. Yes, sir. I believe she had a friend there—in California.

PETER. You don't know who—or where? We're going to America ourselves——

MRS. EDWARDS. She didn't say.

PETER. She left no forwarding address of any kind?

MRS. EDWARDS. Only Thomas Cook in Melbourne, sir—in April.

PETER. Australia?

MRS. EDWARDS. Yes, sir. She's going around the world.

PETER. And nothing until then?

MRS. EDWARDS. Not that I know, sir. I mean not with me.

PETER (*crosses to table L.*). Do you know why Miss Herries left so suddenly?

MRS. EDWARDS (*counters to C.*). No, sir. Her heart was bothering her, I think—and the maid told me she was awful nervous.

PETER. Do you know where that maid is?

MRS. EDWARDS. With Miss Herries, I believe, sir.

PETER. Was Miss Herries being treated by a doctor?

MRS. EDWARDS. Not that I know, sir. I came just before she left—and all I was told was to close the house and wait till Mr. Henry Abbott dismissed me.

PETER. Mr. Henry Abbott? Who's that?

MRS. EDWARDS. He's the agent, sir, in charge of the pictures.

PETER. What do you mean—in charge of them?

MRS. EDWARDS. I believe he's selling them, sir.

PETER (*after a pause*). Is he here now?

MRS. EDWARDS. Yes, sir. Would you like to see him?

PETER. Please.

(*She goes out L.* PETER *takes a cigarette from a case in his pocket, lights it, and crosses R.* HENRY *comes in from up L., stops C.*

HENRY. Mr. Santard?

PETER. How do you do? I believe I saw you here one night—some time ago.

HENRY. Oh, yes. I brought some of my pictures to show Miss Herries——

PETER. Can you throw light on her mysterious disappearance?

HENRY (*laughs*). I think so. Please sit down. (*Indicates L.C. chair.*)

PETER. Thank you. (*Sits chair L.C.*)

HENRY. I'm sorry I wasn't here when you rang up this morning.

PETER. You see, my wife sent her aunt an invitation to our wedding and received a letter from the housekeeper!

HENRY (*crosses to desk. Makes notations on paper on desk*). I'm awfully sorry. I must have been away— on the Continent. Had I been here when your invitation came, I——

PETER. That's all right. What's the old lady up to—sneaking away like that?

HENRY. She did, didn't she? (*Laughs.*) But I can't say I blame her.

PETER. What happened?

HENRY. Well—nothing particularly. She had been fed up for a long time, I think, and she had been planning this trip.

PETER. I understand you are selling her pictures?

HENRY. Just a few—I am also buying others. But I want you to believe that financially I have no interest in the matter.

PETER. Of course.

HENRY. I mean, I am doing this for nothing.

PETER (*slight pause*). Do you know why she didn't come to the wedding?

HENRY. Yes. (*Smiles.*) It isn't difficult. I feel greatly responsible, to an extent. (*Pauses. Crosses in front of desk and sits on it.*) I'm afraid we'll have to turn psychological for a beginning.

PETER. Whatever you say.

HENRY. Well, then—you know something about Miss Herries——

PETER. I met her only once. I liked her immensely.

HENRY. A very fine, gentle, sweet woman.

PETER. That's what I thought——

HENRY. But a lonely woman. I seem to be delivering a lecture on——

PETER. No—go ahead.

HENRY. An old maid, afraid of being a polite nuisance to her friends. A sensitive middle-aged woman—— No relative but a sister—Emily——

PETER (*nods*). My mother-in-law.

HENRY. Whom she hasn't seen for years.

PETER. I wish I could say the same. I can understand that.

HENRY. Well, Miss Herries had a great fondness for my wife——

PETER. Oh——

HENRY (*crosses to C.*). I should explain my position here—Miss Herries is a very generous woman. You probably know that she befriended both my wife and myself——

PETER. No, I didn't.

HENRY. She lent us money—enabled me to make a few commissions—and when my wife was ill kept her here. (PETER *nods*.) I stayed too, of course, and here's where I come in, and why I say I feel great responsibility.

PETER (*leans forward*). I think I understand!

HENRY (*sparring*). Really?

PETER. Please go on.

HENRY. In some way I was seen here, casually by someone, who immediately spread the most damnable silly rumor, that Miss Herries had taken a man to live with her.

PETER. I know. That was Phyllis—my then fiancée. My now wife.

HENRY. I'm sorry.

PETER. You're right. She's damned sorry about it now. Her mother knew she had been here and kept pumping her until Phyllis happened to mention it—just gossip, I thought.

HENRY. I'm afraid so. One of Miss Herries' friends told her and that hurt her so, I believe, that it was the real reason for her "mysterious disappearance," as you say.

PETER. Yes, yes, I see.

HENRY (*crosses to desk—gets list*). So—she went, leaving me certain items in her collection to dispose of. I'm to deposit the money in Blakely's Bank and send a report to Australia in April. It's quite a responsibility.

PETER. Sounds like it.

HENRY (*crosses to C.—*PETER *rises and crosses to meet him*). Here's her list. You can see she's stipulated the minimum amounts to be obtained on each—and quite a few of these prices are pre-war.

PETER. I wouldn't know a thing about it—except that she has some pretty fine stuff.

HENRY (*nods*). Most of it is extremely desirable. But art collectors don't pay as much as they used to.

PETER. I guess you art collectors were the first to feel the pinch of hard times.

HENRY. Both as artist and agent I can tell you, Mr. Santard. You're most emphatically right.

(*They both laugh.*)

PETER. Great stuff, anyway. (*Giving list back to* HENRY—*crosses L.*) I had a fine time here, picking out things I'd like to own.

HENRY. I know! If ever temptation worried me, it did in this house. (*Puts list back on desk.*)

PETER (*pointing to upper L. wall*). There was a swell-looking painting on that wall—— (*Crossing up L. between L.C. chair and table.*)

HENRY. An El Greco. That unfortunately was sold to a museum in Brussels.

PETER. Oh, yes. And a Ming horse.

HENRY. Alas, that too is gone.

PETER (*crosses C.*). There were a few other things that hit me. I remember those two particularly.

HENRY (*smiling*). Well—(*getting list from desk*)—there are a few things, if you feel inclined——

PETER. Not a chance—but let's see anyway. (*Takes list from* HENRY, *looks at it and whistles.*) Whew—I'm just a poor bond salesman——

HENRY (*laughs*). I think Miss Herries might consider a reduction—for a relative.

PETER (*laughs*). Yes, I suppose she might. Oh, say—there's one thing I could be interested in. There was a statue on this table. I forget who did it. (*Points to table L.*)

HENRY (*dressing L. a bit*). A statue?

PETER. I remember—Troubetzkoi!

HENRY. Oh, yes.

PETER. Does that happen to be in stock?

HENRY. Oh, yes. There it is. (*Points up R.*)

PETER (*crosses to upper R.* HENRY *counters up C.*). Oh, there. Yes. Isn't it funny I thought it was—no, you're right. I was a little—you know, the night I was here. (HENRY *smiles.*) In fact, I thought I remembered Miss Herries promising to give it to us for a wedding present. (*Crosses down R.*) But—I suppose she changed her mind after Phyllis spilled that gossip.

HENRY. I'll be glad to remind Miss Herries if you could suggest some tactful method.

PETER (*laughs. Crosses back up R.*). Never mind. Anyway, it doesn't look as nice as it did the night I first saw it. The hell with it.

(*Snaps his fingers. Crosses down R. Doorbell rings.* MRS. EDWARDS *crosses toward the front door.*)

HENRY. I shall tell Miss Herries in my next letter that you called.

PETER. Do that. (*Reflects.*) No—you'd better not. The other half of the family have all decided not to—bother her—until she asks them to.

HENRY. I'm extremely sorry. (MRS. EDWARDS *brings in cable, hands to* HENRY, *who opens it.*) Excuse me.

(MRS. EDWARDS *leaves out L.* HENRY, *crossing to L.C., reads cable without any sign of emotion and puts it in his pocket.*)

PETER (*crosses to desk—puts ou. cigarette*). Well, I'm off. My—wife and I are going to live in America, you know.

HENRY. Indeed.

PETER (*crosses to C.*). I'm going to take charge of a branch out in Kansas City. Ever hear of it?

HENRY. Oh, yes.

PETER. God help me!

HENRY. Good luck, sir!

PETER. Thank you, sir! (*Crosses up C.*) Well, I'll tell the—family about

Miss Herries—not that it matters much, I suppose.

HENRY (*follows* PETER). I shall be here until Miss Herries returns and I'll be glad to do anything I can——

PETER (*laughs*). That's all right. Good-by.

(HENRY *sees* PETER *out.* MR. *and* MRS. EDWARDS *come on and wait until* HENRY *returns. They enter from dining room.* MR. EDWARDS *goes up on platform.* MRS. EDWARDS *goes to above table L.* HENRY *re-enters, still fingering the cablegram. He looks at them a bit triumphantly.*)

MR. EDWARDS (*as* HENRY *enters*). Nicely done, Henry.

HENRY (*crossing to window to watch* PETER *leave*). Yes, I think so. (*Then, handing cable to* EDWARDS. *Crossing to R.C.*) This is interesting.

(EDWARDS *reads.* HENRY *sits at desk.*)

MRS. EDWARDS (*crossing a bit R.*). What is it, Father?

MR. EDWARDS. Feller named Weston cables that his wife, Lucy, was killed in an airplane crash near Marseilles.

MRS. EDWARDS. My goodness——

(MR. EDWARDS *hands cable back to* HENRY.)

HENRY. That settles it. I think that when Miss Herries hears of *this,* things will be much simpler. (*Pauses.*) It also adds a note of permanency to the whole venture. For now Miss Herries has no one but me.

(*Bell.*) That should be Rosenberg. (*Crosses to window and looks out. Then to* EDWARDS.) Let her come down. I want her to meet this chap.

MRS. EDWARDS. Oh, Henry——

HENRY. I'll go out through the basement and come around and let myself in—in a few minutes. Show the man in here. Then you let Miss Herries into this room. Listen carefully. Don't let the man get away if she starts anything. (HENRY *rearranges things on desk.*)

MRS. EDWARDS (*a little fearfully*). Who is it, Henry?

MR. EDWARDS. It's a dealer from Paris.

(*Nodding that it's all right. Doorbell.*)

HENRY (*crossing to dining-room door L.*). Go on. (MR. EDWARDS *goes upstairs.* MRS. EDWARDS *again waits until he has gone up. She looks back at* HENRY *as if a little afraid of this step.*) All right.

(*Reassuringly.* MRS. EDWARDS *goes to the door.* HENRY *lingers until he hears* ROSENBERG'S *voice, then goes out through the door up L.*)

MRS. EDWARDS (*off*). Yes, sir?

MR. ROSENBERG (*off*). Monsieur Henry Abbott.

MRS. EDWARDS (*off*). Yes, sir.

MR. ROSENBERG (*off*). Monsieur Gustav Rosenberg, Bernstein et Fils. My card.

MRS. EDWARDS (*off*). Come in, sir. (*Shows in* MR. ROSENBERG, *a French-*

man.) Mr. Abbott is expected. Will you wait here, sir?

MR. ROSENBERG. Thank you.

(MR. ROSENBERG *looks around the room, spots the Whistler, and comes down to it, putting his hat on table* L. MRS. EDWARDS *backs out* R. *He glances at the windows and sees the shutters and realizes that he cannot get more natural light—examines the canvas—front and back. He takes out his handkerchief, spits on it, and rubs the lower* R., *then the lower* L. *corner of the canvas. He does not find any trace of a signature—which doesn't bother him particularly, however. What does disturb him is the fact that his handkerchief is black with dirt. He is putting his handkerchief back in his pocket and sitting in* L. *chair as* MARY HERRIES *enters the room from the stairs.*)

MARY (*stops on platform—sees* MRS. EDWARDS *off* R., *then looks into room* C.—*on platform*). Who—who are you?

(*She knows that the* EDWARDSES *are listening and that she must play the part she is expected to play. This man, however, is a perfect stranger —he may be one of* HENRY'S *satellites—this may be another trap.*)

MR. ROSENBERG (*rising*). Good afternoon, madame. I am Monsieur Gustav Rosenberg, Bernstein et Fils.

MARY (*crossing down* C.). What are you doing here?

MR. ROSENBERG (*a little puzzled*). I —I am Monsieur Gustav Rosenberg. Monsieur Abbott has invited me to look at this painting.

MARY. Painting?

MR. ROSENBERG. Yes—this painting —this Whistler.

MARY (*crossing in front of* L.C. *chair. Hurt*). No! Oh.

MR. ROSENBERG. What is it, madame; are you ill?

MARY. Oh, no. I'm quite all right. Only sometimes—I forget. (*She must make sure who he is.*) I've even forgotten who you said you were.

MR. ROSENBERG (*now beginning to worry*). Monsieur Rosenberg, madame. Bernstein et Fils, Paris.

MARY. Oh, yes. But are you *really*? (*Suddenly, with more intensity.*) How do I know you are Monsieur Rosenberg, from Paris?

MR. ROSENBERG (*presenting business card*). My card, madame.

MARY (*this is not enough identification*). No!

MR. ROSENBERG. My passport. (*Shows it to her.*)

MARY (*looks at it quickly, realizes that here may be a friend. Then she senses that the others are listening and speaks for their benefit*). Oh. Well, it doesn't make any difference. You'll forget me. Everybody's forgotten me. I'm supposed to be away. Henry writes all my letters.

MR. ROSENBERG (*a bit puzzled*). Pardon, madame?

MARY. No one else sees me. (*She takes a letter from her dress.*) How do you like that picture? (*Points to* HENRY's *painting of the "Ranz des Vaches" on L. wall.*)

MR. ROSENBERG. That? Oh, yes—yes —yes.

MARY (*points at letter which she has taken out of her dress*). Please look at this! (*Then for the benefit of the others.*) It's Henry's picture. (*Puts the letter in his pocket.*) Henry Abbott did it all. *Do you see?*

MR. ROSENBERG. I—I don't know—— (*Reaches into his pocket.*) Madame —what is *this?*

MARY (*pulls his hand away from his pocket*). The cowherd is playing the flute. And the cows are listening. (*Points to the arch.*) *They're listening very carefully, do you see?*

MR. ROSENBERG. Yes—to be sure——

MARY (*points to his pocket*). You *must look at it.*

MR. ROSENBERG. Oh—yes—yes, of course——

MARY. Henry isn't a very good painter. (*Low and pleading for* ROSENBERG *to believe her.*) *He's the very worst sort*—(*her voice rises so the others may hear*)—of a painter.

MR. ROSENBERG. Yes—yes, indeed! (*He looks around, hoping someone will enter.*)

MARY (*pointing to letter*). I'd tell that to anyone—even to *Lucy Weston*—who lives in *Mentone—Mentone*—— (*Then for the benefit of the others.*) But she's too far away. Do you agree with me?

MR. ROSENBERG. Yes, madame—yes. (*Anything to quiet her.*) Please sit down.

MARY (*sits quietly in L.C. chair*). Are you going to wait for Mr. Abbott? Or—(*rises and draws* ROSENBERG *up C.*)—will you *go away now* and come back later?

MR. ROSENBERG. I was told to wait here, madame.

MARY. You could come back later.

MR. ROSENBERG. I am sorry, madame. I have other appointments. I am in London for a few hours only. Please sit down, madame.

(MARY *sits in chair R.C.*)

MARY. But you will remember what I've said about—(*pointing to letter in his pocket*)—the picture?

MR. ROSENBERG. Yes, madame.

(*The front door is heard closing.*)

MARY. Please—help me—*do something!*

(ROSENBERG *crosses up C.* HENRY ABBOTT *enters the room.*)

HENRY. Mr. Rosenberg! (*Shaking hands.*)

MR. ROSENBERG. Ah! Mr. Abbott!

HENRY. You've had a look at the Whistler, I suppose?

MR. ROSENBERG. Yes—I—I have. I am glad you are here.

HENRY (*sees that everything has gone as planned. Crosses to fireplace*).

Yes. (*Crosses to the Whistler.*) Well —what do you think of it?

MR. ROSENBERG (*crosses after* HENRY. MARY *gives* ROSENBERG *a look of pleading*). Oh, yes—yes.

HENRY. Do you think Bernstein et Fils will be interested?

(*All through this,* MARY *is sitting quietly without making a move, watching* MR. ROSENBERG *with desperate hope.*)

MR. ROSENBERG (*a bit distracted by* MARY, *forces himself to discuss the picture*). As I have told you, Monsieur Abbott, Bernstein et Fils are not interested in Whistler—except for this one client.

HENRY. Yes, of course.

MR. ROSENBERG. Like so many Whistlers, it has sunken in and darkened to an extraordinary degree.

HENRY. Undoubtedly a good cleaning and one coat of mastic will bring out any details——

MR. ROSENBERG. Of course—this light—— (*He shrugs, turns* R., *sees* MARY, *turns back to* HENRY, *picks up hat.*) Might I suggest that you have it sent to our London correspondent—Leicester Galleries, Leicester Square, for further examination.

HENRY. Oh, it's genuine, all right.

MR. ROSENBERG. Of course. You will also accompany the painting with the history and the letter of authenticity.

HENRY. Oh, yes.

(MARY *looks pleadingly at* ROSENBERG.)

MR. ROSENBERG. Au 'voir, m'sieur. (*Crosses up between* L.C. *chair and table.*)

HENRY. Good day, Mr. Rosenberg.

MR. ROSENBERG (*crosses up to arch, stops, turns back*). Ah—uh—Mr. Abbott——

HENRY (*goes to him*). Yes?

MR. ROSENBERG. The lady gave me this. (*Produces letter.*) Perhaps it would be better——

HENRY. Oh, yes. Thank you for understanding.

MR. ROSENBERG. Au 'voir, M'sieur Abbott.

HENRY. Au 'voir.

(MR. ROSENBERG *goes.* HENRY *follows him off.* MR. EDWARDS *enters to below table* L. MRS. EDWARDS *to above* L.C. *chair.* ADA *to in front of fireplace.*)

MR. EDWARDS. Well!

HENRY (*re-enters—nods—a close call —then gives letter to* MARY). Here's your letter.

MARY (*low—with despair, still sitting* R.C.). God!

MR. EDWARDS. From listening, I'd have sworn she was——

HENRY. You are to be complimented, Miss Herries. (*Then to* MRS. ED-

WARDS, *crossing to below L.C. chair.*) Take her upstairs.

MARY (*gets up and faces* HENRY, *firmly, resolutely, and with as much strength as she can muster. She speaks evenly and quietly*). Don't be too sure, Henry Abbott. Things end somehow—sometime—— Someone—— It's been too easy for you. How you must despise yourselves! (*Almost a whisper.*) You wretched people—— (*There is a pause.* MARY *starts upstairs.* MRS. EDWARDS *offers to help, but* MARY *draws away.* MARY *goes up the stairs.*)

FADE OUT

EPILOGUE

SCENE—*The lights dim up and we find the scene as it was at the end of the Prologue.* MARY *is seated L.C.—and* MR. FOSTER *is seated R.C.*

MR. FOSTER (*greatly agitated*). Good God—I beg your pardon, Miss Herries—but I mean——

MARY. You do believe me, don't you?

MR. FOSTER. Miss Herries! Really, I—I—I——

MARY. The rain has stopped. Henry will soon be here.

MR. FOSTER (*rising and pacing*). This is dreadful—dreadful. What's to be done?

MARY (*hands him note*). Please take this. Take it.

(FOSTER *looks at the note—then door slam—*FOSTER *hurriedly puts away note.* HENRY *enters and sees* FOSTER.)

HENRY. Hello, Foster. You waited, thank you. I'm sorry to be late. (*He turns on lights and then notices* MARY.) Oh, Aunt Mary! (*He crosses to her.*) Down for your tea, dear?

MARY. Yes.

HENRY. Where is it?

MARY. No one was here.

HENRY. No one here? I don't understand. (*Crosses and rings bell, then crosses to desk.*) Now, Mr. Foster. You want me to sign these papers, don't you?

MR. FOSTER. The signature required by the Inland Revenue.

HENRY. Fine. Where do I sign, Mr. Foster?

MR. FOSTER. Here, sir. This will clear your income tax through June of this year.

HENRY. Till June. (*He starts signing.*)

MR. EDWARDS (*who has entered and put coffee table in front of* MARY. EDWARDS *is in the uniform of the traditional butler*). You rang, sir?

HENRY (*crosses to* MARY *with a protective air*). Yes, Edwards. I will not have you all away from the house at the same time. Miss Herries should never be without someone at her call. I've told you that before.

MR. EDWARDS. We are very sorry, si· but the rain held us up. I had to take Mrs. Edwards to the doctor. She's not feeling well, sir. And we thought——

HENRY. I want it definitely understood that Miss Herries is not to be left alone at any time. You were engaged to attend to Miss Herries' wants at all hours. If that isn't plain I shall have to get someone who will. Make it clear to Mrs. Edwards. And we'll have tea now.

MR. EDWARDS. Yes, sir. Mrs. Edwards is preparing it.

(*He goes toward dining room— stands aside so* MRS. EDWARDS *can come in with tea tray, which she places on coffee table before* MARY. MR. EDWARDS *exits.* HENRY *has gone back to desk immediately.*)

HENRY. Now, then, Mr. Foster. Sorry. (*Resumes signing income tax blanks.*)

FOSTER. That's all right, sir.

MRS. EDWARDS (*after she has placed tea in front of* MARY—*crosses to* C.). I'm sorry about being out, Mr. Abbott.

HENRY. All right, Mrs. Edwards. (*He finishes signing—to* FOSTER. MRS. EDWARDS *exits* L. *on platform.*) Thank you, Mr. Foster.

FOSTER (*picks up papers and puts them in his envelope*). Not at all. (*Crosses down to* MARY.) Good day, madam.

MARY. Oh, you're leaving? Good day, then.

FOSTER (*turns to* HENRY, *who has risen and is at* R. *of desk*). Good day, Mr. Abbott.

HENRY. Good day, Mr. Foster. (MR. FOSTER *starts out up* C. HENRY *lets him go almost out, then stops him.*) Mr. Foster. (FOSTER *stops—looks at* HENRY—*then slowly comes back into room to* HENRY *in front of desk.*) You've never been here before, have you?

FOSTER. No, sir.

HENRY. I'm sorry there was no one here.

MR. FOSTER (*after a moment*). Oh —I understand, Mr. Abbott.

(ADA, *in the costume of a trained nurse, comes downstairs.*)

HENRY. I thought you might not know.

MR. FOSTER. That's quite all right, sir. (*He sees* ADA *arranging* MARY'S *shawl—*ADA *exits* L.) She had me going for a few moments, Mr. Abbott.

(MARY *registers despair.*)

HENRY. Ah, yes. (*He crosses to* MARY—FOSTER *starts up* C. HENRY *stops him.*) Mr. Foster, my aunt is

KIND LADY 779

sometimes left alone—as she was today. Carelessness on the part of the
servants. (*Then a deliberate statement—not a question.*) She gave you
something—a note. (*He holds out
his hand.*)

MR. FOSTER. Oh! (*This is an am-
biguous "oh"—and there is life and
death in the balance. A look passes
between* FOSTER *and* MARY.) No,
sir! Good day, Mr. Abbott.

(*He exits. The door slam after*
FOSTER *is heard.* HENRY *slowly
turns and crosses to* MARY *and stands
looking at her. After a moment* MR.
EDWARDS *enters from dining room.
Crosses to upper C. on platform. He,
too, is puzzled and nervous. With
his head he beckons* MRS. EDWARDS
on from L. She joins MR. EDWARDS
and both look at MARY. *When* MRS.
EDWARDS *has joined* MR. EDWARDS,
ADA *is heard running down the
stairs. She stops at* MR. EDWARDS'

right, frightened. She slowly goes
to the right side of the arch. Then
MR. EDWARDS comes down behind
MARY. He looks at MARY, then at
HENRY.)

MR. EDWARDS. What do you think,
Henry?

(HENRY *does not answer. He is still
watching* MARY. MR. EDWARDS *starts
toward the upper window. Just before he reaches the window—doorbell.* MR. EDWARDS *hurries to upper
window, followed by* ADA *and* MRS.
EDWARDS. HENRY *hurries to downstage window. They all look out.
The doorbell rings, and knocking.
Slowly the* EDWARDSES *and* HENRY
*straighten up and look at each other
—then at* MARY. *Doorbell and knocking again.* MARY *slowly rises from
her chair. She seems to grow in stature. She throws off her shawl.*)

MARY. I'll answer.

CURTAIN

(*On the curtain* MARY *is crossing up C. to go out. The doorbell is ringing
and the knocking is louder and more commanding.*)

Night Must Fall

A Play in Three Acts By

EMLYN WILLIAMS

A drama in three acts by Emlyn Williams. Produced by Sam H. Harris at the Ethel Barrymore Theatre, New York.

CAST OF CHARACTERS

THE LORD CHIEF JUSTICE	Ben Webster
MRS. BRAMSON	May Whitty
OLIVIA GRAYNE	Angela Baddeley
HUBERT LAURIE	Michael Shepley
NURSE LIBBY	Shirley Gale
MRS. TERENCE	Doris Hare
DORA PARKOE	Betty Jardine
INSPECTOR BELSIZE	Mathew Boulton
DAN	Emlyn Williams

Before the play—The Court of Criminal Appeal, London.
Acts I, II, and III—Sitting room of Forest Corner, Mrs. Bramson's Bungalow, Essex, England.

DESCRIPTION OF CHARACTERS

LORD CHIEF JUSTICE: *Sitting in judgment, wearing wig and red robes of office, in the Court of Criminal Appeal.*
MRS. BRAMSON: *She is a fussy, discontented, common woman of fifty-five, old-fashioned both in clothes and coiffure.*
NURSE LIBBY: *A kindly, matter-of-fact young north-country woman in district nurse's uniform.*
OLIVIA GRAYNE: *She is a subdued young woman of twenty-eight, her hair tied severely in a knot, wearing horn-rimmed spectacles.*
HUBERT LAURIE: *He is thirty-five, mustached, hearty, and pompous.*
MRS. TERENCE: *She is the cook, middle-aged, cockney, and fearless.*
DORA: *She is a pretty, stupid, and rather sluttish country girl of twenty, wearing a maid's uniform.*
BELSIZE: *He is an entirely inconspicuous man of fifty, dressed in tweeds: his suavity hides any amount of strength.*
DAN: *He is a young fellow wearing a blue pillbox hat, uniform trousers, a jacket too small for him, and bicycle clips: the stub of a cigarette dangles between his lips. He speaks with a rough accent, indeterminate, but more Welsh than anything else. His personality varies very considerably as the play proceeds: the impression he gives at the moment is one of totally disarming good humor and childlike unself-consciousness. It would need a very close observer to suspect that there is something wrong somewhere—that this personality is completely assumed.*

THE CHARACTERS

(in the order of their appearance)

THE LORD CHIEF JUSTICE
MRS. BRAMSON
OLIVIA GRAYNE   Her niece
HUBERT LAURIE
NURSE LIBBY
MRS. TERENCE   Mrs. Bramson's cook
DORA PARKOE   Her maid
INSPECTOR BELSIZE
DAN

BEFORE THE PLAY

The Court of Criminal Appeal

The action of the play takes place in the sitting room of Forest Corner, Mrs. Bramson's bungalow in Essex.

The time is the present.

ACT ONE

A morning in October.

ACT TWO

Scene I: An afternoon twelve days later.
Scene II: Late afternoon, two days later.

ACT THREE

Scene I: Half an hour later. Nightfall.
Scene II: Half an hour later.

NIGHT MUST FALL

BEFORE THE PLAY

The orchestra plays light tunes until the house lights are turned down; the curtain rises in darkness, accompanied by solemn music. A small light grows in the middle of the stage, and shows the LORD CHIEF JUSTICE *sitting in judgment, wearing wig and red robes of office, in the Court of Criminal Appeal. His voice, cold and disapproving, gradually swells up with the light as he reaches his peroration.*

LORD CHIEF JUSTICE. . . . and there is no need to recapitulate here the arguments for and against this point of law, which we heard in the long and extremely fair summing up at the trial of the appellant at the Central Criminal Court. The case was clearly put to the jury; and it is against sentence of death for these two murders that the prisoner now appeals. Which means that the last stage of this important and extremely horrible case has now been reached. On a later page in the summing up the learned judge said this—(*turning over papers*)—"This case has, through the demeanor of the prisoner in the witness box, obtained the most widespread and scandalous publicity, which I would beg you most earnestly, members of the jury, to forget." I cannot help thinking that the deplorable atmosphere of sentimental melodrama which has pervaded this trial has made the *theater* a more fitting background for it than a court of law; but we are in a court of law, nevertheless, and the facts have been placed before the court. A remarkable and in my opinion praiseworthy feature of the case has been that the *sanity* of the prisoner has never been called into question; and, like the learned judge, the Court must dismiss as mischievous pretense the attitude of this young man who stands convicted of two brutal murders in cold blood. This case has, from beginning to end, exhibited no feature calling for sympathy; the evidence has on every point been conclusive, and on this evidence the jury have convicted the appellant. In the opinion of the Court there is no reason to interfere with that conviction, and this appeal must be dismissed.
(*The chords of solemn music are heard again, and the stage gradually darkens. A few seconds later the music merges into the sound of church bells playing far away, and the lights come on.*)

ACT ONE

The sitting room of Forest Corner, MRS. BRAMSON'S *bungalow in a forest in Essex. A fine morning in October.*

Center back, a small hall; in its left side the front door of the house ("throughout the play, "left" and "right" refer to the audience's left and right"). Thick plush curtains can be drawn across the entrance to the hall; they are open at the moment. Windows, one on each side of the hall, with window seats and net curtains beyond which can be glimpsed the pine trees of the forest. In the left wall, up stage, a door leading to the kitchen. In the left wall, down stage, the fireplace; above it, a cretonne-covered sofa, next to a very solid cupboard built into the wall; below it a cane armchair. In the right wall, up stage, a door leading to MRS. BRAMSON'S *bedroom. In the right wall, down stage, wide-open paned doors leading to the sunroom. Right down stage, next the sunroom, a large dining table with four straight chairs round it. Between the bedroom and the sunroom, a desk with books on it, a cupboard below it, and a hanging mirror on the wall above. Above the bedroom, a corner medicine cupboard. Between the hall and the right window, an occasional table.*

The bungalow is tawdry but cheerful; it is built entirely of wood, with an oil lamp fixed in the wall over the occasional table. The room is comfortably furnished, though in fussy and eccentric Victorian taste; stuffed birds, Highland cattle in oils, antimacassars, and wax fruit are unobtrusively in evidence. On the mantelpiece, an ornate chiming clock. The remains of breakfast on a tray on the table.

MRS. BRAMSON *is sitting in a wheel chair in the center of the room. She is a fussy, discontented, common woman of fifty-five, old-fashioned both in clothes and coiffure;* NURSE LIBBY, *a kindly, matter-of-fact young north-country woman in district nurse's uniform, is sitting on the sofa, massaging one of her hands.* OLIVIA GRAYNE *sits on the old woman's right, holding a book; she is a subdued young woman of twenty-eight, her hair tied severely in a knot, wearing horn-rimmed spectacles; there is nothing in any way remarkable about her at the moment.* HUBERT LAURIE *is sitting in the armchair, scanning the "Daily Telegraph." He is thirty-five, mustached, hearty, and pompous, wearing plus fours and smoking a pipe.*

A pause. The church bells die away.

MRS. BRAMSON (*sharply*). Go on.

OLIVIA (*reading*). ". . . Lady Isabel humbly crossed her attenuated hands upon her chest. 'I am on my way to God,' she whispered, 'to an-swer for all my sins and sorrows.' 'Child,' said Miss Carlyle, 'had I anything to do with sending you from'—(*turning over*)—'East Lynne?' Lady Isabel shook her head and cast down her gaze."

MRS. BRAMSON (*aggressively*). Now that's what I call a beautiful character.

NURSE. Very pretty. But the poor thing'd have felt that much better tucked up in 'ospital instead of lying about her own home gassing her 'ead off——

MRS. BRAMSON. Sh!

NURSE. Sorry.

OLIVIA (*reading*). " 'Thank God,' inwardly breathed Miss Corny. . . . 'Forgive me,' she said loudly and in agitation. 'I want to see Archibald,' whispered Lady Isabel."

MRS. BRAMSON. You don't see many books like *East Lynne* about nowadays.

HUBERT. No, you don't.

OLIVIA (*reading*). " 'I want to see Archibald,' whispered Lady Isabel. 'I have prayed Joyce to bring him to me, and she will not——' "

MRS. BRAMSON (*sharply*). Olivia!

OLIVIA. Yes, Auntie?

MRS. BRAMSON (*craftily*). You're not skipping, are you?

OLIVIA. Am I?

MRS. BRAMSON. You've missed out about Lady Isabel taking up her cross and the weight of it killing her. I may be a fool, but I do know *East Lynne*.

OLIVIA. Perhaps there were two pages stuck together.

MRS. BRAMSON. Very convenient when you want your walk, eh? Yes, I *am* a fool, I suppose, as well as an invalid.

OLIVIA. But I thought you were so much better——

NURSE. You'd two helpings of bacon at breakfast, remember——

MRS. BRAMSON. Doctor's orders. You know every mouthful's agony to me.

HUBERT (*deep in his paper*). There's a man here in Weston-super-Mare who stood on his head for twenty minutes for a bet, and he hasn't come to yet.

MRS. BRAMSON (*sharply*). I thought this morning I'd never be able to face the day.

HUBERT. But last night when you opened the port——

MRS. BRAMSON. I've had a relapse since then. My heart's going like anything. Give me a chocolate.

(OLIVIA *rises and fetches her a chocolate from a large box on the table.*)

NURSE. How does it feel?

MRS. BRAMSON. Nasty. (*Munching her chocolate.*) I *know* it's neuritis.

NURSE. You know, Mrs. Bramson, what you want isn't massage at all, only exercise. Your body——

MRS. BRAMSON. Don't you dictate to me about my body. Nobody here understands my body or anything else about me. As for sympathy, I've forgotten the meaning of the word. (*To* OLIVIA.) What's the matter with your face?

OLIVIA (*startled*). I—I really don't know.

MRS. BRAMSON. It's as long as my arm.

OLIVIA (*dryly*). I'm afraid it's made like that.

(*She crosses the room, and comes back again.*)

MRS. BRAMSON. What are you walking up and down for? What's the matter with you? Aren't you happy here?

OLIVIA. It's a bit lonely, but I'll get used to it.

MRS. BRAMSON. Lonely? All these lovely woods? What *are* you talking about? Don't you like nature?

NURSE. Will that be all for today?

MRS. BRAMSON. I suppose it'll have to be.

NURSE (*rising and taking her bag from the sofa*). Well, I've that confined lady still waiting in Shepperley. (*Going into the hall.*) Toodle-oo!

MRS. BRAMSON. Mind you call again Wednesday. In case my neuritis sets in again.

NURSE (*turning in the hall*). I will that. And if paralysis pops up, let me know. Toodle-oo!

(*She marches cheerily out of the front door.* MRS. BRAMSON *cannot make up her mind if the last re-mark is sarcastic or not. She concentrates on* OLIVIA.)

MRS. BRAMSON. You know, you mustn't think just because this house is lonely you're going to get a rise in salary. Oh, no. . . . I expect you've an idea I'm worth a good bit of money, haven't you? . . . It isn't my money you're after, is it?

OLIVIA (*setting chairs to rights round the table*). I'm sorry, but my sense of humor can't stand the strain. I'll have to go.

MRS. BRAMSON. Can you afford to go?

OLIVIA (*after a pause, controlling herself*). You know I can't.

MRS. BRAMSON. Then don't talk such nonsense. Clear the breakfast things.

(OLIVIA *hesitates, then crosses to the kitchen door.*)

(*Muttering.*) Sense of humor indeed, never heard of such a thing. . . .

OLIVIA (*at the door*). Mrs. Terence, will you clear away?

(*She goes to the left window, and looks out.*)

MRS. BRAMSON. You wait, my girl. Pride comes before a fall. Won't catch a husband with your nose in the air, you know.

OLIVIA. I don't want a husband.

MRS. BRAMSON. Don't like men, I suppose? Never heard of them, I suppose? Don't believe you. See?

OLIVIA (*resigned*). I see. It's going to be a fine day.

MRS. BRAMSON (*taking up "East Lynne" from the table*). It'll cloud over, I expect.

OLIVIA. I don't think so. The trees look beautiful with the sun on them. Everything looks so clean. (*Lifting up three books from the window seat.*) Shall I pack the other half of Mrs. Henry Wood?

MRS. BRAMSON. Mrs. Henry Wood? Who's Mrs. Henry Wood? Pack the other half of Mrs. Henry Wood? What *are* you talking about?

OLIVIA. She wrote your favorite book—*East Lynne*.

MRS. BRAMSON (*looking at her book*). Oh . . . (*Picking a paper out of it.*) What's this? (*Reading ponderously.*) A sonnet. "The flame of passion is not red but white, not quick but slow——"

OLIVIA (*going to her and snatching it from her with a cry*). Don't!

MRS. BRAMSON. Writing *poetry!* That's a hobby and a half, I must say! "Flame of passion . . ." *well!*

OLIVIA (*crossing to the fireplace*). It's only a silly poem I amused myself with at college. It's not meant for anybody but me.

MRS. BRAMSON. You're a dark horse, you are.

(MRS. TERENCE *enters from the kitchen. She is the cook, middle-aged, cockney, and fearless. She carries a bunch of roses.*)

MRS. TERENCE (*grimly*). Would you be wanting anything?

MRS. BRAMSON. Yes. Clear away.

MRS. TERENCE. That's Dora's job. Where's Dora?

OLIVIA. She's gone into the clearing for some firewood.

MRS. BRAMSON. You can't expect the girl to gather firewood with one hand and clear breakfast with the other. Clear away.

MRS. TERENCE (*crossing to the table, under her breath*). All right, you sour-faced old hag.

(HUBERT *drops his pipe.* MRS. BRAMSON *winces and looks away.* MRS. TERENCE *clears the table.*)

HUBERT (*to* OLIVIA). What—what was that she said?

MRS. TERENCE. She 'eard. And then she 'as to save 'er face and pretend she 'asn't. She knows nobody but me'd stay with 'er a day if I went.

MRS. BRAMSON. She oughtn't to talk to me like that. I know she steals my sugar.

MRS. TERENCE. That's a living lie. (*Going round to her.*) Here are your roses.

MRS. BRAMSON. You've cut them too young. I knew you would.

MRS. TERENCE (*taking up her tray and starting for the kitchen*). Then you come out and pick the ones you want, and you'll only 'ave yourself to blame.

MRS. BRAMSON. That's a nice way to talk to an invalid.

MRS. TERENCE. If you're an invalid, I'm the Prince of Wales.

(*She goes back into the kitchen.*)

OLIVIA. Would you like me to read some more?

MRS. BRAMSON. No. I'm upset for the day now. I'd better see she does pick the right roses. (*Wheeling herself, muttering.*) That woman's a menace. Good mind to bring an action against her. She ought to be put away. . . . (*Shouting.*) Wait for me, wait for me!

(*Her voice dies away in the kitchen. The kitchen door closes.* HUBERT *and* OLIVIA *are alone.*)

OLIVIA. That's the fifth action she's threatened to bring this week. (*She crosses to the right window.*)

HUBERT. She's a good one to talk about putting away. Crikey! She'll be found murdered one of these days. . . . (*Suddenly reading from his paper.*) "In India a population of three and a half hundred million is loyal to Britain; now——"

OLIVIA. Oh, Hubert! (*Good humoredly.*) I thought I'd cured you of that.

HUBERT. Sorry.

OLIVIA. You've only had two weeks of her. I've had six.

(*A pause. She sighs restlessly.*)

HUBERT. Fed up?

OLIVIA. It's such a very inadequate expression, don't you think? . . . (*After a pause.*) How bright the sun is today. . . .

(*She is pensive, far away, smiling.*)

HUBERT. A penny for 'em.

OLIVIA. I was just thinking . . . I often wonder on a very fine morning what it'll be like . . . for night to come. And I never can. And yet it's got to. . . . (*Looking at his perplexed face.*) It is silly, isn't it? (DORA *comes in from the kitchen with a duster and crosses toward the bedroom. She is a pretty, stupid, and rather sluttish country girl of twenty, wearing a maid's uniform. She looks depressed.*) Who are those men, Dora?

DORA. What men, miss?

OLIVIA. Over there, behind the clearing.

DORA. Oh. . . . (*Peering past her.*) Oh. 'Adn't seen them. What are they doing poking about in that bush?

OLIVIA (*absently*). I don't know. I saw them yesterday, too, farther down the woods.

DORA (*lamely*). I expect they're looking for something.

(*She goes into the bedroom.*)

HUBERT. She looks a bit off-color, doesn't she?

OLIVIA. The atmosphere must be getting her down too.

HUBERT. I'm wondering if I'm going to be able to stand it myself. Coming over here every day for another week.

OLIVIA (*smiling*). There's nothing to prevent you staying at *home* every day for another week . . . is there?

HUBERT (*still apparently reading his paper*). Oh, yes, there is. What d'you think I invite myself to lunch every day for? You don't think it's the old geyser, do you?

OLIVIA (*smiling*). No.

(*She comes down to the table.*)

HUBERT. Don't want to sound rude, et cetera, but women don't get men proposing to them every day, you know . . . (*Turning over a page.*) Gosh, what a wizard machine——

OLIVIA (*sitting at the left of the table*). I can't think *why* you want to marry me, as a matter of fact. It isn't the same as if I were very pretty or something.

HUBERT. You do say some jolly rum things, Olivia, upon my soul.

OLIVIA. *I'll* tell *you* why, then, if it makes you feel any better. You're cautious; and you want to marry me because I'm quiet. I'd make you a steady wife, and run a home for you.

HUBERT. There's nothing to be ashamed of in being steady. I'm steady myself.

OLIVIA. I know you are.

HUBERT. Then why aren't you keen?

OLIVIA (*after a pause, tolerant but weary*). Because you're an unmitigated bore.

HUBERT. A bore? (*Horrified.*) *Me*, a bore? Upon my word, Olivia, I think you're a bit eccentric, I do really. Sorry to be rude, and all that, but that's put the kibosh on it! People could call me a thing or two, but I've never been called a bore!

OLIVIA. Bores never are. People are too bored with them to call them anything.

HUBERT. I suppose you'd be more likely to say "Yes" if I were an unmitigated bounder?

OLIVIA (*with a laugh*). Oh, don't be silly.

HUBERT (*going to her*). You're a rum girl, Olivia, upon my soul you are. P'raps that's why I think you're so jolly attractive. Like a mouse one minute, and then this straight-from-the-shoulder business. What *is* a sonnet?

OLIVIA. It's a poem of fourteen lines.

HUBERT. Oh, yes, Shakespeare. Never knew you did a spot of rhyming, Olivia! Now that's what I mean about you. . . . We'll have to start calling you Elizabeth Brontë! (*She turns away. He studies her.*) You *are* bored, aren't you? (*He walks to the sunroom. She rouses herself and turns to him impetuously.*)

OLIVIA. I'm being silly, I know—of course I *ought* to get married, and *of course* this is a wonderful chance, and——

HUBERT (*moving to her*). Good egg! Then you will?

OLIVIA (*stalling*). Give me a—another week or two—will you?

HUBERT. Oh. My holiday's up on the twenty-seventh.

OLIVIA. I know I'm being tiresome, but——

MRS. BRAMSON (*in the kitchen*). The most disgraceful thing I've ever heard——

HUBERT. She's coming back. . . .

(OLIVIA *rises and goes to the right window.* HUBERT *hurries into the sunroom.* MRS. BRAMSON *is wheeled back from the kitchen by* MRS. TERENCE, *to the center of the room. She* [MRS. BRAMSON] *has found the pretext for the scene she has been longing to make since she got up this morning.*)

MRS. BRAMSON. Fetch that girl here. This minute.

MRS. TERENCE. Oh, leave the child alone.

MRS. BRAMSON. Leave her alone, the little sneak thief? Fetch her here.

MRS. TERENCE (*at the top of her voice*). Dora! (*Opening the front door and calling into the trees.*) Dora!

OLIVIA. What's Dora done now?

MRS. BRAMSON. Broken three of my Crown Derby, that's all. Thought if she planted them in the rose bed I wouldn't be well enough ever to see them, I suppose. Well, I *have* seen.

MRS. TERENCE (*crossing and calling to the bedroom*). You're wanted.

DORA'S VOICE. What for?

MRS. TERENCE. She wants to kiss you good morning. What d'you think?

(*She collects the tablecloth, fetches a vase from the mantelpiece, and goes into the kitchen.* DORA *enters gingerly from the bedroom, carrying a cup and saucer on a tray.*)

DORA. Did you want me, mum?

MRS. BRAMSON. Crown Derby to you, my girl.

DORA (*uncertain*). Beg pardon, mum?

MRS. BRAMSON. I suppose you think that china came from Marks and Spencer?

DORA. Oh. . . . (*Sniveling.*) Oh . . . oh . . .

OLIVIA (*coming between* DORA *and* MRS. BRAMSON). Come along, Dora, it's not as bad as all that.

DORA. Oh, yes, it is. . . . Oh. . . .

MRS. BRAMSON. You can leave, that's all. You can leave. (*Appalled,* DORA *drops the tray and breaks the saucer.*) That settles it. Now you'll *have* to leave.

DORA (*with a cry*). Oh, please. I . . . (*Kneeling, and collecting broken china.*) Oh, ma'am—I'm not meself, you see. . . . (*Sniveling.*) I'm in—terrible trouble. . . .

MRS. BRAMSON. Have you been stealing?

DORA (*shocked*). Oh, no!

OLIVIA (*after a pause*). Are you going to have a baby?

(*After a pause,* DORA *nods.*)

DORA (*putting the china in her apron*). The idea of me stealing. . . . I do go to Sunday school, anyways. . . .

MRS. BRAMSON. So that's the game. Wouldn't think butter would melt in her mouth. . . . You'll have to go, of course; I can't have that sort of thing in this house. And stop squeaking! You'll bring my heart on again. It's all this modern life. I've always said so. All these films and rubbish.

OLIVIA. My dear auntie, you can't have a baby by just sitting in the pictures.

MRS. BRAMSON. Go away, and don't interfere. (OLIVIA *goes to the left window.* DORA *rises. Triumphantly.*) So you're going to have a child. When?

DORA (*sniffling*). Last August Bank Holiday. . . .

MRS. BRAMSON. What? . . . Oh!

DORA. I 'aven't got a penny only what I earn—and if I lose my job 'ere——

MRS. BRAMSON. He'll have to marry you.

DORA. Oh, I don't think he's keen.

MRS. BRAMSON. I'll *make* him keen. Who is the gentleman?

DORA. A boy I know; Dan his name is—'leas' 'e's not a gentleman. He's a page boy at the Tallboys.

MRS. BRAMSON. The Tallboys? D'you mean that newfangled place all awnings and loud-speakers and things?

DORA. That's rignt. On the by-pass.

MRS. BRAMSON. Just the nice ripe sort of place for mischief, it always looked to me. All those lanterns. . . . What's his character, the good-for-nothing scoundrel?

DORA. Oh, he's nice, really. He done the wrong thing by me, but he's all right, if you know what I mean. . . .

MRS. BRAMSON. No, I don't. Where does he come from?

DORA. He's sort of Welsh, I think. 'E's been to sea too. He's funny, of course. Ever so open. Baby-face they call him. Though I never seem to get 'old of what 'e's thinking, somehow——

MRS. BRAMSON. I'll get hold of what he's thinking, all right. I've had my knife into that sort ever since I was a girl.

DORA. Oh, mum, if I got him to let you speak to him, d'you think I could stay on?

MRS. BRAMSON (*after a pause*). If he marries you at once.

DORA. Shall I—— (*Eagerly.*) As a matter of fact, ma'am, he's gone on a message on his bicycle to Payley Hill this morning, and he said he might pop in to see me on the way back——

MRS. BRAMSON. That's right; nothing like visitors to brighten your mornings, eh? I'll deal with him.

DORA. Yes. . . . (*Going, and turning at the kitchen door—in impulsive relief.*) Oh, ma'am——

MRS. BRAMSON. And I'll stop the Crown Derby out of your wages.

DORA (*crestfallen*). Oh!

MRS. BRAMSON. What were you going to say?

DORA. Well, ma'am, I *was* going to say I don't know how to thank you for your generosity. . . .

(*She goes into the kitchen. The clock chimes.*)

MRS. BRAMSON. Olivia!

OLIVIA. Yes, Auntie?

MRS. BRAMSON. You've forgotten again. Medicine's overdue. Most important.

(OLIVIA *crosses to the medicine cupboard and fetches the medicine.* MRS. TERENCE *comes in from the kitchen with a vase of flowers and barges between the sofa and the wheel chair.*)

MRS. TERENCE (*muttering*). All this furniture . . .

MRS. BRAMSON (*to her*). Did *you* know she's having a baby?

MRS. TERENCE (*coldly*). She did mention it in conversation.

MRS. BRAMSON. Playing with fire, that's the game nowadays.

MRS. TERENCE (*arranging flowers as* OLIVIA *gives* MRS. BRAMSON *her medicine*). Playing with fiddlesticks! We're only young once; that 'ot summer too. She's been a fool, but she's no criminal. And, talking of criminals, there's a p'liceman at the kitchen door.

MRS. BRAMSON. A what?

MRS. TERENCE. A p'liceman. A bobby.

MRS. BRAMSON. What does he want?

MRS. TERENCE. Better ask 'im. I know *my* conscience is clear; I don't know about other people's.

MRS. BRAMSON. But I've never had a policeman coming to see me before!

(DORA *runs in from the kitchen.*)

DORA (*terrified*). There's a man there! From the p'lice! 'E said something about the Tallboys! 'E—'e 'asn't come about me, 'as 'e?

MRS. TERENCE. Of course he 'asn't——

MRS. BRAMSON. He may have.

MRS. TERENCE. Don't frighten the girl; she's simple enough now.

MRS. BRAMSON (*sharply*). It's against the law, what she's done, isn't it? (*To* DORA.) Go back in there till he sends for you.

(DORA *creeps back into the kitchen.*)

OLIVIA (*at the left window*). He isn't a policeman, as a matter of fact. He must be a plain-clothes man.

MRS. TERENCE (*sardonically*). Scotland Yard, I should think.

(BELSIZE *is seen outside, crossing the left window to the front door.*)

MRS. BRAMSON. That place in those detective books? Don't be so silly.

MRS. TERENCE. He says he wants to see you very particular——

(*A sharp rat-tat at the front door.*)

(*Going to the hall.*) On a very particular matter. . . . (*Turning on* MRS. BRAMSON.) And don't you start callin' me silly! (*Going to the front door, and opening it.*) This way, sir.

(BELSIZE *enters, followed by* MRS. TERENCE. *He is an entirely inconspicuous man of fifty, dressed in tweeds; his suavity hides any amount of strength.*)

BELSIZE. Mrs. Bramson? I'm sorry to break in on you like this. My card. . . .

MRS. BRAMSON (*taking it, sarcastically*). I suppose you're going to tell me you're from Scotland Ya—— (*She sees the name on the card.*)

BELSIZE. I see you've all your wits about you!

MRS. BRAMSON. Oh. (*Reading incredulously.*) Criminal Investigation Department!

BELSIZE. A purely informal visit, I assure you.

MRS. BRAMSON. I don't like having people in my house that I don't know.

BELSIZE (*the velvet glove*). I'm afraid the law sometimes makes it necessary.

(MRS. TERENCE *gives him a chair next the table. He sits.* MRS. TERENCE *stands behind the table.*)

MRS. BRAMSON (*to her*). You can go.

MRS. TERENCE. I don't want to go. I might 'ave to be arrested for stealing sugar.

BELSIZE. Sugar? . . . As a matter of fact, you might be useful. Any of you may be useful. Mind my pipe?

(MRS. BRAMSON *blows in disgust and waves her hand before her face.*)

MRS. BRAMSON. Is it about my maid having an illegitimate child?

BELSIZE. I beg your pardon? . . . Oh no! That sort of thing's hardly in my line, thank God. Lonely spot. (*To* MRS. TERENCE.) Long way for you to walk every day, isn't it?

MRS. TERENCE. I don't walk. I cycle.

BELSIZE. Oh.

MRS. BRAMSON. What's the matter?

BELSIZE. I just thought if she walked she might use some of the paths, and have seen—something.

MRS. BRAMSON.) Something of what?

MRS. TERENCE.) Something?

BELSIZE. I'll tell you. I——

(*A piano is heard in the sunroom, playing the "Merry Widow" waltz.*)

(*Casually.*) Other people in the house?

MRS. BRAMSON (*calling shrilly*). Mr. Laurie!

(*The piano stops.*)

HUBERT'S VOICE (*as the piano stops, in the sunroom*). Yes?

MRS. BRAMSON (*to* OLIVIA, *sourly*). Did *you* ask him to play the piano?

(HUBERT *comes back from the sunroom.*)

HUBERT (*breezily*). Hello, house on fire or something?

MRS. BRAMSON. Very nearly. This is Mr.—er—Bel——

BELSIZE. Belsize.

MRS. BRAMSON (*dryly*). Of Scotland Yard.

HUBERT. Oh. (*Apprehensive.*) It isn't about my car, is it?

BELSIZE. No.

HUBERT. Oh. (*Shaking hands affably.*) How do you do?

BELSIZE. How do you do, sir.

MRS. BRAMSON. He's a friend of Miss Grayne's here. Keeps calling.

BELSIZE. Been calling long?

MRS. BRAMSON. Every day for two weeks. Just before lunch.

HUBERT. Well——

OLIVIA (*sitting on the sofa*). Perhaps I'd better introduce myself. I'm Olivia Grayne, Mrs. Bramson's niece. I work for her.

BELSIZE. Oh, I see. Thanks. Well now . . .

HUBERT (*sitting at the table, effusively*). I know a chap on the Stock Exchange who was taken last year and shown over the Black Museum at Scotland Yard.

BELSIZE (*politely*). Really——

MRS. BRAMSON. And what d'you expect the policeman to do about it?

HUBERT. Well, it was very interesting, he said. Bit ghoulish, of course——

BELSIZE. I expect so. . . . (*Getting down to business.*) Now I wonder if any of you've seen anything in the least out of the ordinary round here lately? Anybody called—anybody strange wandering about in the woods—overheard anything?

(*They look at one another.*)

MRS. BRAMSON. The only visitor's been the doctor—and the district nurse.

MRS. TERENCE. Been ever so gay.

HUBERT. As a matter of fact, funny thing did happen to me. Tuesday afternoon it was, I remember now.

BELSIZE. Oh?

HUBERT (*graphically*). I was walking back to my cottage from golf, and I heard something moving stealthily behind a tree, or a bush, or something.

BELSIZE (*interested*). Oh, yes?

HUBERT. Turned out to be a squirrel.

MRS. BRAMSON (*in disgust*). Oh! . . .

HUBERT. No bigger than my hand! Funny thing to happen, I thought.

BELSIZE. Very funny. Anything else?

HUBERT. Not a thing. By Jove, fancy walking in the woods and stumbling over a dead body! Most embarrassing!

MRS. TERENCE. I've stumbled over bodies in them woods afore now. But they wasn't dead. Oh, no.

MRS. BRAMSON. Say what you know, and don't talk so much.

MRS. TERENCE. Well, I've told 'im all I've seen. A bit o' love now and again. Though 'ow they make do with all them pine needles beats me.

BELSIZE. Anything else?

MRS. BRAMSON. Miss Grayne's always moping round the woods. Perhaps *she* can tell you something.

OLIVIA. I haven't seen anything, I'm afraid. Oh—I saw some men beating the undergrowth.

BELSIZE. Yes, I'm coming to that. But no tramps, for instance?

OLIVIA. N-no, I don't think so.

HUBERT. "Always carry a stick's" my motto. I'd like to see a tramp try anything on with me. Ah-ha! Swish!

MRS. BRAMSON. What's all the fuss about? Has there been a robbery or something?

BELSIZE. There's a lady missing.

MRS. TERENCE. Where from?

BELSIZE. The Tallboys.

MRS. BRAMSON. That Tallboys again——

BELSIZE. A Mrs. Chalfont.

MRS. TERENCE. Chalfont? Oh, yes! Dyed platinum blonde—widow of a colonel, so she says, livin' alone, so she says, always wearin' them faldalaldy openwork stockings. Fond of a drop too. That's 'er.

HUBERT. Why, d'you know her?

MRS. TERENCE. Never set eyes on 'er. But you know how people talk. Partial to that there, too, I'm told.

MRS. BRAMSON. What's that there?

MRS. TERENCE. Ask me no questions, I'll tell you no lies.

BELSIZE (*quickly*). Well, anyway, Mrs. Chalfont left the Tallboys last Friday afternoon, without a hat, went for a walk through the woods in this direction, and has never been seen since.

(*He makes his effect.*)

MRS. BRAMSON. I expect she was so drunk she fell flat and never came to.

BELSIZE. We've had the woods pretty well thrashed. (*To* OLIVIA.) Those would be the men you saw. Now she was . . .

HUBERT (*taking the floor*). She may have had a brain storm, you know, and taken a train somewhere. That's not uncommon, you know, among people of her sort. (*Airing knowl-*

edge.) And if what we gather from our friend here's true—and she's both a dipsomaniac *and* a nymphomaniac——

MRS. BRAMSON. Hark at the walking dictionary!

BELSIZE. We found her bag in her room; and maniacs can't get far without cash, however dipso or nympho they may be.

HUBERT. Oh.

BELSIZE. She was a very flashy type of wo—she *is* a flashy type, I should say. At least I hope I should say.

MRS. BRAMSON. What d'you mean? Why d'you hope?

BELSIZE. Well . . .

OLIVIA. You don't mean she may be —she mayn't be alive?

BELSIZE. It's possible.

MRS. BRAMSON. You'll be saying she's been murdered next!

BELSIZE. That's been known.

MRS. BRAMSON. Lot of stuff and nonsense. From a policeman too. Anybody'd think you'd been brought up on penny dreadfuls.

(OLIVIA *turns and goes to the window.*)

BELSIZE (*to* MRS. BRAMSON). Did you see about the fellow being hanged for the Ipswich murder? In last night's papers?

MRS. BRAMSON. I've lived long enough not to believe the papers.

BELSIZE. They occasionally print facts. And murder's occasionally a fact.

HUBERT. Everybody likes a good murder, as the saying goes! Remember those trials in the *Evening Standard* last year? Jolly interesting. I followed——

BELSIZE (*rising*). I'd be very grateful if you'd all keep your eyes and ears open, just in case. (*Shaking hands.*) Good morning—good morning—good morning, Mrs. Bramson. I must apologize again for intruding—— (*He turns to* OLIVIA, *who is still looking out of the window.*) Good morning, Miss . . . er . . .

(*A pause.*)

OLIVIA (*starting*). I'm so sorry.

BELSIZE. Had you remembered something?

OLIVIA. Oh, no.

MRS. BRAMSON. What were you thinking, then?

OLIVIA. Only how—strange it is.

BELSIZE. What?

OLIVIA. Well, here we all are, perfectly ordinary English people. We woke up—— No, it's silly.

MRS. BRAMSON. Of course it's silly.

BELSIZE (*giving* MRS. BRAMSON *an impatient look*). No, go on.

OLIVIA. Well, we woke up this morning thinking, "Here's another day." We got up, looked at the weather, and talked; and here we all are, still talking. . . . And all that time——

MRS. BRAMSON. My dear girl, who are you to expect a policeman——

BELSIZE (*quelling her sternly*). If you please! I want to hear what she's got to say. (*To* OLIVIA.) Well?

OLIVIA. All that time—there may be something—lying in the woods. Hidden under a bush, with two feet just showing. Perhaps one high heel catching the sunlight, with a bird perched on the end of it; and the other—a stockinged foot, with blood —that's dried into the openwork stocking. And there's a man walking about somewhere, and talking, like us; and he woke up this morning, and looked at the weather. . . . And he killed her. . . . (*Smiling, looking out of the window.*) The cat doesn't believe a word of it, anyhow. It's just walking away.

MRS. BRAMSON. Well!

MRS. TERENCE. Ooh, Miss Grayne, you give me the creeps! I'm glad it *is* morning, that's all I can say. . . .

BELSIZE. I don't think the lady can quite describe *herself* as ordinary, after that little flight of fancy!

MRS. BRAMSON. Oh, that's nothing; she writes poetry. Jingle, jingle——

BELSIZE. I can only hope she's wrong, or it'll mean a nice job of work for us! Well, if anything funny happens, nip along to Shepperley police station. Pity you're not on the phone. Good morning. . . . Good morning. . . .

MRS. TERENCE. This way.

(*She follows* BELSIZE *into the hall.*)

BELSIZE. No, don't bother. . . . Good morning.

(*He goes out.* MRS. TERENCE *shuts the door after him.*)

MRS. BRAMSON (*to* HUBERT). What are *you* staring at?

HUBERT (*crossing to the fireplace*). Funny, I can't get out of my mind what Olivia said about the man being somewhere who's done it.

MRS. TERENCE (*coming into the room*). Why, Mr. Laurie, it might be you! After all, there's nothing in your face that *proves* it isn't!

HUBERT. Oh, come, come! You're being a bit hard on the old countenance, aren't you?

MRS. TERENCE. Well, 'e's not going to walk about with bloodshot eyes and a snarl all over his face, is he?

(*She goes into the kitchen.*)

HUBERT. That's true enough.

MRS. BRAMSON. Missing woman indeed! She's more likely than not at this very moment sitting in some saloon bar. Or the films, I shouldn't wonder. (*To* OLIVIA.) Pass me my wool, will you?

(OLIVIA *crosses to the desk. A knock at the kitchen door;* DORA *appears, cautiously.*)

DORA. *Was* it about me?

OLIVIA. Of course it wasn't.

DORA (*relieved*). Oh. . . . Please, mum, 'e's 'ere.

MRS. BRAMSON. Who?

DORA. My boy fr—my gentleman friend, ma'am, from the Tallboys.

MRS. BRAMSON. I'm ready for him. (*Waving aside the wool which* OLIVIA *brings to her.*) The sooner he's made to realize what his duty is, the better, I'll give him baby-face!

DORA. Thank you, ma'am.

(*She goes out through the front door.*)

HUBERT. What gentleman? What duty?

OLIVIA. The maid's going to have a baby. (*She crosses and puts the wool in the cupboard of the desk.*)

HUBERT. Is she, by Jove! . . . Don't look at me like that, Mrs. Bramson! I've only been in the county two weeks. . . . But is *he* from the Tallboys?

MRS. BRAMSON. A page boy or something of the sort.

(DORA *comes back to the front door, looks back, and beckons. She is followed by* DAN, *who saunters past her into the room. He is a young fellow wearing a blue pillbox hat, uniform trousers, a jacket too small for him, and bicycle clips; the stub of a cigarette dangles between his lips. He speaks with a rough accent, indeterminate, but more Welsh than anything else.*
*His personality varies very considerably as the play proceeds; the im-*pression he gives at the moment is one of totally disarming good humor and childlike unself-consciousness. It would need a very close observer to suspect that there is something wrong somewhere—that this personality is completely assumed.* DORA *shuts the front door and comes to the back of the sofa.*)

MRS. BRAMSON (*sternly*). Well?

DAN (*saluting*). Mornin', all!

MRS. BRAMSON. So you're Baby-face?

DAN. That's me. (*Grinning.*) Silly name, isn't it? (*After a pause.*) I must apologize to all and sundry for this fancy dress, but it's my working togs. I been on duty this mornin', and my hands isn't very clean. You see, I didn't know as it was going to be a party.

MRS. BRAMSON. Party?

DAN (*looking at* OLIVIA). Well, it's ladies, isn't it?

HUBERT. Are you shy with ladies?

DAN (*smiling at* OLIVIA). Oh, yes.

(OLIVIA *moves away coldly.* DAN *turns to* MRS. BRAMSON.)

MRS. BRAMSON (*cutting*). You smoke, I see.

DAN. Yes. (*Taking the stub out of his mouth with alacrity and taking off his hat.*) Oh, I'm sorry. I always forget my manners with a cigarette when I'm in company. . . . (*Pushing the stub behind his ear, as* OLIVIA *crosses to the armchair.*) I always been clumsy in people's houses. I am sorry.

MRS. BRAMSON. You know my maid, Dora Parkoe, I believe?

DAN. Well, we have met, yes. (*With a grin at* DORA.)

MRS. BRAMSON (*to* DORA). Go away!

(DORA *creeps back into the kitchen.*)

You walked out with her last August Bank Holiday?

DAN. Yes. . . . Excuse me smiling, but it sounds funny when you put it like that, doesn't it?

MRS. BRAMSON. You ought to be ashamed of yourself.

DAN (*soberly*). Oh, I am.

MRS. BRAMSON. How did it happen?

DAN (*embarrassed*). Well . . . we went . . . did *you* have a nice Bank Holiday?

MRS. BRAMSON. Answer my question!

HUBERT. Were you in love with the wench?

DAN. Oh, yes!

MRS. BRAMSON (*triumphantly*). *When* did you first meet her?

DAN. Er—Bank Holiday morning.

MRS. BRAMSON. Picked her up, I suppose?

DAN. Oh, no, I didn't pick her up! I asked her for a match, and then I took her for a bit of a walk, to take her mind off her work——

HUBERT. You seem to have succeeded.

DAN (*smiling at him, then catching* MRS. BRAMSON's *eye*). I've thought about it a good bit since, I can tell you. Though it's a bit awkward talking about it in front of strangers; though you all look very nice people; but it is a *bit* awkward——

HUBERT. I should jolly well think it is awkward for a chap! Though of course, never having been in the same jam myself——

MRS. BRAMSON. I haven't finished with him yet.

HUBERT. In that case I'm going for my stroll. . . .

(*He makes for the door to the hall.*)

OLIVIA. You work at the Tallboys, don't you?

DAN. Yes, miss. (*Grinning.*) Twenty-four hours a day, miss.

HUBERT (*coming to* DAN's *left*). Then perhaps you can tell us something about the female who's been murdered?

(*An unaccountable pause.* DAN *looks slowly from* OLIVIA *to* HUBERT *and back again.*)

Well, *can* you tell us? You know there was a Mrs. Chalfont staying at the Tallboys who went off one day?

DAN. Yes.

HUBERT. And nobody's seen her since?

DAN. I know.

MRS. BRAMSON. What's she like?

DAN (*to* MRS. BRAMSON). But I thought you said—or somebody said —something about—a murder?

HUBERT. Oh, we ·don't *know*, of course, but there *might* have been, mightn't there?

DAN (*suddenly effusive*). Yes, there might have been, yes!

HUBERT. Ever seen her?

DAN. Oh, yes. I used to take cigarettes an' drinks for her.

MRS.   BRAMSON   (*impatiently*). What's she *like*?

DAN. What's she like? (*To* MRS. BRAMSON.) She's—on the tall side. Thin ankles, with one o' them bracelets on one of 'em. (*Looking at* OLIVIA.) Fair hair——

(*A sudden thought seems to arrest him. He goes on looking at* OLIVIA.)

MRS. BRAMSON. Well? Go on!

DAN (*after a pause, in a level voice*). Thin eyebrows, with white marks, where they was pulled out, to be in the fashion, you know. Her mouth —a bit thin as well, with red stuff painted round it, to make it look more; you can rub it off, I suppose. Her neck—rather thick. (*Laughs a bit loud; and then stops. After a pause.*) She's—very lively. (*With a quick smile that dispels the atmosphere he has unaccountably created.*) You can't say I don't keep my eyes skinned, can you?

HUBERT. I should say you do! A living portrait, if ever there was one, what? Now——

MRS. BRAMSON (*pointedly*). Weren't you going for a walk?

HUBERT. So I was, by Jove! Well, I'll charge off. Bye-bye.

(*He goes out of the front door.*)

OLIVIA (*her manner faintly hostile*). You're very observant.

DAN. Well, the ladies, you know . . .

MRS. BRAMSON. If he weren't so observant, that Dora mightn't be in the flummox she is now.

DAN (*cheerfully*). That's true, ma'am.

OLIVIA (*rising*). You don't sound very repentant.

DAN (*as she crosses, stiffly*). Well, what's done's done's my motto, isn't it?

(OLIVIA *goes into the sunroom. He makes a grimace after her and holds his left hand out, the thumb pointing downward.*)

MRS. BRAMSON. And what does that mean?

DAN. She's a nice bit of ice for next summer, isn't she?

MRS. BRAMSON. You're a proper one to talk about next summer, when Dora there'll be up hill and down dale with a perambulator. Now look here, young man, immorality——

(MRS. TERENCE *comes in from the kitchen.*)

MRS. TERENCE. The butcher wants paying. And 'e says there's men ferreting at the bottom of the garden looking for that Mrs. Chalfont and do you know. about it.

MRS. BRAMSON (*furious*). Well, they won't ferret long, not among my pampas grass! (*Calling.*) Olivia! . . . Oh, that girl's never there. (*Wheeling herself furiously toward the kitchen as* MRS. TERENCE *makes a move to help her.*) Leave me alone. I don't want to be pushed into the nettles today, thank you. (*Shouting loudly as she disappears into the kitchen.*) Come out of my garden, you! Come out!

MRS. TERENCE (*looking toward the kitchen as* DAN *takes the stub from behind his ear and lights it*). Won't let me pay the butcher, so I won't know where she keeps 'er purse; but I do know, so put that in your pipe and smoke it!

DAN (*going to her and jabbing her playfully in the arm*). They say down at the Tallboys she's got enough inside of 'er purse too.

MRS. TERENCE. Well, nobody's seen it open. If *you* 'ave a peep inside, young fellow, you'll go down in 'istory, that's what you'll do. . . . (DAN *salutes her. She sniffs.*) Something's boiling over.

(*She rushes back into the kitchen as* OLIVIA *comes back from the sun-room.*

OLIVIA. Did Mrs. Bramson call me, do you know?

(*A pause. He surveys her from under drooping lids, rolling his cigarette on his lower lip.*)

DAN. I'm sorry, I don't know your name.

OLIVIA. Oh. . . .

(*She senses his insolence, goes self-consciously to the desk and takes out the wool.*)

DAN. Not much doin' round here for a girl, is there? (*No answer.*) It is not a very entertaining quarter of the world for a young lady, is it?

(*He gives it up as a bad job.* DORA *comes in from the kitchen.*)

DORA (*eagerly*). What did she . . . (*Confused, seeing* OLIVIA.) Oh, beg pardon, miss. . . .

(*She hurries back into the kitchen.* DAN *jerks his head after her with a laugh and looks at* OLIVIA.)

OLIVIA (*arranging wool at the table*). I'm not a snob, but, in case you ever call here again, I'd like to point out that though I'm employed by my aunt, I'm not quite in Dora's position.

DAN. Oh, I hope not. (*She turns away, confused. He moves to her.*) Though I'll be putting it all right for Dora. I'm going to marry her. And I——

OLIVIA (*coldly*). I don't believe you.

DAN (*after a pause*). You don't like me, do you?

OLIVIA. No.

DAN (*with a smile*). Well, everybody else does!

OLIVIA (*absorbed in her wool-sorting*). Your eyes are set quite wide apart, your hands are quite good. I don't really know what's wrong with you.

(DAN *looks at his outspread hands. A pause. He breaks it, and goes nearer to her.*)

DAN (*persuasively*). You know, I've been looking at you too. You're lonely, aren't you? I could see——

OLIVIA. I'm sorry, it's a waste of time doing your stuff with me. I'm not the type. (*Crossing to the desk and turning suddenly to him.*) Are you playing up to Mrs. Bramson?

DAN. Playin' up?

OLIVIA. It crossed my mind for a minute. You stand a pretty poor chance there, you know.

DAN (*after a pause, smiling*). What d'you bet me?

(OLIVIA *turns from him, annoyed, and puts the wool away.* MRS. BRAMSON *careers in from the kitchen in her chair.*)

MRS. BRAMSON. They say they've got permits to look for that silly woman —who are *they*, I'd like to know? If there's anything I hate, it's these men who think they've got authority.

OLIVIA. I don't think they're quite as bad as men who think they've got charm.

(*She goes back into the sunroom.* DAN *whistles.*)

MRS. BRAMSON. What did she mean by that?

DAN. Well, it's no good her thinkin' *she's* got any, is it?

MRS. BRAMSON (*sternly*). Now, young man, what about Dora? I——

DAN. Wait a minute. (*Putting his hat on the table and going to her.*) Are you sure you're comfortable like that? Don't you think, Mrs. Bramson, you ought to be facin' a wee bit more this side, toward the sun more, eh? (*He moves her chair round till she is in the center of the room, facing the sunroom.*) You're looking pale, you know. (*As she stares at him, putting the stub in an ash tray on the table.*) I am sorry. Excuse rudeness. Another thing, Mrs. Bramson—you don't mind me sayin' it, do you?—but you ought to have a rug, you know. This October weather's very treacherous.

MRS. BRAMSON (*blinking*). Pale? Did you say pale?

DAN. Washed out. (*His wiles fully turned on, but not overdone in the slightest.*) The minute I saw you just now, I said to myself, now there's a lady that's got a lot to contend with.

MRS. BRAMSON. Oh. Well, I have. Nobody knows it better than me.

DAN. No, I'm sure. . . . Oh, it must be terrible to watch everybody else striding up and down enjoying everything, and to see everybody tasting the fruit——

(*As she looks at him, appreciation of what he is saying grows visibly in her face.*)

I'm sorry. (*Diffidently.*) I didn't ha' ought to say that.

MRS. BRAMSON. But it's true! As true as you are my witness, and nobody else—— (*Pulling herself together.*) Now look here, about that girl——

DAN. Excuse me a minute. (*Examining her throat, like a doctor.*) Would you mind sayin' something?

MRS. BRAMSON (*taken aback*). What d'you want me to say?

DAN. Yes.

MRS. BRAMSON. Yes. What?

DAN. There's a funny twitching in your neck when you talk—very slight, of course—nerves, I expect—— But I hope your doctor knows all about it. D'you mind if I ask what your ailments are?

MRS. BRAMSON. Hadn't you better sit down?

DAN (*sitting*). Thank you.

MRS. BRAMSON. Well, I have the most terrible palpitations. I——

DAN. Palpitations! (*Whistling.*) But the way you get about!

MRS. BRAMSON. Oh?

DAN. It's a pretty bad thing to have, you know. D'you know that nine women out of ten in your position'd be just sittin' down givin' way?

MRS. BRAMSON. Would they?

DAN. Yes, they would! I do know, as a matter of fact. I've known people with palpitations. Somebody very close to me. (*After a pause, soberly.*) They're dead now.

MRS. BRAMSON (*startled*). Oh!

DAN. My mother, as a matter of fact. (*With finely controlled emotion, practically indistinguishable from the real thing.*) I can just remember her.

MRS. BRAMSON. Oh?

DAN. She died when I was six. I know that, because my dad died two years before that.

MRS. BRAMSON (*vaguely*). Oh.

DAN (*studying her*) As a matter o' fact——

MRS. BRAMSON. Yes?

DAN. Oh, no, it's a daft thing——

MRS. BRAMSON (*the old tart note creeping back*). Come along now! Out with it!

DAN. It's only fancy, I suppose, but you remind me a bit of her.

MRS. BRAMSON. Of your mother? (*As he nods simply, her sentimentality stirring.*) Oh . . .

DAN. Have *you* got a son?

MRS. BRAMSON (*self-pityingly*). I haven't anybody at all.

DAN. Oh. But I don't like to talk too much about my mother. (*Putting a finger unobtrusively to his eye.*) Makes me feel—sort of sad. . . . (*With a sudden thought.*) She had the same eyes very wide apart as you, and—and the same very good hands.

MRS. BRAMSON (*looking interestedly at her fingers*). Oh? . . . And the same palpitations?

DAN. And the same palpitations. You don't mind me talking about your health, do you?

MRS. BRAMSON. No.

DAN. Well, d'you know, you ought to get used to letting *other* people do things for you.

MRS. BRAMSON (*a great truth dawning on her*). Yes!

DAN. You ought to be *very* careful.

MRS. BRAMSON. Yes! (*After a pause, eying him as he smiles at her.*) You're a funny boy to be a page boy.

DAN (*shyly*). D'you think so?

MRS. BRAMSON. Well, now I come to talk to you, you seem so much better class—I mean, you know so much of the world——

DAN. I've knocked about a good bit, you know. Never had any advantages, but I always tried to do the right thing.

MRS. BRAMSON (*patronizingly*). I think you deserve better—— (*Sharply again.*) Talking of the right thing, what about Dora?

DAN (*disarming*). Oh, I know I'm to blame; I'm not much of a chap, but I'd put things straight like a shot if I had any money. But, you see, I work at the Tallboys, get thirty bob a week, with tips—but listen to me botherin' you with my worries and rubbish the state you're in. Well!

MRS. BRAMSON. No, I can stand it. (*OLIVIA comes back from the sun-room. Pursing her lips reflectively.*) I've taken a liking to you.

DAN. Well—(*looking round at OLIVIA*)—that's very kind of you, Mrs. Bramson.

MRS. BRAMSON. It's the way you talked about your mother. That's what it was.

DAN. Was it?

OLIVIA (*at the left window*). Shall I pack these books?

DAN (*going to her with alacrity, taking the parcel from her*). I'll post them for you.

OLIVIA. Oh. . . .

DAN. I'm passing Shepperley post office on the bike before post time tomorrow morning. With pleasure!

MRS. BRAMSON. Have you got to go back?

DAN. Now? Well, no, not really. I've finished on duty now I done that errand, and this is my half day.

MRS. BRAMSON (*imperiously*). Stay to lunch.

DAN (*apparently taken aback, after a look at OLIVIA*). Well, I don't like to impose myself——

MRS. BRAMSON. In the kitchen, of course.

DAN. Oh, I know——

MRS. BRAMSON. There's plenty of food! Stay to lunch!

DAN. Well, I don't know. All right, so long as you let me help a bit this morning. . . . Don't you want some string for this? Where's it kep'?

MRS. BRAMSON. That woman knows. In the kitchen somewhere.

DAN. Through here?

(*He tosses the books on the sofa and hurries into the kitchen.* MRS. BRAMSON *holds out her hands and studies them with a new interest.*)

MRS. BRAMSON. That boy's got understanding.

OLIVIA. Enough to marry Dora?

MRS. BRAMSON. You ought to learn to be a little less bitter, my dear. Never hook a man if you don't. With him and that Dora, I'm not so sure it wasn't six of one and half a dozen of the other. I know human nature, and, mark my word, that boy's going to do big things.

(*A scurry in the garden.* MRS. TERENCE *rushes in from the front door, madly excited.*)

MRS. TERENCE. The paper boy's at the back gate, and says there's a placard in Shepperley, and it's got "News of the World—Shepperley Mystery" on it!

MRS. BRAMSON. What!

OLIVIA. They've got it in the papers!

MRS. TERENCE. They've got it in the papers! D'ye want any? (*Beside herself.*)

MRS. BRAMSON. Catch him quick!

MRS. TERENCE. First time I ever 'eard of Shepperley being in print before—hi!

(*She races out of the front door.*)

MRS. BRAMSON. Running around the house shouting like a lunatic! Sensation mad! Silly woman!

(DORA *runs in from kitchen.*)

DORA. They've got it in the papers!

MRS. BRAMSON. Go away!

MRS. TERENCE (*off*). I've bought three!

MRS. BRAMSON (*shouting*). Be QUIET!

(MRS. TERENCE *runs back with three Sunday newspapers and gives one to* OLIVIA *and one to* MRS. BRAMSON.)

OLIVIA (*sitting left of the table*). I expect it is a bit of an event.

MRS. TERENCE (*leaning over the table, searching in her paper*). 'E says they're sellin' like ninepins——

MRS. BRAMSON (*turning pages over, impatiently*). Where *is* it? . . .

MRS. TERENCE. Oh, I expect it's nothing after all. . . .

OLIVIA. Here it is. (*Reading.*) "Disappeared mysteriously . . . woods round the village being searched" . . . then her description . . . tall . . . blonde. . . .

MRS. TERENCE. Blonde? I should think she is. . . . I can't find it!

OLIVIA. Here's something: "A keeper in the Shepperley woods was closely questioned late last night, but he had heard nothing, beyond a woman's voice in the woods on the afternoon in question, and a man's voice, probably with her, singing 'Mighty Lak a Rose.' Inquiries are being pursued. . . ."

MRS. BRAMSON. "Mighty Lak a Rose." What rubbish!

MRS. TERENCE. Oh yes. It's the 'eadline in this one. (*Humming the tune absently as she reads.*) "Don't know what to call you, but you're mighty lak a rose." . . . Those men have done rummaging in the garden, anyway.

MRS. BRAMSON. I must go this minute and have a look at my pampas grass. And if they've damaged it I'll bring an action.

MRS. TERENCE. Fancy Shepperley bein' in print.

MRS. BRAMSON. Wheel me out, and don't talk so much.

MRS. TERENCE (*maneuvering her through the front door*). I could talk me 'ead off and not talk as much as some people I could mention.

(OLIVIA *is alone. A pause. She spreads her paper on the table and finds* DAN's *hat under it. She picks it up and looks at it;* DAN *comes in from the kitchen with a ball of tangled string, a cigarette between his lips. He is about to take the books into the kitchen, when he sees her. He crosses to her.*)

DAN. Excuse me. (*Taking the hat from her, cheerfully.*) I think I'll hang it in the hall, same as if I was a visitor. . . . (*He does so, then takes up the books, sits on the sofa, and begins to unravel the string. A pause.*) You don't mind me stayin' and havin' a bit o' lunch in the kitchen, do you?

OLIVIA. It's not for me to say. As I told you before, I'm really a servant here.

DAN (*after a pause*). You're not a very ordinary servant, though, are you?

OLIVIA (*turning over a page*). N-no. . . .

DAN. Neither am I. (*He unpicks a knot, and begins to hum absent-mindedly. The humming gradually resolves itself into faint singing.*) "I'm a pretty little feller . . . everybody knows . . ."

(OLIVIA *looks up; a thought crosses her mind. She turns her head and looks at him.*)

The curtain begins to fall slowly.

(*Singing, as he intently unravels the string.*) "Don't know what to call me—but I'm mighty lak a rose. . . ."

THE CURTAIN IS DOWN

ACT TWO

SCENE I

An afternoon twelve days later. The weather is a little duller.

MRS. BRAMSON *is sitting on the right of the table in her invalid chair, puzzling out a game of patience. She has smartened up her appearance in the interval and is wearing purple and earrings.* OLIVIA *is sitting opposite her, smoking a cigarette, a pencil and pad on the table in front of her; she is pondering and writing. A portable gramophone on a small table next the desk is playing the H.M.V. dance record of "Dames."*

A pause. MRS. BRAMSON *coughs. She coughs again, and looks at* OLIVIA, *waving her hand before her, clearing away billows of imaginary smoke.*

OLIVIA. I'm sorry. Is my cigarette worrying you?

MRS. BRAMSON (*temper*). Not at all. I like it!

(OLIVIA *stubs out her cigarette with a resigned look and goes on making notes.* DAN *enters from the kitchen, keeping time to the music, carrying a bunch of roses, wearing overalls over flannel trousers and a brown golf jacket, and smoking. He goes to the fireplace and clumps the roses into a vase on the mantelpiece, humming the tune. He crosses to the gramophone, still in rhythm,* MRS. BRAMSON *keeping time skittishly with her hands. He turns off the gramophone and looks over* OLIVIA'S *shoulder at what she is writing.*)

DAN (*singing*). "Their home addresses . . . and their caresses . . . linger in my memory of . . . those beautiful dames" . . . (*His hand to his forehead.*) That's me!

(OLIVIA *looks at him coldly and continues her notes.*)

MRS. BRAMSON. It won't come out. . . .

(DAN *shrugs his shoulders, stands behind* MRS. BRAMSON'S *chair, and studies her play.* OLIVIA *follows his example from her side.*)

OLIVIA (*pointing to two cards*). Look.

MRS. BRAMSON (*infuriated*). I saw that! Leave me alone, and don't interfere.

(*A pause.* DAN *makes a quick movement and puts one card on another.*)

(*Pleased and interested, quite unconscious of the difference in her attitude.*) Oh, yes, dear, of course.

OLIVIA (*as* MRS. BRAMSON *makes a move*). No, that's a spade.

MRS. BRAMSON (*sharply*). No such thing; it's a club. It's got a wiggle on it.

DAN. They both got wiggles on 'em. (*Pointing to another card.*) This is a club.

MRS. BRAMSON. Oh yes, dear, so it is!

OLIVIA (*writing*). The ironmonger says there *were* two extra gallons of paraffin not paid for.

MRS. BRAMSON. And they *won't* be paid for either—not if I have to go to law about it.

(*A pause. She coughs absently.*)

DAN. I'm sorry. Is my cigarette worrying you?

MRS. BRAMSON. No, no, dear. (*This has its effect on* OLIVIA. DAN *sits on the left of the table, where "East Lynne" is open on the table.*) I'm sick of patience.

DAN (*reading laboriously*). "You old-fashioned child——"

MRS. BRAMSON. What?

DAN. *East Lynne.*

MRS. BRAMSON. Oh.

DAN (*reading*). " 'You old-fashioned child!' retorted Mrs. Vane. 'Why did you not put on your diamonds?' 'I—did—put on my diamonds,' stammered Lady Isabel. 'But I—took them off again.' 'What on earth for?' " That's the other lady speaking there——

MRS. BRAMSON. Yes, dear.

DAN. " 'What on earth for?'. . . 'I did not like to be too fine,' answered Lary Isabel, with a laugh—(*turning over*)—"and a blush. 'They glittered so! I feared it might be thought I had put them on to look fine.' "

MRS. BRAMSON (*absently*). Good, isn't it?

DAN (*flicking ash*). Oh, yes, reelistic. (*Reading.*) " 'I see you mean to set up among that class of people who pree-tend to dee-spise ornyment,' scornfully ree-marked Mrs. Vane. 'It is the ree-finement of aff-affectation, Lady Isabel——' "

(*An excited knock at the kitchen door.* DORA *enters.* DAN *turns back the page and surveys what he has been reading, scratching his head.*)

MRS. BRAMSON (*the old edge to her voice*). What is it?

DORA. Them men's in the wood again.

MRS. BRAMSON. What men?

DORA. The men lookin' for that Mrs. Chalfont.

(*A pause.* DAN *hums "Dames" under his breath.*)

MRS. BRAMSON. You don't mean to tell me they're still at it? But they've been pottering about since . . . When was that day Mr. Dan left the Tallboys?

DORA (*stressing a little bitterly*). Mister Dan?

DAN (*smiling*). Ahem!

DORA. *Mister* Dan first came to work for you, mum, a week last Monday.

MRS. BRAMSON. Well, I think it's a disgrace——

DORA. *I*'ve found something!

(*DAN's humming stops abruptly; he swivels round and looks at DORA, his face unseen by the audience. OLIVIA and MRS. BRAMSON stare at DORA; a pause.*)

MRS. BRAMSON. *You*'ve found something?

OLIVIA. What?

DORA (*excited*). This!

(*She holds out her left arm and lets fall from her fist the length of a soiled belt. A pause. OLIVIA puts down her pencil and pad, goes to her, and looks at the belt.*)

OLIVIA. Yes, of course, it's mine! I missed it last week. . . .

MRS. BRAMSON (*balked of excitement*). Oh, yes, I thought I recognized it. . . . What nonsense! . . .

(*DAN looks at her chuckling.*)

DORA (*going, dolefully*). I'm ever so disappointed.

(*She goes into the kitchen. OLIVIA goes to the armchair by the fireplace.*)

MRS. BRAMSON. She'll be joining Scotland Yard next. . . . Go on, dear.

DAN (*reading*). "'It is the ree-finement of affectation, Lady Isabel ——'"

(*The clock chimes.*)

(*Clapping his hands, to MRS. BRAMSON.*) Ah!

MRS. BRAMSON (*pleased*). Oh, Danny . . .

(*He hurries to the medicine cupboard and pours medicine into a spoon. HUBERT comes in from the front door.*)

HUBERT (*eagerly*). Have you heard?

MRS. BRAMSON (*eagerly*). What?

HUBERT. Dora's found a belt!

MRS. BRAMSON (*disappointed again*). Oh . . . it was Olivia's.

HUBERT. I say, what a shame!

MRS. BRAMSON. Tch, tch! . . . all this sensation-mong—— (*DAN drowns her speech by deftly pouring the spoonful of medicine down her throat. He pushes her chocolate box toward her, and strides briskly into the hall.*) Horrid. . . .

DAN (*taking a soft hat from the rack and putting it on*). Good for you, though, the way you are. . . .

MRS. BRAMSON. Yes, dear.

DAN (*coming into the room, and beginning to take off his overalls*). And now it's time for your walk. (*Smiling at OLIVIA.*) It's all right, I got trousers on. . . . (*Peeling the overalls over his feet, and tossing them on to the left window seat.*) Listen to me talking about your walk, when you'll be in a chair all the time. (*Chuckling, to HUBERT.*) That's funny, isn't it! (*Going to MRS. BRAMSON.*) Come on, I got your shawl and your rug in the hall. . . .

MRS. BRAMSON (*as he wheels her into the hall*). Have you got my pills?

DAN. I got them in my pocket.

MRS. BRAMSON. And my chocolates?

DAN. I got them in my pocket too. Here's your hat—better put it on yourself.

MRS. BRAMSON. Yes, dear.

DAN. And here's your shawl.

MRS. BRAMSON. It isn't a shawl, it's a cape.

DAN. Well, I don't know, do I? And I carry your rug on my shoulder. (*To the others.*) See you later! Be good! (*Shutting the front door, his voice dying as the chair passes the left window.*) Down this way today. . . . (*A pause.* HUBERT *and* OLIVIA *look at each other.*)

OLIVIA (*suddenly*). What do *you* think of him?

HUBERT (*a little taken aback*). Him? Grannie's white-headed boy, you mean? Oh, he's all right. (*Heavily.*) A bit slow on the uptake, of course. I wish he'd occasionally take that fag end out of his mouth.

OLIVIA. He does. For *her*.

HUBERT. That's true. That's why he's made such a hit with her. Funny I haven't been able to manage it. In two weeks too—it's uncanny.

OLIVIA. Uncanny? I think it's clever.

HUBERT. You don't think he's a wrong 'un, do you?

OLIVIA. What do we know about him?

HUBERT. Why, his Christian name ——

OLIVIA. And that's all.

HUBERT. He looks pretty honest.

OLIVIA. Looks? (*After a pause.*) It's rather frightening to think what a face can hide. . . . I sometimes catch sight of one looking at me. Careful lips, and blank eyes. . . . And then I find I'm staring at myself in the glass, and I realize how successfully I'm hiding the thoughts I know so well. And then I know we're all—strangers. Windows with blinds, and behind them—secrets. What's behind *his* eyes? (*After a pause, with a smile.*) You're quite right, it *is* morbid.

HUBERT. D'you think he's a thief or something? By Jove, I left my links on the washstand before lunch ——

OLIVIA. He's acting every minute of the time. I know he is! But he's acting pretty well, because I don't know *how* I know. . . . He's walking about here all day, and talking a little, and smiling, and smoking cigarettes. Impenetrable—that's what it is! What's going on—in his mind? What's he thinking of? (*Vehemently.*) He *is* thinking of something! All the time! What is it?

(DAN *enters from the front door and smiles broadly at them.*)

DAN. Anybody seen my lady's pills? It's a matter of life and death. . . . I thought *I* had 'em.

(HUBERT *chuckles.*)

OLIVIA (*after a pause, in a level voice*). Oh, yes. They're in the top drawer of the desk. I'm so sorry.

DAN. Thank you. (*He salutes her, goes to the desk, and takes out the pills. They watch him.*)

MRS. BRAMSON (*off*). Danny!

DAN. Oh, yes, here they are.

HUBERT (*to say something*). Is she feeling off color again?

DAN (*on his way to the front door*). Off color? She's never been on it, man! To hear her go on you'd think the only thing left is artificial respiration, *and* chocolates. (*Laughing, and calling.*) Coming! (*He goes, shutting the front door behind him.*)

HUBERT. No, really you have to laugh!

OLIVIA. But what you've just seen —that's exactly what I mean! It's acting! He's not being himself for a minute—it's all put on for our benefit, don't you see?

HUBERT (*banteringly*). D'you know, I think you're in love with him.

OLIVIA (*with rather more impatience than is necessary*). Don't be ridiculous.

HUBERT. I was only joking.

OLIVIA. He's common and insolent, and I dislike him intently.

(MRS. TERENCE *comes in from the kitchen.*)

MRS. TERENCE. What'll you 'ave for tea, scones or crumpets? Can't make both.

OLIVIA. What d'*you* think of Dan?

MRS. TERENCE. Dan? Oh, 'e's all right. Bit of a mystery.

HUBERT. Oh.

MRS. TERENCE (*shutting the kitchen door and coming into the middle of the room*). Terrible liar, o' course. But then a lot of us are. Told me he used to 'unt to 'ounds and 'ave 'is own pack. Before 'e went up in the world and went as a page boy, I suppose.

OLIVIA (*to* HUBERT). You see? He wouldn't try that on with us, but couldn't resist it with her.

HUBERT. I wonder how soon the old girl'll get his number? Oh, but fair play, we're talking about the chap as if he were the most terrible——

MRS. TERENCE. Why, what's 'e done?

HUBERT. Exactly.

OLIVIA. I don't know, but I feel so strongly . . . Is Dora there? . . . (*Calling cautiously.*) Dora!

MRS. TERENCE. Oh, she won't know anything. She's as 'alf-witted as she's lazy, and that's sayin' a lot. She'd cut 'er nose off to stop the dustbin smelling sooner than empty it, she would.

(DORA *comes in from the kitchen, wiping her hands on her apron.*)

DORA. Did somebody say Dora?

OLIVIA. Has Dan said any more about marrying you?

DORA. No. *She* 'asn't brought it up again, either.

OLIVIA. Does he talk to you at all?

DORA (*perplexed*). Oh, only how-do-you-do and beg-your-pardon. I've never really spent any time in 'is company, you see. Except o' course ——

HUBERT. Quite. What's your idea of him?

DORA. Oh. . . . (*Moving to the center of the room.*) 'E's all right. Takes 'is fun where 'e finds it. And leaves it. . . . Cracks 'imself up, you know. Pretends 'e doesn't care a twopenny, but always got 'is eye on what you're thinking of 'im—if you know what I mean.

OLIVIA. Yes, I do. That incredible vanity. They always have it. Always.

HUBERT. Who?

(*A pause.*)

OLIVIA. Murderers.

(*A pause. They stare at her.*)

HUBERT. Good God! . . .

MRS. TERENCE. D'you mean . . . this woman they're looking for?

OLIVIA. I'm sure of it.

MRS. TERENCE. But 'e's such a—such a ordinary boy——

OLIVIA. That's just it—and then he's suddenly so—extraordinary. I've felt it ever since I heard him sing that song—I told you——

HUBERT. That "mighty-lak-a-rose" thing, you mean? Oh, but it's a pretty well-known one——

OLIVIA. It's more than that. I've kept on saying to myself: No, murder's a thing we read about in the papers; it isn't real life; it can't touch us. . . . But it can. And it's here. All round us. In the forest—in this house. We're—living with it. (*After a pause, rising decisively.*) Bring his luggage in here, will you, Mrs. Terence?

MRS. TERENCE (*staggered*). 'Is luggage? (*Recovering, to* DORA.) Give me a 'and.

(*Wide-eyed, she goes into the kitchen, followed by* DORA.)

HUBERT. I say, this is a bit thick, you know—spying——

OLIVIA (*urgently*). We may never have the house to ourselves again.

(*She runs to each window and looks out across the forest.* MRS. TERENCE *returns carrying luggage: one large and one small suitcase.* DORA *follows, lugging an old-fashioned thick leather hatbox.* MRS. TERENCE *places the suitcases on the table;* DORA *plants the hatbox in the middle of the floor.*)

MRS. TERENCE (*in a conspiratorial tone*). This is all.

HUBERT. But look here, we can't do this——

(OLIVIA *snaps open the lid of the larger suitcase with a jerk. A pause. They look, almost afraid.* DORA *moves to the back of the table.*)

MRS. TERENCE (*as* OLIVIA *lifts it gingerly*). A dirty shirt.

HUBERT. That's all right.

OLIVIA. A clean pair of socks, packet of razor blades.

HUBERT. We shouldn't be doing this—I feel as if I were at school again——

MRS. TERENCE. Singlet . . .

OLIVIA. Half ticket to Shepperley Palais de Danse . . .

MRS. TERENCE. Oh, it's a proper 'aunt!

DORA. Oh, 'ere's a pocketbook. With a letter. (*She gives the letter to* MRS. TERENCE *and the pocketbook to* OLIVIA.)

HUBERT. Look here, this is going a bit too far—you can't do this to a chap——

MRS. TERENCE (*taking the letter from the envelope*). Don't be silly, dear, your wife'll do it to you 'undreds of times. . . . (*Sniffing the note paper.*) Pooh. (*Reading, as they crane over her shoulder.*) "Dear Baby-Face, my own . . ." Signed Lil. . . .

OLIVIA. What awful writing.

MRS. TERENCE (*reading, heavily*). ". . . Next time you strike Newcastle, O.K. by me, baby. . . ." Ooh!

HUBERT. Just another servant girl. . . . Sorry, Dora. . . .

DORA (*lugubriously*). O.K.

OLIVIA (*rummaging in the pocketbook*). Bus ticket to Thorburton, some snaps . . .

MRS. TERENCE. Look at her *bust!*

OLIVIA. Here's a group. . . . Look, Hubert. . . .

(HUBERT *joins her in front of the table.*)

HUBERT. This wench is rather fetching.

MRS. TERENCE (*crowding between them*). Look at 'er! . . . The impudence, 'er being taken in a bathing suit!

DORA. He's not in this one, is 'e?

HUBERT (*impressed*). Oh, I say, there *she* is!

MRS. TERENCE } Who?
DORA

HUBERT. The missing female! In front of the tall man. . . . You remember the photograph of her in the *Mirror?*

DORA. It's awful to think she may be dead. Awful!

MRS. TERENCE. Looks ever so sexy, doesn't she?

DORA. 'Ere's one of a little boy——

OLIVIA. How extraordinary!

HUBERT. What?

OLIVIA. It's himself.

DORA. The little Eton collar. Oh, dear, ever so sweet, isn't it?

MRS. TERENCE. Now that's what I call a real innocent face. . . .

HUBERT (*going to the center of the room*). Well, that's that. . . .

OLIVIA. Wait a minute, wasn't there another one? (*Seeing the hatbox.*) Oh, yes. . . .

HUBERT (*lifting it on to a chair*). Oh, this; yes. . . .

DORA. Old-fashioned, isn't it?

MRS. TERENCE. I should think he got it from a box room at the Tall-boys——

OLIVIA (*puzzled*). But it looks so extraordinary—— (*She gives a sudden gasp.*)

(*They look at her. She is staring at the box. A pause.*)

HUBERT. What is it?

OLIVIA. I don't know. . . . Suppose there is something inside it?

(*A pause. They stare at her, fascinated by her thought. The front door bangs. They are electrified into action, but it is too late. It is DAN. He goes briskly to the table.*)

DAN. She wants to sit in the sun now and have a bit of *East Lynne*. Talk about changin' your mind—— (*He sees the suitcases on the table before him, and is motionless and silent. A pause. The others dare not move. He finally breaks the situation, takes up "East Lynne" from the table, and walks slowly back to the front door. He stops, looks round at HUBERT, smiles, and comes down to him. His manner is normal—too normal.*) Could I have it back, please? It's the only one I got.

HUBERT. Oh, yes, of course. . . . (*Handing him the pocketbook.*)

DAN (*taking it*). Thank you very much.

HUBERT. Not at all. I—— (*To OLIVIA.*) Here, you deal with this. It's beyond me.

DAN (*to him*). Did you see the picture of me when I was a little fellow?

HUBERT. Yes. . . . Very jolly.

DAN (*turning to MRS. TERENCE*). Did *you*? It was in the inside of my wallet.

MRS. TERENCE. Oh, was it?

DAN. Yes. Where I should be keeping my money, only any bit of money I have I always keep *on* me. (*Turning to HUBERT.*) Safer, don't you think?

HUBERT (*smiling weakly*). Ye-es.

DAN. I only keep one ten-bob note. in this wallet, for emergencies. (*Looking.*) That's funny. It's gone. (*He looks at HUBERT. The others look blankly at one another.*) I expect I dropped it somewhere. . . . What did you think of the letter?

HUBERT. Letter?

DAN. You got it your hand.

HUBERT. Well, I didn't—er——

DAN. Means well, does Lil; but we had a row. (*Taking back the letter.*) She would spy on me. And if there's anythin' I hate, it's spyin'. Don't you agree?

HUBERT. Ye-es.

DAN. I'd sooner have anythin' than a spy. (*To MRS. TERENCE.*) Bar a murderer, o' course. (*A pause. He is arranging his property in his wallet.*)

HUBERT (*incredulous*). What—what did you say?

DAN (*turning to him, casually*). Bar a murderer, o' course.

(OLIVIA *steps forward.* MRS. TERENCE *steps back from the chair on which the hatbox has been placed.*)

OLIVIA (*incisively*). Talking of murder, do you know anything about Mrs. Chalfont's whereabouts at the moment?

(DAN *turns to her, and for the first time sees the hatbox. He stands motionless. A pause.*)

DAN. Mrs. Who?

OLIVIA. You can't pretend you've never heard of her.

DAN (*turning to* HUBERT, *recovering himself*). Oh, Mrs. Chalfont's whereabouts! I thought she said her name was Mrs. Chalfontswear. (*Profusely.*) Silly. Swear—about— couldn't think——

OLIVIA. Well?

DAN (*still looking at* HUBERT, *brightly, after a pause*). I've nothin' to go on, but I think she's been murdered.

HUBERT. Oh, you do?

DAN. Yes, I do.

MRS. TERENCE. Who by?

DAN. They say she had several chaps on a string, and—— (*Suddenly.*) There was one fellow, a London chap, a bachelor, very citified—with a fair must—— (*He stares at* HUBERT.)

HUBERT (*touching his mustache unconsciously*). What are you looking at me for?

DAN. Well, you wasn't round these parts the day she bunked, was you?

HUBERT. Yes, I was, as a matter of fact.

DAN (*significantly*). Oh.

MRS. BRAMSON'S VOICE (*calling in the garden*). Danny!

HUBERT (*flustered*). What in God's name are you getting at?

(DAN *smiles and shrugs his shoulders regretfully at him, and goes out through the front door.* OLIVIA *sits at the table.*)

MRS. TERENCE (*to* HUBERT, *perplexed*). Are you sure you didn't do it, sir?

HUBERT. I'm going out for a breath of air.

(*He takes his hat and stick as he goes through the hall, and goes out through the front door.*)

MRS. TERENCE (*to* OLIVIA). You don't still think——

OLIVIA. I won't say any more. I know how silly it sounds.

(DORA *runs into the kitchen, sniveling.*)

MRS. TERENCE (*to* OLIVIA). The way you worked us all up! Doesn't it all go to show——

(She hears DAN *return, and looks round apprehensively. He goes to the table slowly and looks at the two suitcases.)*

DAN *(smiling, to* MRS. TERENCE*).* Would you mind please givin' me a hand with the tidyin' up? . . . *(Taking up the suitcases.)* And carryin' the other one? . . . *(Going into the kitchen, followed by* MRS. TERENCE *carrying the hatbox.)* Looks as if we're goin' on our holidays, doesn't it?

*(*OLIVIA *is alone for a moment. She stares before her, perplexed.* DAN *returns. She looks away. He looks at her, his eyes narrowed. A pause. Studying her, he takes from a pocket of his jacket a formidable-looking clasp knife, unclasps it, and tests the blade casually with his fingers. He glances at the mantelpiece, crosses to it, takes down a stick, and begins to sharpen the end of it.* OLIVIA *watches him. A pause.)*

OLIVIA. Did you do it?

(He whittles at the stick.)

DAN. You wouldn't be bad-lookin' without them glasses.

OLIVIA. It doesn't interest me very much what I look like.

DAN. Don't you believe it. . . . *(Surveying the shavings in the hearth.)* Tch! . . . Clumsy. . . . *(Looking round, and seeing a newspaper lying on the table.)* Ah. . . . *(He crosses to the table. Smiling, with the suspicion of a mock bow.)* Excuse me. *(He unfolds the newspaper on the table and begins to whittle the stick over it.)*

OLIVIA. You're very conceited, aren't you?

DAN *(reassuringly).* Yes.

OLIVIA. And you *are* acting all the time, aren't you?

DAN *(staring at her, as if astonished).* Actin'? Actin' what? *(Leaning over the table, on both arms.)* Look at the way I can look you in the eyes. I'll stare you out.

OLIVIA *(staring into his eyes).* I have a theory it's the criminals who *can* look you in the eyes, and the honest people who blush and look away.

DAN *(smiling).* Oh. . . .

OLIVIA *(after a pause, challenging).* It's a very blank look, though, isn't it?

DAN *(smiling).* Is it?

OLIVIA. You *are* acting, aren't you?

DAN *(after a pause, in a whisper, almost joyfully).* Yes!

OLIVIA *(fascinated).* And what are you like when you stop acting?

DAN. I dunno, it's so long since I stopped.

OLIVIA. But when you're alone?

DAN. Then I act more than ever I do.

OLIVIA. Why?

DAN. I dunno; 'cause I like it. *(Breaking the scene, pulling a chair round to the table.)* Now what d'ye say if *I* ask a question or two for a change? *(Sitting in the chair, facing her.)* Just for a change. . . . Why can't you take a bit of an interest in some other body but me?

OLIVIA (*taken aback*). I'm not interested in you. Only you don't talk. That's bound to make people wonder.

DAN. I can talk a lot sometimes. A drop o' drink makes a power o' difference to me. (*Chuckling.*) You'd be surprised. Ah. . . . (*He returns to his work.*)

OLIVIA. I wonder if I would.

DAN. I know you would.

OLIVIA. I think I can diagnose you all right.

DAN. Carry on.

OLIVIA. You haven't any feelings at all. (*He looks slowly up at her. She has struck home.*) But you live in a world of your own—a world of your own imagination.

DAN. I don't understand so very well, not bein' so very liter-er-airy.

OLIVIA. You follow me perfectly well.

(*He shrugs his shoulders, laughs, and goes on whittling.*)

DAN. D'you still think there's been a bit o' dirty work?

OLIVIA. I don't know what to think now. I suppose not.

DAN (*intent on his work, his back to the audience*). Disappointed?

OLIVIA. What on earth do you mean?

DAN. Disappointed?

OLIVIA (*laughing, in spite of herself*). Yes, I suppose I am.

DAN. Why?

OLIVIA (*the tension at last relaxed*). Oh, I don't know. . . . Because nothing much has ever happened to me, and it's a dull day, and it's the depths of the country. . . . I don't know. . . .

(*A piercing scream from the bottom of the garden. A pause.*)

MRS. BRAMSON (*shrieking from the other side of the house*). Danny! . . . Danny!

(*The clatter of footsteps in the garden.* DORA *runs in from the hall, breathless and terrified.*)

DORA. They're diggin' . . . in the rubbish pit.

OLIVIA. Well?

DORA. There's something sticking out.

OLIVIA. What?

DORA. A hand—somebody's hand! Oh, Miss Grayne—somebody's hand. . . .

(*She runs whimpering into the kitchen, as* OLIVIA *rises and runs to the left window and looks out.*)

MRS. BRAMSON'S VOICE (*calling off*). Danny!

(*DAN rises slowly, his back to the audience.* OLIVIA *turns and suddenly sees him. Horror grows in her face. The blare of music. The lights dim out.*)

SCENE II

The music plays in darkness for a few bars, then the curtain rises again. The music fades away.

Late afternoon, two days later. OLIVIA *is seated above the table snipping long cuttings from newspapers and pasting them into a ledger. A knock at the front door. She starts nervously. Another knock.* MRS. TERENCE *comes in from the kitchen carrying a smoothing iron.*

MRS. TERENCE. If it's them police again, I'll bash their helmets in with this. If it lands me three months, I will.

OLIVIA. They're from Scotland Yard, and they don't wear helmets.

MRS. TERENCE. Then they're going to get 'urt. (*Going into the hall.*) I can tell by their looks what they think. And they better not think it, neither.

OLIVIA. And what do they think?

MRS. TERENCE (*over her shoulder*). They think it's me. I *know* they think it's me.

(*She goes into the hall and opens the front door.*)

HUBERT (*outside*). Good afternoon, Mrs. Terence.

MRS. TERENCE. Oh, come in, sir. (*Coming back into the room.*) It's a civilian for a change.

(*She is followed by* HUBERT.)

HUBERT (*to* OLIVIA). I say, this is all getting pretty terrible, isn't it?

OLIVIA. Yes, terrible.

MRS. TERENCE. Oh, terrible, terrible. There's one word for it; it's terrible. Forty-eight hours since they found 'er. They'll never get 'im now.

HUBERT. Terrible. . . .

MRS. TERENCE. There was another charabanc load just after two o'clock. All standin' round the rubbish 'eap eatin' sandwiches. Sensation, that's what it is.

OLIVIA. Would you like some food, Hubert?

HUBERT. Well, I——

MRS. TERENCE. They're still looking for the 'ead.

HUBERT (*to* OLIVIA, *with a slight grimace*). No, thanks. I had lunch.

MRS. TERENCE. Mangled, she was, mangled. . . . Did you see your name in the *Express*, sir?

HUBERT. I—er—did catch a glimpse of it, yes.

MRS. TERENCE. Little did you think, sir, when you was digging that pit for my rubbish, eh? 'E may 'ave been *watchin'* you digging it. Ooh! I have to sit in my kitchen and think about it.

HUBERT. Then why don't you leave?

MRS. TERENCE (*indignantly*). How can I leave, with the whole village waitin' on me to tell 'em the latest? (*Going toward the kitchen.*) I 'eard 'er 'ead must have been off at one stroke. One stroke.

HUBERT. Really.

MRS. TERENCE (*turning at the door*). She wasn't interfered with, though.

(*She goes into the kitchen.*)

HUBERT. How they all love it. How's the old lady bearing up in the old invalid chair, eh?

OLIVIA. She's bursting out of it with health. And loving it more than anybody. This is my latest job—a press-cutting book. There was a picture of her in the *Chronicle* yesterday; she bought twenty-six copies.

HUBERT (*taking his pipe out*). She'll get to believe she did it herself in the end. . . . Is she in?

OLIVIA. She's gone over to Breakerly to interview a local paper.

HUBERT. The lad pushing the go-cart? . . . He's the devoted son all right, isn't he?

OLIVIA (*after a pause*). I don't talk to him much.

HUBERT. Nice fellow. I've thought a lot about that prying into his things —pretty bad show, really, you know. (*Going to the left window.*) I wonder if they'll ever nab him?

OLIVIA (*with a start*). What do you mean?

HUBERT. The fellow who did it. . . . Wonder what he's doing now.

OLIVIA. I wonder.

HUBERT. Damn clever job, you know, quietly. . . . That was a rum touch, finding that broken lipstick in the rubbish heap. . . . You know, the fact they still have no idea where this woman's head is——

OLIVIA (*convulsively*). Don't. . . .

HUBERT. Sorry.

OLIVIA (*after a pause*). It's a bit of a strain.

HUBERT (*earnestly*). Then why don't you leave?

OLIVIA. I—I couldn't afford it.

HUBERT. But you *could,* if you married me! Now, look here—— (*Going to her.*) You said you'd tell me to-day. So here I am—er—popping the question again. There's nothing much to add, except to go over the old ground again, and say that I'm not what you'd call a terribly brainy chap, but I am straight.

OLIVIA. Yes, I know.

HUBERT. Though, again, I'm not the sort that gets into corners with a pipe and never opens his mouth from one blessed year's end to the other. I can talk.

OLIVIA. Yes, you can.

HUBERT. An all-round chap, really— that's me.

OLIVIA. Yes.

HUBERT. Well?

OLIVIA. I'm sorry, Hubert, but I can't.

HUBERT. 'You can't? But you told me that day we might make a go of it, or words to that effect.

OLIVIA. I've thought it over since then, and I'm afraid I can't.

(*A pause.*)

HUBERT. What's changed you?

OLIVIA. Nothing's changed me, Hubert. I've just thought the matter over, that's all.

(*A pause. He crosses toward the fireplace.*)

HUBERT. Is it another man?

OLIVIA (*startled*). Don't be silly. (*Collecting herself.*) What man could I possibly meet, cooped up here?

HUBERT. Sorry. Can't be helped. Sorry.

DAN (*in the garden*). There we are. Nice outing, eh?

OLIVIA. So am I.

(*The front door opens and* DAN *wheels in* MRS. BRAMSON. *He is as serene as ever, but more animated than before. He is dressed the same as in the previous scene, and is smoking his usual cigarette.* HUBERT *sits at the table.*)

DAN (*hanging up her rug in the hall*). Back home again. I put your gloves away——

MRS. BRAMSON (*as he wheels her in*). I feel dead. (*To* HUBERT.) Oh, it's you. . . . I feel dead.

DAN (*sitting beside her on the sofa, full of high spirits*). Don't you be a silly old 'oman, you look as pretty as a picture—strawberries and cream in your face, and not a day over forty; and when I've made you a nice cup of tea you'll be twenty-five in the sun and eighteen with your back to the light, so you think yourself lucky!

MRS. BRAMSON (*as he digs her in the side*). Oh, Danny, you are a terror! (*To the others.*) He's been at me like this all the way. I must say it keeps me alive.

DAN (*as she hands him her hat and cape*). But you feel dead. I get you.

MRS. BRAMSON (*kittenish*). Oh, you caution! You'll be the death of me!

DAN (*wagging his finger at her*). Ah-ha! (*Hanging up her things in the hall.*) Now what'd you like a drop of in your tea—gin, whisky, liqueur, brandy, or a nice dollop of sailor's rum, eh?

MRS. BRAMSON. Just listen to him! Now don't make me laugh, dear, because there's always my heart.

DAN (*sitting beside her again*). You've lost your heart, you know you have, to the little feller that pushes your pram—you know you have!

MRS. BRAMSON (*laughing shrilly*). Pram! Well! (*Her laugh cut short.*)

It's wicked to laugh, with this—this thing all round us.

DAN (*sobering portentously*). I forgot. (*As she shivers.*) Not in a draft, are you? (*Shutting the front door and coming down to* HUBERT.) D'you remember, Mr. Laurie, me pulling your leg about you havin' done it? Funniest thing out! . . . Talk about laugh!

MRS. BRAMSON (*fondly*). Tttt! . . .

DAN (*a glint of mischief in his eyes*). I think I better get the tea before I get into hot water.

(*He goes toward the kitchen.*)

OLIVIA. Mrs. Terence is getting the tea.

DAN (*at the door*). She don't make tea like me. I'm an old sailor, Miss Grayne. Don't you forget that.

(*He goes into the kitchen.*)

OLIVIA. I'm not interested, I'm afraid.

MRS. BRAMSON (*wheeling herself to the front of the table*). Look here, Olivia, you're downright rude to that boy, and if there's one thing that never gets a woman anywhere, it's rudeness. What have you got against him?

HUBERT. Surely he's got more to say for himself today than when I met him before?

MRS. BRAMSON. Oh, he's been in rare spirits all day.

HUBERT. Johnny Walker, judging by the whiff of breath I got just now.

MRS. BRAMSON. Meaning whisky?

HUBERT. Yes.

OLIVIA. I've never heard you make a joke before, Hubert.

HUBERT. Didn't realize it was one till I'd said it. Sorry.

MRS. BRAMSON. It's not a joke; it's a libel. (*A knock at the front door.*) Come in. (NURSE LIBBY *enters from the front door.*) The boy's a teetotaler.

HUBERT. Sorry; my mistake.

NURSE. Good afternoon. Shall I wait for you in your bedroom?

MRS. BRAMSON. Yes. I feel absolutely dead.

NURSE (*turning at the bedroom, eagerly*). Anything new re the murder?

HUBERT. I believe her head was cut off at one stroke.

NURSE (*brightly*). Oh, poor thing.

(*She goes into the bedroom.* DAN *returns from the kitchen, carrying a tray of tea and cakes.*)

DAN. There you are, fresh as a daisy. Three lumps, as per usual, and some of the cakes you like——

MRS. BRAMSON (*as he pours out her tea*). Thank you, dear. Let me smell your breath. (*After smelling it.*) Clean as a whistle. Smells of peppermints.

OLIVIA. Yes. There were some in the kitchen.

HUBERT. Oh.

MRS. BRAMSON (*to* HUBERT, *as* DAN *pours out two more cups*). So you won't stay to tea, Mr.—er——

HUBERT. Er—(*rising*)—no, thank you. . . . (DAN *sits in* HUBERT'S *chair*.) I think I'll get off before it's dark. Good-by, Mrs. Bramson. Good-by, Mr.—er——

DAN (*grinning and saluting*). Dan. Just Dan. (*He opens the press-cutting ledger.*)

HUBERT (*to* OLIVIA). Good-by.

OLIVIA (*rises*). Good-by, Hubert. I'm sorry.

(DAN *raises his cup as if drinking a toast to* MRS. BRAMSON. *She follows suit.*)

HUBERT. Can't be helped. It'll get dark early today, I think. Funny how the evenings draw in this time of year. Good night.

DAN. Good night.

HUBERT (*to* OLIVIA). Good-by.

OLIVIA. Good-by. (*She goes to the right window seat.*)

MRS. BRAMSON. Johnny Walker, indeed! Impertinence!

DAN (*drinking tea and scanning press cuttings*). Johnny Walker?

MRS. BRAMSON. Never you mind, dear. Any more of those terrible people called? Reporters? Police?

DAN (*gaily*). There's a defi-nite fallin' off in attendance today. Sunday, I expect,

MRS. BRAMSON. Hush, don't talk like that, dear.

DAN. Sorry, mum.

MRS. BRAMSON. And don't call me "mum"!

DAN. Well, if I can't call you Mrs. Bramson, what can I call you?

MRS. BRAMSON. If you were very good, I might let you call me—mother!

DAN (*mischievously, his hand to his forehead*). O.K., Mother.

MRS. BRAMSON (*joining in his laughter*). Oh, you are in a mood today! (*Suddenly, imperiously.*) I want to be read to now.

DAN (*crossing to the desk, in mock resignation*). Your servant, Mother o' mine. . . . What'll you have? *The Channings? The Red Court Farm?*

MRS. BRAMSON. I'm tired of them.

DAN. Well . . . oh! (*Taking a large Bible from the top of the desk.*) What about the Bible?

MRS. BRAMSON. The Bible?

DAN. It's Sunday, you know. I was brought up on it!

MRS. BRAMSON. So was I . . . *East Lynne's* nice, though.

DAN. Not as nice as the Bible.

MRS. BRAMSON (*doubtfully*). All right, dear; makes a nice change. . . . Not that I don't often dip into it.

DAN. I'm sure you do. (*Blowing the dust off the book.*) Now where'll I read?

MRS. BRAMSON (*unenthusiastic*). At random's nice, don't you think, dear?

DAN. At random . . . Yes. . . .

MRS. BRAMSON. The Old Testament.

DAN (*turning over leaves thoughtfully*). At random in the Old Testament's a bit risky, don't you think so?

(MRS. TERENCE *comes in from the kitchen.*)

MRS. TERENCE (*to* MRS. BRAMSON). The paper boy's at the back door and says you're in the *News of the World* again.

MRS. BRAMSON (*interested*). Oh! . . . (*Simulating   indifference.*) That horrible boy again, when the one thing I want is to blot the whole thing out of my mind.

MRS. TERENCE. 'Ow many copies d'you want?

MRS. BRAMSON. Get three.

MRS. TERENCE. *And* 'e says there's a placard in Shepperley with your name on it.

MRS. BRAMSON. What does it say?

MRS. TERENCE. "Mrs. Bramson Talks."

(*She goes back toward the kitchen.*)

MRS. BRAMSON. Oh. (*As* MRS. TERENCE *reaches the kitchen door.*) Go at once into Shepperley and order some. At once!

MRS. TERENCE. Can't be done.

MRS. BRAMSON. Can't be done? What d'you mean, can't be done? It's a scandal. What are you paid for?

MRS. TERENCE (*coming back, furious*). I'm not paid! And 'aven't been for two weeks! And I'm not coming tomorrow unless I am! Put that in your copybook and blot it.

(*She goes back into the kitchen, banging the door.*)

MRS. BRAMSON. Isn't paid? Is she mad? (*To* OLIVIA.) Are you mad? Why don't you pay her?

OLIVIA (*coming down*). Because you don't give me the money to do it with.

MRS. BRAMSON. I—(*fumbling at her bodice*)—wheel me over to that cupboard.

(OLIVIA *is about to do so, when she catches* DAN's *eye.*)

OLIVIA (*to* DAN, *pointedly*). Perhaps *you'd* go into the kitchen and get the paper from Mrs. Terence?

DAN (*after a second's pause, with a laugh*). Of course I will, madam! Anythin' you say! Anythin' you say!

(*He careers into the kitchen, still carrying the Bible.* MRS. BRAMSON *has fished up two keys on the end of a long black tape.* OLIVIA *wheels her over to the cupboard above the fireplace.*)

OLIVIA. If you give me the key, I'll get it for you.

MRS. BRAMSON. No fear! (*She unlocks the cupboard; it turns out to be a small but very substantial safe. Unlocking the safe, muttering to herself.*) Won't go into Shepperley, indeed . . . never heard of such impertinence. . . . (*She takes out a cashbox from among some deeds, unlocks it with the smaller key, and takes out a mass of five-pound and pound notes.*) The way these servants—— What are you staring at?

OLIVIA. Isn't it rather a lot of money to have in the house?

MRS. BRAMSON. "Put not your trust in banks" is my motto, and always will be.

OLIVIA. But that's hundreds of pounds! It——

MRS. BRAMSON (*handing her two notes*). D'you wonder I wouldn't let you have the key?

OLIVIA. Has anybody else asked you for it?

MRS. BRAMSON (*locking the cashbox and putting it back in the safe*). I wouldn't let a soul touch it. Not a soul. Not even Danny. (*She snaps the safe, locks it, and slips the keys back into her bosom.*)

OLIVIA. Has *he* asked you for it?

MRS. BRAMSON. It's enough to have those policemen prying, you forward girl, without——

OLIVIA (*urgently*). Please! Has he?

MRS. BRAMSON. Well, he did offer to fetch some money yesterday for

the dairy. But I wouldn't give him the key! Oh, no!

OLIVIA. Why?

MRS. BRAMSON. Do I want to see him waylaid and attacked, and my key stolen? Oh, no, I told him, that key stays on me——

OLIVIA. Did he—know how much money there is in there?

MRS. BRAMSON. I told him! Do you wonder I stick to the key? I said—what *is* the matter with you, all these questions?

OLIVIA. Oh, it's no use——

(*She goes to the armchair below the fireplace and sits in it.* DAN *returns from the kitchen, with a copy of the "News of the World," the Bible tucked under his arm, a cigarette stub between his lips.*)

DAN. He says they're sellin' like hot cakes! (*Handing the paper to* MRS. BRAMSON.) There you are, I've found the place for you—whole page, headlines an' all.

MRS. BRAMSON. Oh, yes.

(DAN *stands with one knee on the sofa, and turns over the pages of his Bible.*)

(*Reading breathlessly, her back to the fireplace.*) ". . . The Victim's Past" . . . with another picture of me underneath! (*Looking closer, dashed.*) Oh, taken at Tunbridge the year before the war; really it isn't right. (*To* OLIVIA, *savoring it.*) "The Bungalow of Death! . . . Gruesome finds. . . . Fiendish mur-

derer still at large. . . . The
enigma of the missing head . . .
where is it buried?" . . . Oh, yes!
(*She goes on reading silently to herself.*)

DAN (*suddenly, in a clear voice*).
". . . Blessed is the man . . . that
walketh not in the counsel of the
ungodly . . . nor standeth in the
way of sinners . . . nor sitteth in
the seat of the scornful. . . ."

MRS. BRAMSON (*impatiently*). Oh,
the print's too small.

DAN (*firmly*). Shall I read it to you?

MRS. BRAMSON. Yes, dear, do. . . .

(*He shuts the Bible with a bang,
throws it on the sofa, and takes the
paper from her.* OLIVIA *watches him
intently; he smiles at her slowly and
brazenly as he shakes out the paper.*)

DAN (*reading laboriously*). ". . .
The murderer committed the crime
in the forest most—in the forest,
most likely strippin' beforehand——"
(DORA *comes in from the kitchen,
and stands at the door, arrested by
his reading. She is dressed in Sunday best. Reading.*) ". . . and
cleansin' himself afterwards in the
forest lake——"

MRS. BRAMSON. Tch! tch!

DAN (*reading*). ". . . He buried the
body shallow in the open pit, cun-
nin'ly chancin' it bein' filled, which
it was next day, the eleventh——"
(*Nodding at* OLIVIA.) That was the
day 'fore I come here.

MRS. BRAMSON. So it was.

DAN (*reading*). "The body was
nude. Attempts had been made to—
turn to foot of next column." (*Doing so.*)—"Attempts had been made
to era—eradicate fingerprints with a
knife. . . ." (*Far away, the tolling
of village bells. Reading.*) ". . .
The head was severed by a skilled
person, possibly a butcher. The
murderer——" (*He stops suddenly,
raises his head, smiles, takes the cigarette stub, puts it behind his ear,
and listens.*)

OLIVIA. What's the matter?

MRS. BRAMSON. Can you hear something? Oh, I'm scared.

DAN. I forgot it was Sunday. . . .
They're goin' to church in the vil-
lages. All got up in their Sunday
best, with prayer books, and the
organ playin', and the windows
shinin'. Shinin' on holy things, because holy things isn't afraid of the
daylight.

MRS. BRAMSON. But, Danny, what
on earth are you——

DAN (*quelling her*). But all the time
the daylight's movin' over the floor,
and by the end of the sermon the
air in the church is turnin' gray.
And people isn't able to think of
holy things so much no more, only
of the terrible things that's goin' on
outside, that everybody's readin'
about in the papers! (*Looking at*
OLIVIA.) Because they know that
though it's still daylight, and everythin's or'nary and quiet, today will
be the same as all the other days,
and come to an end, and it'll be
night. . . . (*After a pause, coming
to earth again with a laugh at the
others, throwing the newspaper on
the sofa.*) I forgot it was Sunday!

MRS. BRAMSON (*overawed*). Good gracious, what's come over you, Danny?

DAN (*with exaggerated animation*). Oh, I speechify like anything when I'm roused! I used to go to Sunday school, see, and the thoughts sort of come into my head. Like as if I was readin' off a book! (*Slapping his Bible.*)

MRS. BRAMSON. Dear, dear. . . . You should have been a preacher. You should!

(DAN *laughs loudly and opens the Bible.*)

DORA (*going to the table and collecting the tea tray*). I never knew 'e 'ad so many words in 'is 'ead.

MRS. BRAMSON (*suddenly*). I want to lie down now, and be examined.

DAN (*rising*). Anything you say, Mother o' mine. Will you have your medicine in your room as well, eh?

MRS. BRAMSON. Yes, dear. . . . Olivia, you *never* got a new bottle yesterday!

DAN (*as he wheels her into her bedroom*). I got it today while you were with the chap. . . . Popped in at the chemist's.

MRS. BRAMSON. Oh, thank you, dear. The one by the mortuary? . . . Oh, my back. . . . Nurse! . . .

(*Her voice is lost in the bedroom. The daylight begins to fade. The church bells die away.*)

DORA. My sister says all this is wearin' me to a shadow.

OLIVIA. It is trying, isn't it?

DORA. You look that worried, too, Miss Grayne.

OLIVIA. Do I?

DORA. As if you was waiting for something to 'appen.

OLIVIA. Oh?

DORA. Like an explosion. A bomb, or something.

OLIVIA (*smiling*). I don't think that's very likely. . . . (*Lowering her voice.*) Have you talked to Dan at all this week?

DORA. Never get the chance. 'E's too busy dancin' attendance on Madame Crocodile. . . . (DAN *comes back from the bedroom, his cigarette stub between his lips. Going toward the kitchen.*) I'm off. You don't catch me 'ere after dark.

DAN. Why, will ye be late for courting?

DORA. If I was, they'd wait for me. Good afternoon, Miss Grayne. Good afternoon . . . sir.

DAN (*winking at* OLIVIA). Are you sure they'd wait?

DORA. You ought to know.

(*She goes into the kitchen.* DAN *and* OLIVIA *are alone.* DAN *crosses to the sofa with a laugh, humming gaily.*)

DAN. "Their home addresses . . . and their caresses . . ."

(*He sits on the end of the sofa.*)

OLIVIA. You've been drinking, haven't you?

DAN (*after a pause, quizzically*). You don't miss much, do you?

OLIVIA (*significantly*). No.

DAN (*rubbing his hands*). I've been drinking, and I feel fine! . . . (*Brandishing the Bible.*) You wouldn't like another dose of reading?

OLIVIA. I prefer talking.

DAN (*putting down the Bible*). Carry on.

OLIVIA. Asking questions.

DAN (*catching her eye*). Carry on! (*He studies his outspread hands.*)

OLIVIA (*crisply*). Are you sure you were ever a sailor? Are you sure you weren't a butcher?

(*A pause. He looks at her, slowly, then breaks the look abruptly.*)

DAN (*rising with a smile and standing against the mantelpiece*). Aw, talkin's daft! *Doin's* the thing!

OLIVIA. You can talk too.

DAN. Aw, yes! D'you hear me just now? She's right, you know, I should ha' been a preacher. I remember, when I was a kid, sittin' in Sunday school—catching my mother's eye where she was sitting by the door, with the sea behind her; and she pointed to the pulpit, and then to me, as if to say, that's the place for you. . . . (*Far away, pensive.*) I never forgot that.

(*A pause.*)

OLIVIA. I don't believe a word of it.

DAN. Neither do I, but it sounds wonderful. (*Leaning over her, confidentially.*) I never saw my mam, and I never had a dad, and the first thing I remember is—Cardiff Docks. And you're the first 'oman I ever told that, so you can compliment yourself. Or the drink. (*Laughing.*) I think it's the drink.

OLIVIA. You *do* live in your imagination, don't you?

DAN (*reassuringly*). Yes. It's the only way to bear with the awful things you have to do.

OLIVIA. What awful things?

DAN. Well—— (*Grinning like a child and going back to the sofa.*) Ah-ha! I haven't had as much to drink as all that! (*Sitting on the sofa.*) Ah-ha! . . .

OLIVIA. You haven't a very high opinion of women, have you?

(*DAN makes a gesture with his hands, pointing the thumbs downward with a decisive movement.*)

DAN. Women don't have to be drunk to talk. You don't talk that much, though; fair play. (*Looking her up and down, insolently.*) You're a dark horse, you are. (*A pause. She rises abruptly and stands at the fireplace, her back to him. She takes off her spectacles.*) Ye know, this isn't the life for you. What is there to it? Tell me that!

OLIVIA (*somberly*). What is there to it?

DAN. Yes.

OLIVIA. Getting up at seven, mending my stockings or washing them, having breakfast with a vixenish old woman and spending the rest of the day with her, in a dreary house in the middle of a wood, and going to bed at eleven. I'm plain, I haven't got any money, I'm shy, and I haven't got any friends.

DAN (*teasing*). Don't you *like* the old lady?

OLIVIA. I could kill her.

(*A pause. She realizes what she has said.*)

DAN (*with a laugh*). Oh, no, you couldn't! . . . Not many people have it in them to kill people. . . . Oh, no!

(*She looks at him. A pause. He studies the palms of his hands, chuckling to himself.*)

OLIVIA. And what was there to *your* life at the Tallboys?

DAN. My life? Well. . . . The day don't start so good, with a lot of stuck-up boots to clean, and a lot of silly high heels all along the passage waitin' for a polish, and a lot of spoons to clean that's been in the mouths of gapin' fools that looks through me as if I was a dirty window hadn't been cleaned for years. . . . (*Throwing his stub into the fire in a sudden crescendo of fury.*) Orders, orders, orders; go here, do this, don't do that, you idiot, open the door for me, get a move on—I was never meant to take orders, never! Down in the tea place there's an old white beard wigglin'. "Waiter, my tea's stone cold." (*Furiously.*) I'm not a waiter, I'm a millionaire, and everybody's under me! . . . And just when I think I got a bit o' peace—(*his head in his hands*)—there's somebody . . . lockin' the bedroom door—(*raising his head*)—won't let me get out; talk, talk, talk, won't fork out with no more money, at me, at me, at me, won't put no clothes on, calls me everythin', lie on the floor and screams and screams, so nothin' keeps that mouth shut only. (*A pause.*) It's rainin' out of the window, and the leaves is off the trees . . . Oh, Lord . . . I wish I could hear a bit o' music—(*smiling, slowly*). And I do, inside o' myself! And I have a drop of drink, and everything's fine! (*Excited.*) And when it's the night . . .

OLIVIA (*with a cry*). Go on!

(*A pause. He realizes she is there, and turns slowly and looks at her.*)

DAN (*wagging his finger with a sly smile*). Aha! I'm too fly for you! You'd like to know, wouldn't you? Aha! Why would you like to know? (*Insistently, mischievously.*) Why d'you lie awake . . . all night?

OLIVIA. Don't! I'm frightened of you!

DAN (*triumphantly, rising and facing her, his back half to the audience*). Why?

OLIVIA (*desperate*). How do you know I lie awake at night? Shall I tell you why? Because you're awake yourself! You can't sleep, can you? (*Triumphantly, in her turn.*) You can't sleep! There's one thing that keeps you awake, isn't there? One thing you've pushed into the back of your mind, and you can't do any more about it, and you never will. . . . And do you know what it is? It's a little thing. A box. Only a box. But it's . . . rather heavy. . . .

(DAN *looks at her. A long pause. He jerks away with a laugh and sits at the sofa again.*)

DAN (*quietly, prosaically*). The way you was going through my letters the other day—that had to make me smile. . . . (*His voice dies away. Without warning, as if seeing something in his mind which makes him lose control, he shrieks loudly, clapping his hands over his eyes; then he is silent. He recovers slowly and stares at her. After a pause, in a measured voice.*) It's the only thing that keeps me awake, mind you! The only thing! (*Earnestly.*) But I don't know what to do. You see, nothing worries me, nothing in the world, only . . . I don't like a pair of eyes staring at me—(*his voice trailing away*)—with no look in them. I don't know what to do . . . I don't know. (*Without warning he bursts into tears. She sits beside him and seems almost about to put her arms about him. He feels she is there, looks into her eyes, grasps her arm, then pulls himself together abruptly. Rising.*) But it's the only thing! I live by myself—(*clapping his chest*)—inside here—and all the rest of you can go hang! After I've made a use of you, though! Nothing's going to stop me! I feel fine! I—— (BELSIZE *crosses outside. A sharp knock at the front door. She half rises. He motions her to sit again. With his old swagger.*) All right! Anybody's there, I'll deal with 'em—I'll manage myself all right! You watch me!

(*He goes to the front door and opens it.*)

BELSIZE (*at the door, jovially*). Hello, Dan! How's things?

DAN (*letting him in and shutting the door*). Not so bad.

(*He brings* BELSIZE *into the room.*)

BELSIZE (*as* OLIVIA *goes*). Afternoon, Miss Grayne!

OLIVIA (*putting on her spectacles*). How do you do?

(*She makes an effort to compose herself and hurries across to the sunroom.* BELSIZE's *attitude is one of slightly exaggerated breeziness;* DAN's *is one of cheerful naïveté almost as limpid as on his first appearance.*)

BELSIZE. Bearing up, eh?

DAN. Yes, sir, bearin' up, you know.

BELSIZE. We haven't scared you all out of the house yet, I see!

DAN. No chance!

BELSIZE. All these bloodcurdlers, eh?

DAN. I should say so!

BELSIZE. No more news for me, I suppose?

DAN. No chance!

BELSIZE. Ah . . . too bad! Mind if I sit down?

DAN (*pointing to the sofa*). Well, this is the nearest you get to comfort in this house, sir.

BELSIZE. No, thanks, this'll do. (*Sitting on a chair at the table, and indicating the cuttings.*) I see you keep apace of the news?

DAN. I should say so! They can't hardly wait for the latest on the case in this house, sir.

BELSIZE. Ah, well, it's only natural. . . . I got a bit of a funny feeling bottom of my spine myself crossing by the rubbish heap.

DAN. Well, will you have a cigarette, sir? . . . (*His hand to his jacket pocket.*) Only a Woodbine——

BELSIZE. No, thanks.

DAN (*after a pause*). Would you like to see Mrs. Bramson, sir?

BELSIZE. Oh, plenty of time. How's she bearing up?

DAN. Well, it's been a bit of a shock for her, them finding the remains of the lady at the bottom of her garden, you know.

BELSIZE. The remains of the lady! I wish you wouldn't talk like that. I've seen 'em.

DAN (*looking over his shoulder at the cuttings*). Well, you see, I haven't.

BELSIZE. You know, I don't mind telling you, they reckon the fellow that did this job was a bloodstained clever chap.

DAN (*smiling*). You don't say?

BELSIZE (*casually*). He was blackmailing her, you know.

DAN. Tch! tch! Was he?

BELSIZE. Whoever he was.

DAN. She had a lot of fellows on a string, though, didn't she?

BELSIZE (*guardedly*). That's true.

DAN. Though this one seems to have made a bit more stir than any of the others, don't he?

BELSIZE. Yes. (*Indicating the cuttings.*) Regular film star. Made his name.

DAN (*abstractedly*). If you *can* make your name without nobody knowin' what it is, o' course.

BELSIZE (*slightly piqued*). Yes, of course. . . . But I don't reckon he's been as bright as all that.

DAN (*after a slight pause*). Oh, you don't?

BELSIZE. No! They'll nab him in no time.

DAN. Oh . . . Mrs. Bramson'll be that relieved. And the whole country besides. . . .

BELSIZE. Look here, Dan, any self-respecting murderer would have taken care to mutilate the body to such a degree that nobody could recognize it, and here we come and identify it first go! (DAN *folds his arms and looks thoughtful.*) Call that clever? . . . What d'you think?

(DAN *catches his eye and crosses to the sofa.*)

DAN. Well, sir, I'm a slow thinker, I am, but though it might be clever to leave the lady unide—unide——

BELSIZE. Unidentified.

DAN (*sitting on the edge of the sofa*). Thank you, sir. (*Laboriously.*) Well, though it be clever to leave the lady unidentified and not be caught, hasn't it been more clever to leave her identified and still not be caught?

BELSIZE. Why didn't you sleep in your bed on the night of the tenth?

(*A pause.* DAN *stiffens almost imperceptibly.*)

DAN. What you say?

BELSIZE. Why didn't you sleep in your bed on the night of the murder?

DAN. I did.

BELSIZE (*lighting his pipe*). You didn't.

DAN. Yes, I did. Oh—except for about half an hour—that's right. I couldn't sleep for toffee and I went up the fire escape—I remember thinkin' about it next day when the woman was missing, and trying to remember if I could think of anything funny——

BELSIZE. What time was that? (*He rises, crosses to the fireplace, and throws his match into it.*)

DAN. Oh, about . . . Oh, you know how you wake up in the night and don't know what time it is. . . .

BELSIZE (*staring at him doubtfully*). Mmm . . .

DAN. I could never sleep when I was at sea, neither, sir.

BELSIZE. Mmm. (*Suddenly.*) Are you feeling hot?

DAN. No.

BELSIZE. Your shirt's wet through.

DAN (*after a pause*). I've been sawin' some wood.

BELSIZE. Why didn't you tell us you were having an affair with the deceased woman?

DAN. Affair? What's that?

BELSIZE. Come along, old chap, I'll use a straighter word if it'll help you. But you're stalling. She was seen by two of the maids talking to you in the shrubbery. Well?

(*A pause.* DAN *bursts into tears, but with a difference. His breakdown a few minutes ago was genuine; this is a good performance, very slightly exaggerated.* BELSIZE *watches him dispassionately, his brows knit.*)

DAN. Oh, sir, it's been on my conscience ever since . . .

BELSIZE. So you did have an affair with her?

DAN. Oh, no, sir, not that! I avoided her ever after that day she stopped me, sir! . . . You see, sir, a lady stayin' where I was workin', and for all I knew married, and all the other fellers she'd been after, and the brazen way she went on at me. . . . You're only human, aren't you, sir, and when they asked me about her, I got frightened to tell about her stopping me. But now you know about it, sir, it's a weight off my mind, you wouldn't believe! . . .

(*Rising, after seeming to pull himself together.*) As a matter of fact, sir, it was the disgust-like of nearly gettin' mixed up with her that was keepin' me awake at nights.

BELSIZE. I see. You're a bit of a milksop, aren't you?

DAN (*apparently puzzled*). Am I, sir?

BELSIZE. Yes. . . . That'll be all for today. I'll let you off this once.

DAN. I'm that relieved, sir!

BELSIZE (*crossing to the table for his hat*). But don't try and keep things from the police another time.

DAN. No chance!

BELSIZE. They always find you out, you know.

DAN. Yes, sir. Would you like a cup o' tea, sir?

BELSIZE. No, thanks. I've got another inquiry in the village. . . . (*Turning back, with an afterthought.*) Oh, just one thing—might as well just do it, we're supposed to with all the chaps we're questioning, matter of form—if you don't mind. I'll have a quick look through your luggage. Matter of form. . . .

DAN. Oh, yes.

BELSIZE. Where d'you hang out?

DAN (*tonelessly*). Through the kitchen—here, sir. . . . First door facin' . . .

BELSIZE. First door facing——

DAN. You can't miss it.

BELSIZE. I'll find it.

DAN. It's open, I think. (BELSIZE *goes into the kitchen. A pause.* DAN *looks slowly round the room. Turning mechanically to the kitchen door.*) You can't miss it. . . .

(*A pause. The noise of something being moved beyond the kitchen.* DAN *sits on the sofa with a jerk, looking before him. His fingers beat a rapid tattoo on the sides of the sofa. He looks at them, rises convulsively, and walks round the room, grasping chairs and furniture as he goes round. He returns to the sofa, sits, and begins the tattoo again. With a sudden wild automatic movement he beats his closed fists in rapid succession against the sides of his head.* BELSIZE *returns, carrying the hatbox.*)

BELSIZE (*crossing and placing the hatbox on the table*). This one's locked. Have you got the key?

(DAN *rises and takes a step into the middle of the room. He looks at the hatbox at last.*)

DAN (*in a dead voice*). It isn't mine.

BELSIZE. Not yours?

DAN. No.

BELSIZE. Oh? . . . Whose is it, then?

DAN. I dunno. It isn't mine.

(OLIVIA *stands at the sunroom door.*)

OLIVIA. I'm sorry, I thought . . . Why, Inspector, what are you doing with my box?

BELSIZE. Yours?

OLIVIA. Yes! It's got all my letters in it!

BELSIZE. But it was in . . .

OLIVIA. Oh, Dan's room used to be the box-room.

BELSIZE. Oh, I see. . . .

OLIVIA. I'll keep it in my wardrobe; it'll be safer there. . . .

(*With sudden feverish resolution, she picks up the box and carries it into the kitchen.* DAN *looks the other way as she passes him.*)

BELSIZE. I'm very sorry, miss. (*Scratching his head.*) I'm afraid I've offended her.

DAN (*smiling*). She'll be all right, sir. . . .

BELSIZE. Well, young feller, I'll be off. You might tell the old lady I popped in, and hope she's better.

DAN (*smiling and nodding*). Thank you, sir. . . . Good day, sir.

BELSIZE. Good day.

(*He goes out through the front door into the twilight, closing it behind him.*)

DAN. Good day, sir. . . .

(*A pause.* DAN *crumples to the floor in a dead faint.*)

QUICK CURTAIN

ACT THREE

SCENE I

Half an hour later. The light has waned; the fire is lit and throws a red re-flection into the room. DAN *is lying on the sofa, eyes closed.* NURSE LIBBY *sits at the end of the sofa holding his pulse.* MRS. TERENCE *stands behind the sofa with a toby jug of water.*

NURSE. There, lovey, you won't be long now. . . . Ever so much steadier already. . . . What a bit o' luck me blowin' in today! . . . Tt! tt! Pouring with sweat, the lad is. Whatever's he been up to?

MRS. TERENCE. When I walked in that door and saw 'im lyin' full stretch on that floor everything went

topsy-wopsy. (*Pressing the jug to* DAN's *lips.*) It did! The room went round and round. . . .

NURSE (*as* DAN *splutters*). Don't choke 'im, there's a love.

MRS. TERENCE. D'you know what I said to meself when I saw 'im lyin' there?

NURSE. What?

MRS. TERENCE. I said, "That murderer's been at 'im," I said, "and it's the next victim." I did!

NURSE. So you would! Just like the pictures. . . . 'Old your 'ead up, love.

MRS. TERENCE (*as* NURSE LIBBY *supports* DAN'S *head.*) Got a *nice* face, 'asn't he?

NURSE. Oh, *yes!* . . . (*As* DAN'S *eyes flicker.*) Shh, he's coming to. . . . (DAN *opens his eyes and looks at her.*) Welcome back to the land of the living!

MRS. TERENCE. Thought the murderer'd got you!

(*A pause.* DAN *stares, then sits up abruptly.*)

DAN. How long I been like that?

NURSE. We picked you up ten minutes ago, and I'd say it was twenty minutes before that, roughly like, that you passed away.

MRS. TERENCE. Passed away? Don't frighten the boy! Whatever come over you, dear?

DAN. I dunno. Felt sick, I think. (*Recovering himself.*) Say no more about it, eh? Don't like swinging the lead. . . . (*His head in his hand.*)

MRS. TERENCE. Waiting 'and and foot on Madame Crocodile, enough to wear King Kong out. . . .

NURSE. That's better, eh?

DAN. Is it really getting dark?

MRS. TERENCE. It's a scandal the way the days are drawin' in. 'Ave another sip——

DAN (*as she makes to give him more water, to* NURSE LIBBY). You haven't such a thing as a nip of brandy?

NURSE (*opening her bag*). Yes, lovey, I nearly gave you a drop just now——

(DAN *takes a flask from her and gulps; he takes a second mouthful. He gives it back, shakes himself, and looks before him.*)

MPS. TERENCE. Better?

DAN. Yes. . . . Clears the brain no end. . . . Makes you understand better. . . . (*His voice growing in vehemence.*) Makes you see what a damn silly thing it is to get the wind up about anything. *Do* things! Get a move on! Show 'em what you're made of! Get a move on! . . . Fainting, indeed. . . . Proper girl's trick, I'm ashamed of myself. . . . (*Looking round, quietly.*) The light's going. . . . The daytime's as if it's never been; it's dead. . . . (*Seeing the others stare, with a laugh.*) Daft, isn't it?

(DORA *brings in an oil lamp from the kitchen; she is wearing her outdoor clothes. She crosses to the table, strikes a match with her back to the audience, and lights the lamp, then the wall lamp. The twilight is dispelled.*)

NURSE (*shutting her bag, rising*). You'll be all right; a bit light-headed after the fall, I expect. (*Going to the hall.*) Well, got an abscess the other side of Turneyfield, *and* a slow puncture. So long, lovey.

DAN (*sitting up*). So long!

NURSE. Be good, all!

(*She bustles out of the front door. A pause. DAN sits looking before him, drumming his fingers on the sofa.*)

DORA (*closing the right window curtains*). What's the matter with him?

MRS. TERENCE. Conked out.

DORA. Conked out? Oh, dear. . . . D'you think 'e see'd something? I'll tell you what it is!

MRS. TERENCE (*closing the left window curtains*). What?

DORA. The monster's lurking again.

(*Mechanically DAN takes a box of matches and a cigarette from his pocket.*)

MRS. TERENCE. I'll give you lurk, my girl, look at the egg on my toby! Why don't you learn to wash up, instead of walkin' about talking like three halfpennyworth of trash?

DORA. I can't wash up properly in that kitchen, with that light. Them little oil lamps isn't any good except to set the place on fire.

(*She goes into the kitchen. DAN drums his fingers on the sofa. MRS. BRAMSON wheels herself from the bedroom.*)

MRS. BRAMSON. I dropped off. Why didn't somebody wake me? Have I been missing something?

MRS. TERENCE. That Inspector Belsize called.

MRS. BRAMSON (*testily*). Then why didn't somebody wake me? Dan, what did he want?

DAN. Just a friendly call.

MRS. BRAMSON. You seem very far away, dear. What's the matter with you? . . . Dan!

DAN. Bit of an 'eadache, that's all.

MRS. BRAMSON. Doesn't make you deaf, though, dear, does it?

MRS. TERENCE. Now, now, turnin' against the apple of your eye; can't 'ave that goin' on——

(*A sharp knock at the front door. DAN starts up and goes toward the hall.*)

MRS. BRAMSON (*to MRS. TERENCE*). See who it is.

MRS. TERENCE (*at the front door, as DAN is about to push past her*). Oh . . . it's only the paraffin boy. . . . (*To the boy outside, taking a can from him.*) And you bring stuff on a Saturday night another time.

(*DAN is standing behind MRS. BRAMSON's chair.*)

MRS. BRAMSON. I should think so——

(*MRS. TERENCE comes into the room. DAN strikes a match for his cigarette.*)

MRS. TERENCE (*with a cry*). Oh! Can't you see this is paraffin? (*She puts the can on the floor just inside the hall.*)

MRS. BRAMSON. You went through my side like a knife——

MRS. TERENCE. If people knew what to do with their money, they'd put electric light in their 'omes 'stead of dangerin' people's lives.

(*She goes into the kitchen.* DAN *stares before him, the match flickering.*)

MRS. BRAMSON (*blowing out the match*). You'll burn your fingers! Set yourself on fire! Absent-minded! . . . I woke up all of a cold shiver. Had a terrible dream.

DAN (*mechanically*). What about?

MRS. BRAMSON. Horrors. . . . I'm freezing. Get me my shawl off my bed, will you, dear? . . . (*As he does not move.*) My shawl, dear!

(DAN *starts, collects himself, and smiles his most ingratiating smile.*)

DAN. I *am* sorry, mum. In the Land of Nod, I was! Let me see, what was it your highness was after? A shawl? No sooner said than done. . . . You watch me! One, two, three!

(*He runs into the bedroom.*)

MRS. BRAMSON. Silly boy . . . silly boy . . . (OLIVIA *comes in quickly from the kitchen. She is dressed to go out and carries a suitcase.*) Where are you off to?

OLIVIA. I—I've had a telegram. A friend of mine in London's very ill.

MRS. BRAMSON. What's the matter with her?

OLIVIA. Pneumonia.

MRS. BRAMSON. Where's the telegram?

OLIVIA. I—I threw it away.

MRS. BRAMSON. Where d'you throw it?

OLIVIA. I—I——

MRS. BRAMSON. You haven't had any telegram.

OLIVIA (*impatiently*). No, I haven't!

MRS. BRAMSON. What's the matter with you?

OLIVIA. I can't stay in this house tonight.

MRS. BRAMSON. Why not?

OLIVIA. I'm frightened.

MRS. BRAMSON. Oh, don't be.

OLIVIA. Listen to me. I've never known before what it was to be terrified. But when I saw today beginning to end, and tonight getting nearer and nearer, I felt my finger tips getting cold. And I knew it was fright—stark fright. I'm not a fool, and I'm not hysterical, but I've been sitting in my room looking at myself in the glass, trying to control myself, telling myself what are real things, and what aren't. I don't know any longer. The day's over. The forest's all round us. Anything may happen. . . . You shouldn't stay in this house tonight. That's all.

MRS. BRAMSON (*blustering*). It's very silly of you, trying to scare an old woman with a weak heart. What have you got to be frightened of?

OLIVIA. There's been a murder, you know.

MRS. BRAMSON. Nobody's going to murder *you!* Besides, we've got Danny to look after us. He's as strong as an ox, and no silly nerves about him. What *is* it you're afraid of?

OLIVIA. I——

MRS. BRAMSON. Sly, aren't you? Where are you staying tonight?

OLIVIA. In Langbury, with Hubert Laurie and his sister.

MRS. BRAMSON. Not too frightened to make arrangements with *him,* eh?

OLIVIA. Arrangements?

MRS. BRAMSON. Well, some people would call it something else.

OLIVIA (*losing her temper*). Oh, won't you see . . .

MRS. BRAMSON. I'm very annoyed with you. How are you going to get there?

OLIVIA. Walking.

MRS. BRAMSON. Through the forest? Not too frightened for that, I see.

OLIVIA. I'd rather spend tonight in the forest than in this house.

MRS. BRAMSON. That sounds convincing, I must say. Well, you can go, but when you come back, I'm not so sure I shall answer the door. Think that over in the morning.

OLIVIA. The morning?

DAN'S VOICE (*in the bedroom, singing*). ". . . their home addresses . . . and their caresses . . . linger in my memory of those beautiful dames . . ."

(OLIVIA *listens, holding her breath; she tries to say something to* MRS. BRAMSON, *and fails. She makes an effort, and runs out of the front door. It bangs behind her.* DAN *comes back from the bedroom, carrying a shawl.*)

DAN (*over-casual*). What was that at the door?

MRS. BRAMSON. My niece. Gone for the night, if you please.

DAN. Gone—for the night? (*He stares before him.*)

MRS. BRAMSON. Would you believe it? Says she's frightened. (*A pause.*) Come along with the shawl, dear. I'm freezing.

DAN (*with a laugh, putting the shawl round her*). Don't know what's up with me——

(*He goes to the table and looks at a newspaper.* MRS. TERENCE *comes in from the kitchen, her coat on.*)

MRS. TERENCE. Well, I must go on me way rejoicin'.

MRS. BRAMSON. Everybody seems to be going. What *is* all this?

MRS. TERENCE. What d'you want for lunch tomorrow?

MRS. BRAMSON. Lunch tomorrow? Let me see. . . .

DAN. Lunch? Tomorrow? . . . (*After a pause.*) What about a nice little steak?

MRS. BRAMSON. A steak? Let me see. . . . Yes, with baked potatoes——

DAN. And a nice roly-poly puddin', the kind you like?

MRS. BRAMSON. I think so.

MRS. TERENCE. Something light. O.K. Good night.

(*She goes back into the kitchen.* DAN *scans the newspaper casually.*)

MRS. BRAMSON (*inquisitive*). What are you reading, dear?

DAN (*breezily*). Only the múrder again. About the clues that wasn't any good.

MRS. BRAMSON (*suddenly*). Danny, d'you think Olivia's a thief?

DAN. Shouldn't be surprised.

MRS. BRAMSON. What!

DAN. Her eyes wasn't very wide apart.

MRS. BRAMSON (*working herself up*). Goodness me—my jewel box! What a fool I was to let her go. My earrings. The double-faced——

(*She wheels herself furiously into her bedroom.* DORA, *her hat and coat on, comes in from the kitchen in time to see her go.*)

DORA. What's up with her?

DAN (*still at his paper*). Thinks she's been robbed.

DORA. Oh, is that all? That's the fourth time this month she's thought that. One of these days something *will* 'appen to her, and will I be pleased? Oh, baby! . . . Where's Mrs. Terence?

DAN. Gone, I think.

DORA (*frightened*). Oh, law, no! (*Calling.*) Mrs. Terence!

MRS. TERENCE (*calling, in the kitchen*). Ye-es!

DORA. You 'aven't gone without me, 'ave you?

MRS. TERENCE (*appearing at the kitchen door, spearing a hatpin into her hat*). Yes, I'm 'alfway there. What d'you think?

DORA. You did give me a turn! (*Going to the table and taking the box.*) I think I'll 'ave a choc. (*Walking toward the hall.*) I couldn't 'ave walked a step in those trees all by myself. Coming?

DAN (*suddenly*). I'd have come with you with pleasure, only I'm going the other direction. Payley Hill way.

MRS. TERENCE (*surprised*). You going out?

DORA. Oh?

DAN (*in the hall, putting on hat and mackintosh*). Yes. I still feel a bit funny.

MRS. TERENCE. But you can't leave 'er 'ere by herself!

DORA. She'll scream the place down!

DAN (*over-explanatory*). I asked her this very minute, and she don't seem to mind. You know what she is. Said it'd do me good, and won't hear of me stayin'. It's no good arguin' with her.

(DORA *puts the chocolates down on the occasional table. She and* MRS. TERENCE *follow* DAN *into the hall.*)

DORA. No good arguin' with her—don't I know it!

MRS. TERENCE. You 'ave a nice long walk while you get the chance; you wait on 'er too much. (*Closing the plush curtains so that they are all out of sight.*) Ooh, ain't it dark? Got the torch, Dora?

DORA. O.K., honey.

MRS. TERENCE. Laws, I'd be frightened goin' off by meself. . . . Well, we'd best 'urry, Dora. . . . Good night, Dan. Pity you aren't coming our way——

DAN'S VOICE. See you in the morning! Good night!

DORA'S VOICE. O.K.! . . . Toodle-oo!

(*The door bangs. A pause.*)

DAN'S VOICE (*outside the left window*). Good night!

MRS. TERENCE'S VOICE (*outside the right window*). Good night!

DORA (*same*). Good night!

(*Silence.*)

MRS. TERENCE (*farther away*). Good night!

DORA (*same*). Good night!

(MRS. BRAMSON *comes trundling back from the bedroom in her chair.*)

MRS. BRAMSON. Good night here, good night there; anybody'd think it was the night before Judgment Day. What's the matter with . . . (*Seeing the room is empty.*) Talking to myself. Wish people wouldn't walk out of rooms and leave me high and dry. Don't like it. (*She wheels herself round to the table. A pause. She looks round impatiently.*) Where's my chocolates? (*She looks round again, gets up out of her chair for the first time in the play, walks quite normally across the room to the mantelpiece, sees her chocolates are not there, walks up to the occasional table, and takes up the box.*) That girl's been at them again. . . . (*She walks back to her chair, carrying the chocolates, and sits in it again. She begins to munch. She suddenly stops, as if she has heard something.*) What's that? (*She listens again. A cry is heard far away.*) Oh, God! Danny! (*The cry is repeated.*) Danny! (*The cry is heard a third time.*) It's an owl. . . . Oh, Lord! (*She falls back in relief, and eats another chocolate. The clock strikes the half-hour. Silence. The silence gets on her nerves. After a pause, calling softly.*) Danny! . . . (*As there is no answer.*) What's the boy doing in that kitchen? (*She takes up the newspaper, sees a headline, and puts it down hastily. She sees the Bible on the table, opens it, and turns over pages. After a pause, suddenly.*) I've got the jitters. I've got the jitters. I've got the jitters. . . . (*Calling loudly.*) Danny! (*She waits; there is complete silence. She rises, walks over to the kitchen door, and flings it wide open. Shouting.*) Danny! (*No reply.*) He's gone. . . .

They've all gone. . . . They've left me. . . . (*Losing control, beating her hands wildly on her Bible.*) Oh, Lord, help a poor old woman. . . . They've left me! (*Tottering to the sunroom.*) Danny . . . where are you? . . . Danny . . . I'm going to be murdered! I'm going to be murdered! . . . Danny . . . (*Her voice rising, until she is shrieking hysterically.*) Danny! Danny! Danny! (*She stops suddenly. Footsteps on the gravel outside the front door. In a strangled whisper.*) There's something outside—something outside—— Oh, heavens! (*Staggering across to the sofa.*) Danny, where are you? Where are you? There's something outs—— (*The front door bangs. She collapses on the sofa, terrified, her enormous Bible clasped to her breast.*) Oh, Lord, help me . . . help me . . . Oh, Lord, help me. . . . (*Muttering, her eyes closed.*) . . . Forgive us our trespasses . . . (*The curtains are suddenly parted. It is* DAN, *a cigarette between his lips. He stands motionless, his feet planted apart, holding the curtains. There is murder in his face. She is afraid to look, but is forced to at last.*) Danny. . . . Oh. . . . Oh. . . .

DAN (*smiling, suddenly normal and reassuring*). That's all right. . . . It's only Danny. . . .

MRS. BRAMSON. Thank God . . . (*Going off into laughing hysterics.*) Ah . . . ah . . . ah . . . (DAN *throws his cigarette away, lays his hat on the occasional table, throws his mackintosh on the left window seat, and sits beside her, patting her, looking round to see no one has heard her cries.*) I'll never forgive you, never. Oh, my heart! Oh—oh—oh——

(*He runs across to the medicine cupboard and brings back a brandy bottle and two glasses.*)

DAN. Now have a drop of this. . . . (*As she winces at the taste.*) Go on, do you good. . . . (*As she drinks.*) I am sorry, I am really. . . . You see, they wanted me to see them to the main path, past the rubbish heap, see, in case they was frightened. . . . Now that's better, isn't it?

(*They are seated side by side on the sofa.*)

MRS. BRAMSON. I don't know yet. . . . Give me some more. . . . (*He pours one out for her, and for himself. They drink.*) All alone, I was. . . . (*Her face puckering with self-pity.*) Just an old woman calling for help—(*her voice breaking*)—and no answer.

DAN (*putting the bottle on the floor beside him*). Poor old mum, runnin' about lookin' for Danny——

MRS. BRAMSON (*sharply*). I wasn't running about as much as all that. Oh, the relief when I saw your face——

DAN. I bet you wasn't half glad, eh?

MRS. BRAMSON. You're the only one that understands me, Danny, that's what you are.

DAN (*patting her*). That's right.

MRS. BRAMSON. I don't have to tell you everything I've been through. I don't have to tell you about my husband, how unkind and ungodly he was—I wouldn't have minded so much him being ungodly, but oh, he *was* unkind. . . . (*Sipping.*) And I don't have to tell *you* how unkind he was. You know. You just know—whatever else I've not been, I was *always* a great one on psychology.

DAN. You was. (*He takes her glass and fills it again and his own.*)

MRS. BRAMSON. I'm glad those other people have gone. Awful screeching common women. Answer back, answer back, answer back. . . . Isn't it time for my medicine? (*He hands her glass back. They both drink.* DAN *sits smiling and nodding at her.*) That day you said to me about me reminding you of your mother. . . . (DAN *slowly begins to roll up his sleeves a little way.*) These poets and rubbishy people can think all they like about their verses and sonnets and such—that girl Olivia writes sonnets—would you believe it——

DAN. Fancy.

MRS. BRAMSON. They can think all they like, that was a beautiful thought. (*Her arm on his shoulder.*) And when you think you're just an ignorant boy, it's—it's startling.

DAN (*with a loud laugh*). That's right.

MRS. BRAMSON. I'll never forget that. Not as long as I live. . . . (*Trying to stem her tears.*) I want a chocolate now.

DAN. Right you are! . . . (*Placing her glass and his own on the floor and walking briskly to the table.*) A nice one with a soft center, the kind you like. Why, here's one straight away. (*He walks slowly to the back of the sofa. In a level voice.*) Now shut your eyes—open your mouth.

MRS. BRAMSON (*purring*). Oh, Danny. . . . You're the only one. . . . (*She shuts her eyes. He stands behind her and puts the chocolate into her mouth. His fingers close slowly and involuntarily over her neck: she feels his touch, and draws both his hands down, giggling, so that his face almost touches hers. Maudlin.*) What strong hands they are. . . . You're a pet, my little chubby-face, my baby-face, my Danny. . . . Am I in a draft? (*A pause.* DAN *draws his hands slowly away, walks to the back, and shuts the plush curtains.*) I've got to take care of myself, haven't I?

DAN (*turning slowly and looking at her*). You have.

(*He picks up the paraffin can briskly and goes toward the kitchen.*)

MRS. BRAMSON. What are you——

DAN. Only takin' the paraffin tin in the kitchen.

MRS. BRAMSON (*half to herself*). That girl should have carried it in. Anything to annoy me. Tomorrow—— (*Turning and seeing that he is gone.*) Danny! (*Shrieking suddenly.*) Danny!

(DAN *runs back from the kitchen.*)

DAN. What's the matter?

(*He looks hastily toward the hall to see no one has heard.*)

MRS. BRAMSON. Oh dear, I thought——

DAN (*sitting on the back of the sofa*). I was only putting the paraffin away. Now—— (*He leans over the sofa, and raises his arm slowly.*)

MRS. BRAMSON (*putting her hand on his arm*). I think I'll go to bed now.

DAN (*after a pause, dropping his arm*). O.K.

MRS. BRAMSON. And I'll have my supper tray in my room. (*Petulantly.*) Get me back into my chair, dear, will you?

DAN (*jerkily*). O.K.

(*He crosses to the invalid chair.*)

MRS. BRAMSON. Has she put the glass by the bed for my teeth?

DAN (*bringing over the chair*). I put it there myself.

(*He helps her into the chair and pulls it over toward the bedroom.*)

MRS. BRAMSON (*suddenly, in the middle of the room*). I want to be read to now.

DAN (*after a pause of indecision*). O.K. (*Clapping his hands effusively.*) What'll you have? The old East Lynne?

MRS. BRAMSON. No, I don't feel like anything sentimental tonight.

DAN (*looking toward the desk*). What'll you have, then?

MRS. BRAMSON. I think I'd like the Bible.

(*A pause. He looks at her.*)

DAN. O.K.

MRS. BRAMSON (*as he goes smartly to the sofa, fetches the Bible, pulls up a chair to the right of her, sits, and looks for the place*). That piece you were reading. . . . It's Sunday. . . . Isn't that nice? All the aches and pains quiet for once—pretty peaceful.

DAN (*reading*). "Blessed is the man that walketh not in the counsel of the ungodly, nor standeth in the way of sinners, nor sitteth in the seat of the scornful . . ."

MRS. BRAMSON (*drowsily*). You read so nicely, Danny.

DAN. Very kind of you, my lady. (*Reading a little breathlessly.*) "But his delight is in the Law of the Lord; and in His law doth he meditate day and night——"

MRS. BRAMSON. Sh!

DAN. What?

MRS. BRAMSON. What's that?

DAN. Can you hear something?

MRS. BRAMSON. Yes! A sort of—thumping noise. . . . (*She looks at him suddenly, leans forward, and puts her right hand inside his jacket.*) Why, Danny, it's you! It's your heart—beating! (*He laughs.*) Well! Are you all right, dear?

DAN. Fine. I been running along the path, see? (*Garrulously.*) I been out of training, I suppose. When I was at sea I never missed a day running round the decks, o' course.

MRS. BRAMSON (*sleepily*). Of course.

DAN (*speaking quickly, as if eager to conjure up a vision*). I remember those mornings—on some sea—very misty pale it is, with the sun like breathing silver where he's comin' up across the water, but not blowing on the sea at all. And the seagulls standing on the deck rail looking at themselves in the water on the deck, and only me about and nothing else.

MRS. BRAMSON (*nodding sleepily*). Yes.

DAN. And the sun. Just me and the sun.

MRS. BRAMSON (*nodding*). There's no sun now, dear; it's night!

(*A pause. He drums his fingers on the Bible.*)

DAN. Yes—it's night now. (*Reading, feverishly.*) "The ungodly are not so, but are like the chaff which the wind driveth away——"

MRS. BRAMSON. I think I'll go to bye-byes. We'll have the rest tomorrow, shall we? (*Testily.*) Help me, dear, help me, you know what I am——

DAN (*drumming his fingers; suddenly, urgently*). Wait a minute. I —I've only got two more verses——

MRS. BRAMSON. Hurry it up, dear. I don't want to wake up in the morning with a nasty cold.

DAN (*reading slowly*). ". . . Therefore the ungodly shall not stand in the judgment, nor sinners in the congregation of the righteous. . . . For the Lord knoweth the way of the righteous. But the way of the ungodly . . . shall perish . . ." (*A pause. He shuts the Bible loudly, and lays it on the table.* MRS. BRAMSON *can hardly keep awake.*) That's the end.

MRS. BRAMSON. Is it? . . . Ah, well, it's been a long day——

DAN. Are you quite comfortable?

MRS. BRAMSON. A bit achy. Glad to get to bed. Hope that woman's put my bottle in all right. Bet she hasn't ——

DAN. Sure you're comfortable? Wouldn't you like a cushion back of your head?

MRS. BRAMSON. No, dear, just wheel me——

DAN (*rising*). I think you'll be more comfortable with a cushion. (*Rising, humming.*) "I'm a pretty little feller, everybody knows . . . dunno what to call me . . ."

(*He goes deliberately across, humming, and picks up a large black cushion from the sofa. His hands close on the cushion, and he stands silent a moment. He moves slowly back to the other side of her; he stands looking at her, his back three quarters to the audience and his face hidden; he is holding the cushion in both hands.*)

(MRS. BRAMSON *shakes herself out of sleep and looks at him.*)

MRS. BRAMSON. What a funny look on your face, dear. Smiling like that. (*Foolishly.*) You look so kind. (*He begins to raise the cushion slowly.*) So kind . . . (*Absently.*) What are you going to do with that cushion?

(*The lights dim gradually into complete darkness, and the music grows into a thunderous crescendo.*)

SCENE II

The music plays a few bars, then dies down proportionately as the lights come up again.

Half an hour later. The scene is the same, with the same lighting; the room is empty and the wheel chair has been removed.

DAN *comes in from the sunroom, smoking the stub of a cigarette. He crosses smartly, takes the bottle and glasses from the floor by the sofa and places them on the table, pours himself a quick drink, places the bottle on the floor next the desk, throws away his stub, takes another cigarette from his pocket, puts it in his mouth, takes out a box of matches, and lights a match. The clock chimes. He looks at it, seems to make a decision, blows out the match, throws the matchbox on the table, takes* MRS. BRAMSON'S *tape and keys from his trouser pocket, crosses quickly to the safe by the fireplace, opens it, takes out the cashbox, sits on the sofa, unlocks the cashbox, stuffs the keys back into his trousers, opens the cashbox, takes out the notes, looks at them, delighted, stuffs them into his pocket, hurries into the sunroom, returns a second later with the empty invalid chair, plants it in the middle of the room, picks up the cushion from the floor above the table, looks at it a moment, arrested, throws it callously on the invalid chair, hurries into the kitchen, returns immediately with the paraffin, sprinkles it freely over the invalid chair, places the can under the table, lifts the paraffin lamp from the table, and is just about to smash it over the invalid chair when there is the sound of a chair falling over in the sunroom. His face inscrutable, he looks toward it. He carries the lamp stealthily to the desk, puts it down, looks round, picks a chair from near the table, and stands at the sunroom door with the chair held high above his head.*

The stagger of footsteps; OLIVIA *stands in the doorway to the sunroom. She has been running through the forest; her clothes are wild, her hair has fallen about her shoulders, and she is no longer wearing her spectacles. She looks nearly beautiful. Her manner is quiet, almost dazed. He lowers the chair slowly and sits on the other side of the table. A pause.*

OLIVIA. I've never seen a dead body before. . . . I climbed through the window and nearly fell over it. Like a sack of potatoes, or something. I thought it was at first. And that's murder. (*As he looks up at her.*) But it's so ordinary, I came back . . . (*As he lights his cigarette.*) . . . expecting . . . ha—(*laughing hysterically*)—I don't know, and here I find you, smoking a cigarette. You might have been tidying the room for the night. It's so—ordinary. (*After a pause, with a cry.*) Why don't you *say* something?

DAN. I thought you were goin' to stay the night at that feller's.

OLIVIA. I was.

DAN. What d'you come back for?

OLIVIA (*the words pouring out*). To find you out. You've kept me guessing for a fortnight. Guessing hard. I very nearly knew, all the time. But not quite. And now I do know.

DAN. Why was you so keen on finding me out?

OLIVIA (*vehemently, coming to the table*). In the same way any sane, decent-minded human being would want—would want to have you arrested for the monster you are!

DAN (*quietly*). What d'you come back for?

OLIVIA. I—I've told you. (*He smiles at her slowly and shakes his head. She sits at the table and closes her eyes.*) I got as far as the edge of the wood. I could see the lights in the village. . . . I came back. (*She buries her head in her arms.* DAN *rises, looks at her a moment regretfully, puts away his cigarette, and stands with both hands over the invalid chair.*)

DAN (*casually*). She didn't keep any money anywhere else, did she?

OLIVIA. I've read a lot about evil——

(DAN *realizes his hands are wet with paraffin and wipes them on his trousers.*)

DAN. Clumsy.

OLIVIA. I never expected to come across it in real life.

DAN (*lightly*). You didn't ought to read so much. I never got through a book yet. But I'll read you all right. (*Crossing to her, leaning over the table, and smiling at her intently.*) You haven't had a drop to drink, and yet you feel as if you had. You never knew there was such a secret part inside of you. All that book-learnin' and moral-me-eye here and social-me-eye there—you took that off on the edge of the wood same as if it was an overcoat, and you left it there!

OLIVIA. I hate you! I—hate you!

DAN (*urgently*). And same as anybody out for the first time without their overcoats, you feel as light as air! Same as I feel, sometimes—only I never had no overcoat. (*Excited.*) Why, this is my big chance! You're the one I can tell about meself! Oh, I'm sick o' hearin' how clever everybody else is—I want to tell 'em how clever *I* am for a change! . . . Money I'm goin' to have, and people doin' what they're told, and *me* tellin' them to do it! There was a 'oman at the Tallboys, wasn't there? She wouldn't be told, would she? She thought she was up 'gainst a soft fellow in a uniform, didn't she? She never knew it was *me* she was dealin' with—(*striking his chest in a paroxysm of elation*)—me! And this old girl treatin' me like a son 'cause I made her think she was a chronic invalid—ha! She's been more use to me tonight—(*tapping the notes in his jacket pocket smartly*)—than she has to any other body all her life. Stupid, that's what people are—stupid. If those two hadna' been stupid they might be breathin' now; you're not stupid; that's why I'm talkin' to you. (*With exaggerated self-possession.*) You said just now murder's ordinary. Well, it isn't ordinary at all, see? And I'm not an ordinary chap.

There's one big difference 'tween me and other fellows that try this game. I'll *never be found out.* 'Cause I don't care a—— (*Snapping his fingers grandly.*) The world's goin' to hear from me. That's me. (*Chuckling.*) You wait. . . . (*After a pause.*) But you can't wait, can you?

OLIVIA. What do you mean?

DAN. Well, when I say I'll never be found out, what I mean is, no living soul will be able to tell any other living soul about me. (*Beginning to roll up a sleeve, nonchalantly.*) Can you think of anybody—who can go tomorrow—and tell the police the fire at Forest Corner wasn't an accident at all?

OLIVIA. I—I can.

DAN. Oh, no, you can't.

OLIVIA. Why can't I?

DAN. Well, I'm up against a very serious problem, I am. But the answer to it is as simple as pie to a feller like me, simple as pie. (*Rolling up the other sleeve a little way.*) She isn't going to be the only one— found tomorrow—in the fire at Forest Corner. (*After a pause.*) Aren't you frightened? You ought to be! (*Smiling.*) Don't you think I'll do it?

OLIVIA. I know you will. I just can't realize it.

DAN. You know, when I told you all that about meself just now, I'd made up my mind then about you. (*Moving slowly after her, round the table, as she steps back toward the win-* *dow.*) That's what I am, see? I make up me mind to do a thing, and I do it. You remember that first day when I come in here? I said to me-self then, There's a girl that's got her wits about her; she knows a thing or two; different from the others. I was right, wasn't I? You —— (*Stopping abruptly, and looking round the room.*) What's that light in here?

OLIVIA. What light?

DAN. There's somebody in this room's holdin' a flashlight.

OLIVIA. It can't be in this room. . . . It must be a light in the wood.

DAN. It can't be.

(*A flashlight crosses the window curtains.* OLIVIA *turns and stares at it.*)

OLIVIA. Somebody's watching the bungalow. . . .

(*He looks at her, as if he did not understand.*)

DAN (*fiercely*). Nobody's watching! . . . (*He runs to the window. She backs into the corner of the room.*) I'm the one that watches! They've got no call to watch me! I'll go out and tell them that, an' all! (*Opening the curtains in a frenzy.*) I'm the one that watches! (*The light crosses the window again. He stares, then claps his hands over his eyes. Backing to the sofa.*) Behind them trees. (*Clutching the invalid chair.*) Hundreds back of each tree. . . . Thousands of eyes. The whole damn world's on my track! . . . (*Sitting on the edge of the sofa, listening.*)

What's that? . . . Like a big wall fallin' over into the sea. . . . (*Closing his hands over his ears convulsively.*)

OLIVIA (*coming down to him*). They mustn't come in.

DAN (*turning to her*). Yes, but— (*staring*)—you're lookin' at me as if you never see'd me before.

OLIVIA. I never have. Nobody has. You've stopped acting at last. You're real. Frightened. Like a child. (*Putting her arm about his shoulders.*) They mustn't come in.

DAN. But everythin's slippin' away. From underneath our feet. Can't *you* feel it? Starting slow . . . and then hundreds of miles an hour. . . . I'm goin' backwards! . . . And there's a wind in my ears, terrible blowin' wind. . . . Everything's going past me, like the telegraph poles. . . . All the things I've ever seen . . . faster and faster . . . backward —back to the day I was born. (*Shrieking.*) I can see it coming . . . the day I was born! . . . (*Turning to her, simply.*) I'm goin' to die. (*A pause. A knock at the front door.*) It's getting cold. (*Another knock, louder. She presses his head to her.*)

OLIVIA. It's all right. You won't die. I'll tell them I *made* you do it. I'll tell lies—I'll tell——

(*A third and louder knock at the front door. She realizes she must answer, goes into the hall, opens the front door, and comes back, hiding DAN from view.*)

BELSIZE (*in the hall*). Good evening. . . . Sorry to pop back like this—— (*He comes into the room, followed by DORA and MRS. TERRENCE, both terrified. Looking around.*) Everything looks all right here.

MRS. TERENCE. I tell you we *did* 'ear her! Plain as plain! And we'd gone near a quarter of a mile——

DORA. Plain as plain——

MRS. TERENCE. Made my blood run cold. "Danny!" she screamed. "Danny, where are you?" she said. She wanted 'im back, she did, to save 'er——

DORA. Because she was bein' murdered. I knew it! I'd never a' run like that if I 'adn't 'eard——

BELSIZE. We'll soon find out who's right. . . . Now then—— (*As OLIVIA steps aside behind the sofa.*) Hello, Dan!

DAN (*quietly, rising and standing by the fireplace*). Hello.

BELSIZE (*standing behind the invalid chair*). Second time today, eh? . . .

DAN. That's right.

BELSIZE. How's the old lady?

DAN (*after a pause*). Not so bad, thanks, Inspector! Gone to bed, and says she didn't want to be disturbed ——

BELSIZE. Smell of paraffin.

DAN (*with a last desperate attempt at bluster*). You know what she's like, Inspector, a bit nervy these days—— (*As BELSIZE goes to the bed-*

room and flashes a light into it.) I'd no sooner got round the corner she screamed for me—"Danny, Danny, Danny!" she was screamin'— "Danny," she calls me, a pet name for Dan, that is—— (*As* BELSIZE *goes into the sunroom. Rambling on mechanically.*) I told her so then. I said, "It's dangerous, that's what it is, havin' so much paraffin in the house." That paraffin—she shouldn't ha' so much paraffin in the house—— (*His voice trails away. Silence.* BELSIZE *comes back, his face intent, one hand in coat pocket. A pause.*)

BELSIZE (*to* OLIVIA). What are you doing here?

OLIVIA. I'm concerned in——

DAN (*loudly, decisively, silencing her*). It's all right. (*Crossing to* BELSIZE *and swaggering desperately, in front of the women.*) I'm the feller. Anything I'm concerned in, I run all by myself. If there's going to be any putting me on a public platform to answer any questions, I'm going to do it by myself—(*looking at* OLIVIA)—or not at all. I'll manage myself all right——

BELSIZE. I get you. Like a bit of lime-light, eh?

DAN (*smiling*). Well . . .

BELSIZE (*as if humoring him*). Let's have a look at your hands, old boy, will you?

(*With an amused look at* OLIVIA, DAN *holds out his hands. Without warning* BELSIZE *claps a pair of handcuffs over his wrists.* DAN *stares at them a moment, then sits on the sofa and starts to pull at them furi-*ously over his knee. He beats at them wildly, moaning and crying like an animal. He subsides gradually, looks at the others, and rises.*)

DAN (*muttering, holding his knee*). Hurt meself. . . .

BELSIZE. That's better. . . . Better come along quietly. . . . (*He goes up toward the hall.* DAN *follows him, and takes his hat from the occasional table. As he puts it on he catches sight of his face in the mirror. To the others crisply, during this.*) I've a couple of men outside. I'll send 'em in. See that nothing's disturbed. . . . Coming, old chap?

DORA. What's 'e doin'?

MRS. TERENCE. He's lookin' at himself in the glass. . . .

(*A pause.*)

DAN (*speaking to the mirror*). This is the real thing, my boy. Actin'. . . . That's what she said, wasn't it? She was right, you know. I've been playin' up to you, haven't I? I showed you a trick or two, didn't I? . . . But this is the real thing. (*Swaying.*) Got a cigarette? . . . (*Seeing* OLIVIA.) You're not goin' to believe what she said? About helpin' me?

BELSIZE (*humoring him*). No. (*Putting a cigarette between* DAN's *lips and lighting it.*) Plenty of women get a bit hysterical about a lad in your position. You'll find 'em queuing up all right when the time comes. Proposals of marriage by the score.

DAN (*pleased*). Will they?

BELSIZE. Come along——

(DAN *turns to follow him.* DORA *is in the way.*)

DAN. Oh, yes, I forgot about you. . . . (*Smiling with a curious detached sadness.*) Poor little fellow. Poor little chap. . . . (*Looking round.*) You know, I'd like somethin' now I never wanted before. A long walk, all by meself. And just when I can't have it. (*Laughing.*) That's contrary, isn't it?

BELSIZE (*sternly*). Coming?

DAN (*looking at* OLIVIA). Just comin'. (*He goes to* OLIVIA, *takes out his cigarette, puts his manacled arms round her, and kisses her suddenly and violently on the mouth. He releases her with an air of bravado, puts back his cigarette, and looks at her.*) Well, I'm goin' to be hanged in the end. . . . But they'll get their money's worth at the trial. You wait!

(*He smiles, and raises his hand to his hatbrim with the old familiar jaunty gesture of farewell. He walks past* BELSIZE *and out through the front door.* BELSIZE *follows him. The bang of the front door.* OLIVIA *falls to the sofa.*)

(*The sound of* DORA'S *sobbing.*)

CURTAIN

Angel Street

A Victorian Thriller in Three Acts By

PATRICK HAMILTON

CAUTION

Angel Street *was first produced at the John Golden Theatre, New York, by Shepard Traube (in association with Alexander H. Cohen).*

A Victorian Thriller By

PATRICK HAMILTON

STAGED BY MR. TRAUBE

CAST

(In order of appearance.)

Mrs. Manningham	Judith Evelyn
Mr. Manningham	Vincent Price
Nancy	Elizabeth Eustis
Elizabeth	Florence Edney
Rough	Leo G. Carroll

The entire action of the play occurs in a house on Angel Street, located in the Pimlico district of London. The time is 1880.

ACT ONE

Late afternoon.

ACT TWO

Immediately afterward.

ACT THREE

Later the same night.

STORY OF THE PLAY

IT tells the demoniac story of the Manninghams of Angel Street. Under the guise of kindliness, handsome Mr. Manningham is torturing his wife into insanity. He accuses her of petty aberrations that he has arranged himself; and since her mother died of insanity, she is more than half convinced that she, too, is going out of her mind. While her diabolical husband is out of the house, a benign police inspector visits her and ultimately proves to her that her husband is a maniacal criminal suspected of a murder committed fifteen years ago in the same house, and that he is preparing to dispose of her. Then starts the game of trying to uncover the necessary evidence against Mr. Manningham. It is a thrilling and exciting melodramatic game.

DESCRIPTION OF CHARACTERS

MR. MANNINGHAM: *He is tall, good-looking, about forty-five. He is heavily mustached and bearded and perhaps a little too well dressed. His manner is suave and authoritative, with a touch of mystery and bitterness.*

MRS. MANNINGHAM: *She is about thirty-four. She has been good-looking, almost a beauty—but now she has a haggard, wan, frightened air, with rings under her eyes, which tell of sleepless nights and worse.*

ELIZABETH: *She is a stout, amiable, subservient woman of fifty.*

NANCY: *She is a self-conscious, pretty, cheeky girl of nineteen.*

ROUGH: *He is middle-aged—greying, short, wiry, active, brusque, friendly, overbearing. He has a low, warm chuckle and completely dominates the scene from the beginning.*

ANGEL STREET

ACT ONE

THE scene is a living room on the first floor of a four-storied house in a gloomy and unfashionable quarter of London, in the latter part of the last century. The room is furnished in all the heavily draped and dingy profusion of the period, and yet, amidst this abundance of paraphernalia, an air is breathed of poverty, wretchedness, and age.

Fireplace down R. Door at R. above fireplace leading to little room. Settee R., L. of fireplace with stool in front of it. Table C. with chairs R. and L. of it. Window at L. Desk in front window with chairs back and above it. Secretary against wall up R. Lamp on table C. Sliding double doors at back L.C. leading to hall, to L. the front door, to R. the servants' quarters. A circular stair leading to the upper floors is at back up R.C. Chairs down R. and L.

The curtain rises upon the rather terrifying darkness of the late afternoon —the zero hour, as it were, before the feeble dawn of gaslight and tea. In front of the fire, on the sofa, MANNINGHAM is stretched out and sleeping heavily. He is tall, good-looking, about forty-five. He is heavily mustached and bearded and perhaps a little too well dressed. His manner is suave and authoritative, with a touch of mystery and bitterness. MRS. MANNINGHAM is sitting sewing on the chair L. of the C. table. She is about thirty-four. She has been good-looking, almost a beauty—but now she has a haggard, wan, frightened air, with rings under her eyes, which tell of sleepless nights and worse. Big Ben strikes five. The curtain rises.

Pause. From the street below, in the distance, can be heard the intermittent jingling of a muffin man ringing his bell.

MRS. MANNINGHAM listens to this sound for a few moments, furtively and indecisively, almost as though she is frightened even of this. Then she looks toward the sound down in the street. Then to the bell cord by the L.C. door, which she pulls. Then back to her sewing, which she gathers up and puts into a box, at the same time taking a purse therefrom. There is a knock at the door, and ELIZABETH, the cook and housekeeper, enters. She is a stout, amiable, subservient woman of about fifty. Signaling that her husband is asleep, MRS. MANNINGHAM goes over and whispers to her at the door, giving her some money from the purse. ELIZABETH goes out closing the doors.

MR. MANNINGHAM (whose eyes have opened but whose position has not changed a fraction of an inch). What are you doing, Bella?

MRS. MANNINGHAM. Nothing, dear. (MRS. MANNINGHAM crosses quietly and quickly to the secretary with her sewing and starts back to the doors.) Don't wake yourself. (There is a pause. She starts to window.)

MR. MANNINGHAM (whose eyes are closed again). What are you doing, Bella? Come here.

MRS. MANNINGHAM (after hesitating, going to him). Only for tea, my dear. Muffins—for tea. (*She takes his hand.*)

MR. MANNINGHAM. Muffins—eh?

MRS. MANNINGHAM. Yes, dear. He only comes so seldom—I thought I might surprise you.

MR. MANNINGHAM. Why are you so apprehensive, Bella? I was not about to reproach you.

MRS. MANNINGHAM (*nervously releasing her hand*). No, dear. I know you weren't.

MR. MANNINGHAM. That fire's in ashes. Ring the bell, will you, Bella dear, please?

MRS. MANNINGHAM. Yes. (*Is going over to bell, but stops.*) Is it merely to put coal on, my dear? I can do that.

MR. MANNINGHAM. Now then, Bella. We've had this out before. Be so good as to ring the bell.

MRS. MANNINGHAM. But, dear—Lizzie's out in the street. Let me do it. I can do it so easily. (*She comes over to do it.*)

MR. MANNINGHAM (*stopping her with outstretched hand*). No, no, no, no, no. Where's the girl? Let the girl come up if Lizzie's out.

MRS. MANNINGHAM. But, my dear ——

MR. MANNINGHAM. Go and ring the bell, please, Bella—there's a good child. (*MRS. MANNINGHAM gives in and goes back to ring the bell.*) Now, come here. (*She does so.*)

What do you suppose the servants are for, Bella? (*MRS. MANNINGHAM does not answer. There is a pause; then gently.*) Go on. Answer me. (*He rises.*) What do you suppose servants are for?

MRS. MANNINGHAM (*shamefacedly and scarcely audible, merely dutifully feeding him*). To serve us, I suppose, Jack.

MR. MANNINGHAM. Precisely. Then why——

MRS. MANNINGHAM. But I think we should consider them a little, that's all.

MR. MANNINGHAM. Consider them? There's your extraordinary confusion of mind again. You speak as though they work for no consideration. I happen to consider Elizabeth to the tune of sixteen pounds per annum. (*Crosses to MRS. MANNINGHAM.*) And the girl ten. Twenty-six pounds a year all told. And if that is not consideration of the most acute and lively kind, I should like to know what is.

MRS. MANNINGHAM. Yes, Jack. I expect you are right.

MR. MANNINGHAM. I have no doubt of it, my dear. It's sheer weak-mindedness to think otherwise. (*Pause as he crosses and looks in the mirror and she crosses to window and looks out into the street.*) What's the weather doing? Is it still as yellow?

MRS. MANNINGHAM. Yes, it seems to be denser than ever. Shall you be going out in this, Jack dear?

MR. MANNINGHAM. Oh—I expect so. Unless it gets very much worse after tea. (*There is a knock at the door.* MRS. MANNINGHAM *hesitates. There is another knock.*) Come in. (*He crosses and sits on sofa.*)

(ENTER NANCY, *the maid. She is a self-conscious, pretty, cheeky girl of nineteen. He turns and looks at* MRS. MANNINGHAM.)

NANCY (*stands looking at both, as* MRS. MANNINGHAM *hesitates to tell her why she rang the bell*). Oh, I beg your pardon. I thought the bell rang.

MR. MANNINGHAM. Yes, we rang the bell, Nancy. (*Pause.*) Go on, my dear, tell her why we rang the bell.

MRS. MANNINGHAM. Oh—yes—— We want some coal on the fire, Nancy, please.

(NANCY *looks at her impudently and then, with a little smile and toss of the head, goes over to put coal on the fire.*)

MR. MANNINGHAM (*after pause*). And you might as well light the gas, Nancy. This darkness in the afternoon is getting beyond endurance.

NANCY. Yes sir. (*With another barely discernible little smile, she gets the matches and goes to light the two incandescent mantles on each side of the fireplace.*)

MR. MANNINGHAM (*watches her as she lights the second mantle*). You're looking very impudent and pretty this afternoon, Nancy. Do you know that?

NANCY. I don't know at all, sir, I'm sure.

MR. MANNINGHAM. What is it? Another broken heart added to your list?

NANCY. I wasn't aware of breaking any hearts, sir.

MR. MANNINGHAM. I'm sure that's not true. And that complexion of yours. That's not true, either. I wonder what mysterious lotions you've been employing to enhance your natural beauties.

NANCY. I'm quite natural, sir, I promise you. (*Crosses to light lamp on C. table.*)

MR. MANNINGHAM. But you do it adroitly, I grant you that. What are your secrets? Won't you tell us the name of your chemist? Perhaps you could pass it on to Mrs. Manningham—(*a quick look by* NANCY *at* MRS. MANNINGHAM)—and help banish her pallor. She would be most grateful, I have no doubt.

NANCY. I'd be most happy to, I'm sure, sir.

MR. MANNINGHAM. Or are women too jealous of their discoveries to pass them on to a rival?

NANCY. I don't know, sir. Will that be all you're wanting, sir?

MR. MANNINGHAM. Yes. That's all I want, Nancy—— (*She stops.*) Except my tea.

NANCY. It'll be coming directly, sir. (*Goes out L.C. and leaves door open.*)

MRS. MANNINGHAM (*after a pause, reproachfully rather than angrily, moving to below table*). Oh, Jack, how can you treat me like that?

MR. MANNINGHAM. But, my dear, you're the mistress of the house. It was your business to tell her to put the coal on.

MRS. MANNINGHAM. It *isn't* that! It's humiliating me like that. As though I'd do anything to my face, and ask for *her* assistance if I did.

MR. MANNINGHAM. But you seem to look on servants as our natural equals. So I treated her as one. (*Pause as he sits down on settee and picks up newspaper.*) Besides, I was only trifling with her.

MRS. MANNINGHAM. It's strange that you can't see how you hurt me. That girl laughs at me enough already.

MR. MANNINGHAM. Laughs at you? What an idea. What makes you think she laughs at you?

MRS. MANNINGHAM. Oh—I know that she does in secret. In fact, she does so openly—more openly every day.

MR. MANNINGHAM. But, my dear— if she does that, doesn't the fault lie with you?

MRS. MANNINGHAM (*pause*). You mean that I'm a laughable person?

MR. MANNINGHAM. I don't mean anything. It's you who read meanings into everything, Bella dear. I wish you weren't such a perfect little silly. Come here and stop it. I've just thought of something rather nice.

MRS. MANNINGHAM. Something nice? What have you thought of, Jack?

MR. MANNINGHAM. I shan't tell you unless you come here.

MRS. MANNINGHAM (*going over and sitting on chair R. of table*). What is it, Jack? What have you thought of?

MR. MANNINGHAM. I read here that Mr. MacNaughton—the celebrated actor—is in London for another season.

MRS. MANNINGHAM. Yes. I read that. What of it, Jack?

MR. MANNINGHAM. What of it? What do you suppose?

MRS. MANNINGHAM. Oh, Jack dear. Do you mean it? Would you take me to see MacNaughton? You wouldn't take me to see MacNaughton, would you?

MR. MANNINGHAM. I not only would take you to see MacNaughton, my dear. I am going to take you to see MacNaughton. That is, if you want to go.

MRS. MANNINGHAM (*rises*). Oh, Jack! What heaven—what heaven!

MR. MANNINGHAM. When would you like to go? You have only three weeks, according to his advertisement.

MRS. MANNINGHAM (*to back of sofa and over* MR. MANNINGHAM's *shoulder*). Oh—what perfect heaven! Let me see. Do let me see!

MR. MANNINGHAM. There. You see? You can see him in comedy or tragedy—according to your choice. Which would you prefer, Bella—the comedy or the tragedy?

MRS. MANNINGHAM. Oh—it's so hard to say! Either would be equally wonderful. (*Crosses around back of settee to R. end and below.*) Which would you choose, if you were me?

MR. MANNINGHAM. Well—it depends —doesn't it?—upon whether you want to laugh or whether you want to cry.

MRS. MANNINGHAM. Oh—I want to laugh. But then, I should like to cry, too. In fact, I should like to do both. Oh, Jack, what made you decide to take· me? (*Sits on stool and leans against* MR. MANNINGHAM.)

MR. MANNINGHAM. Well, my dear, you've been very good lately, and I thought it would be well to take you out of yourself.

MRS. MANNINGHAM. Oh, Jack dear. You have been so much kinder lately. Is it possible you're beginning to see my point of view?

MR. MANNINGHAM. I don't know that I ever differed from it, did I, Bella?

MRS. MANNINGHAM. Oh, Jack dear. It's true. It's true. (*Looks at him.*) All I need is to be taken out of myself—some little change—to have some attention from you. Oh, Jack, I'd be better—I could really try to be better—you know in what way—if only I could get *out* of myself a little more.

MR. MANNINGHAM. How do you mean, my dear, exactly, *better*?

MRS. MANNINGHAM (*looks away*). You know—you know in what way, dear. About all that's happened lately. We said we wouldn't speak about it.

MR. MANNINGHAM (*drawing away and looking away*). Oh no—don't let's speak about that.

MRS. MANNINGHAM. No, dear, I don't want to—but what I say is so important. I *have* been better—even in the last week. Haven't you noticed it? And why is it? Because you have stayed in and been kind to me. The other night when you stayed in and played cards with me, it was like old days, and I went to bed feeling a normal, happy, healthy human being. And then the day after, when you read your book to me, Jack, and we sat by the fire, I felt all my love for you coming back then, Jack. And I slept that night like a child. All those ghastly dreads and terrible, terrible fears seemed to have vanished. And all just because you had given me your time and taken me from brooding on myself in this house all day and night.

MR. MANNINGHAM (*as he raises up her head off his shoulder*). I wonder if it is that—or whether it's merely that your medicine is beginning to benefit you?

MRS. MANNINGHAM. No, Jack dear, it's not my medicine. I've taken my medicine religiously—haven't I taken it religiously? Much as I detest it! It's more than medicine that I want. It's the medicine of a sweet, sane mind, of interest in something. Don't you see what I mean?

MR. MANNINGHAM. Well—we *are* talking about gloomy subjects, aren't we?

MRS. MANNINGHAM (*sitting on settee*). Yes. I don't want to be gloomy, dear—that's the last thing I want to be. I only want you to understand. Say you understand.

MR. MANNINGHAM (*turns to her*). Well, dear. Don't I seem to? Haven't I just said I'm taking you to the theater?

MRS. MANNINGHAM (*close to him again*). Yes, dear—yes, you have. Oh, and you've made me so happy—so happy, dear.

MR. MANNINGHAM. Well, then, which is it to be—the comedy or the tragedy? You must make up your mind.

MRS. MANNINGHAM (*with exulting solemnity*). Oh, Jack, which shall it be? (*Rising and crossing to down C. and showing her pleasure with delighted gestures.*) What shall it be? It matters so little! It matters so wonderfully little! I'm going to the play! (*To L.C., then to back of C. table and to back of settee and throws her arms around him and kisses him.*) Do you understand that, my husband! I'm going to the play! (*There is a knock on the L.C. door.* MRS. MANNINGHAM *crosses to the fireplace.*) Come in. (*Enter* NANCY, *carrying tray. Pause, as she starts to desk L.*) No, Nancy, I think we'll have it on the table today.

NANCY (*still with impudence*). Oh —just as you wish, madam.

(*Pause, as she puts tray on table C., arranges cups, and puts books, etc., on one side.*)

MRS. MANNINGHAM (*at mantelpiece*). Tell me, Nancy—if you were being taken to the play, and had to choose between comedy and tragedy, which would *you* choose?

NANCY. No, madam? Oh—I'd go for the comedy all the time.

MRS. MANNINGHAM. Would you? Why would you choose the comedy, Nancy?

NANCY. I like to laugh, madam, I suppose.

MRS. MANNINGHAM. Do you? Well —I daresay you're right. I must bear it in mind. Mr. Manningham's taking me next week, you see.

NANCY. Oh yes? I hope you enjoy it. I'll bring the muffins directly. (*Goes out, leaves the doors open, and turns to the R.*)

(*As* NANCY *goes out,* MRS. MANNINGHAM *puts out her tongue at her.* MANNINGHAM *sees this.*)

MR. MANNINGHAM. My dear—what are you doing?

MRS. MANNINGHAM (*as she crosses to the foot of the stairs*). The little beast! Let her put that in her pipe and smoke it.

MR. MANNINGHAM. But what has she done?

MRS. MANNINGHAM. Ah—you don't know her. She tries to torment and score off me all day long. You don't see these things. A man wouldn't. (MR. MANNINGHAM *rises.*) She thinks me a poor thing. And now she can suffer the news that you're taking me to the theater.

MR. MANNINGHAM. I think you imagine things, my dear.

MRS. MANNINGHAM. Oh no, I don't. We've been too familiar with her. (*Arranging chairs, in an emotionally happy state.*) Come along, my dear. You sit one side and I the other—like two children in the nursery.

MR. MANNINGHAM (*stands with back to fire*). You seem wonderfully pleased with yourself, Bella. I must take you to the theater more often, if this is the result.

MRS. MANNINGHAM (*sitting L. of table*). Oh, Jack—I wish you could.

MR. MANNINGHAM. I don't really know why we shouldn't. I used to like nothing so much when I was a boy. In fact, you may hardly believe it, but I even had an ambition to be an actor myself at one time.

MRS. MANNINGHAM (*lifting teapot*). I can well believe it, dear. Come along to your tea now.

MR. MANNINGHAM (*as he moves up back of the settee*). You know, Bella, that must be a very superb sensation. To take a part and lose yourself entirely in the character of someone else. I flatter myself I could have made an actor.

MRS. MANNINGHAM (*pouring tea*). Why, of course, my dear. You were cut out for it. Anyone can see that.

MR. MANNINGHAM (*crosses slowly L. behind settee*). No—do you think so—seriously? I always felt a faint tinge of regret. Of course, one would have required training, but I believe I should have made out—and might

have reached the top of the tree for all I know.

"To be or not to be. That is the question.
Whether 'tis nobler in the mind to suffer
The slings and arrows of outrageous fortune,
Or to take arms—against a sea of troubles,
And, by opposing, end them."

(NANCY *enters, sets the muffin dish down on table during the recitation, and goes out.*)

MRS. MANNINGHAM (*after* NANCY *exits*). You see how fine your voice is? Oh—you've made a great mistake.

MR. MANNINGHAM (*crosses to R. of table. Lightly*). I wonder.

MRS. MANNINGHAM. Then if you had been a famous actor, I should have had a free seat to come and watch you every night of my life. And then called for you at the stage door afterward. Wouldn't that have been paradise?

MR. MANNINGHAM (*as he sits R. of table*). A paradise of which you would soon tire, my dear. I have no doubt that after a few nights you would be staying at home again, just as you do now.

MRS. MANNINGHAM. Oh no, I wouldn't. I should have to keep my eye on you for all the hussies that would be after you.

MR. MANNINGHAM. There would be hussies after me, would there? That is an added inducement, then.

MRS. MANNINGHAM. Yes—I know it, you wretch. But you wouldn't escape me. (*Lifting cover of muffin dish.*) They look delicious. Aren't you glad I thought of them? (*Passes the salt.*) Here's some salt. You want heaps of it. Oh, Jack dear, you must forgive me chattering on like this, but I'm feeling so happy.

MR. MANNINGHAM. I can see that, my dear.

MRS. MANNINGHAM. I'm being taken to the play, you see. Here you are. I used to adore these as a child, didn't you? (*Offers muffin to* MR. MAN-NINGHAM.) I wonder how long it is since we had them? (MR. MANNING-HAM *looks up C. at wall.*) We haven't had them since we've been married, anyway. Or have we? Have we?

MR. MANNINGHAM. I don't know, I'm sure. (*Suddenly rising, looking at the wall upstage, and speaking in a calm, yet menacing way.*) I don't know—Bella——

MRS. MANNINGHAM (*after pause, dropping her voice almost to a whisper*). What is it? What's the matter? What is it now?

MR. MANNINGHAM (*walking over to fireplace in front of settee and speaking with his back to her*). I have no desire to upset you, Bella, but I have just observed something very much amiss. Will you please rectify it at once, while I am not looking, and we will assume that it has not happened.

MRS. MANNINGHAM. Amiss? What's amiss? For God's sake don't turn your back on me. What has happened?

MR. MANNINGHAM. You know perfectly well what has happened, Bella, and if you will rectify it at once I will say no more about it.

MRS. MANNINGHAM. I don't know. I don't know. You have left your tea. Tell me what it is. Tell me.

MR. MANNINGHAM. Are you trying to make a fool of me, Bella? What I refer to is on the wall behind you. If you will put it back, I will say no more about it.

MRS. MANNINGHAM. The wall behind me? What? (*Turns.*) Oh—yes. The picture has been taken down—— Yes—— The picture—— Who has taken it down? Why has it been taken down?

MR. MANNINGHAM. Yes. Why has it been taken down? Why, indeed. You alone can answer that, Bella. Why was it taken down before? Will you please take it from wherever you have hidden it and put it back on the wall again?

MRS. MANNINGHAM. But I haven't hidden it, Jack. (*Rises.*) I didn't do it. Oh, for God's sake look at me. I didn't do it. I don't know where it is. Someone else must have done it.

MR. MANNINGHAM. Someone else? (*Turning to her.*) Are you suggesting perhaps that I should play such a fantastic and wicked trick?

MRS. MANNINGHAM. No, dear, no! But someone else. (*Going to him.*) Before God, I didn't do it! Someone else, dear, someone else.

MR. MANNINGHAM (*shaking her off*). Will you please leave go of me. (*Walking over to bell.*) We will see about "someone else."

MRS. MANNINGHAM (*crossing to front of settee*). Oh, Jack—don't ring the bell. Don't ring it. Don't call the servants to witness my shame. It's not my shame, for I haven't done it—but *don't* call the servants! Tell them not to come. (*He has rung the bell. She goes to him.*) Let's talk of this between ourselves! Don't call that girl in. Please!

MR. MANNINGHAM (*shaking her off violently*). Will you please leave go of me and sit down there! (*She sits in chair above the desk. He goes to fireplace.*) Someone else, eh? Well— we shall see. (MRS. MANNINGHAM, *in chair, sobs.*) You had better pull yourself together, hadn't you? (*There is a knock at the door.*) Come in. (*Enter* ELIZABETH L.C. *and leaves the doors open.*) Ah, Elizabeth. Come in please, Elizabeth. Shut the door. (*Pause as she does so.*) Well, come in, come into the room. (*Pause as* ELIZABETH *crosses to the back of the chair L. of the table.*) Now, Elizabeth, do you notice anything amiss in this room? —Look carefully around the walls and see if you notice anything amiss. (*Pause as* ELIZABETH *looks around the room, and when she sees the space of the missing picture she stands still.*) Well, Elizabeth, what do you notice?

ELIZABETH. Nothing, sir. Except the picture's been taken down.

MR. MANNINGHAM. Exactly. The picture has been taken down. You noticed it at once. Now was that picture in its place when you dusted the room this morning?

ELIZABETH. Yes sir. It was, sir. I don't understand, sir.

MR. MANNINGHAM. Neither do I, Elizabeth, neither do I. And now, before you go, just one question. Was it you who removed that picture, Elizabeth?

ELIZABETH. No sir. Of course I ain't, sir.

MR. MANNINGHAM. You did not. And have you ever, at any time, removed that picture from its proper place?

ELIZABETH. No sir. Never, sir. Why should I, sir?

MR. MANNINGHAM. Indeed, why should you?—And now please, Elizabeth, will you kiss that Bible, will you, as a token of your truthfulness, fetch that Bible from my desk? (*Pause.* ELIZABETH *hesitates. Then she does so.*) Very well, you may go. (*She starts to the desk with Bible, and* MANNINGHAM *motions to her to put it on C. table.*) And please send Nancy in here at once.

ELIZABETH. Yes sir. (*Opens doors, goes out, closes doors, looking at both.*)

MRS. MANNINGHAM (*going to him*). Jack—spare me that girl. Don't call her in. I'll say anything. I'll say that I did it. I did it, Jack, I did it. Don't have that girl in. Don't!

MR. MANNINGHAM. Will you have the goodness to contain yourself? (*There is a knock at the L.C. door.* MRS. MANNINGHAM *sits in chair below fireplace.*) Come in.

NANCY (*opens doors, enters, and leaves doors open. Crossing to settee*). Yes sir. Did you want me?

MR. MANNINGHAM. Yes, I do want you, Nancy. If you will look at the wall behind you, you will see that the picture has gone.

NANCY (*going upstage*). Why. My word. So it has. (*Turns.*) What a rum go! (*Turns to* MANNINGHAM.)

MR. MANNINGHAM. I did not ask for any comment on your part, Nancy. Kindly be less insolent and answer what I ask you. Did *you* take that picture down, or did you not?

NANCY. Me? Of course I didn't. (*Comes to him slyly.*) What should I want to move it for, sir?

MR. MANNINGHAM. Very good. Now will you kiss that Bible lying there, please, as a solemn oath that you did not—and you may go.

NANCY. Willingly, sir. (*She does so, and places Bible on C. table again with a little smile.*) If I'd done it I'd've——

MR. MANNINGHAM. That is all, Nancy. You may go. (NANCY *goes out and closes doors. Going to Bible as if to replace it on the desk.*) There! (*As he crosses down L. and faces* MRS. MANNINGHAM.) I think we may now be said to have demonstrated conclusively——

MRS. MANNINGHAM (*rises; crossing L. to him*). Give me that Bible! Give it to me! Let me kiss it, too! (*Snatches it from him.*) There! (*Kisses it.*) There! Do you see? (*Kisses it.*) There! Do you see that I kiss it?

MR. MANNINGHAM (*as he puts out his hand for the Bible*). For God's

sake be careful what you do. Do you desire to commit sacrilege above all else?

MRS. MANNINGHAM. It is no sacrilege, Jack. Someone else has committed sacrilege. Now see—I swear before God Almighty that I never touched that picture. (*Kisses it.*) There! (*She comes close to him.*)

MR. MANNINGHAM (*he grabs Bible*). Then, by God, you are mad, and you don't know what you do. You unhappy wretch—you're stark gibbering mad—like your wretched mother before you.

MRS. MANNINGHAM. Jack—you promised you would never say that again.

MR. MANNINGHAM (*crosses R. Pause.*) The time has come to face facts, Bella. (*Half turns to her.*) If this progresses you will not be much longer under *my* protection.

MRS. MANNINGHAM (*crossing to him*). Jack—I'm going to make a last appeal to you. I'm going to make a last appeal. I'm desperate, Jack. Can't you see that I'm desperate? If you can't, you must have a heart of stone.

MR. MANNINGHAM (*turns to her*) Go on. What do you wish to say?

MRS. MANNINGHAM. Jack—(*crosses to front of settee*)—I may be going mad, like my poor mother—but if I am mad, you have got to treat me gently. Jack—before God—I never lie to you knowingly. If I have taken down that picture from its place I have not known it. *I have not known it.* If I took it down on those other occasions I did not know it, either. (*Turns and crosses to C.*) Jack, if I steal your things—your rings—your keys—your pencils and your handkerchiefs, and you find them later at the bottom of my box, as indeed you do, then I do not know that I have done it—— Jack, if I commit these fantastic, meaningless mischiefs—so meaningless—(*a step toward him*)—why should I take a picture down from its place? (*Pause.*) If I do all these things, then I am certainly going off my head, and must be treated kindly and gently so that I may get well. (*Crosses to him.*) You must bear with me, Jack, bear with me—not storm and rage. God knows I'm trying, Jack, I'm trying! Oh, for God's sake, believe me that I'm trying and be kind to me!

MR. MANNINGHAM. Bella, my dear—have you any idea where that picture is now?

MRS. MANNINGHAM. Yes, yes, I suppose it's behind the cupboard.

MR. MANNINGHAM. Will you please go and see?

MRS. MANNINGHAM (*vaguely*). Yes —yes. (*Crosses below him, goes R. to upper end of secretary, and produces it.*) Yes, it's here.

MR. MANNINGHAM (*reproachfully. As he crosses to the desk, places the Bible on it, and crosses up L.*) Then you did know where it was, Bella. *Turns to her.*) You did know where it was.

MRS. MANNINGHAM (*as she starts toward him*). No! No! I only supposed it was! I only supposed it was because it was found there before!

It was found there twice before. Don't you see? I *didn't* know—I didn't!

MR. MANNINGHAM. There is no sense in walking about the room with a picture in your hands, Bella. Go and put it back in its proper place.

MRS. MANNINGHAM (*pause as she hangs the picture on wall—she comes to the back of the chair R. of table*). Oh, look at our tea. We were having our tea with muffins——

MR. MANNINGHAM. Now, Bella, I said a moment ago that we have got to face facts. And that is what we have got to do. I am not going to say anything at the moment, for my feelings are running too high. In fact, I am going out immediately, and I suggest that you go to your room and lie down for a little in the dark.

MRS. MANNINGHAM. No, no—not my room. For God's sake don't send me to my room! (*Grabbing chair.*)

MR. MANNINGHAM. There is no question of sending you to your room, Bella. (*Crosses to her.*) You know perfectly well that you may do exactly as you please.

MRS. MANNINGHAM. I feel faint, Jack. (*He goes quickly to her and supports her.*) I feel faint——

MR. MANNINGHAM. Very well. (*Leading her to settee and she sinks down with her head to L. end.*) Now, take things quietly and come and lie down, here. Where are your salts? (*Crosses to secretary, gets salts, and returns to her back of set-*

tee.) Here they are. (*Pause.*) Now, my dear, I am going to leave you in peace.

MRS. MANNINGHAM (*eyes closed, reclining*). Have you got to go? Must you go? Must you always leave me alone after these dreadful scenes?

MR. MANNINGHAM. Now, no argument, please. I had to go in any case after tea, and I'm merely leaving you a little earlier, that's all. (*Pause. Going into wardrobe and returning with undercoat on.*) Now is there anything I can get for you?

MRS. MANNINGHAM. No, Jack dear, nothing. You go.

MR. MANNINGHAM. Very good. (*Goes toward his hat and overcoat, which are on the chair above desk, and stops.*) Oh, by the way, I shall be passing the grocer and I might as well pay that bill of his and get it done with. Where is it, my dear? I gave it to you, didn't I?

MRS. MANNINGHAM. Yes, dear. It's on the secretary. (*Half rising.*) I'll——

MR. MANNINGHAM (*crossing to secretary*). No, dear—don't move— don't move. I can find it. (*At secretary and begins to rummage.*) I shall be glad to get the thing off my chest. Where is it, dear? Is it in one of these drawers?

MRS. MANNINGHAM. No—it's on top. I put it there this afternoon.

MR. MANNINGHAM. All right. We'll find it—we'll find it. Are you sure it's here, dear? There's nothing here except some writing paper.

MRS. MANNINGHAM (*half rising and speaking suspiciously*). Jack, I'm quite sure it *is* there. Will you look carefully?

MR. MANNINGHAM (*soothingly*). All right, dear. Don't worry. I'll find it. Lie down. It's of no importance, I'll find it. No, it's not here. It must be in one of the drawers.

MRS. MANNINGHAM (*She has rushed to the secretary*). It is not in one of the drawers! I put it out here on top! You're not going to tell me *this* has gone, are you? ⎱ (*Together.*)

MR. MANNINGHAM (*speaking at the same time*). My dear. Calm yourself. Calm yourself.

MRS. MANNINGHAM (*searching frantically*). I laid it out here myself! Where is it? (*Opening and shutting drawers.*) Where is it? Now you're going to say I've hidden this!

MR. MANNINGHAM (*walking away to L. end of settee*). My God!— What new trick is this you're playing upon me?

MRS. MANNINGHAM (*at R. lower end of settee*). It was there this afternoon! I put it there! This is a plot! This is a filthy plot! You're all against me! It's a plot! (*She screams hysterically.*)

MR. MANNINGHAM (*coming to her and shaking her violently*). Will you control yourself! Will you control yourself! (*Pause until she calms down.*) Listen to me, madam, if you utter another sound I'll knock you down and take you to your room and lock you in darkness for a week. I have been too lenient with you, and I mean to alter my tactics.

MRS. MANNINGHAM (*sinks to her knees*). Oh, God help me! God help me!

MR. MANNINGHAM. May God help you, indeed. Now listen to me. I am going to leave you until ten o'clock. (*He lifts her up.*) In that time you will recover that paper and admit to me that you have lyingly and purposely concealed it—if not, you will take the consequences. (*Pause as he places her in the chair down R. and he crosses L. to above desk.*) You are going to see a doctor—(*he stops and turns to* BELLA)—madam, more than one doctor—(*puts his hat on and throws his coat over his arm*)—and they shall decide what this means. Now do you understand me?

MRS. MANNINGHAM. Oh God—be patient with me. If I am mad, be patient with me.

MR. MANNINGHAM. I have been patient with you and controlled myself long enough. It is now for you to control yourself, or take the consequences. Think upon that, Bella. (*Goes to L.C. doors and opens them.*)

MRS. MANNINGHAM. Jack—Jack—don't go—Jack—— You're still going to take me to the theater, aren't you?

MR. MANNINGHAM. What a question to ask me at such a time. No,

madam, emphatically, I am not. You play fair by me, and I'll play fair by you. But if we are going to be enemies, you and I, you will not prosper, believe me. (*Goes out.*)

(*Short pause and then a door slams. Whimperingly,* MRS. MANNINGHAM *rises, aiding herself by the mantel, and crosses up to the secretary, searching through the drawers, then crosses to C., looks at the picture at up C., and shudders. Then, turning to C. table, she takes up the pitcher of water from the tea tray, crosses to the secretary, opens the upper door of the secretary, gets a glass, then opens a drawer and takes out a paper of medicine. She takes this medicine and follows it with a drink of water. This is, obviously, incredibly nasty and almost chokes her. She staggers over to the C. table and replaces the pitcher of water and then turns down the table lamp. Then, crossing to the settee, she sinks down on it with her head toward the fireplace and sobs. She mutters, "Peace—Peace—Peace." She breathes heavily as a clock in the house strikes six. Pause. There is a knock at the door. She does not hear it. There is another knock and* ELIZABETH *enters L.C.*)

ELIZABETH. Madam—Madam—— (*She crosses down to back of settee.*)

MRS. MANNINGHAM. Yes!—Yes!— What is it, Elizabeth? Leave me alone.

ELIZABETH (*peering through the darkness*). Madam, there's somebody called.

MRS. MANNINGHAM. Who is it? I don't want to be disturbed.

ELIZABETH. It's a gentleman, madam —he wants to see you.

MRS. MANNINGHAM. Tell him to go, Elizabeth. He wants to see my husband. My husband's out.

ELIZABETH. No, madam—he wants to see you. You must see him, madam.

MRS. MANNINGHAM. Oh, leave me alone. Tell him to go away. I want to be left alone.

ELIZABETH. Madam, madam. I don't know what's going on between you and the master, but you've got to hold up, madam. You've got to hold up.

MRS. MANNINGHAM. I am going out of my mind, Elizabeth. That's what's going on.

ELIZABETH (leaning over back of settee with her arms around MRS. MANNINGHAM). Don't talk like that, madam. You've got to be brave. You mustn't go on lying here in the dark, or your mind will go. You must see this gentleman. It's you he wants— not the master. He's waiting to see you. Come, madam, it'll take you out of yourself.

MRS. MANNINGHAM. Oh, my God— what new torment is this? I'm not in a fit state, I tell you.

ELIZABETH (crosses to back of C. table). Come, madam, I'll turn up the light. (She does so. Then ELIZABETH picks up box of matches and, crossing to the desk lamp, lights it.) There. Now you'll be all right.

MRS. MANNINGHAM. Elizabeth! What have you done? I can't have anyone in. I'm not fit to be seen.

ELIZABETH. You look all right, madam. You mustn't take on so. Now—I'll call him in. (Goes to the door and can be heard calling, "Will you come in, please, sir?")

(The door is heard to slam. MRS. MANNINGHAM rises, half paralyzed, then runs over to the mirror above the mantelpiece and adjusts her hair. Stands with her back to the fireplace, waiting. ELIZABETH returns, holding back the door. DETEC-TIVE ROUGH enters. He is middle-aged—greying, short, wiry, active, brusque, friendly, overbearing. He has a low, warming chuckle and completely dominates the scene from the beginning.)

ROUGH. Thank you. Ah—good evening. (As he crosses down to L. end of settee.) Mrs. Manningham, I believe—— How are you, Mrs. Manningham? (Chuckling, offers his hand.)

MRS. MANNINGHAM (shaking hands). How do you do? I'm very much afraid——

ROUGH. You're very much afraid you don't know me from Adam? That's about the root of the matter, isn't it?

(ELIZABETH goes out L.C., closing the doors.)

MRS. MANNINGHAM. Oh no—it's not that—but no doubt you have come to see my husband?

ROUGH (who is still holding her hand and looking at her appraisingly). Oh no! You couldn't be further out. (Chuckling.) On the contrary, I have chosen this precise moment to call when I knew your husband was out. May I take off my things and sit down? (*Starts to remove his coat.*)

MRS. MANNINGHAM. Why, yes, I suppose you may.

ROUGH. You're a good deal younger and more attractive than I thought, you know. But you're looking very pale. Have you been crying?

MRS. MANNINGHAM. Really—I'm afraid I don't understand at all.

ROUGH. You will do so, madam, very shortly. (*Goes L.C. and begins to remove scarf.*) You're the lady who's going off her head, aren't you? (*Chuckles. To lower end of desk. He puts his hat on the desk and is removing his scarf and overcoat.*)

MRS. MANNINGHAM (*terrified*). What made you say that? (*Goes toward him. Stops at C.*) Who are you? What have you come to talk about?

ROUGH. Ah, you're running away with things, Mrs. Manningham, and asking me a good deal I can't answer at once. (*Taking off coat and putting it on chair down L. and then crosses to down L.C.*) Instead of that, I am going to ask you a question or two. Now, please, will you come here and give me your hands? (*Pause. She obeys.*) Now, Mrs. Manningham, I want you to take a good look at me, and see if you are not looking at someone to whom you can give your trust. I am a perfect stranger to you, and you can read little in my face besides that. But I can read a great deal in yours.

MRS. MANNINGHAM (*pause*). What? What can you read in mine?

ROUGH. Why, madam, I can read the tokens of one who has traveled a very long way upon the path of sorrow and doubt—and will have, I fear, to travel a little further yet before she comes to the end. But I fancy she is coming toward the end, for all that. Come now, are you going to trust me and listen to me?

MRS. MANNINGHAM (*pause*). Who are you? God knows I need help.

ROUGH (*still holding her hands*). I very much doubt whether God knows anything of the sort, Mrs. Manningham. If He did, I believe He would have come to your aid before this. But I am here, and so you must give me your faith.

MRS. MANNINGHAM (*withdraws her hands and withdraws a step*). Who are you? Are you a doctor?

ROUGH. Nothing so learned, ma'am. Just a plain police detective.

MRS. MANNINGHAM (*shrinks away*). Police detective?

ROUGH. Yes. Or was some years ago. (*Crossing to chair L. of table.*) At any rate, still detective enough to see that you've been interrupted in your tea. Couldn't you start again, and let me have a cup? (*He stands back of chair L. of table and holds it for her.*)

MRS. MANNINGHAM. Why, yes—yes. I will give you a cup. It only wants water. (*She begins to busy herself with hot water, cup, pot, etc., throughout the ensuing conversation.*)

ROUGH (*crosses around above table and to back of chair R. of it*). You never heard of the celebrated Sergeant Rough, madam? Sergeant Rough, who solved the Claudesley Diamond Case—Sergeant Rough, who hunted down the Camberwell dogs—Sergeant Rough, who brought Sandham himself to justice. (*He has his hand on back of chair as he looks at her.*) Or were all such sensations before your time?

MRS. MANNINGHAM (*looking up at* ROUGH). Sandham? Why, yes—I have heard of Sandham—the murderer—the Throttler.

ROUGH. Yes—madam—Sandham the Throttler. And you are now looking at the man who gave Sandham to the man who throttled him. And that was the common hangman. In fact, Mrs. Manningham—you have in front of you one who was quite a personage in his day—believe it or not.

MRS. MANNINGHAM (*as she adds water to the tea*). I quite believe it. Won't you sit down? I'm afraid it won't be very hot.

ROUGH. Thank you. (*Sitting.*) How long have you been married, Mrs. Manningham?

MRS. MANNINGHAM (*pouring tea*). Five years—and a little.

ROUGH. Where have you lived during all that time, Mrs. Manningham? Not here, have you?

MRS. MANNINGHAM (*putting milk in his cup and passing it to him*). No—

first we went abroad—then we lived in Yorkshire, and then six months ago my husband bought this house.

ROUGH. You bought it?

MRS. MANNINGHAM. Yes. I had a bit of money. My husband thought this was an excellent investment.

ROUGH (*taking cup*). You had a bit of money, eh? That's very good. And does your husband always leave you alone like this in the evenings?

MRS. MANNINGHAM. Yes. He goes to his club, I believe, and does business.

ROUGH. Oh yes. (*He is stirring his tea, thoughtfully.*)

MRS. MANNINGHAM. Yes——

ROUGH. And does he give you a free run of the whole house while he's out?

MRS. MANNINGHAM. Yes—— Well, no—not the top floor. Why do you ask?

ROUGH. Ah—not the top floor.

MRS. MANNINGHAM. No—no—— Will you have some sugar?

ROUGH. Thanks.

MRS. MANNINGHAM (*bending over eagerly to answer his questions*). What were you saying?

ROUGH (*as he takes sugar. Lightly and chuckling*). Before I go any further, Mrs. Manningham, I must tell you there's a leakage in this household. You have a maid called Nancy?

MRS. MANNINGHAM. Yes—yes——

ROUGH. And Nancy walks out of an evening with a young man named Booker in my employ. I only live a few streets away from you, you know.

MRS. MANNINGHAM. Oh yes?

ROUGH (*with a chuckle*). Well, there is hardly anything which goes on in this house which is not described in detail to Booker, and from that quarter it reaches me.

MRS. MANNINGHAM. I knew it! I knew she talked. Now I know it, she shall be dismissed.

ROUGH. Oh no—no such retribution is going to overtake her at the moment, Mrs. Manningham. In fact, I fancy you are going to be heavily in debt to your maid, Nancy. If it were not for her indiscretions I should not be here now, should I?

MRS. MANNINGHAM. What do you mean? What is this mystery? You must not keep me in the dark. What is it?

ROUGH. I'm afraid I shall have to keep you in the dark for a little, Mrs. Manningham, as I am still quite far down in the dark myself. Can I have another lump of sugar in this?

MRS. MANNINGHAM. Yes. (*Passes bowl to him.*)

ROUGH. Thank you. (*Pause*). We were talking about the top floor.

(*Helping himself to several lumps.*) There is a bedroom above this, and above that again *is* the top floor? Is that right?

MRS. MANNINGHAM. Yes. But it's shut up. When we first took the house, my husband said we would not need the upstairs quarters—until there were children.

ROUGH. You've never been up to the top floor, Mrs. Manningham? (*Pause.*)

MRS. MANNINGHAM. No one goes up there.

ROUGH. Not even a servant to dust?

MRS. MANNINGHAM. No.

ROUGH. Rather funny?

MRS. MANNINGHAM (*pause*). Funny? (*Pause.*) I don't know. (*But she does think so.*)

ROUGH. I think it is. Now, Mrs. Manningham, to ask a personal question. When did you first get the notion into your head that your reason was playing you tricks?

MRS. MANNINGHAM (*about to drink her tea. Pause. Looks at* ROUGH *and then sets her cup down*). How did you know?

ROUGH. Never mind how I know. When did it begin?

MRS. MANNINGHAM. I always had that dread. My mother died insane, when she was quite young. When she was my age. But only in the last six months, in this house—things began to happen——

ROUGH. Which are driving you mad with fear?

MRS. MANNINGHAM (*gasping*). Yes. Which are driving me mad with fear.

ROUGH. Is it the house itself you fear, Mrs. Manningham?

MRS. MANNINGHAM. Yes. I suppose it is. I hate the house. I always did.

ROUGH. And has the top floor got anything to do with it?

MRS. MANNINGHAM. Yes, yes, it has. That's how all this dreadful horror began.

ROUGH. Ah—now you interest me beyond measure. Do tell me about the top floor.

MRS. MANNINGHAM. I don't know what to say. It all sounds so incredible. It's when I'm alone at night. I get the idea that—somebody's walking about up there—(*looking up*)—up there. At night, when my husband's out—I hear noises, from my bedroom, but I'm too afraid to go up.

ROUGH. Have you told your husband about this?

MRS. MANNINGHAM. No. I'm afraid to. He gets angry. He says I imagine things which don't exist.

ROUGH. It never struck you, did it, that it might be your own husband walking about up there?

MRS. MANNINGHAM. Yes—that *is* what I thought—but I thought I must be mad. (*As she turns to* ROUGH.) Tell me how you know.

ROUGH. Why not tell me first how *you* knew, Mrs. Manningham.

MRS. MANNINGHAM (*she rises and goes toward fireplace*). It's true, then! It's true. I knew it. I knew it! When he leaves this house he comes back. He comes back and walks up there above—up and down—up and down. (*Turns to fireplace.*) He comes back like a ghost. How does he get up there?

ROUGH (*rises, crosses to* MRS. MANNINGHAM). That's what we're going to find out, Mrs. Manningham. But there are such commonplace resources as roofs and fire escapes, you know. Now please don't look so frightened. Your husband is no ghost, believe me, and you are very far from mad. (*Pause.*) Tell me now, what made you first think it was him?

MRS. MANNINGHAM. It was the light —the gaslight—it went down and it went up—— (*Starts to cry.*) Oh, thank God I can tell this to someone at last. I don't know who you are, but I must tell you. (*Crosses to* ROUGH.)

ROUGH (*takes her hands*). Now try to keep calm. You can tell me just as well sitting down, can't you? Won't you sit down? (*He moves back.*)

MRS. MANNINGHAM. Yes—yes. (*She sits down on R. end of settee.*)

ROUGH (*looks around*). The light, did you say? Did you see a light from a window?

MRS. MANNINGHAM. No. In this house I can tell everything by the light of the gas. You see the mantel there. Now it's burning full. But if an extra light went on in the kitchen or someone lit it in the bedroom, then this one would sink down. It's the same all over the house.

ROUGH. Yes—yes—that's just a question of insufficient pressure, and it's the same in mine. But go on, please.

MRS. MANNINGHAM (*pause*). Every night, after he goes out, I find myself waiting for something. Then all at once I look round the room and see that the light is slowly going down. Then I hear tapping sounds— persistent tapping sounds. At first I tried not to notice it, but after a time it began to get on my nerves. I would go all over the house to see if anyone had put on an extra light, but they never had. It's always at the same time—about ten minutes after he goes out. That's what gave me the idea that somehow *he* had come back and that it was *he* who was walking about up there. I go up to the bedroom, but I daren't stay there because I hear noises overhead. I want to scream and run out of the house. I sit here for hours, terrified, waiting for him to come back, and I always know when he's coming, always. Suddenly the light goes up again, and ten minutes afterward I hear his key in the lock—(*a look at L.C. doors*)—and he's back again.

ROUGH (*lightly—chuckling*). How very strange, indeed. You know, Mrs. Manningham, you should have been a policeman.

MRS. MANNINGHAM. Are you laughing at me? Do you think I imagine everything, too?

ROUGH. Oh no! I was merely praising the keenness of your observation. I not only think you are right in your suppositions, I think you have made a very remarkable discovery, and one which may have very far-reaching consequences.

MRS. MANNINGHAM. Far-reaching? How?

ROUGH. Well, let's leave that for the moment. (*Moves closer to her.*) Tell me, that is not the only cause, is it, which has lately given you reason to doubt your sanity? (*Pause.*) Has anything else been happening? (*Pause.*) Don't be afraid to tell me.

MRS. MANNINGHAM. Yes, there are other things. I hardly dare speak of them. It has been going on for so long. This business of the gas has only brought it to a head. It seems that my mind and memory are beginning to play me tricks.

ROUGH. Tricks? What sort of tricks? When?

MRS. MANNINGHAM. Incessantly— but more and more of late. He gives me things to look after, and when he asks for them they are gone and can never be found. Then he misses his rings, or his studs, and I will hunt the place for them, and he will find them lying hidden at the bottom of my workbox. Twice the door of that room—(*turning and looking at door up R.*)—was found locked with the key vanished. That was also found at the bottom of my box. Only today, before you came, that picture had been taken from the wall and hidden. (*He looks around at picture.*) Who could have done it but myself? I try to remember. (*He turns to her.*) I break my heart trying to remember. But I can't. Oh, and then there was that terrible business about the dog——

ROUGH. The dog?

MRS. MANNINGHAM. We have a little dog. A few weeks ago it was found with its paw hurt. He believes—— Oh God, how I tell you what he believes—that I had hurt the dog. He does not let the dog near me now. He keeps it in the kitchen and I am not allowed to see it! I begin to doubt, don't you see? I begin to believe I imagine everything. Perhaps I do. Are you here? Is this a dream, too? Who are you? (*Rises.*) I'm afraid they are going to lock me up.

ROUGH. Do you know, Mrs. Manningham, it has occurred to me that you'd be all the better for a little medicine.

MRS. MANNINGHAM. Medicine. Are you a doctor? You're not a doctor, are you?

ROUGH (*chuckling*). No, I'm not a doctor, but that doesn't mean that a little medicine would do you any harm.

MRS. MANNINGHAM. But I have medicine. He makes me take it. It does me no good, and I hate it. How can medicine help a mind that's ill?

ROUGH. Oh—but mine's an exceptional medicine. I have some with me now. You must try it.

MRS. MANNINGHAM. What medicine is it?

ROUGH (*he rises and goes over L.*). You shall sample it and see. (*At C.*) You see, it has been employed by humanity, for several ages, for the purpose of the instantaneous removal of dark fears and doubts. That seems to fit you, doesn't it? (*Crosses to L. to coat, then turns to her.*)

MRS. MANNINGHAM. The removal of doubt. How could a medicine effect that?

ROUGH. Ah—that we don't know. The fact remains that it does. Here we are. (*Produces what is obviously a bottle of whisky and crosses to L. of C. table.*) You see, it comes from Scotland. Now, madam, have you such a thing handy as two glasses or a couple of cups?

MRS. MANNINGHAM (*crosses to L. end of settee*). Why—are you having some too?

ROUGH. Oh yes. I am having some above all things. We could use these cups, if you like.

MRS. MANNINGHAM. No. (*She goes to secretary and brings out two glasses and crosses to R. of C. table.*) I will get two——

ROUGH. Ah—thank you—the very thing. Now we shan't be long.

MRS. MANNINGHAM. What is it? I so dislike medicine. What does it taste like?

ROUGH. Delicious! Something between ambrosia and methylated spirits. Do you mean to say you've never tasted good scotch whisky, Mrs. Manningham?

MRS. MANNINGHAM. Whisky? But I must not take whisky. I can't do that!

ROUGH (*pouring it out*). You underestimate your powers, Mrs. Manningham. You see, I don't want you thinking you can't trust your reason. This will give you faith in your reason like nothing else. Now for some water. All right, this will do. (*Takes water from pitcher and pours it into the glasses.*) There! (*Hands glass to her.*) Tell me—(*is pouring water into his own*)—did you ever hear of the Cabman's Friend, Mrs. Manningham?

MRS. MANNINGHAM. The Cabman's Friend?

ROUGH. Yes. How nice to see you smile. Here's your very good health. (*Drinks.*) Go on—— (*She drinks.*) There—is it so nasty?

MRS. MANNINGHAM. No. I rather like it. My mother used to give us this as children when we had the fever.

ROUGH. Ah, then you're a hardened whisky drinker. But you'll enjoy it better sitting down.

MRS. MANNINGHAM. Yes. (*Sitting down on chair below fireplace. He drinks.*) What were you saying? Who is the Cabman's Friend?

ROUGH. Ah. The Cabman's Friend. (*Crosses to her.*) You should ask me who *was* the Cabman's Friend, Mrs Manningham, for she was an old lady who died many years ago. (*Pause, as he puts whisky on mantelpiece.*)

MRS. MANNINGHAM. An old lady years ago? What has she to do with me?

ROUGH. A great deal, I fancy—(*crosses to R. end of settee*)—if you will follow me patiently. Her name was Barlow—Alice Barlow—and she was an old lady of great wealth, and decided eccentricities. In fact, her principal mania in life was the protection of cabmen. You may think that an extraordinary hobby, but in her odd way she did a lot of good. She provided these men with shelters, clothing, pensions, and so forth, and that was her little contribution to the sum of the world's happiness; or rather her little stand against the sum of the world's pain. There is a great deal of pain in this world, Mrs. Manningham, you know. (*Crosses to upper end of fireplace.*) Well, it was not my privilege to know her, but it was my duty, on just one occasion, to see her. (*Turns to her.*) That was when her throat was cut open, and she lay dead on the floor of her own house.

MRS. MANNINGHAM. Oh, how horrible! Do you mean she was murdered?

ROUGH. Yes. (*Crosses to R. end of settee.*) She was murdered. I was only a comparatively young officer at the time. It made an extremely horrible, in fact I may say lasting, impression on me. You see, the murderer was never discovered but the motive was obvious enough. Her husband had left her the Barlow rubies—(*crosses to L. end of settee*)—and it was well known that she kept them, without any proper precautions, in her bedroom on an upper floor. (*Turns to her.*) She lived alone except for a deaf servant in the basement. Well, for that she paid the penalty of her life.

MRS. MANNINGHAM. But I don't see——

ROUGH. There were some sensational features about the case. The man seemed to have got in at about ten at night, and stayed till dawn. Apart, presumably, from the famous rubies, there were only a few trinkets taken, but the whole house had been turned upside down, and in the upper room every single thing was flung about or torn open. Even the cushions of the chairs were ripped up with his bloody knife, and the police decided that it must have been a revengeful maniac as well as a robber. I had other theories, but I was a nobody then, and not in charge of the case.

MRS. MANNINGHAM. What were your theories?

ROUGH (crossing up R.). Well, it seemed to me, from all that I gathered here and there, that the old lady might have been an eccentric, but that she was by no means a fool. It seemed to me—(crossing to back of settee)—that she might have been one too clever for this man. We presume he killed her to silence her, but what then? What if she had not been so careless? (Slowly crossing to her.) What if she had got those jewels cunningly hidden away in some inconceivable place, in the walls, floored down, bricked in, maybe? What if the only person who could tell him where they were was lying dead on the floor? Would not that account, Mrs. Manningham, for all that strange confusion in which the place was found? (Crossing back of settee to C.) Can't you picture

him, Mrs. Manningham, searching through the night, ransacking the place, hour after hour, growing more and more desperate, until at last the dawn comes and he has to slink out into the pale street, the blood and wreckage of the night· behind? (Turns to her.) And the deaf servant down in the basement sleeping like a log through it all.

MRS. MANNINGHAM. Oh, how horrible! How horrible indeed! And was the man never found?

ROUGH. No, Mrs. Manningham, the man was never found. Nor have the Barlow rubies ever come to light.

MRS. MANNINGHAM. Then perhaps he found them after all, and may be alive today.

ROUGH. I think he is almost certainly alive today, but I don't believe he found what he wanted. That is, if my theory is right.

MRS. MANNINGHAM. Then the jewels may still be where the old lady hid them?

ROUGH. Indeed, Mrs. Manningham, if my theory is right the jewels must still be where she hid them. The official conclusion was quite otherwise. The police, naturally and quite excusably, presumed that the murderer had got them, and there was no reopening of matters in those days. Soon enough the public forgot about it. I almost forgot about it myself. But it would be funny, wouldn't it, Mrs. Manningham, if after all these years I should turn out to be right?

MRS. MANNINGHAM. Yes, yes, indeed. But what has this to do with me?

ROUGH. Ah, that is the whole question, Mrs. Manningham. What, indeed? What has the obscure murder of an old lady fifteen years ago to do with an attractive, though I am afraid at present somewhat pale and wan, young woman who believes she is going out of her mind? Well, I believe there is a link, however remote, wild and strange it may be, and that is why I am here.

MRS. MANNINGHAM. It's all so confusing. Won't you——

ROUGH. Do you conceive it possible, Mrs. Manningham, that that man might never have given up hope of one day getting at the treasure which lay there?

MRS. MANNINGHAM. Yes. Yes. Possibly. But how——

ROUGH. Can you conceive that he may have waited years—gone abroad, got married even, until at last his chance came to resume the search begun on that terrible night? (*Crossing down to her.*) You don't follow where I am leading at all, do you, Mrs. Manningham?

MRS. MANNINGHAM. Follow you? I think so.

ROUGH. You know, Mrs. Manningham, of the old theory that the criminal always returns to the scene of his crime.

MRS. MANNINGHAM. Yes?

ROUGH. Ah yes, but in this case there is something more than morbid compulsion—— There is real treasure there to be unearthed if only he can search again, search methodically,

without fear of interruption, without causing suspicion. And how would he do that? (*All at once she rises.*) Don't you think—— What's the matter, Mrs. Manningham?

MRS. MANNINGHAM (*as she looks at brackets and backs away to R.C.*). Quiet! Be quiet! He has come back! Look at the light! It is going down! (*Pause as light sinks.*) Wait! There! (*Pause.*) He has come back, you see. (*As she looks up at ceiling.*) He is upstairs now.

ROUGH. Dear me, now. How very odd that is. How very odd, indeed.

MRS. MANNINGHAM (*whispering*). He is in the house, I tell you. You must go. He will know you are here. You must go.

(*Warn curtain.*)

ROUGH. How dark it is. (*Crosses down to R. end of settee.*) You could hardly see to read.

MRS. MANNINGHAM. You must go. He is in the house. Please go.

ROUGH (*quickly coming to her and taking her arms in his hands*). Quiet, Mrs. Manningham, quiet! You have got to keep your head. ·Don't you see my meaning, yet? Don't you understand that this was the house?

MRS. MANNINGHAM. House? What house?

ROUGH. The old woman's house, Mrs. Manningham. This house, here, these rooms, these walls. Fifteen years ago Alice Barlow lay dead on the floor in this room. Fifteen years ago the man who murdered her ransacked this house—below and above—but could not find what he sought. What if he is still searching, Mrs. Manningham? (*Indicating upstairs.*) What if he is up there—still searching? Now do you see why you must keep your head?

MRS. MANNINGHAM. But my husband, my husband is up there!

ROUGH (*drops her arms*). Precisely that, Mrs. Manningham. Your husband. (*Going for her drink on mantelpiece.*) You see, I am afraid you are married to a tolerably dangerous gentleman. (*Takes second glass off mantel and crosses to her.*) Now drink this quickly, as we have a great deal to do.

(*He stands there, holding out glass to her. She remains motionless.*)

THE CURTAIN FALLS

ACT TWO

No *time has passed.* MRS. MANNINGHAM *takes the whisky from* ROUGH *in a mechanical way and stares at him.*

MRS. MANNINGHAM. This house—— How do you know this was the house?

ROUGH. Why, ma'am, because I was on the case, and came here myself, that's all.

MRS. MANNINGHAM. The idea is mad. I have been married five years. How can you imagine my husband is—what you imagine he may be?

ROUGH. Mrs. Manningham——

MRS. MANNINGHAM. Yes? (*Pause.*)

ROUGH. When the police came into this place fifteen years ago, as you can understand, there was a great deal of routine work to be done— interviewing of relatives and friends and so forth. Most of that was left to me.

MRS. MANNINGHAM. Well?

ROUGH. Well, amongst all the acquaintances and relatives, nephews and nieces, etc., that I interviewed, there happened to be a young man of the name of Sydney Power. I suppose you have never heard that name at all, have you?

MRS. MANNINGHAM. Power?

ROUGH. Yes, Sydney Power. It conveys nothing to you?

MRS. MANNINGHAM. Sydney Power. No——

ROUGH. Well—(*crosses to L. of table and turns to* MRS. MANNINGHAM *and during the following speech pours himself out another drink*)—he was a kind of distant cousin, apparently much attached to the old lady, and even assisting her in her good works. The only thing was that I remembered his face. Well, I saw that face again just a few weeks ago. It took me a whole day to recollect where I had seen it before, but at last I remembered.

MRS. MANNINGHAM. Well—what of it? What if you did remember him?

ROUGH. It was not much my remembering Mr. Sydney Power, Mrs. Manningham. What startled me was the lady on his arm and the locality in which I saw him.

MRS. MANNINGHAM. Oh—who was the lady on his arm?

ROUGH. You were the lady on his arm, Mrs. Manningham—(turning toward window and crossing up C.) —and you were walking down this street.

MRS. MANNINGHAM (crossing to R. of table). What are you saying? Do you mean you think my husband— my husband is this Mr. Power?

ROUGH. Well, not exactly, for if my theories are correct—— (He drinks.)

MRS. MANNINGHAM. What are you saying? (Sits.) You stand there talking riddles. You are so cold. You are as heartless and cold as he is.

ROUGH (coming down to L. of table). No, Mrs. Manningham, I am not cold, and I am not talking riddles. (Puts his drink on table.) I am just trying to preserve a cold— (sits)—and calculating tone, because you are up against the most awful moment in your life, and your whole future depends on what you are going to do in the next hour.

Nothing less.
for your fre
for the mom

MRS. MANN

ROUGH (
her). You
mind, Mrs. Manning...
You are slowly, methodically, sy tematically being *driven* out of your mind. And why? Because you are married to a criminal maniac who is afraid you are beginning to know too much—a criminal maniac who steals back to his own house at night, still searching for something he could not find fifteen years ago. Those are the facts, wild and incredible as they may seem. (Crossing to table.) His name is no more Manningham than mine is. He is Sydney Power and he murdered Alice Barlow in this house. Afterward he changed his name, and he has waited all these years, until he found it safe to acquire this house in a legal way. He then acquired the empty house next door. Every night, for the last few weeks, he has entered that house from the back, climbed up onto its roof, and come into this house by the skylight. I know that because I have seen him do it. (Crossing to back of settee.) You have watched the gaslight, and without knowing it been aware of the same thing. (Pause as he crosses up C. then down to chair L. of table.) He is up there now. Why—(crossing to L.C.) —he should employ this mad, secretive, circuitous way of getting at what he wants, God Himself only knows. For the same reason, perhaps, that he employs this mad, secretive, circuitous way of getting rid of you: that is, by slowly driving you mad and into a lunatic asylum.

MANNINGHAM. Why?

ROUGH. The fact that you had some money, enough to buy this house, is part of it, I expect. For now that he's got that out of you he doesn't need you any longer. (*Crosses and sits L. of table.*) Thank God you are not married to him, and that I have come here to save you from the workings of his wicked mind.

MRS. MANNINGHAM. Not married? Not married? He married me.

ROUGH. I have no doubt he did, Mrs. Manningham. (*Rises and turns away to L.*) Unfortunately, or rather fortunately—(*turns to her*)—he contracted the same sort of union with another lady many years before he met you. Moreover, the lady is still alive, and the English law has a highly exacting taste in monogamy. You see, I have been finding things out about Mr. Sydney Power. (*A look at the ceiling.*)

MRS. MANNINGHAM. Are you speaking the truth? (*Rises.*) My God—are you speaking the truth? Where is this wife now?

ROUGH (*crossing to L.C.*) I'm afraid she is the length of the world away—on the continent of Australia, to be precise, where I know for a fact he spent two years. Did you know that?

MRS. MANNINGHAM. No. (*Pause. She crosses to front of settee and faces fireplace.*) I—did—not—know—that.

ROUGH. Ah yes. If only I could find her, things would be easier, and that's the whole root of the matter,

Mrs. Manningham—(*crossing to back of settee*)—so far I am only dealing in guesses and *half facts*. I have got to have evidence, and that is why I came to see you. *You have got to give me the evidence* or *help* me find it.

MRS. MANNINGHAM (*turning upstage and facing ROUGH*). This is my husband. Don't you understand—this is my husband. He married me. Do you ask me to betray the man who married me?

ROUGH. By which you mean, of course, the man who has betrayed you into thinking that you are married to him—don't you?

MRS. MANNINGHAM. But I'm married to him. You must go. I must think this out. You must go. I must cling to the man I married. Mustn't I?

ROUGH. Indeed, cling to him by all means, but do not imagine you are the only piece of ivy on the garden wall. You can cling to him if you desire, as his fancy women in the low resorts of the town cling to him. This is the sort of wall you have to cling to, ma'am.

MRS. MANNINGHAM (*sits on settee*). Women? What are you suggesting?

ROUGH. I'm not suggesting anything. I am only telling you what I have seen. He comes to life at night, this gentleman upstairs, in more ways than one. (*Crossing to C.*) I have made it my business to follow him on some of his less serious excursions, and I can promise you he has a taste in *unemployed actresses* which he is at no pains to conceal.

MRS. MANNINGHAM (*after pause*). God in heaven!—what *am* I to believe?

ROUGH (*crossing to L. end of settee*). Mrs. Manningham, it is hard to take everything from you, but you are no more tied to this man, you are under no more obligation to him, than those wretched women in those places. You must learn to be thankful for that.

MRS. MANNINGHAM (*pause*). What do you want me to do? What do you want?

ROUGH (*pause as he crosses down and sits*). I want his papers, Mrs. Manningham—his identity. There is some clue somewhere in this house, and we have got to get at it. (*Looking around the room,* ROUGH *has now completely changed his tone.*) Where does he keep his papers?

MRS. MANNINGHAM (*rises*). Papers? I know of no papers. Unless his bureau——

ROUGH (*rises—crosses at C. around L. end of settee and looks around room and to R.*). Yes. His bureau? His bureau?

MRS. MANNINGHAM. Yes. There. (*Points to desk L. As he crosses and is above table.*) But he keeps it always locked. (*He stops at L.C.*) I have never seen it open.

ROUGH. Ah—he keeps it locked, does he?

MRS. MANNINGHAM. It is just his desk—his bureau——

ROUGH (*crosses L. above desk and around to back of it*). Very well. We will have a look inside.

MRS. MANNINGHAM. But it is locked. How can you, if it is locked?

ROUGH. Oh—it doesn't look so very formidable. You know, Mrs. Manningham, one of the greatest regrets of my life is that fate never made me one of two things—one was a gardener—(*going to overcoat, to fetch ring of keys and implements*) —the other a burglar—both quiet occupations, Mrs. Manningham. As for burgling, I think, if I'd started young and worked my way up, I should have been a genius. (*Crosses back to desk.*) Now let's have a look at this.

MRS. MANNINGHAM (*crossing to him at desk*). But you must not touch this. He will know what you have done.

ROUGH. Come now, ma'am. You're working with me, aren't you—not against me? (*Looks at desk.*) Yes— yes—— Now do you mind if I take off my coat? I'm a man who never feels at work until his coat's off. (*He is taking off his coat and hanging on chair down L., revealing a pink fancy shirt.*) Quite a saucy shirt, don't you think? You didn't suspect I was such a dandy, did you? Now. (*Sits at desk and gets out keys.*) Let's have a real look at this.

MRS. MANNINGHAM (*after a pause. As she crosses up C. facing R.*). But you must not tamper with that. He will know what you have done.

ROUGH. Not if we are clever enough. And this one here doesn't even ask for cleverness. You see, Mrs. Manningham, there are all manner of ——

(*Light comes up.*)

MRS. MANNINGHAM (*she looks at brackets and crosses to above desk*). Stop—stop talking. Haven't you noticed? Haven't you noticed something?

ROUGH. Noticed? I've only——

MRS. MANNINGHAM. Stop! Yes—I was right. Look. Can't you see? The light! It's going up. He's coming back.

ROUGH. The light?

MRS. MANNINGHAM. Quiet! (*Pause, after which the light slowly goes up in a tense silence. Whispering.*) There. It's come back. You see. (*Crossing to L.C.*) You must go. Don't you see? He's coming back. He's coming back and you must go!

ROUGH (*rises*). God bless my soul. This looks as if the unexpected *has* entered in.

MRS. MANNINGHAM. Yes. He *always* does the unexpected. I never know what he'll do. You must go. (*Crosses to upper end of desk.*)

ROUGH (*without moving, looking up ruminatively*). I wonder. Yes. Well, well. (*Puts the keys in his pocket and begins to put on his coat.*) Now —will you go and ring that bell for Elizabeth?

MRS. MANNINGHAM. Elizabeth. Why do you want her?

ROUGH. Do as I say, and ring the bell. At once. Please. Or you can go and fetch her if you like. (MRS. MANNINGHAM *crosses up and rings bell.*) Now let me see.

MRS. MANNINGHAM. Go, please!— Go, please do! You must go at once. (*Crossing to above desk.*) Why do you want Elizabeth?

ROUGH (*picks up overcoat, puts it on, then his scarf, and crosses below desk to her*). All in good time. He's not going to jump through the window, you know. In fact he can't be round at our front door in less than five- minutes—unless he's a magician. Now, can you see anything I've missed?

MRS. MANNINGHAM. No. No. (*Turns and sees whisky bottle and crosses and gets it and gives it to ROUGH.*) Yes, the whisky here.

ROUGH. Oh yes. I told you you'd make a good policeman. Don't forget the glasses.

MRS. MANNINGHAM. Oh, do go, please, please go.

(ELIZABETH *enters L.C.* MRS. MANNINGHAM *puts glasses away in secretary and slowly crosses down R.*)

ROUGH. Ah—Elizabeth—come here, will you?

ELIZABETH (*crosses to ROUGH*). Yes sir?

ROUGH. Elizabeth, you and I have got to do a little, quite calm, but rather quick thinking. You've told me you're anxious to help your mistress, Elizabeth?

ELIZABETH. Why, yes sir, I told you I was, sir. But what's it all about?

ROUGH. Are you anxious to help your mistress, blindly, without asking any questions?

ELIZABETH. Yes sir. But you see——

ROUGH. Come now, Elizabeth. Are you or are you not?

ELIZABETH (after pause, looking at MRS. MANNINGHAM, in quiet voice). Yes sir.

ROUGH. Good. Now, Elizabeth, Mrs. Manningham and I have reason to suppose that in about five minutes' time the master is returning to this house. He mustn't see me leaving. Would you be good enough to take me down to your kitchen and hide me away for a short space of time? You can put me in the oven if you like.

ELIZABETH. Yes sir. But you see—— ⎫

MRS. MANNINGHAM (as he crosses to window and looks out). You must go. You must go. He won't see you if you go now. ⎬ (Together.)

ROUGH. What were you saying, Elizabeth?

ELIZABETH. Yes sir. You could come to the kitchen. But—Nancy's down there, sir.

ROUGH. Nancy! What the devil's this now? I thought this was Nancy's afternoon off. Was it not arranged that I should come when Nancy was away?

ELIZABETH (agitated). Yes sir. But for some reason she's stayed on. I think she's got a young man, and I couldn't make her go, could I, sir? If I'd done that, I'd've——

ROUGH. All right—all right. Then she was here when I came, and she knows I am here—is that it?

ELIZABETH. Oh no. She was in the scullery when I answered the door, and I said it was a man who had come to the wrong house. She hasn't no idea, sir, and I'm——

ROUGH. All right. All right. (Quickly crossing below the table to R.C.) That's better news. But it means you can't entertain me in the kitchen. (At down R.C. turns to ELIZABETH.) Now where are you going to hide me, Elizabeth? Make up your mind quickly.

ELIZABETH. I don't know, sir. Unless you go to the bedroom. Mine and Nancy's, I mean.

ROUGH (crossing up to R. of ELIZABETH). That sounds altogether entrancing! Shall we go there now?

ELIZABETH (coming to him. MRS. MANNINGHAM goes L.). Yes sir, but supposing Nancy went up there before she goes out?

ROUGH. You're a good soul and you think of everything, Elizabeth. (Going to up R.C.) Where does this lead to, and what's the matter with this?

ELIZABETH (crossing to ROUGH). It's where he dresses, where he keeps his clothes. Yes sir. Go in there, sir. He won't see you there. There's a big wardrobe there, at the back.

ROUGH (going toward up R. door). Excuse me. (Goes through door up R.)

MRS. MANNINGHAM (*crossing to C.*). Oh, Elizabeth.

ELIZABETH (*crosses to* MRS. MANNINGHAM). It's all right, ma'am. Don't take on so. It'll be all right.

MRS. MANNINGHAM. I'm sure he ought to go.

ELIZABETH. No, ma'am. He knows best. (ROUGH *enters from up* R.) He's bound to know best.

ROUGH (*as he trots across to upper end of window for a peep*). Perfect accommodation. (*Has seen something.*) Yes, there he is. (*Crossing to* MRS. MANNINGHAM.) Now we really have got to hurry. Get off to bed, Mrs. Manningham, quick. And you, Elizabeth, go to your room. You can't get downstairs in time. Hurry, please. Elizabeth, turn down that lamp.

(ELIZABETH *does so. He goes to turn down gas.*)

MRS. MANNINGHAM. To bed? Am I to go to bed?

ROUGH (*really excited for the first time*). Yes, quick. He's coming. Don't you understand? Go there and stay there. You have a bad head-ache—(*cross to fireplace and start to turn down upper gas bracket*) —a bad headache. (*Quite angry, turning from gas of downstage bracket.*) Will you go, in heaven's name!

(MRS. MANNINGHAM *goes upstairs and* ELIZABETH *exits* L.C. *and to the* R., *leaving the doors open as* ROUGH *turns down the gas in the downstage bracket. There is a light from the hall through the open*

doors. ROUGH *crosses to the* L. *end of the settee, pauses a moment, watching the hall, then nimbly on tiptoes crosses up to the open doors and listens. After a short pause there is the sound of the front door closing. He stiffens and starts to quietly trot to the up* R. *door and, as he reaches up* R.C., *feels his head, discovers his hat missing, and, turning quickly, trots to the desk, gets his hat, puts it on as he quickly crosses to up* R. *door and exits. There is a short pause and* MR. MANNINGHAM *appears in the doorway, peers into the room, and enters, closes the doors and looks up the stairway, then crosses to upstage bracket, turns it up, then to the downstage bracket and turns it up. Then he goes back of the settee, puts his hat on the settee, crosses to the bell, and rings it. Then leisurely he starts to the fireplace. As he reaches the settee* ELIZABETH *opens the doors and enters.*)

ELIZABETH. Did you ring, sir?

MR. MANNINGHAM (*turning to* ELIZABETH). Yes, I did. (*Without yet saying why he has rung he removes his coat and places it over settee and then comes and stands with his back to the fireplace.*) Where is Mrs. Manningham, Elizabeth?

ELIZABETH. I think she's gone to bed, sir. I think she had a bad head-ache and went to bed.

MR. MANNINGHAM. Oh, indeed. And how long has she been in bed, do you know?

ELIZABETH. She went just a little while ago, sir—I think, sir.

MR. MANNINGHAM. Oh. I see. Then we must be quiet, mustn't we? Walk about like cats.—Can you walk about like a cat, Elizabeth?

ELIZABETH (*trying to smile*). Yes sir. I think so, sir.

MR. MANNINGHAM (*mincing upstage*). Very well, Elizabeth. Walk about like a cat. All right. That's all.

ELIZABETH. Yes sir. Thank you, sir.

(*Just as* ELIZABETH *is going to exit, he calls her back.*)

MR. MANNINGHAM. Er—Elizabeth.

ELIZABETH (*coming back*). Yes sir? (MANNINGHAM *is again silent.*) Did you call, sir?

MR. MANNINGHAM. Yes. Why haven't you cleared away the tea-things?

ELIZABETH (*crossing to above table*). Oh—I'm sorry, sir. I was really just about to, sir.

MR. MANNINGHAM (*crossing L. to L.C.*). Yes. I think you had better clear away the tea-things, Elizabeth.

ELIZABETH. Yes sir. (*After pause, putting a dish on the tray.*) Excuse me, sir, but were you going to have some supper, sir?

MR. MANNINGHAM (*crossing to desk*). Oh yes. I am going to have supper. The question is, am I going to have supper here?

ELIZABETH. Oh yes, sir. Are you having it out, sir?

MR. MANNINGHAM. Yes, I am having it out. (MANNINGHAM *takes off his undercoat and puts it carefully over a chair L. of table. He is beginning to undo his tie.*) I have come back to change my linen.

(*He is undoing his collar. There is a pause.*)

ELIZABETH (*looks up and realizes his coat is off*). Do you want a fresh collar, sir? Shall I get you a fresh collar?

MR. MANNINGHAM. Why, do you know where my collars are kept?

ELIZABETH. Why, yes, sir. In your room, there, sir. Shall I get you one, sir?

MR. MANNINGHAM. What a lot you know, Elizabeth. And do you know the sort of collar I want tonight?

ELIZABETH. Why, yes, sir—I think I know the sort of collar, sir.

MR. MANNINGHAM (*as he crosses up back of settee*). Then all I can say is you know a great deal more than I do. No—I think you must let me choose my own collar. (*Turns to* ELIZABETH.) That is, if I have your permission, Elizabeth.

ELIZABETH (*gazing at him*). Yes sir —yes sir——

(MANNINGHAM *crosses to door up R. and exits.* ELIZABETH *puts on the table the plate she is holding and lowers her head, remaining motionless in suspense. Not a sound comes from the other room, and nearly a quarter of a minute goes by. At last* MANNINGHAM *comes out in a per-*

fectly leisurely way. He is putting his tie on and crosses down to mirror over fireplace, looking at himself in the mirror during the ensuing conversation.)

MR. MANNINGHAM. What did you think about Mrs. Manningham tonight, Elizabeth?

ELIZABETH. Mrs. Manningham, sir? In what way do you mean, sir?

MR. MANNINGHAM. Oh—just as regards her general health, Elizabeth.

ELIZABETH. I don't know, sir. She certainly seems very unwell.

MR. MANNINGHAM. Yes. I doubt if you can guess to what extent she is unwell. (*Turns to* ELIZABETH.) Or are you beginning to guess?

ELIZABETH. I don't know, sir.

MR. MANNINGHAM (*crossing to back of settee*). I'm afraid I was compelled to drag you and Nancy into our troubles tonight. Perhaps I should not have done that.

ELIZABETH. It all seems very sad, sir.

MR. MANNINGHAM (*smiling and somewhat appealingly as he takes a step toward* ELIZABETH). I'm at my wits' end, Elizabeth. You know that, don't you?

ELIZABETH. I expect you are, sir.

MR. MANNINGHAM. I have tried everything—kindness, patience, cunning, even harshness—to bring her to her senses. But nothing will stop these wild, wild hallucinations; nothing will stop these wicked pranks and tricks.

ELIZABETH. It seems very terrible, sir.

MR. MANNINGHAM. You don't know a quarter of it, Elizabeth. You only see what is forced upon your attention—as it was tonight. You have no conception of what goes on all the time. (*He is looking at his tie in his hand.*) No—not this one, I think—— (*Starts to up R. door.*)

ELIZABETH. Do you want another tie, sir?

MR. MANNINGHAM (*stops and turns to* ELIZABETH). Yes. (*He strolls again into the other room.* ELIZABETH *turns and watches the up R. door intently. After a pause he comes out with another tie. As he enters* ELIZABETH *quickly turns to tea table. He crosses down to fireplace mirror. He is putting his tie on during the ensuing conversation.*) I suppose you know about Mrs. Manningham's mother, Elizabeth?

ELIZABETH. No sir. What of her, sir?

MR. MANNINGHAM. Not of the manner in which she died?

ELIZABETH. No sir.

MR. MANNINGHAM. She died in the madhouse, Elizabeth, without any brain at all in the end.

ELIZABETH. Oh, sir!—How terrible, sir.

MR. MANNINGHAM. Yes, terrible indeed. The doctors could do nothing. (*Pause. Turns to* ELIZABETH.) You know, don't you, that I shall have to bring a doctor to Mrs. Manningham before long, Elizabeth? (*As he crosses to L. below table and to L. of it and gets his undercoat.*) I have fought against it to the last, but it can't be kept a secret much longer.

ELIZABETH. No sir—no sir.

MR. MANNINGHAM (*putting on his undercoat*). I mean to say, you know what goes on. You can testify to what goes on, can't you?

ELIZABETH. Indeed, sir. Yes.

MR. MANNINGHAM. Indeed, you may *have* to testify in the end. Do you realize that? (*Pause. Sharp.*) Eh?

ELIZABETH (*looking quickly up at him*). Yes sir. I would only wish to help you both, sir.

MR. MANNINGHAM (*crossing below table to settee, gets coat and puts it on, crosses to mirror and adjusts coat*). Yes, I believe you there, Elizabeth. You're a very good soul. I sometimes wonder how you put up with things in this household—this dark household. I wonder why you do not go. You're very loyal.

ELIZABETH (*looking at him in an extraordinary way. He cannot see her*). Always loyal to you, sir. Always loyal to you.

MR. MANNINGHAM. There now, how touching. I thank you, Elizabeth. (*Crosses back of settee to* ELIZABETH.) You will be repaid later for what you have said, and repaid in more ways than one. You understand that, don't you?

ELIZABETH. Thank you, sir. I only want to serve, sir.

MR. MANNINGHAM (*crosses back of settee, gets hat*). Yes, I know that. Well, Elizabeth, I am going out. In fact, I'm even going to try to be a little gay. Can you understand that, or do you think it is wrong?

ELIZABETH. Oh no, sir. No. You should get all the pleasure you can, sir, while you can.

MR. MANNINGHAM. I wonder—yes—I wonder—it's a curious existence, isn't it? Well—good night, Elizabeth. (*Goes off L.C. and to L.*)

ELIZABETH. Good night, sir—good night.

(MANNINGHAM *has left the door open.* ELIZABETH *quickly crosses up to door and looks after him. After a pause* ROUGH *comes forth and* ELIZABETH *turns to him. He and* ELIZABETH *stand there looking at each other. At last* ROUGH *goes to the window and looks out. The door is heard slamming.*)

ROUGH (*coming back to* ELIZABETH). He was right when he said you would be repaid, Elizabeth. Though not in the way he thinks. (*Taking off hat, puts it on desk, then his overcoat and muffler and puts them on chair down L. Pause.*) Will you go and get Mrs. Manningham?

ELIZABETH. Yes sir. I'll get her, sir. (*Starts to stairs.*)

(ROUGH *gets implements out of overcoat pocket.* MRS. MANNINGHAM *comes downstairs.*)

ROUGH. Ah—there you are.

MRS. MANNINGHAM. I saw him go.

(ELIZABETH *takes tray and exits L.C. to R.*)

ROUGH. Now we must get back to work.

MRS. MANNINGHAM. What did he want? What did he come back for?

ROUGH. He only came to change his clothes. Turn up the lamp, will you? (MRS. MANNINGHAM *does so, and comes to him as he again reaches desk.*) Now let's have another look at this.

MRS. MANNINGHAM (*crosses to desk*). What if he comes back again? There is no light to warn us now.

ROUGH. Oh, you've realized that, have you? Well, Mrs. Manningham, we've just got to take that risk. (*Takes his keys from pocket.*) This is going to be child's play, I fancy. Just a little patience—a little adroitness in the use—— (*The front door slams.*) What's that? Go and have a look, will you? (MRS. MANNINGHAM *crosses to the window.*) We seem to be rather bothered this evening, don't we?

MRS. MANNINGHAM. It's all right. It's only Nancy. I forgot. She usually goes out at this time.

ROUGH. She uses the front door—does she?

MRS. MANNINGHAM. Oh yes. Indeed she does. She behaves like the mistress in this house.

ROUGH. A saucy girl. (*The top of the bureau opens.*) Ah—here we are. Next to a key there's nothing a lock appreciates like kindness.

MRS. MANNINGHAM. Will you be able to close it again?

ROUGH. Yes. No damage done. There we are. (*Pulls the upstage drawer out and puts it up on top of desk.* MRS. MANNINGHAM *turns away to R.*) Now. Let's see. Doesn't seem much here. (*Picks up brooch.*) And when she got there the cupboard was bare—and so the poor detective——

MRS. MANNINGHAM. What is that in your hand? What is that in your hand?

ROUGH (*holding up a brooch*). Why, do you recognize this?

MRS. MANNINGHAM. Yes! My brooch! Yes! Is there anything else there? What else is there?—Look, my watch! Oh God, it's my watch!

ROUGH. This also is your property, then? (*He is watching her.*)

MRS. MANNINGHAM. Yes. Both of them. This watch I lost a week ago —my brooch has been missing three months. And he said he would give me no more gifts because I lost them. He said that in my wickedness—(*he looks in drawer*)—I hid them away! Inspector, is there anything else? (*Pause. She crosses to upper end of the desk and looks over his shoulder.*) Is there a bill there? (*He looks up at her.*) Is there a grocery bill?

ROUGH (*searching drawer*). A grocery bill?—No—there doesn't seem to be. (*He has pulled out a letter which he drops on the desk.*)

MRS. MANNINGHAM (*picking up letter*). One moment—one moment.

This letter!—this letter! (*She goes on reading it.*) It's from my cousin —my cousin——

ROUGH. Is your husband's correspondence with your relations very much to the point at the moment, Mrs. Manningham?

MRS. MANNINGHAM. You don't understand. (*Speaking rapidly.*) When I was married I was cast off by all my relations. I have not seen any of them since I was married. They did not approve my choice. I have longed to see them again more than anything in the world. When we came to London—to this house—I wrote to them, I wrote to them twice. There never was any answer. Now I see why there never was any answer. (*Dazed.*) This letter is to me. It's from my cousin.

ROUGH (*cynically*). Yet you never got it. Now you're beginning to understand, Mrs. Manningham?

MRS. MANNINGHAM (*as she crosses to chair L. of table and sits*). Listen. Let me read to you what he says. Let me read it to you. (*Feverishly.*) "Dear Cousin—All of us were overjoyed to hear from you again." (*Looks up at* ROUGH.) Overjoyed, do you hear that? (*Returns to reading the letter.*) He goes on to say that his family are in Devonshire and that they have gone to the country. He says we must meet and recapture old ties. (*She is showing signs of great emotion.*) He says that they all want to see me—that I must go and stay with them—that they will give me—that they will give me their Devonshire cream to fatten my cheeks and their fresh air to bring the sparkle back to my eyes—they

will give me—they'll give me—— (*Breaking down.* ROUGH *crosses to her.*) Dear God, they wanted me back! They wanted me back all the time!

ROUGH (*coming to her as she cries softly*). Poor child. You shall have your Devonshire cream and you shall have the fresh air to bring the sparkle back into your eyes. (*She looks up at him.*) Why, I can see a sparkle in them already. If you will be brave now and trust me, you will not have to wait long. Are you going to trust me?

MRS. MANNINGHAM. Thank you, Inspector, for bringing me this letter. (ROUGH *crosses up and to back of desk.*) What do you wish me to do?

ROUGH. For the moment, nothing. Tell me. This drawer here. It seems to me to have a special lock. Has it ever been open to your knowledge?

MRS. MANNINGHAM (*hesitantly*). No.

ROUGH. No?—I suspected as much. Yes, this is a tougher proposition, I'm afraid. (*He goes to his overcoat and produces an iron instrument.*)

MRS. MANNINGHAM (*rising and crossing to C. to stop him*). What are you going to do? Are you going to force it?

ROUGH (*calmly*). If I possibly can. I don't know that——

MRS. MANNINGHAM (*crossing to desk*). But you must not do that. You must not. What shall I say when my husband comes back?

ROUGH (*ironically. Getting his jimmy from coat*). I have no idea *what* you will say when he comes back, Mrs. Manningham. But then I have no idea what you will do, Mrs. Manningham, if I have no evidence to remove you from his loving care for good.

MRS. MANNINGHAM (*torn with doubts*). Oh God. I am afraid. What can I do?

ROUGH (*sharply*). There is only one thing we *can* do—go ahead. If we go back now, we are lost. I am going to force it and gamble on finding something. Are you with me?

MRS. MANNINGHAM (*tormented as she studies him*). But, don't you see—— All right. Force it! Force it! But be quick. (*She turns away to up R.*)

ROUGH. There's no hurry, madam. He's quite happy where he is. Now I don't like violent methods—of this sort—it makes me feel like a dentist. There—— (*There's a sound of splitting wood.*) All over now. Now let's have a look.

MRS. MANNINGHAM (*after pause in which she watches him. As he pulls out the drawer*). Is there anything there? Is there anything there?

ROUGH (*looking at papers*). No, I don't see anything yet—I don't see anything. Wait a minute—— No—no —— What's this? (*As he picks up a bundle of papers.*) Mr. Manningham—Mr. Manningham—Mr. Manningham——

MRS. MANNINGHAM. Is there nothing?

ROUGH. No—not a thing. We have lost our gamble, ma'am, I'm afraid.

MRS. MANNINGHAM (*frightened*). Oh, dear me, what are we to do? What are we to do? (*Crosses to C.*)

ROUGH (*crossing above the desk to her*). Some rapid thinking at the moment. Don't have any fear, Mrs. Manningham. I've been in many a tighter corner than this. Let's get those things back to begin with, shall we? Give me the watch and the brooch. (*Takes watch and brooch.*) We must put them back where they were. (*Starts up back of desk.*)

MRS. MANNINGHAM. Yes—here they are.

ROUGH. Here on the right, was it not?

MRS. MANNINGHAM. Yes. There— that's right. There.

ROUGH (*holding up brooch*). A nice piece of jewelry. When did he give you this?

MRS. MANNINGHAM. Soon after we were married. But it was only secondhand.

ROUGH. Secondhand, eh? I'm afraid you got everything secondhand from this gentleman, Mrs. Manningham. Well—that's all right. (*He puts brooch in drawer and drawer back in desk.*) Now I must lock this up again—(*closes the second drawer*) —if I can. (*About to lock first drawer.*) Secondhand, did you say? How did you know that brooch was secondhand, Mrs. Manningham?

MRS. MANNINGHAM. There's an affectionate inscription to someone else inside.

ROUGH (*vaguely*). Oh—is there? (*Opens first drawer.*) Why didn't you tell me that?

MRS. MANNINGHAM. Why—I only found it myself a little while ago.

ROUGH (*as he takes out brooch*). Oh—really. Do you know, I have a feeling I have seen this somewhere before? Where is this inscription you speak of?

MRS. MANNINGHAM. It is a sort of trick. I only discovered it by accident. You pull the pin at the back. It goes to the right—(*he follows directions*)—and then to the left. It opens out like a star.

ROUGH (*crossing to C. As he opens it*). Oh yes—yes. Ah—here we are. Yes. (*As he sits L. of table and takes out his jeweler's glass.*) How very odd. What are these spaces here?

MRS. MANNINGHAM (*crosses to L. C.*). There were some beads in it, but they were all loose and falling out—so I took them out.

ROUGH. Oh—there were some beads in it, but they were all loose and falling out—so you took them out. (*Pause.*) Have you got them, by any chance?

MRS. MANNINGHAM. Yes. (*Pause. He shows interest.*) I think so. I put them in a vase.

ROUGH. May I see them, please?

MRS. MANNINGHAM. Yes. (*Goes to mantelpiece. Crosses below settee. He rises and goes up back of table.*) They should still be here.

ROUGH. There should be nine altogether, I think.

MRS. MANNINGHAM. Yes, that's right, I think there were. Yes. (*Takes vase down from upper end of mantel.*) Here they are. Here are some of them, at any rate.

ROUGH (*crossing to her*). Let me see, will you?—Ah—thank you. (*Gets the rubies and quietly crosses to back of table and puts rubies in the brooch.*) Try and find them all, will you? (*She goes back to mantel.*) Did you happen to read this inscription at any time, ma'am?

MRS. MANNINGHAM. Yes, I read it. Why?

ROUGH (*reading*). "Beloved A.B. from C.B. Eighteen fifty-one." (*Looking up at her.*) Does nothing strike you about that?

MRS. MANNINGHAM. No. What of it? What should strike me?

ROUGH. Really, I should have thought that as simple as A.B.C. Have you got the others? There should be four more.

MRS. MANNINGHAM (*crossing back to him*). Yes. Here they are.

ROUGH. Thank you. (*Takes them.*) That's the lot. (*He is putting them in brooch on the table.*) Now tell me this—have you ever been embraced by an elderly detective in his shirt sleeves?

MRS. MANNINGHAM. What do you mean?

ROUGH. For that is your immediate fate at the moment. (*Puts down brooch and comes to her.*) My dear Mrs. Manningham. (*Kisses her.*) My dear, dear Mrs. Manningham! (*Steps back from her and takes her hands.*) Don't you understand?

MRS. MANNINGHAM. No, what are you so excited about?

ROUGH (*leaves her and picks up brooch*). There, there you are, Mrs. Manningham. The Barlow rubies—complete. Twelve thousand pounds' worth before your very eyes! (*Crosses to her and gives her brooch.*) Take a good look at them before they go to the Queen.

MRS. MANNINGHAM. But it couldn't be—it couldn't. They were in the vase all the time. (*She glances toward mantel, then back at him.*)

ROUGH. Don't you see? Don't you see the whole thing? *This* is where the old lady hid her treasure—in a common trinket she wore all the day. I knew I had seen this somewhere before. And where was that? (*Crossing to L.C.*) In portraits of the old lady—when I was on the case. She wore it on her breast. I remember it clearly, though it was fifteen years ago. Fifteen years! (*Crosses to* MRS. MANNINGHAM.) Dear God in Heaven, am I not a wonderful man!

MRS. MANNINGHAM. And I had it all the time. I had it all the time.

ROUGH. And all because he could not resist a little common theft along with the big game. Well, it is I who am after the big game now. (*He shows signs of going.*)

MRS. MANNINGHAM (*crosses to front of table*). Are you going?

ROUGH. Oh yes, I must certainly go. (*Begins to collect his coat and things.*) And very quickly at that.

MRS. MANNINGHAM. Where are you going? Are you going to leave me? What are you going to do?

ROUGH. I am going to move Heaven and earth—Mrs. Manningham—and if I have any luck I—— (*Looking at his watch.*) It's very early yet. What time do *you* think he'll be back?

MRS. MANNINGHAM. I don't know. He's not usually in till eleven.

ROUGH. Yes. So I thought. Let's hope so. That will give me time. Here, give me that. Have you closed it? (*Takes brooch.*) We will put it back where we found it. (*He crosses above desk to upstage drawer.*)

MRS. MANNINGHAM (*follows to upper end of desk*). But what are you going to do?

ROUGH. It's not exactly what I am going to do. It's what the government is going to do in the person of Sir George Raglan. Yes, ma'am. Sir George Raglan. No one less. The power above all the powers that be. (*Puts brooch in drawer—closes and locks drawer.*) He knows I am here tonight, you see. But he didn't know I was going to find what I have found. (*Pause. Looks at broken drawer.*) Yes—we've done for that, I'm afraid. Well, we must just risk it, that's all. (*Tries to force broken drawer into place.*) Now, Mrs. Manningham, you will serve the ends of justice best by simply going to bed. (*Crosses to* MRS. MANNINGHAM.) Do you mind going to bed?

MRS. MANNINGHAM. No. I will go to bed. (*She starts upstairs.*)

(*Warn curtain.*)

ROUGH. Good. Go there and stay there. Your headache is worse. Remember, be ill. Be anything. But stay there, you understand. I'll let myself out. (*Crosses up to L.C. door.*)

MRS. MANNINGHAM (*suddenly. Comes downstairs and crosses to* ROUGH). Don't leave me. Please don't leave me. I have a feeling—— Don't leave me.

ROUGH. Feeling? What feeling?

MRS. MANNINGHAM. A feeling that something will happen if you leave me. I'm afraid. I haven't the courage.

ROUGH. Have the goodness to stop making a fool of yourself, Mrs. Manningham. Here's your courage. (*He gives her whisky, taking it from pocket.*) Take some more of it, but don't get tipsy and don't leave it about. (*Pause—crosses up to doors.*) Good-by. (*He is at L.C. doors, opens them and is about to exit.*)

MRS. MANNINGHAM. Inspector.

ROUGH (*turns to her*). Yes.

MRS. MANNINGHAM (*summoning courage*). All right. Good-by. (*She starts up the stairs.*)

ROUGH (*pause. As he exits*). Good-by. (*Shuts the door. Pause as she stops on the stairs and glances around the room.* ROUGH *suddenly opens the door.*) Mrs. Manningham!

MRS. MANNINGHAM. Yes.

(ROUGH *motions to her to go upstairs. She does so and he watches her.*)

ROUGH. Good-by.

(*When she is out of sight around the curve on the stairs he exits and closes the doors.*)

THE CURTAIN FALLS

ACT THREE

The time is eleven the same night. The room is in darkness, but the L.C. door is open and a dim light in the passage outside can be seen. There is the sound of the front door shutting. Footsteps can be heard, and MANNINGHAM *appears outside. He stops to turn out the light in the passage. He enters the room and goes to the lamp on the C. table and turns it up. Then he lights the two brackets and crosses to table up R. and puts his hat on it. He goes in a slow and deliberate way over to the bell cord and pulls it. He is humming to himself as he goes over to the fireplace.*

NANCY *puts her head round the L.C. door. She has only just come in and is dressed for out-of-doors.*

NANCY. Yes sir. Did you ring, sir?

MR. MANNINGHAM. Yes, Nancy, I did ring. It seems that the entire household has gone to bed without leaving me my milk and without leaving me my biscuits.

NANCY. Oh, I'm sorry, sir. They're only just outside. I'll bring them in! (*Turns to door, then stops and turns to* MR. MANNINGHAM.) Mrs. Manningham usually gets them, doesn't she, sir? Cook's in bed and I've only just come in.

MR. MANNINGHAM. Quite, Nancy. Then perhaps you will deputize for Mrs. Manningham and bring them into the room.

NANCY. Certainly, sir.

MR. MANNINGHAM. And after you do that—(*she stops in doorway*)—Nancy, will you go upstairs and tell Mrs. Manningham that I wish to see her down here?

NANCY. Yes sir. Certainly, sir. (*Exits L.C. and turns to R.*)

(MR. MANNINGHAM *walks into room up R.* NANCY *returns. She has milk in a jug, a glass and biscuits on a tray, and puts them on the table. She goes upstairs. He enters from room up R., crosses slowly to above table, then over to desk.* NANCY *comes downstairs and stops at the foot of the stairs.*)

MR. MANNINGHAM. Well, Nancy?

NANCY. She says she has a headache, sir, and is trying to sleep.

MR. MANNINGHAM. Oh—she still has a headache, has she?

NANCY. Yes sir. Is there anything else you want, sir?

MR. MANNINGHAM. Did you ever know a time when Mrs. Manningham did not have a headache, Nancy?

NANCY. No sir. Hardly ever, sir.

MR. MANNINGHAM (*turns to* NANCY). Do you usually perform your domestic tasks in outdoor costume, Nancy?

NANCY. I told you, sir. I've only just come in, and I heard the bell by chance.

MR. MANNINGHAM. Yes, that's just the point.

NANCY. How do you mean, sir?

MR. MANNINGHAM. Will you be so good as to come closer, Nancy, where I can see you. (NANCY *comes downstage a step. They look at each other in a rather strange way.*) Have you any idea of the time of the day, or rather night, Nancy?

NANCY. Yes sir. It's a little after eleven, sir.

MR. MANNINGHAM. Are you aware that you came in half a minute, or even less, before myself?

NANCY. Yes sir. I thought I saw you, sir.

MR. MANNINGHAM. Oh—you thought you saw me. Well, I certainly saw you.

NANCY (*looking away*). Did you, sir?

MR. MANNINGHAM. Have you ever reflected, Nancy, that you are given a great deal of latitude in this house?

NANCY. I don't know, sir. I don't know what latitude means.

MR. MANNINGHAM. Latitude, Nancy, means considerable liberty—liberty to the extent of two nights off a week.

NANCY (*pause*). Yes sir.

MR. MANNINGHAM. Well, that's all very well. It is not so well, however, when you return as late as the master of .the house. We ought to keep up some pretenses, you know.

NANCY. Yes sir. We must. (*She makes to go.*)

MR. MANNINGHAM. Nancy.

NANCY (*stops*). Yes sir?

MR. MANNINGHAM (*in a more human tone*). Where the devil have you been tonight, anyway?

NANCY (*pause—turns to him*). Only with some friends, sir.

MR. MANNINGHAM. You know, Nancy, when you say friends, I have an extraordinary idea that you mean gentlemen friends.

NANCY (*looking at him*). Well, sir, possibly I might.

MR. MANNINGHAM. You know, gentlemen friends have been known to take decided liberties with young ladies like yourself. Are you alive to such a possibility?

NANCY. Oh no, sir. Not with me. I can look after myself.

MR. MANNINGHAM. Are you always so anxious to look after yourself?

NANCY. No sir, not always, perhaps.

MR. MANNINGHAM. You know, Nancy, pretty as your bonnet is, it is not anything near so pretty as your hair beneath it. Won't you take it off and let me see it?

NANCY (*as she removes hat and crosses to R. of chair R. of table*). Very good, sir. It comes off easy enough. There—is there anything more you want, sir?

MR. MANNINGHAM. Yes. Possibly. Come here, will you, Nancy?

NANCY (*pause*). Yes sir. (*Drops hat on chair R. of table. Coming to him.*) Is there anything you want, sir? (*Changing tone as he puts his arms on her shoulders.*) What do you want? Eh—what do you want? (MANNINGHAM *kisses* NANCY *in a violent and prolonged manner. There is a pause in which she looks at him, and then she kisses him as violently.*) There! Can she do that for you? Can she do that?

MR. MANNINGHAM. Who can you be talking about, Nancy?

NANCY. You know who I mean all right.

MR. MANNINGHAM. You know, Nancy, you are a very remarkable girl in many respects. I believe you are jealous of your mistress.

NANCY. She? She's a poor thing. There's no need to be jealous of her.

You want to kiss me again, don't you? Don't you want to kiss me? (MR. MANNINGHAM *kisses* NANCY.) There! That's better than a sick headache—ain't it?—a sick headache and a pale face all the day.

MR. MANNINGHAM. Why, yes, Nancy, I believe it is. I think, however, don't you, that it would be better if you and I met one evening in different surroundings?

NANCY. Yes. Where? I'll meet you when you like. You're mine now—ain't you?—'cos you want me. You want me—don't you?

MR. MANNINGHAM. And what of you, Nancy? Do you want me?

NANCY. Oh yes! I always wanted you, ever since I first clapped eyes on you. I wanted you more than all of them.

MR. MANNINGHAM. Oh—there are plenty of others?

NANCY. Oh yes—there's plenty of others.

MR. MANNINGHAM. So I rather imagined. And only nineteen.

NANCY. Where can we meet? Where do you want us to meet?

MR. MANNINGHAM (*slowly crossing to front of settee and facing fireplace*). Really, Nancy, you have taken me a little by surprise. I'll let you know tomorrow.

NANCY (*crossing to front of table*). How'll you let me know, when she's about?

MR. MANNINGHAM (*quietly, half turning to Nancy*). Oh, I'll find a

way, Nancy. I don't believe Mrs. Manningham will be here tomorrow.

NANCY. Oh? Not that I care about her. (*Crossing to him.*) I'd like to kiss you under her very nose. That's what I'd like to do.

MR. MANNINGHAM. All right, Nancy. Now you had better go. I have some work to do.

NANCY. Go? I don't want to go.

MR. MANNINGHAM (*turns away from her*). There, run along. I have some work to do.

NANCY. Work? What are you going to work at? What are you going to do?

MR. MANNINGHAM (*turns to* NANCY). Oh—I'm going to write some letters. Then I—— Go along, Nancy, that's a good girl.

NANCY. Oh, very well, sir. You shall be master for a little more. (*Her arms around his neck. Kisses him.*) Good night, Your Lordship. (*Starts to door L.C. and picks up her hat on the way.*)

MR. MANNINGHAM. Good night.

NANCY (*at door stops and turns to him*). When shall you let me know tomorrow?

MR. MANNINGHAM. When I find time, Nancy, when I find time. Good night.

NANCY. Good night! (*Goes out into the hall L.C.—closes doors.*)

(MANNINGHAM *crosses above settee to back of desk and sits down. He rises and crosses to the secretary, gets some papers, crosses back to the desk, and sits down again. He takes up the pen and begins to write. He stops and takes out his key ring, which is on the other end of his watch chain, and unlocks the upstage drawer, then turns to unlock the downstage drawer. He stops as he discovers it has been forced and quickly rises. He turns to the upstage drawer, opens it, and rummages through it. He then looks toward the stairs, crosses below the desk, and stops at up L.C., turns and goes to the bell rope, pulls it, and goes back of desk and takes a quick look at both drawers, then closes them.*)

NANCY (*re-enters*). Yes? What is it now?

MR. MANNINGHAM. Nancy, will you please go upstairs and take a message for me to Mrs. Manningham?

NANCY. Yes. What do you want me to say?

MR. MANNINGHAM. Will you please tell her that she is to come down here this instant, whether she is suffering from a sick headache or any other form of ailment.

NANCY. Just like that, sir?

MR. MANNINGHAM. Just like that, Nancy.

NANCY. With the greatest of pleasure, sir. (*Goes upstairs.*)

(MANNINGHAM *looks at the drawer again carefully. He walks over to the fireplace and stands with his back to it, waiting.*)

NANCY (*returns. On the bottom step*). She won't come. She doesn't mean to come.

MR. MANNINGHAM (*steps forward*). What do you mean, Nancy—she won't come?

NANCY. She said she can't come— she's not well enough. She's just shamming, if you ask me.

MR. MANNINGHAM. Really? Then she forces me to be undignified. (*Walking over to the stairs.*) All right, Nancy, leave it to me.

NANCY. The door's locked. She's got it locked. I tried it.

MR. MANNINGHAM. Oh—really—the door is locked, is it? Very well—— (*He starts up the stairs past her to the fifth step.*)

NANCY. She won't let you in. I can tell by her voice. She's got it locked and she won't open it. Are you going to batter it in?

MR. MANNINGHAM (*turns, comes down to* NANCY). No—perhaps you are right, Nancy. (*Crosses above desk to chair. Sits and starts to write.*) Let us try more delicate means of attaining our ends. Perhaps you will take a note to this wretched imbecile and slip it under her door.

NANCY. Yes, I'll do that. (*Coming to desk.*) What are you going to write?

MR. MANNINGHAM. Never mind what I am going to write. I'll tell you what you can do, though, Nancy.

NANCY. Yes? What?

MR. MANNINGHAM. Just go down to the basement and bring the little dog here, will you?

NANCY (*starts out, stops and turns*). The dog?

MR. MANNINGHAM. The dog, yes.

NANCY. What's the game? What's the idea with the dog?

MR. MANNINGHAM. Never mind. Just go and get it, will you?

NANCY (*starts to L.C. door*). All right.

MR. MANNINGHAM. Or on second thought perhaps you need not get the dog. (*She stops. Turns to him.*) We will just let it be supposed we have the dog. That will be even more delicate still. Here you are, Nancy. (*She crosses to desk.*) Please go and put this under the door.

NANCY (*pause*). What's the idea? What have you written in this?

MR. MANNINGHAM. Nothing very much. Just a little smoke for getting rats out of holes. There. Run along.

NANCY. You're a rum beggar, ain't you? (*At stairs.*) Can't I look?

MR. MANNINGHAM. Go on, Nancy.

(NANCY *goes up. Left alone*, MANNINGHAM *shuts and locks the top of his desk. Then he comes down and carefully places an armchair facing the fireplace—as though he is staging some ceremony. He looks around the room. Then he takes up his place in front of the fire and waits.* NANCY *comes downstairs.*)

NANCY. She's coming. It's done the trick all right.

MR. MANNINGHAM. Ah—so I thought. Very well, Nancy. Now I shall be obliged if you will go to bed at once.

NANCY. Go on. What's the game? What's the row about?

MR. MANNINGHAM. Nancy, will you please go to bed?

NANCY (*coming forward, to him*). All right, I'm going. (*Crosses to him, her arms around him. Kisses him.*) Good night, old dear. Give her what for, won't you?

MR. MANNINGHAM. Good night, Nancy.

NANCY. Ta-ta.

(MRS. MANNINGHAM *appears and stands on the stairs.* MRS. MANNINGHAM *says nothing.* NANCY *goes out L.C. and leaves door ajar. After a long pause* MANNINGHAM *goes to the door and looks to see that* NANCY *is not there, closes it. He comes back and, standing again with his back to the fireplace, looks at her.*)

MR. MANNINGHAM. Come and sit down in this chair, please, Bella.

MRS. MANNINGHAM (*unmoving*). Where is the dog? Where have you got the dog?

MR. MANNINGHAM. Dog? What dog?

MRS. MANNINGHAM. You said you had the dog. Have you hurt it? Let me have it. Where is it? Have you hurt it again?

MR. MANNINGHAM. Again? This is strange talk, Bella—from you—after what you did to the dog a few weeks ago. Come and sit down here.

MRS. MANNINGHAM. I do not want to speak to you. I am not well. I thought you had the dog and were going—to hurt it. That is why I came down.

MR. MANNINGHAM. The dog, my dear Bella, was merely a ruse to compel you to pay me a visit quietly. Come and sit down where I told you.

MRS. MANNINGHAM (*starts upstairs*). No. I want to go.

MR. MANNINGHAM (*shouting*). Come and sit down where I told you!

MRS. MANNINGHAM (*coming downstage to back of table*). Yes—yes— what do you want?

MR. MANNINGHAM. Quite a good deal, Bella. Sit down and make yourself comfortable. We have plenty of time.

MRS. MANNINGHAM (*as she crosses back toward stairs*). I want to go. You cannot keep me here. I want to go.

MR. MANNINGHAM (*calmly*). Sit down and make yourself comfortable, Bella. We have plenty of time.

MRS. MANNINGHAM (*going to chair L. of table C. which he did not indicate and which is nearer the door and sits*). Say what you have to say.

MR. MANNINGHAM. Now you are not sitting in the chair I indicated, Bella.

MRS. MANNINGHAM. What have you to say?

MR. MANNINGHAM. I have to say that you are not sitting in the chair I indicated. Are you afraid of me that you desire to get so near the door?

MRS. MANNINGHAM. No, I am not afraid of you.

MR. MANNINGHAM. No? Then you have a good deal of courage, my dear. However, will you now sit down where I told you?

MRS. MANNINGHAM (*rises slowly and crosses below table*). Yes. (*Pause.*)

MR. MANNINGHAM (*as she crosses*). Do you know what you remind me of, Bella, as you walk across the room?

MRS. MANNINGHAM (*at L. end of settee—stops*). No. What do I remind you of?

MR. MANNINGHAM. A somnambulist, Bella. Have you ever seen such a person?

MRS. MANNINGHAM (*a step toward him*). No, I have never seen one.

MR. MANNINGHAM. Haven't you? Not that funny, glazed, dazed look of the wandering mind—the body that acts without the soul to guide it? I have often thought you had that look, but it's never been so strong as tonight.

MRS. MANNINGHAM (*crosses to R. chair*). My mind is not wandering.

MR. MANNINGHAM. No?—When I came in, Bella, I was told that you had gone to bed.

MRS. MANNINGHAM. Yes. I had gone to bed.

MR. MANNINGHAM. Then may I ask why you are still fully dressed? (*She does not answer.*) Did you hear what I said?

MRS. MANNINGHAM. Yes, I heard what you said.

MR. MANNINGHAM. Then will you tell me why, since you had gone to bed, you are still fully dressed?

MRS. MANNINGHAM. I don't know.

MR. MANNINGHAM. You don't know? Do you know anything about anything you do?

MRS. MANNINGHAM. I don't know. I forgot to undress.

MR. MANNINGHAM. You forgot to undress. A curious oversight, if I may say so, Bella. (*Leaning over her.*) You know, you give me the appearance of having had a rather exciting time since I last saw you. Almost as though you have been up to something. Have you been up to anything?

MRS. MANNINGHAM. No. I don't know what you mean.

MR. MANNINGHAM (*straightens up*). Did you find that bill I told you to find?

MRS. MANNINGHAM. No.

MR. MANNINGHAM (*goes to milk on table*). Do you remember what I said would happen to you if you did not find that bill when I returned tonight?

MRS. MANNINGHAM. No.

MR. MANNINGHAM. No? (*Is pouring milk into glass.*) No? (*She refuses to answer.*) Am I married to a dumb woman, Bella, in addition to all else? The array of your physical and mental deficiencies is growing almost overwhelming. I advise you to answer me.

MRS. MANNINGHAM. What do you want me to say?

MR. MANNINGHAM. I asked you if you remembered something. (*Going back to fireplace with glass of milk.*) Go on, Bella—what was it I asked you if you remembered?

MRS. MANNINGHAM. I don't understand your words. You talk round and round. My head is going round and round.

MR. MANNINGHAM (*at fireplace*). It is not necessary for you to tell me, Bella. I am just wondering if it might interrupt its gyratory motion for a fraction of a second and concentrate upon the present conversation. (*Sips milk.*) And please, what was it I a moment ago asked you if you remembered?

MRS. MANNINGHAM (*labored*). You asked me if I remembered what you said would happen to me if I did not find that bill.

MR. MANNINGHAM. Admirable, my dear Bella! Admirable! We shall make a great logician of you yet—a Socrates—a John Stuart Mill! You shall go down to history as the shining mind of your day. That is, if your present history does not altogether submerge you—take you away from your fellow creatures.

And there is a danger of that, you know, in more ways than one. (*Milk on mantel.*) Well—what did I say I would do if you did not find that bill?

MRS. MANNINGHAM (*choked*). You said you would lock me up.

MR. MANNINGHAM. Yes. And do you believe me to be a man of my word? (*Pause in which she does not answer. Crossing back of settee to C.*) You see, Bella, in a life of considerable and varied experience I have hammered out a few principles of action. In fact, I actually fancy I know how to deal with my fellow men. I learned it quite early actually —at school, in fact. There, you know, there were two ways of getting at what you wanted. One was along an intellectual plane, the other along the physical. If one failed, one used the other. I took that lesson into life with me. Hitherto, with you, I have worked, with what forbearance and patience I leave you to judge, along the intellectual plane. (*Crosses down and over to her.*) The time has come now, I believe, to work along the other as well. You will understand that I am a man of some power—— (*She suddenly looks at him.*) Why do you look at me, Bella? I said I am a man of some power and determination, and as fully capable in one direction as in the other.—I will leave your imagination to work on what I mean.— However, we are really digressing. (*Starts to L., crossing back of table.*) You did not find the bill I told you to find.

MRS. MANNINGHAM. No.

MR. MANNINGHAM. Did you look for it? (*He moves toward desk.*)

MRS. MANNINGHAM. Yes.

MR. MANNINGHAM. Where did you look for it?

MRS. MANNINGHAM. Oh, around the room.

MR. MANNINGHAM. Around the room. Where around the room? (*Pause. At desk. As he bangs on the desk with his right hand.*) In my desk, for instance?

MRS. MANNINGHAM. No—not in your desk.

MR. MANNINGHAM. Why not in my desk?

MRS. MANNINGHAM. Your desk is locked.

MR. MANNINGHAM. Do you imagine you can lie to me?

MRS. MANNINGHAM. I am not lying.

MR. MANNINGHAM (*crosses to C. of desk*). Come here, Bella.

MRS. MANNINGHAM (*coming to him*). What do you want?

MR. MANNINGHAM (*pause*). Now, listen to me. Your dark, confused, rambling mind has led you into playing some pretty tricks tonight— has it not?

MRS. MANNINGHAM. My mind is tired. (*She starts to stairs.*) I want to go to bed.

MR. MANNINGHAM. Your mind indeed is tired. Your mind is so tired that it can no longer work at all. You do not think. You dream. (*He slowly starts toward her.*) Dream all day long. Dream everything. Dream maliciously and incessantly. Don't you know that by now? (*She starts to give way.*) You sleepwalking imbecile, what have you been dreaming tonight—where has your mind wandered—that you have split—(*pounds on desk*)—open my desk? What strange diseased dream have you had tonight—eh?

MRS. MANNINGHAM. Dream? Are you saying I have dreamed—dreamed all that happened?

MR. MANNINGHAM. All that happened when, Bella? Tonight? Of course you dreamed all that happened—or rather all that didn't happen.

MRS. MANNINGHAM. Dream—tonight —are you saying I have dreamed? (*Pause.*) Oh God—have I dreamed? Have I dreamed again?

MR. MANNINGHAM. Have I not told you?

MRS. MANNINGHAM (*storming*). I haven't dreamed. I haven't. Don't tell me I have dreamed. In the name of God, don't tell me that!

MR. MANNINGHAM (*speaking at the same time and forcing her down into small chair L*). Sit down and be quiet. Sit down! (*More quietly and curiously.*) What was this dream of yours, Bella? You interest me.

MRS. MANNINGHAM. I dreamt of a man—(*hysterical*)—I dreamt of a man——

MR. MANNINGHAM (*now very curious*). You dreamed of a man, Bella? What man did you dream of, pray?

MRS. MANNINGHAM. A man. A man that came to see me. Let me rest! Let me rest!

MR. MANNINGHAM. Pull yourself together, Bella. What man are you talking about?

MRS. MANNINGHAM. I dreamed a man came in here.

MR. MANNINGHAM (*as he grasps her neck and slowly raises her*). I know you dreamed it, you gibbering wretch! I want to know more about this man of whom you dreamed. Do you hear! Do you hear me?

MRS. MANNINGHAM. I dreamed—I dreamed——

(*She looks off at door up R., transfixed.* MANNINGHAM *turns and looks as* ROUGH *enters door up R.* MANNINGHAM *releases her and she sinks back into the chair.*)

ROUGH (*as he crosses to chair R. of table*). Was I any part of this curious dream of yours, Mrs. Manningham?—Perhaps my presence here will help you to recall it.

MR. MANNINGHAM (*after pause. Crossing to L.C.*). May I ask who the devil you are, and how you got in?

ROUGH (*crosses back of chair*). Well, who I am seems a little doubtful. Apparently I am a mere figment of Mrs. Manningham's imagination. As for how I got in, I came in, or rather I came back—or better still, I effected an entrance a few minutes before you, and I have been hidden away ever since.

MR. MANNINGHAM. And would you be kind enough to tell me what you are doing here?

ROUGH (*hands on chair back*). Waiting for some friends, Mr. Manningham, waiting for some friends. Don't you think you had better go up to bed, Mrs. Manningham? You look very tired.

MR. MANNINGHAM. Don't you think you had better explain your business, sir?

ROUGH. Well, as a mere figment, as a mere ghost existing only in your wife's mind, I can hardly be said to have any business. Tell me, Mr. Manningham, can you see me? (*Spreading his hands as he makes a complete turn.*) No doubt your wife can, but it must be difficult for you. Perhaps if she goes to her room I will vanish, and you won't be bothered by me any more.

MR. MANNINGHAM. Bella. Go to your room. (*She rises, staring at both in turn, in apprehension and wonderment, goes to the stairs.*) I shall find out the meaning of this and deal with you in due course.

MRS. MANNINGHAM. I——

MR. MANNINGHAM. Go to your room. I will call you down later. I have not finished with you yet, madam.

(MRS. MANNINGHAM *looks at both again and goes upstairs.*)

ROUGH (*pause. To chair down R.*). You know, I believe you're wrong there, Manningham. I believe that is just what you have done.

MR. MANNINGHAM. Done what?

ROUGH. Finished with your wife, my friend. (*He sits down easily in armchair.*)

MR. MANNINGHAM (*crosses to front of table*). Now, sir—will you have the goodness to tell me your name and your business if any?

ROUGH. I have no name, Manningham, in my present capacity. I am, as I have pointed out, a mere spirit. Perhaps a spirit of something that you have evaded all your life—but in my case, only a spirit. Will you have a cigar with a spirit? We may have to wait some time.

MR. MANNINGHAM. Are you going to tell me your business, sir, or am I going to fetch a policeman and have you turned out?

ROUGH (*rises. Puts cigar back in pocket*). Ah—an admirable idea. I could have thought of nothing better myself. Yes, fetch a policeman, Manningham, and have me turned out. (*Pause.*) Why do you wait?

MR. MANNINGHAM. Alternatively, sir, I can turn you out myself.

ROUGH (*standing and facing him*). Yes. But why not fetch a policeman?

MR. MANNINGHAM (*after pause*). You give me the impression, sir, that you have something up your sleeve. Will you go on with what you were saying?

ROUGH. Yes, certainly. Where was I? Yes. (*Pause.*) Excuse me, Manningham, but do you get the same impression as myself?

(*Light starts down.*)

MR. MANNINGHAM. What impression?

ROUGH (*goes upstage, looking at downstage bracket*). An impression that the light is going down in this room?

MR. MANNINGHAM. I have not noticed it.

ROUGH. Yes—surely. There—— (*Crosses to L.C. then down to L. of table. The light goes slowly down. As* ROUGH *moves* MANNINGHAM *keeps his eyes on him.*) Eerie, isn't it? Now we are almost in the dark. Why do you think that has happened? You don't suppose a light has been put on somewhere else? You don't suppose there are other spirits—fellow spirits of mine—spirits surrounding this house now—spirits of justice, even, which have caught up with you at last, Mr. Manningham?

MR. MANNINGHAM (*a step upstage and his hand on the back of chair R. of table*). Are you off your head, sir?

ROUGH. No sir. Just an old man seeing ghosts. It must be the atmosphere of this house. (*Backing away to L.C. as he looks about.*) I can see them everywhere. It's the oddest thing. Do you know one ghost I can see, Mr. Manningham? You could hardly believe it.

MR. MANNINGHAM. What ghost do you see, pray?

ROUGH. Why, it's the ghost of an old woman, sir—an old woman who once lived in this house, who once lived in this very room. Yes—in this very room. What things I imagine!

MR. MANNINGHAM. What are you saying?

ROUGH. Remarkably clear, sir, I see it. An old woman getting ready to go to bed—here in this very room— an old woman getting ready to go up to bed at the end of the day. Why! There she is. She sits just there. (*Points to chair R. of table.* MANNINGHAM *removes his hand from the chair.*) And now it seems I see another ghost as well. (*Pause. He is looking at* MANNINGHAM.) I see the ghost of a young man, Mr. Manningham—a handsome, tall, well-groomed young man. But this young man has murder in his eyes. Why, God bless my soul, he might be you, Mr. Manningham—he might be you! (*Pause.*) The old woman sees him. Don't you see it all? She screams—screams for help—screams before her throat is cut—cut open with a knife. (*Crosses downstage.*) She lies dead on the floor—the floor of this room—of this house. There! (*Pointing to floor in front of table. Pause.*) Now I don't see that ghost any more.

MR. MANNINGHAM. What's the game, eh? What's your game?

ROUGH (*confronting* MANNINGHAM). But I still see the ghost of the man. I see him, all through the night, as he ransacks the house, hour after hour, room after room, ripping everything up, turning everything out, madly seeking the thing he cannot find. Then years pass and where is he? (*Goes to table C.*) Why, sir, is he not back in the same house, the house he ransacked, the house he searched—and does he not now stand before the ghost of the woman he killed—in the room in which he killed her? A methodical man, a patient man, but perhaps he has waited too long. For justice has waited too, and here she is, in my person, to exact her due. And justice found, my friend, in one hour what you sought for fifteen years and still could not find. See here. Look what she found. (*Goes below desk around to drawer.*) A letter which never reached your wife. Then a brooch which you gave your wife but which she did not appreciate. How wicked of her! But then she didn't know its value. How was she to know that it held the Barlow rubies! There! (*Coming below desk to* MANNINGHAM. *Opening it out.*) See. Twelve thousand pounds' worth before your eyes! There you are, sir. You killed one woman for those and tried to drive another out of her mind. And all the time they lay in your own desk, and all they have brought you is a rope around your neck, Mr. Sydney Power!

MR. MANNINGHAM (*pause*). You seem, sir, to have some very remarkable information. Do you imagine you are going to leave this room with such information in your possession? (*Going up to L.C. doors as though to lock them.*)

ROUGH (*away to down L.*). Do you imagine, sir, that you are going to leave this room without suitable escort?

MR. MANNINGHAM. May I ask what you mean by that?

ROUGH. Only that I have men in the house already. Didn't you realize they had signaled their arrival from above, your own way in, Mr. Manningham, when the lights went down?

MR. MANNINGHAM (*pause. He looks at* ROUGH). Here you. What the devil's this? (*He rushes to the door, where two* POLICEMEN *are standing.*) Ah, gentlemen—come in. Come in. Make yourselves at home. Here. (*He makes a plunge. They grab him.*) Leave go of me, will you? Here. Leave go of me! Here's a fine way of going on. Here's a fine way!

(*A struggle ensues.* ROUGH, *seeing help is needed, jerks down the bell cord. With this they secure* MANNINGHAM. ROUGH *kicks him in the shins. He falls.*)

ROUGH (*taking paper from his pocket. Going up to* MANNINGHAM). Sydney Charles Power, I have a warrant for your arrest for the murder of Alice Barlow. I should warn you that anything you may say now may be taken down in writing and used as evidence at a later date. Will you accompany us to the station in a peaceful manner? You will oblige us all, and serve your own interests best, Power, by coming with us quietly. (MANNINGHAM *renews struggle.*) Very well—take him away.

(*They are about to take him away when* MRS. MANNINGHAM *comes down the stairs. There is a silence.*)

MRS. MANNINGHAM. Inspector Rough——

(*The two* POLICEMEN *turn so that* MANNINGHAM *faces* MRS. MANNINGHAM.)

ROUGH (*going to her*). Yes, my dear, now don't you think you'd better——

MRS. MANNINGHAM (*in a weak voice*). Inspector——

ROUGH. Yes.

MRS. MANNINGHAM. I want to speak to my husband.

ROUGH. Now, surely, there's nothing to be——

MRS. MANNINGHAM. I want to speak to my husband.

ROUGH. Very well, my dear, what do you want to say?

MRS. MANNINGHAM. I want to speak to him alone.

ROUGH. Alone?

MRS. MANNINGHAM. Yes, alone. Won't you please let me speak to him alone? I beg of you to allow me. I will not keep him long.

ROUGH (*pause*). I don't quite understand. Alone? (*Pause.*) Very well. You may speak to him alone. (*He crosses to chair R. of table. To* POLICEMEN.) Very well. Make him fast in this chair. (*He signifies that they are to tie him to chair. They do so and exit L.C.*) This is anything but in order—but we will wait outside. (MRS. MANNINGHAM *crosses to desk.* ROUGH *examines fastenings on* MANNINGHAM *and crosses up to door, L.C.*) I'm afraid you must not be long, Mrs. Manningham.

MRS. MANNINGHAM. I do not want you to listen.

ROUGH. No, I will not listen. (ROUGH *hesitates, then exits L.C.*)

(MRS. MANNINGHAM *looking at her husband. At last she goes over to L.C. door, locks it, and then comes to him.*)

MRS. MANNINGHAM. Jack! Jack! What have they done to you? What have they done?

MR. MANNINGHAM (*struggling at his bonds, half whispering*). It's all right, Bella. You're clever, my darling. Terribly clever. Now get something to cut this. I can get out through the dressing-room window and make a jump for it. Can you fetch something?

MRS. MANNINGHAM (*hesitating. Crossing to him*). Yes—yes. I can get something. What can I get?

MR. MANNINGHAM. I've just remembered—there's a razor in my dressing room. Quick! Can you get it, Bella?

MRS. MANNINGHAM (*feverishly*). Razor—yes—I'll get it for you.

MR. MANNINGHAM. Hurry—yes. In my dresser. Hurry—quick and get it.

(*She goes into room up R., talking and mumbling, and comes back with the razor and crosses to desk. As she takes the razor from case, a scrap of paper falls to the floor. She stoops to pick it up, almost unconsciously tidy. She glances at it and a happy smile illuminates her face.*)

MRS. MANNINGHAM (*joyously*). Jack! Here's the grocery bill! (*She comes to him, the grocery bill in one hand, the razor in the other. She is half weeping, half laughing.*) You see, dear, I didn't lose it. I told you I didn't!

MR. MANNINGHAM (*uncomfortably*). Cut me loose, Bella.

MRS. MANNINGHAM (*she stares at him for a moment, then at the grocery bill, then back at him*). Jack—how did this get in here? You said that I—— (*Her voice trails off; a wild look comes into her eyes.*)

MR. MANNINGHAM (*trying to placate her with charm*). I must have been mistaken about the bill. Now—quickly, dear, use the razor! Quick! (*She stares at him for a moment, then moves a step closer. His look falls upon the razor. He glances up at her and a momentary hint of terror comes into his face. He draws back in the chair.*)

MRS. MANNINGHAM. Razor? What razor? (*She holds it up, under his face.*) You are not suggesting that this is a razor I hold in my hand? Have you gone mad, my husband?

MR. MANNINGHAM. Bella, what are you up to?

MRS. MANNINGHAM (*with deadly rage that is close to insanity*). Or is it I who am mad? (*She throws the razor from her.*) Yes. That's it. It's I. Of course it was a razor. Dear God—I have lost it, haven't I? I am always losing things. And I can never find them. I don't know where I put them.

MR. MANNINGHAM (*desperately*). Bella.

(*Warn curtain.*)

MRS. MANNINGHAM. I must look for it, mustn't I? Yes—if I don't find it you will lock me in my room—you will lock me in the madhouse for my mischief. (*Her voice is compressed with bitterness and hatred.*) Where could it be now? (*Turns and looks around to R.*) Could it be behind the picture?. Yes, it must be there! (*She goes to the picture swiftly and takes it down.*) No, it's not there—how strange! I must put the picture back. I have taken it down, and I must put it back. There. (*She puts it back askew.*) Where now shall I look? (*She is raging like a hunted animal. Turns and sees the desk.*) Where shall I look? The desk. Perhaps I put it in the desk. (*Goes to the desk.*) No—it is not there—how strange! But here is a letter. Here is a watch. And a bill—— See, I've found them at last. (*Going to him.*) You see! But they don't help you, do they? And I am trying to help you, aren't I?—to help you escape—— But how can a mad woman help her husband to escape? What a pity—— (*Getting louder and louder.*) If I were not mad I could have helped you—if I were not mad, whatever you had done, I could have pitied and protected you! But because I am mad I have hated you, and because I am mad I am rejoicing in my heart—without a shred of pity —without a shred of regret—watching you go with glory in my heart!

MR. MANNINGHAM (*desperately*). Bella!

MRS. MANNINGHAM. Inspector! Inspector! (*Up to door—pounds on door then flings it open.*) Come and take this man away! Come and take this man away! (ROUGH *and the others come in swiftly.* MRS. MANNINGHAM *is completely hysterical and goes down to lower end of desk.*) Come and take this man away!

(ROUGH *gestures to the men. They remove* MANNINGHAM. MRS. MANNINGHAM *stands apart, trembling with homicidal rage.* ROUGH *takes her by the shoulders sternly. She struggles to get away. He slaps her across the face. She is momentarily stunned.* ELIZABETH *enters, quickly takes in the situation, gets a glass of water from table up R. and brings it down to* MRS. MANNINGHAM *and gives her a drink.* ROUGH *stands at L.C. watching them for a second and——*)

ROUGH (*his eyes on* MRS. MANNINGHAM, *whose wild fury has resolved in weeping. He leads her to chair L. of table where she sits*). Now, my dear, come and sit down. You've had a bad time. I came in from nowhere and gave you the most horrible evening of your life. Didn't I? The most horrible evening of anybody's life, I should imagine.

MRS. MANNINGHAM. The most horrible? Oh no—the most wonderful. Far and away the most wonderful.

CURTAIN